NORWAY

NOR

Originated and developed by
BATO TOMASEVIC

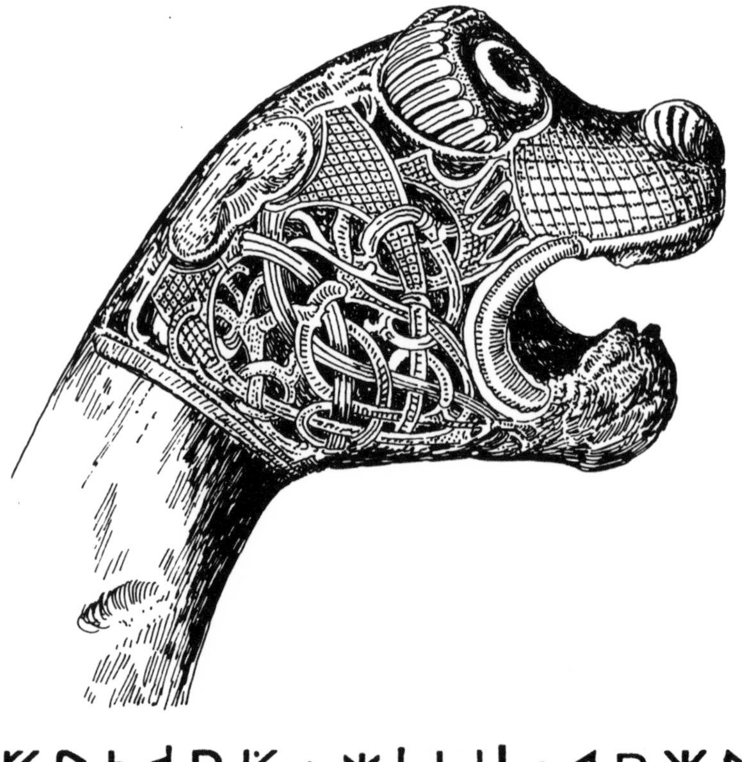

ᚠᚢᚦᚬᚱᚴ : ᚼᚾᛁᛅ' : ᛏᛒᛘᛚ

Text by
GUNVALD OPSTAD

Designed by
GANE ALEKSIC

SMITHMARK

For SMITHMARK Editions
© World copyright 1991

H. Aschehoug & Co. (W. Nygaard) / Flint River Press Ltd.

First published in the United States in 1991
by SMITHMARK Publishers Inc,
112 Madison Avenue, New York,
NY 10016

ISBN: 0-8317-6449-X

Text by
GUNVALD OPSTAD

Translated by
ANNABELLE DESPARD

Captions by
RAGNAR FRISLID

Editors:
EGIL A. KRISTOFFERSEN
MADGE PHILLIPS

Printed and bound in Yugoslavia by
DELO, Ljubljana

SMITHMARK books are available for bulk
purchase for sales and premium use. For
details write or telephone the Manager of
Special Sales, SMITHMARK Publishers Inc.,
112 Madison Avenue, New York, NY 10016.
(212) 532-6600.

CONTENTS

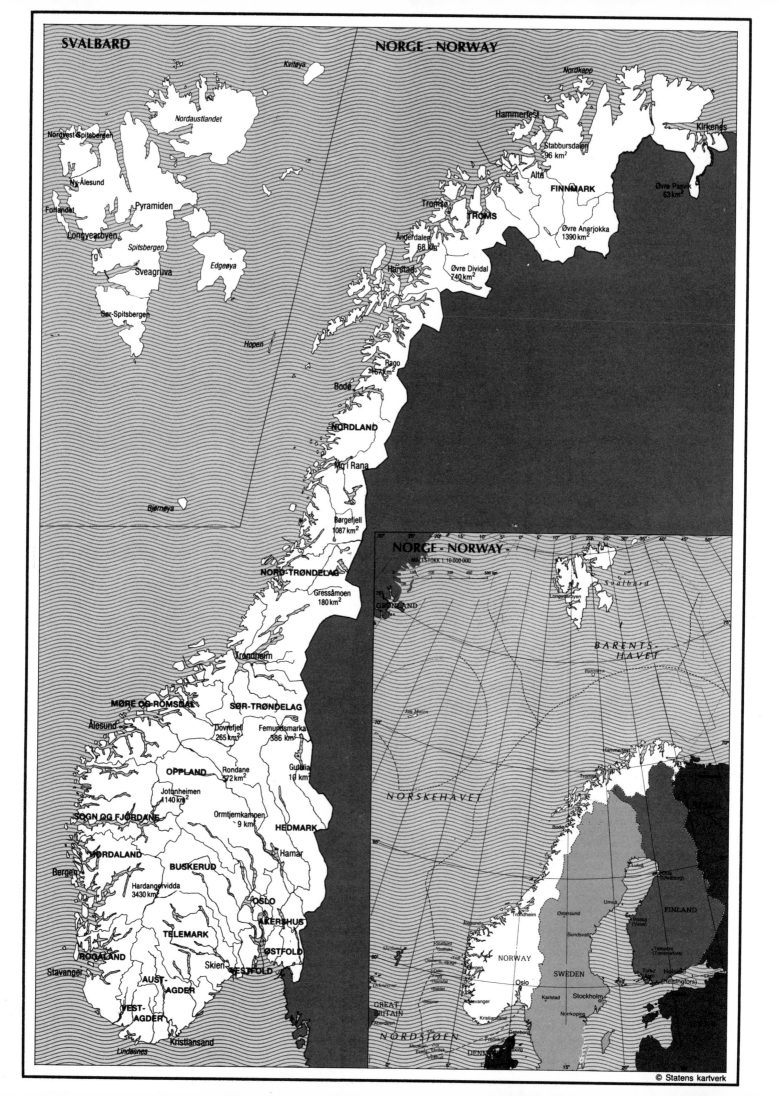

SVALBARD

NORGE - NORWAY

Kvitøya

Nordaustlandet

Nordvest-Spitsbergen

Ny-Ålesund

Forlandet

Pyramiden

Longyearbyen

Spitsbergen

g

Sveagruva

Edgeøya

Sør-Spitsbergen

Hopen

Bjørnøya

Nordkapp

Hammerfest

Kirkenes

Stabbursdalen
96 km²

Alta

FINNMARK

Øvre Pasvik
63 km²

Tromsø

TROMS

Øvre Anarjokka
1390 km²

Anderdalen
68 km²

Harstad

Øvre Dividal
740 km²

Rago
167 km²

Bodø

NORDLAND

Mo i Rana

Børgefjell
1087 km²

NORD-TRØNDELAG

Gressåmoen
180 km²

Trondheim

MØRE OG ROMSDAL

SØR-TRØNDELAG

Ålesund

Dovrefjell
265 km²

Femundsmarka
386 km²

OPPLAND

Rondane
572 km²

Gutulia
10 km²

Jotunheimen
1140 km²

Ormtjernkampen
9 km²

HEDMARK

SOGN OG FJORDANE

HORDALAND

BUSKERUD

Hamar

Bergen

Hardangervidda
3430 km²

OSLO

AKERSHUS

TELEMARK

ØSTFOLD

ROGALAND

Skien

VESTFOLD

Stavanger

AUST-AGDER

VEST-AGDER

Lindesnes

Kristiansand

NORGE - NORWAY
MÅLESTOKK 1:10 000 000
100 200 300 400 500 km

Svalbard

Longyearbyen

GRØNLAND

BARENTS-HAVET

Bjørnøya

Jan Mayen

NORSKEHAVET

Hammerfest

Tromsø

Bodø

FINLAND

Trondheim

Østersund

Umeå

Ålesund

Sundsvall

NORWAY

SWEDEN

Bergen

Oslo

Karlstad

Stockholm

Stavanger

Kristiansand

Norrköping

GREAT BRITAIN

Aberdeen

NORDSJØEN

DENMARK

THE NORWEGIANS

CHAPTER ONE deals with the difficult problem of describing 4,233,116 individuals who live more scattered around than most people in Europe.

Mrs and Mr Typical Norwegian, Kari and Ola Nordmann, who are they? In 1990 there were 4,233,116 different answers to that question. Ola Nordmann is not, of course, that real person living near Oslo who has trouble every time he tries to pay by cheque, because all banks in Norway use his name in their advertisements demonstrating how Ola the Norwegian should fill in a cheque correctly. No, I think of that ordinary, average couple who inhabit this extraordinarily extended piece of land, 1,752 kilometres (1,088 miles) from north to south, but only 6.5 kilometres (4 miles) wide in the middle.

"The people are extremely friendly and helpful. People trust each other entirely, and they never lock their houses. The fishermen build their own boats and make all their tackle," reported the Italian nobleman and merchant Pietro Querini, after being stranded on the island of Røst in Lofoten in the north of Norway in January 1432.

"The Norwegians have fire and temperament and are open, plain-spoken and forthright without being insolent. They never flatter their superiors, but show suitable respect. The normal manner of salutation is to shake hands, and when we gave them or paid them a coin or two, they shook our hands heartily and genuinely, not bowing or putting their thanks into words," wrote the English archdeacon William Coxe, in his travel journal in 1784.

"A general slowness and a fondness for bad food are the only poor qualities we have detected in the Norwegian. He is, for example, ridiculously honest, and he is kind and hospitable," wrote the Englishmen J. A. Lees and W. J. Clutterbuck, in their travelogue *Three in Norway by Two of Them* in 1882.

"The Norwegian is by nature (compared with Frisian smallholders) introverted and reserved, slow in thinking and in action, and in addition suspicious of strangers. Therefore: do not be hasty. Take things calmly." Thus Hitler exhorted the German troops who were to occupy Norway in 1940.

"Norwegians are so unsophisticated, refreshing, open and warm," said the violinist Iona Brown, Artistic Director of the Academy of St Martin-in-the-Fields chamber orchestra, in 1986.

"You are so one-track minded. All Norwegians think alike and talk about the same things: work and money, drinking and their next holiday," said a Yugoslav in 1987 after having stayed in Norway for a long time.

True – all too true!

In addition to the fact that 50 murders are committed in Norway each year, that 100,000 Norwegians are so harassed at work that 100 of them commit suicide annually, that 400,000 people get stomach ulcers in the course of their lives, that 400,000 get diarrhoea each year because of impurities in the drinking water, that there are 100,000 in hospital queues, that hospitals are closed because of lack of funds, that care for the elderly is so poor that even 101-year-olds are sent home, that two billion kroner is paid out in social benefits per year, that 25,000 people need social benefits in Oslo alone, that 7,000 a year are arrested for drug abuse, 100 people die of an overdose, and around 500 prostitute themselves to get drugs, that one billion is lost in thefts from shops, that tax evasion and insurance swindles each amounts to 15 billion, that 60,000 cars are stolen or broken into and there is no guarantee that you can report the crime immediately as telephone booths are vandalized to the tune of 25 million kroner per year. (100 kroner = c. $ 1.50 or £ 0.90 in 1991.)

All this has to be mentioned at this early stage to give a balanced picture.

Ola Nordmann could be that man standing shivering on Karl Johan, Oslo's main street, with frost in his beard and a drip under his nose, staring blindly at beaches, palms and glittering sunlight on the travel agent's Florida poster. Kari Nordmann could well be that liberated topless woman who lies in glittering sunlight on Sjøsanden beach in Mandal, suntanned and carefree, while her child plays in the sand. Ola Nordmann could equally be the Sámi (Lapp) on his snowscooter on Finnmarksvidda, for Norway is also the Sámiland (Lappland). Or he could belong to the number of travellers, tinkers and gypsies who have lived among us with their own language for many hundreds of years. It is, in fact, quite an undertaking to explain what Norway is and what Norwegians are.

Yet if we are to draw up some common characteristics, it would be these: Norwegians do not march in step like the Germans, nor do they move in flocks like the Japanese, but they go about singly like goats. They have vast expanses of country on all sides to wander around in, and what exciting and varied country it is! Norwegians have more breathing space than most: there are 13 people to each square kilometre in Norway, while there are 89 in Yugoslavia, 100 in France, 228 in Great Britain, and 18,121 in Monaco!

Yet while Kari and Ola are born with the proverbial skis on and grow up with rucksacks on their backs, they have fully surrendered to the Anglo-American influence that assails them day and night. This makes them a confused mixture of country bumpkin and wordly-wise, one foot in the potato-patch and the other on the aircraft steps – and may heaven help them from doing the splits.

After all, it's not as if they hadn't been abroad before; in fact, as long ago as the Viking age. Norway claims to have 'discovered' America, as Europeans so arrogantly say of lands whose peoples, in their innocence, were never aware of being discovered. In 1964 President Lyndon B. Johnson proclaimed 9 October an official flagday throughout the U.S.A. in honour of Leif Eriksson. The only trace of him is to be seen in the foundations of some dwellings in Newfoundland and Leif Eriksson

Drive in Brooklyn. Amerigo Vespucci, who arrived 500 years later, had the entire continent named after him. This should really have been called South Eriksson and North Eriksson! But that's how things are for explorers from the provinces. Norway can, however, boast a large piece of Antarctic ice that is called Queen Maud Land, after a Norwegian queen.

Thor Heyerdahl never staked a claim to Easter Island; nor Liv Ullman to the Mid-West, which she conquered in Jan Troell's epic film on the Scandinavian emigration to the U.S.A. However, in the telephone directory in Minneapolis, Minnesota, there are 10 pages of Olsons. And Olson is the son of Ola Nordmann.

Despite their small number and out-of-the-way country, there are occasions when Norwegians have unshakeable confidence that they are the best. How else to explain their fervent missionary activity? In proportion to the size of its population, Norway has more missionaries than any other country in the world. In 1987, 1,369 of them were sent out to 56 different countries! Most of these are paid for by voluntary contributions through organizations such as the Norwegian Mission Society, founded in 1842. At the Annual General Meeting in 1987 it was said that the missionary's territory is no longer south of the Equator. Now it is Europe's turn to be brought to Christianity. The first Norwegian missionaries have already been sent to France, and after that Portugal, Italy and Austria lie open to them.

Norway is reckoned to be the most puritan of the Scandinavian countries. Ninety per cent of the population belongs to the State Church, established at the Reformation in 1536, but only 37 per cent open their Bibles in the course of the year. There are 600 free congregations with 150,000 members in Norway, 18,000 Catholics, and 8,000 Muslims.

A Norwegian is by nature shy, and modesty is also a characteristic of the country's non-Christian population. In the eyes of Americans and Southern Europeans, the whole of Scandinavia is collectively an exponent of Swedish sin. Yet pornography has never been legal in Norway, and has never been sold openly, as in Sweden and Denmark. What goes on under the counter is a different story. To do things furtively is more in accordance with our nature. When Ola Nordmann needed to buy rubber contraceptives in the 60s, he discreetly placed two fingers on the counter at the barber's, and while he modestly kept his glance averted, the barber stooped to look into his drawer and brought out the much-needed two dozen. Today condoms are available in 2,500 shops, in supermarkets and at petrol stations. Accessibility follows geographical patterns of morality. It is easiest to buy condoms in Akershus, near Oslo, and in the north, most difficult in the west and south.

In the 60s it was shameful to produce a child out of wedlock in Norway. Up to 1973 common law marriage was illegal. However, it seems that this ruling slept more soundly than the couples themselves, for out of the 50,000 children born each year in Norway, one in four is born out of wedlock. In Finnmark every second child has unmarried parents, and in Oslo every third. This does not mean that Norwegians are much less moral than in earlier years; they have merely found another way of life. In 1986 70,000 were registered as co-habiting without being married, and the real figures must be much higher. In 1970 15 per cent of the population consisted of single persons, today it is 40 per cent. Around the turn of the century each family comprised on average 4.3 persons; today it is 2.5. Kari gives birth to an average 1.7 children, too few to keep up the population. In the north the population is already

9. Where fjords block the advance of motorists, car ferries take over, as here in Geiranger fjord.
(Husmo-Foto)

strongly on the decline, while the figures show an increase in the east and in the 'oil counties' of west Norway. To counteract this we are living longer. Life expectancy today is 80 years for women and 73 for men. We are also growing. The average Norwegian recruit to the armed services towers 1.79 metres (5 ft.10 inches) above sea level, the tallest ever.

How do Kari and Ola live?

The answer is very well indeed. The houses are so thoroughly insulated that experts are becoming concerned at the possible dangers of not letting air in! Kari and Ola like to live by themselves, in their own small nuclear unit, without any interference from the rest of the family. Grandma is placed in a home – if there is room for her. This is one of the most surprising things to foreigners. Care for the aged is a major unsolved problem of the welfare state. Out of the country's 1.5 million private dwellings, 640,000 are detached houses, 275,000 are flats, 160,000 farms, 160,000 terraced houses, and 70,000 are semi-detached. But as mortgages and bank rates soar out of all proportion, it is increasingly difficult to buy a home, especially for the young. Many Norwegians simply cannot pay their rent, and some 80,000 receive housing benefits from the State.

Norwegians are obsessed by furniture. Everyone spends on average 1,500 kroner per year on furniture, while Europeans in 15 other countries spend a mere third of this amount. Much of it is IKEA i.e. make-it-yourself furniture from the Swedish mail order firm that each year prints 44 million catalogues in 10 languages for 18 countries. Foreigners are amazed at the amount of furniture Norwegians manage to cram into their houses. Though the government appeals to the population to reduce consumption, Mr and Mrs Nordmann just go on spending: on freezers and washing-machines, tumbledriers and microwave ovens, stereos and CD equipment.

There are now 1.9 million cars on the roads. This means 2.5 persons per car in Norway, compared with 2.2 in West Germany and 1.4 in the USA. There are 200,000 Fords and Opels in the country, 150,000 VWs and Volvos, but only 40 Rolls-Royces and 32 Packards, one Bombardier and one Büssing, whatever that might be.

Many people own cabins and have pleasure craft that cost almost as much as a house. So there is plenty of money around. The level of spending is high, and the consumer mentality is spreading, not least among the younger generation. Young people of today, between the ages of eight and 24, spend an average 1,000 kroner a month on themselves. This can easily be seen by looking in the mail box. Nowhere is superfluous consumption as apparent as there! Every day the poor Norwegian has to empty his mail box of wads of leaflets advertising everything from package tours to magnet rings against hay fever, from sentimental novels to courses in Advanced Yoga. Each year the Post Office delivers 550 million commercial offers, with or without an address. Each household receives 320 of these missives in the course of a year. In addition there will be as many from the local store or local organizations. If Kari and Ola co-habit and have different family names, they will receive double the amount of junk mail. No wonder they have taken out bank loans for up to 250 billion kroner to make ends meet. It is poor consolation to know that they can deduct 30 billion kroner in interest off their income tax.

If they are not satisfied with what they have bought, they can complain to the consumer's Ombudsman. He has offices throughout the country, and received 130,000 complaints in 1986. Children can register complaints with the Ombudsman for children, while matters of sexual discrimination can go to the equal rights Ombudsman. Life in Norway is highly regulated. This is seen as a blessing in a welfare state, the expression of a healthy social democratic concern for one's fellow men, even if the rules do become somewhat bureaucratic at times.

Norway is fairly broad-minded as far as animal rights go, permitting both battery hens and pork factories, with the pigs eating and mating on demand as well as artificially. Yet in many high-rise flats it is forbidden to keep pets. With our strongly developed sense of hygiene, we never cease to wonder at the pigs and hens let loose in villages in more southerly climates.

We do, however, accept animals as symbols. They are acceptable at a distance. Swamped as we are in Walt Disney fauna, it is surely an acceptable face of nationalism to start looking for what is essentially Norwegian in our animal kingdom. The State Radio asked the people to proclaim the National Fish, whereupon one group of wits lobbied for the hagfish, an eel that most people would vote the most repulsive form of marine life. Needless to say, the State Radio made sure that the title went to the cod. It is hardly elevating to remember the choice of the dipper as the National Bird. It is now in danger of being made extinct by acid rain from England and the Continent, a fate that also threatens fish in all the lakes in southern Norway.

Recently a considerable effort has been made to have the small Norwegian pony proclaimed National Animal. This horse came from the steppes of Russia some 4,000 years ago, and has worked very hard as a packhorse in the west of Norway and in the timber forests of eastern Norway. Good-natured, modest in its demands, with short legs and a happy disposition, it has become a favourite in Norwegian children's songs. But it too, alas, is in danger of dying out. A generation ago we had 70,000 *Fjordings* or Norwegian ponies, today there are only 5,000 left. Friends of the Fjording want it to replace the lion on the Norwegian coat of arms!

It seems that it is in his diet that the Norwegian has succumbed most to foreign influence in recent years. Cafés have traditionally been small dour rooms with plastic table-tops, metal chairs, and silent people, serving neither beer nor spirits, only tired cheese sandwiches, bland stew, fish balls or meat loaf with stewed cabbage and boiled potatoes – and all closing at five in the afternoon. Nowadays, the main items on the diet of those under 30 are potato crisps and Coke, and there are trendy cafés everywhere with marble table-tops and rock music, pizzas and pasta, hamburgers and cappuchino. All this compelled Ragnvald Hidle from the puritan Jæren district to sit down and write to his newspaper in the oil town Stavanger:

"We live in strange times when all things foreign and weird are made out to be so wonderful. Foreign names and foreign fancy food enjoy an exaggerated reputation. Perhaps there is reason to ask as Henrik Ibsen did: 'Is the greatest then so great?' There are many of us who cannot get to good teetotal places where we can buy good plain Norwegian country fare: porridge, dumplings, meat balls, *lefse*, waffles, pancakes and decent bread rolls. We should get together and start a decent old-fashioned *matstove*, a café for those who care about dialect preservation, the Bible Society, clean-living young people and others..."

That I would call a true Norwegian sentiment! But what is Norwegian and what is not Norwegian in the realm?

The national musical instrument is the harding fiddle, but young people listen to 'A-Ha', the Norwegian pop group that topped charts all over the world in the 80s – singing in English! Yet a Norwegian swells with pride when he sees members of the group wearing the true, all-Norwegian hand-knitted Setesdal sweater. Cod-liver oil is Norwegian, lurking in the fridge as a terror to all children, part of the staple diet for 130 years. Reindeer horn is also Norwegian, ground for medical purposes, but strangely enough used more as an aphrodisiac in the Far East than in Norway.

Then there is *smalahove,* a singed sheep's head that smiles up at you from its plate, which is the traditional festive dish of the west. We shall refrain from saying too much about this, out of consideration for the nation's good name and reputation. We shall return to the dried fish later, also to aquavit.

Our aim with this book is to follow Kari and Ola through history, through their lives, through the seasons, through the country. Let us hasten to bring to your notice yet another Norwegian phenomenon before others do so: the duvet, or *dyne.* That too has a long tradition. As early as 1799 the French officer Jacques-Louis de Bougrenet de la Tocnaye wrote in his journal *Promenade en Norvège:*

"In Sweden one is seldom given more than a light cotton blanket as a covering, even in winter. In this country one buries oneself in a huge eiderdown, even in summer. I for my part cannot keep this over me for more than a quarter of an hour without being bathed in sweat."

Nordmanns forbundet, or the Norseman Federation has members all over the world. The General Secretary Johan Fr. Heyerdahl tells us what genuinely Norwegian things Norwegian-Americans want sent over.

"I have sent many stones and pieces of rock over the pond to those who wished to have a piece of Norwegian granite in the foundations of their house. And duvets. Norwegian-Americans cannot do without them once they have tried them on a visit to Norway..."

Norwegians are very kind – at a distance. As a country we hold the world record in giving aid to developing countries. Yet it is a different story when we are asked to receive refugees from Iran and Sri Lanka. The General Secretary of *Nordmanns forbundet* has a comment on this:

"We need all the inspiration we can get from outside in this small country of ours. I feel there is an alarming attitude of 'Go it alone'. What has created this fear of other countries, cultures and customs, of foreign influences? Just look at our lack of hospitality! We have a lot to learn from the Americans. In the U.S.A. you are invited to have a cup of coffee – and you get a cup of coffee. Getting to know each other is the essential thing."

Just to get some things straight:

Some foreigners wonder about the 'houses' they see beside Norwegian roads. They look like log cabins, but they are very low and have no windows. Do not expect to be invited in. These are woodpiles, layers of logs that will give warmth through the long winter nights when we live up to the ideal of hospitality described in our first book of etiquette *Håvamål* that goes back nearly a thousand years:

"Fire he needs who has come in cold about the knee."

They certainly needed some warmth about the knee, those first people who came to this bleak country.

HISTORY

CHAPTER TWO tells about how the first Norsemen settled next to the icecap, sailed off course and 'discovered' America, but decided to return home and become Social Democrats.

The first settlers probably arrived 10,000 to 11,000 years ago, and they must have been tough. How else could they have come to Norway? Northern Europe has been covered by ice four times in the course of the past million years, and the last ice age was then in retreat. They came to the foot of the glacier, in hide boats and hollowed-out tree trunks, driven by curiosity, or perhaps chased from their homelands. Some may have come overland. A bare strip of land is thought to have remained in both the south and north of Norway throughout the last ice age, and there are experts who believe that a tribe could have survived the long winter there, living like the Eskimos have done until recent times.

Some settled in the south, others in the north. Scientists cannot agree as to who came first; it seems that archaeologists are as regionally biased as anybody else. One site found near the Oslo fjord is assumed to date back 10,000 years. But the richest finds are in the west and north of Norway. These nomadic hunters made their first tools of antler and bone. In his history of Norway, Professor Andreas Holmsen reflects on the uses of these tools:

"(They) fully covered the needs of primitive people. They could make boats of wood and hide and row among the skerries and islands, they could shoot seals and whales with their excellent bone harpoons, and they could fish with hooks or spears of bone. Inland they could kill game, such as reindeer, moose, deer, bears and wild horses, with bows and arrows or with javelins. On the seashore they could gather shellfish with their bare hands, and we know that they had ways of catching sea birds and animals without any implements at all."

Holmsen goes on to describe how these small groups of fishermen and hunters lived their lives, independent of the outside world, and on the whole independent of one another. Yet it does not mean that they were not in touch, or closed to external influences, which would necessarily have come from the east, since they had not yet set out to sea westwards.

After 5,000 years the Norseman started to till the soil and keep domestic animals. He was then visited by warring Indo-European invaders who poured into Europe at that time. It is thought that this led to the development of some form of warrior class. After all, the Vikings must have got their ferocious nature from somewhere.

By A.D. 700 they were fully fledged and raring to go. The homestead and the clan were by now well established, and society was properly divided into masters and serfs, as shown by the medieval Frostating Law, which states that he who pokes out the eyes of another shall pay a fine of a farm and 12 head of cattle, two horses and two slaves. By now neighbourhood feuds were the accepted pastime and passion, the Viking ships had been invented, and general fury was at boiling-point.

They were now ready and could overcome half Europe, invade Ireland and take on England (though it was actually the Danes who did that), they could found Russia (or was it a Swede who did that?) and they could discover America (that we do know was a Norwegian, even if in his heart he was perhaps Icelandic or a Greenlander). When it comes to claiming great deeds we have elastic notions of nationality.

What drove them to this? What makes people abandon hearth and home, concubines and swine, in order to court the dangers of the unknown, drink themselves into a frenzy, rape, loot and pillage, and generally make themselves at home in another land?

It seems there were three reasons:
1) They had killed someone and needed to flee.
2) They had no clue as to where they were sailing.
3) They were bored.

All this emerges clearly from the saga of the discovery of America. It is well known that Leif Eriksson discovered America (though in all truth another man got there first, the Viking Bjarne Herjolvsson, but he couldn't be bothered to step ashore!).

Leif Eriksson's father was a Norseman, Eric the Red, who had had to flee Norway because he had killed a man. He went to Iceland, where he committed more murders and had to move further west on the island. There he had a major dispute with a neighbour who had borrowed some timber from him, which led to his being outlawed, and going over the sea to the larger island further west again.

Leif Eriksson's father never reached America, but it is quite clear that he was the founder of the modern American advertising business. According to the saga: "He called the country he had found Greenland, as he said it would make people want to travel there if the country had a good name."

Leif Eriksson, the discoverer of America, had actually aimed to go to Greenland. He had been home to Norway on a visit and had taken on the task of converting Greenland to Christianity for the king of Norway, Olav Tryggvason.

The Vinland Saga relates:
"Now Leif put out to sea and he sailed for a long time and found land that he did not know before. There, there were wheatfields which were self-sown, and wine-trees grew there. There were trees which are called *massur,* and of all these things they collected samples."

Leif had a half-sister, Frøydis, and she later visited Vinland with her brothers Helge and Finnboge, who had just come from Norway. This description of their visit to Leif's huts in Newfoundland provides definite proof that boredom was the mainspring of Viking violence:

"Now winter came and the brothers spoke about playing games in order to pass the time, and this they did until they started quarrelling.

Then they gave up the games and did not visit each other, and so things went on for some time.''

It ended with Frøydis having every man in the next house killed, including her own brothers:

"Thus the men were slain but the women were left, and nobody would kill them. Then said Frøydis, 'Let me have an axe'. So it was done, and she struck at the five women, and did not leave off until they were all dead.'' So goes the saga, which also relates how Frøydis promised to kill anyone who told tales once they were back in Greenland. If boredom led to episodes of this kind in a domestic setting, what kind of treatment must have lain in store for total strangers?

In the 1960s, Norwegian archaeologist Anne Stine Ingstad discovered at L'Anse aux Meadows in Newfoundland what are assumed to be the remains of the *Leifsbuene,* or Leif's huts, with a spinning wheel of soapstone and a Viking ornament, a find that is considered one of the most worthy of preservation in the world after the Egyptian Pyramids.

It was around the year 1000 that the natives of Newfoundland, the *Skrælingers* or Weaklings, as the saga calls them, found out the disadvantages of being in the path of the Vikings. Leif's brother Torvald came across the first nine natives, and "took them all prisoner except one, who got away in his boat. They killed the other eight, and then they went back to the hill and looked about them.'' Another Viking, Torfinn Karlsevne, and his men were sailing homewards and "on their way they came upon some *Skrælingers* asleep, dressed in skins. They had with them birch-bark sacks containing food and animal bones mixed with blood. Karlsevne and his men concluded they must be outlaws, and killed them.'' That was the way we discovered America.

By 790 the fun had started in Europe. Three Norwegian ships came

Medieval painting showing scenes from the life of St Olav. Drawing by Magnus Petersen.

10. The impressive Vigeland Sculpture Park is one of Oslo's biggest attractions. It is the work of a single artist: sculptor Gustav Vigeland. (Pål Hermansen/ Samfoto/NN)

11. Vigeland Park, which forms part of Frogner Park in Oslo, contains about 190 sculptural works, most depicting human beings and made of bronze or granite. (Husmo-Foto) ▷

12. Oslo is a city with its face turned to the sea. The medieval castle of Akershus and the City Hall are familiar landmarks for anyone sailing into the capital. (Husmo-Foto) ▷ ▷

to England. The king's man rode out to meet them, but in their customary manner the Vikings struck him down. That is all the Anglo-Saxon Chronicle has to relate about the matter. The next attack, on 8 June 793, was on St Cuthbert's monastery at Lindisfarne, the religious centre of Northumberland. The Vikings fell upon the defenceless monks and nuns, killed some of them, drowning a few, slaughtering their cattle and carting the meat on board ship. The honourable saga of the Vikings had started. The rest is well known.

They had already settled on the islands north of Scotland: the Shetland (Hjaltland) and Orkney Isles. From there they moved north to the Faroes and south to northern Scotland (Sudrland) and the Hebrides (Sudrøyene). Anyone who happened to be on the islands was unceremoniously ousted. There are still 100,000 Norse place names in the Shetlands, where the farmers spoke Norwegian right up to the beginning of the nineteenth century!

In the 820s the Irish coastland was full of Vikings. By 850 most of the Celtic region was Norwegian. In the Golden Age of Dublin, around 950, there was a Norwegian king in each district, a Norwegian chieftain in each town, and a Norwegian warrior in each house. On the Isle of Man, a *ting* or assembly is still held each summer at Tynwald according to the old Norwegian custom. This has been an unbroken tradition since 979, and the British monarch or royal representative has to turn up.

The voyages of destruction went south through the rivers of France, round Spain and into the Mediterranean. In France and southern Europe the Norwegian and Danish Vikings operated together, while in Constantinople they met the Swedes, who had arrived there by way of the rivers of Russia. Towards the end of the ninth century the Vikings' grip embraced virtually the whole of Europe.

They wrought havoc on the coastlands around the North Sea, the English Channel and the Bay of Biscay. They held the Frisian Islands, and they sailed up the Elbe and the Rhine. They burnt Hamburg, laid waste to Cologne, Aachen and Koblenz, and forced their way up the River Mosel to Trier. They pitched camp on the estuaries of the Loire and Seine and went on voyages of plunder to Orleans and Paris. In the 880s the Seine was invaded by a Viking fleet so large (700 ships with 40,000 men) that the vessels covered the river for a distance of 20 kilometres (12 miles) from Paris. There was no greater invasion of Europe from the north until the discovery of Majorca by package tourists 1100 years later! The Norsemen made their way to Toulouse and conquered Bordeaux, fought the Moors at Lisbon, and took possession of Seville before they were themselves defeated. They even visited the west coast of Morocco. While in the Mediterranean, they made raids into Africa, Spain and France. All this was in addition to colonizing Iceland and Greenland.

The Viking era lasted from around 800 to 1050. Its greatest influence was in seven places: the kingdoms of Dublin and Man, the earldom of the Orkneys, and the settlements of the Shetlands, Faroes, Iceland and Greenland. In France Normandy got its name from the Norsemen, and the reputation for quarrelsomeness lasted for a long time. When our friend the French officer Jacques de la Tocnaye travelled around Norway 200 years ago, he noted in his journal:

"In latter years the government has tried to stay the passion for litigation that is as characteristic of Norwegians as of their descendants in France. In each town there are now two courts of arbitration where the parties have to meet before their case can be brought to court..."

15. The climax of Constitution Day in Oslo is the children's parade, which ends in front of the Royal Palace, where the king greets the children from the balcony. (Mittet)

16. Nearly every school has its band, and they all practise incessantly in spring, in preparation for the great event – the children's parade on 17 May. (Mittet)

17. Constitution Day, 17 May, with its parades and festivities, may become too much for a small girl. When that happens, father's shoulders are the best resting place, and ensure the best view of what is going on. (Mittet)

17

18. Patient citizens of Oslo lining up for the bus in snowy weather near the city's cathedral. (Husmo-Foto)

19. Though Oslo is a coastal city, its position at the end of a long fjord gives it a continental climate with cold winters and heavy snow. (Husmo-Foto)

20. Thanks to the Gulf Stream, winters are milder along the Norwegian coast than anywhere else on a similar latitude, and winter clouds deposit more rain and sleet than snow. This is the town of Ålesund. (Knut Enstad)

19

The Vikings had their own mythology and cosmology, the remains of which can still be found in Norway. We say: "There goes Thor with his hammer" when we hear thunder. The Christian daily paper *Vart Land* has Odin's messengers, the ravens Hugin and Munin, depicted above its satire column, and in the North Sea many of the oil fields and rigs bear names from Viking mythology, such as Valhalla, Balder, Hod, Heidrun, Sleipner.

There is no founder as such of the Norse beliefs, and no set of dogma. However, there is an epic of creation, with the two first human beings, Ash and Alder, and there is the apocalyptic vision of the end of the world, Ragnarok. The world tree, Yggdrasil, was central to the Viking religion, which had much in common with Greek mythology. Thor was the most popular god, riding across the skies, hammer in hand, in his goat-drawn chariot. The one-eyed Odin, god of war, rode the eight-legged horse Sleipnir, and received fallen warriors in Valhalla, where they awoke to new life and new battles. Frøya was the goddess of love, and Iduna the giver of eternel youth. The home of the gods, the Aesir, was in Asgard. The humans dwelt in Midgard while the giants, the Jotuns, lived in Utgard, the wild country of Jotunheimen (the present name of Norway's central mountain range).

A strong streak of fatalism permeated the Viking outlook and also their superstition, their belief in elves and fates, goblins and trolls. All these are found in Norwegian folk tales. People still believed in trolls and supernatural beings until the recent past.

Historians tell us not to judge our ancestors by our own standards, but by theirs. So we will be careful of labelling our hero kings murderers, torturers, and arsonists. Yet it was no straight-forward matter when the old Viking kings made up their minds to introduce their subjects to the gentle teachings of Jesus, the 'White Christ' as they called him.

One of the men who converted Norway to Christianity was Olav Tryggvason, perhaps the most fabled king in Norway's history, 'the most beautiful, the greatest and strongest and the most widely renowned athlete of all Norsemen', according to Snorre Sturlason, writer of the Icelandic Prose Saga. King Olav's special prowess was running on the oars of a ship outside the hull. His life was a fable in itself. He was born on a small island, a mere rock, when his mother was fleeing from Norway to the east. Before he reached his uncle in Holmgard (now Novgorod in the U.S.S.R.) he was sold twice as a slave in Estonia; first when he was three years old for a goat, and the second time for a good cloak. His guardian was killed because he was too old to become a slave. Later Olav met the murderer, and the nine-year-old struck him with his axe so that it remained stuck in his skull. As soon as Olav was old enough he went west. He raided and slaughtered whenever he could: Bornholm, Friesland, Germany and England were in his path. He killed people in the Scilly Isles too, but it was there that he was converted to Christianity. After this, he energetically converted Norway, slaying those who were unwilling to receive the Word of Christ. This is how he went about it in Tønsberg, Norway's oldest town:

"King Olav had all these men gathered in a room and had it all well laid out; prepared a great feast for them and gave them strong drink; and when they were drunk Olav had the place set on fire and burnit and all the folk who were therein, except Øyvind Kelde, who got away through the smoke hole." Fortunately he was captured and put on a rock on the west coast, Skratteskjær, where he drowned slowly as the tide rose.

26. The traditional ski-jumping competition at Holmenkollen in Oslo is a kind of national holiday in Norway, as well as a major event on the international winter sports calendar. It has been held every year since 1892, except for the Second World War. (Kim Hart/ Samfoto)

In this manner Norway received the Christian faith.

The other heroic king, Olav Haraldsson (St Olav) used the same method. He let some die and others were mutilated, as the saga tells us. One of life's unsolved mysteries is how he reconciled his missionary activity with the commandment 'Thou shalt not kill'. What is clear is that he was regarded as a saint after his death, and is always called Saint Olav in Norway. The number of statues unveiled in his honour increases, and a play is performed each year in his memory at Stiklestad in Trøndelag, where he was slain in battle. Olsok, 29 July, is commemorated as a special day in his honour.

Before we leave the Vikings it is only fair to mention the good things about them: their excellent laws, their trading activities, their skill in boatbuilding and in fashioning beautiful ornaments, which are still being discovered. Not long ago an extraordinary treasure trove of Viking jewels was literally turned up from under a stone in Grimstad in south Norway.

The country's modern history dates from 1814. Norway was united as one kingdom shortly before the year 900, and flourished in the high Middle Ages – politically, culturally and economically. From 1537 to 1814 Norway was subject to Danish sovereignty, with severe consequences for our language, social organization and history. We gained our independence on 17 May 1814, but only conditionally: we were forced into a union with Sweden and acquired a Swedish king. The nineteenth century was a century of nationalism for Norway.

The rebellious young poetic genuis Henrik Wergeland, who was

Lithograph of Bergen from about 1800.

described as tall, broad-shouldered, red-cheeked, often on horseback, often drunk, argumentative and fanatical, put all his energy into promoting our independence. He Norwegianized the language, and challenged the king of Sweden by introducing the celebration of 17 May.

P. Chr. Asbjørnsen and Jørgen Moe, following the example of the Brothers Grimm in Germany, collected Norwegian folk tales, and the grammarian Ivar Aasen formed the New Norwegian written language based on Norwegian dialects, an antidote to the dominant Danish language. Artists such as J. C. Dahl, Adolph Tidemand and Hans Gude painted in what has been termed the 'national Romantic' style.

In the political field the left-wing party of the day — *Venstre* — was organized to fight for Norwegian independence and for an extension of suffrage, at that time restricted to professional and wealthy people. The parliamentary system was introduced in 1884; one man one vote in 1898; one woman one vote in 1913. By then the struggle for independence had borne fruit. On the 7 June 1905 Norway became independent of Sweden and chose her own king, the Danish Prince Carl, who took the name Haakon VII.

In this century Norwegian political life has to a great degree been dominated by the struggle for a just distribution of social benefits. The influence of the Left gave way to that of the Labour Party, *Arbeiderpartiet*, which after leaving a somewhat revolutionary past behind it, at least on paper, took office in 1935 in a more or less forced coalition with the Agrarian Party, *Bondepartiet*.

Norway kept out of the First World War, but was occupied by the Germans in the Second. A startled Norwegian people had to stand by and watch an unprepared country being invaded by a force of 10,000 Germans, increasing to 400,000 in the next five years, blasting their way into rocks and cliffs and turning the whole of Norway into a fortress — *Festung Norwegen*.

The small Nazi party (*Nasjonal Samling*) had never had any real influence, yet on the evening of 9 April 1940, the people of Norway heard on their radio an oddly awkward and feeble voice attempting to sound masterful and resolute announcing that the Norwegian Nazi Party had taken over the government of Norway. With this act of usurpation the speaker gave a new name to the concept of treason in all languages: quisling.

Vidkun Quisling, clergyman's son and politician, is still something of a mystery to the Norwegian people. He was undoubtedly of brilliant intelligence, but a fanatic and a dreamer. As a young man he had worked for Fridtjof Nansen providing aid to refugees in Russia, and at the beginning of the 30s he had been minister of defence in the Agrarian Party government. In 1933 he founded the Norwegian Nazi Party. His hour of triumph came in 1940, though he had to play second fiddle all through the war to Hitler's *Reichskommisar für die besetzen Norwegischen Gebiete*, Joseph Terboven, banker and *gauleiter*, who had had the honour of having Hitler as best man at his wedding. Quisling was installed as 'Minister President', though he preferred the German-style *Fører*, and expended great energy in ineffectual efforts to coerce the Norwegian people into embracing Nazism. The king and the country's lawful government went into exile, and took up their position against the Germans from London. At home a clandestine military resistance army, the Home Front, was gradually built up, while the man in the street had his own ways of showing resistance to the occupier. Haakon VII's insignia, a red woollen cap *(nisselua)*, and a paper-clip on the lapel were small pinpricks against the occupying forces, yet they found their mark: "From my experience of working in a bank I know that one uses paper clips to fasten documents that one wishes to lay aside. The act of wearing paper clips seems to me to be one of cutting truth: the ex-king and his exile government are in truth stapled together and laid aside!" These were the words of *Reichskommisar* Terboven in his 1 May speech in 1941.

Radios were confiscated, the press was 'Nazified', and stringent food rationing introduced. Some 1,700 Norwegians were killed and wounded in the fighting of 1940. Altogether 10,000 men and women lost their lives at home or abroad in the Second World War. In addition 27,000 Russians died in Norway, either during the liberation of the north of Norway in 1944, or as prisoners of war in German camps. In 1942, 5,000 Yugoslavs were deported by the German Nazis to Norway; only 1,700 survived.

There are more than 20 Yugoslav war cemeteries in Norway, of which the largest is in Botn in Nordland, where 1,657 are buried.

Around 40,000 Norwegians were imprisoned during the war, 19,000 of them in Grini, the prison camp near Oslo, while 8,000 were deported to Germany and German-occupied countries. Among these were Trygve Bratteli and Einar Gerhardsen, later to become prime ministers. Half the prisoners died in captivity. Very few Norwegian Jews survived the war. Altogether 366 Norwegians were executed in Norway and Germany.

Many towns and villages were burnt to the ground, and the entire counties of North Troms and Finnmark were devastated as part of the Germans' scorched-earth policy. The inhabitants were forcibly evacuated south, but 23,000 defied the order and stayed behind, many hiding in caves.

The post-war trials were conducted in a calm manner, and the severity of the punishments diminished with time. The Nazi Party had 55,000 members, 46,000 of whom were later punished for treason. Twelve German and 25 Norwegian Nazis were executed. One of these was Quisling. The German *Reichskommisar* Joseph Terboven committed suicide at Skaugum, the residence of the Norwegian crown prince that he had occupied. Capital punishment has since been abolished in Norway.

Around 9,000 children were born of German fathers in Norway during the war. It was not until the 1980s that they dared to come out publicly and organize themselves. Their mothers had their heads shaved in the chaotic outbreak of peace in May 1945.

Present-day Norway is still characterized by a social democratic way of thinking which has its roots in the lean 30s and also in the spirit of co-operation that went into rebuilding Norway after the war. The former road worker Prime Minister Einar Gerhardsen went straight to the hearts of the Norwegian people with his sober life-style and speech of the common man. Ola Nordmann was proud when he read in the paper that the prime minister and his wife had been spotted on their summer holiday in Italy – in a small tent on a camp-site.

From 1935 until 1963 Norway had a succession of Labour governments, interrupted only by the war. Since 1963 the Labour Party has alternated in office with the Conservatives (in coalition). However, the Conservatives have moved closer to Labour, and Labour closer to the right, so that it is becoming difficult to distinguish between the two major parties. The great period of egalitarianism has made its impact. People no longer address each other by the formal *De*, but use the familiar *du*. The title *Herr* seems to be used by Norwegians as a term of polite abuse.

Some feel the authorities have too much say in regulating the smallest detail of people's lives, but that seems to be an inherited failing among Norwegians. The central authorities have delegated much decision-making, and the country is divided into 18 counties and 454 boroughs, Oslo being both county and borough. The Storting (Parliament) has 165 members, and usually works in plenary sessions, but for certain legislative matters is divided into two chambers, the larger Odelsting and the smaller Lagting.

Each Friday the king meets with the cabinet, which means that ministers make their decisions in the presence of the king. He himself has no political power, but plays an important role as a unifying symbol.

Unlike her neighbours, Norway has never had a large aristocracy, and since 1821 the nobility has been abolished. The first aristocracy was established in the Middle Ages, but died out partly because of the Black Death, partly because a large number became yeoman farmers. A new aristocracy arose in the seventeenth century, many of whose members were descended from Fru Inger of Østraat in Trøndelag, the lady about whom Ibsen wrote a play. A few were elevated to the peerage through their property: Count Ulrik Frederik Gyldenløve of Laurvigen (Larvik), Count Peder Griffenfeldt of Tunsberg (later Jarlsberg), and Baron Ludvig Rosenkrantz of Rosendal in Sunnhordaland, south of Bergen. The family seats at Larvik and Rosendal are now museums, while the manor at Jarlsberg is lived in and run by the eleventh generation of the family in direct line from the first owner. There are still some great landowners, one of them being Harald Løvenskiold' who owns an extensive part of the enormous forest area around Oslo, Nordmarka.

In recent years a new 'aristocracy' has emerged, veritable dynasties of politicians, not least from within the Labour Party. There is also an accumulation of power in the Trades Union Congress (LO – *Landsorganisasjonen*), which has 35 unions and around 870,000 members. Its counterparts, the employers in industry and crafts, have recently amalgamated their organizations into the NHO *(Næringslivets Hovedorganisasjon)*, comprising 1,500 companies and 425,000 employees. However, wage settlements are often left to the politicians.

The international student revolt of 1968 had a strong impact on Norway, less perhaps because of the importance of its main instigator, the small Maoist Communist Party, AKP-ml, than because of the overreaction of the Conservative press! Whatever the cause, Norway experienced an upsurge of radicalization in the 1970s and early 80s, a spate of labour disputes and demonstrations. Women, pro-abortionists, gays and environmentalists hurled themselves into the fray, battling for their rights, while blue- and white-collar workers, even the clergy, put forward pay claims. There was also the biggest farmers' demonstration ever.

The law declaring homosexuality illegal was repealed in 1972. In 1981 Norway became the first country in the world to pass a law banning discrimination on the grounds of religion, race or sexual proclivity. Gays have their own organization, the Norwegian Federation of 1948. Yet it is one thing to clamp down on overt discrimination, less easy to root out covert discrimination. There was great consternation in the 1980s when a prominent Conservative female politician came out openly as the lover of the woman who was Secretary General of the Norwegian Federation of 1948. She was not re-elected to Parliament. As in other countries, gays are deeply involved in the AIDS debate. By September 1990, 176 cases of AIDS had been registered in Norway; 122 of these have died.

If we are to sum up the main events of post-war Norway, we are left with four dates. In 1949 Norway became a member of NATO after plans failed for a Scandinavian defence union. No passports are required when travelling between the Nordic countries, there is a common labour market, mutual social security schemes, and a considerable reduction of tariffs between the countries. But that is the full extent of the co-operation. On the whole developments have been slow. By 1987 they had, for instance, not been able to come to an agreement on a common Nordic TV-satellite.

The second event, in 1967, attracted less attention, but was of great importance for the individual. A national pensions scheme was intro-duced, the greatest single social reform in our history. Its aim was to give Norwegians security from cradle to grave, and 20 years later it was to provide the main means of subsistence for one quarter of the population.

On 23 December 1969, the first workable oil well was discovered in the North Sea, and Ola Nordmann turned into an oil sheik.

Lastly, on 22 September 1972, a referendum decided against Nor-way becoming a member of the European Economic Community. This issue split the nation into two camps, forcing every level of argument into the field and causing enmity between brother and brother, father and son. It is understandable that until the end of the 80s, the Norwe-gians avoided any further discussion of the matter. But at the beginning of the 90s, the European connection is again the hottest political ques-tion. And maybe the mood has changed, so that Norway in a few years may seek EC membership.

It may fairly be said of the post-war period that things have moved in an evolutionary rather than a revolutionary way. Having completed reconstruction work, Norway developed a mania for centralization. Any opportunity to amalgamate was seized; farms, schools, boroughs, banks, dairies, private companies and public institutions were formed into larger units. Thousands of small children had to be picked up by bus rather than walk to the nearest village school. Thousands of workers had to commute long distances to get to work. The country has altogether changed course from one that was socialist-inspired to one that is more purely capitalist and profit-oriented.

There has been liberalization within the domains of the media, licensing laws and the health service. One of the most hotly debated issues of the past decade has been privatization of the public health service. Norway must surely be said to have one of the world's best health services, aiming to treat everyone alike, regardless of status. Any complaints put forward about our health service would seem absurd to someone in Cochabamba or Calcutta. Yet while hospital queues are growing and some hospitals have so little money that they refuse to take in new patients, no politician dares to raise the level of taxation to solve the welfare crisis.

Norway's Social Democrats still call their party the Labour Party, unlike their fellows in Sweden and Denmark. The trouble is that real labourers are not so thick on the ground: they have all turned into consultants, shop assistants and computer salesmen.

The benefits have been reaped, the welfare state is more or less a reality, and the country finds itself at a crossroads.

THE LAND

CHAPTER THREE tells of the amazing variety of our beautiful countryside and how people from Sunnmøre put their money in the bank, while those living in the north invest theirs in Danish pastries.

We don't want to sound boastful, but we must say that the Norwegian landscape is unique. It is so wild, so unspoilt (well, up to a point...) and so varied! There is continuous change, from the wide farmlands of Trøndelag, and east Norway with its large well-kept farms surrounded by dark threatening forests, to the sheltered idyllic Sørlandet; from the wind-blown shores of Jæren, via the towering mountains and plummeting fjords of the west to the weatherbeaten coast of the north with small fishing villages clinging to the rock face; while as a last outpost to the east lie the mighty wastes of Finnmark, wrapped in the dark of total night – or lit by the midnight sun.

As varied as the landscape is the population, even though the last decades have seen a sad tendency towards centralization. "Rural Norway is in the process of turning into a lanky thinly-populated town, while Oslo is a big city whose face is spotty with puberty," declared the Grand Old Man of Norwegian poetry, Rolf Jacobsen, on his eightieth birthday in 1987.

South Norway is divided lengthwise by Langfjellene (literally the Long Mountains), and crosswise by Dovrefjell. These Norwegian mountains are extremely hard. Indeed Dovre is the very symbol of the Norwegian bedrock. 'Faithful, and of one accord, until Dovre fall' was the motto of our political forebears who gathered in 1814 to found the Constitution.

East Norway is a country of long, sloping valleys, large parishes, and forests that stretch deep into Sweden. Here, as elsewhere, primary industries have given way to service industries, tourism and commercial enterprise. Yet this in the land of the big farmers, and the part of the country with the most marked class differences.

Small towns are dotted along the coast of the Oslo fjord, for the south (Sørlandet) is especially the holiday paradise of Norway, with its unique archipelago, skerries and creeks. This is traditionally an outgoing part of the world; that is, the men go to sea, while the women stay home and look after the house. And yet the south and the west have the reputation of being the most puritanical areas, with their chapels, temperance movements and religious dissenters. This may of course be changing, but the myth remains, and when the state television wants someone to put forward ultra-conservative views, they inevitably find someone from the south.

More stones must have been picked up from the Jæren plain than anywhere else in Norway, and the farmer from Jæren is reckoned to be the country's most painstaking. Today he also makes money from oil, as Rogaland and particularly Stavanger is the main base for the Norwegian oil industry.

The landscape up the west coast must be the most beautiful we have, with long stretches of fjord feeling their way inland under perpendicular rock faces where small farms have maintained a precarious foothold through the ages. You can still see these dwellings in Geirangerfjorden, where all the cruise ships pass. Today most of them are deserted. The French officer Jacques de la Tocnaye tells us in his journal of 1799, *Promenade en Norvège*, what it was like to live in the west:

"On small shelves 700 to 800 feet in the air we see farms which are only accessible if you first climb vertically up a 30- to 40-foot ladder and then clamber up the rocks. The ladder descends straight into the sea, and is firmly attached, so that you can moor your boat to it. With some amazement one notes animals grazing on these shelves, even cows that can only have been conveyed up there as sucking calves on the back of their owner. Bishop Pontoppidan must be right when he relates how a coffin has to be lowered by rope for a burial."

Roads that can be used even in winter have been built across the mountains from east to west, shielded by snow screens and with numerous tunnels. Yet every winter the radio makes announcements about blocked roads and snowed-in cars. Even the Bergen train gets stuck on the Finse plateau between Oslo and Bergen.

The roads have been straightened wherever possible. But take your car up the Trollstigen road in Romsdal or down the old zig-zag route in Måbødalen in Hardanger, and you will get some idea of what it was like to be a driver in Norway in the infancy of the motorcar. It was in these parts that drivers from flat Denmark looked around for locals to take their place at the wheel!

It may be true that Norway is in the process of becoming one continuous town, as our great poet expressed it, and Oslo is certainly in its puberty: '... that strange city no one escapes from until it has left its mark on him...' as Knut Hamsun wrote in his first novel *Hunger* in the days when the town was still called Christiania. While Copenhagen with its 100,000 citizens in 1800 and Stockholm with 75,000 were reckoned among the great cities of the Continent, Oslo with its population of 12,000 was still a hamlet, a Lilliput on the outskirts of Europe. Today the city has 450,000 citizens and, though still provincial, it has gained an international touch here and there. Immigrants from the Third World run small corner stores — the ones Norwegians closed as unprofitable, and the main street, Karl Johan, is now changed beyond recognition with seething life, musicians and street vendors. As the capital city, Oslo is the seat of the most important institutions: Parliament, government offices, the lawcourts and the royal palace.

In recent times, the capital has been trying to emulate Manhattan by constructing oversized modern buildings in central commercial areas, like Aker Brygge and Grønland/Vaterland. But still it has charm. In the core of the city lies the quadrangular grid of streets founded by the

29. Varden, high above Molde, offers a magnificent view of the town, and the 87 mountain peaks that form the Romsdal Alps on the other side of the fjord. (Husmo-Foto)

30. Stavanger, Norway's oil capital, has old waterfront houses that conceal restaurants and modern boutiques behind their quaint façades. (Husmo-Foto) ▷

31. The Nidaros Cathedral in Trondheim, built between 1100 and 1300, was an important site of pilgrimage in medieval Europe. (Husmo-Foto) ▷ ▷

42. In November the sun can still be
seen on the mountains around
Hammerfest, before winter darkness
descends on this town, the most
northerly in the world. (O. Åsheim/
Samfoto)

43. Ålesund on the west coast is
above all a fishing community. After
a big fire in 1904, the centre was
rebuilt in Art Noveau style. (T. Bølstad/
Samfoto)

44. Norway's southern coast usually
has quite mild winters, but sometimes
a spell of cold weather may cause
trouble for seagoing traffic, as here in
the harbour of Risør. (M. Løberg/
Samfoto)

45

45. The old city bridge with its distinctive 'portals' connects the two halves of Trondheim, on either side of the river Nidelva. (Husmo-Foto)

46. Arendal is a busy seaside town and a centre for cruising and holidaying on the sunny south coast of Norway. (Mittet)

47. The Nidaros Cathedral in Trondheim, the largest medieval building in Scandinavia. Before the Refcrmation in 1536, it was the seat of an archbishop. (Husmo-Foto) ▷

48. Molde is known as the city of roses, and the 'Rose Girl', by sculptress Ragnhild Butenschøn, has her basket filled with golden roses in summertime. Large parts of the town were destroyed during the war (in 1940), so that Molde today has much modern architecture, like the church in the background. (Husmo-Foto) ▷ ▷

49. Along the sounds and inlets under the jagged peaks of the Lofoten mountains nestle small fishing communities with characteristic old houses. (R. Frislid/NN) ▷ ▷ ▷

Danish-Norwegian Renaissance monarch Christian IV, whose name the city bore for so long. Since those days Oslo has steadily expanded, eating up the surrounding fields in the last century, and now extending its suburbs well into neighbouring boroughs. You get out there by underground and local trains, but don't lose heart if no one talks to you! Not that Oslo dwellers are slow and taciturn. It's just that they bear in them a dream of forests and lonely mountain spaces that they try to relive as often as they can.

And they do have the opportunity, for the city is surrounded by extensive and wonderful woodland, in fact one of the largest areas of forest in Norway. People use this forestland, Nordmarka or Marka, both summer and winter. On a fine day there can be over 100,000 people in Nordmarka; in winter they take the train to the northern edge of the forest and ski the 40 to 50 kilometres (25 to 30 miles) home. Nordmarka is sacred to Oslo-dwellers with its thousands of snow crystals glittering against the winter light, its birdsong fading in the pale summer nights, the blue anemones of spring, or when Nature puts on her glowing autumn garments. When hydroelectric developers wanted to lay their hands on Marka in 1946, 40,000 people protested in front of the City Hall — and they won!

But is it not rainy Bergen that is Norway's number one city — at least according to people from Bergen? "I'm not from Norway; I'm from Bergen" they sing in their characteristic dialect. So what is Bergen? It is Bryggen, the Wharf — its earlier name, German Wharf, was dropped in 1945 after the occupation, though it dates from the Hanseatic time. With its wooden buildings in a style unchanged since the Middle Ages, it is a collection of intriguing small houses that creep up the hillsides. It is a city of extraordinary military bands of small boys (*Buekorpsene*) that march out with wooden guns and awake the town with drumbeats every Sunday morning. Bergen is the city under the seven hills, with the waters of Puddefjorden and Vågen stretching right up to the fish market. For it was fish that made the town, dried fish from the north that was shipped on from Bergen. Bergen was one of the most important Hanseatic towns, a relic of which is the large number of foreign names.

Trondheim, too, has an aura of history. An ancient site of pilgrimage, it was the seat of an archbishopric that covered Norway, the Hebrides and the Isle of Man, the Orkney and Shetland Islands, Iceland and Greenland. Scandinavia's most magnificent cathedral, Nidarosdomen, is a monument to this. High in the air like a pinnacled saint stands Olav Tryggvason, founder of the town and brutal missionary. His later descendant, Olav Haraldson, did actually become a saint, and is the reason for all the pilgrimages. Like Bergen, Trondheim is a university town, especially proud of its technological university. Trondheim and Bergen compete for the position of second most important city of Norway.

And now to north Norway. To any one from the south this seems an infinite distance away. Just take a look at the map. When you get to Bodø, you're only half-way up. You have to lay four maps of Denmark in a row to get from Trondheim in mid-Norway to Kirkenes furthest north-east.

Most 'southerners' know little about north Norway. They may have been to the Canaries or Majorca, but it's unlikely they will have visited Neiden or Brøstadbotn. Which is a pity, for the north has scenery as wild and as unexpected as that of the west. One of the greatest experiences is

50. A granite lion guards the building of the Storting, Norway's national assembly. (Husmo-Foto)

to travel by the coastal express (*Hurtigruta*) and see the cliff face of Lofoten rising sheer above Vestfjorden. It is by following the coastline that you can see how Norway was made. The coast will give you proof of the Norwegians' amazing ability to find a foothold in the smallest cracks. Wherever there is a few spare feet of beachline under a rock face, you can be sure someone has staked his claim to it and planted his state-mortgaged house. There, with his fishing-smack, he abandons himself to the sea and his own devices, the fog-horn and the lighthouse beam.

Along the whole coastline there are lighthouses guiding ships to safety. Yet the lighthouse keeper is a disappearing breed, and now only 65 out of Norway's 200 lighthouses are manned. When the rationalization programme is completed, there will be even fewer. Even the horn, background music to seafaring people on foggy nights, is threatened in our age of advanced technology.

There are 33 lifeboats ready to go out to ships in distress. These have been paid for with money raised through sales and raffles by a thousand organizations working voluntarily for the Life Boat Society throughout Norway.

The north Norwegian journalist, Arthur Arntzen, said something very beautiful about life on the north Norwegian coast when interviewed by the Oslo paper *Aftenposten*:

"As a journalist I have on a couple of occasions found myself present in a fishing village when boats with five or six men have gone down. But grief takes a strange shape in these outlying places. It is not hysterical. There is a calmness in grief in places like this. I noticed there were no tears over losing a son or a father. As if they accepted that his days were over – that what had been had been good. This uprightness and firmness is perhaps learnt from living close to the sea and the mighty forces of nature. So unlike town . . ."

He also said something about another side of the northerner, his amazingly inventive language, something the writer Knut Hamsun took south. If you take the oaths away from a northerner, you take half his language, Arntzen said.

The north is not without cities. There is Hammerfest, the northern-most town in the world. And there is Tromsø, the 'Paris of the North', the liveliest town in Norway, with its marvellous people, its university, its famous Mack beer, and its Arctic cathedral. There is, of course, the tundra where reindeer feed, and where the Såmi pitch camp, but you also find more gentle wooded landscapes in this wild territory, in the Pasvik Valley on the Russian border, or in Målselv or Bardufoss in Troms. Then you have extraordinary natural phenomena such as the Torghatten mountain with a hole in it, and the Moskenes whirlpool, the mælstrom described by both Edgar Allan Poe and Jules Verne.

There is also Nordkapp, the most northerly plateau in the world, visited yearly by some 100,000 tourists who want to see the midnight sun. Weather permitting! On 1 July 1987, there was a snowstorm on Nordkapp. Unfortunately the Norwegian sense of inferiority has man-ifested itself here too. With the south already overrun by holiday parks with dinosaurs, Gullivers and Donald Duck shows, it seems that the Scandinavian mega-corporations, SAS and Kosmos, decided that Nord-kapp wasn't selling properly. They therefore blasted out some hundred tons of rock to make way for restaurants and other facilities. One of these is a huge screen, curved 200 degrees, where Nordkapp can be artificaly experienced in 3D and stereo sound. There is also a grotto and a tunnel that leads to a 10-metre-wide (33-foot) panoramic window of the sea. From Nordkapp the tourists can link up directly with America's number one amusement park in Florida – via a Walt Disney satellite. "They have ruined everything," said a German tourist, who wept when he saw what was being done to Nordkapp in 1987. In 1990 an extensive area of the plateau was turned into a parking lot, where hundreds of his compatriots, video-cameras made ready, sleep in their campers, waiting for the midnight sun. But the northerner lets these things happen, even when the authorities ask him to stay away from the North Cape so as not to disturb the tourists!

"The northerner is Norway's dreamer and fantast, the one who cuts a dash. I wonder whether he is not in many ways the incarnation of the soul of Norway? When a *Sunnmøring* comes home after a trip to the fishing grounds, he has earned 400 kroner. He puts 400 kroner in the bank. When a northener comes home from a fishing trip, he has earned 200 kroner. He spends 20 on a silk scarf for his sweetheart, and the rest on Danish pastries! His personal motto is: 'One must have a little enjoyment in life'."

This is taken from the 1965 novel *Rubicon* by one of Norway's most translated post-war novelists, Agnar Mykle. Coming from a Sunnmøre family from the west and having lived in the north, he ought to know what he is talking about.

People from Sunnmøre are said to be the most industrious in

Medieval stave church, Borgund, western Norway.

Norway. Who else would dream of starting a furniture industry in a part of the world where hardly a tree grows? Meanwhile the northerners keep up the myth of the pastries. North Norway has always been dependent on the south. In olden days the fishermen of the north had to sell their catch in Bergen. The Frenchman Jacques de la Tocnaye described the results of this a couple of centuries ago:

"The tradesmen are skilful at tempting them, and never let them go home without a hefty debt, and as they buy everything on credit, this can mount up to 20,000 rix-dollars (a silver coin worth 4 kroner). As security they stake their farms with live and dead stock, thus putting themselves entirely in the power of the tradespeople. These take care to renew the loans, so that the fishermen never become free."

It is the people from Sunnmøre who make the profit from the fish in the north — at least according to the fishermen from the north. Our present fisheries policy is formed in the east to benefit the west. Western Norway has built up a large sea-going fishing fleet, while the man from Finnmark sticks close to the shore with his hand-held line and lead sinker. Finnmark has once more become a crofting community compared with the rich west country, they say.

Not only that. North Norway is becoming depopulated. The drop of 10,000 in the region's population in the last five years alone is the largest since the nineteenth century. In Finnmark there are 1,000 fewer people each year. This hurts in a county with only 75,000 inhabitants.

It is essential to keep up the population of the north because of the fish and the possible oil resources in the Barents Sea. Much political debate in recent years has been concerned with how to stop the population drifting away. Newpapers in the south are continually refer-ring to the lack of skilled persons in the north. We hear about all the vacant teaching jobs in secondary schools, about police constables being posted north to Vardø, and about the only doctor in Berlevåg 'escaping' from the strain.

It is indeed quite a transition for someone from, say, Toten, to become parish priest in Loppa, an island right out in the Arctic Ocean. Toten is reputed to be the most introspective and inbred place in Norway. 'Damn Norway – long live Toten' is the stock saying. On Loppa Bård Jahr Pettersen has to cater for the spiritual welfare of a parish that is spread over 11 hamlets, many of them accessible only by boat. There are seven churches in the parish and he has to conduct 112 church services, 20 funerals, up to 10 weddings and the confirmation of 50 young souls. One church service can take as long as 11 hours with the journey there and back.

Many suggestions have been made for political solutions to the north Norway question, and a number of 'Finnmark Deals' have been launched to provide decent conditions for the population. Some say taxation should be removed, others say that more should be spent on aid for regional development. Some occupational groups already receive state support – health workers, teachers and administrators – but not the girls who slice fillets of cod in icy rooms. And what Finnmark really needs is girls – girls and people with education. Many feel that the main priority should be education and research. There is a tendency for people who study in the region to stay there.

The tradition of the south providing aid to the north is a venerable one. Under a bequest made in 1621 by a clergyman's wife, Ingeborg Mikkeldatter, 500 kilos (1,100 pounds) of flour were to be handed out to the poor and needy of Øksnes every Christmas in perpetuity, bought with the interest on the 300 old Norwegian dollars she left as a legacy. These 500 kilos of flour are still being sent to Nordland from Vaksdal Mills in Bergen!

The local government minister in 1987, William Engseth, is from the north himself, but told the northerners to stop moaning and groaning. He says that the north is a land of opportunity, but its people must have the sense to make use of their resources, investing in fishing, fish farms, minerals and tourism. The air is clean and there is plenty of hunting and fishing. He does not think that the plans for the north should be drawn up by people sitting in Oslo, but that they should be made on the northerners' own terms. And he thinks it is nonsense to believe anyone will establish themselves on a rock in the north for 50 weeks a year in order to lie on a Mediterranean beach for two weeks. He was here referring to the Soviet practice of using free holidays in the south to tempt people to move to the Kola Peninsula, where they also receive higher wages and better housing than their compatriots in more central regions. The result is that the population in the north of the Soviet Union has increased. Today there are almost a million people living on the Kola Peninsula, 450,000 of them in Murmansk, the large Arctic city near the border with Finnmark.

Today many people in Finnmark want to build a 40-kilometre (25-mile) railway line from Kirkenes to the Soviet industrial city Nikel, which is connected by rail to the rest of the Soviet Union. Nikel (population 300,000) is easily visible from the hills in the Pasvik Valley. There is already lorry traffic between the two towns. Kirkenes intends to invest heavily in increased trade with the U.S.S.R.

The town also wants to take on ship repairs for the Russians. The linchpin of industry in Kirkenes is the state-owned mining company A/S Sydvaranger, now in danger of being closed down, as it is proving too costly to extract the necessary iron ore. A/S Sydvaranger has therefore partly amalgamated with the giant Finnish shipyard Wärtilä and started KIMEK, the engineering works at Kirkenes, which aims at having the Soviet fleet as its main customer. The Russians certainly have enough ships to repair if you count all their fishing vessels, ice-breakers and floating oil installations.

This is Norway, from east to west, north to south, wilderness and waste, oil kingdom and city. You can reach it all, by car and boat, by train

Medieval farm drawn by Ken Ole Moen after excavations in Handøy, northern Norway.

or plane. There are 4,200 kilometres (2,600 miles) of railway from Oslo to Stavanger, Bergen and Bodø. The Nordland railway is planned to reach Harstad, but is unlikely ever to get there. The country has 85,000 kilometres (53,000 miles) of public road — 50 times the length of the country stretched out. This road network includes 225 car ferries. Norway is the land of the car ferry: many memories of summer holidays include long waits in narrow fjords, with refreshments from the ice-cream shop and children on the quay selling baskets of freshly picked strawberries and cherries. Some 50 million passengers a year travel by boat in Norway, and 45 million of them are car ferry passengers. The others take small boats to outlying islands and into fjords where there are no roads.

Annually, 275,000 passengers sail on the *Hurtigruta*, the coastal express. This is an adventure in itself! 'The world's most beautiful coastal route' takes you from Bergen to Kirkenes through narrow straits and over the open sea, past rocky islands and cliffs, stopping at 36 ports of call, summer and winter. Before air travel this was the only year-round southbound route. Today airways have brought the northern region closer to the capital and to the Continent — if you can afford to fly. Less than five per cent of the total Norwegian passenger transport in 1984 was airborne.

If the Norwegian mainland has not satisfied your need for wild countryside, there are still the islands to the north, although it is hardly desirable to expand tourist activity in those areas. 'Svalbard discovered' was reported by the Icelanders in 1194, and since 1925 Norway has had sovereignty over this island in the Barents Sea.

The Svalbard Treaty, with around 40 nations as signatories, opened the island to development and enterprise from nations other than Norway. Today Russians and Norwegians both have coalmines on Svalbard, living there without much communication. The Norwegians' main base is Longyearbyen, where the midnight sun shines from April, and where there is a school and a hospital, a flight to Norway two or three times a week, and satellite radio, television and telephone. In 1985 there were 1,386 Norwegians on Svalbard, 2,549 Russians, 11 Poles, and eight of other nationalities. The Russians are based in Barentsburg.

Though not publicized, there is tourism on Svalbard, including ski scooter trips in temperatures as low as minus 35 °C, and the limited accommodation of the Norwegian mining company has up to 70,000 guest nights. People also stay through the winter on the meteorological stations on the other islands besides Svalbard: Jan Mayen, Bjørnøya (Bear Island) and Hopen. Every Christmas the newspapers telephone from the mainland to find out if the Christmas mail has arrived and to get stories about 'overwinterers' who have had to use frying-pans to ward off polar bears trying to break into their huts. There have been 50 serious confrontations between polar bears and humans since the polar bear became a protected species in 1973. Svalbard is the only place in Norway where rabies has been registered, carried by the Arctic fox, reindeer and seals, though not by polar bears. There are at least 10,000 Arctic foxes on the island.

There are those who dream of Svalbard turning into a kind of Arctic centre, with two international airports, a Hilton hotel, oil and gaspipes to the mainland, and a permanent road linking the two island 'metropolises'. This is likely to remain a dream. Unless, of course, someone from Sunnmøre does something about it.

THE SÅMI

CHAPTER FOUR is the story of how the Norwegians conquered Lappland, and how the Såmi miraculously managed to salvage some of their cultural identity.

I confess I am a Såmi, said one of the participants at a conference of Coast Såmi in Finnmark in 1982. Confess! This reveals the full extent of the discrimination against the Såmi; this proves the success of the majority in oppressing them; this shows how long the Norwegians had been telling them they belonged to an inferior race. And yet there was promise in the word. He did confess rather than deny he was a Såmi, as his people had done for so long to avoid discrimination.

The Såmi language still lives! To a Norwegian it is an exciting experience to hear children chattering in Såmi in the streets of the village of Kautokeino. You get the feeling of being among the Quechua Indians in an Andean village, let's say in Appillapampa in Bolivia!

Three tribes meet in the north: the Såmi (Lapps), the Finns and the Norwegians. No-one has yet traced a connection between the Komsa people who lived in Finnmark 10,000 years ago and the population of Finnmark today, yet of the three races, it was most likely the Såmi who came first.

They appear in the writings of the Roman historian Tacitus in the year A.D. 100. The north Norwegian chieftain Ottar of Helgeland related in the ninth century how he collected taxes from the Lapps in the north. Exploitation can be traced back a long way. So can the first of many derogatory descriptions that were to pursue them through the ages:

"Even in the summer there is much snow, and just as they do not differ much from wild beasts in judgement, nor do they eat anything but the raw flesh of wild animals. They make their clothing of skins." This was written by the Lombard historian Paul around the year 800.

They were an independent people, living in their own country, Såmiid Ædnan, and they knew no boundaries. Within their own territory they had their own little communities, or *siida*, consisting of 40 to 300 people. There were enormous common lands for hunting and fishing open to all. They lived under skies that compelled a mystic worship of nature, with the glowing sun pursuing them from around the horizon all summer, but disappearing in winter and leaving them in darkness on the endless tundra, alone with the silence, the wolf howls and the fantastic, ever-changing northern lights, the cold and biting snowstorms, and the sea that beats more fiercely against the east coast of Finnmark than most

51. The U-shaped valleys and fjords were carved out by ice, and glaciers still hang above the narrow valleys. This is the famous Briksdalsbreen at Olden in Njordfjord. (Husmo-Foto)

other places in the world. Even the coastal express sometimes has to seek harbour.

This was the life of the Lapps, hunters and fishermen, at one with nature, at peace with their gods. The rivers and fjords were teeming with fish, cloudberries grew on the ground, and the reindeer grazed on the tundra, finding their own summer and winter pastures — they were not yet tamed.

No-one knows the origin of the Lapps or Såmi. In their own mythical tradition, as told by the Såmi author Ailo Gaup, the Sun's daughter was the mother of the sons of the sons of the Sun, the heroes of legend. From the sons of the Sun descended the shaman of the *siida*, the *noiade*, priest and medicine man of the village, wise man and healer, conjuring up spirits with his supernatural powers. He officiated at the animal sacrifices that were made outdoors in front of a sacred stone, the *sieidia*, or a carved wooden deity. Able to speak to the spirits, he could get in touch with ancestors and bring feritility, good reindeer pasture, good hunting and plentiful fish. The *noiade* of the Såmi was akin to the Tadiber of the Samoyeds, the Angakod of the Inouits, and the medicine man of the North American Indian tribes. The Såmi had many gods: for birth and well-being, for the heavens, and for the air. The *noiade* had two aids when worshipping: the monotone chant — the *joik* — and the runic drum — *runebommen*.

The *joik* was originally a religious song and formed part of the identity of the Såmi, each person having his own separate *joik*. The runic drum could be as large as three metres (10 feet) across and was inscribed with the entire cosmology of the Såmi: the gods in their universe, the humans in theirs, the sun, the moon, the stars, and the tundra. When the *noiade* beat the drum he used a piece of reindeer antler and some antler figures, which he laid on top of the drumskin. His prophecies were based on the way the antler figures performed during the drumming. To get properly into contact with the spirits, he had to work himself up into a state of ecstasy. The name of the solar deity was Bæivve, and the symbol of the sun was in the centre of the runic drum. Fire sacrifices were also made to the sun. There were many manifestations of solar worship, something that is perfectly comprehensible to anyone who has experienced the Finnmark tundra by midnight sun.

Right up to recent times there has been a strong fear of the Såmi's magic powers, of his sorcerer's arts, his ability to cast a spell over 'both Weather and Water', as the poet and clergyman Peter Dass wrote in his *Nordland Trumpet* in the seventeenth century.

Less than enchanted with the Såmi culture were their neighbours. The Norwegians were only there for the material benefits of the north, the furs and the fish, the feathers, the eider-down, and the game. More and more Norwegians moved north and were joined by Swedes and Finns, Karelians and Russians. They brought with them taxation, trade, colonization and a demand for territory.

Many came carrying a Bible. The Lapp religion was looked upon as idolatry and devil-worship, and Christianity was imposed by law. The death penalty was prescribed for Lapps who would not give up their religion, and their shamans, the *noiades*, could be burnt at the stake for refusing to convert.

In the eighteenth century, the 'Apostle of Finnmark', Thomas von Westen, carried out his inquisition of the Lapps, burning their altars and destroying the runic drums. A missionary in the Lofoten Islands burnt 40

52. New types of sport have reached the Norwegian mountains in winter, for instance, paragliding by means of snow scooters. The picture is from Tyin in the Jotunheim mountain massif. (Husmo-Foto) ▷

53

53. *Riding has became a winter sport, and for many people makes a pleasant change from skiing. Many hotels keep a string of Fjording or Iceland ponies, hardy breeds that make headway through the snow.* (Husmo-Foto)

54. *The horse has enjoyed a renaissance as a riding animal and for the traditional sledge ride, made with burning torches on winter evenings.* (Husmo-Foto) ▷

55. When summer comes, those who miss the snow can cross a glacier on a mountain hike, as in this picture, where the route to Norway's highest peak, Gald høpiggen, (2,469 metres, 8,073 feet) leads across the glacier of Styggebreen. (Hêlge Sunde) ▷ ▷

56. Reflected by a shining white wall of snow, the Easter sun is twice as brilliant. (Husmo-Foto) ▷ ▷ ▷

Lapp altars in the course of only two weeks. The priest forbade the *joik,* and demanded that the children be baptized with Norwegian or biblical names, despite the stong tradition of family name among the Sámi. This enforced conversion to Christianity was part of the struggle between the national states over Lappland, as they then called it. The Norwegians had built both a fortress and a church in Vardø in the fourteenth century. By the end of the seventeenth century there were Norwegian churches in all places of any importance in Finnmark. The Russian Orthodox Church came to East Finnmark in the sixteenth century, and there is still a small Orthodox chapel in Neiden. The Swedish Church came later.

The Danish-Norwegian Renaissance king, Christian IV, went right up to the Kola Peninsula in 1599 in order to levy taxes, and at the same time the Russians from Novgorod considered the whole of Finnmark as their taxable property. The Sámi were squeezed by double exploitation, Sámiid Ædnan was drained of resources, and by the seventeenth century Lapp society had disintegrated.

Immigration continued. In the eighteenth century waves of Finns came to Lyngen, Alta and Tana, driven by famine in the forests of Finland. There was fish to attract them to the coast, while the valleys were now opened up to agriculture and grazing. The most intense period of immigration was in the 1860s, when some fishing villages became one hundred per cent Finnish. By then the national states were no longer content with taxing the Sámi; they had also occupied their territory.

In the Middle Ages the northern states had not drawn up any boundaries in the north. Before 1750 the land of the Sámi was described as 'the Lapp nation', or as a 'foreign nation' that did not belong to the kingdom. Then the neighbouring states simply divided up this nation among themselves. Sweden and Norway decided upon their border through Sámi territory in 1751. The nomadic 'Reindeer Sámi' were permitted to move their herds over the new border as before, but the rights of the other tribes to use the land of their forefathers went unrecognized. The border between Norway and Russia was demarcated in 1826. Thus the whole of the country was swallowed up by the conquerors. The Sámi had to adapt to the existence of a minority group, submitting to colonial powers that followed the classic pattern in destroying their ethnic identity.

While the white man in North America used the semblance of a contract to cheat the Indians of their territory, the Norwegians did not even bother to do that. In 1843 the Ministry of Finance established that there was no Crown property in Finnmark; five years later the Ministry proclaimed the whole county the property of the Crown, without any kind of negotiations with the Sámi. ''Finnmark proper has from ancient times been considered as belonging to the King or the State, because it was originally only inhabited by a nomad people, the Lapps, who have no permanent habitations,'' the Ministry pronounced, and concluded that ''Finnmark has from the most ancient times been considered a colony.''

So the Sámi were driven away by Norwegian settlers.

From 1902 they were not even granted permission to buy their own land if they could not speak Norwegian. This discriminating law was not repealed until 1965. The most urgent task of the colonial power was to get rid of the native language. The Church vacillated in its attitude: some clergymen thought the Sámi should be converted in their own language, while others wanted to eradicate it entirely.

An extraordinary figure in the history of the Sámi is the Swedish

63. The mountains have no shortage of hotels and tourist stations, big and small, all of them packed with happy skiers in the winter and Easter vacations. This picture is from the central valley of Gudbrandsdal in southern Norway. (Husmo-Foto)

botanist and priest Lars Levi Læstadius, who started an exceedingly pietistic revival movement in the last century: the Læstadian movement, as it has been called. He moralized and chastized the Såmi, taking on the role of both father and teacher to the impoverished farmers and nomad Lapps. He hated excess and drunkenness, and especially the liquor that wrought havoc among the Såmi. He called it 'liquid Devil's shite'. But he spoke to the Såmi in their own language and respected them for what they were. For this reason he still has supporters and some congregations follow his teachings, for instance in Alta, Ibostad and Lyngen.

His teachings were to some extent behind the so-called Kautokeino Rising of 1852, when 30 adults and 19 children attacked members of the Swedish-Norwegian upper class. The Læstadian movement demanded total abstinence, and did to a certain degree curb the Såmi's drinking of spirits. This strict religion, with its insistence on penance and contrition, often assumed ecstatic forms. During the services people worked themselves into a state of frenzy, laughing and crying out. It did not help matters when the bishop sent the masterful clergyman Nils Joachim Christian Vibe Stockfleth to sort things out. He was a man who liked his drink and was generous in sharing his brandy keg with the Såmi he met on his visitations.

There were more of his kind. ''There were idle and self-satisfied clergymen who lived in ease and luxury with scarcely a thought for their poor parishioners. Some were drawn in reindeer sleds from one wind-blown chapel to the next, often so drunk when they arrived that they had to be tipped out of the sled and lugged into the warmth of the chapel like a carcase of meat.'' This is how Tor Edvin Dahl described them in Norway's cultural history.

The Rev. Stockfleth personally beat up the 'enthusiasts' in Kautokeino using his pastoral cane. He dismissed the Såmi constable from office and installed a Swede who was held to be a scoundrel. When the parish priest, who was much disliked, went so far as to take lodgings with the hated liquor retailer, the Såmi's religious indignation boiled over and they took action. They horsewhipped the sinful Norwegians and killed both the constable and the publican, though they spared the life of the priest – out of a deep respect for religion.

A trial followed: 33 persons were tried, 27 convicted, and five condemned to death, though three of them were pardoned. Aslak Haatta and Mons Somby were beheaded in Alta on 14 October 1854. One of the 'enthusiasts' had already been beaten to death by guards while the

Lapps hunting on skis. Illustration to Olaus Magnus: 'History of the Nordic Peoples', Rome 1555.

prisoners were being transferred from Kautokeino to the prison in Alta. The central powers sent an infantry unit of 50 men to Alta to restore law and order – an act that was to be repeated over a century later.

The great Norwegianization process started in the 1850s and lasted well into our age. Såmi children were forced to learn Norwegian at school, and their own language was presented as inferior. It was not until 1967 that Norwegian law gave teachers the opportunity to use Såmi as an auxiliary language, and only in 1985 was it legalized as a teaching medium in school. Many who come from Såmi homes speak little Norwegian when they start school. The result of the linguistic coercion has been that only about half the Såmi population is literate. Norwegianization was not confined to the school system. Norwegians assumed power at all levels of society, buildings and properties were given Norwegian names, and the official language was Norwegian even in places that were entirely Såmi.

The result of this degradation was predictable. At the 1891 census 20 per cent of the population of Troms and Finnmark declared they were Såmi; by 1970 the figure was four per cent.

Yet there is hope for change. On 29 May 1987, a milestone in Såmi history, the Storting passed a new Såmi Law, stating for the first time that there are two population groups in Norway and that the State has a duty to ensure that the Såmi population can preserve its own culture and language. This law was the result of two factors. One was the growing interest in aboriginal peoples and the conditions of minority groups that emerged all over the world in the 1960s. The other was the clash between the promoters of hydroelectric development schemes and environmentalists in 1970 and in the 1980s that culminated in serious unrest in Finnmark. A force of 600 policemen collected from all over the country was sent by troop carrier to remove the conservationists who were out to save the Alta-Kautokeino river; these were Såmi, 'Greens', and intellectuals, who linked themselves together to form great human chains on the building site.

The environmentalists had previously staged demonstrations against hydroelectric schemes in the south, but in Alta their interests coincided with those of the ethnic minority. In the initial plans of 1968 the whole Såmi community of Masi was to have been submerged. Even in the more moderate plans put forward ten years later, many sites that were an important part of the Såmi cultural heritage were threatened, as was some magnificent landscape and valuable pastureland. In the 1970s

Reindeer sledge, 'like a boat or shoe'. Illustration to Olaus Magnus: 'History of the Nordic Peoples', Rome 1555.

there were many demonstrations against the scheme, and Alta became the country's most contentious issue. In Oslo a group of Såmi went on hunger-strike in front of the Parliament buildings, and devout Såmi women squatted in Prime Minister Gro Harlem Brundtland's office, praying and singing hymns, until they were removed by the police.

The conflict that brought strife right into people's families culminated on 14 January 1981, when the 600 policemen from the troop ship *Janina* forcibly removed the 'chain gang'. Altogether 900 people were arrested. Many hundreds were fined. Half those arrested were from the north of Norway, the rest from the south, from Finland and elsewhere. Some of the activists keep the police summons, framed, as a memento.

By 1987 the 115-metre-high (377-foot) dam was finished – ahead of schedule – ready to provide 30,000 families with power. Gro Harlem Brundtland, who was prime minister during the Alta fight, and since has been called the 'world minister of the environment' because of her work as chairman for the United Nations environmental report, caused some consternation in 1990 when she told Norwegian papers that it had not been necessary to build the dam! Until the Såmi Law was passed in 1987, the Såmi were one of the few minority groups in Europe that had no legal recognition. This law establishes that "the State is bound to ensure that the Såmi population have the material conditions in which to foster their own culture and maintain their language, as well as influence over the physical and economic basis of their culture." In practical terms, the law allows for a Såmi parliament – a *ting*. (In neighbouring Finland there has been the equivalent of this since 1973.) This is to deal with Såmi matters, starting by advising government, county and local authorities, and assuming more authority with time. The Såmi parliament – or *Såmeting* – consists of 39 members, chosen from 13 geographical constituencies, based on a population census of the Såmi. Anyone who regards himself as a Såmi can put himself on the electoral roll.

The highly controversial issue of the Såmi's rights to land and water is not touched by the Såmi Law. It is an exceedingly complicated matter. Before the Nordic states occupied their territory, the Såmi had many traditional rights of the kind that nomadic people need in order to survive: rights relating to grazing reindeer and cattle, salmon fishing, catching whales and seals, felling timber, gathering hay and peat from common land, picking cloudberries, collecting eggs and feathers. As these rights have never been sold, the activists assert that the Såmi still own them. The problem is how to reclaim them in a society so totally changed from that of the ancient Såmiid Ædnan. There is no reason to believe that the colonial power will give up its acquisitions without a struggle.

The Såmi are as politically divided as any other people, and their reaction to the new legislation was not unanimous. It is hardly a simple task to create unity in a minority at such an advanced stage of Norwegianization. The superstructure of the Såmi is a Nordic Såmi Conference, held every third year in Sweden, Finland and Norway by turns. The Russian Såmi do not take part. There is nonetheless no real separatist movement, though there are some who claim that the Såmi should have their own independent state.

There are an estimated 50,000 Såmi in the world today: 2,000 on the Kola Peninsula in the Soviet Union, 5,000 in Finland, 15,000 in Sweden, and 30,000 in Norway. The exact figure is difficult to ascertain, as the borders between the different population groups are undefined, and many will not admit to being Såmi. As a young man from Guovdageaidnu (Kautokeino) put it: "I am a Såmi; I own reindeer. But my brother is not a Såmi; he is a car mechanic."

How extensive the land of the Såmi once was remains a matter of academic debate. There are still at least nine different Såmi dialects, found from the Kola Peninsula in the U.S.S.R. to Elga in south Norway. Not all Såmi understand each other's dialect. Also some dialect areas are very small: Lulesåmi is spoken by only 2,000 people from Lulea in Sweden to Hamarøy in Norway, childhood home of Knut Hamsun.

It is a common misconception that only the lasso-throwing, colourfully dressed reindeer-owner is a Såmi. Even in the most exclusively Såmi areas, only 20 per cent of the population is involved in keeping reindeer. Only a couple of thousand Såmi altogether keep reindeer in Norway. Until the Second World War their way of life was more or less the same as when the reindeer was tamed in the seventeenth century. Since the war there have been drastic changes for the Såmi, as for other Norwegians. River boats have been equipped with outboard motors, and Finnmark is the county in Norway with the greatest number of the motorized ski-scooters that have replaced the reindeer sled. Yet it is among the Reindeer Såmi that the Såmi culture has been best preserved. The reindeer follow the same paths, and the knowledge of weather, beasts, and countryside that it takes to move 100,000 reindeer every year is not learnt in five minutes, but over generations. The animals are moved from their winter grazing on the Finnmark tundra to the coast, where the calving takes place and where the animals need to be watched day and night. From there they go to summer pastures and then back again. These huge migrations occasionally lead to conflict with the locals, as in 1987 when the population of Nordkyn tried to deter thousands of reindeer from crossing over Hopsland to their summer pastures. They were impeding road construction works . . .

It is the reindeer herdsman who has kept his beautiful jackét (kofte) as an everyday garment. The Såmi from Hattfjelldal and Snåsa in the south, who also keep reindeer, wear theirs for festive occasions only. Except in Nesseby and Tysfjord, the Coast Såmi have let theirs go out of use, and when they wanted to reconstruct their kofte in the 1980s, they had to go to the Norwegian Folk Museum in Oslo to find the model.

It is the Coast Såmi who constitute the greater part of the Såmi population in Finnmark: 75 per cent in the census of 1930. By 1950 there were hardly any of them who would admit their origin. They were the ones who were exposed to the most brutal Norwegianization and have suffered the harshest fate. Once they regarded themselves as the true Såmi. Trappers, fishermen and small farmers, they lived off the resources the coast had to offer. Trade with Russia meant a great deal to them and kept them self-sufficient, but this ceased after the Russian Revolution. Then came the motorboat that needed capital investment and made their fishing methods obsolete. Finally there was the Second World War, when Finnmark was burnt and their entire existence disrupted.

What does the future hold in store for these people? At the end of the 1980s a Norwegian national newspaper used the original Såmi place names for the first time: Gaivoudna for Kåfjord, Deatnu for Tana. In 1987 these names were used when local authorities issued job advertisements: Guovdageaidnu Suohkan it said (Kautokeino Council), with a Lapp tent in its coat of arms. The Church, which from time to time has shown a positive attitude to the Såmi language, has bilingual services in

Nesseby, Tana, Karasjok and Kautokeino, and sometimes in other parishes. It is on the cards that Såmi will be the official language of most central Såmi councils, and Kautokeino already favours employing applicants with a knowledge of the language.

In 1855 half the population of Finnmark spoke Såmi. Today less than 10 per cent in the county speak this ancient language, which has 100 words for reindeer but none for war. How is it to survive the onslaught of the media?

Såmi Radio is of course a good means of communication. Part of the national network of the Norsk Rikskringkasting, it puts out daily news bulletins in Såmi in the north and in the capital. Nearly twice as many Såmi live in Oslo as in Karasjok and Kautokeino! The radio provides the only link with the outer world for the nomadic Såmi, and there was a great response to the information service introduced in 1987 which gave the Såmi the opportunity to ring in and warn other families if the reindeer track was so bad that the animals should be herded by a different route. Yet the Reindeer Såmi constitute less than one tenth of the total Såmi population. The Såmi Radio station in Karasjok also puts out a news programme in Norwegian to give listeners all over the country some idea of what is happening in the Såmi areas. In addition, it is supposed to produce TV programmes for the national network, but lacks money to make more than a couple a year. Såmi children have to learn Norwegian if they are to understand children's television at all.

There is no great tradition in written Såmi. An alphabet was published in Sweden in 1619, and Luther's Catechism in North Såmi and Norwegian in 1728. All told, there can be no more than a thousand books and publications in the language. Some Såmi authors have published their works in Norwegian. Among the first was Matti Aikio, with his realistic stories from the turn of the century. Now we have the poet Ailo Gaup and the novelist Annok Sarri Nordrå. In 1987 Ole Henrik Magga from Kautokeino presented the first doctoral dissertation in the Såmi language at the University of Oslo. That was where he was taught for the first time in his own mother tongue!

There is a Såmi newspaper in Karsjok, *Såmi Aigi*, and in the 80s, Såmi publishers were printing books for Såmi children in their own language.

An internationally acclaimed manifestation of the Såmi spirit was the first full-length Såmi film *Ofelav (The Pathfinder)*, made by Nils Gaup in 1987, about a band of maurauders who preyed on the Såmi in the Viking era. This film, nominated for an Oscar award, had the suspense of a modern action thriller combined with elements from the Såmi world of beliefs and imagination. Many of its actors came from the Såmi theatre group Beaiccas (The Sun), founded in Kautokeino in 1979.

The *joik*, the Såmi folksong, has enjoyed a renaissance through composers of modern music like John Persen, and through the outstanding Såmi folk singer Mari Boine Persen and her interpretations with jazz musicians such as the world-famous tenor saxophonist Jan Garbarek.

Yet not all Såmi dare admit to their culture. In 1987 Kautokeino Council tried to introduce an official *joik*, just as other boroughs have their town or city song, but colonial power still held sway. The same year this age-old, traditional mode of singing was still forbidden by law in Såmi schools.

No one can say that Norway's imperialist policy towards Såmiid Ædnan has not been successful.

THE MONARCHY

CHAPTER FIVE is about the Norwegian royal house and particularly about King Olav V who died in January 1991, aged 87, a monarch who was born with his skis on.

On the winter evening when the announcement was broadcast that the old king was dead, the people of Oslo started to gather outside the royal palace. With them they brought candles and flowers that they silently placed in the snow in the palace square. During the whole of the vigil the wintery square glowed with light and colour as the people mourned their dead king. And this scene repeated itself every night until after the funeral.

On the old king's death his only son, Crown Prince Harald, automatically became Harald V. At his side was Crown Princess Sonja, born a commoner, the daughter of an Oslo merchant, and now the country's new queen. There is no longer any coronation ceremony, and the only formal occasion that marked the transition from one reign to the next was the new monarch's reception in the Storting, Norway's national assembly, where he pledged an oath of loyalty to the Constitution.

There are few republicans in Norway, and even the most fervent of these bore no ill-will towards the old king himself. When he arrived at the annual Holmenkollen ski-jumping contest, a comfortable, elderly gentleman in blue plus-fours, knitted stockings, old-fashioned blue anorak and peaked cap with the emblem of the ski association, it was a signal to the whole country that the most important winter festival had started. That keen skiing enthusiast would then bring out pencil and paper to note down the scores, in total disregard of computer screens and other modern contraptions. Was he not after all a fully qualified judge? Had he not jumped at Holmenkollen in 1922 and 1923, and attended the competition almost uninterruptedly since 1911?

No wonder he was the favourite of ski-mad Norwegians. They sing 'God save our gracious King', forgetting that it is an imported anthem. Nor is the present Norwegian monarchy of long standing. For centuries we were subjects of foreign monarchs. There were no descendants of the Norwegian line left when the present monarchy was introduced in 1905, so a Danish prince, married to his English cousin, was brought over to our royal palace. The palace was not particularly grand either, as it had been intended as a guest residence for the Swedish king. It should in fact have been much larger; the idea was for an H-shaped building, but through lack of funds it ended up as a U. Even that was not completed until 1849.

64. Agriculture and fishing are the main means of livelihood in most of the parishes along the fjords in Troms county, as here at Altæided. (R. Frislid/NN)

Swedes, who have seen much grander things, tend to laugh at our palace, but we think it looks quite good on the hilltop above the city's main street. And if it makes the Swedes feel better, they can console themselves with the fact that it is Karl Johan, king of the Swedish/Norwegian union, who is mounted on a bronze charger and surveys the avenue that has been give his name.

The Danish prince, Carl, and his English princess, Maud, came here in 1905, after he had been elected King Haakon VII in a plebiscite. As sovereign he wielded little actual power, but was held in great respect. In a seafaring nation it may have helped towards his popularity that King Haakon VII had been a sailor himself and had tattoos on his arm. It was during wartime exile in London that he really became the people's king, a symbol of resistance to German occupation. A photograph that has become part of our history shows him and his son, Crown Prince Olav, under a birch tree in Molde during the dramatic flight of 1940. (Queen Maud had died in 1938.) At home in Norway small boys carved his initials between Nazi posters — an H with a 7 in it. When he came back to the capital after the war, on 7 June 1945, there was a rejoicing in Oslo such as had never been seen or heard before.

By then Crown Prince Olav had already returned to the country as chief of defence. As a fully trained officer he was well prepared for the task. From the age of eighteen he had participated in cabinet meetings, and during the war he had pleaded Norway's cause in Britain, just as the Swedish-born Crown Princess Märtha had done in the U.S.A., to which she had escaped with the children, Ragnhild, Astrid and Harald.

Crown Princess Märtha died in 1954, and when King Haakon was taken ill in 1955, Crown Prince Olav was appointed regent. On his father's death two years later, he ascended the throne with the same motto: 'Everything for Norway'.

We had had Olavs as kings before, dating back to the time when Harald Hairfaired united the kingdom of Norway. There were Olavs who converted the country to Christianity so that heads were rolling in all directions, Olavs who excelled as sportsmen. Olav V was one of the latter. However, unlike Olav Tryggvason, who ran on the oars while his men were rowing, Olav V preferred to stay inside the boat and win Olympic medals and other coveted sailing trophies.

He himself handed out royal trophies to the sportmen of the year, and always turned up at the annual ski marathon, Birkebeineren, commemorating the time eight hundred years ago when his predecessor, King Haakon Haakonsson, was carried as a child by skiers over the mountains from Lillehammer to Rena. There are 5,700 participants who ski the 55 kilometres (34 miles) of blood, sweat and blisters. In 1994 the entire skiing world will compete in the surroundings of Lillehammer — during the Olympic Winter Games.

In his book The Final Testament of 1974, the outspoken Russian Premier Nikita Khrushchev provides some amusing descriptions of his visit to the king in 1964:

"We then travelled to Norway, which is also a monarchy. Of course I paid my respects to the Norwegian sovereign. I had been told that his late father had had such a strong belief in democracy that he used to take the tram to a place where he liked to fish, and that the other passengers often mistook him for an ordinary citizen. I'm not absolutely certain it is true that he behaved so democratically, but this was the story.

"I had been prepared for my meeting with the king, for he had

65. Canoeing down foaming rivers is an exciting passtime that tempts young people to measure their strength and skill against the forces of nature, as here on the river Sjoa. (Husmo-Foto) ▷

66

66. The char with its tomato-coloured
belly is a tempting catch for the ice
fisherman, who lies flat on the ice,
peering down through the hole,
waiting to strike at the right moment.
(Dag Kjelsaas/NN/Samfoto)

67. Fishing through a hole in the ice
of a lake is an activity that attracts
Norwegians of all ages, especially in
March and April, when the sun begins
to warm. (Rolf Sørensen/NN/Samfoto)

rather a strange physical defect. My advisors said that he could begin laughing out loud for no apparent reason. He did not laugh because there was anything amusing, he just had this peculiarity or disease. If he were to start laughing in my presence, I must therefore take no notice – as if I had not heard it.

"We were driven to a building that did not look like a palace at all. There was nothing royal about it. It could not be compared with the palaces of our czars which I have visited in Leningrad and Peterhof, not least the palace of Catherine the Great, or of Paul at Tsarskoe Selo. The Norwegian palace looked like the house of any successful capitalist. At the door we were greeted by a man in a kind of khaki-coloured uniform. He ushered me into an office, showed me to a chair, and we sat down. Suddenly it occurred to me that this was the king. One could easily have mistaken him for the gardener," said Nikita Khrushchev.

What Khrushchev perhaps did not realize is that Olav was by no means impecunious. On the contrary, he was one of the richest men in Norway, second only to Olav Thon, who went to Oslo from Hallingdal after the war to sell fox pelts and ended up as the largest property owner in the country – worth two billion kroner in 1987. The Oslo paper *Dagbladet* estimated that Olav was worth one billion, after assessing his wealth and property in 1987. The Norwegian royal family therefore ranks as the sixth richest in Europe, wealthier than those of Sweden and Denmark, but unable to compete with the British monarchy, whose fortune is reckoned to be 22 billion kroner, according to the British expert H. B. Brooks-Baker in *Burke's Peerage*.

The Norwegian monarch owns estates in the United Kingdom worth 660 million kroner, left by Queen Maud. In Norway he owns Kongeseteren, the fairytale castle in Nordmarka that was part of the gift of the Norwegian people to King Haakon on his coronation in 1905. This was where King Olav resided during the skiing festival in Holmenkollen, and it was here that he died after suffering a heart atack. There is also Prinsehytta, the royal chalet in Jotunheimen, a gift from the Swedish king to Olav when he came of age. Olav himself bought a summer house, Bloksberg, near Hankø, for the sailing, but in his later years stayed on board the royal yacht when taking part in regattas.

The monarch's property also includes the extraordinary Solstraaleø (Sunshine Isle), in Sunnhordaland, a gift from the English family of Musgrove which fell out of favour with British royalty in Victorian times and settled in Norway. The island, though, is overgrown and seldom visited.

The palace, the summer residence at Bygdøy, Oscarshall castle on the Oslo fjord, the manor of Ledaal near Stavanger, Gamlehaugen near Bergen and Stiftsgården in Trondheim, where the king stays on his visits, all these are owned by the State.

The late King Olav also held shares to the total value of more than five million kroner in a number of leading Swedish concerns. For his duties as king he received 8.4 million kroner from the Civil List in 1987. Of this 60 percent went on salaries for staff, and much of the remainder was used for official occasions and the upkeep of property.

As the son of a seaman and a keen sailor himself, King Olav had an especially weak spot for the royal yacht *Norge*, a gift from the Norwegian people on his 75th birthday in 1947. She was originally a luxury yacht called *Philante*, built for the British aeroplane magnate Sopwith in 1937. During the war the ship was on active service for three years.

79. Hang-gliding over Ringerike, north of Oslo. This peaceful yet exhilarating way of flying, taking off from mountain peaks or steep hillsides, now has many devotees. (Helge Sunde/Samfoto)

King Olav's three children all married commoners. Ragnhild, the eldest, is married to a shipowner's son and industrial magnate in Brazil, Erling S. Lorentzen. The second daughter, Astrid, is the wife of an Oslo businessman, Johan B. Ferner. Both princesses live relatively quiet lives away from the glare of the media.

The new royal couple, King Harald and Queen Sonja, both born in 1937, were married in 1968. When Harald saw the light of day, he was the first Norwegian prince to be born in the country since 1370. He was the youngest of King Olav's children, but he inherited the throne, for conservative Norway has not got around to introducing equal rights with regard to royalty.

Unperturbed by the fact that there are female monarchs in both England and Denmark, the Norwegian Constitution until recently stated:

"The line of succession is lineal and agnatic, so that only the legitimate male issue of a male may inherit."

There is every indication that King Harald was made aware of the necessary qualifications for being a Norwegian monarch when very young. At the ripe age of three he appeared at Holmenkollen for the first time. At the age of six he was sent into exile in America, where he refused to go to the barber's or have his hair cut; he was to be the new Harald Hairfaired who would save Norway! He returned to Norway with the royal family on 7 June 1945, and followed in his father's footsteps, being educated at Oxford, and in the army at home, becoming both general and admiral. We shall have to wait some time before we see a conscientious objector on the throne!

Whilst a royal bachelor, Harald naturally kept the press in business, and he was married off to quite a few princesses in his time. However, he himself chose a young girl from a department store in Oslo, Sonja Haraldsen. It is not clear whether this accorded with his father's wishes. The outspoken Jens Haugland, former minister of justice, wrote in his diary that 'the King asked Trygve Lie to speak to Crown Prince Harald and get him to marry according to his rank', but the former Secretary General of the United Nations refused to become involved.

After a glorious royal wedding in 1968, the couple settled at Skaugum, a large farm in Asker outside Oslo, given to King Olav as a wedding present by Norway's ambassador in Spain, Fritz Wedel Jarlsberg. It is a farm of 100 acres of cultivated land, some 50 acres of pastureland, and some not too profitable forests. There is a staff of 20, which includes four footmen. As king and queen, they continue to live on the farm.

The royal couple have two children, Märtha Louise, born in 1971, and Haakon Magnus, born in 1973. Both perform folk dances merrily, and represent the royal family in a way that touches all hearts. Of the two it is again the younger, the boy, who will inherit the throne. In 1990 Parliament decided to change the Constitution in order to legalize female succession, but made it clear that the existing order should be kept for Prince Haakon Magnus.

How did Norway receive a queen who had no blue blood in her veins? They have taken her to their hearts, according to the popular press. It is universally agreed that they are an easy democratic couple. Harald is a good yachtsman like his father, a keen fisherman and a good shot, working at improving his performance with grouse shooting courses. The new queen is an outdoor girl and a good skier, who has competed incognito in the most strenuous of races, such as the Holmenkollen ski marathon. No wonder she is accepted in a skiing country!

Medieval abbey seals.

WOMANPOWER

CHAPTER SIX is about the liberated Norwegian woman, about the Viking Frøydis who whetted her sword on her breasts, and about Prime Minister Gro Harlem Brundtland who formed a world-record-breaking women's cabinet.

It caused quite an international stir when doctor and politician Gro Harlem Brundtland in 1986 formed a minority government for the Norwegian Labour Party. Eight of the 18 ministers were women, herself included. She had held the office once before, serving as Norway's first women prime minister for some months in 1981. But at that time she had only three female cabinet ministers, and created more of a sensation by introducing academics into the Labour Party leadership. As a qualified physician, and the daughter of a doctor and former cabinet minister, she signalled the beginning of the end of a long tradition of working-class Labour Party politicians who derived their learning from the university of life. Thanks to her exceedingly hasty temper, revealed both on and off the air, the press was soon calling her 'the Harridan of Bygdøy', a nickname that gave vent to a good deal of male chauvinism on the part of political commentators. Bygdøy, where she lives, is incidentally one of the most desirable parts of Oslo.

Norwegians could with great satisfaction watch her take her place as the leading Nordic politician on the world stage.

She is not the first women to sort things out for the men! While by no means wanting to compare their methods, we ought perhaps to mention what Eric the Red's daughter Frøydis did when she met the *Skrælingers* in Vinland and her male companions' courage failed:

"Frøydis came out and saw Karlsevne and his men running away. She cried: 'Why are you fleeing from these miserable creatures? I would have thought that great fellows like you could knock them down like cattle! If I only had a weapon, I believe I would fight better than any of you!' But they did not heed what she said. Frøydis ran after them, but was too slow as she was with child. She followed the others into the woods, but the *Skrælingers* were behind her. She found a dead man in the wood. It was Torbrand Snorreson, with a stone lodged in his skull. Beside him lay his sword, and she raised it to defend herself. As the *Skrælingers* approached, she uncovered her breasts and whetted her sword on them."

The saga of Eric the Red recounts that the natives were so horrified they ran to their boats and rowed away!

Experts differ in their opinions as to the real condition of Norwegian women at this time of expansion for the country. Of course the sagas mostly tell us about upper-class women: queens, and the wives and daughters of chieftains. Seven hundred years before the Viking era, the Roman historian Tacitus wrote that 'the women follow their men into battle, caring for the wounded'. He was amazed that so many women mastered runes, and he was surprised by the sexual morality of the Nordic barbarians, who held that a girl without her virginity was disgraced, and by the mutual respect between men and women. Snorre Sturlason, the Icelandic saga-writer, names many wise and capable women, but only one who spoke up in the council.

The Viking era was the foremost age of slavery in Norwegian history. Many of the estimated 75,000 slaves were brought home as booty after raids. One of the Edda poems from this time, *Rigstula,* gives

Edvard Munch: Sitting Nude, 1896, charcoal, pencil and watercolour.

us a picture of Tir, a woman slave, arriving at the farm with muddy boots, sunburnt arms and a hooked nose. It then describes how she baked flat bread. The Arabian writer and explorer Ahmed ibn Fadlan tells us that the Nordic Vikings in Russia had many women slaves about them. Sometimes these were burnt with orgiastic ritual on the funeral pyre of their deceased lord. That female slaves were sacrificed and placed at their queen's side we know from the Oseberg ship, the Viking vessel found in Vestfold and now to be seen at Bygdøy in Oslo. A woman slave could be given away, sold, hired out, and even killed by her owner without it being considered murder in the eyes of the law. If she stole anything worth even one øre, she was to have one ear cut off. On repeating the offence, she lost the other. At the third offence she lost her nose. A woman slave who had given birth was let off work until she was strong enough to carry two buckets of water from the well.

The battle for women's rights in Norway started in the middle of the nineteenth century, inspired partly by the novel *Amtmannens Døtre* by Camilla Collett, sister of the rebel poet Henrik Wergeland. For women of the middle class it was important to secure the right to education, while for working-class women it was more important to be able to make a living and to limit the number of pregnancies. For both these groups the aim was to get the vote — achieved in 1913, fifteen years after universal suffrage for men.

The great wave of women's liberation that swept through the western world in the 1970s made a clear impact in Norway. As in other places it was a two-pronged movement, driven by the 'New Feminists', who emphasized the raising of women's consciousness at all levels, including the sexual, while the more Marxist 'Women's Front' concentrated on the economic aspect, their banners proclaiming: 'No class struggle without female struggle, no female struggle without class struggle.' Both factions fought for equal rights in every area, with specific demands for more crèches, the right to abortion, equal opportunities in education, equal pay for equal work.

When Gro Harlem Brundtland formed her 'women's cabinet' in 1986, it was part of a long process that is still not complete. Norway could have had women cabinet ministers as early as 1916, and yet it was not until 1945 that the first, the Communist Kirsten Hansteen, took office. Most of Harlem Brundtland's female ministers were in charge of areas of special interest to women, such as education, health, law, the environment, consumer affairs and overseas aid. The toughest job was perhaps the one given to Gunhild Øyangen, arts graduate and farmer's wife from Trøndelag, who was placed in charge of the traditionally male-dominated Ministry of Agriculture.

If you look at the way jobs and elected offices are distributed in Norway, you will still see a clear male domination. In 1987 only one in four councillors was female. Out of the two million employed in the country, only 44 per cent are women, most of them in typically female jobs. This is also reflected in their wages. Men still earn more than women, despite the accepted principle of equal pay for equal work. Men get the top jobs, and they make all the major decisions, even in 'female' occupations. In the postal service, for instance, more women are employed than men. Yet there is no female director, and there are only four women among the country's 135 postmasters. A mere four per cent of professors in Norway are women, only 10 per cent of the civil servants in the police force, only 16 per cent of self-employed persons in business. Only 27 per cent of the girls who have the right to inherit a farm are certain that they will indeed take it over.

Girls still prefer the traditional female occupations, according to a survey carried out by the University of Trondheim. They want to be 1) hairdressers or beauticians, 2) tourist guides, 3) hospital nurses, 4) children's nurses, 5) veterinary surgeons, 6) cooks, 7) physicians, 8) civil engineers and engineers, 9) lawyers, 10) computer operators.

Boys on the other hand want to be 1) mechanics, 2) engineers, 3) farmers, 4) pilots, 5) computer operators, 6) electricians, 7) carpenters, 8) cooks, 9) directors or managers, 10) policemen.

There is some light in the gloom. More women than men continue with further education beyond secondary school: 40 per cent of women and 25 per cent of men. The percentage of women in the male-dominated colleges has doubled in recent years and is now 42 at the National College of Agricultural Engineering, 33 at the College of Business Administration and Economics, and 24 at Norway's College of Technology.

Some women have broken down barriers and made Norwegian history. In 1961 Ingrid Bjerkaas was ordained as Norway's first woman minister of the Church of Norway. In 1968 Lily Bølviken became the first

Poster by Edvard Munch for Henrik Ibsen's 'Peer Gynt', Paris 1896.

woman High Court judge. In 1974 Ebba Lodden became regional commissioner, and was thus the most important 'man' in the county. In 1987 Siri Skare became Norway's first woman Air Force pilot, though she was not permitted to fly fighter planes. In the same year we find Ellen Holager Andenæs in charge of the uniformed branch of the Oslo police, and Ellen Stensrud elected as the first woman leader of the powerful, male-dominated Oslo Engineering Workers' Union, the largest in the country with 13,000 members.

In recent years it is mostly women who have put Norway on the map in the field of sport. These include marathon runners Grete Waitz and Ingrid Kristiansen, and the women's national handball and soccer teams.

The most entrenched opposition to equal rights for women is to be found in the Church and in Christian organizations. Members of the clergy have carried out boycott action if a female minister officiates, and a female resident curate was prevented from conducting the Christmas service because the male organist refused to play. The mighty Norwegian Lutheran Home Mission Society is against women priests as 'contrary to the Word of God', and there are still bishops in the Norwegian Church who refuse to ordain women priests. But attitudes in general have changed. Just after the Second World War almost half the population was against women priests, while today 90 per cent are in favour. So it is really only a question of time before the first woman bishop takes up her crozier.

In 1978 the first Equal Rights Law was passed, banning discrimination in the treatment of men and women. The following year the equal rights Ombudsman, Eva Kolstad, was appointed to see that the law was carried out, for instance in matters of employment. Farm girls have changed the ancient system of odal tenure of land and the allodial law so that now it is the eldest child who inherits a farm, not necessarily the eldest boy, as before.

A new abortion law gives women the right to take the final decision on terminating a pregnancy. The law on names has also been changed, so that a baby born in Norway today is automatically given the mother's family name. If the parents wish the child to have the father's name, they must specifically state this.

In 1981 the world's first children's Ombudsman was appointed, whose job it is to see that children's rights are respected. A law passed in 1987 forbids adults to perform any act of violence towards children. It states that spanking and clips over the ear are forbidden, though light, reprimanding smacking is permitted – but it is not quite clear how you are to distinguish between the two.

In recent years the struggle against pornography, abuse of women, incest and rape have been dominant female issues in Norway. There are 50 centres for battered women in the country, and the Oslo health board runs a reception centre for rape victims.

The Norwegian woman is not out of the urban mould, accustomed to ball-gowns, powder puffs and smelling salts. She has been formed by hard labour, on the coast, high in the mountains, and on steep hillsides – not the kind to swoon, or wilt in ebe face of adversity.

"They are all dressed in black. The men's costume is not distinguished other than by some large buttons similar to those worn by our lackeys, but the women wear a hideous skirt that barely reaches the knee. It clings tightly around the hips and has a great many pleats at the bottom, not unlike the wide pantaloons worn by Dutch seamen. If our *Parisiennes* had had such garments, they would have had no need of all the transparent materials so fashionable of late. They are as revealing of the body's contours as if they had been naked. And yet I will insist on this being the most unattractive garment I have ever seen," our friend Jacques de la Tocnaye reported from Trøndelag in 1799.

Other aspects of Norwegian life seem to have appealed more to this somewhat narrow-minded officer. He writes of west Norway:

"The women prepare the food. The men say grace and sit down in a corner where they eat their fill in peace and quiet. When they have finished the women sit down in another corner and eat whatever is left over. I will not maintain that this is particularly gallant behaviour, but it does prove again that Norwegian women, with the exception of those in Trondheim and Christiania (Oslo), know how to accord their husbands the respect due to them."

So things must have made some progress in the course of two centuries. However, the concept of equal rights is probably not uppermost in everyday life. In most homes it is the woman who does the cooking, though the husband may undertake some domestic chores. It is remarkable how many homes installed dishwashers as soon as the male took his place at the kitchen sink! And it is not only in the urban homes of intellectuals that we see a new division of labour. In the country it was customary for the woman to have sole responsibility for the cows and milking. It was considered degrading for the husband to go into the cowshed. Today men and women share most of the work. Yet our antiquated legal system will not acknowledge this. In 1987 a court ruled that a farmer's earnings were greater than his wife's, the reason being that he could also drive a tractor!

It is not possible to give a single description that covers all Norwegian women of today. They are as varied as the landscape. There is an ocean of difference in attitude, life style and experience between the fisherman's wife working with bait in a Lofoten fishery and the office girl at her computer in fashionable Bygdøy Allé in Oslo.

Southern Europeans do not distinguish between different Scandinavian women, but lump them all together. This may have started with the Nordic woman as portrayed in the films of Ingmar Bergman and other Swedish film directors of the 50s: beautiful blonde girls who danced through the summer, frankly proclaiming their sexuality.

But of course there is a difference between the women, as there is between all the people of Scandinavia. The Norwegian woman never became feminist in the same way as the Danish. She did not spend her summers in women's camps, or discuss her sex life openly with journalists, or even in private. Nor does the Norwegian woman organize her life as meticulously and rationally as the Swedish woman seems to do, in everything from vegetarian food to sexual diet.

Above all the Norwegian girl is a friend and a comrade, whether she lives in a town or in the country, by the coast or in the mountains. It is therefore strange that she has stepped out of the traditional female role well known from more southerly countries, where the woman sacrifices herself for her parents-in-law and does not consign them to an old people's home. It may be a weakness in Norwegian social democracy, or it may be a sign of strength. Perhaps it is an indication that we are only half-way along our road to social welfare: the new woman has fulfilled herself, the old woman has been left out in the final reckoning.

84. The area of the Lofoten
archipelago, with spawning cod
beneath the glittering surface and
snowclad mountains reaching skyward,
is as attractive for painters as it is for
fishermen. (Husmo-Foto)

85. Most of the Norwegian fishing
fleet consists of small, but very
seaworthy boats. (Husmo-Foto)

86. The fish market, which begins where the harbour ends, offers the Bergen housewife live fish and other delicacies from the sea. (Helge Sunde)

87. The capelin, a small fish of the smelt family, is very important for Norwegian fisheries: when the capelin approaches the shore to spawn, the cod follows. In addition, this fish is an important resource of the fishing industry in its own right. (Husmo-Foto)

88. During the main fishing season, in late winter and early spring, vessels from many parts of the country converge on Lofoten. (Hugo Henriksen/Samfoto)

87

89

90

89. Far out at sea, beyond the Lofoten archipelago in northern Norway, lies the small community of Røst with its multitude of islets, many of them famous for their colonies of sea birds. (Hans Hvide Bang/Samfoto/NN)

90. A large proportion of the goods transported in Norway is carried by boat. Small cargo vessels are a common sight among the thousands of skerries and isles scattered off the coast. (R. Frislid/NN)

91. A summer's night in the north
with the light of the midnight sun
shining on distant mountains: Lyngen
fjord backed by the Lyngen Alps. (R.
Frislid/NN)

92. With all its fjords and bays and
inlets, the Norwegian coastland has
a total length of 21,000 kilometres
(13,000 miles). Everywhere along the
shore fishing boats, big and small, are
a feature of the scene. (R. Frislid/NN)

93. The flat North Cape plateau, high
above the ice-cold Polar Sea, teems
with tourists all summer. The
elongated promontory of
Knivskjellodden (in the foreground)
stretches even farther north than the
North Cape. (Husmo-Foto)

SEASONS AND CELEBRATIONS

CHAPTER SEVEN relates what Kari and Ola do with themselves all year round, when, what and how they celebrate, and what they like to drink.

What exactly do Kari and Ola Nordmann do up there under the glacier all the year? What do they get up to? What do they celebrate? Let's start with the winter straight away and get it over and done with.

Even if Ola Nordmann has by now 10,000 years of experience of the snow, he is caught off guard every single year. People in the mountainous regions are not really taken by surprise; they have a natural relationship with both snow and ice and take them as they come – sometime in early autumn.

But when the snow has settled inland for about a month, a strange thing happens. It starts snowing near the coast, where the journalists live and where the newspapers are printed. What a sensation! The dramatic headlines totally ignore the inland areas. 'Winter has set in! Total chaos on the roads! Snowploughs caught in blizzard!' And indeed there are long traffic jams with cars that won't start and petrol stations that have run out of tow ropes and are besieged by people who have decided to change from summer to winter tyres. In Norway it is normal to use studded tyres in winter, something visiting Danes forget, which leaves them standing at the bottom of the hills, blocking the road with their lorries. Studded tyres wear out the asphalt and make a mess of the surroundings, but they do save lives.

When it has finished snowing, it is time for the cold weather to set in. And there is nothing whatsoever to be said in favour of a Norwegian winter when the temperature sinks to minus 30° C or lower. There are some places that always have the record for the coldest temperatures, for instance Østerdalen and inland Finnmark. Yet it can feel just as cold at minus 20° C on the wet and stormy coastline as at 40° below zero in the still winter landscape of mountainous Røros.

The effects are the same. When you want to start the car to let the snowplough through you discover that the lock is frozen so you can't get in, the bonnet won't open, the batteries are flat, and the windscreen is impossible to see through. In the houses the pipes freeze, lavatories are blocked, and in draughty buildings old people have to stay in bed to keep warm. 'Log angels' deliver free firewood to the elderly, construction workers are made redundant, forestry work ceases, railway points freeze, mountain passes are closed, ships weighed down by ice have to seek a harbour. Even the Oslo fjord sometimes freezes over, so that you

94. The narrow fjords of western Norway, with their steep sides and waterfalls plunging into the sea, are among the most popular destinations of foreign tourists. This picture is from Geiranger fjord. (Husmo-Foto)

can walk right out to sea, where the icebreaker struggles to clear a shipping lane.

At this point extraordinary things can happen. While the whole of southern Norway is stamping its feet to keep warm, we hear that the temperature has made a leap above zero on Svalbard, the island jammed up against the North Pole. Northern Norway can experience a variation of temperature of up to 40 °C in the course of a day!

One gets used to everything – even winter. Kari prefers woollen undergarments and high boots to nylon tights and a weak bladder. The Norwegian winter is so beautiful, and snow is essential for Christmas, the greatest time of celebration for Norwegians. So Jacques de la Tocnaye discovered in 1799:

"At Christmastide the Norwegians like feasting and celebrating with their friends. To make it quite clear how hospitable they are and how essential it is that everyone is happy, they even set up a sheaf of oats on a pole outside the barn door, to give the birds something to eat. The sheaf remains hanging until it falls of its own accord, and no one would dream of using it to entice the birds so they could be caught and eaten." Only a French gourmet could voice such a thought!

The Christmas sheaves are still to be seen, hanging outside farm-houses and on the balcony of high-rise blocks, and the robin redbreast features in the sheaf on all the Christmas cards Norwegians send each other.

The festive season is well prepared for. By September the restaur-ants are trying to work up a Christmas appetite in their customers with firtree-shaped advertisements tempting them with 'Christmas sausage, Christmas ham, Christmas anchovies, Christmas pork, Christmas ale, etc, etc.' – in short, the legendary Christmas spread, *julebord*.

In the days before Christmas tension increases dramatically. Every-thing has to be ready by Christmas Eve. By then all cakes must be baked, all stars hung up in the windows and on the front door, and all gifts must be wrapped. The Norwegians have their main celebration on Christmas Eve. For many people it is the only day in the year when they go to church. It is the day when the whole family holds each other by the hand and proceeds round the tree singing the old familiar carols, while mother and father have tears in their eyes as they think back to the Christmases of their childhood.

But the Christmas tree is Danish! In Norway, land of forests, 30 per cent of the one million or so Christmas trees sold are imported from Denmark, despite the fact that they are twice as expensive as the Norwegian ones. The reason is that the Danes have managed to grow a tree that does not shed its needles as easily as the untidier domestic product. So in the past ten years the Danes have captured a large chunk of the Norwegian Christmas-tree market. Yet forestry research is being carried out, and there is hope that one day the honour of the country may be restored. In any case, many of the Norwegian Christmas hymns are also of Danish origin.

Father Christmas, however, is Norwegian. At least so children from all over the world believe, to judge from the letters that get sent to the Chief Tourist Officer in Oslo.

Christmas dinner is highly traditional, but varies according to reg-ion. 'In the barn sits Father Christmas with his porridge' is one of the more popular seasonal songs. It was for long a custom to put out a plateful of porridge both in the festive season and at other times for

Father Christmas, or *Nissen*. He is not the large American-style Santa, but a small gnome-like, grey-bearded, homespun creature.

The usual Christmas Eve dinner in the east of Norway consists of roast pork, meat rissoles, sausages and sauerkraut, with cream of cloudberries or creamed rice for dessert. There is an almond hidden in the rice, which brings the lucky finder an extra gift. Beer and aquavit will be drunk, unless it is a teetotal family. In the west, the menu is salted and dried ribs of mutton, mashed swedes, potatoes, beer and aquavit. The meat will have been smoked over a layer of birch sprigs placed at the bottom of the pot. In the south many people eat steamed cod on Christmas Eve, accompanied by red wine. The special dish *lutefisk* is also served at Christmas time. This is made of dried cod prepared in a special potash lye, traditionally made from birch ash. It used to be said that the lye is particularly strong at Christmas if the wife is bad-tempered.

The Lapps eat saddle of reindeer at Christmas, served with white bread, a great rarity and delicacy in former times. But in our Norwegianized era both *lutefisk* and pork have invaded the homes of the Såmi.

Many take a holiday in the days between Christmas and New Year. On New Year's Eve the Norwegians let their hair down again. At midnight there is a carnival atmosphere in the ice-cold winter. Boats blow their horns in the harbour and people rush out into the winter night, onto their balconies or into the street — to let off fireworks to the tune of 100 million kroner. There are strict regulations about letting off rockets, and one is supposed to obtain a licence from the police. On New Year's Eve every Norwegian breaks the law.

The month of January closes with a somewhat more prosaic event, the filling in of the income-tax return form, the annual report to the tax authorities on how much you earned in the past year.

It is dark in Norway in winter, especially in the north, where the sun disappears completely below the horizon to make up for having stayed up all day and all night in the summer. The soul of the north Norwegian grows restless when the fantastic sunlight again appears on the horizon after the dark season. In Tromsø they celebrate 'Sun Day', and locals go up into the hills from where they can look to the south. People drink 'sun coffee' and eat cakes, the fire brigade provides hot chocolate, cream and buns for its men, while others exchange their usual packed lunch for Danish pastries and cocoa. Some of the more optimistic outdoor restaurants venture a pre-season opening. School children used to get the day off to celebrate the return of the sun. Now they have cocoa and buns and a carnival before running out at noon into the first spindly rays from the guest of honour peeping out between the peaks of Balsfjord.

The true Nordic sun worship is to be seen at Easter! After people have spent all winter shovelling snow, and the children have just exchanged their winter boots for shoes that allow them to lift their feet off the ground, you would think they would have had enough of winter. Far from it. The 10,000-year-old yearning for the glacier must still be in the Norseman's bones. Every Easter there is a mass migration when 800,000 Norwegians pack a thermos, sandwiches, oranges and a detective novel in their rucksack, bring out their skis and set off for the mountains. The Norwegian State Railway has its peak season, buses have their roofs piled high with skis, and the Red Cross and other bodies stand by with teams of 10,000 or more voluntary First Aid helpers, divers, glacier climbers, mountain rescue dogs, helicopters and planes, ready to save people who get lost or caught in avalanches on their holiday. Even so, help does not always arrive in time.

Every fourth household has a cottage in the mountains or by the sea. In addition, the Norwegian Tourist Association has huts scattered all over the country. The energetic have 16,000 kilometres (10,000 miles) of track to explore. In the Tourist Association huts there is always room, even if it means sleeping in the sauna. Many people spend their Easter holiday skiing from hut to hut. Often these are self-service, that is, the guests help themselves to the food they need and leave the money. No-one is around to check up on this — the Tourist Association trusts its members. Recently, however, there have been cases of non-payment, resulting in a loss of six to eight per cent every year, so the Association threatens to stop this unique tradition of Norwegian hospitality.

It has always been a status symbol to return from the Easter holiday with a tanned face. And however much of a welfare state Norway may be, Easter in the mountains is still for the healthy and — well-off. Predictably, statistics show that the larger a family's income, the more chance of them going away on holiday. Norway has the world's longest Easter break, with a public holiday on Maundy Thursday, Good Friday, half Saturday, and Easter Sunday and Monday. Those who stay at home can also enjoy solving crime mysteries, as for some extraordinary reason Easter and who-dunnits have become synonymous. There is always a thriller serialized on TV in Holy Week.

The fact that Norwegians are born with skis on has affected their behaviour at times other than at Easter.

Skis must have been in use in Siberia and in Europe about four or five thousand years ago. A Greek fifth-century source tells us of Lapps skiing, and the Norse sagas portray both heroes and heroines on skis. The goddess Skadi could shoot with her bow and arrow while on skis, which should give her the credit for having started the biathlon.

The oldest pairs consisted of one long and one short ski, the shorter being covered in hide to give a powerful kick. Skiing as a sport did not really get going until the appearance in the eighteenth century of the Telemark ski, which was narrow in the middle and had a raised tip. It was superseded by the laminated skis of the 1930s, and from 1970 all Norwegians have been born with plastic skis on. But there are still wooden skis to be seen, treasured by wooden-ski enthusiasts. who are looked upon as freaks when they appear on the slopes dressed in quaint knickerbockers. Young skiers of today look more like astronauts, equipped with special skis, special helmets and space suits from the age of

Snowcastle under attack. Illustration to Olaus Magnus 'History of the Nordic Peoples', Rome 1555.

three. However, the late 80s ushered in a nostalgic return to the old Telemark way of skiing.

The father of skiing as we know it, Sondre Norheim, came from Telemark, where his childhood home, in Morgedal, is today a museum. He taught people to ski in Norway and in the U.S.A., to which he emigrated in 1884. Another native of Telemark, Jon Torsteinson Rue, otherwise known as Snowshoe Thompson, became legendary in the last century when for twenty years he brought the mail on skis over the Sierra Nevada from Placerville in California to Virginia City in Nevada.

Our most famous ski hero is perhaps Fridtjof Nansen, the polar scientist, who skied over Greenland in 1888, and later tried to ski to the North Pole with his companion Hjalmar Johansen. After these two had spent a year together in the icy wastes, and saved each other's life more than once, Nansen went so far as to suggest that they should address each other by the familiar *du*, which should dispel the idea that Norwegians are a reserved people. Roald Amundsen was a hero of the same calibre, planting the Norwegian flag on the South Pole in 1911.

More attainable is the feat of Olaf Rye, who 180 years ago jumped 9.5 metres (30 feet) at Eidsborg, which must be reckoned as the first Norwegian ski-jumping record. Norwegians have always been very keen on jumping, provided they win. They usually did to begin with, when there were more modest requirements as to style and length.

The greatest winter sports event for Norwegians is the Holmenkollen competition, the jumping event that counts as our second national day. When the Olympic Games were held in Norway in 1952, there were 120,000 spectators at Holmenkollen. Every year Holmenkollen Sunday is a great festival, with tens of thousands of people going up there on foot or by tram, with a thermos in their rucksack, to the accompaniment of brass bands. From the tender age when Norwegians first toddle forth on small skis, the great dream is to win the jumping at Holmenkollen. The event gets tremendous media coverage, and the winner is a national hero — until the next year.

All winter long people take long ski trips, into the forests, over the mountains — a wonderful thing to do when snow crystals glitter and powder snow is scattered from the trees. Cross-country skiing events are popular all over the country, the Birkebeiner run being the most famous.

In recent years alpine skiing has become a national sport, for those who can afford the equipment. There are 500 ski lifts set up for the nation's 450,000 downhill skiers, in Hemsedal, at Geilo, in Voss, in Trysil, and many other places. Norwegians are not yet quite sure of themselves when it comes to this Continental fashion, so they have called the new ski resort near Oslo 'Norefjell *Alpine* Village'.

Skating was the great spectator sport in Norway for as long as Norwegians got the medals, especially when they won every time as they did with Hjalmar 'Hjallis' Andersen, gold-medallist in the 1952 Olympic Games. He will remain forever Norway's King of Skating, and Sonja Henie the Queen.

Spring comes late to this elongated country of ours. It is a melancholic season, when the people of Jaeren look out for the lapwing, when children play hopscotch, and the Minister of Transport announces special restrictions due to the frost. The frost sits deep in the ground, and the roads cannot take heavy loads in the spring thaw.

May Day is celebrated by the Labour movement in Norway, as in other countries. It is also the day when anti-socialists cause a good deal of irritation by not hoisting their flags and by demonstratively working on their farms or in the garden.

A day celebrated by everyone is 17 May — in honour of Norway's Constitution of 1814. There can be no other country in the world that celebrates its national day in such a manner. For days beforehand, brass bands can be heard in every school and on every street, practising patriotic songs and all the marches to be played in this otherwise unmilitary country. Now the red and the blue *Russ* make their noisy appearance, the thousands of students celebrating the end of twelve years of school with their specially painted red or blue cars, their ribald newspapers, their beerdrinking competitions, and their Miss Russ awards. The ones dressed in blue have attended commercial high school, the ones in red have graduated from other high schools.

At a very early hour small children start blowing their 17 May trumpets in the street and waving their flags. Foreign visitors are especially impressed by the children's procession in Oslo, when tens of thousands of schoolchildren with bands and flags parade up Karl Johan Street to greet the king on his balcony. The day provides an explosion of colour in this country of granite.

When Ola and Kari wake up from their winter hibernation they feel the need to get out into the garden. Norwegians love their gardens: 66 per cent of households have their own, 23 per cent have access to communal gardens, and only 11 per cent have to make do with balcony boxes.

Midsummer Night's Eve, 23 June, has been another great festivity for many hundreds of years. The old Frostating Law from the twelfth century prescribed how *Jonsok* was to be celebrated, and gave detailed instructions as to how the farmer should brew his St Hans or St John beer. On the coast, thousands of little boats go out to the small islands where huge bonfires are lit, and there is dancing to the accordion (or blaring rock music) until sunrise. A romantic calm descends on Ola and Kari Nordmann when the sea lies still and the birds briefly go to rest. Next morning they have a headache.

Soccer is the great spectator sport in the summer, although interest has dwindled somewhat in the past few years. Norwegian football is still in the transition stage between amateur and professional. The country insists on 'non-amateur' or semi-professional status, which means that players should, at least in theory, have a job that brings in more than they get from playing football. Yet Norwegian soccer has gone international and has to call on professionals from all over Europe when the national team is picked. There are now concrete plans to make the game fully professional.

Norway is above all a country that goes in for sports and athletic pursuits for the masses. Sports associations have 1.7 million members, more than one per household! There are many different mass meetings. The greatest soccer festival is the Norway Cup in Oslo, when 1,100 youth teams compete, among them guests from all over the world. In recent years mass running events have become popular: the Oslo Marathon with 8,000 competitors, the Oslo Centre Race that draws 12,000 participants, and others. The great trial of strength is the annual cycle race from Trondheim to Oslo. The fastest do the 554-kilometre (344-mile) stretch in 14 hours, the slowest take a couple of days. In addition mass walks are arranged all over the country.

In fact, walking, hiking or rambling, call it what you will — they call it a *tur* – is a Norwegian speciality. Every evening after the News, Kari and Ola go for a little stroll in the neighbourhood. Every weekend the woods and forests are filled with Norwegians with a knapsack and thermos flask, pushing the baby and with the dog on a lead. You name it, the Norwegians will have a *tur* for it: by car or boat, sailing, scouting, fishing, mountain climbing, a *tur* for Sunday and one for gathering every conceivable berry in the forest.

In July Kari and Ola go away for their annual vacation. They water their plants, lock the door, putting their boots outside to make burglars think they are at home, and forget their house or flat for the next three or four weeks. Many simply go to their family in the country, others go walking in the mountains or on a boating holiday to the south of Norway. In the Oslo fjord and in the south there is teeming life in the summer, when tens of thousands of people spend their holidays on board their boats or in the numerous camp sites along the coast. Many foreigners hire cabins in Norway. Keen anthropologists have calculated that 4,050 million nights were spent in private cabins in 1984, while only 11 million were spent in hotels.

But many people also go the opposite way, from the countryside to the cities. According to a Tourist Board list, the most popular attractions are the Vigelandsanlegget sculpture park and the Holmenkollen ski-jump area in Oslo, the Fløybanen climbing tramway in Bergen, the Tusenfryd amusement park, the Viking Museum and the Kon-Tiki Museum in Oslo, the Kristiansand animal park, and the Nidarosdomen Cathedral in Trondheim.

A large number of Norwegians prefer to go to southern climes in the summer – if they haven't already been there in the winter. Tour operators tempt the public with around 50 destinations in 20 countries, and 400,000 yearly succumb. Many go to the Canary Islands, where they find waiters who speak Norwegian – or at least Swedish. More and more opt to buy their own house in Spain or the South of France, especially pensioners fleeing from the Nordic winter.

One rather special 'package tour' is to 'Costa del Ilseng' near Hamar. Ilseng is a work camp for drunken drivers, many of whom spend their three-week 'holiday' on carpentry, assembling lamps, or wrapping cakes of soap, rather than drinking wine and eating grilled pork in Las Palmas. Around 7,000 Norwegians were sentenced for drunken driving in 1984. It has been reckoned that 200,000 drivers a year take to the road with 6.5 times more than the prescribed limit of alcohol (0.50) in the bloodstream. What else do we do in summer? Young people who have worked to save money in the first weeks of summer, go Inter-Railing at the end of the holiday. In 1986, 16,000 young people took advantage of this scheme for cut-price travel on the railways of Europe.

The bees buzz in the fields, the waves lap against the shore, a sleepy wind meanders through city streets, and the Norwegian summer goes by. A hectic strawberry season is followed by the blueberry season, when Kari and Ola are to be seen in the woods, heads down, bottoms up, snipping away with their special berry-pickers. Haymaking is followed by potato picking, and then one day there is a breath of autumn in the air, the trees turn yellow, and the leaves begin to fall.

The frost sets in the ground, it is hard underfoot, soon the first flakes of snow are swirling in the air, and Norwegians can once more let themselves be caught by surprise at the onset of winter – for the 10,001st time!

Whatever the season or cause for celebration, *Skål!* is the toast.

Foreigners are always immensely amused by Norwegian drinking laws. And one can't get away from the humour in laws that permit you to buy a whole crate of beer at the local store, but not one bottle on its own. Or when a local inhabitant is refused a drink on the terrace of the local hotel, while his good friend from the neighbouring town can order as much as he likes. This is the tail-end of a tradition of fighting the evils of alcoholism that was inaugurated a century ago by such pioneers Asbjørn Kloster, whose statue you can see in Stavanger — a campaign that meets with little enthusiasm today.

Norwegians have extraordinarily long and strong traditions in drinking and drunkenness. Snorre tells us that our great hero of Viking times, Olav Tryggvason, got people drunk so he could set fire to their houses if they refused to become Christians.

"They longed for the intoxicating drink as a bear longs for honey," runs another description of the Vikings, who would travel great distances in foreign parts in order to get wine while on their plundering trips to the Mediterranean. "Rich merchants live well and drink fairly heavily," wrote Jacques de la Tocnaye. Europeans must have learnt the art of distilling liquor some time after the end of the Viking period, but spirits were first introduced into Norway by Archbishop Olav Engelbrektsson in Trondheim in 1530. Once in the country, distilling apparatus became as normal a part of household equipment as pots and pans.

It just had to go wrong for the drink-crazy Norwegians. The battle against the Demon was launched in the middle of the sixteenth century, when it became forbidden to serve spirits (hard liquor) on Sundays and holidays — a law that stands to this day. Despite all regulations, people went on making spirits, first from grain, then from potatoes when they were introduced in the eighteenth century. At about that time distilling became illegal, though the law was repealed in 1816. Once more consumption increased dramatically, reaching 16 litres of spirits per citizen in 1833 (one litre = nearly two pints). It was this that led to the temperance movement.

In 1848 a law on the manufacture and processing of spirits put an end to home distilling. In its place legal, industrial distilling was established. Whereas in 1832 there were 10,000 registered distilleries in the country, a couple of decades later only 40 were left. The number of establishments licensed for the sale and serving of spirits was halved, and by 1851 the consumption of spirits had fallen to six litres per head.

From 1916 to 1927 prohibition was enforced, for some years including even fortified wine. Since 1922 the State has had a monopoly of the distribution and sale of wines and spirits in the country, and since 1927 over the production of spirits as well. Today six distilleries deliver spirits to the Wine Monopoly, about two million litres a year altogether. Some 2,000 farmers send potatoes to be distilled. The Wine Monopoly carries out production in Hamar, Oslo, Bergen and Trondheim, and runs 95 shops.

In latter years there has been a relaxation in alcohol legislation. It is still not possible to buy wine in the local store, as in Denmark and most other European countries. But whereas only half the population of Norway could buy beer in their own parish in 1955, this is now possible for 97.3 per cent of the population, and about 50 per cent live in areas that have a Wine Monopoly outlet.

What does Ola Nordmann drink? In this respect, he is pretty much

a creature of habit: it is not permitted to advertise alcohol to introduce new brands, just as tobacco advertising is forbidden. (A law passed in 1988 also restricts smoking at work or in public places.) However, the grapevine works in such a way that fashions in drinking change from time to time. His increased affluence has also given him a more refined palate: it is no longer the one standard 'red' that is served at a big dinner.

Norwegians do not really drink very much — at least officially. According to 1985 statistics, France had a consumption of 13.3 litres of spirits per habitant, while Norway was right at the bottom of the league with 4.2 litres. For instance, Kari and Ola drank only 48 litres of beer each in 1985 (as against 172 litres of milk!), while West Germans drank 146 litres, East Germans 142, Czechs 131, and the Danes 121 litres of beer. And beer does have a longstanding tradition in Norway. The communal bowl of ale was found in all homes. Brewing was ritual and mystical. The ingredients were barley malt, juniper and hops, and sometimes grated potatoes. When the yeast was added, the Norwegian was supposed to start yelling — to make the beer stronger. But while it was fermenting, one had to be careful not to stamp one's feet, bang doors or talk in a loud voice, as this could stop the process.

Many still brew their own beer for Christmas and other occasions, yet home brewing generally is on the decline: most people get their supply at the supermarket. Norwegian beer does not have the same worldwide fame as Danish Tuborg or Carlsberg. However, the breweries of Schou, Frydenlund and Ringnes in Oslo, Hansa in Bergen, and Mack in Tromsø have maintained the traditions of the southern European brewers who once came to teach us how to make beer. Rather successfully in fact: at an exclusive contest in Belgium in 1987, the small Nordland Brewery from Bodø was proclaimed the best in the world.

Norwegians are modest wine drinkers, downing a mere five litres on average in 1986, while the Portuguese drank 87 and the French 80. The Wine Monopoly stocks a wide range of good wines from most producer countries. A little wine is also produced in Norway, mostly from locally-grown fruit such as rhubarb, cherries, redcurrants. Home production is increasingly popular, mainly using wine kits from the wine producers. For some strange reason there is no law against this.

The Russians have their vodka, the Dutch their Genever, and the Norwegians their *akevitt, aqua vitae*, Latin for 'water of life'. Aquavit is a spiced liquor, made from the potato — the grape of the north — according to ancient and secret recipes that include cumin, fennel, coriander, bitter-orange peel, aniseed, and the essence of 50 other herbs and spices. It has to be stored in an oak cask that has previously contained sherry. If the aquavit is to be really good it has to travel at least two or three months on a Wilh. Wilhelmsen ship that crosses the Equator. For many years the passage was to Australia, but now the route has been changed. However, the effect is the same: the motion and the variations in temperature make the aquavit extra mature.

It is estimated that home distilling increased from 1.2 litres in 1956 to 4.4 litres in 1986, that is, to more than one litre per Norwegian.

There were 6,800 sentences for drunken driving in 1985 (3.9 for every 1,000 cars) and 32,284 arrests for drunken behaviour. We are now talking mainly about Ola Nordmann — only 2,500 of those arrested were women. Even if Ola Nordmann drinks the least in Europe, he drinks the fastest! The Saturday-night binge is a well-known national phenomenon. Considering the price of drink in Norway, cirrhosis of the liver is quite a status symbol.

105. Norway is a mountainous land, two thirds of it lying above or north of the timber line. In Jotunheimen, the central mountain massif in southern Norway, many peaks rise well above 2,000 metres (6,000 feet). (R. Frislid/NN)

FARMING AND FISHING

CHAPTER EIGHT is about the Norwegian farmer who tills his land in the short summer and is paid the same as a factory worker, and the Norwegian fisherman who braves the cruel sea.

The Norwegian farmer, who is he?

Is he the splendid, proud, silent man, the loner, the *Übermensch* as we know him from novelist Trygve Gulbranssen's trilogy of the 1930s, *Beyond Sing the Woods*, a work translated into 30 languages and filmed several times?

Or is he like Isak Sellanraa, in Knut Hamsun's *Growth of the Soil*, who breaks the ground with the sweat of his brow, and ends up so wealthy he can go out into the pasture and count his horse!

Foreigners have made various attempts to describe him through the centuries. Our French travelling companion, Jacques de la Tocnaye, met him on his journey in 1799 after coming back over the mountains to the eastern part of the country:

"The people on this side of the mountains seem to belong to another category altogether, and this becomes increasingly obvious the further east you travel. They are as friendly and generous as the people of Bergen are quarrelsome and greedy. Further inland you find wealthier, in fact, some very wealthy farmers, some of whom behave in a highly polished manner. These people do not deserve to be called peasants, for in other countries they would be considered gentlemen."

About a century later in their classic travelogue *Three in Norway – by Two of Them*, J.A. Lees and W.J. Clutterbuck describe the natives as "immeasurably slow. We have studied these people and have come to the conclusion that nothing we do can make them increase their pace, while on the contrary it takes very little to make them slow down. When it comes to old people, it is indeed a rarity to see them move at all. Norwegian boys are so lively and full of explosive energy that they are never satisfied unless they are in at least three places at once. But when they attain the age of fifteen and their parents let them eat their fill, their restlessness completely disappears and gives way to a kind of apathetic paralysis." The Englishmen had collected these observations from the mountain villages around Jotunheimen.

After yet another century, the general secretary of the Farmers' Union, Hans Haga, asserted in 1986: "Our farmers are tradition-bound and conservative, and so proud of their roots that innovation is difficult for them."

It is quite clear that the farm itself and the consciousness of ancient traditions have meant a great deal in this country, where agriculture has been carried on for at least 6,000 years, and where there have been farms for perhaps 2,500 years. Burial grounds on the old farms tell us about these worthy freeholders and their authoritative wives. The deep ruts made by horses' hooves from farm to farm show the close contact between the ancient homesteads, and the fortified villages of the Iron Age point to the farmers' need to protect themselves against intruders. The more cut-off the mountain village or the valley, the stronger the family pride. It was no coincidence that the Norwegian Nazis' romantic cult of old rural traditions gained most adherents in isolated areas such as Valle in Setesdal, Finsland in Vest-Agder, Tolga, Dovre and other mountain villages in east Norway.

Not much of the country bumpkin is left in the modern Norwegian farmer. He is young, dynamic and well-educated. He wears a suit, carries a briefcase, and is an expert on battery hens, bacon factories, greenhouses, accountancy and pesticides! According to the Conservative paper *Aftenposten*, he is the richest farmer in the world. This is partly due to the fact that he has been good at organizing himself. There are two main unions for farmers, one for the big and one for the small: the Farmers' Union and the Farmer and Smallholders' Union. There is also a powerful Forestry Union and co-operatives for everything from fertilizers to milk production. They even have one of the greatest youth organizations in the country, 4H, which stands for a clear Head, a warm Heart, clever Hands and good Health. It has 25,000 members – and there are only 100,000 farmers in Norway.

No-one can claim that a country so far north, with such meagre soil and so short a summer, is ideal for agriculture. But when Ola Nordmann was hungry during the German occupation in the Second World War, he realized the importance of being self-sufficient in food. Politicians therefore decided, when faced with the task of building Norway up again after the war, that agriculture should get the same opportunities as other areas of production. In 1975 it was even established by law that agricultural workers were to have the same wages as industrial workers, and farmers' incomes were heavily boosted by state subsidies. In 1987, however, the Labour Party discovered that the subsidies had not had the desired effect. On the contrary, they had made the rich farmers in the fertile eastern areas even richer, while smallholders, particularly farmers in outlying districts, had not reaped the same benefit from the subsidies. While the State had favoured the large farms, leading to a certain extent to surplus production, each year 3,000 small farms were being abandoned. This could hardly be said to counteract the flight from the countryside and did lead to some shift in priorities.

Norway is not alone in supporting agriculture. In 1987, the 24 OECD countries used the equivalent of 1,000 billion kroner to help farmers, and the cost to EEC countries of storing the surplus production alone amounted to more than the total agricultural subsidies of Norway. The other OECD countries try desperately to reduce outlays for farm support, despite massive protests from farmers. In Norway the response to the retrenchment of 1987 was the biggest farmers' demonstration ever held. From hill farms, plains, valleys and coastal areas some 10,000 poured into the capital and marched to Youngstorvet, the traditional battlesite of the Labour movement. Their slogans were: 'Keep your village alive!', 'If the farmer goes, the country dies!', 'Stop witch-hunting farmers!' They were tired, they said, of being ostracized and described as parasites.

When pointing out the differences between farmers in 1799, Jacques de la Tocnaye said he thought the inland farmers were easier to get on with than the 'fish-eaters' of the coast: "Up here in the mountain valleys, where the warmth of the sun is reflected from the hills, the grain ripens more quickly than by the coast, and it follows that people are much more content. Nonetheless, most people live by the coast, where they drag out their days, imagining that they would die of grief if they could not look out to sea."

The crofter in Finnmark has as little in common with the rich farmer of the east as does the smallholder on the west coast who has for generations carried the hay on his back from outlying patches of pasture-land. In 1985 the net income of each farm in the eastern areas was 228,200 kroner, compared with 245,300 in Jæren and 143,600 in north Norway. In fact, the west coast farmer has now rationalized and taken his cow off the farm, turning to strawberry production and salmon farming instead!

The annual general meeting of the local dairy used to be the place where you could see the Norwegian small farmer in his element. In a convival atmosphere that had a whiff of the barnyard, the farmers would meet in the school or chapel to drink coffee and discuss milk prices. When it came to the price of milk, the Norwegian farmer was on sure ground, yet he had to argue against well-spoken dairy specialists who had been to agricultural college. But the farmers had to watch the small homesteads disappear and a milk factory take over. They had to capitulate to rationalization experts who promised ten øre more per litre if only they could bring about a merger with the dairy in the next village, which again could be amalgamated with the county dairy, which could be taken over by the district dairy. Now there are only 19 dairy companies left, and the Norwegian Milk Board won't give up until the whole thing is one vast company.

Farms are also decreasing in number, but getting larger and more efficient: in 1939 there were 215,000, by 1985 only 105,000. Today's farm averages 23 acres with 22 head of cattle and 66 sheep, as against seven and 17 respectively a generation ago. Though 3,000 farms disappear every year, the total acreage has been stable in recent years as farms have been taken over by other farms, or because the surviving farmers rent any spare land.

If we include Svalbard, we have a total area of 100 million acres, of which only 9.5 million are farmed and 66 million consist of workable forestry land. Half the farmed area is pastureland or used for grazing, though one third of the land provides 30 per cent of the grain eaten in Norway. The politicians say we must grow more food, and that the aim is to be self-sufficient in meat, potatoes and storable vegetables. Norwegian produce, including fish and meat, makes up 53 per cent of the total calory intake. The rest has to be imported.

Forestry has also undergone a drastic rationalization process since the war. The horse and sleigh have been replaced by the tractor on the forest road, and the local sawmill is a thing of the past. The largest company for the conversion of wood products is Norwegian Forestry Industries, started in 1966 by the organization of forestry owners and 13,000 shareholders. Today the company has a turnover of 3 billion kroner, mainly in the field of newsprint. Some nine million cubic metres (11.8 cubic yards) of timber, mostly coniferous, were felled annually in Norway in the 1980s. Half of this went to sawmills and wood products, the rest for wood pulp and chemical pulp. Nothing is as friendly and evocative of home comfort as chimney smoke on a still, frosty morning, but most people today heat their houses by oil or electricity. Of all the nine million cubic metres of timber, only 300,000 are used for firewood.

When autumn comes, primitive instincts are awakened in Ola Nordmann, and it is no longer safe to go out into the countryside! When the men gather at first light with their guns and red caps, it becomes clear that the elk hunt must be the Norwegian tradition closest to the ancient heathen rituals of the hunting tribe. In some places the school gives the children a day off so that the eldest sons can be in on the sacrificial killing from a tender age. In 1985, 25,000 elks were brought down by 32,000 hunters. Many also hit other things, such as tractors and horses. Though the statistics keep quiet about this, the press does not. The local papers give detailed reports on the hunting with the names of the good marksmen and the weight of the dead animal, thereby confirming the importance of the hunt as a tradition.

Big-game hunting in Norway brought in five million kilos (4,910 tons) of meat in 1985, while small-game or general hunting brought in one million kilos. The total volume of meat from livestock breeding comes to 180 million kilos (176,000 tons), which means that game accounts for 3.5 per cent of Norway's total meat consumption. Notwithstanding all this hunting, it is a fact that the numbers of elk, reindeer and deer have increased tenfold since the war.

The strange thing is that while rural areas are being depopulated in Norway, there are more and more hunters. In the decade up to 1985, the number rose from 120,000 to 185,000, 4,000 of whom were women. Some relate this to increased affluence, as more people can afford to go hunting. Grouse shooting has become a mass sport: 80,000 people go out every year, and in 1985 they bagged 700,000 grouse and ptarmigan. As the sport becomes more popular, the hunter runs the risk of no longer being the great hero he was to the ancient tribes. In fact, he may well be looked upon as a despoiler of the countryside and a status-seeker.

There are foxes, bears, wolves and wolverines in the woods, though you may not meet them when out walking. A hundred years ago bears were to be found in forests all over Norway, and most villages could boast of a hunter who had shot a prestigious total, but by 1965 there were perhaps less than 50 left. At the beginning of the 1970s bears,

Kitchen utensils from the Oseberg ship. Viking Age.

wolves and wolverines became protected species, and the numbers of bears and wolverines have increased accordingly. Today there are probably 250 bears and 200 wolverines. Most of the former are in the wooded areas between Sweden and Norway, though the occasional one is sighted in every county except Vestfold. Wolverines are usually to be found where there are reindeer, but they rove over the whole country. There is no danger now of either of these species becoming extinct.

Wolves are a rarer breed. After the war they were to be found in the north, while the south was reckoned to be wolf-free. Lately the wolf has had to give way to the motorized ski-scooter in the north, though a pack of about 30 has grown up in the forests of the south between Glåmdalen and Värmland in Sweden. In Finland there is a very much larger pack of about 200 animals.

Not all farmers love these predators, which caused damage and loss of livestock worth about 7 million kroner in 1986. The wolverine is the worst sinner, killing 200 reindeer and 2,000 sheep a year. The bear will also attack sheep, and then the farmer gets his gun and goes out with a special licence from the Royal Ministry of Agriculture.

From now on wildlife should be even better protected. Norway has signed the Council of Europe's convention aimed at safeguarding flora and fauna, and has worked out a comprehensive plan for the protection of bears, wolverines and wolves. Six special areas have been designated, covering one third of the country, where animals can roam in safety. So now it's up to them to stick to the regulations!

Fishing, along with hunting, is the most ancient occupation in Norway. Since being washed ashore under the edge of the ice some 10,000 years ago with fish hook and harpoon of bone and antler in his hide boat, the fisherman here has become used to fending for himself in the struggle against wind and weather and sea – the mysterious ocean that hides so much and where every creature is part of a chain: the whale and the seal linked to the large fish, the large fish to the smaller, the small fish to animal plankton, and animal plankton to plant plankton...

He went to the nearest coast and to the most distant waters for his catch, and as time went by the number of fishermen grew. The hide boat and bone tackle were replaced by sail and steam, harpoon guns and depth charges. In the 1880s up to 33,000 men took part in the legendary cod fishing off the Lofoten Islands. In the 1930s, 10,000 Norwegians were working on the other side of the globe, in the floating whale factories of the Antarctic.

New kinds of animals came, old kinds of fish disappeared, and the Norwegian fisherman did not always display the greatest wisdom. He was still learning the hard way as recently as 1987, when he found his nets full of seals. There had been seals in Eastern Finnmark for many years, but now the whole northern part of Norway was suddenly invaded by these creatures that ate the cod and ruined equipment for the Lofoten fishermen.

There are an estimated four million Greenland seals in the world, half of them in Newfoundland, the rest on the East Ice of the Barents Sea and the West Ice off Greenland. In the winter of 1986–87, around half a million turned up on the Norwegian coast, and 50,000 of them were caught in the fishing nets and filled up one refrigerator plant after another – in place of the fish that were nowhere to be seen! It was a total catastrophe. Many of the seals had fatty tissue of a mere 20 millimetres (less than an inch), which is the minimum they need not to freeze to death. Since each seal eats about five kilos (11 lbs) of fish a day, this vast number consumed about 75,000 tons a month — more than the whole Lofoten season's catch. These seals were ravenously hungry.

The seal was not the only one to go hungry. Leif and Trond Fredriksen, fishermen from Svolvær, the largest town in Lofoten, were interviewed by *Dagbladet* in 1987, six weeks into the Lofoten fishing season. After yet another day with a 'black sea', this is what father and son had to say:

"We have no explanation for what is happening. It is frightening. Many fishermen are really scared. We just don't know what to do with ourselves. What little cod we have caught is without liver or roe, and practically without guts. It is black inside and emaciated. On the Finnmark coast some of the fish we caught had their snouts worn down from eating seaweed, for want of anything better. We have had bad times in Lofoten before, but this is different. This is serious. Today we caught not one fish in 35 nets..."

At the same time a deathly silence fell over the bird rocks on Bjørnøya (Bear Island) in the Barents Sea. In 1986 there were 400,000 common guillemots nesting there. The following year only one tenth were left. The decrease had long been noticeable in Troms and West Finnmark. The sea birds were so short of food, so desperate, that at least 100,000 guillemots drowned in the cod fishing nets off Outer Troms.

How could this happen? What were the reasons for this seal invasion, for the starvation, the dead birds, and the catastrophe which brought nature to such a cruel imbalance and resulted in the government paying compensation to fishermen? There was a heated discussion about this for some months. Most people were of the opinion that the Barents Sea had simply been fished out. The food chain here consists of plankton, herring, capelin, cod, haddock, saithe, whale and seal, with man straddling the pyramid. Oceanographers had warned against drawing too heavily on the capelin, the small fish that is the food of both the cod and the seal, yet the authorities allowed for a large quota. The result was that the capelin population sank from 2.6 million tons to less than 100,000 tons in the years 1984 to 1987, while the cod population decreased in direct proportion. Then large fishing trawls swept the Barents Sea clean of capelin. The larder was bare. The chain had been broken. Hence the starving cod and the wandering seal.

"It is gross overfishing. It is almost unbelievable that the authorities allowed the trawling fleet to wipe out the capelin. It is one of the most direct causes of the ecological catastrophe we can see approaching. But it seems as if it is the authorities that understand the least," said the Fredriksens, two generations of fishermen from Svolvær.

They are two of Norway's 30,000 professional fishermen. Thirty years ago there were twice as many. Half the fishermen are from the north of Norway, but only two out of three have fishing as a full-time occupation.

As one can see, the catch varies a good deal, according to the whims of the authorities and Mother Nature. Normally Norwegian fishermen haul 2.5 million tons of fish yearly out of the sea. That means that Norway, with one thousandth of the world population, has three to four per cent of the world's fishing. Only Japan, the Soviet Union, China, the U.S.A. and Chile fish more than Norway. About one third of the total catch consists of capelin, while cod, saithe and herring make up about one tenth each. Shrimp fishing produces just under 100,000 tons. We export 90 per cent of the fish, mainly to EC countries, the U.S.A. and

Japan. This brings in almost nine billion kroner, and represents 10 per cent of our total exports apart from ships and petroleum. Only about five per cent of the fish is distributed fresh; 20 per cent is frozen, and about 60 per cent is used in manufacturing oil, fishmeal and other products.

The average Norwegian eats 38 kilos (83.6 pounds) of fish a year, less than a third in its fresh form. This includes the popular mackerel in tomato sauce, and the favourite Norwegian dishes – incomprehensible to all foreigners – fishballs and fishpudding!

The catch is mostly from the Norwegian coastal zone and outside the 200-mile limit from the Svalbard area and near Jan Mayen. Less than 15 per cent is fished in other countries' zones.

There are approximately 25,000 fishing boats, two-thirds of them open and used only during a short part of the year for coastal fishing for cod and sprat, herring, lobster and crab. It is the large boats that make the profits.

The industry is exceedingly well regulated. Norway was the first country in the world to set up a separate Fisheries Ministry, in 1946, and has its own state bank for fishermen. The 20,000-member-strong Norwegian Fishermen's Association can demand state subsidies if the catch is not good enough, a practice that seems to have become permanent.

In the inter-war years the price of fish varied from day to day and from village to village. There are no fish auctions in Norway as in other countries. In many fishing villages there was only one buyer and he set the price. The Depression in the 30s was hard on fishermen, but in 1936 they were guaranteed a minimum price for fish that was to be salted or dried, and in 1938 they acquired their 'constitution', the Raw Fish Act, which enabled them to sell the fish through their own joint companies. They now sell through Norway's Raw Fish Association, which has its establishments along the entire coastline from Finnmark to Nordmøre, as well as 13 other sales companies.

Today there are about 700 centres of the fish industry in Norway, employing around 16,000 people. Drying and salting of fish is carried out along large stretches of the coast, much as in the days when the Italian nobleman and merchant Pietro Querini landed on the windblown island of Røst in Lofoten in 1431. He was on his way from Crete to Flanders with a cargo of wine, but seems to have navigated as erratically as the Vikings who found themselves in America. He was, however, so enthusiastic about the Norwegian stockfish that he informed the Pope about it, and thus opened up a unique new market for the Norwegians.

'Stockfish – Viking food with a long tradition!' advertise the Norwegian fish exporters, and underline the differences between salted fish, klipfish and stockfish. Salted fish is decapitated, gutted and skinned, has its backbone removed, and is laid in brine for a minimum of three weeks before it can be sold, either whole or in fillets. The saltfish is used as the raw material for the klipfish, which is fish cleaned, salted and dried. In former years it was dried in the open on the cliff (klippe), hence the name. Today the drying takes place in a special warm-air unit. The first klipfish was dried at the time when Columbus went to America. In the seventeenth century it became an important Norwegian export. Today bacalao is part of the diet in many Catholic countries, especially Portugal, Brazil and Italy. Stockfish is unsalted fish dried in the open solely by wind and sun. This is what one sees hanging on the drying racks in Norwegian fishing villages.

108

108. Long distances and difficult weather conditions for boats and motor vehicles make the airplane invaluable, especially in northern Norway. This is the airfield at Båtsfjord, Finnmark. (Husmo-Foto)

109. Out to the oil field:
a drilling rig being towed out of
Oslo − fjord. (Hans Hvide Bang/
Samfoto/NN) ▷

110. Oil drilling rig at Gansfjorden,
Stavanger. Platforms for deep-sea
drilling have become a new speciality
of the shipbuilding industry. (Husmo-
Foto) ▷ ▷

Despite regulations and good organization, some fishermen are more equal than others, and this difference is not likely to diminish in the future. Today there are nine factory ships in the Norwegian fishing fleet, but in the next few years we can reckon on a large number of saltfish and freezer trawlers with refrigeration plants being converted into fish factories. This will be beneficial to the shipowners of Møre, but will weaken the fishermen of the north — or so they fear.

The fishing smack owner Stein Hansen told *Dagbladet* how this aspect of the North-South conflict hits the individual, as in Øyhellsundet in Lofoten, where experts urged that the herring be protected, but the authorities let the 'large-scale' fishermen get them.

"It's almost like war," said Stein Hansen from Gratangen, come all the way from his home village to fish his legal quota. "We small fishermen are chased away, while these huge trawlers pump up everything they come across. Soon there will be no more herring here, mark my words!"

The herring is an unreliable visitor! No one knows when he's coming, no one knows when he's going. But when he does turn up, he creates quite a stir! The herring appears on the Scandinavian coast in periodical large waves of migration. The last great wave of winter herring came to Norway in the 1950s, when 2,800 vessels and 25,000 men were employed in fishing for the herring. The largest shoals came to the west coast, but herring oil factories were to be found right up into the Oslo fjord, 'smelling of money'. In one single year, 1956, 1.7 million tons were caught. Fantastic!

And then there was all that came in its wake. There was a boom in fish barrels, and in small sawmills all round the coast people were busy making barrel staves. Others worked day and night to pack the fish into the barrels so that it lay there in layers, properly gutted, belly up, in such strong brine that a potato with a nail in it could stay afloat. That was how it should be!

But people are greedy, and well-equipped. In modern times fishermen have gone out to meet the herring on the banks with drift nets and seines. By the end of the 60s all the herring had been fished, and many small towns on the west coast found themselves in difficulties. The herring was totally protected for some years, and more than half the herring oil factories closed down. However, the stock is increasing again according to old hands who had large catches of herring in the North Sea in 1987.

Herring was the poor man's food. Salmon, on the other hand, is the rich man's food! Ola Nordmann's aim is to turn the salmon into a domestic animal. In the 1960s he began in a small way to breed salmon commercially. One fish farm after another appeared in Norwegian fjords and creeks, and salmon-breeding was hailed as the new economic wonder. The new 'coastal aristocracy' grew rich. In 1986, 40,000 tons of salmon worth around two billion kroner were exported to 20 countries; 99 per cent of the fish had been bred commercially. There were up to 700 hatcheries, 5,000 people were directly employed in fish farming, and 2,000 more were queueing up to start sea farms. Many Norwegians had also become involved in fish farms abroad.

But it is not easy to tame the salmon. *Salmo salmar* is used to having the whole Atlantic around him, and when confined in a small space, he suffers from stress, cold water vibriosis, and lice, ending up having to be cured with large doses of antibiotics and nerve gas. New dangers are

118. Tranøy lighthouse in Hamarøy (Nordland county) is one of nearly 100 manned lighthouses along the coast. On clear summer nights in northern Norway, the lighthouses are not lit. (R. Frislid/ NN)

always lurking. During the frightening environmental catastrophe of 1988, when the Skagerrak was invaded by poisonous algae that killed all fish, the fish farmers had to flee further north with their hatcheries. Fish farmers now put their trust in a vaccine against cold water vibriosis or 'Hitra disease', as it is called in Norway, and they are planning to breed other kinds of fish such as halibut and turbot, catfish and plaice.

The fishmonger in the famous Bergen fish market has taken up the challenge and now puts up a large notice advertising 'Wild salmon'!

And still we have the wild cod. From time immemorial cod have swum to the coast by the millions to spawn, from Lopphavet to Trøndelag, but in particular on the north side of Vestfjorden, from Lødingen to Røst, giving cause for the adventure that is the richest in tradition and lore: the Lofoten fishery.

There have been mass migrations to the Lofoten fishery, there have been fabulous catches, and there have been black years.

"They came from the west country. From Trøndelag, Nordland Troms and Finmark they came. There were fishermen, cooks, rookies, baitsmen, menders of nets as well as of bicycles, peddlers, Jews and jewellers, fire-and-brimstone preachers, and conjurors. Each had his own idea of Lofoten and what he could get there. They were after fish that would give them the kind of money they had never had before. This was in the order of things, whether they made a living from pulling an oar or selling pastries and cheap watches to the fishermen." The north Norwegian folklorist and author Frank A. Jenssen gives us this description in his colourful book on the Lofoten fishery.

In 1895 the greatest number of fishermen ever seen in Lofoten, 32,600 in all, brought in 125,000 tons of spawning cod. The peak was in 1947, when 20,500 men caught 146,000 tons. In the 1980s only about 4,000 people were taking advantage of the Lofoten fishing season, and the catch was around 50,000 tons. When the great seal invasion came in 1987, the results were so poor that buyers had to get in fish from far away in order to cover the Italian market.

The organization of the Lofoten fishery goes back a long way. In the Viking period there were laws to ensure that the chieftains got their share of the catch. Most of the dried fish that was brought into Bergen a thousand years ago came from Lofoten. At the beginning of the eighteenth century all the fishing was done with a hand-held line, which Norwegian fishermen today call the *juksa*. Then, a few decades later, came the long line and the use of nets, so the authorities had to divide up the fishing grounds.

The traditional vessel was the *fembøring*, an open boat with five pairs of oars, or the *attring* with four pairs or eight oars, both of them square-rigged and narrow, like a Viking ship. In 1905 the motor boat started to take over. Then, after the Second World War, came radar, the echo sounder, sonar, all excellent means of plotting the whereabouts of the fish, and these were followed by the hydraulic winch to hoist the catch on board, and satellite-linked navigation that can help steer the boat to within yards of the shoal.

Today it is the fishermen themselves who determine how the sea is to be divided up, and the fish is caught with hand-held lines, long lines, nets, and trawls. Out on the fishing grounds there is a difference between the rich and the poor, between those who hold a single line in their hands and those with large nets.

In his book, Jenssen describes them all, and everything in connection with the Lofoten fishery: its drinking traditions and the women who at one time in the last century made an immoral living. Above all he describes today's participants — from the fisherman with his hand-held line and jig with red woollen thread or rubber worm who growls that 'trawling is dirty fishing', to the fishery magnate Arne W. Johansen, who owns the whole of Stamsund and lives in a palace by north Norwegian standards. Also included are the tongue cutters, that little closed shop of children between the ages of eight and sixteen who cut out the cods' tongues in accordance with unwritten medieval laws. In his book, there is the lifeboat that comes to the rescue of vessels with nets in their propellors. There is the boiler that in an infernal atmosphere heats up cod liver oil to 970°C in seven minutes. He presents the Fisherman's Retreat that serves waffles and the Word of God, the fishery protection inspectors who have police authority in matters concerning the fishing grounds, the women who toil in the bait rooms and on board. He tells us about the feast that follows the first catch of spawning cod, with a special soup called *mølje*, served with roe, liver, stomach, blood, beer and aquavit.

He describes the stockfish taster, Lofoten's counterpart of the connoisseur wine taster, who has held an official position since 1716, after Querini had told His Holiness about the stockfish of Røst. The taster ensures that all fish sent to Rome or other places are of top quality. He has to rely on his nose, his eyes and his tastebuds to determine to which of the 26 classes each fish belongs. There is a true Italian ring to the names of the categories: *Vestre Piccolo, Vestre Piccolo Piccolo, Vestre*

Illustration (by the authors) to 'Three in Norway by Two of Them', by J.A. Lees and W.J. Clutterbuck, first published in 1882, reprinted by Aschehoug in 1988.

Demi Magro, Anakona Vestre, Grand Premier – and *Ragno*, the jewel of them all, the spawning cod with golden belly and translucent sides.

There is still cod to be had in the Barents Sea, say the experts; there is in fact a great deal of cod, if only it gets enough capelin to feed on and escapes yet another invasion of seals. But these prophecies are not always matched by the experience of the fishermen.

Because of the seal disaster of 1987, many Norwegians wanted to step up sealhunting, which had all but come to a halt. In the 1970s Norwegians caught 300,000 seals a year in the East Ice and West Ice. In 1987 only five or six state-subsidized ships went off to kill some 10,000 animals – a decrease due to international protests and threats of boycott because of the way seal cubs were culled: hunters battered the baby seals to death using a club on their little skulls.

But what happened to the Norwegian whaler? He too is giving up. Whaling has been carried on since prehistoric times. Basques caught whales in the Bay of Biscay in the ninth century, the English and Dutch off Svalbard in the seventeenth, and in the eighteenth, the Americans started their whaling activities. Norwegians have hunted for whales for as long as they have lived in Norway.

In the old days whale fishing meant hurling a hand harpoon from a rowing boat after small whales that, when captured, would float on their own blubber. It was not until 1868, when the Norwegian whaler Svend Foyn invented the harpoon gun and developed the steam-driven whaling ship, that whaling really took off. It increased so dramatically that from 1904 the whale had to be protected along the Norwegian coast.

After this the Norwegians threw themselves into a merciless hunt for whales in the Antarctic, with the result that the creature was near extinction by the 1960s, though it must be said that the Norwegians were not the only ones to blame. Before 1912 there were seven whaling stations on South Georgia, four of them Norwegian. Thousands upon thousands of whalers from the towns in Vestfold went south. At the beginning of the 1930s there were 41 Norwegian whaling factories and six shore stations in the South Atlantic. In the middle of the 1930s as many as 17,000 whales were harpooned by Norwegians in the Antarctic, and the gigantic mammals, weighing up to 150 tons, were pumped full of air and towed to the floating whale factories. At times Norway produced 80 per cent of the world's whale oil.

Large whales were still being hunted after the Second World War, but by 1960 there were not many left. The blue whale became a protected species in 1963, the baleen whale in 1964, and the fin whale in the southern hemisphere in 1977. Norway closed its last whaling station in the Antarctic in 1968.

Since the 1920s Norway has been catching minke whale commercially, with a peak catch of 4,000 whales a year. In the 1980s this activity was drastically reduced, and in 1987, 53 boats, mainly from Nordland, were licensed to catch 375 whales.

When Prime Minister Gro Harlem Brundtland presented the United Nations environmental report *Our Common Future* in London in 1987, the Greenpeace organization asked her to put her own house in order and stop that year's massacre of whales, the 'barbaric environmental vandalism' that is anathema to the international community. And she promised. She declared that all commercial Norwegian whaling was to cease after the 1987 season, in accordance with the statutes of the International Whaling Commission, and under pressure from the U.S.A.

SEAMEN AND SHIPPING

CHAPTER NINE is the story of the Norwegian seaman who sailed Norway from poverty to riches, and the shipowners who kicked him out when he became too expensive.

No-one is the subject of so much touching emotion as the rookie, the young boy who packed his bags, waved farewell to his mother, dried a tear, and left his small village in the mountains or by the coast. When he returned six months later he was a fully-fledged sailor, the hero of his peer group, having had his initiation in the storms of Biscay and the brothels of Hamburg.

For over a century women have been sitting in the Seaman's Missions knitting garments for those brave unknown boys away at sea, gifts that have been collected and handed out by the Norwegian Seaman's Church when the ship reached harbour.

It is hardly surprising that Ola Nordmann feels the sea in his bones considering that his long country has 2,650 kilometres (1,645 miles) of coastline following the most direct route from the Swedish to the Russian border. If you take in every bay and creek and stretch that distance out, you will have travelled 21,347 kilometres (13,256 miles), or almost half way round the world.

Norwegian children have always been taught that their country has the world's greatest tonnage of shipping in proportion to the population. We have all been brought up on pictures of ships in foreign ports, in Houston and Durban, San Francisco and Hong Kong. For years the newspapers gave exact positions of all Norwegian ships around the world, so that mother and father could send their letters to the nearest seaman's church.

Yet Norwegian shipping has had its ups and downs.

The first setback came in the thirteenth century when Viking ships were unable to compete with the beamier, decked Hanseatic trading vessels. In the sixteenth century the Dutch came in search of timber, and later that century Norwegian shipping picked up again. By the nineteenth century shipping provided a good revenue for the country.

The last century was the age of sail. Sailing ships were anchored so close together in the Norwegian harbours that small boys could run dry-footed across them. The tonnage increased from 100,000 in 1830 to 1.4 millions in 1890. Today Norway has only three square-rigged tall ships left as a reminder of those days. Then came ships driven by steam and engines, there were two world wars, and in the last war the whole merchant fleet was put at the service of the Allies.

The world fleet increased from 80 million registered tons in 1948 to 290 million in 1973, and at that time Norway with her one thousandth of the world population had 10 per cent of the world tonnage. In the 1970s each Norwegian had on average 7,000 tons, each Briton 600, each Japanese 375, and each American 70 tons.

Then came the big shock. In 1973 oil prices rose, trade generally was on the way down, and there were far too many tankers in the world! One ship after another was laid up. At the beginning of the 80s around 50 giant tankers were in their moorings – 40 per cent of the Norwegian tanker fleet.

The Norwegian shipowners then agreed among themselves that their own seamen had become too expensive, making Norway uncompetitive on the world market. They found that it would be cheaper to bring in people from the Third World who would be willing to sign on for a fraction of a Norwegian's pay. By this means they could save 4 million kroner per ship per year, or 1.2 billion for the whole fleet.

But then the ships could no longer sail under the Norwegian flag so they would have to fly a so-called 'flag of convenience', from Liberia, Panama, Bahamas or some other tax haven. Norwegian seamen have always despised ships registered under such flags. On board these vessels, the men have been treated indifferently, with none of the rights Norwegian seamen have fought for concerning pay, conditions and safety regulations. Sometimes the people taken on board were made to sign two contracts, one that could be shown to ITF, the International Transport Workers Federation, and one that laid down their real conditions.

But Norwegian shipowners had made up their minds to register abroad. In the mid-80s the Conservative government softened the restrictions on this, and by 1987, 455 Norwegian-owned vessels of 14.57 million tons deadweight were sailing under flags of convenience, while only 512, amounting to 9.76 million tons, were registered at home. The largest shipping lines applied for permission to register abroad, including the giant Bergesen line, whose tonnage equalled one third of the remaining Norwegian fleet. Not even our large cruise ships were spared, ships that for years had sailed from Miami with the Norwegian flag rippling in the wind. This was even the fate of Norway's flagship, the S/S *Norway*, formerly the French liner *France*.

By the beginning of 1987 Norway had for the first time dropped out

Horce-racing on ice. Illustration to Olaus Magnus: 'History of the Nordic Peoples', Rome 1555.

of the list of the ten most important shipping nations in the world. A decade before she had been listed fourth. Registration abroad coincided with a total collapse of the oil-rig and supply-ship market. Thousands of seamen were laid off and made redundant.

The Norwegian sailor was in danger of becoming obsolete. In October 1986 the Seaman's Union marched in silent protest through the streets of Oslo. And then they got even more reason to protest.

In 1930 the shipowner Erling Dekke Naess had registered his whale factory *Viking* in Panama. This was for him the start of a glorious shipping career abroad. In the 50s and 60s his Panama-registered fleet was estimated to be the third largest in the world. His activities brought him recognition that varied from his being called 'Public Enemy Number One' and 'pirate', to the award of the Royal Order of St Olav, and an honorary doctorate of the University of Bergen. In a speech in Oslo in January 1984, he suggested that Norway set up her own international ship register. At this point the country still had a merchant fleet with a tonnage of about 32 million tons deadweight. The flight from the flag had started, but was not yet catastrophic.

Nobody then believed that such an improbable idea would ever become a reality in Norway! But in the autumn of 1986 the proposal was put in all seriousness before the annual general meeting of the shipowners' federation, and on 1 July 1987, the Norwegian International Ship Register (NIS) was established in Bergen at record speed, following the most bitter discord in Norway for many years. It gave shipowners the right to fire Norwegian seamen on NIS ships and to hire foreign seamen at Third World rates; it also granted tax exemption to foreign investors in NIS. Some 10,000 seamen were sacrificed in order to improve the health of Norwegian shipping.

The day after the register had been established, the first NIS registered ship, M/S *Norcan* of the Stenersen line, called at Bergen. The temporary Norwegian crew had been put ashore in Rotterdam the day before and replaced by Indians. "We can't afford Norwegians. They demand one month at sea and one ashore, while the Asians stay at sea for nine months and ask for less pay," said shipowner Sigmund Stenersen to a Bergen newspaper. The Indian crew members received 3,000 kroner a month, the Norwegian sailors got 8,600.

If not for the sailor, for the shipowner NIS was a big success. After three years, three-quarters of the Norwegian merchant fleet was registered in NIS, and Norway was again one of the most important shipping nations in the world. In May 1990, the fleet consisted of 1,460 vessels with a total 51.5 million tons deadweight. Of these, 837 ships (37.2 million tons deadweight) were registrered in the NIS, and only 262 ships (1.7 million tons deadweight) were in the national register and had kept their Norwegian crews. There were still 365 ships (12.6 tons deadweight) sailing under flags of convenience.

The Norwegian Seaman's Mission is now at a loss. Since 1864 it has provided Norwegian seamen with waffles and the Gospel, reading rooms and mail from home, in its many churches all over the world. There are still 23 of these, and there are no plans to phase them out. Some 2,000 seaman's mission societies, run by increasingly aged women, still send their Christmas gifts to young boys out in the unknown. Now the mission has new target groups: oil workers in the North Sea, students and Norwegian residents abroad. But there is hardly any use in sending parcels to Ola Nordmann the sailor. He is no longer to be found in the seaman's church. He is sitting at the Job Centre hoping for new work.

ECONOMIC TRENDS

119. *The common guillemot and the kittiwake live in the protected bird colony of Ålesund. Bird colonies are to be found all along the coasts, but are most numerous in northern Norway, where hundreds of thousands of seabirds breed. (Roger Engvik)*

CHAPTER TEN is about the Norwegian factory worker, about waterfalls and hydroelectricity, profits and losses,. and about industrial life that became so chaotic that no-one knew any longer who owned whom.

When Dad was young the factory was unchanging. It was somewhere he took his lunch box and thermos flask to every day, regular as clockwork, shift after shift, year after year, making something that had always been made there, for the very same owners and with the very same workmates. The factory was as solid as a rock. The Stock Exchange report on the radio was something you heard as an even, monotonous background noise while you had your afternoon nap, as stimulating as the weather report. And a savings bank was still the modest building in the station town or fishing village, founded by the village's grandparents and run in their spare time by the fathers.

But after the Oslo Stock Exchange had lived a quiet life on the outskirts of Europe for many years, it plunged into a wild rollercoaster ride in the unprecedented boom of the 1980s when newly rich financiers and old companies bought each other up right, left and centre, leaving no-one untouched. Directors who had always displayed wisdom and decorum in interviews, now presided over extraordinary general meetings in a climate 'tainted by mutual accusation, slander and mistrust as deep as the ocean'. A pack of young men in ties and loud-checked suits suddenly appeared, hot on the trail of the new money to be found in media companies and fashion retailing, estate agencies and industrial enterprises. Soup producers started making asphalt, mining companies published weekly magazines, shares changed hands so quickly that poor old Ola no longer knew who owned him when he came to the factory in the morning.

'Cannibals of the business world' was how former prime minister, Per Borten, described these new heroes of the Norwegian media age. The result of the Stock Exchange's wild go-go days was that the Government had to pass a new Stock Exchange Law, reinforcing public control of the activity and bringing in more rigorous punishment for offenders. Most people were relieved that the legislation came when it did. All these things happened just as Norway found herself in the oil age. In the 1980s it was hardly possible to give a survey of business and finance valid for more than one week!

120. *The fjords of western Norway are narrow, but stretch far inland, as here at Geiranger, where tourists can admire the mountains from the deck of a cruise ship. (Mittet)* ▷

121. *At the foot of steep mountains and barely sheltered from the mighty ocean lie the small fishing communities of Outer Troms. This is Gryllefjord on the island of Senja. (O. Åsheim/ Samfoto)* ▷ ▷

The old Norsemen, like people in other countries, had to bring out the resources from wherever they were: fish from the sea, game from the moors, trees from the forest, and iron ore from the hillside. In the Viking age furs and pelts were the most important export articles, superseded by stockfish in the thirteenth century. As time went by, many settlements grew up where rivers met the sea, preferably where there was also another resource nearby.

Rivers and waterfalls are the salient features of the Norwegian landscape. The playful streams are where boys build mills, their own wooden turbines that whirl round and round. The waterfalls are mysterious, thundering, frightening, the home of the river sprite *Nøkken*, the creature of the underworld who teaches young boys to play the fiddle. It was not without reason that Ibsen let certain of his characters vanish into the waterfall.

The waterfall became the Norseman's prime helpmate in the centuries that followed, not least for grinding corn and cutting timber. Each farm had to have its own flourmill and sawmill. The water-driven sawmill first came into use in Norway in the sixteenth century. Soon vast amounts of timber products were being exported to England and the Netherlands, so much so that huge oak forests were destroyed in the south. There was a clear need for restriction, and in 1668 royal charters were granted to 664 sawmills to provide sawn timber for export. The others had permission to provide only for local needs.

Next came mining. In 1524 the first royal charter was given to a copper mine in Seljord in Telemark. Then came the silver mines, run by German mining experts brought to the country by the Danish king. They worked the Norwegian peasantry hard, and forced them to provide both coal and wood for the mines.

The Renaissance king, Christian IV, founded the ironworks at Bærum and Fossum near Oslo, the silverworks at Kongsberg and the copper industry of Røros. Eventually there were 15 ironworks, their names to be seen on iron stoves in old Norwegian houses.

In the distinctive mountain town of Røros, which is among the most worthy of conservation in Europe, huge slag heaps are a reminder of the miners' toil in the pits. The writer Johan Falkberget has immortalized their lives in his novels. The English social economist and population expert Thomas Robert Malthus travelled in Norway in 1799 and left this contemporary description of life in Røros:

"The miners work from Monday morning till Friday noon. In this period they live in a building near the mines, and on Friday they go home to their wives and children. If, by working extra hard, they finish the stipulated work before time, they can go home earlier. Usually they work from 4 a.m. until 5 p.m., except for meal times and for two hours from 10 to 12... When we left the mine, we went to see the house where the miners are lodged during the week, and I think I have never seen more pitiable accommodation. Almost a hundred men are crammed together in a room that measures 8 × 9 yards. They sleep on narrow bunks in a kind of scaffolding that runs along the walls. The bunks looked no wider than two feet, and we saw neither bedding nor covering. Many of the men were sleeping as we entered the room. They never take off their clothes from Monday to Friday." These were Malthus's impressions, recorded in the light of a miner's lamp.

A century later he could have switched on the electric light. Norway's first commercial hydroelectricity plant started up in Skien

131. By means of 12 mighty curves around waterfalls and ravines the Trollstigen road helps motorists to ascend 800 metres (2,600 feet) up the mountainside. This road in the Romsdalen district of western Norway, completed in 1936, took 20 years to build.
(Mittet)

in 1885. Hammerfest, the northernmost town in the world, was the first in the world to get electric street lights, in 1890. Our waterfalls have made Norway, with its warm rooms and well-lit streets on a cold winter's night, the country that consumes the most energy per capita in the world. In 1983 each human being used on average under 2,000 kilowatt-hours of electricity a year. Yugoslavs used 3,000, West Germans 6,000, North Americans 10,000, Icelandics, Swedes and Canadians roughly 15,000 each. Norwegians used 22,000. Ola Nordmann does not turn off the light when he leaves a room.

The encyclopædia *Nordisk Conversationslexicon* was not quite correct when it pronounced in 1871 that electric light 'is hardly suitable to use for ordinary illumination, as it is so expensive, and also so intense that one contracts inflammation of the eye merely from seeing it for a few minutes'.

For a long time the development of hydroelectricity met no resistance whatsoever. The plants were small, the power was essential, the future lay in electricity, and we all wanted it. But as the waterfalls disappeared and the sites made more and more unsightly scars on areas of outstanding natural beauty, people started to realize the value of what was being lost. Environmentalists intensified their protests in the 1960s, and Norway's largest waterfall and her great pride, Vøringsfossen, was partially saved. The watershed in the attitude to hydroelectric power development came around 1970, but the great battle was to be the fight for the Alta-Kautokeino river ten years later.

Just after the Second World War there were 2,000 electricity plants. Since then only very large projects have been constructed. Today there are 425 such plants in the country, producing 105 TerraWatt hours a year (1 TWh = one thousand million kilowatt hours). Much of Norway's water power is still unexploited. If everything were to be tapped, it would be possible to reach an output of 550 TWh a year. In the mid-80s it was reckoned that it would only pay to develop 172 TWh. At that point 25 TWh were left untouched for environmental reasons. Experts estimate that from now on it will be cheaper to exploit the natural gas in the North Sea than the remaining waterfalls.

Experiments have been made with wave power on the west coast, but this will hardly be significant before the turn of the century. Wind power has been rejected as a possibility so far, but solar energy has been tried out on a small scale. Any plans to develop nuclear power in Norway were scrapped after the Chernobyl accident in the Soviet Union in 1986. No-one in Norway can tell you what is to replace the natural gas when it runs out one day.

The true industrial revolution in Norway began in the 1850s, when textile production started up by the Aker river in Oslo. Hjula Mill was the best known. Wood pulp and chemical pulp factories were opened in forestry areas. In Skien the Union company was started, and the Grenland district came to be one of Norway's most densely populated and most polluted areas. In 1891 Sarpsborg, using British capital, inaugurated its pulp and paper factory Borregaard, destined to be the pride of Norwegian industry for a century to come.

The real bonanza in Norwegian industrial development was due to another waterfall, Rjukanfossen. At a dinner party given by the future prime minister, Gunnar Knudsen, in 1903, the engineer Sam Eyde and professor Kristian Birkeland got talking. The former had access to a vast supply of hydroelectric power. He had founded Elkem, an electrochemical company, and he was convinced that it would be possible to produce artificial fertilizer from nitrogen in the atmosphere, if only he could direct a flash of lightning, an electric flame fierce enough for the extraction process. Birkeland had just hit upon this – the previous week! The outcome was the founding in 1905 of the Norwegian hydroelectric nitrogen company that became Norsk Hydro, the taming of the spectacular Rjukan Falls, and the factories built in Notodden and Rjukan.

Needless to say, Rjukan, a small place at the bottom of Vestfjord valley under the towering Gausta peak, was rapidly transformed: its population had increased to 8,000 by 1920. Northern Europe's first passenger cableway was installed to lift people out of the narrow valley up into the light and air. The place flourished, people were happy and life went on – for some decades. Rjukan is most famous for the events that took place there on 27 February 1943, when the Norwegian Resistance sabotaged Norsk Hydro's heavy water plant in order to prevent Hitler from developing the atomic bomb.

More electrometallurgical and electrochemical plants were to be built in this country so rich in waterfalls. Vast plants with smelting furnaces and rolling-mills were squeezed into small communities, spewing their smoke up the hillsides and their waste products into the sea. Much of this industry produced iron alloys for reinforcing other metals. Some factories had private backing, others were state enterprises that aimed at keeping the population distributed throughout the country. The engineering industry was now well under way; the fish products and high technology industries were to follow.

The towns had their own specialities. Christian Bjelland made Stavanger into a sardine town, Helly J. Hansen made raincoats in Moss, Jonas Øgland bicycles in Sandnes, the Viking Company made rubber boots in Askim. The Sunnmørings make furniture, Mustad & Co. at Gjøvik sell fish-hooks all over the world, and Jordan's toothbrushes are exported to 80 countries, beaten on the market only by Colgate and Gillette. The toothpicks on Thai Airlines are made in the small forest village of Flisa in Solør.

Despite all this, in 1986 the government had to draw the conclusion that Norway is still a poorly developed industrial nation, mostly deliver-

Farmers fishing, drying and smoking salmon. Illustration to Olaus Magnus: 'History of the Nordic Peoples', Rome 1555.

ing semi-manufactures that are finished elsewhere. The raw material is brought here, where water-power is cheap, and sent on in an unfinished state. Nor is there much chance of expansion within the market. The leading industrial nations are now concentrating on brain power and information technology. The semi-manufacturing countries are likely to be left behind, exposed to fluctuations in the market, as many raw material producers have been for a long time.

Norwegian industry has become more international in recent years. In 1985 the majority of shares in about 1,800 companies were in foreign hands, while Norwegians had interests in 4,400 foreign companies all over the world.

With traditional industries such as shipbuilding, fishing and mining in decline, Ola Nordmann has had to look around for new ways of making a living, whether in fish farms, tourism, fashion, the media or computers. Sometimes it works, sometimes it does not. In many ways Norway is the land of small firms. There are 181,000 of them, often run by one man and his wife. Some 40 per cent of production is accounted for by firms employing less than 100 people.

However, it is the large companies that count! Listed according to turnover, the largest firms in the mid-80s were Statoil, Norsk Hydro, Esso, Philips, the insurance company Storebrand-Norden, the state-owned telecommunications Televerket, Shell and Elf. The highest net profits were made by eight oil companies, followed by Den norske Creditbank and Televerket. Den norske Creditbank was later to suffer heavy losses, not least through ill-judged placing of shares. Norsk Hydro had the highest number of employees – 26,400, followed by the state postal service (25,100) and Televerket (21,200).

Among the world's largest companies outside the U.S.A., Statoil is ranked number 78 and Norsk Hydro 101. Statoil is part of the oil chapter in our saga of Norway and the Norwegians. And what happened to Norsk Hydro after that historic dinner in 1903, when the lightning flashed between Sam Eyde and Kristian Birkeland? The process developed by the two of them to extract artificial fertilizer from the air proved to be too power-intensive, and was replaced at the end of the 1920s by the German Haber-Bosch process. The Rjukan plant was rebuilt, and Norsk Hydro created Norway's largest industrial works, Porsgrunn Fabrikker, on Herøya, in the Grenland area. In the 1960s electric power was replaced by oil, and the plant once more had to be tailored to meet petrochemical-based production. Norsk Hydro became an oil company itself, started operating in the North Sea, bought up petrol stations, and planned the production of gas.

Before the Second World War, Ardalstangen and Øvre Ardal were two peaceful, humble villages as far as you can get up the Sognefjord, at the foot of Jotunheimen, surrounded by peaks of up to 1,300 metres (over 4,000 feet) on all sides. During the war the German occupation forces started work on an aluminium plant there. After the war the Norwegian State took over the unfinished project and carried on with the Ardal plant, taking into account the population factor and the effect on the small community. Ardal was a typical example of post-war industrial development in Norway.

Forty years later Ardal and Sunndal were amalgamated with the aluminium division of Norsk Hydro, which already owned the smelting works at Karmøy in the west. Hydro Aluminium became the second largest aluminium company in Europe, supplying 600,000 tons a year, with 50 plants at home and abroad, and a total workforce of 12,000 in 12 countries. In Norway the company controls the key industries of many small towns.

In addition, Norsk Hydro is behind the artificial fertilizer produced at Glomfjord in Nordland and in France, magnesium in Canada, fish farmed in Ireland, Iceland and Scotland, ammunition made at the Norwegian Dyno industries, the chocolate from Freia and Marabou, and a great deal else – with total assets of 41 billion kroner in 1985. The concern accounted for 17 per cent of the total value of the companies quoted on the Stock Exchange in 1986. The State owns 51 per cent of the shares, 10.4 are privately owned by Norwegians, and 38.6 by foreign investors. Yet the small town of Rjukan, where it all started, is now a dying community, unless it is to be artificially revived by hotels, motels and sportels, chalets and skilifts high up on the plateau beneath Gausta-toppen.

Norway's largest private industrial concern is Aker-Norcem, which started as a mechanical workshop in 1842 and a cement plant in 1892, and now has a workforce of 14,000 and a turnover of 10 billion kroner a year. Its entrepreneurial activities range over the whole world, and it has helped to make concrete platforms for the oil rigs in the North Sea, through Norwegian Contractors.

Illustration to 'Three in Norway by Two of Them' by J.A. Lees and W.J. Clutterbuck, 1882.

The Kværner business, opened in 1848 by the brothers Jens and Andreas Jensen as Myrens Workshop in an old smithy near Akerselva in Oslo, is one of the world's largest makers of hydroelectric turbines, a pioneer in wave power, and supplier to the oil industry, in particular through Rosenberg Verft in Stavanger.

Elektrisk Bureau employs 10,000 people in 17 different plants in Norway, has interests in 12 countries, and touches every Norwegian directly — through his telephone.

Elkem, which branched out from Christiania Spigerverk and the company founded by Sam Eyde in 1904, produces steel, ferro-alloys, aluminium and many kinds of manufactured goods in 25 different places in Norway, from Finnmark to Lista.

Borregaard has now become Orkla-Borregaard and produces everything from chemical pulp and paper to washing powder, biscuits, sausages and women's magazines, and it is one of the big shareholders in the Norwegian newspaper world.

Norwegian state enterprises do not exactly flourish. Not that there are many of them. Some were established for defence reasons: the armaments factory at Kongsberg in 1814, the Horten naval shipyard in 1849, and the Raufoss munitions factory in 1896. After the last world war it became vital for Norway to be self-sufficient in steel. The State therefore bought a substantial part of the mining company A/S Sydvaranger in Kirkenes, on the Soviet border.

Norway's really great national effort was the founding of A/S Norsk Jernverk, the ironworks in Mo i Rana, a small town that after the war had a population of 9,000. The idea was to make use of the raw materials from the Rana mines, take in coal from Svalbard, give the northerners something to keep them in the area; in fact it was to be the epitome of industrial development according to all the principles of social democracy.

The town grew big and strong, thanks to the iron foundry, and it gradually increased in size to 26,000 inhabitants. Of these, 5,500 were directly employed by the ironworks in the middle of the 70s, and the whole town of Mo was dependent on it. The State owned 80 per cent of the shares, Elkem 20 per cent.

But the ironworks made a loss. Over a period of five years alone the State had to contribute three billion kroner to keep it going, despite the company having laid off a thousand men in the same period. In 1989 the production of ore-based iron stopped in Mo, after 30 years. Now it is only in Svalbard that the authorities have no qualms about subsidizing the mines. They are essential to maintaining our sovereignty in the north.

The State is loosening its grip on many state-owned companies. Televerket has been divided into two parts, one a monopoly, the other competitive. The state broadcasting company Norsk Rikskringkasting has become an independent body, and the postal service is also to be given economic freedom. Conservative politicians wish to sell off Norsk Hydro to private investors — so far without luck.

At the start of the 90s, it must be conceded that the idea of solidarity is not as widespread in social democracy as it was in the hard years after the war. Today it is profit that counts. Norway now has the highest level of unemployment since the depression years of the 30s.

News reports on corruption have become a part of our daily life, not least in the capital, where in 1990 the lord mayor had to withdraw after being criticized for mixing private and municipal interests.

The Norwegians have lost their innocence, if they ever had any.

STRIKING IT RICH

CHAPTER ELEVEN tells the tale of Ola Nordmann who turned into an oil tycoon, and how Americans and Spaniards, Portuguese and Mexicans helped him to get oil out of the North Sea.

Ever since the day Edwin L. Drake first struck oil in Pennsylvania in 1859, petroleum had been something remote from the average Norwegian. To seamen who shipped the oil, from Texas and Abadan, it was a reality, but for the landlubber petrol was something in a can, maybe in a tank, to heat cold houses in the winter. The paraffin barrel on its rack in the garden was part of the Norwegian scene.

But then, in the late 1960s, someone claimed to have found oil in the North Sea! Since then, Norwegians have been fed with a daily diet of information about sectors and drilling, rigs and OPEC meetings.

Norway has three per cent of the gas reserves and 1.5 per cent of the oil reserves in the world — on her doorstep, so to speak. The oil adventure has completely changed Norwegian ideas about industry and has made young men aim at a career 'in oil' instead of at sea.

We started south of the 62nd parallel and constructed a big, floating 'city' far south in the North Sea, Ekofisk, and another just outside Bergen, Statfjord. There are many large and small oilfields between them. In 1986 oil and gas were produced from 12 fields in all in the North Sea by means of 19 production platforms and a sea-bed construction. Many fields have not yet been exploited, such as the large Troll field that in a few years' time will supply half Europe with natural gas. By 1987 it was estimated that all the oil and gas south of the 62nd parallel had been recorded and the search for oil has since moved further north. On the Haltenbanken shelf, off mid-Norway, a large deposit of gas has been found. The big question now is how much is yet to be discovered in the Barents Sea and on Svalbard.

Ola Nordmann was sceptical in 1962 when foreigners turned up wanting to investigate what was at the bottom of the North Sea. The background to this was that gas had been found in the Netherlands. "Search, but don't drill," the Norwegians said at the beginning. But in 1965 the first permission to drill was granted.

Norway had by then proclaimed her sovereignty over the Norwegian Continental Shelf and the North Sea had been divided between Norway, Denmark and Great Britain according to a centre-line principle.

In the summer of 1966 the first hole was drilled on the Norwegian

132. A Norwegian farmer and his horse. The Fjord horse (Fjording) is a breed that has much in common with the European wild horse, with its standing mane and black stripe from head to tail. (Husmo-Foto)

Continental Shelf. It was dry. But 1968 saw the first commercially exploitable find on the Cod field. On 23 December 1969, the Ekofisk field was discovered, and in 1971 the first well was put into production. The oil adventure had really begun.

But the Norwegians had no idea what to do when they were suddenly thrown into the oil age. Even if they could transport the oil, they couldn't get it up from the sea-bed. Consequently, 91 per cent of the projects were handled by foreigners, and foreigners were wholly responsible for operations when the first sectors were divided up. It was Spaniards, Portuguese and Mexicans who developed Ekofisk. Until 1970 Norway had to import ordinary workers as well as experts. The Norwegians had enough to do coping with the on-shore industry. In the mid-80s all the production fields were still being operated by foreign companies. The North Sea was a new Texas! To make up for this the Norwegians gave the fields names taken from Norse mythology and folk tales.

As early as 1969 the government had claimed the right to a share in all the commercially exploitable fields on the Norwegian Shelf. In 1972 the Norwegian Petroleum Directorate and the state oil company Statoil were established to take charge of all the Norwegian interests. As time went by the Norwegians took an increasingly active part.

The first finds created a real Klondyke atmosphere in Norway. Everyone wanted to buy shares, everyone wanted to speculate in the 'black gold' of the sea. But it soon turned out to be more difficult than anticipated to raise the capital and acquire the know-how for the enormously expensive production. The way most Norwegians benefited from the oil bonanza was not from gains on the Stock Exchange but indirectly, through the general increase in revenue brought in by Statoil. The comments of the director of Statoil became almost as significant as those of the prime minister – perhaps because we did not hear him so often.

In the twenty years that have gone by since the start, Statoil has grown into one of Scandinavia's leading industrial concerns with about 10,000 on the payroll. It pumps up 50 million tons of oil a year, and is involved in some way in everything that goes on in the North Sea. Statoil is the operator of the Statfjord and Gullfaks fields, runs the gigantic Statepipe system, and is responsible for shipping the crude oil from Statfjord; it runs the refineries at Mongstad and at Bamble, it has bought up about a thousand petrol stations in Denmark and Sweden, and controls 27 per cent of the Norwegian market.

The other great Norwegian oil company, Norsk Hydro, created from the giant company founded by Sam Eyde and Kristian Birkeland in 1905, is 51 per cent state-owned. The company has been involved in the North Sea since the beginning of the oil adventure, in particular in the Ekofisk, Frigg and Gullfaks fields. It owns a large part of the great petro-chemical installations at Bamble in Telemark, runs petrol stations in Sweden, and is involved in the planning of a vast gas power station in the west of Norway.

The only privately-owned Norwegian company found fit to operate on the Norwegian Shelf is Saga Petroleum. But despite its 55,000 shareholders, it has been unable to manage without considerable help from industry. The Swedish mega company Volvo owns 20 per cent of the shares, and Saga wishes to increase foreign investment to 40 per cent. Appropriately, it is Saga that is to expand the Snorre field. After all, it was Snorre who gave Norway the sagas!

133. Forestry is highly mechanized, but some farmers still prefer the horse when moving timber to the collection stations, where it is taken over by tractors or trucks for further transportation. (Husmo-Foto) ▷

134. As far up the dizzy heights as grass can grow, the sheep will follow. This is Vengedalen in the Romsdalen district. (R. Frislid/ NN) ▷ ▷

139. *On farms in western Norway
with their steep slopes, the sturdy
little Fjording is almost indispensable.*
(Husmo-Foto)

140. The wood-burning stove and the coffee pot have a very important place in the small huts which used to be the home of forestry workers for most of the week. Today, new roads make it possible for them to drive daily to the forests. (Husmo-Foto)

141. Grey, weather-beaten log cabins with turf roofs are typical of the old dairy farm. But the equipment hanging on the wall shows that the milking machine has found its way even here. (R. Frislid/NN)

142. Modern forestry is based on clear felling of larger or smaller areas, which appreciably alters the appearance of woodlands. (Pål Hermansen/Samfoto/NN)

143. Upland dairy farms are still worked in some places. Hay from such farms is an important supplement to winter fodder. This dairy farm is at Innfjorden, in the western district of Romsdalen. (R. Frislid/NN)

144. Forested hills are typical of the scenery in the interior of eastern Norway, as here near Lake Krøderen. (R. Frislid/ NN) ▷

There is also a third private company, the Norwegian Petroleum Company. When oil fever was at its height, it had to hire the largest cinema in Oslo to conduct its annual general meetings. It is still one of the companies with the largest number of shares on the Oslo Stock Exchange (58,000 in all), but it showed a loss in 1986, when the shares were worth only half their nominal value and the company waited in vain for a chance to operate in Norwegian territorial waters.

Anyone who flies over the North Sea will see that production platforms vary. Steel platforms were the first to be used. To ensure stability, supports, 50 to 100 metres (140–280 feet) in length, were thrust down into the sea-bed from the platform legs. Gravity-base structures are another type, usually great concrete platforms held in place by their own weight. The most famous of these are the Norwegian-constructed Condeep platforms, the first of which was placed in a depth of 70 metres (200 feet) on the Ekofisk field in 1970. But operations at greater depths require new kinds of platform, one type being a floating steel platform attached to the sea-bed by a length of steel tubing. Saga Petroleum is planning to use this type of platform on the Snorre field, due to go into production from 1992. It is already in operation on the British Hutton field in the North Sea.

Technical developments have also made it possible to eliminate the production platform. A system of this kind is used on North East Frigg. The so-called production valves are placed in a steel frame on the sea-bed, and production is operated from a control platform that receives radio signals from the Frigg field. This may be the future pattern of oil development in the Barents Sea, a development that is hardly visible on the surface, unlike the steel and concrete cities that populate the North Sea.

Three types of raw material are obtained: dry gas (methane gas with small parts of ethane and propane), wet gas (ethane, propane and butane gas) and crude oil.

Oil and gas are brought ashore partly by ship, partly through pipelines on the sea-bed. The tankers fuel from loading buoys connected to the production platforms. These loading buoys are vast, the one at Statfjord A being 182 metres (654 feet) high. The pipelines have a diameter of up to 125 centimetres (36 inches) and convey oil to most countries around the North Sea.

From Ekofisk the oil is piped to Teesside in England and the natural gas to Emden in West Germany. The gas goes from Frigg in two parallel gas pipes to St Fergus in Scotland. From Murchison the wet gas and oil is taken to Sullom Voe in the Shetlands and the dry gas to St. Fergus. In the autumn of 1986, Prime Minister Gro Harlem Brundtland officially inaugurated the Statepipe system, Norway's most ambitious industrial project as well as the world's greatest offshore transport system for gas, and the main artery connecting the North Sea both to Norway and to the pipelines of the Continent. The pipeline stretches 880 kilometres (550 miles) under the sea.

Yet another vast pipeline is to be laid in the 1990s, from the rich fields of Troll and Sleipner to Zeebrugge in Belgium, altogether 830 kilometres (515 miles), or 1,300 (810 miles) if you count all the side lines that lead the oil off to the various customers: Ruhrgass, BEB and Thyssengas in Germany, Gasunie in Holland, Distrigaz in Belgium, and Gaz de France.

Back on shore the Norwegians are constantly aware of the oil. Huge

145. Autumn and late winter are times for felling timber. Forestry is an important industry in Norway: up to 10 million cubic metres (13 million cubic yards) of timber are cut each year. (A. Normann/ Samfoto)

rigs are towed in and out of the fjords, old-established shipyards are wiped off the map or remodelled to serve the oil industry, and small villages are transformed into industrial sites. The most intensive activity takes place in Stavanger, Norway's oil city, which has 150,000 people living within half an hour's drive of the city centre. The old brisling town now has the highest house prices in Norway, since 10 international and two Norwegian companies are based there. Oil tanks and pipelines have proliferated in many other places: Slagentangen in Vestfold, Rafnes in Bamble, Sola in Rogaland, Mongstad in North Hordaland.

The oil refinery in Mongstad, now owned by Statoil, started up in 1975 and is capable of supplying tankers of up to 300,000 tons. For Statoil's new crude oil terminal there, 2.6 million cubic metres (53 million cu.ft.) of stone have to be blasted out of the rock – the same amount that went to the building of the Cheops pyramid in Egypt. The terminal and the refinery together make it the country's greatest land-based industrial project ever, originally estimated to cost 7 billion kroner. It is to receive 90 per cent of all the oil from the Statfjord and Gullfaks fields, and will supply all Statoil's petrol stations, which sell one out of five gallons of petrol sold in Scandinavia.

But in 1987 the Mongstad project turned into Norway's greatest industrial scandal when it was found to have exceeded the building estimate by 5 billion kroner, an amount so astronomical that the wits of the press immediately introduced a new monetary unit, 'the mong'!

The great Statepipe system goes ashore in Kårstø, which has become one of Norway's busiest ports with 250 ships calling in each year. The North Sea gas is brought in here and the wet gas is separated and sent on to the U.S.A., Sweden and other countries. The dry gas is transported to Ekofisk and from there by pipeline to Emden in West Germany.

Now Statoil, in co-operation with the state-run company Statskraft, is to build a gas-fuelled power station at Kårstø, while Norsk Hydro plans another at Karmøy. The oil from Oseberg is to be brought ashore further up the west coast, at Sture in Øygarden. A third gas power station is to be built in mid-Norway, based on Haltenbanken gas, and a gas pipe is likely to be extended into Sweden, which is committed to phasing out its nuclear power stations by the year 2010.

In short, Ola Nordmann is claiming more and more of the oil action. In 1977 there were 27,500 people involved in oil production offshore and on land. Of these, 21 per cent were foreigners. In 1987 the number had

Illustration (by the authors) to 'Three in Norway by Two of Them' by J.A. Lees and W.J. Clutterbuck, 1882.

increased to 64,300 while the number of foreigners had fallen to six per cent. On 29 January 1987, a red letter day in Norwegian oil history, Ola Nordmann was able to send out the first 100 per cent Norwegian-produced barrel of oil from the Gullfaks A platform. It had been planned and constructed by Norwegians under the combined ownership of three Norwegian companies: Statoil, Saga and Norsk Hydro. It was also the first rig to have Norwegian as the working language.

Until the mid 1980s all was well in the oil country of Norway. The 'black gold' flowed, the gas poured out, investments were huge (33 billion in 1986), but so were returns. The standard of living reached a new peak, and unemployment was among the lowest in Europe. Ola Nordmann took off to the Canaries for his holidays and traded in his old Volvo for the latest model. Then he was jolted into remembering that he was not alone in the world! There was a drastic fall in the internationally-set oil price, upon which he had based all his activities. Fluctuations in oil income signalled the danger of being solely dependent upon this industry. Nor does oil and fossil fuel last for ever. At the present rate of exploitation, the Norwegian oil bonanza should be over by the turn the century. If the companies are allowed to have their way, 75 per cent of the oil reserves will have run out by that time. However, we do have enough gas (almost half the total reserves of Europe) to last another century. It is highly probable that Norway has reserves of up to 10 billion tons of oil equivalents, including those in the Barents Sea. But the waters of the north are among the most rigorous in the world, with severe winter storms, continuous darkness and an exceedingly harsh climate. Exploitation will be very costly.

The north of Norway felt sadly left behind in the oil age. It was therefore a subject of general rejoicing when the Norwegian sector of the Barents Sea was cleared for drilling in 1987 and when the government that same year gave out the first three concessions in the Barents Sea to Statoil, Norsk Hydro and Saga Petroleum. At last north Norway was to get its share of the riches. At last people would stop moving away!

The Russians had been drilling for oil and gas in the Barents Sea from the early 80s and begun production in 1987. In June of that year, Ross Rig started exploratory drilling in the Norwegian sector. A month later the first sample was seen on the deck, brought up from 1,000 metres deep in the Finnmark West field, and Saga Petroleum could announce its find. It smelled of oil! Some days later, though, it proved to smell more of gas. And it is still not worth extracting gas so far north.

Oil has brought great riches to Norway, and also great unhappiness. The worst disaster happened on 27 March 1980, when the Alexander L. Kielland hotel platform toppled over into the sea, taking 124 people with it. Only 89 were saved.

One special danger is uncontrolled blow-outs on the rigs. The first occurred on 22 April 1977, when the oil burst up like a geyser spurting 60 metres (200 feet) into the air from the Bravo platform. The 100 men on board were evacuated. After a week the American 'well-killer' Red Adair managed to stop the blow-out. The environmental organization Greenpeace has published a report showing that a blow-out not stopped within 100 days would cause pollution to the Norwegian coastline costing between two and five billion kroner.

It is tempting to speculate about what is to be done with all the rigs when the oil adventure is over. It will cost 75 billion kroner just to remove the platforms from Ekofisk and Statfjord.

INTERNATIONAL ASPECTS

CHAPTER TWELVE tells us what it is like to be new in a foreign land, how Ola and Kari Nordmann get on in international company, and how they try to hold on to their culture.

Norway – for Norwegians?
The Norwegians' relationship to the rest of the world is somewhat complicated. Maybe not so much when we travel, as when the rest of the world comes to us. We aren't used to that at all. Up to the Second World War Norway lay secluded and totally innocent of all involvement. That whole villages in Finnmark were Finnish did not concern the south at all: Finnmark was so far away, and the Finns were inconspicuous. They were, after all, white. And Lapps were only something you read about in romantic novels. Around 1950 there were only two black people domiciled in Norway: one a drummer, the other a singer. Thirty years on, Norwegian papers were filled daily with stories of refugees and racial prejudice, and 32 nations were represented on the staff of the Grand Hotel in Oslo alone!

Once upon a time the Norwegian himself experienced what it was like to be an immigrant. Between 1825, when Cleng Persson led the first batch of immigrants from Rogaland on the sloop *Restauration,* and 1930, over 850,000 Norwegians set out for America. In the peak year of 1882, as many as 28,804 left the barren rocks of Norway to seek their fortune in 'God's own country'. The majority settled in the Mid-West, Minnesota and North Dakota, which are dotted with Norwegian place names. They also went to Texas, Seattle and Brooklyn in New York. They built Norwegian churches, and produced Norwegian newspapers – over 400 of these, some of them still in existence. Even if they were immigrants, they kept their identity and were proud of their origins. It was of course a matter of sòme irritation that there were already people there who owned the land: those 'obnoxious heathens' who would not let themselves be driven away, 'cannibals' perpetrating 'unspeakable acts of violence', as the Norwegians wrote home in their letters from America in the nineteenth century. It evokes unmistakable echoes of the descriptions the Vikings gave of the *Skrælingers* in Vinland 800 years earlier: ''They were black, ugly creatures, with ugly hair on their hands, wide eyes and broad faces.''

When Peter Minuit, governor of the colony of New Holland, bought Manhattan in 1626 to found New Amsterdam (later New York), it was a Norwegian – Cornelius Sand – who served as his interpreter in the transaction that cost a few beads and baubles. Where the Indians hunted for buffalo there now live almost as many people with a Norwegian heritage as there are in Norway itself. In Seattle Norwegians fish in the old fishing places of the native Americans. The white man and his wife did not arrive there until 1851.

The Norwegian found his place in the world, but did he accept foreigners in return? The Constitution of 1814 stated that 'Jews are still banned from entering the country'. This clause was not removed until 1851, after persistent campaigning by the poet and human rights activist Henrik Wergeland. But even when Jews were allowed in, not everybody wished them welcome.

"To a great extent these Jews make a living from illicit trading, mainly in clocks, and partly through card games. They are people without a nation although they have been in Norway for many years... I can only suppose that most of them can be bought for whatever purposes providing they get money from it." This was a confidential note from a policeman to the Norwegian Ministry of Justice during the First World War.

Around 400 refugees came into Norway between the wars, although there is a memo from the Ministry stating that 'in principle our policy is to close the borders to refugees. If we relax this, we will have a host of them upon us'.

There are several special reasons why Norway ought to have a positive policy on this issue. One is Fridtjof Nansen, the humanist and polar scientist who in 1921 was appointed the first High Commissioner for Refugees. Under his leadership, assistance was extended to 450,000 refugees and displaced persons after the First World War. He also helped hundreds of thousands of Russians who had fled the Revolution. All these people were saved thanks to a piece of paper that bore his name — the Nansen passport. Another reason is that tens of thousands of Norwegians themselves had to escape the country during the German occupation, making their way to Sweden, Britain, the U.S.A. and elsewhere.

Today there are between 15 and 23 million refugees in the world. Some 16,000, from 70 national groups in all, have been admitted to Norway since the Second World War. About 1,500 foreigners, mainly Poles, chose to stay on in Norway when the war ended. Two years later 550 Jewish refugees came from camps in Germany and Poland. After the Hungarian Rising we took in 1,500 Hungarian refugees, joined in recent years by many Asians, mainly Vietnamese, but also Tamils and Iranians. Of the Latin Americans, many are from Chile.

Norway is the Scandinavian country that has accepted the lowest number of refugees: in 1985 we admitted 774 asylum-seekers, while the Danes took in 10,000 and Sweden 15,000. In 1987 the number had risen to 8,500. Since then Norway has passed a controversial Aliens Law that is far more restrictive but should not affect 'genuine' refugees. Once admitted, they will enjoy greater legal protection through the new legislation, but only a quarter of those who apply can count on getting political asylum. In 1986 almost 60 per cent were admitted on humanitarian grounds. This group must from now on reckon on being sent out of the country. Norway has, however, committed herself to taking in 1,000 United Nations quota refugees.

The State set up a separate Aliens Office on 1 January 1988, at the same time establishing new reception centres for refugees in Oslo,

Kristiansand, Bergen, Trondheim and Stavanger. The idea is for these centres to hand over refugees to the care of local communities, who will be refunded up to a certain level. In practice, very few local authorities are willing to accept them, and indeed no-one seems prepared for the task. In the meantime there are 1,000 refugees waiting to be placed.

Some locations are considered unsuitable for refugees even though they offer housing and jobs. Båtsfjord, a fishing village in the far north of Finnmark, was turned down when it asked for 10 refugees, even though people from Finnmark are generous and used to seeing new faces. After all, people from all over the world come to work in its Båtsfjord fish factory – in 1987, 20 nations were represented! But the refugee secretariat said 'no' because Finnmark is so far north and the Tamils, from so far south, might feel out of place on the wharf in a snowstorm. However, the minister of social affairs intervened personally and Båtsfjord was sent its refugees – who are doing fine!

The local social workers who have to handle the cases lack the necessary knowledge about the refugees' background and culture. Nor do they have the time and resources to see that the refugees are trained or given a job. In consequence many have simply ended up living on welfare. If they get a job it is rarely compatible with their qualifications. A study made in 1980 showed that 32 per cent of university-trained Africans and 22 per cent of Latin Americans worked in shops, petrol stations, etc. in Oslo, as against only three per cent of Norwegian university graduates.

Many asylum-seekers have to wait months for a decision as to where they are to be placed, and are meanwhile lodged in hotels and boarding houses all over the country.

In 1986 400 reports of racial discrimination were made to the Anti-Racism Centre in Oslo. Many of these were clearly cases of institutional racism, some even involving the police. The police headquarters in Oslo received nearly 100 reports of racism, but all the cases were dismissed. The first encounter a refugee has with Norway is often with the immigration control at Fornebu Airport near Oslo, which in recent years has come in for a good deal of criticism.

Racist agitation increased in the late 80s and the papers were full of letters expressing prejudice towards immigrants. Incidents were reported in many parts of the country, including the Hedmark village of Brumunddal, where a Pakistani had his shop blown up by racist youths.

These negative examples are not the whole story. Not all Norwegians are racially prejudiced. On the contrary, there are always people ready to defend anyone who is discriminated against. But the Gallup polls show that Ola and Kari Nordmann may not be as tolerant as they make out. 'Norway – mainly for Norwegians' was how *Aftenposten* summed up the results of a poll on immigrants in 1985. A later opinion poll showed that 51 per cent of Norwegians did not think the country should accept more than the 6,000 refugees stipulated for the year. Only eight per cent were in favour of receiving more.

Some come, others go. In 1986, 16,211 Norwegians took up residence abroad. At the same time 23,383 foreigners moved here, over half of them Europeans. In 1987 there were altogether 115,000 foreigners in Norway, mainly Danes, Britons and Swedes, but also 8,000 Pakistanis.

Norway introduced an immigration ban in 1975. However, the experts point out that without immigration Norway will have a population of only 3.5 million by the year 2050, as against 4.1 million today.

With net immigration of 4,000 a year, by 2050 we will arrive at the same level as Sweden has today. In Sweden every tenth citizen is an immigrant.

Aid to developing countries increased from 9.6 million kroner in 1962 to 6.2 billion kroner in 1987. Norway provides 1.5 per cent of the total aid given in the world. And recent investigations prove that 85 per cent of the people are in favour of this. If we compare figures for 1984, we find that Norway contributed 1.2 per cent of her Gross National Product to development aid, the Netherlands did the same, while Denmark gave 0.85, Sweden 0.80, France 0.36, Great Britain 0.33 and the U.S.A. 0.24 per cent.

While Norwegians have long maintained close, and mostly amicable ties with their Scandinavian neighbours, before *glasnost* and *perestroika* they were almost without contact with their next-door neighbour in the north, the Soviet Union. Once in a while there was a tourist trip over the border, across the Pasvik River. There was not much traffic on a higher level either. When the Norwegian prime minister visited the Soviet Union in 1986, she was the first premier to do so since 1974. Nor had any of her Soviet counterparts been here between 1971, when Alexei Kosygin came to Norway, and 1988, when Prime Minister Ryshkov paid a visit.

But then things began changing very fast; the frontier was opened to a certain extent, and people started visiting one another. In 1990, President Mikhail Gorbachev was awarded the Nobel Peace Prize!

Yet from the other direction, from the mighty nation across the Atlantic, an unprecedented stream of influences pours into the small houses in the Pasvik Valley every minute of the day, in the form of sounds and images, cartoons and news flashes, rock music and mass-produced daydreams from Denver, Colorado.

Norwegians have not always felt at ease, squeezed between two superpowers. Not that many people normally go around thinking about the military situation. Though Norway has always been a loyal member of NATO, she has opposed the establishment of military bases, and the storage of nuclear warheads on her territory in peacetime.

Norway has her own mobilization forces in case of emergency. These consist of 325,000 men, or 7.7 per cent of the population, the highest number in any NATO nation. There are only 1,000 enlisted soldiers in the Norwegian Army, most of them serving with the United Nations contingent in the Middle East.

When Ola Nordmann is nineteen years old he has to do military service, twelve months in the Army, or fifteen in the Navy or Air Force. Conscientious objection to military service is possible on certain grounds, and 2,500 young people every year do alternative civil service.

The 'knorr', a shorter and beamier vessel than the Viking warship, the 'dakkar', was used by Viking explorers and settlers of Iceland, Greenland and North America. About 20 metres (50 feet) in length, it could carry some 30 people and a few head of livestock.

There are about 21,400 national servicemen in Norway. Until they are forty-four they will have to put up with being summoned periodically for refresher training and sleeping in a tent, unless they are transferred to the Home Guard. An extension of the resistance movement against the Germans in the Second World War, the Home Guard consists of 90,000 men from all over the country, who would be sent to engage in guerilla warfare in an emergency. Equipped with loaded AG-3 guns, they meet every year for six days' training.

The Chernobyl nuclear disaster, on 26 April 1986, awakened Norway abruptly. In the event, the fallout reached Norway only after two days, but no-one knew how to cope with the situation. Contradictory statements were issued by the authorities and experts, many of them intended to comfort and reassure the general public. There is still a measure of disagreement among the experts. Some of them concluded that the effects had not been dramatic in Norway, and that it was quite safe to eat reindeer meat containing 20,000 becquerels, as long as one did not eat too much. Four years later, a high level of radioactivity was still to be found in sheep and reindeer. In 1990, farmers in some areas had to feed 150,000 sheep a special diet for up to eight weeks before slaughter to reduce the content in the meat to 600 becquerels.

But threats to the environment and human health appeared long before Chernobyl. For too many years Norway has been used as a dumping ground for industrial waste from the Continent and the British Isles. Thousands of lakes have had all life destroyed by acid rain. There are 400,000 freshwater lakes in Norway, covering an area that is larger than the farmland. As late as the 1950s, there were fish in every brook and pond, and small boys could catch them with their bare hands. Now the lakes of southern Norway have been polluted with sulphuric acid, 90 per cent of which comes from outside the country's borders.

A United Nations report in 1987 held Great Britain responsible for 43 per cent of the sulphuric pollution in the south of Norway and 36 per cent of the carbon dioxide. Even in the north of Norway British industry is the second greatest cause of pollution, appreciably ahead of local industry in this respect.

The sea will perhaps soon be as moribund as the rivers and lakes. In 1986 half the seaweed off the coast stretching from Nordmøre to Finnmark proved to be dead. If this continues we face an environmental catastrophe and a threat to both the fish and the human population of the coast.

During the great algae disaster in the summer of 1988, millions of fish died in their hatcheries and out in the Skagerrak and North Sea, and thousands of dead seals floated in to land. The German rivers Rhine, Elbe and Mosel alone carry 38 million tons of zinc, 13,500 tons of lead, 5,600 tons of copper and varying amounts of arsenic, cadmium, mercury and even radioactive waste into the sea every year, according to the American journal *Newsweek*'s survey of the disaster. In addition, 145 million tons of ordinary sewage are dumped every year.

The Norwegians themselves are not free from blame. Because of discharge from Norwegian industry, 18 Norwegian fjords are heavily polluted. The worst hit are Iddefjorden near Halden and Kristiansand harbour and fjord. Health authorities in these areas warned people not to eat fish or seafood. Sørfjorden in Hardanger had already been labelled the stretch of water with the highest metal content in the world. At the end of this narrow fjord lies Odda, one of those Norwegian industrial

148. The porch of a stave church is usually supported by carved wooden pillars, as at Hopperstad church, Sogn, western Norway. (R. Frislid/NN)

149. Stave churches are usually ornamented with elaborate woodcarving. This is a detail from Vågåmo church in the Gundbrandsdalen valley. (R. Frislid/NN)

150. Although rebuilt, Vågåmo stave church has retained many of its original details. (R. Frislid/NN)

160

160. *The churches of the mountain and forest communities usually occupy an imposing site, even if they are not very impressive in size and architecture. From Sollia in the east Norwegian valley of Østerdalen.* (R. Frislid/NN)

161. People tend to move from
isolated communities to more populous
places, and many small farms are left
abandoned today, particularly in
northern Norway, as here at
Ballangen, Nordland county.
(R. Frislio/NN)

towns that grew up where freshwater ran into the sea. For years the zinc plant Norzink spewed 100,000 tons of heavy metal waste into the sea annually, although now its waste matter is transported to huge rock caverns. The Norwegian share in the company is in fact modest: Norzinc is owned by the Swedish firm Boliden and the British BP International, and most of the produce is exported. For the small community of 8,000 inhabitants the factory is, of course, of vital importance, but industrial jobs have a price. By now it is impossible to cultivate shellfish anywhere in the entire Hardanger fjord.

Not all pollution comes from the south. The Soviet nickel works, built in Nikel only six kilometres (3.7 miles) from the Norwegian border, is slowly killing the environment around Kirkenes and in the beautiful and fertile Pasvik Valley in Finnmark. The factory pumps out more noxious sulphur dioxide than the total of emissions by Norwegian industry – up to 320,000 tons a year. The inhabitants of the Pasvik Valley have recorded scorched trees, rust and dead moss and lichen, the staple food of reindeer. The people of Finnmark fear for their salmon rivers, and both Neiden and Grense Jacobselv are on the danger list.

One would imagine that at least Svalbard, 'the land of icy coast', had a clean bill of health, but the spectre of pollution has arrived there too. The clean Arctic winter is a myth. The Norwegian Institute of Air Pollution concluded in 1987, after five years of research, that Svalbard has as much sulphur dioxide and sulphate in the air as the rest of northern Scandinavia, despite the fact that there are no local causes of pollution on the island. The industrial fallout can be traced to both northern U.S.S.R. and to Europe. Even dust from the Gobi and Sahara deserts can be found at an altitude of 4,000 metres (13,000 feet).

Norway has the supremacy on Svalbard, and this is on the whole respected by the signatories to the Svalbard Treaty, although in these northern waters open to European Community fishing vessels, situations somewhat reminiscent of a 'cod war' can arise.

The Barents Sea is the area where Norway faces her most important challenge in foreign policy. Despite the negotiations on fishing boundaries that have been carried on between Norway and the Soviet Union since 1974, they have not yet been able to agree. Nor have the two countries reached accord on how the continental shelf should be divided up between them.

It can hardly be any easier for Norway to hold on to her possessions on the far side of the world, in the Antarctic. Norwegians are usually proud of the fact that they have never had colonies, or at least have only penguins and walrusses as their subjects. In fact, the country lays claim to Bouvet Island, Peter I's Land and Queen Maud Land, the last an icy waste seven times the size of Norway. However, the ice cap, which is up to 3,000 metres (10,000 feet) thick, could conceal valuable metals.

Norwegians have always had an indomitable urge to ski to the South Pole. Roald Amundsen was the first to get there on 14 December 1911. After that, we busied ourselves hunting whales and annexing territories in the Antarctic. Peter I's Land was seen for the first time by the Russian Bellinghause expedition in 1821, and was given the name of the czar. Yet it was the whaling captain Nils Larsen who went ashore in 1929 and planted the Norwegian flag there. Two years previously the Norwegians had laid claim to Bouvet Island. In 1939 Queen Maud Land was formally taken over.

The only snag about these territories, some 15,000 kilometres

162. The town of Lillehammer, some 200 kilometres (125 miles) north of Oslo, is a centre of the arts and tourism, and a busy town all year round. It is the venue of the Winter Olympic Games of 1994. (Pål Hermansen/Samfoto/NN)

(nearly 10,000 miles) away from the Norwegian Parliament, is that no other countries recognize our right to them, or that of any other state claiming to own land in the Antarctic. The vast continent is divided up like a cake between Australia, Great Britain, Argentina, Chile, New Zealand, France and Norway. According to the terms of the Antarctic Treaty that came into effect in 1961, it is impossible for any country to lay claims to the area, carry out any form of military activity, conduct nuclear tests or dump nuclear waste there.

Enough about our foreign policy!

I will not deny that there are things that preoccupy Norwegians more than the Antarctic in their relationship to the rest of the world. There are, for instance, many of us who worry about what will happen to Norwegian culture under the massive Anglo-American influence that is swamping us. The most pessimistic predict that the Norwegian language will not survive for more than thirty years under the impact.

Norwegians have always gathered ideas from the rest of the world. Just look at Norwegian architecture! The solid, traditional timbered houses that you can still see in the valleys, and in places like the Norwegian Folk Museum in Oslo and Maihaugen in Lillehammer, have been giving way to one international style after another. The small houses along the coast are the result of century-long contact across the North Sea with England and the Netherlands, but have been adapted to Norwegian reality by our master builders, whose skills were formed by wind and weather. Round the turn of the century came the Swiss chalet style with dragon heads and carving, later to be supplanted by its very opposite, severe and rectangular functionalism, *funkis* as it is called in Norway. Today Post-Modernism has softened the lines of large buildings with cheerful colours and a free mixing of styles.

Housing estates get more and more similar: three-quarters of all newly built small houses consist of boring, prefabricated square units, constructed on the drawing board by the manufacturers, delivered ready to be placed on their foundations and painted in the colours of the year by Ola and Kari and their friends.

We have always lived on the outskirts of Europe. While the Swedes got their first university in 1477, and the Danes in 1479, we did not get ours until 1811. While our neighbours with their royal courts could look back on centuries of theatre, opera and ballet, we had to wait for our own national theatre until 1899. We got our national opera in 1958 (with no opera house), and our college of music in 1973.

Our only painter who is truly internationally known, Edvard Munch, had to go to Germany to gain recognition before he was acknowledged at home. Our great dramatist, Henrik Ibsen, had to seek refuge in the south of Europe for twenty-seven years because this mountain country was too narrow for him. And our great composer, Edvard Grieg, had to study in Germany before he could write his famous and truly Norwegian Concerto in A-minor, composed in Denmark. In after times we honour them with museums!

Right up to our day many Norwegian artists have had to go abroad to study. In particular we have exported singers; Kirsten Flagstad, Ingrid Bjoner and Aase Nordmo Løvberg are well-known names in the opera world. Jazz musicians like singer Karin Krog and tenor saxophonist Jan Garbarek have won international fame through festivals and recordings, even if they have stayed at home. The Oslo Philharmonic Orchestra under the Soviet conductor Mariss Jansons and the Norwegian Chamber

Medieval convent seal.

Orchestra under the Briton Iona Brown have also received international acclaim. The painter and sculptor Kjell Erik Killi Olsen, sculptor Bard Breivik, and textile artist Jan Groth are making a name for themselves abroad.

There is no particular wish to isolate ourselves. We translate a mass of foreign literature, and we cultivate our international connections through the Bergen festivals, the festival of church music in Kristiansand, the jazz festivals in Kongsberg and Molde, and the graphics festival in Fredrikstad. But after the experience of being subjected to foreign powers for centuries, it is natural that we would like to have a say when our fate is to be decided – as we had in 1972 when we said 'no' to the EEC. Yet the traditional Norwegian sense of inferiority combined with an increasing lack of historical awareness has brought out an abject and uncritical admiration of all things American, especially in the tabloid press. This cultural state of puberty in a young and uncertain nation has given free rein to the commercial pop industry. A random list of the week's top-selling LP's printed in the Oslo paper *Dagbladet* one winter's day could produce only six titles in Norwegian and four in Swedish out of 50 albums. The rest were Anglo-American. French and German pop music is rarely heard in Norway. Very few rock groups sing in Norwegian, for if one is to make one's way in the world, like 'A-Ha', it has to be in English.

The traditional Norwegian national instrument, the harding fiddle, can hardly compete against this pressure, despite its beautiful, but complicated music, full of ornaments and embellishments. Our contemporary composers have fared better, and Arne Nordheim and the Italian-born Antonio Bibalo are continually having their great dramatic works or ballets performed abroad. Our senior composer, Harald Sæverud of Bergen, is more popular than ever. Thanks to state subsidies, most of our contemporary music is accessible on LP records.

The State has recognized the consequences of the fact that Norway is a small and exposed linguistic area, and has taken measures to ensure the country keeps its scattered population, its language and its culture. Post-war cultural policy has been to send on tour films, paintings and sculpture, theatre and music, to all corners of the country. The state-run rural cinema used to visit 1,000 small places a year in its heyday, before the arrival of the video. The touring theatre, Riksteatret, and the travelling art gallery went all over the country, the state concert society organized both local concerts and tours. Each district had its own library, and even the district of Oslo sent round a book bus. People not only borrow books; the commercial publishers' own book club became a roaring success, selling 48 million books in the course of its first 25 years – 30 to each Norwegian home!

From the 70s the cultural policy has been one of decentralization and democratization. Regional theatres have been set up in many towns, and there are arts centres run by the artists themselves. The government has introduced grants, and 485 artists received guaranteed incomes in 1987. To support writers, the State buys 1,000 copies of all new Norwegian works of fiction, which it distributes among the libraries of the country.

Foreigners probably know Norwegian literature best through the works of Henrik Ibsen and Knut Hamsun, Trygve Gulbranssen and Agnar Mykle. The children's authors Alf Prøysen, Thorbjørn Egner and Anne-Cath Vestly also have readers all over the word.

Of the 2,500 books published yearly in Norway, 300 are works of fiction. The most translated among recent prose writers are Knut Faldbakken, Vera Henriksen, Bjørg Vik and Herbjørg Wassmo. Olav H. Hauge, Rolf Jacobsen and Jan Erik Vold are reckoned as the most important poets today.

Kari and Ola Nordmann also read magazines, journals and, of course, newspapers. There are some 160 newspapers with a circulation of 3.2 million in this country with only 1.5 million households. There is some measure of state support to sustain such a varied press. The state broadcasting company, Norsk Rikskringkasting, had a monopoly on radio and TV transmissions in the country until the 1980s. Since then the air has been free for all.

It may not strengthen us culturally that our small country has two official languages of equal standing, in addition to the less prestigious Såmi. In the Viking days we all spoke Old Norse, much as they do in Iceland today. Then the Danes forced their language on us through four centuries of supremacy. This Danish/Norwegian is our main language today. It has become more Norwegian in time, losing much of the pomposity of the old administrative ruling class, but it has never absorbed the smile that is to be found in modern Danish. The other language, New Norwegian, built up from our dialects and formed by Ivar Aasen in the nineteenth century, is richer and more melodious. Many of our greatest writers have used New Norwegian, including Olav Duun and Tarjei Vesaas, who have perhaps been the most European of us all. Citizens can demand official forms written in the language of their choice. Norsk Rikskringkasting is obliged to put out 25 per cent of its programmes in New Norwegian. Of the 454 local authorities in the country, 114 (with a population of 500,000) have chosen New Norwegian as their official language, 181 (with 1.6 million) have chosen Danish/Norwegian, while 159 (with 2 million) remain neutral.

The two languages are very similar, and the official language policy in our century has been to amalgamate them into one common laguage. This has aroused a long and bitter language dispute that is still going on. Today the opponents ought really to bury the hatchet and join forces in the battle against Americanization and other foreign influences. This has already had some bizarre consequences: the laundry or *vaskeri* has turned into a *vaskoteque*, while the barber's shop has become a *klippoteque*. Whatever next?

Perhaps more Norwegian than anything else is the earth closet or outdoor latrine, that small house with a heart carved in the door and the coronation portrait from Trondheim in 1906 on the wall. Whether it is a two-seater or a six-man privy with a small seat for the children, the thunderbox has been literally the seat of Ola Nordmann's growth and development. Here he could sit in peace and quiet while snowstorms howled or bees hummed in the bluebells. This has been his spiritual home, this is where he worked out his philosophy. Today the outdoor privy is on its way out. It has had its own book written, and it has its own fan club, *Gammeldassens venner* (Friends of the Old Loo). It won't be long before it becomes an antique. One thing is certain though: it will be a black day for Norwegian culture when the tourist officers try to attract their customers with a *shitoteque*. Though you never know!

In the mid-1980s the state-owned Norwegian oil company Statoil sent a letter to Norway's Fishermen's Union in English. The sturdy fishermen accepted the challenge, and answered – in Old Norse!

Important Dates

c. 8000 BC	Earliest traces of Stone Age hunters and fishermen, and rock carvings.
3000–2500 BC	Farming peoples settle in east Norway.
1500–500 BC	Bronze Age.
500 BC	Iron Age begins.
3rd c AD	Earliest runic inscriptions.
5th–7th c	Migrations and unquiet times, hill forts for defence.
9th c	Small clan-based states with judicial assemblies develop.
800–1050	The Viking Age. Settlements founded in Ireland, Great Britain, France, Iceland, Greenland and northern isles. Voyages to Vinland (North American cons to Vinland (North American coast). Plundering raids in the Mediterranean.
c. 900	Development of regional courts of law based on the representative system, and a defence system based on the people's duty to build, maintain and man ships.
c. 900	King Harald I Fairhaired unites much of Norway.
995–1000	Reign of Olaf I Tryggvason, who forcibly converts his subjects to Christianity. He dies in battle against King Sweyn I of Denmark.
1015–30	Reign of Olaf II Haraldsson, first king of all Norway. By force and with the help of Anglo-Saxon missionaries he completes the conversion of his people. After his death in battle against Norwegian allies of Canute, king of Denmark and England, he is sanctified as St Olaf.
1066	Harald III Hardraade (Hardruler) invades northern England and is killed at Stamford Bridge in battle against King Harold Godwinson of England, three days before the landing of William of Normandy near Hastings.
1152	Archbishopric is founded at Nidaros (Trondheim), where a great cathedral is built.
12th and 13th c	Great social changes. Rapid growth of population, and rise of secular and clerical aristocracy. Freeholders become tenants.
1130–1240	Civil wars.
1217–63	Reign of Haakon IV Haakonsson, who establishes a strong and united kingdom after a century of civil wars. Royal administration and control of Norwegian settlements strengthened. Trade flourishes with the settlement of German merchants in Bergen and elsewhere.
1263–80	Reign of Magnus V Lagabøter (Lawmender), who creates a national code of laws.
1349	The Black Death kills one to two thirds of the population, thus devastating the economy and weakening the state.

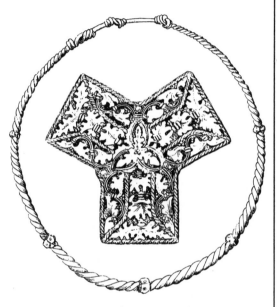

Typical examples of Viking craftsmanship in fashioning gold jewelry.

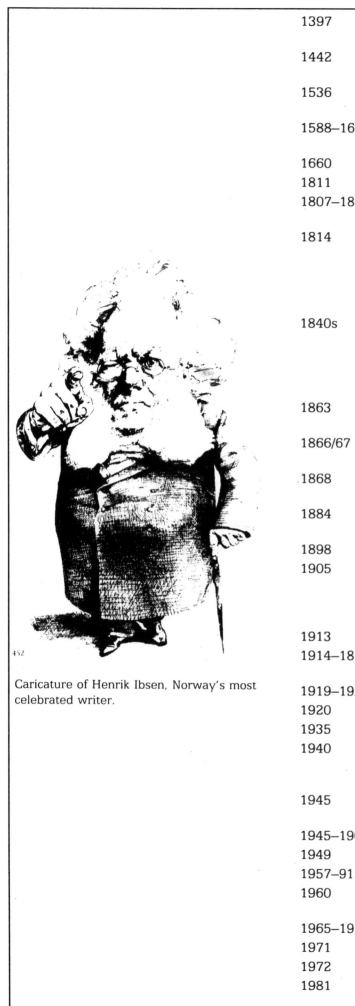

Caricature of Henrik Ibsen, Norway's most celebrated writer.

1397	Union with Denmark and Sweden under Eric of Pomerania, following the death of Olaf IV (1387), last of the old royal line.
1442	Christopher III of Denmark accepted as Norwegian king. Danish monarchs henceforth rule the country until 1814.
1536	Norwegians accept the Reformation (Evangelical Lutheran Church).
1588–1648	Reign of Christian IV, who rebuilds Oslo (Christiania) after a great fire. Rapid development of mining and lumber mills.
1660	The king gains absolute power.
1811	Foundation of Oslo University in the reign of Frederick VI.
1807–1814	Denmark-Norway take part in the Napoleonic wars as French allies. Blockade and famine in Norway.
1814	Denmark cedes Norway to Sweden. Norwegians declare themselves independent. A national assembly works out a democratic constitution. Norway is forced to accept union with Sweden under the Swedish crown, but retains its own constitution and parliament. Civil servants form the dominant class in society.
1840s	Ivar Aasen creates the New Norwegian written language (Nynorsk) on the basis of dialects. Henrik Wergeland (1808–1845), poet and social reformer, writes his finest lyrical poetry. National romanticism strongly influences art and literature. Decade of social reforms.
1863	Birth of Edvard Munch (d. 1944), Norway's greatest painter and graphic artist.
1866/67	Henrik Ibsen (1828–1906) publishes *Brand* and *Peer Gynt*, the first of his major plays.
1868	Edvard Grieg (1843–1907) composes his famous Piano Concerto.
1884	The parliamentary system strengthens the power of the Storting (Parliament).
1898	Universal male suffrage.
1905	Union with Sweden dissolved by decision of the Storting and a national plebiscite. A second plebiscite is four to one in favour of a monarchy over a republic. Prince Charles (Carl) of Denmark becomes king as Haakon VII.
1913	Female suffrage.
1914–18	Norway remains neutral in World War I, but her shipping aids Great Britain.
1919–1927	Alcohol prohibition.
1920	Norwegian sovreignty over Svalbard recognized.
1935	First Labour government.
1940	German invasion (April 9). King Haakon and government move to London. Vidkun Quisling installed as 'minister president' (1942) and Josef Terboven as 'Reichskommissar'.
1945	Norway liberated (May). Labour Party returned to power in general election.
1945–1965	Labour Party in power.
1949	Norway joins NATO.
1957–91	Reign of Oaf V.
1960	Norway a founder member of the European Free Trade Association (EFTA).
1965–1971	Non-socialist coalition government.
1971	First oil well starts production in the Ekofisk field.
1972	Referendum rejects membership of the Common Market (EEC).
1981	First woman prime minister, Gro Harlem Brundtland, heads Labour government.
1991	Harald V ascends the throne.

Photographs:

B. AREKLETT/SAMFOTO/NN (77)

O. ÅSHEIM/SAMFOTO (41, 121)

HANS HVIDE BANG/SAMFOTO/NN (7, 8, 89, 97, 104, 109)

HANS HVIDE BANG/SAMFOTO (95, 100)

JØRN BØHMER OLSEN, R. SØRENSEN/NN (96)

T. BØLSTAD/SAMFOTO (43)

JOHAN BRUN/NN (60, 135, 136)

SVEIN-ERIK DAHL/SAMFOTO (22, 23, 118, 157, 158, 159)

O. D. ENERSEN/SAMFOTO/NN (74, 76)

ROGER ENGVIK (119, 123)

KNUT ENSTAD (20)

BETTEN FOSSE/SAMFOTO (116)

F. FRIBERG/NN (61)

RAGNAR FRISLID/NN (49, 64, 75, 90–92, 98, 101, 102, 106, 111, 127, 134, 141, 143, 144, 146, 148–156, 160, 161)

A. O. GAUTESTAD/NN (68)

KIM HART/SAMFOTO (26, 41, 72)

HUGO HENRIKSEN/SAMFOTO (88)

PÅL HERMANSEN/SAMFOTO/NN (10, 59, 99, 103, 122, 124–126, 128–130, 142, 162)

HUSMO-FOTO (1–5, 11, 12, 14, 18, 19, 21, 24, 25, 28–34, 36, 38, 45, 47, 48, 50–54, 56, 57, 63, 65, 71, 80–85, 87, 93, 94, 107, 108, 113, 133, 138, 139, 140, 147)

DAG KJELSAAS/NN/SAMFOTO (66)

KNUDSENS FOTOSENTER (69)

R. LISLERUD/SAMFOTO (40)

M. LØBERG/SAMFOTO (44, 112)

M. LØBERG/SAMFOTO/NN (13)

MITTET (15–17, 46, 58, 62, 114, 120, 131)

A. NORMANN/SAMFOTO (145)

OLA RØE/SAMFOTO (78)

PER-ANDERS ROSENKVIST/SAMFOTO (115)

ROLF SØRENSEN/NN/SAMFOTO (67)

HELGE SUNDE (6, 35, 37, 39, 55, 86, 117)

HELGE SUNDE/SAMFOTO (27, 73, 79, 137)

TORE WUTTUDAL/NN/SAMFOTO (70)

Index

Index of Tables

College Physics

SEVENTH EDITION

College Physics

SEVENTH EDITION

Francis W. Sears
Late Professor Emeritus
Dartmouth College

Mark W. Zemansky
Late Professor Emeritus
City College of the City University of New York

Hugh D. Young
Professor of Physics
Carnegie-Mellon University

ADDISON-WESLEY PUBLISHING COMPANY

Reading, Massachusetts   Menlo Park, California   New York
Don Mills, Ontario   Wokingham, England   Amsterdam   Bonn
Sydney   Singapore   Tokyo   Madrid   San Juan

Sponsoring Editor: Stuart W. Johnson
Production Services: Sherry Berg
Text Design: Catherine L. Johnson
Cover Design: Marshall Henrichs
Illustrator: Oxford Illustrators, Ltd.
Technical Art Consultant: Loretta Bailey
Copy Editor: Barbara Willette
Manufacturing Supervisor: Roy Logan

Library of Congress Cataloging-in-Publication Data

Sears, Francis Weston, 1898–
   College physics / Francis W. Sears, Mark Zemansky, Hugh D. Young.
  — 7th ed.
     p.   cm.
   Includes index.
   ISBN 0-201-17285-2
   1. Physics.   I. Zemansky, Mark Waldo, 1900–   II. Young, Hugh
D.   III. Title.
QC23.S369   1990
530—dc20   89-34377
                                                                          CIP

9 10-RNT-00 99 98 97

Preface

This new edition of *College Physics* represents the most comprehensive revision in the long, successful history of the book. My most important objective has been to make the book more "user-friendly." To accomplish this I have used a more relaxed and informal prose style than in previous editions, and I have included many new features that will help students learn from the book.

While carrying out this revision, I have tried very hard to preserve the qualities and features that users of previous editions have found useful. The basic goal is unchanged: providing a broad, rigorous introduction to physics at the beginning college level. This book is intended for students whose mathematics preparation includes high-school algebra and trigonometry but no calculus. The primary emphasis is on physical principles and the development of problem-solving ability, rather than on historical background or specialized applications. The complete text may be taught in an intensive two-semester course, and the book is also adaptable to a wide variety of shorter courses.

Here are some of the most important new features in this edition:

Table of Contents

After careful consideration and consultation with many users of our book, I have reorganized the chapters on mechanics. These chapters now conform to the usual order in introductory courses, beginning with kinematics and dynamics and treating statics later as a special case of dynamics. Getting students into the study of motion immediately will enhance motivation for the study of physics, through frequent contact with everyday experience.

Problems

The end-of-chapter problem collections have been extensively revised. Each collection is now grouped into three categories: *Exercises,* single-concept problems that can be keyed to specific sections of the text; *Problems*, usually requiring two or more nontrivial steps for their solution; and *Challenge Problems*, intended to challenge the strongest students. The number of problems has grown by 402; the total number is now 1,863. In addition, there is a list of thought-provoking questions at the end of each chapter, about 700 questions in all. The revision of the problem collections was carried out by Professor A. Lewis Ford (Texas A&M University), with the assistance of Mr. Craig Watkins (Massachusetts Institute of Technology). Professor Lawrence Coleman (University of California, Davis) also contributed many new problems.

Problem-Solving Strategies

The remark heard most often in the freshman Physics classroom is: "I understood the material, but I couldn't do the problems!" To respond to this universal cry for help, I have included in each chapter one or more sections called *Problem-Solving Strategy,* where I list specific suggestions for developing a methodical and systematic approach to solving problems. My most important objective in this book is to help students learn to apply physical principles to a wide variety of problems, and these new strategy sections should be a substantial help.

Chapter Introductions

Each chapter now begins with an introductory paragraph that summarizes the content of the chapter and relates it to what has gone before and what will come later. These paragraphs will enhance continuity and perspective for users of the book by encouraging them to look both backward and forward in order to see clearly the interrelations of various areas of physics and the beauty and fundamental unity of the subject.

Mathematical Level

The level of mathematical sophistication has not changed substantially from previous editions. Some of the challenge problems invite the student to stretch his mathematical ability, especially in situations requiring numerical approximations.

Changes in Subject Matter

Many topics have been added or treated in greater depth than in previous editions. A few examples are:

gravitational field,
automotive power,

damped and forced oscillations,

Maxwell–Boltzmann distribution,

sign conventions for Kirchhoff's rules,

Maxwell's equations,

circular apertures and resolving power,

superconductivity,

band theory of solids.

The elasticity chapter has been rewritten so that each type of stress is introduced at the same time as its corresponding strain. The treatment of fluid mechanics has been condensed and reduced from two chapters to one. The treatment of acoustic phenomena has been shortened, as has the treatment of magnetic materials. The material on quantum effects and quantum theory has been reorganized and extensively rewritten to provide a more logical progression of new concepts.

Units and Notation

In this edition, SI units are used almost exclusively. English units are retained in a few examples and problems in the first half of the book, but only SI units are used in the second half. The joule is used as the standard unit of energy of all forms, including heat. In examples, units are always carried through all stages of numerical calculations. As usual, boldface symbols are used for vector quantities, and in addition boldface $+$, $-$, and $=$ signs are used to remind the student at every opportunity of the crucial distinctions between operations with vectors and those with numbers.

Flexibility

This book is adaptable to a wide variety of course outlines. Many instructors will find that it contains too much material for a one-year course, and the format has been designed to facilitate tailoring the book to individual needs by omitting certain chapters or sections. For example, any or all of the chapters on relativity, fluid mechanics, acoustics, electromagnetic waves, optical instruments, and several others can be omitted without loss of continuity. In addition, some sections that are unusually challenging or somewhat out of the mainstream have been identified with an asterisk preceding the section title. These too may be omitted without loss of continuity.

Conversely, however, topics such as osmosis, surface tension, physiological effects of electric currents, and humidity that until recently have been regarded as of peripheral importance have now come to the fore again in the life sciences, earth and space sciences, and environmental problems. An instructor who wishes to stress these kinds of applications will find this text a useful source for discussion of the appropriate principles.

In any case, instructors should not feel constrained to work straight through the book from cover to cover. Many chapters are, of course, inherently sequential in nature, but within this general limitation I would encourage instructors to select from among the contents those chapters that fit their needs, omitting material that is not relevant for the objectives of a particular course.

Supplements

A textbook should stand on its own feet. Yet many students benefit from supplementary materials designed to be used with the text. With this thought in mind, we offer a *Study Guide,* a *Solutions Manual,* and *Computer-Based Instruction.*

The *Study Guide,* prepared by Professors Barney Sandler and Daria Bouadana, includes for each chapter a summary, a list of basic terms, programmed quizzes, step-by-step solutions of example problems, and a programmed test.

The *Solutions Guide,* prepared by Professor A. Lewis Ford, includes completely worked-out solutions for about one third of the problems in the book. (Answers to all odd-numbered problems are listed at the end of the book.)

The *Computer-Based Instruction,* written by Professor Joseph Priest (Miami University, Ohio), is designed to help students master basic concepts. These interactive programs have been used in recent years by thousands of students and have proven to be a very effective alternative to the traditional modes of learning. The software runs on the IBM PC and the Apple II series.

Instructional Aids

We also offer several aids for the instructor:

A booklet containing answers to all even-numbered problems, available only to instructors, can be obtained from the publisher.

With this new edition, we are pleased to offer a computerized testing program. AWTest can generate virtually an infinite number of problems using a random-number process. In addition, this program has an add/edit feature that allows instructors to customize the program to their particular needs.

Reviewers

Many of the changes in this edition are a direct result of recommendations from colleagues who have used earlier editions with their students. The views and suggestions collected through reviews, written questionnaires, telephone surveys, and discussion groups have been invaluable. In addition to those named in connection with the problem revisions,

I gratefully acknowledge the very helpful and valuable contributions of the following people:

Robert L. Anderson (University of Georgia)

Paul Avery (University of Florida)

Daria Bouadana (New York City Technical College)

Robert Beck Clark (Texas A&M University)

Lawrence Coleman (University of California, Davis)

Sally E. Cummins (Barnard College)

John S. Eck (University of Toledo)

Allan Edwards (University of Georgia)

Norma Eison (C.U.N.Y., Brooklyn College)

Edward Fry (Texas A&M University)

Kenneth Hardy (Florida International University)

Robert Hart (S.U.N.Y., Binghamton)

John L. Hubisz (College of the Mainland)

Sanford Kern (Colorado State University)

Jean Krisch (University of Michigan, Ann Arbor)

Marles L. McCurdy (Tarrant County Junior College)

Marcus T. McEllistrem (University of Kentucky)

Arunajallam Nadasen (Michigan State University)

Jacob Neuberger (Queens College)

Arnold D. Pickar (Portland State University)

Lawrence S. Pinsky (University of Houston)

Michael Ram (S.U.N.Y., Buffalo)

Barney Sandler (New York City Technical College)

Balkrishna R. Tambe (Southern College of Technology)

C.C. Trail (Brooklyn College)

James B. Whitenton (Southern College of Technology)

Robert L. Wild (University of California, Riverside)

Mark E. Williams (Southwestern College)

Professor William Cloud (Eastern Illinois University) has read page proofs for the entire book, checking for accuracy in the typography, computations, numbering of equations, section references, and figures, and innumerable other details. His meticulous work has been a great help in making the book as error-free as possible.

With the departure of Professors Sears and Zemansky from this life, I have assumed sole responsibility for the book. I feel a little like a violin-maker who is asked to take a Stradivarius apart and repair it. It is an honor to be asked to do it, but it is also an awesome responsibility. I have taken great care to remain true to the original spirit of this text, while making it as useful for today's students as the first edition was for its users a few decades ago.

Acknowledgments

I owe a special debt of gratitude to my colleagues at Carnegie-Mellon, especially Professors Robert Kraemer, Bruce Sherwood, and Helmut Vogel, for many stimulating discussions about physics pedagogy, and to Professor Vogel for major contributions to the high-energy physics material. Finally, it is a joy to express my gratitude to my wife Alice and our children Gretchen and Rebecca for their love, support, and emotional sustenance during the writing of this new edition.

As always, I welcome communications from students and professors, especially when they concern errors or deficiencies that you find in this edition. I have written the best book I know how to write; I hope it will help you to teach and learn physics. In turn, you can help me by letting me know what still needs to be improved!

Pittsburgh, Pennsylvania   H.D.Y.

Contents

5

Applications of Newton's Laws 94

6

Circular Motion and Gravitation 124

7

Work and Energy 146

8

Impulse and Momentum 181

9

Rotational Motion 207

10

Equilibrium of a Rigid Body 245

11

Periodic Motion 261

27

Capacitance and Dielectrics 602

28

Current, Resistance, and Electromotive Force 622

29

Direct-Current Circuits 648

30

Magnetic Field and Magnetic Forces 671

31

Sources of Magnetic Field 701

32

Electromagnetic Induction 726

33

Inductance 747

34

Alternating Currents 765

35

Electromagnetic Waves 788

36

The Nature and Propagation of Light 811

37

Images Formed by a Single Surface 839

38

Lenses and Optical Instruments 861

39

Interference and Diffraction 889

40

Relativistic Mechanics 923

College Physics

SEVENTH EDITION

Models, Measurements, and Vectors

The study of physics is an adventure. You will find it challenging, sometimes frustrating, occasionally painful, and often richly rewarding and satisfying. It will appeal to your sense of beauty as well as to your rational intelligence. Our present understanding of the physical world has been built on foundations laid by scientific giants such as Galileo, Newton, Maxwell, and Einstein. You can share their excitement of discovery when you learn to use physics to solve practical problems and to gain insight into everyday phenomena. Above all, you will come to see physics as a towering achievement of the human intellect in its quest to understand the world we all live in.

Our journey through the world of physics begins with *mechanics*, the study of motion and its causes. Everyday experience offers us many examples of mechanical principles, so this is a natural starting point. First, we ponder a little about the nature of physical theory and the role of idealized models in representing physical systems. Then we introduce several elements of the *language* of physics that we will need throughout our study.

The first item of language is the matter of *units*. When we measure a quantity, such as a length or a time interval, we express the result in terms of some standard unit, such as the kilometer or the second. We need to become familiar with systems of units and their notations, and we also need procedures for converting quantities from one unit system to another, for example, "miles per hour" to "meters per second." A related concept is the *precision* of a number, often described by means of *significant figures*. We also consider ways of approaching problems in which precise calculations are unnecessary or perhaps impossible but rough *estimates* can be interesting and useful.

Finally, we study several aspects of *vector algebra*. We use vectors to describe and analyze many physical quantities, such as velocity and force, that have directions as well as magnitudes.

1–1
Introduction

Physics is an *experimental* science. Figure 1–1 shows two famous experimental facilities. Physicists observe the phenomena of nature and try to find and invent patterns and principles that relate these phenomena. These patterns are called physical theories or, when they are very broad and well established, physical laws. The development of physical theory requires creativity at every stage, from the design of an experiment to the drawing of conclusions from the result. According to legend, Galileo Galilei (1564–1642) experimented with objects of different weights dropped from the top of the Leaning Tower of Pisa; he found that they all fell at very nearly the same rate. For this experiment, Galileo first had to recognize that it was important to use objects with different weights; then he had to make the inductive leap from his observations to the principle, or theory, that the acceleration of a falling body is independent of its weight.

The development of physical theory is always a two-way street that starts and ends with observations or experiments. This development

(a)   (b)

1–1

Two research laboratories. (a) The Cathedral of Pisa (Italy), with the Baptistry in the foreground, the Cathedral behind it, and the famous Leaning Tower at the far right. According to legend, Galileo studied the motion of freely falling bodies by dropping them from the tower. He is also alleged to have gained insights into pendulum motion by observing the swinging of the hanging chandeliers in the Cathedral. The nearly parabolic dome of the Baptistry produces interesting acoustical effects. (Art Resource, New York.) (b) The Hubble Space Telescope. When this 2.4-m reflecting telescope is placed in orbit 500 km above the surface of the earth, it will permit observation of celestial objects 100,000,000 times fainter in brightness than the faintest objects visible with the best earth-based telescope. (Courtesy Lockheed Corporation.)

often takes a devious path, involving blind alleys, wrong guesses, and the discarding of unsuccessful theories in favor of more promising ones. No theory is ever regarded as the final or ultimate truth; there is always the possibility that new observations will require revision of a theory. It is in the nature of physical theory that we can *disprove* a theory by finding a phenomenon that is inconsistent with it, but we can never prove that a theory is always correct.

Getting back to Galileo, suppose we drop a feather and a cannonball. They certainly *do not* fall at the same rate. This does not mean that Galileo was wrong; it means that his theory was incomplete. One complicating feature is air resistance. If we drop the feather and the cannonball *in vacuum*, then they *do* fall at the same rate. Galileo's theory has a range of validity, namely, those bodies that are heavy enough that air resistance has almost no effect. A feather or a parachute is clearly not within this range.

Every physical theory has a range of validity and a boundary outside which it is not applicable. Often, a new development in physics has the effect of extending the range of validity of a principle. For example, Galileo's work with falling bodies was greatly extended half a century later by Newton's laws of motion and law of gravitation.

An essential part of the interplay of theory and experiment is learning how to apply physical principles to a variety of practical problems. At various points in our study we will discuss systematic problem-solving procedures that will help you to set up problems and carry out solutions efficiently and accurately. Learning to solve problems is absolutely essential; you don't *know* physics unless you can *do* physics. This means not only learning the general principles, but also learning how to apply them in a variety of specific situations.

1–2
Idealized Models

In everyday conversation the word **model** often means either a small-scale replica, such as a model railroad, or a human body that displays articles of clothing (or the absence thereof). In physics, a *model* is a simplified version of a physical system that would be too complicated to analyze in full without the simplifications.

Here is an example. We want to analyze the motion of a baseball thrown through the air. How complicated can we make this problem? The ball is not perfectly spherical, nor perfectly rigid; it flexes a little and spins as it moves through the air. Wind and air resistance influence its motion, the earth is rotating beneath it, its weight varies a little as its distance from the center of the earth changes, and so on. If we try to include all these things, the analysis gets pretty hopeless. Instead, we go in the opposite direction. We neglect the size and shape of the ball, representing it as a point object. We neglect air resistance and make the ball move in vacuum; we forget about the earth's rotation, and we make the weight exactly constant. *Now* we have a problem that is simple enough to deal with. The ball is now a point moving along a simple parabolic path; we will analyze this model in detail in Chapter 3.

The main point is that we have to overlook several minor and inconsequential effects in order to concentrate on the most important features of the motion. That's what we mean by making an idealized model of the system. Of course, we have to be careful not to neglect *too much*. If we ignore the effect of gravity completely, then when we throw the ball, it travels in a straight line and disappears into space, never to be seen again. A lot of judgment and creativity are required to construct a model that simplifies a system without throwing out its essential features. We don't want to throw the baby out with the bathwater!

When we analyze a system or predict its behavior on the basis of a model, we always need to remember that the validity of our predictions is limited by the validity of the model. If the model represents the real system quite precisely, then we expect predictions made from it to agree quite closely with the actual behavior of the system. Going back to Pisa with Galileo once more, we see that his prediction about falling bodies corresponded to an idealized model that does not include the effects of air resistance, the rotation of the earth, and the variation of weight with height. This model works well for a bullet and a cannonball, less well for a feather.

The concept of idealized models is of the utmost importance in all of physical science and technology. In applying physical principles to complex systems, we always make extensive use of idealized models, and it is important to be aware of the assumptions we are making. Indeed, the principles of physics themselves are stated in terms of idealized models; we speak about point masses, rigid bodies, ideal insulators, and so on. Idealized models will play a crucial role in our discussion of physical theories and their applications to specific problems throughout this book.

1-3
Standards and Units

Any number that is used to describe a physical phenomenon quantitatively is called a **physical quantity.** Some physical quantities are so fundamental that we can define them only by describing a procedure for measuring them. Such a definition is called an **operational definition.** In other cases we define a physical quantity by describing a way to *calculate* the quantity from other quantities that we can measure. In the first case we might use a ruler to measure a distance, or a stopwatch to measure a time interval. In the second case we might define the average speed of a moving object as the distance traveled (measured with a ruler) divided by the time of travel (measured with a stopwatch).

When we measure a quantity, we always compare it with some reference standard. When we say that a rope is 30 meters long, we mean that it is 30 times as long as a meter stick, which is defined to be 1 meter long. We call such a standard a **unit** of the quantity. The meter is a unit of distance, and the second is a unit of time. When we use a number to describe a physical quantity, it is essential to specify the unit we are using; to describe a distance simply as "30" would have no meaning.

To make precise measurements, we need definitions of the units of measurement that do not change and that can be duplicated by observers in various locations. When the metric system was established in 1791 by the Paris Academy of Sciences, the **meter** was originally defined as one ten-millionth of the distance from the equator to the North Pole, and the **second** as the time for a pendulum 1 meter long to swing from one side to the other.

These definitions were cumbersome and hard to duplicate precisely, and in more recent years they have been replaced by more refined definitions. Since 1889 the definitions of the basic units have been established by an international organization, the General Conference on Weights and Measures. The system of units defined by this organization is based on the metric system, and since 1960 it has been known officially as the **International System** or SI (the abbreviation for the French equivalent, Système International).

From 1889 until 1967 the unit of time was defined in terms of the length of the day, directly related to the time of the earth's rotation. The present standard, adopted in 1967, is much more precise. It is based on an atomic clock, such as the one shown in Fig. 1–2. This instrument uses the energy difference between the two lowest energy states of the cesium atom. Electromagnetic radiation (microwaves) of precisely the proper frequency causes transitions from one of these states to the other. One second is defined as the time required for 9,192,631,770 cycles of this radiation.

In 1960 an atomic standard for the meter was also established. It used the wavelength of the orange-red light emitted by atoms of krypton (^{86}Kr) in a glow discharge tube; 1 meter was defined as 1,650,763.73 of these wavelengths. In November 1983 the standard was changed again,

1–2
NBS-6 is the latest of six generations of primary atomic frequency standards developed by the National Bureau of Standards (NBS). Consisting of a 6-m cesium beam tube, NBS-6 achieves an accuracy of better than one part in 10^{13} and, when operated as a clock, can keep time to within 3 millionths of a second per year. (Courtesy National Bureau of Standards.)

in a more radical way. The new definition of the meter is the distance light travels in 1/299,792,458 second. This has the effect of defining the speed of light to be precisely 299,792,458 m·s^{-1}; we then define the meter to be consistent with this number and with the above definition of the second. The reason for this change is that at present we can measure the speed of light and intervals of time much more precisely than distances.

The standard of *mass* is the mass of a particular cylinder of platinum-iridium alloy. Its mass is defined to be 1 **kilogram,** and it is kept at the International Bureau of Weights and Measures at Sèvres, near Paris. An atomic standard of mass has not yet been adopted because at present we cannot measure masses on an atomic scale with as great precision as on a macroscopic scale.

Once the fundamental units have been defined, it is easy to introduce larger and smaller units for the same physical quantities. In the metric system these other units are always related to the fundamental units by multiples of 10 or 1/10. Thus one kilometer (1 km) is 1000 meters, one centimeter (1 cm) is 1/100 meter, and so on. We usually express the multiplicative factors in exponential notation; $1000 = 10^3$, $1/1000 = 10^{-3}$, and so on. With this notation,

$$1 \text{ km} = 10^3 \text{ m}, \qquad 1 \text{ cm} = 10^{-2} \text{ m}.$$

The names of the additional units are always derived by adding a **prefix** to the name of the fundamental unit. For example, the prefix "kilo-," abbreviated k, always means a unit larger by a factor of 1000; thus

$$1 \text{ kilometer} = 1 \text{ km} = 10^3 \text{ meters} = 10^3 \text{ m},$$

$$1 \text{ kilogram} = 1 \text{ kg} = 10^3 \text{ grams} = 10^3 \text{ g},$$

$$1 \text{ kilowatt} = 1 \text{ kW} = 10^3 \text{ watts} = 10^3 \text{ W}.$$

Table 1–1 lists the standard SI prefixes with their meanings and abbreviations. We note that most of these are multiples of 10^3.

When pronouncing unit names with prefixes, always accent the *first* syllable: KIL-o-gram, KIL-o-meter, CEN-ti-meter, and MIC-ro-meter. (In English-speaking countries, kilometer is sometimes pronounced kil-OM-eter.)

Here are several examples of the use of multiples of 10 and their prefixes. Some additional time units are also included.

$1 \text{ nanometer} = 1 \text{ nm} = 10^{-9} \text{ m}$ (a few times the size of an atom)

$1 \text{ micrometer} = 1 \text{ } \mu\text{m} = 10^{-6} \text{ m}$ (size of some bacteria and cells)

$1 \text{ millimeter} = 1 \text{ mm} = 10^{-3} \text{ m}$ (point of a ballpoint pen)

$1 \text{ centimeter} = 1 \text{ cm} = 10^{-2} \text{ m}$ (diameter of your little finger)

$1 \text{ kilometer} = 1 \text{ km} = 10^3 \text{ m}$ (a ten-minute walk)

$1 \text{ microgram} = 1 \text{ } \mu\text{g} = 10^{-9} \text{ kg}$ (mass of a 1-mm length of hair)

$1 \text{ milligram} = 1 \text{ mg} = 10^{-6} \text{ kg}$ (mass of a grain of salt)

$1 \text{ gram} = 1 \text{ g} = 10^{-3} \text{ kg}$ (mass of a paper clip)

$1 \text{ nanosecond} = 1 \text{ ns} = 10^{-9} \text{ s}$ (time for light to travel 0.3 m)

TABLE 1–1   Prefixes for powers of ten

Power of ten	Prefix	Abbreviation
10^{-18}	atto-	a
10^{-15}	femto-	f
10^{-12}	pico-	p
10^{-9}	nano-	n
10^{-6}	micro-	μ
10^{-3}	milli-	m
10^{-2}	centi-	c
10^3	kilo-	k
10^6	mega-	M
10^9	giga-	G
10^{12}	tera-	T
10^{15}	peta-	P
10^{18}	exa-	E

1 microsecond = 1 μs = 10^{-6} s (time for a PC to do an addition)

1 millisecond = 1 ms = 10^{-3} s (time for sound to travel 0.35 m)

1 minute   = 1 min = 60 s

1 hour   = 1 hr = 3600 s

1 day   = 1 day = 86,400 s

Finally, we mention the British system of units. These units are used only in the United States and a few other countries, and in most of these they are being replaced by SI. British units are now officially *defined* in terms of SI units, as follows:

Length: 1 inch = 2.54 cm (exactly).

Force: 1 pound = 4.448221615260 newtons (exactly).

The fundamental British unit of time is the second, defined the same way as in SI. In physics, British units are used only in mechanics and thermodynamics; there is no British system of electrical units.

In this book we use SI units for all examples and problems, but in the early chapters we occasionally give approximate equivalents in British units. As you do problems using SI units, try to think of the approximate equivalents in British units, but also try to think in SI as much as you can. A lot of U.S. industry has already converted to metric standards; we speak about 4-liter engines, 50-mm lenses, 35-mm film, 750-mL wine bottles, and so on. The use of SI in everyday life is not far off.

1-4
Unit Consistency and Conversions

We use equations to express relations among physical quantities that are represented by algebraic symbols. Each algebraic symbol always denotes both a number and a unit. For example, d might represent a distance of 10 m, t a time of 5 s, and v (for velocity) a speed of 2 m/s or 2 m·s^{-1}. (In this book we usually use negative exponents with units to avoid use of the fraction bar.)

An equation must always be **dimensionally consistent.** You can't add apples and pomegranates; two terms may be added or equated only if they have the same units. For example, if a body moving with constant speed v travels a distance d in a time t, these quantities are related by the equation

$$d = vt. \tag{1-1}$$

If d is measured in meters, then the product vt must also be expressed in meters. Using the above numbers as an example, we may write

$$10 \text{ m} = (2 \text{ m·s}^{-1})(5 \text{ s}).$$

Because the unit s^{-1} (= 1/s) cancels the unit s in the last factor, the product vt does have units of meters, as it must. In calculations, units are treated just like algebraic symbols with respect to multiplication and division.

When a problem requires calculations using numbers with units, always write the numbers with the correct units and carry the units through the calculation as in the example above. This provides a very useful check for calculations. If at some stage in a calculation you find that an equation or an expression has inconsistent units, you know you have made an error somewhere. In this book we will always carry units through all calculations, and we strongly urge you to follow this practice when you solve problems.

PROBLEM-SOLVING STRATEGY: *Unit Conversions*

Units are multiplied and divided just like ordinary algebraic symbols. This fact provides a convenient procedure for converting a quantity from one set of units to another. The key to the procedure is the fact that we can use equality to represent the same physical quantity when we express it in two different units. For example, to say that 1 min = 60 s does not mean that the number 1 is equal to the number 60; it means that 1 min represents the same physical time interval as 60 s. Thus we may multiply a quantity by 1 min and then divide it by 60 s, or multiply by the quantity (1 min/60 s), without changing its physical meaning. To find the number of seconds in 3 min, we write

$$3 \text{ min} = (3 \text{ min})\left(\frac{60 \text{ s}}{1 \text{ min}}\right) = 180 \text{ s}.$$

This makes sense; the second is a smaller unit than the minute, so there are more seconds than minutes in the same time interval.

Example 1–1   American women in the age group 19 to 22 years have an average height of 5 ft 4 in. What is this height in centimeters? In meters?

Solution   We first express the height in inches:

$$5 \text{ ft} = \left(\frac{12 \text{ in.}}{1 \text{ ft}}\right)(5 \text{ ft}) = 60 \text{ in.},$$

$$5 \text{ ft 4 in.} = 5 \text{ ft} + 4 \text{ in.} = 60 \text{ in.} + 4 \text{ in.} = 64 \text{ in.}$$

Then

$$64 \text{ in.} = \left(\frac{2.54 \text{ cm}}{1 \text{ in.}}\right)(64 \text{ in.}) = 163 \text{ cm}.$$

(We have rounded the product to the nearest centimeter.) Finally,

$$163 \text{ cm} = \left(\frac{1 \text{ m}}{100 \text{ cm}}\right)(163 \text{ cm}) = 1.63 \text{ m}.$$ ■

Example 1–2   A woman drives a car in Germany at 50 km·hr^{-1} (50 kilometers per hour). Express this speed in meters per second and miles per hour.

Solution

$$50 \text{ km·hr}^{-1} = (50 \text{ km·hr}^{-1})\left(\frac{1000 \text{ m}}{1 \text{ km}}\right)\left(\frac{1 \text{ hr}}{3600 \text{ s}}\right) = 13.9 \text{ m·s}^{-1},$$

$$50 \text{ km·hr}^{-1} = (50 \text{ km·hr}^{-1})\left(\frac{1 \text{ mi}}{1.609 \text{ km}}\right) = 31.1 \text{ mi·hr}^{-1}. \quad ■$$

1–5
Precision and Significant Figures

Measurements always have uncertainties. When we measure a distance with an ordinary ruler, it is usually reliable only to the nearest millimeter, while with a precision micrometer caliper we can measure distances dependably to 0.01 mm or even better. We often indicate the precision of a number by writing the number, the symbol ±, and a second number indicating the likely uncertainty. If the diameter of a steel rod is given as 56.47 ± 0.02 mm, this means that the true value is unlikely to be less than 56.45 mm or greater than 56.49 mm.

We can also express precision in terms of the maximum likely fractional or percent uncertainty. A resistor labeled "47 ohms ± 10%" probably has a true resistance differing from 47 ohms by no more than 10% of 47 ohms, that is, about 5 ohms. The resistance is probably between 42 and 52 ohms. In the steel rod example above, the fractional uncertainty is (0.02 mm)/(56.47 mm) or about 0.00035; the percent uncertainty is (0.00035)(100%) or about 0.035%.

Here is a shorthand that is sometimes used to denote precision. The number 1.6454(21) means 1.6454 ± 0.0021. The numbers in parentheses show the uncertainty in the final digits of the main number.

When we use numbers having uncertainties or errors to compute other numbers, the computed numbers are also uncertain. It is especially important to understand this when comparing a number obtained from measurements with a value obtained from a theoretical prediction. Suppose you want to verify the value of π, the ratio of the circumference to the diameter of a circle. The true value of this ratio, to ten digits, is 3.141592654. To make your own calculation, you draw a large circle and measure its diameter and circumference to the nearest millimeter, obtaining the values 135 mm and 424 mm. You punch these into your calculator and obtain the quotient 3.140740741. Does this agree with the true value or not?

To answer this question, we must first recognize that at least the last six digits in your answer are meaningless because they imply greater precision than is possible with your measurements. The number of meaningful digits in a number is called the number of **significant figures;** usually, a numerical result has no more significant figures than the numbers from which it is computed. Thus your value of π has only three significant figures and should be stated simply as 3.14 or possibly as

3.141 (rounded to four figures). Within the limit of three significant figures, your value does agree with the true value.

In the examples and problems in this book we usually assume that the numerical values we give are precise to three or at most four significant figures, and thus your answers should use at most four significant figures. You may do the arithmetic with a calculator having a display with five to ten digits. But you should *not* give a ten-digit answer for a calculation using numbers with three significant figures. To do so is not only unnecessary; it is genuinely wrong because it misrepresents the precision of the results. Always round your answer to keep only the correct number of significant figures, or in doubtful cases one more at most. Thus in Example 1–2 the result should have been stated as 13.9 or 14 m·s^{-1}. Of course, significant figures provide only a crude representation of the reliability of a number. The fractional uncertainty of 104 is not appreciably less than that of 96, despite the difference in the number of significant figures. When a better representation of uncertainty is needed, more sophisticated statistical methods are used.

In calculations with very large or very small numbers we can show significant figures much more easily by using powers-of-ten notation, sometimes called **scientific notation.** The distance from the earth to the sun is about 149,000,000,000 m, but writing the number in this form gives no indication of the number of significant figures. Certainly not all 12 are significant! Instead, we move the decimal point 11 places to the left (corresponding to dividing by 10^{11}) and multiply by 10^{11}. That is,

$$149{,}000{,}000{,}000 \text{ m} = 1.49 \times 10^{11} \text{ m}.$$

In this form it is clear that the number of significant figures is three. In scientific notation the usual practice is to express the quantity as a number between 1 and 10 multiplied by the appropriate power of 10.

We can use the same technique when we multiply or divide very large or very small numbers. For example, the energy E corresponding to the mass m of an electron is given by Einstein's equation

$$E = mc^2, \tag{1–2}$$

where c is the speed of light. The appropriate numbers are $m = 9.11 \times 10^{-31}$ kg and $c = 3.00 \times 10^8$ m·s^{-1}. We find

$$\begin{aligned} E &= (9.11 \times 10^{-31} \text{ kg})(3.00 \times 10^8 \text{ m·s}^{-1})^2 \\ &= (9.11)(3.00)^2(10^{-31})(10^8)^2 \text{ kg·m}^2\text{·s}^{-2} \\ &= (82.0)(10^{[-31+(2\times 8)]}) \text{ kg·m}^2\text{·s}^{-2} \\ &= 8.20 \times 10^{-14} \text{ kg·m}^2\text{·s}^{-2}. \end{aligned}$$

Most calculators use scientific notation and do this addition of exponents automatically for you; but you should be able to do such calculations by hand when necessary. Incidentally, the value used for c has three significant figures even though two of them are zeros. To greater accuracy, $c = 2.997925 \times 10^8$ m·s^{-1}. It would *not* be correct to write $c = 3.000 \times 10^8$ m·s^{-1}. Do you see why?

Here is an exception to the general rules about significant figures. When an integer or a fraction occurs in a general equation, that number is regarded as having infinitely great precision. For example, in the equation $v^2 = v_0{}^2 + 2a(x - x_0)$, which is Eq. (2–13) in Chapter 2, the "2" is precisely 2, with no uncertainty at all, and can be written as 2.0000000000000 if the occasion demands.

1–6
Estimates and Orders of Magnitude

We have talked about the importance of knowing the precision of numbers that represent physical quantities. But there are also situations in which even a very crude estimate of a quantity may give us useful information. There are cases where we know how to calculate a certain quantity but have to guess at the data we need for the calculation. Or the calculation may be too complicated to carry out exactly, so we make some crude approximations. In either case our result is also a guess, but many times such a guess is useful, even if it is uncertain by a factor of two or ten or more. Such calculations are often called **order-of-magnitude** calculations or estimates.

Example 1–3   You are writing an international espionage novel in which the hero escapes across the border with a billion dollars worth of gold in his suitcase. Is this possible? Would that amount of gold fit in the suitcase? Would it be too heavy to carry?

Solution   Gold sells for around $400 an ounce. On a particular day the price might be $200 or $600, but never mind. An ounce is about 30 grams. Actually, an ordinary (avoirdupois) ounce is 28.35 g; an ounce of gold is a troy ounce, which is 9.45% more. Again, never mind. Ten dollars worth of gold has a mass somewhere around 1 gram, so a billion (10^9) dollars worth is a hundred million (10^8) grams, or a hundred thousand (10^5) kilograms. This corresponds to a weight in British units of around 200,000 lb, or a hundred tons. Whether the precise number is 50 tons or 200 doesn't matter; either way, our hero is not about to carry it across the border in a suitcase.

We can also estimate the *volume* of this gold. If its density were the same as that of water (1 g·cm^{-3}), the volume would be 10^8 cm^3 or 100 m^3. But gold is a heavy metal; we might guess its density as ten times that of water. Gold is actually 19.3 times as dense as water. But guessing ten, we find a volume of 10 m^3. Visualize ten cubical stacks of gold bricks, each one meter on a side, and ask whether it would fit in a suitcase!   ■

Problems 1–14 through 1–26 at the end of this chapter are of the estimating or "order-of-magnitude" variety. Some are silly, and most require guesswork for the needed input data. Don't try to look up a lot of data; make the best guesses you can. Even when they are off by a factor of ten, the results can be useful and interesting.

1–7
Vectors and Vector Addition

Some physical quantities, such as time, temperature, mass, density, and electric charge, can be described completely by a single number with a unit. Many other quantities, however, have a *directional* quality and cannot be described by a single number. A familiar example is velocity; to describe the motion of a body, we must say not only how fast it is moving but also in what direction. To fly from Chicago to New York, the plane has to head east, not south. Force is another example; when we push or pull on a body, we exert a force on it. To describe a force, we need to describe the direction in which it acts as well as its magnitude, or "how hard" the force pushes or pulls.

When a physical quantity is described by a single number, we call that quantity a **scalar quantity.** A quantity that has both a *magnitude* (the "how much" or "how big" part) and a *direction* in space is called a **vector quantity.** Calculations with scalar quantities use the operations of ordinary arithmetic, but calculations with vector quantities are somewhat different. Vector quantities play an essential role in all areas of physics, so let's start right away to learn more about what vectors are and how they combine.

We start with the simplest of all vector quantities, **displacement.** Displacement is simply a change in position of a point. (The point may be a model to represent a particle.) In Fig. 1–3a we represent the change of position from point P_1 to point P_2 by a line from P_1 to P_2, with an arrowhead at P_2 to represent the direction of motion. Displacement is a vector quantity because we must state not only how far the particle moves, but also in what direction. A displacement of 3 km north from a given starting point doesn't get us to the same place as a displacement of 3 km southeast.

We usually represent a displacement by a single letter, such as A in Fig. 1–3a. In this book we always print vector symbols in boldface type to remind you that vector quantities have different properties from scalar quantities. In handwriting, vector symbols are usually underlined or written with an arrow above, as shown in Fig. 1–3c, to indicate that they represent vector quantities. When you write a symbol for a vector quantity, *always* decorate it in one of these ways. If you don't distinguish between scalar and vector quantities in your notation, you probably won't make the distinction in your thinking either, and hopeless confusion will result.

Displacement is always a straight line segment, directed from the starting point to the end point, even though the actual path of the particle may be curved. In Fig. 1–4, when the particle moves along the curved path shown from P_1 to P_2, the displacement is still the vector A shown. Also, when it continues on to P_3 and then returns to P_1, the displacement for the entire trip is zero.

The vector from point P_3 to point P_4 in Fig. 1–3b has the same length and direction as the one from P_1 to P_2. These two displacements are equal, even though they start at different points. By definition, two vector quantities are equal if they have the same magnitude (length) and

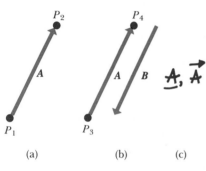

1–3
(a) Vector A is the displacement from point P_1 to point P_2. (b) The displacement from P_3 to P_4 is equal to that from P_1 to P_2, but displacement B is the negative of displacement A.

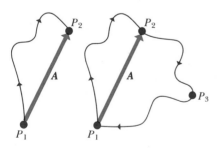

1–4
A displacement is always a straight line segment, directed from the starting point to the endpoint, even if the actual path is curved. When a point ends at the same place it started, the displacement is zero.

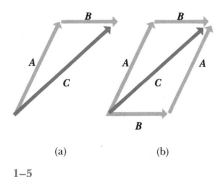

1–5
(a) Vector **C** is the vector sum of vectors **A** and **B**. (b) The order in vector addition is immaterial.

direction, no matter where they are located in space. The vector **B,** however, is not equal to **A** because its direction is *opposite* to that of **A.** We define the *negative* of a vector as a vector having the same magnitude but opposite direction to the original vector. The negative of vector quantity **A** is denoted as **−A,** and we use a boldface minus to emphasize the vector nature of the quantities. Thus the relation between **A** and **B** may be written as **A = −B** or **B = −A.** When two vectors **A** and **B** have opposite directions, we say that they are *antiparallel*. Note that we also use a boldface equals sign to emphasize that equality of two vector quantities is not the same relationship as equality of scalar quantities. Two vector quantities are equal only when they have the same magnitude *and* the same direction.

We represent the **magnitude** of a vector quantity (its length, in the case of a displacement vector) by the same letter used for the vector but in light italic type rather than boldface italic. An alternative notation is the vector symbol with vertical bars on both sides. Thus

$$\text{(Magnitude of } A) = A = |A|. \tag{1–3}$$

By definition, the magnitude of a vector quantity is a scalar quantity (a single number) and is always positive. We also note that a vector can never be equal to a scalar because they are different kinds of quantities. The expression "**A** = 6 m" is just as wrong as "2 oranges = 3 apples" or "6 lb = 7 km!"

Now suppose a particle undergoes a displacement **A,** followed by a second displacement **B,** as shown in Fig. 1–5a. The final result is the same as though the particle had started at the same initial point and undergone a single displacement **C,** as shown. We call displacement **C** the **vector sum** of displacements **A** and **B;** the relationship is expressed symbolically as

$$C = A + B. \tag{1–4}$$

The boldface plus sign emphasizes that adding two vector quantities requires a geometrical process and is not the same operation as adding two scalar quantities such as 2 + 3 = 5.

If we make the displacements **A** and **B** in the reverse order, as in Fig. 1–5b, with **B** first and **A** second, the result is the same, as the figure shows. Thus

$$C = B + A$$

and

$$A + B = B + A. \tag{1–5}$$

This shows that the order of the terms in the sum doesn't matter.

Figure 1–5b also suggests an alternative graphical representation of the vector sum; when vectors **A** and **B** are both drawn with their tails at the same point, vector **C** is the diagonal of a parallelogram constructed with **A** and **B** as two adjacent sides.

The vector sum is often called the **resultant;** thus the vector sum **C** of vectors **A** and **B** can be called the resultant displacement.

Figure 1–6 shows a special case in which two vectors **A** and **B** are parallel, as in Fig. 1–6a, or antiparallel, as in Fig. 1–6b. When the vectors

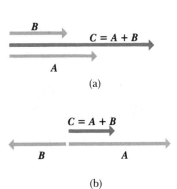

1–6
Vector sums of (a) two parallel vectors and of (b) two antiparallel vectors.

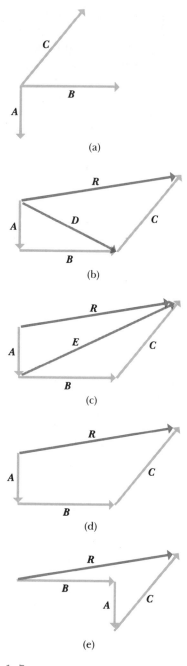

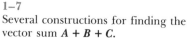

1–7
Several constructions for finding the vector sum $A + B + C$.

are parallel, the magnitude of the vector sum equals the *sum* of the magnitudes of A and B; when they are antiparallel, it equals the *difference* of their magnitudes.

When we need to add more than two vectors, we may first find the vector sum of any two, add this vectorially to the third, and so on. This process is shown in Fig. 1–7. Figure 1–7a shows three vectors A, B, and C. In Fig. 1–7b, vectors A and B are first added, giving a vector sum D; vectors C and D are then added by the same process to obtain the vector sum R:

$$R = A + B + C = D + C.$$

Alternatively, we can first add B and C, as in Fig. 1–7c, to obtain vector E, and then add A and E to obtain R:

$$R = A + B + C = A + E.$$

We don't even need to draw vectors D and E; all we need to do is draw the given vectors in succession, with the tail of each at the head of the one preceding it, and complete the polygon by a vector R from the *tail* of the first to the *head* of the last vector, as shown in Fig. 1–7d. The order makes no difference; Fig. 1–7e shows a different order, and we invite you to try others.

Diagrams for addition of displacement vectors don't have to be drawn actual size. Often, we will use a scale similar to those used for maps, in which the distance on the diagram is proportional to the actual distance, such as 1 cm for 5 km. When we work with other vector quantities with different units, such as force or velocity, we *must* use a scale. In a diagram for force vectors we might use a scale in which a vector 1 cm long represents a force of magnitude 5 N. (The newton, abbreviated N, is the SI unit of force.) A 20-N force would then be represented by a vector 4 cm long with the appropriate direction.

A vector quantity such as a displacement can be multiplied by a scalar quantity (an ordinary number). The displacement $2A$ is a displacement (vector quantity) in the same direction as the vector A but twice as long. The scalar quantity used to multiply a vector may also be a physical quantity having units. For example, you may be familiar with the relationship $F = ma$; force F (a vector quantity) is equal to the product of mass m (a scalar quantity) and acceleration a (a vector quantity). The magnitude of the force is equal to the mass multiplied by the magnitude of the acceleration, and the unit of the magnitude of force is the product of the unit of mass and the unit of the magnitude of acceleration. The direction of F is the same as that of a.

We have already mentioned the special case of multiplication by -1: $(-1)A = -A$ is by definition a vector having the same magnitude as A but opposite direction. This provides the basis for defining vector subtraction. We define the difference $A - B$ of the two vectors A and B to be the vector sum of A and $-B$:

$$A - B = A + (-B). \tag{1–6}$$

The boldface $+$, $-$, and $=$ signs remind us of the vector nature of these operations.

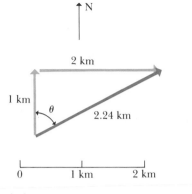

1–8
Scale vector diagram for the ski trip of
Example 1–4.

Example 1–4   A cross-country skier skis 1.0 km north and then 2.0 km east.

a) How far and in what direction is she from the starting point?

b) What are the magnitude and direction of her resultant displacement?

Solution

a) Figure 1–8 is a scale diagram. By careful measurement, we find that the distance from the starting point is about 2.2 km and the angle θ is about 63°. But it is much more accurate to *calculate* the result. The vectors in the diagram form a right triangle, and we can find the length of the hypotenuse by using the theorem of Pythagoras:

$$\sqrt{(1.0 \text{ km})^2 + (2.0 \text{ km})^2} = 2.24 \text{ km}.$$

The angle θ can be found with a little simple trigonometry. By definition of the tangent function,

$$\tan \theta = \frac{2.0 \text{ km}}{1.0 \text{ km}}, \qquad \theta = 63.4°.$$

b) The magnitude of the resultant displacement is just the distance we found in part (a), 2.24 km. We can describe the direction as 63.4° east of north, or 26.6° north of east. Take your choice!   ■

1–8
Components of Vectors

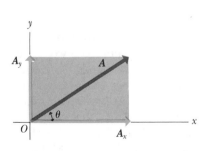

1–9
Vectors A_x and A_y are the rectangular component vectors of A in the directions of the x- and y-axes.

We need to develop efficient and general methods for adding vectors. In Example 1–4 (Section 1–7) we added two vectors by drawing and measuring a scale diagram and by calculations based on the properties of right triangles. Measuring a diagram offers only very limited precision. Calculation offers much greater precision, limited only by the precision of the input data. But our example was a special case in which the two vectors were perpendicular. With an angle other than 90° or with more than two vectors we would get into repeated trigonometric solutions of oblique triangles, which can get horribly complicated. So we need a simple but more general approach.

Addition and subtraction of vectors are usually carried out by the use of **components.** To define what we mean by components, we begin with a rectangular (cartesian) coordinate axis system as in Fig. 1–9. We can represent any vector lying in the xy-plane as the sum of a vector parallel to the x-axis and a vector parallel to the y-axis. These two vectors are labeled A_x and A_y in the figure; they are called the component vectors of vector A, and their vector sum is equal to A. In symbols,

$$A = A_x + A_y. \tag{1–7}$$

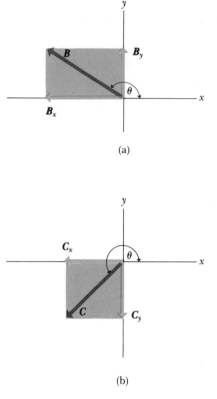

(a)

(b)

1–10

Components of a vector may be positive or negative numbers.

By definition, each component vector lies along a coordinate-axis direction. Thus we need only a single number to describe each one. For example, the number A_x is, apart from a possible negative sign, the magnitude of the component vector A_x. We further specify that the number A_x is positive when the vector A_x points in the positive axis direction and negative when in the opposite direction. The two numbers A_x and A_y are called simply the components of A.

If we know the magnitude A of the vector A and its direction, given by angle θ in Fig. 1–9, we can calculate the components. From the definitions of the trigonometric functions,

$$\frac{A_x}{A} = \cos \theta \qquad \text{and} \qquad \frac{A_y}{A} = \sin \theta;$$

$$A_x = A \cos \theta \qquad \text{and} \qquad A_y = A \sin \theta. \tag{1–8}$$

These equations are correct when the angle θ is measured counterclockwise from the positive x-axis, a common convention. If θ is a different angle, the relationships are different. Be careful!

In Fig. 1–10, the component B_x is negative because its direction is opposite to that of the positive x-axis. This is consistent with Eq. (1–8); the cosine of an angle in the second quadrant is negative. B_y is positive, but both C_x and C_y are negative.

We can describe a vector completely by giving either its magnitude and direction or its x- and y-components. Equations (1–8) show how to find the components if we know the magnitude and direction. Or if we are given the components, we can find the magnitude and direction. Applying the Pythagorean theorem to Fig. 1–9, we find

$$A = \sqrt{A_x{}^2 + A_y{}^2}. \tag{1–9}$$

Also, from the definition of the tangent of an angle,

$$\tan \theta = \frac{A_y}{A_x}$$

and

$$\theta = \arctan \frac{A_y}{A_x}. \tag{1–10}$$

There is one slight complication in using Eq. (1–10) to find θ. Suppose $A_x = 2$ m and $A_y = -2$ m; then $\tan \theta = -1$. But there are two angles having tangents of -1, namely, 135° and 315° (or $-45°$). To decide which is correct, we have to look at the individual components; because A_x is positive and A_y is negative, the angle must be in the fourth quadrant; thus $\theta = 315°$ (or $-45°$) is the correct value. Most pocket calculators give $\arctan (-1) = -45°$; in this case that is correct, but if instead we have $A_x = -2$ m and $A_y = 2$ m, then the correct angle is 135°. You should always draw a sketch to check which of the two possibilities is the correct one.

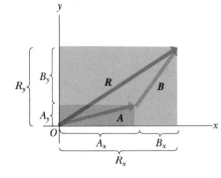

1–11
R_x is the x-component of the vector sum **R** of vectors **A** and **B** and is equal to the sum of the x-components of **A** and **B**. The y-components are similarly related.

Now let's see how we can use components to calculate the vector sum of several vectors. The component method requires only right triangles and simple computations, and it can be carried out with great precision. Here is the basic idea. Figure 1–11 shows two vectors **A** and **B** and their vector sum (resultant) **R,** along with x- and y-components of all three vectors. You can see from the diagram that the x-component R_x of the vector sum is simply the sum $(A_x + B_x)$ of the x-components of the vectors being added. The same is true for the y-components. In symbols,

$$R_x = A_x + B_x,$$
$$R_y = A_y + B_y. \tag{1–11}$$

Once we know the components of **A** and **B,** perhaps by using Eqs. (1–8), we can compute the components of the vector sum **R**. Then if the magnitude and direction of **R** are needed, we can obtain them from Eqs. (1–9) and (1–10).

This procedure for finding the sum of two vectors can easily be extended to any number of vectors. Let **R** be the vector sum of **A, B, C, D, E, ...** Then

$$R_x = A_x + B_x + C_x + D_x + E_x + \cdots,$$
$$R_y = A_y + B_y + C_y + D_y + E_y + \cdots. \tag{1–12}$$

In general, some of the components are positive and some are negative, so you must be careful about signs when evaluating the sums in Eqs. (1–12).

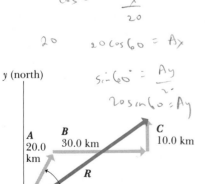

1–12
Three successive displacements **A, B,** and **C** and the resultant or vector sum displacement **R = A + B + C.**

Example 1–5   The pilot of a private plane flies 20.0 km in a direction 60° north of east, then 30.0 km straight east, then 10.0 km straight north. How far and in what direction is the plane from the starting point?

Solution   Figure 1–12 is a diagram showing the vector sum and a set of coordinate axes. We have chosen the x-axis as east and the y-axis as north, the usual choice for maps. Let **A** be the first displacement, **B** the second, **C** the third, and **R** the vector sum or resultant displacement. Eyeballing the diagram, we estimate that R is about 50 km, at an angle of about 30° north of east. We can later check this estimate against our calculated results.

The components of **A** are

$$A_x = (20.0 \text{ km})(\cos 60°) = 10.0 \text{ km},$$

$$A_y = (20.0 \text{ km})(\sin 60°) = 17.3 \text{ km}.$$

The following table shows the components of all the displacements, the addition of components, and the other calculations.

Distance	Angle	x-component	y-component
A = 20.0 km	60°	10.0 km	17.3 km
B = 30.0 km	0°	30.0 km	0
C = 10.0 km	90°	0	10.0 km
		R_x = 40.0 km	R_y = 27.3 km

$$R = \sqrt{(40.0 \text{ km})^2 + (27.3 \text{ km})^2} = 48.4 \text{ km},$$

$$\theta = \arctan \frac{27.3 \text{ km}}{40.0 \text{ km}} = 34.3°.$$

Alternatively, we can find θ first, as above, and then use Eqs. (1–8) to find R:

$$R = \frac{R_x}{\cos \theta} = \frac{40.0 \text{ km}}{\cos 34.3°} = 48.4 \text{ km},$$

or

$$R = \frac{R_y}{\sin \theta} = \frac{27.3 \text{ km}}{\sin 34.3°} = 48.4 \text{ km}.$$

We have talked only about vectors that lie in the xy-plane, but the component method works just as well for vectors having any direction in space. We introduce a z-axis perpendicular to the xy-plane; then in general a vector A has components A_x, A_y, and A_z in all three coordinate directions. The magnitude A is given by

$$A = \sqrt{A_x{}^2 + A_y{}^2 + A_z{}^2} \tag{1–13}$$

This whole discussion of vector addition has centered around combining displacement vectors, but the method is also applicable to many other vector quantities. In Chapter 4 we will study the concept of *force*. We will make extensive use of the fact that forces can be combined according to the same methods of vector addition that we have used with displacement.

Questions

1–1 What are the units of the number π?

1–2 The rate of climb of a mountain trail was described in the guidebook as 150 meters per kilometer. How can this be expressed as a number with no units?

1–3 Suppose you are asked to compute the cosine of 3 meters. Is this possible?

1–4 Hydrologists describe the rate of volume flow of rivers in "second-feet." Is this unit technically correct? If not, what would be a correct unit?

1–5 A highway contractor stated that in building a bridge deck he had poured 200 yards of concrete. What do you think he meant?

1–6 Does a vector having zero length have a direction?

1–7 What is your weight in newtons?

1–8 What is your height in centimeters?

1–9 What physical phenomena (other than a pendulum or cesium clock) could be used to define a time standard?

1–10 Could some atomic quantity be used for a definition of a unit of mass? What advantages or disadvantages would this have compared to the 1-kg platinum cylinder kept at Sèvres?

1–11 How could you measure the thickness of a sheet of paper with an ordinary ruler?

1–12 Can you find two vectors with different lengths that have a vector sum of zero? What length restrictions are required for three vectors to have a vector sum of zero?

1–13 What is the displacement when a bicyclist travels from the north side of a circular race track of radius 500 meters to the south side? When she makes one complete circle around the track?

1–14 What are the units of volume? Suppose a student tells you a cylinder of radius r and height h has volume given by $\pi r^3 h$. Explain why this cannot be correct.

1–15 An angle (measured in radians) is a number with no units, since it is a ratio of two lengths. Think of other geometrical or physical quantities that are unitless.

1–16 Can you find a vector quantity that has components different from zero but a magnitude of zero?

1–17 One sometimes speaks of the "direction of time," evolving from past to future. Does this mean that time is a vector quantity?

Exercises

Section 1–3 Standards and Units

Section 1–4 Unit Consistency and Conversions

1–1 Starting with the definition 1.00 in. = 2.54 cm, compute the number of miles in one kilometer.

1–2 The density of water is 1.00 g·cm^{-3}. What is this value in kilograms per cubic meter?

1–3 The piston displacement of a certain automobile engine is given as 2.50 L (2.50 liters). Using only the facts that 1.00 L = 1000 cm^3 and 1.00 in. = 2.54 cm, express this volume in cubic inches.

1–4 If one Deutschmark (the West German unit of currency) is worth 55.0 cents and gasoline costs 1.30 Deutschmarks per liter, what is its cost in dollars per gallon? Use the conversion factors in Appendix E. How does your answer compare to the cost of gasoline in the United States?

1–5 Compute the number of seconds in a day (24 hours), and in a year (365 days).

1–6 The Concorde is the fastest airliner used for commercial service; it can cruise at 1450 mi·hr^{-1} (about twice the speed of sound, or in other words Mach 2).

a) What is the cruise speed of the Concorde in mi·s^{-1}?

b) What is the cruise speed of the Concorde in m·s^{-1}?

1–7 The gasoline consumption of a small car is 15.0 km·L^{-1} (1 L = 1 liter). How many miles per gallon is this? Use the conversion factors in Appendix E.

1–8 The speed limit on a highway in Lower Slobbovia was given as 120,000 furlongs per fortnight. How many miles per hour is this? (One furlong is 1/8 mile, and a fortnight is 14 days. A furlong originally referred to the length of a plowed furrow.)

Section 1–5 Precision and Significant Figures

1–9 Estimate the percent error in measuring

a) a distance of about 20 cm with a meter stick;

b) a mass of about 15 g with a chemical balance;

c) a time interval of about 6 min with a stopwatch.

1–10 What is the percent error in each of the following approximations to π?

a) 22/7   b) 355/113

1–11 What is the fractional error in the approximate statement 1 yr = $\pi \times 10^7$ s? (Assume that a year is exactly 365 days.)

1–12 An angle is given, to one significant figure, as 5°, meaning that its value is between 4.5° and 5.5°. Find the corresponding range of possible values of the cosine of the angle. Is this a case in which there are more significant figures in the result than in the input data?

1–13 The mass of the earth is 5.98×10^{24} kg, and its radius is 6.38×10^6 m. Compute the density of the earth, using powers-of-ten notation and the correct number of significant figures. (The density of an object is defined as its mass divided by its volume. The formula for the volume of a sphere is given in Appendix B.)

Section 1–6 Estimates and Orders of Magnitude

1–14 How many hairs do you have on your head?

1–15 A box of typewriter paper is $11'' \times 17'' \times 9''$; it is marked "10 M." Does that mean it contains ten thousand or ten million sheets?

1–16 What total volume of air does a person breathe in a lifetime? How does that compare with the volume of the Houston Astrodome?

1–17 If all the gasoline burned in cars and trucks in the United States in one year were placed in a cubical tank, how big would the tank be?

1–18 Could the water supply needs of Los Angeles be met by hauling water in by truck? By railroad?

1–19 How many kernels of corn does it take to fill a 1-L (one-liter) soft-drink bottle?

1–20 How many drops of water are in all the oceans?

1–21 What is the total length of film in a two-hour feature movie? What is the diameter of the reel if the film is all on a single reel?

1–22 How many times does a human heart beat during a lifetime? How many gallons of blood does it pump?

1–23 How much would it cost to paper the continental United States with dollar bills?

1–24 If you filled your room with rocks, what would they weigh? What if you filled it with crumpled newspapers?

1–25 How many dollar bills would have to be stacked up to reach the moon? Would that be cheaper than building and launching a spacecraft?

1–26 How many cars can pass through a two-lane tunnel through a mountain in 1 hour?

Section 1–7 Vectors and Vector Addition

1–27 A bug starts at the center of a 12-in. phonograph record and crawls along a straight radial line to the edge. While this is happening, the record turns through an angle of 45°. Draw a sketch of the situation and describe the magnitude and direction of the bug's final displacement from its starting point.

1–28 A postal employee drives a delivery truck 1.25 mi north, then 4.44 mi east, then 3.58 mi northwest (at 45° between north and west). Determine the magnitude and direction of the resultant displacement by drawing a scale diagram.

1–29 Use a scale drawing to find the magnitude and direction of

a) the vector sum $A + B$;

b) the vector difference $A - B$

for the vectors A and B given in Fig. 1–13.

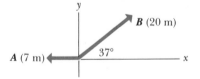

FIGURE 1–13

1–30 A spelunker is surveying a cave. He follows a passage 210 m straight east, then 80 m in a direction 60.0° west of north, then 150 m at 45.0° west of south. After a fourth unmeasured displacement he finds himself back where he started. Use a scale drawing to determine the fourth displacement (magnitude and direction).

Section 1–8 Components of Vectors

1–31 Use a scale drawing to find the x- and y-components of the following vectors. In each case the magnitude of the vector and the angle, measured counterclockwise, that it makes with the +x-axis are given.

a) magnitude 9.40 m, angle 60.0°;

b) magnitude 15.0 km, angle 315°;

c) magnitude 4.60 cm, angle 143°.

1–32 Compute the x- and y-components of each of the vectors A, B, and C that are given in Fig. 1–14.

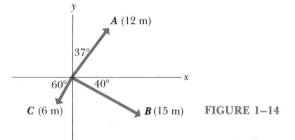

FIGURE 1–14

1–33 Find the magnitude and direction of the vector represented by each of the following pairs of components:

a) $A_x = 3.20$ cm, $A_y = -5.15$ cm;

b) $A_x = -5.48$ m, $A_y = -9.60$ m;

c) $A_x = -2.10$ km, $A_y = 6.85$ km.

1–34 Vector A has components $A_x = -2.20$ cm, $A_y = 3.64$ cm; and vector B has components $B_x = 4.90$ cm, $B_y = -5.72$ cm. Find

a) the components of the vector sum $A + B$;

b) the magnitude and direction of $A + B$;

c) the components of the vector difference $A - B$;

d) the magnitude and direction of $A - B$.

1–35 A disoriented physics professor drives 5.18 km east, then 6.20 km north, then 2.05 km west. Find the magnitude and direction of the resultant displacement, using the method of components.

1–36 A postal employee drives a delivery truck 1.25 mi north, then 4.44 mi east, then 3.58 mi northwest (at 45°

between north and west). Use the method of components to determine the resultant displacement (magnitude and direction).

1–37 Use the method of components to find the magnitude and direction of

a) the vector sum **A** + **B**;

b) the vector difference **A** − **B**

for the vectors **A** and **B** given in Fig. 1–13.

Problems

1–38 One standard of frequency is the radio waves generated by the hydrogen maser. These waves have a frequency of 1,420,405,751.786 hertz. (Hertz is a special name for cycles per second.) A clock controlled by a hydrogen maser is off by only 1 s in 100,000 years. For the following questions, use only three significant figures. (The large number of significant figures for the frequency was given to illustrate the remarkable precision to which it has been measured.)

a) What is the time for one cycle of the radio wave?

b) How many cycles occur in 1 hour?

c) How many cycles would have occurred during the age of the earth, which is estimated to be 4600 million years?

d) By how many seconds would a hydrogen maser clock be off during the lifetime of the earth?

1–39 Vector **A** is 5.80 cm long and is 60.0° above the x-axis in the first quadrant. Vector **B** is 5.80 cm long and is 60.0° below the x-axis in the fourth quadrant. Find the magnitude and direction of

a) the vector sum **A** + **B**;

b) the vector difference **A** − **B**;

c) the vector difference **B** − **A**.

1–40 A vector **A** of length 7.40 m makes an angle of 53.1° with a vector **B** of length 5.60 m. Find the magnitude of the vector difference **A** − **B** and the angle it makes with vector **A**.

1–41 Vector **M**, of magnitude 4.75 cm, is at 58.0° counterclockwise from the +x-axis. It is added to vector **N**, and the resultant is a vector of magnitude 4.75 cm, at 39.0° counterclockwise from the +x-axis. Find

a) the components of **N**;

b) the magnitude and direction of **N**.

1–42 A spelunker is surveying a cave. He follows a passage 210 m straight east, then 80 m in a direction 60.0° west of north, then 150 m at 45.0° west of south. After a fourth unmeasured displacement he finds himself back where he started. Use the method of components to determine the fourth displacement (magnitude and direction).

1–43 Two points P_1 and P_2 are described by their x- and y-coordinates, (x_1, y_1) and (x_2, y_2), respectively. Show that the components of the displacement **A** from P_1 to P_2 are $A_x = x_2 - x_1$ and $A_y = y_2 - y_1$. Also derive expressions for the magnitude and direction of this displacement.

1–44 A sailor in a small sailboat encounters shifting winds. She sails 2.00 km east, then 3.40 km northeast, then an additional distance in an unknown direction. Her final position is 6.68 km directly east of the starting point. Find the magnitude and direction of the third leg of the voyage.

1–45 A cross-country skier skies 7.40 km in the direction 30.0° west of south, then 2.80 km in the direction 45.0° north of west, and finally 6.00 km in the direction 22.0° east of north. To then return to his starting point, how far and in what direction must he travel?

Challenge Problems

1–46 Physicists, mathematicians, and others often deal with large numbers. The number 10^{100} has been given the whimsical name *googol* by mathematicians. (See Edward Kasner and J. R. Newman in *The World of Mathematics*, Vol. 3 (1988), edited by J. R. Newman. New York: Simon and Schuster.) Let us compare some large numbers in physics with the googol. (*Note:* The

following problem requires numerical values that can be found in the appendixes of the book, with which you should become familiar.)

a) Approximately how many atoms make up the earth? For simplicity, take the average atomic mass of the atoms to be 14 g·mole^{-1}. Avogadro's number gives the number of atoms in a mole.

b) Approximately how many neutrons are in a neutron star? Neutron stars are made up of neutrons and have approximately twice the mass of the sun.

c) In one theory of the origin of the universe, the universe at a very early time had a density (mass divided by volume) of 10^{15} g·cm^{-3} and a radius approximately equal to the present distance from the earth to the sun. Assuming that 1/3 of the particles were protons, 1/3 were neutrons, and the remaining 1/3 were electrons, how many particles then made up the universe?

1–47 When two vectors A and B are drawn from a common point, the angle between them is θ.

a) Show that the magnitude of their vector sum is given by

$$\sqrt{A^2 + B^2 + 2AB \cos \theta}.$$

b) If A and B have the same magnitude, under what circumstances does their vector sum have the same magnitude as A or B?

c) Derive a result analogous to that in (a) for the magnitude of the vector difference $A - B$.

d) If A and B have the same magnitude, under what circumstance does $A - B$ have this same magnitude?

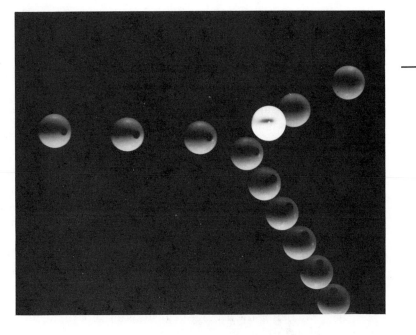

2

Motion along a Straight Line

Our study of physics begins with *mechanics*, the study of the relationships among force, matter, and motion. In this chapter and the next, we discuss mathematical methods for describing motion, and in later chapters we explore the relationship of motion to force. The part of mechanics concerned with describing motion is called **kinematics.**

Often, we can think of a moving body as a *particle*. The particle is a **model** for the body. It provides a simplified, idealized description of the position and motion of the body when effects such as rotation and change of shape are not important.

Motion is a continuous change of position. The simplest case is motion of a particle along a straight line. We will always take that line to be a **coordinate axis.** The position of the body is described by its displacement from the origin of coordinates. Displacement is a vector quantity, as we discussed in Chapter 1. In motion of a particle along a line that is a coordinate axis, only one component of displacement is different from zero, and the particle's position is described by a single **coordinate.** The velocity and acceleration vectors also have only one component, along the coordinate axis. In Chapter 3 we will consider more general motions in space, in which the particle has two or three coordinates and the velocity and acceleration vectors have two or three nonzero components.

2–1
Average Velocity

Suppose a hockey player skates the puck down the center line of the ice toward the opposition's net. The puck moves along a straight line; we will use this line as the x-axis of our coordinate system, as shown in Fig. 2–1. The origin O is at the center of the rink. The puck's distance from the origin is given by the coordinate x, which varies with time. Suppose that 4 seconds (4.0 s) after face-off, the puck is at point P, 5.0 m from the origin, and that at 6.0 s after face-off it is at point Q, 13.0 m from the origin. Then it has traveled a distance of (13.0 m − 5.0 m) = 8.0 m in a time of (6.0 s − 4.0 s) = 2.0 s. We define its **average velocity** during this interval to be a vector quantity whose x-component is the change in x divided by the time, that is, (8.0 m)/(2.0 s) = 4.0 m·s^{-1}.

Let's generalize this. At time t_1 the puck is at point P, with coordinate x_1, and at time t_2 it is at point Q, where its coordinate is x_2. The displacement during the time interval from t_1 to t_2 is the vector from P to Q; the x-component of this vector is $(x_2 - x_1)$, and all other components are zero. We define the average velocity as a vector in the direction from P to Q, with an x-component v_{av} given by

$$v_{av} = \frac{x_2 - x_1}{t_2 - t_1}. \tag{2–1}$$

This is the x-component of the average velocity vector; all other components are zero.

Changes in quantities, such as $(x_2 - x_1)$ and $(t_2 - t_1)$, occur so often throughout physics that it is worthwhile to use a special notation. From now on we will use the Greek letter Δ to represent a *change* in any quantity. Thus we write

$$\Delta x = x_2 - x_1. \tag{2–2}$$

Be sure you understand that Δx is *not* the *product* of Δ and x. It is a *single symbol*, and it means "the change in the quantity x." This is the x-component of displacement of the particle. With this same notation we denote the time interval from t_1 to t_2 as $\Delta t = t_2 - t_1$.

We can now express the x-component of **average velocity** as the ratio of the x-component of displacement Δx to the time interval Δt. As above, we represent this quantity by the letter v with a subscript "av" to signify

2–1
A hockey puck moving on the x-axis.

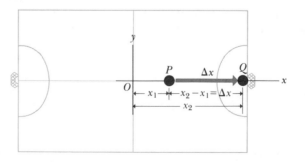

average value. Thus

$$v_{\mathrm{av}} = \frac{x_2 - x_1}{t_2 - t_1} = \frac{\Delta x}{\Delta t}. \tag{2-3}$$

In some cases, v_{av} is negative. Suppose that in our initial example the puck is moving toward the origin, with $x_1 = 13.0$ m and $x_2 = 5.0$ m. Then the x-component of average velocity is -4.0 m·s^{-1}. Whenever x is positive and decreasing or negative and becoming more negative, the particle is moving toward the left in Fig. 2–1, and v_{av} is negative.

As we have mentioned, average velocity is a vector quantity, and Eq. (2–3) defines the x-component of this vector. In this chapter, all vectors have *only* x-components. We will often call x the displacement and v_{av} the *average velocity*, remembering that these are really the x-components of vector quantities that in straight-line motion have *only* x-components. In Chapter 3, displacement, velocity, and acceleration vectors will have two or three nonzero components.

It doesn't matter whether the speed of the hockey puck is or is not constant during the time interval $\Delta t = t_2 - t_1$. It may have started from rest, reached a maximum speed, and then slowed down. But to calculate the average velocity, we need only the total displacement $\Delta x = x_2 - x_1$ and the total time interval $\Delta t = t_2 - t_1$.

2–2
Instantaneous Velocity

Even when a particle speeds up or slows down, we can still define a velocity at any one specific instant of time or at one specific point in the path. Such a velocity is called **instantaneous velocity,** and it needs to be defined carefully.

Suppose we want to find the instantaneous velocity of the hockey puck in Fig. 2–1 at the point P. We can take the second point Q to be closer and closer to the first point P, and we can compute the average velocity over these shorter and shorter displacements and time intervals. Although both Δx and Δt become very small, their quotient does not necessarily become small. We then define the instantaneous velocity at P as the value that this series of average velocities approaches as the time interval becomes very small and Q becomes closer and closer to P.

In mathematical language the instantaneous velocity is called the **limit** of $\Delta x/\Delta t$ as Δt approaches zero or the **derivative** of x with respect to t. We use the symbol v with no subscript for instantaneous velocity, so

$$v = \lim_{\Delta t \to 0} \frac{\Delta x}{\Delta t}. \tag{2-4}$$

We assume that Δt is positive (i.e., t_2 is a later time than t_1), so v has the same algebraic sign as Δx. If the positive x-axis points to the right, as in Fig. 2–1, a positive value of v means motion toward the right, and a negative value toward the left. If in Fig. 2–1 the particle is to the right of O but is moving toward the left, then it has a positive x and a negative v.

A particle to the left of O moving toward the right has a negative x and a positive v. Can you see what the situation is when *both* x and v are negative?

Instantaneous velocity, like average velocity, is a vector quantity, and Eq. (2–4) defines its x-component. In straight-line motion, all other components are zero, and in this case we will often call v the instantaneous velocity. When we use the term *velocity* we always mean instantaneous rather than average velocity unless we state otherwise.

If we express distance in meters and time in seconds, velocity is expressed in meters per second (m·s^{-1} or m/s). Other common units of velocity are kilometers per hour (km·hr^{-1}), feet per second (ft·s^{-1}), miles per hour (mi·hr^{-1}), and knots (1 knot = 1 nautical mile or 6080 ft per hour).

Example 2–1   A cheetah is crouched in ambush 20 m to the east of an observer's blind (see Fig. 2–2). At time $t = 0$ the cheetah charges an antelope in a clearing 50 m east of the observer. The cheetah runs along a straight line; the observer estimates that during the first 2 s of the attack, the cheetah's coordinate x varies with time according to the equation $x = 20$ m $+ (5$ m·s$^{-2})t^2$.

a) Find the displacement of the cheetah during the interval between $t_1 = 1$ s and $t_2 = 2$ s.

At time $t_1 = 1$ s, the cheetah's position x_1 is

$$x_1 = 20 \text{ m} + (5 \text{ m·s}^{-2})(1 \text{ s})^2 = 25 \text{ m}.$$

At time $t_2 = 2$ s, the position x_2 is

$$x_2 = 20 \text{ m} + (5 \text{ m·s}^{-2})(2 \text{ s})^2 = 40 \text{ m}.$$

The displacement during this interval is

$$x_2 - x_1 = 40 \text{ m} - 25 \text{ m} = 15 \text{ m}.$$

b) Find the average velocity during this time interval:

$$v_{av} = \frac{40 \text{ m} - 25 \text{ m}}{2 \text{ s} - 1 \text{ s}} = \frac{15 \text{ m}}{1 \text{ s}} = 15 \text{ m·s}^{-1}.$$

c) Find the instantaneous velocity at time $t_1 = 1$ s by taking first $\Delta t = 0.1$ s, then 0.01 s, then 0.001 s.

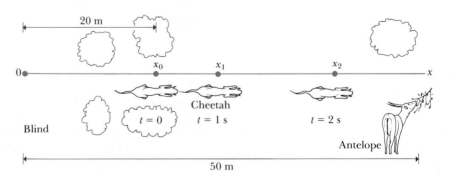

2–2
A cheetah attacking an antelope from ambush.

When $\Delta t = 0.1$ s, $t_2 = 1.1$ s and

$$x_2 = 20 \text{ m} + (5 \text{ m·s}^{-2})(1.1 \text{ s})^2 = 26.05 \text{ m}.$$

The average velocity during this interval is

$$v_{av} = \frac{26.05 \text{ m} - 25 \text{ m}}{1.1 \text{ s} - 1 \text{ s}} = 10.5 \text{ m·s}^{-1}.$$

We invite you to follow this same pattern to work out the average velocities for the 0.01-s and 0.001-s intervals. The results are 10.05 m·s^{-1} and 10.005 m·s^{-1}. As Δt gets smaller and smaller, the average velocity gets closer and closer to 10.0 m·s^{-1}, and we conclude that the instantaneous velocity at time $t = 1$ s is 10.0 m·s^{-1}.   ∎

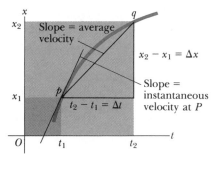

2–3
Coordinate–time graph of the motion shown in Fig. 2–1. The average velocity between t_1 and t_2 equals the slope of the line pq. The instantaneous velocity at P equals the slope of the tangent at p.

The term **speed** is used to denote distance traveled divided by time, on either an average or an instantaneous basis. Thus speed is a scalar quantity, not a vector; it has no direction. If a race car makes one lap around the Indianapolis race track (2.5-mi circumference) in 1.00 min (= 1/60 hr), its average speed is (2.5 mi)/(1/60 hr) = 150 mi·hr^{-1}. Its instantaneous speed may or may not be constant, but its velocity is certainly not constant because it changes direction at the turns. At the end of one lap the race car is back where it started, so its average *velocity* for one lap is zero!

We can get added insight into the concepts of average and instantaneous velocity by plotting a graph with position x on the vertical axis and time t on the horizontal axis, that is, a graph of x as a function of t. Such a graph is shown in Fig. 2–3. The curve in this figure *does not* represent the path of the particle in space; the path is a straight line. Rather, the graph is a pictorial representation of the relationship of position and time. Point p on the graph corresponds to the particle being at point P in Fig. 2–1 (with coordinate x_1) at time t_1. Point q on the graph corresponds to point Q.

For the interval t_1 to t_2 the average velocity $v_{av} = \Delta x/\Delta t$ is the ratio of the vertical change Δx to the horizontal change Δt; these are the vertical and horizontal sides of the right triangle in Fig. 2–3, with hypotenuse from p to q. We call the ratio of these two sides the **slope** of the line joining points p and q.

As point Q approaches point P in Fig. 2–1, point q approaches point p in Fig. 2–3. In the limit when Δt approaches zero, the slope of the line pq equals the slope of the *tangent line* to the curve at point p. We can determine this slope by drawing the tangent line at p and constructing a right triangle with the tangent line as its hypotenuse. The ratio of the vertical side (with distance units) to the horizontal side (with time units) is the slope of the tangent line and is equal to the instantaneous velocity at p. *The instantaneous velocity at any point on a coordinate–time graph equals the slope of the tangent line to the graph at that point.* When the tangent slopes upward to the right, its slope is positive, the velocity is positive, and the motion is in the direction of increasing x. When the tangent slopes downward to the right, the velocity is negative. At a point where the tangent is horizontal, its slope is zero and the velocity is zero.

Note that as we go from p to q in Fig. 2–3, the slope of the tangent line *decreases*; this shows that the puck is slowing down as it moves from P to Q.

2–3
Average and Instantaneous Acceleration

When the velocity of a moving body changes with time, we say that the body has an *acceleration*. Just as velocity is a quantitative description of the rate of change of position with time, so acceleration is a quantitative description of the rate of change of velocity with time. Like velocity, acceleration is a vector quantity. In straight-line motion its only nonzero component is along the coordinate axis.

Considering again the motion of a particle along the x-axis, we suppose that at time t_1 the particle is at point P and has x-component of velocity v_1 and that at a later time t_2 it is at point Q and has x-component of velocity v_2.

We define the **average acceleration** a_{av} of the particle, as it moves from P to Q, to be a vector quantity whose x-component is the ratio of the change in the x-component of velocity $\Delta v = v_2 - v_1$ to the time interval $\Delta t = t_2 - t_1$.

$$a_{av} = \frac{v_2 - v_1}{t_2 - t_1} = \frac{\Delta v}{\Delta t}. \tag{2–5}$$

In straight-line motion we will usually call a_{av} the average acceleration, rather than the x-component of average acceleration.

Example 2–2   An astronaut has left the space shuttle on a tether line to test a new personal maneuvering device. Her on-board partner measures her velocity before and after certain maneuvers, as follows:

a) $v_1 = 0.8$ m·s^{-1}, $v_2 = 1.2$ m·s^{-1}; (speed increases)
b) $v_1 = 1.6$ m·s^{-1}, $v_2 = 1.2$ m·s^{-1}; (speed decreases)
c) $v_1 = -0.4$ m·s^{-1}, $v_2 = -1.0$ m·s^{-1}; (speed increases)
d) $v_1 = -1.6$ m·s^{-1}, $v_2 = -0.8$ m·s^{-1}. (speed decreases)

If $t_1 = 2$ s and $t_2 = 4$ s in each case, find the average acceleration for each set of data.

Solution

a) $a_{av} = \dfrac{1.2 \text{ m·s}^{-1} - 0.8 \text{ m·s}^{-1}}{4 \text{ s} - 2 \text{ s}} = 0.2$ m·s^{-2};

b) $a_{av} = \dfrac{1.2 \text{ m·s}^{-1} - 1.6 \text{ m·s}^{-1}}{4 \text{ s} - 2 \text{ s}} = -0.2$ m·s^{-2};

c) $a_{av} = \dfrac{-1.0 \text{ m·s}^{-1} - (-0.4 \text{ m·s}^{-1})}{4 \text{ s} - 2 \text{ s}} = -0.3 \text{ m·s}^{-2};$

d) $a_{av} = \dfrac{-0.8 \text{ m·s}^{-1} - (-1.6 \text{ m·s}^{-1})}{4 \text{ s} - 2 \text{ s}} = +0.4 \text{ m·s}^{-2}.$

When the acceleration has the *same* direction as the initial velocity, the astronaut goes faster; when it is in the opposite direction, she slows down. When she moves in the negative direction with increasing speed (c), her acceleration is negative; when she moves in the negative direction with decreasing speed (d), her acceleration is positive. ■

We can now define **instantaneous acceleration,** following the same procedure that we used for instantaneous velocity. Consider this situation: A sports car driver has just entered the final straightaway at the Grand Prix. He reaches point P at time t_1, moving with velocity v_1. He passes point Q, closer to the finish line, at time t_2 with velocity v_2, as shown in Fig. 2–4.

To define instantaneous acceleration at point P, we take the second point Q in Fig. 2–4 to be closer and closer to the first point P, so the average acceleration is computed over shorter and shorter intervals of time. The instantaneous acceleration at point P is the limit approached by the average acceleration when point Q is taken closer and closer to point P.

$$a = \lim_{\Delta t \to 0} \frac{\Delta v}{\Delta t}. \tag{2–6}$$

Instantaneous acceleration plays an essential role in the laws of mechanics. From now on when we use the term *acceleration*, we will always mean instantaneous acceleration, not average acceleration.

If we express velocity in meters per second and time in seconds, then acceleration is in meters per second per second $(\text{m·s}^{-1}\text{·s}^{-1})$. This is usually written as m·s^{-2} and is read "meters per second squared."

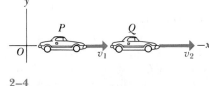

2–4
Car moving on the x-axis.

Example 2–3   Suppose the velocity v of the car in Fig. 2–4, at any time t, is given by the equation

$$v = 10 \text{ m·s}^{-1} + (2.0 \text{ m·s}^{-3})t^2.$$

a) Find the change in velocity of the car in the time interval between $t_1 = 2$ s and $t_2 = 5$ s.

We substitute the values of t into the equation. At time $t_1 = 2$ s,

$$v_1 = 10 \text{ m·s}^{-1} + (2 \text{ m·s}^{-3})(2 \text{ s})^2$$
$$= 18 \text{ m·s}^{-1}.$$

At time $t_2 = 5$ s,

$$v_2 = 10 \text{ m·s}^{-1} + (2 \text{ m·s}^{-3})(5 \text{ s})^2$$
$$= 60 \text{ m·s}^{-1}.$$

The change in velocity Δv is therefore

$$\Delta v = v_2 - v_1 = 60 \text{ m·s}^{-1} - 18 \text{ m·s}^{-1}$$
$$= 42 \text{ m·s}^{-1}.$$

The corresponding time interval is $\Delta t = 5 \text{ s} - 2 \text{ s} = 3 \text{ s}$.

b) Find the average acceleration in this time interval.

$$a_{av} = \frac{v_2 - v_1}{t_2 - t_1} = \frac{42 \text{ m·s}^{-1}}{3 \text{ s}} = 14 \text{ m·s}^{-2}.$$

c) Find the instantaneous acceleration at time $t_1 = 2$ s by taking Δt to be first 0.1 s, then 0.01 s, then 0.001 s.

When $\Delta t = 0.1$ s, $t_2 = 2.1$ s and

$$v_2 = 10 \text{ m·s}^{-1} + (2.0 \text{ m·s}^{-3})(2.1 \text{ s})^2 = 18.82 \text{ m·s}^{-1},$$

$$\Delta v = 0.82 \text{ m·s}^{-1},$$

and

$$a_{av} = \frac{0.82 \text{ m·s}^{-1}}{0.1 \text{ s}} = 8.2 \text{ m·s}^{-2}.$$

We invite you to repeat this pattern for $\Delta t = 0.01$ s and 0.001 s; the results are $a_{av} = 8.02 \text{ m·s}^{-2}$ and 8.002 m·s^{-2}, respectively. As Δt gets smaller and smaller, the average acceleration gets closer and closer to 8.0 m·s^{-2}, and we conclude that the instantaneous acceleration at $t = 2.0$ s is 8.0 m·s^{-2}. ■

We can get added insight into the concepts of average and instantaneous acceleration by plotting a graph with velocity v on the vertical axis and time t on the horizontal axis. Such a graph is shown in Fig. 2–5. The points on the graph corresponding to points P and Q in Fig. 2–4 are labeled p and q. The average acceleration during this interval is represented by the slope of the line pq, computed by using the appropriate scales and units of the graph. As point Q in Fig. 2–4 approaches point P, point q in Fig. 2–5 approaches point p, and the slope of the line pq approaches the slope of the line tangent to the curve at point p. Thus *the instantaneous acceleration at any point on the graph equals the slope of the line tangent to the curve at that point.* In Fig. 2–5 the instantaneous acceleration varies with time. Automotive engineers sometimes call the time rate of change of acceleration the "jerk."

A few remarks about the *sign* of acceleration may be helpful. When the acceleration and velocity of a body have the same sign, the body is speeding up. If both are positive, the body moves in the positive direction with increasing speed. If both are negative, the body moves in the negative direction with a velocity that becomes more and more negative with time, and again the body's speed increases.

When v and a have opposite signs, the body is slowing down. If v is positive and a is negative, the body moves in the positive direction with decreasing speed. If v is negative and a is positive, the body moves in the

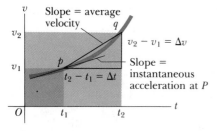

2–5
Velocity–time graph of the motion shown in Fig. 2–4. The average acceleration between t_1 and t_2 equals the slope of the line pq. The instantaneous acceleration at P equals the slope of the tangent at p.

negative direction with a velocity that is becoming less negative, and again the body slows down.

The term *deceleration* is sometimes used either for a negative value of a or for a decrease in speed. Because of this ambiguity, it is best to avoid this term. We do not use it in this book; instead we recommend careful attention to the interpretation of the algebraic sign of a in relation to that of v.

2–4
Motion with Constant Acceleration

The simplest accelerated motion is straight-line motion with *constant* acceleration, when the velocity changes at the same rate throughout the motion. The graph of velocity as a function of time is then a straight line, as in Fig. 2–6. The velocity changes by equal amounts in equal time intervals, and the slope of the graph is constant. In this case it is easy to derive equations for position x and velocity v as functions of time. Let's start with velocity. In Eq. (2–5) we can replace the average acceleration a_{av} by the constant (instantaneous) acceleration a. We then have

$$a = \frac{v_2 - v_1}{t_2 - t_1}. \qquad (2\text{–}7)$$

Now let $t_1 = 0$ and let t_2 be any arbitrary later time t. We use the symbol v_0 for the velocity at the initial time $t = 0$; the velocity at any later time t is v. Then Eq. (2–7) becomes

$$a = \frac{v - v_0}{t - 0}, \qquad \text{or} \qquad v = v_0 + at. \qquad (2\text{–}8)$$

We can interpret this equation as follows: The acceleration a is the constant rate of change of velocity, that is, the change in velocity per unit time. The term at is the product of the change in velocity per unit time, a, and the time interval t. Therefore it equals the *total* change in velocity from the initial time $t = 0$ to the later time t. The velocity v at any time t then equals the initial velocity v_0 (at $t = 0$) plus the change in velocity at. Graphically, we can consider the height v of the graph in Fig. 2–6 at any time t as the sum of two segments: one with length v_0 equal to the initial velocity, the other with length at equal to the change in velocity during time t.

Next we want to derive an equation for the position x of a particle moving with constant acceleration. To do this, we make use of two different expressions for the average velocity v_{av} during the interval from $t = 0$ to any later time t. First, when the acceleration is constant and the velocity–time graph is a straight line, as in Fig. 2–6, the velocity changes at a uniform rate. In this case the average velocity throughout any time interval is the simple arithmetic average of the velocities at the beginning and end of the interval. For the time interval 0 to t,

$$v_{av} = \frac{v_0 + v}{2}. \qquad (2\text{–}9)$$

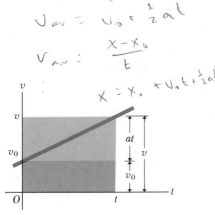

$$V_{av} = \frac{V_o + V}{2}$$

$$V = V_o + at$$

$$V_{av} = \frac{1}{2}\left(V_o + V_o + at\right)$$

$$V_{av} = V_o + \tfrac{1}{2}at$$

$$V_{av} = \frac{x - x_o}{t}$$

$$x = x_o + V_o t + \tfrac{1}{2}at^2$$

2–6
Velocity–time graph for straight-line motion with constant acceleration.

(This is *not* true in general when the acceleration is not constant and the velocity–time graph is a curve, as in Fig. 2–5.) We also know that v, the velocity at any time t, is given by Eq. (2–8). Substituting that expression for v into Eq. (2–9), we find

$$v_{av} = \tfrac{1}{2}(v_0 + v_0 + at)$$

$$= v_0 + \tfrac{1}{2}at. \tag{2–10}$$

We can also get an expression for v_{av} from the definition given by Eq. (2–1). We call the position at time $t = 0$ the *initial position* and denote it x_0. The position at the later time t is called simply x. Thus for the time interval $\Delta t = t - 0$ and the corresponding displacement $x - x_0$, Eq. (2–1) gives

$$v_{av} = \frac{x - x_0}{t}. \tag{2–11}$$

Finally, we equate Eqs. (2–10) and (2–11) and simplify the resulting equation:

$$v_0 + \tfrac{1}{2}at = \frac{x - x_0}{t},$$

or

$$x = x_0 + v_0 t + \tfrac{1}{2}at^2. \tag{2–12}$$

This equation states that if at the initial time $t = 0$ a particle is at position x_0 and has velocity v_0, its new position x at any later time t is the sum of three terms: its initial position x_0 plus the distance $v_0 t$ it would move if its velocity were constant plus an additional distance $\tfrac{1}{2}at^2$ caused by the changing velocity.

We may also combine Eqs. (2–8) and (2–12) to obtain a relation for x, v, and a that does not contain t. We first solve Eq. (2–8) for t and then substitute the resulting expression into Eq. (2–12) and simplify:

$$t = \frac{v - v_0}{a},$$

$$x = x_0 + v_0\left(\frac{v - v_0}{a}\right) + \tfrac{1}{2}a\left(\frac{v - v_0}{a}\right)^2.$$

Transfer the term x_0 to the left side and multiply through by $2a$:

$$2a(x - x_0) = 2v_0 v - 2v_0^2 + v^2 - 2v_0 v + v_0^2,$$

or, finally,

$$v^2 = v_0^2 + 2a(x - x_0). \tag{2–13}$$

We can obtain one additional useful relationship by equating the two expressions for v_{av}, Eqs. (2–9) and (2–11), and multiplying through by t. Doing this, we obtain

$$x - x_0 = \frac{v_0 + v}{2}\, t. \tag{2–14}$$

(handwritten at top)
$at = v - v_0$
$v_{avg} = \dfrac{v + v_0}{2} = \dfrac{at + 2v_0}{2} = v_0 + \dfrac{at}{2}$

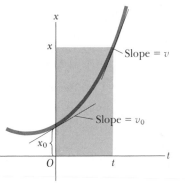

2–7
Coordinate–time graph for motion with constant acceleration.

(figure labels: x, x, x_0, O, t, Slope = v, Slope = v_0)

We note that Eq. (2–14) does not contain the acceleration a. This is sometimes a convenience when a is not given in the problem.

Equations (2–8), (2–12), (2–13), and (2–14) are the *equations of motion with constant acceleration*. Any kinematic problem involving motion of a particle on a straight line with constant acceleration can be solved by using these equations.

The curve in Fig. 2–7 is a graph of the coordinate x as a function of time for motion with constant acceleration for a case in which v_0 and a are positive. That is, it is a graph of Eq. (2–12); the curve is a *parabola*. The slope of the tangent at $t = 0$ equals the initial velocity v_0, and the slope of the tangent at any time t equals the velocity v at that time. The slope continuously increases with t, and measurements would show that the *rate* of increase with t is constant.

PROBLEM-SOLVING STRATEGY: *Motion with Constant Acceleration*

1. It is essential to decide at the beginning of a problem where the origin of coordinates is and which axis direction is positive. The choices are usually made on the basis of convenience; it is often easiest to place the particle at the origin at time $t = 0$. A diagram showing these choices is always helpful.

2. Once you have chosen the positive axis direction, the positive directions for velocity and acceleration are also determined. It would be inconsistent to define x as positive to the right of the origin and velocities toward the left as positive.

3. In constant-acceleration problems it always helps to make a list of quantities such as x, x_0, v, v_0, and a. In general, some of these will be known and some unknown. Write down those that are known. When possible, select an equation from Eqs. (2–8), (2–12), (2–13), and (2–14) that contains only one of the unknowns; solve for the unknown, then substitute the known values and compute the value of the unknown.

4. It often helps to restate the problem in prose first and then translate the prose description into symbols and equations. *When* does the particle arrive at a certain point? (That is, at what value of t?) *Where* is the particle when its velocity has a certain value? (That is, what is the value of x when v has the specified value?) In the following example we ask "Where is the motorcyclist when his velocity is 5 m·s^{-1}?" Translated into symbols, this becomes "What is the value of x when $v = 5$ m·s^{-1}?"

5. Take a hard look at your results to see whether they make sense. Are they within the general range of magnitudes you expected?

(handwritten, left column)
$v_2 = v_0 + at$
$5 = 3 + (4)(t)$
$\tfrac{1}{2}5 = t$

$x = 5 + 3(\tfrac{1}{2}) + \tfrac{1}{2}(4)(\tfrac{1}{2})^2$

7

Example 2–4   A motorcyclist heading east through a small Iowa town accelerates as he passes the signpost at $x = 0$ marking the city limits. His acceleration is constant, $a = 4$ m·s^{-2}. At time $t = 0$ he is 5 m east of the signpost and has a velocity of $v = 3$ m·s^{-1}.

(handwritten: $v_0 = 3,\ x_0 = 5$)

a) Find his position and velocity at time $t = 2$ s.

b) Where is he when his velocity is 5 m·s^{-1}?

(handwritten)
a) $x = x_0 + v_0 t + \tfrac{1}{2}at^2 = 5 + 3(2) + \tfrac{1}{2}(4)(2)^2$
   $v = v_0 + at = 3 + 2(1) = \underline{11} = 5 + 6 + 8 = $ *(circled)* 19

Solution   We take the signpost as the origin of coordinates, and the positive *x*-axis points east. At the initial time $t = 0$ the initial position is $x_0 = 5$ m, and the initial velocity is $v_0 = 3$ m·s^{-1}. With reference to Eqs. (2–8), (2–12), (2–13), and (2–14), we have

$$x_0 = 5 \text{ m},$$

$$v_0 = 3 \text{ m·s}^{-1},$$

$$a = 4 \text{ m·s}^{-2}.$$

a) We want to know the position and velocity (i.e., the values of *x* and *v*) at the later time $t = 2$ s. From Eq. (2–12), which gives position *x* as a function of time *t*, we have

$$x = x_0 + v_0 t + \tfrac{1}{2} a t^2$$
$$= 5 \text{ m} + (3 \text{ m·s}^{-1})(2 \text{ s}) + \tfrac{1}{2}(4 \text{ m·s}^{-2})(2 \text{ s})^2$$
$$= 19 \text{ m}.$$

From Eq. (2–8), which gives velocity *v* as a function of time *t*, we have

$$v = v_0 + at$$
$$= 3 \text{ m·s}^{-1} + (4 \text{ m·s}^{-2})(2 \text{ s})$$
$$= 11 \text{ m·s}^{-1}.$$

b) We want to know the value of *x* when $v = 5$ m·s^{-1}. From Eq. (2–13), we have

$$v^2 = v_0{}^2 + 2a(x - x_0),$$

$$(5 \text{ m·s}^{-1})^2 = (3 \text{ m·s}^{-1})^2 + 2(4 \text{ m·s}^{-2})(x - 5 \text{ m}),$$

$$x = 7 \text{ m}.$$

Alternatively, we may use Eq. (2–8) to find first the *time* when $v = 5$ m·s^{-1}:

$$5 \text{ m·s}^{-1} = 3 \text{ m·s}^{-1} + (4 \text{ m·s}^{-2})(t),$$

$$t = \tfrac{1}{2} \text{ s}.$$

Then from Eq. (2–12), we have

$$x = 5 \text{ m} + (3 \text{ m·s}^{-1})(\tfrac{1}{2} \text{ s}) + \tfrac{1}{2}(4 \text{ m·s}^{-2})(\tfrac{1}{2} \text{ s})^2$$
$$= 7 \text{ m}. \qquad \blacksquare$$

A special case of motion with constant acceleration occurs when the acceleration is zero. The *velocity* is then constant, and the equations of motion become simply

$$v = v_0 = \text{constant},$$

$$x = x_0 + vt.$$

Example 2–5   A motorist passes a school-crossing corner, where the speed limit is 10 m·s^{-1} (about 22 mi·hr^{-1}), traveling with constant velocity of 20 m·s^{-1}. A police officer on a motorcycle, stopped at the corner, starts off in pursuit with constant acceleration of 2.0 m·s^{-2}.

a) How much time elapses before the motorcycle overtakes the car?

b) What is the motorcycle's speed when it overtakes the car?

c) What is the total distance traveled when the motorcycle overtakes the car?

handwritten: a) $20t = \frac{1}{2}(2)t^2 = \not{2}t \cdot t$

Solution   The car and motorcycle both move with constant acceleration, so we can use the formulas we have developed. Take the origin at the school corner, so $x_0 = 0$ for both. Let x_c be the position of the car and x_m be the position of the motorcycle at any time. Then applying Eq. (2–12) to each, we find

$$x_c = (20 \text{ m·s}^{-1})t,$$

handwritten: $v_2 = at +$
$(2 \cdot) (2) = 40$

$$x_m = \tfrac{1}{2}(2.0 \text{ m·s}^{-2})t^2.$$

a) At the time the motorcycle catches the car, they must be at the same position, so at this time, $x_c = x_m$. Equating the two expressions above, we have

$$(20 \text{ m·s}^{-1})t = \tfrac{1}{2}(2.0 \text{ m·s}^{-2})t^2,$$

or

$$t = 0, \ 20 \text{ s}.$$

There are *two* times when the car and motorcycle have the same x-coordinate; the first is the time ($t = 0$) when the car passes the motorcycle at the corner, and the second is the time when the motorcycle catches up.

b) From Eq. (2–8) we know that the motorcycle's speed at any time is given by

$$v = (2.0 \text{ m·s}^{-2})t,$$

so when $t = 20$ s, we find $v = 40$ m·s^{-1}. When the motorcycle overtakes the car, it is traveling twice as fast as the car.

c) In 20 seconds the distance traveled by the car is

$$x_c = (20 \text{ m·s}^{-1})(20 \text{ s}) = 400 \text{ m},$$

and the distance traveled by the motorcycle is

$$x_m = \tfrac{1}{2}(2.0 \text{ m·s}^{-2})(20 \text{ s})^2 = 400 \text{ m}.$$

We knew, of course, that these distances had to be equal. Why? ∎

2–5
Freely Falling Bodies

The most familiar example of motion with (nearly) constant acceleration is that of a body falling toward the earth. The motion of a falling body under the influence of the earth's gravity is often called **free fall;** it has held the attention of philosophers and scientists since ancient times. Aristotle thought (erroneously) that heavy objects fall faster than light objects, in proportion to their weight. Galileo argued that the motion of a falling body should be independent of its weight. Suppose, said Galileo, that we tie a light object and a heavy object together and drop them. Will the light object's supposed slower speed slow the heavier object down, so that the speed of the two together is *less than* the heavy body alone? Or will the two together, constituting a heavier body, fall *faster* than the heavy body alone? The only resolution of this paradox is the conclusion that the motion of a falling body is *independent* of its weight. We mentioned in Section 1–1 the supposed connection of this matter to the Leaning Tower of Pisa.

In more recent times the motion of falling bodies has been studied with great precision. When air resistance can be neglected, we find that all bodies at a particular location fall with the same acceleration, regardless of their size or weight. If the distance of fall is small in comparison to the radius of the earth, the acceleration is constant throughout the fall. In the following discussion we neglect the effects of air resistance and the decrease of acceleration with increasing altitude. We call this idealized motion *free fall*, although it includes rising as well as falling motion.

The constant acceleration of a freely falling body is called the **acceleration due to gravity,** the *acceleration of gravity*, or (most accurately) the *acceleration of free fall*, and we denote its magnitude with the letter g. At or near the earth's surface, the value of g is approximately 9.8 m·s^{-2}, 980 cm·s^{-2}, or 32 ft·s^{-2}. Because it is the magnitude of a vector quantity, g is always a *positive* number. On the surface of the moon the acceleration of gravity is caused by the attractive force of the moon rather than the earth, and $g = 1.67$ m·s^{-2}. Near the surface of the sun, $g = 274$ m·s^{-2}.

In the following examples we use the constant-acceleration equations developed in Section 2–4. We suggest that you review the problem-solving strategies in that section before you study these examples.

Example 2–6   A bullet is dropped from the Leaning Tower of Pisa; it starts from rest and falls freely. Compute its position and velocity after 1, 2, 3, and 4 s. Take the origin 0 at the starting point, the y-axis vertical, and the upward direction as positive.

Solution   The initial coordinate y_0 and the initial velocity v_0 are both zero. The acceleration is downward (in the negative y-direction), so $a = -g = -9.8$ m·s^{-2}.

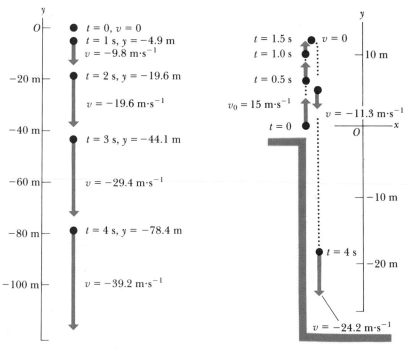

2–8
Position and velocity of a freely falling
body.

2–9
Position and velocity of a body thrown
vertically upward.

From Eqs. (2–12) and (2–8), with x replaced by y, we get

$$y = v_0 t + \tfrac{1}{2}at^2 = 0 + \tfrac{1}{2}(-g)t^2 = (-4.9 \text{ m·s}^{-2})t^2,$$

$$v = v_0 + at = 0 + (-g)t = (-9.8 \text{ m·s}^{-2})t.$$

When $t = 1$ s, $y = (-4.9 \text{ m·s}^{-2})(1 \text{ s})^2 = -4.9$ m, and $v = (-9.8 \text{ m·s}^{-2})(1 \text{ s}) = -9.8 \text{ m·s}^{-1}$. The body is therefore 4.9 m below the origin (y is negative) and has a downward velocity (v is negative) of magnitude 9.8 m·s^{-1}.

The position and velocity at 2, 3, and 4 s are found in the same way. The results are shown in Fig. 2–8; check the numerical values for yourself. ■

Example 2–7 Suppose you throw a ball vertically upward from the cornice of a tall building, and it leaves your hand with an upward speed of 15 m·s^{-1}. On its way back down, it just misses the cornice. In Fig. 2–9, the downward path is displaced a little to the right from its actual position for clarity. Find (a) the position and velocity of the ball 1 s and 4 s after leaving your hand; (b) the velocity when the ball is 5 m above the cornice; (c) the maximum height reached and the time at which it is reached. Take the origin ($y = 0$) at the elevation at which the ball leaves your hand, and let the y-axis be vertical and positive upward.

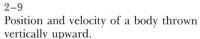

Solution The initial position y_0 is zero. The initial velocity v_0 is $+15$ m·s^{-1}, and the acceleration is $a = -9.8$ m·s^{-2}. The velocity at any time is

$$v = v_0 + at = 15 \text{ m·s}^{-1} + (-9.8 \text{ m·s}^{-2})t. \tag{2-15}$$

The position at any time is

$$y = v_0 t + \tfrac{1}{2}at^2 = (15 \text{ m·s}^{-1})t + \tfrac{1}{2}(-9.8 \text{ m·s}^{-2})t^2. \tag{2-16}$$

The velocity at any position is given by

$$v^2 = v_0{}^2 + 2ay = (15 \text{ m·s}^{-1})^2 + 2(-9.8 \text{ m·s}^{-2})y. \tag{2-17}$$

a) When $t = 1$ s, Eqs. (2–16) and (2–15) give

$$y = +10.1 \text{ m}, \qquad v = +5.2 \text{ m·s}^{-1}.$$

The ball is 10.1 m above the origin (y is positive), and it has an upward velocity (v is positive) of 5.2 m·s^{-1} (less than the initial velocity, as expected).

When $t = 4$ s, again from Eqs. (2–16) and (2–15),

$$y = -18.4 \text{ m}, \qquad v = -24.2 \text{ m·s}^{-1}.$$

The ball has passed its highest point and is 18.4 m *below* the origin (y is negative). It has a *downward* velocity (v is negative) of magnitude 24.2 m·s^{-1}. Note that it is not necessary to find the highest point reached or the time at which it was reached. The equations of motion give the position and velocity at *any* time, whether the ball is on the way up or the way down.

b) When the ball is 5 m above the origin,

$$y = +5 \text{ m}$$

and, from Eq. (2–17),

$$v^2 = 127 \text{ m}^2 \text{·s}^{-2}, \qquad v = \pm 11.3 \text{ m·s}^{-1}.$$

The ball passes this point *twice*, once on the way up and again on the way down. The velocity on the way up is $+11.3$ m·s^{-1}, and on the way down it is -11.3 m·s^{-1}.

c) At the highest point, $v = 0$. Hence, from Eq. (2–17),

$$0 = (15 \text{ m·s}^{-1})^2 - (19.6 \text{ m·s}^{-2})y.$$

and

$$y = 11.5 \text{ m}.$$

We can now find the time at the highest point from Eq. (2–15), setting $v = 0$:

$$0 = 15 \text{ m·s}^{-1} + (-9.8 \text{ m·s}^{-2})t,$$

$$t = 1.53 \text{ s}.$$

Alternatively, to find the maximum height, we may ask first *when* the maximum height is reached. That is, at what t is $v = 0$?

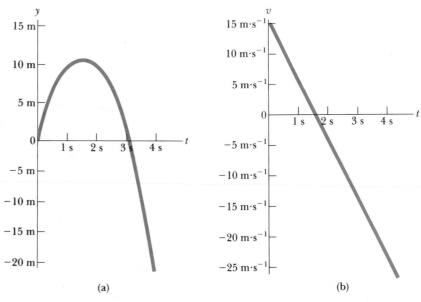

(a)   (b)

2–10
Graphs of y and v as functions of t for Example 2–7.

As was just shown, $v = 0$ when $t = 1.53$ s; substituting this value of t back into Eq. (2–16), we find

$$y = (15 \text{ m·s}^{-1})(1.53 \text{ s}) + \tfrac{1}{2}(-9.8 \text{ m·s}^{-2})(1.53 \text{ s})^2$$
$$= 11.5 \text{ m}.$$

Although at the highest point the velocity is instantaneously zero, the *acceleration* at this point is still -9.8 m·s^{-2}. The ball stops for an instant, but its velocity is continuously changing; the acceleration is constant throughout.

Figure 2–10 shows graphs of position and velocity as functions of time for this problem. Note that the graph of v versus t has a constant negative slope; the acceleration is negative on the way up, at the highest point, and on the way down.　■

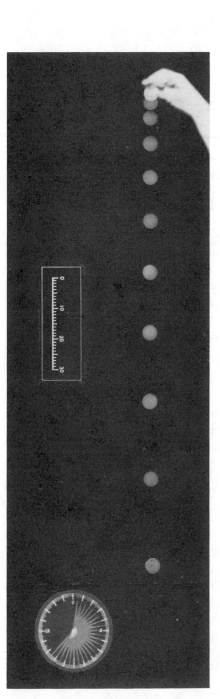

2–11
Multiflash photograph (retouched) of freely falling golf ball.

Figure 2–11 is a multiple-flash photograph of a falling golf ball, taken with a stroboscopic light source. This light source produces a series of intense flashes at equal time intervals. Each flash is so short (a few millionths of a second) that there is no blur in the image of even a rapidly moving body. As each flash occurs, the position of the ball at that instant is recorded on the film. The average velocity of the ball between any two flashes is proportional to the distance between corresponding images in the photograph. The increasing distances between images show that the velocity is continuously increasing; the ball accelerates. Careful measurement shows that the change in velocity is the same in each time interval, showing that the acceleration is *constant*.

2–6
Relative Velocity

We always describe the position and velocity of a body with reference to a particular coordinate system. When we speak of the velocity of a moving car, we usually mean its velocity with respect to the earth. But suppose we throw a ball inside a moving bus. An observer in the bus sees the motion differently than an observer standing on the ground beside the bus. So we speak of the ball's velocity relative to the bus and its velocity relative to the ground, or more generally of the **relative velocity** of one body relative to another.

Suppose a long train of flatcars is moving to the right along a straight level track, as in Fig. 2–12. Such trains are used in the Alps to transport automobiles through long tunnels. Suppose a daredevil is driving a car toward the right along the flatcars. In Fig. 2–12, v_{FE} represents the velocity of the flatcars F relative to the earth E, and v_{AF} the velocity of the automobile A relative to the flatcars. In any time interval the total displacement of the automobile relative to the earth is the sum of its displacement relative to the flatcars and their displacement relative to the earth. Thus the automobile's velocity relative to the earth, v_{AE}, is equal to the *sum* of the relative velocities v_{AF} and v_{FE}:

$$v_{AE} = v_{AF} + v_{FE}. \qquad (2\text{--}18)$$

If we take the x-axis to lie along the railroad track, with the positive direction to the right, then both v_{FE} and v_{AF} are positive quantities. Thus if the flatcars are traveling relative to the earth with $v_{FE} = 30$ km·hr^{-1}, and the automobile is traveling relative to the flatcars with $v_{AF} = 40$ km·hr^{-1}, the velocity (v_{AE}) of the automobile relative to the earth is 70 km·hr^{-1}.

In straight-line motion the velocity v_{AE} is the *algebraic* sum of v_{AF} and v_{FE}. Thus if the automobile were traveling to the *left* with a velocity of 40 km·hr^{-1} relative to the flatcars, $v_{AF} = -40$ km·hr^{-1}, and the velocity of the automobile relative to the earth would be -10 km·hr^{-1}; that is, it would be traveling to the left, relative to the earth.

PROBLEM-SOLVING STRATEGY: *Relative Velocity*

Note the order of the double subscripts on the velocities; v_{AB} always means "velocity of A relative to B." In writing equations such as Eq. (2–18), make sure that the first subscript on the left side of the equation is the same as the first subscript in the *first* term on the right and that the second on the left is the same as the second in the *last* term on the right. Also, adjacent subscripts in adjacent terms on the right must match. Thus

$$v_{AE} = v_{AB} + v_{BC} + v_{CD} + v_{DE}.$$

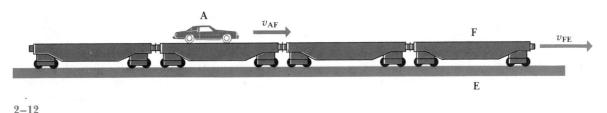

2–12
Vector v_{FE} is the velocity of the flatcars F relative to the earth E, and v_{AF} is the velocity of automobile A relative to the flatcars.

Example 2–8   A woman is driving a car at 65 km·hr^{-1} on a straight, level road where the speed limit is 40 km·hr^{-1}. She is spotted by a motorcycle officer, who accelerates in pursuit. By the time the driver sees the motorcycle's flashing blue light in her rear-view mirror, the motorcycle is traveling at 80 km·hr^{-1}. What is the motorcycle's velocity relative to the car?

Solution   Let the car be C, the motorcycle M, and the earth E. Then

$$v_{CE} = 65 \text{ km·hr}^{-1} \quad \text{and} \quad v_{ME} = 80 \text{ km·hr}^{-1},$$

and we want to find v_{MC}.

From the rule for combining velocities,

$$v_{ME} = v_{MC} + v_{CE}.$$

Thus

$$80 \text{ km·hr}^{-1} = v_{MC} + 65 \text{ km·hr}^{-1},$$

$$v_{MC} = 15 \text{ km·hr}^{-1},$$

and the officer is pulling up behind the driver at 15 km·hr^{-1}.

Note that the relative velocities would be the same if the motorcycle were ahead of the car. The relative *positions* of the bodies do not matter. The velocity of M relative to C would still be +15 km·hr^{-1}, but the officer would now be pulling away from the driver at this rate instead of approaching from behind. ∎

In more general motion, where the velocities do not all lie along a straight line, we have to use vector addition to combine velocities. We will consider relative velocity more generally at the end of Chapter 3.

Questions

2–1 When a particle moves in a circular path, how many coordinates are required to describe a position, assuming that the radius of the circle is given?

2–2 What is meant by the statement that space is three-dimensional?

2–3 Does the speedometer of a car measure speed or velocity?

2–4 Some European countries have highway speed limits of 100 km·hr^{-1}. What is the equivalent number of miles per hour?

2–5 A student claims that a speed of 60 mi·hr^{-1} is the same as 88 ft·s^{-1}. Is this relationship exact or only approximate?

2–6 In a given time interval, is the total displacement of a particle equal to the product of the average velocity and the time interval, even when the velocity is not constant?

2–7 Under what conditions is average velocity equal to instantaneous velocity?

2–8 When one flies in an airplane at night in smooth air, there is no sensation of motion even though the plane may be moving at 800 km·hr^{-1} (500 mi·hr^{-1}). Why is this?

2–9 An automobile is traveling north. Can it have a velocity toward the north and at the same time have an acceleration toward the south? Under what circumstances?

2–10 A ball is thrown straight up in the air. What is its acceleration at the instant it reaches its highest point?

2–11 Is the acceleration of a car greater when the accelerator is pushed to the floor or when the brake pedal is pushed hard?

2–12 Under constant acceleration, the average velocity of a particle is half the sum of its initial and final velocities. Is this still true if the acceleration is *not* constant?

2–13 A baseball is thrown straight up in the air. Is the acceleration greater while it is being thrown or after it has been thrown?

2–14 How could you measure the acceleration of an automobile by using only instruments located within the automobile?

2–15 If the initial position and initial velocity of a vehicle are known and a record is kept of the acceleration at each instant, can its position after a certain time be computed from these data? Explain how this might be done.

Exercises

Section 2–1   Average Velocity

2–1 In 1954, Roger Bannister became the first human to run a mile in less than 4 minutes. Suppose that a runner on a straight track covers a distance of 1.00 mi in exactly 4.00 min. What is the magnitude of his average velocity in

  a) mi·hr^{-1};   b) ft·s^{-1}?

2–2 A hiker travels in a straight line for 40 min with an average velocity of magnitude 1.25 m·s^{-1}. What distance does he cover during this time?

2–3 You normally drive on the freeway between San Francisco and Sacramento at an average speed of 105 km·hr^{-1} (65 mi·hr^{-1}), and the trip takes 2 hr and 10 min. On a rainy day you slow down and drive the same distance at an average speed of 80 km·hr^{-1} (50 mi·hr^{-1}). How much longer does the trip take?

2–4 A mouse moves along a straight line; its distance x from the origin at any time t is given by the equation $x = (8.5 \text{ cm·s}^{-1})t - (2.5 \text{ cm·s}^{-2})t^2$. Find the average velocity of the mouse in the interval from $t = 0$ to $t = 1.0$ s and in the interval from $t = 0$ to $t = 4.0$ s.

2–5 A car is traveling in a straight line along a road. Its distance x from a stop sign is given as a function of time t by the equation $x = (2.00 \text{ m·s}^{-2})t^2 + (0.250 \text{ m·s}^{-3})t^3$. Calculate the average velocity of the car for the following time intervals:

  a) $t = 0$ to $t = 2.00$ s;

  b) $t = 0$ to $t = 4.00$ s;

  c) $t = 2.00$ s to $t = 4.00$ s.

Section 2–2   Instantaneous Velocity

2–6 A physics professor leaves her house and walks along the sidewalk toward campus. After 5 min she realizes that it is raining and returns home. Her distance from her house as a function of time is shown in Fig. 2–13. At which of the labeled points is her velocity:

  a) zero?

  b) constant and positive?

  c) constant and negative?

  d) increasing in magnitude?

  e) decreasing in magnitude?

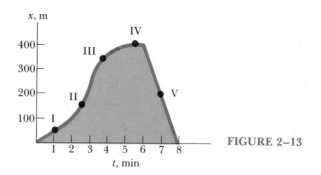

FIGURE 2–13

2–7 Consider the motion described in Example 2–1. Assume that the equation given for $x(t)$ applies even for times slightly greater than 2 s.

a) Calculate the average velocity of the cheetah for the time intervals

i) $t = 0$ to $t = 1.00$ s;

ii) $t = 0$ to $t = 2.00$ s.

b) Calculate the magnitude of the instantaneous velocity of the cheetah at time $t = 2.00$ s. Compare your result to the instantaneous velocity at $t = 1.00$ s that was calculated in the example.

2–8 A hobbyist is testing a new model rocket engine by using it to propel a cart along a model railroad track. He determines that its motion along the x-axis is described by the equation $x = (0.160 \text{ m·s}^{-2})t^2$. Compute the magnitude of the instantaneous velocity of the cart at time $t = 3.00$ s. Do this by letting Δt be 0.1 s, 0.01 s, and 0.001 s. Determine the limiting value to which the results are approaching.

Section 2–3   *Average and Instantaneous Acceleration*

2–9 A test driver at Incredible Motors, Inc., is testing a new model car having a speedometer calibrated to read m·s^{-1} rather than mi·hr^{-1}. The following series of speedometer readings was obtained during a test run.

Time (s)	0	2	4	6	8	10	12	14	16
Velocity (m·s^{-1})	0	0	2	5	10	15	20	22	22

a) Compute the average acceleration during each 2-s interval. Is the acceleration constant? Is it constant during any part of the time?

b) Make a velocity–time graph of the data above, using scales of 1 cm = 1 s horizontally, and 1 cm = 2 m·s^{-1} vertically. Draw a smooth curve through the plotted points. By measuring the slope of your curve, find the magnitude of the instantaneous acceleration at times $t = 8$ s, 13 s, and 15 s.

2–10 A girl is riding a skateboard on a level sidewalk. Her velocity v at any time t is given by $v = 4.00 \text{ m·s}^{-1} - (0.500 \text{ m·s}^{-3})t^2$. Calculate her average acceleration for the following time intervals:

a) $t = 0$ to $t = 2.00$ s;

b) $t = 0$ to $t = 6.00$ s;

c) $t = 2.00$ s to $t = 6.00$ s.

2–11 In Example 2–3, calculate the magnitude of the instantaneous acceleration of the car at time $t = 3.00$ s. Compare your result to the value at $t = 2.00$ s that was calculated in the example.

2–12 An astronaut has left Spacelab V to test a new space scooter for use in constructing Space Habitat I. His partner measures the following velocity changes, each taking place in a 10.0-s interval. What are the magnitude, the algebraic sign, and the direction of the average acceleration in each interval? Assume that the positive direction is to the right.

a) At the beginning of the interval the astronaut is moving toward the right along the x-axis at 20.0 m·s^{-1}, and at the end of the interval he is moving toward the right at 5.0 m·s^{-1}.

b) At the beginning he is moving toward the left at 5.0 m·s^{-1}, and at the end he is moving toward the left at 20.0 m·s^{-1}.

c) At the beginning he is moving toward the left at 20.0 m·s^{-1}, and at the end he is moving toward the right at 20.0 m·s^{-1}.

2–13 Figure 2–14 is a graph of the coordinate x of a spider crawling along the x-axis. Sketch a graph of its velocity and acceleration as functions of time.

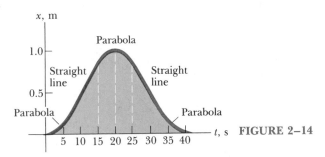

FIGURE 2–14

2–14 An automobile has velocity v given as a function of time t by $v(t) = \alpha + \beta t^2$, where $\alpha = 4.00$ m·s^{-1} and $\beta = 0.200$ m·s^{-3}. Calculate:

a) the average acceleration for the time interval $t = 0$ to $t = 5.00$ s;

b) the magnitude of the instantaneous acceleration for

i) $t = 0$;

ii) $t = 5.00$ s.

Calculate the instantaneous acceleration in the following way. In each case, let Δt first equal 0.1 s, then 0.01 s, and finally 0.001 s. Determine the limiting value that the results are approaching.

Section 2–4   *Motion with Constant Acceleration*

2–15 The makers of a certain automobile advertise that it can accelerate from 15.0 to 50.0 mi·hr^{-1} in 10.0 s. Assume that the acceleration is constant. Compute

a) the acceleration in ft·s^{-2};

b) the distance the car travels in this time.

2–16 An airplane travels 800 m down the runway before taking off. If it starts from rest, moves with constant acceleration, and becomes airborne in 20.0 s, what is its speed, in $m \cdot s^{-1}$, when it takes off?

2–17 The fastest time for a 440-yd race from a standing start is 7.08 s, according to the 1984 *Guinness Book of World Records*. This was done on a 1200-cc motorcycle in 1980. Assuming constant acceleration:

a) What was the acceleration of the cycle (in $ft \cdot s^{-2}$)?

b) What was the final speed of the cycle (in $ft \cdot s^{-1}$)?

c) With this acceleration, how much time would it take to go from 0 to 55.0 $mi \cdot hr^{-1}$?

2–18 An antelope running with constant acceleration covers the distance between two points 60.0 m apart in 6.00 s. Its speed as it passes the second point is 15.0 $m \cdot s^{-1}$.

a) What is its speed at the first point?

b) What is the acceleration?

2–19 The graph in Fig. 2–15 shows the velocity of a motorcycle police officer plotted as a function of time.

a) Find the instantaneous acceleration at times $t = 3$ s, at $t = 7$ s, and at $t = 11$ s.

b) How far does the officer go in the first 5 s? The first 9 s? The first 13 s?

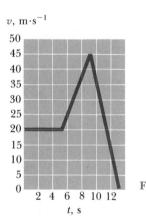

v, $m \cdot s^{-1}$

FIGURE 2–15

2–20 The "reaction time" of the average automobile driver is about 0.7 s. (The reaction time is the interval between the perception of a signal to stop and the application of the brakes.) If an automobile can slow down with an acceleration of -12.0 $ft \cdot s^{-2}$, compute the total distance covered in coming to a stop after a signal is observed

a) from an initial velocity of 15.0 $mi \cdot hr^{-1}$ (in a school zone);

b) from an initial velocity of 55.0 $mi \cdot hr^{-1}$.

2–21 A hypothetical spaceship takes a straight-line path from the earth to the moon, a distance of about 400,000 km. Suppose it accelerates at 10.0 $m \cdot s^{-2}$ for the first 20.0 min of the trip, then travels at constant speed until the last 20.0 min, when it accelerates at -10.0 $m \cdot s^{-2}$, just coming to rest as it reaches the moon.

a) What is the maximum speed attained?

b) What fraction of the total distance is traveled at constant speed?

c) What total time is required for the trip?

2–22 Figure 2–16 is a graph of the acceleration of a model railroad locomotive moving on the x-axis. Sketch the graphs of its velocity and coordinate as functions of time if $x = 0$ and $v = 0$ when $t = 0$.

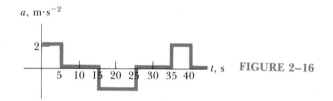

a, $m \cdot s^{-2}$

FIGURE 2–16

2–23 A subway train starts from rest at a station and accelerates at a rate of 1.60 $m \cdot s^{-2}$ for 8.0 s. It runs at constant speed for 70.0 s, and slows down at -2.50 $m \cdot s^{-2}$ until it stops at the next station. Find the *total* distance covered.

Section 2–5   Freely Falling Bodies

2–24

a) If a flea can jump to a height of 0.750 m, what is its initial speed as it leaves the ground?

b) For how much time is it in the air?

2–25 A brick is dropped from the roof of a building. The brick strikes the ground after 5.00 s.

a) How tall, in meters, is the building?

b) What is the magnitude of the brick's velocity just before it reaches the ground?

2–26 A hot-air balloonist, rising vertically with a constant velocity of magnitude 8.00 $m \cdot s^{-1}$, releases a sandbag at an instant when the balloon is 20.0 m above the ground.

a) Compute the height above ground and velocity of the sandbag at the following times after its release: 0.500 s, 2.00 s.

b) How many seconds after its release does the bag strike the ground?

c) With what magnitude of velocity does it strike?

2–27 A student throws a water balloon vertically downward from the top of a building. The balloon leaves the thrower's hand with a speed of 15.0 m·s^{-1}.

a) What is its speed after falling for 2.00 s?

b) How far does it fall in 2.00 s?

c) What is the magnitude of its velocity after falling 10.0 m?

2–28 A rock is thrown vertically upward with a speed of 12.0 m·s^{-1} from the roof of a building that is 60.0 m above the ground.

a) In how many seconds after being thrown does the rock strike the ground?

b) What is the speed of the rock just before it strikes the ground?

2–29 An egg is thrown nearly vertically upward from a point near the cornice of a tall building. It just misses the cornice on the way down and passes a point 120 ft below its starting point 5.00 s after it leaves the thrower's hand.

a) What is the initial speed of the egg?

b) How high does it rise above its starting point?

c) What is the magnitude of its velocity at the highest point?

d) What are the magnitude and direction of its acceleration at the highest point?

2–30 A ball is thrown vertically upward from the ground with a speed of 36.0 m·s^{-1}.

a) At what time after being thrown does the ball have a velocity of 12.0 m·s^{-1} upward?

b) At what time does it have a velocity of 12.0 m·s^{-1} downward?

c) When is the displacement of the ball zero?

d) When is the velocity of the ball zero?

e) What are the magnitude and direction of the acceleration while the ball is moving upward?

f) What are the magnitude and direction of the acceleration while it is moving downward?

g) What are the magnitude and direction of the acceleration when it is at the highest point?

2–31 The rocket-driven sled Sonic Wind No. 2, used for investigating the physiological effects of large accelerations, runs on a straight, level track that is 3500 ft long. Starting from rest, it can reach a speed of 1000 mi·hr^{-1} in 1.80 s.

a) Compute the acceleration in ft·s^{-2}, assuming that it is constant.

b) What is the ratio of this acceleration to that of a free falling body, g?

c) What is the distance covered in 1.80 s?

d) A magazine article states that at the end of a certain run the speed of the sled decreased from 632 mi·hr^{-1} to zero in 1.40 s and that during this time its passenger was subjected to more than 40 times the pull of gravity (that is, the acceleration was greater than 40g). Are these figures consistent?

2–32 Suppose the acceleration of gravity were only 2.0 m·s^{-2} instead of 9.8 m·s^{-2}.

a) Estimate the height to which you could jump vertically from a standing start if you could jump to 0.75 m when g = 9.8 m·s^{-2}.

b) How high could you throw a baseball if you could throw it 18 m when g = 9.8 m·s^{-2}?

c) Estimate the maximum height of a window from which you would care to jump to a concrete sidewalk below if for g = 9.8 m·s^{-2} you would be willing to jump from a height of 4.0 m, which is the typical height of a first-story window.

Section 2–6 Relative Velocity

2–33 A railroad flatcar is traveling to the right at a speed of 12.0 m·s^{-1} relative to a person standing on the ground. A motor scooter is being ridden on the flatcar. What is the velocity (magnitude and direction) of the motor scooter relative to the flatcar if its velocity relative to the person on the ground is

a) 18.0 m·s^{-1} to the right?

b) 1.5 m·s^{-1} to the left?

c) zero?

2–34 A "moving sidewalk" in an airport terminal building moves at a speed of 1.00 m·s^{-1} and is 90.0 m long. If a woman steps on at one end and walks with a speed of 2.00 m·s^{-1} relative to the moving sidewalk, how much time does she need to reach the opposite end if she walks

a) in the same direction the sidewalk is moving?

b) in the opposite direction?

2–35 Two piers A and B are located on a river; B is 1400 m downstream from A. Two men must make round trips from pier A to pier B and return. One man is to row a boat at a constant speed of 5.80 km·hr^{-1} relative to the water, and the other man is to walk on the shore at a constant speed of 5.80 km·hr^{-1}. The velocity of the river is 3.20 km·hr^{-1} in the direction from A to B. How much time does it take each man to make the round trip?

Problems

2–36 It has been found that the human body can survive a negative acceleration trauma incident (sudden stop) if the magnitude of the acceleration is less than 250 m·s^{-2} (approximately $25g$'s). If you are in an automobile accident with an initial speed of 80.0 km·hr^{-1} (50 mi·hr^{-1}) and are stopped by an airbag that inflates from the dashboard, over what distance must the airbag stop you for you to survive the crash?

2–37 A typical world-class male sprinter will accelerate to his maximum speed in 4.0 s. If such a runner finishes a 100-m race in 9.0 s, what is the runner's average acceleration during the first 4.0 s of the race?

2–38 A car is initially stopped at a traffic light. It then travels along a straight road such that its distance x from the light is given by $x = bt^2 + ct^3$, where $b = 1.50 \text{ m·s}^{-2}$ and $c = 0.0200 \text{ m·s}^{-3}$.

a) Calculate the average velocity of the car for the time intervals $t = 0$ to $t = 5.00$ s and $t = 0$ to $t = 10.0$ s.

b) Calculate the magnitude of the instantaneous velocity of the car at

   i) $t = 5.00$ s;

   ii) $t = 10.0$ s.

   In each case, do this by taking $\Delta t = 0.1$ s, 0.01 s, and 0.001 s, and then determine the limiting value.

2–39 A sled starts from rest at the top of a hill and slides down with constant acceleration. At some later time it is 32.0 m from the top; two seconds after that it is 50.0 m from the top, two seconds later it is 72.0 m from the top, and two seconds later it is 98.0 m from the top.

a) What is the average velocity of the sled during each of the 2.00-s intervals after passing the 32.0-m point?

b) What is the acceleration of the sled?

c) What is the speed of the sled when it passes the 32.0-m point?

d) How much time did it take to go from the top to the 32.0-m point?

e) How far does the sled go during the first second after passing the 32.0-m point?

2–40 A simple reaction time test can be made by using a meter stick. A meter stick is held vertically above your hand, with the lower end between your thumb and first finger. On seeing the meter stick released, you grab it with these two fingers. Your reaction time can be calculated from the distance the meter stick falls, read directly from the point where your fingers grabbed it.

a) Derive a relationship for your reaction time in terms of this measured distance, d.

b) If the measured distance is 24.5 cm, what is the reaction time?

2–41 You are on the roof of the physics building, 96.0 m above the ground. Your physics professor, who is 1.8 m tall, is walking beside the building at a constant speed of 1.20 m·s^{-1}. If you wish to drop an egg on your professor's head, where should the professor be when you release the egg?

2–42 The engineer of a passenger train traveling at 25.0 m·s^{-1} sights a freight train whose caboose is 200 m ahead on the same track. The freight train is traveling in the same direction as the passenger train with a speed of 15.0 m·s^{-1}. The engineer of the passenger train immediately applies the brakes, causing a constant acceleration of -0.100 m·s^{-2}, while the freight train continues with constant speed.

a) Will there be a collision?

b) If so, where will it take place?

2–43 At the instant the traffic light turns green, an automobile that has been waiting at an intersection starts ahead with a constant acceleration of 2.50 m·s^{-2}. At the same instant a truck, traveling with a constant speed of 15.0 m·s^{-1}, overtakes and passes the automobile.

a) How far beyond its starting point does the automobile overtake the truck?

b) How fast is the automobile traveling when it overtakes the truck?

2–44 A student determined to test the law of gravity for herself walks off a skyscraper 200 m high, stopwatch in hand, and starts her free fall (zero initial velocity). Five seconds later, Superman arrives at the scene and dives off the roof to save the student.

a) What must the magnitude of Superman's initial velocity be so that he catches the student just before the ground is reached? (Assume that Superman's acceleration is that of any free-falling body.)

b) If the height of the skyscraper is less than some minimum value, even Superman can't save the student. What is this minimum height?

2–45 An automobile and a truck start from rest at the same instant, with the automobile initially at some distance behind the truck. The truck has a constant acceleration of 2.00 m·s^{-2}, and the automobile an acceleration of 2.60 m·s^{-2}. The automobile overtakes the truck after the truck has moved 125 m.

a) How much time does it take the automobile to overtake the truck?

b) How far was the automobile behind the truck initially?

c) What is the speed of each when they are abreast?

2–46 A celebrated jumping frog jumps vertically upward. It has a speed of 3.46 m·s^{-1} when it reaches one half its maximum height.

a) How much does it rise?

b) What are its velocity and acceleration 0.750 s after it jumps?

2–47 A football is kicked vertically upward from the ground, and a student gazing out of the window sees it moving upward past her at 12.0 m·s^{-1}. The window is 15.0 m above the ground.

a) How high does the football go above ground?

b) How much time does it take to go from a height of 15.0 m to its highest point?

2–48 A marble is dropped, and then 1.00 s later and from a point 8.00 m lower a second marble is dropped. When are the two marbles 20.0 m apart?

2–49 A ball is released from rest at the top of an inclined plane 15.0 m long and reaches the bottom 3.00 s later. At the same instant that the first ball is released, a second ball is projected upward along the plane from its bottom with a certain initial speed. The second ball is to travel part way up the plane, stop, and return to the bottom so that it arrives simultaneously with the first ball. Both balls have the same constant acceleration.

a) Find the acceleration of the balls.

b) What must be the initial speed of the second ball?

c) How far up the plane does the second ball travel?

2–50 A juggler performs in a room whose ceiling is 4.00 m above the level of his hands. He throws an apple vertically upward so that it just reaches the ceiling.

a) With what initial speed does he throw the apple?

b) How much time is required for the apple to reach the ceiling?

He throws a second apple upward with the same initial speed at the instant that the first apple is at the ceiling.

c) How much time after the second apple is thrown do the two apples pass each other?

d) When the apples pass each other, how far are they above the juggler's hands?

2–51 A flowerpot falls off a window sill and past another window directly below. It takes 0.40 s to pass the lower window, which is 2.00 m high. How far is the top of the window below the sill of the window above?

2–52 The driver of a car wishes to pass a truck that is traveling at a constant speed of 20.0 m·s^{-1} (about 45 mi·hr^{-1}). The car initially is also traveling at 20.0 m·s^{-1}. The car's maximum acceleration in this speed range is 0.50 m·s^{-2}. Initially, the vehicles are separated by 25.0 m, and the car pulls back into the truck's lane after it is 25.0 m ahead of the truck. The car is 3.5 m long, and the truck is 10.5 m. If the car's acceleration is a constant 0.50 m·s^{-2},

a) how much time is required for the car to pass the truck?

b) what distance does the car travel during this time?

c) what is the final speed of the car?

2–53 A stone is dropped from the top of a tall cliff (with zero initial speed), and 1.00 s later a second stone is thrown vertically downward with a speed of 16.0 m·s^{-1}. How far below the top of the cliff will the second stone overtake the first?

Challenge Problems

2–54 A delivery truck's velocity v at any time t is given by

$$v(t) = (4.00 \text{ m·s}^{-2})t + (3.00 \text{ m·s}^{-4})t^3.$$

Use the definition of instantaneous acceleration, Eq. (2–6), to calculate the truck's acceleration *as a function of time*. Do this as follows. Let $t_1 = t$ and $t_2 = t + \Delta t$. Use Eq. (2–5) to calculate a_{av} for the time interval t_1 to t_2.

Then in your expression for a_{av}, let Δt get very small, which carries out the $\lim_{\Delta t \to 0}$ operation of Eq. (2–6).

2–55 A student is running to catch the campus shuttle bus, which is stopped at the bus stop. The student is running at a constant speed of 6.0 m·s^{-1}; she can't run any faster. When the student is still 60.0 m from the bus, it starts to pull away. The bus moves with a constant acceleration of 0.18 m·s^{-2}.

a) For how much time and how far does the student have to run before she overtakes the bus?

b) When she reaches the bus, how fast is the bus traveling?

c) Sketch a graph showing $x(t)$ for both the student and the bus. Take $x = 0$ to be the initial position of the student.

d) The equations that you used in part (a) to find the time have a second solution, corresponding to a later time for which the student and bus will again be at the same place if they continue their specified motions. Explain the significance of this second solution. How fast will the bus be traveling at this point?

e) If the student's constant speed is 4.0 m·s^{-1}, does she catch the bus?

f) What is the *minimum* speed the student must have to just catch up with the bus? For what time and what distance does she have to run in that case?

2–56 An alert hiker sees a boulder fall from the top of a distant cliff and notes that it takes 1.50 s for the boulder to fall the last third of the way to the ground.

a) What is the height of the cliff in meters?

b) If in part (a) you get two roots to a quadratic equation and use one for your answer, what does the other root represent?

2–57

a) Suppose cars are lined up bumper to bumper at a red light. Assume that each car is 4.60 m in length. When the light turns green, the first car accelerates at 1.22 m·s^{-2}. When this car is 5.00 m in front of the second car, the second car begins to accelerate at 1.22 m·s^{-2}. When the second car is 5.00 m in front of the third car, the third begins to accelerate at 1.22 m·s^{-2}. This continues in similar fashion for the fourth and fifth cars and so on. If the light stays green for a minute and a half (90.0 s), how many cars have made it to the beginning of the intersection before the light turns red again?

b) Now assume instead that the cars stopped at the red light are spaced such that there is 5.00 m between each pair of cars. If, when the light turns green, each car immediately accelerates at 1.22 m·s^{-2} for 10.0 s and then goes at constant speed, how many cars make it to the beginning of the intersection before the light turns red again? Assume as in part (a) that the light is green for 90.0 s and that each car is 4.60 m long. Compare your answer to that of part (a); you might find the results surprising.

2–58 A ball is thrown straight up from the edge of the roof of a building. A second ball is dropped from the roof 2.00 s later.

a) If the height of the building is 60.0 m, what must be the initial speed of the first ball if both are to hit the ground at the same time?

Consider the same situation, but now let the initial speed v_0 of the first ball be given and treat the height h of the building as an unknown.

b) What must the height of the building be for both balls to reach the ground at the same time for each of the following values of v_0:

i) 13.0 m·s^{-1};

ii) 19.2 m·s^{-1}?

c) If v_0 is greater than some value v_{max}, there is *no* value of h for which both balls hit the ground at the same time. Solve for v_{max}. The value v_{max} has a simple physical interpretation. What is it?

d) If v_0 is less than some value v_{min}, there is *no* value of h for which both balls hit the ground at the same time. Solve for v_{min}. The value v_{min} also has a simple physical interpretation. What is it?

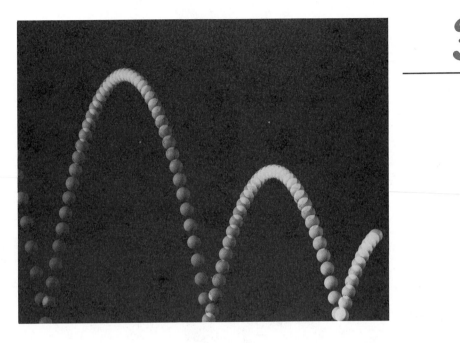

Motion in a Plane

In Chapter 2 we studied motion along a straight line. Now we broaden our discussion to include motion along a curved path that lies in a plane. A few familiar examples are the flight of a thrown or batted baseball, a projectile shot from a gun, a ball whirled in a circle at the end of a cord, the motion of the moon or a satellite around the earth, and the motion of the planets around the sun. To describe these motions, we need to generalize the kinematic language of Chapter 2. The vector quantities displacement, velocity and acceleration no longer lie along a single line, and we need to use the methods of vector algebra that we learned in Chapter 1.

The content of this chapter, like that of the preceding one, is classified as *kinematics*; we are concerned only with *describing* motion, not with relating motion to its causes. But the language that we learn here will be an essential tool in later chapters when we use Newton's laws of motion to study the relation between force and motion.

3–1
Average and Instantaneous Velocity

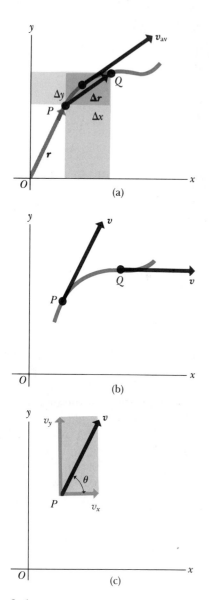

(a)

(b)

(c)

3–1
(a) The displacement Δr between points P and Q has components Δx and Δy. The average velocity v_{av} has the same direction as Δr. (b) The instantaneous velocity v at each point is always tangent to the path at that point. (c) Components of the instantaneous velocity at P are shown.

To begin our study of motion in a plane, we consider the situation of Fig. 3–1a. A particle moves along a curved path in the xy-plane; points P and Q represent the positions of the particle at two different times. We can describe the position of the particle at P by means of the displacement vector r from the origin O to P; we call r the **position vector** of the particle. The components of r are simply the coordinates x and y; make sure you understand why this is so.

As the particle moves from P to Q, its *displacement* is the change Δr in the position vector r, as shown in Fig. 3–1a. The x- and y-components of Δr are the quantities Δx and Δy, as shown.

The particle moves from P to Q during a time interval Δt. We define the **average velocity** v_{av} during this interval as a vector quantity equal to the displacement divided by the time interval:

$$v_{av} = \frac{\Delta r}{\Delta t}. \qquad (3\text{–}1)$$

That is, the average velocity is a vector quantity having the same direction as Δr and a magnitude equal to the magnitude of Δr divided by Δt. The magnitude of Δr is always the straight-line distance from P to Q, regardless of the actual shape of the path taken by the particle. Thus the average velocity would be the same for any path that would take the particle from P to Q in the time interval Δt.

We define the **instantaneous velocity** v at point P just as we did in Chapter 2. We let the interval Δt become smaller and smaller; the instantaneous velocity at P is the *limit* that the average velocity approaches when $\Delta t \to 0$ and point Q moves closer and closer to point P.

$$\text{Instantaneous velocity} = v = \lim_{\Delta t \to 0} \frac{\Delta r}{\Delta t}. \qquad (3\text{–}2)$$

As point Q approaches point P, the *direction* of the vector Δr becomes tangent to the path at P. *The instantaneous velocity vector at any point is tangent to the path at that point.* The instantaneous velocities at points P and Q are shown in Fig. 3–1b. Just as in Chapter 2, we define average velocity with reference to a finite time interval, while instantaneous velocity describes the motion at a specific point and at a specific instant of time.

It follows from Eq. (3–1) that the components $(v_x)_{av}$ and $(v_y)_{av}$ of average velocity are the corresponding components of displacement, divided by Δt. That is,

$$(v_x)_{av} = \frac{\Delta x}{\Delta t}, \qquad (v_y)_{av} = \frac{\Delta y}{\Delta t}. \qquad (3\text{–}3)$$

Similarly, the instantaneous rates of change of x and y, denoted by v_x and v_y, are equal to the x- and y-components, respectively, of instantaneous velocity v:

$$v_x = \lim_{\Delta t \to 0} \frac{\Delta x}{\Delta t}, \qquad v_y = \lim_{\Delta t \to 0} \frac{\Delta y}{\Delta t}. \qquad (3\text{–}4)$$

The magnitude v of the instantaneous velocity v is given by the Pythagorean theorem:

$$v = |v| = \sqrt{v_x{}^2 + v_y{}^2}, \qquad (3\text{–}5)$$

and the angle θ in Fig. 3–1c by

$$\tan \theta = \frac{v_y}{v_x}. \qquad (3\text{–}6)$$

Thus we can represent velocity, a vector quantity, either in terms of its components or in terms of its magnitude and direction, just as with other vector quantities such as displacement and force. The *direction* of the instantaneous velocity of a particle at any point is *always* tangent to the path at that point.

Example 3–1   A particle has x and y coordinates (4.0 m, 2.0 m) at time $t_1 = 2.0$ s and coordinates (7.0 m, 6.0 m) at time $t_2 = 2.5$ s. Find (a) the components of average velocity and (b) the magnitude and direction of the average velocity, during this time interval.

Solution

a) We have $\Delta x = 7.0$ m $-$ 4.0 m $= 3.0$ m, $\Delta y = 6.0$ m $-$ 2.0 m $=$ 4.0 m, and $\Delta t = 0.5$ s. To find the components, we use Eqs. (3–3):

$$(v_x)_{av} = \frac{3.0 \text{ m}}{0.5 \text{ s}} = 6.0 \text{ m·s}^{-1},$$

$$(v_y)_{av} = \frac{4.0 \text{ m}}{0.5 \text{ s}} = 8.0 \text{ m·s}^{-1}.$$

b) The magnitude of v_{av} is the square root of the sum of the squares of the components:

$$|v_{av}| = \sqrt{(v_x)_{av}{}^2 + (v_y)_{av}{}^2}$$
$$= \sqrt{(6.0 \text{ m·s}^{-1})^2 + (8.0 \text{ m·s}^{-1})^2} = 10.0 \text{ m·s}^{-1}.$$

Alternatively, the magnitude of v_{av} is the distance between the points (5.0 m) divided by the time interval (0.5 s), or 10.0 m·s^{-1}.

The direction of v_{av} is most easily described by its angle, measured counterclockwise from the positive x-axis. Calling this angle θ, we have

$$\tan \theta = \frac{8.0 \text{ m·s}^{-1}}{6.0 \text{ m·s}^{-1}}, \qquad \theta = 53.1°. \qquad \blacksquare$$

3–2
Average and Instantaneous Acceleration

In Fig. 3–2a the vectors v_1 and v_2 represent the instantaneous velocities, at points P and Q, of a particle moving in a curved path. At each point the instantaneous velocity is tangent to the path, so the directions of the two velocities are different. Their magnitudes may also be different if, for example, the particle is moving faster at Q than at P. The displacement from P to Q occurs during a time interval Δt.

We define the **average acceleration** a_{av} of the particle during this interval as the *vector change in velocity*, $\Delta v = v_2 - v_1$, divided by the time interval Δt:

$$\text{Average acceleration} = a_{av} = \frac{\Delta v}{\Delta t}. \tag{3–7}$$

But just what is Δv? It is the vector difference $v_2 - v_1$:

$$\Delta v = v_2 - v_1 \quad \text{or} \quad v_2 = v_1 + \Delta v.$$

Thus v_2 is the vector sum of the original velocity v_1 and the change Δv. This relationship is shown in Fig. 3–2b. Average acceleration is a vector quantity with the same direction as the vector Δv. The average acceleration vector a_{av} is shown in Fig. 3–2a.

We now define the **instantaneous acceleration** a at point P as the limit that the average acceleration approaches when point Q becomes closer and closer to point P and both Δv and Δt approach zero:

$$\text{Instantaneous acceleration} = \mathbf{a} = \lim_{\Delta t \to 0} \frac{\Delta v}{\Delta t}. \tag{3–8}$$

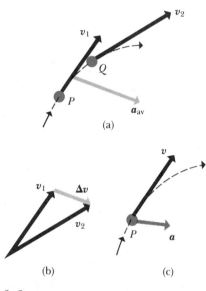

3–2
(a) The vector $a_{av} = \Delta v/\Delta t$ represents the average acceleration between P and Q. (b) Construction for obtaining $\Delta v = v_2 - v_1$. (c) Instantaneous acceleration a at point P. Vector v is tangent to the path; vector a points toward the concave side of the path.

The instantaneous acceleration vector at point P is shown in Fig. 3–2c. Note that it does *not* have the same direction as the velocity vector; in general there is no reason why it should. Looking at the vector diagram in Fig. 3–2c, we see that the acceleration vector must always lie on the *concave* side of the curved path. In the next section we will discuss components of the acceleration vector.

3–3
Components of Acceleration

We often represent the acceleration of a particle in terms of the components of this vector quantity. Figure 3–3 again shows the motion of a particle as described in a rectangular coordinate system. During a time interval Δt the velocity of the particle changes by an amount Δv, with components Δv_x and Δv_y. So we can represent the average acceleration a_{av} in terms of its x- and y-components:

$$(a_x)_{av} = \frac{\Delta v_x}{\Delta t}, \qquad (a_y)_{av} = \frac{\Delta v_y}{\Delta t}. \tag{3–9}$$

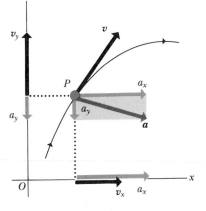

3–3
The acceleration a is resolved into its components a_x and a_y.

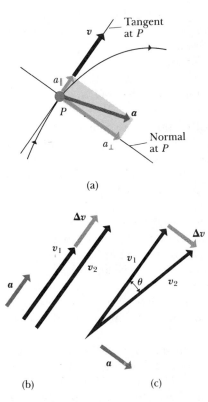

(a)

(b)   (c)

3–4
(a) The acceleration is resolved into a component $a_\parallel$ parallel or *tangent* to the path and a component $a_\perp$ perpendicular or *normal* to the path. (b) When a is parallel to v, the magnitude of v increases, but its direction does not change. (c) When a is perpendicular to v, the direction of v changes, but its magnitude is constant.

Similarly, the x- and y-components of instantaneous acceleration, a_x and a_y, are

$$a_x = \lim_{\Delta t \to 0} \frac{\Delta v_x}{\Delta t}, \qquad a_y = \lim_{\Delta t \to 0} \frac{\Delta v_y}{\Delta t}. \qquad (3\text{–}10)$$

If we know the components a_x and a_y, we can find the magnitude and direction of the acceleration vector a, just as with velocity.

Example 3–2   In Example 3–1 (Section 3–1), suppose that at time $t_1 = 2.0$ s the particle has components of velocity $v_x = 1.0$ m·s^{-1} and $v_y = 3.0$ m·s^{-1} and that at time $t_2 = 2.5$ s the components are $v_x = 4.0$ m·s^{-1} and $v_y = 3.0$ m·s^{-1}. Find (a) the components and (b) the magnitude and direction of the average acceleration during this interval.

Solution

a) The change in v_x is $(4.0$ m·s$^{-1} - 1.0$ m·s$^{-1}) = 3.0$ m·s^{-1}, so the x-component of average acceleration during the interval $\Delta t = 0.5$ is

$$(a_x)_{av} = \frac{3.0 \text{ m·s}^{-1}}{0.5 \text{ s}} = 6.0 \text{ m·s}^{-2}.$$

The change in v_y is zero, so $(a_y)_{av}$ in this interval is also zero.

b) The vector a_{av} has only an x-component. The vector points in the $+x$-direction and has magnitude 6.0 m·s^{-2}. ■

When a particle moves in a curved path, it is sometimes useful to represent its acceleration in terms of components $a_\perp$ and $a_\parallel$, in directions **normal** (perpendicular) and **tangential** (parallel) to the path, as shown in Fig. 3–4a. Because these components are defined with reference to the direction of the path rather than with stationary coordinate axes, they do not have constant directions in space. These components have a very direct physical meaning, however. The parallel component $a_\parallel$ corresponds to a change in the *magnitude* of the velocity vector v (i.e., a change in speed), while the normal component $a_\perp$ is associated with a change in the *direction* of the velocity.

Figure 3–4 shows two special cases. In Fig. 3–4b the acceleration a is *parallel* to the velocity v_1. Then because a gives the rate of change of velocity, the change in v during a small time interval Δt is a vector Δv having the same direction as a and hence the same direction as v_1. Thus the velocity v_2 at the end of Δt, given by $v_2 = v_1 + \Delta v$, is a vector having the same direction as v_1 but different magnitude.

In Fig. 3–4c the acceleration a is *perpendicular* to the velocity v. In a very small time interval Δt, the change Δv is a vector very nearly perpendicular to v_1, as shown. Again $v_2 = v_1 + \Delta v$, but in this case, v_1 and v_2 have different directions. As Δt approaches zero, the angle θ in the figure also approaches zero, Δv becomes perpendicular to *both* v_1 and v_2, and v_1 and v_2 have the same magnitude.

Thus when a is *parallel* to v, its effect is to change the magnitude of v but not its direction; when a is *perpendicular* to v, its effect is to change the direction of v but not its magnitude. In general, a may have components *both* parallel and perpendicular to v, but the above statements are still valid for the individual components. In particular, when a particle travels along a curved path with constant speed, its acceleration is not zero, even though the magnitude of v does not change. In this case the acceleration is always perpendicular to v at each point. When a particle moves in a circle with constant speed, the acceleration is at each instant directed toward the center of the circle. We will work out the details of this special case in Section 3–5.

3–4
Projectile Motion

A **projectile** is any body that is given an initial velocity and then follows a path determined by the effects of gravitational acceleration and air resistance. A batted baseball, a thrown football, an object dropped from an airplane, and a bullet shot from a rifle are all examples of projectiles. The path followed by a projectile is called its *trajectory*. Free fall (Section 2–5) is a special case of projectile motion in which trajectory is a vertical straight line.

Our idealized model for this class of problems consists of a single particle with an acceleration due to gravity that is constant in both magnitude and direction. We neglect the effects of air resistance and the curvature and rotation of the earth. In this model, as in all models, we neglect minor details in order to focus on the essential features of the motion.

The acceleration due to gravity is always straight down; it has no horizontal component. Thus projectile motion is a combination of *horizontal* motion with constant *velocity* and *vertical* motion with constant *acceleration*. The horizontal and vertical motions are independent and can be analyzed separately. That is, we can express all the vector relationships in terms of separate equations for the horizontal and vertical components, and the actual motion is the superposition of these separate motions.

We will use a coordinate system with the x-axis horizontal and the y-axis vertically upward. The y-component of acceleration is the acceleration due to gravity, just as in Section 2–5. The x-component of acceleration is zero; the horizontal component of velocity is constant. Thus the components of a are

$$a_x = 0, \qquad a_y = -g. \tag{3–11}$$

The negative sign for a_y is needed because the positive y-axis is upward, while the acceleration due to gravity is downward. Remember that g is always a *positive* number; we will usually assume that $g = 9.80 \text{ m·s}^{-2}$.

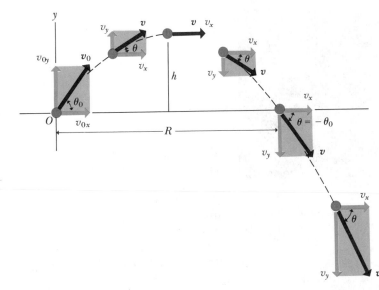

3–5
Trajectory of a body projected with an initial velocity v_0 at an angle of departure θ_0. *The distance R is the* horizontal range, and h is the maximum height.

All of this means that in projectile motion, each coordinate varies with constant-acceleration motion, and we can use Eqs. (2–8), (2–12), (2–13), and (2–14) directly. Suppose that at time $t = 0$ our particle is at the point (x_0, y_0) and that at this time its velocity components have the initial values v_{0x} and v_{0y}. The components of acceleration are $a_x = 0$, $a_y = -g$. Considering the x motion first, we substitute v_x for v, v_{0x} for v_0, and 0 for a in Eqs. (2–8) and (2–12). We find

$$v_x = v_{0x}, \tag{3–12}$$

$$x = x_0 + v_{0x}t. \tag{3–13}$$

For the y motion we substitute y for x, v_y for v, v_{0y} for v_0 and $-g$ for a:

$$v_y = v_{0y} - gt, \tag{3–14}$$

$$y = y_0 + v_{0y}t - \tfrac{1}{2}gt^2. \tag{3–15}$$

Usually, it is simplest to take the initial position as the origin; in this case, $x_0 = y_0 = 0$. This point might be, for example, the position of a ball at the instant it leaves the thrower's hand or the position of a bullet at the instant it leaves the gun barrel.

Figure 3–5 shows the path of a projectile that passes through the origin at time $t = 0$. The position, velocity, and velocity components are shown at a series of times separated by equal intervals. The x-component of acceleration is zero, so v_x is constant, while v_y changes by equal amounts in equal times, corresponding to constant y-acceleration.

We can also represent the initial velocity v_0 by its magnitude v_0 (the initial speed) and its angle θ_0 with the positive x-axis. In terms of these quantities, the components v_{0x} and v_{0y} of initial velocity are

$$v_{0x} = v_0 \cos \theta_0,$$

$$v_{0y} = v_0 \sin \theta_0. \tag{3–16}$$

3-6
Stroboscopic photograph of a bouncing golf ball, showing parabolic trajectories after each bounce. Successive images are separated by equal time intervals, as in Fig. 3–5. Each peak in the trajectories is lower than the preceding one because of energy loss during the "bounce" or collision with the horizontal surface. (Dr. Harold Edgerton, M.I.T., Cambridge, Massachusetts.)

Using these relations in Eqs. (3–12) through (3–15) and setting $x_0 = y_0 = 0$, we find

$$x = (v_0 \cos \theta_0)t, \tag{3–17}$$

$$y = (v_0 \sin \theta_0)t - \tfrac{1}{2}gt^2, \tag{3–18}$$

$$v_x = v_0 \cos \theta_0, \tag{3–19}$$

$$v_y = v_0 \sin \theta_0 - gt. \tag{3–20}$$

These equations describe the position and velocity of the projectile in Fig. 3–5 at any time t.

We can get a variety of additional information from these equations. For example, the distance r of the projectile from the origin at any time (the magnitude of the position vector r) is given by

$$r = \sqrt{x^2 + y^2}. \tag{3–21}$$

The projectile's speed (the magnitude of its velocity) at any time is

$$v = \sqrt{v_x{}^2 + v_y{}^2}. \tag{3–22}$$

The *direction* of the velocity, in terms of the angle θ it makes with the positive x-axis, is given by

$$\tan \theta = \frac{v_y}{v_x}. \tag{3–23}$$

The velocity vector v is tangent to the trajectory at each point.

We can derive an equation for the shape of the trajectory, in terms of x and y, by eliminating t. We find $t = x/(v_0 \cos \theta_0)$ and

$$y = (\tan \theta_0)x - \frac{g}{2v_0{}^2 \cos^2 \theta_0}x^2. \tag{3–24}$$

Don't worry about the details of this equation; the important point is its general form. The quantities v_0, $\tan \theta_0$, $\cos \theta_0$, and g are constants, so the equation has the form

$$y = ax - bx^2,$$

where a and b are constants. This is the equation of a *parabola*. In projectile motion, with our simple model, the trajectory is always a parabola. Figure 3–6 shows parabolic trajectories of a bouncing golf ball.

PROBLEM-SOLVING STRATEGY: *Projectile Problems*

The strategies used in Sections 2–4 and 2–5 for straight-line, constant-acceleration problems are also useful here.

1. Define your coordinate system. Make a sketch showing your axes; label the positive direction for each axis and show the location of the origin. We suggest that you consistently take the positive y-direction as upward rather than switching directions from one problem to the next.

2. Make lists of known and unknown quantities. In some problems the components (or magnitude and direction) of initial velocity will be given, and

you can use Eqs. (3–17) through (3–20) to find the coordinates and velocity components at some later time. In other problems you may be given two points on the trajectory and be asked to find the initial velocity. Be sure you know which quantities are given and which are to be found.

3. It often helps to state the problem in prose and then translate into symbols. For example, *when* does the particle arrive at a certain point? (That is, at what value of t?) *Where* is the particle when its velocity has a certain value? (That is, what are the values of x and y when v_x or v_y has the specified value?)

4. At the highest point in a trajectory, $v_y = 0$. So the question "When does the projectile reach its highest point?" translates into "What is the value of t when $v_y = 0$?" Similarly, if $y_0 = 0$, then "When does the projectile return to its initial elevation?" translates into "What is the value of t when $y = 0$?" And so on.

5. Resist the temptation to break the trajectory into segments and analyze each one separately. You don't have to start all over, with a new axis system and a new time scale, when the projectile reaches its highest point. It is usually easier to set up Eqs. (3–17) through (3–20) at the start and use the same axes and time scale throughout the problem.

Example 3–3   A motorcycle stunt rider rides off the edge of a cliff with a horizontal velocity of magnitude 5.0 m·s^{-1}. Find the rider's position and velocity after $\frac{1}{4}$ s. (See Fig. 3–7.)

Solution   The coordinate system is shown in Fig. 3–7. We know the following: $x_0 = 0$, $y_0 = 0$, $v_{0x} = 5.0$ m·s^{-1}, $v_{0y} = 0$, $a_x = 0$, $a_y = -g = -9.8$ m·s^{-2}.

Where is the motorcycle at $t = \frac{1}{4}$ s? The answer is contained in Eqs. (3–17) and (3–18). When $t = \frac{1}{4}$ s, the x- and y-coordinates are

$$x = v_{0x}t = (5.0 \text{ m·s}^{-1})(\tfrac{1}{4} \text{ s}) = 1.25 \text{ m},$$

$$y = -\tfrac{1}{2}gt^2 = -\tfrac{1}{2}(9.8 \text{ m·s}^{-2})(\tfrac{1}{4} \text{ s})^2 = -0.306 \text{ m}.$$

The negative value of y shows that at this time the motorcycle is *below* its starting point.

What is the distance from the origin at this time? From Eq. (3–21),

$$r = \sqrt{x^2 + y^2} = \sqrt{(1.25 \text{ m})^2 + (-0.306 \text{ m})^2} = 1.29 \text{ m}.$$

What is the velocity at time $t = \frac{1}{4}$ s? From Eqs. (3–19) and (3–20), the components of velocity at time $t = \frac{1}{4}$ s are

$$v_x = v_{0x} = 5.0 \text{ m·s}^{-1},$$

$$v_y = -gt = (-9.8 \text{ m·s}^{-2})(\tfrac{1}{4} \text{ s}) = -2.45 \text{ m·s}^{-1}.$$

From Eq. (3–22), the speed (magnitude of the velocity) at this time is

$$v = \sqrt{v_x^2 + v_y^2} = 5.57 \text{ m·s}^{-1}.$$

From Eq. (3–23), the angle θ of the velocity vector is

$$\theta = \arctan \frac{v_y}{v_x} = \arctan \frac{-2.45 \text{ m·s}^{-1}}{5.0 \text{ m·s}^{-1}} = -26.1°.$$

At this time the velocity is 26.1° *below* the horizontal. ∎

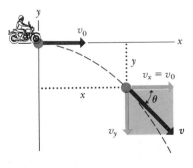

3–7
Trajectory of a body projected horizontally.

Example 3–4   In Fig. 3–5, suppose the projectile is a home-run ball hit with an initial speed $v_0 = 50$ m·s^{-1} at an initial angle $\theta_0 = 53.1°$. The ball is probably struck a meter or so above ground level, but we neglect this distance and assume it starts at ground level ($y_0 = 0$). Then

$$v_{0x} = v_0 \cos \theta_0 = (50 \text{ m·s}^{-1})(0.60) = 30 \text{ m·s}^{-1},$$

$$v_{0y} = v_0 \sin \theta_0 = (50 \text{ m·s}^{-1})(0.80) = 40 \text{ m·s}^{-1}.$$

a) Find the position of the ball, and the magnitude and direction of its velocity, when $t = 2.0$ s.

Using the coordinate system shown in Fig. 3–5, we want to find x, y, v_x, and v_y at time $t = 2.0$ s. From Eqs. (3–17) through (3–20),

$$x = (30 \text{ m·s}^{-1})(2.0 \text{ s}) = 60 \text{ m},$$

$$y = (40 \text{ m·s}^{-1})(2.0 \text{ s}) - \tfrac{1}{2}(9.8 \text{ m·s}^{-2})(2.0 \text{ s})^2 = 60.4 \text{ m},$$

$$v_x = 30 \text{ m·s}^{-1},$$

$$v_y = 40 \text{ m·s}^{-1} - (9.8 \text{ m·s}^{-2})(2.0 \text{ s}) = 20.4 \text{ m·s}^{-1},$$

$$v = \sqrt{v_x^2 + v_y^2} = 36.3 \text{ m·s}^{-1},$$

$$\theta = \arctan \frac{20.4 \text{ m·s}^{-1}}{30 \text{ m·s}^{-1}} = \arctan 0.680 = 34.2°.$$

b) Find the time when the ball reaches the highest point of its flight, and find its height h at this point.

At the highest point the vertical velocity v_y is zero. When does this happen? Call the time t_1; then

$$v_y = 0 = 40 \text{ m·s}^{-1} - (9.8 \text{ m·s}^{-2})t_1,$$

$$t_1 = 4.08 \text{ s}.$$

The height h at this time is the value of y when $t = 4.08$ s:

$$h = (40 \text{ m·s}^{-1})(4.08 \text{ s}) - \tfrac{1}{2}(9.8 \text{ m·s}^{-2})(4.08 \text{ s})^2 = 81.6 \text{ m}.$$

Alternatively, we can use the constant-acceleration formula

$$v_y^2 = v_{0y}^2 + 2a_y(y - y_0) = v_{0y}^2 - 2g(y - y_0).$$

At the highest point, $v_y = 0$ and $y = h$. Substituting these in, along with $y_0 = 0$, we find

$$0 = (40 \text{ m·s}^{-1})^2 - 2(9.8 \text{ m·s}^{-2})h$$

and

$$h = 81.6 \text{ m}.$$

c) Find the *horizontal range R*, that is, the horizontal distance from the starting point to the point at which the ball hits the ground.

First, *when* does the ball hit the ground? When $y = 0$! Call this time t_2; then, from Eq. (3–18),

$$y = 0 = (40 \text{ m·s}^{-1})t_2 - \tfrac{1}{2}(9.8 \text{ m·s}^{-2})t_2^2.$$

This is a quadratic equation for t_2; it has two roots,

$$t_2 = 0 \quad \text{and} \quad t_2 = 8.16 \text{ s}.$$

There are two times at which $y = 0$; $t_2 = 0$ is the time the ball *leaves* the ground, and $t_2 = 8.16$ s is the time of its return. This is exactly twice the time to reach the highest point, so the time of descent equals the time of ascent. (This is *always* true if the starting and end points are at the same elevation. Can you prove this?)

The horizontal range R is the value of x when the ball returns to the ground, that is, when $t = 8.16$ s:

$$R = v_{0x}t_2 = (30 \text{ m·s}^{-1})(8.16 \text{ s}) = 245 \text{ m}.$$

The ball really *is* a home run! The vertical component of velocity at this point is

$$v_y = 40 \text{ m·s}^{-1} - (9.8 \text{ m·s}^{-2})(8.16 \text{ s}) = -40 \text{ m·s}^{-1}.$$

That is, v_y has the same magnitude as the initial vertical velocity v_{0y} but the opposite direction. Since v_x is constant, the angle *below* the horizontal at this point equals the initial angle θ_0.

d) If the ball does not hit the ground, it continues to travel on *below* its original level. Maybe there is a big hole where the landing point ought to be, or the playing field might be located atop a flat-topped hill that drops off steeply on one side. Then negative values of y, corresponding to times greater than 8.16 s, are possible. Can you compute the position and velocity at a time 10 s after the start, corresponding to the last position shown in Fig. 3–5? The results are

$$x = 300 \text{ m}, \qquad y = -90 \text{ m},$$

$$v_x = 30 \text{ m·s}^{-1}, \qquad v_y = -58 \text{ m·s}^{-1}. \qquad \blacksquare$$

Example 3–5 In Fig. 3–8, William Tell's son shoots an arrow from ground level at an apple hanging in a tree. At the same instant he shoots, the apple starts to drop straight down from the tree. Show that the arrow's path curves just enough for it to hit the apple, regardless of its initial velocity.

Solution We have to prove that there is some time when the apple and the arrow have the same x- and y-coordinates. First let's ask when the x-coordinates are the same. For the apple, $x = d$ at *all* times, and x for the arrow is given by Eq. (3–17): $x = (v_0 \cos \theta_0)t$. When these are equal, $d = (v_0 \cos \theta_0)t$, or

$$t = \frac{d}{v_0 \cos \theta_0}.$$

Now we ask whether y_{apple} and y_{arrow} are also equal at this time; if they are, we have a hit. The apple is in one-dimensional free-fall, and its

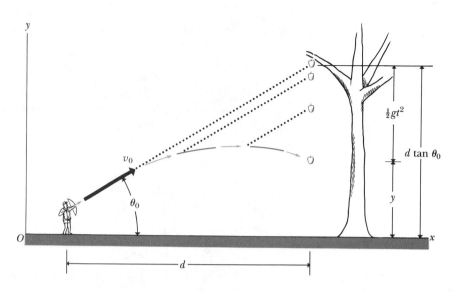

3–8
Trajectory of an arrow shot directly at a freely falling apple.

position at any time is given by Eq. (2–12), with appropriate symbol changes. The initial height is $d \tan \theta_0$, and we find

$$y_{\text{apple}} = d \tan \theta_0 - \tfrac{1}{2}gt^2.$$

For the arrow we use Eq. (3–18):

$$y_{\text{arrow}} = (v_0 \sin \theta_0)t - \tfrac{1}{2}gt^2.$$

So we see that if $d \tan \theta_0 = (v_0 \sin \theta_0)t$ at the time when the two x's are equal, we have a hit. To prove that this does happen, we replace t with the above expression for t; the right side of the equation then becomes

$$(v_0 \sin \theta_0)t = (v_0 \sin \theta_0)\, \frac{d}{v_0 \cos \theta_0} = d \tan \theta_0.$$

Thus we have proved that at the time the x-coordinates are equal, the y-coordinates are also equal; an arrow aimed at the initial position of the apple always hits it, no matter what v_0 is.   ■

Example 3–6   For a projectile launched with speed v_0 at initial angle θ_0, derive general expressions for the maximum height h and range R shown in Fig. 3–5. For a given v_0, what value of θ_0 gives maximum height? Maximum range?

Solution   We follow the same pattern as in Example 3–4, part (b). First, for a given θ_0, *when* does the projectile reach its highest point? At this point $v_y = 0$, so the time t_1 at the highest point ($y = h$) is given by

$$v_y = v_0 \sin \theta_0 - gt_1 = 0, \qquad t_1 = \frac{v_0 \sin \theta_0}{g}.$$

Next, in terms of v_0 and θ_0, what is the value of y at this time? From Eq. (3–18),

$$h = v_0 \sin \theta_0 \, \frac{v_0 \sin \theta_0}{g} - \tfrac{1}{2}g\left(\frac{v_0 \sin \theta_0}{g}\right)^2 = \frac{v_0^2 \sin^2 \theta_0}{2g}. \quad (3\text{–}25)$$

If we vary θ_0, the maximum value of h occurs when $\sin \theta_0 = 1$ and $\theta = 90°$; that is, when the projectile is launched straight up. That's what we should expect. If it is launched horizontally, $\theta_0 = 0$ and the maximum height is zero!

To derive a general expression for the range, we first find an expression for the time t_2 when the projectile returns to the ground. At that time $y = 0$ and, from Eq. (3–18),

$$t_2(v_0 \sin \theta_0 - \tfrac{1}{2}gt_2) = 0.$$

The two roots of this quadratic equation for t_2 are $t_2 = 0$ (launch time) and $t_2 = 2v_0 \sin \theta_0/g$. The range R is the value of x at the second time. From Eq. (3–17),

$$R = (v_0 \cos \theta_0) \frac{2v_0 \sin \theta_0}{g}.$$

We can now use the trigonometric identity $2 \sin \theta_0 \cos \theta_0 = \sin 2\theta_0$ to rewrite this as

$$R = \frac{v_0{}^2 \sin 2\theta_0}{g}. \qquad (3\text{–}26)$$

The maximum value of $\sin 2\theta_0$, namely unity, occurs when $2\theta_0 = 90°$, or $\theta_0 = 45°$, and this angle gives the maximum range for a given initial speed.

Note: We don't recommend memorizing Eqs. (3–25) and (3–26). They are applicable only in the special circumstances we have described. In particular, Eq. (3–26) can be used *only* when launch and landing heights are equal. There are many end-of-chapter problems to which these equations are *not* applicable. ■

Example 3–7   The quarterback wants to throw a football at 20 m·s^{-1} to a receiver 30 m away; at what angle should he throw it?

Solution   We want the range to be 30 m. Solving Eq. (3–26) for θ_0, we find

$$\theta_0 = \tfrac{1}{2} \arcsin \frac{Rg}{v_0{}^2}$$

$$= \tfrac{1}{2} \arcsin \frac{(30 \text{ m})(9.80 \text{ m·s}^{-2})}{(20 \text{ m·s}^{-1})^2}$$

$$= \tfrac{1}{2} \arcsin 0.735.$$

There are *two* values of θ_0 between 0 and 90° satisfying this equation; $\arcsin 0.735 = 47.3°$ or $132.7°$, giving $\theta_0 = 23.7°$ or $66.3°$. Both these angles give the same range, although the time of flight and the maximum height are greater for the higher-angle trajectory. Incidentally, the sum of these two values of θ_0 is exactly 90°. This is *not* a coincidence; can you prove this? (See Problem 3–31.) ■

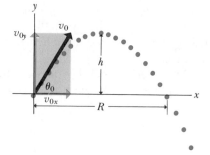

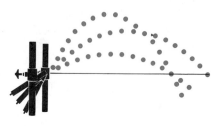
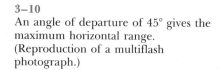

3–9
Trajectory of a body projected at an angle with the horizontal. (Reproduction of a multiflash photograph.)

3–10
An angle of departure of 45° gives the maximum horizontal range. (Reproduction of a multiflash photograph.)

Figure 3–9 is copied from a multiflash photograph of the trajectory of a ball; x- and y-axes and the initial velocity vector have been added. The horizontal distances between consecutive positions are all equal, showing that the horizontal velocity component is constant. The vertical distances first decrease and then increase, showing that the vertical motion is accelerated.

Figure 3–10 is made from a composite photograph of three trajectories of a ball projected from a spring gun with angles of 30°, 45°, and 60°. The initial speed v_0 is approximately the same in all three cases. The horizontal ranges are nearly the same for the 30° and 60° angles, and the range for 45° is greater than either.

3–5
Circular Motion

We talked about components of acceleration in Section 3–3. When a particle moves along a curved path, the direction of its velocity must change. Thus it *must* have a component of acceleration perpendicular (normal) to the path, even if its speed is constant. When a particle moves in a circle with constant speed, the motion is called **uniform circular motion.** In this case there is no component of acceleration parallel (tangent) to the path; otherwise, the speed would change. The component of acceleration normal to the path, which causes the direction of the velocity to change, is related in a simple way to the speed of the particle and the radius of the circle. Our next project is to derive this relation. Keep in mind that this problem is different from the situation in Section 3–4, in which the acceleration was constant in magnitude and direction. Here the acceleration is perpendicular to the velocity at each instant, and the direction of the velocity changes continuously. Thus the direction of the acceleration also changes continuously.

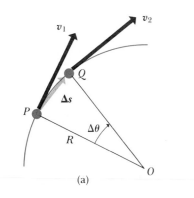

(a)

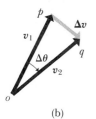

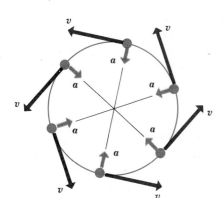

(b)

3–11
Construction for finding change in velocity, Δv, of a particle moving in a circle.

Figure 3–11a shows a particle moving in a circular path of radius R with center at O. The particle moves from P to Q, with displacement Δs, in a time Δt. The vector change in velocity Δv during this time is shown.

The triangles OPQ and opq in Fig. 3–11 are *similar*, since both are isosceles triangles and the angles labeled $\Delta\theta$ are the same. Ratios of corresponding sides are equal, and

$$\frac{\Delta v}{v_1} = \frac{\Delta s}{R}$$

or

$$\Delta v = \frac{v_1}{R}\Delta s.$$

The magnitude of the average acceleration a_{av} during Δt is therefore

$$a_{av} = \frac{\Delta v}{\Delta t} = \frac{v_1}{R}\frac{\Delta s}{\Delta t}.$$

The magnitude a of the *instantaneous* acceleration a at point P is the limit of this expression as point Q is taken closer and closer to point P:

$$a = \lim_{\Delta t \to 0}\frac{v_1}{R}\frac{\Delta s}{\Delta t} = \frac{v_1}{R}\lim_{\Delta t \to 0}\frac{\Delta s}{\Delta t}.$$

But the limit of $\Delta s/\Delta t$ is the speed v_1 at point P. Also, P can be any point of the path, so we can drop the subscript from v_1 and let v represent the speed at any point. Then

$$a_{\perp} = \frac{v^2}{R}. \tag{3–27}$$

We have added the subscript $\perp$ as a reminder that the direction of the instantaneous acceleration is always perpendicular to the instantaneous velocity and thus to a tangent line to the circle at each point.

Thus we have found that *the magnitude of the instantaneous acceleration is equal to the square of the speed divided by the radius of the circle. Its direction is perpendicular to v and inward along the radius.* Because the acceleration is always directed toward the center of the circle, it is sometimes called **centripetal acceleration.** The word *centripetal* is derived from two Greek words meaning "seeking the center." Figure 3–12 shows the directions of the velocity and acceleration vectors at several points for a particle moving with uniform circular motion.

The magnitude of the acceleration in uniform (constant-speed) circular motion can also be expressed in terms of the **period** τ of the motion, the time for one revolution. If a particle travels once around the circle, a distance of $2\pi R$, in a time τ, its speed v is given by

$$v = \frac{2\pi R}{\tau}. \tag{3–28}$$

3–12
Velocity and acceleration vectors of a particle in uniform circular motion.

Thus Eq. (3–27) can also be written as

$$a_\perp = \frac{4\pi^2 R}{\tau^2}. \tag{3–29}$$

Example 3–8   A car traveling at a constant speed of 20 m·s^{-1} rounds a curve of radius 100 m. What is its acceleration?

Solution   The magnitude of the acceleration is given by Eq. (3–27):

$$a_\perp = \frac{v^2}{R} = \frac{(20 \text{ m·s}^{-1})^2}{100 \text{ m}} = 4.0 \text{ m·s}^{-2}.$$

The direction of a at each instant is perpendicular to the velocity and directed toward the center of the circle.   ■

Example 3–9   In a carnival ride, the passengers travel in a circle of radius 5.0 m, making one complete circle in 4.0 s. What is the acceleration?

Solution   The speed is the circumference of the circle divided by the period τ (the time for one revolution).

$$v = \frac{2\pi R}{\tau} = \frac{2\pi(5.0 \text{ m})}{4.0 \text{ s}} = 7.85 \text{ m·s}^{-1}.$$

The centripetal acceleration is

$$a_\perp = \frac{v^2}{R} = \frac{(7.85 \text{ m·s}^{-1})^2}{5.0 \text{ m}} = 12.3 \text{ m·s}^{-2}.$$

Or, from Eq. (3–29),

$$a_\perp = \frac{4\pi^2(5.0 \text{ m})}{(4.0 \text{ s})^2} = 12.3 \text{ m·s}^{-2}.$$

As in the preceding example, the direction of a is always toward the center of the circle. The magnitude of a is greater than g, the acceleration due to gravity, so this is quite a wild ride!   ■

We have assumed throughout this discussion that the particle's speed is constant. If the speed varies, Eq. (3–27) still gives the *normal* component of acceleration, but in that case there is also a *tangential* component of acceleration. From the discussion at the end of Section 3–3 we see that the tangential component of acceleration is equal to the rate of change of speed:

$$a_\parallel = \lim_{\Delta t \to 0} \frac{\Delta v}{\Delta t}. \tag{3–30}$$

3–6
Relative Velocity

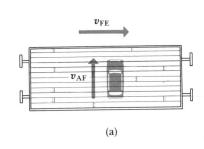

(a)

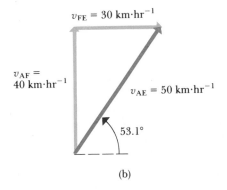

(b)

3–13
(a) An automobile being driven across a moving railroad flatcar. (b) Velocity vector diagram showing how the automobile's velocity v_{AE} relative to the earth is related to its velocity v_{AF} relative to the flatcar and the flatcar's velocity v_{FE} relative to the earth.

In Section 2–6 we introduced the concept of **relative velocity** for motion along a straight line. It is easy to extend this concept to include motion in a plane or in space. Suppose that the automobile in Fig. 2–12 is traveling not in the same direction as the train, but perpendicular to this direction, *across* the flatcars. In any time interval the displacement of the automobile relative to the earth is the vector sum of its displacement relative to the flatcars and their displacement relative to the earth. Thus the *velocity* v_{AE} of the automobile A relative to the earth E is the vector sum of its velocity v_{AF} relative to the flatcars F and their velocity v_{FE} relative to the earth. That is, Eq. (2–18) is a special case of the more general *vector* equation:

$$v_{AE} = v_{AF} + v_{FE}. \tag{3–31}$$

Suppose the automobile is moving across the flatcars at 40 km·hr^{-1} and they are moving relative to the earth at 30 km·hr^{-1}. The appropriate vector diagram is shown in Fig. 3–13. The automobile's velocity relative to the earth is 50 km·hr^{-1} at an angle of 53° to the direction of the train's motion.

We can extend Eq. (3–31) to include any number of relative velocities. For example, if a bug B crawls along the floor of the automobile with a velocity v_{BA} relative to the automobile, the bug's velocity relative to the earth is the vector sum of its velocity relative to the automobile and that of the velocity of the automobile relative to the earth:

$$v_{BE} = v_{BA} + v_{AE}.$$

Combining this with Eq. (3–31), we find

$$v_{BE} = v_{BA} + v_{AF} + v_{FE}. \tag{3–32}$$

This equation illustrates the general rule for combining relative velocities.

 PROBLEM-SOLVING STRATEGY: Relative Velocity

The strategy introduced in Section 2–6 is also useful here.

1. Write each velocity with a double subscript, *in the proper order*, as "velocity of (first subscript) relative to (second subscript)."

2. In Eq. (3–32) the first subscript on the left side is the same as the *first* subscript of the *first* velocity in the sum on the right side. The second subscript on the left side is the same as the last subscript on the last velocity in the sum. The second subscript of each velocity except the last in the sum is the same as the first subscript of the next term in the sum. This sounds complicated, but referring to Eq. (3–32) will help you to see how it works.

Any of the relative velocities in an equation such as Eq. (3–31) can be transferred from one side of the equation to the other, with its sign reversed. Thus Eq. (3–31) can be written

$$v_{AF} = v_{AE} - v_{FE}. \qquad (3\text{–}33)$$

The velocity of the automobile relative to the flatcar equals the *vector difference* between the velocities of automobile and flatcar, each relative to the earth.

One more point to note is that the velocity of body A relative to body B, v_{AB}, is the negative of the velocity of B relative to A, v_{BA}:

$$v_{AB} = -v_{BA}.$$

That is, v_{AB} is equal in magnitude and opposite in direction to v_{BA}. If in Section 2–6 the automobile is traveling to the *right* at 40 mi·hr^{-1} relative to the flatcars, the flatcars are traveling to the *left* at 40 mi·hr^{-1} relative to the automobile. Also note that if we replace $-v_{FE}$ by v_{EF} in Eq. (3–33), we have the same pattern of subscripts as described in the Problem-Solving Strategy.

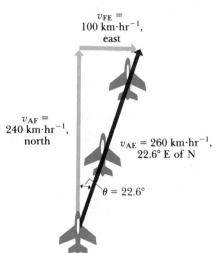

$v_{FE} =$ 100 km·hr^{-1}, east

$v_{AF} =$ 240 km·hr^{-1}, north

$v_{AE} = 260$ km·hr^{-1}, 22.6° E of N

$\theta = 22.6°$

3–14
Vector diagram for aircraft flying north, wind blowing east, and resultant velocity vector of the plane.

Example 3–10 The compass of an airplane indicates that it is headed due north, and its airspeed indicator shows that it is moving through the air at 240 km·hr^{-1}. If there is a wind of 100 km·hr^{-1} from west to east, what is the velocity of the aircraft relative to the earth?

Solution Let subscript A refer to the airplane and subscript F to the moving air (which now plays the role of the flatcar in Fig. 3–13). Subscript E refers to the earth. The information given is:

$$v_{AF} = 240 \text{ km·hr}^{-1}, \qquad \text{due north},$$
$$v_{FE} = 100 \text{ km·hr}^{-1}, \qquad \text{due east},$$

and we want to find the magnitude and direction of v_{AE}:

$$v_{AE} = v_{AF} + v_{FE}.$$

The three relative velocities and their relationship are shown in Fig. 3–14. It follows from this diagram that

$$v_{AE} = 260 \text{ km·hr}^{-1}, \qquad \theta = \arctan \frac{100 \text{ km·hr}^{-1}}{240 \text{ km·hr}^{-1}} = 22.6° \text{ E of N.} \quad \blacksquare$$

Example 3–11 In Example 3–10, in what direction should the pilot head to travel due north? What will then be his velocity relative to the earth? (Assume that the wind velocity and the magnitude of his airspeed are the same as in Example 3–10.)

Solution Now the information given is:

$$v_{AF} = 240 \text{ km·hr}^{-1}, \qquad \text{direction unknown},$$
$$v_{FE} = 100 \text{ km·hr}^{-1}, \qquad \text{due east}.$$

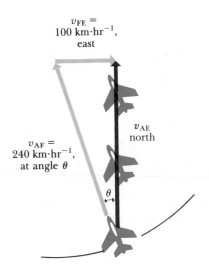

$v_{FE} = 100 \text{ km·hr}^{-1}$, east

$v_{AF} = 240 \text{ km·hr}^{-1}$, at angle θ

v_{AE} north

θ

3–15
The resultant vector v_{AF} shows the direction in which the pilot should point the plane in order to have the plane travel due north.

We want to find v_{AE}; its magnitude is unknown, but we know that its direction is due north. Note that both this and the preceding example require us to determine two unknown quantities. In Example 3–10 these were the *magnitude and direction* of v_{AE}; in this example the unknowns are the direction of v_{AF} and the *magnitude* of v_{AE}.

The three relative velocities must still satisfy the *vector equation*

$$v_{AE} = v_{AF} + v_{FE}.$$

The appropriate vector diagram is shown in Fig. 3–15. We find

$$v_{AE} = \sqrt{(240 \text{ km·hr}^{-1})^2 - (100 \text{ km·hr}^{-1})^2} = 218 \text{ km·hr}^{-1},$$

$$\theta = \arcsin \frac{100 \text{ km·hr}^{-1}}{240 \text{ km·hr}^{-1}} = 22.6°.$$

The pilot should head 22.6° west of north, and his ground speed is then 218 km·hr^{-1}. ∎

Questions

3–1 A simple pendulum (a mass swinging at the end of a string) swings back and forth in a circular arc. What is the direction of its acceleration at the ends of the swing? At the midpoint?

3–2 A football is thrown in a parabolic path. Is there any point at which the acceleration is parallel to the velocity? Perpendicular to the velocity?

3–3 When a rifle is fired at a distant target, the barrel is not lined up exactly on the target. Why not? Does the angle of correction depend on the distance of the target?

3–4 The acceleration of a falling body is measured in an elevator traveling upward at a constant speed of 9.8 m·s^{-1}. What result is obtained?

3–5 One can play catch with a softball in an airplane in level flight just as though the plane were at rest. Is this still possible when the plane is making a turn?

3–6 A package is dropped out of an airplane in level flight. If air resistance could be neglected, how would the motion of the package look to the pilot? To an observer on the ground?

3–7 No matter what the initial velocity, the motion of a projectile (neglecting air resistance) is *always* confined to a single plane. Why?

3–8 If a jumper can give himself the same initial speed regardless of the direction in which he jumps (forward or straight up), how is his maximum vertical jump (high jump) related to his maximum horizontal jump (broad jump)?

3–9 A manned space-flight projectile is launched in a parabolic trajectory. A man in the capsule feels weightless. Why? In what sense is he weightless?

3–10 The maximum range of a projectile occurs when it is aimed at 45° if air resistance is neglected. Is this still true if air resistance is included? If not, is the optimum angle greater or less than 45°? Why?

3–11 A passenger in a car rounding a sharp curve is thrown toward the outside of the curve. What force throws her in this direction?

3–12 In uniform circular motion, what is the *average* velocity during one revolution? The average acceleration?

3–13 In uniform circular motion the acceleration is perpendicular to the velocity at every instant, even though both change continuously in direction. Is there any other motion having this property, or is uniform circular motion unique?

3–14 If an artificial earth satellite is in an orbit with a period of exactly one day, how does its motion look to an observer on the rotating earth? (Such an orbit is said to be *geosynchronous;* most communications satellites are placed in such orbits.)

3–15 Raindrops hitting the side windows of a car in motion often leave diagonal streaks. Why? What about diagonal streaks on the windshield? Is the explanation the same or different?

3–16 In a rainstorm with a strong wind, what determines the best position in which to hold an umbrella?

Exercises

Section 3–1   Average and Instantaneous Velocity

3–1 A squirrel has x- and y-coordinates (2.68 m, 3.44 m) at time $t_1 = 0$ and coordinates (−5.50 m, 8.12 m) at time $t_2 = 4.00$ s. For this time interval, find

a) the components of the average velocity;

b) the magnitude and direction of the average velocity.

3–2 An elephant is at the origin of coordinates at time $t_1 = 0$. For the time interval from $t_1 = 0$ to $t_2 = 20.0$ s the average velocity of the elephant has components $(v_x)_{av} = 4.2$ m·s^{-1} and $(v_y)_{av} = -5.8$ m·s^{-1}. At time $t_2 = 20.0$ s,

a) what are the x- and y-coordinates of the elephant?

b) how far is the elephant from the origin?

Section 3–3   Components of Acceleration

3–3 A jet plane at time $t_1 = 0$ has components of velocity $v_x = 180$ m·s^{-1}, $v_y = -120$ m·s^{-1}. At time $t_2 = 20.0$ s the velocity components are $v_x = 110$ m·s^{-1}, $v_y = 40$ m·s^{-1}. For this time interval, calculate

a) the components of the average acceleration;

b) the magnitude and direction of the average acceleration.

3–4 A dog playing in an open field has components of velocity $v_x = 4.5$ m·s^{-1} and $v_y = 2.20$ m·s^{-1} at $t_1 = 10.0$ s. For the time interval from $t_1 = 10.0$ s to $t_2 = 20.0$ s the average acceleration of the dog has magnitude 0.62 m·s^{-2} and direction 52.0° counterclockwise from the $+x$-axis. At $t = 20.0$ s,

a) what are the x- and y-components of the velocity of the dog?

b) what are the magnitude and direction of the velocity of the dog?

Section 3–4   Projectile Motion

3–5 A tennis ball rolls off the edge of a table top 1.00 m above the floor and strikes the floor at a point 2.60 m horizontally from the edge of the table.

a) Find the time of flight.

b) Find the magnitude of the initial velocity.

c) Find the magnitude and direction of the velocity of the ball just before it strikes the floor. Draw a diagram to scale.

3–6 A golf ball is hit horizontally from a tee at the edge of a cliff. Its x- and y-coordinates are given as functions of time by

$$x = (32.0 \text{ m·s}^{-1})t, \qquad y = -(4.90 \text{ m·s}^{-2})t^2.$$

a) Compute the x- and y-coordinates at times $t = 0$, 1.00 s, 2.00 s, 3.00 s, and 4.00 s. Plot these positions on graph paper and sketch the trajectory.

b) Determine the ball's initial velocity vector and its acceleration vector.

c) Find the x- and y-components of the velocity at time $t = 2.00$ s. Plot the velocity vector at the appropriate point on the trajectory obtained in part (a). Is the velocity tangent to the trajectory?

3–7 An airplane flying horizontally at a speed of 150 m·s^{-1} drops a box from an elevation of 2000 m.

a) How much time is required for the box to reach the earth?

b) How far does it travel horizontally while falling?

c) Find the horizontal and vertical components of its velocity when it strikes the earth.

d) Where is the airplane when the box strikes the earth, if the speed of the airplane remains constant?

3–8 A physics book slides off a horizontal table top with a speed of 2.80 m·s^{-1}. It is observed to strike the floor in 0.650 s. Find

a) the height of the table top above the floor;

b) the horizontal distance from the edge of the table to the point where the book strikes the floor;

c) the horizontal and vertical components of its velocity and the magnitude and direction of its velocity when it reaches the floor.

3–9 A marksman fires a .22-caliber rifle horizontally at a target; the bullet has a muzzle velocity with magnitude 750 ft·s^{-1}. How much does the bullet drop in flight if the target is

a) 50.0 yd away?   b) 150.0 yd away?

3–10 A football is thrown with an initial upward velocity component of 15.0 m·s^{-1} and a horizontal velocity component of 18.0 m·s^{-1}.

a) How much time is required to reach the highest point of the trajectory?

b) How high is this point?

c) How much time (after being thrown) is required for the ball to return to its original level? How does this compare with the time calculated in part (b)?

d) How far has it traveled horizontally during this time?

3–11 A baseball is thrown at an angle of 53.1° above the horizontal with an initial speed of 50.0 m·s^{-1}.

a) At what *two* times is the baseball at a height of 25.0 m above the point from which it was thrown?

b) Calculate the horizontal and vertical components of the baseball's velocity at each of the two times calculated in part (a).

c) What are the magnitude and direction of the baseball's velocity when it returns to the level from which it was thrown?

3–12 A batted baseball leaves the bat at an angle of 30.0° above the horizontal and is caught by an outfielder 375 ft from the plate. Assume that the height of the point where it was struck by the bat equals the height of the point where it was caught.

a) What is the initial speed of the ball?

b) How high does it rise above the point where it struck the bat?

3–13 Suppose the departure angle θ_0 in Fig. 3–8 is 14.0° and the distance d is 5.00 m. Where do the arrow and apple meet if the initial speed of the arrow is

a) 25.0 m·s^{-1}?

b) 15.0 m·s^{-1}?

Sketch both trajectories.

c) What happens if the initial speed of the arrow is 6.0 m·s^{-1}?

3–14 A man stands on a roof of a building that is 40.0 m tall and throws a rock with a velocity of 60.0 m·s^{-1} at an angle of 41.0° above the horizontal. Calculate:

a) the maximum height, above the roof, reached by the rock;

b) the magnitude of the velocity of the rock just before it strikes the ground;

c) the horizontal distance from the base of the building to the point where the rock strikes the ground.

Section 3–5   Circular Motion

3–15 A Ferris wheel with radius 15.0 m is turning about a horizontal axis through its center; the linear speed of a passenger on the rim is constant and equal to 9.00 m·s^{-1}.

a) What are the magnitude and direction of the acceleration of a passenger as she passes through the lowest point in her circular motion?

b) How much time does it take the Ferris wheel to make one revolution?

3–16 The earth has a radius of 6.38×10^6 m and turns around once on its axis in 24.0 hr. What is the radial acceleration of an object at the equator of the earth, in units of m·s^{-2}?

3–17 The radius of the earth's orbit around the sun (assumed circular) is 1.49×10^{11} m, and the earth travels around this orbit in 365 days.

a) What is the magnitude or the orbital velocity of the earth, in m·s^{-1}?

b) What is the radial acceleration of the earth toward the sun, in m·s^{-2}?

3–18 A model of a helicopter rotor has four blades, each 2.50 m in length from the central shaft to the blade tip, and is rotated in a wind tunnel at 1800 rev·min^{-1}.

a) What is the linear speed of a blade tip in meters per second?

b) What is the radial acceleration of a blade tip expressed as a multiple of the acceleration of gravity, g?

Section 3–6   Relative Velocity

3–19 A passenger on a ship traveling due east with a speed of 24.0 knots observes that the stream of smoke from the ship's funnels makes an angle of 20.0° with the ship's wake. The wind is blowing from south to north. Assume that the smoke acquires a velocity (with respect to the earth) equal to the velocity of the wind as soon as it leaves the funnels. Find the magnitude of the velocity of the wind in knots. (A knot is a unit of speed used by sailors; 1 knot = 1.852 km·hr^{-1}.)

3–20 An airplane pilot wishes to fly due north. A wind of 66.0 km·hr^{-1} (about 40 mi·hr^{-1}) is blowing toward the west.

a) If the flying speed of the plane (its speed in still air) is 290.0 km·hr^{-1} (about 180 mi·hr^{-1}), in what direction should the pilot head?

b) What is the speed of the plane over the ground?

Illustrate with a vector diagram.

3–21 A river flows due north with a speed of 1.5 m·s^{-1}. A man rows a boat across the river; his velocity relative to the water is 3.0 m·s^{-1} due east. The river is 1000 m wide.

a) What is his velocity relative to the earth?

b) How much time is required to cross the river?

c) How far north of his starting point does he reach the opposite bank?

3–22

a) In what direction should the rowboat in Exercise 3–21 be headed in order to reach a point on the opposite bank directly east from the starting point?

b) What is the magnitude of the velocity of the boat relative to the earth?

c) How much time is required to cross the river?

▪ *Problems*

3–23 The coordinates of a model airplane moving in the *xy*-plane are given as functions of time by $x = 8.00$ m $- (4.00$ m·s$^{-1})t$ and $y = (1.50$ m·s$^{-2})t^2$. Calculate the magnitude and direction of the airplane's average velocity for the following time intervals:

a) $t = 0$ to $t = 2.0$ s;

b) $t = 0$ to $t = 4.0$ s.

3–24 A bird flies in the *xy*-plane with a velocity vector with components given by $v_x = 12.0$ m·s$^{-1} - (5.00$ m·s$^{-3})t^2$ and $v_y = (8.00$ m·s$^{-2})t$.

a) Calculate the *x*- and *y*-components of the average acceleration of the bird for the time interval $t = 0$ to $t = 1.00$ s. Also calculate the magnitude and direction of this average acceleration.

b) Repeat the calculation for the time interval $t = 0$ to $t = 3.00$ s.

3–25 A player kicks a football at an angle of 40.0° with the horizontal, with an initial speed of 12.0 m·s^{-1}. A second player standing at a distance of 30.0 m from the first (in the direction of the kick) starts running to meet the ball at the instant it is kicked. How fast must he run in order to catch the ball just before it hits the ground?

3–26 A girl throws a water-filled balloon at an angle of 50.0° with a speed of 15.0 m·s^{-1}. A car is advancing toward the girl at a constant speed of 8.00 m·s^{-1}. If the balloon is to hit the car, how far away should the car be when the balloon is thrown?

3–27 According to the *Guinness Book of World Records*, the longest home run ever measured was hit by Roy "Dizzy" Carlyle in a minor league game and travelled 618 ft before landing on the ground outside the ballpark.

a) Assuming that the ball's initial velocity was 55.0° above the horizontal and neglecting air resistance, what would the initial speed of the ball need to be to produce such a home run if the ball is hit at a point 3.00 ft above ground level? Assume that the ground is perfectly flat.

b) How far above a fence 10.0 ft in height would the ball be if the fence is 380 ft from home plate?

3–28 An airplane diving at an angle of 36.9° below the horizontal drops a bag of sand from an altitude of 1200 m. The bag is observed to strike the ground 6.00 s after its release.

a) What is the speed of the plane?

b) How far does the bag travel horizontally during its fall?

c) What are the horizontal and vertical components of its velocity just before it strikes the ground?

3–29 A baseball thrown at an angle of 60.0° above the horizontal strikes the vertical wall of a building 45.0 m away at a point 20.0 m above the point from which it was thrown.

a) Find the magnitude of the initial velocity of the baseball (the velocity with which it is thrown).

b) Find the magnitude and direction of the velocity of the baseball just before it strikes the building.

3–30 A snowball rolls off a roof that slopes downward at an angle of 40°, as shown in Fig. 3–16. The edge of

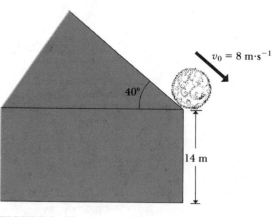

FIGURE 3–16

the roof is 14.0 m above the ground, and the snowball has a speed of 8.00 m·s^{-1} as it rolls off the roof.

a) How far from the edge of the house does the snowball strike the ground if it doesn't strike anything else while falling?

b) A man 2.00 m tall is standing 6.00 m from the edge of the house. Will he be hit by the snowball?

3–31 Prove that a projectile launched at angle θ_0 has the same range as one launched with the same speed at angle $(90° - \theta_0)$.

3–32 A rock is thrown from the roof of a building with a velocity v_0 at an angle of θ from the horizontal. The building has height h. Calculate the magnitude of the velocity of the rock just before it strikes the ground, and show that this speed is independent of θ.

3–33 A physics professor did daredevil stunts in his spare time. His last stunt was to attempt to jump across a river on a motorcycle (Fig. 3–17). The takeoff ramp was inclined at 53.0°, the river was 40.0 m wide, and the far bank was 15.0 m lower than the top of the ramp. The river itself was 100 m below the ramp. What should his speed have been at the top of the ramp to have just made it to the edge of the far bank?

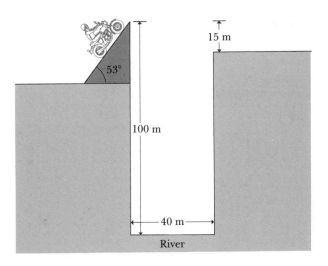

FIGURE 3–17

 Challenge Problems

3–39 A projectile is given an initial velocity with magnitude v_0 at an angle ϕ above the surface of an incline, which is in turn inclined at an angle θ above the horizontal (see Fig. 3–18). Calculate the distance, measured along the incline, from the launch point to where the

3–34 A movie stuntwoman drops from a helicopter that is 40.0 m above ground and is moving with a constant velocity whose components are 10.0 m·s^{-1} upward and 20.0 m·s^{-1} horizontal and toward the east. Where on the ground (relative to the position of the helicopter when she drops) should the stuntwoman have placed the foam mats that will break her fall?

3–35 In an action-adventure film the hero is supposed to throw a grenade from his car, which is going 60.0 km·hr^{-1}, to his enemy's car, which is going 110 km·hr^{-1}. The enemy's car is 14.6 m in front of the hero's when he lets go of the grenade. If the hero throws the grenade so that its initial velocity relative to the hero is at an angle of 45.0° above the horizontal, what should be the magnitude of the velocity? The cars are both traveling in the same direction on a level road. Find the magnitude of the velocity both relative to the hero and relative to the earth.

3–36 When a train's speed is 15.0 m·s^{-1} eastward, raindrops that are falling vertically with respect to the earth make traces that are inclined 30.0° to the vertical on the windows of the train.

a) What is the horizontal component of a drop's velocity with respect to the earth? With respect to the train?

b) What is the magnitude of the velocity of the raindrop with respect to the earth? With respect to the train?

3–37 An airplane pilot sets a compass course due west and maintains an air speed of 240 km·hr^{-1}. After flying for 0.500 hr she finds herself over a town that is 190 km west and 35 km north of her starting point.

a) Find the wind velocity in magnitude and direction.

b) If the wind velocity is 90.0 km·hr^{-1} due south, in what direction should the pilot set her course to travel due west? Take the same air speed of 240 km·hr^{-1}.

3–38 A motorboat travels 24.0 km·hr^{-1} relative to the earth in the direction 37.0° north of east. If the velocity of the boat due to the wind is 3.20 km·hr^{-1} eastward and that due to the current is 6.40 km·hr^{-1} southward, what are the magnitude and direction of the velocity of the boat due to its own power?

object strikes the incline. Your answer will be in terms of v_0, g, θ, and ϕ. (*Note:* You might be interested in the three different methods of solution that are presented by I. R. Lapidus in *Amer. Jour. of Phys.*, Vol. 51 (1983), pp. 806 and 847. See also H. A. Buckmaster in *Amer.*

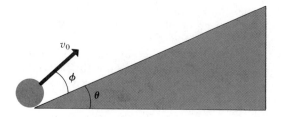

FIGURE 3–18

Jour. of Phys., Vol. 53 (1985), pp. 638–641, for a thorough study of this and some similar problems.)

3–40 Refer to the previous problem.

a) An archer on ground of constant upward slope of 30.0° aims at a target 50.0 m farther up the incline. The arrow in the bow and the bull's-eye at the center of the target are each 1.50 m above the ground. The initial velocity of the arrow just after it leaves the bow has magnitude 36.0 m·s^{-1}. At what angle above the *horizontal* should the archer aim to hit the bull's-eye? If there are two such angles, calculate the smaller of the two. You might have to solve the equation for the angle by iteration, that is, by trial and error. How does the angle compare to that required when the ground is level, with zero slope?

b) Repeat the above for ground of constant *downward* slope of 30.0°.

3–41 An object is traveling in a circle of radius $R = 4.00$ m with a constant speed of $v = 10.0$ m·s^{-1}. Let v_1 be the velocity vector at time t_1 and v_2 be the velocity vector at time t_2. Consider $\Delta v = v_2 - v_1$ and $\Delta t = t_2 - t_1$. Recall that $a_{av} = \Delta v/\Delta t$. For $\Delta t = 0.500$ s, 0.100 s, and 0.0500 s, calculate the magnitude and direction (relative to v_1) of the average acceleration a_{av}. Compare your results to the general expression for the instantaneous acceleration a for uniform circular motion that is derived in the text.

3–42 A man is riding on a flatcar traveling with a constant speed of 9.10 m·s^{-1} (Fig. 3–19). He wishes to throw a ball through a stationary hoop 4.90 m above the height of his hands so that the ball will be moving horizontally as it passes through the hoop. He throws the ball with a speed of 14.0 m·s^{-1} with respect to himself.

a) What must be the vertical component of the initial velocity of the ball?

b) How many seconds after he releases the ball does it pass through the hoop?

c) At what horizontal distance in front of the hoop must he release the ball?

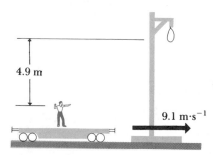

4.9 m

9.1 m·s^{-1}

FIGURE 3–19

Newton's Laws of Motion

In the two preceding chapters we have studied *kinematics*, the language for *describing* motion. We are now ready to tackle problems in **dynamics,** involving the relation of motion to its causes. Along with the kinematic quantities displacement, velocity, and acceleration, we will use the concepts of *force* and *mass*. In the special case when a body is in *equilibrium*, its acceleration is zero. Such special cases are grouped under the subheading *statics*.

All the principles of dynamics can be wrapped up in a neat package containing three statements called *Newton's laws of motion*. The first law states that when the vector sum of forces on a body is zero, the acceleration of the body is also zero. The second law relates force to acceleration when the vector sum of forces is *not* zero, and the third law is a relation be-

tween the forces that two interacting bodies exert on each other.

Newton's laws are *empirical* laws, deduced from experiment; they cannot be derived from anything more fundamental. They were clearly stated for the first time by Sir Isaac Newton (1642–1727), who published them in 1686 in his *Philosophiae Naturalis Principia Mathematica* (Mathematical Principles of Natural Philosophy). Many other scientists before Newton contributed to the foundations of mechanics, especially Galileo Galilei (1564–1642), who died the same year Newton was born. Indeed, Newton himself said, "If I have been able to see a little farther than other men, it is because I have stood on the shoulders of giants."

4–1
Force

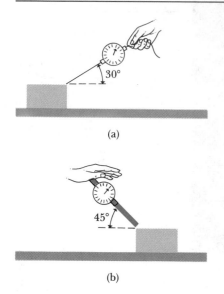

4–1
Force may be exerted on the box by either (a) pulling it or (b) pushing it.

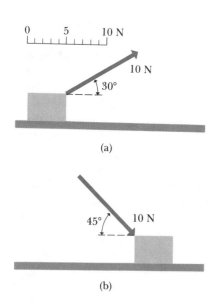

4–2
Force diagram for the forces acting on the box in Fig. 4–1.

The concept of **force** provides a quantitative description of the interaction of two bodies. When you push on a car that is stuck in the snow, you exert a force on it; a locomotive exerts a force on the train it is pulling or pushing, and so on. When a force involves direct contact between two bodies, we call it a *contact force*. There are also forces, including gravitational and electrical forces, that act even when the bodies are separated by empty space. The force of gravitational attraction that the earth exerts on a body is called the *weight* of the body. Viewed on an atomic scale, contact forces result principally from the electrical attractions and repulsions of the electrons and nuclei in the atoms of the materials.

Force is a *vector* quantity; to describe a force, we need to describe the *direction* in which it acts as well as its *magnitude*, the quantity that describes "how much" or "how hard" the force pushes or pulls. The SI unit of the magnitude of force is the *newton*, abbreviated N. In Section 4–4 we will define the newton in terms of the meter, the kilogram, and the second. In the cgs metric system the unit of force is the *dyne*, equal to 10^{-5} N. In the British system the unit of force is the *pound* (abbreviated lb), sometimes called the *pound-force* (abbreviated lbf). One pound is *defined* to be precisely 4.448221615260 newtons.

A familiar instrument for measuring forces is the spring balance. It consists of a coil spring, enclosed in a case for protection, with a pointer attached to one end. When forces are applied to the ends of the spring, it stretches; the amount of stretch depends on the force. We can make a scale and calibrate such an instrument by using a number of identical bodies with weights of exactly 1 N each. When two, three, or more of these are suspended simultaneously from the balance, the total force stretching the spring is 2 N, 3 N, and so on, and the corresponding positions of the pointer can be labeled 2 N, 3 N, and so on. Then we can use the spring balance to measure the magnitude of an unknown force. We can also make a similar instrument that measures pushes instead of pulls.

Suppose we slide a box along the floor by pulling it with a string or pushing it with a stick, as in Fig. 4–1. We are applying a force to the box, and this force is related to the motion of the box. The forces in the two cases can be represented as in Fig. 4–2; in each case the labels indicate the magnitude and direction of the force, and the lengths of the arrows (drawn to some scale, such as 1 cm = 5 N) also show the magnitude.

What happens when *two* forces, represented by the vectors F_1 and F_2 in Fig. 4–3, are applied at the same time to a point A of a body? Experiment shows that the effect of these two forces acting together is the same as the effect of a single force equal to the *vector sum* $R = F_1 + F_2$ of the original forces. This single force R is often called the **resultant** of the two forces. So we see that the vector sum, which we defined in Section 1–7 for displacement vectors, is also applicable to force vectors. More generally, the effect of any number of forces applied at a point on a body is the same as the effect of a single force equal to the vector sum, or resultant, of the forces.

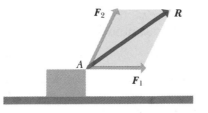

4-3
A force represented by the vector **R**, equal to the vector sum of F_1 and F_2, produces the same effect as the forces F_1 and F_2 acting simultaneously.

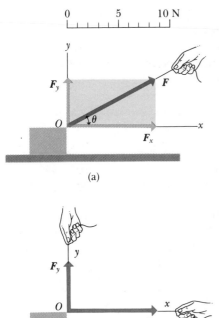

(a)

(b)

4-4
The inclined force **F** may be replaced by its rectangular components F_x and F_y. $F_x = F \cos \theta$, $F_y = F \sin \theta$.

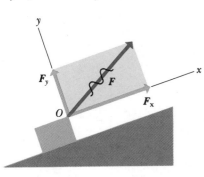

4-5
F_x and F_y are the rectangular components of **F**, parallel and perpendicular to the sloping surface of the inclined plane.

The fact that forces can be combined by vector addition is of the utmost importance, and we will use this fact many times in later chapters. This fact allows us to represent a force by means of *components*, as we did with displacements in Section 1–8. In Fig. 4–4a, force **F** acts on a body at point O. The component vectors of **F** in the directions Ox and Oy are F_x and F_y. When F_x and F_y are applied simultaneously, as in Fig. 4–4b, the effect is exactly the same as the effect of the original force. *Any force can be replaced by its components, acting at the same point.*

As a numerical example, let

$$F = 10.0 \text{ N}, \qquad \theta = 30°.$$

Then

$$F_x = F \cos \theta = (10.0 \text{ N})(0.866) = 8.66 \text{ N},$$

$$F_y = F \sin \theta = (10.0 \text{ N})(0.500) = 5.00 \text{ N},$$

and the effect of the original 10.0-N force is equivalent to a force to the right with magnitude 8.66 N and a lifting force with magnitude 5.00 N applied at the same time.

There is no law that says our coordinate axes have to be vertical and horizontal. Figure 4–5 shows a box being pulled up a loading ramp by a force **F**, represented by its components F_x and F_y, parallel and perpendicular to the sloping surface of the ramp. The wiggly line drawn through the force vector **F** shows that we have replaced it by its x- and y-components.

We will often need to find the vector sum (resultant) of several forces acting on a body. We will use the Greek letter Σ (capital "sigma," equivalent to the Roman S) as a shorthand notation for a sum. If the forces are labeled F_1, F_2, F_3, and so on, and their resultant is **R**, then we abbreviate the operation as

$$R = F_1 + F_2 + F_3 + \cdots = \sum F, \qquad (4\text{-}1)$$

where **Σ**F is read as "sum of the forces." The component version of Eq. (4–1) is the pair of equations

$$R_x = \sum F_x,$$
$$R_y = \sum F_y, \qquad (4\text{-}2)$$

where ΣF_x is the sum of the x-components, and so on. Each component may be positive or negative; be careful with signs when you evaluate the sums in Eqs. (4–2). Equation (4–1) uses a boldface **Σ** as a reminder that the sum is a vector sum, and Eqs. (4–2) use a lightface Σ because components are ordinary numbers.

Once we have R_x and R_y, we can find the magnitude and direction of R. The magnitude is

$$R = \sqrt{R_x^2 + R_y^2},$$

and the angle θ between R and the x-axis can be found from the relation $\tan \theta = R_y/R_x$. The components R_x and R_y may be positive or negative, and the angle θ may be in any of the four quadrants.

Example 4–1   In Fig. 4–6a, three forces F_1, F_2, F_3 lying in the xy-plane act at point O. Let $F_1 = 120$ N, $F_2 = 200$ N, $F_3 = 150$ N, $\theta = 60°$, and $\phi = 45°$. Find the x- and y-components of the resultant or vector sum R, and find its magnitude and direction.

Solution   The computations can be arranged systematically as in the following table.

Force	Angle	x-component	y-component
$F_1 = 120$ N	0	+120 N	0
$F_2 = 200$ N	60°	+100 N	+173 N
$F_3 = 150$ N	45°	−106 N	−106 N

$$R_x = \sum F_x = 114 \text{ N}, \qquad R_y = \sum F_y = 67 \text{ N},$$

$$R = \sqrt{(114 \text{ N})^2 + (67 \text{ N})^2} = 132 \text{ N},$$

$$\alpha = \arctan \frac{67 \text{ N}}{114 \text{ N}} = \arctan 0.588 = 30.4°.$$

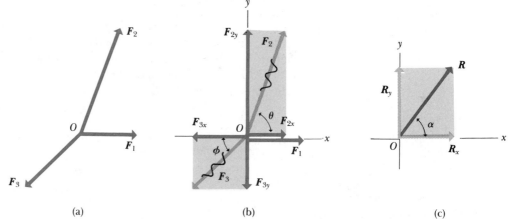

(a)   (b)   (c)

4–6
Vector R, the resultant of F_1, F_2, and F_3, is obtained by the method of rectangular resolution. The rectangular components of R are $R_x = \Sigma F_x$ and $R_y = \Sigma F_y$.

4–2
Equilibrium and Newton's First Law

When a force acts on a body, it can change the state of motion of the body. A body that is initially at rest can start to move, for example. When several forces act at the same time, their effects can compensate for or cancel one another. When this happens, there is *no* change in the motion, and we say that the body is in **equilibrium.** This means that it either remains at rest or moves in a straight line with constant velocity.

In Fig. 4–7 a small body such as a hockey puck rests on a horizontal surface with negligible friction, such as an air-hockey table or a slab of wet ice. Our idealized model for the body is a single point. If the body is initially at rest and a single force F_1 acts on it, as in Fig. 4–7a, the body starts to move. If the body is in motion at the start, the force makes it speed up, slow down, or change direction, depending on the direction of the force. In any of these cases the body is *not* in equilibrium.

Now suppose we apply a second force F_2, as in Fig. 4–7b, equal in magnitude to F_1 but opposite in direction. When we do the experiment, we find that the body is then in equilibrium. If it is at rest at the start, it remains at rest; if it is initially moving, it continues to move in the same direction with constant speed. In this case the two forces are negatives of each other, $F_2 = -F_1$, and their vector sum is zero.

$$R = F_1 + F_2 = 0.$$

For brevity, we speak of two forces as being "equal and opposite" when they have equal magnitudes and opposite directions.

We can generalize this result to a body with any number of forces acting on it. When a body is in equilibrium, the vector sum, or resultant, of all the forces acting on it must be zero. Each component of the resultant must therefore be zero. Hence for a body in equilibrium

$$R = \sum F = 0. \qquad (4-3)$$

Also, since each component of R must be zero,

$$\sum F_x = 0,$$
$$\sum F_y = 0. \qquad (4-4)$$

When Eqs. (4–4) are satisfied, the body is in equilibrium, provided that it may be represented as a point or that all the forces acting on it are applied at the same point.

This condition for equilibrium is called *Newton's first law of motion.* Newton's original statement, translated from the Latin of the *Principia*, was:

> Every body continues in its state of rest, or of uniform motion in a straight line, unless it is compelled to change that state by forces impressed on it.

Newton's first law of motion states that when no force is applied to a body, it either remains at rest or moves with constant velocity in a

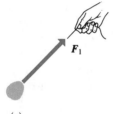

F_1

(a)

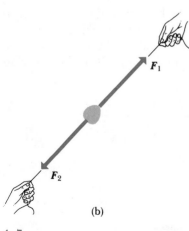

F_1

F_2

(b)

4–7
A small body acted on by two forces is in equilibrium if the forces are equal in magnitude and opposite in direction.

straight line. It follows that *once a body has been set in motion, no force is needed to keep it moving.*

This statement may seem to be contradicted by everyday experience. Suppose you push a book along a horizontal tabletop with your hand. After you stop pushing it (and applying a force to it), it does *not* continue to move indefinitely; it slows down and eventually stops. To keep it moving uniformly, you have to continue to push it. But this is because as the book slides, the tabletop applies a frictional force to it in a direction *opposite* to the book's motion. The smoother the surfaces of the book and table, the smaller the frictional force and the smaller the force we need to apply to keep the book moving. The first law states that if we could eliminate the frictional force completely, we would need *no* forward force at all to keep the book moving, once it had been started. The law also states that when the *resultant* force on the book is zero, as it is when the resisting frictional force is balanced by an equal forward force, the book continues to move uniformly. In other words, to keep the book moving with constant velocity, *zero resultant force is equivalent to no force at all.*

4–3
Mass and Newton's Second Law

When a body is at rest, some other body has to apply a push or pull to it to make it start to move. Similarly, to slow down or stop a body that is already in motion also requires a force. To change the *direction* of motion of a moving body, we have to apply a sideways force, that is, in a direction different from the direction of motion. Each of these processes (speeding up, slowing down, or changing direction) involves a change in either the magnitude or the direction of the velocity. In each case the body has an *acceleration*, and a force must act on it to cause this acceleration.

Here are several fundamental experiments. A small body, which we may model as a particle, rests on a level, frictionless surface and moves to the right along the x-axis of a coordinate system, as in Fig. 4–8a. We apply a constant horizontal force *F* to the body. This force might be supplied by a spring balance, as described in Section 4–1, with the spring

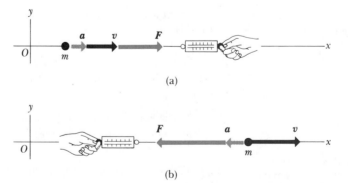

(a)

(b)

4–8
The acceleration *a* is proportional to the force *F* and is in the same direction as the force.

stretched a constant amount. We find that during the time the force is acting, the velocity of the body changes at a constant rate; that is, the body moves with *constant acceleration*. If the magnitude of the force is changed, the acceleration changes in the same proportion. Doubling the force doubles the acceleration, halving the force halves the acceleration, and so on. When the force is removed, the acceleration becomes zero; the body then moves with constant velocity, as we discussed in Section 4–2. The *rate of change* of velocity for a given body is directly proportional to the force acting on the body.

In Fig. 4–8b the velocity of the body is also toward the right, but the *force* is toward the left. Under these conditions the body moves more and more slowly to the right until it stops. It then reverses its direction of motion and begins to move more and more rapidly toward the left. During this entire process the direction of the acceleration is toward the *left*, in the same direction as the force *F.* Hence the *magnitude* of the acceleration is proportional to that of the force, and the *direction* of the acceleration is the *same* as that of the force, regardless of the direction of the velocity.

Because the acceleration of a body is directly proportional to the force exerted on it, the *ratio* of the force to the acceleration is a constant, regardless of the magnitude of the force. We call this ratio the inertial mass or simply the **mass** of the body, denoted by m. That is, $m = F/a$, or

$$F = ma. \tag{4–5}$$

We can think of the mass of a body as the *force per unit of acceleration*. For example, if the acceleration of a certain body is 5 m·s^{-2} when the force is 20 N, the mass of the body is

$$m = \frac{20 \text{ N}}{5 \text{ m·s}^{-2}} = 4 \text{ N·(m·s}^{-2})^{-1},$$

and a force of magnitude 4 N must act on the body for each m·s^{-2} of acceleration.

When a large force is needed to give a body a certain acceleration, the mass of the body is large; if only a small force is needed for the same acceleration, the mass is small. The greater the mass, the more the body "resists" being accelerated. Thus the mass of a body is a quantitative measure of the property that in everyday life we call *inertia*.

We can use Eq. (4–5) to compare and thus measure masses. Suppose we apply a certain force F to a body having a known mass m_1 and we find an acceleration a_1. We then apply the *same* force to another body having an unknown mass m_2, and we find an acceleration a_2. Then, according to Eq. (4–5),

$$m_1 a_1 = m_2 a_2,$$

or

$$\frac{m_2}{m_1} = \frac{a_1}{a_2}. \tag{4–6}$$

The ratio of the masses is the inverse of the ratio of the accelerations.

When two bodies with masses m_1 and m_2 are fastened together, the mass of the composite body is always found to be $m_1 + m_2$. This additive property of mass may seem obvious, but it has to be verified experimentally. The concept of mass is one way to define "quantity of matter" in a precise way.

So far we have talked about a particle moving along a straight line (the x-axis), with a force that also lies along this direction. This is a special case, of course. The force may also have a component in the y-direction, and the particle's path may curve. Also, more than one force may act on the particle. So we need to generalize our formulation to include motion in a plane or in space and the possibility of several forces acting simultaneously.

A fundamental natural law, confirmed by many experiments, is that *when several forces act on a particle at the same time, the acceleration is the same as would be produced by a single force equal to the vector sum of these forces.* This sum is usually most conveniently handled by use of the method of components. Thus when several forces act on a particle moving along the x-axis,

$$\sum F_x = ma_x. \tag{4–7}$$

When a particle moves in a plane, with position described by coordinates (x, y), its velocity is a vector quantity with components v_x and v_y equal to the time rates of change of x and y, respectively. Its acceleration is a vector quantity with components a_x and a_y equal to the rates of change of v_x and v_y, respectively. Then a more general formulation of the relation of force to acceleration is

$$\sum F_x = ma_x,$$
$$\sum F_y = ma_y. \tag{4–8}$$

This pair of equations is equivalent to the single vector equation

$$\sum \mathbf{F} = m\mathbf{a}. \tag{4–9}$$

We write the left-hand side explicitly as $\Sigma \mathbf{F}$ to emphasize that the acceleration is determined by the resultant of all the forces acting on the particle. If the particle moves in three dimensions, then Eqs. (4–8) include a third equation for the z-components, $\Sigma F_z = ma_z$.

Equation (4–9), or the equivalent pair of equations (4–8), is the mathematical statement of Newton's *second law of motion.* The acceleration of a body (the rate of change of its velocity) is equal to the vector sum (resultant) of all forces acting on the body, divided by its mass. The acceleration has the same direction as the resultant force.

In this chapter we consider only straight-line motion, and we always take the line to be a coordinate axis. In these problems, $\mathbf{v}$ and $\mathbf{a}$ have components only along this axis. Individual forces may have components along directions other than this axis, but the *sum* of these other components will always be zero. In Chapter 5 we will consider more general motion in which v_y, a_y, and ΣF_y need not be zero.

4–4
Systems of Units

Before we can put Newton's second law to work in practical problems, we need to discuss the *units* that we use to measure force, mass, and acceleration. From the equation $\Sigma F = ma$ it is clear that a force of one unit gives a mass of one unit an acceleration of one unit, no matter what system we use. Thus the three units cannot be chosen independently; once we choose units for mass and acceleration, the unit of force is determined.

In this book our principal unit system is the International System (SI), which we introduced in Section 1–3. This system is used worldwide, not only for scientific work but also for commerce and industry. The United States and England are among the few nations that do not use SI units exclusively; England and much of U.S. industry are in the process of converting.

In Section 1–3 we described the definitions of the basic SI units, the meter, the kilogram, and the second. We now define the SI unit of force as *the magnitude of force that gives an acceleration of* 1 m·s^{-2} *to a body with mass one kilogram.* This unit of force is called one **newton** (1 N). Thus in SI units,

$$F \text{ (N)} = m \text{ (kg)} \times a \text{ (m·s}^{-2})$$

and

$$1 \text{ N} = 1 \text{ kg·m·s}^{-2}.$$

These are very useful relationships to remember; we will use them often in the next several chapters.

In the *centimeter-gram-second* (cgs) system, the unit of mass is one gram (1 g), equal to 1/1000 kg, and the unit of acceleration is 1 cm·s^{-2}. The unit of force is called *one dyne* (abbreviated as *dyn*); 1 dyne gives 1 gram an acceleration of 1 cm·s^{-2}. Since 1 kg = 10^3 g and 1 m·s^{-2} = 10^2 cm·s^{-2}, it follows that 1 N = 10^5 dyn. In the cgs system,

$$F \text{ (dyn)} = m \text{ (g)} \times a \text{ (cm·s}^{-2}) \quad \text{and} \quad 1 \text{ dyn} = 1 \text{ g·cm·s}^{-2}.$$

The British system is defined somewhat differently. We first select a unit of force, the pound (or pound-force), abbreviated lb (or lbf). Then we define the unit of mass as *the mass of a body whose acceleration is* 1 ft·s^{-2} *when the resultant force on the body is* 1 lb. This unit of mass in the British system is called *one slug.*

$$F \text{ (lb)} = m \text{ (slugs)} \times a \text{ (ft·s}^{-2}) \quad \text{and} \quad 1 \text{ lb} = 1 \text{ slug·ft·s}^{-2}.$$

The pound is used in everyday life to describe a quantity of matter (for example, a pound of butter); but properly speaking, it is a unit of *force* or *weight*. Thus a pound of butter is an amount having a *weight* of 1 lb. A useful fact in converting between SI and British units is that a body with a *mass* of 1 kg has a *weight* of about 2.2 lb (more precisely, 2.2046 lb).

The units of force, mass, and acceleration in the three systems are summarized in Table 4–1.

TABLE 4–1

System of units	Force	Mass	Acceleration
SI	newton (N)	kilogram (kg)	m·s^{-2}
cgs	dyne (dyn)	gram (g)	cm·s^{-2}
British	pound (lb)	slug	ft·s^{-2}

Here is an important problem-solving tip. Because of the above definitions, units of force are equivalent to units of mass times acceleration; for example, $1 \text{ N} = 1 \text{ kg·m·s}^{-2}$. When you check equations for consistency of units, it is always appropriate to replace "N" wherever it appears by "kg·m·s^{-2}." Similarly, 1 lb can always be replaced by 1 slug·ft·s^{-2}.

4–5
Mass and Weight

In the introductory discussion of force in Section 4–1 we mentioned that the **weight** of a body on earth, a familiar kind of force, is the result of the earth's gravitational attraction for the body. We will study gravitational interactions in detail in Chapter 6, but we need some preliminary discussion now. The terms *mass* and *weight* are often misused and interchanged in everyday conversation; it is absolutely essential for you to understand clearly the distinctions between these two physical quantities.

Mass, as we have seen, characterizes the *inertial* properties of a body. The greater the mass, the greater the force needed to cause a given acceleration; this meaning is reflected in Newton's second law, $\Sigma \boldsymbol{F} = m\boldsymbol{a}.$ Weight, on the other hand, is a *force*, exerted on a body by the pull of the earth or some other large body. Everyday experience shows us that bodies having large mass also have large weight; a cart loaded with bricks is hard to get rolling because of its large mass, and it is also hard to lift off the ground because of its large weight. On the moon the cart would be just as hard to get rolling, but it would be easier to lift. So what exactly *is* the relationship between mass and weight?

The answer to this question, according to legend, came to Newton as he sat under an apple tree watching the apples fall. A freely falling body has an acceleration equal to g; and because of Newton's second law, this requires a force. If a 1-kg body falls with an acceleration of 9.8 m·s^{-2}, the required force has magnitude

$$F = ma = (1 \text{ kg})(9.8 \text{ m·s}^{-2}) = 9.8 \text{ kg·m·s}^{-2} = 9.8 \text{ N}.$$

But the force that makes the body accelerate downward is the gravitational pull of the earth, that is, the *weight* of the body. Any body with a mass of 1 kg *must* have a weight of 9.8 N to give it the acceleration we observe when it is in free fall. More generally, a body with mass m must have weight with magnitude w given by

$$w = mg. \tag{4–10}$$

Although we have introduced g as the acceleration of a freely falling body, its significance goes deeper than that. It represents an entity called *gravitational field*. We will study gravitational field in detail in Chapter 6, but here is a brief preview. The earth, the moon, or any other massive body sets up in the space around it a force field called a gravitational field. This field has the property that it exerts a force on any particle that is present in the field. Gravitational field is a vector quantity. Its magnitude, denoted by g, may vary from one point to another; its direction is the same as that of the force it exerts on a particle in the field. A particle with mass m in a gravitational field with magnitude g experiences a gravitational force with magnitude mg in the direction of the field.

The value of g varies somewhat from point to point on the earth's surface, from about 9.78 to 9.82 m·s^{-2}. There are several reasons for this. The earth is not perfectly spherical but is flattened at the poles and is a little fatter in the southern hemisphere than in the northern. Its density is not uniform, and the gravitational force depends on elevation, that is, on the distance from the center of the earth. There are further complications associated with its rotation and orbital motion; these make the observed acceleration of free fall slightly different from the actual gravitational field at a given point.

At a point where $g = 9.80$ m·s^{-2}, the weight of a standard kilogram is $w = 9.80$ N. At a different point, where $g = 9.78$ m·s^{-2}, the weight is $w = 9.78$ N but the mass is still 1 kg. The weight of a body varies from one location to another; the mass does not. If we take a standard kilogram to the surface of the moon, where the acceleration of free fall (equal to the gravitational field at the moon's surface) is 1.67 m·s^{-2}, its weight is 1.67 N but its mass is still 1 kg.

The weight of a body is a force, a vector quantity, and we can write Eq. (4–10) as a vector equation:

$$\mathbf{w} = m\mathbf{g}. \tag{4–11}$$

It is important to understand that the weight of a body, as given by Eq. (4–11), acts on the body *all the time*, whether it is actually in free fall or not. The gravitational field is there all the time, whether or not the body is moving. When a 1-kg body hangs suspended from a string, it is in equilibrium, and its acceleration is zero. But its weight is still acting on it and is given by Eq. (4–11). In this case the string pulls up on the body, applying an upward force. The *vector sum* of the forces is zero, and the body is in equilibrium.

There are various ways to measure the mass of a body. One way is to use the relationship $m = F/a$; we apply a known force to the body, measure its acceleration, and compute the mass as the ratio of force to acceleration. This method, or a variation of it, is used to measure the masses of atomic and subatomic particles and of astronauts in orbiting space stations.

Another method is to use a comparison technique, finding by trial some other body or collection of bodies of known mass, whose total mass is equal to that of the given body. Usually, it is easier to compare *weights* than masses. If the weights of two bodies at a given location are equal, their masses are also equal. Balances can be used to determine with great precision (up to 1 part in 10^6) when the weights of two bodies are equal and hence when their masses are equal. This method doesn't work in the zero-gravity environment of outer space. Why not?

The concept of mass plays two rather different roles in mechanics. The weight of a body, the gravitational force acting on it, is proportional to its mass, so mass is *the property of matter that causes bodies to exert gravitational forces on each other*. We may call this property *gravitational mass*. On the other hand, Newton's second law tells us that the force (which need not be gravitational) needed to cause a certain acceleration of a body is proportional to its mass. This inertial property of the body may be called its *inertial* mass.

So how do we know that the *gravitational* mass of a particular particle has to be the same as its *inertial* mass? Experiment! Extraordinarily precise experiments have established with a precision of better than 1 part in 10^{12} that in fact the two *are* the same. If we have to push twice as hard on body A as on body B to cause a given acceleration, then the *weight* of A at a given location is precisely twice that of body B at the same location. This equivalence is also the fundamental reason that the acceleration of free fall is independent of mass.

Finally, we remark that the SI units for mass and weight are often misused in everyday life. Incorrect expressions such as "This box weighs 6 kg" are nearly universal. What is meant, of course, is that the *mass* of the box, probably determined indirectly by *weighing*, is 6 kg. This usage is so common that there is probably no hope of straightening things out, but be sure you recognize that the term *weight* is often used when *mass* is meant. To keep your own thinking clear, be careful to avoid that kind of mistake!

4–6
Newton's Third Law

A force acting on a body is always the result of its interaction with another body. During this interaction, forces act on *both* bodies; I can't push on you unless you push back on me at the same time. Whenever one body exerts a force on another, the second body exerts simultaneously on the first a force that is equal in magnitude and opposite in direction to the force of the first on the second. It is impossible to have a single isolated force. A force on a body must be applied by some other body or bodies, and the second body experiences an equal and opposite force.

This property of forces is Newton's *third law of motion*. In his words,

> To every action there is always opposed an equal reaction; or, the mutual actions of two bodies upon each other are always equal, and directed to contrary parts.

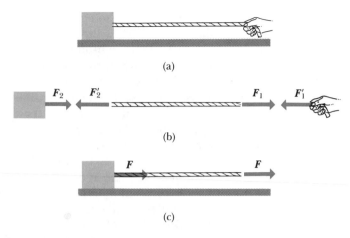

4–9
(a) A person pulls on a rope attached to a block. The forces that the rope exerts on the block and on the person are shown. (b) Separate diagrams showing the forces acting on the block, on the rope, and on the person. (c) If the rope is in equilibrium so that $F'_2 = -F_1$, the rope can be considered to transmit a force from the person to the block and vice versa.

The forces that two interacting bodies exert on each other are often called an **action** and a **reaction.** This does not imply that one is cause and the other result. *Either* force may be considered the action and the other the reaction.

Here is an example. A person pulls on one end of a rope attached to a box, as in Fig. 4–9. The box may or may not be in equilibrium. The resulting action–reaction pairs of horizontal forces are shown in the figure. (The forces all act along the line of the rope; the force vectors have been offset from this line to show them more clearly.) Vector F_1 represents the force exerted *on* the rope *by* the person. Its reaction is the equal and opposite force F'_1 exerted *on* the person *by* the rope. Vector F_2 represents the force exerted on the box by the rope. The reaction to it is the equal and opposite force F'_2 exerted on the rope by the box:

$$F'_1 = -F_1, \qquad F'_2 = -F_2. \tag{4–12}$$

It is very important to realize that the forces F_1 and F'_2, although they are opposite in direction and have the same line of action, are *not* an action–reaction pair. Both of these forces act on the *same* body (the rope); an action and its reaction *must* always act on *different* bodies. Furthermore, the forces F_1 and F'_2 are not necessarily equal in magnitude. These forces both act on the rope, and applying Newton's second law to the rope gives

$$F_1 + F'_2 = m_{\text{rope}}a_{\text{rope}}.$$

If the box and rope are accelerating to the right, the rope is not in equilibrium. In that case, F_1 has greater magnitude than F'_2. Only in the special case when the rope is in equilibrium are the forces F_1 and F'_2 equal in magnitude, but this is an example of Newton's *first* law, not his *third*. Even when the rope is accelerating, the action–reaction forces F_1 and F'_1 are still equal in magnitude to *each other*, as are F_2 and F'_2, from Newton's *third* law, but then F_1 is *not* equal in magnitude to F'_2.

In the special case when the rope is in equilibrium, or when we can consider it as massless, then F'_2 equals $-F_1$ because of Newton's *first* or *second* law. Also, F'_2 *always* equals $-F_2$ by Newton's *third* law, so in this special case, F_2 also equals F_1. We can then view the rope as "transmitting" to the box, without change, the force the person exerts on it, as in Fig 4–9c. This is a useful point of view, but you have to remember that it is valid only when the rope is massless or in equilibrium.

A body, such as the rope in Fig. 4–9, that has pulling forces applied at its ends is said to be in **tension.** The tension at any point equals the magnitude of force acting at that point. In Fig. 4–9b the tension at the right-hand end of the rope equals the magnitude of F_1 (or of F'_1), and the tension at the left-hand end equals the magnitude of F_2 (or of F'_2). If the rope is in equilibrium and if no forces act except at its ends, the tension is the same at both ends and throughout the rope. If the magnitudes of F_1 and F_2 are 50 N each, the tension in the rope is 50 N (*not* 100 N). Resist the temptation to add the two forces; remember that the total force $F_1 + F'_2$ on the rope in this case is zero!

Finally, we emphasize again a fundamental truth: The two forces in an action–reaction pair *never* act on the same body. Remembering this general principle can often help you avoid confusion about action–reaction pairs.

4–7
Examples

Here are several simple one-dimensional applications of Newton's laws. As you study them, watch for applications of the following strategy.

PROBLEM-SOLVING STRATEGY: *Newton's Laws*

1. Always define your coordinate system; a diagram showing the location of the origin and the positive axis direction is always helpful. If you know the direction of the acceleration, it is often convenient to take that as your positive direction.

2. Be consistent with signs. If the x-axis is horizontal and the right-hand end is defined as positive, then velocity, acceleration, and force components to the right are also positive.

3. In applying Newton's laws, always concentrate on a specific body. Draw a diagram showing all the forces (magnitudes and directions) acting *on* this body, but *do not* include forces that the body exerts on any other body. Such a diagram is called a **free-body diagram.** The acceleration of the body is determined by the forces acting *on* it, not by the forces it exerts on something else.

4. Identify the known and unknown quantities, and give each unknown an algebraic symbol.

5. Always check for unit consistency; use the conversion $1 \text{ N} = 1 \text{ kg·m·s}^{-2}$ when appropriate.

We will expand this strategy in Chapter 5 to deal with more complex problems. It is important for you to use it consistently from the start, however, to develop good habits in the systematic analysis of problems.

Example 4–2   A constant horizontal force with magnitude 2 N acts on a box of mass 4 kg resting on a level frictionless surface. What is the acceleration of the box?

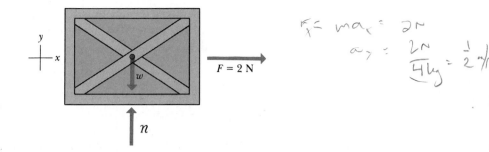

handwritten:
$F = ma_x = 2N$
$a_y = \frac{2N}{4kg} = \frac{1}{2} \, m/$

4–10
Free-body diagram for Example 4–2, showing side view of box.

Solution We take the $+x$-axis in the direction of the horizontal force. The free-body diagram (Fig. 4–10) includes this force and the two vertical forces, the weight w of the box and the upward supporting force n exerted on it by the surface. The acceleration is given by Newton's second law, Eq. (4–7); there is only one horizontal force, and we have

$$\sum F_x = ma_x, \qquad 2 \text{ N} = (4 \text{ kg})a,$$

$$a = \frac{F}{m} = \frac{2 \text{ N}}{4 \text{ kg}} = 0.5 \text{ N·kg}^{-1} = 0.5 \text{ (kg·m·s}^{-2})\text{·kg}^{-1} = 0.5 \text{ m·s}^{-2}.$$

The force is constant, so the acceleration is also constant. If we are given the initial position and velocity of the box, we can find the velocity and position at any later time from the equations of motion with constant acceleration. There is no vertical acceleration, so we know that the two vertical forces must sum to zero. ∎

Example 4–3 A student shoves a lab notebook of mass 0.2 kg toward the right along a level lab bench. As the book leaves contact with the student's hand, it has an initial velocity of 0.4 m·s^{-1}. As it slides, it slows down because of the horizontal friction force exerted on it by the bench top. It slides a distance of 1.0 m before coming to rest. What are the magnitude and direction of the friction force acting on it?

Solution Suppose the book slides along the x-axis in the $+x$-direction, starting at the point $x_0 = 0$ with the given initial velocity. A free-body diagram is shown in Fig. 4–11. We assume that the friction force is constant. The acceleration is then constant also; from Eq. (2–13) we have

$$v^2 = v_0^2 + 2ax,$$

$$0 = (0.4 \text{ m·s}^{-1})^2 + (2a)(1.0 \text{ m}),$$

$$a = -0.08 \text{ m·s}^{-2}.$$

handwritten: $v_0 = .4 \, m/s$

$v_0 = 0.4 \text{ m·s}^{-1}$

4–11
Free-body diagram for Example 4–3, showing side view of lab notebook.

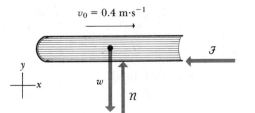

The negative sign means that the acceleration is toward the *left* (although the velocity is toward the right). The x-component $\mathcal{F}$ of the friction force on the book is

$$\mathcal{F} = ma = (0.2 \text{ kg})(-0.08 \text{ m·s}^{-2}) = -0.016 \text{ N}.$$

Again the negative sign shows that the force on the book is directed toward the left. ∎

Example 4–4   A machine part with a mass of 5 kg slides along a rail aligned with the x-axis; its acceleration is given as a function of time by

$$a = 6 \text{ m·s}^{-2} - (3 \text{ m·s}^{-3})t.$$

Find the force acting on the body, as a function of time. What is the force at time $t = 5$ s? For what times is the force positive? Negative? Zero?

Solution   The free-body diagram is just like the one for Example 4–2. From Newton's second law,

$$F = ma = (5 \text{ kg})[6 \text{ m·s}^{-2} - (3 \text{ m·s}^{-3})t]$$
$$= 30 \text{ N} - (15 \text{ N·s}^{-1})t.$$

At time $t = 5$ s the force is $30 \text{ N} - (15 \text{ N·s}^{-1})(5 \text{ s}) = -45 \text{ N}$. The force (as well as the acceleration) is zero when $6 \text{ m·s}^{-2} - (3 \text{ m·s}^{-3})t = 0$; that is, when $t = 2$ s. When $t < 2$ s, F is positive; when $t > 2$ s, F is negative. ∎

Example 4–5   A flowerpot having a mass of 10 kg is suspended by a chain from the ceiling. What is its weight? What force (magnitude and direction) does the chain exert on it? What is the tension in the chain? Assume that the weight of the chain itself is negligible.

Solution   Separate free-body diagrams for the flowerpot and the chain are shown in Fig. 4–12. We take the positive y-axis to be upward, as shown. The magnitude of the weight of the pot is given by Eq. (4–10):

$$w = (10 \text{ kg})(9.8 \text{ m·s}^{-2}) = 98 \text{ N}.$$

The y-component of this force is -98 N. The upward force exerted by the chain has magnitude T. The pot is in equilibrium, so the vector sum of forces acting on it must be zero. In particular, the sum of the y-components is

$$\sum F_y = T + (-98 \text{ N}) = 0, \qquad T = 98 \text{ N}.$$

Thus the chain must pull *up* with a force T of magnitude 98 N. By Newton's third law, the pot pulls *down* on the chain with a force of 98 N. The chain is also in equilibrium. We have assumed that the chain is weightless, so an upward force of 98 N must act on the chain at its top end to make the vector sum of forces on the *chain* equal zero. The tension in the chain is 98 N. ∎

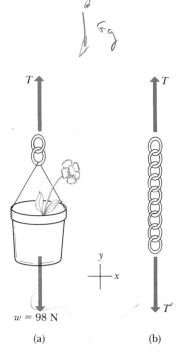

4–12
Free-body diagrams for Example 4–5.
(a) Forces acting on the flowerpot;
(b) forces acting on the chain. Each body is in equilibrium, and the sum of the forces on each must be zero. The weight of the chain is assumed to be negligible.

4–8
Inertial Frames of Reference

We always describe the motion of a body as it is seen by a particular observer, usually associated with some other body. The motion of a body looks different to different observers. A passenger in an airplane making its takeoff run is at rest relative to an observer on the airplane but is moving faster and faster relative to an observer standing on the earth. Any such observer, with coordinate axes and instruments to measure distance and time, is called a **frame of reference.** A coordinate system moving with the airplane is one frame of reference; a system that is stationary on earth is another.

Let's look at the passenger's motion in a frame of reference attached to the airplane. While the plane is accelerating down the runway, a passenger feels the back of his seat pushing him forward, but he remains at rest relative to the airplane. Therefore Newton's first law does not describe the situation correctly; a forward force acts on the passenger, but he does not accelerate relative to the airplane. That is, he remains at rest relative to the airplane.

Suppose, on the other hand, that the passenger is standing in the aisle on roller skates. This is unlikely but not inconceivable. When the takeoff run starts, the passenger starts to roll *backward* relative to the plane, even though no backward force acts on him. Again Newton's first law is not obeyed. So what's wrong?

The point is that Newton's first law is obeyed in some frames of reference and not in others. We now define an **inertial frame of reference** as a frame of reference in which Newton's first law *is* obeyed. Relative to an inertial frame, a body *does* remain at rest or move uniformly in a straight line when no force (or no resultant force) acts on it.

An airplane accelerating during takeoff is evidently *not* an inertial frame. We will often consider a reference frame attached to the earth to be an inertial frame, although it is not precisely so because of effects related to the earth's rotation and other motions. But if a frame of reference *is* inertial, then a second frame moving uniformly (that is, with constant speed in a straight line, without rotation) relative to it is *also* inertial. The reason is that any body in uniform motion, as seen by an observer in the first frame, will also appear to an observer in the second frame to be in uniform motion. The velocities measured by the two observers are not the same, but each is constant. But if the second frame accelerates relative to the first, then a body that the first observer sees moving with constant velocity will appear to the second observer to be accelerating. In that case, at least one of the frames must be noninertial.

This discussion shows that there is no single, unique inertial frame of reference. There are infinitely many, but the motion of any one relative to any other is uniform in the above sense. It follows that there is no such thing as "absolute rest" or "absolute motion." An airplane in steady flight is just as suitable an inertial frame of reference as the earth. You could play "catch" on the plane, if the flight attendant would let you, and the ball wouldn't behave any differently than when the plane is parked at the loading ramp.

In most of this book we assume that the earth is an adequate approximation to an inertial frame of reference. This assumption is then part of the idealized model that we construct for a mechanics problem. When a body at rest relative to the earth begins to move, or when a moving body speeds up, slows down, or changes direction, we know that a force must be acting on it, or perhaps several forces with a vector sum or *resultant* that is different from zero. The body's acceleration and the resultant force are related by Newton's second law. Like the first law, it is obeyed only in inertial frames of reference.

Questions

4–1 When a heavy weight is lifted by a string that is barely strong enough, the weight can be lifted by a steady pull, but if the string is jerked it will break. Why?

4–2 When a car accelerates, starting from rest, where is the force applied to the car to cause its acceleration? By what other body is the force exerted?

4–3 When a car stops suddenly, the passengers are thrown forward, away from their seats. What force causes this motion?

4–4 For medical reasons it is important for astronauts in outer space to determine their body mass at regular intervals. Devise a scheme for measuring body mass in a zero-gravity environment.

4–5 In SI units, suppose the fundamental units had been chosen to be force, length, and time instead of mass, length, and time. What would be the units of mass, in terms of the fundamental units?

4–6 When a bullet is fired from a gun, what is the origin of the force that accelerates the bullet?

4–7 Why can a person dive into water from a height of 10 m without injury, while a person who jumps off the roof of a 10-m building and lands on a concrete street is likely to be seriously injured?

4–8 A passenger in a bus notices that a ball that has been at rest in the aisle suddenly starts to move toward the rear of the bus. Think of two different possible explanations, and devise a way to decide which is correct.

4–9 Two bodies on the two sides of an equal-arm balance exactly balance each other. If the balance is placed in an elevator and given an upward acceleration, do they still balance?

4–10 If a woman in an elevator drops her briefcase but it does not fall to the floor, what can she conclude about the elevator's motion?

4–11 Suppose you are sealed inside a box on the planet Vulcan. After some time you notice that objects do not fall to the floor when released. How can you determine whether you and the box are in free fall or whether the Vulcans have somehow found a way to turn off the force of gravity?

4–12 Automotive engineers, in discussing the vertical motion of an automobile driving over a bump, call the rate of change of the acceleration the "jerk." Why is this a useful quantity in characterizing the riding qualities of an automobile?

Exercises

Section 4–1   Force

4–1 A raccoon pushes a tin box along the floor as in Fig. 4–1b with a force of 35.0 N that points downward at an angle of 30.0° below the horizontal. Using a scale of 1 cm = 5 N, find the horizontal and vertical components of the force by the graphical method. Check your results by calculating the components.

4–2 Two men pull horizontally on ropes attached to a post; the angle between the ropes is 38.0°. If man A exerts a force of 68.0 lb and man B a force of 50.0 lb, find the magnitude of the resultant force and the angle it makes with A's rope.

4–3 A man is dragging a trunk up the loading ramp of a mover's truck. The ramp has a slope angle of 20.0°, and the man pulls upward with force F whose direction makes an angle of 30.0° with the ramp.

a) How large a force F is necessary in order for the component F_x parallel to the plane to be 28.0 N?

b) How large will the component F_y then be?

4–4 Two forces, F_1 and F_2, act at a point. The magnitude of F_1 is 9.00 N, and its direction is 60.0° above the x-axis in the first quadrant. The magnitude of F_2 is 6.00 N, and its direction is 53.0° below the x-axis in the fourth quadrant.

a) What are the x- and y-components of the resultant force?

b) What is the magnitude of the resultant?

c) What is the magnitude of the vector difference $F_1 - F_2$?

Section 4–5   *Mass and Weight*

4–5

a) What is the mass of a book that weighs 3.00 N at a location where $g = 9.80$ m·s^{-2}?

b) At the same location, what is the weight of a dog whose mass is 12.0 kg?

4–6

a) What is the mass of a radio that weighs 6.00 lb at a location where $g = 32.0$ ft·s^{-2}?

b) At the same location, what is the weight of a television set whose mass is 0.900 slug?

4–7 At the surface of Mars the acceleration due to gravity is $g = 3.70$ m·s^{-2}. A watermelon weighs 45.0 N at the surface of the earth. What are its mass and weight on the surface of Mars?

Section 4–6   *Newton's Third Law*

4–8 Imagine that you are holding a book weighing 6 N at rest on the palm of your hand. Complete the following sentences:

a) A downward force of magnitude 6 N is exerted on the book by _____.

b) An upward force of magnitude _____ is exerted on _____ by the hand.

c) Is the upward force in part (b) the reaction to the downward force in part (a)?

d) The reaction to the force in part (a) is a force of magnitude _____, exerted on _____ by _____. Its direction is _____.

e) The reaction to the force in part (b) is a force of magnitude _____, exerted on _____ by _____. Its direction is _____.

f) The forces in parts (a) and (b) are equal and opposite because of Newton's _____ law.

g) The forces in parts (b) and (e) are equal and opposite because of Newton's _____ law.

Suppose now that you exert an upward force of magnitude 8 N on the book.

h) Does the book remain in equilibrium?

i) Is the force exerted on the book by the hand equal and opposite to the force exerted on the book by the earth?

j) Is the force exerted on the book by the earth equal and opposite to the force exerted on the earth by the book?

k) Is the force exerted on the book by the hand equal and opposite to the force exerted on the hand by the book?

Finally, suppose that you snatch your hand away while the book is moving upward.

l) How many forces then act on the book?

m) Is the book in equilibrium?

4–9 A bottle is given a push along a tabletop and slides off the edge of the table. Neglect air resistance.

a) What forces are exerted on the bottle while it is falling from the table to the floor?

b) What is the reaction to each force; that is, on what body and by what body is the reaction exerted?

Section 4–7   *Examples*

4–10 Boxes of several sizes rest on a frozen pond, which serves as a frictionless horizontal surface.

a) If a fisherman applies a force with magnitude 26.0 N to a box and produces an acceleration of 8.50 m·s^{-2}, what is the mass of the box?

b) What magnitude of force is required to give a 500-kg box an acceleration of 1.60 m·s^{-2}?

c) If a force with magnitude 58.0 N is applied to a box with mass 120 kg, what acceleration is produced?

4–11 World-class sprinters can accelerate out of the starting blocks with an acceleration that is nearly horizontal and of magnitude 15 m·s^{-2}. How much horizontal force does an 80-kg sprinter apply during his start to produce this acceleration?

4–12 A .22 rifle bullet, traveling at 360 m·s^{-1}, strikes a block of soft wood, which it penetrates to a depth of 0.150 m. The mass of the bullet is 2.40 g. Assume a constant retarding force.

a) How much time is required for the bullet to stop?

b) What force, in newtons, does the wood exert on the bullet?

4–13 A crate with mass 1.20 slugs initially at rest on a frictionless horizontal plane is acted on by a horizontal force of 14.0 lb.

a) What acceleration is produced?

b) How far does the crate travel in 10.0 s?

c) What is its speed at the end of 10.0 s?

4–14 A hockey puck with mass 0.250 kg is at rest at the origin $x = 0$ on a frictionless horizontal surface. At time $t = 0$ a player applies a force of 0.160 N to the puck, parallel to the x-axis; the player continues to apply this force until $t = 5.00$ s.

a) What are the position and speed of the puck at $t = 5.00$ s?

b) If the same force is again applied at $t = 15.0$ s, what are the position and speed of the puck at $t = 20.0$ s?

4–15 A dockworker applies a constant horizontal force of 54.0 N to a block of ice on a smooth horizontal plane. The block starts from rest and is observed to move 80.0 m in 5.00 s.

a) What is the mass of the block of ice?

b) If the worker stops pushing at the end of 5.00 s, how far does the block move in the next 5.00 s?

4–16 A force in the x-direction varies in time according to $F = (400 \ \text{N·s}^{-1})t - (150 \ \text{N·s}^{-3})t^3$. This force is applied to a large aluminum girder of mass 500 kg that is being moved into position for assembly as part of a space station.

a) What is the acceleration of the girder as a function of time?

b) For what range of times is the acceleration positive?

4–17 An electron (mass = 9.11×10^{-31} kg) leaves one end of a TV picture tube with zero initial speed and travels in a straight line to the accelerating grid which is 1.00 cm away. It reaches the grid with a speed of $4.00 \times 10^6 \ \text{m·s}^{-1}$. If the accelerating force is constant, compute

a) the acceleration;

b) the time to reach the grid;

c) the accelerating force, in newtons.

(The gravitational force on the electron may be neglected.)

Problems

4–18 Two forces F_1 and F_2 act on an object such that the resultant force R has a magnitude equal to that of F_1 and makes an angle of 90.0° with F_1. Let $F_1 = R = 25.0$ N. Find the magnitude of the second force, and its direction (relative to F_1).

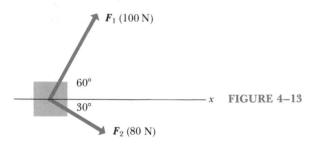

FIGURE 4–13

4–19 Two adults and a child want to push a crate in the direction marked x in Fig. 4–13. The two adults push with forces F_1 and F_2, whose magnitudes and directions are indicated in the figure. Find the magnitude and direction of the *smallest* force that the child should exert.

4–20 The resultant of four forces is 1200 N in the direction 30.0° west of north. Three of the forces are 400 N, 60.0° north of east; 200 N, south; and 400 N, 53.0° west of south. Find the magnitude and direction of the fourth force.

4–21 The three forces shown in Fig. 4–14 act on an object located at the origin.

a) Find the x- and y-components of each of the three forces.

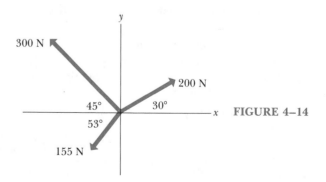

FIGURE 4–14

b) Find the magnitude and direction of the resultant of these forces.

c) Find the magnitude and direction of a fourth force that must be added to make the resultant force zero. Indicate the fourth force by a diagram.

4–22 A loaded elevator with very worn cables has a total mass of 1600 kg, and the cables can withstand a maximum total tension of 24,000 N.

a) What is the maximum upward acceleration for the elevator if the cables are not to break?

b) What is the answer to part (a) if the elevator is taken to the moon, where $g = 1.67$ m·s^{-2}?

4–23 According to the *Guinness Book of World Records*, basketball player Darrell Griffith holds the record for the standing vertical jump, with a jump of 1.2 m (4 ft). If Griffith weighs 890 N (200 lb) and the time of the jump before his feet leave the ground is 0.5 s, what is the average force he applies to the ground?

4–24 A 70.0-kg man climbs a vertical rope that is attached to the ceiling. The weight of the rope can be neglected. Calculate the tension in the rope if the man

a) climbs at a constant rate;

b) hangs motionless on the rope;

c) accelerates up the rope at 0.40 m·s^{-2};

d) slides down the rope with a downward acceleration of 0.40 m·s^{-2}.

4–25 An 80.0-kg man steps off a platform 3.20 m above the ground. He keeps his legs straight as he falls, but at the moment his feet touch the ground his knees begin to bend, and his torso moves an additional 0.60 m before coming to rest.

a) What is his speed at the instant his feet touch the ground?

b) What is the acceleration of his torso as he slows down if the acceleration is assumed to be constant?

c) What force do his feet exert on the ground while he slows down? Express this force in newtons and also as a multiple of his weight.

4–26 A parachutist relies on the drag force of her parachute to reduce her acceleration toward the earth. If she has a mass of 50.0 kg and her parachute drag supplies an upward force of 380 N, what is her acceleration?

Challenge Problem

4–27 If a beach ball with mass 0.0800 kg is thrown vertically upward in a vacuum, so there is no drag force on it, it reaches a height of 10.0 m. If the ball is thrown upward with the same initial velocity but in air instead of vacuum, its maximum height is 8.4 m. What is the drag force on the ball, assuming that it is constant during the upward motion of the ball?

5

Applications of Newton's Laws

Newton's laws of motion form the foundation for all of classical mechanics, including statics (the study of bodies in equilibrium) and dynamics (the general relationships between force and motion). In this chapter we present no new fundamental principles, but rather an opportunity to learn to apply Newton's laws to a variety of practical problems. We begin with a look at the various kinds of forces found in nature. Then we study the contact force between two bodies, including friction forces. Next we consider bodies in equilibrium, with an analysis that uses Newton's first and third laws and some vector language from Chapter 1. Finally, we work with Newton's second law, analyzing in detail the relationships between force and motion for bodies that are *not* in equilibrium. Along the way, we develop problem-solving strategies that can be used for both statics and dynamics problems.

5–1
Forces in Nature

Our present-day understanding of the physical world includes four distinct classes of forces. Two are familiar in everyday experience. The other two are concerned with interactions of fundamental particles and cannot be observed with the unaided senses.

Of the two familiar classes of force, **gravitational interactions** were the first to be studied in detail. The *weight* of a body results from the earth's gravitational attraction acting on it. The sun's gravitational attraction for the earth is responsible for making the earth move in a nearly circular orbit around the sun instead of the straight-line path it would follow if there were no force. Indeed, one of Newton's great achievements was to recognize that the motions of the planets around the sun and the free fall of objects on earth are both the result of gravitational forces. In Chapter 6 we will study gravitational interactions in greater detail, and we will analyze their vital role in the motions of planets and satellites.

The second familiar class of forces, **electromagnetic interactions,** includes electric and magnetic forces. When you run a comb through your hair, you can then use it to pick up bits of paper or fluff; this interaction is the result of electric charge on the comb. Magnetic forces occur in interactions between magnets or between a magnet and a piece of iron. These may seem to fall in a different category, but magnetic interactions are actually the result of electric charges in motion. Indeed, in an electromagnet an electric current in a coil of wire causes magnetic interactions. We will study electric and magnetic interactions in detail in the second half of this book.

These two interactions differ enormously in their strength. The electrical repulsion between two protons at a given distance is stronger than their gravitational attraction by a factor of the order of 10^{36}. Gravitational forces play no significant role in atomic or molecular structure. But in bodies of astronomical size, positive and negative charges are usually present in nearly equal amounts; the resulting electrical interactions nearly cancel out. Gravitational interactions alone remain, and they are the dominant influence in the motion of planets and also in the internal structure of stars.

The other two classes of interactions are less familiar. One, the **strong interaction,** is responsible for holding the nuclei of atoms together. Nuclei contain electrically neutral and positively charged particles; the charged particles repel each other, and a nucleus could not be stable if it were not for the presence of an attractive force of a different kind that counteracts the repulsive electrical interactions. In this context the strong interaction is also called the *nuclear force*. It has shorter range than electrical interactions, but within its range it is much stronger. The strong interaction is also responsible for the creation of exotic unstable particles in high-energy particle collisions.

Finally, there is the **weak interaction;** it plays no direct role in the behavior of ordinary matter, but it is of vital importance in interactions among fundamental particles. The weak interaction is responsible for beta decay, the emission of an electron (beta particle) from a radioactive nucleus by conversion of a neutron into a proton, an electron, and a neutrino. The weak interaction is also responsible for the decay of many unstable particles produced in high-energy collisions of fundamental particles.

Since about 1970, attempts have been made to understand all four classes of interactions on the basis of a single unified theory called a *grand unified theory* (GUT). Such theories are still speculative, and there are many unanswered questions. The experimental evidence of the last decade or so tends to support a unified theory of the electromagnetic and weak interactions. The entire area is a very active field of current research.

5–2
Contact Forces and Friction

When two bodies interact by direct contact (touching) of their surfaces, the interaction forces are called **contact forces.** On a microscopic level these forces result from electromagnetic interactions of charged particles of the atoms in the bodies. But in this chapter we will simply *describe* the interaction behavior of macroscopic bodies in terms of contact forces, without going into their electromagnetic basis.

To begin, let's think about a body sliding across a surface. It might be, for example, the lab notebook sliding across the bench in Example 4–3 (Section 4–7). To analyze the motion of the body, we need to know the forces acting on it. One of these is the force applied to the book by the surface; we call this force the *contact force*. Every contact force can always be represented in terms of a component perpendicular to the surface and a component parallel to the surface. We call the perpendicular component the **normal force,** denoted by $\mathcal{n}$. (*Normal* is a synonym for *perpendicular*.) The component parallel to the surface is the **friction force,** denoted by $\mathcal{f}$. By definition, $\mathcal{n}$ and $\mathcal{f}$ are always perpendicular. We use special script symbols for these quantities to emphasize their special role in representing the contact force. In addition, use of the script letter $\mathcal{n}$ avoids confusion with the abbreviation for newton, N.

If the body could slide without any resistance at all, there would be *no* friction force. In the real world this is an unattainable idealization, although driving a car on wet ice comes fairly close! A "frictionless surface" is a useful concept in idealized models of mechanical systems in which the friction force is negligibly small. In that case the contact force has *only* a normal component and is perpendicular to the surface.

The direction of the friction force on each interacting body is opposite to the motion of that body relative to the other. When a book slides from left to right along a tabletop, the friction force on it acts to the left. According to Newton's third law, the book applies to the table a force of equal magnitude, directed to the right; it tries to drag the table along with it.

The *magnitude* of the friction force usually increases when the normal force increases. There is more resistance to sliding when the surfaces are pushed more firmly together; this principle is used in automotive braking systems. In many cases the magnitude $\mathcal{F}$ of the friction force is found to be approximately *proportional* to the magnitude n of the normal force; in such cases we represent the relation by the equation

$$\mathcal{F}_k = \mu_k n, \tag{5–1}$$

where μ_k is a constant called the **coefficient of kinetic friction.** The adjective "kinetic" and the corresponding subscript k refer to the fact that the two surfaces are moving relative to each other.

The friction force and the normal force are always perpendicular, so Eq. (5–1) is *not* a vector equation but a relation between the *magnitudes* of the two forces.

The coefficient of kinetic friction depends on the materials and the surfaces. For Teflon on steel, μ_k is about 0.04; for rubber tires on rough dry concrete, μ_k can be as large as 1.0. The more slippery the surface, the smaller the coefficient of friction. Table 5–1 shows a few representative values of μ_k. Friction forces can also depend on the relative *velocity* of the interacting bodies; we will ignore that complication here in order to concentrate on the simplest cases.

TABLE 5–1	**Coefficients of friction**	
Materials	**Static, μ_s**	**Kinetic, μ_k**
Steel on steel	0.74	0.57
Aluminum on steel	0.61	0.47
Copper on steel	0.53	0.36
Brass on steel	0.51	0.44
Zinc on cast iron	0.85	0.21
Copper on cast iron	1.05	0.29
Glass on glass	0.94	0.40
Copper on glass	0.68	0.53
Teflon on Teflon	0.04	0.04
Teflon on steel	0.04	0.04
Rubber on concrete (dry)	1.0	0.8
Rubber on concrete (wet)	0.30	0.25

Friction forces may also act when there is *no* relative motion. For example, when we push on a heavy packing case, trying to slide it across the floor, the case may not move because the floor exerts an equal and opposite friction force on the case. This is called a **static friction** force $\mathcal{F}_s$.

Figure 5–1 shows a box at rest on a horizontal surface. Its weight w and the upward normal force n exerted on it by the surface have equal magnitude, and it is in equilibrium. Now we attach a rope to the box as in

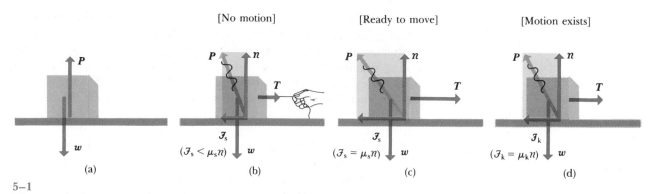

5–1
The magnitude of the friction force $\mathcal{F}_s$ is less than or equal to $\mu_s n$ when there is no relative motion and is equal to $\mu_k n$ when there is motion.

Fig. 5–1b and gradually increase the tension T in the rope. At first the box remains at rest because the force of static friction $\mathcal{F}_s$ is equal in magnitude and opposite in direction to the force T. As T increases, $\mathcal{F}_s$ also increases, staying equal in magnitude to T. (In each part of the figure the vector P represents the total contact force on the box, the vector sum of the normal and friction forces.)

When T reaches a certain critical value, the box suddenly "breaks loose" and starts to slide. This means that the force of static friction $\mathcal{F}_s$ is limited to a certain *maximum* value. When the applied force T exceeds the maximum friction force, the forces become unbalanced and the box starts to slide. Figure 5–1c is the force diagram when T is just below its critical value. If T exceeds this value, the box is no longer in equilibrium.

For a given pair of surfaces the maximum value of $\mathcal{F}_s$ depends on the normal force n; when n increases, the maximum friction force also increases, and a greater force is needed to make the box start to slide. In some cases the maximum value of $\mathcal{F}_s$ is approximately *proportional* to n; we call the proportionality factor μ_s the **coefficient of static friction.** The actual force of static friction can have any magnitude between zero (when there is no other force parallel to the surface) and a maximum value given by $\mu_s n$. In symbols,

$$\mathcal{F}_s \leq \mu_s n. \tag{5–2}$$

The equality sign holds only when the applied force T, parallel to the surface, has reached the critical value at which motion is about to start (Fig. 5–1c). When T is less than this value (Fig. 5–1b), the inequality sign holds. In that case we have to use the equilibrium conditions ($\Sigma F = 0$) to find $\mathcal{F}_s$. As soon as sliding starts, the friction force usually *decreases* because, as Table 5–1 shows, the coefficient of kinetic friction is usually *less* than the coefficient of static friction for any given pair of surfaces.

Table 5–1 lists values only for solids. Liquids and gases show frictional effects also, but the simple equation $\mathcal{F} = \mu n$ does not hold. Friction between two surfaces separated by a layer of liquid or gas is determined by the *viscosity* of the fluid. If a body can be made to slide on a layer of gas, friction can be made very small. A familiar laboratory example of this principle is the linear air track, shown in Fig. 5–2a. The

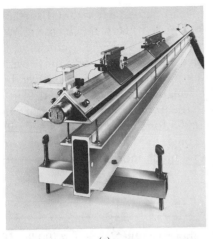

(a)

(b)

5-2
(a) The Ealing–Stull linear air track. Inverted Y-shaped sliders ride on a layer of air streaming through many fine holes in the inverted V-shaped surface. (b) The Ealing–Daw two-dimensional air table. Plastic pucks slide on a cushion of air issuing from more than a thousand minute holes in the tabletop. (Courtesy of the Ealing Corporation.)

frictional force is velocity-dependent, but at typical speeds the effective coefficient of friction is of the order of 0.001. A similar device is the frictionless air table shown in Fig. 5–2b. The pucks are supported by an array of small air jets about 2 cm apart. Two-dimensional collisions can be demonstrated on this table. The same principle is used in "air-hockey" games.

Example 5–1 Suppose the body shown in Fig. 5–1 is a 500-N crate full of home exercise equipment that a delivery company has just unloaded in your driveway. You find that to get it moving toward your garage, you have to push with a horizontal force of magnitude 200 N, but that once it is moving, you can keep it moving at constant speed with only 100 N. What are the coefficients of static and kinetic friction?

Solution When you are getting the crate moving, the appropriate force diagram is Fig. 5–1c. Remember that w, $\mathcal{N}$, and $\mathcal{F}$ are the *magnitudes* of the forces; some of the components have negative signs. For example, the magnitude of the weight is w, but its y-component is $-w$. Using the data above with the equilibrium conditions, Eqs. (4–4), we have

$$\sum F_y = \mathcal{N} + (-w) = \mathcal{N} - 500 \text{ N} = 0, \qquad \mathcal{N} = 500 \text{ N},$$

$$\sum F_x = T + (-\mathcal{F}_s) = 200 \text{ N} - \mathcal{F}_s = 0, \qquad \mathcal{F}_s = 200 \text{ N}.$$

$$\mathcal{F}_s = \mu_s \mathcal{N} \qquad \text{(motion about to start)}.$$

Hence

$$\mu_s = \frac{\mathcal{F}_s}{\mathcal{N}} = \frac{200 \text{ N}}{500 \text{ N}} = 0.40.$$

After the crate starts to move, the forces are as in Fig. 5–1d, and we have

$$\sum F_y = \mathcal{N} + (-w) = \mathcal{N} - 500 \text{ N} = 0, \qquad \mathcal{N} = 500 \text{ N},$$

$$\sum F_x = T + (-\mathcal{F}_k) = 100 \text{ N} - \mathcal{F}_k = 0, \qquad \mathcal{F}_k = 100 \text{ N}.$$

$$\mathcal{F}_k = \mu_k \mathcal{N} \qquad \text{(motion occurs)}.$$

Hence

$$\mu_k = \frac{\mathcal{F}_k}{\mathcal{N}} = \frac{100 \text{ N}}{500 \text{ N}} = 0.20. \qquad \blacksquare$$

Example 5–2 In Example 5–1, what is the friction force if the crate is at rest on the surface and a horizontal force of 50 N is applied to it?

Solution We have

$$\sum F_x = T + (-\mathcal{F}_s) = 50 \text{ N} - \mathcal{F}_s = 0. \qquad \text{(First law)}$$

$$\mathcal{F}_s = 50 \text{ N}.$$

In this case, $\mathcal{F}_s < \mu_s \mathcal{N}$. $\blacksquare$

It is a lot easier to move a heavy load across a horizontal surface using rollers or a cart with wheels than to slide it. How much easier? We can define a coefficient of rolling friction μ_r for a wheeled vehicle; μ_r is the ratio of the horizontal force needed to make the body move with constant speed on a flat surface, to the upward normal force exerted by the surface (equal in this case to the weight of the vehicle and load). Transportation engineers call this ratio the *tractive resistance*. Typical values of tractive resistance are 0.002 to 0.003 for steel wheels on steel rails and 0.01 to 0.02 for rubber tires on concrete. These values show one reason why railroad trains are in general much more fuel-efficient than highway trucks.

Example 5–3 A 1200-kg car weighs about 12,000 N (about 2700 lb). If the tractive resistance is $\mu_r = 0.01$, what horizontal force is needed to make the car move with constant speed?

Solution From the definition of tractive resistance, a horizontal force of $(0.01)(12,000 \text{ N}) = 120 \text{ N}$ (about 27 lb) is required. ∎

In addition to tractive resistance, rolling vehicles experience air drag. Air-resistance forces usually increase proportionally to the square of the speed. They are often negligible at low speeds but comparable to or greater than tractive resistance at highway speeds.

5–3
Equilibrium of a Particle

In this section we consider several problems involving the **equilibrium** of particles. The essential physical principle is Newton's first law: When a particle is at rest in an inertial frame of reference, the vector sum of all the forces acting on it must be zero. In symbols,

$$\sum F = 0. \tag{5–3}$$

We will usually use this in component form:

$$\sum F_x = 0,$$
$$\sum F_y = 0. \tag{5–4}$$

As in all problem-solving, a systematic approach is always helpful. We strongly recommend that you study the application of the following strategy in our examples and that you try to apply it in solving assigned problems.

PROBLEM-SOLVING STRATEGY: *Equilibrium of a Particle*

1. Make a simple sketch of the apparatus or structure, showing dimensions and angles.

2. Choose some body that is in equilibrium. Draw a diagram of this body by itself, without including the other bodies that interact with it. Show with arrows (use a colored pencil or pen) *all* of the forces exerted *on* it by other bodies. Don't forget the body's weight, the force the earth exerts on it. This diagram is called the *force diagram* or **free-body diagram.** *Do not* show, in the free-body diagram of a chosen body, any of the forces exerted *by it* on other bodies.

3. Draw a set of coordinate axes and represent each force acting on the particle in terms of its components. Cross out lightly those forces that have been replaced by their components. Often, one particular choice of axes can simplify the problem considerably. For example, when there is friction it is usually simplest to take the axes in the

directions of the normal and frictional forces, even when these are not vertical and horizontal.

4. Set the algebraic sum of all *x*-forces (or force components) equal to zero, and the algebraic sum of all *y*-forces (or components) equal to zero. This provides two independent equations, which can be solved simultaneously for two unknown quantities, which may be forces, angles, distances, etc.

5. If there are two or more bodies, repeat Steps 2 through 4 for the other bodies until you have as many independent equations as the number of unknown quantities.

6. Whenever possible, look at your results and ask whether they make sense. When the result is a symbolic expression or formula, try to think of special cases (particular values or extreme cases for the various quantities) for which you can *guess* what the results ought to be. Check to see that your formula works in these particular cases.

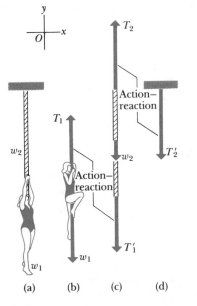

5–3
(a) Gymnast hanging at rest from vertical rope. (b) The gymnast is isolated, and all forces acting on her are shown. (c) Forces on the rope. (d) Downward force on the ceiling. Lines connect action–reaction pairs.

In diagrams it is often convenient to label force vectors with symbols that represent their *magnitudes*; in print we use light italic letters for these. The direction of each force can usually be found from the diagram, perhaps with the help of a labeled angle. Then when you find components of vectors, be careful to add a negative sign to any component that points in a negative axis direction.

Example 5–4   A gymnast has just begun climbing up a rope hanging from a gymnasium ceiling, as in Fig. 5–3a. She stops, suspended from the lower end of the rope by her hands. Her weight is 600 N, and the weight of the rope is 100 N. Analyze the forces on the gymnast and on the rope.

Solution   Figure 5–3b is a free-body diagram for the gymnast. The forces acting on her are her weight w_1 and the upward force T_1 exerted on her by the rope. We take the *x*-axis to be horizontal and the *y*-axis to be vertically upward; then there are no *x*-components of force. The *y*-components are those associated with the forces T_1 and w_1. Force T_1 acts in the positive *y*-direction, and its *y*-component is just the magnitude T_1, a positive (scalar) quantity. But w_1 acts in the negative *y*-direction, and its *y*-component is the *negative* of the magnitude w_1. Thus the algebraic sum of *y*-components is $T_1 + (-w_1)$. Then from the equilibrium condition,

$\Sigma F_y = 0$, we have

$$\sum F_y = T_1 + (-w_1) = 0,$$

$$T_1 = w_1. \quad \text{(First law)}$$

The tension at the bottom of the rope equals the gymnast's weight, which is certainly not surprising.

The forces w_1 and T_1 are *not* an action–reaction pair, although they are equal in magnitude and opposite in direction and have the same line of action. The weight w_1 is the earth's attractive force on the gymnast. Its reaction is the equal and opposite attractive force exerted *on* the earth *by* the gymnast. This force does not act *on* the gymnast, so it does not appear in the free-body diagram for the gymnast.

The reaction to the force T_1 is a downward force, T_1', of equal magnitude, exerted on the rope by the gymnast:

$$T_1 = T_1'. \quad \text{(Third law)}$$

The force T_1' is shown in Fig. 5–3c, which is the free-body diagram for the rope. The other forces on the rope are its own weight w_2 and the upward force T_2 exerted on its upper end by the ceiling. The y-component of T_2 is positive, while those of w_2 and T_1' are negative. The rope is also in equilibrium, so

$$\sum F_y = T_2 + (-w_2) + (-T_1') = 0,$$

$$T_2 = w_2 + T_1'. \quad \text{(First law)}$$

The reaction to T_2 is the downward force T_2' in Fig. 5–3d, exerted on the ceiling by the rope:

$$T_2 = T_2'. \quad \text{(Third law)}$$

With the numbers given, the gymnast's weight w_1 is 600 N, and the weight of the rope w_2 is 100 N. Then

$$T_1 = w_1 = 600 \text{ N},$$

$$T_1' = T_1 = 600 \text{ N},$$

$$T_2 = w_2 + T_1' = 100 \text{ N} + 600 \text{ N} = 700 \text{ N},$$

$$T_2' = T_2 = 700 \text{ N}.$$

The tension is greatest at the top of the rope, where it must support the weights of both the rope and the gymnast. ∎

Example 5–5 In Fig. 5–4a, a hanging lamp of weight w hangs from a cord that is knotted at point O to two other cords, one fastened to the ceiling and the other to the wall. We want to find the tensions in these three cords, assuming the weights of the cords to be negligible.

Solution To use the conditions of equilibrium to determine unknown forces (in this case, the tensions in the cords), we have to identify some body that is in equilibrium and on which the desired forces act. The suspended lamp is one such body; as shown in the preceding examples, the tension T_1 in the vertical cord supporting the lamp is equal in magni-

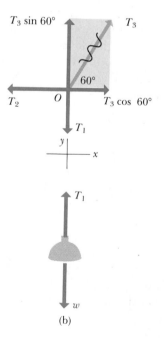

5–4
(a) A lamp of weight w is suspended from a cord knotted at O to two other cords. (b) Free-body diagrams for the lamp and for the knot, showing the components of force acting on each.

tude to the weight of the lamp. The other cords do not exert forces on the lamp (because they are not attached directly to it), but they do act on the knot at O. So let's consider the *knot* as a particle in equilibrium; the weight of the knot itself is negligible.

Free-body diagrams for the lamp and the knot are shown in Fig. 5–4b, where T_1, T_2, and T_3 are the *magnitudes* of the forces shown; the directions of these forces are indicated by the vectors on the diagram. An x–y coordinate axis system is also shown, and the force of magnitude T_3 has been resolved into its x- and y-components.

Considering the lamp first, we note that there are no x-components of force. The y-component of force exerted by the cord is in the positive y-direction and is just T_1. The y-component of the weight is in the negative y-direction and is $-w$. The equilibrium condition for the lamp, that the algebraic sum of y-components of force must be zero, is

$$T_1 + (-w) = 0, \quad \text{or} \quad T_1 = w.$$

The tension in the vertical cord equals the weight of the lamp; no surprises so far!

We now consider the knot at O. There are both x- and y-components of force acting on it, so there are two separate equilibrium conditions. The algebraic sum of the x-components must be zero, and the algebraic sum of y-components must separately be zero. (Note that x- and y-components are *never* added together in a single equation.) We find

$$\sum F_x = 0: \quad T_3 \cos 60° - T_2 = 0.$$

$$\sum F_y = 0: \quad T_3 \sin 60° - T_1 = 0.$$

Because $T_1 = w$, the second equation can be rewritten as

$$T_3 = \frac{T_1}{\sin 60°} = \frac{w}{\sin 60°} = 1.155w.$$

We can now use this result in the first equation:

$$T_2 = T_3 \cos 60° = (1.155w) \cos 60° = 0.577w.$$

Thus all three tensions can be expressed as multiples of the weight w of the lamp, which we assume is known. To summarize,

$$T_1 = w,$$

$$T_2 = 0.577w,$$

$$T_3 = 1.155w.$$

If the lamp's weight is $w = 50.0$ N, then

$$T_1 = 50.0 \text{ N},$$

$$T_2 = (0.577)(50.0 \text{ N}) = 28.9 \text{ N},$$

$$T_3 = (1.155)(50.0 \text{ N}) = 57.7 \text{ N}.$$

We note that T_3 is greater than the weight of the lamp. If this seems strange, note that T_3 must be large enough that its vertical component is equal to w in magnitude; thus T_3 itself must have somewhat *larger* magnitude than w. ∎

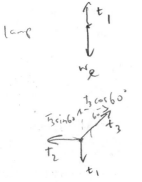

lamp

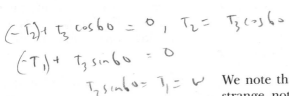

$(-T_2) + T_3 \cos 60 = 0 \,, \quad T_2 = T_3 \cos 60$

$(-T_1) + T_3 \sin 60 = 0$

$T_3 \sin 60 = T_1 = w$ ✓

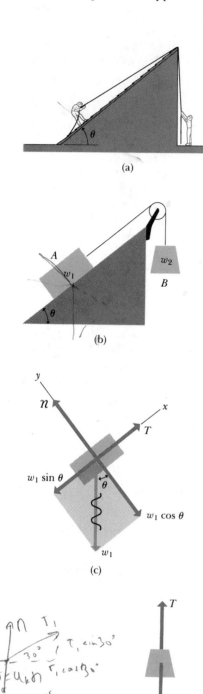

(a)

(b)

(c)

(d)

5-5
Forces on a body in equilibrium on a frictionless inclined plane. (a) The physical situation; (b) idealized model of situation; (c) free-body diagram for body A; (d) free-body diagram for body B.

$T_1 \cos 30° = f = \mu_k n = 0.2 n$

$T_1 \sin 30° + n = 500 N$

Example 5–6   A roof repairman with weight w_1 is trying to find a leak in an icy, perfectly frictionless roof with slope angle θ, as shown in Fig. 5–5a. He is secured by a rope with negligible mass that passes over the top and down the vertical side of the building. The other end of the rope is held by his helper (weight w_2) on the ground. The helper finds that to hold the man on the roof, he must put his full weight on the rope. If we know the weight w_1 of the roofer, what is the weight w_2 of the helper?

Solution   We represent the situation by the idealized model shown in Fig. 5–5b, where A is the roofer and B the helper. Free-body diagrams for the two bodies are shown in Fig. 5–5c and Fig. 5–5d. We label the forces with light italic symbols representing the *magnitudes* of these forces. The forces on body B are its weight w_2 and the force T exerted on it by the rope. Because it is in equilibrium,

$$T + (-w_2) = 0, \qquad T = w_2.$$

Body A is acted on by its weight w_1, the force T exerted on it by the rope, and the force n exerted on it by the plane. We use the same symbol T for the tensions at both ends of the rope because they are the same. The pulley, which corresponds to the frictionless top edge of the roof, changes the directions of the forces exerted by the rope but not their magnitudes. There is no friction, so the contact force can have no component along the plane that would resist the motion of the body on the plane. Hence it must be perpendicular or *normal* to the surface of the plane, and we call it n.

It is simplest to choose x- and y-axes parallel and perpendicular to the surface of the plane, because then only the weight w_1 needs to be resolved into components. The conditions of equilibrium for body A give

$$\sum F_x = T - w_1 \sin \theta = 0,$$
$$\sum F_y = n - w_1 \cos \theta = 0.$$

As a specific example, suppose $w_1 = 800$ N and $\theta = 30°$. Then

$$w_2 = T = w_1 \sin \theta = (800\ \text{N})(0.500) = 400\ \text{N},$$

and

$$n = w_1 \cos \theta = (800\ \text{N})(0.866) = 693\ \text{N}.$$

Note carefully that *if there is no friction*, the same weight w_2 of 400 N is required for equilibrium, whether the system remains at rest or moves with constant speed in *either* direction. This is *not* the case when friction is present.   ■

Example 5–7   In Example 5–1 (Section 5–2), suppose you try to move your crate full of exercise equipment by tying a rope around it and pulling upward on the rope at an angle of 30° above the horizontal. How hard do you have to pull to keep the crate moving with constant velocity? Assume $w = 500$ N and $\mu_k = 0.20$.

Solution   Figure 5–6 is a free-body diagram showing the forces on the crate. We note that the normal force n is *not* equal in magnitude to the weight of the crate because the force exerted by the rope has an additional vertical component that tends to lift the crate off the floor. From

$n = 5 t_1 \cos 30$

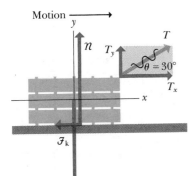

Motion ⟶

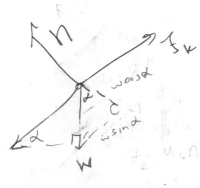

($\mathcal{F}_k = 0.2n$)

5–6
Forces on a crate being dragged to the right on a level surface at constant speed.

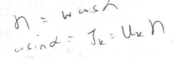

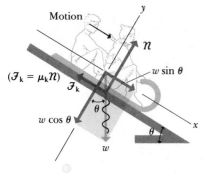

5–7
Forces on a toboggan sliding down a hill (with friction) at constant speed.

the equilibrium conditions,

$$F_x = T \cos 30° + (-\mathcal{F}_k) = T \cos 30° - 0.20n = 0,$$

$$F_y = T \sin 30° + n + (-500 \text{ N}) = 0.$$

These are two simultaneous equations for the two unknown quantities T and n. To solve them, we can eliminate one unknown and solve for the other. There are many ways to do this; here is one: Rearrange the second equation to the form

$$n = 500 \text{ N} - T \sin 30°.$$

Substitute this expression for n back into the first equation:

$$T \cos 30° - 0.20(500 \text{ N} - T \sin 30°) = 0.$$

Finally, solve this equation for T, then substitute the result back into either of the original equations to obtain n. The results are

$$T = 103 \text{ N}, \qquad n = 448 \text{ N}.$$

Note that the normal force is *less* than the weight and that the tension required is a little greater than what we needed (100 N) when we pulled horizontally. But work the problem again using $\theta = 11°$; if you do it right, you'll find $T = 98$ N. Try it! Does this result surprise you?   ∎

Example 5–8   A toboggan loaded with vacationing students (total weight w) slides down a long, snow-covered slope with a coefficient of kinetic friction μ_k. The slope has just the right angle to make the toboggan slide with constant speed. Derive an expression for the slope angle in terms of w and μ_k.

Solution   Figure 5–7 shows the free-body diagram. The forces on the toboggan are its weight w and the normal and frictional components of the contact force exerted on it by the plane. We take axes perpendicular and parallel to the surface of the plane and represent the weight in terms of its components in these two directions, as shown. The equilibrium conditions in component form are

$$\sum F_x = w \sin \theta + (-\mathcal{F}_k) = w \sin \theta - \mu_k n = 0,$$

$$\sum F_y = n + (-w \cos \theta) = 0.$$

Hence

$$\mu_k n = w \sin \theta, \qquad n = w \cos \theta.$$

Dividing the first of these equations by the second, we find

$$\mu_k = \frac{\sin \theta}{\cos \theta} = \tan \theta.$$

It follows that any body, regardless of its weight, slides down an inclined plane with a constant speed if the tangent of the slope angle of the plane equals the coefficient of kinetic friction. This result gives us a simple experimental method for measuring the coefficient of kinetic friction. Note that the greater the coefficient of friction, the steeper the plane has to be for the body to slide with constant velocity; this is just what we should expect.   ∎

5–4
Applications of Newton's Second Law

We are now ready to discuss **dynamics** problems, showing applications of Newton's second law to systems that are *not* in equilibrium. In this case,

$$\sum F = ma. \tag{5–5}$$

We will usually use this relation in component form:

$$\sum F_x = ma_x,$$
$$\sum F_y = ma_y. \tag{5–6}$$

The problem-solving strategy that we suggest below is very similar to our strategy for equilibrium problems in Section 5–3. We urge you to study it carefully, watch for its applications in our examples, and use it when you tackle the end-of-chapter problems.

PROBLEM-SOLVING STRATEGY: *Newton's Second Law*

1. Focus your attention on a particular moving body. You will apply Newton's second law to this body.

2. Draw a free-body diagram. Be sure to include all the forces acting *on* the chosen body, but be equally careful *not* to include any force exerted *by* the body on some other body. Some of the forces may be unknown; label these with algebraic symbols. Usually, one of the forces will be the body's weight, which you will usually label as *mg*. If a numerical value of mass is given, you can compute the corresponding weight.

3. Show your coordinate axes explicitly in the free-body diagram, and then determine components of forces with reference to these axes. When a force is represented in terms of its components, cross out the original force so as not to include it twice. If you know the direction of the acceleration, it is usually best to take its direction as that of either the *x*- or *y*-axis. When there are two or more bodies, you can use a separate axis system for each body; you don't *have* to use the same axis system for all the bodies.

4. If more than one body is involved, the above steps must be carried out for each body. In addition, the motions of the bodies may be related. For example, they may be connected by a rope. Express these relations in algebraic form as relations between the accelerations of the various bodies.

5. Write the Newton's-second-law equations, Eqs. (5–6), for each body, and solve to find the unknown quantities.

6. Check particular cases or extreme values of quantities, when possible, and compare the results for these particular cases with your intuitive expectations. Ask, "Does this result make sense?"

Example 5–9   A 10.0-kg block of ice is at rest on a horizontal surface. What constant horizontal force *T* do we need to apply to give it a velocity of 4.0 m·s^{-1} at the end of 2.0 s? The friction force between the block and the surface is constant and equal to 5.0 N.

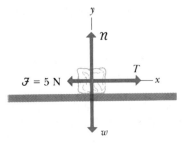

5–8
Force diagram for block in Example 5–9.

Solution Figure 5–8 shows a free-body diagram and a coordinate system. We can find the unknown force by using Eqs. (5–6) if we can find the acceleration, so let's start there. The y-component of acceleration is zero, and we can get the x-component from the velocity data. (The forces are all constant, so a_x is also constant.) We find

$$a_x = \frac{v - v_0}{t} = \frac{4.0 \text{ m·s}^{-1} - 0}{2.0 \text{ s}} = 2.0 \text{ m·s}^{-2}.$$

The sum of the x-components of force is

$$\sum F_x = T + (-\mathcal{F}).$$

(Note that the *magnitude* of the friction force, $\mathcal{F} = 5.0$ N, is a positive quantity but that the *component* of this force in the x-direction is negative, equal to $-\mathcal{F}$ or -5.0 N.) So Newton's second law gives

$$T + (-\mathcal{F}) = ma_x,$$
$$T = ma_x + \mathcal{F},$$
$$= (10.0 \text{ kg})(2.0 \text{ m·s}^{-2}) + 5.0 \text{ N} = 25 \text{ N}.$$

We need 5.0 N to overcome friction and 20 N more to give the block of ice the specified motion.

Note that we did not need the y-components at all in this problem. Here they are anyway:

$$a_y = 0,$$
$$\sum F_y = n + (-w) = 0,$$
$$n = w = mg = (10.0 \text{ kg})(9.8 \text{ m·s}^{-2}) = 98 \text{ N}. \quad ■$$

Example 5–10   An elevator and its load, shown in Fig. 5–9, have a total mass of 800 kg. The elevator is originally moving downward at 10 m·s^{-1}, and it is brought to rest with constant acceleration in a distance of 25 m. Find the tension T in the supporting cable.

Solution Again we can find the acceleration; this time we use the constant-acceleration formula $v^2 = v_0^2 + 2a(y - y_0)$. Taking the positive y-axis upward, we have $v_0 = -10$ m·s^{-1}, $v = 0$, and $y - y_0 = -25$ m. Then

$$(0)^2 = (-10 \text{ m·s}^{-1})^2 + 2a_y(-25 \text{ m}),$$
$$a_y = +2.0 \text{ m·s}^{-2}.$$

Note that even though the velocity is downward, the acceleration is upward, corresponding to downward motion with decreasing speed.

Now we are ready to use Newton's second law:

$$\sum F_y = T + (-w) = ma_y,$$
$$T = w + ma_y = mg + ma_y$$
$$= (800 \text{ kg})(9.8 \text{ m·s}^{-2}) + (800 \text{ kg})(2.0 \text{ m·s}^{-2}) = 9440 \text{ N}.$$

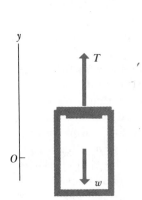

5–9
The resultant vertical force is $T - w$.

The tension must be 1600 N *greater* than the weight to cause the elevator to stop its descent.   ∎

Example 5–11   In Example 5–10, what force do a passenger's feet exert downward on the floor if the passenger's mass is 80.0 kg?

Solution   We first find the force the floor exerts *on* the passenger's feet, which is the reaction force to the force asked for. The forces on the passenger are his weight $(80.0 \text{ kg})(9.80 \text{ m·s}^{-2}) = 784$ N and the upward force F applied by the floor. The passenger's acceleration is the same as the elevator's, and Newton's second law gives

$$F + (-784 \text{ N}) = (80.0 \text{ kg})(2.00 \text{ m·s}^{-2}) = 160 \text{ N}$$

and

$$F = 944 \text{ N}.$$

While the elevator is stopping, the passenger pushes down on the floor with a force of 944 N, 160 N more than his weight. The passenger *feels* a greater strain in his legs and feet than when the elevator is stationary or moving with constant velocity.   ∎

Let's generalize this result. A passenger with mass m rides in an elevator with acceleration a. What force does the passenger exert on the floor? We invite you to follow the same analysis as above to show that

$$F = m(g + a),$$

where F is the magnitude of the action-reaction pair representing the floor-passenger interaction. When a is positive, the elevator is accelerating upward and F is greater than the passenger's weight $w = mg$; when it is accelerating downward, F is less than the weight. If the passenger doesn't know the elevator is accelerating, he may have the feeling that his weight is changing; indeed, if the passenger is standing on a bathroom scale, it reads F, not w. (Why?) We can think of F as the passenger's *apparent* weight. With upward acceleration, the apparent weight is greater than the true weight, and the passenger feels heavier; with downward acceleration he feels lighter. This is a real effect; try taking a few steps inside an elevator that is starting to move up or down after a stop.

The extreme case occurs when the elevator has a downward acceleration $a = -g$, that is, when it is in free fall. In that case, $F = 0$ and the passenger seems to be weightless. It is in this sense that an astronaut orbiting the earth in a space capsule is said to be "weightless." The effect of this condition is exactly the same as though the body were in outer space with no gravitational force at all. The physiological effect of prolonged weightlessness is an interesting medical problem that is being actively explored. Gravity plays an important role in blood distribution in the body; one reaction to weightlessness is a decrease in blood volume through increased excretion of water. In some cases, astronauts returning to earth have experienced temporary impairment of their sense of balance and a greater tendency toward motion sickness.

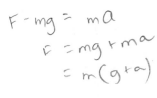

$$F - mg = ma$$
$$F = mg + ma$$
$$= m(g + a)$$

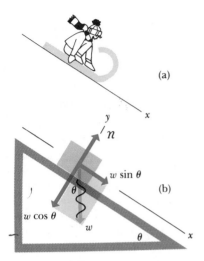

5-10
(a) A body on a frictionless inclined plane. (b) Free-body diagram.

Example 5–12   Let's go back to the toboggan. (Remember Example 5–8?) The hill slopes at a constant angle θ, and this time the toboggan is so well waxed that there is no friction at all. What is its acceleration?

Solution   The only forces acting on the toboggan are its weight w and the normal force n exerted by the hill (Fig. 5–10b). Take axes parallel and perpendicular to the surface of the hill and resolve the weight into x- and y-components. Then

$$\sum F_x = w \sin \theta.$$

From $\Sigma F_x = ma_x$ we have

$$w \sin \theta = ma_x,$$

and since $w = mg$,

$$a_x = g \sin \theta.$$

The mass does not appear in the final result, which means that *any* body, regardless of its mass, slides down a frictionless inclined plane with an acceleration of $g \sin \theta$. In particular, when $\theta = 0$, $a_x = 0$, and when the plane is vertical, $\theta = 90°$ and $a_x = g$, as we should expect.

Note again that we did not need the y-components; we know that $a_y = 0$, so $\Sigma F_y = 0$ and

$$n = mg \cos \theta.$$

We don't need this result here, but it will be useful in the next example!

■

Example 5–13   Consider the same toboggan, but this time it isn't as well waxed, and there is a coefficient of kinetic friction μ_k. As the toboggan moves down the hill, it still accelerates, but not as much as before. How much?

Solution   The free-body diagram now has an additional force $\mathcal{F}_k$ in the $-x$-direction, as shown in Fig. 5–11. It is given by $\mathcal{F}_k = \mu_k n$, and at the end of Example 5–12 we found that $n = mg \cos \theta$. So $\mathcal{F}_k = \mu_k mg \cos \theta$. Newton's second law for the x-components then gives

$$mg \sin \theta + (-\mu_k\, mg \cos \theta) = ma_x,$$

$$a_x = g(\sin \theta - \mu_k \cos \theta).$$

Does this result make sense? Here are some tests. First, if the hill is *vertical*, $\theta = 90°$; then $\sin \theta = 1$, $\cos \theta = 0$, and $a_x = g$: free fall, just what we would expect. Second, on a hill at angle θ with *no* friction, $\mu_k = 0$ and $a_x = g \sin \theta$. That's the same situation as in Example 5–12, and we get the same result; that's encouraging! Then suppose that $a_x = 0$; in that case there is just enough friction to make the toboggan move with constant velocity. Our result then gives

$$\sin \theta = \mu_k \cos \theta \quad \text{and} \quad \mu_k = \tan \theta.$$

This agrees with our result from Example 5–8; good! Finally, note that

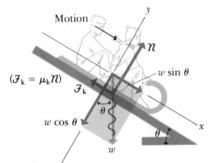

5-11
Toboggan accelerating down a hill, with friction.

there may be so much friction that $\mu_k \cos \theta$ is actually greater than $\sin \theta$; in that case, a_x is negative; if we give the toboggan an initial downhill push, it will slow down and eventually stop. ■

We have pretty much beaten the toboggan problem to death, but there is an important lesson to be learned. We started out with a simple problem and then extended it to more and more general situations. Our most general result *contains* all the previous ones as special cases; and that's a nice, neat package! Don't memorize this package, because its usefulness is limited to this one specific problem. But do try to understand how we obtained it and what it means.

One final variation that you may want to try out is the case in which we give the toboggan an initial push *up* the hill. The direction of the friction force is now reversed, so the acceleration is different from the downhill value. It turns out that the expression for a_x is the same as before except that the minus sign becomes plus. Can you prove this?

Example 5–14   In Fig. 5–12a we pull a 4.0-kg cart along a horizontal frictionless surface with a 0.50-kg rope, applying a force $F = 9.0$ N to the rope. Find the acceleration of the system and the tension at the point where the rope is fastened to the cart.

Solution   Once again, only x-components are relevant. We can proceed in either of two ways.

Method 1: Consider the cart and rope as a composite body with a total mass of 4.50 kg. A 9-N force gives this body an acceleration of $(9.0 \text{ N})/(4.5 \text{ kg}) = 2.0 \text{ m·s}^{-2}$. Then, looking at the 4.0-kg cart by itself, we see that to give it an acceleration of 2.0 m·s^{-2} requires a force

$$T = (4.0 \text{ kg})(2.0 \text{ m·s}^{-2}) = 8.0 \text{ N}.$$

Then the net forward force on the *rope* is $9.0 \text{ N} - 8.0 \text{ N} = 1.0 \text{ N}$. This corresponds to a mass of 0.50 kg accelerating at 2.0 m·s^{-2}, the same acceleration as that of the cart.

If this method seems slightly acrobatic, let's go a little more slowly.

Method 2: Write an equation of motion for the cart and another for the rope, using a and T for the unknown acceleration and tension. For

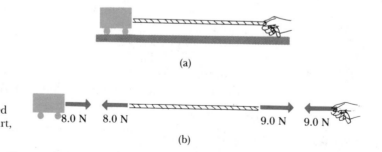

(a)

5–12

(a) A person pulls on a rope attached to a cart. (b) Forces acting on the cart, the rope, and the person's hand.

8.0 N   8.0 N   9.0 N   9.0 N

(b)

the ca

$$T = (4.0 \text{ kg})a,$$

and for the pe

$$9.0 \text{ N} - T = (0.5 \text{ kg})a.$$

These are two taneous equations for T and a. An easy way to solve them is to subst the first equation for T into the second and then solve for a. We le the details for you to work out; the results are again $a = 2.0 \text{ m·s}^{-2}$ and $= 8.0 \text{ N}$.

Note that an essential element in either solution is the fact that the two bodies in our system have the same acceleration. We can apply Newton's second law to either body separately or to the composite system as a whole. ∎

Example 5–15   In Fig. 5–13 a block with mass m_1 and weight $w_1 = m_1g$ moves on a level, frictionless surface. It is connected by a light, flexible string passing over a small frictionless pulley to a hanging block of mass m_2 and weight $w_2 = m_2g$. Find the acceleration of each block and the tension in the string.

Solution   The two bodies have different motions, so we *must* consider them separately, with a free-body diagram and $\mathbf{\Sigma F = ma}$ equations for each. Figure 5–13 shows a free-body diagram and a coordinate system for each body. There is no friction in the pulley, and the string is considered massless, so the tension T in the string is the same throughout; it applies a force of magnitude T to each block. For the block on the surface, Newton's second law gives

$$\sum F_x = T = m_1 a_x,$$
$$\sum F_y = n + (-m_1g) = m_1 a_y = 0,$$

and for the hanging block,

$$\sum F_y = m_2 g + (-T) = m_2 a_y.$$

We note that it is perfectly all right to use different coordinate axes for the two bodies. Here it is convenient to take the $+y$-direction as downward for m_2, so both bodies move in positive axis directions.

Now if the string doesn't stretch, the speeds of the two bodies at any instant are equal, so their accelerations have the same magnitude. That is, a_x for m_1 equals a_y for m_2. We can denote this common magnitude simply as a. (The directions of the two accelerations are different, of course.) The two Newton's-second-law equations are then

$$T = m_1 a,$$
$$m_2 g + (-T) = m_2 a.$$

These are two simultaneous equations for the unknowns T and a. An easy way to solve them is to add the two equations; this eliminates T,

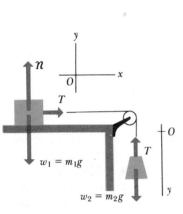

5–13
Force diagram for a block on a frictionless horizontal surface and for the hanging block.

giving

$$m_2 = m_1a + m_2a = (m_1 + m_2)a$$

and

$$a = \frac{m_2}{m_1 + m_2}g.$$

Substituting this back into the first equation, we get

$$T = \frac{m_1m_2}{m_1 + m_2}g.$$

We see that the tension T is *not* equal to the weight m_2g of mass m_2 but is *less* by a factor of $m_1/(m_1 + m_2)$. Further thought shows that T *cannot* be equal to m_2g; if it were, m_2 would be in equilibrium, and it isn't!

Now let's check some special cases. If $m_1 = 0$, we would expect that m_2 would fall freely and there would be no tension in the string. The equations do give $T = 0$ and $a = g$ for this case. Also, if $m_2 = 0$, we expect no tension and no acceleration; for this case the equations give $T = 0$ and $a = 0$. Thus in these two cases the general analytical results agree with our intuitive expectations. Again, don't memorize these formulas, but concentrate on understanding how we obtained them and what they mean. ∎

Example 5–16   Figure 5–14a represents a simple *accelerometer*. A small body is hung from a string attached to point P on the ceiling of a car. When the system has an acceleration a toward the right, the string makes an angle θ with the vertical. In a practical instrument, some form of damping is needed to keep the string from swinging when the acceleration changes. For example, the system might hang in a tank of oil. You can make a primitive version of this device by tying a thread to the ceiling light in a car, tying a key or nearly any other small object to the other end, and using a protractor. The problem: Given m and θ, what is the acceleration a?

Solution   As shown in the free-body diagram, Fig. 5–14b, two forces act on the body: its weight $w = mg$ and the tension T in the string. The sum of the horizontal components of force is

$$\sum F_x = T \sin \theta,$$

and the sum of the vertical components is

$$\sum F_y = T \cos \theta + (-mg).$$

The x-acceleration is the acceleration a of the system, and the y-acceleration is zero. Hence

$$T \sin \theta = ma,$$

$$T \cos \theta = mg.$$

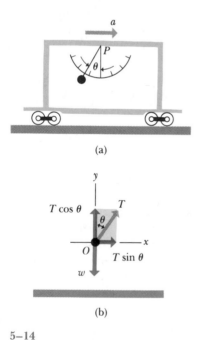

(a)

(b)

5–14
(a) A simple accelerometer. (b) The forces on the body are w and T.

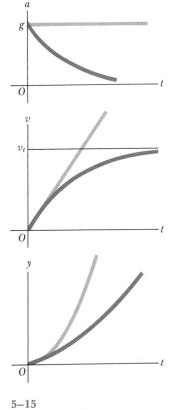

5–15
Graphs of acceleration, velocity, and position versus time for a body falling in a viscous fluid, shown as solid color curves. The light color curves show the corresponding relations if there is *no* viscous friction.

When we divide the first equation by the second, we get

$$a = g \tan \theta.$$

The acceleration a is proportional to the tangent of the angle θ. When $\theta = 0$, the acceleration is zero; when $\theta = 45°$, $a = g$, and so on. We note that θ can never be 90° because that would require an infinite acceleration. Also note that this result is independent of the mass of the body. ∎

Example 5–17 Sometimes a frictional force opposing the motion of a body is not constant but increases with the body's speed. Two familiar examples are air resistance on a falling body and the viscous resisting force on a body falling through a liquid. Suppose we drop a penny into a deep pond. For small speeds the liquid opposes the motion with a resisting force f that is approximately proportional to the penny's speed v:

$$f = kv, \tag{5–7}$$

where k is a proportionality constant that depends on the dimensions of the penny and the properties of the fluid. Taking the positive direction to be downward and neglecting any force associated with buoyancy in the fluid, we find that the net downward force is $mg - kv$; Newton's second law gives

$$mg - kv = ma. \tag{5–8}$$

When the penny first starts to move and $v = 0$, the resisting force is zero, and the initial acceleration is $a = g$. As the speed increases, the resisting force also increases, until finally it equals the weight in magnitude. At this time the acceleration becomes zero, and there is no further increase in speed. The final speed is called the **terminal speed,** v_t. To derive an expression for v_t, we substitute $v = v_t$ and $a = 0$ into Eq. (5–8) and solve for v_t; we find

$$v_t = \frac{mg}{k}. \tag{5–9}$$

Figure 5–15 shows graphs of acceleration, velocity, and position as functions of time. Deriving the details of these graphs requires methods of calculus. ∎

In high-speed motion through air, the resisting force is approximately proportional to v^2 rather than to v; it is then called *air drag* or simply *drag*. Falling raindrops, airplanes, and cars moving at high speed all experience air drag. In this case, Eq. (5–7) is replaced by $f = Kv^2$. We invite you to prove that the terminal speed is then given by

$$v_t = \sqrt{\frac{mg}{K}}, \tag{5–10}$$

and that the units of the constant K are $\text{N·s}^2\text{·m}^{-2}$ or kg·m^{-1}.

Example 5–18   For a human body falling though air the numerical value of the constant K in Eq. (5–10) is found to be about 0.25 kg·m^{-1}. If an 80-kg skydiver jumps out of an airplane and reaches terminal velocity before she opens her parachute, what is her terminal velocity?

Solution   From Eq. (5–10),

$$v_t = \sqrt{\frac{(80 \text{ kg})(9.8 \text{ m·s}^{-2})}{0.25 \text{ kg·m}^{-1}}} = 56 \text{ m·s}^{-1},$$

or about 125 mi·hr^{-1}.   ∎

Questions

5–1 Can a body be in equilibrium when only one force acts on it?

5–2 A helium balloon hovers in midair, neither ascending nor descending. Is it in equilibrium? What forces act on it?

5–3 If the two ends of a rope in equilibrium are pulled with forces of equal magnitude and opposite direction, why is the total tension in the rope not zero?

5–4 A horse is hitched to a wagon. Since the wagon pulls back on the horse just as hard as the horse pulls on the wagon, why doesn't the wagon remain in equilibrium, no matter how hard the horse pulls?

5–5 A clothesline is hung between two poles, and then a shirt is hung near the center. No matter how tightly the line is stretched, it always sags a little at the center. Explain why.

5–6 A man sits in a chair that is suspended from a rope. The rope passes over a pulley suspended from the ceiling, and the man holds the other end of the rope in his hands. What is the tension in the rope, and what force does the chair exert on the man?

5–7 How can pushing *down* on a bicycle pedal make the bicycle move *forward*?

5–8 A car is driven up a steep hill at constant speed.

Discuss all the forces acting on the car. In particular, what pushes it up the hill?

5–9 Can the coefficient of friction ever be greater than unity? If so, give an example; if not, explain why not.

5–10 A block rests on an inclined plane with enough friction to prevent sliding down. To start the block moving, is it easier to push it up the plane, down the plane, or sideways? Why?

5–11 In pushing a box up a ramp, is it better to push horizontally or to push parallel to the ramp?

5–12 In stopping a car on an icy road, is it better to push the brake pedal hard enough to "lock" the wheels and make them slide or to push gently so that the wheels continue to roll? Why?

5–13 When one stands with bare feet in a wet bathtub, the grip feels fairly secure, and yet a catastrophic slip is quite possible. Discuss this situation with respect to the two coefficients of friction.

5–14 The horrible squeak made by a piece of chalk held at the wrong angle against a blackboard results from alternate sticking and slipping of the chalk against the blackboard. Interpret this phenomenon in terms of the two coefficients of friction. Can you think of other examples of "slip–stick" behavior?

Exercises

Section 5–2   Contact Forces and Friction

5–1 A small crate with a mass of 0.80 slug is being pushed on a horizontal surface with a constant speed of 15.0 ft·s^{-1} by a stockroom worker. The coefficient of kinetic friction between the crate and the surface is 0.20.

a) What horizontal force must be applied by the worker to maintain the motion?

b) If the force calculated in part (a) is removed, how soon does the crate come to rest?

5–2 A box of bananas weighing 25.0 N rests on a horizontal surface. The coefficient of static friction between the box and the surface is 0.40, and the coefficient of kinetic friction is 0.20.

a) If no horizontal force is applied to the box and the box is at rest, how large is the friction force exerted on the box?

b) How great is the friction force if a horizontal force of 6.0 N is exerted on the box and the box is initially at rest?

c) What is the minimum horizontal force that will start the box in motion?

d) What is the minimum horizontal force that will keep the box in motion once it has been started?

e) If a horizontal force of 15.0 N is applied to the box, how great is the friction force?

5–3 In a physics lab experiment a 10.0-kg box is pushed across a flat table by a horizontal force F.

a) If the box is moving at a constant speed of 3.50 m·s^{-1} and the coefficient of kinetic friction is 0.14, what is the magnitude of the force F?

b) What is the magnitude of F if the box is accelerating with a constant acceleration of 0.220 m·s^{-2}?

c) How would your answers to parts (a) and (b) change if the experiments were performed on the moon, where $g = 1.67$ m·s^{-2}?

5–4 A hockey puck leaves a player's stick with a speed of 14.0 m·s^{-1} and slides 32.0 m before coming to rest. Find the coefficient of friction between the puck and the ice.

5–5

a) If the coefficient of friction between tires and dry pavement is 0.80, what is the shortest distance in which an automobile can be stopped by locking the brakes when traveling at 22.0 m·s^{-1} (about 50 mi·hr^{-1})?

b) On wet pavement the coefficient of friction may be only 0.25. How fast should you drive on wet pavement in order to be able to stop in the same distance as in part (a)?

(*Note:* Locking the brakes is *not* the safest way to stop.)

5–6 Find the ratio of the stopping distance of an automobile on wet concrete with the wheels locked ($\mu_k = 0.25$) to the stopping distance of the same automobile stopped by tractive friction only (where the tractive resistance $\mu_r = 0.0120$). Assume the same initial speed for both cases.

5–7 Air pressure greatly affects the tractive resistance of bicycle tires. To study this effect, two tires are set rolling with the same initial speed of 6.00 m·s^{-1} along a long, straight road, and the distance each travels before its speed is reduced by half is measured. One tire is inflated to a pressure of 40 psi, and the other is at 105 psi. The low-pressure tire goes 45.6 m, and the high-pressure tire goes 213.2 m. What is the tractive resistance μ_r for each? Assume that the net horizontal force is due to tractive friction only.

Section 5–3   Equilibrium of a Particle

5–8 In each of the situations in Fig. 5–16 the blocks suspended from the rope have weight w. The pulleys are frictionless. Calculate in each case the tension T in the rope in terms of the weight w.

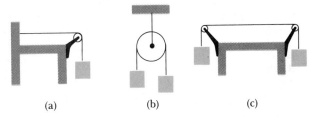

(a)   (b)   (c)

FIGURE 5–16

5–9 Two 20.0-N weights are suspended at opposite ends of a rope that passes over a light, frictionless pulley. The pulley is attached to a chain that goes to the ceiling.

a) What is the tension in the rope?

b) What is the tension in the chain?

5–10 A picture frame hung against a wall is suspended by two wires attached to its upper corners. If the two wires make the same angle with the vertical, what must this angle be if the tension in each wire is equal to the weight of the frame? (Neglect any friction between the wall and the picture frame.)

5–11 Figure 5–17 illustrates a mountaineering technique called a Tyrolean traverse. A rope is stretched tightly between two points, and the climber slides across the rope. The climber's weight is 700 N, and the breaking strength of the rope (typically 11-mm-diameter nylon) is 22,000 N.

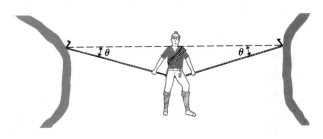

FIGURE 5–17

a) If the angle θ is 15.0°, find the tension in the rope.

b) What is the smallest value the angle θ can have if the rope is not to break?

5–12 Find the tension in each cord in Fig. 5–18 if the weight of the suspended object is w.

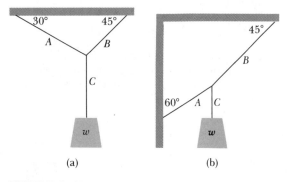

(a)   (b)

FIGURE 5–18

5–13 In Fig. 5–19 the tension in the diagonal string is 30.0 N.

a) Find the magnitudes of the horizontal forces F_1 and F_2 that must be applied to hold the system in the position shown.

b) What is the weight of the suspended block?

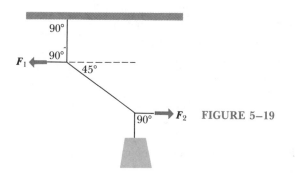

FIGURE 5–19

5–14 A tether ball leans against the post to which it is attached, as shown in Fig. 5–20. If the string to which the ball is attached is 1.80 m long, the ball has a radius of 0.200 m, and the ball has a mass of 0.500 kg, what

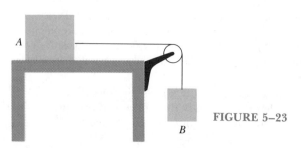

FIGURE 5–20

are the tension in the rope and the force the pole exerts on the ball? Assume that there is so little friction between the ball and the pole that friction can be neglected. (The string is attached to the ball such that a line along the string passes through the center of the ball.)

5–15 Two blocks, each with weight w, are held in place on a frictionless incline as shown in Fig. 5–21. In terms of w and the angle θ of the incline, calculate the tension in

a) the rope connecting the blocks;

b) the rope that connects block A to the wall.

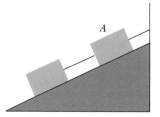

FIGURE 5–21

5–16 A man is pushing a piano weighing 420 lb at constant velocity up a ramp that is inclined at 34.0° above the horizontal. Neglect friction. If the force applied by the man is parallel to the incline, calculate the magnitude of this force.

5–17 Two crates connected by a rope lie on a horizontal surface as shown in Fig. 5–22. Crate A has weight w_A, and crate B has weight w_B. The coefficient of kinetic friction between the crates and the surface is μ_k. The crates are pulled to the right at constant velocity by a horizontal force P. In terms of w_A, w_B, and μ_k, calculate

a) the magnitude of the force P;

b) the tension in the rope connecting the blocks.

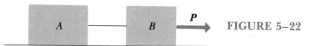

FIGURE 5–22

5–18 Consider the system shown in Fig. 5–23. The coefficient of kinetic friction between block A (weight

w_A) and the tabletop is μ_k. Calculate the weight w_B of the hanging block required if this block is to descend at constant speed once it has been set into motion.

5–19 In emergency situations with major blood loss, the doctor will order the patient placed in the Trendelberg position, which is to raise the foot of the bed to get maximum blood flow to the brain. If the coefficient of static friction between the typical patient and the bed sheets is 1.8, what is the maximum angle at which the bed can be tilted with respect to the floor before the patient begins to slide?

5–20 A child pushes on a box resting on the floor. The box weighs 260 N, and the child is pushing down on the box with a force that makes an angle of 45.0° with the horizontal, as shown in Fig. 4–1b. If the smallest force the child can apply that gets the box moving is 150 N, what is the coefficient of static friction between the box and the floor?

5–21 A safe weighing 2500 N is to be lowered at constant speed down skids 4.80 m long, from a truck 2.40 m high.

a) If the coefficient of kinetic friction between safe and skids is 0.30, will the safe need to be pulled down or held back?

b) How great a force parallel to the skids is needed?

5–22

a) If a force with magnitude 95.0 N parallel to the surface of a 20.0° ramp will push a 120-N mailbag up the ramp at constant speed, what force parallel to the ramp will push it down at constant speed?

b) What is the coefficient of kinetic friction?

5–23 A large crate with weight w rests on a horizontal floor. The coefficients of friction between the crate and the floor are μ_s and μ_k. A man pushes downward at an angle θ below the horizontal on the crate with a force $\boldsymbol{P}$.

a) What magnitude of force $\boldsymbol{P}$ is required to keep the crate moving at constant velocity?

b) If μ_s is larger than some critical value, the man cannot start the crate moving no matter how hard he pushes. Calculate this critical value of μ_s.

5–24 Two blocks, A and B, are placed as in Fig. 5–24 and connected by ropes to block C. Both A and B weigh 30.0 N each, and the coefficient of kinetic friction between each block and the surface is 0.50. Block C descends with constant velocity.

a) Draw two separate force diagrams showing the forces acting on A and on B.

b) Find the tension in the rope connecting blocks A and B.

c) What is the weight of block C?

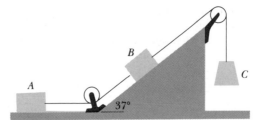

FIGURE 5–24

Section 5–4 Applications of Newton's Second Law

5–25 The first two steps in the solution of Newton's second law problems are to select an object for analysis and then to draw free-body diagrams for that object. Draw a free-body diagram for each of the following situations:

a) a mass M sliding down a frictionless inclined plane of angle θ;

b) a mass M sliding up a frictionless inclined plane of angle θ;

c) a mass M sliding up an inclined plane of angle θ with kinetic friction present;

d) masses M and m sliding down an inclined plane of angle θ with friction present, as shown in Fig. 5–25a. Here draw free-body diagrams for both m and M. Identify the forces that are action–reaction pairs.

e) Draw free-body diagrams for masses m and M shown in Fig. 5–25b. Identify all action–reaction pairs. There are frictional forces between all surfaces in contact. The pulley is frictionless and massless.

In all cases, be sure you have the correct direction of the forces and are completely clear on what object is causing each force in your free-body diagram.

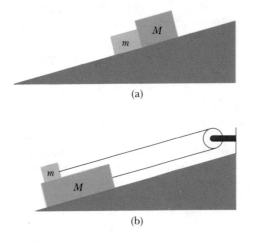

(a)

(b)

FIGURE 5–25

5-26 A 6.00-kg bucket of water is accelerated upward by a cord whose breaking strength is 74.0 N. Find the maximum upward acceleration that can be given to the bucket without breaking the cord.

5-27 An elevator with a mass of 2000 kg descends with an acceleration of 2.50 m·s^{-2}. What is the tension in the supporting cable?

5-28 A train (an engine plus four cars) is accelerating at 3.50 ft·s^{-2}. If the mass of each car is 2700 slugs and if each car has negligible frictional forces acting on it, what is

a) the force of the engine on the first car?

b) the force of the first car on the second car?

c) the force of the second car on the third car?

d) the force of the third car on the fourth car?

e) What would these same four forces be if the train were slowing down with an acceleration of -3.50 ft·s^{-2}. When solving, note the importance of selecting the correct set of cars as your object.

5-29 A large fish hangs from a spring balance supported from the roof of an elevator.

a) If the elevator has an upward acceleration of 2.45 m·s^{-2} and the balance reads 60.0 N, what is the true weight of the fish?

b) Under what circumstances will the balance read 35.0 N?

c) What will the balance read if the elevator cable breaks?

5-30 A transport plane is to take off from a level landing field with two gliders in tow, one behind the other. The mass of each glider is 1500 kg, and the friction force or drag on each may be assumed to be constant and equal to 2000 N. The tension in the towrope between the transport plane and the first glider is not to exceed 10,000 N.

a) If a speed of 40.0 m·s^{-1} is required for takeoff, what minimum length of runway is needed?

b) What is the tension in the towrope between the two gliders while they are accelerating for the takeoff?

5-31

a) A large rock rests upon a rough horizontal surface. A bulldozer pushes on the rock with a horizontal force T that is slowly increased, starting from zero. Draw a graph with T along the x-axis and the friction force $\mathcal{F}$ along the y-axis, starting at $T = 0$ and showing the region of no motion, the point at which the rock is ready to move, and the region where the rock is moving.

b) A block with weight w rests on a rough horizontal plank. The slope angle of the plank θ is gradually increased until the block starts to slip. Draw two graphs, both with θ along the x-axis. In one graph, show the ratio of the normal force to the weight, n/w, as a function of θ. In the second graph, show the ratio of the friction force to the weight, $\mathcal{F}/w$. Indicate the region of no motion, the point at which the block is ready to move, and the region where the block is moving.

5-32 A 5.00-kg block slides down a plane inclined at 40.0° to the horizontal. Find the acceleration of the block

a) if the plane is frictionless;

b) if the coefficient of kinetic friction is 0.20.

5-33 A packing crate rests on a loading ramp that makes an angle θ with the horizontal. The coefficient of kinetic friction is 0.40, and the coefficient of static friction is 0.80.

a) As the angle θ is increased, find the minimum angle at which the crate starts to slip.

b) At this angle, find the acceleration (in m·s^{-2}) once the crate has begun to move.

c) How much time is required for the crate to slip 8.00 m along the ramp?

5-34 Which way does the accelerometer in Fig. 5-14a deflect under the following conditions?

a) The cart is moving toward the right with increasing speed.

b) The cart is moving toward the right with decreasing speed.

c) The cart is moving toward the left with increasing speed.

5-35 Which way does the accelerometer in Fig. 5-14a deflect under the following conditions?

a) The cart is at rest on a sloping surface.

b) The cart is given an initial velocity up a frictionless inclined plane. It first moves up, then stops, and then moves down. What is the deflection in each stage of the motion?

5-36 A box with mass m is dragged across a rough level floor having a coefficient of kinetic friction μ_k by a rope which is pulled upward at an angle θ above the horizontal with a force of magnitude F. In terms of m, μ_k, θ, F, and g, obtain expressions for

a) the normal force;

b) the frictional force;

c) the acceleration of the box;

d) the magnitude of force required to move the box with constant speed.

5-37 A block with mass 8.00 kg resting on a horizontal surface is connected by a cord passing over a light, frictionless pulley to a hanging block with mass 6.00 kg. The coefficient of kinetic friction between the block and the horizontal surface is 0.50. After the blocks are released, find

a) the acceleration of each block;

b) the tension in the cord.

5–38 A drag force with magnitude $f = Kv^2$ acts on a falling raindrop.

a) Show that the SI units of K are kg·m^{-1}.

b) Show that the falling raindrop reaches a terminal speed given by Eq. (5–10).

5–39 A 600-N man stands on a bathroom scale in an elevator. As the elevator starts moving, the scale reads 900 N.

a) Find the acceleration of the elevator (magnitude and direction).

b) What is the acceleration if the scale reads 350 N?

c) If the scale reads zero, should the man worry? Explain.

Problems

5–40 In Fig. 5–26, a person lifts a weight w by pulling down on a rope with a force F. The upper pulley is attached to the ceiling by a chain, and the lower pulley is attached to the weight by another chain. In terms of w, find the tension in each chain and the force F if the weight is lifted at constant speed. Assume the weights of the rope, pulleys, and chains to be negligible.

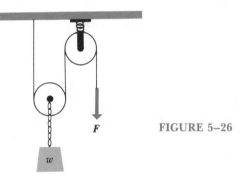

F   FIGURE 5–26

5–41 Figure 5–27 shows a technique called rappelling, used by mountaineers for descending vertical rock

15°

FIGURE 5–27

faces. The climber sits in a rope seat, and the rappel rope slides through a friction device attached to this seat. Suppose that the rock is perfectly smooth (no friction) and that the climber's feet push horizontally onto the rock. If the climber's weight is 600 N, find the tension in the rope and the force the climber's feet exert on the rock face.

5–42 A physics student playing with an air hockey table (just a frictionless surface) gives the puck a velocity of 15.0 ft·s⁻¹ along the length (5.50 ft) of the table at one end. By the time it has reached the other end the puck has drifted 1.40 in. to the right but still has a velocity along the length of 15.0 ft·s⁻¹. She concludes correctly that the table is not level and correctly calculates its inclination from the above information. What does the student get for the angle of inclination?

5–43 A refrigerator with weight w is being pushed up an incline at constant velocity by a man who applies a force **P**. The surface of the incline is at an angle θ above the horizontal. *Neglect friction*. If the force **P** is *horizontal*, calculate its magnitude in terms of w and θ.

5–44 If the coefficient of static friction between a table and a rope is μ_s, what fraction of the rope can hang over the edge of the table without the rope sliding?

5–45 A dictionary is pulled to the right at constant velocity by a 10.0-N force pulling upward at 30.0° above the horizontal. The coefficient of kinetic friction between the dictionary and the surface is 0.40. What is the weight of the dictionary?

5–46

a) Block A in Fig. 5–28 weighs 100 N. The coefficient of static friction between the block and the surface on which it rests is 0.40. The weight w is 30.0 N, and the system is in equilibrium. Find the friction force exerted on block A.

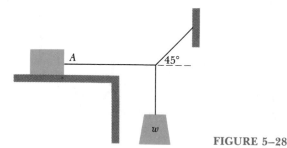

FIGURE 5–28

b) Find the maximum weight w for which the system will remain in equilibrium.

5–47 A window washer pushes his scrub brush up a vertical window at constant velocity by applying a force $\boldsymbol{P}$ as shown in Fig. 5–29. The brush weighs 9.00 N, and the coefficient of kinetic friction is $\mu_k = 0.40$. Calculate

a) the magnitude of the force $\boldsymbol{P}$;

b) the normal force exerted by the window on the brush.

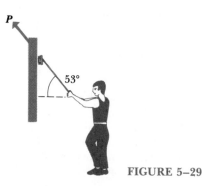

FIGURE 5–29

5–48 A block weighing 100 N is placed on an inclined plane with slope angle 30.0° and is connected to a hanging block of weight w by a cord passing over a small, frictionless pulley, as in Fig. 5–30. The coefficient of static friction is 0.52, and the coefficient of kinetic friction is 0.20.

a) Find the weight w for which the 100-N block moves up the plane at constant speed, once it has been set in motion.

b) Find the weight w for which it moves down the plane at constant speed.

c) For what range of values of w does the block remain at rest if it is released from rest?

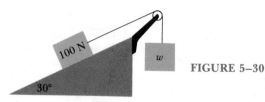

FIGURE 5–30

5–49 Block A, with weight w, slides down an inclined plane S of slope angle 37.0° at a constant velocity while the plank B, also having weight w, rests on top of A. The plank is attached by a cord to the top of the plane (Fig. 5–31).

a) Draw a diagram of all the forces acting on block A.

b) If the coefficient of kinetic friction is the same between the surfaces A and B and between S and A, determine its value.

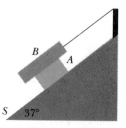

FIGURE 5–31

5–50 Block A in Fig. 5–32 weighs 4.20 N, and block B weighs 8.40 N. The coefficient of kinetic friction between all surfaces is 0.30. Find the magnitude of the horizontal force $\boldsymbol{P}$ necessary to drag block B to the left at constant speed

a) if A rests on B and moves with it;

b) if A is held at rest, as in Fig. 5–32b.

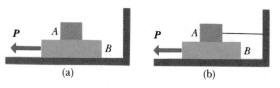

(a)   (b)

FIGURE 5–32

5–51 Block A in Fig. 5–33 weighs 4.20 N, and block B weighs 8.40 N. The coefficient of kinetic friction between all surfaces is 0.30. Find the magnitude of the horizontal force $\boldsymbol{P}$ necessary to drag block B to the left at constant speed if A and B are connected by a light flexible cord passing around a fixed frictionless pulley.

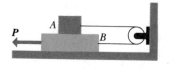

FIGURE 5–33

5–52 A woman attempts to push a box of books with weight w up a ramp inclined at an angle θ above the horizontal. The coefficients of friction between the ramp and the box are μ_s and μ_k. The force $\boldsymbol{P}$ applied by the woman is *horizontal*.

a) If μ_s is greater than some critical value, the woman cannot start the box moving up the ramp no matter how hard she pushes. Calculate this critical value of μ_s.

b) Assume that μ_s is less than this critical value. What magnitude of force must the woman apply to keep the box moving up the ramp at constant velocity?

5–53 A 20.0-kg box rests on the flat floor of a truck. The coefficients of friction between the box and floor are $\mu_s = 0.15$ and $\mu_k = 0.10$. The truck stops at a stop sign and then starts to move with an acceleration of 2.00 m·s^{-2}. If the box is 4.00 m from the rear of the truck when it starts, how much time elapses before the box falls off the rear of the truck? How far does the truck travel in this time?

5–54 A 150-kg crate is released from an airplane traveling due east at an altitude of 9000 m with a ground speed of 120 m·s^{-1}. The wind applies a constant force on the crate of 250 N directed horizontally in the opposite direction to the plane's flight path. Where and when (with respect to the release location and time) does the crate hit the ground?

5–55 A truck traveling down a 10.0° slope is slowing down with an acceleration of magnitude 2.00 m·s^{-2}. A box weighing 900 N is resting on the back of the truck.

a) Will the box slide forward on the truck bed if the coefficient of static friction between the box and the truck bed is 0.30?

b) If your answer in part (a) is yes, what will be the acceleration of the box relative to the truck bed if the coefficient of kinetic friction is 0.22?

5–56 A 40.0-kg packing case is initially at rest on the floor of a truck. The coefficient of static friction between the case and the truck floor is 0.30, and the coefficient of kinetic friction is 0.20. Before each acceleration given below, the truck is traveling due east at constant speed. Find the magnitude and direction of the friction force acting on the case

a) when the truck accelerates at 3.00 m·s^{-2} eastward;

b) when it accelerates at 2.20 m·s^{-2} westward.

5–57 Two blocks connected by a cord passing over a small, frictionless pulley rest on frictionless planes, as shown in Fig. 5–34.

a) Which way does the system move?

b) What is the acceleration of the blocks?

c) What is the tension in the cord?

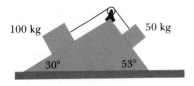

FIGURE 5–34

5–58 A book whose mass is 2.00 kg is projected up a long 30.0° incline with an initial speed of 16.0 m·s^{-1}. The coefficient of kinetic friction between the book and the plane is 0.30.

a) Find the magnitude of the friction force acting on the book as it moves up the plane.

b) For how much *time* does the book move up the plane?

c) How *far* does the book move up the plane?

d) How much time does it take the book to slide from its position in part (c) back to its starting point?

e) With what speed does it arrive at this point?

f) If the mass of the book were 5.00 kg instead of 2.00 kg, would the answers in the preceding parts be different?

5–59 In terms of m_1, m_2, and g, find the acceleration of each block in Fig. 5–35. There is no friction anywhere in the system.

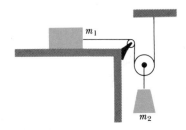

FIGURE 5–35

5–60 Block A in Fig. 5–36 has a mass of 4.00 kg, and block B has a mass of 20.0 kg. The coefficient of kinetic friction between B and the horizontal surface is 0.10.

a) What is the mass of block C if block B is moving to the right with an acceleration of 2.00 m·s^{-2}?

b) What is the tension in each cord when block B has the acceleration stated above?

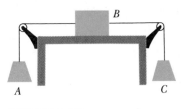

FIGURE 5–36

5–61 The two blocks in Fig. 5–37 are connected by a heavy, uniform rope with a mass of 4.00 kg. An upward force of 200 N is applied as shown.

a) What is the acceleration of the system?

b) What is the tension at the top of the heavy rope?

c) What is the tension at the midpoint of the rope?

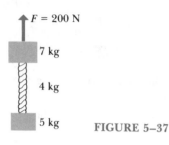

FIGURE 5–37

5–62 The masses of blocks A and B in Fig. 5–38 are 20.0 kg and 10.0 kg, respectively. They are initially at rest on the floor and are connected by a weightless string passing over a weightless and frictionless pulley. An upward force F is applied to the pulley. Find the accelerations a_1 of block A and a_2 of block B when F is

  a) 124 N,   b) 294 N,   c) 424 N.

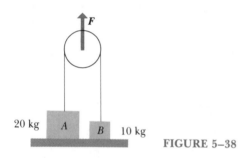

FIGURE 5–38

5–63 Two objects with masses 6.00 kg and 2.00 kg, respectively, hang 1.00 m above the floor from the ends of a cord 4.00 m long passing over a frictionless pulley. Both objects start from rest. Find the maximum height reached by the 2.00-kg object.

5–64 Two blocks with masses 4.00 kg and 8.00 kg, respectively, are connected by a string and slide down a 30.0° inclined plane, as in Fig. 5–39. The coefficient of kinetic friction between the 4.00-kg block and the plane is 0.20; that between the 8.00-kg block and the plane is 0.40.

  a) Calculate the acceleration of each block.

  b) Calculate the tension in the string.

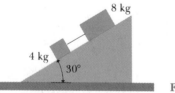

FIGURE 5–39

5–65 What acceleration must the cart in Fig. 5–40 have in order that the block A does not fall? The coefficient of static friction between the block and the cart is

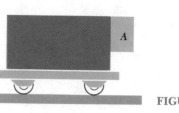

FIGURE 5–40

μ_s. How would the behavior of the block be described by an observer on the cart?

5–66 A man with mass 90.0 kg stands on a platform with mass 50.0 kg. He pulls on the free end of a rope that runs over a pulley on the ceiling and has its other end fastened to the platform. With what force does he have to pull to give himself and the platform an upward acceleration of 1.00 m·s^{-2}?

5–67 A 20.0-kg monkey has a firm hold on a light rope that passes over a frictionless pulley and is attached to a 20.0-kg bunch of bananas, as shown in Fig. 5–41. The monkey looks upward, sees the bananas, and starts to climb the rope to get at the bananas.

  a) As the monkey climbs, do the bananas move up, move down, or remain at rest?

  b) As the monkey climbs, does the distance between the monkey and the bananas decrease, increase, or remain constant?

  c) The monkey releases its hold on the rope. What about the distance between the monkey and the bananas while the monkey is falling?

  d) Before reaching the ground, the monkey grabs the rope to stop its fall. What do the bananas do?

FIGURE 5–41

5–68 A rock with mass $m = 5.00$ kg falls from rest in a viscous medium. The rock is acted on by a net constant downward force of 30.0 N (a combination of gravity and the buoyant force exerted by the medium) and by a viscous retarding force proportional to its speed and with magnitude $(5.00 \ \text{N·s·m}^{-1})v$, where v is the speed in meters per second. (See Example 5–17.)

a) Find the initial acceleration, a_0.

b) Find the acceleration when the speed is $3.00 \ \text{m·s}^{-1}$.

c) Find the speed when the acceleration equals $0.100a_0$.

d) Find the terminal speed, v_t.

Challenge Problems

5–69 A box with weight w is pulled at constant speed along a level floor by a force $\boldsymbol{P}$ that pulls upward at an angle ϕ above the horizontal. The coefficient of kinetic friction between the floor and box is μ_k.

a) In terms of ϕ, μ_k, and w, calculate P.

b) For $w = 400$ N and $\mu_k = 0.300$, calculate P for ϕ ranging from 0° to 90° in increments of 10°. Sketch a graph of P versus ϕ. From your graph, estimate the value of ϕ for which the P required to maintain constant speed is a minimum.

5–70

a) A wedge with mass M rests on a frictionless horizontal tabletop. A block with mass m is placed on the wedge, as shown in Fig. 5–42a. There is no friction between the block and the wedge. The system is released from rest. Calculate

i) the acceleration of the wedge;

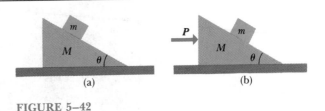

(a)   (b)

FIGURE 5–42

ii) the horizontal and vertical components of the acceleration of the block.

Do your answers reduce to the correct results when M is very large?

b) The wedge and block are as in part (a). Now a horizontal force $\boldsymbol{P}$ is applied to the wedge, as in Fig. 5–42b. What magnitude must $\boldsymbol{P}$ have if the block is to remain at constant height above the tabletop?

6

Circular Motion and Gravitation

In Chapter 5 we learned how to apply Newton's laws to several simple statics and dynamics problems. In this chapter we continue our study of dynamics, concentrating especially on *circular motion*. Bodies move in circular paths in a wide variety of situations, such as cars on racetracks, rotating machine parts, and the motions of planets and satellites; it is worthwhile to study this special class of motions in detail. We also return to *gravitational* interactions for a detailed study of Newton's law of gravitation. This law plays a central role in planet and satellite motion, and it also provides a fuller understanding of the concept of *weight*. We explored the *kinematics* of circular motion in Section 3–5; we suggest that you review that section now to help you understand what is to come.

6–1
Force in Circular Motion

When a particle moves in a circular path of radius R with constant speed v, the motion is called **uniform circular motion.** We showed in Section 3–5 that in this motion the particle has an acceleration directed always toward the center of the circle, perpendicular to the instantaneous velocity. This is called **centripetal acceleration;** its magnitude, as derived in Section 3–5, is

$$a_\perp = \frac{v^2}{R}.$$ (6–1)

The symbol $\perp$ is a reminder that at each point the acceleration is perpendicular to the instantaneous velocity. The **period** τ is the time for one revolution; it is given by

$$\tau = \frac{2\pi R}{v}.$$ (6–2)

In terms of the period, the centripetal acceleration can also be expressed as

$$a_\perp = \frac{4\pi^2 R}{\tau^2}.$$ (6–3)

Circular motion, like all other motion of a particle, is governed by Newton's second law. The particle's acceleration toward the center of the circle must be caused by a net *force* also directed radially toward the center. The magnitude of the radial acceleration is given by v^2/R, so the magnitude of the net radial force F on a particle of mass m must be

$$F = ma_\perp = m\frac{v^2}{R}.$$ (6–4)

Here's a familiar example. We tie a small object, such as a key, to a string and whirl it in a circle. The string has to pull constantly toward the center of the circle. If it breaks, then the inward force no longer acts, and the object flies off along a tangent to the circle.

When several forces act on a body in uniform circular motion, their *vector sum* must have the magnitude given by Eq. (6–4) and must be directed toward the center of the circle. The force in Eq. (6–4) is sometimes called *centripetal force*. This term tends to imply that this force is somehow different from ordinary forces, and it really isn't. The term *centripetal* refers to the fact that in uniform circular motion the direction of the velocity changes in such a way that the acceleration vector is always directed toward the center of the circle. The net force that causes this acceleration must also point toward the center; hence the term centripetal. In the equation $\Sigma \boldsymbol{F} = m\boldsymbol{a}$, the sum of forces must include only the real physical forces, pushes or pulls exerted by strings, rods, gravitation, and so on; the quantity $m(v^2/R)$ does *not* appear in $\Sigma \boldsymbol{F}$ but rather is the $m\boldsymbol{a}$ side of the equation.

PROBLEM-SOLVING STRATEGY: *Circular Motion*

1. The strategies for dynamics problems outlined at the beginning of Section 5–4 are equally applicable here, and we suggest that you reread them before beginning your study of the examples below.

2. A serious peril in circular motion problems is the temptation to regard $m(v^2/R)$ as a *force*, as though the body's circular motion somehow generates an extra force in addition to the real physical forces exerted by strings, contact with other bodies, gravitation, or whatever. *Resist this temptation!* It may help to draw the free-body diagram with *green* arrows for the forces and a *red* arrow for the acceleration. Then in the $\Sigma F = ma$ equations, write the force terms in green and the $m(v^2/R)$ term in red. This may sound silly, but if it helps, do it!

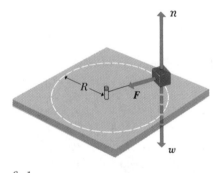

6–1
A body revolving uniformly in a circle on a horizontal frictionless surface.

Example 6–1   A small plastic box having a mass of 0.200 kg revolves uniformly in a circle on a horizontal frictionless surface such as an air-hockey table. It is attached by a cord 0.200 m long to a pin set in the surface. If the box makes two complete revolutions per second, find the force F exerted on it by the cord. (See Fig. 6–1.)

Solution   The period is $\tau = (1.00 \text{ s})/(2 \text{ rev}) = 0.500$ s. The circumference of the circle is $2\pi(0.200 \text{ m}) = 1.26$ m, so the speed is $v = (1.26 \text{ m})/(0.500 \text{ s}) = 2.51 \text{ m·s}^{-1}$. The speed could also be determined by using Eq. (6–2). The magnitude of the centripetal acceleration is

$$a_\perp = \frac{v^2}{R} = \frac{(2.51 \text{ m·s}^{-1})^2}{0.200 \text{ m}} = 31.6 \text{ m·s}^{-2}.$$

Alternatively, we may use Eq. (6–3). The period is $\tau = (1 \text{ s})/(2 \text{ rev}) = 0.500$ s, and

$$a_\perp = \frac{4\pi^2(0.200 \text{ m})}{(0.500 \text{ s})^2} = 31.6 \text{ m·s}^{-2}.$$

The body has no vertical acceleration, so the forces n and w are equal and opposite. The only force toward the center of the circle is the tension F in the cord, and

$$F = ma = (0.200 \text{ kg})(31.6 \text{ m·s}^{-2})$$
$$= 6.32 \text{ N.} \qquad \blacksquare$$

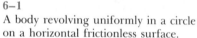

Example 6–2   An inventor who dares to be different proposes to make a pendulum clock with a mass m at the end of a thin wire of length L. Instead of swinging back and forth, the pendulum mass moves in a horizontal circle with constant speed v, with the wire making a constant angle θ with the vertical direction. Assuming that the time τ for one revolution (i.e., the period) is known, find the tension T in the wire and the angle θ.

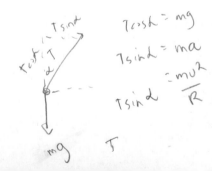

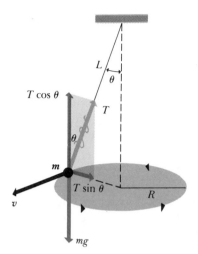

6–2
A conical pendulum.

$$v = \frac{2\pi R}{\tau}$$

Solution　A free-body diagram and a coordinate system are shown in Fig. 6–2. The center of the circular path is at the center of the shaded area, *not* at the top end of the wire. The forces on the system in the position shown are the weight mg and the tension T in the wire. The tension has a horizontal component $T \sin \theta$ and a vertical component $T \cos \theta$. (The force diagram in Fig. 6–2 is exactly like that in Fig. 5–14b, but in this case the acceleration a is the *radial* acceleration, v^2/R.) The system has no vertical acceleration, so the sum of the vertical components of force is zero. The horizontal force must equal the mass m times the radial (centripetal) acceleration. Thus the $\Sigma \mathbf{F} = m\mathbf{a}$ equations are

$$T \sin \theta = m\frac{v^2}{R}, \qquad T \cos \theta - mg = 0.$$

These are two simultaneous equations for the unknowns T and θ. An easy way to eliminate T is to divide the first of these equations by the second; the result is

$$\tan \theta = \frac{v^2}{gR}. \qquad (6\text{–}5)$$

Also, the radius R of the circle is given by $R = L \sin \theta$, and the speed is the circumference $2\pi L \sin \theta$ divided by the period τ:

$$v = \frac{2\pi L \sin \theta}{\tau}.$$

We use these relations to eliminate R and v from Eq. (6–5), obtaining

$$\cos \theta = \frac{g\tau^2}{4\pi^2 L}$$

or

$$\tau = 2\pi\sqrt{\frac{L \cos \theta}{g}}. \qquad (6\text{–}6)$$

　　Once we know θ, we can find the tension T from $T = mg/\cos \theta$. For a given length L, $\cos \theta$ decreases and θ increases as τ becomes smaller. The angle can never be 90°, however; this would require that $\tau = 0$ and $v = \infty$. This system is called a *conical pendulum* because it is shaped like a pendulum but the suspending wire traces out a cone. It would not make a very good clock because the period depends on θ in such a direct way.

　　You may be tempted to add to the forces in Fig. 6–2 an extra outward force to "keep the body out there" at angle θ or to "keep it in equilibrium." Perhaps you have heard the term *centrifugal force*; centrifugal means "fleeing from the center." Resist that temptation! First, the body *doesn't* stay "out there"; it is in constant motion around its circular path. Its velocity is constantly changing in direction, it accelerates, and it is *not* in equilibrium. Second, if there *were* an additional outward ("centrifugal") force to balance the inward force, there would then be *no* net inward force to cause the circular motion, and the body would move in a straight line, not a circle. If you were rotating with the body, you might *think* there was an extra force and that the body was in equilibrium, but this is because you would then be in a noninertial frame of reference. In an inertial frame of reference there is no such thing as centrifugal force, and we promise not to mention this term again.　■

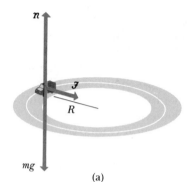

(a)

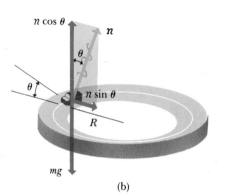

(b)

6-3
(a) Forces on a vehicle rounding a
curve on a level track. (b) Forces when
the track is banked.

Example 6–3   The driver of a truck is rounding a flat, unbanked curve
of radius R. If the coefficient of friction between tires and road is μ_s,
what is the maximum speed v at which the driver can take the curve
without sliding?

Solution   Figure 6–3a shows a free-body diagram for the situation. The
acceleration v^2/R toward the center of the curve must be caused by the
friction force $\mathcal{F}$, and there is no vertical acceleration. Thus we have

$$\mathcal{F} = m\frac{v^2}{R}, \qquad n - mg = 0.$$

The first equation shows that the friction force *needed* increases with
speed. But the maximum friction force *available* is $\mathcal{F} = \mu_s n = \mu_s mg$,
and this determines the maximum speed. Combining these relations to
eliminate $\mathcal{F}$, we find

$$\mu_s mg = m\frac{v^2}{R},$$

or

$$v = \sqrt{\mu_s g R}. \tag{6–7}$$

If $\mu_s = 0.50$ and $R = 25$ m, then

$$v = \sqrt{(0.50)(9.8 \text{ m·s}^{-2})(25 \text{ m})} = 11.1 \text{ m·s}^{-1},$$

or about 25 mi·hr^{-1}. This is the maximum speed; if we take the curve
more slowly than this, the friction force is *less than* $\mu_s mg$. Why do we use
the coefficient of *static* friction for a moving truck? What happens when
we try to go *faster* than this maximum speed?   ■

Example 6–4   An engineer proposes to rebuild the curve in Example
6–3, banking it so that at a certain speed v, *no* friction at all is needed for
the truck to make the curve. At what angle θ should it be banked?

Solution   The free-body diagram is shown in Fig. 6–3b. The normal
force n is no longer vertical but is perpendicular to the roadway at an
angle θ with the vertical. Thus it has a vertical component $n \cos \theta$ and a
horizontal component $n \sin \theta$, as shown. We want to get around the
curve without relying on friction, so no friction force is included. The
horizontal component of n must now cause the acceleration v^2/R; there
is no vertical acceleration. Thus

$$n \sin \theta = \frac{mv^2}{R}, \qquad n \cos \theta - mg = 0.$$

Dividing the first of these equations by the second, we find

$$\tan \theta = \frac{v^2}{gR}. \tag{6–8}$$

If $R = 25$ m and $v = 11.1$ m·s^{-1}, as in Example 6–3, then

$$\theta = \arctan \frac{(11.1 \text{ m·s}^{-1})^2}{(9.8 \text{ m·s}^{-2})(25 \text{ m})} = 26.7°.$$

The banking angle depends on the speed and the radius. For a given radius, no one angle is correct for all speeds. In the design of highways and railroads, curves are banked for the *average speed* of the traffic over them. The same considerations apply to the correct banking angle of an airplane when it makes a turn in level flight. We also note that the banking angle is given by the same expression as that for the angle of a conical pendulum, Eq. (6–5) in Example 6–2. In fact, the free-body diagrams of Figs. 6–2 and 6–3b are identical. ∎

6–2
Motion in a Vertical Circle

In all the examples in Section 6–1 the body moved in a horizontal circle. Motion in a vertical circle is no different in principle, but the weight of the body has to be treated carefully. The following example will show what we mean.

Example 6–5 In a carnival ride, such as a Ferris wheel, a passenger moves in a vertical circle of radius R with constant speed v. Assuming that the seat remains upright during the motion, derive expressions for the force the seat exerts on the passenger at the top of the circle, and at the bottom.

Solution Figure 6–4 is a diagram of the situation, with free-body diagrams for the two positions. We take the positive direction as upward in both cases. Let F_1 be the force the seat applies to the passenger at the top of the circle, and let F_2 be the force at the bottom. At the top the acceleration has magnitude v^2/R, but its vertical component is negative because its direction is downward, toward the center of the circle. So the $\Sigma F = ma$ equation at the top is

$$F_1 + (-mg) = -m\frac{v^2}{R},$$

or

$$F_1 = m\left(g - \frac{v^2}{R}\right).$$

$\Sigma F_y = 0 =$

$mg - F_1 = \dfrac{mv^2}{R}$

$F_1 = m\left(g - \dfrac{v^2}{R}\right)$

At the top the upward force the seat applies to the passenger is smaller in magnitude than the passenger's weight. If the ride goes fast enough that $g - v^2/R$ becomes zero, the seat applies *no* force, and the passenger is about to become airborne. If v becomes still larger, F_1 becomes negative; this means that a *downward* force is needed to keep the passenger in the seat. This could be supplied by a seat belt pulling down on the passenger, or we could glue the passenger to the seat.

At the bottom the acceleration is upward, and the equation of motion is

$$F_2 + (-mg) = +m\frac{v^2}{R},$$

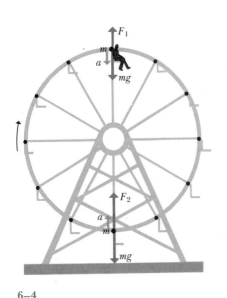

6–4
Forces and acceleration for a passenger on a Ferris wheel.

or

$$F_2 = m\left(g + \frac{v^2}{R}\right).$$

At this point the upward force provided by the seat is always *greater than* the passenger's weight. You feel the seat pushing up on you more firmly than when you are at rest.

As a specific example, suppose the passenger's mass is 60 kg, the radius of the circle is $R = 8.0$ m, and the wheel makes one revolution in 10 s. The speed is the circumference divided by the time for one revolution, $v = (2\pi)(8.0 \text{ m})/(10 \text{ s}) = 5.03 \text{ m·s}^{-1}$, and

$$\frac{v^2}{R} = \frac{(5.03 \text{ m·s}^{-1})^2}{8.0 \text{ m}} = 3.16 \text{ m·s}^{-2}.$$

The two forces are

$$F_1 = (60 \text{ kg})(9.8 \text{ m·s}^{-2} - 3.16 \text{ m·s}^{-2}) = 398 \text{ N},$$
$$F_2 = (60 \text{ kg})(9.8 \text{ m·s}^{-2} + 3.16 \text{ m·s}^{-2}) = 778 \text{ N}.$$

The passenger's weight is 588 N, and F_1 and F_2 are about 30% less than and greater than the weight, respectively.   ∎

When we tie a string to an object and whirl it in a vertical circle, this analysis is not directly applicable; v isn't constant in this case because at every point except the top and bottom there is a component of force (and therefore of acceleration) tangent to the circle. Even worse, we can't use the constant-acceleration formulas to relate the speeds at various points because *neither* the magnitude nor the direction of the acceleration is constant. The necessary speed relations are best obtained by using energy relations; we will return to such problems in Chapter 7.

6–3
Newton's Law of Gravitation

The *weight* of a body, the force that attracts it toward the earth (or whatever celestial body it is near) is an example of gravitational attraction. In this section we will explore gravitation in more detail. Newton discovered the **law of gravitation** during his study of the motions of planets around the sun, and he published it in 1686. It may be stated as follows:

> *Every particle of matter in the universe attracts every other particle with a force that is directly proportional to the product of the masses of the particles and inversely proportional to the square of the distance between them.*

Translating this into an equation, we have

$$F_g = G\frac{m_1 m_2}{r^2}, \tag{6–9}$$

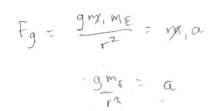

at earth's surface, object₂ w/ mass = m_1, r = radius of earth.

$$F_g = \frac{g m_1 m_E}{r^2} = m_1 a$$

$$\frac{g m_E}{r^2} = a$$

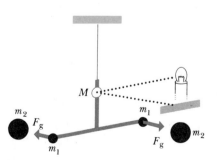

6–5

Principle of the Cavendish balance.

where F_g is the magnitude of the gravitational force on either particle, m_1 and m_2 are their masses, r is the distance between them, and G is a fundamental physical constant called the **gravitational constant.** The numerical value of G depends on the system of units used.

The gravitational attraction forces always act along the line joining the two particles, and they form an action–reaction pair. Even when the masses of the particles are different, the two interaction forces have equal magnitude.

We have spoken of interaction forces between two *particles*. It turns out that the interaction of any two bodies having spherical symmetry (such as solid spheres or spherical shells) is the same as though we concentrated all the mass of each at its center, effectively replacing each spherical body with a particle at the center. Thus if we model the earth as a homogeneous sphere of mass m_E, the force exerted by it on a small body with mass m, at a distance r from its center, is

$$F_g = G\frac{m m_E}{r^2}, \tag{6–10}$$

provided that the body lies outside the earth, that is, that r is greater than the radius of the earth. A force of the same magnitude is exerted *on* the earth by the body. In Chapter 25 we will learn how to prove the above statements about spheres in connection with analogous problems with electric charge.

At points *inside* the earth the situation is different. If we could drill a hole to the center of the earth and measure the force of gravity on a body at various depths, we would find that the force *decreases* as we approach the center, rather than increasing as $1/r^2$. As the body enters the interior of the earth (or other spherical body), some of the earth's mass is on the side of the body opposite from the center and pulls in the opposite direction. Exactly at the center the gravitational force on the body is zero.

To determine the value of the gravitational constant G, we have to *measure* the gravitational force between two bodies of known masses m_1 and m_2 at a known distance. For bodies of reasonable size the force is extremely small, but it can be measured with an instrument called a *torsion balance*, used by Sir Henry Cavendish in 1798 to determine G. The same type of instrument was also used by Charles Augustin de Coulomb to study forces of electrical and magnetic attraction and repulsion.

The Cavendish balance consists of a light, rigid rod shaped like an inverted T (Fig. 6–5), supported by a very thin vertical quartz fiber. Two small spheres, each of mass m_1, are mounted at the ends of the horizontal arms of the T. When we bring two large spheres, each of mass m_2, to the positions shown, the attractive gravitational forces twist the T through a small angle. To measure the angle, we shine a beam of light on a mirror M fastened to the T; the reflected beam strikes a scale, and as the T twists, the reflected beam moves along the scale.

After calibrating the instrument with a known force, we can measure gravitational forces and thus determine G. The value is found to be (in SI units)

$$G = 6.673 \times 10^{-11} \text{ N·m}^2\text{·kg}^{-2}.$$

Gravitational forces combine vectorially. If each of two masses exerts a force on a third, the *total* force on the third mass is the vector sum of the individual forces of the first two. Example 6–8 makes use of this property.

Example 6–6   The mass m_1 of one of the small spheres of a Cavendish balance is 0.00100 kg, the mass m_2 of one of the large spheres is 0.500 kg, and the center-to-center distance between each large sphere and the nearer small one is 0.0500 m. Find the gravitational force on each sphere due to the nearest other sphere.

Solution   The magnitude of each force is

$$F_g = (6.67 \times 10^{-11} \text{ N·m}^2\text{·kg}^{-2}) \frac{(0.00100 \text{ kg})(0.500 \text{ kg})}{(0.0500 \text{ m})^2}$$

$$= 1.33 \times 10^{-11} \text{ N},$$

or about one hundred-billionth of a newton! *Reminder:* The two bodies experience the *same* magnitude of force, even though their masses are very different.   ■

Example 6–7   Suppose one large and one small sphere in Example 6–6 are detached from the apparatus and placed 0.0500 m (between centers) from each other at a point in space far removed from all other bodies. What is the acceleration of each, relative to an inertial system?

Solution   The force on each sphere has the same magnitude that we found in Example 6–6. The acceleration a_1 of the smaller sphere is

$$a_1 = \frac{F_g}{m_1} = \frac{1.33 \times 10^{-11} \text{ N}}{1.00 \times 10^{-3} \text{ kg}} = 1.33 \times 10^{-8} \text{ m·s}^{-2}.$$

The acceleration a_2 of the larger sphere is

$$a_2 = \frac{F_g}{m_2} = \frac{1.33 \times 10^{-11} \text{ N}}{0.500 \text{ kg}} = 2.67 \times 10^{-11} \text{ m·s}^{-2}.$$

The two accelerations are *not* equal, and they are not constant because the gravitational forces increase as the spheres start to move toward each other.   ■

Example 6–8   Some of the masses from Example 6–6 are arranged as shown in Fig. 6–6. Find the magnitude and direction of the total force exerted on the small sphere by both large ones.

Solution   We use the principle of superposition; the total force on the small sphere is the vector sum of the two forces due to the two individual large spheres. We can compute the vector sum by using components, but first we find the magnitudes of the forces. The force F_1 on the small mass

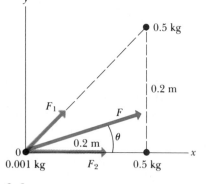

6–6
The total gravitational force on the 0.001-kg mass is the vector sum of the forces exerted by the two 0.5-kg masses.

due to the upper large one is

$$F_1 = \frac{(6.67 \times 10^{-11} \text{ N·m}^2\text{·kg}^{-2})(0.500 \text{ kg})(0.00100 \text{ kg})}{(0.200 \text{ m})^2 + (0.200 \text{ m})^2}$$

$$= 4.17 \times 10^{-13} \text{ N},$$

and the force F_2 due to the lower large mass is

$$F_2 = \frac{(6.67 \times 10^{-11} \text{ N·m}^2\text{·kg}^{-2})(0.500 \text{ kg})(0.00100 \text{ kg})}{(0.200 \text{ m})^2}$$

$$= 8.34 \times 10^{-13} \text{ N}.$$

The x- and y-components of these forces are

$$F_{1x} = (4.17 \times 10^{-13} \text{ N}) \cos 45° = 2.95 \times 10^{-13} \text{ N},$$

$$F_{1y} = (4.17 \times 10^{-13} \text{ N}) \sin 45° = 2.95 \times 10^{-13} \text{ N},$$

$$F_{2x} = 8.34 \times 10^{-13} \text{ N},$$

$$F_{2y} = 0.$$

The components of the total force on the small mass are

$$F_x = 11.29 \times 10^{-13} \text{ N},$$

$$F_y = 2.95 \times 10^{-13} \text{ N}.$$

The magnitude of this force is

$$F = \sqrt{(11.29 \times 10^{-13} \text{ N})^2 + (2.95 \times 10^{-13} \text{ N})^2}$$

$$= 1.17 \times 10^{-12} \text{ N},$$

and its direction is

$$\theta = \arctan \frac{2.95 \text{ N}}{11.29 \text{ N}} = 14.6°. \qquad \blacksquare$$

We can now define the **weight** of a body more generally as *the total gravitational force exerted on the body by all other bodies in the universe.* When the body is near the surface of the earth, we can neglect all other gravitational forces and consider the weight as being due entirely to the earth's attraction. At the surface of the moon, weight is the gravitational attraction of the moon, and so on. Thus if we again model the earth as a homogeneous sphere of radius R and mass m_E, the weight w of a small body of mass m at or near its surface (i.e., at a distance from the surface that is much smaller than R) is

$$w = F_g = \frac{Gmm_E}{R^2}. \qquad (6\text{--}11)$$

But we also know from the discussion of Section 4–5 that the weight w of a body is its mass m times the acceleration g of free fall (and that g is also the gravitational field at the position of the mass). That is, $w = mg$.

Equating this with Eq. (6–11) and dividing by m, we find

$$g = \frac{Gm_E}{R^2}. \tag{6–12}$$

Because this result does not contain m, the acceleration due to gravity is independent of mass. We already knew that, of course, but this analysis shows how this conclusion follows from the law of gravitation. Furthermore, we can measure all the quantities in Eq. (6–12) except for m_E, so this relation allows us to compute the mass of the earth. We first solve Eq. (6–12) for m_E, obtaining

$$m_E = \frac{gR^2}{G}.$$

Taking $R = 6380$ km $= 6.38 \times 10^6$ m, and $g = 9.80$ m·s^{-2}, we find

$$m_E = 5.98 \times 10^{24} \text{ kg}.$$

We need the value of G to make this calculation; this is why Cavendish referred to his measurement of G as "weighing the earth."

The weight of a given body decreases inversely with the square of its distance from the earth's center. For example, at a radial distance $2R$ from the center we should replace R^2 in Eq. (6–11) by $(2R)^2$. At this distance the weight is one quarter of its value at the earth's surface.

The *apparent* weight of a body on earth differs slightly from the earth's gravitational force because the earth rotates and is therefore not precisely an inertial frame of reference. We have ignored this effect in the above discussion and have assumed that the earth *is* an inertial system.

*6–4
Gravitational Field

We can restate Newton's law of gravitation in a useful way, using the concept of **gravitational field.** Instead of calculating the interaction forces between two masses by using Eq. (6–9) directly, we consider a two-stage process. A mass creates a *gravitational field* in the space around it. The gravitational field then exerts a force on the second mass.

But what *is* a gravitational field, and how do we know when one is present? We can use a test mass m as a detector of gravitational field. We take the mass to various points and measure the gravitational force that acts on it at each point. We then *define* the gravitational field g at each point as the gravitational force F_g experienced by the test mass m when it is at that point, divided by the mass. Thus

$$g = \frac{F_g}{m}. \tag{6–13}$$

To say it another way, at a point where the gravitational field is g, the force F_g on a mass m is given by

$$F_g = mg. \tag{6–14}$$

Force is a vector quantity, so gravitational field is also a vector quantity; Eqs. (6–13) and (6–14) are vector equations.

In Example 6–8, instead of calculating directly the forces on the 0.001-kg body by the large bodies, we may take the point of view that the large bodies create a *gravitational field* at the location of the small body and that the field exerts a force on any mass located at the point.

The gravitational field g caused by a point mass M, at a distance r away from it, has magnitude

$$g = \frac{GM}{r^2} \qquad (6-15)$$

and is directed toward the point mass. When several masses are located in the vicinity of a point, the *total* gravitational field at this point is the *vector sum* of the gravitational fields caused by the separate masses. Once we know the field at a point, we can quickly calculate the gravitational force on any body located at that point.

In general, gravitational field varies from point to point. Thus it is not a single vector quantity but rather a whole collection of vector quantities, one vector associated with each point in space. It is an example of a *vector field*. Another familiar example of a vector field is the velocity in a flowing fluid; different parts of the fluid have different velocities, and we speak of the *velocity field* in the fluid. When we study electricity and magnetism in the second half of this book, we will work a lot with electric and magnetic fields, which are both vector fields.

We have used the same symbol (g) for gravitational field that we have been using for the acceleration of free fall. This is not an accident. Indeed, in an inertial frame of reference the acceleration of free fall at any point is *equal* to the gravitational field at that point. When the force $F_g = mg$ is the *only* force acting on a body with mass m, then Newton's second law gives $F = ma$, and the acceleration is $a = g$. In particular, when g is the gravitational field of earth, the gravitational force F_g is simply the *weight* w of the body, and we obtain the familiar relation $w = mg$, which is Eq. (4-11).

Example 6–9   In Example 6–8, find the magnitude of the gravitational field at the location of the 0.001-kg mass.

Solution   From Eq. (6–13), the gravitational field at this point has magnitude

$$g = \frac{11.7 \times 10^{-13} \text{ N}}{0.00100 \text{ kg}} = 11.7 \times 10^{-10} \text{ m·s}^{-2}.$$

The direction of the field is the same as that of the force on the small body.   ■

Example 6–10   A ring-shaped body with radius a has total mass M. Find the gravitational field at point P, a distance x from the center, along the line through the center of the ring and perpendicular to its plane.

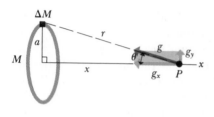

6–7
Gravitational field of a ring of mass M and radius a.

Solution The situation is shown in Fig. 6–7. We imagine the ring as divided into small segments Δs; we call the mass of a segment ΔM. At point P this segment produces a gravitational field with magnitude

$$g = \frac{G\,\Delta M}{r^2} = \frac{G\,\Delta M}{x^2 + a^2}.$$

The component of this field along the x-axis is given by

$$g_x = -g\cos\theta = -\frac{G\,\Delta M}{x^2 + a^2}\,\frac{x}{\sqrt{x^2 + a^2}} = -\frac{G\,\Delta M x}{(x^2 + a^2)^{3/2}}. \quad (6\text{–}16)$$

Now x is the same for every segment around the ring, so to find the *total* x-component of gravitational field from all the mass elements ΔM, we simply sum all the ΔM's to obtain the *total* mass M. The result is

$$g_x = -\frac{GMx}{(x^2 + a^2)^{3/2}}. \quad (6\text{–}17)$$

The y-component of gravitational field at point P is zero because the y-components of field produced by two segments at opposite sides of the ring cancel each other, and the contributions of all such pairs added over the entire ring add to zero.

Equation (6–17) shows that at the center of the ring ($x = 0$) the total gravitational field is zero. We should expect this; mass elements on opposite sides pull in opposite directions, and their fields cancel. Also, when x is much larger than a, we can neglect a in the denominator of Eq. (6–17); the expression then becomes approximately equal to GM/x^2. This shows that at distances (x) much greater than the size (a) of the ring it appears as a point mass.   ∎

6–5
Satellite Motion

Artificial satellites orbiting the earth are a familiar fact of contemporary life, and we know that they differ only in scale, not in principle, from the motion of our moon around the earth or the motion of the moons of Jupiter. But we still have to deal with questions such as "What holds that thing up there, anyway?" So it is worthwhile to see what we can do about applying Newton's laws and the law of gravitation to the analysis of satellite motion. We can do quite a lot!

For starters, think back to the discussion of projectile motion in Section 3–4. In Example 3–3 a motorcycle rider rides horizontally off the edge of a cliff, launching himself into a parabolic path that presumably ends at the surface of the earth. If he survives and repeats the experiment with increased launch speed, he will land farther from the starting point. We can imagine him launching himself with great enough speed that the earth's curvature becomes significant; as he falls, the earth curves away beneath him; and if he is going fast enough, he may be able to go right on around the earth and never land!

Figure 6–8a shows a variation on this theme. We launch a projectile from point *A* in the direction *AB*, tangent to the earth's surface. Trajectories (3) to (7) show the effect of increasing the initial speed. Trajectory (3) just misses the earth, and the projectile has become an earth satellite. Its speed when it returns to point *A* is the same as its initial speed; if there is no retarding force (such as air resistance), it repeats its motion indefinitely.

Trajectories (1) through (5) are ellipses or segments of ellipses; trajectory (4) is a special case of an ellipse, namely, a circle. Trajectories (6) and (7) are not closed orbits; for these the projectile never returns to its starting point, but "escapes" permanently from the earth.

A circular orbit is the simplest case and the only one we will analyze in detail. Many manmade satellites have nearly circular orbits, and the orbits of the planets around the sun are also nearly circular. We know that a particle in uniform circular motion with speed *v* and radius *r* has

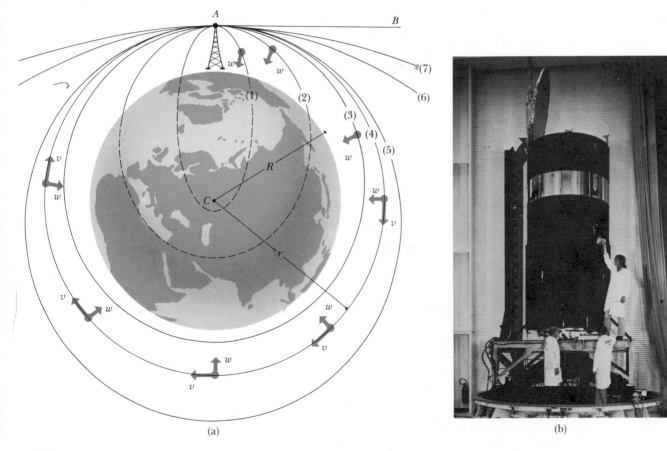

(a)   (b)

6–8
(a) Trajectories of a body projected from point *A* in the direction *AB* with different initial velocities. Orbits (1) and (2) would be completed as shown if the earth were a point mass at *C*. (b) A communications satellite before launch. The main body is 2.16 m in diameter and 2.82 m in height. Solar-energy collector panels on the sides and a parabolic antenna at the end can be seen. (Courtesy Hughes Aircraft Co.)

an acceleration, with magnitude $a_\perp = v^2/r$, directed always toward the center of the circle. For a satellite, the *force* that provides this acceleration is the gravitational attraction of the earth (mass m_E) for the satellite (mass m). If the radius of the circular orbit, measured from the *center* of the earth, is r, then the gravitational force is given by $F_g = Gm_Em/r^2$. Using Newton's second law, we equate this to the product of the satellite's mass m and its acceleration v^2/r:

$$\frac{Gmm_E}{r^2} = \frac{mv^2}{r}.$$

Solving this for v, we find

$$v = \sqrt{\frac{Gm_E}{r}}. \tag{6-18}$$

This relation shows that we can't choose the orbit radius r and the speed v independently; they have to be related by Eq. (6–18). It also shows that the satellite's motion does not depend on its mass m because m doesn't appear in Eq. (6–18).

We can also derive a relation between the orbit radius r and the *period* τ, the time for one revolution. The speed v is the distance $2\pi r$ traveled in one revolution, divided by the time τ for one revolution. Thus

$$v = \frac{2\pi r}{\tau}. \tag{6-19}$$

We can obtain an expression for τ by solving this for τ and combining it with Eq. (6–18):

$$\tau = \frac{2\pi r}{v} = 2\pi r\sqrt{\frac{r}{Gm_E}} = \frac{2\pi r^{3/2}}{\sqrt{Gm_E}}. \tag{6-20}$$

Equations (6–18) and (6–20) show that larger orbits correspond to slower speeds and longer periods. The proportionality of τ to the three-halves power of r was discovered by Johannes Kepler. You can check it using the data on the solar system in Appendix F. For example, the orbit radius of Uranus is about twice that of Saturn, so its period ought to be about $(2)^{3/2}$ times (about 2.83) as long as that of Saturn. Check it out!

Example 6–11 Suppose you want to place the communications satellite shown in Fig. 6–8b into a circular orbit 300 km above the earth's surface. What must be its speed, its period, and its radial acceleration? The earth's radius is 6380 km = 6.38×10^6 m, and its mass is 5.98×10^{24} kg. (See Appendix F.)

Solution The radius of the orbit is

$$r = 6380 \text{ km} + 300 \text{ km} = 6680 \text{ km} = 6.68 \times 10^6 \text{ m}.$$

From Eq. (6–18),

$$v = \sqrt{\frac{(6.67 \times 10^{-11}\ \text{N·m}^2\text{·kg}^{-2})(5.98 \times 10^{24}\ \text{kg})}{6.68 \times 10^6\ \text{m}}}$$

$$= 7730\ \text{m·s}^{-1}.$$

From Eq. (6–20),

$$\tau = \frac{2\pi(6.68 \times 10^6\ \text{m})}{7730\ \text{m·s}^{-1}} = 5430\ \text{s} = 90.5\ \text{min}.$$

The radial acceleration is

$$a_{\perp} = \frac{v^2}{r} = \frac{(7730\ \text{m·s}^{-1})^2}{6.68 \times 10^6\ \text{m}} = 8.94\ \text{m·s}^{-2}.$$

This is somewhat less than the value of the free-fall acceleration g at the earth's surface and is, in fact, equal to the value of g at a height of 300 km above the earth's surface. ∎

We have talked mostly about manmade earth satellites, but the same analysis is applicable to the circular motion of *any* body under its gravitational attraction to a stationary body. Other familiar examples are our moon, the moons of Jupiter, and the planets orbiting the sun in nearly circular paths. The rings of Saturn, shown in Fig. 6–9, are composed of small particles in circular orbits around the planet.

Indeed, the study of planetary motion played a pivotal role in the early development of physics. Johannes Kepler (1571–1630) spent several painstaking years analyzing the motions of the planets, basing his work on remarkably precise measurements made by the Danish astronomer Tycho Brahe (1546–1601) *without the aid of a telescope*. (The telescope was invented in 1608.) Kepler discovered that the orbits of the planets are (nearly circular) ellipses and that the period of a planet in its orbit is proportional to the three-halves power of the orbit radius, as Eq. (6–20) shows.

But it remained for Isaac Newton (1642–1727) to show, with his laws of motion and law of gravitation, that this behavior of the planets could be understood on the basis of the very same physical principles he had developed to analyze *terrestrial* motion. Newton recognized that the falling apple (Section 4–5) was pulled to the earth by gravitational attraction. But to arrive at the $1/r^2$ form of the law of gravitation, he had to do something much subtler; he had to take Brahe's observations of planetary motions, as systematized by Kepler, and show that Kepler's rules demanded a $1/r^2$ force law.

From our historical perspective 300 years later, there is absolutely no doubt that this **Newtonian synthesis,** as it has come to be called, is one of the greatest achievements in the entire history of science, certainly comparable in significance to the development of quantum mechanics, the theory of relativity, and the understanding of DNA in our own century. It was an astonishing leap in understanding, made by a giant intellect!

6–9
The rings of Saturn, photographed from Voyager 1 on November 1, 1980, from a distance of 700,000 km. Individual particles move in circular orbits, with periods given by Eq. (6–20), using Saturn's mass. The outer portions of the rings take more time for one revolution than the inner portions. (Courtesy of Jet Propulsion Laboratory/NASA.)

*6–6
The Centrifuge

The centrifuge is an important laboratory tool for separating particles from a liquid having a different density from that of the particles. Muddy water is a familiar example. In still water, mud particles settle to the bottom, but the process may take several hours or days because the terminal speeds of the particles, given by Eq. (5–9) ($v_t = mg/k$), are extremely small.

We can speed up the process greatly by whirling the container at high speed. The particles move approximately in circles, with speed v and acceleration v^2/r. When they reach their terminal speed v_t *relative to the fluid*, the resisting force of the fluid on a particle, given by Eq. (5–7) ($f = kv_t$), must equal the mass m of a particle times its acceleration v^2/r. The terminal speed v_t of the particles relative to the fluid is then given by

$$v_t = \frac{mv^2/r}{k}. \tag{6–21}$$

Thus the terminal speed or *sedimentation rate* is increased by a factor of $(v^2/r)/g$, which may be many thousands.

Centrifuges are used to separate cream from milk, blood cells from plasma, silt from river water, macromolecules from solutions, and in many other ways. In one type of laboratory centrifuge the specimen is placed in a test tube in a motor-driven rotor that holds it at an angle while rotating at high speed.

Example 6–12   A centrifuge rotates at 9000 rev·min⁻¹, and the specimen is 10 cm from the axis. What is its acceleration? By what factor is the sedimentation rate increased?

Solution   The specimen moves in a circle of radius 0.100 m and circumference $2\pi(0.100 \text{ m}) = 0.628$ m. It rotates 9000 times per minute, or $9000/60 = 150$ times per second. Its speed is $v = (0.628 \text{ m})(150 \text{ s}^{-1}) = 94.2 \text{ m·s}^{-1}$. Its acceleration is

$$a = \frac{v^2}{r} = \frac{(94.2 \text{ m·s}^{-1})^2}{0.100 \text{ m}} = 8.88 \times 10^4 \text{ m·s}^{-2}.$$

Thus the sedimentation rate is increased by a factor of

$$\frac{a}{g} = \frac{8.88 \times 10^4 \text{ m·s}^{-2}}{9.80 \text{ m·s}^{-2}} = 9060.$$ ∎

▪ *Questions*

6–1 "It's not the fall that hurts you; it's the sudden stop at the bottom."

Translate this saying into the language of Newton's laws of motion.

6–2 If action and reaction are always equal in magnitude and opposite in direction, why don't they always cancel each other and leave no net force for acceleration of the body?

6–3 Scales for weighing objects can be classified as those that use springs and those using standard weights to balance unknown weights. Which group would have greater accuracy when used in an accelerating elevator? When used on the moon? Does it matter whether you are trying to determine mass or weight?

6–4 Because of air resistance, two objects of unequal mass do *not* fall at precisely the same rate. If two bodies of identical shape but unequal mass are dropped simultaneously from the same height, which one reaches the ground first?

6–5 In discussing the Cavendish balance, a student claimed that the reason the small pivoted masses move toward the larger stationary masses rather than the larger toward the smaller is that the larger masses exert a stronger gravitational pull than the smaller. Please comment.

6–6 Since the earth is constantly attracted toward the sun by the gravitational interaction, why does it not fall into the sun and burn up?

6–7 A student wrote: "The only reason an apple falls downward to meet the earth instead of the earth falling upward to meet the apple is that the earth is much more massive and so exerts a much greater pull." Please comment.

6–8 Cavendish described his measurement of the gravitational constant G as "weighing the earth." This is an apt description not of the experiment itself but of the significance of the result. Why?

6–9 In uninformed discussions of satellites, one hears questions such as: "What keeps the satellite moving in its orbit?" and "What keeps the satellite up?" How do you answer these questions? Are your answers applicable to the moon?

6–10 A certain centrifuge is claimed to operate at 100,000 g. What does this mean?

Exercises

Section 6–1   Force in Circular Motion

6–1 A stone with a mass of 2.50 kg is attached to one end of a string 0.80 m long, breaking strength 500 N, and is whirled in a horizontal circle on a frictionless tabletop. The other end of the string is held stationary. Find the maximum speed the stone can attain without breaking the string.

6–2 A flat (unbanked) curve on a highway has a radius of 240 m. A car rounds the curve at a speed of 28.0 m·s⁻¹. What is the minimum coefficient of friction that will prevent sliding?

6–3 A highway curve with radius 900 ft is to be banked so that a car traveling 55.0 mi·hr⁻¹ will not skid sideways even in the absence of friction. At what angle should the curve be banked?

6–4 A small button placed on a record of diameter 12.0 in. will revolve with the record when it is brought up to a speed of 33⅓ rev·min⁻¹, provided that the button is no more than 5.0 in. from the axis.

a) What is the coefficient of static friction between the button and the record?

b) How far from the axis can the button be placed, without slipping, if the turntable rotates at 45.0 rev·min⁻¹?

6–5 The "Giant Swing" at a county fair consists of a vertical central shaft with a number of horizontal arms attached at its upper end. Each arm supports a seat suspended from a cable 6.50 m long, with the upper end of the cable fastened to the arm at a point 4.00 m from the central shaft.

a) Find the time of one revolution of the swing if the cable supporting a seat makes an angle of 30.0° with the vertical.

b) Does the angle depend on the weight of the passenger for a given rate of revolution?

6–6 One of the problems for humans living in outer space is the fact that they are weightless. One way around this problem is to design space stations as shown in Fig. 6–10 and have them spin about their center at a constant rate. This creates artificial gravity. If the diameter of the space station is 1400 m, how many revolutions per minute are needed for the artificial gravity acceleration to be 9.80 m·s⁻²?

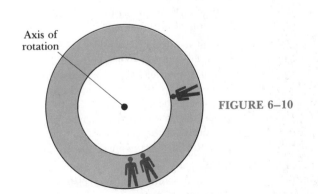

Axis of rotation

FIGURE 6–10

Section 6–2   Motion in a Vertical Circle

6–7 A bowling ball weighing 16.0 lb is attached to the ceiling by a 15.0-ft rope. The ball is pulled to one side and released; it then swings back and forth as a pendulum. As the rope swings through the vertical, the speed of the bowling ball is 18.0 ft·s^{-1}.

a) What is the acceleration of the bowling ball, in magnitude and direction, at this instant?

b) What is the tension on the rope at this instant?

6–8 A cord is tied to a pail of water, and the pail is swung in a vertical circle with radius 1.40 m. What must be the minimum speed of the pail at the highest point of the circle if no water is to spill from the pail?

6–9 A stunt pilot who has been diving vertically at a speed of 180 m·s^{-1} pulls out of the dive by changing his course to a circle in a vertical plane.

a) What is the minimum radius of the circle if the acceleration at the lowest point is not to exceed "6.00g"? (The plane's speed at this point is 180 m·s^{-1}.)

b) What is the *apparent* weight of a 90.0-kg pilot at the lowest point of the pullout?

6–10 The radius of a Ferris wheel is 8.00 m, and it makes one revolution in 12.0 s.

a) Find the *apparent* weight of an 80.0-kg passenger at the highest and lowest points.

b) What would be the time for one revolution if her apparent weight at the highest point were zero?

c) What would then be her *apparent* weight at the lowest point?

Section 6–3   Newton's Law of Gravitation

6–11 A communications satellite with a mass of 350 kg is in a circular orbit with a radius of 40,000 km, measured from the center of the earth. What is the gravitational force on the satellite, and what fraction is this of its weight at the surface of the earth?

6–12 What is the ratio of the gravitational pull of the sun on the moon to that of the earth on the moon? Use the data in Appendix F. What is the significance of the result for the motion of the moon?

6–13 In an experiment using the Cavendish balance to measure the gravitational constant G it is found that a mass of 0.800 kg attracts another sphere of mass 4.00 × 10^{-3} kg with a force of 1.30 × 10^{-10} N when the distance between the centers of the spheres is 4.00 × 10^{-2} m. The acceleration of gravity at the earth's surface is 9.80 m·s^{-2}, and the radius of the earth is 6380 km. Compute the mass of the earth from these data.

6–14 The mass of the moon is about 1/81, and its radius 1/4, that of the earth. Compute the acceleration due to gravity on the moon's surface from these data.

6–15 A 0.100-kg point mass is located on the line between a 5.00-kg and a 10.0-kg point mass. It is 3.00 m to the right of the 5.00-kg mass and 7.00 m to the left of the 10.0-kg mass. What are the magnitude and direction of the force on the 0.100-kg mass?

Section 6–4   Gravitational Field

6–16 What are the magnitude and direction of the gravitational force on a 0.100-kg point mass placed at a point where the gravitational field has components $g_x = -3.25$ m·s^{-2} and $g_y = +5.80$ m·s^{-2}?

6–17 The gravitational force F on a 0.0100-kg test mass is found to have components $F_x = -0.395$ N and $F_y = 0.256$ N at a certain point. What are the components of the gravitational field vector at that point?

6–18 What is the magnitude of the gravitational field 1.80 m from a 5.00-kg point mass?

6–19 What are the magnitude and direction of the gravitational field at a point midway between two point masses, one with mass m_1 and the other with mass m_2, where $m_2 > m_1$? The two point masses are a distance d apart.

Section 6–5   Satellite Motion

6–20 What is the period of revolution of a manmade satellite with mass m that is orbiting the earth in a circular path of radius 9380 km (about 3000 km above the surface of the earth)?

6–21 To launch a satellite in a circular orbit 900 km above the surface of the earth, what orbital speed must be given to the satellite?

6–22 An earth satellite moves in a circular orbit with an orbital speed of 7550 m·s^{-1}.

a) Find the time of one revolution.

b) Find the radial acceleration of the satellite in its orbit.

Section 6–6   The Centrifuge

6–23 A sample of blood is located 15.0 cm from the axis of a centrifuge.

a) How many revolutions per minute must the centrifuge make if the sedimentation rate is to be increased by a factor of 3000?

b) What then is the radial acceleration of the sample?

6–24 A large centrifuge rotates at 8000 rev·min^{-1}.

a) What must be the distance of the specimen from the axis if it is to have a radial acceleration of 2.00 × 10^5 m·s^{-2}?

b) By what factor is the sedimentation rate increased because of the rotation of the centrifuge?

Problems

6–25 Consider a roadway banked as in Example 6–4, where there is a coefficient of static friction of 0.35 and a coefficient of kinetic friction of 0.25 between the tires and the roadway. The radius of the curve is $R = 42$ m.

a) If the banking angle is $\theta = 25.0°$, what is the *maximum* speed the automobile can have before sliding *up* the banking?

b) What is the *minimum* speed the automobile can have in order not to slide *down* the banking?

6–26 You are riding in a school bus. As the bus rounds a flat curve, a lunch box with a mass of 0.500 kg suspended from the ceiling of the bus by a 1.60-m-long string is found to be in equilibrium when the string makes an angle of 37.0° with respect to the vertical. In this position the lunch box is 50.4 m from the center of curvature of the curve. What is the speed v of the bus?

6–27 In the ride "Spindletop" at the Six Flags Over Texas amusement park, people stand against the inner wall of a hollow vertical cylinder with radius 3.0 m. The cylinder starts to rotate, and when it reaches a constant rotation rate of 0.70 rev·s^{-1}, the floor on which people are standing drops about 0.5 m. The people remain pinned against the wall.

a) Draw a force diagram for a person in this ride after the floor has dropped.

b) What minimum coefficient of static friction is required if the person in the ride is not to slide downward to the new position of the floor?

c) Does your answer in part (b) depend on the mass of the passenger?

(*Note:* When the ride is over, the cylinder is slowly brought to rest; as it slows down, people slide down the walls to the floor.)

6–28 A curve with a 150-m radius on a level road is banked at the correct angle for a speed of 15.0 m·s^{-1}. If an automobile rounds this curve at 30.0 m·s^{-1}, what is the minimum coefficient of friction between tires and road needed so that the automobile will not skid?

6–29 You are driving with a friend who is sitting to your right on the passenger side of the front seat. You would like to be closer to your friend and decide to use physics to achieve your romantic goal by making a quick turn.

a) Which way (to the left or to the right) should you turn the car to get your friend to slide toward you?

b) If the coefficient of static friction between your friend and the car seat is 0.55 and you keep driving at a constant speed of 15 m·s^{-1}, what is the maximum radius you could make your turn and still have your friend slide your way?

6–30 The 4.00-kg block in Fig. 6–11 is attached to a vertical rod by means of two strings. When the system rotates about the axis of the rod, the strings are extended as shown in the diagram.

a) How many revolutions per minute must the system make for the tension in the upper string to be 90.0 N?

b) What is then the tension in the lower string?

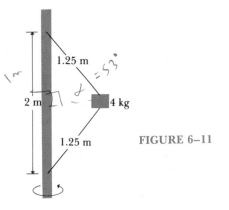

1.25 m

2 m

1 m

=53°

4 kg

1.25 m   **FIGURE 6–11**

6–31 The asteroid Toro was discovered in 1964. Its radius is about 5.0 km.

a) Assuming that the density (mass per unit volume) of Toro is the same as that of the earth, find its total mass and find the acceleration due to gravity at its surface.

b) Suppose an object is to be placed in a circular orbit around Toro, with a radius just slightly larger than the asteroid's radius. What is the speed of the object? Could you launch yourself into orbit around Toro by running?

6–32 A physics major is working to pay his college tuition by performing in a traveling carnival. He rides a motorcycle inside a hollow steel sphere with a radius of 12.0 m. The surface of the sphere is full of holes so that the audience can see in. After gaining sufficient speed, he travels in a vertical circle. The physics major has a mass of 60.0 kg, and his motorcycle has a mass of 40.0 kg.

a) What minimum speed must he have at the top of the circle if the tires of the motorcycle are not to lose contact with the steel sphere?

b) At the bottom of the circle his speed is twice the value calculated in part (a). What is the magnitude of the normal force exerted on the motorcycle by the steel sphere at this point?

6–33 A spaceship travels from the earth directly toward the sun. At what distance from the center of the earth do the gravitational forces of the sun and the earth on the ship exactly cancel each other out? Use the data in Appendix F.

6–34 Two spheres, each with a mass of 6.40 kg, are fixed at points A and B (Fig. 6–12). Find the magnitude and direction of the initial acceleration of a sphere with a mass of 0.0100 kg if it is released from rest at point P and acted on only by forces of gravitational attraction of the spheres at A and B.

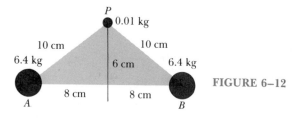

FIGURE 6–12

6–35 Three point masses are fixed at the positions shown in Fig. 6–13.

a) Calculate the x- and y-components of the gravitational field at point P, which is at the origin of coordinates, due to these three point masses.

b) What would be the magnitude and direction of the force on a 0.0250-kg mass placed at P?

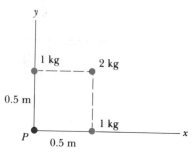

FIGURE 6–13

6–36 Two point masses are located at x–y coordinates as follows: 3.00 kg at (1.00 m, 0) and 4.00 kg at (0, −0.500 m).

a) What are the components of the gravitational field at the origin due to these two point masses?

b) What will be the magnitude and direction of the gravitational force on a 0.0300-kg test mass placed at the origin?

6–37 Several satellites are moving in a circle in the earth's equatorial plane. They are at such a height above the earth's surface that they always remain above the same point. Find the altitude of these satellites above the earth's surface. (Such an orbit is said to be *geosynchronous*.)

Challenge Problems

6–38 A ball is held at rest at position A in Fig. 6–14 by two light strings. The horizontal string is cut, and the ball starts swinging as a pendulum. Point B is the farthest to the right that the ball reaches as it swings back and forth. What is the ratio of the tension in the supporting string in position B to its value at A before the horizontal string was cut?

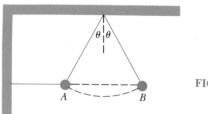

FIGURE 6–14

6–39 A small block with mass m is placed inside an inverted cone that is rotating about a vertical axis such that the time for one revolution of the cone is τ (see

Fig. 6–15). The walls of the cone make an angle θ with the vertical. The coefficient of static friction between the block and the cone is μ_s. If the block is to remain at a constant height h above the apex of the cone, what are the maximum and minimum values of τ?

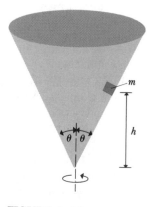

FIGURE 6–15

6–40 A bead can slide without friction on a circular hoop with a radius of 0.100 m in a vertical plane. The hoop rotates at a constant rate of 3.00 rev·s^{-1} about a vertical diameter, as in Fig. 6–16.

a) Find the angle θ at which the bead is in vertical equilibrium. (Of course it has a radial acceleration toward the axis.)

b) Is it possible for the bead to "ride" at the same elevation as the center of the hoop?

c) What will happen if the hoop rotates at 1.00 rev·s^{-1}?

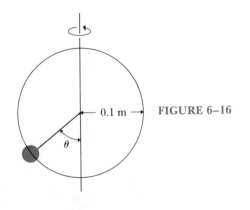

0.1 m →   FIGURE 6–16

7

Work and Energy

Energy is one of the most important unifying concepts in all of physical science. Its importance stems from the principle of **conservation of energy,** which states that in any isolated system the total energy (including all forms of energy) is constant, no matter what happens within the system. In this chapter we concentrate on mechanical energy, which is associated with the motion and position of mechanical systems. The concepts of work and kinetic energy, and the relationship between them, are central in this analysis. Potential energy simplifies work calculations with some kinds of forces. Power characterizes work or transfer of energy into or out of a system per unit time.

7–1
Conservation of Energy

The concept of **energy** appears throughout every area of physics, yet it is difficult to define in a general way just what energy *is*. This concept is the cornerstone of a fundamental law of nature called *conservation of energy*. Conservation laws, including conservation of mass, energy, momentum, angular momentum, electric charge, and others, play vital roles in every area of physics and help to unify the subject.

A familiar conservation law is conservation of *mass* in chemical reactions. Many experiments have shown that the total *mass* of the material participating in a chemical reaction is always the same (within the limits of experimental precision), before and after the reaction. This generalization is called the principle of *conservation of mass*, and it is obeyed in all chemical reactions.

Something analogous happens in collisions between bodies. For a body of mass m moving with speed v we can define a quantity $\frac{1}{2}mv^2$ called the *kinetic energy* of the body. When two highly elastic or "springy" bodies (such as two hard steel ball bearings) collide, we find that the individual speeds change but that the total kinetic energy (the sum of the $\frac{1}{2}mv^2$ quantities) is the same after the collision as before. We say that kinetic energy is *conserved* in such collisions.

When two soft, deformable bodies, such as two balls of putty or chewing gum, collide, we find that kinetic energy is *not* conserved. But something else happens; the bodies become *warmer*. Even better, it turns out that there is a definite relationship between the rise in temperature and the loss of kinetic energy. We can define a new quantity, *internal energy*, that increases with temperature in a definite way so that the *sum* of kinetic energy and internal energy *is* conserved in these collisions.

We can also define additional forms of energy that enable us to extend the principle of conservation of energy to broader and broader classes of phenomena. The astonishing thing is that in *every* situation in which it seems that the total energy in all known forms is *not* conserved, it has been found possible to identify a new form of energy so that the *total* energy, including the new form, *is* conserved. There is energy associated with heat, elastic deformations, electric and magnetic fields, and, according to the theory of relativity, even mass itself. Conservation of energy is a *universal* conservation principle; no exception has ever been found.

In this chapter we are concerned mostly with *mechanical* energy, associated with motion, position, and deformation of bodies. In some interactions, mechanical energy is conserved; in others, mechanical energy is converted to other forms or another form of energy is converted to mechanical energy. In Chapters 15 and 18 we will study in detail the relation of mechanical energy to heat, and in later chapters we will encounter still other forms of energy.

7–2
Work

In everyday usage the word *work* means any activity that requires muscular or mental exertion. Physicists use the term in a much more specific sense involving a *force* acting on a body while the body undergoes a *displacement*. When a body undergoes a displacement with magnitude s along a straight line while a constant force with magnitude F, directed along the same line, acts on it, we define the **work** W done by the force as

$$W = Fs. \tag{7–1}$$

Work turns out to be directly related to changes in kinetic energy, so it is a very useful concept.

What if the force doesn't have the same direction as the displacement? In Fig. 7–1 a constant force F makes an angle θ with the displacement. We take the component of F in the direction of the displacement s, and we define the work as the product of this component and the magnitude of the displacement. The component of F in the direction of s is $F \cos \theta$, so

$$W = (F \cos \theta)s. \tag{7–2}$$

By definition the component of F *perpendicular* to s does no work.

We calculate work using two vector quantities (force and displacement), but work itself is a *scalar* quantity. A 5-N force toward the east acting on a body that moves 6 m to the east does exactly the same work as a 5-N force toward the north acting on a body that moves 6 m to the north. Work can be positive or negative. When the force has a component in the *same direction* as the displacement (and θ is between $0°$ and $90°$), $\cos \theta$ in Eq. (7–2) is positive, and the work W is *positive*. When it has a component *opposite* to the displacement, θ is between $90°$ and $180°$, $\cos \theta$ is negative, and the work is *negative*. When the force is *perpendicular* to the displacement, $\theta = 90°$ and the work done by the force is *zero*.

Note that we always speak of work done *by* a specific force. It's easy to get confused, especially when you're dealing with an interaction between two bodies, so always be sure to specify exactly what force is doing the work you are talking about. When a body is lifted, the work done on the body by the lifting force is positive; when a spring is stretched, the work done by the stretching force is positive. But the work done by the *gravitational* force on a body being lifted is *negative* because the (downward) gravitational force is opposite to the (upward) displacement. You may think it is "hard work" to hold a brick out at arm's length, but you aren't doing any work on the brick, in the technical sense, because there is no motion! Even when you walk on a level floor while carrying the brick, you do no work on the brick because the (vertical) supporting force has no component in the direction of the (horizontal) motion. When a body slides along a surface, the work done by the normal force acting on the body is zero, and when a body moves in a circle, the work done by the centripetal force on the body is also zero.

The *unit* of work in any system is the unit of force multiplied by the unit of distance. In SI units, in which the unit of force is the newton and

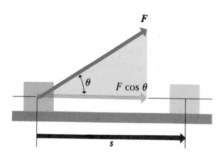

7–1
The work done by the force F during a displacement s is $(F \cos \theta)s$.

the unit of distance is the meter, the unit of work is the *newton meter* (N·m). This combination appears so often in mechanics that we give it a special name, the **joule** (abbreviated J, pronounced "jewel"):

$$1 \text{ joule} = (1 \text{ newton})(1 \text{ meter}) \qquad \text{or} \qquad 1 \text{ J} = 1 \text{ N·m.}$$

In the cgs system the unit of work is the dyne-centimeter, also called the *erg*. Because $1 \text{ dyn} = 10^{-5} \text{ N}$ and $1 \text{ cm} = 10^{-2} \text{ m}$,

$$1 \text{ erg} = 10^{-7} \text{ J.}$$

In the British system the unit of work is the *foot-pound* (ft·lb). The following conversions are useful:

$$1 \text{ J} = 0.7376 \text{ ft·lb}, \qquad 1 \text{ ft·lb} = 1.356 \text{ J.}$$

When several forces act on a body, we can use Eq. (7–1) or Eq. (7–2) to compute the work done by each separate force. Then, because work is a scalar quantity, the *total* work W_{tot} done by all the forces is the algebraic sum of the quantities of work done by the individual forces. An alternative route to finding the total work W_{tot} is to compute the vector sum (resultant) of the forces and then use this vector sum as F in Eq. (7–2).

Example 7–1   Figure 7–2 shows a worker dragging a crate along a horizontal surface by applying a constant force F at an angle θ to the direction of motion. The other forces on the crate are its weight w, the upward normal force n exerted by the surface, and the friction force $\mathcal{F}$. What is the work done by each force when the crate moves a distance s along the surface to the right? What is the *total* work done by all the forces?

Solution   The component of F in the direction of motion is $F \cos \theta$. The work done by F is

$$W_F = (F \cos \theta)s.$$

The forces w and n are both at right angles to the displacement, so they do no work on the crate:

$$W_w = 0, \qquad W_n = 0.$$

The friction force $\mathcal{F}$ is opposite to the displacement, so the work done by the friction force is

$$W_{\mathcal{F}} = \mathcal{F}s \cos 180° = -\mathcal{F}s.$$

The total work W_{tot} done by all forces on the crate is the algebraic sum of the work done by the individual forces:

$$W_{tot} = W_F + W_w + W_n + W_{\mathcal{F}}$$
$$= (F \cos \theta)s + 0 + 0 - \mathcal{F}s = (F \cos \theta - \mathcal{F})s.$$

But $(F \cos \theta - \mathcal{F})$ is the horizontal component of the *resultant* force on the crate; the vertical component of the resultant is zero. Thus the total work done by all the forces is equal to the work done by the resultant force.

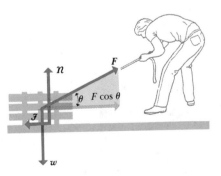

7–2
A crate on a rough horizontal surface moving to the right under the action of a force F inclined at an angle θ.

Suppose that $F = 50$ N, $\mathcal{F} = 15$ N, $\theta = 37°$, and $s = 20$ m. Then

$$W_F = (F \cos \theta)s$$
$$= (50 \text{ N})(\cos 37°)(20 \text{ m}) = 800 \text{ N·m},$$
$$W_{\mathcal{F}} = -\mathcal{F}s$$
$$= (-15 \text{ N})(20 \text{ m}) = -300 \text{ N·m},$$
$$W_{\text{tot}} = W_F + W_{\mathcal{F}} = 500 \text{ N·m}.$$

As a check, we express the total work as

$$W_{\text{tot}} = (F \cos \theta - \mathcal{F})s$$
$$= (40 \text{ N} - 15 \text{ N})(20 \text{ m}) = 500 \text{ N·m}. \quad \blacksquare$$

Once more, for emphasis: When several forces act on a body, there are always two equivalent ways to calculate the total work. We may calculate the work done by each force separately and take the algebraic sum, or we may compute the vector sum (resultant) of the forces and compute the work done by the resultant.

7–3
Work Done by a Varying Force

In Section 7–2 we defined work done by a *constant* force. But what happens when you stretch a coil spring? To stretch it more, you have to pull harder, so the force is *not* constant as the spring is stretched. We need to be able to compute work done by a force that varies during the displacement.

Here's how we do it. Suppose a particle moves along the x-axis, from x_a to x_b, under the action of a force directed along the axis but varying with the particle's position. Figure 7–3a shows a graph of the force magnitude as a function of the particle's coordinate x. To find the work done by this force, we divide the displacement into short segments Δx_1, Δx_2, and so on, as in Fig. 7–3b. We approximate the varying force by a force that is constant within each segment. The force has approximately the value F_1 in segment Δx_1, F_2 in segment Δx_2, and so on. The work done

7–3
(a) Curve showing how F varies with x.
(b) If the area is partitioned into small rectangles, their sum is approximately equal to the total work done during the displacement; the greater the number of rectangles used, the closer is the approximation.

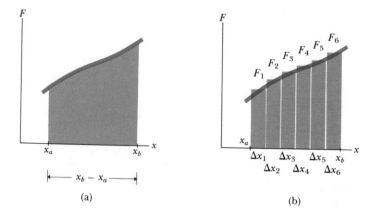

(a)   (b)

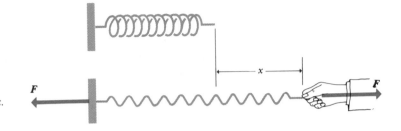

7–4
The force to stretch a spring is
proportional to its elongation: $F = kx$.

by the force in the first segment is then $F_1 \Delta x_1$, in the second $F_2 \Delta x_2$, and
so on. The *total* work is

$$W = F_1 \Delta x_1 + F_2 \Delta x_2 + \cdots. \qquad (7\text{–}3)$$

But the products $F_1 \Delta x_1$, $F_2 \Delta x_2$, ..., are the *areas* of the vertical
strips in Fig. 7–3b, so the total work is represented by the total area of
these strips. As we make the subdivisions smaller and smaller, this total
area becomes more and more nearly equal to the shaded area between
the smooth curve and the x-axis bounded by vertical lines at x_a and x_b. So
on a graph of force as a function of position, the total work done by the
force is represented by the area under the curve between the initial and
final positions.

Now let's get back to our stretched spring. To keep a spring stretched
an amount x beyond its unstretched length, we have to apply a force with
magnitude F at each end, as shown in Fig. 7–4. If the elongation is not
too great, we find that F is directly proportional to x:

$$F = kx, \qquad (7\text{–}4)$$

where k is a constant called the **force constant** (or spring constant) of the
spring. The fact that elongation is directly proportional to force, for
elongations that are not too great, was discovered by Robert Hooke in
1678 and is known as **Hooke's law.** We will discuss it more fully in a later
chapter. It really shouldn't be called a *law* because it is a statement about
a specific device, not a fundamental law of nature.

Suppose now that we apply equal and opposite forces to the ends of
the spring and gradually increase the forces, starting from zero. We hold
the left end stationary; the force at this end does no work. The force at
the moving end *does* do work. Figure 7–5 is a graph of F as a function of
x (the elongation of the spring). The work done by F when the elongation goes from zero to a maximum value X is represented by the shaded
triangular area. The area of a triangle is half the base (X) times the
altitude (kX), so the total work done by F is

$$W = \tfrac{1}{2}(X)(kX) = \tfrac{1}{2}kX^2. \qquad (7\text{–}5)$$

The work is therefore proportional to the *square* of the final elongation X. When the elongation is doubled, the work increases by a factor of
four. Another view of this relationship is that the total work W is equal to
the *average* force $\tfrac{1}{2}kX$ multiplied by the total displacement X.

The spring also exerts a force on the hand, which moves during the
stretching process. The displacement of the hand is the same as that of
the moving end of the spring, but the force on it is the negative of the

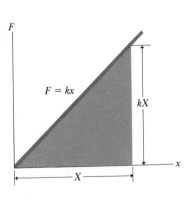

7–5
The work done in stretching a spring
is equal to the area of the shaded
triangle.

force on the spring because the two forces form an action–reaction pair. Thus the work done *on the hand* is the negative of the work done on the spring, namely, $-\frac{1}{2}kX^2$. In work calculations we must always take care to specify on which body the work is being done.

If the spring has spaces between the coils, Hooke's law holds for compression as well as stretching. In this case the work done on the spring in compressing it a distance X is also given by Eq. (7–5).

Example 7–2   A woman weighing 600 N steps on a bathroom scale containing a heavy spring. The spring is compressed 1.0 cm under her weight. Find the force constant of the spring and the total work done on it during the compression.

Solution   From Eq. (7–4),

$$k = \frac{F}{x} = \frac{600 \text{ N}}{0.010 \text{ m}} = 60{,}000 \text{ N·m}^{-1}.$$

Then from Eq. (7–5),

$$W = \tfrac{1}{2}kX^2 = \tfrac{1}{2}(60{,}000 \text{ N·m}^{-1})(0.010 \text{ m})^2 = 3.0 \text{ N·m} = 3.0 \text{ J.}   ■$$

When we change the elongation or compression of a spring from x_1 to x_2, the total work we do on the spring is

$$W = \tfrac{1}{2}kx_2{}^2 - \tfrac{1}{2}kx_1{}^2,$$

provided that $x = 0$ corresponds to zero elongation or compression, as above. (Can you prove this?)

The definition of work can be further generalized to include a force that varies in direction as well as magnitude and a displacement that may occur along a curved path. In Fig. 7–3 we take F to mean the component of force along the direction of the displacement Δx, and the various Δx's can be segments of a curved path. We will not need these further generalizations; they often involve methods of integral calculus.

7–4
Work and Kinetic Energy

In Section 7–2 we promised to work out the relation between work and kinetic energy. Without that relationship the concept of work wouldn't be of much use. So now it's time to make good on that promise. We begin with a body of mass m moving along the x-axis under the action of a constant resultant force of magnitude F directed along the axis. The body's acceleration is constant and is given by Newton's second law, $F = ma$. Suppose the speed increases from v_1 to v_2 while the body undergoes a displacement s. Using the constant-acceleration equation, Eq. (2–13), and replacing v_0 by v_1, v by v_2, and $(x - x_0)$ by s, we have

$$v_2{}^2 = v_1{}^2 + 2as,$$

$$a = \frac{v_2{}^2 - v_1{}^2}{2s}$$

When we multiply this equation by m, we find

$$ma = F = m\frac{v_2{}^2 - v_1{}^2}{2s},$$

and

$$Fs = \tfrac{1}{2}mv_2{}^2 - \tfrac{1}{2}mv_1{}^2. \tag{7–6}$$

The product Fs is the work W_{tot} done by the resultant force F. The quantity $\tfrac{1}{2}mv^2$, one half the product of the mass of the body and the square of its speed, is called its **kinetic energy,** K:

$$K = \tfrac{1}{2}mv^2. \tag{7–7}$$

The first term on the right side of Eq. (7–6) is the final kinetic energy of the body, $K_2 = \tfrac{1}{2}mv_2{}^2$, and the second term is the initial kinetic energy, $K_1 = \tfrac{1}{2}mv_1{}^2$. The difference between these terms is the *change* in kinetic energy, so Eq. (7–6) says that *the work done by the resultant external force on a body is equal to the change in kinetic energy of the body*:

$$W_{\text{tot}} = K_2 - K_1 = \Delta K. \tag{7–8}$$

This result is called the **work–energy theorem;** it is the cornerstone for most of what follows in this chapter. We will often write it as $W_{\text{tot}} = \Delta K$, where $\Delta K = K_2 - K_1$ is the change in kinetic energy.

Kinetic energy, like work, is a *scalar* quantity. It can never be negative; work can be either positive or negative. The kinetic energy of a moving body depends only on its speed (the *magnitude* of its velocity) but not on the *direction* of its motion. A body moving north at 5 m·s^{-1} has the same kinetic energy as the same body moving east at 5 m·s^{-1}. The *change* in kinetic energy during any displacement is determined by the total work done by all the forces acting on the body. When this work W_{tot} is *positive*, the particle speeds up during the displacement, K_2 is greater than K_1, and the kinetic energy *increases*. When the total work is *negative*, the kinetic energy *decreases*, and when $W_{\text{tot}} = 0$, K is *constant*.

A reminder: In Eq. (7–8), W_{tot} is the work done by the *resultant* force, the *vector sum* of *all* the forces acting on the body. Alternatively, we can calculate the work done by each separate force; W_{tot} is then the *algebraic sum* of all these quantities of work. Example 7–1 (Section 7–2) illustrates these two alternatives.

Although we derived Eq. (7–8) for the special case of a *constant* resultant force, it is true even when the force varies with position. To prove this, we divide the total displacement x into a large number of small segments Δx, just as in the calculation of work done by a varying force. The change of kinetic energy in segment Δx_1 is equal to the work $F_1 \, \Delta x_1$, and so on; the total change of kinetic energy is the sum of the changes in the individual segments and is thus equal to the total work done during the entire displacement.

In SI units, m is measured in kilograms and v in meters per second. From Eq. (7–8), kinetic energy must have the same units as work. To verify this, we recall that $1 \text{ N} = 1 \text{ kg·m·s}^{-2}$, so

$$1 \text{ J} = 1 \text{ N·m} = 1 \ (\text{kg·m·s}^{-2})\text{·m} = 1 \text{ kg·m}^2\text{·s}^{-2}.$$

The joule is the SI unit of *both* work and kinetic energy and, as we will see later, of all kinds of energy. In the cgs system, with m in grams and v in centimeters per second, we have

$$1 \text{ erg} = 1 \text{ dyn·cm} = 1 \text{ g·cm·s}^{-2}\text{·cm} = 1 \text{ g·cm}^2\text{·s}^{-2}.$$

In the British system,

$$1 \text{ ft·lb} = 1 \text{ ft·slug·ft·s}^{-2} = 1 \text{ slug·ft}^2\text{·s}^{-2}.$$

PROBLEM-SOLVING STRATEGY: *Work and Kinetic Energy*

1. Make a list of all the forces acting on the body, and calculate the work done by each force. In some cases, one or more forces may be unknown; represent the unknowns by algebraic symbols. Be sure to check signs; when a force has a component in the *same* direction as the displacement, its work is positive; when the direction is opposite to the displacement, the work is negative. When force and displacement are perpendicular, the work is zero.

2. Add the amounts of work done by the separate forces to find the total work. Again be careful with signs. Sometimes, though not often, it may be easier to calculate the resultant (vector sum) of the forces first, and then find the work done by the resultant force.

3. List the initial and final kinetic energies K_1 and K_2. If a quantity such as v_1 or v_2 is unknown, express it in terms of the corresponding algebraic symbol.

4. Use the relationship $W_{\text{tot}} = K_2 - K_1 = \Delta K$; insert the results from the above steps and solve for whatever unknown is required.

Example 7–3   We consider again the crate in Fig. 7–2 and the numbers at the end of Example 7–1. We found that the total work done by all the forces is 500 N·m = 500 J. Hence the kinetic energy of the body must increase by 500 J. Suppose the initial speed v_1 is 4 m·s^{-1} and the mass of the body is 10 kg. What is the final speed?

Solution   Steps 1 and 2 of the strategy have been done in Example 7–1. The initial kinetic energy is

$$K_1 = \tfrac{1}{2}mv_1{}^2 = \tfrac{1}{2}(10 \text{ kg})(4 \text{ m·s}^{-1})^2 = 80 \text{ J}.$$

Equation (7–8) gives

$$K_2 = K_1 + W = 80 \text{ J} + 500 \text{ J} = 580 \text{ J},$$
$$K_2 = \tfrac{1}{2}(10 \text{ kg})v_2{}^2 = 580 \text{ J},$$

and

$$v_2 = 10.8 \text{ m·s}^{-1}.$$

Note that this problem can also be done without the use of work and energy considerations. We can find the acceleration from $F = ma$ and then use the equations of motion with constant acceleration to find v_2:

$$a = \frac{F}{m} = \frac{40 \text{ N} - 15 \text{ N}}{10 \text{ kg}} = 2.5 \text{ m·s}^{-2}.$$

Then

$$v_2{}^2 = v_1{}^2 + 2as = (4 \text{ m·s}^{-1})^2 + 2(2.5 \text{ m·s}^{-2})(20 \text{ m})$$
$$= 116 \text{ m}^2\text{·s}^{-2},$$
$$v_2 = 10.8 \text{ m·s}^{-1}.$$

This is the same result as the one we obtained with the work–energy approach, but there we avoided the intermediate step of finding the acceleration. You will find several other examples and problems in this chapter that *can* be done without using energy considerations but are *easier* when energy methods are used. Also, when a problem can be done by two different methods, doing it both ways is a good way to check your work.   ∎

7–5
Gravitational Potential Energy

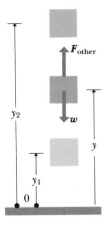

7–6
Work done by the gravitational force w during the motion of an object from one point in a gravitational field to another. Vertical displacement is from height y_1 to y_2.

In this section we want to apply the work–energy theorem to work done on a body by the gravitational force acting on it, that is, by its weight. In the process we will develop an important and useful new concept, *potential energy*, which is energy associated with the *position* of a body. To begin, let's consider a body with mass m that moves along the (vertical) y-axis, as shown in Fig. 7–6. The forces acting on it are its weight, with magnitude $w = mg$, and possibly some other forces; we call the resultant of the other forces F_{other}. When the body moves from a height y_1 above the origin to a greater height y_2, the weight and displacement are in opposite directions, and the work W_{grav} done on the body by its weight is

$$W_{\text{grav}} = Fs \cos 180° = -w(y_2 - y_1) = -(mgy_2 - mgy_1). \quad (7\text{–}9)$$

The work is negative, as we should expect. But this expression also gives the correct work when the body moves *downward* (so y_2 is *less than* y_1); in that case, W_{grav} is positive. It also gives the correct result when y_1 or y_2 or both are negative, corresponding to positions *below* the origin. Check it out and verify that these statements are true.

So we can express W_{grav} in terms of the values of the quantity mgy at the beginning and end of the displacement. This quantity, the product of the weight mg and the height y above the origin of coordinates is called the **gravitational potential energy,** U:

$$U = mgy. \quad (7\text{–}10)$$

Its initial value is $U_1 = mgy_1$, and its final value is $U_2 = mgy_2$. We can express the work W_{grav} done by the gravitational force during the displacement from y_1 to y_2 as

$$W_{grav} = U_1 - U_2 = -\Delta U. \qquad (7\text{-}11)$$

The negative sign in front of ΔU is essential. Remember that ΔU always means the final value minus the initial value. When the body moves down, y decreases, the gravitational force does *positive* work, and the potential energy *decreases*. When the body moves up, the work is negative and the potential energy increases.

To see what all this is good for, suppose for the moment that the body's weight is the *only* force acting on it, so that $\boldsymbol{F}_{other} = \boldsymbol{0}$. The body may be in free fall, or maybe we threw it into the air. Let its speed at y_1 be v_1 and its speed at y_2 be v_2. The work–energy theorem, Eq. (7–8), says $W_{tot} = K_2 - K_1$; in this case, $W_{tot} = W_{grav} = U_1 - U_2$. Putting these together, we get

$$U_1 - U_2 = K_2 - K_1,$$

which we can rewrite as

$$K_1 + U_1 = K_2 + U_2$$

or

$$\tfrac{1}{2}mv_1{}^2 + mgy_1 = \tfrac{1}{2}mv_2{}^2 + mgy_2. \qquad (7\text{-}12)$$

We now define $K + U$ to be the *total mechanical energy* (kinetic plus potential) of the system; let's call it E. Then $E_1 \,(= K_1 + U_1)$ is the total energy at y_1, and $E_2 \,(= K_2 + U_2)$ is the total energy at y_2. Equation (7–12) says that when the body's weight is the only force doing work on it, $E_1 = E_2$. That is, E is constant; it has the same value at y_1 and y_2 and at all points during the motion. In this situation *the total mechanical energy is constant or conserved*. This is our first example of the principle of **conservation of energy.**

When we throw a ball into the air, it slows down on the way up as kinetic energy is converted to potential energy. On the way back down, potential energy is converted back to kinetic energy, and the ball speeds up. But the total energy, kinetic plus potential, is the same at every point in the motion.

Example 7–4   You throw a 0.200-kg ball straight up in the air, giving it an initial upward velocity of magnitude 20.0 m·s^{-1}. Use conservation of energy to find how high it goes.

Solution   The only force doing work on the ball after it leaves your hand is its weight, and we can use Eq. (7–12). Let's take the origin at the starting point; then $y_1 = 0$. At this point, $v_1 = 20.0$ m·s^{-1}. We want to find the height at which it stops and begins to fall back to earth, so $v_2 = 0$

and y_2 is unknown. Eq. (7–12) gives

$$\tfrac{1}{2}(0.200 \text{ kg})(20.0 \text{ m·s}^{-1})^2 + (0.200 \text{ kg})(9.80 \text{ m·s}^{-2})(0)$$
$$= \tfrac{1}{2}(0.200 \text{ kg})(0)^2 + (0.200 \text{ kg})(9.80 \text{ m·s}^{-2})y_2,$$

$$y_2 = 20.4 \text{ m}.$$

Note that the mass divides out, as we should expect; we learned in Chapter 2 that the motion of a body in free fall doesn't depend on its mass. Also, it would have been better problem-solving technique to substitute the values $y_1 = 0$ and $v_2 = 0$ in Eq. (7–12) and then solve algebraically for y_2 to get

$$y_2 = \frac{v_1^{\;2}}{2g}$$

and substitute in the numerical values only at the very end. This saves arithmetic and also gives us a result that we recognize as one we could have derived using Eq. (2–13).   ◾

Another important point about potential energy is that it doesn't matter where we put the origin. If we shift the origin for y, y_1 and y_2 change, but the *difference* $(y_1 - y_2)$ does not. It follows that although U_1 and U_2 change, the difference $(U_1 - U_2)$ is the same as before. The choice of origin is arbitrary; the physically significant quantity is not the value of U at a particular point, but only the *difference* in U between two points.

When there are other forces acting on the body in addition to its weight, then F_{other} in Fig. 7–6 is *not* zero. The total work W_{tot} is then the sum of the gravitational work W_{grav}, still given by Eq. (7–11), and the work done by F_{other}, which we will call W_{other}. That is, $W_{\text{tot}} = W_{\text{grav}} + W_{\text{other}}$. Equating this to the change in kinetic energy, we have

$$W_{\text{other}} + W_{\text{grav}} = K_2 - K_1. \tag{7–13}$$

Also, from Eq. (7–11), $W_{\text{grav}} = U_1 - U_2$, so

$$W_{\text{other}} + U_1 - U_2 = K_2 - K_1,$$

which we can rearrange in the form

$$K_2 + U_2 = K_1 + U_1 + W_{\text{other}}.$$

Finally, using the appropriate expressions for the various energy terms, we obtain

$$\tfrac{1}{2}mv_2^{\;2} + mgy_2 = \tfrac{1}{2}mv_1^{\;2} + mgy_1 + W_{\text{other}}. \tag{7–14}$$

This result says that *the work done by all the forces* **except the gravitational force** *equals the change in the total mechanical energy* $K + U$ *of the body.* When W_{other} is positive, the total mechanical energy increases, and $K_2 + U_2$ is greater than $K_1 + U_1$. When W_{other} is negative, the mechanical energy decreases. In the special case in which $W_{\text{other}} = 0$, as when there are no forces other than the body's weight, the total mechanical energy is constant, and we are back to Eq. (7–12).

PROBLEM-SOLVING STRATEGY: *Conservation of Mechanical Energy I*

1. Decide what the initial and final states (i.e., positions and velocities) of the system are; use the subscript 1 for the initial state and 2 for the final state.

2. Define your coordinate system, particularly the level at which $y = 0$. You will use this to compute potential energies. Equation (7–10) assumes that the positive direction for y is upward; we suggest that you use this choice consistently.

3. Make a list of the initial and final kinetic and potential energies, that is, K_1, K_2, U_1, and U_2. In general, some of these will be known and some unknown. Use algebraic symbols for any unknown coordinates or velocities.

4. Identify all nongravitational forces that do work. A free-body diagram is often helpful. Calculate the work W_{other} done by all these forces. If some of the needed quantities are unknown, represent them by algebraic symbols.

5. Use Eq. (7–14) to relate these quantities. If there is no nongravitational work, this is the same as Eq. (7–12). Then solve to find whatever unknown quantity is required.

6. Keep in mind, here and in later sections, that each force must be represented either in U or in W_{other} but never in both places. The gravitational work is included in ΔU, so it would be wrong to include it again in W_{other}.

Example 7–5   In Example 7–4, suppose your hand moves up 0.50 m while giving the ball its upward velocity of 20 m·s^{-1}.

a) Assuming that your hand exerts a constant upward force on the ball, find the magnitude of that force.

b) Find the speed of the ball at a point 15 m above the point where it leaves your hand.

Solution

a) Let point 1 be the point where your hand first starts to move, and point 2 be the point where the ball leaves your hand. With the same coordinate system as before, we have $y_1 = -0.50$ m and $y_2 = 0$. Then

$$U_1 = mgy_1 = (0.20 \text{ kg})(9.8 \text{ m·s}^{-2})(-0.50 \text{ m}) = -1.0 \text{ J},$$

$$U_2 = mgy_2 = (0.20 \text{ kg})(9.8 \text{ m·s}^{-2})(0) = 0,$$

$$K_1 = 0,$$

$$K_2 = \tfrac{1}{2}mv_2{}^2 = \tfrac{1}{2}(0.20 \text{ kg})(20 \text{ m·s}^{-1})^2 = 40 \text{ J}.$$

Let P be the upward force your hand applies to the ball as you throw it. The work W_{other} is the work done by this force. According to Eq. (7–14),

$$40 \text{ J} + 0 = 0 + (-1.0 \text{ J}) + W_{other},$$

$$W_{other} = 41 \text{ J}.$$

The kinetic energy of the ball increases by 40 J, and its potential energy increases by 1 J; the sum is equal to W_{other}.

If P is constant, then

$$W_{\text{other}} = P(y_2 - y_1),$$

and

$$P = \frac{W_{\text{other}}}{y_2 - y_1} = \frac{41 \text{ J}}{0.50 \text{ m}} = 82 \text{ N}.$$

b) Let point 3 be at the 15-m height. Then $y_3 = 15$ m, and v_3 is to be determined. Between points 2 and 3, $W_{\text{other}} = 0$. We have $U_3 = (0.20 \text{ kg})(9.8 \text{ m·s}^{-2})(15 \text{ m}) = 29$ J and $K_3 = \frac{1}{2}(0.20 \text{ kg})v_3^2$. Equation (7–12) gives

$$K_2 + U_2 = K_3 + U_3,$$

$$40 \text{ J} + 0 = \tfrac{1}{2}(0.20 \text{ kg})v_3^2 + 29 \text{ J},$$

and

$$v_3 = \pm 10 \text{ m·s}^{-1}.$$

The significance of the plus-or-minus sign is that the ball passes this point *twice*, once on the way up and again on the way down. Its *potential* energy at this point is the same whether it is moving up or down. Hence its kinetic energy is the same, and its *speed* is the same. The algebraic sign of the velocity is plus when the ball is moving up and minus when it is moving down. ■

In all our examples so far, the body has moved along a straight vertical line; what happens when the path is a slanted or curved path, as in Fig. 7–7a? The work done by the gravitational force during this displacement is still given by Eq. (7–9) or (7–11):

$$W_{\text{grav}} = U_1 - U_2 = mgy_1 - mgy_2.$$

To prove this, we divide the path into small segments Δs; a typical one is shown in Fig. 7–7b. The work done in this segment is the component of displacement in the direction of the force, multiplied by the magnitude of the force. As Fig. 7–7b shows, the vertical component of displacement has magnitude $\Delta s \cos \theta = \Delta y$, so the work done by w is

$$-mg \, \Delta s \, \cos \theta = -mg \, \Delta y.$$

This is the same as though the body had been displaced straight up a distance Δy. This is true for every segment, so the *total* work done by the gravitational force depends only on the *total* vertical displacement $(y_2 - y_1)$. It is given by $-mg(y_2 - y_1)$ and is independent of any horizontal motion that may occur.

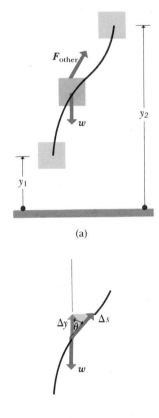

(a)

(b)

7–7
(a) A displacement along a curved path. (b) The work done by the gravitational force w depends only on the vertical component of displacement Δy.

Example 7–6 A child slides down a curved playground slide that is one quadrant of a circle of radius R, as in Fig. 7–8. If she starts from rest and there is no friction, find her speed at the bottom of the slide.

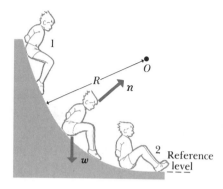

7–8
A child sliding down a frictionless curved slide. The child's mass is 25 kg.

Solution Resist the temptation to use the equations of motion with constant acceleration; the acceleration isn't constant because the slope becomes smaller and smaller as the child descends. However, if there is no friction, the only force other than the child's weight is the normal force n exerted by the slide. The work done by this force is zero because at each point it is perpendicular to the small element of displacement near that point. Thus $W_{\text{other}} = 0$, and mechanical energy is conserved. Take point 1 at the starting point and point 2 at the bottom of the slide, where $y = 0$. Then $y_1 = R$, $y_2 = 0$, and

$$K_2 + U_2 = K_1 + U_1,$$
$$\tfrac{1}{2}mv_2{}^2 + 0 = 0 + mgR,$$
$$v_2 = \sqrt{2gR}.$$

The speed is the same as if the child had fallen *vertically* through a height R.

As a numerical example, let $R = 3.00$ m. Then

$$v = \sqrt{2(9.80 \text{ m·s}^{-2})(3.00 \text{ m})} = 7.67 \text{ m·s}^{-1}.$$ ■

Example 7–7 In Example 7–6, suppose that the slide is not frictionless and that the child's speed at the bottom is only 3.00 m·s^{-1}. What work was done by the frictional force acting on the child?

Solution In this case, $W_{\text{other}} = W_{\mathcal{F}}$; from Eq. (7–14),

$$
\begin{aligned}
W_{\mathcal{F}} &= \tfrac{1}{2}mv_2{}^2 - \tfrac{1}{2}mv_1{}^2 + mgy_2 - mgy_1 \\
&= \tfrac{1}{2}(25.0 \text{ kg})(3.00 \text{ m·s}^{-1})^2 - 0 + 0 \\
&\quad - (25.0 \text{ kg})(9.80 \text{ m·s}^{-2})(3.00 \text{ m}) \\
&= 112 \text{ J} - 735 \text{ J} = -623 \text{ J}.
\end{aligned}
$$

The work done by the friction force is -623 J, and the total mechanical energy *decreases* by 623 J. The mechanical energy of a body is *not* conserved when friction forces act on it. (Do you see why $W_{\mathcal{F}}$ has to be negative?)   ■

Example 7–8 If there is no air resistance, the only force acting on a ball after it is thrown is its weight, and the mechanical energy of the ball is constant. Figure 7–9 shows two trajectories with the same initial speed (and thus the same total energy) but with different initial angles. At all points at the same elevation the potential energy is the same; hence the kinetic energy is the same, and the speed is the same.   ■

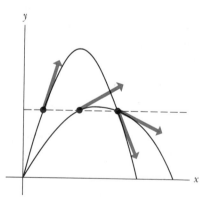

7–9
For the same initial speed, the speed is the same at all points at the same elevation.

We have been assuming all along that the gravitational force on a body (its weight) is constant. But we know from Section 6–3 that the earth's gravitational force on a body of mass m is given more generally by

$$F_{\text{g}} = \frac{Gmm_{\text{E}}}{r^2}, \tag{7–15}$$

where m_E is the mass of the earth and r is the distance of the body from the earth's center. In problems in which r changes enough that the gravitational force can't be considered as constant, we have to revise our discussion of potential energy.

At this point we have to quote a result that really needs integral calculus for a proper derivation. The result is this: When a body of mass m moves under the action of the earth's gravitational force, as given by Eq. (7–15), from a point at a distance r_1 from the center of the earth to a point at a distance of r_2, the total work done by the gravitational force is

$$W_{\text{grav}} = \frac{Gmm_E}{r_2} - \frac{Gmm_E}{r_1}. \tag{7-16}$$

The path doesn't have to be a straight line; the work depends only on the initial and final values of r.

We want to define the corresponding potential energy U so that $W_{\text{grav}} = U_1 - U_2$, as before; comparing this with Eq. (7–16), we see that the appropriate definition is

$$U = -\frac{Gmm_E}{r}. \tag{7-17}$$

Note that when r increases, the force does negative work and U increases (i.e., becomes less negative). When r decreases, the body "falls" toward earth, the gravitational work is positive, and the potential energy decreases (i.e., becomes more negative). One slightly peculiar feature of Eq. (7–17) is that U is always negative. The reason for this is that U is zero when the mass m is infinitely far away from the earth; this is quite a different choice from making $U = 0$ at some arbitrary height as we did before. But we have learned that the choice of zero point is arbitrary and that only *differences* of U from one point to another are significant, so negative values of U should not be too alarming.

Armed with Eq. (7–17), we can now use our energy relations for problems in which the $1/r^2$ behavior of the earth's gravitational force has to be included.

Example 7–9   In Jules Verne's story "From the Earth to the Moon" (written in 1865), three men were shot to the moon in a shell fired from a giant cannon sunk in the earth in Florida. What muzzle velocity would be needed (a) to raise the shell (total mass m) to a height above the earth equal to the earth's radius; (b) to escape from the earth completely? To simplify the calculation, neglect the gravitational pull of the moon.

Solution

a) The only force doing work is the gravitational force, so $W_{\text{other}} = 0$ and $K_1 + U_1 = K_2 + U_2$. Let point 1 be the starting point and point 2 be the point of maximum height, where $v = 0$. If the radius of the earth is R, then $r_1 = R$ and $r_2 = 2R$. Also, $v_2 = 0$, and v_1 is to be determined. The energy-conservation equation gives

$$\frac{1}{2}mv_1{}^2 - G\frac{mm_E}{R} = 0 - G\frac{mm_E}{2R}.$$

Rearranging this and using numerical values from Appendix F, we find

$$v_1 = \sqrt{\frac{Gm_E}{R}} = \sqrt{\frac{(6.67 \times 10^{-11}\ \text{N}\cdot\text{m}^2\cdot\text{kg}^{-2})(5.98 \times 10^{24}\ \text{kg})}{6.38 \times 10^6\ \text{m}}}$$
$$= 7920\ \text{m}\cdot\text{s}^{-1}\ (= 17{,}715\ \text{mi}\cdot\text{hr}^{-1}).$$

b) When v_1 is the escape velocity, $r_1 = R$, $r_2 = \infty$, and $v_2 = 0$ (because we want the body to barely reach $r_2 = \infty$ with no kinetic energy left over). Then

$$\frac{1}{2}mv_1{}^2 - G\frac{mm_E}{R} = 0$$

or

$$v_1 = \sqrt{\frac{2Gm_E}{R}} = \sqrt{\frac{2(6.67 \times 10^{-11}\ \text{N}\cdot\text{m}^2\cdot\text{kg}^{-2})(5.98 \times 10^{24}\ \text{kg})}{6.38 \times 10^6\ \text{m}}}$$
$$= 1.12 \times 10^4\ \text{m}\cdot\text{s}^{-1}\ (= 25{,}050\ \text{mi}\cdot\text{hr}^{-1}).$$

The speed of an earth satellite in a circular orbit of radius just slightly greater than R is, from Eq. (6–18), the same as the result of part (a). The escape velocity is larger than this by exactly a factor of $\sqrt{2}$. ∎

Finally, Eq. (7–16) can be rewritten as

$$W_{\text{grav}} = Gmm_E\frac{r_1 - r_2}{r_1 r_2}.$$

If the body stays close to the earth, then in the denominator we may replace r_1 and r_2 by R, the earth's radius, obtaining

$$W_{\text{grav}} = Gmm_E\frac{r_1 - r_2}{R^2}.$$

But according to Eq. (6–12), $g = Gm_E/R^2$, and we obtain

$$W_{\text{grav}} = mg(r_1 - r_2),$$

which agrees with Eq. (7–9) with the y's replaced by r's. We see that Eq. (7–9) may be considered a special case of the more general Eq. (7–16).

7–6
Elastic Potential Energy

We can use the concept of potential energy to calculate work done by *elastic* forces such as the spring we discussed in Section 7–3. Figure 7–10 shows the spring from Fig. 7–4, with its left end held stationary and its right end attached to a body with mass m that can move along the x-axis.

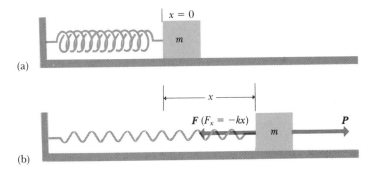

7–10
As an applied force P produces an extension x of a spring, an elastic restoring force F also acts on the mass m. The x-component of F is $F_x = -kx$.

The body is at $x = 0$ when the spring is neither stretched nor compressed. A force P is applied, and the mass undergoes a displacement. How much work does the spring force do on the mass?

In Section 7–3 we found that the work we must do *on* the spring to stretch it from an elongation x_1 to a greater elongation x_2 is given by $\frac{1}{2}kx_2^2 - \frac{1}{2}kx_1^2$, where k is the force constant of the spring. The spring force *on the mass* is the negative of the force acting *on the spring*, so the work the spring does on the mass is just the negative of this expression. In a displacement from x_1 to x_2 the spring does an amount of work W_{el} given by

$$W_{el} = \tfrac{1}{2}kx_1^2 - \tfrac{1}{2}kx_2^2,$$

where the subscript "el" stands for *elastic*.

Following the same procedure as for gravitational work, we define **elastic potential energy** as

$$U = \tfrac{1}{2}kx^2. \qquad (7\text{--}18)$$

We can express the work W_{el} done on the body by the elastic force in terms of the change in potential energy:

$$W_{el} = \tfrac{1}{2}kx_1^2 - \tfrac{1}{2}kx_2^2 = U_1 - U_2. \qquad (7\text{--}19)$$

When x increases, W_{el} is *negative* and U *increases*; when x decreases, W_{el} is positive and U *decreases*. If the spring can be compressed as well as stretched, then x is negative for compression. But U is positive for both positive and negative x, and Eqs. (7–18) and (7–19) are valid for both cases. When $x = 0$, $U = 0$; this is the equilibrium position of the system.

The work–energy theorem says that $W_{tot} = K_2 - K_1$. If the spring force is the *only* force that does work on the body, then

$$W_{tot} = W_{el} = U_1 - U_2.$$

The work–energy theorem then gives us

$$K_1 + U_1 = K_2 + U_2$$

and

$$\tfrac{1}{2}mv_1^2 + \tfrac{1}{2}kx_1^2 = \tfrac{1}{2}mv_2^2 + \tfrac{1}{2}kx_2^2. \qquad (7\text{--}20)$$

In this case the total energy $E = K + U$ is *conserved*.

When there are other forces that also do work on the mass, we call their work W_{other}, as before. Then the total work is $W_{tot} = W_{el} + W_{other}$,

and the work–energy theorem gives

$$W_{el} + W_{other} = K_2 - K_1.$$

The work done by the spring is still $W_{el} = U_1 - U_2$, so again

$$K_2 + U_2 = K_1 + U_1 + W_{other}$$

and

$$\tfrac{1}{2}mv_2{}^2 + \tfrac{1}{2}kx_2{}^2 = \tfrac{1}{2}mv_1{}^2 + \tfrac{1}{2}kx_1{}^2 + W_{other}. \qquad (7\text{--}21)$$

This equation shows that *the work done by all the forces* **except the elastic force** *equals the change in the total mechanical energy $E = K + U$ of the body.* When W_{other} is positive, E increases; when W_{other} is negative, E decreases.

Finally, when we have *both* gravitational and elastic forces (when a body hangs at the end of a spring in a gravitational field, for example), we can still use the relationship

$$K_2 + U_2 = K_1 + U_1 + W_{other}, \qquad (7\text{--}22)$$

but now U_1 and U_2 are the initial and final values of the *total* potential energy, including both gravitational and elastic forces, that is, $U = U_{grav} + U_{el}$. If the gravitational and elastic forces are the *only* forces that do work on the body, then $W_{other} = 0$; in that special case we have again

$$K_1 + U_1 = K_2 + U_2.$$

Figure 7–11 shows a spectacular example of transformations between kinetic energy and gravitational and elastic potential energies.

7–11

Stroboscopic photograph of a pole-vaulter. The athlete's initial kinetic energy is partly converted to elastic potential energy in the flexed pole, then to gravitational potential energy as he rises and clears the bar, then back to kinetic energy as he drops on the other side. The elastic and gravitational forces are conservative. (Dr. Harold Edgerton, M.I.T., Cambridge, Massachusetts.)

PROBLEM-SOLVING STRATEGY: Conservation of Energy II

The strategy outlined in Section 7–5 is equally useful here. In the list of kinetic and potential energies in Step 3, include both gravitational and elastic potential energies when appropriate. Remember that every force that does work must be represented *either* in U or in W_{other}, but *never* in both places. The work done by the gravitational and elastic forces is accounted for by their potential energies; the work of the other forces, W_{other}, has to be included separately. In some cases there will be "other" forces that do no work, as we mentioned in Section 7–2.

Example 7–10 In Fig. 7–10 a body with mass $m = 4.00$ kg sits on a frictionless horizontal plane, connected to a spring with force constant $k = 24.0$ N·m^{-1}. We pull on the body, stretching the spring 0.500 m, and release the body with no initial velocity. The body begins to move back toward its equilibrium position $(x = 0)$. What is its velocity when $x = 0.300$ m?

Solution As the body starts to move, potential energy is converted into kinetic energy. The spring force is the only force doing work on the body, so $W_{other} = 0$, and we may use Eq. (7–20). Here is a list of the energy quantities:

$$K_1 = \tfrac{1}{2}(4.00 \text{ kg})(0)^2 = 0,$$

$$U_1 = \tfrac{1}{2}(24.0 \text{ N·m}^{-1})(0.500 \text{ m})^2 = 3.00 \text{ J},$$

$$K_2 = \tfrac{1}{2}(4.00 \text{ kg})v_2{}^2,$$

$$U_2 = \tfrac{1}{2}(24.0 \text{ N·m}^{-1})(0.300 \text{ m})^2 = 1.08 \text{ J}.$$

Then from Eq. (7–20),

$$0 + 3.00 \text{ J} = \tfrac{1}{2}(4.00 \text{ kg})v_2{}^2 + 1.08 \text{ J},$$

and

$$v_2 = \pm 0.98 \text{ m·s}^{-1}.$$

What is the physical significance of the plus-or-minus sign?
Please note that this problem *cannot* be done by using the equations of motion with constant acceleration because the spring force varies with position. The energy method, by contrast, offers a simple and elegant solution. ∎

Example 7–11 For the system of Example 7–10, suppose the body is initially at rest at $x = 0$, with the spring unstretched. Then we apply a constant force P of magnitude 10.0 N to the body. What is the speed of the body when it has moved to $x = 0.500$ m?

Solution Again, we don't have constant acceleration. (Do you see why not?) But we can still use energy relations. Here is a list of the energy quantities:

$$K_1 = 0, \qquad K_2 = \tfrac{1}{2}(4.00 \text{ kg})v_2^2,$$

$$U_1 = 0, \qquad U_2 = \tfrac{1}{2}(24.0 \text{ N·m}^{-1})(0.500 \text{ m})^2 = 3.00 \text{ J},$$

$$W_{\text{other}} = (10.0 \text{ N})(0.500 \text{ m}) = 5.00 \text{ J}.$$

Putting the pieces together, we find

$$K_2 + U_2 = K_1 + U_1 + W_{\text{other}}$$

$$\tfrac{1}{2}(4.00 \text{ kg})v_2^2 + 3.00 \text{ J} = 0 + 0 + 5.00 \text{ J},$$

$$v_2 = 1.00 \text{ m·s}^{-1}.$$ ∎

Example 7–12   In Example 7–11, suppose the force P is removed when the body has moved 0.500 m. How much *farther* does the body move before coming to rest?

Solution   The elastic force is now the only force, and total mechanical energy $(K + U)$ is conserved. The kinetic energy at the 0.500-m point is $\tfrac{1}{2}mv^2 = 2.00$ J, and the potential energy is $\tfrac{1}{2}kx^2 = 3.00$ J. The total energy is therefore 5.00 J (equal to the work done by the force P). When the body comes to rest at x_{max}, its kinetic energy is zero, so its potential energy must be 5.00 J:

$$\tfrac{1}{2}kx_{\text{max}}^2 = \tfrac{1}{2}(24.0 \text{ N·m}^{-1})x_{\text{max}}^2 = 5.00 \text{ J},$$

$$x_{\text{max}} = 0.645 \text{ m}.$$

So the body moves 0.145 m farther after the force is removed.   ∎

Example 7–13   A brick with mass m, initially at rest, is dropped from a height h onto a spring with force constant k, as shown in Fig. 7–12. Find the maximum distance d that the spring is compressed. ·

Solution   The gravitational and elastic forces are the only forces acting on the brick, and the total mechanical energy $E = K + U$ is conserved. The brick is released from rest, so $v_1 = 0$ and $K_1 = 0$. At the instant when maximum compression occurs, the brick comes to rest again, so $K_2 = 0$. Thus the *total* (gravitational plus elastic) potential energy is the same at the beginning and at the end. The brick drops a *total* distance $h + d$, so $U_{\text{grav}} = mg(h + d)$ at the beginning and $U_{\text{grav}} = 0$ at the end. The elastic potential energy is zero at the beginning; and at the end, $U_{\text{el}} = \tfrac{1}{2}kd^2$. Equating these two quantities, we find

$$mg(h + d) = \tfrac{1}{2}kd^2, \qquad \text{or} \qquad d^2 - \frac{2mg}{k}d - \frac{2mgh}{k} = 0.$$

We solve this for d, using the quadratic formula, to find

$$d = \frac{1}{2}\left[\frac{2mg}{k} \pm \sqrt{\left(\frac{2mg}{k}\right)^2 + \frac{8mgh}{k}} \right].$$

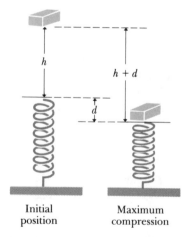

Initial position   Maximum compression

7–12
The total fall of the brick is $h + d$.

The positive root is the one we want; the negative root corresponds to the height to which the brick and spring would rebound if they were fastened together after contact. ∎

7–7
Conservative and Dissipative Forces

When gravitational and elastic forces act on a body, the work they do can be expressed in terms of a change in potential energy. This work depends only on the endpoints of the motion; and if these are the only forces acting on the body, the total mechanical energy $E = K + U$ is *conserved*. We call these forces **conservative forces.**

Another feature of conservative forces is that their work is always *reversible*. When we throw a ball up in the air, it slows down as kinetic energy is converted into potential energy. But on the way down, the conversion is reversed, and the ball speeds up as potential energy is converted back to kinetic energy. If there is no air resistance, the ball lands just as fast as it was thrown. If we shove a body against a spring bumper, the spring compresses and slows the body down; but then it bounces back, and if there is no friction, the body bounces away with the same speed and kinetic energy it had at the beginning. Again, there is a two-way conversion from kinetic to potential energy and back.

Gravitational forces show yet another property of conservative forces. We may move from point 1 to point 2 by different paths, but the work done by the gravitational force is the same for all of the paths. For example, in a uniform gravitational field the work depends only on the change in height. If a body moves around a closed path, ending at the same point where it started, the total work done by the gravitational field is zero!

The work done by a conservative force always has these properties:

1. It is equal to the difference between the initial and final values of a *potential energy* function.
2. It is reversible.
3. It is independent of the path of the body and depends only on the starting and ending points.
4. When the starting and ending points are the same, the total work is zero.

Not all forces are conservative; consider the friction force acting on a body that slides on a stationary surface. There is no potential-energy function; when the body slides in one direction and then back to its original position, the total work done on it by the friction force is *not* zero. When the direction of motion reverses, so does the friction force, and it does *negative* work in *both* directions. When a body slides across a surface with decreasing speed (and decreasing kinetic energy), the lost kinetic energy cannot be recovered by reversing the motion or in any other way, and mechanical energy is *not* conserved.

Such a force is called a *nonconservative force* or a **dissipative force.** To describe the associated energy relations, we have to introduce additional kinds of energy and a more general energy-conservation principle. When a body slides on a rough surface, the surface becomes hotter; the energy associated with this change in the state of the material is called *internal energy.* In later chapters we will study the relation of internal energy to temperature changes, heat, and work. This is the heart of the area of physics called *thermodynamics.*

Example 7–14   Let's look again at Example 7–7 (Section 7–5), in which a body is acted on by a dissipative friction force. The body starts with 735 J of potential energy, and at the end it has 112 J of kinetic energy. The work $W_{\mathscr{f}}$ done by the friction force is −623 J. As the body slides down the track, the surfaces become warmer; the same temperature changes could have been produced by adding 623 J of heat to the bodies. Thus their *internal* energy increases by 623 J; the sum of this energy and the final mechanical energy equals the initial mechanical energy, and the total energy of the system (including nonmechanical forms of energy) is conserved.   ∎

7–8
Power

Time considerations are not involved in the definition of work. When you lift a body weighing 100 N through a vertical distance of 0.5 m, you do 50 J of work whether it takes you 1 second, 1 hour, or 1 year to do it. Often, though, we need to know how quickly work is done. The time rate at which work is done or energy is transferred is called **power.** Like work and energy, power is a *scalar* quantity.

When a quantity of work ΔW is done during a time interval Δt, the **average power** P_{av} is defined as

$$P_{\mathrm{av}} = \frac{\Delta W}{\Delta t}. \tag{7-23}$$

If the rate at which work is done is not constant, this ratio may vary; in this case we define *instantaneous power* P as the limit of this quotient as $\Delta t \to 0$:

$$P = \lim_{\Delta t \to 0} \frac{\Delta W}{\Delta t}. \tag{7-24}$$

The SI unit of power, the joule per second ($J \cdot s^{-1}$), is called the **watt** (W). The kilowatt (1 kW = 10^3 W) and the megawatt (1 MW = 10^6 W) are also commonly used. In the British system, in which work is expressed in foot-pounds and time in seconds, the unit of power is the foot-pound per second. A larger unit called the *horsepower* (hp) is also used:

$$1 \text{ hp} = 550 \text{ ft·lb·s}^{-1}$$
$$= 33{,}000 \text{ ft·lb·min}^{-1}.$$

That is, a 1-hp motor running at full load does 33,000 ft·lb of work every minute. A useful conversion factor is

$$1 \text{ hp} = 746 \text{ W} = 0.746 \text{ kW}.$$

The watt is a familiar unit of *electrical* power; a 100-W light bulb converts 100 J of electrical energy into light and heat each second. But there is nothing inherently electrical about the watt; a light bulb could be rated in horsepower, and many automobile manufacturers now rate their engines in kilowatts rather than horsepower.

Power units can be used to define new units of work or energy. The *kilowatt-hour* (kWh) is the usual commercial unit of electrical energy. One kilowatt-hour is the total work done in 1 hour (3600 s) when the power is 1 kilowatt (10^3 J·s^{-1}), so

$$1 \text{ kWh} = (10^3 \text{ J·s}^{-1})(3600 \text{ s}) = 3.6 \times 10^6 \text{ J} = 3.6 \text{ MJ}.$$

The kilowatt-hour is a unit of *work* or *energy*, not power.

It is a curious fact of life that although energy is an abstract physical quantity, it has a price! We don't buy a newton of force or a meter per second of velocity, but a kilowatt-hour of energy is sold at a definite price. In the form of electrical energy, a kilowatt-hour usually costs from one half cent to around ten cents, depending on location and amount purchased.

When a force acts on a moving body, it does work on the body (unless the force and velocity are always perpendicular). The corresponding power can be expressed in terms of force and velocity. Suppose a force F acts on a body while it undergoes a displacement of magnitude Δs. If $F_\parallel$ is the component of F tangent to the path, then the work is given by $\Delta W = F_\parallel \Delta s$, and the average power is

$$P_{av} = \frac{F_\parallel \Delta s}{\Delta t} = F_\parallel \frac{\Delta s}{\Delta t} = F_\parallel v_{av}. \qquad (7\text{–}25)$$

We define instantaneous power as the limit of this as $\Delta t \to 0$:

$$P = F_\parallel v, \qquad (7\text{–}26)$$

where v is the magnitude of the instantaneous velocity.

Example 7–15   A jet airplane engine develops a thrust (a forward force on the plane) of 15,000 N (roughly 3000 lb). When the plane is flying at 300 m·s^{-1} (roughly 600 mph), what horsepower does the engine develop?

Solution

$$P = Fv = (1.50 \times 10^4 \text{ N})(300 \text{ m·s}^{-1}) = 4.50 \times 10^6 \text{ W}$$

$$= (4.50 \times 10^6 \text{ W})\left(\frac{1 \text{ hp}}{746 \text{ W}}\right) = 6030 \text{ hp.} \qquad \blacksquare$$

Example 7–16   As part of a charity fund-raising drive, a Chicago marathon runner of mass 50.0 kg runs up the stairs to the top of the Sears tower, the tallest building in the United States (443 m), in 15.0 minutes. What is her average power output in watts? In kilowatts? In horsepower?

Solution   The total work is

$$W = mgh = (50.0 \text{ kg})(9.80 \text{ m·s}^{-2})(443 \text{ m}) = 2.17 \times 10^5 \text{ J.}$$

The time is 15 min = 900 s, so the average power is

$$P_{av} = \frac{2.17 \times 10^5 \text{ J}}{900 \text{ s}} = 241 \text{ W} = 0.241 \text{ kW} = 0.323 \text{ hp.}$$

Alternatively, the average vertical component of velocity is (443 m)/(900 s) = 0.492 m·s^{-1}, so the average power is

$$P_{av} = Fv_{av} = (mg)v_{av}$$
$$= (50.0 \text{ kg})(9.80 \text{ m·s}^{-2})(0.492 \text{ m·s}^{-1}) = 241 \text{ W.} \qquad \blacksquare$$

*7–9
Automotive Power

Energy relations in a gasoline-powered automobile provide a familiar and interesting example of some of the energy and power concepts in this chapter. First, burning 1 liter of gasoline provides about 3.5×10^7 J of energy. Not all of this is converted to *mechanical* energy; the laws of thermodynamics, which we will encounter in Chapters 18 and 19, impose fundamental limitations on the efficiency of converting heat to mechanical energy or work. In a typical car engine, two thirds of the heat from gasoline combustion is wasted in the cooling system and the exhaust. Another 20% or so is converted to mechanical energy but is lost in friction in the drive train or is used by accessories such as electric-power generators, air-conditioners, and power steering. This leaves about 15% of the energy to propel the car.

Most of this energy is used to overcome rolling friction and air resistance; each of these can be described in terms of a force that resists the motion of the car. We described rolling friction in Section 5–2 in terms of an effective coefficient of rolling friction called *tractive resistance* μ_r. A typical value of μ_r for rubber tires on hard pavement is 0.015. For a 1000-kg compact car weighing about 10,000 N, the resisting force of rolling friction is thus

$$F_{roll} = (0.015)(10,000 \text{ N}) = 150 \text{ N.}$$

This force is nearly independent of car speed.

The air resistance force F_{air} increases rapidly with speed; the relationship can be expressed approximately by the equation

$$F_{air} = \tfrac{1}{2}CA\rho v^2, \tag{7-27}$$

where A is the silhouette area of the car (seen from the front), ρ is the density of air (about 1.2 kg·m^{-3} at ordinary temperatures), v is the car's speed, and C is a dimensionless constant called the *drag coefficient* that depends on the shape of the moving body. A typical value of C for a car designed with moderate attention to aerodynamics is 0.50 (but some cars go as low as $C = 0.35$ or so). Assuming $A = 2.0$ m^2 for our car, we find an air-resistance force of

$$F_{air} = \tfrac{1}{2}(0.50)(2.0 \text{ m}^2)(1.2 \text{ kg·m}^{-3})v^2$$
$$= (0.60 \text{ N·s}^2\text{·m}^{-2})v^2.$$

In a residential speed zone, where $v = 10$ m·s^{-1} (about 22 mi·hr^{-1}), the air-resistance force is about

$$F_{air} = (0.60 \text{ N·s}^2\text{·m}^{-2})(10 \text{ m·s}^{-1})^2 = 60 \text{ N}.$$

At a moderate speed of 15 m·s^{-1} (34 mi·hr^{-1}), F_{air} is 135 N, and at a highway speed of 30 m·s^{-1} (67 mi·hr^{-1}) it is 540 N. Thus at slow speeds, air resistance is less important than rolling friction. At moderate speeds they are comparable, and at highway speeds, air resistance dominates.

What does this mean in terms of the *power* needed from the engine? In constant-speed driving, the forward force supplied by the driven wheels must just balance the sum of these two resisting forces, and the power is this force multiplied by the velocity. For our hypothetical car the power needed for constant speed v is

$$P = (F_{roll} + F_{air})v$$
$$= [150 \text{ N} + (0.60 \text{ N·s}^2\text{·m}^{-2})v^2]v. \tag{7-28}$$

You can do the arithmetic yourself; for the three speeds mentioned above, you will find the following results:

v, m·s^{-1}	F_{roll}, N	F_{air}, N	F_{tot}, N	P, kW	P, hp
10	150	60	210	2.10	2.81
15	150	135	285	4.28	5.73
30	150	540	690	20.7	27.7

Now, how is all this related to fuel consumption? Let's look at the 15 m·s^{-1} case. The power required is 4.28 kW = 4280 J·s^{-1}. In 1 hour (3600 s) the total energy required is

$$(4280 \text{ J·s}^{-1})(3600 \text{ s}) = 1.54 \times 10^7 \text{ J}.$$

During that hour the car travels a distance of

$$(15 \text{ m·s}^{-1})(3600 \text{ s}) = 5.4 \times 10^4 \text{ m} = 54 \text{ km}.$$

Now, as we explained above, only 15% of the 3.5×10^7 J of energy obtained by burning 1 liter (1 L) of gasoline is available to propel the car,

so the available energy per liter is

$$(0.15)(3.5 \times 10^7 \text{ J·L}^{-1}) = 5.25 \times 10^6 \text{ J·L}^{-1}.$$

So the amount of fuel consumed in 1 hour (54 km) is actually

$$(1.54 \times 10^7 \text{ J})/(5.25 \times 10^6 \text{ J·L}^{-1}) = 2.93 \text{ L}.$$

That amount of gasoline gets us 54 km, so the fuel consumption per unit distance is (54 km)/(2.93 L) = 18.4 km·L^{-1}, or about 43.3 miles per gallon.

The power required for a steady 15 m·s^{-1} is 4.28 kW, but the power required for acceleration and hill-climbing may be much greater. Suppose the car accelerates from zero to 30 m·s^{-1} in 20 s. The final kinetic energy (with $m = 1000$ kg) is

$$K = \tfrac{1}{2}mv^2 = \tfrac{1}{2}(1000 \text{ kg})(30 \text{ m·s}^{-1})^2 = 4.5 \times 10^5 \text{ J}.$$

The average power required is

$$P_{\text{av}} = \frac{4.5 \times 10^5 \text{ J}}{20 \text{ s}} = 2.25 \times 10^4 \text{ W} = 22.5 \text{ kW} = 30.2 \text{ hp}.$$

Thus this relatively rapid acceleration requires five times as much power as cruising at a steady moderate speed.

What about hill-climbing? A 5% grade, which is about the maximum found on most interstate highways, rises 5 meters for every 100 meters of horizontal distance. A car driving at 15 m·s^{-1} up a 5% grade is gaining elevation at the rate of (0.05)(15 m·s^{-1}) = 0.75 m·s^{-1}. To lift a car weighing 10,000 N at this rate requires a power of

$$P = Fv = (10{,}000 \text{ N})(0.75 \text{ m·s}^{-1})$$
$$= 7500 \text{ J·s}^{-1} = 7.50 \text{ kW} = 10.0 \text{ hp}.$$

The *total* power required is this amount plus the 4.28 kW needed to maintain 15 m·s^{-1} on a level road, that is,

$$P_{\text{tot}} = 7.50 \text{ kW} + 4.28 \text{ kW} = 11.78 \text{ kW}.$$

Finally, let's compare these energy and power quantities with some purely *thermal* considerations. This is a little premature; we will study the relationship of heat to mechanical energy in detail in later chapters, but here's a little preview. We will learn that to heat 1 kg of water from 0°C to to 100°C requires an energy input to the water of 4.18 × 10^5 J. Thus the 3.5 × 10^7 J obtained from 1 L of gasoline is enough to heat (3.5 × 10^7 J)/ (4.18 × 10^5 J·kg^{-1}) = 83.7 kg of water from freezing to boiling. That's not a whole lot of water, only about 23 gallons. So the amount of energy needed to heat 23 gallons of water from freezing to boiling is enough to push our car more than 18 km! Does that surprise you?

 Questions

7–1 An elevator is hoisted by its cables at constant speed. Is the total work done on the elevator positive, negative, or zero?

7–2 A rope tied to a body is pulled, causing the body to accelerate. But according to Newton's third law, the body pulls back on the rope with an equal and opposite force. Is the total work done then zero? If so, how can the body's kinetic energy change?

7–3 In Fig. 7–9 the projectile has the same initial kinetic energy in each case. Why does it not then rise to the same maximum height in each case?

7–4 Are there any cases in which a frictional force can *increase* the mechanical energy of a system? If so, give examples.

7–5 An automobile jack is used to lift a heavy weight by exerting a force that is much smaller in magnitude than the weight. Does this mean that less work is done than if the weight had been lifted directly?

7–6 A compressed spring is clamped in its compressed position and is then dissolved in acid. What becomes of its potential energy?

7–7 A child standing on a playground swing can increase the amplitude of his motion by "pumping up," pulling back on the swing ropes at the appropriate points during the motion. Where does the added energy come from?

7–8 In a siphon, water is lifted above its original level during its flow from one container to another. Where does it get the needed potential energy?

7–9 A woman bounces on a trampoline, going a little higher with each bounce. Explain how she increases her total mechanical energy.

7–10 Is it possible for the second hill on a roller coaster track to be higher than the first? What would happen if it were higher?

7–11 Does the kinetic energy of a car change more when it speeds up from 10 to 15 m·s^{-1} or from 15 to 20 m·s^{-1}?

7–12 A car accelerates from an initial speed to a greater final speed while the engine develops constant power. Is the acceleration greater at the beginning of this process or at the end?

7–13 Time yourself while running up a flight of steps, and compute your maximum power in horsepower. Are you stronger than a horse?

7–14 When a constant force is applied to a body moving with constant acceleration, is the power of the force constant? If not, how would the force have to vary with speed for the power to be constant?

7–15 An advertisement for a power saw states: "This power tool uses the energy of the motor to stop the blade rotation within 5 seconds after the switch is turned off." Is this an accurate statement? Please explain.

■ *Exercises*

Section 7–2   Work

7–1 A fisherman reels in 20.0 m of line while pulling in a fish that exerts a constant resisting force of 16.0 N. If the fish is pulled in at constant speed, how much work is done on it by the tension in the line?

7–2 A physics book is pushed 1.20 m along a horizontal tabletop by a horizontal force of 2.00 N. The opposing force of friction is 0.400 N.

a) How much work is done on the book by the 2.00-N force?

b) What is the work done on the book by the friction force?

7–3 A water skier is pulled by a tow rope behind a boat. He skies off to the side, and the rope makes an angle of 20.0° with his direction of motion. The tension in the rope is 120 N. How much work is done on the skier by the rope during a displacement of 250 m?

7–4 A factory worker pushes a 50.0-kg crate a distance of 8.00 m along a level floor, at constant speed, by pushing horizontally on it. The coefficient of kinetic friction between the crate and floor is 0.25.

a) What magnitude of force must the worker apply?

b) How much work is done on the crate by this force?

c) How much work is done by friction?

d) How much work is done by the normal force? By gravity?

7–5 In Exercise 7–4, suppose the worker pushes downward at an angle of 30.0° below the horizontal.

a) What magnitude of force must the worker apply to move the crate at constant speed?

b) How much work is done on the crate by this force when the crate is pushed a distance of 8.00 m?

c) How much work is done on the crate by friction during this displacement?

d) How much work is done by the normal force? By gravity?

7–6 The old oaken bucket that hangs in a well has a mass of 6.75 kg. We slowly pull it up a distance of 5.00 m by pulling horizontally on a rope passing over a pulley at the top of the well.

a) How much work do we do in pulling the bucket up?

b) How much work is done by the gravitational force acting on the bucket?

7–7 A 28.0-lb suitcase is pulled up a frictionless plane inclined at 30.0° to the horizontal by a force *P* with a magnitude of 18.0 lb and acting parallel to the plane. If the suitcase travels 15.0 ft along the incline, calculate

a) the work done on the suitcase by the force P,

b) the work done by the gravity force,

c) the work done by the normal force,

d) the total work done on the suitcase.

7–8 An 8.00-kg package slides 2.00 m down a surface that is inclined at 53.0° below the horizontal. The coefficient of kinetic friction between the package and the surface is $\mu_k = 0.40$. Calculate

a) the work done by friction on the package,

b) the work done by gravity,

c) the work done by the normal force,

d) the total work done on the package.

Section 7–3   Work Done by a Varying Force

7–9 The end of a spring with force constant k is at $x = 0$ when no force is applied to it.

a) In terms of x_1 and k, how much force must be applied to the end of the spring to stretch it to $x = x_1$?

b) To stretch it to $x = x_2$?

c) How much work is done by the force that stretches the end of the spring from x_1 to x_2?

7–10 A force of 80.0 N is observed to stretch a certain spring a distance of 0.400 m beyond its unstretched length.

a) What magnitude of force is required to stretch the spring 0.100 m beyond its unstretched length? To compress the spring 0.200 m?

b) How much work must be done to stretch the spring 0.100 m beyond its unstretched length? How much work to compress the spring 0.200 m from its unstretched length?

7–11 A force in the positive x-direction acts on a refrigerator with a mass of 90.0 kg. The magnitude of the force varies with the x-coordinate of the refrigerator according to the equation $F = (45.0 \text{ N·m}^{-1})x$. How much work does this force do when the refrigerator moves from $x_1 = 2.0$ m to $x_2 = 8.0$ m?

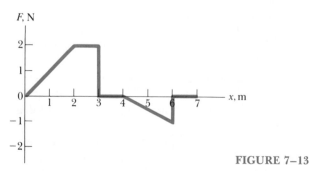

FIGURE 7–13

7–12 A force F that is parallel to the x-axis acts on a block of ice. The magnitude of the force varies with the x-coordinate of the block as shown in Fig. 7–13. Calculate the work done on the block of ice by the force F when the block moves from $x = 0$ to $x = 7.0$ m.

Section 7–4   Work and Kinetic Energy

7–13

a) Compute the kinetic energy of a 1200-kg automobile traveling at 20 km·hr^{-1}.

b) By what factor does the kinetic energy increase if the speed is doubled?

7–14 Compute the kinetic energy, in joules, of a 12.0-g rifle bullet traveling at 250 m·s^{-1}.

7–15 A baseball pitcher is throwing a fast ball, which has a speed (leaving his hand) of 42.0 m·s^{-1}. The mass of the baseball is 0.180 kg. How much work has the pitcher done on the ball in throwing it?

7–16 A television set with a mass of 1.40 slugs is initially at rest on a frictionless horizontal surface. It is then pulled 4.0 ft by a horizontal force of magnitude 25.0 lb. Use the work–energy relation (Eq. 7–8) to find its final speed.

7–17 A little red wagon with a mass of 4.60 kg moves in a straight line on a frictionless horizontal surface. It has an initial speed of 10.0 m·s^{-1} and then is pulled 4.0 m by a force with a magnitude of 18.0 N in the direction of the initial velocity.

a) Use the work–energy relation to calculate the wagon's final speed.

b) Calculate the acceleration produced by the force. Use this acceleration in the kinematic relations of Chapter 2 to calculate the wagon's final speed. Compare this result to that obtained in part (a).

7–18 A sled with a mass of 8.00 kg moves in a straight line on a frictionless horizontal surface. At one point in its path its speed is 4.00 m·s^{-1}, and after it has traveled 9.00 m its speed is 7.00 m·s^{-1} in the same direction. Use the work–energy relation to find the magnitude of the force acting on the sled, assuming that this force is constant and that it acts in the direction of the motion of the sled.

7–19 A force with magnitude 30.0 N acts on a 1.20-kg soccer ball moving initially in the direction of the force with a speed of 4.00 m·s^{-1}. Over what distance must the force act to change the ball's speed to 6.00 m·s^{-1}?

7–20 A small block with a mass of 0.0500 kg is attached to a cord passing through a hole in a frictionless horizontal surface, as in Fig. 7–14. The block is originally revolving at a distance of 0.200 m from the hole with a speed of 0.70 m·s^{-1}. The cord is then pulled from below, shortening the radius of the circle in which

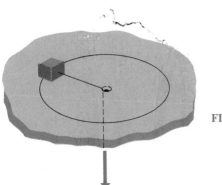

FIGURE 7–14

the block revolves to 0.100 m. At this new distance the speed of the block is observed to be 1.40 m·s⁻¹. How much work was done by the person who pulled on the cord? (Note that the tension in the cord *changes* as the radius is shortened.)

7–21 A car is traveling on a level road with speed v_0 at the instant when the brakes are applied. Assume that the wheels are locked and the car is skidding, so the friction force between the tires and road is kinetic friction with coefficient μ_k.

a) Use the work–energy relation (Eq. 7–8) to calculate the minimum stopping distance of the car in terms of v_0, μ_k, and the acceleration g due to gravity.

b) It is observed that the car stops in a distance of 120 ft if $v_0 = 35.0$ mi·hr⁻¹. What is the stopping distance if $v_0 = 60.0$ mi·hr⁻¹? Assume that μ_k and hence the kinetic friction force remain the same.

Section 7–5   Gravitational Potential Energy

7–22 A 9.00-kg sack of flour is lifted vertically at a constant speed of 4.00 m·s⁻¹ through a height of 12.0 m.

a) How great a force is required?

b) How much work is done on the sack by the lifting force? What becomes of this work?

7–23 What is the potential energy of a 900-kg elevator at the top of the Empire State Building, 380 m above street level? Assume that the potential energy at street level is zero.

7–24 You and your bicycle have a combined mass of 95.0 kg. When you reach the base of an overpass, you are traveling along the road at 3.00 m·s⁻¹. If the vertical height of the overpass is 5.20 m and your speed at the top is 1.50 m·s⁻¹, how much work have you done in getting to the top? (Ignore work done by friction and any inefficiency in the bike or your legs.)

7–25 A barrel with a mass of 80.0 kg is suspended by a vertical rope 12.0 m long.

a) What horizontal force is necessary to hold the bar-

rel in a position displaced sideways 4.0 m from its initial position, as shown in Fig. 7–15?

b) How much work is done on the barrel by the force that moves it to this position?

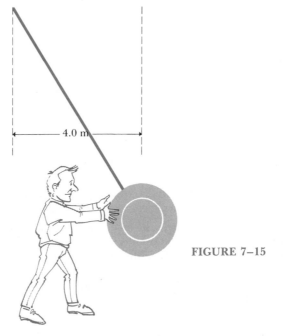

4.0 m

FIGURE 7–15

7–26 A baseball is thrown from the roof of a 120-ft-tall building with an initial velocity of magnitude 60.0 ft·s⁻¹ and at an angle of 37.0° above the horizontal.

a) What is the speed of the ball just before it strikes the ground? Use energy methods.

b) What would be the answer in part (a) if the initial velocity was at an angle of 37.0° *below* the horizontal?

7–27 A small rock with a mass of 0.100 kg is released from rest at point A, which is at the top edge of a hemispherical bowl with radius $R = 0.600$ m (Fig. 7–16). When it reaches point B at the bottom of the bowl, the rock is observed to have speed $v = 1.80$ m·s⁻¹. Calculate the *work* done by friction on the rock when it moves from A to B. (*Note:* The friction force is not constant. You can easily solve for the friction *work* but not for the friction *force*.)

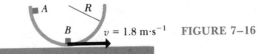

A R

B $v = 1.8$ m·s⁻¹   FIGURE 7–16

7–28 A small rock with mass m is fastened to a massless string of length 0.80 m to form a pendulum. The pendulum is swinging so as to make a maximum angle of 60.0° with the vertical. What is the speed of the rock when the string passes through the vertical position?

7–29 A 5.00-kg dictionary is pushed up a frictionless plane inclined upward at 30.0° to the horizontal. It is pushed 2.00 m along the incline by a constant 100-N force parallel to the plane. If its speed at the bottom is 3.00 m·s^{-1}, what is its speed at the top? Use energy methods.

7–30 A 12.0-kg microwave oven is pushed 14.0 m up the sloping surface of a ramp inclined upward at an angle of 37.0° above the horizontal, by a constant force F of magnitude 120 N acting parallel to the surface of the ramp. The coefficient of kinetic friction between the oven and ramp is 0.25.

a) What is the work done by the force F?

b) What is the work done by the friction force?

c) Compute the increase in potential energy of the oven.

d) Use your answers to parts (a), (b), and (c) to calculate the increase in kinetic energy of the oven.

e) Use $\Sigma F = ma$ to calculate the acceleration of the oven. Assuming that the oven is initially at rest, use the acceleration to calculate the oven's speed after traveling 14.0 m. Compute from this the increase in kinetic energy of the oven, and compare to your answer in part (d).

7–31 The asteroid Toro, discovered in 1964, has a radius of about 5.00 km and a mass of about 2.00 × 10^{15} kg. Use the results of Example 7–9 to calculate the magnitude of the escape velocity for an object at the surface of Toro. Could a person reach this speed just by running?

7–32 Use the results of Example 7–9 to calculate the magnitude of the escape velocity for an object

a) from the surface of the moon;

b) from the surface of Saturn.

c) Why is the escape velocity for an object independent of the object's mass?

7–33 An artillery shell with mass m is shot vertically upward from the surface of the earth. If the shell's initial speed is 5.00 × 10^3 m·s^{-1}, to what height above the surface of the earth will it rise? (Neglect the effect of the drag force exerted by the air so that the only force on the shell is assumed to be gravity.)

Section 7–6   Elastic Potential Energy

7–34 A force of 900 N stretches a certain spring a distance of 0.100 m.

a) What is the potential energy of the spring when it is stretched 0.100 m?

b) Compressed 0.0500 m?

7–35 A force of 750 N stretches a certain spring a distance of 0.150 m. What is the potential energy of the spring when a 60.0-kg mass hangs vertically from it?

7–36 A slingshot will shoot a 10-g BB 40.0 m straight up.

a) How much potential energy is stored in the slingshot's rubber band?

b) With the same potential energy stored in the rubber band, how high can the slingshot shoot a 20-g BB?

7–37 A 1.50-kg book is dropped from a height of 0.60 m onto a spring with force constant $k =$ 1960 N·m^{-1}. Find the maximum distance the spring will be compressed.

7–38 You are asked to design spring bumpers for the walls of a parking garage. A freely rolling 1200-kg car moving at 0.50 m·s^{-1} is to compress the spring no more than 0.080 m before stopping. What should be the force constant of the spring?

7–39 A spring having a force constant $k = 300$ N·m^{-1} rests on a frictionless horizontal surface. One end is in contact with a stationary wall, and a 4.00-kg can of beans is pushed against the other end, compressing the spring 0.100 m. The can is then released with no initial velocity.

a) What is the can's speed when the spring returns to its uncompressed length?

b) What is the can's speed when the spring is still compressed 0.060 m?

7–40 A block with a mass of 5.00 kg is moving at 8.00 m·s^{-1} along a frictionless horizontal surface toward a spring with force constant $k = 500$ N·m^{-1} that is attached to a wall (Fig. 7–17). Find the maximum distance the spring is compressed. The spring has negligible mass.

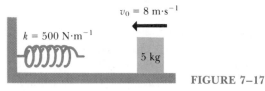

$$v_0 = 8 \text{ m·s}^{-1}$$

$k = 500$ N·m^{-1}

5 kg

FIGURE 7–17

7–41 A brick with a mass of 0.400 kg is pressed against a vertical spring with force constant $k = 500$ N·m^{-1} such that the spring is compressed 0.200 m. When the brick is released, how high does it rise from this position? (The brick and the spring are *not* attached. The spring has negligible mass.)

7–42 A 2.00-kg block is pushed against a spring with force constant $k = 400$ N·m^{-1}, compressing it 0.180 m. The block is then released and moves along a frictionless horizontal surface and then up a frictionless incline with slope angle 37.0° (Fig. 7–18).

a) What is the speed of the block as it slides along the horizontal surface after having left the spring?

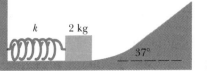

FIGURE 7–18

b) How far does the block travel up the incline before starting to slide back down?

7–43 The spring of a spring-gun has force constant $k = 600$ N·m^{-1}. The spring is compressed 0.0500 m, and a ball with mass 0.0400 kg is placed in the horizontal barrel against the compressed spring. The spring is then released, and the ball is propelled out of the barrel.

a) Compute the speed with which the ball leaves the gun if friction forces are negligible.

b) Determine the speed of the ball as it leaves the end of the barrel if a constant friction force of 11.0 N acts on the ball while it travels the 0.0500 m along the barrel. Note that in this case the maximum speed does not occur at the end of the barrel.

Section 7–8   Power

7–44 At 7.00 cents per kilowatt-hour, what does it cost to operate a 10.0-hp motor for 8.00 hr?

7–45 A tandem (two-person) bicycle team must overcome a force of 34.0 lb to maintain a speed of 30.0 ft·s^{-1}. Find the power required per rider, assuming that they each contribute equally. Express your answer in horsepower.

7–46 The total consumption of electrical energy in the United States is about 1.0×10^{19} joules per year.

a) What is the average rate of electrical energy consumption, in watts?

b) If the population of the United States is 240 million, what is the average rate of electrical energy consumption per person?

c) The sun transfers energy to the earth by radiation at a rate of approximately 1.4 kW per square meter of surface. If this energy could be collected and converted to electrical energy with 100% efficiency, how great an area (in square kilometers) would be required to supply the electrical energy used by the United States?

7–47 A man whose mass is 85.0 kg walks up to the third floor of a building. This is a vertical height of 15.0 m above the street level.

a) By how much has he increased his potential energy?

b) If he climbs the stairs in 20.0 s, what is his rate of working in watts?

7–48 The hammer of a pile driver has a weight of 1100 lb and must be lifted a vertical distance of 4.00 ft in 3.00 s. What horsepower engine is required?

7–49 A ski tow is to be operated on a 25.0° slope 300 m long. The rope is to move at 12.0 km·hr^{-1}, and power must be provided for 60 riders at one time, with an average mass per rider of 70.0 kg. Estimate the power required to operate the tow.

7–50 The engine of a motor boat delivers 30.0 kW to the propeller while the boat is moving at 15.0 m·s^{-1}. What would be the tension in the towline if the boat were being towed at the same speed?

7–51 The Grand Coulee Dam is 1270 m long and 170 m high. The electrical power output from generators at its base is approximately 2000 MW. How many cubic meters of water must flow over the dam per second to produce this amount of power? (The density, or mass per unit volume, of water is 1.00×10^3 kg·m^{-3}.)

Section 7–9   Automotive Power

7–52 The engine of an automobile develops 30.0 kW (40 hp) when the automobile is traveling at 50.0 km·hr^{-1}.

a) What is the resisting force acting on the automobile, in newtons?

b) If the resisting force is proportional to the velocity, what power will drive the car at 25.0 km·hr^{-1}? At 100 km·hr^{-1}? Give your answers in kilowatts and in horsepower.

7–53

a) If 30.0 hp are required to drive a 1200-kg automobile at 50.0 km·hr^{-1} on a level road, what is the total retarding force due to friction, air resistance, and so on?

b) What power is necessary to drive the car at 50.0 km·hr^{-1} up a 10% grade (i.e., a hill rising 10.0 m vertically in 100 m horizontally)?

c) What power is necessary to drive the car at 50.0 km·hr^{-1} *down* a 2% grade?

d) Down what percent grade would the car coast at 50.0 km·hr^{-1}?

7–54 For a touring bicyclist the drag coefficient is 1.00, the frontal area is 0.463 m^2, and the tractive resistance is $\mu_r = 4.5 \times 10^{-3}$. The rider weighs 680 N, and her bike weighs 125 N.

a) To maintain a speed of 14.0 m·s^{-1} (about 31 mph) on a level road, what must the rider's power output be?

b) For racing, the same rider uses a different bike, one with a tractive resistance of 3.0×10^{-3} and a weight of 75 N. She also crouches down, reducing her drag coefficient to 0.88 and reducing her frontal area to 0.366 m². What then must her power output be to maintain a speed of 14.0 m·s⁻¹?

c) For the situation in part (b), what power output is required to maintain a speed of 7.0 m·s⁻¹? Note the great drop in power requirement when the speed is only halved. (See "The Aerodynamics of Human-Powered Land Vehicles," *Scientific American*, December 1983. The article discusses aerodynamic speed limitations for a wide variety of human-powered vehicles.)

Problems

7–55 A projectile with mass m is fired from a gun with a muzzle velocity of magnitude v_0 at an angle of θ above the horizontal. Neglecting air resistance and using energy methods, find the maximum height attained by the projectile.

7–56 The system of Fig. 7–19 is released from rest with the 12.0-kg block 3.00 m above the floor. Use the principle of conservation of energy to find the speed with which the block strikes the floor. Neglect friction and the inertia of the pulley.

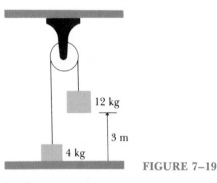

12 kg

3 m

4 kg

FIGURE 7–19

7–57 A meter stick, pivoted about a horizontal axis through its center, has a metal clamp with a mass of 3.00 kg attached to one end and a second clamp with a mass of 1.00 kg attached to the other. The mass of the meter stick can be neglected. The system is released from rest with the stick horizontal. What is the speed of each clamp as the stick swings through a vertical position?

7–58 A car in an amusement park ride rolls without friction around the loop-the-loop track shown in Fig. 7–20. It starts from rest at point A at a height h above the bottom of the loop.

a) What is the minimum value of h (in terms of R) such that the car moves around the loop without falling off at the top (point B)?

b) If $h = 2.75R$ and $R = 25.0$ m, compute the speed, radial acceleration, and tangential acceleration of the passengers when the car is at point C, which is at the end of a horizontal diameter. Show these acceleration components in a diagram, approximately to scale.

7–59 A man with a mass of 90.0 kg sits on a platform suspended from a moveable pulley as shown in Fig. 7–21 and raises himself at constant speed by a rope passing over a fixed pulley. The platform and the pulleys have negligible mass. Assuming no friction losses, find

a) the force the man must exert;

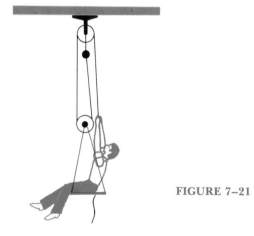

FIGURE 7–21

b) the increase in his energy when he raises himself 2.00 m. Answer by calculating his increase in potential energy and also by computing the product of the force on the rope and the length of the rope passing through his hands.

7–60 A skier starts at the top of a very large frictionless spherical snowball, with a very small initial velocity, and skis straight down the side. At what point does she lose contact with the snowball and fly off at a tangent? That is, at the instant when she loses contact with the snowball, what angle does a radial line from the center of the snowball to the skier make with the vertical?

7–61 A small block of ice with a mass of 0.550 kg is placed against a horizontal compressed spring mounted on a horizontal tabletop that is 1.90 m above the floor. The spring has a force constant $k = 2940$ N·m⁻¹ and is

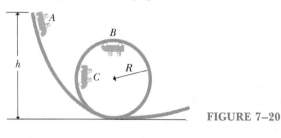

FIGURE 7–20

initially compressed 0.045 m. The spring is released, and the block slides along the table, off the edge, and travels to the floor. If there is negligible friction between the ice and the table, what is the speed of the block of ice when it reaches the floor?

7–62 A ball with a mass of 0.500 kg is tied to a string with length 1.50 m, and the other end of the string is tied to a rigid support. The ball is held straight out horizontally from the point of support, with the string pulled taut, and is then released.

a) What is the speed of the ball at the lowest point of its motion?

b) What is the tension in the string at this point?

7–63 A rock is tied to a cord, and the other end of the cord is held fixed. The rock is given an initial tangential velocity that causes it to rotate in a vertical circle. Prove that the tension in the cord at the lowest point exceeds that at the highest point by six times the weight of the rock.

7–64 Consider the system shown in Fig. 7–22. The coefficient of kinetic friction between the 8.00-kg block and the tabletop is $\mu_k = 0.25$. Neglect the mass of the rope and of the pulley, and assume that the pulley is frictionless. Use energy methods to calculate the speed of the 6.00-kg block after is has descended 2.00 m, starting from rest.

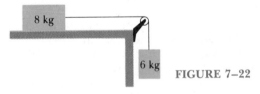

FIGURE 7–22

7–65 In a truck-loading station at a post office a 2.00-kg package is released from rest at point A on a track that is one quadrant of a circle of radius 2.40 m (Fig. 7–23). It slides down the track and reaches point B with a speed of 4.00 m·s^{-1}. From point B it slides on a level surface a distance of 3.50 m to point C, where it comes to rest.

a) What is the coefficient of kinetic friction on the horizontal surface?

b) How much work is done on the package by friction as it slides down the circular arc from A to B?

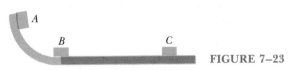

FIGURE 7–23

7–66 A pump is required to lift 800 kg (about 200 gallons) of water per minute from a well that is 14.0 m deep and eject it with a speed of 30.0 m·s^{-1}.

a) How much work is done per minute in lifting the water?

b) How much in giving it kinetic energy?

c) What power engine is needed?

7–67 The human heart is a powerful and extremely reliable pump. Each day it takes in and discharges about 7500 L of blood. If the work done by the heart is equal to the work required to lift this amount of blood a height equal to that of the average American female (1.63 m), and if the density (mass per unit volume) of blood is the same as that of water (1.00×10^3 kg·m^{-3}),

a) how much work does the heart do in a day?

b) what is its power output in watts?

7–68 A rock is thrown straight up from the surface of the asteroid Toro (see Exercise 7–31) with a speed of 20.0 m·s^{-1}, which is greater than the escape speed. What is the speed of the rock when it is far from Toro? Neglect the gravitational forces due to all other astronomical objects.

7–69 A hammer with mass m is dropped from a height h above the earth's surface. This height is not necessarily small in comparison with the radius R_E of the earth. If air resistance is neglected, derive an expression for the speed v of the hammer when it reaches the surface of the earth. Your expression should involve h, R_E, and m_E, the mass of the earth.

7–70 A block with a mass of 2.50 kg is forced against a horizontal spring of negligible mass, compressing the spring a distance 0.200 m. When released, the block moves on a horizontal tabletop a distance 1.00 m before coming to rest. The spring constant k is 150 N·m^{-1} (Fig. 7–24). What is the coefficient of kinetic friction, μ_k, between the block and the table?

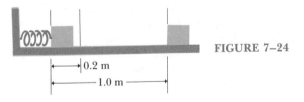

FIGURE 7–24

0.2 m

1.0 m

7–71 An 80.0-kg man jumps from a height of 3.00 m onto a platform mounted on springs. As the springs compress, the platform is pushed down a maximum distance of 0.200 m below its initial position, and then it rebounds. The platform and springs have negligible mass.

a) What is the man's speed at the instant the platform is depressed 0.100 m?

b) If the man had just stepped gently onto the platform, how far would it have been pushed down?

7–72 If a fish is attached to a vertical spring and slowly lowered to its equilibrium position, it is found to stretch the spring by an amount d. If the same fish is attached to the unstretched spring and then allowed to fall from rest, through what maximum distance does it stretch the spring? (*Hint:* Calculate the force constant of the spring in terms of the distance d and the mass m of the fish.)

7–73 A 0.500-kg block *attached* to a spring of length 0.600 m and force constant $k = 40.0$ N·m^{-1} is at rest at point A on a frictionless horizontal surface (Fig. 7–25). A constant horizontal force $P = 20.0$ N is applied to the block and moves the block to the right along the surface.

a) What is the speed of the block when it reaches point B, which is 0.250 m to the right of point A?

b) When the block reaches point B, the force P is suddenly removed. In the subsequent motion, how close does the block get to the wall?

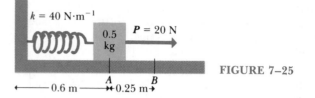

FIGURE 7–25

7–74 A wooden block with a mass of 5.00 kg is placed against a compressed spring at the bottom of an incline of slope 37.0° (point A). When the spring is released, it projects the block up the incline. At point B, a distance of 6.00 m up the incline from A, the block is observed to have a velocity with magnitude 8.00 m·s^{-1}, directed up the incline. The coefficient of kinetic friction between the block and incline is $\mu_k = 0.40$. Calculate the amount of potential energy that was initially stored in the spring.

■ *Challenge Problems*

7–75 There are two equations from which a change in the gravitational potential energy U of a mass m can be calculated. One is $U = mgy$ (Eq. 7–10). The other is $U = -G(mm_E/r)$ (Eq. 7–17). As shown in Section 7–5, the first equation is correct only if g is a constant over the change in height Δy. The second is always correct. Actually, g is never exactly constant over any change in height, but the variation may be so small that we ignore it. Consider the difference in U between a mass at the earth's surface and a distance h above it using both equations, and find for what height h (Eq. 7–10) is in error by 1%. Express this h as a fraction of the earth's radius, and also obtain a numerical value for it.

7–76 On an incline a 2.00-kg block is released 4.00 m from a long spring with force constant $k = 60.0$ N·m^{-1} that is attached at the bottom of the incline, as shown in Fig. 7–26. The incline makes an angle of 53.0° with the horizontal, and the coefficients of friction between the block and the incline are $\mu_s = 0.40$ and $\mu_k = 0.20$.

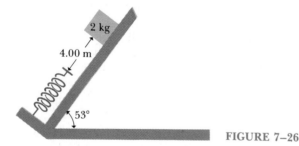

FIGURE 7–26

a) What is the speed of the block just before it reaches the spring?

b) What will be the maximum compression of the spring?

c) The block rebounds back up the incline. How close does it get to its initial position?

7–77 A shaft is drilled from the surface to the center of the earth. The gravitational force on an object of mass m that is inside the earth at a distance r from the center has magnitude $F = mgr/R_E$, where R_E is the radius of the earth, and points toward the center of the earth. If an object is released in the shaft at the surface of the earth, what speed will it have when it reaches the center of the earth?

7–78 An object has several forces acting on it. One of these forces is F, a force in the $+x$-direction whose magnitude depends on the y-coordinate of the object according to the equation $F = (3.00$ N·m$^{-1})y$. Calculate the work done by this force for each of the following displacements of the object:

a) The object starts at the point $x = 0$, $y = 4.00$ m and moves parallel to the x-axis to the point $x = 2.00$ m, $y = 4.00$ m.

b) The object starts at the point $x = 2.00$ m, $y = 0$ and moves in the y-direction to the point $x = 2.00$ m, $y = 4.00$ m.

c) The object starts at the origin and moves on the line $y = 2x$ to the point $x = 2.00$ m, $y = 4.00$ m.

Impulse and Momentum

The preceding chapter was devoted to the concepts of work and energy and to the principle of conservation of energy, one of the great conservation principles of physical science. In this chapter we develop an equally fundamental conservation law, conservation of *momentum*. We introduce two new concepts, impulse and momentum, and we use Newton's laws to develop simple relations between them. This formulation is especially useful for impacts and collisions, in which very large forces act for short times and cause sudden changes in motion of a body.

8–1
Impulse and Momentum

This chapter is about impulse and momentum; let's begin by defining these new quantities. Suppose a particle with mass m is moving at some instant with velocity v, while a force F acts on it. We define the **momentum** of the particle, which we denote by p, as

$$p = mv. \tag{8-1}$$

Momentum is a *vector quantity*. We define **impulse** with reference to the force F and a time interval $t_2 - t_1 = \Delta t$ during which it acts. Denoting impulse by J, we define the impulse of a constant force F acting from time t_1 to t_2 as

$$J = F(t_2 - t_1) = F\,\Delta t. \tag{8-2}$$

Impulse, like momentum, is a vector quantity.

These definitions seem arbitrary, but it is easy to develop a simple relationship that shows their usefulness. Let's begin with a simple case, straight-line motion along the x-axis, with a constant force along the axis. Then the force, velocity, and acceleration have only x-components, and we can denote them simply as F, v, and a. In this case, momentum and impulse also have only x-components. When the force F is constant, the acceleration a is also constant. If the particle has velocity v_0 at the initial time $t = 0$, then its velocity v at a later time t is given by

$$v = v_0 + at,$$

where a is determined from $F = ma$. When we multiply this equation by m and replace ma by F, we get

$$mv = mv_0 + Ft,$$

or

$$Ft = mv - mv_0. \tag{8-3}$$

The left side of this equation is equal to the x-component of the impulse of the force between the initial time $t = 0$ and the later time t, and the right side is the *change* in the x-component of momentum during the same interval. There is nothing special about the two times $t = 0$ and t. If the particle has velocity v_1 at time t_1 and velocity v_2 at time t_2, then

$$F(t_2 - t_1) = mv_2 - mv_1 \tag{8-4}$$

Thus *the change of momentum during any time interval equals the impulse of the force during that interval.* Keep in mind that Eq. (8–4) is really a relationship for the x-components of the vector quantities impulse and momentum. In straight-line motion we will often call mv the momentum of the particle, just as we called v the velocity in Chapter 2, when in both cases we really mean the x-components of these vector quantities.

Example 8–1   A particle with a mass of 2 kg moves along the x-axis with an initial velocity of 3 m·s^{-1}. A force $F = -6$ N (i.e., in the negative x-direction) is applied for a period of 3 s. Find the final velocity.

Solution   From Eq. (8–4),

$$(-6 \text{ N})(3 \text{ s}) = (2 \text{ kg})v_2 - (2 \text{ kg})(3 \text{ m·s}^{-1}),$$

or

$$v_2 = -6 \text{ m·s}^{-1}.$$

The particle's final velocity is in the negative x-direction.   ■

The SI unit of impulse is 1 N·s, and the unit of momentum is 1 kg·m·s^{-1}. Because 1 N = 1 kg·m·s^{-2}, we have

$$1 \text{ N·s} = (1 \text{ kg·m·s}^{-2})(1 \text{ s}) = 1 \text{ kg·m·s}^{-1}.$$

That is, the units of impulse and momentum are the same. Indeed, they *have* to be the same if Eq. (8–4) is to be dimensionally consistent.

Example 8–2   A hockey puck with a mass of 0.10 kg moves along the x-axis on a frictionless ice surface with an initial velocity of 20 m·s^{-1}. Find its final velocity in each of the following cases:

a) A force $F = 0.20$ N acts for 5 s;

b) A force of 0.20 N acts for 5 s, and then a force of -0.40 N acts for the next 5 s;

c) A force of 0.20 N acts for 5 s, and then a force of -0.10 N acts for 10 s.

Solution

a) The impulse is $J = (0.20 \text{ N})(5 \text{ s}) = 1.0$ N·s. From Eq. (8–4),

$$1.0 \text{ N·s} = (0.10 \text{ kg})v_2 - (0.10 \text{ kg})(20 \text{ m·s}^{-1}),$$

$$v_2 = 30 \text{ m·s}^{-1}.$$

b) The total impulse is

$$J = (0.20 \text{ N})(5 \text{ s}) + (-0.40 \text{ N})(5 \text{ s}) = -1.0 \text{ N·s}.$$

From Eq. (8–4),

$$-1.0 \text{ N·s} = (0.10 \text{ kg})v_2 - (0.10 \text{ kg})(20 \text{ m·s}^{-1}),$$

$$v_2 = 10 \text{ m·s}^{-1}.$$

The impulse is negative, and the puck's velocity in the $+x$-direction decreases.

c) The total impulse is

$$J = (0.20 \text{ N})(5 \text{ s}) + (-0.10 \text{ N})(10 \text{ s}) = 0.$$

The total impulse is zero; there is no net momentum change, so $v_2 = 20$ m·s^{-1}. While the forces are acting, the velocity increases and decreases, but the final value is the same as the initial value.   ■

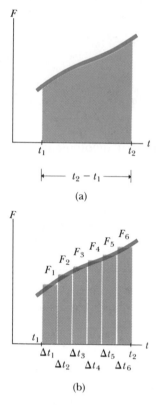

$t_2 - t_1$

(a)

(b)

8–1

(a) Graph showing how the force F varies with time t. (b) The area of the first rectangle, $F_1 \, \Delta t_1$, is approximately equal to the impulse of the force during Δt_1, and the total area under the curve between t_1 and t_2 is the total impulse during this interval.

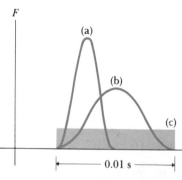

8–2

Force–time graph for Example 8–3.

We can generalize this discussion to the case in which the force F acting on the particle is not constant. Suppose F keeps the same direction but its magnitude F varies with time. We divide the total time interval into a large number of intervals Δt; the total impulse is the sum of the $F \, \Delta t$ products. We can plot a graph of F as a function of t, as shown in Fig. 8–1. Then the magnitude of the total impulse from time t_1 to t_2 is represented by the area under the curve between t_1 and t_2. The figure also shows how to define the magnitude of the *average* force F_{av} during this interval. We define F_{av} so that $F_{av}(t_2 - t_1)$ is equal to the impulse of the actual time-varying force during the same interval. Then the rectangular area bounded by t_1, t_2, and F_{av} equals the area under the curve representing the actual force. For *any* force, constant or not,

$$J = F_{av}(t_2 - t_1) = mv_2 - mv_1. \qquad (8–5)$$

Example 8–3   A ball with a mass of 0.40 kg is thrown against a brick wall. It hits the wall moving horizontally to the left at 30 m·s^{-1}, and it rebounds horizontally to the right at 20 m·s^{-1}. Find the impulse of the force exerted on the ball by the wall. If the ball is in contact with the wall for 0.010 s, find the average force on the ball during the impact.

Solution   Take the x-axis as horizontal and the positive direction to the right. The initial momentum of the ball is

$$p_1 = mv_1 = (0.40 \text{ kg})(-30 \text{ m·s}^{-1}) = -12 \text{ kg·m·s}^{-1}.$$

The final momentum is

$$p_2 = mv_2 = +8.0 \text{ kg·m·s}^{-1}.$$

The *change* in momentum is

$$p_2 - p_1 = mv_2 - mv_1 = 8.0 \text{ kg·m·s}^{-1} - (-12 \text{ kg·m·s}^{-1})$$
$$= 20 \text{ kg·m·s}^{-1} = J.$$

Hence the impulse of the force exerted on the ball was 20 kg·m·s^{-1} = 20 N·s. Since the impulse is *positive*, the force is toward the right.

The time variation of the force may be similar to one of the curves in Fig. 8–2. The force is zero before impact, rises to a maximum, and then decreases to zero when the ball loses contact with the wall. If the ball is relatively rigid, like a baseball or a golf ball, the time of collision is small and the maximum force is large, as in curve (a). If the ball is softer, like a tennis ball, the collision time is larger and the maximum force is less, as in curve (b). In any case, the *area* under the curve represents the impulse $J = 20$ N·s.

If the collision time is 0.01 s, then from Eq. (8–5),

$$F_{av}(0.01 \text{ s}) = 20 \text{ N·s}, \qquad F_{av} = 2000 \text{ N}.$$

This average force is represented by the horizontal line (c) in Fig. 8–2.

Figure 8–3 is a stroboscopic photograph showing the impact of a tennis ball and racket during a serve. ∎

Example 8–4   Suppose the ball in Example 8–3 is a soccer ball with a mass of 0.40 kg. Initially, it is moving to the left at 30 m·s⁻¹, but then it is kicked and given a velocity at 45° upward and to the right, with a magnitude of 30 m·s⁻¹. Find the impulse of the force and the average force, assuming a collision time of 0.010 s.

Solution   The velocities are not along the same line, and we have to be careful to treat momentum and impulse as vector quantities, using their x- and y-components. Taking the x-axis horizontally to the right and the y-axis vertically upward, we find the following velocity components:

$$v_{1x} = -30 \text{ m·s}^{-1}, \qquad v_{1y} = 0,$$
$$v_{2x} = v_{2y} = (0.707)(30 \text{ m·s}^{-1}) = 21 \text{ m·s}^{-1}.$$

The x-component of impulse is equal to the x-component of momentum change, and the same is true for the y-components:

$$J_x = m(v_{2x} - v_{1x})$$
$$= (0.40 \text{ kg})[21 \text{ m·s}^{-1} - (-30 \text{ m·s}^{-1})]$$
$$= 20.4 \text{ kg·m·s}^{-1},$$

$$J_y = m(v_{2y} - v_{1y})$$
$$= (0.40 \text{ kg})(21 \text{ m·s}^{-1} - 0)$$
$$= 8.4 \text{ kg·m·s}^{-1}.$$

The components of average force on the ball are

$$F_x = J_x/\Delta t = 2040 \text{ N}, \qquad F_y = J_y/\Delta t = 840 \text{ N}.$$

The magnitude and direction of the average force are

$$F_{av} = \sqrt{(2040 \text{ N})^2 + (840 \text{ N})^2} = 2.2 \times 10^3 \text{ N},$$

$$\theta = \arctan \frac{840 \text{ N}}{2040 \text{ N}} = 25°,$$

where θ is measured upward from the $+x$-axis. ∎

8–3
Multiflash stroboscopic photograph of a tennis racket hitting a ball during a serve. The exposure rate was 300 pictures per second. The ball is in contact with the racket for approximately 0.01 s. The ball flattens noticeably on both sides, and the frame of the racket bends and vibrates during and after the impact. (Dr. Harold Edgerton, M.I.T., Cambridge, Massachusetts.)

The relationship between impulse and momentum change has a superficial resemblance to the work–energy theorem we developed in Chapter 7, but there are important differences. First, impulse is a product of a force and a *time* interval, while work is a product of force and a *distance* and depends on the angle between force and displacement. Impulse and momentum are *vector* quantities, while work and kinetic energy are *scalars*. Even in straight-line motion, in which only one component of a vector is involved, force and velocity may have components along this line that are either positive or negative.

8–2
Conservation of Momentum

The concept of momentum can be very useful in situations in which we have two or more interacting bodies. Let's consider first an idealized system consisting of two bodies that interact with each other but not with anything else—two skaters on a perfectly frictionless ice rink, for example. Each body exerts a force on the other, so the momentum of each body changes. According to Newton's third law, the forces the bodies exert on each other are always equal in magnitude and opposite in direction. Thus the *impulses* given to the two bodies in any time interval are also equal and opposite, and therefore the *momentum changes* of the two bodies are equal and opposite.

We define the **total momentum** of the system, **P,** as the *vector sum* of momenta of the bodies in the system:

$$P = mv_1 + mv_2 = p_1 + p_2. \tag{8–6}$$

If the change in momentum of one body is exactly the negative of that of the other, then the change in the *total* momentum must be zero. *When two bodies interact only with each other, their total momentum is constant.* This statement is the principle of **conservation of momentum.**

When we are considering a system that includes several interacting bodies, we can classify the forces acting on the bodies as internal and external. A force that one body in the system exerts on another is called an **internal force,** and a force exerted on one of the bodies in the system by some agency outside the system is an **external force.** When no external forces act on a system, we call it an **isolated system.** An alternative statement of the principle of conservation of momentum is: *The total momentum of an isolated system is constant.* More generally, if there are external forces but their vector sum is zero, the total momentum is still constant. The *internal* forces can change the momentum of an individual body within the system, but they cannot change the *total* momentum of the system.

The principle of conservation of momentum is one of the most fundamental and important principles in mechanics. In some respects it is more general than the principle of conservation of mechanical energy. For example, it is valid even if the internal forces are not conservative, while mechanical energy is conserved only when they are *conservative.* In this chapter we will see situations in which both momentum and mechanical energy are conserved and others in which only momentum is conserved.

PROBLEM-SOLVING STRATEGY: *Conservation of Momentum*

Momentum is a vector quantity; you *must* use vector addition to compute the total momentum of a system. Using components is usually the simplest method.

1. Define your coordinate system. Sketch the coordinate axes, including the positive direction for each. Often it is easiest to choose the x-axis to have the direction of one of the initial velocities.

2. Draw a sketch including the coordinate axes and vectors representing all known velocity vectors. Label the vectors with magnitudes, angles, components, or whatever information is given, and give algebraic symbols to all unknown magnitudes, angles, or components.

3. Compute the x- and y-components of momentum of each body, both before and after the collision, impact, or other interaction, using the relations $p_x = mv_x$ and $p_y = mv_y$. Even when all the velocities lie along a line (such as the x-axis), the components of velocity along this line can be positive or negative; be careful with signs!

4. Write an equation equating the total *initial* x-component of momentum to the total *final* x-component of momentum. Write another

equation for the y-components. These two equations express conservation of momentum in component form. Some of the components will be expressed in terms of symbols representing unknown quantities.

5. Solve these equations to determine whatever results are required. In some problems you will have to convert from the x- and y-components of a velocity to its magnitude and direction, or the reverse.

6. Remember that the x- and y-components of velocity or momentum are *never* added together in the same equation.

7. In some problems, energy considerations give additional relationships among the various velocities, as we will see later in this chapter.

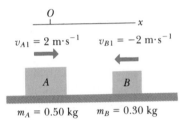

8–4
Two gliders collide on a linear air track, as in Example 8–5. The masses and initial velocities are shown.

Example 8–5   Figure 8–4 shows two gliders moving toward each other on a linear air track. The total vertical force on each glider is zero; the resultant force on each glider is the horizontal force exerted on it by the other glider. The combination is an isolated system, and its total momentum is constant.

After the gliders collide, B moves away with a final velocity of +2.0 m·s⁻¹. What is the final velocity of A?

Solution   Take the x-axis to lie along the air track, with the positive direction to the right. Let the final velocity of A be v_{A2}. Then we write an equation showing the equality of the total momentum (x-component) before and after the collision:

$$(0.50 \text{ kg})(2.0 \text{ m·s}^{-1}) + (0.30 \text{ kg})(-2.0 \text{ m·s}^{-1})$$
$$= (0.50 \text{ kg})v_{A2} + (0.30 \text{ kg})(+2.0 \text{ m·s}^{-1}).$$

Solving this equation for v_{A2}, we find $v_{A2} = -0.40$ m·s⁻¹.   ■

Example 8–6   A marksman holds a 3.00-kg rifle loosely in his hands and fires a bullet of mass 5.00 g with a muzzle velocity $v_B = 300$ m·s⁻¹. What is the recoil velocity v_R of the rifle? What is the final kinetic energy of the bullet? Of the rifle?

Solution   We consider an idealized model in which the forces the marksman exerts on the rifle are negligible, so the rifle and bullet can be considered an isolated system. Then the total momentum of the system is zero both before and after firing. Take the positive x-axis to be the direction the rifle is aimed; then conservation of the x-component of momentum gives

$$0 = (0.00500 \text{ kg})(300 \text{ m·s}^{-1}) + (3.00 \text{ kg})v_R,$$

$$v_R = -0.500 \text{ m·s}^{-1}.$$

The negative sign means that the recoil velocity is in the direction opposite to that of the bullet.

The kinetic energy of the bullet is

$$K_B = \tfrac{1}{2}(0.00500 \text{ kg})(300 \text{ m·s}^{-1})^2 = 225 \text{ J},$$

and the kinetic energy of the rifle is

$$K_R = \tfrac{1}{2}(3.00 \text{ kg})(0.500 \text{ m·s}^{-1})^2 = 0.375 \text{ J}.$$

The bullet acquires much greater kinetic energy than the rifle; the reason is that it moves much farther than the rifle during the interaction, and the interaction force on it does more *work* than on the rifle. In fact, we see that the ratio of the two kinetic energies, 600:1, is equal to the inverse ratio of the masses. It can be shown that this always happens in recoil situations; we leave the proof as a problem. The two interaction forces act for equal *times*, so their impulses are equal in magnitude, and the momentum changes are equal and opposite.   ■

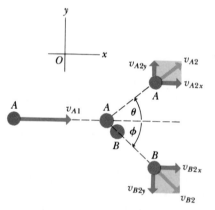

8–5
Velocity vector diagram for Example 8–7.

Example 8–7   Figure 8–5 shows two chunks of ice sliding on a frictionless frozen pond. Chunk A, with mass $m_A = 5.0$ kg, moves with initial velocity $v_{A1} = 2.0$ m·s^{-1} parallel to the x-axis. It collides with chunk B, which has mass $m_B = 3.0$ kg and is initially at rest. After the collision the velocity of A is found to be $v_{A2} = 1.0$ m·s^{-1} in a direction making an angle $\theta = 30°$ with the initial direction. What is the final velocity of B?

Solution   The total momentum of the system is the same before and after the collision. The velocities are not all along a single line, and we have to treat momentum as a *vector* quantity, using components of each momentum in the x- and y-directions. Then momentum conservation requires that the sum of the x-components before the collision must equal the sum after the collision, and similarly for the y-components. Just as with force equilibrium problems, we write a separate equation for each component. For the x-components (before and after) we have

$$(5.0 \text{ kg})(2.0 \text{ m·s}^{-1}) + (3.0 \text{ kg})(0)$$
$$= (5.0 \text{ kg})(1.0 \text{ m·s}^{-1})(\cos 30°) + (3.0 \text{ kg})v_{B2x},$$
$$v_{B2x} = 1.9 \text{ m·s}^{-1}.$$

Similarly, conservation of the y-component of total momentum gives

$$(5.0 \text{ kg})(0) + (3.0 \text{ kg})(0) = (5.0 \text{ kg})(1.0 \text{ m·s}^{-1})(\sin 30°) + (3.0 \text{ kg})v_{B2y},$$

from which

$$v_{B2y} = -0.83 \text{ m·s}^{-1}.$$

The magnitude of v_{B2} is

$$v_{B2} = \sqrt{(1.9 \text{ m·s}^{-1})^2 + (-0.83 \text{ m·s}^{-1})^2} = 2.1 \text{ m·s}^{-1},$$

and the angle of its direction from the positive x-axis is

$$\phi = \arctan \frac{-0.83 \text{ m·s}^{-1}}{1.9 \text{ m·s}^{-1}} = -24°.   ■$$

8–3
Inelastic Collisions

The term *collision* usually means an interaction between two bodies in which there is a very strong interaction that lasts a relatively short time. If the interaction forces are much larger than any external forces, we can model the system as an isolated system, neglecting the external forces entirely. Two cars colliding at an icy intersection are a good example. Even two cars colliding on dry paving can be treated as an isolated system if the interaction forces are much larger than the friction forces of tires against pavement.

When the interaction forces between the bodies are *conservative*, the total *kinetic energy* of the system is the same after the collision as before. Such a collision is called an **elastic collision.** A collision between two hard steel balls or two ivory billiard balls is almost completely elastic. Figure 8–6 shows a model for an elastic collision. When the bodies collide, the spring is momentarily compressed, and some of the original kinetic energy is momentarily converted to elastic potential energy. Then the bodies bounce apart, the spring expands, and this potential energy is reconverted to kinetic energy.

A collision in which the total kinetic energy after the collision is *less* than that before the collision is called an **inelastic collision.** In one kind of inelastic collision the colliding bodies stick together and move *as a unit* after the collision. In Fig. 8–6 we could replace the spring with a ball of chewing gum that squashes and sticks the two bodies together. A ball of gum striking a window shade, a bullet embedding itself in a block of wood, and two cars colliding and bending their fenders are examples of inelastic collisions.

Let's do a little general analysis of an inelastic collision in which the two bodies (A and B) stick together after the collision. Their two final velocities are then equal:

$$v_{A2} = v_{B2} = v_2.$$

Conservation of momentum gives the relation

$$m_A v_{A1} + m_B v_{B1} = (m_A + m_B)v_2. \qquad (8\text{–}7)$$

If we know the masses and initial velocities, we can compute the final velocity.

The total kinetic energy of a system after an inelastic collision is always less than that before the collision. Suppose, for example, that a body having mass m_A and initial velocity v_1 collides inelastically with a body of mass m_B that is initially at rest. After the collision the two bodies have a common velocity v_2, given by Eq. (8–8):

$$v_2 = \frac{m_A}{m_A + m_B} v_1. \qquad (8\text{–}8)$$

The kinetic energies K_1 and K_2 before and after the collision, respectively, are

$$K_1 = \tfrac{1}{2} m_A v_1^2, \qquad K_2 = \tfrac{1}{2}(m_A + m_B)\left(\frac{m_A}{m_A + m_B}\right)^2 v_1^2,$$

8–6
Body A (with spring) and body B approach each other on a frictionless surface.

so the ratio of final to initial kinetic energy is

$$\frac{K_2}{K_1} = \frac{m_A}{m_A + m_B}.$$ (8–9)

The right side is always less than unity because the denominator is always greater than the numerator. Even when the initial velocity of m_B is not zero, it is not hard to prove that the kinetic energy after an inelastic collision is always less than before.

Please note: We don't recommend memorizing Eqs. (8–8) and (8–9). We derived them only to prove that kinetic energy is always lost in this kind of collision.

Example 8–8   Suppose that in the collision in Fig. 8–4 the two bodies stick together after the collision; the masses and initial velocities are as shown. Find the final velocity, and compare the initial and final kinetic energies.

Solution   From momentum conservation,

$$(0.50 \text{ kg})(2.0 \text{ m·s}^{-1}) + (0.30 \text{ kg})(-2.0 \text{ m·s}^{-1}) = (0.50 \text{ kg} + 0.30 \text{ kg})v_2,$$

and

$$v_2 = 0.50 \text{ m·s}^{-1}.$$

Since v_2 is positive, the system moves to the right after the collision. The kinetic energy of body A before the collision is

$$\tfrac{1}{2}m_A v_{A1}^2 = \tfrac{1}{2}(0.50 \text{ kg})(2.0 \text{ m·s}^{-1})^2 = 1.0 \text{ J},$$

and that of body B is

$$\tfrac{1}{2}m_B v_{B1}^2 = \tfrac{1}{2}(0.30 \text{ kg})(-2.0 \text{ m·s}^{-1})^2 = 0.60 \text{ J}.$$

The total kinetic energy before the collision is therefore 1.6 J. Note that the kinetic energy of body B is positive, although its velocity v_{B1} and its momentum $m v_{B1}$ are both negative.

The kinetic energy after the collision is

$$\tfrac{1}{2}(m_A + m_B)v_2^2 = \tfrac{1}{2}(0.50 \text{ kg} + 0.30 \text{ kg})(0.50 \text{ m·s}^{-1})^2 = 0.10 \text{ J}.$$

The final kinetic energy is only 1/16 of the original, and 15/16 is "lost" in the collision.

The energy isn't really lost, of course; it is converted from mechanical energy to various other forms. If there is a ball of chewing gum between the masses, it squashes irreversibly and becomes warmer. If the masses couple together like two freight cars, the energy goes into elastic waves that are eventually dissipated. If there is a spring between the bodies that is compressed when they lock together, then the energy is stored as potential energy of the spring. In all of these cases the *total* energy of the system is conserved, although *kinetic* energy is not. However, in an isolated system, momentum is *always* conserved, whether the collision is elastic or not.   ∎

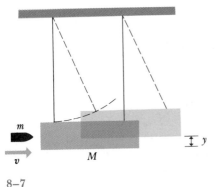

Example 8–9   Figure 8–7 shows a *ballistic pendulum*, a system for measuring the speed of a bullet. The bullet is fired into a block of wood, making a completely inelastic collision with it. The momentum of the system just after the collision equals the original momentum of the bullet, but the *velocity* is very much smaller and can be measured more easily. We can analyze this event in two stages; the first is the embedding of the bullet in the block, and the second is the subsequent swinging of the block on its string. As we will see, momentum is conserved in the first stage, energy in the second.

As Fig. 8–7 shows, the pendulum, a wood block with mass M, hangs vertically by two strings. A bullet with mass m and velocity v strikes the block and embeds itself in it. If the collision time is very small in comparison with the time of swing of the pendulum, the supporting strings remain practically vertical during the collision. Hence no external horizontal forces act on the system during the collision, and the horizontal momentum is conserved. Then if V represents the velocity of bullet and block just after the collision, momentum conservation gives

$$mv = (m + M)V, \qquad v = \frac{m + M}{m}V.$$

The kinetic energy of the system just after impact is $K = \frac{1}{2}(m + M)V^2$.

After the collision the block and bullet move as a unit. The only forces are the weight (a conservative force) and the string tensions (which do no work). So during the swing of the pendulum to the right, mechanical energy is conserved. The pendulum comes to rest at a height y, where its initial kinetic energy has all become potential energy; then it starts to swing back down. At the highest point,

$$\tfrac{1}{2}(m + M)V^2 = (m + M)gy, \qquad V = \sqrt{2gy},$$

so we find

$$v = \frac{m + M}{m}\sqrt{2gy}.$$

By measuring m, M, and y we can compute the original velocity v of the bullet.

Suppose $m = 5.00$ g $= 0.00500$ kg, $M = 2.00$ kg, and $y = 3.00$ cm $= 0.0300$ m. Then, working backward, we find the velocity V of the block just after impact:

$$V = \sqrt{2(9.80 \text{ m·s}^{-2})(0.0300 \text{ m})} = 0.767 \text{ m·s}^{-1}.$$

Then we use momentum conservation to find the bullet's velocity v just before impact:

$$(0.00500 \text{ kg})v = (2.00 \text{ kg} + 0.00500 \text{ kg})(0.767 \text{ m·s}^{-1}),$$

$$v = 307 \text{ m·s}^{-1}.$$

The kinetic energy just before impact is $\frac{1}{2}(0.00500 \text{ kg})(307 \text{ m·s}^{-1})^2 = 236$ J, while just after impact it is $\frac{1}{2}(2.005 \text{ kg})(0.767 \text{ m·s}^{-1})^2 = 0.589$ J. Nearly all the kinetic energy disappears as the wood splinters and the bullet becomes hotter.   ■

8–4
Elastic Collisions

Now let's look at an *elastic* collision between two bodies A and B, assuming again that they are an isolated system. We start with a head-on collision, in which all the velocities lie along the same line. Later we will consider more general collisions.

Because the system is isolated, momentum is conserved. The new feature for elastic collisions is that the interaction forces are *conservative*, so kinetic energy is also conserved. From conservation of kinetic energy we have

$$\tfrac{1}{2}m_A v_{A1}^2 + \tfrac{1}{2}m_B v_{B1}^2 = \tfrac{1}{2}m_A v_{A2}^2 + \tfrac{1}{2}m_B v_{B2}^2,$$

and from conservation of momentum we have

$$m_A v_{A1} + m_B v_{B1} = m_A v_{A2} + m_B v_{B2}.$$

If the masses and initial velocities are known, these two equations can be solved simultaneously to find the two final velocities. The general solution is a little complicated, so we will concentrate on a particular case, in which one body is at rest before the collision.

Suppose mass m_B is initially at rest. Think of it as a target for m_A to hit. We can then simplify the velocity notation, letting v be the initial velocity of A, and v_A and v_B the final velocities of A and B. Then the kinetic energy and momentum conservation equations are, respectively,

$$\tfrac{1}{2}m_A v^2 = \tfrac{1}{2}m_A v_A^2 + \tfrac{1}{2}m_B v_B^2, \tag{8–10}$$

$$m_A v = m_A v_A + m_B v_B. \tag{8–11}$$

Assuming that the masses and v are known, we may solve for v_A and v_B. This involves some fairly strenuous algebra, but it's worth it. No pain, no gain! The simplest approach is somewhat indirect and uncovers an additional interesting feature of elastic collisions along the way.

We first rearrange Eqs. (8–10) and (8–11) as follows:

$$m_B v_B^2 = m_A(v^2 - v_A^2) = m_A(v - v_A)(v + v_A), \tag{8–12}$$

$$m_B v_B = m_A(v - v_A). \tag{8–13}$$

We now divide Eq (8–12) by Eq. (8–13) to obtain

$$v_B = v + v_A. \tag{8–14}$$

We now substitute this back into Eq. (8–13) to eliminate v_B, and then solve for v_A:

$$m_B(v + v_A) = m_A(v - v_A),$$

$$v_A = \frac{m_A - m_B}{m_A + m_B}\, v. \tag{8–15}$$

Finally, we substitute this result back into Eq. (8–14) to obtain

$$v_B = \frac{2m_A}{m_A + m_B}\, v. \tag{8–16}$$

The calculation has been a little tedious, but there's no substitute for persistence!

Now we can interpret the results. Suppose that A is a ping-pong ball and B is a bowling ball. Then we expect A to bounce off with a velocity nearly equal to the original value but in the opposite direction, and we expect B's velocity to be much smaller. Indeed, when m_A is much smaller than m_B, the fraction in Eq. (8–15) is approximately equal to (-1), and the fraction in Eq. (8–16) is much smaller than unity. We challenge you to invent a similar check for the opposite case, in which A is the bowling ball and B the ping-pong ball.

Another interesting case is that of *equal* masses. If $m_A = m_B$, then Eqs. (8–15) and (8–16) give $v_A = 0$ and $v_B = v$. That is, the first body stops and the second leaves with the same velocity the first had before the collision. This phenomenon is familiar to all pool players.

Now comes the surprise bonus. Equation (8–14) can be rewritten as

$$v = v_B - v_A. \tag{8–17}$$

Now $v_B - v_A$ is just the velocity of B relative to A after the collision, and v, apart from sign, is the velocity of B relative to A before the collision. *The relative velocity has the same magnitude before and after the collision.* Although we have proved this only for one special case, it turns out to be a general property of *all* elastic collisions, even when both bodies are moving initially and the velocities do not all lie along the same line. This result provides an alternative definition of an elastic collision: *In an elastic collision the relative velocity of the two bodies has the same magnitude before and after the collision. Whenever this condition is satisfied, the total kinetic energy is also conserved.*

Example 8–10   Suppose the collision shown in Fig. 8–4 is elastic. What are the velocities of A and B after the collision?

Solution   From conservation of momentum,

$$(0.50 \text{ kg})(2.0 \text{ m·s}^{-1}) + (0.30 \text{ kg})(-2.0 \text{ m·s}^{-1})$$
$$= (0.50 \text{ kg})v_{A2} + (0.30 \text{ kg})v_{B2},$$
$$0.50v_{A2} + 0.30v_{B2} = 0.40 \text{ m·s}^{-1}.$$

(In the last equation we divided through by the unit "kg.") From the relative velocity relation for an elastic collision,

$$v_{B2} - v_{A2} = -(v_{B1} - v_{A1})$$
$$= -(-2.0 \text{ m·s}^{-1} - 2.0 \text{ m·s}^{-1}) = 4.0 \text{ m·s}^{-1}.$$

Solving these equations simultaneously, we find

$$v_{A2} = -1.0 \text{ m·s}^{-1},$$
$$v_{B2} = 3.0 \text{ m·s}^{-1}.$$

Both bodies reverse their directions of motion; A moves to the left at 1.0 m·s^{-1}, and B moves to the right at 3.0 m·s^{-1}. The total kinetic energy after the collision is

$$\tfrac{1}{2}(0.50\ \text{kg})(-1\ \text{m·s}^{-1})^2 + \tfrac{1}{2}(0.30\ \text{kg})(3\ \text{m·s}^{-1})^2 = 1.6\ \text{J}.$$

This equals the total kinetic energy before the collision, as expected. ■

When an elastic collision is not head-on, the velocities are not all parallel to one coordinate axis. If they all lie in a plane, each final velocity has two unknown components, and there are four unknowns in all. Conservation of energy and conservation of the x- and y-components of momentum give only three equations. There are infinitely many combinations of final velocities that satisfy these equations. To determine the final velocities uniquely, we need additional information, such as the direction or magnitude of one of the final velocities.

Example 8–11   In Fig. 8–5, suppose body A has mass $m_A = 5.0$ kg and body B has mass $m_B = 3.0$ kg. Body A has an initial velocity of 4.0 m·s⁻¹ in the positive x-direction and a final velocity of 2.0 m·s⁻¹ in an unknown direction. Find the final speed v_{B2} of body B and the angles θ and ϕ in the figure, assuming that the collision is elastic.

Solution   The initial and final kinetic energies are equal:

$$\tfrac{1}{2}(5.0\ \text{kg})(4.0\ \text{m·s}^{-1})^2 = \tfrac{1}{2}(5.0\ \text{kg})(2.0\ \text{m·s}^{-1})^2 + \tfrac{1}{2}(3.0\ \text{kg})v_{B2}{}^2,$$

and

$$v_{B2} = 4.47\ \text{m·s}^{-1}.$$

Conservation of the x- and y-components of total momentum gives, respectively,

$$(5.0\ \text{kg})(4.0\ \text{m·s}^{-1}) = (5.0\ \text{kg})(2.0\ \text{m·s}^{-1})\cos\theta$$
$$+ (3.0\ \text{kg})(4.47\ \text{m·s}^{-1})\cos\phi,$$

$$0 = (5.0\ \text{kg})(2.0\ \text{m·s}^{-1})\sin\theta - (3.0\ \text{kg})(4.47\ \text{m·s}^{-1})\sin\phi.$$

These are two simultaneous equations for θ and ϕ; the simplest solution is to eliminate ϕ as follows: We solve the first equation for $\cos\phi$ and the second for $\sin\phi$; we then square each equation and add; since $\sin^2\phi + \cos^2\phi = 1$, this eliminates ϕ and leaves an equation that we can solve for $\cos\theta$ and hence for θ. We can then substitute this value back into either of the two equations and solve the result for ϕ. We leave the details for you to work out as a problem; the results are

$$\theta = 36.9°, \qquad \phi = 26.5°. \qquad ■$$

The examples in this section and the preceding one show that we can classify collisions according to energy considerations. A collision in which kinetic energy is conserved is called *elastic*. A collision in which the total kinetic energy decreases is called *inelastic*. We have discussed inelastic collisions in which the two bodies stick together. There are also inelastic collisions in which some kinetic energy is lost but the two bodies *do not* reach a common final velocity. There are also cases in which the final kinetic energy is *greater* than the initial value. Rifle recoil, discussed in Example 8–6 (Section 8–2) is an example.

Finally, momentum conservation can sometimes be applied even to systems that are not really isolated. It may happen that there are some external forces acting on the colliding bodies but that they are small in comparison to the internal forces during the collision. Then we may use a model that neglects the external forces during the actual collision.

8–5
Center of Mass

We can restate the principle of conservation of momentum in a useful way by introducing the concept of **center of mass.** Suppose we have several particles, with masses m_1, m_2, and so on. Let the coordinates of m_1 be (x_1, y_1), those of m_2 be (x_2, y_2), and so on. We define the center of mass of the system as the point having coordinates (X, Y) given by

$$X = \frac{m_1 x_1 + m_2 x_2 + m_3 x_3 + \cdots}{m_1 + m_2 + m_3 + \cdots},$$

$$Y = \frac{m_1 y_1 + m_2 y_2 + m_3 y_3 + \cdots}{m_1 + m_2 + m_3 + \cdots}. \qquad (8\text{--}18)$$

In statistical language the center of mass is a *weighted average* position of the particles.

The x- and y-components of velocity of the center of mass, V_x and V_y, are the rates of change of X and Y; from Eqs. (8–18), these are

$$V_x = \frac{m_1 v_{1x} + m_2 v_{2x} + m_3 v_{3x} + \cdots}{m_1 + m_2 + m_3 + \cdots},$$

$$V_y = \frac{m_1 v_{1y} + m_2 v_{2y} + m_3 v_{3y} + \cdots}{m_1 + m_2 + m_3 + \cdots}. \qquad (8\text{--}19)$$

These equations are equivalent to the single vector equation

$$\mathbf{V} = \frac{m_1 \mathbf{v}_1 + m_2 \mathbf{v}_2 + m_3 \mathbf{v}_3 + \cdots}{m_1 + m_2 + m_3 + \cdots}. \qquad (8\text{--}20)$$

We denote the *total* mass $m_1 + m_2 + \cdots$ by M; we can then rewrite Eq. (8–20) as

$$M\mathbf{V} = m_1 \mathbf{v}_1 + m_2 \mathbf{v}_2 + m_3 \mathbf{v}_2 + \cdots = \mathbf{P}. \qquad (8\text{--}21)$$

The right side is simply the total momentum $\mathbf{P}$ of the system; we have proved that *the total momentum is equal to the total mass times the velocity of the center of mass.* It follows that for an isolated system, in which the total momentum is constant, the velocity of the center of mass is also constant.

8–8
The center of the mass of this wrench is marked with an X. The total external force acting on the wrench is zero. As it spins on a smooth horizontal surface, the center of mass moves in a straight line with constant velocity. (*PSSC Physics*, 2e, 1965; D. C. Heath and Company, Inc., with Education Development Center, Inc., Newton, Mass.)

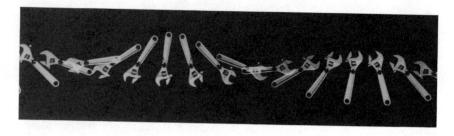

Proceeding one additional step, we note that the *rates of change* of the various velocities, that is, the accelerations, are related in the same way:

$$M\boldsymbol{A} = m_1\boldsymbol{a}_1 + m_2\boldsymbol{a}_2 + m_3\boldsymbol{a}_3 + \cdots, \qquad (8\text{–}22)$$

where $\boldsymbol{A}$ is the acceleration of the center of mass. Now $m_1\boldsymbol{a}_1$ is equal to the vector sum of forces on the first particle, and so on, and the right side of Eq. (8–22) is equal to the vector sum of *all* the forces on *all* the particles. Just as we did in Section 8–2, we may classify each force as internal or external; because of Newton's third law, the internal forces all cancel in pairs. That is, $\boldsymbol{\Sigma F} = \boldsymbol{\Sigma F}_{\text{ext}} + \boldsymbol{\Sigma F}_{\text{int}}$, and $\boldsymbol{\Sigma F}_{\text{int}} = \boldsymbol{0}$ from Newton's third law. What survives on the right side is only the sum of the *external* forces, and we have

$$\sum \boldsymbol{F}_{\text{ext}} = M\boldsymbol{A}. \qquad (8\text{–}23)$$

That is, *when a body or a collection of particles is acted on by external forces, the center of mass moves just as though all the mass were concentrated at that point and it were acted on by a resultant force equal to the sum of the external forces on the system.*

For example, suppose we mark the center of mass of an adjustable wrench, which is some point partway down the handle. We then slide the wrench with a spinning motion across a smooth tabletop, as in Fig. 8–8. The motion appears complicated, but the center of mass follows a straight line, as though all the mass were concentrated at that point. As another example, suppose a shell traveling in a parabolic trajectory explodes in flight, splitting into two fragments with equal mass, as shown in Fig. 8–9. The fragments follow new parabolic paths, but the center of mass continues on the original parabolic trajectory, just as though all the mass were still concentrated at that point. A Fourth of July skyrocket exploding in air is a spectacular example.

This property of the center of mass is important in the analysis of the motion of rigid bodies, in which we describe the motion of a body as a

8–9
A shell explodes in flight. The fragments follow individual parabolic paths, but the center of mass continues on the same trajectory as the shell's path before exploding.

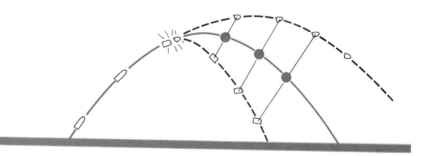

combination of motion of the center of mass and rotational motion about an axis through the center of mass. We will return to this topic in Chapter 9.

Finally, we note again that for an *isolated* system, $\Sigma \mathbf{F}_{ext} = \mathbf{0}$. In this case, Eq. (8–23) shows that the acceleration $\mathbf{A}$ of the center of mass is zero, so its velocity $\mathbf{V}$ is constant, and from Eq. (8–21) the total momentum $\mathbf{P}$ is also constant. This reaffirms our statement in Section 8–2 that the total momentum of an isolated system is constant.

In principle, the position of the center of mass of a body can always be calculated by regarding it as a collection of particles and using Eqs. (8–18). In practice, these calculations can become quite complex. Usually, we will deal with symmetric bodies in which the center of mass lies at the geometric center. We will discuss other calculation techniques in Chapter 10 in connection with the related concept of *center of gravity*.

Example 8–12   A 2.0-kg body and a 3.0-kg body are moving along the x-axis. At a particular instant the 2.0-kg body is 1.0 m from the origin and has a velocity of 3.0 m·s^{-1}, and the 3.0-kg body is 2.0 m from the origin and has a velocity of -1.0 m·s^{-1}. Find the position and velocity of the center of mass, and also find the total momentum.

Solution   From Eqs. (8–18),

$$X = \frac{(2.0 \text{ kg})(1.0 \text{ m}) + (3.0 \text{ kg})(2.0 \text{ m})}{2.0 \text{ kg} + 3.0 \text{ kg}} = 1.6 \text{ m},$$

and from Eq. (8–19) the x-component of the center-of-mass velocity is

$$V_x = \frac{(2.0 \text{ kg})(3.0 \text{ m·s}^{-1}) + (3.0 \text{ kg})(-1.0 \text{ m·s}^{-1})}{2.0 \text{ kg} + 3.0 \text{ kg}} = 0.60 \text{ m·s}^{-1}.$$

The total x-component of momentum is

$$P_x = (2.0 \text{ kg})(3.0 \text{ m·s}^{-1}) + (3.0 \text{ kg})(-1.0 \text{ m·s}^{-1}) = 3.0 \text{ kg·m·s}^{-1}.$$

Alternatively, from Eq. (8–21),

$$P_x = (5.0 \text{ kg})(0.60 \text{ m·s}^{-1}) = 3.0 \text{ kg·m·s}^{-1}. \qquad \blacksquare$$

---

*8–6

Rocket Propulsion

Rocket propulsion offers an interesting application of momentum and impulse considerations. A rocket is propelled by rearward ejection of burned fuel that initially was in the rocket. The forward force on the rocket is the reaction to the backward force on the ejected material. The mass of the rocket decreases as material is ejected. As a simple example, we consider a rocket fired in outer space, where there is no gravitational

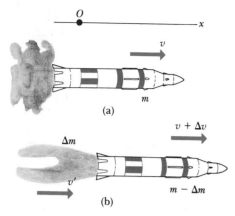

(a)

(b)

8–10

(a) Rocket at time t after takeoff, with mass m and upward velocity v. Its momentum is mv. (b) At time $t + \Delta t$ the mass of the rocket (and unburned fuel) is $m - \Delta m$, its velocity is $v + \Delta v$, and its momentum is $(m - \Delta m)(v + \Delta v)$. The ejected gas has momentum $\Delta m(v - v_r)$.

field and no air resistance. We choose our x-axis to be along the rocket's direction of motion.

Figure 8–10a shows the rocket at a time t after takeoff, when its mass is m and its velocity relative to our coordinate system is v. The total momentum at this instant is mv. In a short time interval Δt, a mass Δm of burned fuel is ejected from the rocket. Let v_r be the speed of this material *relative to the rocket*. The velocity v' of the fuel relative to our coordinate system is then

$$v' = v - v_r,$$

and its momentum is

$$\Delta m \, v' = \Delta m(v - v_r).$$

At the end of the time interval Δt, the mass of rocket and unburned fuel has decreased to $m - \Delta m$, and its velocity has increased to $v + \Delta v$. Its momentum at this time is

$$(m - \Delta m)(v + \Delta v).$$

Thus the *total* momentum (rocket plus ejected fuel) at time $t + \Delta t$ is

$$(m - \Delta m)(v + \Delta v) + \Delta m(v - v_r).$$

Figure 8–10b shows the rocket and ejected fuel at this time.

According to our initial assumption, the rocket and fuel are an isolated system; the total momentum of the system must be the same at time t and at time $t + \Delta t$:

$$mv = (m - \Delta m)(v + \Delta v) + \Delta m(v - v_r),$$

which can be simplified to

$$m \, \Delta v = \Delta m \, v_r + \Delta m \, \Delta v.$$

When Δt is small, we can neglect the term $\Delta m \, \Delta v$ because it is a product of two small quantities and thus is much smaller than the other terms. Dropping this term, dividing by Δt, and rearranging, we find

$$m\frac{\Delta v}{\Delta t} = v_r\frac{\Delta m}{\Delta t}. \tag{8–24}$$

Now $\Delta v/\Delta t$ is the acceleration of the rocket, so the left side of this equation (mass times acceleration) equals the resultant force F, or *thrust*, on the rocket.

$$F = v_r\frac{\Delta m}{\Delta t}. \tag{8–25}$$

The thrust is proportional both to the relative velocity, v_r, of the ejected fuel and to the mass of fuel ejected per unit time, $\Delta m/\Delta t$.

The acceleration of the rocket is

$$a = \frac{\Delta v}{\Delta t} = \frac{v_r \, \Delta m}{m \, \Delta t}. \tag{8–26}$$

The rocket's mass m decreases continuously while the fuel is being consumed. If v_r and $\Delta m/\Delta t$ are constant, the acceleration increases until all the fuel is consumed.

Example 8–13   In the first second of its flight, a rocket ejects 1/60 of its mass with a relative velocity of 2400 m·s^{-1}. What is the acceleration of the rocket?

Solution   We have $\Delta m = m/60$, $\Delta t = 1$ s. From Eq. (8–26),

$$a = \frac{\Delta v}{\Delta t} = \frac{2400 \text{ m·s}^{-1}}{(60)(1 \text{ s})} = 40 \text{ m·s}^{-2}.$$

At the start of the flight, when the velocity of the rocket is zero, the ejected fuel is moving to the left, relative to our coordinate system, at 2400 m·s^{-1}. At the end of the first second the rocket is moving at 40 m·s^{-1}, and the fuel's speed relative to our system is 2360 m·s^{-1}. We could now compute the acceleration at $t = 1$ s (using the decreased rocket mass), find the velocity at $t = 2$ s, and so on, stepping through the calculation one second at a time until all the fuel is burned up. As the mass decreases, the acceleration in successive 1-s intervals increases. We would find that after about 22 s the rocket's velocity in our coordinate system passes 2400 m·s^{-1}. The burned fuel ejected after this time therefore moves *forward*, not backward, in our system. We could improve the precision of our calculations by taking smaller time intervals; to go to the limit as each interval approaches zero would require calculus methods.

In the early days of rocket propulsion, people who didn't understand conservation of momentum thought that a rocket couldn't function in outer space because "it doesn't have anything to push against." On the contrary, rockets work *best* in outer space! Figure 8–11 shows a dramatic example of rocket propulsion.   ∎

8–11
Launch of a space shuttle, a dramatic example of rocket propulsion. Successful launch and landing of the space shuttle are the first steps toward feasibility of a manned space station in orbit around the earth. Despite a catastrophic setback, research and progress continue. (Courtesy NASA, Kennedy Space Center.)

Questions

8–1 Suppose you catch a baseball, and then someone invites you to catch a bullet with the same momentum or with the same kinetic energy. Which would you choose?

8–2 In splitting logs with a hammer and wedge, is a heavy h████ ████ore effective than a lighter hammer? Why?

8–3 W██ ████ge, heavy truck collides with a passenger ca██ ██ occupants of the car are much more likely to be h██ ██ the truck driver. Why?

8–4 A████ █████pped on the floor is more likely to brea█ ███ ███r is concrete than if it is wood. Why?

8–5 "█████ ████ fall that hurts you; it's the sudden stop at the█████████iscuss.

8–6 W█████████son fires a rifle or shotgun, it is advisable to hold the butt firmly against the shoulder rather than a bit away from it, to minimize the impact on the shoulder. Why?

8–7 When a catcher in a baseball game catches a fast ball, he does not hold his arms rigid, but relaxes them so that the mitt moves several inches while the ball is being caught. Why is this important?

8–8 When rain falls from the sky, what becomes of its momentum as it hits the ground? Is your answer also valid for Newton's famous apple?

8–9 A man stands in the middle of a perfectly smooth, frictionless frozen lake. He can set himself in motion by throwing things, but suppose he has nothing to throw. Can he propel himself to shore *without* throwing anything?

8–10 A machine gun is fired at a steel plate. Is the average force on the plate from the bullet impact greater if the bullets bounce off or if they are squashed and stick to the plate?

8–11 How do Mexican jumping beans work? Do they violate conservation of momentum? Of energy?

8–12 Early critics of Robert Goddard, a pioneer in the use of rocket propulsion, claimed that rocket engines could not be used in outer space where there is no air for the rocket to push against. How would you answer such criticism? Would the criticism be valid for a jet engine in an ordinary airplane?

8–13 In a zero-gravity environment, can a rocket-propelled spaceship ever attain a speed greater than the relative speed with which the burnt fuel is exhausted?

■ Exercises

Section 8–1   Impulse and Momentum

8–1

a) What is the momentum of a 10,000-kg truck whose speed is 30.0 m·s^{-1}?

b) What speed must a 5,000-kg truck attain in order to have

    i) the same momentum?

    ii) the same kinetic energy?

8–2 A block of ice with a mass of 2.50 kg is moving on a frictionless, horizontal surface. At $t = 0$ the block is moving to the right with a velocity of magnitude 8.00 m·s^{-1}. Calculate the velocity of the block (magnitude and direction) after each of the following forces has been applied for 5.00 s:

a) a force of 5.00 N, directed to the right;

b) a force of 7.00 N, directed to the left.

8–3 A bullet with a mass of 0.0050 kg and moving with a speed of 400 m·s^{-1} penetrates a distance of 0.0800 m into a wooden block firmly attached to the earth. Assume that the force that stops it is constant. Use a coordinate system for which the direction of the initial velocity of the bullet is the positive x-direction. Compute

a) the acceleration of the bullet,

b) the accelerating force,

c) the time of the acceleration,

d) the impulse of the force.

Compare the answer to part (d) with the initial momentum of the bullet.

8–4 A baseball has mass 0.200 kg.

a) If the velocity of a pitched ball has a magnitude of 35.0 m·s^{-1}, and after the ball is batted the velocity is 55.0 m·s^{-1} in the opposite direction, find the change in momentum of the ball and the impulse applied to it by the bat.

b) If the ball remains in contact with the bat for 2.00 × 10^{-3} s, find the average force applied by the bat.

8–5 A baseball with a mass of 0.250 kg is struck by a bat. Just before impact, the ball is traveling horizontally at 40.0 m·s^{-1}, and it leaves the bat traveling in the opposite direction at an angle of 30.0° above horizontal with a speed of 55.0 m·s^{-1}. If the ball and bat are in contact for 4.00 × 10^{-3} s, find the horizontal and vertical components of the average force on the ball.

8–6 A golf ball with a mass of 0.080 kg initially at rest is given a speed of 50 m·s^{-1} when it is struck by a club. If the club and ball are in contact for 1.5 × 10^{-3} s, what average force acts on the ball? Is the effect of the ball's weight during the time of contact significant?

Section 8–2   Conservation of Momentum

8–7 On a frictionless, horizontal surface, block A having a mass of 3.00 kg is moving to the right toward block B having a mass of 5.00 kg, which is initially at rest. After the collision, block A has a velocity of 1.20 m·s^{-1} to the left, and block B has velocity 5.40 m·s^{-1} to the right.

a) What was the speed of block A before the collision?

b) Calculate the change in the total kinetic energy of the system that occurs in the collision.

8–8 An 80.0-kg man standing on ice throws a 0.400-kg ball horizontally with a speed of 30.0 m·s^{-1}. With what speed and in what direction will the man begin to move if there is no friction between his feet and the ice?

8–9 You are standing on a sheet of ice that covers a parking lot; there is negligible friction between your feet and the ice. A friend throws you a ball that is traveling horizontally at 15.0 m·s^{-1}. Your mass is 80.0 kg.

a) If you catch the ball, with what speed do you and the ball move afterward?

b) If the ball hits you and bounces off so that afterward it is moving horizontally 15.0 m·s^{-1} in the opposite direction, what is your speed after the collision?

8–10 A railroad handcar is moving along straight, frictionless tracks. In each of the following cases the car initially has a total mass (car and contents) of 200 kg and is traveling east with a velocity of magnitude 4.00 m·s⁻¹. Find the *final velocity* of the car in each of the three cases.

a) A 40.0-kg mass is thrown sideways out of the car with a velocity of magnitude 2.00 m·s⁻¹ relative to the car.

b) A 40.0-kg mass is thrown backward (to the west) out of the car with a velocity of magnitude 4.00 m·s⁻¹ relative to the *initial* motion of the car.

c) A 40.0-kg mass is thrown into the car with a velocity of magnitude 6.00 m·s⁻¹ relative to the ground and opposite in direction to the velocity of the car.

8–11 Ice hockey star Wayne Gretzky is skating at 13.0 m·s⁻¹ toward a defender, who is in turn skating at 5.0 m·s⁻¹ toward Gretzky. Gretzky's weight is 756 N; that of the defender is 900 N. Immediately after the collision, Gretzky is moving at 3.00 m·s⁻¹ in his original direction. Neglect external horizontal forces applied by the ice to the skaters during the collision.

a) What is the velocity of the defender immediately after the collision?

b) Calculate the change in total kinetic energy of the two players.

8–12 Block *A* in Fig. 8–12 has a mass of 1.00 kg, and block *B* has a mass of 2.00 kg. The blocks are forced together, compressing a spring *S* between them, and the system is released from rest on a level, frictionless surface. The spring is not fastened to either block and drops to the surface after it has expanded. Block *B* acquires a speed of 0.900 m·s⁻¹.

a) What is the final speed of block *A*?

b) How much potential energy was stored in the compressed spring?

FIGURE 8–12

8–13 An open-topped freight car with a mass of 10,000 kg is coasting without friction along a level track. It is raining very hard, and the rain is falling vertically downward. The car is originally empty and moving with a speed of 3.00 m·s⁻¹. What is the speed of the car after it has traveled long enough to collect 1000 kg of rainwater?

8–14 One of James Bond's adversaries is standing on a frozen lake; there is no friction between his feet and the ice. He throws his steel-lined hat with a velocity of 30.0 m·s⁻¹ at 37.0° above the horizontal, hoping to hit James. If his mass is 160 kg and that of his hat is

9.00 kg, what is the magnitude of his horizontal recoil velocity?

8–15 A hockey puck *B* rests on a smooth ice surface and is struck by a second puck *A*, which was originally traveling at 20.0 m·s⁻¹ and which is deflected 30.0° from its original direction (Fig. 8–13). Puck *B* acquires a velocity at 45.0° with the original velocity of *A*. The pucks have the same mass.

a) Compute the speed of each puck after the collision.

b) What fraction of the original kinetic energy of puck *A* is dissipated during the collision?

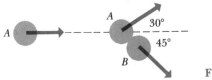

FIGURE 8–13

8–16 A ball with a mass of 0.600 kg is initially at rest. It is struck by a second ball having a mass of 0.400 kg, initially moving with a velocity of 0.250 m·s⁻¹ toward the right along the x-axis. After the collision the 0.400-kg ball has a velocity of 0.200 m·s⁻¹ at an angle of 36.9° above the x-axis in the first quadrant. Both balls move on a frictionless, horizontal surface.

a) What are the magnitude and direction of the velocity of the 0.600-kg ball after the collision?

b) What is the change in the total kinetic energy of the two balls as a result of the collision?

Section 8–3 *Inelastic Collisions*

8–17

a) An empty freight car with a mass of 10,000 kg rolls at 5.00 m·s⁻¹ along a level track and collides with a loaded car with a mass of 20,000 kg, standing at rest with brakes released. Friction can be neglected. If the cars couple together, find their speed after the collision.

b) Find the decrease in kinetic energy as a result of the collision.

c) With what speed should the loaded car be rolling toward the empty car for both to be brought to rest by the collision?

8–18 On a horizontal frictionless table, a 3.00-kg block moving 5.00 m·s⁻¹ to the right collides with an 8.00-kg block moving 1.50 m·s⁻¹ to the left.

a) If the two blocks stick together, what is the final velocity (magnitude and direction)?

b) How much mechanical energy is dissipated in the collision?

8–19 Three identical boxcars are coupled together and are moving at a constant speed of 20.0 m·s^{-1} on a level, frictionless track. They collide with another (identical) boxcar that is initially at rest and couple to it, so the four cars roll on as a unit. Friction can be neglected.

a) What is the speed of the four cars?

b) What percentage of the kinetic energy of the boxcars is dissipated in the collision?

8–20 An 18.0-kg fish moving horizontally to the right at 2.40 m·s^{-1} swallows a 2.0-kg fish that is swimming to the left at 6.80 m·s^{-1}. What is the speed of the large fish immediately after its lunch if the forces exerted on the fishes by the water can be neglected?

8–21 A 5.00-g bullet is fired horizontally into a 2.00-kg wooden block resting on a horizontal surface. The coefficient of kinetic friction between block and surface is 0.20. The bullet remains embedded in the block, which is observed to slide 0.105 m along the surface before stopping. What was the initial speed of the bullet?

8–22 A 2000-kg automobile going eastward on Illinois Avenue at 50.0 km·hr^{-1} collides with a 4000-kg truck which is going northward *across* Illinois Avenue at 20.0 km·hr^{-1}. If they become coupled on collision, what are the magnitude and direction of their velocity immediately after the collision? (Friction forces between the cars and the road can be neglected during the collision.)

8–23 A 10.0-g rifle bullet is fired with a speed of 600 m·s^{-1} into a ballistic pendulum with a mass of 5.00 kg suspended from a cord 0.800 m long. Compute

a) the vertical height through which the pendulum rises,

b) the initial kinetic energy of the bullet,

c) the kinetic energy of the bullet and pendulum immediately after the bullet becomes embedded in the pendulum.

Section 8–4   Elastic Collisions

8–24 A 10.0-g marble rolls to the left with a velocity of magnitude 0.400 m·s^{-1} on a smooth, level surface and makes a head-on collision with a larger 30.0-g marble rolling to the right with a velocity of magnitude 0.100 m·s^{-1}. If the collision is perfectly elastic, find the velocity of each marble after the collision. (Since the collision is head-on, all the motion is along a line.)

8–25 A 0.300-kg block is moving to the right on a horizontal, frictionless surface with a speed of 0.60 m·s^{-1}. It makes a head-on collision with a 0.200-kg block that

is moving to the left with a speed of 1.20 m·s^{-1}. Find the final velocity (magnitude and direction) of each block if the collision is elastic. (Since the collision is head-on, all motion is along a line.)

8–26 Supply the details of the calculation of θ and ϕ in Example 8–11.

Section 8–5   Center of Mass

8–27 Find the position of the center of mass of the earth–moon system. Use the data in Appendix F.

8–28 Three particles have the following masses and coordinates: (a) 2.00 kg, (4.00 m, 1.00 m); (b) 3.00 kg, (1.00 m, −4.00 m); (c) 4.00 kg, (−6.00 m, 5.00 m). Find the coordinates of the center of mass of the system.

8–29 A 1000-kg automobile is moving along a straight highway at 30.0 m·s^{-1}. Another car, with a mass of 2000 kg and a speed of 20.0 m·s^{-1}, is 30.0 m ahead of the first and is traveling in the same direction.

a) Find the position of the center of mass of the two automobiles.

b) Find the total momentum from the above data.

c) Find the speed of the center of mass.

d) Find the total momentum, using the speed of the center of mass. Compare your result with that of part (b).

Section 8–6   Rocket Propulsion

8–30 A small rocket burns 0.0400 kg of fuel per second, ejecting it as a gas with a velocity relative to the rocket of magnitude 5000 m·s^{-1}.

a) What force does this gas exert on the rocket?

b) Would the rocket operate in free space?

c) If it would operate in free space, how would you steer it? Could you brake it?

8–31 A rocket is fired from an orbiting space station, where the gravitational field is very small. If the rocket has an initial mass of 5000 kg and ejects gas at a relative velocity of magnitude 2000 m·s^{-1}, how much gas must it eject in the first second to have an initial acceleration of 30.0 m·s^{-2}?

8–32 A rocket is fired in deep space, where there is no gravitational field. In the first second it ejects 1/80 of its mass as exhaust gas and has an acceleration of 50.0 m·s^{-2}. What is the speed of the exhaust gas relative to the rocket?

Problems

8–33 Find the average recoil force on a machine gun firing 120 shots per minute. The mass of each bullet is 10.0 g, and the muzzle speed is 600 m·s^{-1}.

8–34 A steel ball having a mass of 0.0800 kg is dropped from a height of 4.00 m onto a horizontal steel slab. The collision is elastic, and the ball rebounds to its original height.

a) Calculate the impulse delivered to the ball during impact.

b) If the ball is in contact with the slab for 1.50 × 10^{-3} s, find the average force on the ball during impact.

8–35 Objects A (mass 3.00 kg), B (mass 4.00 kg), and C (mass 2.00 kg) are sliding on a horizontal, frictionless surface and are approaching the origin as shown in Fig. 8–14. The initial velocities of A and B are given in the figure. All three objects arrive at the origin at the same time. What must be the x- and y-components of the initial velocity of C if all three objects are to end up at rest after the collision?

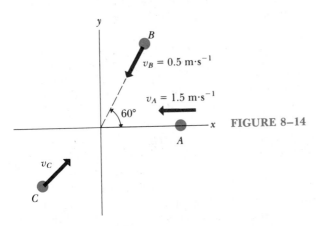

$v_B = 0.5$ m·s^{-1}

$v_A = 1.5$ m·s^{-1}

60°

FIGURE 8–14

8–36 A tennis ball weighing 0.500 N has velocity v_1 with components $v_{1x} = 18.0$ m·s^{-1} and $v_{1y} = -5.00$ m·s^{-1} before being struck by a racket. The racket applies a force F with components $F_x = -600$ N and $F_y = 250$ N that we will assume to be constant during the 4.00 × 10^{-3} s that the racket and ball are in contact.

a) What are the x- and y-components of the impulse of the force applied to the ball?

b) What are the x- and y-components of the final velocity of the ball?

8–37 A bullet with a mass of 5.00 g is shot *through* a 1.00-kg wood block suspended on a string 2.000 m long. The center of mass of the block is observed to rise a distance of 0.40 cm. Find the speed of the bullet as it emerges from the block if its initial speed is 300 m·s^{-1}.

8–38 A station wagon traveling west collides with a pickup truck traveling north. They stick together as a result of the collision. The station wagon has a mass of 1400 kg, and the pickup truck has a mass of 900 kg. A police officer estimates from the skid marks that immediately after the collision the combined object was traveling at 12.0 m·s^{-1} in a direction 37.0° west of north. Calculate the speeds of the station wagon and pickup just before the collision.

8–39 A bullet with a mass of 4.00 g, traveling in a horizontal direction with a velocity of magnitude 500 m·s^{-1}, is fired into a wooden block with a mass of 1.00 kg that is initially at rest on a level surface. The bullet passes through the block and emerges with its speed reduced to 100 m·s^{-1}. The block slides a distance of 0.200 m along the surface from its initial position.

a) What is the coefficient of kinetic friction between block and surface?

b) What is the decrease in kinetic energy of the bullet?

c) What is the kinetic energy of the block at the instant after the bullet passes through it?

8–40 A rifle bullet with a mass of 0.010 kg strikes and embeds itself in a block of mass 0.990 kg, which rests on a frictionless, horizontal surface and is attached to a coil spring, as shown in Fig. 8–15. The impact compresses the spring 10.0 cm. Calibration of the spring shows that a force of 1.50 N is required to compress the spring 1.00 cm.

a) Find the magnitude of the velocity of the block just after impact.

b) What was the initial speed of the bullet?

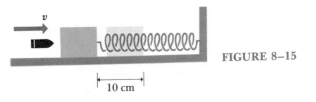

v

FIGURE 8–15

10 cm

8–41 A block with a mass of 0.300 kg, sliding to the right with a velocity of magnitude 0.120 m·s^{-1} on a smooth, level surface, makes a perfectly elastic head-on collision with a block with mass m that is initially at rest. After the collision the velocity of the 0.300-kg block is 0.040 m·s^{-1} in the same direction as its initial velocity. Find

a) the velocity (magnitude and direction) of the block of mass m after the collision;

b) the mass m.

8–42 Two railroad cars roll along and couple with a third car, which is initially at rest. These three roll along and couple to a fourth. This process continues until the speed of the final collection of railroad cars is one-tenth the speed of the initial two railroad cars. All the cars are identical. Ignoring friction, how many cars are in the final collection of cars?

8–43 Consider the following recoil situation. Initially, there is a combined object with mass $m_A + m_B$, at rest at the origin. Then, because of some internal force, the object breaks into two pieces. One piece, mass m_A, travels off to the left with speed v_A. The other piece, mass m_B, travels off to the right with speed v_B.

a) Use conservation of momentum to solve for v_B in terms of m_A, m_B, and v_A.

b) Use the results of part (a) to show that $K_A/K_B = m_B/m_A$, where K_A and K_B are the kinetic energies of the two pieces.

8–44 A stone with a mass of 0.100 kg rests on a frictionless horizontal surface. A bullet of mass 2.50 g, traveling horizontally at 500 m·s^{-1}, strikes the stone and rebounds horizontally at right angles to its original direction with a speed of 300 m·s^{-1}.

a) Compute the magnitude and direction of the velocity of the stone after it is struck.

b) Is the collision perfectly elastic?

8–45 A neutron with mass m collides elastically with a nucleus of mass M, which is initially at rest. Show that if the neutron's initial kinetic energy is K_0, the maximum kinetic energy that it can *lose* during the collision is

$$4mMK_0/(M + m)^2.$$

(*Hint:* The maximum energy loss occurs in a head-on collision.)

8–46 The results of a one-dimensional elastic collision between two objects, where object B is initially at rest, are given by Eqs. (8–15) and (8–16). It was shown in Section 8–4 that when m_A is much less than m_B these equations give $v_A \approx -v$ and $v_B \approx 0$ and that when $m_A = m_B$ the equations give $v_A = 0$ and $v_B = v$. Make a similar

analysis for the following special cases:

a) the case when m_A is much larger than m_B;

b) $m_A = 2m_B$;

c) $m_B = 2m_A$.

8–47 A man and a woman are sitting in a sleigh that is at rest on frictionless ice. The weight of the man is 800 N, the weight of the woman is 600 N, and that of the sleigh is 1200 N. The people suddenly see a poisonous spider on the floor of the sleigh and jump out. The man jumps to the left with a velocity of 4.00 m·s^{-1} at 30.0° above the horizontal, and the woman jumps to the right at 8.00 m·s^{-1} at 37.0° above the horizontal. Calculate the horizontal velocity (magnitude and direction) that the sleigh has after they jump out.

8–48 A neutron with a mass of 1.67×10^{-27} kg, moving with a speed of 4.50×10^4 m·s^{-1}, makes a head-on collision with a boron nucleus with a mass of 17.0×10^{-27} kg, which is originally at rest.

a) If the collision is completely inelastic, so the neutron and boron nucleus stick together, what is the final kinetic energy of the system expressed as a fraction of the original kinetic energy, K_0?

b) If the collision is perfectly elastic, what fraction of the neutron's original kinetic energy is transferred to the boron nucleus?

8–49 A man with a mass of 80.0 kg stands up in a 30.0-kg canoe of length 5.00 m. He walks from a point 0.50 m from one end to a point 0.50 m from the other end. If resistance to motion of the canoe in the water can be neglected, how far does the canoe move during this process?

8–50 A uniform steel rod 0.600 m in length is bent in a 90° angle at its midpoint. Determine the position of its center of mass. (*Hint:* The mass of each side of the angle may be assumed to be concentrated at its center.)

8–51 You are standing on a concrete slab, which in turn is resting on a frozen lake. Assume that there is no friction between the slab and the ice. The slab has a weight five times your weight. If you begin walking forward at 1.50 m·s^{-1}, relative to the ice, with what speed, relative to the ice, does the slab move?

8–52 Two men, James and Charles, are standing on the smooth surface of a frozen pond. Charles has a mass of 60.0 kg, and James has a mass of 90.0 kg. They are 20.0 m apart and hold the ends of a light rope that is stretched between them. Midway between the two men a loaded revolver lies on the ice. James pulls on the rope, and as a result slides toward the revolver. When James has moved 3.0 m, how far, and in what direction, has Charles moved?

Challenge Problems

8–53 A small steel ball moving with speed v_0 in the positive x-direction makes a perfectly elastic noncentral collision with an identical ball originally at rest. After impact, the first ball moves with speed v_1 in the first quadrant at an angle θ_1 with the x-axis, and the second moves with speed v_2 in the fourth quadrant at an angle θ_2 with the x-axis.

a) Write the equations expressing conservation of linear momentum in the x-direction and in the y-direction.

b) Square these equations and add them.

c) At this point, introduce the fact that the collision is perfectly elastic.

d) Prove that $\theta_1 + \theta_2 = \pi/2$. (You have shown that this equation is obeyed in any elastic collision between objects of equal mass, when one object is initially at rest.)

8–54 In Exercise 8–15, suppose the collision is perfectly elastic and A is deflected 30.0° from its initial direction. Find the final speed of each puck and the direction of B's final velocity. (*Hint:* Use the relation derived in part (d) of Problem 8–53.)

8–55 Fission, the process that supplies energy in nuclear power plants, occurs when a heavy nucleus is split into two medium-sized nuclei. One such reaction would occur if a neutron colliding with a ^{235}U nucleus split that nucleus into a ^{141}Ba nucleus and a ^{92}Kr nucleus. In this reaction, two neutrons also would be split off from the original ^{235}U. Before the collision we have the arrangement in Fig. 8–16a. After the collision we have the Ba nucleus moving in the $+z$-direction and the Kr nucleus in the $-z$-direction. The three neutrons are

moving in the xy-plane as shown in Fig. 8–16b. If the incoming neutron has an initial velocity with magnitude 4.00×10^6 m·s^{-1} and a final velocity with magnitude 2.00×10^6 m·s^{-1} in the directions shown, what are the speeds of the other two neutrons, and what can you say about the speeds of the Ba and Kr nuclei? (The mass of the Ba nucleus is approximately 2.3×10^{-25} kg, and that of Kr is about 1.5×10^{-25} kg.)

8–56 A frame with a mass of 0.200 kg, when suspended from a certain coil spring, is found to stretch the spring 0.100 m. A lump of putty with a mass of 0.400 kg is dropped from rest onto the frame from a height of 0.300 m (Fig. 8–17) and sticks to it. Find the maximum distance the frame moves downward.

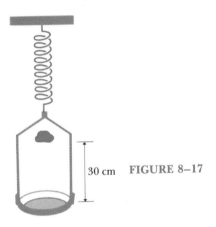

30 cm   **FIGURE 8–17**

8–57 A 20.0-kg projectile is fired at an angle of 60.0° above the horizontal and with a muzzle velocity of magnitude 160 m·s^{-1}. At the highest point of its trajectory the projectile explodes into two fragments with equal mass, one of which falls vertically with zero initial speed.

a) How far from the point of firing does the other fragment strike if the terrain is level?

b) How much energy was released during the explosion?

8–58 Block A, mass m_A, is moving on a frictionless horizontal surface in the $+x$-direction with velocity v_{A1} and makes an elastic collision with block B, mass m_B, that is initially at rest. The collision is head-on, so both blocks move along the x-axis after the collision.

a) Calculate the velocity of the center of mass (CM) of the two-block system before the collision.

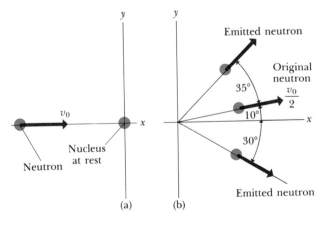

FIGURE 8–16

b) Consider a coordinate system whose origin is at the CM and moves with it. Is this an inertial reference frame?

c) What are the initial velocities u_{A1} and u_{B1} of the two blocks in this CM reference frame, and what is the total momentum in this frame?

d) Use conservation of momentum and energy, applied in the CM frame, to relate the final momentum of each block to its initial momentum and hence the final velocity of each block to its initial velocity. Your results should show that a one-dimensional elastic collision has a very simple description in CM coordinates.

e) Let $m_A = 2.00$ kg, $m_B = 4.00$ kg, and $v_{A1} = 3.00$ m·s^{-1}. Find the CM velocities u_{A1} and u_{B1}, apply the simple result found in part (d), and transform back to velocities in a stationary frame to find the final velocities of the blocks. Does your result agree with Eqs. (8–15) and (8–16)?

8–59 Two asteroids with masses m_A and m_B are moving with velocities v_A and v_B with respect to an astronomer in a space vehicle.

a) Show that the total kinetic energy as measured by the astronomer is

$$K = \tfrac{1}{2}MV^2 + \tfrac{1}{2}(m_A v'_A{}^2 + m_B v'_B{}^2),$$

with V and M defined as in Section 8–5, $v'_A = v_A - V$, and $v'_B = v_B - V$. In this expression the total kinetic energy of the two asteroids is the energy associated with their center of mass plus that associated with the internal motion relative to the center of mass.

b) If the asteroids collide, what is the *minimum* possible kinetic energy they can have after the collision, as measured by the astronomer?

9

Rotational Motion

In the opening chapters we talked mostly about the motion of *particles*. Real-world bodies can be more complicated; they can rotate, and they can deform as the forces that act on them stretch, twist, and squeeze them. In this chapter and the next we introduce a more general model, a body that has a definite size and definite shape and that can have rotational as well as translational motion. For the present we continue to neglect deformations; we assume that the body has a perfectly definite and unchanging shape and size. We call this idealized model a **rigid body;** the study of rotational motion of a rigid body is the principal subject of this chapter. We begin with kinematic language for *describing* rotational motion, and then we develop dynamic principles relating the forces on the body to its rotational motion. This development involves several new physical quantities, including torque, moment of inertia, and angular momentum. Many aspects of rotational motion are directly analogous to straight-line motion of a particle. We postpone until Chapter 12 a detailed study of the deformations of real-world bodies when forces act on them.

9–1

Angular Velocity and Acceleration

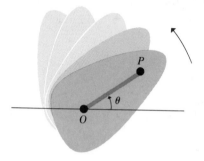

9–1
Body rotating about a fixed axis through point O.

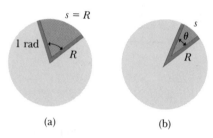

(a)   (b)

9–2
An angle θ in radians is defined as the ratio of the arc s to the radius R.

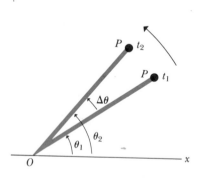

9–3
Angular displacement $\Delta\theta$ of a rotating body.

Let's think first about a rigid body that rotates about a stationary axis; it might be a motor shaft, a chunk of roast beef on a barbecue skewer, or a merry-go-round. In Fig. 9–1 a rigid body rotates about a stationary line passing through point O, perpendicular to the plane of the diagram. Line OP is a line in the body that rotates with it. The angle θ describes the rotational position of the body and serves as a *coordinate* for rotational motion.

Usually, we will measure the angle θ in **radians.** As shown in Fig. 9–2a, one radian (1 rad) is the angle subtended at the center of a circle by an arc of length equal to the radius of the circle. The circumference is 2π times the radius, so there are 2π (about 6.283) radians in one complete revolution (360°). Hence

$$1 \text{ rad} = \frac{360°}{2\pi} = 57.3°,$$

$$360° = 2\pi \text{ rad} = 6.28 \text{ rad},$$

$$180° = \pi \text{ rad} = 3.14 \text{ rad},$$

$$90° = \pi/2 \text{ rad} = 1.57 \text{ rad},$$

and so on.

In Fig. 9–2b an angle θ is subtended by an arc of length s on a circle of radius R; θ (in radians) is equal to s divided by R:

$$\theta = \frac{s}{R}, \qquad s = R\theta. \tag{9–1}$$

An angle in radians is the quotient of two lengths, so it is a pure number, without units. If $s = 1.5$ m and $R = 1$ m, then $\theta = 1.5$ rad, but to say simply $\theta = 1.5$ would be equally correct.

We can describe rotational *motion* of a rigid body in terms of the rate of change of θ. In Fig. 9–3 a reference line OP in a rotating body makes an angle θ_1 with the stationary horizontal line Ox at time t_1. At a later time t_2 the angle has changed to θ_2. We define the **average angular velocity** of the body ω_{av} in the time interval $\Delta t = t_2 - t_1$ as the ratio of the angular displacement $\Delta\theta = \theta_2 - \theta_1$, to Δt:

$$\omega_{av} = \frac{\Delta\theta}{\Delta t}. \tag{9–2}$$

The **instantaneous angular velocity** ω is the limit of ω_{av} as Δt approaches zero:

$$\omega = \lim_{\Delta t \to 0} \frac{\Delta\theta}{\Delta t}. \tag{9–3}$$

Because the body is rigid, *all* lines in it rotate through the same angle in the same time, and every part of the body has the same angular velocity.

If the angle θ is in radians, the unit of angular velocity is 1 radian per second (1 rad·s^{-1} or simply 1 s^{-1}). Other units, such as the revolution per minute (rev·min^{-1} or rpm), are often used. Two useful conversions are

$$1 \text{ rev·s}^{-1} = 2\pi \text{ rad·s}^{-1}$$

and

$$1 \text{ rev·min}^{-1} = 1 \text{ rpm} = \frac{2\pi}{60} \text{ rad·s}^{-1}.$$

When the angular velocity of a rigid body changes, it has an *angular acceleration*. If ω_1 and ω_2 are the instantaneous angular velocities at times t_1 and t_2, we define the **average angular acceleration** α_{av} as

$$\alpha_{av} = \frac{\omega_2 - \omega_1}{t_2 - t_1} = \frac{\Delta\omega}{\Delta t}, \tag{9–4}$$

and the **instantaneous angular acceleration** α as the limit of ω_{av} as $\Delta t \to 0$.

$$\alpha = \lim_{\Delta t \to 0} \frac{\Delta\omega}{\Delta t}. \tag{9–5}$$

The unit of angular acceleration is 1 rad·s^{-2} or 1 s^{-2}.

We usually use Greek letters for angular kinematic quantities: θ for angular position, ω for angular velocity, and α for angular acceleration. These are analogous to x for position, v for velocity, and a for acceleration, respectively, in straight-line motion. In each case, velocity is the rate of change of position, and acceleration is the rate of change of velocity.

9–2
Rotation with Constant Angular Acceleration

In Chapter 2 we found that analyzing straight-line motion is particularly simple in the special case in which the acceleration is *constant*. This is also true of rotational motion; when the angular acceleration is constant, we can derive equations for angular velocity and angular position with exactly the same procedure that we used in Section 2–4. We suggest that you review that section before continuing.

Let ω_0 be the initial angular velocity (at time $t = 0$) of a rigid body, and let ω be its angular velocity at any later time t. The angular acceleration α is constant and equal to the average value for any interval. Using Eq. (9–4) with the interval from 0 to t, we find

$$\alpha = \frac{\omega - \omega_0}{t - 0} \quad \text{or} \quad \omega = \omega_0 + \alpha t. \tag{9–6}$$

The product αt is the total *change* in ω between $t = 0$ and the later time t; the angular velocity ω at time t is the sum of the initial value ω_0 and this total change.

To derive an equation for the angular position θ as a function of time, we proceed just as we did in Section 2–4. The angular velocity changes at a uniform rate, so its average value between 0 and t is the average of the initial and final values, that is,

$$\omega_{av} = \frac{\omega_0 + \omega}{2};$$

(9–7)

Combining this with Eq. (9–6), we find

$$\omega_{av} = \tfrac{1}{2}(\omega_0 + \omega_0 + \alpha t)$$

$$= \omega_0 + \tfrac{1}{2}\alpha t.$$

(9–8)

We also know that ω_{av} is the total angular displacement $(\theta - \theta_0)$ in the time interval from 0 to t, divided by $t - 0$:

$$\omega_{av} = \frac{\theta - \theta_0}{t - 0}.$$

(9–9)

Finally, we equate Eqs. (9–8) and (9–9) and simplify the resulting equation:

$$\omega_0 + \tfrac{1}{2}\alpha t = \frac{\theta - \theta_0}{t},$$

or

$$\theta = \theta_0 + \omega_0 t + \tfrac{1}{2}\alpha t^2.$$

(9–10)

This equation states that if at the initial time $t = 0$ the body has been rotated to angular position θ_0 and has angular velocity ω_0, then its angular position θ at any later time t is the sum of three terms: its initial angular position θ_0, plus the rotation $\omega_0 t$ that it would have if the angular velocity were constant, plus an additional rotation $\tfrac{1}{2}\alpha t^2$ caused by the changing angular velocity.

Still pursuing the same path as in Section 2–4, we can combine Eqs. (9–6) and (9–10) to obtain a relation between θ and ω that does not contain t. In view of the perfect analogy between straight-line and rotational quantities, it is legitimate simply to take Eq. (2–13) and replace each straight-line quantity by its rotational analog, obtaining

$$\omega^2 = \omega_0{}^2 + 2\alpha(\theta - \theta_0).$$

(9–11)

If this discussion doesn't convince you of the validity of Eq. (9–11), feel free to invent a detailed derivation analogous to the development that led to Eq. (2–13). We leave that task for you as a problem.

Keep in mind that all of this discussion is valid *only* in the special case in which the angular acceleration is *constant*; be careful not to try to apply these equations to problems in which α is *not* constant. Table 9–1 shows the analogy between Eqs. (9–6), (9–10), and (9–11) for motion with constant angular acceleration and the corresponding equations for motion with constant linear acceleration.

TABLE 9–1   Comparison of linear and angular motion with constant acceleration

Motion with constant linear acceleration	Motion with constant angular acceleration
$a = \text{constant}$	$\alpha = \text{constant}$
$v = v_0 + at$	$\omega = \omega_0 + \alpha t$
$x = x_0 + v_0 t + \frac{1}{2}at^2$	$\theta = \theta_0 + \omega_0 t + \frac{1}{2}\alpha t^2$
$v^2 = v_0^2 + 2a(x - x_0)$	$\omega^2 = \omega_0^2 + 2\alpha(\theta - \theta_0)$
$x - x_0 = \frac{1}{2}(v + v_0)t$	$\theta - \theta_0 = \frac{1}{2}(\omega + \omega_0)t$

Example 9–1   The angular velocity of a bicycle wheel is 4.00 rad·s^{-1} at time $t = 0$, and its angular acceleration is constant and equal to 2.00 rad·s^{-2}. A spoke OP on the wheel is horizontal at time $t = 0$.

a) What angle does this spoke make with the horizontal at time $t = 3.00$ s?

b) What is the wheel's angular velocity at this time?

Solution   We can use Eqs. (9–6) and (9–10) to find θ and ω at any time in terms of the given initial conditions.

a) The angle θ is given as a function of time by

$$\theta = \theta_0 + \omega_0 t + \frac{1}{2}\alpha t^2$$
$$= 0 + (4.00 \text{ rad·s}^{-1})(3.00 \text{ s}) + \frac{1}{2}(2.00 \text{ rad·s}^{-2})(3.00 \text{ s})^2$$
$$= 21.0 \text{ rad} = \frac{21.0}{2\pi} \text{ rev} = 3.34 \text{ rev.}$$

The body turns through three complete revolutions plus an additional 0.34 rev or $(0.34 \text{ rev})(2\pi \text{ rad·rev}^{-1}) = 2.15 \text{ rad} = 123°$. The line OP thus turns through 123° and makes an angle of 57° with the horizontal.

b) In general, $\omega = \omega_0 + \alpha t$. At time $t = 3.0$ s,

$$\omega = 4.00 \text{ rad·s}^{-1} + (2.00 \text{ rad·s}^{-2})(3.00 \text{ s}) = 10.0 \text{ rad·s}^{-1}.$$

Alternatively, from Eq. (9–11),

$$\omega^2 = \omega_0^2 + 2\alpha(\theta - \theta_0)$$
$$= (4.00 \text{ rad·s}^{-1})^2 + 2(2.00 \text{ rad·s}^{-2})(21.0 \text{ rad})$$
$$= 100 \text{ rad}^2\text{·s}^{-2},$$
$$\omega = 10.0 \text{ rad·s}^{-1}. \qquad \blacksquare$$

9–3
Relation between Angular and Linear Velocity and Acceleration

As part of our detailed analysis of rigid body rotation, we need to develop relations between the rotational motion of a rigid body and the motion of an individual particle within the body. First, when a rigid body rotates about a stationary axis, every particle in the body moves in a circular path. The circle lies in a plane perpendicular to the axis, with its center on the axis. It is useful to represent the acceleration of a particle in terms of its normal (radial) and tangential components, as we discussed in Section 3–3.

The speed of a particle in a rotating rigid body is directly proportional to the body's angular velocity. In Fig. 9–4, point P is a distance r away from the axis of rotation, and it moves in a circle of radius r. When the angle θ increases by a small amount $\Delta\theta$ in a time interval Δt, the particle moves through an arc length $\Delta s = r\,\Delta\theta$. If $\Delta\theta$ is very small, the arc is nearly a straight line, and the average speed of the particle is given by

$$v_{av} = \frac{\Delta s}{\Delta t} = r\,\frac{\Delta\theta}{\Delta t}.$$

In the limit, as $\Delta t \to 0$, this becomes

$$v = r\omega. \tag{9–12}$$

The *direction* of the particle's velocity is tangent to its circular path at each point.

If the angular velocity changes by $\Delta\omega$, the particle's speed changes by an amount Δv given by

$$\Delta v = r\,\Delta\omega.$$

This corresponds to a component of acceleration $a_{\parallel}$ tangent to the circle. If these changes take place in a small time interval Δt, then

$$(a_{\parallel})_{av} = \frac{\Delta v}{\Delta t} = r\,\frac{\Delta\omega}{\Delta t},$$

and, in the limit, as $\Delta t \to 0$,

$$a_{\parallel} = r\alpha, \tag{9–13}$$

where $a_{\parallel}$ is the **tangential component of acceleration** of a point at a distance r from the axis.

The **radial component of acceleration** of the point, as worked out in Section 3–5, is $a_{\perp} = v^2/r$. We can also express this in terms of ω by using Eq. (9–12):

$$a_{\perp} = \frac{v^2}{r} = \omega^2 r. \tag{9–14}$$

This is true at each instant *even when ω and v are not constant.*

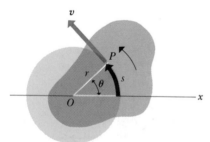

9–4
The distance s moved through by point P equals $r\theta$.

The tangential and radial components of acceleration of a point P in a rotating body are shown in Fig. 9–5. Their vector sum is the acceleration a, as shown.

9–5
Nonuniform rotation about a fixed axis through point O. The tangential component of acceleration of point P, $a_{\parallel}$, equals $r\alpha$; the radial component $a_{\perp}$ equals $\omega^2 r$.

Example 9–2 A discus thrower turns with angular acceleration $\alpha = 50$ rad·s^{-2}, moving the discus in a circle of radius 0.80 m. Find the radial and tangential components of acceleration of the discus and the magnitude of its acceleration at the instant when the angular velocity is 10 rad·s^{-1}.

Solution We model the discus as a particle moving in a circular path. The acceleration components are given by Eqs. (9–13) and (9–14):

$$a_{\perp} = \omega^2 r = (10 \text{ s}^{-1})^2(0.80 \text{ m}) = 80 \text{ m·s}^{-2},$$

$$a_{\parallel} = r\alpha = (0.80 \text{ m})(50 \text{ s}^{-2}) = 40 \text{ m·s}^{-2}.$$

The magnitude of the acceleration vector is

$$a = \sqrt{a_{\perp}^2 + a_{\parallel}^2} = 89 \text{ m·s}^{-2},$$

or about nine times the acceleration due to gravity. Note that when we use Eqs. (9–13) and (9–14), we *must* express the angular quantities in radians. In unit cancellations we may drop out "radians" when it is convenient because an angle expressed in radians is a unitless number. ∎

9–4
Kinetic Energy and Moment of Inertia

A rotating rigid body consists of mass in motion, so it has kinetic energy. We can express the kinetic energy of a rotating body in terms of its angular velocity and a new quantity called *moment of inertia*. To develop this relationship, we think of the body as made up of a lot of particles. The speed v of each particle is given by Eq. (9–12), $v = r\omega$, where ω is the body's angular velocity and r is the distance of a particular particle from the axis of rotation (equal to the radius of the circle in which it moves). Different particles have different values of r, but ω is the same for all. If the first particle has mass m_1 and distance from the axis r_1, its kinetic energy K_1 is

$$K_1 = \tfrac{1}{2}m_1 v_1^2 = \tfrac{1}{2}m_1 r_1^2 \omega^2.$$

The *total* kinetic energy K of the body is the sum of the kinetic energies of all the particles:

$$K = \tfrac{1}{2}m_1 r_1^2 \omega^2 + \tfrac{1}{2}m_2 r_2^2 \omega^2 + \cdots$$
$$= \tfrac{1}{2}(m_1 r_1^2 + m_2 r_2^2 + \cdots)\omega^2.$$

The quantity in parentheses, obtained by multiplying the mass of each particle by the square of its distance from the axis and adding these products, is called the **moment of inertia** I of the body.

$$I = m_1r_1{}^2 + m_2r_2{}^2 + \cdots = \sum mr^2. \tag{9-15}$$

In terms of moment of inertia I, the rotational kinetic energy K of a rigid body is

$$K = \tfrac{1}{2}I\omega^2. \tag{9-16}$$

This is analogous to the expression for kinetic energy of a particle:

$$K = \tfrac{1}{2}mv^2.$$

In these expressions, moment of inertia is analogous to mass, and angular velocity ω is analogous to velocity v.

In SI units the unit of moment of inertia is 1 kilogram-meter^2 (1 kg·m^2).

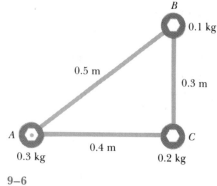

9–6
A strangely shaped machine part.

Example 9–3   An engineer is designing a one-piece machine part consisting of three heavy connectors linked by light molded struts, as in Fig. 9–6. The connectors can be considered as massive particles connected by massless rods.

a) What is the moment of inertia of this machine part about an axis through point A, perpendicular to the plane of the diagram?

b) What is the moment of inertia about an axis coinciding with rod BC?

c) If the body rotates about an axis through A perpendicular to the plane of the diagram, with angular velocity $\omega = 4.0$ rad·s^{-1}, what is its rotational kinetic energy?

Solution

a) The particle at point A lies *on* the axis. Its distance r *from* the axis is zero, and it contributes nothing to the moment of inertia. Therefore, from Eq. (9–15),

$$\begin{aligned} I = \sum mr^2 &= (0.10 \text{ kg})(0.50 \text{ m})^2 + (0.20 \text{ kg})(0.40 \text{ m})^2 \\ &= 0.057 \text{ kg·m}^2. \end{aligned}$$

b) The particles at B and C both lie on the axis, so neither contributes to the moment of inertia; only A contributes, and we have

$$I = \sum mr^2 = (0.30 \text{ kg})(0.40 \text{ m})^2 = 0.048 \text{ kg·m}^2.$$

c) From Eq. (9–16),

$$K = \tfrac{1}{2}I\omega^2 = \tfrac{1}{2}(0.057 \text{ kg·m}^2)(4.0 \text{ rad·s}^{-1})^2 = 0.456 \text{ J.} \qquad \blacksquare$$

The results of parts (a) and (b) show that the moment of inertia of a body depends on the location of the axis. We can't just say, "The moment

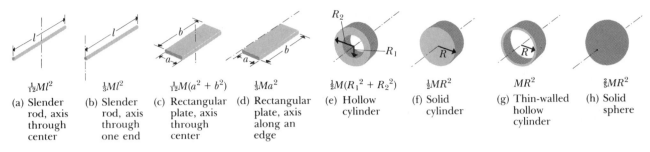

$\frac{1}{12}Ml^2$

(a) Slender rod, axis through center

$\frac{1}{3}Ml^2$

(b) Slender rod, axis through one end

$\frac{1}{12}M(a^2 + b^2)$

(c) Rectangular plate, axis through center

$\frac{1}{3}Ma^2$

(d) Rectangular plate, axis along an edge

$\frac{1}{2}M(R_1^2 + R_2^2)$

(e) Hollow cylinder

$\frac{1}{2}MR^2$

(f) Solid cylinder

MR^2

(g) Thin-walled hollow cylinder

$\frac{2}{5}MR^2$

(h) Solid sphere

9–7
Moments of inertia. For each body the axis is shown as a broken line.

of inertia of this body is 0.048 kg·m²"; we have to say, "The moment of inertia of this body *with respect to axis BC* is 0.048 kg·m²."

In Example 9–3 we represented the body as several point masses, and we evaluated the sum in Eq. (9–15) directly. When the body is a *continuous* distribution of matter, such as a solid cylinder or plate, methods of integral calculus have to be used to evaluate the sums. Figure 9–7 gives moments of inertia for several familiar shapes in terms of the masses and dimensions.

You may be tempted to try to compute the moment of inertia of a body by assuming that all the mass is concentrated at the center of mass and then multiplying the total mass by the square of the distance from the center of mass to the axis. Resist that temptation; it doesn't work! For example, when a uniform thin rod of length L and mass M is pivoted about an axis through one end, perpendicular to the rod, the moment of inertia is $I = ML^2/3$. If we took the mass as concentrated at the center, a distance $L/2$ from the axis, we would obtain the *incorrect* result $I = M(L/2)^2 = ML^2/4$.

Now that we have learned how to calculate the kinetic energy of a rotating rigid body, we can apply the energy principles of Chapter 7 to rotational motion. Next, we consider some strategy and some examples.

PROBLEM-SOLVING STRATEGY: *Rotational Energy*

1. We suggest that you review the problem-solving strategy outlined in Section 7–5; it is equally useful here. The only new idea is that the kinetic energy K is expressed in terms of the moment of inertia I and angular velocity ω of the body instead of its mass m and speed v. We can then use work–energy relations and conservation of energy, where appropriate, to find relations involving position and motion of a rotating body.

2. The kinematic relations of Section 9–3, particularly Eqs. (9–12) and (9–13), are often useful, especially when a rotating cylindrical body functions as any sort of pulley. Example 9–4 illustrates this point.

Example 9–4   A light, flexible, nonstretching rope is wrapped several times around a solid cylinder of mass 50 kg and diameter 0.12 m, which rotates about a stationary horizontal axis, held by frictionless bearings, as

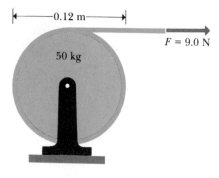

9-8
A rope unwinds from a cylinder. The force F does work and increases the kinetic energy of the cylinder.

shown in Fig. 9–8. The free end of the rope is pulled with a constant force of magnitude 9.0 N for a distance of 2.0 m. If the cylinder is initially at rest, find its final angular velocity and the final speed of the rope.

Solution   Because no energy is lost in friction, the final kinetic energy $K = \frac{1}{2}I\omega^2$ of the cylinder is equal to the work $W = Fd$ done by the force, which is (9.0 N)(2.0 m) = 18 J. From Fig. 9–7, the moment of inertia is

$$I = \tfrac{1}{2}MR^2 = \tfrac{1}{2}(50 \text{ kg})(0.060 \text{ m})^2 = 0.090 \text{ kg·m}^2.$$

The work–energy relation then gives

$$18 \text{ J} = \tfrac{1}{2}(0.090 \text{ kg·m}^2)\omega^2,$$

$$\omega = 20 \text{ rad·s}^{-1}.$$

The final speed of the rope is equal to the final tangential speed v of the cylinder, which is given by Eq. (9–12):

$$v = r\omega = (0.060 \text{ m})(20 \text{ rad·s}^{-1}) = 1.2 \text{ m·s}^{-1}. \qquad \blacksquare$$

Example 9–5   We wrap a light, flexible rope around a solid cylinder with mass M and radius R, which rotates with no friction about a stationary horizontal axis, as in Fig. 9–9. We tie the free end of the rope to a mass m and release the mass with no initial velocity at a distance h above the floor. Find the speed of mass m and the angular velocity of the cylinder just as mass m strikes the floor.

Solution   Initially, the system has no kinetic energy ($K_1 = 0$). We take the potential energy to be zero when m is at floor level; then $U_1 = mgh$ and $U_2 = 0$. There are no nonconservative forces, so $W_{\text{other}} = 0$ and $K_1 + U_1 = K_2 + U_2$. (The rope does no net work; at one end the force and displacement are in the same direction, and at the other end they are in opposite directions. So the total work done by both ends of the rope is zero.) Just before m hits the floor, both this mass and the cylinder have kinetic energy. The total kinetic energy K_2 at that time is

$$K_2 = \tfrac{1}{2}mv^2 + \tfrac{1}{2}I\omega^2.$$

Now, according to Fig 9–7, the moment of inertia of the cylinder is $I = \frac{1}{2}mR^2$. Furthermore, v and ω are related by $v = R\omega$, since the speed of mass m must be equal to the tangential speed at the outer surface of the cylinder. Using these relations and equating the initial and final total energies, we find

$$0 + mgh = \tfrac{1}{2}mv^2 + \tfrac{1}{2}(\tfrac{1}{2}MR^2)\left(\frac{v}{R}\right)^2 = \tfrac{1}{2}(m + \tfrac{1}{2}M)v^2,$$

$$v = \sqrt{\frac{2gh}{1 + M/2m}}.$$

When M is much larger than m, v is very small, as we would expect. When M is much smaller than m, v is nearly equal to the speed of a body in free fall with initial height h, namely, $\sqrt{2gh}$. $\qquad \blacksquare$

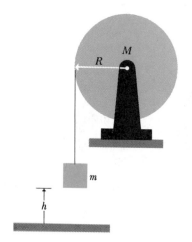

9-9
As the cylinder rotates, the rope unwinds and mass m drops.

9–5
Torque

In studying the dynamics of a particle we made extensive use of Newton's second law, $\Sigma F = ma$. Now we need to develop an analogous relation between the *angular acceleration* of a rotating rigid body and the forces acting on it. This relation involves a new concept, *torque*, which is a measure of the tendency of a force to cause a rotation of the body on which it acts. This tendency depends on the magnitude and direction of the force and also on the location of the point where it acts. For example, it is easier to push a door open by pushing near the doorknob side than near the hinge side. Torque is always defined with reference to a specific *axis* of rotation.

Figure 9–10 shows a body that can rotate about an axis perpendicular to the plane of the figure, through point O. It is acted on by two forces F_1 and F_2. The tendency of force F_1 to cause a rotation about the axis through O depends on both the magnitude F_1 of the force and the perpendicular distance l_1 between the line of action of the force (i.e., the line along which the force vector lies) and the axis. If $l_1 = 0$, there is *no* tendency to cause rotation. To understand the role of the distance l_1, think of a wrench handle; we can turn a tight bolt more easily by using a long-handled wrench than by using a short-handled one. The distance l_1 is called the **moment arm** (or *lever arm*) of force F_1 about the axis through O, and the product $F_1 l_1$ is called the **torque** or **moment** of the force about point O, denoted by the Greek letter Γ (capital "gamma"). The terms *torque* and *moment* are synonymous; we will usually use *torque*, but *moment arm* is the more usual term for the distance l_1.

$$\Gamma = Fl. \tag{9–17}$$

The moment arm of F_1 is the perpendicular distance OA or l_1, and the moment arm of F_2 is the perpendicular distance OB or l_2. When the line along which a force acts passes through the axis of rotation, the moment arm for that force is zero, and its torque with respect to that axis is zero.

Force F_1 tends to cause *counterclockwise* rotation about the axis, while F_2 tends to cause *clockwise* rotation. To distinguish between these directions of rotation, we will usually use the convention that *counterclockwise torques are positive and clockwise torques are negative*. Hence the torque Γ_1 of the force F_1 about the axis through O is

$$\Gamma_1 = +F_1 l_1,$$

and the torque Γ_2 of F_2 is

$$\Gamma_2 = -F_2 l_2.$$

In problems involving torques in this and the following chapter we use the symbol

to indicate the choice of positive direction of rotation. The SI unit of torque is the newton-meter. This happens to be the same as the unit of

9–10
The moment or torque of a force about an axis is the product of the force and its moment arm.

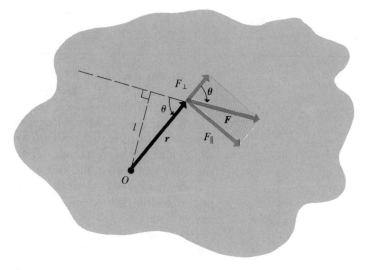

9–11
Several equivalent ways to calculate torque with respect to point O.
$\Gamma = Fl = Fr \sin \theta = F_{\parallel} r$.

work or energy, but ordinarily the joule is *not* used as a unit of torque.

Often one of the important forces acting on a body is its *weight*. This force is not concentrated at a single point but is distributed over the entire body. Nevertheless, we can always calculate the corresponding torque about any axis by assuming all the weight to be concentrated at the *center of mass* of the body. We postpone proof of this statement until Chapter 10, but meanwhile we will use it in some of the problems here.

Figure 9–11 shows that there are several alternative ways to calculate the torque of a force F applied at a point with position vector r (from the chosen axis through O). We can find the moment arm l and use $\Gamma = Fl$, or we can determine the angle θ and use $\Gamma = rF \sin \theta$. Finally, we can represent F in terms of a component $F_{\perp}$ along the direction of r and a component $F_{\parallel}$ at right angles, as shown by the light-colored vectors. This notation may appear to be backward, but it is consistent with the discussion in Section 3–3. If the point at which the force is applied moves in a circle with radius r centered at O, then $F_{\parallel}$ is tangent to that circle, and $F_{\perp}$ is perpendicular to the tangent line. Then $F_{\parallel} = F \sin \theta$, and

$$\Gamma = F_{\parallel} r = r(F \sin \theta) = Fl.$$

The component $F_{\perp}$ has no torque with respect to O because its moment arm with respect to that point is zero. Whenever the line of action of a force goes through the point we are using to calculate torques, the torque of that force is zero.

9–6
Torque and Angular Acceleration

We are now ready to develop the fundamental dynamic relation for rotational motion of a rigid body. We will prove that the angular acceleration of a rotating body is directly proportional to the sum of the torques with respect to the axis of rotation. The proportionality factor is the moment of inertia.

To develop this relationship, we again imagine the body as being made up of a large number of particles; the first particle on our list has mass m_1 and distance r_1 from the axis. We represent the *total force* acting on this particle in terms of a component $F_{1\perp}$ that acts along the radial direction and a component $F_{1\parallel}$ that is tangent to the circle of radius r_1 in which the particle moves as the body rotates. Newton's second law for the tangential components is

$$F_{1\parallel} = m_1 a_{1\parallel}. \tag{9–18}$$

Now $a_{1\parallel}$ can be expressed in terms of the angular acceleration α, according to Eq. (9–13): $a_{1\parallel} = r_1 \alpha$. Using this relation and multiplying both sides of Eq. (9–18) by r_1, we obtain

$$F_{1\parallel} r_1 = m_1 r_1^{\,2} \alpha. \tag{9–19}$$

But $F_{1\parallel} r_1$ is just the *torque* of the force, and $m_1 r_1^{\,2}$ is the moment of inertia of the particle. The component $F_{1\perp}$ acts along a line passing through the axis and so has no torque with respect to the axis. Equation (9–19) can be rewritten as

$$\Gamma_1 = I_1 \alpha.$$

We may write an equation like this for every particle in the body and add all these equations. The left side of the resulting equation is the sum of all the torques acting on all the particles, and the right side is the total moment of inertia $I = I_1 + I_2 + \cdots$, multiplied by α, which is the same for every particle. Thus for the entire body,

$$\sum \Gamma = I\alpha. \tag{9–20}$$

Now let's think about the forces. The force $\boldsymbol{F}$ on each particle is the vector sum of external and internal forces, as we defined these in Section 8–2. The two internal forces that any pair of particles exert on each other are an action–reaction pair; according to Newton's third law, they have equal magnitude and opposite direction. Assuming that they act along the line joining the two particles, their moment arms with respect to any axis are also equal, so the torques for each such pair add to zero. Indeed, *all* the internal torques add to zero, so the sum $\Sigma\Gamma$ includes only the torques of the *external* forces.

Equation (9–20) is the rotational analog of Newton's second law, $\boldsymbol{\Sigma F} = m\boldsymbol{a}.$ It provides the basis for relating the rotational motion of a rigid body to the forces acting on it.

PROBLEM-SOLVING STRATEGY: *Rotational Dynamics*

The strategy that we recommend for problems in rotational dynamics is very similar to that used in Section 5–4 for applications of Newton's laws:

1. Select a body for analysis. You will apply $\Sigma F = ma$ or $\Sigma\Gamma = I\alpha$, or sometimes both, to this body.

2. Draw a free-body diagram. Be sure to include all the forces acting *on* the chosen body, but be equally careful *not* to include any force exerted *by* the body *on* some other body. Some of the forces may be unknown; label them with algebraic symbols. Often, one of the forces will be the body's weight; it is useful to label it immediately as mg

rather than w. If a numerical value of mass is given, the corresponding numerical value of weight may be computed.

3. Choose coordinate axes for each body, and also indicate a positive sense of rotation for each rotating body. If you know the direction of α in advance, it is usually easiest to pick that as the positive sense of rotation. When appropriate, determine components of force with reference to the chosen axes. When a force is represented in terms of its components, cross out the original force so as not to include it twice.

4. If more than one body is involved, carry out the above steps for each body. Some problems will include bodies that have translational motion and others that have rotational motion. There may also be *geometrical* relations between the motions of two or more bodies. Express these in algebraic form, usually as relations between two accelerations or an acceleration and an angular acceleration.

5. Write the appropriate dynamic equations, mentioned in Step 1 above. Write a separate equation of motion for each body, and then solve the equations to find the unknown quantities. Often, this involves solving a set of simultaneous equations.

6. Check special cases or extreme values of quantities when possible, and compare the results for these particular cases with your intuitive expectations. Ask, "Does this result make sense?"

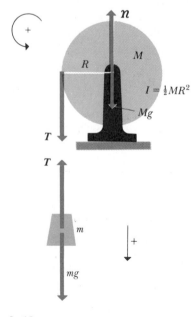

Example 9–6   Consider the same situation as in Example 9–4 (Section 9–4). We wrap a rope several times around a uniform solid cylinder of diameter 0.12 m and mass 50 kg, pivoted so it can rotate about its axis. What is the angular acceleration when the rope is pulled with a force of 9.0 N? What is the acceleration of the rope?

Solution   The torque is $\Gamma = Fl = (0.060 \text{ m})(9.0 \text{ N}) = 0.54 \text{ N·m}$, and from Fig. 9–7f the moment of inertia is $I = \frac{1}{2}MR^2 = \frac{1}{2}(50 \text{ kg})(0.060 \text{ m})^2 = 0.090 \text{ kg·m}^2$. The angular acceleration α is

$$\alpha = \frac{\Gamma}{I} = \frac{0.54 \text{ N·m}}{0.090 \text{ kg·m}^2} = 6.0 \text{ rad·s}^{-2}.$$

We invite you to check the units in this equation and make sure they come out right. The acceleration of the rope is given by Eq. (9–13):

$$a = r\alpha = (0.060 \text{ m})(6.0 \text{ rad·s}^{-2}) = 0.36 \text{ m·s}^{-2}.$$

Can you use this result to determine the speed of the rope after it has been pulled 2.0 m? Try it, and compare your result with Example 9–4, in which we used work and energy considerations. ∎

Example 9–7   In Example 9–5 (Section 9–4), find the acceleration of mass m and the angular acceleration of the cylinder.

Solution   We have to treat the two bodies separately. Figure 9–12 shows a free-body diagram for each body. We take the positive sense of rotation for the cylinder to be counterclockwise and the positive direction for the coordinate of m to be downward. Newton's second law applied to m gives

$$mg - T = ma.$$

The force Mg and the force n exerted by the bearing act along lines through the axis of rotation and thus have no torque with respect to that

9–12
Free-body diagrams for Example 9–7.

axis. Applying Eq. (9–20) to the cylinder gives

$$RT = I\alpha = \tfrac{1}{2}MR^2\alpha.$$

Now for the kinematic relation: At any instant, every point of the string moves with the same velocity, including the point at which the string is tangent to the cylinder. Thus the velocity of the mass and string at any instant is equal to the tangential velocity of a point on the surface of the cylinder. It follows that the acceleration a of mass m must equal the tangential acceleration of a point on the surface of the cylinder, which, according to Eq. (9–13), is given by $a_\parallel = R\alpha$. We use this to replace $(R\alpha)$ with a in the cylinder equation, divide by R, and substitute the resulting expression for T into the equation of motion for m. This eliminates T from the equations, and when we carry out the algebra, we obtain

$$mg - \tfrac{1}{2}Ma = ma, \qquad a = \frac{mg}{m + M/2} = \frac{g}{1 + M/2m}.$$

We note that the tension in the rope is *not* equal to the weight mg of mass m; if it were, m could not accelerate. From the above relations,

$$T = mg - ma = \frac{mg}{1 + 2m/M}.$$

When M is much larger than m, the tension is nearly equal to mg, and the acceleration is correspondingly much less than g. When M is zero, $T = 0$ and $a = g$; the mass then falls freely.

If mass m starts from rest at a height h above the floor, its velocity v when it strikes the ground is given by $v^2 = v_0{}^2 + 2ah$. In this case, $v_0 = 0$ and

$$v = \sqrt{2ah} = \sqrt{\frac{2gh}{1 + M/2m}}.$$

This is the same result that we obtained from energy considerations in Section 9–4. ∎

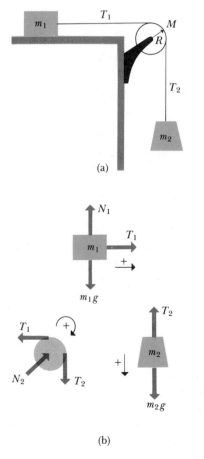

(a)

(b)

9–13
(a) System for Example 9–8. (b) Free-body diagrams.

Example 9–8   In Fig. 9–13a, mass m_1 slides without friction on the horizontal surface, the pulley is in the form of a thin cylindrical shell (with massless spokes) with mass M and radius R, and the string turns the pulley without slipping. Find the acceleration of each mass, the angular acceleration of the pulley, and the tension in each part of the string.

Solution   Figure 9–13b shows free-body diagrams and coordinate systems for the three bodies involved. We note that the mass of the pulley plays an essential role. The two tensions T_1 and T_2 *cannot* be equal; if they were, the pulley could not have an angular acceleration. Hence to label the tension in both parts of the string as simply T would be a serious error.

The equations of motion for masses m_1 and m_2 are

$$T_1 = m_1a_1, \tag{9–21}$$

$$m_2g - T_2 = m_2a_2. \tag{9–22}$$

The unknown normal force N_2 acting on the axis of the pulley has no torque with respect to the axis of rotation. From Fig. 9–7g the moment of inertia of the pulley is $I = MR^2$, and its equation of motion is

$$T_2R - T_1R = I\alpha = (MR^2)\alpha. \qquad (9\text{–}23)$$

Assuming that the string does not stretch or slip, we have the additional *kinematic* relations

$$a_1 = a_2 = R\alpha. \qquad (9\text{–}24)$$

(The accelerations of m_1 and m_2 have different directions but the same magnitude.)

Equations (9–21) through (9–24) are five equations for the five unknowns a_1, a_2, α, T_1, and T_2. (Equation (9–24) is actually two equations.) So we have as many equations as unknowns. To solve them, we first use Eq. (9–24) to eliminate a_2 and α from Eqs. (9–21) through (9–23). We then have three equations for the three unknowns T_1, T_2, and a_1:

$$T_1 = m_1 a_1,$$

$$m_2 g - T_2 = m_2 a_1,$$

$$T_2 - T_1 = Ma_1.$$

The easiest way to solve these is simply to *add* the three equations, which eliminates T_1 and T_2, and then to solve for a_1. The result is

$$a_1 = \frac{m_2 g}{m_1 + m_2 + M}.$$

We can then substitute this back into Eqs. (9–21) and (9–22) to find the tensions. The results are

$$T_1 = \frac{m_1 m_2 g}{m_1 + m_2 + M}, \qquad T_2 = \frac{(m_1 + M)m_2 g}{m_1 + m_2 + M}.$$

Let's check some special cases to see whether these results make sense. First, if either m_1 or M is much larger than m_2, the accelerations are very small, and T_2 is approximately $m_2 g$. But if m_2 is much *larger* than either m_1 or M, the acceleration is approximately g. Both results are what we should expect. Can you think of other special cases to check? ■

*9–7

Rotation about a Moving Axis

We can extend our analysis of the dynamics of rotational motion (Section 9–6) to some cases in which the axis of rotation moves, that is, both translational and rotational motion occur at once. Familiar examples of such motion include a ball rolling down a hill and a yo-yo unwinding at the end of a string. The key to this more general analysis, which we will not derive in detail, is that $\Sigma\Gamma = I\alpha$ remains valid when the axis of rotation moves *if the axis passes through the center of mass of the body and does not change its direction.*

Another useful relationship, which we also state without proof, is an expression for the total kinetic energy of a rigid body that has both translational and rotational motion. For a body of mass M, moving with a center-of-mass velocity V and rotating with angular velocity ω about an axis through the center of mass, the *total kinetic energy K* of the body is the sum of the kinetic energies of the separate motions:

$$K = \tfrac{1}{2}MV^2 + \tfrac{1}{2}I_c\omega^2, \tag{9–25}$$

where I_c is the moment of inertia about the axis through the center of mass.

PROBLEM-SOLVING STRATEGY: *Rotation about a Moving Axis*

The strategy outlined in Section 9–6 is equally useful here. There is one new wrinkle: When a body undergoes translational and rotational motion at the same time, we need two separate equations of motion *for the same body*. One of these is based on $\mathbf{\Sigma F} = M\mathbf{A}$ for the translational motion of the center of mass. We showed in Section 8–5 that for a body with total mass M the acceleration $\mathbf{A}$ of the center of mass is the same as that of a point mass M, acted on by all the forces on the actual body. The other equation of motion is based on $\Sigma\Gamma = I_c\alpha$ for the rotational motion about the axis through the center of mass, with moment of inertia I_c. In addition, there is often a geometric relation between the two motions, such as a wheel that rolls without slipping or a string that unwinds from a pulley while turning it.

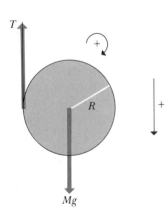

9–14
A cylinder rotates and drops as the string unwinds.

Example 9–9   We wrap a string several times around a solid cylinder with mass M and radius R. We hold the end of the string stationary while releasing the cylinder with no initial motion. The string unwinds but does not slip as the cylinder drops and rotates (like a primitive yo-yo). Find the downward acceleration of the cylinder and the tension in the string.

Solution   Figure 9–14 shows a free-body diagram for the situation, including the choice of positive coordinate directions. The equation for the translational motion of the center of mass is

$$Mg - T = MA. \tag{9–26}$$

The moment of inertia for an axis through the center of mass is $I_c = \tfrac{1}{2}MR^2$, and the equation for rotational motion about the axis through the center of mass is

$$TR = I_c\alpha = \tfrac{1}{2}MR^2\alpha. \tag{9–27}$$

In addition, if the string unwinds without slipping, the linear displacement of the center of mass in any time interval equals R times the angular displacement. This gives us the kinematic relations

$$V = R\omega \tag{9-28}$$

and

$$A = R\alpha. \tag{9-29}$$

We now use Eq. (9–29) to eliminate α from Eq. (9–27) and then solve Eqs. (9–26) and (9–27) simultaneously for T and A. The results are amazingly simple:

$$A = \frac{2}{3}g, \qquad T = \frac{1}{3}Mg. \qquad \blacksquare$$

Example 9–10   In the situation of Example 9–9, use energy considerations to find the speed V of the center of mass of the cylinder after it has dropped a distance h.

Solution   The potential energies are $U_1 = Mgh$ and $U_2 = 0$. The initial kinetic energy K_1 is zero, and the final kinetic energy K_2 is given by Eq. (9–25):

$$K_2 = \tfrac{1}{2}MV^2 + \tfrac{1}{2}I_c\omega^2.$$

But $\omega = V/R$ from Eq. (9–28), and $I_c = \tfrac{1}{2}MR^2$, so

$$K_2 = \tfrac{1}{2}(\tfrac{1}{2}MR^2)\left(\frac{V}{R}\right)^2 + \tfrac{1}{2}MV^2 = \tfrac{3}{4}MV^2.$$

Finally, we use $K_1 + U_1 = K_2 + U_2$:

$$Mgh = \frac{3}{4}MV^2,$$

and

$$V = \sqrt{\frac{4}{3}gh}.$$

We can also get this result by using the constant-acceleration formula $V^2 = V_0{}^2 + 2Ah$, using the acceleration from Example 9–9. Try it! $\blacksquare$

Example 9–11   A solid bowling ball rolls without slipping down a ramp inclined an angle θ to the horizontal. What is its acceleration?

Solution   Figure 9–15 shows a free-body diagram, with positive coordinate directions indicated. The moment of inertia, from Fig. 9–7h, is $I = \tfrac{2}{5}MR^2$. The equations of motion for translational motion and for rotation about the axis through the center of mass, respectively, are

$$Mg \sin \theta - \mathcal{F} = MA, \tag{9-30}$$

$$\mathcal{F}R = I\alpha = \left(\frac{2}{5}MR^2\right)\alpha. \tag{9-31}$$

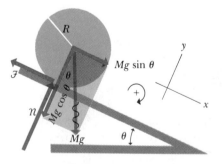

9–15
Free-body diagram for a ball rolling down a plane.

If the ball rolls without slipping, then $A = R\alpha$. We use this to eliminate α and then solve for A and $\mathcal{F}$ to obtain

$$A = \frac{5}{7}g \sin \theta, \qquad \mathcal{F} = \frac{2}{7}Mg \sin \theta.$$

The acceleration is just 5/7 as large as it would be if the ball could *slide* without friction down the slope like the toboggan in Example 5–12 (Section 5–4).

The friction force is needed to prevent slipping and to give the ball its angular acceleration. We can derive an expression for the minimum coefficient of static friction μ_s needed to prevent slipping. The normal force is $\mathcal{n} = Mg \cos \theta$, so to prevent slipping, the coefficient of friction must be at least as great as

$$\mu_s = \frac{\mathcal{F}}{\mathcal{n}} = \frac{\frac{2}{7}mg \sin \theta}{mg \cos \theta} = \frac{2}{7} \tan \theta.$$

If the plane is tilted only a little, θ is small, and only a small value of μ_s is needed to prevent slipping; but as the angle increases, the required value of μ_s increases, as we might expect intuitively.

Finally, suppose μ_s is *not* large enough to prevent slipping. Then we have a whole new ball game, so to speak. Equations (9–30) and (9–31) are still valid, but because the ball now slides as it rotates, there is no longer a definite relation between A and α. Now $\mathcal{F}$ in Eq. (9–31) is a kinetic friction force, given by $\mathcal{F} = \mu_k \mathcal{n} = \mu_k Mg \cos \theta$, and the center-of-mass acceleration is

$$A = g(\sin \theta - \mu_k \cos \theta),$$

just as in Example 5–13.   ■

9–8
Work and Power in Rotational Motion

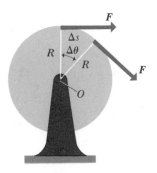

9–16
A force applied to a rotating body does work on the body.

A force applied to a rotating body does *work* on the body. This happens in many real-life situations, such as a rotating motor shaft driving a power tool or some other machine. We can express this work in terms of torque and angular displacement.

Suppose a force F acts at the rim of a pivoted wheel of radius R, as shown in Fig. 9–16, while the wheel rotates through a small angle $\Delta\theta$ during a small time interval Δt. Assume that the intervals are small enough that we may consider the force to be constant in magnitude. By definition, the work done by the force F is $\Delta W = F \, \Delta s$. But $\Delta s = R \, \Delta\theta$, so

$$\Delta W = FR \, \Delta\theta.$$

Now FR is the *torque* Γ due to the force F, and

$$\Delta W = \Gamma \, \Delta\theta. \tag{9–32}$$

If the torque is constant while the angle changes by a finite amount from θ_1 to θ_2, then

$$W = \Gamma(\theta_2 - \theta_1). \tag{9–33}$$

That is, *the work done by a constant torque equals the product of the torque and the angular displacement.* Angular displacement (in radians) is a pure number, without units. In SI units, in which Γ is expressed in newtons·meters (N·m), the work is in joules. Equation (9–33) is the rotational analog of Eq. (7–1) for the work done by a force in a straight-line displacement.

The force in Fig. 9–16 has no component along the *radial* direction. If there were such a component, it would do no work because the displacement of the point of application has no radial component. Similarly, a radial component of force would make no contribution to the torque. Hence Eqs. (9–32) and (9–33) are still correct even when F does have a radial component.

When we divide both sides of Eq. (9–32) by the time interval Δt, we find

$$\frac{\Delta W}{\Delta t} = \Gamma \frac{\Delta \theta}{\Delta t}.$$

But $\Delta W / \Delta t$ is the rate of doing work, or *power*, and $\Delta \theta / \Delta t$ is angular velocity ω. Hence

$$P = \Gamma \omega. \tag{9–34}$$

When a torque Γ acts on a body that rotates with angular velocity ω, its power (rate of doing work) is the product of torque and angular velocity. This is the analog of the relation $P = Fv$ that we developed in Section 7–8 for particle motion.

Example 9–12   The crankshaft of an automobile engine rotates at 3600 rpm and transmits 80 hp from the engine to the rear wheels. Compute the torque developed by the engine.

Solution   We first find ω (in radians per second) and convert the power to watts; then we use Eq. (9–34):

$$\omega = \frac{(3600 \text{ rev·min}^{-1})(2\pi \text{ rad·rev}^{-1})}{60 \text{ s·min}^{-1}} = 120\pi \text{ rad·s}^{-1},$$

$$80 \text{ hp} = (80 \text{ hp})(746 \text{ W·hp}^{-1}) = 59{,}700 \text{ W},$$

$$\Gamma = \frac{P}{\omega} = \frac{59{,}700 \text{ W}}{120\pi \text{ rad·s}^{-1}} = 158 \text{ N·m}.$$

We could apply this much torque by using a wrench 1 m long and applying a force of 158 N (about 35 lb) to the end of its handle.   ∎

9–9
Angular Momentum and Angular Impulse

The concept of **angular momentum** plays a role in rigid-body rotation that is closely analogous to that of momentum in motion of a particle, and there is a corresponding conservation principle. To introduce this concept, we begin by defining the angular momentum of a particle.

Figure 9–17a shows a particle with mass m moving in the plane of the figure with velocity v and momentum mv. We define the angular momentum L of the particle, with respect to an axis that passes through O and is perpendicular to the plane of the figure, as the product of the magnitude of its momentum ($p = mv$) and the perpendicular distance r from the axis to the line along which the particle's instantaneous velocity lies:

$$\text{Angular momentum} = L = mvr = pr. \qquad (9\text{--}35)$$

This definition is analogous to the definition of torque of a force, with r playing the role of the moment arm.

Now we define the *total* angular momentum of a body of finite size as the sum of the angular momenta of the particles of the body. For a rotating rigid body we can express this in terms of the body's moment of inertia and angular velocity. Figure 9–17b shows a rigid body rotating about an axis through O. Suppose the first particle we consider has mass m_1. Its speed v_1 is related to the angular velocity ω of the body by $v_1 = r_1\omega$. The angular momentum L_1 of this particle is therefore

$$L_1 = m_1 v_1 r_1 = m_1 r_1^2 \omega.$$

The total angular momentum L of the body is the sum of these quantities for all the particles; ω is the same for all, and

$$L = m_1 r_1^2 \omega + m_2 r_2^2 \omega + \cdots = \left(\sum mr^2\right)\omega.$$

But $\sum mr^2$ is just the moment of inertia I of the body about the chosen axis, so the total angular momentum L is simply

$$L = I\omega. \qquad (9\text{--}36)$$

This is analogous to the definition of linear momentum mv for a particle; each is a product of an inertial quantity and a velocity. Thus this definition continues the analogy between linear and angular quantities that we mentioned earlier in the chapter.

In defining angular momentum we need to define a positive and a negative sense of rotation, just as we did for other angular quantities. I is always positive, so the sign of L is the same as that of ω. For example, in Fig. 9–17b, in which the positive direction of rotation is defined to be clockwise, L is positive for clockwise rotations and negative for counterclockwise.

When a constant torque Γ acts on a body having moment of inertia I, for a time interval Δt from t_1 to t_2, the angular velocity changes from ω_1

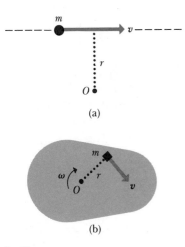

9–17
Angular momentum.

to ω_2, according to the relation

$$\Gamma = I\alpha = I\frac{\Delta\omega}{\Delta t} = I\frac{\omega_2 - \omega_1}{t_2 - t_1}.$$

Rearranging this equation, we obtain

$$\Gamma(t_2 - t_1) = I\omega_2 - I\omega_1 = L_2 - L_1 = \Delta L. \qquad (9\text{-}37)$$

The product of the torque and the time interval during which it acts is called the **angular impulse** of the torque; we denote this quantity by J_θ.

$$\text{Angular impulse} = J_\theta = \Gamma(t_2 - t_1). \qquad (9\text{-}38)$$

This quantity is the rotational analog of the impulse of a force, which was defined in Section 8–1. Equation (9–37) states that *the angular impulse acting on a body equals the change of angular momentum of the body about the same axis,* or $J_\theta = \Delta L$.

We can restate the basic dynamic relation for rigid-body rotation, given by Eq. (9–20), in terms of angular momentum. We rewrite Eq. (9–37) as

$$\Gamma = \frac{L_2 - L_1}{t_2 - t_1} = \frac{\Delta L}{\Delta t}. \qquad (9\text{-}39)$$

That is, the torque on a body, with respect to a specified axis, equals the rate of change of angular momentum of the body with respect to that axis. If there are several torques acting on the body, we generalize Eq. (9–39) to

$$\sum \Gamma = \frac{\Delta L}{\Delta t}. \qquad (9\text{-}40)$$

This equation is exactly correct when the torques are constant. When the torques vary with time, it is strictly correct only in the limit when $\Delta t \to 0$.

Equation (9–40) is particularly useful when we develop the principle of *conservation* of angular momentum in the next section. We have discussed changes in angular momentum that occur when the angular velocity ω of the body changes, but there are also cases in which ω is constant and I changes because of a change of shape or rearrangement of component parts of a body. In cases in which I is not constant, Eq. (9–20) is not valid. But the angular momentum is still given at each instant by $L = I\omega$, and the rate of change of angular momentum is still given by Eq. (9–40). The next section includes some examples in which we have to take this more general view.

9–10
Conservation of Angular Momentum

Here is the **principle of conservation of angular momentum.** When two bodies A and B interact with each other but not with anything else, their total angular momentum with respect to any specified axis is constant (conserved). Under these conditions, A and B together form an *isolated*

9–18
Conservation of angular momentum.

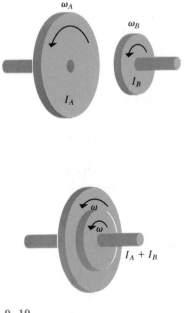

9–19
An impulsive torque acts when two rotating disks engage.

system; we have used this concept before, in Section 8–2. So we can also say that *the total angular momentum of an isolated system is conserved.*

Here's the proof: Suppose body A exerts a force on body B; call this force F_B and the corresponding torque (with respect to whatever axis we choose) Γ_B. This torque, according to Eq. (9–40), is equal to the rate of change of angular momentum of B:

$$\Gamma_B = \frac{\Delta L_B}{\Delta t}.$$

At the same time, body B exerts a force F_A on body A, with a corresponding torque Γ_A, and

$$\Gamma_A = \frac{\Delta L_A}{\Delta t}.$$

According to Newton's third law, the two forces are equal and opposite, so $F_A + F_B = 0$. Furthermore, if the forces act along the same line, their moment arms with respect to the chosen axis are equal. Thus the *torques* of these two forces are equal and opposite, and $\Gamma_A + \Gamma_B = 0$. So if we add the two previous equations, we find

$$\frac{\Delta L_A}{\Delta t} + \frac{\Delta L_B}{\Delta t} = 0,$$

or, because $L_A + L_B$ is the *total* angular momentum L of the system,

$$\frac{\Delta L}{\Delta t} = 0. \qquad (9\text{–}41)$$

That is, the total angular momentum of the system is constant, or *conserved*, as we asserted at the start.

A circus acrobat, a diver, and a skater performing a pirouette on the toe of one skate all take advantage of this principle. Suppose an acrobat has just left a swing as in Fig. 9–18, with arms and legs extended and with a counterclockwise angular momentum. When he pulls his arms and legs in, his moment of inertia I becomes much smaller. His angular momentum $I\omega$ remains constant and I decreases, so his angular velocity ω increases. When a skater spins with arms outstretched and then pulls her arms in, her angular velocity increases as her moment of inertia decreases. In each case we are seeing conservation of angular momentum in an isolated system.

Example 9–13   Figure 9–19 shows two disks with moments of inertia I_A and I_B; initially, they are rotating with constant angular velocities ω_A and ω_B, respectively. We then push the disks together with forces acting along the axis, so as not to apply any torque on either disk. The disks rub against each other and eventually reach a common final angular velocity ω. Derive an expression for ω.

Solution   The two disks are an isolated system. The only torque acting on either disk is the torque applied by the other disk; there are no external torques. Thus the total angular momentum of the system is the same before and after they are pushed together. At the end they rotate together as one body with total moment of inertia $I = I_A + I_B$ and angular velocity ω; conservation of angular momentum gives

$$I_A\omega_A + I_B\omega_B = (I_A + I_B)\omega$$

and

$$\omega = \frac{I_A\omega_A + I_B\omega_B}{I_A + I_B}.$$

Example 9–14   In Example 9–13 (Fig. 9–19), suppose disk A has a mass of 2.0 kg, a radius of 0.20 m, and an initial angular velocity of 50 rad·s^{-1} (about 500 rpm) and that disk B has a mass of 4.0 kg, a radius of 0.10 m, and an initial angular velocity of 200 rad·s^{-1}. Find the common final angular velocity ω after the disks are pushed into contact. Is kinetic energy conserved during this process?

Solution   The moments of inertia of the two disks are

$$I_A = \tfrac{1}{2}(2.0 \text{ kg})(0.20 \text{ m})^2 = 0.040 \text{ kg·m}^2$$

and

$$I_B = \tfrac{1}{2}(4.0 \text{ kg})(0.10 \text{ m})^2 = 0.020 \text{ kg·m}^2.$$

From conservation of angular momentum we have

$(0.04 \text{ kg·m}^2)(50 \text{ rad·s}^{-1}) + (0.02 \text{ kg·m}^2)(200 \text{ rad·s}^{-1})$

$$= (0.04 \text{ kg·m}^2 + 0.02 \text{ kg·m}^2)\omega,$$

$$\omega = 100 \text{ rad·s}^{-1}.$$

The initial kinetic energy is

$$K_1 = \tfrac{1}{2}(0.04 \text{ kg·m}^2)(50 \text{ rad·s}^{-1})^2 + \tfrac{1}{2}(0.02 \text{ kg·m}^2)(200 \text{ rad·s}^{-1})^2$$
$$= 450 \text{ J}.$$

The final kinetic energy is

$$K_2 = \tfrac{1}{2}(0.04 \text{ kg·m}^2 + 0.02 \text{ kg·m}^2)(100 \text{ rad·s}^{-1})^2 = 300 \text{ J}.$$

Thus one third of the kinetic energy was lost during this "angular collision," the rotational analog of an inelastic collision. We should not expect kinetic energy to be conserved, even though the resultant external force and torque are zero, since nonconservative (frictional) internal forces act while the two disks are rubbing together, gradually approaching a common angular velocity.

9–20
Conservation of angular momentum about a fixed axis.

Example 9–15   In Fig. 9–20 a man stands at the center of a turntable, holding his arms extended horizontally, with a 5.0-kg dumbbell in each hand. He is set rotating about a vertical axis, making one revolution in 2.0 s. Find the man's new angular velocity if he drops his hands to his sides. The moment of inertia of the man (without the dumbbells) may be assumed to be constant and equal to 6.0 kg·m². The dumbbells are 1.0 m from the axis initially, and 0.20 m from it at the end.

Solution   If we neglect friction in the turntable, no external torques act about the vertical axis, and the angular momentum about this axis is constant; that is,

$$I_1\omega_1 = I_2\omega_2,$$

where I_1 and ω_1 are the initial moment of inertia and angular velocity and I_2 and ω_2 are the final values. In each case, $I = I_{man} + I_{dumb}$.

$$I_1 = 6.0 \text{ kg·m}^2 + 2(5.0 \text{ kg})(1.0 \text{ m})^2 = 16 \text{ kg·m}^2,$$

$$I_2 = 6.0 \text{ kg·m}^2 + 2(5.0 \text{ kg})(0.20 \text{ m})^2 = 6.4 \text{ kg·m}^2,$$

$$\omega_1 = 2\pi\left(\frac{1 \text{ rev}}{2 \text{ s}}\right) = \pi \text{ rad·s}^{-1}.$$

From conservation of angular momentum,

$$(16 \text{ kg·m}^2)(\pi \text{ rad·s}^{-1}) = (6.4 \text{ kg·m}^2)\omega_2,$$

$$\omega_2 = 2.5\pi \text{ rad·s}^{-1} = 1.25 \text{ rev·s}^{-1}.$$

That is, the angular velocity more than doubles.
    The initial kinetic energy is

$$K_1 = \tfrac{1}{2}(16 \text{ kg·m}^2)(\pi \text{ rad·s}^{-1})^2 = 79 \text{ J}.$$

The final kinetic energy is

$$K_2 = \tfrac{1}{2}(6.4 \text{ kg·m}^2)(2.5\pi \text{ rad·s}^{-1})^2 = 197 \text{ J}.$$

Where did the extra energy come from?   ∎

Example 9–16   A door 1.0 m wide, with a mass of 15 kg, is hinged at one side so that it can rotate without friction about a vertical axis. A bullet with a mass of 10 g and a speed of 400 m·s^{-1} is fired into the door, perpendicular to the plane of the door, and embeds itself at the exact center. Find the angular velocity of the door just after the bullet embeds itself. Is kinetic energy conserved?

Solution   There is no external torque about the axis defined by the hinges, so angular momentum about this axis is conserved. The initial angular momentum of the bullet is given by Eq. (9–35):

$$L = mvr = (0.010 \text{ kg})(400 \text{ m·s}^{-1})(0.50 \text{ m}) = 2.0 \text{ kg·m}^2\text{·s}^{-1}.$$

This is equal to the final angular momentum $I\omega$, where $I = I_{door} + I_{bullet}$. From Fig. 9–7d,

$$I_{door} = \frac{ML^2}{3} = \frac{(15 \text{ kg})(1.0 \text{ m})^2}{3} = 5.0 \text{ kg·m}^2.$$

The moment of inertia of the bullet is

$$I_{bullet} = mr^2 = (0.010 \text{ kg})(0.50 \text{ m})^2 = 0.0025 \text{ kg·m}^2.$$

Conservation of angular momentum requires that $mvr = I\omega$, or

$$2.0 \text{ kg·m}^2\text{·s}^{-1} = (5.0 \text{ kg·m}^2 + 0.0025 \text{ kg·m}^2)\omega,$$

$$\omega = 0.40 \text{ rad·s}^{-1}.$$

The collision of bullet and door is inelastic because there are nonconservative forces acting during the impact. Thus we do not expect energy to be conserved. To check, we calculate initial and final kinetic energies:

$$K_1 = \tfrac{1}{2}mv^2 = \tfrac{1}{2}(0.010 \text{ kg})(400 \text{ m·s}^{-1})^2 = 800 \text{ J};$$

$$K_2 = \tfrac{1}{2}I\omega^2 = \tfrac{1}{2}(5.0025 \text{ kg·m}^2)(0.40 \text{ rad·s}^{-1})^2 = 0.40 \text{ J}.$$

The final kinetic energy is only 1/2000 of the initial value!   ∎

*9–11
Vector Representation of Angular Quantities

A rotational quantity associated with an axis of rotation, such as angular velocity, angular momentum, or torque, can be represented by a *vector* lying along that axis. Thus we can define angular velocity as a vector quantity ω having a magnitude equal to the number of radians through which the body turns per unit time and a direction along the axis of rotation.

A vector lying along a given line can have either of two opposite directions on that line. It is customary to define the angular velocity vector as having the direction in which a screw with a right-hand thread would advance if the screw turned with the body, as shown in Fig. 9–21. Alternatively, wrap the fingers of your right hand around the axis, with your fingers pointing in the direction of rotation; your thumb then points in the direction of the vector ω.

Similarly, a symmetric body turning about its axis of symmetry has a vector angular momentum L directed along its axis, parallel to the angular velocity vector. For such a body we can write the *vector* relationship

$$L = I\omega, \tag{9–42}$$

where I is the moment of inertia about the axis of rotation. Deriving this equation would be beyond our scope, but we note that it is valid *only* when the axis of rotation is a symmetry axis of the body, such as a motor shaft or the axle of a turning wheel. When a body rotates about an axis that is *not* a symmetry axis, such as a disk with an axis through its center but not perpendicular to its plane, the angular momentum vector does not have the same direction as the angular velocity. As a result, a body rotating with constant angular velocity *does not* have constant angular momentum. This makes the body tend to wobble, and torques must be supplied by the bearings supporting the body to prevent wobbling. A general analysis of rigid-body motion is a problem of considerable complexity.

We can also define a vector torque. A torque tends to cause a rotation about a certain axis, the axis about which the body would begin to rotate

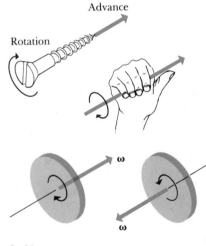

9–21
Vector angular velocity of a rotating body.

if it were initially at rest with only the torque under consideration acting on it. We define torque to be a vector with the direction of this axis and a magnitude given by our previous definition of torque. The right-hand rule described above determines which way the vector points along the axis.

With these generalized definitions of torque and angular momentum as vector quantities, the generalized relation between torque and angular momentum turns out to be

$$\sum \Gamma = \frac{\Delta L}{\Delta t}. \qquad (9\text{--}43)$$

We have not needed this generalized equation thus far in this chapter because when the axis of rotation always keeps the same direction, only one component of angular velocity is different from zero. Such rotational motion is analogous to motion of a particle along a straight line. But Eq. (9–43) also includes the possibility that Γ and L may have different directions. In that case, L and $\Delta L/\Delta t$ have different directions, and the direction of the axis of rotation may change. In such situations it is essential to consider the vector nature of the various angular quantities.

We cannot discuss the general formulation of the dynamics of rotation in detail here, but here is an example of its application. Figure 9–22 shows a familiar toy gyroscope. We set the flywheel spinning by wrapping a string around its shaft and pulling. When the shaft is supported at only one end, as shown in the figure, one possible motion is a steady circular motion of the axis in a horizontal plane. This is an interesting

9–22
Vector ΔL is the change in angular momentum produced in time Δt by the moment Γ of the force w. Vectors ΔL and Γ are in the same direction.

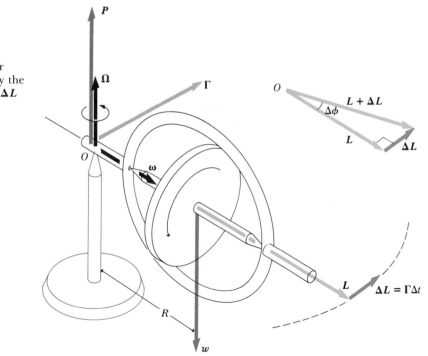

phenomenon and quite unexpected if you haven't seen it before; intuition suggests that the free end of the axis should simply drop if it isn't supported. Vector angular momentum considerations provide the key to understanding this behavior.

The forces acting on the gyroscope are its weight w, acting downward at the center of mass, and the upward force P at the pivot point O. If these forces acted on a body that was initially *at rest*, they would cause a rotation about a horizontal axis perpendicular to the gyroscope's axis; the associated torque Γ is in the direction shown, and the gyroscope axis would drop. However, the body is *not* at rest, and the effect of this torque is not to *initiate* a rotational motion but to *change* a motion that already exists. At the instant shown, the body has a definite, nonzero angular momentum described by the vector L, and the *change* ΔL in angular momentum in a short time interval following this is given by Eq. (9–43). Thus ΔL has the same direction as Γ. After time Δt the angular momentum is $L + \Delta L$, and, as the vector diagram shows, this means that the gyroscope axis has turned through a small angle $\Delta \phi$ given by $\Delta \phi = |\Delta L|/|L|$. Thus the motion of the axis is consistent with the torque–angular momentum relationship. This motion of the axis is called **precession.**

The rate at which the axis precesses, $\Delta \phi/\Delta t$, is called the *precession angular velocity*; denoting this quantity by Ω, we find

$$\Omega = \frac{\Delta \phi}{\Delta t} = \frac{|\Delta L|/|L|}{\Delta t} = \frac{\Gamma}{L} = \frac{wR}{I\omega}. \qquad (9\text{--}44)$$

Thus the precession angular velocity is *inversely* proportional to the angular velocity of spin about the axis. A rapidly spinning gyroscope precesses slowly, and as it slows down, the precession angular velocity *increases*!

Now let's return to the question of why the unsupported end of the axis does not fall. The reason is that the upward force P exerted on the gyroscope by the pivot is just equal in magnitude to its weight w. The resultant vertical *force* is zero, and the vertical acceleration of the center of mass is zero. However, the resultant *torque* of these forces is *not* zero, and the angular momentum changes.

If the gyroscope is not rotating initially, it has no initial angular momentum L. In that case its angular momentum ΔL after a time Δt is just the angular momentum it acquires from the torque acting on it, and it has the same direction as the torque. In other words, the gyroscope then rotates about an axis through O in the direction of the vector Γ, and the axis drops. But if it is originally rotating, the *change* in its angular momentum produced by the torque adds vectorially to the large angular momentum it already has, and since ΔL is horizontal and perpendicular to L, the result is a motion of precession, with both the angular momentum vector and the axis remaining horizontal.

This example gives us a glimpse of the richness of the dynamics of rotational motion, which can involve some very complex phenomena. In the next chapter we consider a *simpler* set of problems involving the *equilibrium* of rigid bodies.

Questions

9–1 What is the difference between tangential and radial acceleration for a point on a rotating body?

9–2 A flywheel rotates with constant angular velocity. Does a point on its rim have a tangential acceleration? A radial acceleration? Are these accelerations constant? In magnitude? In direction?

9–3 A flywheel rotates with constant angular acceleration. Does a point on its rim have a tangential acceleration? A radial acceleration? Are these accelerations constant? In magnitude? In direction?

9–4 Can a single force applied to a body change both its translational and rotational motion?

9–5 How might you determine experimentally the moment of inertia of an irregularly shaped body?

9–6 Can you think of a body that has the same moment of inertia for all possible axes? For all axes passing through a certain point? What point?

9–7 A cylindrical body has mass M and radius R. Is it ever possible for its moment of inertia to be greater than MR^2?

9–8 To maximize the moment of inertia of a flywheel while minimizing its weight, what shape should the flywheel have?

9–9 In tightening cylinder-head bolts in an automobile engine the critical quantity is the *torque* applied to the bolts. Why is this more important than the actual *force* applied to the wrench handle?

9–10 The flywheel of an automobile engine is included to increase the moment of inertia of the engine crankshaft. Why is this desirable?

9–11 A solid ball and a hollow ball with the same mass and radius roll down a slope. Which one reaches the bottom first?

9–12 A solid ball, a solid cylinder, and a hollow cylinder roll down a slope. Which reaches the bottom first? Last? Does it matter whether the radii are the same?

9–13 When an electrical motor is turned on, it takes longer to come up to final speed if there is a grinding wheel attached to the shaft. Why?

9–14 Experienced cooks can tell whether an egg is raw or hard-boiled by rolling it down a slope (taking care to catch it at the bottom). How is this possible?

9–15 Consider the idea of an automobile powered by energy stored in a rotating flywheel, which can be "recharged" by using an electric motor. What advantages and disadvantages would such a scheme have, compared to more conventional drive mechanisms? Could as much energy be stored as in a tank of gasoline? What factors would limit the maximum energy storage?

9–16 An electric grinder coasts for a minute or more after the power is turned off, while an electric drill coasts for only a few seconds. Why is there a difference?

9–17 Part of the kinetic energy of a moving automobile is in rotational motion of its wheels. When the brakes are applied hard on an icy street, the wheels lock, and the car starts to slide. What becomes of the rotational kinetic energy?

Exercises

Section 9–1   Angular Velocity and Acceleration

9–1

a) What angle in radians is subtended by an arc 5.00 m in length on the circumference of a circle whose radius is 2.00 m? What is this angle in degrees?

b) The angle between two radii of a circle with radius 1.50 m is 0.600 rad. What length of arc is intercepted on the circumference of the circle by the two radii?

c) An arc 45.0 cm in length on the circumference of a circle subtends an angle of 42.0°. What is the radius of the circle?

9–2 Compute the angular velocity in radians per second of the crankshaft of an automobile engine that is rotating at 3800 rev·min^{-1}.

9–3 A merry-go-round is being pushed by a child. The angle the merry-go-round has turned through varies with time according to $\theta(t) = (3.00 \text{ rad·s}^{-1})t + (0.0500 \text{ rad·s}^{-3})t^3$.

a) Calculate the average angular velocity for the time intervals $t = 0$ to $t = 2.00$ s and $t = 0$ to $t = 5.00$ s.

b) Use Eq. (9–3) to calculate the magnitude of the instantaneous angular velocity at

   i) $t = 2.00$ s;

   ii) $t = 5.00$ s.

In each case, do this by taking $\Delta t = 0.1$ s, 0.01 s, and 0.001 s and then deducing the limiting value.

9–4 A bicycle tire rotates with an angular velocity that is given by $\omega(t) = 4.00$ rad·s^{-1} $-$ $(0.800$ rad·s$^{-3})t^2$.

a) Calculate the average angular acceleration for the time intervals $t = 0$ to $t = 1.00$ s and $t = 0$ to $t = 2.00$ s.

b) Use Eq. (9–5) to calculate the magnitude of the instantaneous angular acceleration at

   i) $t = 1.00$ s;

   ii) $t = 2.00$ s.

In each case, do this by taking $\Delta t = 0.1$ s, 0.01 s, and 0.001 s and then deducing the limiting value.

Section 9–2   Rotation with Constant Angular Acceleration

9–5 Derive Eq. (9–11) by combining Eqs. (9–6) and (9–10) to eliminate t.

9–6 A bicycle wheel has an initial angular velocity of 2.20 rad·s^{-1}. If its angular acceleration is constant and equal to 0.200 rad·s^{-2}, what is its angular velocity after it has turned through 3.50 revolutions?

9–7 A wheel turns with constant angular acceleration 0.640 rad·s^{-2}.

a) How much time does it take to reach an angular velocity of 8.00 rad·s^{-1}, starting from rest?

b) Through how many revolutions does the wheel turn in this time interval?

9–8 An electric motor is turned off, and its angular velocity decreases uniformly from 900 rev·min^{-1} to 400 rev·min^{-1} in 5.00 s.

a) Find the angular acceleration in revolutions per second squared and the number of revolutions made by the motor in the 5.00-s interval.

b) How many more seconds are required for the motor to come to rest if the angular acceleration remains constant at the value calculated in part (a)?

9–9 A circular saw blade 0.60 m in diameter starts from rest and accelerates with constant angular acceleration to an angular velocity of 180 rad·s^{-1} in 4.50 s. Find the angular acceleration and the angle through which the blade has turned.

9–10 A flywheel whose angular acceleration is constant and equal to 3.00 rad·s^{-2} rotates through an angle of 100 rad in 5.00 s. What was the angular velocity of the flywheel at the beginning of the 5.00-s interval?

9–11 A flywheel requires 3.00 s to rotate through 186 rad. Its angular velocity at the end of this time is 108 rad·s^{-1}. Find

a) the angular velocity at the beginning of the 3.00-s interval;

b) the constant angular acceleration.

Section 9–3   Relation between Angular and Linear Velocity and Acceleration

9–12

a) A cylinder 0.150 m in diameter rotates in a lathe at 620 rev·min^{-1}. What is the tangential speed of the surface of the cylinder?

b) The proper tangential speed for machining cast iron is about 0.600 m·s^{-1}. At how many revolutions per minute should a piece of stock 0.0800 m in diameter be rotated in a lathe to produce this tangential speed?

9–13 Find the required angular velocity of an ultracentrifuge in revolutions per minute for the radial acceleration of a point 1.00 cm from the axis to equal $200{,}000g$ (i.e., $200{,}000$ times the acceleration of gravity).

9–14 A wheel rotates with a constant angular velocity of 16.0 rad·s^{-1}.

a) Compute the radial acceleration of a point 0.500 m from the axis, from the relation $a_\perp = \omega^2 r$.

b) Find the tangential speed of the point, and compute its radial acceleration from the relation $a_\perp = v^2/r$.

9–15 A flywheel with a radius of 0.300 m starts from rest and accelerates with constant angular acceleration of 0.750 rad·s^{-2}. Compute the magnitude of the tangential acceleration, the radial acceleration, and the resultant acceleration of a point on its rim

a) at the start;

b) after it has turned through $60°$;

c) after it has turned through $120°$.

9–16 An electric fan blade 3.00 ft in diameter is rotating about a fixed axis with an initial angular velocity of 0.50 rev·s^{-1}. The angular acceleration is 2.00 rev·s^{-2}.

a) Compute the angular velocity after 1.00 s.

b) Through how many revolutions has the blade turned in this time interval?

c) What is the tangential speed of a point on the tip of the blade at $t = 1.00$ s?

d) What is the magnitude of the resultant acceleration of a point on the tip of the blade at time $t = 1.00$ s?

Section 9–4   Kinetic Energy and Moment of Inertia

9–17 Four small spheres, each with a mass of 0.300 kg, are arranged in a square 0.400 m on a side and are connected by light rods, as shown in Fig. 9–23. Find the moment of inertia of the system about an axis

a) through the center of the square, perpendicular to its plane (an axis through point O in the figure);

b) bisecting two opposite sides of the square (an axis along the line AB in the figure).

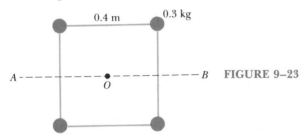

FIGURE 9–23

9–18 Small blocks, each with mass m, are clamped at the ends and at the center of a light rod of length L. Compute the moment of inertia of the system about an axis perpendicular to the rod and passing through a point one third of the length from one end. Neglect the moment of inertia of the light rod.

9–19 Find the moment of inertia of a rod that is 4.00 cm in diameter and 2.00 m long and has a mass of 12.0 kg for the following axes. Use the formulas of Fig. 9–7.

a) About an axis perpendicular to the rod and passing through its center.

b) About an axis perpendicular to the rod and passing through one end.

c) About a longitudinal axis passing through the center of the rod.

9–20 The three objects shown in Fig. 9–24 have equal masses m. Object A is a solid cylinder of radius R. Object B is a hollow, thin cylinder of radius R. Object C is a solid square with length of side $= 2R$. The objects have axes of rotation perpendicular to the page and through the center of mass of each object.

a) Which object has the smallest moment of inertia?

b) Which object has the largest moment of inertia?

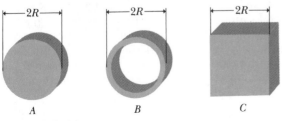

FIGURE 9–24

9–21 A grinding wheel in the shape of a solid disk is 0.200 m in diameter and has a mass of 3.00 kg. The wheel is rotating at 2200 rev·min^{-1} about an axis through its center.

a) What is its kinetic energy?

b) How far would it have to drop in free fall to acquire the same kinetic energy?

9–22 A wagon wheel is constructed as in Fig. 9–25. The radius of the wheel is 0.300 m, and the rim has a mass of 1.20 kg. Each of the four spokes, which lie along a diameter and are 0.600 m long, has a mass of 0.250 kg. What is the moment of inertia of the wheel about an axis through its center and perpendicular to the plane of the wheel? (Use the formulas given in Fig. 9–7.)

FIGURE 9–25

9–23 A light, flexible rope is wrapped several times around a solid cylinder with a weight of 40.0 lb and a radius of 0.750 ft, which rotates without friction about a fixed horizontal axis. The free end of the rope is pulled with a constant force P for a distance of 22.0 ft. What must P be for the final speed of the end of the rope to be 12.0 ft·s^{-1}? (Note that in British units, moment of inertia has units of slugs times feet squared.)

9–24 The flywheel of a gasoline engine is required to give up 300 J of kinetic energy while its angular velocity decreases from 720 rev·min^{-1} to 540 rev·min^{-1}. What moment of inertia is required?

9–25 A light rope is wrapped several times around a large wheel with a radius of 0.400 m, which rotates in frictionless bearings about a stationary horizontal axis, as shown in Fig. 9–9. The free end of the rope is tied to a suitcase with a mass of 15.0 kg. The suitcase is released from rest at a height of 4.00 m above the ground. The suitcase has a speed of 3.50 m·s^{-1} when it reaches the ground. Calculate

a) the angular velocity of the wheel when the suitcase reaches the ground;

b) the moment of inertia I of the wheel.

Section 9–5   Torque

9–26 Forces $F_1 = 8.60$ N and $F_2 = 2.40$ N are applied tangentially to a wheel with a radius of 1.50 m, as shown in Fig. 9–26. What is the net torque on the wheel due to these two forces for an axis perpendicular to the wheel and passing through its center?

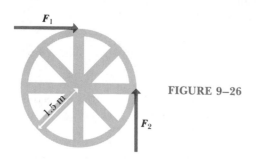

FIGURE 9–26

9–27 Calculate the torque (magnitude and direction) about point O due to the force F in each of the situations sketched in Fig. 9–27. In each case the object to which the force is applied has a length of 4.00 ft and the force $F = 30.0$ lb.

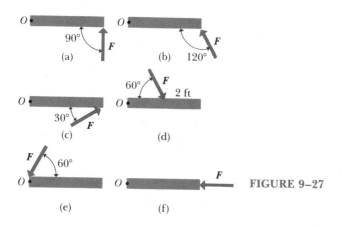

FIGURE 9–27

9–28 Calculate the resultant torque about point O for two forces applied as in Fig. 9–28.

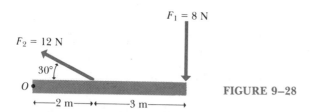

FIGURE 9–28

9–29 A square metal plate 0.180 m on each side is pivoted about an axis through point O at its center and perpendicular to the plate, as shown in Fig. 9–29. Calculate the net torque about this axis due to the three forces shown in the figure if the magnitudes of the forces are $F_1 = 12.0$ N, $F_2 = 16.0$ N, and $F_3 = 18.0$ N.

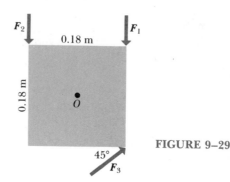

FIGURE 9–29

Section 9–6   Torque and Angular Acceleration

9–30 The flywheel of an engine has moment of inertia 45.0 kg·m².

a) What constant torque is required to bring it up to an angular velocity of 900 rev·min⁻¹ in 10.0 s, starting from rest?

b) What is its final kinetic energy?

9–31 Use the acceleration a calculated in Example 9–6 to determine the speed of the rope after it has been pulled 2.00 m. Compare your result to Example 9–4, in which work and energy considerations are used.

9–32 A grindstone in the shape of a solid disk with a diameter of 0.800 m and a mass of 50.0 kg is rotating at 700 rev·min⁻¹. A tool is pressed against the rim with a normal force of 200 N, and the grindstone comes to rest in 10.0 s. Find the coefficient of kinetic friction between the tool and the grindstone. Neglect friction in the bearings.

9–33 A cord is wrapped around the rim of a flywheel 0.500 m in radius, and a steady pull of 30.0 N is exerted on the cord. The wheel is mounted on frictionless bearings on a horizontal shaft through its center. The moment of inertia of the wheel is 4.00 kg·m². Compute the angular acceleration of the wheel.

9–34 A thin rod with length l and mass M is pivoted about a vertical axis at one end. A force with constant magnitude F is applied to the other end, causing the rod to rotate. The force is maintained perpendicular to the rod and to the axis of rotation. Calculate the angular acceleration α of the rod.

9–35 A bucket of water with a mass of 20.0 kg is suspended by a rope wrapped around a windlass in the form of a solid cylinder 0.400 m in diameter, also with a mass of 20.0 kg. The cylinder is pivoted on a frictionless axle through its center. The bucket is released from rest at the top of a well and falls 20.0 m to the water. Neglect the weight of the rope.

a) What is the tension in the rope while the bucket is falling?

b) With what speed does the bucket strike the water?

c) What is the time of fall?

d) While the bucket is falling, what is the force exerted on the cylinder by the axle?

Section 9–7 Rotation about a Moving Axis

9–36 A string is wrapped several times around the rim of a small hoop with a radius of 0.0800 m and a mass of 0.280 kg. If the free end of the string is held in place and the hoop is released from rest, calculate

a) the tension in the string while the hoop descends as the string unwinds;

b) the time it takes the hoop to descend 0.500 m;

c) the angular velocity of the rotating hoop after it has descended 0.500 m.

9–37 A solid cylinder with a mass of 4.00 kg rolls, without slipping, down a 36.9° slope. Find the acceleration, the friction force, and the minimum coefficient of static friction needed to prevent slipping.

9–38 Repeat part (c) of Exercise 9–36, this time using energy considerations.

Section 9–8 Work and Power in Rotational Motion

9–39 A grindstone in the form of a solid cylinder has a radius of 0.500 m and a mass of 40.0 kg.

a) What torque brings it from rest to an angular velocity of 300 rev·min^{-1} in 10.0 s?

b) Through what angle has it turned during that time?

c) Use Eq. 9–33 to calculate the work done by the torque.

d) What is the grindstone's kinetic energy when it is rotating at 300 rev·min^{-1}? Compare your answer to the result in part (c).

9–40 What is the power output in horsepower of an electric motor turning at 3600 rpm and developing a torque of 4.20 lb·ft?

9–41 A playground merry-go-round has a radius of 4.40 m and a moment of inertia of 245 kg·m^2 and turns with negligible friction about a vertical axle through its center.

a) A child applies a 25.0-N force tangentially to the edge of the merry-go-round for 20.0 s. If the

merry-go-round is initially at rest, what is its angular velocity after this 20.0-s interval?

b) How much work did the child do on the merry-go-round?

c) What is the average power supplied by the child?

9–42 The flywheel of a motor has a mass of 300 kg and a moment of inertia of 580 kg·m^2. The motor develops a constant torque of 2000 N·m, and the flywheel starts from rest.

a) What is the angular acceleration of the flywheel?

b) What is its angular velocity after it makes 4.00 revolutions?

c) How much work is done by the motor during the first 4.00 revolutions?

9–43

a) Compute the torque developed by an airplane engine whose output is 2.40×10^6 W at an angular velocity of 2400 rev·min^{-1}.

b) If a drum of negligible mass, 0.500 m in diameter, were attached to the motor shaft and the power output of the motor were used to raise a weight hanging from a rope wrapped around the drum, how large a weight could be lifted? (Assume that the weight is lifted at constant speed.)

c) With what speed would it rise?

Section 9–9 Angular Momentum and Angular Impulse

9–44 Calculate the angular momentum of a uniform sphere with a radius of 0.120 m and a mass of 14.0 kg if it is rotating about an axis along a diameter at 6.00 rad·s^{-1}.

9–45 What is the angular momentum of the minute hand on a clock about an axis through the center of the clock face if the clock hand has a length of 25.0 cm and a mass of 30.0 g? Take the minute hand to be a slender rod rotating about one end.

9–46 A man with a mass of 70 kg is standing on the rim of a large disk that is rotating at 0.200 rev·s^{-1} about an axis through its center. The disk has a mass of 120 kg and a radius of 4.00 m. Calculate the total angular momentum of the man-plus-disk system. (Assume that the man can be treated as a point.)

9–47 A rock with a mass of 0.800 kg is thrown with speed $v = 12.0$ m·s^{-1}. When it is at point P in Fig. 9–30, what is its angular momentum relative to point O? Assume that the rock travels in a straight line with constant speed.

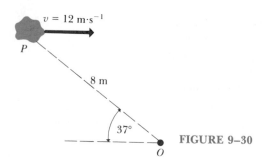

FIGURE 9–30

9–48 A solid wood door 1.00 m wide and 2.00 m high is hinged along one side and has a total mass of 35.0 kg. Initially open and at rest, the door is struck with a hammer at its center. During the blow, an average force of 2000 N acts for 5.00×10^{-3} s. Find the angular velocity of the door after the impact.

Section 9–10 Conservation of Angular Momentum

9–49 On an old-fashioned rotating piano stool, a woman sits holding a pair of dumbbells at a distance of 0.60 m from the axis of rotation of the stool. She is given an angular velocity of 3.00 rad·s^{-1}, after which she pulls the dumbbells in until they are only 0.20 m distant from the axis. The woman's moment of inertia about the axis of rotation is 5.00 kg·m^2 and may be considered constant. Each dumbbell has a mass of 5.00 kg and may be considered a point mass. Neglect friction.

a) What is the initial angular momentum of the system?

b) What is the angular velocity of the system after the dumbbells are pulled in toward the axis?

c) Compute the kinetic energy of the system before and after the dumbbells are pulled in. Account for the difference, if any.

9–50 The outstretched arms of a figure skater preparing for a spin can be considered a slender rod pivoting about an axis through its center. When her arms are brought in and wrapped around her body to execute the spin, they can be considered a thin-walled hollow cylinder. If her original angular velocity is 0.800 rev·s^{-1}, what is her final angular velocity? Her arms have a combined mass of 8.00 kg. When outstretched, they span 1.80 m; when wrapped, they form a cylinder with a radius of 25.0 cm. The moment of inertia of the remainder of the skater's body is constant and equal to 3.00 kg·m^2.

9–51 A puck on a frictionless air-hockey table has a mass of 0.0500 kg and is attached to a cord passing through a hole in the table surface, as in Fig. 9–31. The puck is originally revolving at a distance of 0.300 m from the hole, with an angular velocity of 2.50 rad·s^{-1}. The cord is then pulled from below,

shortening the radius of the circle in which the puck revolves to 0.100 m. The puck may be considered a point mass.

a) What is the new angular velocity?

b) Find the change in kinetic energy of the puck.

c) How much work was done by the person who pulled the cord?

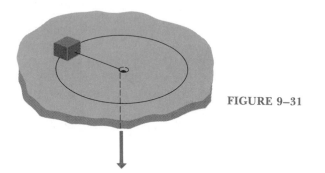

FIGURE 9–31

9–52 In models of stellar evolution, one scenario is for stars to undergo sudden gravitational collapse in which the radius of the star decreases drastically while most of the star's mass is retained. Consider the hypothetical collapse of our sun. Data is given in Appendix F. The present period of rotation of the sun on its axis is 25.0 days. If the sun undergoes gravitational collapse to a new radius of 42.0 km (about 26 mi) while keeping its present mass, calculate its new revolution rate in revolutions per second. (This illustrates one possible model for the formation of pulsars.)

9–53 A turntable rotates about a fixed vertical axis, making one revolution in 6.00 s. The moment of inertia of the turntable about this axis is 1200 kg·m^2. A man with a mass of 80.0 kg, initially standing at the center of the turntable, runs out along a radius. What is the angular velocity of the turntable when the man is 2.00 m from the center? (Assume that the man can be treated as a point.)

9–54 A large wooden turntable in the shape of a flat disk has a radius of 2.00 m and a total mass of 120 kg. The turntable is initially rotating about a vertical axis through its center with an angular velocity of 2.60 rad·s^{-1}. From a very small height a bag of sand with a mass of 100 kg is dropped vertically onto the turntable at a point near the outer edge.

a) Find the angular velocity of the turntable after the sandbag is dropped. (Assume that the bag of sand can be treated as a point mass.)

b) Compute the kinetic energy of the system before and after the sandbag is dropped. Why are these kinetic energies not equal?

9–55 The door in Exercise 9–48 is struck at its center by a handful of sticky mud with a mass of 0.500 kg traveling 14.0 m·s^{-1} just before impact. Find the final angular velocity of the door.

Section 9–11 Vector Representation of Angular Quantities

9–56 The stabilizing gyroscope of a ship is a solid disk with a mass of 50,000 kg; its radius is 2.00 m, and it rotates about a vertical axis with an angular velocity of 900 rev·min^{-1}.

a) How much time is required to bring it up to speed, starting from rest, with a constant power input of 5.20×10^4 W?

b) Find the torque needed to cause the axis to precess in a vertical fore-and-aft plane at the rate of 1.00°·s^{-1}.

9–57 The mass of the rotor of a toy gyroscope is 0.150 kg, and its moment of inertia about its axis is 1.50×10^{-4} kg·m^2. The mass of the frame is 0.0300 kg. The gyroscope is supported on a single pivot, as in Fig. 9–32, with its center of mass a horizontal distance 5.00 cm from the pivot. The gyroscope is precessing in

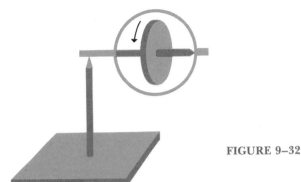

FIGURE 9–32

a horizontal plane at the rate of one revolution in 6.00 s.

a) Find the upward force exerted by the pivot.

b) Find the angular velocity with which the rotor is spinning about its axis, expressed in revolutions per minute.

c) Copy the diagram, and show by vectors the angular momentum of the rotor and the torque acting on it.

Problems

9–58 A 20.0-g weight is attached to the free end of a 1.60-m piece of string that is attached to the ceiling. The weight is pulled to one side so that the string makes a 45.0° angle with the vertical and is then released. What is the angular velocity of the weight when its angular acceleration is zero?

9–59

a) Prove that when a body starts from rest and rotates about a fixed axis with constant angular acceleration, the radial acceleration of a point in the body is directly proportional to its angular displacement.

b) Through what angle has the body turned at the instant when the resultant acceleration of a point makes an angle of 30.0° with the radial direction?

9–60 A meter stick with a mass of 0.200 kg is pivoted about one end so that it can rotate without friction about a horizontal axis. The meter stick is held in a horizontal position and released. As it swings through the vertical, calculate

a) the angular velocity of the stick;

b) the linear speed of the end of the stick opposite the axis.

c) Compare the answer in part (b) to the speed of a particle that has fallen 1.00 m, starting from rest.

9–61 A solid uniform disk with mass m and radius R is pivoted about a horizontal axis through its center, and a small object with mass m is attached to the rim of the disk. If the disk is released from rest with the small object at the end of a horizontal radius, find the angular velocity when the small object is at the bottom.

9–62 A magazine article described a passenger bus in Zurich, Switzerland, that derived its motive power from the energy stored in a large flywheel. The wheel was brought up to speed periodically, when the bus stopped at a station, by an electric motor, which could then be attached to the electric power lines. The flywheel was a solid cylinder with a mass of 1000 kg and a diameter of 1.80 m; its top angular velocity was 3000 rev·min^{-1}.

a) At this angular velocity, what is the kinetic energy of the flywheel?

b) If the average power required to operate the bus is 1.86×10^4 W, how long can it operate between stops?

9–63 The flywheel of a punch press has a moment of inertia of 25.0 kg·m^2 and runs at 400 rev·min^{-1}. The flywheel supplies all the energy needed in a quick punching operation.

a) Find the speed in revolutions per minute to which

the flywheel will be reduced by a sudden punching operation requiring 4000 J of work.

b) What must be the constant power supply to the flywheel (in watts) to bring it back to its initial speed in a time of 8.00 s?

9–64 Consider the system sketched in Fig. 9–33. The pulley has a radius of 0.200 m and a moment of inertia of 0.480 kg·m². The rope does not slip on the pulley rim. Use energy methods to calculate the speed of the 4.00-kg block just before it strikes the floor.

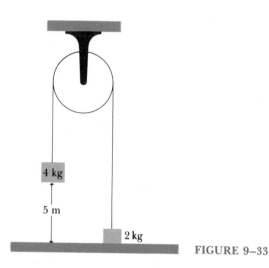

4 kg

5 m

2 kg

FIGURE 9–33

9–65 Consider the system sketched in Fig. 9–34. The pulley has radius R and moment of inertia I. The rope does not slip over the pulley. The coefficient of kinetic friction between block A and the tabletop is μ_k. The system is released from rest, and block B descends. Use energy methods to calculate the speed of block B as a function of the distance d that it has descended.

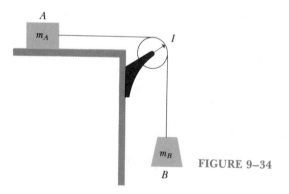

A

m_A

I

m_B

B

FIGURE 9–34

9–66 A constant torque equal to 25.0 N·m is exerted on a pivoted wheel for 12.0 s, during which time the angular velocity of the wheel increases from zero to 100 rev·min⁻¹. The external torque is then removed, and the wheel is brought to rest by friction in its bear-

ings in 100 s. Compute

a) the moment of inertia of the wheel;

b) the magnitude of the friction torque;

c) the total number of revolutions made by the wheel during the entire 112-s time interval.

9–67 A 60.0-kg grindstone is 0.750 m in diameter and has a moment of inertia of 18.0 kg·m². A tool is pressed down on the rim with a normal force of 50.0 N. The coefficient of kinetic friction between the tool and the stone is 0.60, and there is constant friction torque 5.00 N·m between the axle of the stone and its bearings.

a) How much force must be applied normally at the end of a crank handle 0.500 m long to bring the stone from rest to 120 rev·min⁻¹ in 9.00 s?

b) After the grindstone attains an angular velocity of 120 rev·min⁻¹, what normal force is needed at the end of the handle to maintain a constant angular velocity of 120 rev·min⁻¹?

c) How long will it take the grindstone to come from 120 rev·min⁻¹ to rest if it is acted on by the axle friction alone?

9–68 A flywheel 1.00 m in diameter is pivoted on a horizontal axis. A rope is wrapped around the outside of the flywheel, and a steady pull of 50.0 N is exerted on the rope. The flywheel starts from rest, and 10.0 m of rope are unwound in 6.00 s.

a) What is the angular acceleration of the flywheel?

b) What is its final angular velocity?

c) What is its final kinetic energy?

d) What is its moment of inertia?

9–69 Dirk the Dragonslayer is exploring a castle. He is spotted by a dragon, who chases him down a hallway. Dirk runs into a room and attempts to swing the heavy door shut before the dragon gets him. The door is initially perpendicular to the wall, so it must be turned through 90° to close. The door is 3.00 m tall and 1.00 m wide, and it weighs 850 N. The friction at the hinges can be neglected. If Dirk applies a force of 180 N at the edge of the door and perpendicular to it, how much time does it take him to close the door?

9–70 A block with mass $m = 5.00$ kg slides down a surface inclined 37.0° to the horizontal, as shown in Fig. 9–35. The coefficient of kinetic friction is 0.25. A string attached to the block is wrapped around a flywheel on a fixed axis at O. The flywheel has a mass $M = 20.0$ kg, and outer radius $R = 0.200$ m, and a moment of inertia with respect to the axis of 0.400 kg·m².

a) What is the acceleration of the block down the plane?

b) What is the tension in the string?

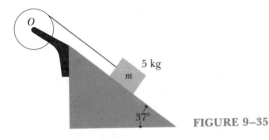

FIGURE 9–35

9–71 Figure 9–36 represents an Atwood's machine. Find the linear accelerations of blocks A and B, the angular acceleration of the wheel C, and the tension in each side of the cord if there is no slipping between the cord and the surface of the wheel. Let the masses of the blocks A and B be 4.00 kg and 2.00 kg, respectively; the moment of inertia of the wheel about its axis be 0.300 kg·m²; and the radius of the wheel be 0.120 m.

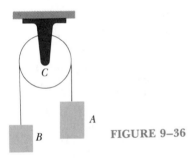

FIGURE 9–36

9–72 A yo-yo is made from two uniform disks, each with mass m and radius R, connected by a light axle of radius b. A string is wound several times around the axle, and then its end is held stationary while the yo-yo is released from rest, dropping as the string unwinds. Find the acceleration of the yo-yo and the tension in the string.

9–73 A lawn roller in the form of a thin-walled hollow cylinder with mass M is pulled horizontally with a constant force F applied by a handle attached to the axle. If it rolls without slipping, find the acceleration and the frictional force.

9–74 A uniform rod with a mass of 0.0300 kg and a length of 0.400 m rotates freely in a horizontal plane about a fixed axis through its center and perpendicular to the rod. Two small objects, each with a mass of 0.0200 kg, are mounted so that they can slide along the rod. They are initially held by catches at positions 0.0500 m on each side of the center of the rod, and the system is rotating at 45.0 rev·min⁻¹. Without otherwise changing the system, the catches are released, and the masses slide outward along the rod and fly off at the ends.

a) What is the angular velocity of the system at the instant when the small masses reach the ends of the rod?

b) What is the angular velocity of the rod after the small masses leave it?

9–75 A solid disk is rolling without slipping on a level surface at a constant speed of 4.00 m·s⁻¹. How far can it roll up a 30.0° ramp before it stops?

9–76 A small block with a mass of 0.800 kg is attached to a cord passing through a hole in a frictionless horizontal surface. The block is originally revolving in a circle with a radius of 0.500 m about the hole, with a tangential speed of 4.00 m·s⁻¹. The cord is then pulled slowly from below, shortening the radius of the circle in which the block revolves. The breaking strength of the cord is 600 N. What is the radius of the circle when the cord breaks?

9–77 Figure 9–37 shows part of a "fly-ball" governor, a speed-controlling device used in old-fashioned steam engines. Each of the steel balls A and B has a mass of 0.200 kg and is rotating about the vertical axis with an angular velocity of 4.00 rad·s⁻¹ at a distance 0.150 m from the axis. Collar C is now forced down until the balls are at a distance 0.0500 m from the axis. How much work must be done to move the collar down?

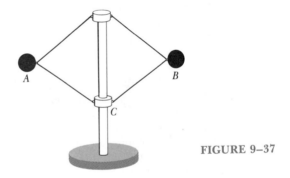

FIGURE 9–37

9–78 A man with a mass of 60.0 kg runs around the edge of a horizontal turntable that is mounted on a frictionless vertical axis through its center. The velocity of the man, relative to the earth, has a magnitude of 3.00 m·s⁻¹. The turntable is rotating in the opposite direction with an angular velocity of magnitude 0.200 rad·s⁻¹ relative to the earth. The radius of the turntable is 2.00 m, and its moment of inertia about the axis of rotation is 400 kg·m². Find the final angular velocity of the system if the man comes to rest, relative to the turntable.

9–79 Disks A and B are mounted on a shaft SS and may be connected or disconnected by a clutch C, as in Fig. 9–38. The moment of inertia of disk A is one half that of disk B. With the clutch disconnected, A is brought up to an angular velocity ω_0. The accelerating

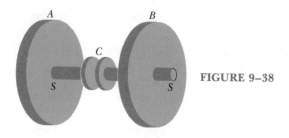

A B

C

S S

FIGURE 9–38

torque is then removed from A, and A is coupled to disk B by the clutch. (Bearing friction may be neglected.) It is found that 3000 J of heat are developed

in the clutch when the connection is made. What was the original kinetic energy of disk A?

9–80 The moment of inertia of the front wheel of a bicycle about its axle is 0.220 kg·m², its radius is 0.360 m, and the forward speed of the bicycle is 5.00 m·s⁻¹. With what angular velocity must the front wheel be turned about a vertical axis to counteract the capsizing torque due to a mass of 60.0 kg, 0.040 m horizontally to the right or left of the line of contact of wheels and ground? (Bicycle riders: Compare your own experience to see whether your answer seems reasonable.)

■ *Challenge Problems*

9–81 The moment of inertia of a sphere with uniform density is $\frac{2}{5}MR^2 = 0.4000MR^2$ (Fig. 9–7). Recent satellite observations show the earth's moment of inertia to be $0.3308MR^2$. The earth has a mantle and a core. The average density (mass per unit volume) of the core is approximately 11.0×10^3 kg·m⁻³; the mantle's average density is 5.00×10^3 kg·m⁻³. The mantle occurs from the earth's surface to a depth of 3600 km, and the remainder is core. For this two-part model of the earth, what is the earth's moment of inertia? Express your answer in terms of M and R as above.

9–82 A demonstration gyroscope wheel is constructed by removing the tire from a bicycle wheel 0.70 m in diameter, wrapping lead wire around the rim, and taping it in place. The shaft projects 0.15 m at each side of the wheel, and a man holds the ends of the shaft in his hands. The mass of the system is 8.00 kg; its entire mass may be assumed to be located at its rim. The shaft is horizontal, and the wheel is spinning about the shaft at 5.00 rev·s⁻¹. Find the magnitude and direction of the force each hand exerts on the shaft

a) when the shaft is at rest;

b) when the shaft is rotating in a horizontal plane about its center at 0.040 rev·s⁻¹;

c) when the shaft is rotating in a horizontal plane about its center at 0.200 rev·s⁻¹.

d) At what rate must the shaft rotate in order that it may be supported at one end only?

9–83 A target in a shooting gallery consists of a vertical square wooden board, 0.200 m on a side and with a mass of 2.50 kg, that is pivoted on an axis along its top edge. The board is struck at the center by a bullet with a mass of 5.00 g that is traveling at 300 m·s⁻¹.

a) What is the angular velocity of the board just after the bullet's impact?

b) What maximum height above the equilibrium position does the center of the board reach before starting to swing down again?

c) What bullet speed would be required for the board to swing all the way over after impact?

9–84 When an object is rolling without slipping, the rolling friction force is much less than the friction force when the object is sliding; a silver dollar will roll on its edge much farther than it will slide on its flat side. (See Section 5–2.) When an object is rolling without slipping on a horizontal surface, one can therefore take the friction force to be zero so that a and α are approximately zero and v and ω are approximately constant. Rolling without slipping means that $v = r\omega$ and $a = r\alpha$. If an object is set into motion on a surface *without* these equalities, sliding (kinetic) friction will act on the object as it slips until rolling without slipping is established. A solid cylinder with mass M and radius R, rotating with angular velocity ω_0 about an axis through its center, is set on a horizontal surface for which the kinetic friction coefficient is μ_k.

a) Draw a free-body force diagram for the cylinder on the surface. Think carefully about the direction of the kinetic friction force on the cylinder. Calculate the accelerations a of the center of mass (CM) and α of rotation about the CM.

b) The cylinder is initially slipping completely, as initially $\omega = \omega_0$ but $v = 0$. Rolling without slipping sets in when $v = R\omega$. Calculate the *distance* the cylinder rolls before slipping stops.

c) Calculate the work done by the friction force on the cylinder as it moves from where it was set down to where it begins to roll without slipping.

10

Equilibrium of a Rigid Body

In Chapter 5 we discussed equilibrium of bodies that can be modeled as *particles*. A particle is in equilibrium whenever the vector sum of the forces acting on it is zero. Now that we have learned the basic principles of rotational dynamics, we can return to the subject of equilibrium to study the more general problem of equilibrium of a rigid body. For such a body, there is a second condition for equilibrium; the sum of the *torques* about any axis must also be zero in order for the body not to have any tendency to rotate. Often one of the forces acting on a rigid body is its weight; we show how to compute the torque due to the weight of a body, using the concept of center of mass from Section 8–5 and the related concept of center of gravity, which we introduce in this chapter.

10–1
The Second Condition for Equilibrium

We learned in Section 5–3 that for a particle acted on by several forces to be in equilibrium, the vector sum of the forces acting on the particle must be zero, $\Sigma F = 0$. This is often called the **first condition for equilibrium.** In terms of components,

$$\sum F_x = 0, \qquad \sum F_y = 0. \tag{10–1}$$

For a rigid body there is a **second condition for equilibrium:**

The sum of the torques of all forces acting on the body, with respect to any specified axis, must be zero.

This condition is needed so that the body has no tendency to begin to *rotate.* The body doesn't actually have to be pivoted about the axis chosen. If a rigid body is in equilibrium, it can't have any tendency to rotate about *any* axis; thus the sum of torques must be zero, *no matter what axis is chosen.*

$$\sum \Gamma = 0 \quad about \; any \; axis. \tag{10–2}$$

Although the choice of axis is arbitrary, we must use the *same* axis to calculate all of the torques. An important element of problem-solving strategy is to pick the axis or axes so as to simplify the calculations as much as possible.

The second condition for equilibrium is based on the dynamics of rotational motion in exactly the same way that the first condition is based on Newton's first law. For a rigid body at rest to remain at rest, it must have no angular acceleration about any axis, so the sum of torques with respect to every axis must be zero. Note that the term *equilibrium* is used here in a more restricted sense than it was for particles. A particle in uniform motion (constant velocity) is in equilibrium. Uniform rotational motion of a rigid body is *not* an equilibrium state because the individual particles in the body have accelerations. However, a rigid body in uniform *translational* motion (without rotation) *is* in equilibrium.

10–2
Center of Gravity

In many equilibrium problems, one of the forces acting on the body is its *weight.* We need to be able to calculate the *torque* of this force with respect to any axis. The problem is that the weight does not act at a single point but is distributed over the entire body. However, we are going to prove that we can always calculate the torque due to the body's weight by assuming that the entire force of gravity (weight) is concentrated at the **center of mass** of the body, which in this context is also called the **center of gravity.** We mentioned this result without proof in Section 9–5, and now we return for a detailed proof.

We assume throughout this discussion that the body is in a *uniform* gravitational field, that is, that the acceleration due to gravity g has the

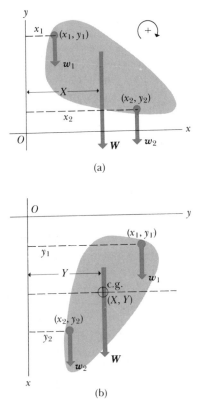

10–1
The body's weight **W** is the resultant of a large number of parallel forces. The line of action of **W** always passes through the center of gravity.

same magnitude and direction at every point in the body. Every particle in the body experiences a gravitational force, and the total weight of the body is the vector sum (resultant) of a large number of parallel forces.

Let's consider the gravitational torque on a flat body of arbitrary shape in the xy-plane, as shown in Fig. 10–1a. We imagine the body as made up of a large number of small particles with weights $w_1, w_2, \cdots,$ with coordinates $(x_1, y_1), (x_2, y_2), \cdots$. The total weight W of the body is

$$W = w_1 + w_2 + \cdots = \sum w.$$

The direction of each gravitational force (the weight of a particle) is straight down, that is, in the $-y$-direction. Each particle's weight also contributes to the total *torque* acting on the body. Computing torques about point O, we see that the torque Γ_1 associated with particle 1 is $\Gamma_1 = w_1 x_1$, the torque for particle 2 is $\Gamma_2 = w_2 x_2$, and so on and that the total torque is

$$\sum \Gamma = \Gamma_1 + \Gamma_2 + \cdots = w_1 x_1 + w_2 x_2 + \cdots = \sum wx.$$

For convenience we are taking *clockwise* torques to be positive; this is opposite to the convention we often used in Chapter 9.

We now ask: Where must we consider the total weight W to act in order for its torque to equal the above expression? Suppose it acts along a line at a distance X to the right of the origin, so its torque is WX. Then X must satisfy the equation

$$w_1 x_1 + w_2 x_2 + \cdots = WX,$$

or

$$X = \frac{w_1 x_1 + w_2 x_2 + \cdots}{w_1 + w_2 + \cdots} = \frac{\sum wx}{\sum w} = \frac{\sum wx}{W}. \qquad (10\text{–}3)$$

We get the correct torque if we assume that the total weight acts along a line determined by Eq. (10–3).

Now we rotate the object and the coordinate axes 90° clockwise, so that the gravitational forces are in the $+x$-direction, as shown in Fig. 10–1b. The total weight W is the same as before, but now it must act along a line a distance Y to the right of the origin in Fig. 10–1b, such that $WY = \Sigma wy$, or

$$Y = \frac{w_1 y_1 + w_2 y_2 + \cdots}{w_1 + w_2 + \cdots} = \frac{\sum wy}{\sum w} = \frac{\sum wy}{W}. \qquad (10\text{–}4)$$

The point of intersection of the lines of action of **W** in the two parts of Fig. 10–1 has coordinates (X, Y) and is called the *center of gravity* of the body. The line of action of **W** *always* passes through the center of gravity; the torque of **W** can always be obtained correctly by taking the entire weight **W** of the body to act at the center of gravity.

If we divide numerator and denominator in Eqs. (10–3) and (10–4) by g and use the fact that $w_1 = m_1 g$, and so on, the right sides of these equations become identical to the equations defining the center of mass in Section 8–5, Eqs. (8–18). Thus *the center of gravity of any body is identical to its center of mass.* We note, however, that the definition of center of gravity makes sense only in a uniform gravitational field, where g has the same value everywhere; otherwise, the w's would depend on position.

The center of *mass*, conversely, is defined independently of any gravitational effect.

We can often use symmetry considerations to locate the center of gravity of a body. The center of gravity of a homogeneous sphere, cube, circular disk, or rectangular plate is at its geometric center. The center of gravity of a right circular cylinder or cone is on the axis of symmetry, and so on.

In some cases we can think of a body as being made up of several pieces that individually have some symmetry that lets us determine their individual centers of gravity. Then we can compute the coordinates of the center of gravity of the combination from Eqs. (10–3) and (10–4), letting w_1, w_2, . . . be the weights of the individual pieces and (x_1, y_1), (x_2, y_2), . . . be the coordinates of their centers of gravity.

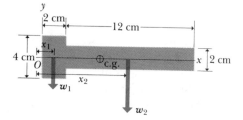

10–2
Machine part for Example 10–1.

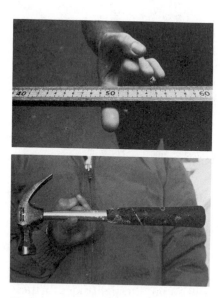

10–3
Locating the center of gravity of a body by balancing. The meter stick balances at its midpoint, but the hammer has a heavy head at one end. (Nancy Rodger, The Exploratorium.)

Example 10–1   Locate the center of gravity of the machine part in Fig. 10–2. The part consists of a disk 4 cm in diameter and 2 cm long attached to a rod 2 cm in diameter and 12 cm long. Both pieces have the same uniform density.

Solution   From symmetry, the center of gravity lies along the axis, and the center of gravity of each part is midway between its ends. The volume of the disk is 8π cm^3, and the volume of the rod is 12π cm^3. Since the weights of the two parts are proportional to their volumes,

$$\frac{w_{\text{disk}}}{w_{\text{rod}}} = \frac{w_1}{w_2} = \frac{8\pi}{12\pi} = \frac{2}{3}, \qquad w_2 = \frac{3}{2}w_1.$$

$$X = \frac{w_1(1 \text{ cm}) + \frac{3}{2}w_1 \,(8 \text{ cm})}{w_1 + \frac{3}{2}w_1} = 5.2 \text{ cm}.$$

The center of gravity is on the axis, 5.2 cm to the right of O.

The center of gravity (center of mass) has several other important properties. First, when a body is in equilibrium in a gravitational field, supported or suspended at a single point, the center of gravity is always directly above or below the point of suspension. If it were anywhere else, the weight would have a torque with respect to this point, and the body could not be in rotational equilibrium. This fact can be used for an experimental determination of the location of the center of gravity of an irregular body. Figure 10–3 shows two examples of locating the center of gravity of a body by finding its balance point.

Second, a force applied to a body at its center of gravity does not tend to cause the body to rotate about an axis through this point, although a force applied at any other point tends to cause both rotational and translational motion. We used this fact implicitly in the examples of Section 9–7.

Third, as we discussed in Section 8–5, the total momentum of a body equals the product of its total mass and its center-of-mass velocity. The acceleration of the center of mass is the same as that of a point mass equal to the total mass of the body, acted on by the resultant external force.   ∎

10–3
Examples

The principles of rigid-body equilibrium are few and simple; the vector sum of the forces on the body must be zero, and the sum of torques about any axis must be zero. The hard part comes when you try to apply these principles to specific problems. Careful and systematic problem-solving methodology always pays off. The following strategy is very similar to the suggestions in Section 5–3 for equilibrium of a particle.

PROBLEM-SOLVING STRATEGY: *Equilibrium of a Rigid Body*

1. Make a sketch of the physical situation, including dimensions.

2. Choose some appropriate body as the body in equilibrium, and draw a free-body diagram showing the forces acting *on* this body and no others. *Do not* include forces exerted *by* this body on other bodies.

3. Draw coordinate axes and specify a positive sense of rotation for torques. Represent forces in terms of their components with respect to the axes you have chosen.

4. Write equations expressing the equilibrium conditions. Remember that $\Sigma F_x = 0$, $\Sigma F_y = 0$, and $\Sigma \Gamma = 0$ are always separate equations; *never* add x- and y-components in a single equation.

5. In choosing an axis to compute torques, note that if a force has a line of action that goes *through* a particular axis, the torque of the force with respect to that axis is zero. You can often eliminate unknown forces or components from the torque equation by a clever choice of axis location. Also remember that when a force is represented in terms of its components, you can compute the torque of that force by finding the torque of each component separately, each with its appropriate moment arm and sign, and adding the results. This is often easier than determining the moment arm of the original force.

6. You always need as many equations as you have unknowns. Depending on the number of unknowns, you may need to compute torques with respect to two or more axes to obtain enough equations. Often, there are several equally good sets of force and torque equations for a particular problem; there is usually no single "right" combination of equations. When you have as many independent equations as unknowns, you can solve the equations simultaneously.

Example 10–2   A hanging flower basket *B* with weight w_2 is hung on a horizontal beam over the edge of a balcony railing, as shown in Fig. 10–4a. The beam rests on the railing and is counterbalanced at its other end by a body with weight w_1. Assuming that the weight of the beam itself is negligible, find the weight w_1 needed to balance the basket, and the total upward force *P* exerted on the beam at point *O*. (This illustrates the principle of *cantilever* construction, by which decks, stairways, and the like can be built over empty space, supported entirely from one side.)

Solution   Figure 10–4b is a free-body diagram for the beam. The first condition for equilibrium ($\Sigma F_y = 0$) gives

$$\sum F_y = P - w_1 - w_2 = 0.$$

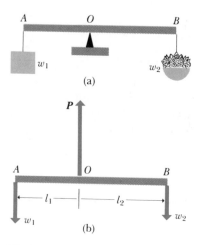

(a)

(b)

10–4
A flower basket cantilevered out over a balcony railing.

Now let's take torques about an axis through O, perpendicular to the diagram; the second condition for equilibrium gives

$$\Sigma \Gamma_O = w_1 l_1 - w_2 l_2 = 0.$$

As an example, suppose that $l_1 = 1.2$ m, $l_2 = 1.6$ m, and $w_2 = 15$ N. From the equations above,

$$w_1 = 20 \text{ N}, \qquad P = 35 \text{ N}.$$

To emphasize the point that the total torque about *any* axis is zero, let's compute torques about an axis through point A:

$$\Sigma \Gamma_A = P l_1 - w_2 (l_1 + l_2)$$
$$= (35 \text{ N})(1.2 \text{ m}) - (15 \text{ N})(2.8 \text{ m}) = 0.$$

The point that we use to compute torques doesn't even have to lie on the rod. To verify this, try calculating the total torque about a point 0.4 m to the left of A and 0.4 m above it. ■

Example 10–3   The ladder in Fig. 10–5a is 10 m long and has a weight of 400 N, with the center of gravity at its center. It leans in equilibrium against a vertical frictionless wall and makes an angle of 53.1° with the horizontal (conveniently forming a 3-4-5 right triangle). Find the magnitudes and directions of the forces F_1 and F_2 in Fig. 10–5b.

Solution   Figure 10–5b shows a free-body diagram. If the wall is frictionless, F_1 is horizontal. The direction of F_2 is unknown; except in special cases, its direction does *not* lie along the ladder. We represent the force F_2 in terms of its (unknown) x- and y-components; then later we can compute the magnitude and direction of F_2. Note that F_{2x} and F_{2y} are the friction and normal components, respectively, of the contact force on the

10–5
(a) A ladder in equilibrium leaning against a frictionless wall. (b) Free-body diagram for the ladder. The force at the base is represented in terms of its x- and y-components.

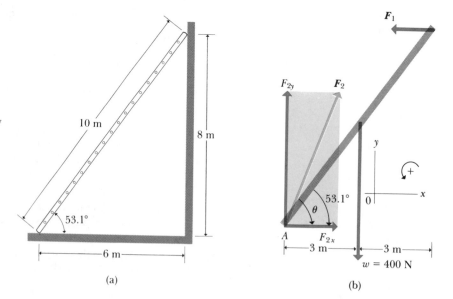

(a)

(b)

ladder at its base. The first condition of equilibrium leads to the equations

$$\sum F_x = F_{2x} - F_1 = 0,$$
$$\sum F_y = F_{2y} - 400 \text{ N} = 0.$$

In applying the second condition for equilibrium we are free to choose an axis through *any* point to compute torques. The equation is simplest if we choose a point that lies on the lines of action of two or more forces because then these forces do not appear in the torque equation. Therefore a logical choice is an axis through point A; the corresponding torque equation is

$$\sum \Gamma_A = F_1(8 \text{ m}) - (400 \text{ N})(3 \text{ m}) = 0.$$

From the second equation above, $F_{2y} = 400$ N, and from the third,

$$F_1 = \frac{1200 \text{ N·m}}{8 \text{ m}} = 150 \text{ N}.$$

Then, from the first equation,

$$F_{2x} = 150 \text{ N}.$$

Hence

$$F_2 = \sqrt{(400 \text{ N})^2 + (150 \text{ N})^2} = 427 \text{ N},$$

$$\theta = \arctan \frac{400 \text{ N}}{150 \text{ N}} = 69.4°.$$

Note that the direction of the force at the base of the ladder is *not* along the length of the ladder. In fact, if you consider torques about the *top* of the ladder, you can see that F_2 must have a torque about this point, so it *cannot* lie along the length of the ladder. ■

Example 10–4 Figure 10–6a shows a human arm lifting a dumbbell, and Fig. 10–6b is a free-body diagram for the forearm, showing the forces involved. The forearm is in equilibrium under the action of the weight w of the dumbbell, the tension T in the tendon connected to the biceps muscle, and the forces exerted on the forearm by the upper arm at the elbow joint. For clarity the tendon force has been displaced away from the elbow farther than its actual position. The weight w and the angle θ are given; we want to find the tendon tension and the two components of force at the elbow (three unknown scalar quantities in all).

Solution First we represent the tendon force in terms of its components T_x and T_y, using the given angle θ and the unknown magnitude T:

$$T_x = T \cos \theta, \qquad T_y = T \sin \theta.$$

We also represent the force at the elbow in terms of its components E_x and E_y. We don't need to know at the beginning whether these are positive or negative. They could come out either way. Next we note that if we take torques about the elbow joint, the resulting torque equation does

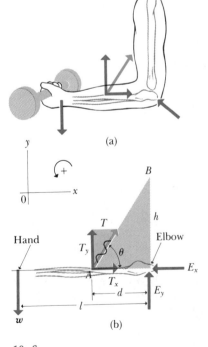

(a)

(b)

10–6
Force diagrams for a human forearm.

not contain E_x, E_y, or T_x because the lines of action of all these forces pass through this point. The torque equation is then simply

$$lw - dT_y = 0.$$

From this we find

$$T_y = \frac{lw}{d} \quad \text{and} \quad T = \frac{lw}{d \sin \theta}.$$

To find E_x and E_y, we could now use the first conditions for equilibrium, $\Sigma F_x = 0$ and $\Sigma F_y = 0$. Instead, for added practice in using torques, we take torques about the point A where the tendon is attached:

$$(l - d)w + dE_y = 0 \quad \text{and} \quad E_y = -\frac{(l - d)w}{d}.$$

The negative sign shows that our initial guess for the direction of E_y was wrong; it is actually vertically *downward*.

Finally, we take torques about point B in the figure:

$$lw - hE_x = 0 \quad \text{and} \quad E_x = \frac{lw}{h}.$$

Please notice how much we have simplified these calculations by using a little ingenuity in choosing the point for calculating torques so as to eliminate one or more of the unknown quantities. In the last step, the force T has no torque about point B; thus when the torques of T_x and T_y are computed separately, they must add to zero. We invite you to check out this statement.

As a specific example, suppose $w = 50$ N, $d = 0.10$ m, $l = 0.50$ m, and $\theta = 80°$. Then $\tan \theta = h/d$, and we find

$$h = d \tan \theta = (0.10 \text{ m})(5.67) = 0.57 \text{ m}.$$

From the previous general results we find

$$T = \frac{(0.50 \text{ m})(50 \text{ N})}{(0.10 \text{ m})(0.98)} = 255 \text{ N},$$

$$E_y = -\frac{(0.50 \text{ m} - 0.10 \text{ m})(50 \text{ N})}{0.10 \text{ m}} = -200 \text{ N},$$

$$E_x = \frac{(0.50 \text{ m})(50 \text{ N})}{0.57 \text{ m}} = 44.1 \text{ N}.$$

The magnitude of the force at the elbow is

$$E = \sqrt{E_x^2 + E_y^2} = 205 \text{ N}.$$

As was mentioned above, we have not explicitly used the first condition for equilibrium, that the vector sum of the forces be zero. As a check, compute ΣF_x and ΣF_y to verify that they really *are* zero. Consistency checks are always a good idea! ∎

10-4
Couples

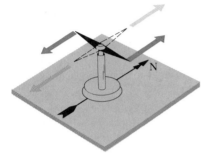

10-7
Forces on the poles of a compass needle.

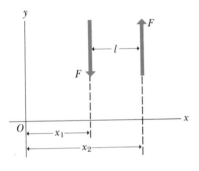

10-8
Two equal and opposite forces having different lines of action are called a *couple*. The torque of the couple is the same about all points and is equal to *Fl*.

Sometimes the forces on a body include two forces with equal magnitude and opposite direction, with lines of action that are parallel but do not coincide. Such a pair of forces is called a **couple.** A common example is a compass needle in the earth's magnetic field, as shown in Fig. 10–7. The north and south poles of the needle are acted on by equal forces, one toward the north and the other toward the south. Except when the needle points in the N–S direction, the two forces do not have the same line of action.

Figure 10–8 shows a couple consisting of two forces, each with magnitude F, separated by a perpendicular distance l. The vector sum of the forces is zero, so this pair of forces has no effect in producing translation (as a whole) of the body on which it acts. The only effect of a couple is to produce rotation.

The total torque of the couple in Fig. 10–8 about an arbitrary point O is

$$\sum \Gamma_0 = x_2 F - x_1 F$$
$$= (x_1 + l)F - x_1 F$$
$$= lF. \qquad (10-5)$$

The distances x_1 and x_2 do not appear in the result, and we conclude that *the torque of a couple is the same about all points in the plane of the forces and is equal to the product of the magnitude of either force and the perpendicular distance between their lines of action.*

A plumber tightening a pipe fitting uses the principle of the couple. The plumber applies a force to the end of the wrench handle and holds the pipe close to the fitting with the free hand, exerting an opposite force. Thus there is no net force sideways on the pipe, which would put a strain on the opposite end, but only a torque tending to screw the two parts together.

Questions

10-1 Mechanics sometimes extend the length of a wrench handle by slipping a section of pipe over the handle. Why is this a dangerous procedure?

10-2 Manuals for car-engine repair always specify the *torque* (moment) to be applied when tightening the cylinder-head bolts. Why is torque specified, rather than the *force* to be applied to the wrench handle?

10-3 Car tires are sometimes "balanced" on a machine that pivots the tire and wheel about the center, by laying weights around the wheel rim until it does not tip

from the horizontal plane. Discuss this procedure in terms of the center of gravity.

10-4 Is it possible for a solid body to have no matter at its center of gravity? Consider, for example, a disk with a hole in the center, an empty bottle, and a hollow cylinder.

10-5 A man climbs a tall, old stepladder that has a tendency to sway. He feels much more unstable when standing near the top than when near the bottom. Why?

10–6 What determines whether a body in equilibrium is stable or unstable? As an example, discuss a cone resting on its base on a horizontal floor; a cone balanced on its point; and a cone lying on its side.

10–7 When a heavy load is placed in the back end of a truck, behind the rear wheels, the effect is to *raise* the front end of the truck. Why?

10–8 When a tall, heavy object, such as a refrigerator, is pushed across a rough floor, what determines whether it slides or tips?

10–9 Why is a tapered water glass with a narrow base easier to tip over than one with straight sides? Does it matter whether the glass is full or empty?

10–10 People sometimes prop open a door by wedging some object in the space between the hinged side of the door and the frame. Explain why this often results in the hinge screws being ripped out.

10–11 Discuss the action of a claw hammer in pulling out nails, in terms of torques.

10–12 In trying to lift an object that is much too heavy to be lifted directly, one often speaks of the importance of "leverage." Discuss this term in relation to moments, and explain how it is related to the concept of leverage in trading stock options and other securities.

10–13 Why is it easier to hold a 10-kg body in your hand at your side than to hold it with your arm extended horizontally?

10–14 In pioneer days, when a Conestoga wagon was stuck in the mud, a person would grasp a wheel spoke and try to turn the wheel, rather than simply pushing the wagon. Why?

10–15 Does the center of gravity of a solid body always lie within the body? If not, give a counterexample.

Exercises

Section 10–2   Center of Gravity

10–1 A ball with radius $r_1 = 0.060$ m and mass $m_1 = 1.00$ kg is attached by a light rod 0.400 m in length to a second ball with radius $r_2 = 0.080$ m and mass $m_2 = 3.00$ kg, as shown in Fig. 10–9. Where is the center of gravity of this system?

0.4 m r_1 m_1 r_2 m_2 FIGURE 10–9

10–2 In Exercise 10–1, suppose the rod is uniform and has a mass of 2.00 kg. Where is the system's center of gravity?

10–3 Three small objects of equal mass are located in the xy-plane at points having coordinates (0.200 m, 0), (0, 0.200 m), and (0.200 m, 0.200 m). Determine the coordinates of the center of gravity.

Section 10–3   Examples

10–4 Two men are carrying a uniform ladder that is 16.0 ft long and weighs 200 lb. If one man applies an upward force equal to 80.0 lb at one end, at what point should the other man lift?

10–5 A heavy electric motor is to be carried by two men by placing it on a light board 2.00 m long. To lift the board with the motor on it, one man must lift at one end with a force of 700 N and the other at the opposite end with a force of 500 N. What is the weight of the motor, and where is its center of gravity located along the board?

10–6 In Exercise 10–5, suppose the board is not light but weighs 300 N, with its center of gravity at its center. The two men each exert the same force as before. What is the weight of the motor in this case, and where is it located?

10–7 A diving board 3.00 m long is supported at a point 1.00 m from the end, and a diver weighing 680 N stands at the free end, as shown in Fig. 10–10. The diving board has uniform cross section and weighs 400 N. Find

a) the force at the support point;

b) the force at the end that is held down.

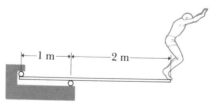

1 m   2 m   FIGURE 10–10

10–8 A uniform trapdoor in the ceiling is hinged at one side; its total weight is 300 N. Find the net upward force needed to begin to open it and the total force exerted on the door by the hinges if

a) the upward force is applied at the center;

b) the upward force is applied at the center of the edge opposite the hinges.

10–9 In Example 10–2, calculate the total torque about a point 0.400 m to the left of A and 0.400 m above it. Show that for the values of w_1 and P calculated in the example, the total torque about this point is zero.

10–10 The horizontal beam in Fig. 10–11 weighs 200 N, and its center of gravity is at its center. Find

a) the tension in the cable;

b) the horizontal and vertical components of the force exerted on the beam at the wall.

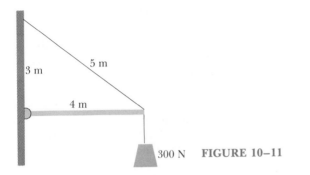

300 N   **FIGURE 10–11**

10–11 Find the tension T in each cable and the magnitude and direction of the force exerted on the strut by the pivot in each of the arrangements in Fig. 10–12. Let the weight of the suspended object in each case be w. Neglect the weight of the strut.

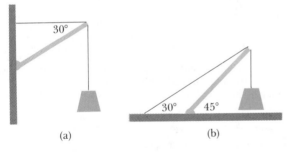

(a)   (b)

FIGURE 10–12

10–12

a) In Example 10–4, show that the torques about point B due to T_x and T_y sum to zero. Do this for the general case rather than for the specific numerical values given at the end of the example.

b) In Example 10–4, show that $\Sigma F_x = 0$ and $\Sigma F_y = 0$. Do this both for the general case and for the specific numerical values given at the end of the example.

10–13 A door 1.00 m wide and 2.50 m high weighs 160 N and is supported by two hinges, one 0.50 m from the top and the other 0.50 m from the bottom.

Each hinge supports half the total weight of the door. Assuming that the door's center of gravity is at its center, find the horizontal components of force exerted on the door by each hinge.

10–14 The boom in Fig. 10–13 is uniform and weighs 3800 N.

a) Find the tension in the guy wire and the horizontal and vertical components of the force exerted on the boom at its lower end.

b) Does the line of action of the force exerted on the boom at its lower end lie along the boom?

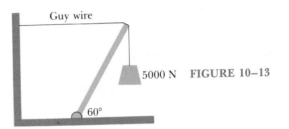

5000 N   **FIGURE 10–13**

Section 10–4   Couples

10–15 Two equal parallel forces of magnitude $F_1 = F_2 = 8$ N are applied to a rod as shown in Fig. 10–14.

a) What should be the distance l between the forces if they are to provide a net torque of 9.00 N·m about the left-hand end of the rod?

b) Is this torque clockwise or counterclockwise?

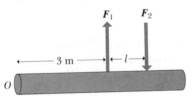

FIGURE 10–14

10–16 Two forces of magnitude $F_1 = F_2 = 5.00$ N are applied to a rod as shown in Fig. 10–15.

a) Calculate the net torque about point O due to these two forces by calculating the torque due to each separate force.

b) Calculate the net torque about point P due to these two forces by calculating the torque due to each separate force.

c) Compare your results to Eq. (10–5).

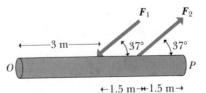

FIGURE 10–15

Problems

10–17 A uniform plank is supported horizontally by a brick at one end and an egg at the other. The plank is 8.00 m long and weighs 60 N, and you weigh 450 N. If a force of 150 N will break the egg, how far from the end of the plank where the brick is can you stand and not break the egg?

10–18

a) In Fig. 10–16 a 6.00-m-long uniform beam is hanging from a point 1.00 m to the right of its center. The beam weighs 50.0 N and makes an angle of 30.0° with the vertical. At the right-hand end of the beam a 100.0-N weight is hung; an unknown weight w hangs at the other end. If the system is in equilibrium, what is w?

b) If the beam makes an angle of 45.0° with the vertical, what is w?

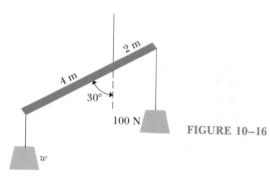

2 m

4 m

30°

100 N

w

FIGURE 10–16

10–19 A uniform plank 15.0 m long, weighing 400 N, rests symmetrically on two supports 8.00 m apart, as shown in Fig. 10–17. A boy weighing 720 N starts at point A and walks toward the right.

a) Construct in the same diagram two graphs showing the upward forces F_A and F_B exerted on the plank at points A and B as functions of the coordinate x of the boy. Let 1 cm = 100 N vertically, and 1 cm = 1.00 m horizontally.

b) From your diagram, how far beyond point B can the boy walk before the plank tips?

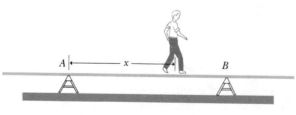

A |← x → B

FIGURE 10–17

c) How far from the right end of the plank should support B be placed so that the boy can walk just to the end of the plank without causing it to tip?

10–20 Your dog Fido is 0.740 m long (nose to hind legs). His fore (front) legs are 0.15 m horizontally from his nose, his center of gravity is 0.15 m horizontally from his hind legs, and he weighs 220 N.

a) How much force does a level floor exert on each of his fore feet, and on each of his hind feet?

b) If Fido picks up a 25-N bone and holds it in his mouth (directly under his nose), what is the force exerted by the floor on each of his fore and each of his hind feet?

10–21 A uniform ladder 10.0 m long, weighing 500 N, leans against a vertical wall, making an angle of 30° with the vertical. A man weighing 800 N climbs up the ladder to a point a vertical distance of 3.00 m above the ground. Where is the center of gravity of the system consisting of the man and the ladder?

10–22 A certain automobile has a wheelbase (distance between front and rear axles) of 2.60 m. If 60.0% of the weight rests on the front wheels, how far behind the front wheels is the center of gravity?

10–23 A horizontal boom 5.00 m long is hinged to a vertical wall at one end, and a 500-N object hangs from its other end. The boom is supported by a guy wire from its outer end to a point on the wall directly above the boom. The weight of the boom can be neglected.

a) If the tension in this wire is not to exceed 1000 N, what is the minimum height above the boom at which it may be fastened to the wall?

b) By how many newtons would the tension be increased if the wire were fastened 0.500 m below this point, if the boom remains horizontal?

10–24 A station wagon weighing 19,600 N has a wheelbase of 3.00 m. Ordinarily, 10,780 N rests on the front wheels and 8820 N on the rear wheels. A box weighing 2500 N is now placed on the tailgate, 1.00 m behind the rear axle. How much total weight now rests on the front wheels? On the rear wheels?

10–25 One end of a meter stick is placed against a vertical wall, as shown in Fig. 10–18. The other end is held by a light cord making an angle θ with the stick. The coefficient of static friction between the end of the meter stick and the wall is 0.40.

a) What is the maximum value the angle θ can have if the stick is to remain in equilibrium?

b) Let the angle θ be 10°. A block of the same weight

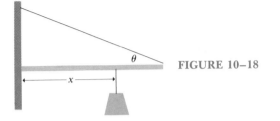

FIGURE 10–18

as the meter stick is suspended from the stick as shown, at a distance x from the wall. What is the minimum value of x for which the stick will remain in equilibrium?

c) When $\theta = 10°$, how large must the coefficient of static friction be so that the block can be attached at the left end of the stick without causing it to slip?

10–26 End A of the bar AB in Fig. 10–19 rests on a frictionless horizontal surface, while end B is hinged. A horizontal force P of magnitude 90.0 N is exerted on end A. Neglect the weight of the bar. What are the horizontal and vertical components of the force exerted by the bar on the hinge at B?

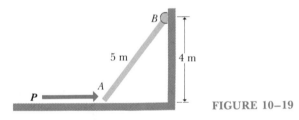

FIGURE 10–19

10–27 A single additional force is to be applied to the bar in Fig. 10–20 to maintain it in equilibrium in the position shown. The weight of the bar can be neglected.

a) What are the horizontal and vertical components of the required force?

b) What is the angle the force must make with the bar?

c) What is the magnitude of the required force?

d) Where should the force be applied?

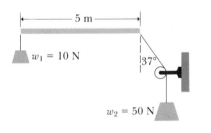

FIGURE 10–20

10–28 A circular disk 0.500 m in diameter, pivoted about a horizontal axis through its center, has a cord wrapped around its rim. The cord passes over a frictionless pulley P and is attached to an object that weighs 240 N. A uniform rod 2.00 m long is fastened to the disk, with one end at the center of the disk. The apparatus is in equilibrium, with the rod horizontal, as shown in Fig. 10–21.

a) What is the weight of the rod?

b) What is the new equilibrium direction of the rod when a second object, weighing 20.0 N is suspended from the other end of the rod, as shown by the broken line? That is, what is then the angle the rod makes with the horizontal?

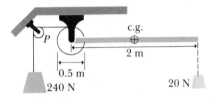

FIGURE 10–21

10–29 A playground equipment company is designing a new swing set with the dimensions shown in Fig. 10–22. For safety the company wants to allow for someone as heavy as 1200 N (about 270 lb) sitting on each of the two seats. Adding an additional safety factor of 30%, they consider the downward force at the top of each end of the swing frame to be 1560 N. At either end, each of the two uniform 3.00-m side pieces weighs 180 N, and they are joined at the top by a frictionless hinge.

a) What vertical force is exerted by the ground on each of the two side pieces?

b) What is the tension in the horizontal rod? (The weight of this rod is negligible.)

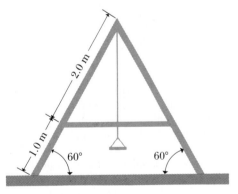

FIGURE 10–22

10–30 A uniform ladder 10.0 m long rests against a frictionless vertical wall with its lower end 6.00 m from the wall. The ladder weighs 400 N. The coefficient of static friction between the foot of the ladder and the ground is 0.40. A man weighing 950 N climbs slowly up the ladder.

a) What is the maximum frictional force that the ground can exert on the ladder at its lower end?

b) What is the actual frictional force when the man has climbed 3.00 m along the ladder?

c) How far along the ladder can the man climb before the ladder starts to slip?

10–31 A roller whose diameter is 1.00 m weighs 520 N. What is the minimum horizontal force necessary to pull the roller over a brick 0.100 m high when the force is applied

a) at the center of the roller?

b) at the top of the roller?

10–32 A gate 4.00 m long and 2.00 m high weighs 300 N. Its center of gravity is at its center, and it is hinged at A and B. To relieve the strain on the top hinge, a wire CD is connected as shown in Fig. 10–23. The tension in CD is increased until the horizontal force at hinge A is zero.

a) What is the tension in the wire CD?

b) What is the magnitude of the horizontal component of the force at hinge B?

c) What is the combined vertical force exerted by hinges A and B?

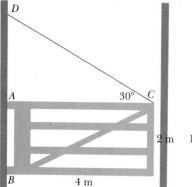

FIGURE 10–23

10–33 You and a friend are carrying a 200-kg crate up a flight of stairs, with you at the lower end. The crate is 2.50 m long and 0.50 m high, and its center of gravity is at its center. The stairs make a 45.0° angle with respect to the floor. The crate is carried also at a 45.0° angle, so its bottom side is parallel to the slope of the stairs, as shown in Fig. 10–24. If the force each of you applies is vertical, what is the magnitude of each of these forces? Is it best to be the person above or below on the stairs?

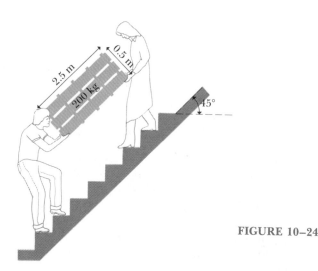

FIGURE 10–24

10–34 The objects in Fig. 10–25 are constructed of uniform wire bent into the shapes shown. Find the position of the center of gravity of each.

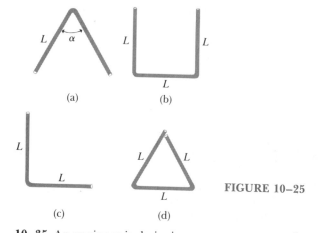

FIGURE 10–25

10–35 An engineer is designing a conveyor system for loading hay bales into a wagon. Each bale has a mass of 25.0 kg and is 0.75 m long, 0.25 m wide, and 0.50 m high. The center of gravity of the bale is at its geometrical center. The coefficient of static friction between a bale and the conveyor belt is 0.30, and the belt moves with constant speed. The situation is shown in Fig. 10–26.

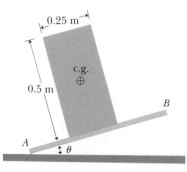

FIGURE 10–26

a) The angle θ of the conveyor is slowly increased. At some critical angle a bale will tip (if it doesn't slip first), and at some different critical angle it will slip (if it doesn't tip first). Find the two critical angles, and determine which is reached first.

b) Would the outcome of part (a) be different if the coefficient of friction were 0.75?

10–36 The hay bale of Problem 10–35 is dragged along a horizontal surface with constant speed by a force **P,** as shown in Fig. 10–27. The coefficient of kinetic friction is 0.30.

a) Find the magnitude of the force **P.**

b) Find the value of h for which the block just begins to tip.

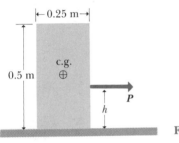

FIGURE 10–27

Challenge Problems

10–38 One end of a post weighing 500 N and with height h rests on a rough horizontal surface with $\mu_s = 0.40$. The upper end is held by a rope fastened to the surface and making an angle of 37.0° with the post, as in Fig. 10–29. A horizontal force **F** is exerted on the post as shown.

a) If the force **F** is applied at the midpoint of the post, what is the largest value it can have without causing the post to slip?

b) How large can the force be, without causing the post to slip, if its point of application is 6/10 of the way from the ground to the top of the post?

c) Show that if the point of application of the force is too high, the post cannot be made to slip, no matter how great the force. Find the critical height for the point of application.

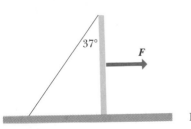

FIGURE 10–29

10–37 A garage door is mounted on an overhead rail, as in Fig. 10–28. The wheels at A and B have rusted so that they do not roll, but rather slide along the track. The coefficient of kinetic friction is 0.40. The distance between the wheels is 2.00 m, and each is 0.50 m in from the vertical sides of the door. The door is uniform and weighs 600 N. It is pushed to the left at constant speed by a horizontal force **P.**

a) If the distance h is 1.50 m, what is the vertical component of the force exerted on each wheel by the track?

b) Find the maximum value that h can have without causing one wheel to leave the track.

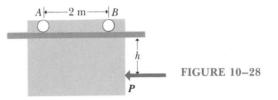

FIGURE 10–28

10–39 Two ladders, 4.00 m and 3.00 m long, respectively, are hinged at point A and tied together by a horizontal rope 0.60 m above the floor, as in Fig. 10–30. The ladders weigh 600 N and 450 N, respectively, and the center of gravity of each is at its center. If the floor is frictionless, find

a) the upward force at the bottom of each ladder;

b) the tension in the rope;

c) the magnitude of the force one ladder exerts on the other at point A.

d) If a load of 1000 N is now suspended from point A, find the tension in the horizontal rope.

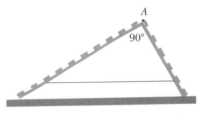

FIGURE 10–30

10–40 A bookcase weighing 1100 N rests on a horizontal surface for which the coefficient of static friction is $\mu_s = 0.35$. The bookcase is 1.80 m tall and 2.00 m wide and has its center of gravity at its geometrical center.

The bookcase rests on four short legs that are each 0.10 m in from the edge of the bookcase. A person pulls on a rope attached to an upper corner of the bookcase with a force P that makes an angle θ with the bookcase, as shown in Fig. 10–31.

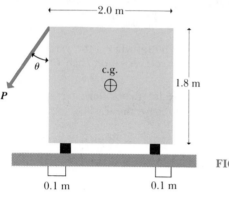

FIGURE 10–31

a) If $\theta = 90°$, so that P is horizontal, show that as P is increased from zero, the bookcase will start to slide before it tips, and calculate the magnitude of P that will start the bookcase sliding.

b) If $\theta = 0°$, so that P is vertical, show that the bookcase will tip over rather than slide, and calculate the magnitude of P that will cause the bookcase to start to tip.

c) Calculate as a function of θ the magnitude of P that will cause the bookcase to start to slide and the magnitude that will cause it to start to tip. What is the smallest value that θ can have for the bookcase to start to slide before it starts to tip?

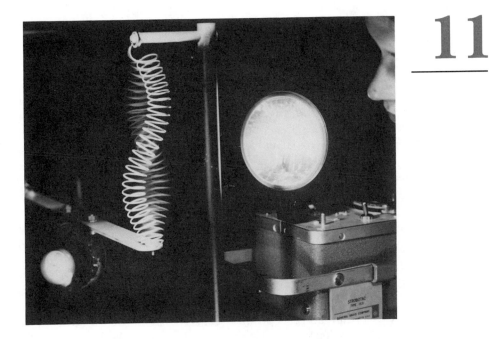

Periodic Motion

In this chapter we consider a class of problems in which a body repeats the same motion over and over again in a repetitive or cyclic pattern. Any such motion is called a **periodic motion** or an **oscillation.** Many familiar examples come to mind: the pendulum of a grandfather's clock, the vibrating strings of a musical instrument, the pistons in a gasoline engine, a child playing on a swing. Less obvious examples are the vibrations of the quartz crystal in a watch, the electromagnetic waves of radio and television transmission, and vibrations of atoms in the crystal lattice of a solid material. Periodic motion plays a vital role in many areas of physics, and studying it will give us an important foundation for later work in several areas.

A mechanical system that undergoes periodic motion always has a stable equilibrium position and a restoring force that tends to move the system back toward equilibrium when it is displaced. But when the system is displaced and released, it overshoots the equilibrium position and goes into a back-and-forth motion on both sides of equilibrium. The pendulum of a grandfather's clock is a familiar example.

11–1
Basic Concepts

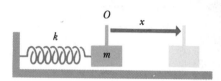

11–1
Model for periodic motion. If the spring obeys Hooke's law, the motion is simple harmonic motion.

One of the simplest systems that can undergo periodic motion is a mass attached to a spring, as shown in Fig. 11–1. The body might be a glider on a linear air track, as described in Section 5–2, moving without friction. The body is attached to one end of a spring, and the other end of the spring is held stationary. Quite a bit of our effort in this chapter will be directed toward understanding the behavior of this system, and we will use it as an idealized model to analyze the main features of periodic motion.

Let x be the displacement of the body from its equilibrium position. When $x = 0$, the spring is neither stretched nor compressed. When the body is displaced to the right, x is positive and the spring stretches. The x-component of force F that the spring exerts on the body is toward the left (the negative x-direction), and F is negative. When the body is displaced to the left, x is negative, the spring is compressed, the force on the body is toward the right (the positive x-direction), again toward equilibrium, and F is positive. Thus the sign of F is always opposite to the sign of x itself, and the spring force is a *restoring force*.

In Section 7–3 we learned that for some springs the force is *directly proportional* to the deformation, at least for small deformations. This proportionality is called Hooke's law. In Fig. 11–1, if the spring obeys Hooke's law, we may represent the relationship of F to x as

$$F = -kx, \tag{11–1}$$

where k is the **force constant** for the spring. The negative sign is needed because we are describing the force the spring exerts *on* the mass, not the force on the spring. Equation (11–1) is valid for both positive and negative x; in both cases, F and x have opposite signs.

Now suppose we displace the body a distance A to the right and then release it, without giving it any initial velocity. The spring pulls the body toward the equilibrium position, and it accelerates in this direction. The acceleration is *not* constant; the force decreases as the body approaches equilibrium. When the body reaches $x = 0$, the force and acceleration become zero, but the body's velocity causes it to "overshoot" the equilibrium position and continue to move to the left. The force then reverses direction; the body slows down and stops, then starts back toward equilibrium again.

In Section 11–2 we will use energy considerations to show that the motion is confined to a range $x = \pm A$ on either side of the equilibrium position and that each complete back-and-forth trip takes the same amount of time. If there were no loss of mechanical energy due to friction, the motion would continue forever. This specific motion, under the influence of a restoring force that is directly proportional to displacement, is called **simple harmonic motion,** abbreviated **SHM.**

Here are some terms that we will use often in this chapter: A complete vibration or **cycle** is one round trip, say, from A to $-A$ and back to A or from 0 to A to 0 to $-A$ to 0. The motion from one side to the other (e.g., A to $-A$) is a half-cycle, not a full cycle.

The **period** of the motion, denoted by τ, is the time required for one cycle.

The **frequency,** denoted by f, is the number of cycles per unit time. The frequency is the reciprocal of the period: $f = 1/\tau$. The SI unit of frequency, the cycle per second, is called the **hertz** (1 Hz = 1 s^{-1}).

The **amplitude,** A, is the maximum displacement from equilibrium, that is, the maximum value of $|x|$. The total overall range of the motion is $2A$.

Simple harmonic motion is the simplest of all periodic motions to analyze. In more complex examples the force may depend on displacement in a more complicated way, but only when it is *directly proportional* to displacement do we use the name "simple harmonic motion." However, many more complex periodic motions are *approximately* simple harmonic if the displacements are small enough. Simple harmonic motion is a *model* that represents many real-life periodic motions, and it is worth analyzing in detail.

11–2
Energy in Simple Harmonic Motion

We would like to obtain expressions for position, velocity, and acceleration as functions of time for a body undergoing simple harmonic motion. The acceleration isn't constant, so we can't use the equations for motion with *constant* acceleration from Chapter 2. In this section we will use energy considerations to derive a relationship between the position and velocity of the body, and in Section 11–3 we will use a geometric construction to derive expressions for x, v, and a as functions of t.

Figure 11–2 shows the vibrating body of Fig. 11–1 at a distance x from its equilibrium position $x = 0$. The mass is m; the body moves along a straight line (the x-axis), and the force component F_x along that line is the elastic restoring force: $F = -kx$.

From Newton's second law, the x-component of acceleration a is given by

$$F_x = -kx = ma$$

or

$$a = -\frac{k}{m}x. \tag{11–2}$$

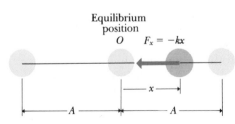

Equilibrium position
$O \quad F_x = -kx$

11–2
Coordinate system and free-body diagram for a body in simple harmonic motion.

At each instant the acceleration is proportional to the negative of the displacement. (Simple harmonic motion is sometimes *defined* as motion having this property.) When x has its maximum positive value A, the acceleration has its maximum negative value $-kA/m$; at the instant when the body passes the equilibrium position its acceleration is zero.

We can use conservation of energy to derive a relationship between the body's position x and velocity v. The elastic restoring force is a *conservative* force, so we can represent the work done by this force in terms of a potential energy $U = \frac{1}{2}kx^2$, just as we did in Section 7–6. The kinetic energy is $K = \frac{1}{2}mv^2$; in Eq. (7–21), $W_{\text{other}} = 0$, so the total energy $E =$

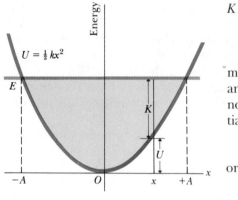

11–3
Relation between total energy E, potential energy U, and kinetic energy K for a body oscillating with SHM.

$K + U$ is constant. That is,

$$E = \tfrac{1}{2}mv^2 + \tfrac{1}{2}kx^2 = \text{constant.} \tag{11–3}$$

The total energy E is also directly related to the amplitude A of the motion. When the body reaches its maximum displacement $\pm A$, it stops and turns back toward equilibrium. At this instant, $v = 0$, so the body has no kinetic energy. The (constant) total energy is thus equal to the potential energy at this point, which is $\tfrac{1}{2}kA^2 = E$. Thus

$$\tfrac{1}{2}mv^2 + \tfrac{1}{2}kx^2 = \tfrac{1}{2}kA^2,$$

or

$$v = \pm\sqrt{\frac{k}{m}}\sqrt{A^2 - x^2}. \tag{11–4}$$

We can use this relation to obtain the velocity (apart from a sign) for any given position.

Figure 11–3 is a graphical representation of Eq. (11–3). Energy is plotted vertically, and the coordinate x is plotted horizontally. The curve represents the potential energy, $U = \tfrac{1}{2}kx^2$; this curve is a parabola. The horizontal line at height E represents the constant total energy of the body. We see that the body's motion is restricted to values of x lying between the points where the horizontal line intersects the parabola. If x were outside this range, the potential energy would exceed the total energy, and that is impossible.

If we draw a vertical line at any value of x within the permitted range, the length of the segment between the x-axis and the parabola represents the potential energy U at that value of x. The length of the segment between the parabola and the horizontal line at height E represents the corresponding kinetic energy K. At the endpoints the energy is all potential, and at the midpoint it is all kinetic. The speed has its maximum value v_{max} at the midpoint:

$$\tfrac{1}{2}mv_{max}^2 = E, \qquad v_{max} = \sqrt{2E/m}. \tag{11–5}$$

Both the maximum potential energy and the maximum kinetic energy are equal to the total energy E (and thus to each other). We can use this fact to relate the maximum velocity to the amplitude:

$$E = \tfrac{1}{2}kA^2 = \tfrac{1}{2}mv_{max}^2, \qquad v_{max} = \sqrt{\frac{k}{m}}A. \tag{11–6}$$

Example 11–1   A spring is mounted as in Fig. 11–1. By attaching a spring balance to the free end and pulling toward the right, we determine that the force is proportional to the displacement and that a force of 4.0 N causes a displacement of 0.020 m. We attach a 2.0-kg body to the end, pull it a distance of 0.040 m, and release it.

a) Find the force constant of the spring.
From Eq. (11–1),

$$k = \left|\frac{F}{x}\right| = \frac{4.0 \text{ N}}{0.020 \text{ m}} = 200 \text{ N·m}^{-1}.$$

b) Find the maximum velocity of the vibrating body.

The maximum velocity occurs at the equilibrium position, where $x = 0$. From Eq. (11–4), for any x,

$$v = \pm\sqrt{\frac{k}{m}}\sqrt{A^2 - x^2},$$

so when $x = 0$,

$$v = v_{max} = \pm\sqrt{\frac{k}{m}}\,A = \pm\sqrt{\frac{200\ \text{N}\cdot\text{m}^{-1}}{2.0\ \text{kg}}}\,(0.040\ \text{m}) = \pm 0.40\ \text{m}\cdot\text{s}^{-1}.$$

This is the same result as Eq. (11–6).

c) Compute the maximum acceleration.

From Eq. (11–2),

$$a = -\frac{k}{m}x.$$

The maximum acceleration occurs at the ends of the path, where $x = \pm A$. Therefore

$$a_{max} = -\frac{k}{m}(\pm A) = -\frac{200\ \text{N}\cdot\text{m}^{-1}}{2.0\ \text{kg}}(\pm 0.04\ \text{m}) = \pm 4.0\ \text{m}\cdot\text{s}^{-2}.$$

d) Determine the velocity and acceleration when the body has moved halfway in to the center from its initial position.

At this point, $x = A/2 = 0.020$ m. From Eq. (11–4),

$$v = -\sqrt{\frac{200\ \text{N}\cdot\text{m}^{-1}}{2.0\ \text{kg}}}\sqrt{(0.040\ \text{m})^2 - (0.020\ \text{m})^2} = -0.35\ \text{m}\cdot\text{s}^{-1}.$$

We have chosen the negative square root because we are told that the body is moving from $x = A$ toward $x = 0$. From Eq. (11–2),

$$a = -\frac{200\ \text{N}\cdot\text{m}^{-1}}{2.0\ \text{kg}}(0.020\ \text{m}) = -2.0\ \text{m}\cdot\text{s}^{-2}. \qquad \blacksquare$$

11–3
Equations of Simple Harmonic Motion

The position–velocity relation given by Eq. (11–4) is useful, but it does not give us the particle's position, velocity, and acceleration as functions of *time*. We can develop these additional relationships with the help of a geometric representation called the **circle of reference.** This representation makes use of a close relationship between SHM and uniform circular motion, which we studied in Section 3–5. The basic idea is shown in Fig. 11–4. Point Q moves counterclockwise around a circle with a radius A that is equal to the amplitude of the actual simple harmonic motion, with constant angular velocity ω (measured in radians per second). Thus ω is the rate of change of the angle ϕ; $\omega = \Delta\phi/\Delta t$.

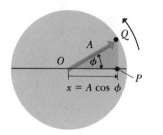

11–4
Coordinate of a body in simple harmonic motion.

The vector from O to Q is the position vector of point Q relative to O; this vector has constant magnitude A and at time t is at an angle ϕ measured counterclockwise from the positive x-axis. As Q moves, this vector rotates counterclockwise with constant angular velocity $\omega = \Delta\phi/\Delta t$. As we will see soon, the horizontal component of this vector represents the actual motion of the body under study. Such a rotating vector is called a **phasor.** (This term was in use long before the invention of the Star Trek stun-gun of similar name!) This representation is also useful in many other areas in which physical quantities have periodic time variations, including ac circuit analysis (Chapter 34) and interference phenomena in optics (Chapter 39).

In Fig. 11–4, point P lies on the horizontal diameter of the circle, directly below Q. We call Q the *reference point*, the circle the *reference circle*, and P the *projection* of Q onto the diameter. The location of P is that of a *shadow* of Q on the x-axis, cast by a light beam parallel to the y-axis. As Q revolves, P moves back and forth along the diameter, staying always directly below (or above) Q. We are about to show that the motion of P is *simple harmonic motion*.

The displacement of P from the origin O at any time t is the distance OP or x; from Fig. 11–4,

$$x = A \cos \phi.$$

If point Q is at the extreme right end of the diameter at time $t = 0$, then $\phi = 0$ when $t = 0$. Because ω is constant, the time variation of ϕ is given by

$$\phi = \omega t$$

and

$$x = A \cos \omega t. \tag{11–7}$$

Now ω, the angular velocity of Q (in radians per second) is related to f, the number of complete revolutions of Q per second. There are 2π radians in one complete revolution, so

$$\omega = 2\pi f. \tag{11–8}$$

Furthermore, the point P makes one complete back-and-forth vibration (one cycle) for each revolution of Q. Hence f is also the number of vibrations per second or the *frequency* of vibration of point P. Thus we can also write Eq. (11–7) as

$$x = A \cos 2\pi f t. \tag{11–9}$$

We can find the instantaneous velocity of P with the help of Fig. 11–5. The reference point Q moves with a tangential velocity given by Eq. (9–12):

$$v_\parallel = \omega A = 2\pi f A.$$

Point P is always directly below or above the reference point, so the velocity v of P at each instant must equal the x-component of the velocity of Q. That is, from Fig. 11–5,

$$v = -v_\parallel \sin \phi = -\omega A \sin \phi;$$

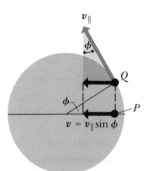

11–5
Velocity in simple harmonic motion.

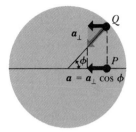

11–6
Acceleration in simple harmonic motion.

and

$$v = -\omega A \sin \omega t = -2\pi f A \sin 2\pi f t. \qquad (11\text{--}10)$$

The minus sign is needed because the direction of the velocity is toward the left. When Q is below the horizontal diameter, the velocity of P is toward the right, but $\sin \phi$ is negative at such points. So the minus sign is needed in both cases. Equation (11–10) gives the velocity of point P at any time.

We can also find the acceleration of point P. Because P is always directly below or above Q, its acceleration must equal the x-component of the acceleration of Q. Point Q moves in a circular path with constant angular velocity ω, and its acceleration is toward the center, with magnitude given by Eq. (9–14):

$$a_\perp = \omega^2 A = 4\pi^2 f^2 A.$$

From Fig. 11–6 the x-component of this acceleration is

$$a = -a_\perp \cos \phi;$$

or

$$a = -\omega^2 A \cos \omega t = -4\pi^2 f^2 A \cos 2\pi f t. \qquad (11\text{--}11)$$

The minus sign is needed because the acceleration is toward the left. When Q is to the left of the center, the acceleration of P is toward the right, but since $\cos \phi$ is negative at such points, the minus sign is still needed. Equation (11–11) gives the acceleration of P at any time.

Now comes the crucial step in showing that the motion of P is simple harmonic. We combine Eqs. (11–7) and (11–11), obtaining

$$a = -\omega^2 x. \qquad (11\text{--}12)$$

Because ω is constant, the acceleration a at each instant equals a negative constant times the displacement x at that instant. But this is just the essential feature of simple harmonic motion, as given by Eq. (11–2); force and acceleration are proportional to the negative of displacement from equilibrium. This shows that the motion of P is indeed simple harmonic!

To make Eqs. (11–2) and (11–12) agree precisely, we must choose an angular velocity ω for the reference point Q such that

$$\omega^2 = \frac{k}{m}. \qquad (11\text{--}13)$$

With that choice, the frequency of motion of Q, and thus of the actual particle P, is given by

$$f = \frac{\omega}{2\pi} = \frac{1}{2\pi}\sqrt{\frac{k}{m}}. \qquad (11\text{--}14)$$

The basic unit for f is cycles per second or simply s^{-1}. In SI units, 1 cycle per second is given the special name *1 hertz* (1 Hz) in honor of Heinrich Hertz, one of the pioneers in investigating electromagnetic waves during the latter part of the nineteenth century.

The *period* τ of the motion (the time for one cycle) is the reciprocal of the frequency: $\tau = 1/f$. Frequency f is the number of cycles per second; period τ is the number of seconds per cycle. From Eq. (11–14),

$$\tau = \frac{1}{f} = 2\pi\sqrt{\frac{m}{k}}. \qquad (11\text{–}15)$$

The general form of Eqs. (11–14) and (11–15) is just what we should expect. When m is large, we expect the motion to be slow and ponderous, corresponding to small f and large τ. A large value of k means a very stiff spring, corresponding to large f and small τ. It may be surprising that these equations *do not* contain the amplitude A of the motion. Suppose we give our spring–mass system some initial displacement, release it, and measure its frequency. Then we stop it, give it a *different* initial displacement, and release it again. We find that the two frequencies are the same. To be sure, the maximum displacement, maximum speed, and maximum acceleration are all different in the two cases, but *not* the frequency.

Indeed, one of the most important characteristics of simple harmonic motion is that *the frequency does not depend on the amplitude of the motion.* This is why a tuning fork vibrates with the same frequency, regardless of amplitude. If it were not for this property of simple harmonic motion, it would be impossible to play most musical instruments in tune. A periodic motion in which the frequency is independent of amplitude is said to be **isochronous.**

Figure 11–7 shows graphs of Eqs. (11–9), (11–10), and (11–11)— the position, velocity, and acceleration—as functions of time. We invite you to check that v at any time is the slope of the x versus t curve and that a at any time is the slope of the v versus t curve.

We can simplify many of the relationships in simple harmonic motion by using the angular velocity ω rather than the frequency f. As Eq. (11–8) shows, the two are related by $\omega = 2\pi f$. Because of this relationship, ω is usually called the **angular frequency** of the motion. In terms of ω we can rewrite Eqs. (11–2) and (11–4) as

$$a_x = -\omega^2 x,$$
$$v = \pm\omega\sqrt{A^2 - x^2}. \qquad (11\text{–}16)$$

In these and most of the other equations of simple harmonic motion, using ω instead of f saves us having to write a lot of factors of 2π. By convention the hertz is *not* used as a unit of angular frequency; the usual unit is the radian per second or simply s^{-1}.

Throughout this discussion we have assumed that the initial position of the particle (at time $t = 0$) is its maximum positive displacement A, but this is not an essential restriction. Different initial positions correspond to different initial positions of the reference point Q. For example, if at time $t = 0$ the phasor OQ makes an angle ϕ_0 with the positive x-axis, then the angle ϕ at time t is given not by $\phi = \omega t$ as before, but by

$$\phi = \phi_0 + \omega t. \qquad (11\text{–}17)$$

The only change in the above discussion is to replace (ωt) in Eqs. (11–7),

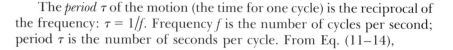

11–7
Graphs of coordinate, velocity, and acceleration of a body moving with simple harmonic motion.

(11–10), and (11–11) by $(\omega t + \phi_0)$. These equations then become

$$x = A \cos (\omega t + \phi_0), \tag{11–18}$$

$$v = -\omega A \sin (\omega t + \phi_0), \tag{11–19}$$

$$a = -\omega^2 A \cos (\omega t + \phi_0) = -\omega^2 x. \tag{11–20}$$

The constant ϕ_0 determines the point in the cycle where we start at time $t = 0$. It is called a **phase angle.** Suppose that at time $t = 0$ the body has an initial position x_0 and an initial velocity v_0. Then from Eqs. (11–18) and (11–19),

$$x_0 = A \cos \phi_0, \tag{11–21}$$
$$v_0 = -\omega A \sin \phi_0.$$

If $\phi_0 = 0$, then $x_0 = A$ and $v_0 = 0$. This corresponds to a motion in which the body is given an initial displacement equal to the amplitude A and released with no initial velocity. But if $\phi_0 = -\pi/2$, then $x_0 = 0$ and $v_0 = \omega A$; this corresponds to starting the body at the equilibrium position $(x = 0)$ by giving it an initial velocity v_0; the amplitude A is then given by $A = v_0/\omega$. The maximum velocity occurs at $x = 0$, so this agrees with Eq. (11–6).

Now suppose we give the body *both* an initial displacement x_0 and an initial velocity v_0. What is the amplitude? The answer is contained in Eqs. (11–21); we can extract it by squaring the first equation, dividing the second equation by ω and squaring it, and adding the two results, using the identity $\sin^2 \phi_0 + \cos^2 \phi_0 = 1$. We invite you to work out the details; the result is

$$A^2 = x_0^2 + \frac{v_0^2}{\omega^2}. \tag{11–22}$$

In this case the amplitude is not equal to the initial displacement. This is reasonable; if at time $t = 0$ the particle has an initial displacement x_0 in the positive direction and also a positive velocity v_0 in that direction, then it will move *farther* in that direction before returning; hence A must be greater than x_0. The frequency and period relations, Eqs. (11–12) and (11–13), are unchanged. Equation (11–22) can also be derived (more easily) from energy considerations; we invite you to carry out that derivation.

If x_0 and v_0 are known, we can also determine the phase angle ϕ_0 from Eqs. (11–21); we divide the first by the second and rearrange the result to obtain

$$\phi_0 = \arctan \frac{-v_0}{\omega x_0}. \tag{11–23}$$

Figure 11–8 shows graphs of x as a function of t for three different motions with the same amplitude and frequency but different phase angles.

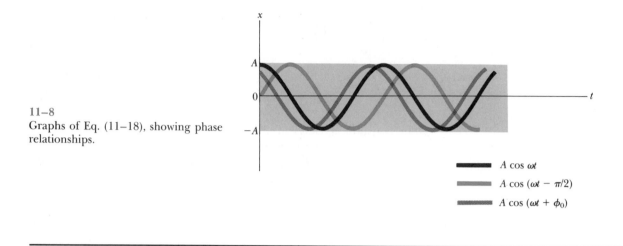

11–8
Graphs of Eq. (11–18), showing phase relationships.

—— $A \cos \omega t$

—— $A \cos (\omega t - \pi/2)$

—— $A \cos (\omega t + \phi_0)$

PROBLEM-SOLVING STRATEGY: *Simple Harmonic Motion*

1. Be careful to distinguish between quantities that represent basic physical properties of the system and quantities that describe a particular motion that occurs when the system is set in motion in a specific way. The physical properties include the mass m, the force constant k, and the quantities derived from these, including the period τ, the frequency f, and the angular frequency $\omega = 2\pi f$. In some problems, m or k, or both, can be determined from other information given about the system. Quantities that describe a particular motion include the amplitude A, the maximum velocity v_{max}, the phase angle ϕ_0, and any quantity representing the position, velocity, or acceleration at a particular time.

2. If the problem involves a relation among position, velocity, and acceleration without reference to time, it is usually easier to use Eqs. (11–2) or (11–4) than to use the general

expression for position as a function of time given by Eq. (11–18).

3. When detailed information about positions, velocities, and accelerations at various times is required, then Eqs. (11–18) through (11–20) must be used. If the body is given an initial displacement x_0 but no initial velocity ($v_0 = 0$), then the amplitude is $A = x_0$, and the phase angle is $\phi_0 = 0$. If it has an initial velocity v_0 but no initial displacement ($x_0 = 0$), the amplitude is $A = v_0/\omega$, and the phase angle is $\phi_0 = -\pi/2$. If the initial position x_0 and initial velocity v_0 are both different from zero, we determine the amplitude and phase angle from Eqs. (11–22) and (11–23).

4. The energy equation, Eq. (11–3), together with the relation $E = \frac{1}{2}kA^2$, sometimes provides a convenient alternative for relations between velocity and position, especially when energy quantities are also required.

Example 11–2   Consider the same system as in Example 11–1 (Section 11–2), with $k = 200$ N·m^{-1} and $m = 2.0$ kg.

a) Find the angular frequency, frequency, and period of the motion.
From Eq. (11–13),

$$\omega = \sqrt{\frac{k}{m}} = \sqrt{\frac{200 \text{ N·m}^{-1}}{2.0 \text{ kg}}} = 10 \text{ s}^{-1},$$

$$f = \frac{\omega}{2\pi} = 1.6 \text{ Hz}, \qquad \tau = \frac{1}{f} = 0.63 \text{ s}.$$

b) If the body is released from rest at $x = 0.040$ m, how much time is required for it to move halfway to the center from the initial position?

   In this case, $\phi_0 = 0$, and the position at any time is given by $x = A \cos (10 \text{ s}^{-1})t$. The required time is determined by the condition

$$\frac{A}{2} = A \cos (10 \text{ s}^{-1})t,$$

from which

$$\cos (10 \text{ s}^{-1})t = \tfrac{1}{2},$$

$$t = \frac{\pi}{30} \text{ s}.$$

Note that the quantity $(10 \text{ s}^{-1})t$ plays the role of an angle, measured always in radians. In numerical calculations you will have to set your calculator on "radians" mode.   ■

Example 11–3   The system in Example 11–1 is given an initial displacement of 0.050 m and an initial velocity of 2.0 m·s^{-1}. Find the amplitude, the phase angle, and the total energy of the motion, and write an equation for the position as a function of time.

Solution   From Eq. (11–22),

$$A = \sqrt{x_0^2 + (v_0/\omega)^2}$$
$$= \sqrt{(0.050 \text{ m})^2 + (2.0 \text{ m·s}^{-1}/10 \text{ s}^{-1})^2} = 0.206 \text{ m}.$$

From Eq. (11–23),

$$\phi = \arctan \frac{-v_0}{\omega x_0}$$
$$= \arctan \frac{-2.0 \text{ m·s}^{-1}}{(10 \text{ s}^{-1})(0.050 \text{ m})} = -76° = -1.3 \text{ rad}.$$

From Eq. (11–3) and the following discussion,

$$E = \tfrac{1}{2}kA^2 = \tfrac{1}{2}(200 \text{ N·m}^{-1})(0.206 \text{ m})^2$$
$$= 4.25 \text{ J}.$$

Alternatively, from the initial conditions,

$$E = \tfrac{1}{2}mv_0^2 + \tfrac{1}{2}kx_0^2$$
$$= \tfrac{1}{2}(2.0 \text{ kg})(2.0 \text{ m·s}^{-1})^2 + \tfrac{1}{2}(200 \text{ N·m}^{-1})(0.050 \text{ m})^2$$
$$= 4.25 \text{ J}.$$

The position at any time is given by Eq. (11–18):

$$x = (0.206 \text{ m}) \cos [(10 \text{ s}^{-1})t - 1.3 \text{ rad}].$$ ■

Example 11–4   In Example 11–2, use the circle of reference to find the time for the displacement from $x = A$ to $x = A/2$, requested in part (b).

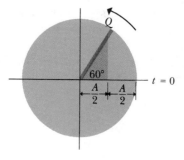

11–9
Phasor diagram for Example 11–4.

Solution While the body moves halfway in, the reference point revolves through an angle of 60° (Fig. 11–9). Since the reference point moves with constant angular velocity and in this example makes one complete revolution during one period ($\tau = \pi/5$ s), the time to rotate through 60° is

$$\frac{1}{6}\frac{\pi}{5}\text{ s} = \frac{\pi}{30}\text{ s} = 0.10\text{ s}. \qquad \blacksquare$$

Suppose we rotate the system of Fig. 11–1 by 90°, so that the mass hangs vertically from the spring in a uniform gravitational field, as in Fig. 11–10a. The motion does not change in any essential way. In Fig. 11–10b a body of mass m hangs in equilibrium from a spring with force constant k. In this position the spring is stretched an amount Δl just great enough that the spring's upward vertical force $k\,\Delta l$ on the body balances its weight mg. In that case,

$$k\,\Delta l = mg.$$

Take $x = 0$ to be the equilibrium position. When the body is at a distance x *above* its equilibrium position, as in Fig. 11–10c, the extension of the spring is $\Delta l - x$. The upward force it exerts on the body is then $k(\Delta l - x)$, and the resultant force F on the body is

$$F = k(\Delta l - x) - mg = -kx,$$

that is, a net downward force of magnitude kx. Similarly, when the body is *below* the equilibrium position, there is a net upward force proportional to x. If the body is set in vertical motion, it oscillates with SHM, with the same angular frequency as though it were horizontal, $\omega = (k/m)^{1/2}$.

11–10
The restoring force on a body suspended by a spring is proportional to the coordinate measured from the equilibrium position.

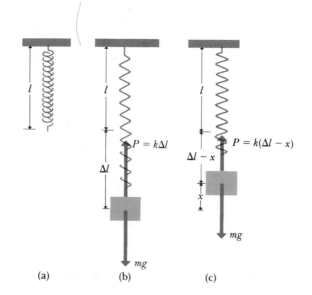

(a)   (b)   (c)

Example 11–5   A body with a mass of 5.0 kg is suspended by a spring, which stretches 0.10 m when the body is attached. The body is then displaced downward an additional 0.050 m and released. Find the amplitude, period, and frequency of the resulting simple harmonic motion.

Solution   Since the initial position is 0.050 m from equilibrium and there is no initial velocity, $A = 0.050$ m. To find the period, we first find the force constant k of the spring. It is stretched 0.10 m by a force of $(5.0 \text{ kg})(9.8 \text{ m·s}^{-2})$, so

$$k = \frac{mg}{\Delta l} = \frac{(5.00 \text{ kg})(9.80 \text{ m·s}^{-2})}{0.100 \text{ m}} = 490 \text{ N·m}^{-1},$$

$$\tau = 2\pi\sqrt{\frac{m}{k}} = 2\pi\sqrt{\frac{5.00 \text{ kg}}{490 \text{ N·m}^{-1}}} = 0.635 \text{ s},$$

$$f = \frac{1}{\tau} = 1.57 \text{ Hz}.$$

■

*11–4
Angular Simple Harmonic Motion

Simple harmonic motion has a direct analog for bodies that undergo *rotational* motion. Suppose a body is pivoted so that it can rotate about an axis and is acted on by a torque that is directly proportional to its angular displacement from some equilibrium position. The balance wheel in a mechanical watch, shown in Fig. 11–11, is such a system. The torque is supplied by a coil spring called the *hairspring*, which is coaxial with the rotation axis. The resulting rotational motion is directly analogous to linear SHM, and the corresponding equations can be written down immediately from our previous analogies between linear and angular quantities.

   Caution: In the following discussion, be careful not to confuse the back-and-forth rotational motion of a body in angular SHM with the steady rotation of point Q in the circle-of-reference representation of SHM.

   A restoring torque Γ proportional to angular displacement θ is expressed by

$$\Gamma = -k'\theta, \tag{11–24}$$

where k' is a proportionality constant analogous to the force constant of a spring; k' is called the *torque constant*. The equation of motion, from $\Gamma = I\alpha$, is

$$-k'\theta = I\alpha, \quad \text{or} \quad \alpha = -\frac{k'}{I}\theta.$$

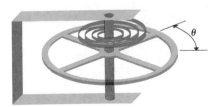

11–11
Balance wheel in a watch. The spring exerts a torque proportional to the angular displacement from the equilibrium position, and the motion is angular simple harmonic motion.

This has the same form as Eq. (11–2), with each linear quantity replaced by its angular analog. So we conclude that the angular frequency ω of an angular harmonic oscillator is given by

$$\omega = \sqrt{\frac{k'}{I}}. \tag{11–25}$$

The corresponding expressions for the frequency f and the period τ are

$$f = \frac{1}{2\pi} \sqrt{\frac{k'}{I}}, \qquad \tau = 2\pi \sqrt{\frac{I}{k'}}. \tag{11–26}$$

This analogy can be extended to develop equations for the angular position, velocity, and acceleration as functions of time. We need to be cautious in our choice of symbols; we must not use ω for the angular velocity of the body (a quantity that varies with time) because we have already used it for the angular frequency of the motion (a constant for any given system). A natural symbol for the body's angular velocity is Ω. Then the appropriate formulas are obtained by replacing x everywhere by θ, v by Ω, and a by α.

We have mentioned that the balance wheel of a watch or mechanical clock is an example of angular harmonic motion. If the hairspring behaves according to Eq. (11–24), the motion is *isochronous*; the period is constant even though the amplitude decreases somewhat as the mainspring unwinds.

11–5
The Simple Pendulum

11–12
Forces on the bob of a simple pendulum.

A **simple pendulum** is an idealized model consisting of a point mass suspended by a weightless, unstretchable string in a uniform gravitational field. When the mass is pulled to one side of its straight-down equilibrium position and released, it oscillates about the equilibrium position. We can now analyze the motion of this system, asking in particular whether it is simple harmonic.

As Fig. 11–12 shows, the path is not a straight line but the arc of a circle with radius L equal to the length of the string. We use as our coordinate the distance x measured along the arc. If the motion is simple harmonic, the restoring force must be directly proportional to x or, since $x = L\theta$, to θ. Is it?

In Fig. 11–12 the forces on the mass are represented in terms of tangential and radial components; the restoring force F is

$$F = -mg \sin \theta. \tag{11–27}$$

The restoring force is therefore proportional *not* to θ but to $\sin \theta$, so the motion is *not* simple harmonic. However, *if the angle θ is small*, $\sin \theta$ is very nearly equal to θ. For example, when $\theta = 0.1$ rad (about 6°), $\sin \theta = 0.0998$, a difference of only 0.2%. With this approximation, Eq. (11–27) becomes

$$F = -mg\theta = -mg\frac{x}{L},$$

or

$$F = -\frac{mg}{L}x. \tag{11–28}$$

The restoring force is then proportional to the coordinate *for small displacements*, and the constant mg/L represents the force constant k. From Eq. (11–13), the angular frequency of a simple pendulum with small amplitude is

$$\omega = \sqrt{\frac{k}{m}} = \sqrt{\frac{mg/L}{m}} = \sqrt{\frac{g}{L}}. \tag{11–29}$$

The corresponding frequency and period relations are

$$f = \frac{\omega}{2\pi} = \frac{1}{2\pi}\sqrt{\frac{g}{L}}, \tag{11–30}$$

$$\tau = \frac{2\pi}{\omega} = \frac{1}{f} = 2\pi\sqrt{\frac{L}{g}}. \tag{11–31}$$

Note that these expressions do not contain the *mass* of the particle; this is because the restoring force, a component of the particle's weight, is proportional to m. Thus the mass appears on both sides of $F = ma$ and cancels out. For small oscillations the period of a pendulum for a given value of g is determined entirely by its length.

An elegant argument invented by Galileo 400 years ago also leads to this conclusion. Make a simple pendulum, said Galileo, measure its period, and then split the pendulum down the middle, string and all. Splitting it should not change the motion, so each half must swing with the same period as the original! Therefore the period cannot depend on the mass.

The dependence on L and g in Eqs. (11–29) through (11–31) is just what we should expect on the basis of everyday experience. A long pendulum has a longer period than a shorter one. Increasing g increases the restoring force, causing the frequency to increase and the period to decrease.

We emphasize again that the motion of a pendulum is only *approximately* simple harmonic. When the amplitude is not small, the departures from simple harmonic motion can be substantial. But how small is "small"? The period can be expressed by an infinite series; when the maximum angular displacement is Θ, the period τ is given by

$$\tau = 2\pi\sqrt{\frac{L}{g}}\left(1 + \frac{1^2}{2^2}\sin^2\frac{\Theta}{2} + \frac{1^2 \cdot 3^2}{2^2 \cdot 4^2}\sin^4\frac{\Theta}{2} + \cdots\right). \tag{11–32}$$

We can compute the period to any desired degree of precision by taking enough terms in the series. We invite you to check that when $\Theta = 15°$ (on either side of the central position), the true period differs from that given by the approximate Eq. (11–31) by less than 0.5%.

The usefulness of the pendulum as a timekeeper depends on the fact that for small amplitudes the motion is *very nearly* isochronous (period independent of amplitude). Thus as a pendulum clock runs down and the amplitude of the swings becomes slightly smaller, the clock still keeps very nearly correct time.

The simple pendulum is also a precise and convenient method for measuring the acceleration of gravity g, since L and τ can be measured easily. Such measurements are often used in geophysics. Local deposits of ore or oil affect the local value of g because their density differs from that of their surroundings. Precise measurements of this quantity over an area being surveyed often furnish valuable information about the nature of underlying deposits.

Example 11–6   Find the period and frequency of a simple pendulum 1.000 m long.

Solution   From Eq. (11–31),

$$\tau = 2\pi \sqrt{\frac{1.000 \text{ m}}{9.800 \text{ m·s}^{-2}}} = 2.007 \text{ s.}$$

Then

$$f = \frac{1}{\tau} = 0.498 \text{ Hz.}$$

The period is almost exactly 2 s; at one time there was a proposal to define the second as half the period of a one-meter pendulum.   ■

---

*11–6
The Physical Pendulum

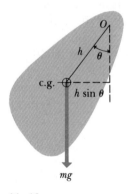

11–13
A physical pendulum.

A **physical pendulum** is any *real* pendulum, as contrasted with the idealized model of the *simple* pendulum, in which all the mass is concentrated at a point. For small oscillations, analyzing the motion of a real pendulum is almost as easy as for a simple pendulum. Figure 11–13 shows a body of irregular shape pivoted so that it can turn without friction about an axis through point O. In the equilibrium position the center of gravity is directly below the pivot; in the position shown in the figure, the body is displaced from equilibrium by an angle θ, which serves as a coordinate for the system. The distance from O to the center of gravity is h, the moment of inertia of the body about the axis through O is I, and the total mass is m. When the body is displaced as shown, the weight mg causes a restoring torque

$$\Gamma = -(mg)(h \sin \theta). \tag{11–33}$$

When released, the body oscillates about its equilibrium position; as in the case of the simple pendulum, the motion is not simple harmonic because the torque Γ is proportional to sin θ rather than to θ itself. However, if θ is small, we can again approximate sin θ by θ, and the motion is approximately harmonic. With this approximation,

$$\Gamma \simeq -(mgh)\theta,$$

and the effective torque constant is

$$k' = -\frac{\Gamma}{\theta} = mgh.$$

We can now use this in Eqs. (11–25) and (11–26) to obtain expressions for the angular frequency and period. The angular frequency is

$$\omega = \sqrt{\frac{k'}{I}} = \sqrt{\frac{mgh}{I}}, \tag{11–34}$$

and the period is

$$\tau = 2\pi\sqrt{\frac{I}{k'}} = 2\pi\sqrt{\frac{I}{mgh}}. \tag{11–35}$$

Example 11–7   Let the body in Fig. 11–13 be a uniform rod of length L, pivoted at one end. Find the period of its motion.

Solution   From Chapter 9 the moment of inertia about an axis through one end is $I = \frac{1}{3}ML^2$. The distance from the pivot to the center of gravity is $h = L/2$. From Eq. (11–35),

$$\tau = 2\pi\sqrt{\frac{\frac{1}{3}mL^2}{mgL/2}} = 2\pi\sqrt{\frac{2L}{3g}}.$$

If the rod is a meter stick ($L = 1.00$ m) and $g = 9.80$ m·s^{-2}, then

$$\tau = 2\pi\sqrt{(2/3)(1.00 \text{ m})/9.80 \text{ m·s}^{-2}} = 1.64 \text{ s}.$$

Note that the period is smaller by a factor of $(2/3)^{1/2} = 0.816$ than the period of a simple pendulum with the same length.   ∎

Example 11–8   A simple pendulum can be considered a special case of a physical pendulum. Show that Eq. (11–35) gives the same expression for its period as Eq. (11–31).

Solution   If the length is L, the moment of inertia is $I = ML^2$, and the distance from the pivot to the center of gravity is $h = L$. Using these expressions in Eq. (11–35), we find

$$\tau = 2\pi\sqrt{\frac{ML^2}{MgL}} = 2\pi\sqrt{\frac{L}{g}},$$

which does indeed agree with Eq. (11–31).   ∎

11–14
The moment of inertia of this connecting rod can be determined by measuring its period of oscillation.

Example 11–9   How can the period of a physical pendulum be used to determine its moment of inertia about its pivot?

Solution   We solve Eq. (11–35) for I:

$$I = \frac{\tau^2 mgh}{4\pi^2}.$$

All the quantities on the right can be measured directly, so we can determine the moment of inertia about some axis for a body with a complicated shape by suspending it about that axis as a physical pendulum and measuring its period of vibration. We can locate the center of gravity by balancing. For example, Fig. 11–14 shows a connecting rod pivoted about a horizontal knife-edge. Suppose that the mass of the rod is 2.00 kg and that when it is set into oscillation, it makes 100 complete vibrations in 120 s, so that $\tau = 120$ s$/100 = 1.20$ s. From the above relation,

$$I = \frac{(1.20 \text{ s})^2 (2.00 \text{ kg})(9.80 \text{ m}\cdot\text{s}^{-2})(0.200 \text{ m})}{4\pi^2} = 0.143 \text{ kg}\cdot\text{m}^2. \quad \blacksquare$$

*11–7
Damped and Forced Oscillations

In the idealized oscillating systems we have discussed thus far, there is no friction. These systems are *conservative*; the total mechanical energy is constant, and a system set into motion continues oscillating forever, with no decrease in amplitude.

Real-world systems always have some friction, however, and oscillations do die out with time unless some means is provided for replacing the mechanical energy lost to friction. A pendulum clock continues to run because the potential energy stored in the spring or weights is used to replace the mechanical energy lost because of friction in the pendulum and the gears. But when the spring "runs down" and no more energy is available, the pendulum swings decrease in amplitude and stop.

The decrease in amplitude caused by dissipative forces is called **damping,** and the corresponding motion is called **damped oscillation.** The suspension system of an automobile is a familiar example of damped oscillations. The shock absorbers provide a velocity-dependent damping force so that when the car goes over a bump, it doesn't continue bouncing forever. For optimal passenger comfort the system should have enough damping that it bounces only once or twice after each bump. As the shocks get old and worn, the damping decreases and the bouncing is more persistent. Not only is this nauseating, but it is bad for steering because the front wheels have less positive contact with the ground. Thus damping is an advantage in this system. But in a system such as a clock or an electrical oscillating system in a radio transmitter, it is usually desirable to have as little damping as possible.

There are many practical situations in which we would like to maintain oscillations of constant amplitude in a damped oscillating system. A familiar example is a child sitting on a swing. We set the system into motion by pulling the child and the swing back from the straight-down equilibrium position and releasing them. If that is all we do, the system oscillates with decreasing amplitude and eventually comes to rest. But by giving the system a little push once each cycle we can maintain a nearly constant amplitude. More generally, we can maintain a constant-amplitude oscillation in a damped harmonic oscillator by applying an oscillating force, that is, a force that varies with time in a periodic or cyclic way. We call this additional force a *driving force*.

The frequency of variation of the force doesn't have to be the same as the natural oscillation frequency of the system. If we apply a periodically varying driving force to the mass of the harmonic oscillator system of Fig. 11–1, the mass undergoes a periodic motion *with the same frequency as that of the driving force*. We call this motion a **forced oscillation** or a *driven oscillation*; it is different from the motion that occurs when the system is simply set into motion and then left alone to oscillate with a natural frequency determined by m and k.

When the frequency of the driving force is *equal* to the natural frequency of the system, we would expect the amplitude of the resulting oscillation to be larger than when the two are very different, and this expectation is borne out by more detailed analysis and experiment. Suppose we apply a force F that varies *sinusoidally* with time, according to

$$F = F_{max} \cos \omega_d t.$$

If we vary the frequency ω_d of the driving force, the amplitude of the resulting forced oscillation varies in an interesting way, as shown in Fig. 11–15. When there is very little damping, the amplitude goes through a

11–15

Graph of the amplitude A of forced oscillation of a damped harmonic oscillator, as a function of the frequency ω_d of the driving force, plotted on the horizontal axis as the ratio of ω_d to the angular frequency $\omega = \sqrt{k/m}$ of an undamped oscillator. Each curve is labeled with the value of a dimensionless quantity that characterizes the amount of damping. As this quantity increases, the peak becomes broader and less sharp and shifts toward lower frequencies. When it is too large, the peak disappears completely.

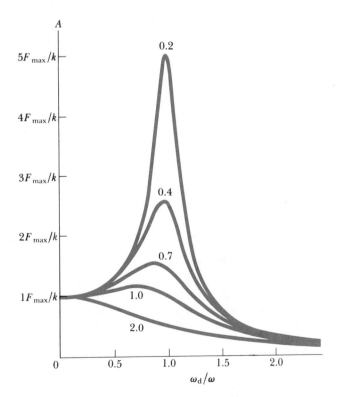

sharp peak as the driving frequency ω_d passes through the natural oscillation frequency ω. When there is more damping, the peak becomes broader and smaller in height and shifts toward lower frequencies.

The fact that there is an amplitude peak at driving frequencies close to the natural frequency of the system is called **resonance.** Physics is full of examples of resonance; building up the oscillations of a child on a swing is one. A vibrating rattle in a car that occurs only at a certain engine speed is another familiar example. You have probably heard of the dangers of a band marching across a bridge; if the frequency of their steps is close to a natural vibration frequency of the bridge, dangerously large oscillations can build up. A tuned circuit in a radio or television receiver responds strongly to waves having frequencies near its resonant frequency, and this is used to select a particular station and reject the others. We will study resonance in electric circuits in detail in Chapter 34.

Questions

11–1 Think of several examples in everyday life of motion that is at least approximately simple harmonic. In what respects does each differ from SHM?

11–2 Does a tuning fork or similar tuning instrument undergo simple harmonic motion? Why is this a crucial question to musicians?

11–3 If a spring is cut in half, what is the force constant of each half? How would the frequency of SHM using a half-spring differ from that using the same mass and the entire spring?

11–4 The analysis of SHM in this chapter neglected the mass of the spring. How does the spring mass change the characteristics of the motion?

11–5 The system shown in Fig. 11–10 is mounted in an elevator, which accelerates upward with constant acceleration. Does the period increase, decrease, or remain the same?

11–6 A highly elastic "superball" bouncing on a hard floor has a motion that is approximately periodic. In what ways is the motion similar to SHM? In what ways is it different?

11–7 How could one determine the force constants of a car's springs by bouncing each end up and down?

11–8 Do the pistons in an automobile engine undergo simple harmonic motion?

11–9 Why is the "springiness" of a diving board adjusted for different dives and different weights of divers? How is the adjustment made?

11–10 In Fig. 11–1, suppose the stationary end of the spring is connected instead to another mass that is equal to the original mass and free to slide along the same line. Could such a system undergo SHM? How would the period compare with that of the original system?

11–11 For the mass–spring system of Fig. 11–1, is there any point during the motion at which the mass is in equilibrium?

11–12 In any periodic motion, unavoidable friction always causes the amplitude to decrease with time. Does friction also affect the *period* of the motion? Give a qualitative argument to support your answer.

11–13 If a pendulum clock is taken to a mountaintop, does it gain or lose time, assuming it is correct at a lower elevation?

11–14 When the amplitude of a simple pendulum increases, should its period increase or decrease? Give a qualitative argument; do not rely on Eq. (11–32). Is your argument also valid for a physical pendulum?

11–15 A pendulum is mounted in an elevator that accelerates upward with constant acceleration. Does the period increase, decrease, or remain the same?

11–16 At what point in the motion of a simple pendulum is the string tension greatest? Least?

11–17 A child on a swing can increase the amplitude of the swing by "pumping up." Where does the extra energy come from? (The answer is not "from the child.")

11–18 Could a standard of time be based on the period of a certain standard pendulum? What advantages and disadvantages would such a standard have in comparison to the actual present-day standard discussed in Section 1–3?

Exercises

Section 11–1   Basic Concepts

11–1 A vibrating object goes through eight complete vibrations in 1.00 s. Find the period of the motion.

11–2 In Fig. 11–1 the mass is displaced 0.120 m from its equilibrium position and released with no initial velocity. After 1.80 s its displacement is found to be 0.120 m on the opposite side, and it has passed the equilibrium position once during this interval. Find

  a) the amplitude,

  b) the period,

  c) the frequency.

11–3

  a) A force of 25.0 N is required to displace the end of a spring 0.120 m. What is the force constant k of the spring?

  b) A spring has force constant $k = 1500$ N·m^{-1}. What force is required to displace the end of the spring 0.080 m?

Section 11–2   Energy in Simple Harmonic Motion

11–4 A spring with force constant $k = 600$ N·m^{-1} is mounted as in Fig. 11–1. An 0.800-kg block attached to the end is undergoing simple harmonic motion with an amplitude 0.075 m. There is no friction force on the block. Compute

  a) the maximum speed of the block;

  b) the speed of the block when it is at $x = 0.030$ m;

  c) the magnitude of the maximum acceleration of the block;

  d) the acceleration of the block when it is at $x = 0.030$ m;

  e) the total mechanical energy of the block at any point in its motion.

11–5 An object with a mass of 0.500 kg is undergoing simple harmonic motion on the end of a horizontal spring with force constant $k = 400$ N·m^{-1}. When the object is 0.012 m from its equilibrium position, it is observed to have a speed of 0.300 m·s^{-1}. What is

  a) the total energy of the object at any point of its motion?

  b) the amplitude of the motion?

  c) the maximum speed attained by the object during its motion?

11–6 An object with a mass of 0.400 kg is undergoing simple harmonic motion with an amplitude of 0.025 m on the end of a horizontal spring. The maximum acceleration of the object is observed to have a magnitude of 15.0 m·s^{-2}. What is

  a) the force constant of the spring?

  b) the maximum speed of the object?

  c) the acceleration (magnitude and direction) of the object when it is displaced 0.012 m to the left of its equilibrium position?

Section 11–3   Equations of Simple Harmonic Motion

11–7 A harmonic oscillator is made using a block with mass 0.500 kg and a spring with unknown force constant. The oscillator is found to have a period of 0.600 s. Find the force constant of the spring.

11–8 A harmonic oscillator has a mass of 4.00 kg and a spring with a force constant of 80.0 N·m^{-1}. Find

  a) the period;

  b) the frequency;

  c) the angular frequency.

11–9 A block of unknown mass is attached to a spring with force constant 200 N·m^{-1} in the arrangement shown in Fig. 11–1. It is found to vibrate with frequency 6.00 Hz. Find

  a) the period;

  b) the angular frequency;

  c) the mass of the block.

11–10 An object is undergoing simple harmonic motion with period $\tau = 0.600$ s. The object initially is at $x = 0$ and has velocity in the positive direction. Use the circle of reference to calculate the time it takes the object to go from $x = 0$ to $x = A/4$.

11–11 An object is undergoing simple harmonic motion with period $(\pi/2)$ s and amplitude $A = 0.200$ m. At $t = 0$ the object is at $x = 0$. How far is the object from the equilibrium position when $t = (\pi/5)$ s?

11–12 Derive Eq. (11–22)

  a) from Eqs. (11–21);

  b) from conservation of energy.

11–13 An object with a mass of 4.00 kg is attached to a spring with force constant $k = 100$ N·m^{-1}. The object is given an initial velocity in the positive direction of magnitude $v_0 = 9.00$ m·s^{-1} and no initial displacement ($x_0 = 0$). Find

a) the amplitude;

b) the phase angle;

c) the total energy of the motion.

d) Write an equation for the position as a function of time.

11–14 Repeat Exercise 11–13, but assume that the object is given an initial velocity -8.00 m·s^{-1} and an initial displacement of $x_0 = +0.200$ m.

11–15 An object is vibrating with simple harmonic motion that has an amplitude of 12.0 cm and a frequency of 4.00 Hz. Compute

a) the maximum magnitude of the acceleration and of the velocity;

b) the acceleration and speed when the coordinate of the object is $x = +5.0$ cm;

c) the time required to move from the equilibrium position directly to a point 9.0 cm distant from it.

11–16 A tuning fork labeled 440 Hz has the tip of each of its two prongs vibrating through a maximum displacement from equilibrium equal to 0.800 mm.

a) What is the maximum speed of the tip of a prong?

b) What is the maximum acceleration of the tip of a prong?

11–17 The scale of a spring balance reading from zero to 180 N is 9.00 cm long. A fish suspended from the balance is observed to oscillate vertically at 2.50 Hz. What is the mass of the fish? Neglect the mass of the spring.

11–18 A block with a mass of 2.00 kg is suspended from a spring having negligible mass and is found to stretch the spring 0.150 m.

a) What is the force constant of the spring?

b) What is the period of oscillation of the block if it is pulled down and released?

11–19 A block with a mass of 3.00 kg hangs from a spring. When displaced from equilibrium, it oscillates with a period of 0.500 s. How much is the spring stretched when the block hangs in equilibrium?

Section 11–4   Angular Simple Harmonic Motion

11–20 The balance wheel of a watch vibrates with an angular amplitude of $\pi/2$ rad and with a period of 0.500 s.

a) Find its maximum angular velocity.

b) Find its angular velocity when its angular displacement is one half its angular amplitude.

c) Find its angular acceleration when its angular displacement is 22.5°.

11–21 A certain alarm clock ticks four times each second, each tick representing half a period. The balance wheel consists of a thin rim of radius 1.50 cm connected to the balance staff by thin spokes of negligible mass. The total mass of the balance wheel is 1.20 g.

a) What is the moment of inertia of the balance wheel?

b) What is the torque constant of the hairspring?

Section 11–5   The Simple Pendulum

11–22 Find the length of a simple pendulum that makes 100 complete swings in 85.0 s at a point where $g = 9.80$ m·s^{-2}.

11–23 A certain simple pendulum has a period on earth of 0.500 s. What is its period on the surface of the moon, where $g = 1.67$ m·s^{-2}?

11–24 A simple pendulum 3.40 m long swings with amplitude 0.200 m.

a) Compute the linear speed v of the pendulum at its lowest point.

b) Compute its linear acceleration a at the ends of its path.

Section 11–6   The Physical Pendulum

11–25 A 1.50-kg monkey wrench is pivoted at one end and allowed to swing as a physical pendulum. The period is 0.750 s, and the pivot is 0.200 m from the center of gravity.

a) What is the moment of inertia of the wrench about an axis through the pivot?

b) If the wrench was initially displaced 0.150 rad from its equilibrium position, what is the angular velocity of the wrench as it passes through the equilibrium position?

11–26 A thin, uniform rod with length L and mass M is pivoted about a perpendicular axis through the rod at a distance $L/5$ from one end. The moment of inertia of the rod about this axis is $(13/75)ML^2$. Find the period of oscillation of the rod.

Problems

11–27 The motion of the piston of an automobile engine is approximately simple harmonic.

a) If the stroke of an engine (twice the amplitude) is 0.120 m, and the engine runs at 3600 rev·min^{-1}, compute the acceleration of the piston at the endpoint of its stroke.

b) If the piston has a mass of 0.400 kg, what resultant force must be exerted on it at this point?

c) What is the speed of the piston, in meters per second, at the midpoint of its stroke?

11–28 An object with a mass of 0.150 kg is acted on by an elastic restoring force with force constant $k = 25.0$ N·m^{-1}.

a) Construct the graph of elastic potential energy U as a function of displacement x over a range of x from -0.300 m to $+0.300$ m. Let 1 cm = 0.1 J vertically and 1 cm = 0.05 m horizontally.

The object is set into oscillation with an initial potential energy of 0.500 J and an initial kinetic energy of 0.200 J. Answer the following questions by reference to the graph:

b) What is the amplitude of oscillation?

c) What is the potential energy when the displacement is one half the amplitude?

d) At what displacement are the kinetic and potential energies equal?

e) What is the speed of the object at the midpoint of its path (that is, at $x = 0$)?

f) What is the initial phase angle ϕ_0 if the initial velocity v_0 is negative and the initial displacement x_0 is positive?

11–29 Four passengers whose combined mass is 250 kg are observed to compress the springs of an automobile by 5.00 cm when they enter the automobile. If the total load supported by the springs is 900 kg, find the period of vibration of the loaded automobile.

11–30 A block is executing simple harmonic motion in a horizontal plane with an amplitude of 0.100 m. At a point 0.060 m away from equilibrium the velocity is ± 0.360 m·s^{-1}.

a) What is the period?

b) What is the displacement when the velocity is ± 0.120 m·s^{-1}?

c) If a small object placed on the oscillating block is just on the verge of slipping at the endpoint of the path, what is the coefficient of static friction between the small object and the block?

11–31 A rubber raft bobs up and down, executing simple harmonic motion due to the waves on a lake. The amplitude of the motion is 2.00 ft, and the period is 4.00 s. A stable dock is next to the raft and is at a level equal to the highest level of the raft. People wish to step off the raft onto the dock but can do so comfortably only if the level of the raft is within 1.00 ft of the dock level. How much time do the people have to get off comfortably during each period of the simple harmonic motion?

11–32 A 0.0100-kg object moves with simple harmonic motion that has an amplitude of 0.240 m and a period of 2.50 s. The x-coordinate is $+0.240$ m when $t = 0$. Compute

a) the x-coordinate of the object when $t = 0.500$ s,

b) the magnitude and direction of the force acting on the object when $t = 0.500$ s,

c) the minimum time required for the object to move from its initial position to the point at which $x = -0.120$ m,

d) the speed of the object when $x = -0.120$ m.

11–33 An object with a mass of 0.100 kg hangs from a long spiral spring. When the object is pulled down 0.100 m below its equilibrium position and released, it vibrates with a period of 1.50 s.

a) What is its speed as it passes through the equilibrium position?

b) What is its acceleration when it is 0.050 m above the equilibrium position?

c) When it is moving upward, how much time is required for it to move from a point 0.050 m below its equilibrium position to a point 0.050 m above it?

d) The motion of the object is stopped, and then the object is removed from the spring. How much does the spring shorten?

11–34

a) A block suspended from a spring vibrates with simple harmonic motion. At an instant when the displacement of the block is equal to one half the amplitude, what fraction of the total energy of the system is kinetic and what fraction is potential? Assume that $U = 0$ at equilibrium.

b) When the block is in equilibrium, the length of the spring is an amount s greater than in the unstretched state. Prove that $\tau = 2\pi\sqrt{s/g}$.

11-35 A 30.0-N force stretches a vertical spring 0.250 m.

a) What mass must be suspended from the spring so that the system will oscillate with a period of $(\pi/4)$ s?

b) If the amplitude of the motion is 0.080 m and the period is that specified in part (a), where is the object and in what direction is it moving $(\pi/12)$ s after it has passed the equilibrium position, moving downward?

c) What force (magnitude and direction) does the spring exert on the object when it is 0.030 m below the equilibrium position, moving upward?

11-36 A block with a mass of 4.00 kg is attached to a coil spring and oscillates vertically in simple harmonic motion. The amplitude is 0.300 m, and at the highest point of the motion the spring has its natural unstretched length. Calculate the elastic potential energy of the spring (take it to be zero for the unstretched spring), the kinetic energy of the block, its gravitational potential energy relative to the lowest point of the motion, and the sum of these three energies, when the body is

a) at its lowest point;

b) at its equilibrium position;

c) at its highest point.

11-37 To measure g in an unorthodox manner, a student places a ball bearing on the concave side of a lens, as shown in Fig. 11-16. She attaches the lens to a simple harmonic oscillator (actually a small stereo speaker) whose amplitude is A and whose frequency f can be varied. She can measure both A and f with a strobe light.

FIGURE 11-16

a) If the ball bearing has a mass m, find an expression for the normal force exerted by the lens on the ball bearing as a function of time. Your result should be in terms of A, f, m, g, and a phase angle ϕ_0.

b) The frequency is slowly increased. When it reaches a value f_b, the ball is heard to bounce. Derive an expression for g in terms of A and f_b.

c) Why is the result in part (b) independent of m?

11-38 The general equation of simple harmonic motion,

$$x = A \cos(\omega t + \phi_0),$$

can be written in the equivalent form

$$x = B \sin \omega t + C \cos \omega t.$$

a) Find the expressions for the amplitudes B and C in terms of the amplitude A and the initial phase angle ϕ_0.

b) Interpret these expressions in terms of a phasor diagram.

11-39 A block with a mass of 0.50 kg sits on top of a block with a mass of 5.00 kg that rests on the floor. The larger block is attached to a horizontal spring that has a force constant 15.0 N·m^{-1}. It is displaced and undergoes simple harmonic motion. What is the largest amplitude the 5.00-kg mass can have for the smaller mass to remain at rest relative to the larger block? The coefficient of static friction between the two blocks is 0.30. There is no friction between the larger block and the floor.

Challenge Problems

11-40 A very interesting, though impractical, example of simple harmonic motion occurs when a particle is dropped down a hole that extends from one side of the earth through its center to the other side. Prove that the motion is simple harmonic and find the period. (*Note:* One needs to use the following property of the gravitational force: The force on an object with mass m due to a spherical mass M with radius R is toward the center of the sphere and has magnitude GmM'/r^2, where r is the distance from the center of M out to the location of point mass m and M' is the mass of that

part of M in the sphere of radius r. Hence if $r > R$, then $M' = M$. But if, for example, $r = R/2$, then $M' = M/8$ because only one eighth the volume and hence one eighth the mass of M is inside the sphere of radius r.)

11-41 Two springs with the same unstretched length but different force constants k_1 and k_2 are attached to a block of mass m on a level, frictionless surface. Calculate the effective force constant k_{eff} in each of the three cases (a), (b), and (c) depicted in Fig. 11-17. (The effective force constant is defined by $\Sigma F = -k_{eff}x$.)

d) A body of mass m, suspended from a spring with a force constant k, vibrates with a frequency f_1. When the spring is cut in half and the same body is suspended from one of the halves, the frequency is f_2. What is the ratio f_2/f_1?

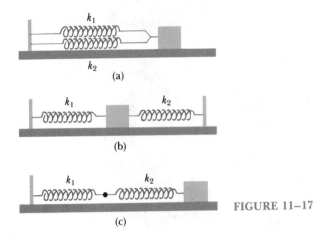

k_1

k_2

(a)

k_1 k_2

(b)

k_1 k_2

(c)

FIGURE 11–17

11–42 Two springs, each with an unstretched length of 0.20 m, are attached to opposite ends of a block of mass m on a level, frictionless surface. Spring 1 on the left-hand side of the block has force constant k_1, and spring 2 on the right-hand side has force constant k_2. The outer ends of the springs are now attached to two pins P_1 and P_2, 0.10 m from the original positions of

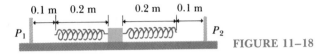

0.1 m   0.2 m   0.2 m   0.1 m

P_1 P_2

FIGURE 11–18

the ends of the springs. (See Fig. 11–18.) Let

$$k_1 = 1.00 \ \text{N·m}^{-1}, \qquad k_2 = 2.00 \ \text{N·m}^{-1}, \qquad m = 0.100 \ \text{kg}.$$

a) Find the length of each spring when the block is in its new equilibrium position after the springs have been attached to the pins.

b) Find the period of vibration of the block if it is slightly displaced from its new equilibrium position and released.

11–43 A block with mass m_1 attached to a horizontal spring with force constant k is moving with simple harmonic motion having amplitude A. At the instant when the block passes through its equilibrium position, a lump of putty of mass m_2 is dropped vertically onto it from a very small height and sticks to it.

a) Find the new period and amplitude.

b) Was there a loss of mechanical energy? If so, where did it go? Calculate the ratio of the final to the initial mechanical energy.

c) What are the answers to part (a) if the putty is dropped on the block when it is at one end of its path?

12

Elasticity

We have used various models to describe bodies in motion or in equilibrium. In the opening chapters our model was usually a *particle* with a position represented by a single geometric point. Then in Chapters 9 and 10 we analyzed the motion and equilibrium of rigid bodies. The rigid body is also an idealized model; a rigid body has a definite size and shape but does not stretch, squeeze, or twist when forces act on it. Of course, real materials always *do* deform when forces act on them; in this chapter we consider the relationships between forces and deformations. The concepts of stress, strain, and elastic modulus help us to describe the elastic properties of materials independently of the dimensions of a particular specimen. When the forces are small enough, the deformation of a material is proportional to the force, but with larger forces the behavior is more complex. For sufficiently large forces, materials can deform irreversibly or break, and we can use the concept of stress to characterize the *strength* of a material. Elastic properties of materials are of tremendous practical importance in the design of buildings, automobiles, and many of the necessities of everyday life.

12–1
Tensile Stress and Strain

The simplest elastic behavior to understand is the stretching of a bar, rod, or wire when its ends are pulled. Figure 12–1a shows a bar having uniform cross-sectional area A, with equal and opposite forces F pulling at its ends. We say that the bar is in **tension.** We have talked about tensions in ropes and strings in earlier chapters; it's the same concept here. Imagine a cross section through the bar perpendicular to its length, as shown by the broken line. Every part of the bar is in equilibrium, so the part to the right of the section must be pulling on the part to the left with a force F, and vice versa. If the forces at the ends are applied uniformly over the end surfaces, then the forces at every other cross section are also distributed uniformly over the section, as shown by the short arrows in Fig. 12–1b. We define the **stress** at this section as the ratio of the force F to the cross-sectional area A:

$$\text{Stress} = \frac{F}{A}. \tag{12–1}$$

We call this stress a **tensile stress** because each part exerts tension on the other.

The SI unit of stress is the newton per square meter (N·m^{-2}). This unit is also given a special name, the **pascal** (abbreviated Pa):

$$1 \text{ pascal} = 1 \text{ Pa} = 1 \text{ N·m}^{-2}.$$

In the British system the logical unit of stress would be the pound per square foot, but the pound per square inch (lb·in^{-2} or psi) is more commonly used. The conversion factors are

$$1 \text{ psi} = 6891 \text{ Pa}, \qquad 1 \text{ Pa} = 1.451 \times 10^{-4} \text{ psi}.$$

The units of stress are the same as those of *pressure*, which we will encounter frequently in later chapters. The pascal is a fairly small unit; air pressure in automobile tires is typically of the order of 2×10^5 Pa, and steel cables are commonly used with tensile stresses of the order of 10^8 Pa.

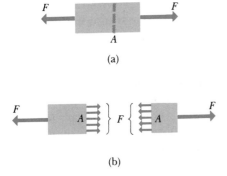

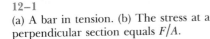

12–1
(a) A bar in tension. (b) The stress at a perpendicular section equals F/A.

Example 12–1   A human biceps (upper arm muscle) may exert a force of the order of 600 N (about 135 lb) on the bones to which it is attached. If the muscle has a cross-sectional area at its center of 50 cm^2 = 0.0050 m^2, and the tendon attaching its lower end to the bones below the elbow joint has a cross section of 0.50 cm^2 = 5.0×10^{-5} m^2, find the tensile stress in each of these cross sections.

Solution   In each case the stress is the force per unit area. For the muscle,

$$\text{Tensile stress} = \frac{600 \text{ N}}{0.0050 \text{ m}^2} = 1.2 \times 10^5 \text{ N·m}^{-2} = 1.2 \times 10^5 \text{ Pa}.$$

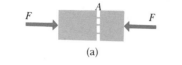

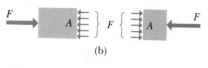

12–2
A bar in compression.

For the tendon,

$$\text{Tensile stress} = \frac{600 \text{ N}}{5.0 \times 10^{-5} \text{ m}^2} = 1.2 \times 10^7 \text{ Pa.} \quad \blacksquare$$

When the forces acting on the ends of a bar are pushes rather than pulls, as in Fig. 12–2a, we say that the bar is in **compression.** The stress on the cross section shown by a broken line is now a **compressive stress;** each portion pushes rather than pulls on the other.

The fractional change of length (stretch) of a body subjected to a tensile stress is called the **tensile strain.** Figure 12–3 shows a bar of natural length l_0 that stretches to a length $l = l_0 + \Delta l$ when equal and opposite forces F are applied to its ends. The elongation Δl does not occur only at the ends; every part of the bar stretches in the same proportion. The tensile strain is defined as the ratio of the elongation Δl to the original length l_0:

$$\text{Tensile strain} = \frac{l - l_0}{l_0} = \frac{\Delta l}{l_0}. \quad (12\text{–}2)$$

Tensile strain is stretch per unit length. It is a ratio of two lengths, and we always measure the two lengths in the same units. Thus strain is a pure (dimensionless) number with no units. The **compressive strain** of a bar in compression is defined in the same way as tensile strain; it is the ratio of the decrease in length to the original length, the squeeze per unit length.

The tensile or compressive *strain* depends on the tensile or compressive *stress*; the harder you pull on something, the more it stretches; and the harder you push, the more it squashes. Robert Hooke (1635–1703), a contemporary of Newton, discovered that when the forces are not too large, this relation is a *direct proportion.* In this case, stress is proportional to strain, and the ratio of stress to strain is constant. This proportionality is called **Hooke's law.**

The quotient of any stress and the corresponding strain is called an **elastic modulus;** and for the particular case of tensile or compressive stress and strain, it is called **Young's modulus,** denoted by Y:

$$Y = \frac{\text{tensile stress}}{\text{tensile strain}} = \frac{\text{compressive stress}}{\text{compressive strain}},$$

$$Y = \frac{F/A}{\Delta l/l_0} = \frac{l_0}{A}\frac{F}{\Delta l}. \quad (12\text{–}3)$$

Strain is a pure number, so the units of Young's modulus are the same as those of stress, namely, force per unit area. Some typical values are listed in Table 12–1. This table also gives values of three other elastic constants that we will discuss in later sections.

When a material stretches, the dimensions *perpendicular* to the stretch become *smaller.* When you stretch a wire or a rubber band, it gets a little thinner as well as longer. When the forces are small enough that Hooke's law is valid, the fractional decrease in width is proportional to

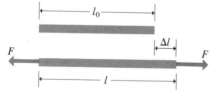

12–3
The longitudinal strain is defined as $\Delta l/l_0$.

TABLE 12-1	**Approximate elastic constants**						
	Young's modulus, Y		Shear modulus, S		Bulk modulus, B		
Material	Pa	lb·in^{-2}	Pa	lb·in^{-2}	Pa	lb·in^{-2}	Poisson's ratio, σ
Aluminum	0.70×10^{11}	10×10^6	0.30×10^{11}	3.4×10^6	0.70×10^{11}	10×10^6	0.16
Brass	0.91×10^{11}	13×10^6	0.36×10^{11}	5.1×10^6	0.61×10^{11}	8.5×10^6	0.26
Copper	1.1×10^{11}	16×10^6	0.42×10^{11}	6.0×10^6	1.4×10^{11}	20×10^6	0.32
Glass	0.55×10^{11}	7.8×10^6	0.23×10^{11}	3.3×10^6	0.37×10^{11}	5.2×10^6	0.19
Iron	1.9×10^{11}	26×10^6	0.70×10^{11}	10×10^6	1.0×10^{11}	14×10^6	0.27
Lead	0.16×10^{11}	2.3×10^6	0.056×10^{11}	0.8×10^6	0.077×10^{11}	1.1×10^6	0.43
Nickel	2.1×10^{11}	30×10^6	0.77×10^{11}	11×10^6	2.6×10^{11}	34×10^6	0.36
Steel	2.0×10^{11}	29×10^6	0.84×10^{11}	12×10^6	1.6×10^{11}	23×10^6	0.19
Tungsten	3.6×10^{11}	51×10^6	1.5×10^{11}	21×10^6	2.0×10^{11}	29×10^6	0.20

the tensile strain. If w_0 is the original width and Δw is the change in width, then

$$\frac{\Delta w}{w_0} = -\sigma \frac{\Delta l}{l_0}, \qquad (12\text{-}4)$$

where σ is a dimensionless constant, different for different materials, called **Poisson's ratio.** For many common materials, σ has a value between 0.1 and 0.3; several representative values are listed in Table 12-1. Similarly, a material under compressive stress bulges at the sides, and again the fractional change in width is given by Eq. (12-4).

Experiments have shown that for many materials the ratio of compressive stress to compressive strain is the same as the ratio of tensile stress to tensile strain. Hence Young's modulus describes the behavior of many (though not all) materials in both tension and compression.

Example 12-2   In a small elevator, a 500-kg load hanging from a steel cable 3.0 m long with a cross section of 0.20 cm^2 is found to stretch the cable 0.40 cm beyond its no-load length. Determine the stress, the strain, and the value of Young's modulus for the steel in the cable.

Solution   We use the definitions of stress, strain, and Young's modulus as given by Eqs. (12-1), (12-2), and (12-3):

$$\text{Stress} = \frac{F}{A} = \frac{(500 \text{ kg})(9.8 \text{ m·s}^{-2})}{2.0 \times 10^{-5} \text{ m}^2} = 2.45 \times 10^8 \text{ Pa};$$

$$\text{Strain} = \frac{\Delta l}{l_0} = \frac{0.0040 \text{ m}}{3.0 \text{ m}} = 0.00133;$$

$$Y = \frac{\text{stress}}{\text{strain}} = \frac{2.45 \times 10^8 \text{ Pa}}{0.00133} = 1.8 \times 10^{11} \text{ Pa}.$$

As the cable stretches, it becomes a little narrower; according to Eq. (12–4),

$$\frac{\Delta w}{w_0} = -(0.19)(0.00133) = -0.000253.$$

We invite you to show that if the cable has a circular cross section, its diameter is about 0.50 cm and the change in diameter when it stretches is about −0.00013 cm. This is not quite within the precision of ordinary micrometer calipers. ■

Young's modulus characterizes the elastic properties of a material under tension or compression in a way that is independent of the size or shape of the particular specimen. We can use it to determine how any specific rod, cable, or spring made of the material will distort under given forces. We may solve Eq. (12–3) for F, obtaining

$$F = \frac{YA}{l_0}\Delta l.$$

Now let's change notation: Label the quantity YA/l_0 as k and call it the **force constant.** Call the elongation x instead of Δl; then we have

$$F = kx.$$

We have seen this relationship before, in Sections 7–3 and 7–6 in connection with work and potential energy for a spring, and again in Chapter 11 in connection with simple harmonic motion. The elongation of a body in tension is *directly proportional* to the stretching force, and the shortening of a body in compression is directly proportional to the compressing force. Hooke's law was originally stated in this form; it was reformulated in terms of stress and strain much later by other physicists.

When a helical or coil spring is stretched or compressed, the stress and strain in the wire are nearly pure *shear* (to be discussed in Section 12–3), but the elongation or compression is still proportional to the stretching or compressing force, within certain limits of maximum force. That is, the equation $F = kx$ is still valid. Of course, a coil spring can be compressed only if there are spaces between the coils.

The units of the force constant are newtons per meter or pounds per foot. The reciprocal of the force constant, that is, the ratio of elongation or compression to force, is called the *compliance* of the spring.

12–2
Bulk Stress and Strain

We have discussed tensile and compressive stresses and strains. A different stress–strain situation occurs when a solid or fluid material is subjected to a uniform pressure over its whole surface. We can describe the resulting deformation in terms of the volume change of the material. A

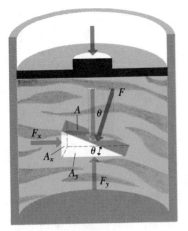

12–4
A fluid under hydrostatic pressure.
The force on a surface in any direction
is normal to the surface.

familiar example is the compression of a gas under pressure. The term *fluid* means a substance that can *flow*, so the term applies to both liquids and gases.

A force transmitted across a cross section of a fluid at rest is always *perpendicular* to that section; if we tried to exert a force parallel to a section, the fluid would slip sideways to counteract the effort. In the language that we will introduce in Section 12–3 there can be no *shear stress* in a fluid at rest. Similarly, when a solid is immersed in a fluid and both are at rest, the forces that the fluid exerts on the surface of the solid are always perpendicular to the surface at each point.

Figure 12–4 shows a fluid in a cylinder with a piston. We apply a downward force to the piston, and this force is transmitted throughout the fluid. If we neglect the weight of the fluid, the force per unit area (pressure) is the same at every point. To prove this, consider the wedge-shaped portion of fluid shown in Fig. 12–4. The only forces on this wedge are those exerted on its imaginary surfaces by the surrounding fluid, and each force must be perpendicular to the corresponding surface. We denote the forces on the three faces by F_x, F_y, and F, as shown. The wedge is in equilibrium, so the vector sum of forces acting on it must be zero. In components,

$$F \sin \theta = F_x, \qquad F \cos \theta = F_y.$$

Also,

$$A \sin \theta = A_x, \qquad A \cos \theta = A_y.$$

Dividing the upper equations by the lower ones, we find

$$\frac{F}{A} = \frac{F_x}{A_x} = \frac{F_y}{A_y}.$$

This shows that the force per unit area is the *same* on all these surfaces. It does not depend on their orientation, and it is always a compression. The force per unit area on any of these surfaces is called the **pressure** p in the fluid,

$$p = \frac{F}{A}, \qquad F = pA. \tag{12–5}$$

The fact that pressure applied to the surface of a fluid is transmitted unchanged to all parts of the fluid is called Pascal's law.

Pressure has the same units as stress; commonly used units include 1 Pa ($= 1 \text{ N·m}^{-2}$) and 1 lb·in^{-2} (1 psi). Also in common use is the **atmosphere,** abbreviated atm. One atmosphere is defined to be the average pressure of the earth's atmosphere at sea level.

1 atmosphere = 1 atm = 1.013×10^5 Pa = 14.7 lb·in^{-2}.

Pressure is a scalar quantity, not a vector quantity; it has no direction. The force acting on any area within, or at the boundary surface of, a fluid at rest is always perpendicular to the area, regardless of the orientation of the area.

If the force per unit area on the surface of a solid body is the same at every point of the surface, and if the force at each point is normal to the surface and directed inward, then the stress at every point *within* the body is a pressure. This is *not* the case in Fig. 12–2, in which forces are applied only at the ends of the bar, but it is automatically the case if a solid is immersed in a fluid under pressure.

Pressure is the *stress* in a volume deformation. The corresponding strain is **volume strain;** it is defined as the fractional change in volume, that is, the ratio of the volume change ΔV to the original volume V_0:

$$\text{Volume strain} = \frac{\Delta V}{V_0}. \tag{12-6}$$

Volume strain is change in volume per unit volume. Like tensile or compressive strain, it is a pure number, without units.

There is a Hooke's-law relation for volume stress and strain. For sufficiently small pressure changes the volume strain is *proportional* to the stress (pressure change). The corresponding elastic modulus (ratio of stress to strain) is called the **bulk modulus,** denoted by B. The general definition of the bulk modulus is the (negative) ratio of a small pressure change Δp to the volume strain $\Delta V/V_0$ (fractional change in volume) it causes:

$$B = -\frac{\Delta p}{\Delta V/V_0}. \tag{12-7}$$

The minus sign is included in the definition of B because an *increase* of pressure always causes a *decrease* in volume. In other words, if Δp is positive, ΔV is negative. The minus sign in Eq. (12–7) makes B itself a positive quantity.

For small pressure changes in a solid or a liquid, we consider B to be constant. The bulk modulus of a *gas,* however, depends on the initial pressure.

The reciprocal of the bulk modulus is called the **compressibility** k. From Eq. (12–7),

$$k = \frac{1}{B} = -\frac{\Delta V/V_0}{\Delta p} = -\frac{1}{V_0}\frac{\Delta V}{\Delta p}. \tag{12-8}$$

Compressibility is the *fractional decrease in volume,* $-\Delta V/V_0$, *for a small increase Δp in pressure.*

TABLE 12–2   Compressibilities of liquids

Liquid	Compressibility, k		
	Pa^{-1}	$(\text{lb}\cdot\text{in}^{-2})^{-1}$	atm^{-1}
Carbon disulfide	93×10^{-11}	64×10^{-7}	94×10^{-6}
Ethyl alcohol	110×10^{-11}	76×10^{-7}	111×10^{-6}
Glycerine	21×10^{-11}	14×10^{-7}	21×10^{-6}
Mercury	3.7×10^{-11}	2.6×10^{-7}	3.8×10^{-6}
Water	45.8×10^{-11}	31.6×10^{-7}	46.4×10^{-6}

Table 12–1 includes values of the bulk modulus. Its units, force per unit area, are the same as those of pressure (and of tensile or compressive stress), and the units of compressibility are those of *reciprocal pressure*, area per unit force. The compressibility of water, from Table 12–2, is 46.4×10^{-6} atm^{-1}. This means that for each atmosphere increase in pressure the volume decreases by 46.4 parts per million.

Example 12–3 The volume of oil contained in a certain hydraulic press is 0.20 m^3 = 200 L. Find the decrease in volume of the oil when it is subjected to a pressure increase of 2.04×10^7 Pa. The compressibility of the oil is 20×10^{-6} atm^{-1}.

Solution Because we are given the compressibility in atm^{-1}, we first convert the pressure to atmospheres:

$$\Delta p = 2.04 \times 10^7 \text{ Pa} = 201 \text{ atm.}$$

Then from Eq. (12–8),

$$\Delta V = -kV_0 \, \Delta p = -(20 \times 10^{-6} \text{ atm}^{-1})(0.2 \text{ m}^3)(201 \text{ atm})$$
$$= -8.0 \times 10^{-4} \text{ m}^3 = -0.80 \text{ L.}$$

This represents a substantial compression of the oil under the action of a very large pressure, nearly 3000 lb·in^{-2}. ■

12–3
Shear Stress and Strain

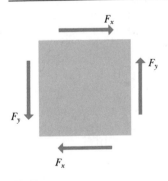

12–5
A body under shear stress.

A third kind of stress is shown in Fig. 12–5. This stress is called **shear stress;** we define it as the force *tangent* to a material surface divided by the area on which the force acts. Shear stress, like the other two types of stress, is a force per unit area. For systems in equilibrium, shear stress can exist only in *solid* materials.

A shear deformation is shown in Fig. 12–6. The gray-shaded outline *abcd* represents an unstressed block of material, and the area *a'b'c'd'* shaded in color shows the same block under stress. In part (a) the centers of the stressed and unstressed block coincide. The deformation in part (b) is the same as that in part (a), but the figure has been shifted to make the edges *ad* and *a'd'* coincide. In shear stress the lengths of the faces remain very nearly constant; all dimensions parallel to the diagonal *ac* increase in length, and those parallel to the diagonal *bd* decrease in length. This type of strain is called a **shear strain;** it is defined as the ratio of the displacement *x* of corner *b* to the transverse dimension *h*:

$$\text{Shear strain} = \frac{x}{h} = \tan \phi. \qquad (12\text{–}9)$$

12–6
Change in shape of a block in shear. The shear strain is defined as x/h.

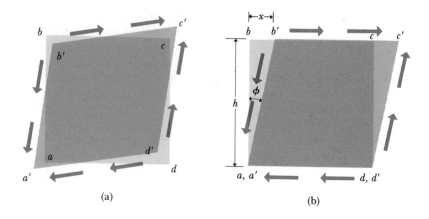

(a)   (b)

In real-life situations, x is nearly always much smaller than h, tan ϕ is very nearly equal to ϕ, and the strain is simply the angle ϕ (measured in radians, of course). Like all strains, shear strain is a pure number with no units because it is a ratio of two lengths.

Once again, we find experimentally that if the forces are not too large, the shear strain is *proportional* to the shear stress. The corresponding elastic modulus (ratio of shear stress to shear strain) is called the **shear modulus,** denoted by S.

$$S = \frac{\text{shear stress}}{\text{shear strain}}$$
$$= \frac{F/A}{x/h} = \frac{hF}{xA} = \frac{F/A}{\phi}, \qquad (12\text{–}10)$$

with x and h defined as in Fig. 12–6.

For most materials the shear modulus is one third to one half as large as Young's modulus. The shear modulus is also called the *modulus of rigidity* or the *torsion modulus*. Representative values of shear modulus are given in Table 12–1. The shear modulus has significance only for *solid* materials. A liquid or gas flows freely under the action of a shear stress, and a fluid at rest cannot sustain such a stress.

Example 12–4   Suppose the object in Fig. 12–6 is a brass plate 1.0 m square and 0.50 cm thick. How large a force F must be exerted on each of its edges if the displacement x in Fig. 12–6b is 0.020 cm? The shear modulus of brass is 0.36×10^{11} Pa.

Solution   The shear stress at each edge is

$$\text{Shear stress} = \frac{F}{A} = \frac{F}{(1.0\ \text{m})(0.0050\ \text{m})} = (200\ \text{m}^{-2})F.$$

The shear strain is

$$\text{Shear strain} = \frac{x}{h} = \frac{2.0 \times 10^{-4}\ \text{m}}{1.0\ \text{m}} = 2.0 \times 10^{-4}.$$

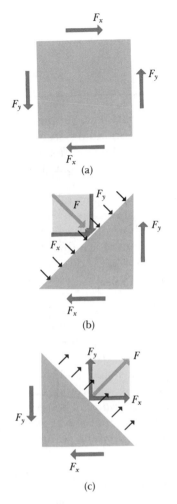

12–7
(a) A body in shear. The stress on one diagonal, part (b), is a pure compression; that on the other, part (c), is a pure tension.

The shear modulus S is

$$S = \frac{\text{stress}}{\text{strain}} = 0.36 \times 10^{11} \text{ Pa} = \frac{(200 \text{ m}^{-2})F}{2.0 \times 10^{-4}},$$

and

$$F = 3.6 \times 10^4 \text{ N}.$$

■

Another aspect of the relations among the elastic constants is that different cross sections in a body have different states of stress. As an example, consider the body under shear stress in Fig. 12–7, acted on by the pairs of forces F_x and F_y distributed over its surfaces. The block in Fig. 12–7a is in equilibrium, and every portion of it must also be in equilibrium. If we consider the triangular piece shown in Fig. 12–7b, the distributed forces over the diagonal face must have a resultant $\mathbf{F}$ whose components are equal in magnitude to F_x and F_y. Thus the stress at the diagonal face is a pure *compression*, even though the stresses at the right and bottom faces are shear stresses. Similarly, the diagonal face shown in Fig. 12–7c is in pure *tension*.

The same thing happens with the stretched bar that we used in Section 12–1 to introduce tensile stress. A cross section perpendicular to the length of the bar has a purely tensile stress, as shown in Fig. 12–1. But suppose we take a cross section at an angle, with area A', as in Fig. 12–8a. The stress at this face has both tensile and shear components, as shown in Fig. 12–8b. The force acting at a particular cross section has a definite direction and magnitude and can be represented by means of its components, but the components are different for different orientations of the section. For a complete general description of the state of stress in a material we have to take three mutually perpendicular cross section orientations and describe the three components of force (per unit area) for each of the three. The resulting set of nine numbers is called the *stress tensor*; this is an example of a class of physical quantities called *tensors*.

The various types of stress, strain, and elastic moduli are summarized in Table 12–3.

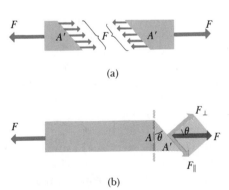

12–8
A bar in tension. The stress at an inclined section (a) can be resolved into (b) a normal stress $F_\perp / A'$ and a tangential or shear stress $F_\parallel / A'$.

TABLE 12–3   Stresses and strains

Type of stress	Stress	Strain	Elastic modulus	Name of modulus
Tension or compression	$\frac{F}{A}$	$\frac{\Delta l}{l_0}$	$Y = \dfrac{F/A}{\Delta l/l_0}$	Young's modulus
Hydrostatic pressure	$p\left(= \dfrac{F}{A}\right)$	$\frac{\Delta V}{V_0}$	$B = -\dfrac{p}{\Delta V/V_0}$	Bulk modulus
Shear	$\frac{F}{A}$	$\tan \phi \approx \phi$	$S = \dfrac{F/A}{\phi}$	Shear modulus

*12–4
Elasticity and Plasticity

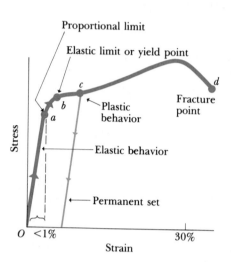

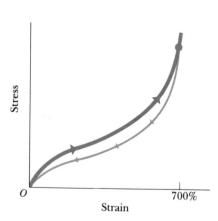

Typical stress–strain diagram for a ductile metal under tension. The horizontal scale is not uniform.

Typical stress–strain diagram for vulcanized rubber, showing elastic hysteresis.

We are now ready to examine the limitations of Hooke's law. Suppose we plot a graph of stress as a function of the corresponding strain. If Hooke's law is obeyed, stress is directly proportional to strain, and the graph is a straight line. Real materials show several types of departures from this idealized behavior.

Figure 12–9 shows a typical stress–strain graph for a metal such as copper or soft iron. The stress in this case is a simple tensile stress, and the strain is shown as the *percent* elongation. The horizontal scale is not uniform. The first portion of the curve, up to a strain of less than 1%, is a straight line, indicating Hooke's-law behavior with stress directly proportional to strain. This straight-line portion ends at point *a*; the stress at this point is called the **proportional limit.**

From *a* to *b*, stress and strain are no longer proportional, and Hooke's law is *not* obeyed. But if the load is removed at any point between *O* and *b*, the curve is retraced, and the material returns to its original length. Up to this point the deformation is *reversible*. When the load is removed, the material returns to its original shape, and the energy put into the material to cause the deformation is recovered. Up to this point the forces exerted by the material are *conservative*. The region *Ob* is called the *elastic* region; in this region the material shows *elastic behavior*. Point *b*, the end of this region, is called the **yield point;** the stress at the yield point is called the **elastic limit.**

When we increase the stress further, the strain continues to increase. But now when we remove the load at some point beyond *b*, say *c*, the material does not come back to its original length. Instead, it follows the thin line in Fig. 12–9. The length at zero stress is now *greater* than the original length; the material has undergone an *irreversible* deformation, and we say that it has a *permanent set*. Further increase of load beyond *c* produces a large increase in strain (even if the stress decreases) until a point *d* is reached at which *fracture* takes place. The behavior of the material from *b* to *d* is called *plastic flow* or *plastic deformation*. A plastic deformation is *irreversible*; when the stress is removed, the material does not return to its original state.

For some materials a large amount of plastic deformation takes place between the elastic limit and the fracture point. Such a material is said to be *ductile*. But if fracture occurs soon after the elastic limit is passed, the metal is said to be *brittle*. A soft iron wire that can have considerable permanent stretch without breaking is ductile, while a steel piano string that breaks soon after its elastic limit is reached is brittle.

Figure 12–10 shows a stress–strain curve for a typical sample of vulcanized rubber that has been stretched to over seven times its original length. There is *no* region of this curve where stress is proportional to strain! The substance, however, is elastic; when the load is removed, the rubber returns to its original length. When the load is gradually removed, the material does *not* retrace the original stress–strain curve but follows the thin curve of Fig. 12–10.

TABLE 12–4	Breaking stresses of materials

Material	Breaking stress (Pa or N·m^{-2})
Aluminum	2.2×10^8
Brass	4.7×10^8
Glass	10×10^8
Iron	3.0×10^8
Phosphor bronze	5.6×10^8
Steel	11.0×10^8

This behavior, in which the curves for increasing and decreasing stress do not coincide, is known as *elastic hysteresis*. When the stress–strain relation has this behavior, the associated forces are *not* conservative; the work done by the material in returning to its original shape is *less* than the work required to deform it. Think of elastic hysteresis as a kind of internal friction in which the material resists any change, either increasing or decreasing, in its strain. The area bounded by the two curves, that is, the area of the *hysteresis loop*, is proportional to the energy dissipated within the elastic material.

Some types of rubber have large elastic hysteresis, and these materials are very useful as vibration absorbers. If a block of such a material is placed between a piece of vibrating machinery and the floor, elastic hysteresis takes place during each cycle of vibration. Mechanical energy is converted to internal energy in the material, causing a rise in its temperature, and only a small amount of vibration energy is transmitted to the floor.

The stress required to cause actual fracture of a material is called the **breaking stress** or the *ultimate strength*. Two materials, such as two types of steel, may have very similar elastic constants but vastly different breaking stresses. Table 12–4 gives a few typical values of breaking stress for several materials in tension.

Questions

12–1 When a wire is bent back and forth, it becomes hot. Why?

12–2 When a wire is stretched, the cross section decreases somewhat from the undeformed value. How does this affect the definition of tensile stress? Should the original or the decreased value be used?

12–3 Is the work required to stretch a metal rod proportional to the amount of stretch? Explain.

12–4 Why is concrete with steel reinforcing rods embedded in it stronger than plain concrete?

12–5 Is the shear modulus of steel greater or less than that of jelly? By roughly what factor?

12–6 Is the bulk modulus for steel greater or less than that of air? By roughly what factor?

12–7 Looking at the molecular structure of matter, discuss why gases are generally more compressible than liquids and solids.

12–8 Climbing ropes used by mountaineers are usually made of nylon. Would a steel cable of equal strength be just as good? What advantages and disadvantages would it have in comparison to nylon?

12–9 How could you measure the force constants of the springs in an automobile?

12–10 In a nylon mountaineering rope, is a lot of mechanical hysteresis desirable or undesirable?

12–11 A spring scale for measuring weight has a spring and a scale that indicates how much the spring stretches under a given weight. Such scales are often illegal in commerce. (Note the inscription "no springs, honest weight" found on some grocery store scales.) Why? (What property of a metal spring could affect its accuracy?)

12–12 Coil springs found in automobile suspension systems are sometimes designed *not* to obey Hooke's law. How can a spring be made so as to achieve this result? Why is it desirable?

12–13 Compare the mechanical properties of a steel cable made by twisting many thin wires together with those of a solid steel wire of the same diameter. What advantages does each have?

12–14 Electric power lines are sometimes made by using wires with steel core and copper jacket or strands of copper and steel twisted together. Why?

12–15 A spring is compressed, clamped in its compressed position, and then dissolved in acid. What becomes of the elastic potential energy?

12–16 When rubber mounting blocks are used to absorb machine vibrations through mechanical hysteresis, as discussed in Section 12–4, what becomes of the energy associated with the vibrations?

Exercises

Section 12–1   Tensile Stress and Strain

12–1 A certain metal rod that is 4.00 m long and 0.50 cm^2 in cross-sectional area is found to stretch 0.20 cm under a tension of 15,000 N. What is Young's modulus for this metal?

12–2 A relaxed biceps muscle requires a force of 25.0 N for an elongation of 4.0 cm, and the same muscle under maximum tension requires a force of 500 N for the same elongation. Find Young's modulus for the muscle tissue under each of these conditions if the muscle is assumed to be a uniform cylinder with a length of 0.200 m and a cross-sectional area of 50.0 cm^2.

12–3 A nylon rope used by mountaineers elongates 1.50 m under the weight of an 80.0-kg climber.

   a) If the rope is 50.0 m in length and 12.0 mm in diameter, what is Young's modulus for this material?

   b) If Poisson's ratio for nylon is 0.20, find the change in diameter under this stress.

12–4 A steel post 15 cm in diameter and 3.00 m long is placed vertically and is required to support a load of 8000 kg. What is

   a) the stress in the post?

   b) the strain in the post?

   c) the change in length of the post?

12–5 A copper wire with length 1.40 m has diameter 3.0 mm. What is the force constant k for this wire?

12–6 A 5.0-kg mass is hung on a vertical steel wire 0.500 m long and 6.0×10^{-3} cm^2 in cross-sectional area. Hanging from the bottom of this mass is a similar steel wire from which is hung a 10.0-kg mass. Compute for each wire the

   a) tensile strain;

   b) elongation.

12–7 A circular steel wire 4.00 m long is to stretch no more than 0.20 cm when a tensile force of 300 N is applied to each end of the wire. What is the minimum diameter of wire required?

12–8 Two round rods, one steel and the other brass, are joined end to end. Each rod is 0.500 m long and 2.00 cm in diameter. The combination is subjected to a tensile force with magnitude 7000 N. What is

   a) the strain in each rod?

   b) the elongation of each rod?

   c) the change in diameter of each rod?

12–9 A 100-kg mass suspended from a wire whose unstretched length l_0 is 4.00 m is found to stretch the wire by 6.0×10^{-3} m. The cross-sectional area of the wire, which can be assumed constant, is 0.10 cm^2.

   a) If the load is pulled down a small additional distance and released, find the frequency at which it vibrates.

   b) Compute Young's modulus for the wire.

Section 12–2   Bulk Stress and Strain

12–10 A specimen of oil having an initial volume of 1000 cm^3 is subjected to a pressure increase of 1.50×10^6 Pa, and the volume is found to decrease by 0.30 cm^3. What is the bulk modulus for the material? The compressibility?

12–11 In the Challenger Deep of the Mariana Trench the depth of seawater is 10.9 km, and the pressure is 1.10×10^8 Pa (about 1.09×10^3 atm).

   a) If a cubic meter of water is taken from the surface to this depth, what is the change in its volume? (Normal atmospheric pressure is about 1.0×10^5 Pa. Assume that k for seawater is the same as the freshwater value given in Table 12–2.)

   b) What is the density, the mass per unit volume, of seawater at this depth? (At the surface, seawater has a density of 1.03×10^3 kg·m^{-3}.)

Section 12–3   Shear Stress and Strain

12–12 In Fig. 12–5, suppose the object is a square steel plate, 10.0 cm on a side and 1.00 cm thick. Find the magnitude of force required on each of the four sides to cause a shear strain of 0.0400.

12–13 Two strips of metal are riveted together at their ends by four rivets, each with diameter 0.400 cm. What is the maximum tension that can be exerted by the riveted strip if the shearing stress on each rivet is not to exceed 6.00×10^8 Pa? Assume that each rivet is to carry one quarter of the load.

Section 12–4   Elasticity and Plasticity

12–14 The elastic limit of a steel elevator cable is 2.75×10^8 Pa. Find the maximum upward acceleration that can be given a 900-kg elevator when it is supported by a cable whose cross-sectional area is 2.00 cm^2 if the stress is not to exceed one quarter of the elastic limit.

12–15 A steel wire has the following properties:

Length = 5.00 m

Cross-sectional area = 0.040 cm^2

Young's modulus = 2.0 × 10^{11} Pa

Shear modulus = 0.84 × 10^{11} Pa

Proportional limit = 3.60 × 10^8 Pa

Breaking stress = 11.0 × 10^8 Pa

The wire is fastened at its upper end and hangs vertically.

a) How great a weight can be hung from the wire without exceeding the proportional limit?

b) How much will the wire stretch under this load?

c) What is the maximum weight that can be supported?

Problems

12–16 A 15.0-kg mass, fastened to the end of a steel wire with an unstretched length of 0.50 m, is whirled in a vertical circle with angular velocity 2.00 rev·s^{-1} at the bottom of the circle. The cross-sectional area of the wire is 0.010 cm^2. Calculate the elongation of the wire when the mass is at the lowest point of the path.

12–17 A copper wire 4.00 m long and 1.00 mm in diameter was given the test below. A load of 20.0 N was originally hung from the wire to keep it taut. The position of the lower end of the wire was read on a scale:

Added load, N	Scale reading, cm
0	3.02
10	3.07
20	3.12
30	3.17
40	3.22
50	3.27
60	3.32
70	4.27

a) Make a graph of these values, plotting the increase in length horizontally and the added load vertically.

b) Calculate the value of Young's modulus.

c) What was the stress at the proportional limit?

12–18 Compressive strength of our bones is important in everyday life. Young's modulus for bone is about 1.0 × 10^{10} Pa. Bone can take only about a 1.0% change in its length before fracturing.

a) What is the maximum force that can be applied to a bone whose minimum cross-sectional area is 3.0 cm^2? (This is approximately the cross-sectional area of a tibia, or shinbone, at its narrowest point.)

b) Estimate from what maximum height a 70-kg person (one weighing about 150 lb) could jump and not fracture the tibia. Take the time between when the person first touches the floor and when he or she has stopped to be 0.020 s, and assume that the stress is distributed equally between the person's two legs.

12–19 A rod 1.05 m long, whose weight is negligible, is supported at its ends by wires A and B of equal length, as shown in Fig. 12–11. The cross-sectional area of A is 1.00 mm^2; that of B is 3.00 mm^2. Young's modulus for wire A is 2.40 × 10^{11} Pa; that for B is 1.60 × 10^{11} Pa. At what point along the bar should a weight w be suspended to produce

a) equal stresses in A and B?

b) equal strains in A and B?

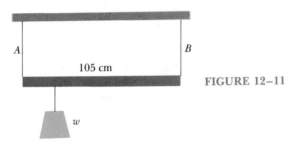

FIGURE 12–11

12–20 An amusement park ride consists of seats attached to cables as shown in Fig. 12–12. Each steel cable has a length of 20.0 m and a cross-sectional area of 7.00 cm^2.

a) What amount is the cable stretched when the ride is at rest? Assume that each seat plus two people seated in it has a total weight of 3000 N.

b) The ride, when turned on, has a maximum angular velocity of 1.40 rad·s^{-1}. How much is the cable then stretched?

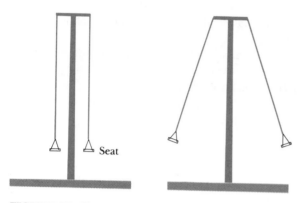

FIGURE 12–12

12–21 A copper rod with a length of 0.800 m and a cross-sectional area of 2.00 cm² is fastened end to end to a steel rod with length L and a cross-sectional area of 1.00 cm². The compound rod is subjected to equal and opposite pulls of magnitude 5.00×10^4 N at its ends.

a) Find the length L of the steel rod if the elongations of the two rods are equal.

b) What is the stress in each rod?

c) What is the strain in each rod?

12–22 A moonshiner produces pure ethanol (ethyl alcohol) late at night and stores it in a stainless steel tank in the form of a cylinder 0.400 m in diameter with a tight-fitting piston at the top. The total volume of the tank is 200 L (0.200 m³). In an attempt to squeeze a lit-

tle more into the tank the moonshiner piles lead bricks on the piston, so the total mass of bricks and piston is 1420 kg. What additional volume of ethanol can the moonshiner squeeze into the tank? (Assume that the wall of the tank is perfectly rigid.)

12–23 In Fig. 12–5, suppose the object is a square aluminum plate 0.200 m on a side. When forces are applied to the four edges, of equal magnitude 3.00×10^6 N each, we want the resulting shear strain to be no greater than 0.0100. What minimum thickness of plate is required?

12–24 A bar with cross-sectional area A is subjected to equal and opposite tensile forces F at its ends. Consider a plane through the bar making an angle θ with a plane at right angles to the bar (Fig. 12–13).

a) What is the tensile (normal) stress at this plane in terms of F, A, and θ?

b) What is the shear (tangential) stress at the plane in terms of F, A, and θ?

c) For what value of θ is the tensile stress a maximum?

d) For what value of θ is the shear stress a maximum?

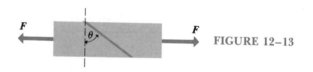

FIGURE 12–13

■ *Challenge Problems*

12–25 A 5.00-kg mass is hung from a vertical steel wire 2.00 m long and 5.00×10^{-3} cm² in cross-sectional area. The wire is securely fastened to the ceiling.

a) Calculate the amount the wire is stretched by the hanging mass.

The mass is very slowly pulled downward 0.0600 cm from its equilibrium position by an external force of magnitude P. Calculate

b) the work done by gravity when the mass moves downward 0.0600 cm;

c) the work done by the force P;

d) the work done by the force the wire exerts on the mass;

e) the change in the elastic potential energy (the

potential energy associated with the tensile stress in the wire) when the mass moves downward 0.0600 cm. Compare the answers in parts (d) and (e).

12–26 The compressibility of sodium is to be measured by observing the displacement of the piston in Fig. 12–4 when a force is applied. The sodium is immersed in an oil that fills the cylinder below the piston. Assume that the piston and walls of the cylinder are perfectly rigid and that there is no friction and no oil leak. Compute the compressibility of the sodium in terms of the applied force F, the piston displacement x, the piston area A, the initial volume of the oil V_0, the initial volume of the sodium v_0, and the compressibility of the oil k_0.

Fluid Mechanics

In this chapter we continue our study of the mechanical properties of real materials. Chapter 12 was concerned with *elastic* properties of materials, and we now study the mechanical properties of fluids. A fluid is any substance that can flow; we use the term for both liquids and gases. We usually think of a gas as easily compressed and a liquid as nearly incompressible, although there are exceptional cases.

Fluid statics is the study of fluids at rest, and fluid dynamics is the study of fluids in motion. We begin with equilibrium situations, including the concepts of density, pressure, buoyancy, and surface tension. The conditions for equilibrium are based on Newton's first law. Fluid dynamics is much more complex and indeed is one of the most complex branches of mechanics. Fortunately, we can represent many important situations with idealized models that are simple enough to permit detailed analysis. Even so, we will barely scratch the surface of this broad and interesting topic.

13–1
Density

The **density** of a material is defined as its mass per unit volume. A homogeneous material has the same density throughout. The SI unit of density is the kilogram per cubic meter (kg·m^{-3}). The cgs unit, the gram per cubic centimeter (g·cm^{-3}), is also widely used. We use the Greek letter ρ (rho) for density. If a mass m of material has volume V, the density ρ is given by

$$\rho = \frac{m}{V}, \qquad m = \rho V. \tag{13–1}$$

Densities of several common solids and liquids at ordinary temperatures are given in Table 13–1. The conversion factor

$$1 \text{ g·cm}^{-3} = 1000 \text{ kg·m}^{-3}$$

is useful. The most dense material found on earth is the metal osmium (22,500 kg·m^{-3} or 22.5 g·cm^{-3}). The density of air is about 1.2 kg·m^{-3} (0.0012 g·cm^{-3}), but the density of white dwarf stars is of the order of 10^9 kg·m^{-3}, and that of neutron stars is of the order of 10^{18} kg·m^{-3}!

The **specific gravity** of a material is the ratio of its density to the density of water; it is a pure (unitless) number. For example, the specific gravity of aluminum is 2.7. "Specific gravity" is a poor term, since it has nothing to do with gravity; "relative density" would be better.

Density measurements are an important analytical technique. For example, we can determine the charge condition of a storage battery by measuring the density of its electrolyte, a sulfuric acid solution. As the battery discharges, the sulfuric acid (H_2SO_4) combines with lead in the battery plates to form insoluble lead sulfate ($PbSO_4$), decreasing the concentration of the solution. The density decreases from about 1.30×10^3 kg·m^{-3} for a fully charged battery to 1.15×10^3 kg·m^{-3} for a discharged battery. Similarly, permanent-type antifreeze is usually a so-

TABLE 13–1	**Densities**			
Material	**Density, kg·m^{-3}**	**Material**	**Density, kg·m^{-3}**
Aluminum	2.7×10^3	Silver	10.5×10^3
Brass	8.6×10^3	Steel	7.8×10^3
Copper	8.9×10^3	Mercury	13.6×10^3
Gold	19.3×10^3	Ethanol	0.81×10^3
Ice	0.92×10^3	Benzene	0.90×10^3
Iron	7.8×10^3	Glycerin	1.26×10^3
Lead	11.3×10^3	Water	1.00×10^3
Platinum	21.4×10^3	Seawater	1.03×10^3

To obtain the densities in grams per cubic centimeter, simply omit the factor of 10^3.

lution of ethylene glycol (density 1.12×10^3 kg·m^{-3}) in water. The glycol concentration determines the freezing point of the solution; it can be found from a simple density measurement. Both these measurements are performed routinely in service stations with the aid of a hydrometer, which measures density by observation of the level at which a calibrated body floats in a sample of the solution. The hydrometer is discussed in Section 13–3.

13–2
Pressure in a Fluid

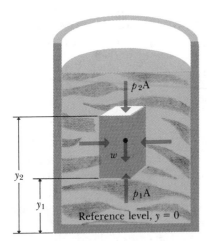

(a)

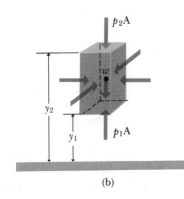

(b)

13–1
Forces on a rectangular element of fluid in equilibrium.

When we introduced the concept of fluid pressure in Section 12–2, we neglected the *weight* of the fluid and assumed that the pressure was the same everywhere in the fluid. This is not really true, of course. Atmospheric pressure is greater at sea level than in high mountains, and the pressure of water in a lake or in the ocean increases with increasing depth below the surface. Thus we need to refine our concept of pressure; we define the **pressure** p at a point in a fluid as the ratio of the normal force ΔF on a small area ΔA around that point, to the area:

$$p = \frac{\Delta F}{\Delta A}, \qquad \Delta F = p\,\Delta A. \qquad (13\text{–}2)$$

If the pressure is the same at all points of a finite plane surface of area A, these equations reduce to Eq. (12–5):

$$p = \frac{F}{A}, \qquad F = pA.$$

We can now derive a general relation between the pressure p at any point in a fluid in a gravitational field and the elevation y of the point. If the fluid is in equilibrium, every volume element is in equilibrium. Consider the rectangular volume shown in Fig. 13–1. The bottom and top surfaces are at elevations y_1 and y_2 above some reference level where $y = 0$. The area of each of these surfaces is A. The height of this volume is $y_2 - y_1$, its volume is $V = (y_2 - y_1)A$, its mass is $m = \rho V = \rho(y_2 - y_1)A$, and its weight is $w = mg = \rho g(y_2 - y_1)A$.

Call the pressure at the bottom surface p_1; then the total upward force on this surface is p_1A. The pressure at the top surface is p_2, and the total downward force on the top surface is p_2A. The fluid in this volume is in equilibrium, so the total y-component of force, including the weight and the forces at the bottom and top surfaces, must be zero. This condition gives

$$p_1A - p_2A - \rho g(y_2 - y_1)A = 0.$$

We can divide out the area A and rearrange, obtaining

$$p_2 - p_1 = -\rho g(y_2 - y_1). \qquad (13\text{–}3)$$

When y_2 is greater than y_1, p_2 is less than p_1, as we would expect. Pressure increases with depth; when we decrease y, we increase p.

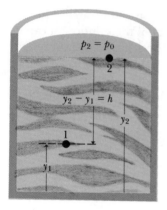

13–2
The pressure at a depth h in a liquid is greater than the surface pressure p_0 by $\rho g h$.

Let's apply this equation to a liquid in an open container, as shown in Fig. 13–2. Take point 1 at any level and let p represent the pressure at this point. Take point 2 at the surface of the liquid, where the pressure is atmospheric pressure. We denote atmospheric pressure by p_0. Then

$$p_0 - p = -\rho g(y_2 - y_1),$$

$$p = p_0 + \rho g h. \tag{13–4}$$

The pressure p at a depth h below the surface is greater than the pressure p_0 at the surface by an amount $\rho g h$. It also follows from Eq. (13–4) that if the pressure at the top surface is increased in any way, say by inserting a piston on the top surface and pressing down on it, the pressure p at any depth must increase by exactly the same amount. This fact was recognized in 1653 by the French scientist Blaise Pascal (1623–1662) and is called **Pascal's law:** *Pressure applied to an enclosed fluid is transmitted undiminished to every portion of the fluid and the walls of the containing vessel.* The pressure depends only on depth; the *shape* of the container does not matter.

The hydraulic jack shown schematically in Fig. 13–3 illustrates Pascal's law. A piston of small cross-sectional area A_1 exerts a force F_1 on the surface of a liquid such as oil. The pressure $p = F_1/A_1$ is transmitted through the connecting pipe to a larger piston of area A_2. Since the pressure is the same in both cylinders,

$$p = \frac{F_1}{A_1} = \frac{F_2}{A_2} \quad \text{and} \quad F_2 = \frac{A_2}{A_1}F_1. \tag{13–5}$$

Thus the hydraulic jack is a force-multiplying device with a multiplication factor equal to the ratio of the areas of the two pistons. Barber chairs, dentist chairs, car lifts and jacks, and hydraulic brakes all use this principle.

In deriving Eq. (13–3) we have assumed that the density ρ of the fluid is constant; this is a reasonable assumption for liquids, which are relatively incompressible, but it is realistic for gases only for short distances. We can use Eq. (13–3) to estimate the variation of atmospheric pressure with height over a distance of a few meters. For example, in a room with a ceiling height of 3.0 m filled with air of uniform density $1.2 \ \mathrm{kg \cdot m^{-3}}$, the difference in pressure between floor and ceiling is

$$\rho g h = (1.2 \ \mathrm{kg \cdot m^{-3}})(9.8 \ \mathrm{m \cdot s^{-2}})(3.0 \ \mathrm{m}) = 35 \ \mathrm{Pa},$$

or about 0.00035 atm. This difference is so small that we usually assume that gas pressure is the same everywhere in a container. But between sea level and the summit of Mount Everest (8882 m above sea level) the density of air changes by nearly a factor of three, and in this case we cannot use Eq. (13–3).

In many practical situations the significant quantity is the *difference* between the pressure inside a container and atmospheric pressure. For example, if the pressure inside a tire is just equal to atmospheric pressure, the tire is flat. When we say that the pressure in a car tire is 32 pounds (actually 32 $\mathrm{lb \cdot in^{-2}}$), we mean that it is *greater* than atmospheric pressure (14.7 $\mathrm{lb \cdot in^{-2}}$) by this amount. The *total* pressure in the tire is

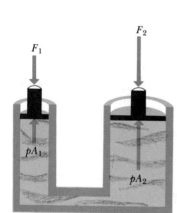

13–3
Principle of the hydraulic jack, an application of Pascal's law.

then 46.7 lb·in^{-2}. The excess pressure above atmospheric pressure is usually called **gauge pressure,** and the total pressure is called **absolute pressure.** Engineers use the abbreviations psig and psia for "pounds per square inch gauge" and "pounds per square inch absolute," respectively.

Normal atmospheric pressure at sea level is

$$p_0 = 1.013 \times 10^5 \text{ Pa} = 14.7 \text{ lb·in}^{-2} = 1 \text{ atm.}$$

Example 13-1   A residential hot water heating system has an expansion tank in the attic, 12 m above the boiler. If the tank is open to the atmosphere, what is the gauge pressure in the boiler? The absolute pressure?

Solution   From Eq. (13–4), the absolute pressure is

$$p = p_0 + \rho g h$$
$$= (1.01 \times 10^5 \text{ Pa}) + (1000 \text{ kg·m}^{-3})(9.8 \text{ m·s}^{-2})(12 \text{ m})$$
$$= 2.19 \times 10^5 \text{ Pa} = 2.16 \text{ atm} = 31.8 \text{ lb·in}^{-2}.$$

The gauge pressure is

$$p - p_0 = (2.19 - 1.01) \times 10^5 \text{ Pa} = 1.18 \times 10^5 \text{ Pa}$$
$$= 1.16 \text{ atm} = 17.1 \text{ lb·in}^{-2}.$$

If the boiler has a pressure gauge, it is always calibrated to read gauge pressure rather than absolute pressure.

We may also estimate the variation in atmospheric pressure over this height. The density of air at sea level and a temperature of 20°C is about 1.2 kg·m^{-3}, about 0.12% of the density of water. If this density were constant over the 12-m height, then the atmospheric pressure at furnace level would be greater than that in the attic by

$$\rho g h = (1.2 \text{ kg·m}^{-3})(9.8 \text{ m·s}^{-2})(12 \text{ m}) = 141 \text{ Pa} = 0.0014 \text{ atm,}$$

or a very small fraction of the pressure calculated above. Thus the variation in air pressure over this height is negligible.   ∎

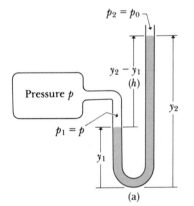

$p_2 = p_0$

$y_2 - y_1$
(h)

Pressure p

$p_1 = p$

y_1

y_2

(a)

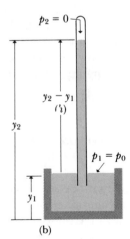

$p_2 = 0$

$y_2 - y_1$
(h)

y_2

$p_1 = p_0$

y_1

(b)

13-4
(a) The open-tube manometer. (b) The barometer.

The simplest pressure gauge is the open-tube manometer, shown in Fig. 13–4a. The U-shaped tube contains a liquid; one end of the tube is connected to the container where the pressure is to be measured, and the other end is open to the atmosphere at pressure p_0. The pressure at the bottom of the left column is $p + \rho g y_1$, and the pressure at the bottom of the right column (the same point) is $p_0 + \rho g y_2$, where ρ is the density of the liquid in the manometer. These are the same point, so these pressures must be equal:

$$p + \rho g y_1 = p_0 + \rho g y_2,$$

and

$$p - p_0 = \rho g(y_2 - y_1) = \rho g h. \tag{13-6}$$

The pressure p is the *absolute pressure*; the difference $p - p_0$ between absolute and atmospheric pressure is the *gauge pressure*. Thus the gauge pressure is proportional to the difference in height of the liquid columns.

The **mercury barometer** is a long glass tube, closed at one end, that has been filled with mercury and then inverted in a dish of mercury, as shown in Fig. 13–4b. The space above the mercury column contains only mercury vapor; its pressure is negligibly small, so the pressure above the mercury column is practically zero. From Eq. (13–4),

$$p_0 = \rho g(y_2 - y_1) = \rho g h. \tag{13–7}$$

Thus the mercury barometer reads atmospheric pressure directly from the height of the mercury column.

We have defined the SI unit of pressure, *1 pascal* (1 Pa), equal to 1 newton per square meter (1 N·m^{-2}). Two related units are the *bar*, defined as 10^5 Pa, and the *millibar*, defined as 10^{-3} bar or 10^2 Pa. Atmospheric pressures are of the order of 1000 millibars; the National Weather Service usually reports atmospheric pressures using this unit.

$$1.013 \times 10^5 \text{ Pa} = 1.013 \text{ bar} = 1013 \text{ millibar} = 1 \text{ atm.}$$

Because mercury manometers and barometers are widely used, pressures are also sometimes described in terms of the height of the corresponding mercury column, as so many "inches of mercury" or "millimeters of mercury" (abbreviated mm Hg). The pressure due to a column of mercury one millimeter high has even been given a special name, *one torr* (after Evangelista Torricelli, inventor of the mercury barometer). Such units depend on the density of mercury, which varies with temperature, and on the value of g, which varies with location. These units are gradually passing out of common use in favor of the pascal.

One common type of blood-pressure gauge, called a *sphygmomanometer*, includes a manometer similar to that shown in Fig. 13–4a. Blood-pressure readings, such as 130/80, refer to the maximum and minimum gauge pressures, measured in millimeters of mercury or torrs. Blood pressure varies with height at different points in the body; the standard reference point is the upper arm, level with the heart. Pressure is also affected by the viscous nature of blood flow, by valves throughout the vascular system, and by the body's changing the diameters of blood vessels.

Example 13–2   Compute the atmospheric pressure p_0 on a day when the height of mercury in a barometer is 76.0 cm.

Solution   The height of the mercury column depends on ρ and g as well as on the atmospheric pressure. As was mentioned, ρ varies with temperature, and g varies with latitude and elevation above sea level. Assuming that $g = 9.80$ m·s^{-2} and $\rho = 13.6 \times 10^3$ kg·m^{-3}, we find that

$$p_0 = \rho g h = (13.6 \times 10^3 \text{ kg·m}^{-3})(9.8 \text{ m·s}^{-2})(0.76 \text{ m})$$
$$= 101,300 \text{ N·m}^{-2} = 1.013 \times 10^5 \text{ Pa.} \qquad \blacksquare$$

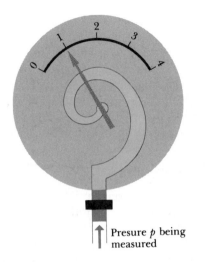

13–5
A Bourdon pressure gauge. The spiral metal tube is attached to a pointer. When the pressure inside the tube increases, the tube straightens out a little, deflecting the pointer on the scale.

Presure p being measured

Another type of pressure gauge, often more convenient than a liquid manometer, is the Bourdon pressure gauge, shown in Fig. 13–5. It consists of a flattened brass tube closed at one end and bent into a circular or spiral shape. The closed end of the tube is connected by a gear and pinion to a pointer that moves over a scale. The open end of the tube is connected to the container where the pressure is to be measured. When pressure increases within the flattened tube, the tube straightens slightly, just as a bent rubber garden hose straightens when the water is turned on. The resulting motion of the closed end is transmitted to the pointer.

*13–3
Buoyancy

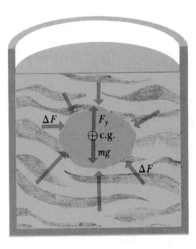

13–6
Archimedes' principle. The upward buoyant force F_y equals the weight of the displaced fluid.

Buoyancy is a familiar phenomenon; a body immersed in water seems to have less weight than in air. When a body is immersed in a fluid that has greater density than the body, the body can *float* in that fluid. The human body floats in water, and a helium-filled balloon floats in air.

Archimedes' principle states: *When a body is wholly or partially immersed in a fluid, the fluid exerts an upward force on the body equal to the weight of the fluid that is displaced by the body.* To prove this principle, we consider an arbitrary portion of fluid at rest. In Fig. 13–6 the irregular outline is the surface bounding this portion of fluid. The arrows represent the forces exerted on the boundary surface by the surrounding fluid.

The entire fluid is at rest and therefore in equilibrium. For the sum of all the y-components of force acting on this portion of fluid to be zero, the sum of the y-components of the surface forces must be equal in magnitude to the weight mg of the fluid inside the surface. Also, the sum of the torques must be zero, so the line of action of the resultant y-component of surface force must pass through the center of gravity of this fluid.

Now we remove the fluid inside the surface and replace it with a solid body having exactly the same shape. The pressure at every point is

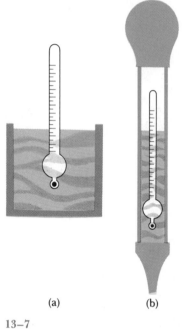

(a)   (b)

13–7
(a) A simple hydrometer.
(b) Hydrometer used as a tester for
battery acid or antifreeze.

exactly the same as before. Therefore the total force exerted on the body by the surrounding fluid is the same and is again equal in magnitude to the weight mg of fluid displaced. We call this upward force the **buoyant force** on the solid body. The line of action of this force again passes through the center of gravity of the displaced fluid.

When a balloon floats in equilibrium in air, its weight must be the same as the weight of the air displaced by the balloon. That is, the average density of a floating balloon must be the same as that of the surrounding air. Similarly, when a submerged submarine is in equilibrium, its average density must be equal to that of the surrounding water.

A body whose average density is less than that of a liquid can float partially submerged at the free upper surface of the liquid. The greater the density of the liquid, the less of the body is submerged. When you swim in seawater (density 1030 kg·m^{-3}), your body floats higher than in fresh water (1000 kg·m^{-3}). Another familiar example is the hydrometer, shown in Fig. 13–7. The calibrated float sinks into the fluid until the weight of the fluid it displaces is exactly equal to its own weight. The hydrometer floats *higher* in denser liquids than in less dense liquids. It is weighted at its bottom end so that the upright position is stable, and a scale in the top stem permits direct density readings.

Figure 13–7b shows a hydrometer that is commonly used to measure density of battery acid or antifreeze. The bottom of the tube is immersed in the liquid; the bulb is squeezed to expel air and then released, like a giant medicine dropper. The liquid rises into the outer tube, and the hydrometer floats in this sample of the liquid.

Example 13–3   A brass block with a mass of 0.500 kg and a density of 8.00×10^3 kg·m^{-3} is suspended from a string. What is the tension in the string if the block is in air? If it is completely immersed in water?

Solution   We neglect the very small buoyant force of *air*; then the tension when the block is in air is just equal to its weight:

$$mg = (0.500 \text{ kg})(9.80 \text{ m·s}^{-2}) = 4.90 \text{ N}.$$

When immersed in water, the block experiences an upward buoyant force equal to the weight of water displaced. Figure 13–8a shows a free-body diagram for the block, including its weight, the tension T, and the upward buoyant force B. To find B, we first find the volume of the block:

$$V = \frac{m}{\rho} = \frac{0.500 \text{ kg}}{8.00 \times 10^3 \text{ kg·m}^{-3}} = 6.25 \times 10^{-5} \text{ m}^3.$$

The weight of this volume of water is

$$\begin{aligned} w = mg &= \rho_{\text{water}} V g \\ &= (1.00 \times 10^3 \text{ kg·m}^{-3})(6.25 \times 10^{-5} \text{ m}^3)(9.80 \text{ m·s}^{-2}) \\ &= 0.612 \text{ N}. \end{aligned}$$

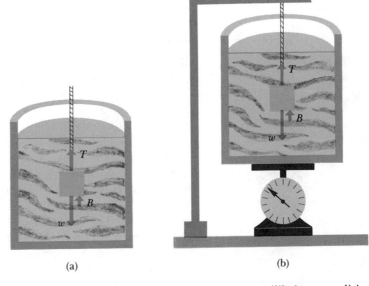

13–8
(a) A brass block hangs in equilibrium, immersed in water, under the action of its weight w, the string tension T, and the buoyant force B. (b) The water container sits on a scale; the scale reading increases when the brass block is immersed.

(a)   (b)

This is equal to the buoyant force B. The equilibrium condition, with the positive y-direction upward, is

$$T + B - w = 0,$$

$$T + 0.612 \text{ N} - 4.90 \text{ N} = 0,$$

$$T = 4.29 \text{ N}.$$

Here is a shortcut leading to the same result: The density of water is less than that of brass by a factor

$$\frac{1.0 \times 10^3 \text{ kg·m}^{-3}}{8.0 \times 10^3 \text{ kg·m}^{-3}} = \frac{1}{8}.$$

That is, the weight of a given volume of water is one eighth that of an equal volume of brass, and the weight of the displaced water is $(1/8)(4.9 \text{ N}) = 0.612 \text{ N}$. ∎

Example 13–4   Suppose you place the water container in Example 13–3 on a scale, as in Fig. 13–8b. How does the scale reading change when the brass is immersed in the water?

Solution   Consider the water and the brass together as a system; its total weight does not change when the brass is immersed. Thus the total supporting force, the vector sum of the tension T and the upward force F of the scale on the container (equal to the scale reading), is the same in both cases. But T decreases by 0.612 N when the brass is immersed, so the scale reading F must *increase* by 0.612 N. Qualitatively, we can see that the scale force *must* increase because when the brass is immersed, the water level in the container rises, increasing the pressure of water on the bottom of the container. ∎

*13–4
Surface Tension

13–9
A paper clip "floating" on water. The clip is supported not by buoyant forces (Section 13–3) but by surface tension of the water. (Nancy Rodger, The Exploratorium.)

What do all the following phenomena have in common? A liquid squeezed from the tip of a medicine dropper emerges not as a continuous stream but as a succession of drops. A paper clip, if placed carefully on a water surface, makes a small depression in the surface and rests there without sinking (Fig. 13–9), even though its density is several times that of water. Some insects can walk on the surface of water; their feet make indentations in the surface but do not penetrate it. When a small clean glass tube is dipped into water, the water rises in the tube, but when the tube is dipped in mercury, the mercury is depressed.

In all these phenomena the surface of the liquid behaves as though it is under *tension*. The situation of Fig. 13–10 shows this effect very directly. We attach a loop of thread to a wire ring, as shown. We dip the ring and thread into a soap solution and remove them, forming a thin film of liquid in which the thread "floats" freely, as shown in Fig. 13–10a. If we then puncture the film inside the loop, the thread springs out into a circular shape as in Fig. 13–10b; the surfaces of the liquid pull radially outward on it, as shown by the arrows. These same forces were acting even before the film was punctured, but then there was film on *both* sides of the thread, and the net force on a section of thread was zero.

Another simple demonstration of surface tension is shown in Fig. 13–11. A piece of wire is bent into a U shape, and a second piece of wire is used as a slider. When the apparatus is dipped in a soap solution and removed, the slider (if its weight w_1 is not too great) is quickly pulled up to the top of the U. We can hold the slider in equilibrium by adding a second weight w_2. Surprisingly, the same total force $F = w_1 + w_2$ will hold the slider at rest in *any* position, regardless of the area of the liquid film; the force does not increase as the surface is stretched farther. This is very different from the elastic behavior of a sheet of rubber, in which the force needed to hold it increases as the sheet is stretched.

The soap film in Fig. 13–11 is very thin, but its thickness is still large in comparison with the size of a molecule. A soap film is made up chiefly

13–10
A wire ring with a flexible loop of thread, dipped in a soap solution, (a) before and (b) after puncturing the surface films inside the loop.

Wire ring

Thread

(a)   (b)

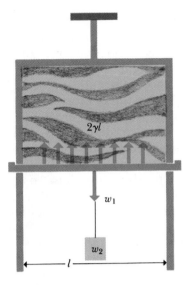

13–11
The horizontal slide wire is in equilibrium under the action of the upward surface force $2\gamma l$ and the downward pull $w_1 + w_2$.

of bulk liquid, bounded by two surface layers several molecules thick. When the slider in Fig. 13–11 is pulled down and the area of the film increases, molecules move from the main body of the liquid into the surface layers. The surface layers are not "stretched" as a rubber sheet would be, but rather more surface is created by molecules moving from the bulk liquid.

Let l be the length of the wire slider. Since the film has two surfaces, the total length along which the surface force acts on the slider is $2l$. The **surface tension** γ in the film is defined as *the ratio of the surface force F to the length d* (perpendicular to the force) *along which the force acts*:

$$\gamma = \frac{F}{d}. \tag{13–8}$$

In this case, $d = 2l$ and

$$\gamma = \frac{F}{2l}.$$

We have previously used the term *tension* in reference to a *force*, but surface tension is a *force per unit length*. The SI unit of surface tension is the newton per meter ($N \cdot m^{-1}$). This unit is not in common use; the usual unit is the cgs unit, the dyne per centimeter ($dyn \cdot cm^{-1}$). The conversion factor is

$$1 \ N \cdot m^{-1} = 1000 \ dyn \cdot cm^{-1}.$$

Some typical values of surface tension are shown in Table 13–2. Surface tension usually decreases as temperature increases; Table 13–2 shows this behavior for water.

A drop of liquid under no external forces, or in free fall in vacuum, is always spherical in shape because the surface is under tension and

TABLE 13–2	Experimental values of surface tension	
Liquid in contact with air	**T, °C**	**Surface tension, dyn·cm^{-1}**
Benzene	20	28.9
Carbon tetrachloride	20	26.8
Ethyl alcohol	20	22.3
Glycerin	20	63.1
Mercury	20	465.0
Olive oil	20	32.0
Soap solution	20	25.0
Water	0	75.6
Water	20	72.8
Water	60	66.2
Water	100	58.9
Oxygen	−193	15.7
Neon	−247	5.15
Helium	−269	0.12

A drop of milk splashes on a hard surface. (Dr. Harold Edgerton, M.I.T., Cambridge, Massachusetts.)

tends to have the minimum possible area. A sphere has smaller surface area for a given volume than any other geometric shape. Figure 13–12 is a beautiful example of the formation of spherical droplets in a very complex phenomenon, the impact of a drop on a rigid surface.

Surface tension causes a pressure difference between the inside and outside of a soap bubble or a liquid drop. A soap bubble consists of two spherical surface films very close together, with a thin layer of liquid between. Surface tension causes the films to tend to contract; but as the bubble contracts, it compresses the inside air, increasing the interior pressure to a point that prevents further contraction.

The excess pressure inside the bubble depends on its radius. To derive the relationship, we assume temporarily that there is no external pressure. Each half of the soap bubble is in equilibrium; we consider the lower half, as shown in Fig. 13–13. At the surface where this half joins the upper half, two forces act, the upward force of surface tension and the downward force due to the pressure of air in the upper half. If the radius of the spherical surface is R, the circumference of the circle along which the surface tension acts is $2\pi R$. (Assuming that the thickness of the bubble is very small, we neglect the difference between inner and outer radii.) The total force of surface tension for each surface (inner and outer) is $\gamma(2\pi R)$, so the total force of surface tension is $(2\gamma)(2\pi R)$. The force due to air pressure is the pressure p times the area πR^2 of the circle over which it acts. For the resultant of these forces to be zero we must have

$$(2\gamma)(2\pi R) = p(\pi R^2),$$

or

$$p = \frac{4\gamma}{R}. \tag{13–9}$$

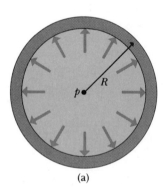

(a)

Now the pressure outside the bubble is in general *not* zero. But from the derivation we can see that Eq. (13–9) gives the *difference* between inside and outside pressure. In the terminology of Section 13–2 this is the *gauge* pressure. If the outside pressure is p_0, then

$$p - p_0 = \frac{4\gamma}{R} \quad \text{(soap bubble).} \tag{13–10}$$

For a liquid drop, which has only *one* surface film, the difference between pressure of the liquid and that of the outside air is half that for a soap bubble:

$$p - p_0 = \frac{2\gamma}{R} \quad \text{(liquid drop).} \tag{13–11}$$

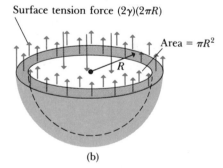

Surface tension force $(2\gamma)(2\pi R)$

Area = πR^2

(b)

(a) Cross section of a soap bubble, showing the two surfaces, the thin layer of liquid, and inside air. (b) Equilibrium of half a soap bubble. The surface-tension force exerted by the other half is $(2\gamma)(2\pi R)$, and the force exerted by the air inside the bubble is the pressure p times the area πR^2.

Example 13–5   Calculate the excess pressure inside a drop of mercury 4.00 mm in diameter at 20°C.

Solution   From Table 13–2,

$$\gamma = 465 \text{ dyn·cm}^{-1} = 465 \times 10^{-3} \text{ N·m}^{-1}.$$

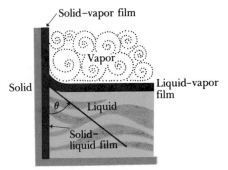

13–14
Surface films exist at the solid–vapor boundary as well as at the liquid–vapor boundary.

From Eq. (13–11),

$$p - p_0 = \frac{2\gamma}{R} = \frac{(2)(465 \times 10^{-3} \text{ N·m}^{-1})}{0.00200 \text{ m}}$$

$$= 465 \text{ N·m}^{-2}$$

$$= 0.00459 \text{ atm.} \qquad \blacksquare$$

Additional surface-tension effects occur when a gas–liquid interface meets a solid surface, such as the wall of a container, as shown in Fig. 13–14. In general the liquid–gas surface curves up or down as it approaches the solid surface, and the angle θ at which it meets the surface is called the **contact angle.** When the surface curves up, as with water and glass, θ is less than 90°; when it curves down, as with mercury and glass, θ is greater than 90°. The first case occurs with a liquid that "wets" or adheres to the solid surface, the second to a nonwetting liquid.

An important surface-tension phenomenon is the elevation or depression of the liquid in a narrow tube, as shown in Fig. 13–15. We call this effect **capillarity;** this term stems from the description of such tubes as *capillary*, which means hairlike. For a liquid that wets the tube, such as water, the contact angle is less than 90°; the liquid *rises* until it reaches an equilibrium height y, as shown in Fig. 13–15a. This height is determined by the requirement that the total surface tension force around the line where the liquid–gas surface meets the solid should just balance the extra weight of the liquid in the tube. The curved liquid surface is called a *meniscus.* Figure 13–15b shows the situation with a nonwetting liquid such as mercury. The contact angle is greater than 90°. The meniscus curves the other way, and the surface is depressed, pulled *down* by the surface-tension forces.

Capillarity is responsible for the absorption of water by paper towels, the rise of melted wax in a candlewick, and many other everyday phenomena. It is also an essential part of many life processes. A familiar example is the rising of water (actually a dilute aqueous solution) from the roots of a plant to its foliage, due partly to capillarity and partly to osmotic pressure developed in the roots. In the higher animals, including humans, blood is pumped through the arteries and veins, but capillarity is still important in the smallest blood vessels, which indeed are called capillaries.

A related phenomenon is that of *negative pressure*. The stress in a liquid is ordinarily *compressive* in nature; but in some circumstances, liquids can sustain *tensile* stresses. Imagine a cylindrical tube, closed at one end and having a tight-fitting piston at the other. We fill the tube completely with a liquid that wets both the inner surface of the tube and the piston face; the molecules of liquid adhere to all the surfaces. If we pull the piston out, we expect that the liquid will pull away from the piston, leaving an empty space. However, if the surfaces are very clean and the liquid very pure, a tensile stress, accompanied by an increase in volume, can be observed. The liquid behaves as though we are stretching it! Adhesive forces prevent it from pulling away from the walls of the container.

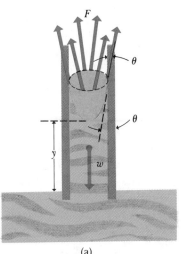

(a)

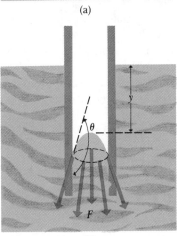

(b)

13–15
Surface-tension forces on a liquid in a capillary tube. The liquid (a) rises if $\theta < 90°$ and (b) is depressed if $\theta > 90°$.

With water, tensile stresses as large as 300 atm have been observed. In the laboratory this situation is highly unstable; a liquid under tension tends to break up into many small droplets. In tall trees, however, negative pressures are a regular occurrence. Negative pressure is thought to be an important mechanism for transport of water and nutrients from the roots to the leaves in the small xylem tubes (diameter of the order of 0.1 mm) in the growing layers of the tree.

13–5
Fluid Flow

We are now ready to consider *motion* of a fluid. This motion can be extremely complex, as shown by the flow of a river in flood or the swirling flames of a campfire. Despite this, some situations can be represented by relatively simple idealized models. An **ideal fluid** is a fluid that is *incompressible* and has no internal friction or viscosity. The assumption of incompressibility is usually a good approximation for liquids, and we may also treat a gas as incompressible whenever the pressure differences from one region to another are not too great. Internal friction in a fluid causes shear stresses when two adjacent layers of fluid move relative to each other, as when the fluid flows inside a tube or around an obstacle. In some cases these shear forces are negligible in comparison with forces arising from gravitation and pressure differences.

The path of an individual element of a moving fluid is called a **flow line.** If the overall flow pattern does not change with time, the flow is called **steady flow.** In steady flow, every element passing through a given point follows the same flow line. In this case the fluid velocity at each point of space remains constant in time, although in general the velocity of a particular particle of the fluid changes in both magnitude and direction during its motion.

A **streamline** is a curve whose tangent at any point is in the direction of the fluid velocity at that point. When the flow pattern changes with time, the streamlines do not coincide with the flow lines, but in steady flow the two sets of lines are identical. Our analysis will be confined to steady-flow situations, in which flow lines and streamlines are identical.

If we construct all of the flow lines passing through the edge of an imaginary element of area, such as the area *A* in Fig. 13–16, these lines enclose a tube called a **flow tube.** From the definition of a flow line, no fluid can cross the side walls of a tube of flow; in steady flow there can be no mixing of the fluids in different flow tubes.

Figure 13–17 shows patterns of fluid flow from left to right around a number of obstacles and in a channel of varying cross section. The photographs were made by injecting dye into water flowing between two closely spaced glass plates. Each obstacle is surrounded by a flow tube. The tube splits into two portions at a *stagnation point* (a point at which the velocity is zero) on the upstream (left) side of the obstacle. These portions rejoin at a second stagnation point on the downstream (right) side. The cross sections of all flow tubes decrease at a constriction and increase again when the channel widens.

13–16
A flow tube bounded by flow lines.

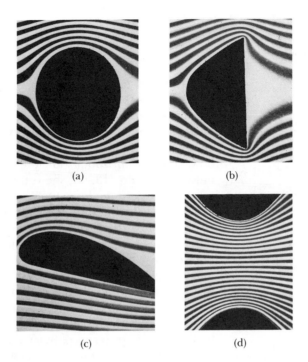

(a)   (b)

(c)   (d)

13–17
(a), (b), (c): Streamline flow around obstacles of various shapes. (d) Flow in a channel of varying cross-sectional area.

The patterns of Fig. 13–17 are typical of **laminar flow,** in which adjacent layers of fluid slide smoothly past each other. At sufficiently high flow rates, or when boundary surfaces cause abrupt changes in velocity, the flow becomes irregular and chaotic; this is called **turbulent flow.** In turbulent flow *there is no steady-state pattern*; the flow pattern continuously changes.

Conservation of mass in fluid flow is embodied in an important relationship called the **continuity equation.** Here is a derivation of this equation for an incompressible fluid in steady flow. Figure 13–18 shows a portion of a flow tube between two stationary cross sections with areas A_1 and A_2. The speeds at these sections are v_1 and v_2. No fluid flows across the side wall of the tube because the fluid velocity is tangent to the wall at every point on the wall. During a time interval Δt the fluid at A_1 moves a distance $v_1 \Delta t$. The volume of fluid ΔV_1 that flows into the tube across A_1 during this interval is the fluid in the cylindrical element with base A_1 and height $v_1 \Delta t$; $\Delta V_1 = A_1 v_1 \Delta t$. If the density of the fluid is ρ, the *mass* Δm_1 flowing in is $\Delta m_1 = \rho A_1 v_1 \Delta t$. Similarly, the mass Δm_2 that flows out across A_2 in the same time is $\Delta m_2 = \rho A_2 v_2 \Delta t$. In steady flow the total mass in the tube is constant, so $\Delta m_1 = \Delta m_2$, and

$$\rho A_1 v_1 \, \Delta t = \rho A_2 v_2 \, \Delta t,$$

or

$$A_1 v_1 = A_2 v_2. \qquad (13\text{–}12)$$

That is, the product Av is constant along any flow tube. When the cross section of a flow tube decreases, as in Fig. 13–17d, the velocity increases.

As an example, if a water pipe with 2-cm diameter is connected to a pipe with 1-cm diameter, can you show that the flow velocity must be four times as great in the 1-cm part as in the 2-cm part?

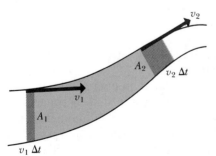

13–18
Flow into and out of a portion of a tube of flow.

13–6
Bernoulli's Equation

We can now use the concepts introduced in Section 13–5, along with the work–energy theorem, to derive an important relationship called **Bernoulli's equation.** This equation relates the pressure, flow velocity, and height for flow of an ideal fluid. We derive it by applying the work–energy theorem to flow of an ideal fluid. When an incompressible fluid flows along a horizontal flow tube of varying cross section, its velocity must change; Eq. (13–12) shows this. Each element of fluid must have an acceleration, and the force that causes this acceleration has to be applied by the fluid surrounding the element.

Because of these accelerations, the pressure must be different in different regions; if it were the same everywhere, the net force on every fluid element would be zero. When a fluid element speeds up, it must move from a region of larger to smaller pressure in order to have a net forward force to accelerate it. When the cross section of a flow tube varies, the pressure *must* vary along the tube, even when there is no difference of elevation. If the elevation also changes, there is an additional pressure difference. Bernoulli's equation relates the pressure difference between two points in a flow tube to changes in both velocity and elevation.

To derive the Bernoulli equation, we apply the work–energy theorem to the fluid in a section of a flow tube. In Fig. 13–19 we consider the fluid that at some initial time lies between the two cross sections a and c. The speed at this end is v_1, and the pressure is p_1. In a small time interval Δt the fluid initially at a moves to b, a distance $\Delta s_1 = v_1 \, \Delta t$, where v_1 is the speed at this end of the tube. In the same time interval the fluid initially at c moves to d, a distance $\Delta s_2 = v_2 \, \Delta t$. The cross-sectional areas at the two ends are A_1 and A_2, as shown. Because of the continuity relation, the volume of fluid ΔV passing *any* cross section during time Δt is $\Delta V = A_1 \, \Delta s_1 = A_2 \, \Delta s_2$.

Let's compute the *work* done on this fluid during Δt. The total force on the cross section at a is $p_1 A_1$, and the force at c is $p_2 A_2$, where p_1 and p_2 are the pressures at the two ends. The net *work* done on the element during this displacement is therefore

$$W = p_1 A_1 \, \Delta s_1 - p_2 A_2 \, \Delta s_2$$
$$= (p_1 - p_2) \, \Delta V. \qquad (13\text{–}13)$$

We need the negative sign in the second term because the force at c is opposite in direction to the displacement.

We now equate this work to the total change in energy, kinetic and potential, of the element. The kinetic energy of the fluid between sections b and c does not change. At the beginning of Δt the fluid between a and b has volume $A_1 \, \Delta s_1$, mass $\rho A_1 \, \Delta s_1$, and kinetic energy $\frac{1}{2}\rho(A_1 \, \Delta s_1)v_1{}^2$. Similarly, at the end of Δt the fluid between c and d has kinetic energy $\frac{1}{2}\rho(A_2 \, \Delta s_2)v_2{}^2$. The net change in kinetic energy ΔK during time Δt is

$$\Delta K = \tfrac{1}{2}\rho \, \Delta V \, (v_2{}^2 - v_1{}^2). \qquad (13\text{–}14)$$

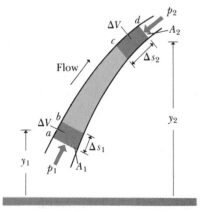

13–19
The net work done on the shaded element equals the increase in its kinetic and potential energy.

What about the change in potential energy? The potential energy of the mass between a and b at the beginning of Δt is $\Delta m\, gy_1 = \rho\, \Delta V\, gy_1$, and the potential energy of the mass between c and d at the end of Δt is $\Delta m\, gy_2 = \rho\, \Delta V\, gy_2$. The net change in potential energy ΔU during Δt is

$$\Delta U = \rho\, \Delta V\, g(y_2 - y_1). \qquad (13\text{--}15)$$

Combining Eqs. (13–13), (13–14), and (13–15) in the work–energy theorem $W = \Delta K + \Delta U$, we obtain

$$(p_1 - p_2)\Delta V = \tfrac{1}{2}\rho\, \Delta V\, (v_2{}^2 - v_1{}^2) + \rho\, \Delta V\, g(y_2 - y_1)$$

or

$$p_1 - p_2 = \tfrac{1}{2}\rho(v_2{}^2 - v_1{}^2) + \rho g(y_2 - y_1). \qquad (13\text{--}16)$$

In this form, Bernoulli's equation states that the work per unit volume of fluid ($p_1 - p_2$) is equal to the sum of the changes in kinetic and potential energies per unit volume that occur during the flow. Or we may interpret Eq. (13–16) in terms of pressures. The second term on the right is the pressure difference caused by the weight of the fluid and the difference in elevation of the two ends. The first term on the right is the additional pressure difference associated with the change of velocity of the fluid.

Equation (13–16) can also be written as

$$p_1 + \rho gy_1 + \tfrac{1}{2}\rho v_1{}^2 = p_2 + \rho gy_2 + \tfrac{1}{2}\rho v_2{}^2. \qquad (13\text{--}17)$$

The subscripts 1 and 2 refer to *any* two points along the flow tube, so Bernoulli's equation may also be written as

$$p + \rho gy + \tfrac{1}{2}\rho v^2 = \text{constant.} \qquad (13\text{--}18)$$

Note carefully that the pressures must be either all absolute pressures or all gauge pressures and that a consistent set of units must be used. In SI units, pressure is expressed in pascals, density in kilograms per cubic meter, and velocity in meters per second.

PROBLEM-SOLVING STRATEGY: *Bernoulli's Equation*

Bernoulli's equation is derived from the work–energy relationship, so it isn't surprising that much of the problem-solving strategy suggested in Sections 7–5 and 7–6 is equally applicable here. In particular:

1. Always begin by identifying clearly points 1 and 2, with reference to Bernoulli's equation.

2. Make lists of the known and unknown quantities in Eq. (13–17). The variables are p_1, p_2, v_1, v_2, y_1, and y_2, and the constants are ρ and g. What is given? What do you need to determine?

3. In some problems you will need to use the continuity equation, Eq. (13–12), to get a relation between the two velocities in terms of cross-sectional areas of pipes or containers. Or perhaps you will know both velocities and will need to determine one of the areas.

4. The volume flow rate $\Delta V/\Delta t$ across any area A is given by $\Delta V/\Delta t = Av$, and the corresponding mass flow rate $\Delta m/\Delta t$ is $\Delta m/\Delta t = \rho Av$. These relations sometimes come in handy.

As you read the following example and the applications discussed in Section 13–7, watch for applications of this strategy.

Example 13–6   Water enters a house through a pipe with an inside diameter of 2.0 cm at an absolute pressure of 4.0×10^5 Pa (about 4 atm). The pipe leading to the second-floor bathroom 5.0 m above is 1.0 cm in diameter. When the flow velocity at the inlet pipe is 4.0 m·s^{-1}, find the flow velocity and pressure in the bathroom.

Solution   Let point 1 be at the inlet pipe and point 2 at the bathroom. The velocity v_2 at the bathroom is obtained from the continuity equation:

$$v_2 = \frac{A_1}{A_2}v_1 = \frac{\pi(1.0 \text{ cm})^2}{\pi(0.5 \text{ cm})^2}(4.0 \text{ m·s}^{-1}) = 16 \text{ m·s}^{-1}.$$

We take $y_1 = 0$ (at the inlet) and $y_2 = 5.0$ m (at the bathroom). We are given p_1 and v_1; we can find p_2 from Bernoulli's equation:

$$\begin{aligned} p_2 &= p_1 - \tfrac{1}{2}\rho(v_2{}^2 - v_1{}^2) - \rho g(y_2 - y_1) \\ &= 4.0 \times 10^5 \text{ Pa} - \tfrac{1}{2}(1.0 \times 10^3 \text{ kg·m}^{-3})(256 \text{ m}^2\text{·s}^{-2} - 16 \text{ m}^2\text{·s}^{-2}) \\ &\quad - (1.0 \times 10^3 \text{ kg·m}^{-3})(9.8 \text{ m·s}^{-2})(5.0 \text{ m}) \\ &= 2.3 \times 10^5 \text{ Pa} = 2.3 \text{ atm.} \end{aligned}$$

Note that when the water is turned off, the second term on the right vanishes, and the pressure rises to 3.5×10^5 Pa.   ■

13–7
Applications of Bernoulli's Equation

Here are several practical applications of Bernoulli's equation.

1. *Fluid statics.* Just as equilibrium of a particle is a special case of **F = ma,** the equations of fluid statics are special cases of Bernoulli's equation when the velocity is zero everywhere. Thus when v_1 and v_2 are zero, Eq. (13–16) reduces to

$$p_1 - p_2 = \rho g(y_2 - y_1), \tag{13–19}$$

which is equivalent to Eq. (13–3).

2. *Speed of efflux: Torricelli's theorem.* Figure 13–20 shows a tank with cross-sectional area A_1, filled to a depth h with a liquid of density ρ. The space above the top of the liquid contains air at pressure p, and the liquid flows out of an orifice with area A_2. How fast does the fluid run out?

We can consider the entire volume of moving fluid as a single flow tube; v_1 and v_2 are the speeds at points 1 and 2. The quantity v_2 is called the *speed of efflux*. The pressure at point 2 is atmospheric pressure, p_0. Applying Bernoulli's equation to points 1 and 2 and taking $y = 0$ at the bottom of the tank, we find

$$p + \tfrac{1}{2}\rho v_1{}^2 + \rho gh = p_0 + \tfrac{1}{2}\rho v_2{}^2,$$

or

$$v_2{}^2 = v_1{}^2 + 2\frac{p - p_0}{\rho} + 2gh.$$

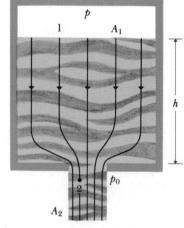

13–20
Flow of a liquid out of an orifice.

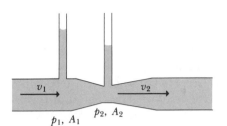

13–21
The Venturi tube.

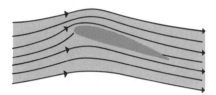

13–22
Flow lines around an airfoil.

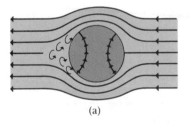

(a)

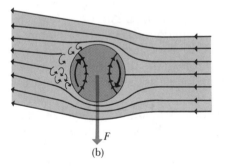

(b)

13–23
(a) Air flow past a stationary ball, showing a symmetric region of turbulence behind ball. (b) Air flow past a spinning ball, showing an asymmetric region of turbulence and deflection of airstream. The net force on the ball is in the direction shown. Motion of the air from right to left relative to the ball corresponds to motion of a ball through still air from left to right.

Ordinarily, A_2 is much smaller than A_1; in this case, $v_1{}^2$ is very much smaller than $v_2{}^2$ and can be neglected. We then find

$$v_2{}^2 = 2\frac{p - p_0}{\rho} + 2gh. \tag{13–20}$$

The speed of efflux v_2 depends on both the pressure difference $(p - p_0)$ and on the height h of the liquid level in the tank. If the top of the tank is open to the atmosphere, there is no excess pressure, $p = p_0$, and $p - p_0 = 0$. In that case we have simply

$$v_2 = \sqrt{2gh} \tag{13–21}$$

That is, *the speed of efflux is the same as the speed a body would acquire in falling freely through a height h.* This is *Torricelli's theorem.* It is valid not only for an opening in the bottom of a container, but also for a hole in a side wall at a depth h below the surface.

3. The *Venturi tube,* shown in Fig. 13–21, is a constriction or throat inserted in a pipeline, with inlet and outlet tapers to avoid turbulence. Bernoulli's equation, applied to the wide and narrow parts of the pipe (with $y_1 = y_2$), becomes

$$p_1 + \tfrac{1}{2}\rho v_1{}^2 = p_2 + \tfrac{1}{2}\rho v_2{}^2.$$

From the continuity equation, the speed v_2 is greater than the speed v_1, so the pressure p_2 in the throat is *less* than p_1. A net force to the right accelerates the fluid as it enters the throat, and a net force to the left slows it as it leaves. The pressures p_1 and p_2 can be measured by attaching vertical side tubes, as shown in the diagram. When we know these pressures and the areas A_1 and A_2, we can compute the velocities and the mass flow rate. When used for this purpose, the device is called a *Venturi meter.* This concept is used in some gasoline engines, where gasoline is sprayed from a nozzle or an injector into a low-pressure region produced in a Venturi throat.

4. *Lift on an aircraft wing.* Figure 13–22 shows flow lines around a cross section of an aircraft wing or an airfoil. The orientation of the wing relative to the flow direction causes the flow lines to crowd together above the wing. This corresponds to increased flow velocity in this region, just as in the throat of a Venturi. Hence the region above the wing has increased velocity and reduced pressure, while below the wing the pressure remains nearly atmospheric. Because the upward force on the underside of the wing is greater than the downward force on the top side, there is a net upward force or *lift.* (This highly simplified discussion ignores the effect of turbulent flow and the formation of vortices; a more complete discussion has to take these into account.)

We can also understand this phenomenon on the basis of Newton's laws. In Fig. 13–22 the air flowing past the wing has a net *downward* change in the vertical component of its momentum, corresponding to the downward force the wing exerts on it. The reaction force *on* the wing is *upward,* as we concluded above.

5. *The curved flight of a spinning ball.* In Fig. 13–23a, a ball is moving through air from left to right. To an observer moving with the center of the ball, the air stream appears to move from right to left, as shown by

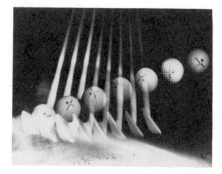

13–24
Stroboscopic photograph of a golf ball being struck by a club. The picture was taken at 1000 flashes per second; the ball rotates once in eight pictures, corresponding to an angular velocity of 125 revolutions per second. (Dr. Harold Edgerton, M.I.T., Cambridge, Massachusetts.)

the flow lines in the figure. Because of the large velocities ordinarily involved, a region of turbulent flow occurs behind the ball, as shown.

When the ball is spinning, as in Fig. 13–23b, the viscosity of air causes layers of air near the ball's surface to be pulled around in the direction of spin. The velocity of air relative to the ball's surface becomes greater at the top of the ball than at the bottom. The region of turbulence becomes asymmetric; turbulence occurs farther forward on the top side than on the bottom. This asymmetry causes a pressure difference; the average pressure at the top of the ball becomes greater than that at the bottom. The corresponding net downward force deflects the ball as shown. In a baseball curve pitch, the ball spins about a nearly vertical axis, and the actual deflection is sideways. In that case, Fig. 13–23b is a *top* view of the situation. Tennis balls with spin behave similarly.

A similar effect occurs with golf balls, which always have "backspin" from impact with the slanted face of the golf club. The resulting pressure difference between the top and bottom of the ball causes a "lift" force that keeps the ball in the air considerably longer than would be possible without spin. A well-hit drive appears from the tee to "float" or even curve *upward* during the initial portion of its flight. This is a real effect, not an illusion. The dimples on the ball play an essential role; because of effects associated with viscosity of air, an undimpled ball has a much shorter trajectory than a dimpled one given the same initial velocity and spin. Figure 13–24 shows the backspin of a golf ball just after it is struck by a club.

13–8
Viscosity

Viscosity is internal friction in a fluid; viscous forces oppose the motion of one portion of a fluid relative to another. Viscosity is the reason it takes effort to paddle a canoe through calm water. An ideal fluid, the model we used to derive the Bernoulli equation, has no viscosity, but in real-life fluids, especially liquids, effects associated with viscosity are often significant. Viscosity plays a vital role in the flow of fluids in pipes, the flow of blood, the lubrication of engine parts, and many other areas of practical importance.

The simplest example of viscous flow is motion of a fluid between two parallel plates, as shown in Fig. 13–25. The bottom plate is stationary, while the top plate moves with constant speed v. The fluid adheres to the surfaces, and the fluid in contact with each surface has the same speed as that surface. The fluid at the top surface has speed v, and the fluid adjacent to the bottom surface is at rest. The speeds of intermediate layers of fluid increase uniformly from one surface to the other, as shown by the arrows.

Flow of this type is called *laminar*. (A lamina is a thin sheet.) In laminar flow, the layers of fluid slide smoothly over one another, and a portion of the fluid, which at some instant has the shape $abcd$, will a moment later take the shape $abc'd'$ and will become more and more distorted as the motion continues. That is, the fluid is in a state of continuously increasing *shear strain*.

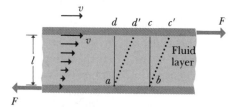

13–25
Laminar flow of a viscous fluid.

To maintain the motion, we have to apply a constant force F to the right on the upper, moving plate, and so indirectly on the upper liquid surface. This force tends to drag the fluid, and the lower plate as well, to the right, so we need an equal force toward the left on the lower plate to hold it stationary. If A is the surface area of each plate, the ratio F/A is the *shear stress* exerted on the fluid.

When a shear stress acts on a *solid*, it causes a deformation of the solid, such as dd' in Fig. 13–25. The shear strain is defined as the ratio of this displacement to the transverse dimension l. Within the elastic limit, the shear stress is proportional to the shear strain, as we discussed in Section 12–3. With a *fluid*, the shear strain continues to increase without limit as long as the stress is applied. The stress depends not on the shear strain, but on its *rate of change*. The strain in Fig. 13–25 (at the instant when the volume of fluid has the shape $abc'd'$) is dd'/ad, or dd'/l. The *rate of change* of strain equals the rate of change of dd' (the speed v of the moving surface) divided by l. That is,

$$\text{Rate of change of shear strain} = \frac{v}{l}.$$

The rate of change of shear strain is also called the *strain rate*.

The **viscosity** of the fluid, denoted by η, is defined as the ratio of the shear stress, F/A, to the rate of change of shear strain:

$$\eta = \frac{\text{shear stress}}{\text{rate of change of shear strain}} = \frac{F/A}{v/l},$$

or

$$F = \eta A \frac{v}{l}. \tag{13–22}$$

For a liquid that flows readily, such as water or gasoline, a relatively small shear stress is needed for a given strain rate. For a liquid such as honey or glycerin, a greater shear stress is needed for the same strain rate, and the viscosity is greater. Viscosities of all fluids are strongly temperature dependent, increasing for gases and decreasing for liquids as the temperature increases. An important goal in the design of oils for engine lubrication is to *reduce* the temperature variation of viscosity as much as possible.

From Eq. (13–22), the unit of viscosity is that of force times distance, divided by area times velocity. The SI unit is

$$1 \text{ N·m·m}^{-2}(\text{m·s}^{-1})^{-1} = 1 \text{ N·s·m}^{-2}.$$

The corresponding cgs unit, 1 dyn·s·cm^{-2}, is the only viscosity unit in common use; it is called 1 **poise**, in honor of the French scientist Jean Louis Marie Poiseuille:

$$1 \text{ poise} = 1 \text{ dyn·s·cm}^{-2} = 10^{-1} \text{ N·s·m}^{-2}.$$

Small viscosities are expressed in *centipoise* ($1 \text{ cp} = 10^{-2}$ poise) or *micropoise* ($1 \text{ } \mu\text{p} = 10^{-6}$ poise). A few typical values are given in Table 13–3.

Not all fluids behave according to the direct proportionality of force and velocity predicted by Eq. (13–22). An interesting exception is blood,

TABLE 13–3   **Typical values of viscosity**

Temperature, C°	Viscosity of castor oil, poise	Viscosity of water, centipoise	Viscosity of air, micropoise
0	53.00	1.792	171
20	9.86	1.005	181
40	2.31	0.656	190
60	0.80	0.469	200
80	0.30	0.357	209
100	0.17	0.284	218

for which velocity increases more rapidly than force. This behavior results from the fact that blood is not a homogeneous fluid but rather a suspension of solid particles in a liquid. As the strain rate increases, these particles deform and become preferentially oriented to facilitate flow. The fluids that lubricate human joints show similar behavior. Some paints cling to the brush but flow when brushed on. A fluid that obeys Eq. (13–22) is called a **Newtonian fluid;** it is a useful (although approximate) model for the behavior of many pure substances. Fluids that are suspensions or dispersions are often non-Newtonian in their viscous behavior.

When a viscous fluid flows in a pipe, as in Fig. 13–26, the flow velocity is different at different points of a cross section. The outermost layer of fluid clings to the walls of the tube, and its velocity is zero. The walls exert a backward drag on this layer, which in turn drags backward on the next layer inward, and so on. If the velocity is not too great, the flow is *laminar*, with a velocity that is greatest at the center and decreases to zero at the walls. The flow is like a lot of telescoping tubes sliding relative to one another, the central tube moving fastest and the outermost tube at rest.

A velocity profile for flow in a cylindrical pipe is shown in Fig. 13–26b. Deriving an equation for the relation of flow velocity v to distance r from the axis of the cylinder requires calculus; the result of the derivation is

$$v = \frac{p_1 - p_2}{4\eta L}(R^2 - r^2). \tag{13–23}$$

The velocity decreases from a maximum value $(p_1 - p_2)R^2/4\eta L$ at the center to zero at the wall. The velocity at each point is proportional to the pressure change per unit length $(p_1 - p_2)/L$, called the **pressure gradient.** The curve in Fig. 13–26b is a graph of Eq. (13–23), with the v-axis horizontal and the r-axis vertical.

Often, we want to know the total volume flow rate through a pipe (total volume per unit time). Equation (13–23) shows that the maximum flow velocity is proportional to R^2, and the *average* velocity over a cross section is also proportional to R^2. The cross-sectional area is πR^2; we expect the volume flow rate $\Delta V/\Delta t$ to be proportional both to the average velocity and to the cross-sectional area and thus to R^4. A detailed deriva-

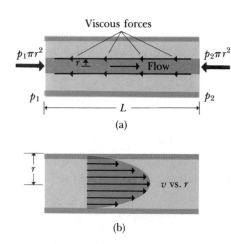

13–26
(a) Forces on a cylindrical element of a viscous fluid. (b) Velocity distribution for viscous flow.

tion, again using calculus, confirms this conclusion; the volume flow rate is given by

$$\frac{\Delta V}{\Delta t} = \frac{\pi}{8} \frac{R^4}{\eta} \frac{p_1 - p_2}{L}. \tag{13–24}$$

This relation was first derived by Poiseuille and is called **Poiseuille's law.** It shows that the volume rate of flow is inversely proportional to viscosity, as we would expect. The volume flow rate is also proportional to the pressure gradient $(p_1 - p_2)/L$, and it varies as the *fourth power* of the radius. If the radius is doubled, the flow rate increases by a factor of 16. This relation is familiar to physicians in connection with hypodermic needles. Needle size is much more important than thumb pressure in determining the flow rate from the needle; doubling the needle diameter has the same effect as increasing the thumb force sixteenfold. Similarly, blood flow in arteries and veins can be controlled over a wide range by relatively small changes in diameter, an important temperature-control mechanism in warm-blooded animals. Relatively slight narrowing of arteries due to arteriosclerosis can result in elevated blood pressure and added strain on the heart muscle.

One more useful relation in viscous fluid flow is the expression for the force F exerted on a sphere of radius r moving with speed v through a fluid with viscosity η. When the flow is laminar, the relationship is simple:

$$F = 6\pi\eta r v. \tag{13–25}$$

We have encountered this kind of velocity-proportional force before, in Example 5–17 (Section 5–4). Equation (13–25) is called **Stokes' law.**

A sphere falling in a viscous fluid reaches a *terminal speed* v_t for which the total force, including the weight of the sphere, the viscous retarding force, and the buoyant force, is zero. Let ρ be the density of the sphere and ρ' the density of the fluid. The weight of the sphere is then $\frac{4}{3}\pi r^3 \rho g$, and the buoyant force is $\frac{4}{3}\pi r^3 \rho' g$; at terminal velocity,

$$\frac{4}{3}\pi r^3 \rho' g + 6\pi\eta r v_t - \frac{4}{3}\pi r^3 \rho g = 0,$$

or

$$v_t = \frac{2}{9}\frac{r^2 g}{\eta}(\rho - \rho'). \tag{13–26}$$

We can determine the viscosity of a fluid from Eq. (13–26) by measuring the terminal velocity of a sphere of known radius and density. Conversely, if we know the viscosity, we can determine the radius of the sphere by measuring the terminal velocity. Robert Millikan used this method to determine the radius of very small electrically charged oil drops by observing free fall in air. He used these drops to measure the charge of an individual electron; we will discuss this landmark experiment further in Section 26–5.

The Stokes'-law force is what keeps clouds in the air. The terminal speed for a water droplet of radius 10^{-5} m is of the order of 1 mm·s^{-1}. At higher speeds the flow often becomes turbulent, and Stokes' law is no longer valid. In air the drag force at highway speeds is approximately proportional to v^2. We have discussed the applications of this relation to skydiving (Example 5–18, Section 5–4) and to air drag of a moving automobile (Section 7–9). Raindrops have terminal speeds of a few meters per second because of air drag; otherwise, they would smash everything in their path!

*13–9
Turbulence

When the speed of a flowing fluid exceeds a certain critical value, the flow is no longer laminar. For a fluid in a pipe the flow pattern we described in Section 13–8 as telescoping tubes breaks down. The pattern becomes extremely irregular and complex, and it changes continuously with time; there is no steady-state pattern. This irregular, chaotic flow is called **turbulence.** Figure 13–27 shows the contrast between laminar and turbulent flow in a few familiar systems.

The transition from laminar to turbulent flow is often very sudden. A flow pattern that is stable at low speeds suddenly becomes unstable when a critical speed is reached. Irregularities in the flow pattern can be caused by roughness in the pipe wall, variations in density of the fluid, and many other factors. At small flow speeds these disturbances are damped out, and the flow pattern tends to maintain its laminar nature. But when the critical speed is reached, the disturbances no longer damp out; instead, they grow until they destroy the entire laminar-flow pattern.

13–27
(a) Laminar flow. (b) Turbulent flow.
(c) First laminar, then turbulent flow.

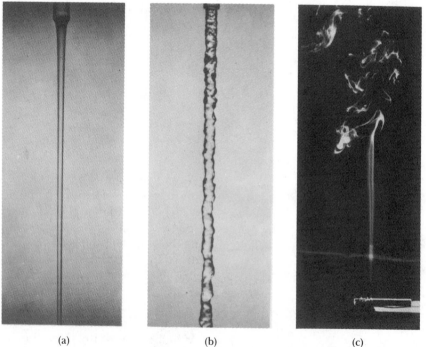

(a)   (b)   (c)

Turbulence poses some profound questions for theoretical physics. The motion of any particular particle in a fluid is presumably determined by Newton's laws. If we know the motion of the fluid at some initial time, shouldn't we be able to predict the motion at any later time? After all, when we launch a projectile, we can compute the entire trajectory if we know the initial position and velocity. How is it that a system that obeys well-defined physical laws can have unpredictable, chaotic behavior?

There is no simple answer to these questions. Indeed, the study of chaotic behavior in deterministic systems is a very active field of research in theoretical physics. The development of supercomputers in recent years has enabled scientists to carry out computer simulations of the behavior of physical systems on a scale that would have been hopeless only a few years ago. The results of such simulations have often guided new developments in the theory of chaotic behavior. A particularly significant result of these studies has been the discovery of common characteristics in the behavior of widely divergent kinds of systems, including turbulent fluid flow, population fluctuations in ecosystems, the growth of crystals, the shapes of coastlines, and many others.

Questions

13–1 A rubber hose is attached to a funnel, and the free end is bent around to point upward. When water is poured into the funnel, it rises in the hose to the same level as in the funnel, despite the fact that the funnel has a lot more water in it than the hose. Why?

13–2 Is the pressure inside a siphon tube greater or less than atmospheric pressure? Does this suggest a limitation on the maximum height over which a siphon can be used?

13–3 How can one instrument function as both a barometer and an altimeter?

13–4 In describing the size of a large ship, one uses such expressions as "it displaces 20,000 tons." What does this mean? Can the weight of the ship be obtained from this information?

13–5 A popular, though expensive, sport is hot-air ballooning, in which a large nylon balloon is filled with air heated by a gas burner at the bottom. Why must the air be heated? How does the balloonist control ascent and descent?

13–6 A rigid lighter-than-air balloon filled with helium cannot continue to rise indefinitely. Why not? What determines the maximum height it can attain?

13–7 Does the buoyant force on an object immersed in water change if the object and the container of water are placed in an elevator that accelerates upward?

13–8 If a person can barely float in seawater, will he or she float more easily in fresh water or be unable to float at all? Why?

13–9 The purity of gold can be tested by weighing it in air and in water. How? Why is it not feasible to make a fake gold brick by gold-plating some cheaper material?

13–10 A possible new technology made feasible by the "zero-gravity" environment of an orbiting space station is the making of metal foam. Why is it easier to make metal foam under zero-g conditions than on earth?

13–11 Why can't a skin diver obtain an air supply at any desired depth by breathing through a "snorkel," a tube connected to a face mask and having its upper end above the water surface?

13–12 Suppose the door of a room makes an airtight but frictionless fit in its frame. Do you think you could open the door if the air pressure on one side were standard atmospheric pressure and that on the other side differed from standard by 1%?

13–13 Is the continuity relation, Eq. (13–12), valid for compressible fluids? If not, is there a similar relation that *is* valid?

13–14 If the velocity at each point in space in steady-state fluid flow is constant, how can a fluid particle accelerate?

13–15 Does the "lift" of an airplane wing depend on altitude?

13–16 How does a baseball pitcher give the ball the spin that makes it curve? Can he make it curve in either direction? Does it matter whether he is right-handed or left-handed? What is a spitball? Why is it illegal?

13–17 In a store-window vacuum cleaner display, a table-tennis ball is suspended in midair in a jet of air blown from the outlet hose of a tank-type vacuum cleaner. The ball bounces around a little but always returns to the center of the jet, even if the jet is tilted. How does this behavior illustrate the Bernoulli relation?

13–18 Why do jet airplanes usually fly at altitudes of about 30,000 ft, though it takes a lot of fuel to climb that high?

13–19 What causes the sharp hammering sound sometimes heard from a water pipe when an open faucet is suddenly turned off?

13–20 When a smooth-flowing stream of water comes out of a faucet, it narrows as it falls, and if it falls far enough it eventually breaks up into drops. Why does it narrow? Why does it break up?

13–21 A tornado consists of a rapidly whirling air vortex. Why is the pressure always much lower in the center than at the outside? How does this condition account for the destructive power of a tornado?

13–22 When paddling a canoe, one can attain a certain critical speed with relatively little effort, and then a much greater effort is required to make the canoe go even a little faster. Why?

13–23 Why does air escaping from the open end of a small pipe make a lot more noise than air escaping at the same volume rate from a large pipe?

Exercises

Section 13–1   Density

13–1 A rectangular block of an unidentified material has dimensions $5.0 \times 15.0 \times 30.0$ cm and a mass of 2.50 kg. What is the density?

13–2 A lead cube has a total mass of 15.0 kg. What is the length of a side?

13–3 A cylindrical aluminum rod has a length of 84.0 cm and a diameter of 0.60 cm. What is its mass?

13–4 A solid metal sphere has a radius of 4.50 cm and a mass of 1.20 kg. What is the density of the sphere if it is uniform?

Section 13–2   Pressure in a Fluid

13–5 A diving bell is to be designed to withstand the pressure of seawater at a depth of 900 m.

  a) What is the gauge pressure at this depth? (Neglect changes in the density of water with depth.)

  b) What is the force due to the deep water on a circular glass window 15.0 cm in diameter?

13–6 What gauge pressure must a pump produce to pump water from the bottom of the Grand Canyon (730-m elevation) to Indian Gardens (1370 m)? Express your results in pascals and in atmospheres.

13–7 The piston of a hydraulic automobile lift is 0.300 m in diameter. What gauge pressure, in pascals, is required to lift a car with a mass of 1200 kg? Also express this pressure in atmospheres.

13–8 A barrel contains a 0.200-m layer of oil floating on water that is 0.300 m deep. The density of oil is 600 kg·m^{-3}.

  a) What is the gauge pressure at the oil–water interface?

  b) What is the gauge pressure at the bottom of the barrel?

13–9 The liquid in the open-tube manometer in Fig. 13–4a is mercury, $y_1 = 3.00$ cm, and $y_2 = 9.00$ cm. Atmospheric pressure is 970 millibars.

  a) What is the absolute pressure at the bottom of the U-shaped tube?

  b) What is the absolute pressure in the open tube at a depth of 6.00 cm below the free surface?

  c) What is the absolute pressure of the gas in the tank?

  d) What is the gauge pressure of the gas in pascals? In torr?

Section 13–3   Buoyancy

13–10 An ore sample weighs 14.00 N in air. When the sample is suspended by a light cord and totally immersed in water, the tension in the cord is 9.00 N. Find the total volume and the density of the sample.

13–11 A solid brass statue weighs 160 N in air.

  a) What is its volume?

  b) The statue is suspended from a rope and totally immersed in water. What is the tension in the rope (the *apparent* weight of the statue in water)?

13–12 A slab of ice floats on a freshwater lake. What minimum volume must the slab have for a 70.0-kg man to be able to stand on it without getting his feet wet?

13–13 When an iceberg floats in seawater, what fraction of its volume is submerged? (The ice, being of glacial origin, is freshwater.)

13–14 A cubical block of wood 10.0 cm on a side floats at the interface between oil and water as in Fig. 13–28,

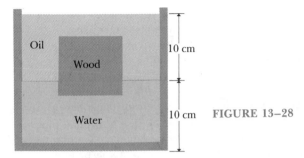

Oil

Wood

10 cm

Water

10 cm   FIGURE 13–28

with its lower surface 2.00 cm below the interface. The density of the oil is 700 kg·m^{-3}.

a) What is the gauge pressure at the upper face of the block?

b) What is the gauge pressure at the lower face of the block?

c) What is the mass of the block?

13–15 A large hollow plastic sphere is held below the surface of a freshwater lake by a cable anchored to the bottom of the lake. The sphere has a volume of 0.300 m^3, and the tension in the cable is 800 N.

a) Calculate the buoyant force exerted by the water on the sphere.

b) What is the mass of the sphere?

c) The cable breaks, and the sphere rises to the surface of the lake. When the sphere comes to rest again, what fraction of its volume will be submerged?

Section 13–4   Surface Tension

13–16 Find the excess pressure

a) inside a water drop with a radius of 1.50 mm;

b) inside a water drop with a radius of 0.0100 mm (typical of water droplets in fog).

Assume that $T = 20°C$.

13–17 Find the gauge pressure in pascals inside a soap bubble 7.00 cm in diameter. The surface tension is 25.0×10^{-3} N·m^{-1}.

Section 13–5   Fluid Flow

13–18 Water is flowing in a pipe of varying cross-sectional area, and at all points the water completely fills the pipe. At point 1 the cross-sectional area of the pipe is 0.080 m^2 and the magnitude of the fluid velocity is 3.00 m·s^{-1}.

a) What is the fluid speed at points in the pipe where the cross-sectional area is

i) 0.060 m^2?

ii) 0.112 m^2?

b) Calculate the volume of water discharged from the open end of the pipe in 1.00 s.

13–19 Water is flowing in a circular pipe of varying cross-sectional area, and at all points the water completely fills the pipe.

a) At one place in the pipe the radius is 0.200 m. What is the magnitude of the water velocity at this point if the volume flow rate in the pipe is 0.400 m^3·s^{-1}?

b) At a second point in the pipe the water velocity has a magnitude of 4.60 m·s^{-1}. What is the radius of the pipe at this point?

Section 13–6   Bernoulli's Equation

Section 13–7   Applications of Bernoulli's Equation

13–20 A circular hole 2.00 cm in diameter is cut in the side of a large water tank, 14.0 m below the water level in the tank. The top of the tank is open to the air. Find

a) the speed of efflux;

b) the volume discharged per unit time.

13–21 A sealed tank containing seawater to a height of 8.00 m also contains air above the water at a gauge pressure of 4.00 atm. Water flows out from a small hole at the bottom. Calculate the efflux speed of the water.

13–22 At a certain point in a horizontal pipeline the liquid's speed is 3.00 m·s^{-1}, and the gauge pressure is 3.00×10^4 Pa. Find the gauge pressure at a second point in the line if the cross-sectional area at the second point is one half that at the first. The liquid in the pipe is water.

13–23 At a certain point in a pipeline the liquid's speed is 5.00 m·s^{-1}, and the gauge pressure is 6.40×10^4 Pa. Find the gauge pressure at a second point in the line 8.00 m lower than the first if the cross-sectional area at the second point is twice that at the first. The liquid in the pipe is water.

13–24 Water flowing in a horizontal pipe discharges at the rate of 4.00×10^{-3} m^3·s^{-1}. At a point in the pipe where the cross-sectional area is 1.00×10^{-3} m^2 the absolute pressure is 1.80×10^5 Pa. What is the cross-sectional area of a constriction in the pipe if the pressure there is reduced to 1.20×10^5 Pa?

13–25 What gauge pressure is required in the city mains for a stream from a fire hose connected to the mains to reach a vertical height of 30.0 m?

13–26 An airplane with a mass of 8000 kg has a wing area of 20.0 m^2. If the pressure on the lower wing surface is 0.600×10^5 Pa during level flight at an elevation of 4000 m, what is the pressure on the upper wing surface?

13–27 Air is streaming horizontally past a small airplane's wings such that the speed is 50.0 m·s⁻¹ over the top surface and 30.0 m·s⁻¹ past the bottom surface. If the plane has a mass of 300 kg and a wing area of 5.00 m², what is the net force (including the effects of gravity) on the airplane? Assume that the density of air is 1.29 kg·m⁻³.

Section 13–8   Viscosity

13–28 Water at 20°C is flowing in a pipe with a radius of 20.0 cm. If the water's speed in the center of the pipe is 2.00 m·s⁻¹ and the flow is laminar, what is the water's speed

   a) 10.0 cm from the center of the pipe (i.e., halfway between the center and the walls)?

   b) at the walls of the pipe?

13–29 Water at 20°C flows through a pipe with a radius of 1.00 cm. If the flow speed at the center of the pipe is 0.300 m·s⁻¹ and the flow is laminar, find the pressure drop along a 2.00-m section of pipe due to viscosity.

13–30 A copper sphere with a mass of 0.20 g is ob-

served to fall with a terminal speed of 6.0 cm·s⁻¹ in an unknown liquid. If the density of copper is 8900 kg·m⁻³ and that of the liquid is 2800 kg·m⁻³, what is the viscosity of the liquid?

13–31 What speed must a gold sphere with radius 3.00 mm have in castor oil at 20°C for the viscous drag force to be one fourth the weight of the sphere?

13–32 Water at 20°C is flowing in a horizontal pipe that is 15.0 m long; the flow is laminar. A pump maintains a gauge pressure of 1200 Pa at a large tank at one end of the pipe. The other end of the pipe is open to the air.

   a) If the pipe has a diameter of 8.00 cm, what is the volume flow rate?

   b) What gauge pressure must the pump provide to achieve the same volume flow rate for a pipe with a diameter of 4.00 cm?

   c) For the pipe in part (a) and the same gauge pressure maintained by the pump, what does the volume flow rate become if the water is at a temperature of 60°C?

■ *Problems*

13–33 The deepest point known in any of the earth's oceans is in the Mariana Trench, 10.92 km deep.

   a) Assuming water to be incompressible, what is the gauge pressure at this depth? Use the density of seawater.

   b) The actual gauge pressure is 1.17×10^8 Pa. Your calculated value of the pressure will be less because the density actually varies with depth. Take your value for the pressure and, using the compressibility of water, find its density at the bottom of the Mariana Trench. What is the percent change in the density of the water?

13–34 A U-shaped tube open to the air at both ends contains some mercury. A quantity of water is carefully

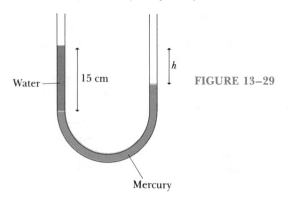

poured into the left arm of the tube until the vertical height of the water column is 15.0 cm, as shown in Fig. 13–29.

   a) What is the gauge pressure at the water–mercury interface?

   b) Calculate the vertical distance h from the top of the mercury in the right-hand arm of the tube to the top of the water in the left-hand arm.

13–35 According to an old advertising claim, a certain small car would float in water.

   a) If the car's mass is 1200 kg and its interior volume is 4.00 m³, what fraction of the car is immersed as it floats? The buoyancy of steel and other materials may be neglected.

   b) As water gradually leaks in and displaces the air in the car, what fraction of the interior volume is filled with water when the car sinks?

13–36 A hydrometer consists of a spherical bulb and a cylindrical stem with cross-sectional area 0.400 cm². The total volume of bulb and stem is 13.2 cm³. When immersed in water, the hydrometer floats with 8.00 cm of the stem above the water surface. In alcohol, 1.00 cm of the stem is above the surface. Find the density of alcohol. (*Note:* This illustrates the accuracy of such a hydrometer. Relatively small density differences give

Water — | 15 cm | h **FIGURE 13–29**

Mercury

rise to relatively large differences in hydrometer readings.)

13–37 The densities of air, helium, and hydrogen (at standard conditions) are 1.29 kg·m^{-3}, 0.178 kg·m^{-3}, and 0.0899 kg·m^{-3}, respectively.

a) What is the volume in cubic meters displaced by a hydrogen-filled dirigible that has a total "lift" of 15,000 kg? (The "lift" is the total mass of the dirigible that can be supported by the buoyant force in addition to the mass of the gas with which it is filled.)

b) What would be the "lift" if helium were used instead of hydrogen? In view of your answer, why is helium the gas that is actually used? (*Hint:* Remember the *Hindenberg.*)

13–38 An open barge is 25 m wide and has a longitudinal cross section as shown in Fig. 13–30. (The dimension not shown in the figure is 25 m.) If the barge is made from 7.5-cm-thick steel plate on each of its four sides and its bottom, what mass of coal can the barge carry without sinking? Is there enough room in the barge to hold this amount of coal? (The density of coal is about 1.5 g·cm^{-3}.)

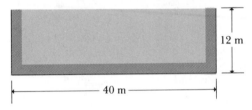

FIGURE 13–30

13–39 Consider an object with height h, mass M, and uniform cross-sectional area A floating upright in a liquid with density ρ.

a) Calculate the vertical distance from the surface of the liquid to the bottom of the floating object at equilibrium.

b) A downward force of magnitude F is applied to the top of the object. At the new equilibrium position, how much farther below the surface of the liquid is the bottom of the object than it was in part (a)? (Assume that F is small enough for some of the object to remain above the surface of the liquid.)

c) Your result in part (b) shows that if the force is suddenly removed, the object will oscillate up and down in simple harmonic motion. Calculate the period of this motion, in terms of the density ρ of the liquid and the mass M and cross-sectional area A of the object.

d) A 1500-kg cylindrical can buoy floats vertically in seawater (density 1.03×10^3 kg·m^{-3}). The diameter of the buoy is 0.800 m. Calculate the additional

distance the buoy will sink when a 100-kg man stands on top.

e) Calculate the period of the resulting vertical simple harmonic motion when the man dives off.

f) Calculate the period of oscillation of an ice cube 4.00 cm on a side floating in water with a density of 1.00×10^3 kg·m^{-3} if it is pushed down and released.

13–40 A piece of wood is 0.500 m long, 0.200 m wide, and 0.040 m thick. Its density is 0.600 g·cm^{-3}. What volume of lead must be fastened underneath to sink the wood in calm water so that its top is just even with the water level? What is the mass of this volume of lead?

13–41 Block A in Fig. 13–31 hangs by a cord from spring balance D and is submerged in a liquid C contained in beaker B. The mass of the beaker is 1.00 kg; the mass of the liquid is 1.50 kg. Balance D reads 2.50 kg, and balance E reads 7.50 kg. The volume of block A is 4.00×10^{-3} m^3.

a) What is the density of the liquid?

b) What will each balance read if block A is pulled up out of the liquid?

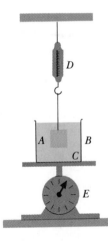

FIGURE 13–31

13–42 In seawater (density 1.03×10^3 kg·m^{-3}), a life preserver with a volume of 0.0500 m^3 will support an 80.0-kg person (average density 920 kg·m^{-3}) with 20% of the person's volume above water when the life preserver is fully submerged. What is the density of the material composing the life preserver?

13–43 A cubical block of wood 0.100 m on a side and with a density of 500 kg·m^{-3} floats in a jar of water. Oil with a density of 600 kg·m^{-3} is poured on the water until the top of the oil layer is 0.0400 m below the top of the block.

a) How deep is the oil layer?

b) What is the gauge pressure at the lower face of the block?

13–44 A block of balsa wood placed in one scale pan of an equal-arm balance is found to be exactly balanced by a 0.0500-kg brass mass in the other scale pan. Find the true mass of the balsa wood if its density is 150 kg·m^{-3}. Neglect the buoyancy of the brass in air. (The density of air is 1.29 kg·m^{-3}.)

13–45 A cubical brass block with sides of length L floats in mercury.

a) What fraction of the block is above the mercury surface?

b) If water is poured on the mercury surface, how deep must the water layer be so that the water surface just rises to the top of the brass block? (Express your answer in terms of L.)

13–46 A piece of gold-aluminum alloy weighs 45.0 N. When the piece of alloy is suspended from a spring balance and completely submerged in water, the balance reads 34.0 N. What is the weight of gold in the alloy if the density of gold is 19.3 g·cm^{-3} and the density of aluminum is 2.70 g·cm^{-3}?

13–47 What radius must a water drop have for the difference between inside and outside pressures to be 0.0200 atm? Assume that $T = 20°C$.

13–48 Water stands at a depth H in a large open tank whose side walls are vertical (Fig. 13–32). A hole is made in one of the walls at a depth h below the water surface.

a) At what distance R from the foot of the wall does the emerging stream of water strike the floor?

b) Let $H = 15.0$ m and $h = 3.00$ m. At what height below the water surface could a second hole be cut so that the stream emerging from it would have the same range as the stream emerging from the first hole?

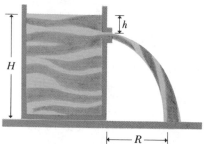

FIGURE 13–32

13–49 A cylindrical vessel, open at the top, is 0.200 m high and 0.100 m in diameter. A circular hole whose cross-sectional area is 1.00 cm^2 is cut in the center of the bottom of the vessel. Water flows into the vessel from a tube above it at the rate of 1.60 × 10^{-4} m^3·s^{-1}. How high will the water in the vessel rise?

13–50 In a horizontal pipeline the pressure difference between the main pipeline and the throat of a Venturi

meter is 2.00 × 10^5 Pa. The cross-sectional areas of the pipe and the constriction are 0.100 m^2 and 0.020 m^2, respectively. How many cubic meters per second are flowing through the pipe? The liquid in the pipe is water.

13–51 Water flows steadily from an open reservoir, as in Fig. 13–33. The elevation of point 1 is 10.0 m, and the elevation of points 2 and 3 is 2.00 m. The cross-sectional area at point 2 is 0.0400 m^2, and at point 3 it is 0.0200 m^2. The area of the reservoir is very large in comparison with the cross-sectional areas of the pipe. Assuming that Bernoulli's equation applies, compute

a) the discharge rate in cubic meters per second;

b) the gauge pressure at point 2.

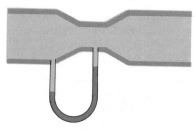

FIGURE 13–33

13–52 The horizontal section of pipe shown in Fig. 13–34 has a cross-sectional area of 40.0 cm^2 at the wider portions and 10.0 cm^2 at the constriction. Water is flowing in the pipe, and the discharge rate from the pipe is 5.00 × 10^{-3} m^3·s^{-1} (5.00 L·s^{-1}). Find

a) the speeds at the wide and the narrow portions;

b) the pressure difference between these portions;

c) the difference in height between the mercury columns in the U-shaped tube.

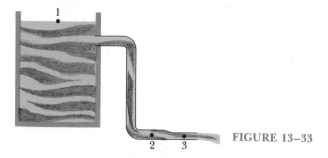

FIGURE 13–34

13–53 Modern airplane design calls for a "lift" due to the net force of the moving air on the wing of about 1000 N per square meter of wing area. Assume that air flows past the wing of an aircraft with streamline flow. If the speed of flow past the lower wing surface is 160 m·s^{-1}, what is the required speed over the upper surface to give a "lift" of 1000 N·m^{-2}? The density of air is 1.29 kg·m^{-3}.

13–54 Two very large open tanks, A and F (Fig. 13–35), both contain the same liquid. A horizontal pipe

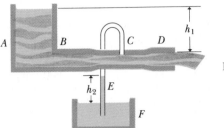

FIGURE 13–35

BCD, having a constriction at *C*, leads out of the bottom of tank *A*, and a vertical pipe *E* opens into the constriction at *C* and dips into the liquid in tank *F*. Assume streamline flow and no viscosity. If the cross-sectional area at *C* is one half that at *D*, and if *D* is a distance h_1 below the level of the liquid in *A*, to what height h_2 does liquid rise in pipe *E*? Express your answer in terms of h_1. Neglect changes in atmospheric pressure with elevation.

13–55 Figure 13–27a shows a liquid flowing from a vertical pipe. Notice that the vertical stream of the liquid has a very definite shape as it flows from the pipe.

a) We will now get the equation for this shape. Assume that the liquid is in free fall once it leaves the pipe and then find an equation for the speed of the liquid as a function of the distance it has fallen. Combining this with the equation of continuity, find an expression for the radius of the stream of liquid.

b) If water flows out of a vertical pipe with a speed of 2.00 m·s^{-1} as it exits from the pipe, how far below the outlet will the radius be one half the original radius of the stream?

13–56

a) With what terminal speed does an air bubble 2.00 mm in diameter rise in a liquid of viscosity 1.50 poise and density 900 kg·m^{-3}? (Assume that the density of air is 1.29 kg·m^{-3}.)

b) What is the terminal speed of the same bubble in water at 20°C?

13–57 The densities of steel and glycerin are 7800 kg·m^{-3} and 1260 kg·m^{-3}, respectively. The viscosity of glycerin at room temperature is 8.30 poise.

a) With what speed is a steel ball 2.50 mm in radius falling in a tank of glycerin at an instant when its acceleration is one half that of a freely falling body?

b) What is the terminal speed of the ball?

13–58 Oil having a viscosity of 3.00 poise and a density of 800 kg·m^{-3} is to be pumped from one large open tank to another through 1.00 km of smooth steel pipe 0.150 m in diameter. The line discharges into the air at

a point 30.0 m above the level of the oil in the supply tank.

a) What gauge pressure, in pascals and in atmospheres, must the pump exert to maintain a flow of 0.0800 m^3·s^{-1}?

b) What is the power consumed by the pump?

13–59 The tank at the left in Fig. 13–36a has a very large cross-sectional area and is open to the atmosphere. The depth $y = 0.600$ m. The cross-sectional areas of the horizontal tubes leading out of the tank are 1.00 cm^2, 0.500 cm^2, and 0.200 cm^2, respectively. The liquid is ideal, having zero viscosity.

a) What is the volume rate of flow out of the tank?

b) What is the speed in each portion of the horizontal tube?

c) What are heights of the liquid in the vertical side tubes?

Suppose that the liquid in Fig. 13–36b has a viscosity of 0.500 poise and a density of 800 kg·m^{-3} and that the depth of liquid in the large tank is such that the volume rate of flow is the same as in part (a). The distance between the side tubes at *c* and *d*, and between those at *e* and *f*, is 0.200 m. The cross-sectional areas of the horizontal tubes are the same in both diagrams.

d) What is the difference in level between the tops of the liquid columns in tubes *c* and *d*?

e) In tubes *e* and *f*?

f) What is the flow speed on the axis of each section of the horizontal tube?

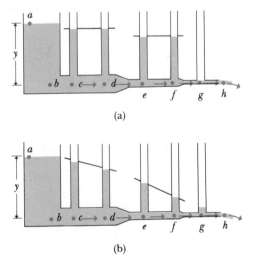

(a)

(b)

FIGURE 13–36

13–60 For an object falling in air, Stokes' law is obeyed only for small speeds. The air drag on an object falling through the earth's atmosphere is more accurately given by $\frac{1}{2}CA\rho v^2$, where *A* is the area of the object perpendicular to the motion, ρ is the density of the air, and C is the drag coefficient. (Refer to Sections 5–4 and 7–9.) C is determined experimentally; for a spherical object having the velocities of this problem it is approximately 0.5. (*Note:* For a graph of the values of C over a wide range of speeds, see J.E.A. John and W. Haberman, *Introduction to Fluid Mechanics* [Englewood Cliffs, N.J.: Prentice-Hall], p. 198.) A ball bearing with radius 0.500 cm and mass 3.00 g is dropped from the top of the Sears Tower in Chicago, which is 443 m tall.

a) Calculate the speed the ball bearing would have at the ground if air resistance were negligible.

b) Taking into account air resistance, what is the terminal speed of the ball bearing? (Assume that the density of air is 1.29 kg·m^{-3}.)

Challenge Problems

13–61 The following is quoted from a letter. How would you reply?

> *It is the practice of carpenters hereabouts, when laying out and leveling up the foundations of relatively long buildings, to use a garden hose filled with water, into the ends of the hose being thrust glass tubes 10 to 12 inches long. The theory is that water, seeking a common level, will be of the same height in both the tubes and thus effect a level. Now the question rises as to what happens if a bubble of air is left in the hose. Our greybeards contend the air will not affect the reading from one end to the other. Others say that it will cause important inaccuracies.*

Can you give a relatively simple answer to this question, together with an explanation? Fig. 13–37 gives a rough sketch of the situation that caused the dispute.

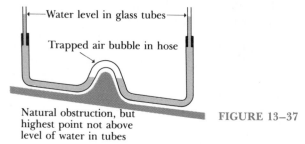

Water level in glass tubes

Trapped air bubble in hose

Natural obstruction, but highest point not above level of water in tubes

FIGURE 13–37

13–62 A U-shaped tube having a horizontal portion of length l (see Fig. 13–38) contains a liquid. What is the difference in height between the liquid columns in the vertical arms if the tube has an acceleration a toward the right? Explain why the difference in height does not depend on the density of the liquid or on the

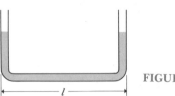

FIGURE 13–38

cross-sectional area of the tube. Would it be the same if the vertical tubes did not have equal cross-sectional areas? Would it be the same if the horizontal portion were tapered from one end to the other?

13–63 A cubical block of wood 0.300 m on a side is weighted so that its center of gravity is at the point shown in Fig. 13–39a, and it floats in water with one half its volume submerged. Compute the restoring torque, the net torque about a horizontal axis perpendicular to the block and passing through its geometrical center, when the block is "heeled" at an angle of 45.0° as in Fig. 13–39b.

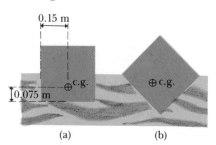

0.15 m

c.g.

0.075 m

c.g.

(a)   (b)

FIGURE 13–39

13–64 A rock with mass $m = 5.00$ kg is suspended from the roof of an elevator by a light cord. The rock is totally immersed in a bucket of water that sits on the floor of the elevator but doesn't touch the bottom or sides of the bucket.

a) When the elevator is at rest, the tension in the cord is 39.0 N. Calculate the volume of the rock.

b) Derive an expression for the tension in the cord when the elevator is accelerating *upward* with an acceleration a. Calculate the tension when $a = 1.60$ m·s^{-2} upward.

c) Derive an expression for the tension in the cord when the elevator is accelerating *downward* with an acceleration a. Calculate the tension when $a = 1.60$ m·s^{-2} downward.

d) What is the tension when the elevator is in free fall, with a downward acceleration equal to g?

13–65 A siphon, as depicted in Fig. 13–40, is a convenient device for removing liquids from containers. To establish the flow, the tube must be initially filled with fluid. Let the fluid have density ρ and let the atmospheric pressure be p_0. Assume that the cross-sectional area of the tube is the same at all points along the tube.

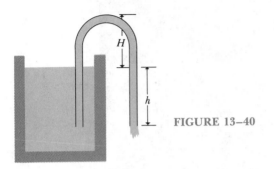

FIGURE 13–40

a) If the lower end of the siphon is a distance h below the surface of the liquid in the container, what is the speed of the fluid at it flows out the lower end of the siphon? (Assume that the container has a very large diameter, and neglect any effects of viscosity.)

b) A curious feature of a siphon is that the fluid initially flows "uphill." What is the greatest height H that the high point of the tube can have and the siphon flow still occur?

14

Temperature and Expansion

With this chapter we begin the study of a broad class of phenomena associated with *temperature* and *heat*. Such diverse topics as expansion joints in bridges, the efficiency of an automobile engine, solar energy, and the design of better refrigerators are all part of this new subject area. We have based our study of mechanics on the three fundamental quantities mass, length, and time. Now we need to introduce the additional fundamental quantity *temperature*. The concept of thermal equilibrium is central to the problem of measuring temperature, and we need to learn something about *thermometers* (temperature-measuring instruments) and the various temperature scales that are in common use. Finally, we consider the expansion and contraction of materials that are caused by temperature changes.

This chapter lays the groundwork for our study of *thermodynamics*, a broad subject concerned with energy transformations and their relationships to the properties of matter. Thermodynamics forms an indispensable part of the foundation of physics, chemistry, the life sciences, and most of contemporary technology.

14–1
Temperature and Thermal Equilibrium

The concept of **temperature** is rooted in qualitative ideas of "hot" and "cold" based on our sense of touch. A body that feels hot usually has a higher temperature than the same body when it feels cold. That's pretty vague, of course, but many properties of matter that we can measure quantitatively depend on temperature. The length of a metal rod increases as the rod becomes hotter. The pressure of gas in a container increases with temperature; a steam boiler may explode if it gets too hot. Electrical properties of materials change with temperature; most metals are poorer electrical conductors when hot than when cold. When a material is extremely hot, it glows "red-hot" or "white-hot," the color depending on its temperature.

All of this behavior can be understood in greater detail on the basis of the *molecular* structure of materials. In Chapter 20 we will look at the relationship between temperature and the energy of molecular motion in detail. It is important to understand, however, that temperature and heat are inherently *macroscopic* concepts. They can and must be defined independently of any detailed molecular picture.

To define temperature *quantitatively*, we need a scheme for assigning numbers to various gradations of hot or cold. We can use any measurable property of a system that varies with its "hotness" or "coldness." A simple example is a liquid such as mercury or ethanol in a bulb attached to a thin tube, as in Fig. 14–1a. When the system becomes hotter, the liquid rises in the tube and the value of L increases. This is, of course, the basic principle of a familiar type of thermometer. Another simple system is a quantity of gas in a constant-volume container, as shown in Fig. 14–1b. The pressure p, measured by the gauge, increases or decreases as the gas becomes hotter or colder. A third example is the electrical resistance R of a conducting wire, which also varies when the wire becomes hotter or colder.

In each of these examples a measurable quantity that changes with the hotness or coldness of the system, such as the length L, the pressure p, or the resistance R, can be used to assign a number to a system to describe how hot it is. Thus each device can be used as a **thermometer.**

There's a problem with these devices, though: In each example the measured quantity indicates the temperature *of the thermometer*. How can such a device be used to measure the temperature of any other body? The answer to this question leads us to the concept of *thermal equilibrium* and an important related principle. First, how do you use a mercury thermometer that is initially at room temperature to measure the temperature of a cup of hot coffee? You stick the thermometer in the coffee; the thermometer becomes hotter, and the coffee cools off a little. You watch the thermometer, and after you see that no further change is taking place as a result of this interaction, you read the thermometer. This *equilibrium* condition, in which the interaction is no longer causing changes in the system, is called **thermal equilibrium.**

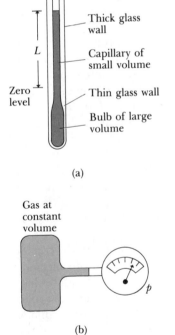

(a)

(b)

14–1
(a) A system whose state is specified by the value of the length L. (b) A system whose state is given by the value of the pressure p.

But how do we know that at thermal equilibrium the thermometer and the coffee have the same temperature? To establish this, we need some additional experiments. Consider the interaction of two systems. System A is the tube-and-liquid system of Fig 14–1a, and system B is the container of gas and pressure gauge of Fig. 14–1b. When the two systems are brought into contact, in general the values of L and p change as the systems move toward thermal equilibrium. Initially, one system is hotter than the other, and each system changes the state of the other.

If the systems are separated by an insulating material or **insulator** such as wood, plastic foam, or fiberglass, they influence each other more slowly. An ideal insulator is defined as a material that permits *no* interactions at all between the two systems. Such an ideal insulator *prevents* the attainment of thermal equilibrium if the two systems are not initially in thermal equilibrium. This is exactly what the insulating material in a camping cooler does. We don't want the cold food inside to warm up and attain thermal equilibrium with the hot summer air outside; the insulation prevents this, although not forever.

Now consider three systems, A, B, and C, as shown in Fig. 14–2. We do not need to specify in detail what they are, but let's suppose that initially they are *not* in thermal equilibrium. Perhaps one is very hot, one is very cold, and the third is lukewarm. We surround the three systems with an insulating box so that they cannot interact with anything except each other.

We also separate systems A and B with an insulating wall, the gray slab in Fig. 14–2a, but we let system C interact with both A and B; we indicate this symbolically in the figure with a thin colored slab, a thermal **conductor.** (A conducting material is one that *permits* thermal interactions between the systems it separates.) We wait until there is no further change as a result of this interaction, that is, until thermal equilibrium is attained. We then remove system C from systems A and B by inserting an insulating wall, as in Fig. 14–2b, and we also remove the insulating wall between A and B, replacing it by a conducting wall. What happens?

Experiment shows that *nothing* happens; the states of systems A and B do not change! Conclusion: If system C is initially in thermal equilibrium with both A and B, then A and B are also in thermal equilibrium with each other. If this result seems trivial and obvious, we caution you not to be too hasty. Intuition can be misleading, and even conclusions that seem obvious have to be tested experimentally.

Two systems in thermal equilibrium with a third system are in thermal equilibrium with each other. This principle is called the **zeroth law of thermodynamics.** This strange-sounding name refers to the fact that the basic principles of thermodynamics are embodied in three statements called the first, second, and third laws of thermodynamics. The principle we have just discussed is fundamental to all of these, although its importance was not clearly recognized until after the others. So it really deserves the name "zeroth law."

The property of any system that determines whether or not it is in thermal equilibrium with another system is its temperature. *Two systems in thermal equilibrium must have the same temperature.* When a thermometer is in thermal equilibrium with another body, reading the temperature of the thermometer also gives the temperature of the other body. When the

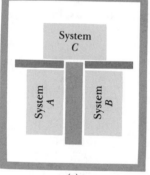

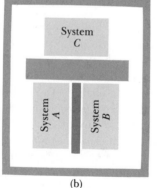

14–2
The zeroth law of thermodynamics. (a) If A and B are each in thermal equilibrium with C, then (b) A and B are in thermal equilibrium with each other. Thick gray layers represent insulating walls; thinner colored layers represent conducting walls.

temperatures of two systems are different, they *cannot* be in thermal equilibrium. A temperature scale, such as the Fahrenheit or Celsius scale, is simply a specific scheme for assigning numbers to temperatures. We will study temperature scales in Section 14–3.

14–2
Thermometers

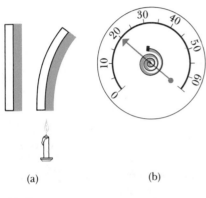

(a)   (b)

14–3
(a) A bimetallic strip bends when it is heated because one metal expands more than the other. (b) A bimetallic strip, usually in the form of a spiral, may be used as a thermometer.

One familiar type of thermometer is the tube-and-liquid type shown in Fig. 14–1a. The liquid is usually mercury or colored ethanol. If we label the liquid level at the freezing temperature of water "zero" and the level at the boiling temperature "100," and if we divide the distance between these two points into 100 equal intervals, we obtain the familiar Celsius scale, which we will discuss in detail in the next section.

Another common type of thermometer contains strips of two different metals welded together, as shown in Fig. 14–3a. Because one metal expands more than the other with temperature increases, the composite strip bends when the temperature changes. In practical thermometers this strip is usually made in the form of a spiral; the outer end is anchored to the thermometer case, and the inner end is attached to a pointer, as shown in Fig. 14–3b. The pointer rotates in response to temperature changes, and a circular scale is provided.

In a *resistance thermometer* we measure the changing electrical resistance of a coil of fine wire. Resistance can be measured with great precision, and the resistance thermometer is one of the most precise instruments for the measurement of temperature. At very low temperatures a small carbon cylinder or a germanium crystal is used instead of a coil of wire.

To measure very high temperatures, an *optical pyrometer* can be used. It measures the brightness of light emitted by a red-hot or white-hot substance. As shown in Fig. 14–4, it consists of a telescope T with a small

14–4
An optical pyrometer. The telescope T is pointed toward the hot body B, and the power supply P is adjusted until the brightness of the filament in the lamp L is the same as that of the hot body. The filter F reduces the overall brightness level. The power supply can be calibrated to read temperature directly.

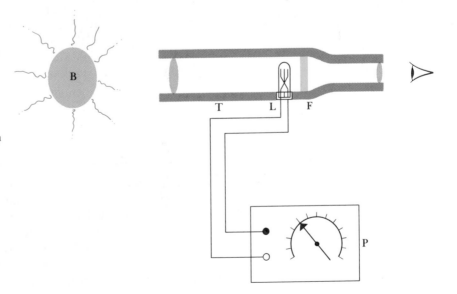

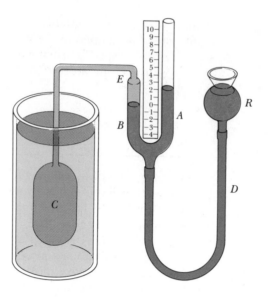

14-5
The constant-volume gas thermometer.

electric light bulb L mounted in the tube. The bulb is connected to a variable power supply P, and the brightness of the bulb is varied until it matches that of the substance being observed. The power-supply adjustment can be calibrated to read temperature directly. No part of the instrument touches the hot substance, so the optical pyrometer can be used at temperatures that would destroy most other thermometers.

Among all temperature-dependent properties or **thermometric properties,** the pressure of a gas kept at constant volume is outstanding in its sensitivity, accuracy, and reproducibility. A constant-volume gas thermometer is shown schematically in Fig. 14–5. The gas, usually helium, is contained in bulb C, and its pressure is measured by the open-tube mercury manometer. As the temperature of the gas increases, the gas expands, forcing the mercury down in tube B and up in tube A. By raising or lowering the mercury reservoir R we can keep the mercury level in B at a reference mark E, thus keeping the volume of the gas constant. The pressure is determined by the difference in mercury levels in tubes A and B. Gas thermometers are used mainly to establish standards and calibrate other thermometers. They are large, bulky, and slow in coming to thermal equilibrium.

14-3
The Celsius and Fahrenheit Scales

The **Celsius temperature scale** (formerly called the *centigrade* scale in English-speaking countries) is defined so that the freezing temperature of pure water at normal atmospheric pressure is zero or 0°C (zero degrees Celsius) and the boiling temperature of pure water at normal atmospheric pressure is 100 or 100°C. We interpolate between or extrapolate beyond these reference temperatures by using one of the thermometers described in Section 14–2. The temperature for a state that is colder than freezing water is a negative number. The Celsius scale is used, both in everyday life and in science and industry, everywhere in the world except for a few English-speaking countries, and even in the United States the Celsius scale is coming into more and more common use.

The temperature scale used in everyday life in the United States is the **Fahrenheit scale.** It places the freezing temperature of water at 32°F (32 degrees Fahrenheit) and the boiling temperature of water at 212°F, both at normal atmospheric pressure. Thus there are 180 degrees between freezing and boiling, compared to 100 on the Celsius scale, and one Fahrenheit degree represents only 100/180 or 5/9 as great a temperature change as one Celsius degree.

To convert temperatures from Celsius to Fahrenheit, we note that a Celsius temperature T_C is the number of Celsius degrees above freezing; to obtain the number of Fahrenheit degrees above freezing, we must multiply this by 9/5. But freezing on the Fahrenheit scale is at 32°F, so to obtain the actual Fahrenheit temperature we must first multiply the Celsius value by 9/5 and then add 32°. Symbolically,

$$T_F = \tfrac{9}{5}T_C + 32°. \tag{14–1}$$

To convert Fahrenheit to Celsius, we solve this equation for T_C, obtaining

$$T_C = \tfrac{5}{9}(T_F - 32°). \tag{14–2}$$

That is, we first subtract 32° to obtain the number of Fahrenheit degrees above freezing and then multiply by 5/9 to obtain the number of Celsius degrees above freezing, that is, the Celsius temperature.

We don't recommend memorizing Eqs. (14–1) and (14–2). Instead, try to understand the reasoning that led to them well enough that you can derive them on the spot when you need them.

We often need to distinguish between an actual temperature on a certain scale and a temperature *interval*, representing a *difference* in the temperatures of two bodies or a *change* of temperature of a body. To make this distinction, we state a temperature *interval* of 10° as 10 C° (10 Celsius degrees) and an actual temperature of 20° as 20°C (20 degrees Celsius). Thus a beaker of water heated from 20°C to 30°C undergoes a temperature change of 10 C°. We will use this notation consistently throughout this book.

Here is a serious problem in defining temperature scales. When two thermometers, such as a liquid-in-tube system and a resistance thermometer, are calibrated so that they agree at 0°C and 100°C, they *do not* necessarily agree at intermediate temperatures. Different thermometric properties such as length and resistance change with temperature in slightly different ways. Thus a temperature scale defined in this way always depends somewhat on the specific properties of the material used in the thermometer.

The most consistent scales are based on a constant-volume gas thermometer with the lowest practical pressures. Low-pressure gas thermometers using various gases are found to agree very closely, and such thermometers are used for high-precision standards. But we are still dependent on the properties of specific materials. Why can't we define a temperature scale that is *completely* independent of material properties? It turns out that we *can* do this; we will return to this fundamental problem in Chapter 19, after we have developed the necessary thermodynamic principles.

The bimetallic strip shown in Fig. 14–3a is used in many *thermostats* for controlling heating and cooling systems. One end of the bimetallic strip is attached to an electrical contact set, which makes or breaks contact as the bimetallic strip bends or straightens in response to temperature changes. This electrical contact turns the furnace or air conditioner on or off so as to maintain a constant temperature.

14–4
The Kelvin Scale

When we calibrate a constant-volume gas thermometer, we use a graph similar to Fig. 14–6, showing the relation between gas pressure p and temperature T. Such a graph suggests that there is a hypothetical temperature at which the gas pressure becomes zero. Surprisingly, this temperature turns out to be the same for many different gases, namely, $-273.15°C$. We can't actually observe this zero-pressure condition, for several reasons. One reason is that gases liquefy and solidify at very low temperatures, and the proportionality of pressure to temperature no longer holds.

We can use this extrapolated zero-pressure temperature to define a new temperature scale with its zero-point at this temperature. This is the basis of the **Kelvin temperature scale,** named after Lord Kelvin (1824–1907). The degrees are the same size as on the Celsius scale, but the zero is shifted so that 0 K = $-273.15°C$ and 273.15 K = $0°C$; that is,

$$T_K = T_C + 273.15°. \tag{14–3}$$

Ordinary room temperature, 20°C, is 20 + 273.15, or about 293 K.

In SI nomenclature, "degree" is not used with the Kelvin scale; the temperature mentioned above is read "293 kelvins," not "degrees Kelvin." We capitalize Kelvin when it refers to the temperature scale, but the *unit* of temperature is the *kelvin*, not capitalized but abbreviated K.

We have introduced the Kelvin scale with reference to the Celsius scale, which has two fixed points, the normal freezing and boiling temperatures of water. However, we can also define the Kelvin scale with reference to a gas thermometer (at very low pressure) by using only a single reference temperature. We define the ratio of any two temperatures T_1 and T_2 on the Kelvin scale as the ratio of the corresponding gas-thermometer pressures p_1 and p_2:

$$\frac{T_2}{T_1} = \frac{p_2}{p_1}. \tag{14–4}$$

To complete the definition, we need only specify the Kelvin temperature of a single specific state. For reasons of precision and reproducibility the state chosen is not a freezing or boiling point but the *triple point* of water. This is the unique condition under which solid water (ice), liquid, and

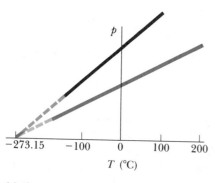

14–6
Graph of pressure versus temperature for two different constant-volume gas thermometers. A straight-line extrapolation predicts that the pressure would become zero at $-273.15°C$ if that temperature could be reached and the proportionality of pressure to temperature held exactly.

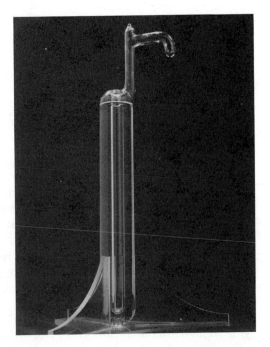

14–7
A cell used to establish the triple-point temperature of water. The cylindrical Pyrex container is nearly filled with water of the highest possible purity and then permanently sealed. Partial freezing of the sealed water leads to the triple-point solid–liquid–vapor equilibrium condition and establishes the triple-point temperature of 0.0100°C or 273.1600 K. Calibrations with a single triple-point cell are precise to within 0.0001 K, and triple-point cells agree with each other within 0.0002 K. (Courtesy National Bureau of Standards.)

water vapor can all coexist together. This occurs at a temperature of 0.01°C and a water-vapor pressure of 610 Pa (about 0.006 atm). The triple-point temperature T_{triple} of water is assigned the value $T_{triple} = 273.16$ K. A cell used to establish the triple-point temperature is shown in Fig. 14–7. Thus with reference to Eq. (14–4), if p_{triple} is the pressure in a gas thermometer at temperature T_{triple} and p is the pressure at some other temperature T, then T is given on the Kelvin scale by

$$T = T_{triple}\frac{p}{p_{triple}}, \qquad (14\text{–}5)$$

with T_{triple} *defined* to be 273.16 K.

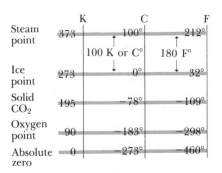

14–8
Relationships among Kelvin, Celsius, and Fahrenheit temperature scales. Temperatures have been rounded off to the nearest degree.

Example 14–1   Suppose a constant-volume gas thermometer has a pressure of 1.50×10^4 Pa at temperature T_{triple} and a pressure of 1.95×10^4 Pa at some unknown temperature T. What is T?

Solution   From Eq. (14–5),

$$T = (273 \text{ K})\frac{1.95 \times 10^4 \text{ Pa}}{1.50 \times 10^4 \text{ Pa}} = 355 \text{ K}$$

$$= 82°\text{C}.$$ ■

The relationships of the three temperature scales discussed above are shown graphically in Fig. 14–8.

The Kelvin scale is called an **absolute temperature scale,** and its zero point is called **absolute zero.** To define more completely what we mean by absolute zero, we need to use thermodynamic principles to be developed in the next several chapters. We will return to this concept in Chapter 19.

14–5
Thermal Expansion

Most solid materials expand when heated. Suppose a rod of material has a length L_0 at some initial temperature T_0. When the temperature increases by an amount ΔT, the length increases by ΔL. Experiment shows that if ΔT is not too large, ΔL is *directly proportional* to ΔT. But ΔL is also proportional to L_0; if two rods made of the same material have the same temperature change, but one rod is initially twice as long as the other, then the *change* in its length is also twice as great. Introducing a proportionality constant α (which is different for different materials), we may express this relation in an equation:

$$\Delta L = \alpha L_0 \, \Delta T. \qquad (14\text{–}6)$$

This shows that if a body has length L_0 at temperature T_0, then its length L at a temperature $T = T_0 + \Delta T$ is given by

$$\begin{aligned} L &= L_0 + \Delta L \\ &= L_0(1 + \alpha \, \Delta T). \end{aligned} \qquad (14\text{–}7)$$

The constant α, which describes the thermal expansion properties of a particular material, is called the *temperature coefficient of linear expansion* or simply the **coefficient of linear expansion.** The units of α are K^{-1} or $(C°)^{-1}$. For most materials, every linear dimension changes according to Eq. (14–6) or (14–7). Thus L could equally well represent the thickness of the rod, the side length of a square sheet, or the diameter of a hole in the material. There are some exceptional cases. Wood, for example, has different expansion properties along the grain and across the grain; and single crystals of material can have different properties along different crystal-axis directions. We exclude these exceptional cases from the present discussion.

The direct proportionality expressed by Eq. (14–6) is not exact; it is *approximately* correct for sufficiently small temperature changes. For a given material, α varies somewhat with the initial temperature T_0 and the size of the temperature interval. Because Eq. (14–6) is at best an approximation, we will ignore this variation. Average values of α for several materials are listed in Table 14–1. Within the precision of these values, we don't need to worry about whether T_0 is 0°C or 20°C or some other temperature. We also note from these values that α is usually a very small number; even for a temperature change of 100 C°, the fractional length change $\Delta L/L_0$ is of the order of 1/1000.

Increasing temperature usually causes increases in *volume*, for both solid and liquid materials. Experiments show that if the temperature change ΔT is not too great (say less than 100 C° or so), the increase in volume ΔV is approximately *proportional* to the temperature change. The volume change is also proportional to the initial volume V_0, as is the case

TABLE 14–1   Coefficient of linear expansion

Material	α, $(C°)^{-1}$
Aluminum	2.4×10^{-5}
Brass	2.0×10^{-5}
Copper	1.7×10^{-5}
Glass	$0.4\text{–}0.9 \times 10^{-5}$
Steel	1.2×10^{-5}
Invar	0.09×10^{-5}
Quartz (fused)	0.04×10^{-5}

TABLE 14–2   **Coefficient of volume expansion**

Solids	β, $(C°)^{-1}$	Liquids	β, $(C°)^{-1}$
Aluminum	7.2×10^{-5}	Ethanol	75×10^{-5}
Brass	6.0×10^{-5}	Carbon disulfide	115×10^{-5}
Copper	5.1×10^{-5}	Glycerin	49×10^{-5}
Glass	$1.2\text{–}2.7 \times 10^{-5}$	Mercury	18×10^{-5}
Steel	3.6×10^{-5}		
Invar	0.27×10^{-5}		
Quartz (fused)	0.12×10^{-5}		

with linear expansion. The relationship can be expressed as follows:

$$\Delta V = \beta V_0 \, \Delta T. \qquad (14\text{–}8)$$

The constant β characterizes the volume expansion properties of a particular material; it is called the *temperature coefficient of volume expansion* or the **coefficient of volume expansion.** The units of β are K^{-1} or $(C°)^{-1}$. Like the coefficient of linear expansion, β varies somewhat with temperature. Equation (14–8) is an approximate relation, valid for sufficiently small temperature changes. For many substances, β decreases at low temperatures. Several values of β in the neighborhood of room temperature are listed in Table 14–2. Note that the values for liquids are much larger than those for solids.

PROBLEM-SOLVING STRATEGY: *Thermal Expansion*

1. Identify which of the quantities in Eq. (14–6) or (14–8) are known and which are unknown. Often, you will be given two temperatures and will have to compute ΔT. Or you may be given an initial temperature T_0 and may have to find a final temperature corresponding to a given length or volume change. In this case, find ΔT first; then the final temperature is $T_0 + \Delta T$.

2. Unit consistency is crucial, as always. L_0 and ΔL (or V_0 and ΔV) must have the same units, and if you use a value of α or β in $(C°)^{-1}$, then ΔT must be in Celsius degrees $(C°)$.

3. Remember that sizes of holes in a material expand with temperature just the same way as any other linear dimension, and the volume of a hole (such as the volume of a container) expands the same way as the corresponding solid shape. If this seems strange, look at it from a molecular viewpoint. All the molecules in the body get a little farther apart when the body expands; when the molecules around the periphery of a hole move farther apart, the hole has to get bigger.

Example 14–2   A surveyor uses a steel measuring tape that is exactly 50.000 m long at a temperature of 20°C. What is its length on a hot summer day when the temperature is 35°C?

Solution   We have $L_0 = 50.000$ m, $T_0 = 20°C$, and $T = 35°C$. From Eq. (14–6),

$$\Delta L = (50 \text{ m})(1.2 \times 10^{-5} \text{ (C°)}^{-1})(35°C - 20°C)$$
$$= 9.0 \times 10^{-3} \text{ m} = 9.0 \text{ mm},$$
$$L = L_0 + \Delta L = 50.000 \text{ m} + 0.009 \text{ m} = 50.009 \text{ m}.$$

Thus the length at 35°C is 50.009 m. Note that L_0 is given to five significant figures but that we need only two of them to compute ΔL.   ∎

Example 14–3   In Example 14–2 the surveyor measures a distance when the temperature is 35°C and obtains the result 35.794 m. What is the actual distance?

Solution   The distance between two successive meter marks on the tape is a little more than a meter, in the ratio (50.009 m)/(50.000 m). Thus the true distance is

$$\frac{50.009 \text{ m}}{50.000 \text{ m}}(35.794 \text{ m}) = 35.800 \text{ m}.$$ ∎

Example 14–4   A glass flask with a volume of 200 cm³ is filled to the brim with mercury at 20°C. How much mercury overflows when the temperature of the system is raised to 100°C? The coefficient of volume expansion of the glass in 1.2×10^{-5} (C°)$^{-1}$.

Solution   Because β is much larger for mercury than for glass, we know that some mercury is going to run over. The increase in the volume of the flask is

$$\Delta V = \beta V_0 \Delta T$$
$$= (1.2 \times 10^{-5} \text{ (C°)}^{-1})(200 \text{ cm}^3)(100°C - 20°C) = 0.19 \text{ cm}^3.$$

The increase in the volume of the mercury is

$$\Delta V = (18 \times 10^{-5} \text{ (C°)}^{-1})(200 \text{ cm}^3)(100°C - 20°C) = 2.9 \text{ cm}^3.$$

The volume of mercury that overflows is

$$2.9 \text{ cm}^3 - 0.19 \text{ cm}^3 = 2.7 \text{ cm}^3.$$ ∎

Water, in the temperature range from 0°C to 4°C, *decreases* in volume with increasing temperature; this is opposite to the behavior of most substances. Between 0°C and 4°C the coefficient of expansion of water is *negative*. Above 4°C, water expands when heated. The density of water is greatest at 4°C. Water also expands when it freezes, unlike most materials.

This anomalous behavior of water has an important effect on plant and animal life in lakes. When a lake cools, the cooled water at the surface flows to the bottom because of its greater density. But when the temperature reaches 4°C, this flow ceases, and the water near the surface

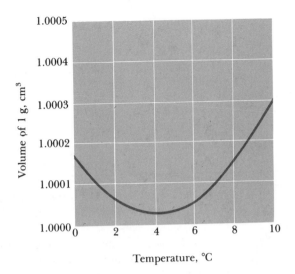

Temperature, °C

14–9
Volume of 1 g of water in the temperature range from 0°C to 10°C. If Eq. (14–8) were obeyed, the curve would be a straight line.

remains colder (and less dense) than that at the bottom. As the surface freezes, the ice floats because it is less dense than water. The water at the bottom remains at 4°C until nearly the entire lake is frozen. If water behaved like most substances, contracting continuously on cooling and freezing, lakes would freeze from the bottom up. Circulation due to density differences would continuously carry warmer water to the surface for efficient cooling, and lakes would freeze solid much more easily. This would destroy all plant and animal life that can withstand cold water but not freezing. All life forms known on earth depend on chemical systems based on aqueous solutions; if water did not have this special property, the evolution of various life forms would have taken a very different course.

The anomalous expansion of water in the temperature range 0°C to 10°C is shown in Fig. 14–9. Table 14–3 covers a wider range of temperatures.

For solid materials there is a simple relation between the volume expansion coefficient β and the linear expansion coefficient α. To derive this relation, we consider a solid body in the form of a rectangular block with dimensions L_1, L_2, and L_3. Its volume V_0 is

$$V_0 = L_1 L_2 L_3.$$

When the temperature increases by ΔT, each linear dimension changes according to Eq. (14–7), and the new volume is

$$
\begin{aligned}
V_0 + \Delta V &= [L_1(1 + \alpha\,\Delta T)][L_2(1 + \alpha\,\Delta T)][L_3(1 + \alpha\,\Delta T)] \\
&= L_1 L_2 L_3 (1 + \alpha\,\Delta T)^3 = V_0 (1 + \alpha\,\Delta T)^3 \\
&= V_0 [1 + 3\alpha\,\Delta T + 3(\alpha\,\Delta T)^2 + (\alpha\,\Delta T)^3].
\end{aligned}
$$

If $\alpha\,\Delta T$ is small, the terms containing $(\alpha\,\Delta T)^2$ and $(\alpha\,\Delta T)^3$ are very small and may be neglected. For example, if $\Delta T = 100$ C° and $\alpha = 10^{-5}$ (C°)$^{-1}$, then $\alpha\,\Delta T = 10^{-3}$ but $(\alpha\,\Delta T)^2 = 10^{-6}$. We drop the two smallest terms and then subtract V_0 from both sides:

$$\Delta V = (3\alpha) V_0 \, \Delta T.$$

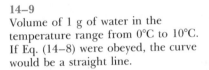

TABLE 14–3   Volume and density of water

T, °C	Volume of 1 g, cm³	Density, g·cm⁻³
0	1.0002	0.9998
4	1.0000	1.0000
10	1.0003	0.9997
20	1.0018	0.9982
50	1.0121	0.9881
75	1.0258	0.9749
100	1.0434	0.9584

Comparing this with Eq. (14–8), we conclude that

$$\beta = 3\alpha. \tag{14–9}$$

We invite you to check this relation for some of the materials listed in Tables 14–1 and 14–2.

*14–6
Thermal Stresses

If we clamp the ends of a rod rigidly to prevent expansion or contraction and then change the temperature, tensile or compressive stresses, called **thermal stresses,** are set up in the rod. The rod would ordinarily expand or contract, but the clamps prevent this. The resulting stresses may become large enough to stress the rod beyond its elastic limit or even beyond its breaking strength. Hence in the design of any structure that is subject to changes in temperature, provision must be made for expansion. Concrete highways usually have cracks between sections, filled with a material that "gives" with temperature changes to permit expansion and contraction of the concrete. Long steam pipes have expansion joints or U-shaped sections of pipe to prevent buckling or stretching with temperature changes. If one end of a steel bridge is rigidly fastened to its abutment, the other end always rests on rollers.

We can compute the thermal stress set up in a rod that is not free to expand or contract. We simply compute the amount the rod would expand (or contract) if it were not held and then compute the stress needed to compress (or stretch) it back to its original length. Suppose that a rod of length L_0 and cross-sectional area A has its ends rigidly fastened while the temperature is reduced (negative ΔT), causing a tensile stress. The fractional change in length if the rod were free to contract would be

$$\frac{\Delta L}{L_0} = \alpha \, \Delta T. \tag{14–10}$$

Both ΔL and ΔT are negative. Since the rod is *not* free to contract, the tension must increase enough to produce an equal and opposite fractional change in length. But from the definition of Young's modulus, Eq. (12–3),

$$Y = \frac{F/A}{\Delta L/L_0}, \qquad \frac{\Delta L}{L_0} = \frac{F}{AY}. \tag{14–11}$$

The tensile force F is determined by the requirement that the *total* fractional change in length, thermal expansion plus elastic strain, must be zero:

$$\alpha \, \Delta T + \frac{F}{AY} = 0,$$

$$F = -AY\alpha \, \Delta T. \tag{14–12}$$

For a decrease in temperature, ΔT is negative, so F is positive. The tensile

stress F/A in the rod is

$$\frac{F}{A} = -Y\alpha \, \Delta T. \qquad (14-13)$$

If, instead, ΔT represents an *increase* in temperature, then F and F/A become negative, corresponding to *compressive* force and stress, respectively.

Thermal stresses can also be induced by nonuniform temperature. Even if a solid body at uniform temperature has no internal stresses, stress may be induced by nonuniform expansion due to temperature differences. Have you ever broken a thick glass container such as a vase by pouring very hot water into it? Thermal stress caused by temperature differences exceeded the breaking stress of the material, and it cracked. Heat-resistant glasses such as Pyrex have exceptionally low expansion coefficients. Usually, they also have high strength, so the container walls can be made thin; this minimizes temperature differences.

Similar phenomena occur with volume expansion. If you fill a bottle completely with water, tightly cap it, and then warm it, the bottle will break because the thermal expansion coefficient for water is much greater than for glass. If a material is enclosed in a very rigid container so that its volume cannot change, then a rise in temperature ΔT is accompanied by an increase in pressure Δp. An analysis similar to that leading to Eq. (14–13) shows that the pressure increase is given by

$$\Delta p = B\beta \, \Delta T, \qquad (14-14)$$

where B is the bulk modulus for the material.

Questions

14–1 Does it make sense to say that one body is twice as hot as another?

14–2 A student claimed that thermometers are useless because a thermometer always registers *its own* temperature. How would you respond?

14–3 What other properties of matter, in addition to those mentioned in the text, might be used as thermometric properties? How could they be used to make a thermometer?

14–4 A thermometer is laid out in direct sunlight. Does it measure the temperature of the air, or of the sun, or what?

14–5 Thermometers sometimes contain red or blue liquid, which is often ethanol. What advantages and disadvantages does this have compared with mercury?

14–6 Could a thermometer similar to that shown in Fig. 14–1a be made by using water as the liquid? What difficulties would this thermometer present?

14–7 What is the temperature of vacuum?

14–8 Is there any particular reason for constructing a

temperature scale with higher numbers corresponding to hotter bodies, rather than the reverse?

14–9 If a brass pin is a little too large to fit in a hole in a steel block, should you heat the pin and cool the block or the reverse?

14–10 When a block with a hole in it is heated, why doesn't the material around the hole expand into the hole and make it smaller?

14–11 Many automobile engines have cast-iron cylinders and aluminum pistons. What kinds of problems can occur if the engine gets too hot?

14–12 When a hot-water faucet is turned on, the flow often decreases gradually before it settles down. This is an annoyance in the shower. Why does it happen?

14–13 Two bodies made of the same material have the same external dimensions and appearance, but one is solid and the other is hollow. When they are heated, is the overall volume expansion the same or different?

14–14 A thermostat for controlling household heating systems often contains a bimetallic element consisting of two strips of different metals, welded together face to face. When the temperature changes, this composite strip bends one way or the other. Why?

14–15 Why is it sometimes possible to loosen caps on screw-top bottles by dipping the cap briefly in hot water?

14–16 The rate at which a pendulum clock runs depends on the length of the pendulum. Would a pendu-lum clock gain time in hot weather and lose in cold or the reverse? Could one design a pendulum, perhaps using two different metals, that would *not* change length with temperature?

14–17 When a rod is cooled but prevented from con-tracting, as in Section 14–6, thermal tension develops. Under these circumstances, does the *thickness* of the rod change? If so, how would the change be calculated?

■ *Exercises*

Section 14–3   *The Celsius and Fahrenheit Scales*

14–1 When the United States finally converts officially to metric units, the Celsius temperature scale will re-place the Fahrenheit scale for everyday use. As a fa-miliarization exercise, find the Celsius temperatures corresponding to

a) a cool room (62.0°F);

b) a hot summer day (92.0°F);

c) a cold winter day (18.0°F).

14–2

a) If you feel sick in France and are told that you have a temperature of 39.0°C, should you be con-cerned?

b) What is normal body temperature on the Celsius scale?

c) At what temperature do the Fahrenheit and Celsius scales coincide?

Section 14–4   *The Kelvin Scale*

14–3 The normal boiling point of liquid nitrogen is −195.81°C. What is this temperature on the Kelvin scale?

14–4 In a rather primitive experiment with a constant-volume gas thermometer the absolute pressure at the triple point of water (0.01°C) was found to be 4.00×10^4 Pa, and the pressure at the normal boiling point (100.0°C) to be 5.40×10^4 Pa. According to these data, what is the temperature of absolute zero on the Celsius scale?

14–5 The ratio of the pressures of a gas at the melting point of lead and at the triple point of water, when the gas is kept at constant volume, is found to be 2.1982. What is the Kelvin temperature of the melting point of lead?

14–6 A gas thermometer of the type shown in Fig. 14–5 registered an absolute pressure corresponding to 8.00 cm of mercury when in contact with water at the triple point. What pressure does it read when in con-tact with water at the normal boiling point?

Section 14–5   *Thermal Expansion*

14–7 A building with a steel framework is 150 m tall when the temperature is 0°C. How much taller is the building on a hot summer day when the temperature is 36.0°C?

14–8 A steel bridge is built in the summer when the temperature is 35.0°C. At the time of construction its length is 80.00 m. What is the length of the bridge on a cold winter day when the temperature is −12.0°C?

14–9 The pendulum shaft of a clock is made of alumi-num. What is the fractional change in length of the shaft when it is cooled from 32.0°C to 7.0°C?

14–10 A metal rod is 80.000 cm long at 20.0°C and 80.032 cm long at 40.0°C. From these data, calculate the average coefficient of linear expansion of the rod for this temperature range.

14–11 To ensure a tight fit, the aluminum rivets used in airplane construction are made slightly larger than the rivet holes and cooled by "dry ice" (solid CO_2) before being driven. If the diameter of a hole is 0.4000 cm, what should be the diameter of a rivet at 20.0°C if its diameter is to equal that of the hole when the rivet is cooled to −78.0°C, the temperature of dry ice? Assume that the expansion coefficient remains con-stant at the value given in Table 14–1.

14–12 A machinist bores a hole 1.800 cm in diameter in a brass plate at a temperature of 20°C. What is the diameter of the hole when the temperature of the plate is increased to 200°C? Assume that the expansion coef-ficient remains constant over this temperature range.

14–13 A glass volumetric flask has a capacity of 500.00 mL at room temperature (20.0°C). What is its capacity at a temperature of 5.0°C if the coefficient of linear expansion for the glass is 1.20×10^{-5} $(C°)^{-1}$?

14–14 A brass cylinder is initially at 20.0°C. At what temperature will its volume be 0.250% larger than it is at 20.0°C?

14–15 A glass flask whose volume is exactly 1000 cm^3 at 0°C is completely filled with mercury at this tempera-ture. When flask and mercury are heated to 100°C,

13.4 cm^3 of mercury overflow. If the coefficient of volume expansion of mercury is 18.0×10^{-5} (C°)$^{-1}$, compute the coefficient of volume expansion of the glass.

14–16 An underground tank with a capacity of 2500 L (2.50 m^3) is filled with ethanol that has an initial temperature of 25.0°C. After the ethanol has cooled off to the temperature of the tank and ground, which is 10.0°C, how much air space will there be above the ethanol in the tank? (Assume that the volume of the tank doesn't change.)

14–17 Use the data of Table 14–3 to find the average coefficient of volume expansion of water in the temperature range

a) 0°C to 4°C;

b) 75°C to 100°C.

Section 14–6   Thermal Stresses

14–18 The cross-sectional area of a steel rod is 3.60 cm^2. What force applied to each end will prevent the rod from contracting when it is cooled from 520°C to 20°C?

14–19 Steel railroad rails 14.0 m long are laid on a winter day when the temperature is −5.0°C.

a) How much space must be left between adjacent rails if they are to just touch on a summer day when the temperature is 39.0°C?

b) If the rails were originally laid in contact, what would be the stress in them on a summer day when the temperature is 39.0°C?

14–20

a) A wire that is 3.00 m long at 20°C is found to increase in length by 2.2 cm when heated to 520°C. Compute its average coefficient of linear expansion for this temperature range.

b) Find the stress in the wire if it is attached between two supports (zero tension) at 520°C and cooled to 20°C without being allowed to contract. Young's modulus for the wire is 3.0×10^{11} Pa.

14–21

a) A block of steel at an initial pressure of 1.00 atm and a temperature of 20.0°C is kept at constant volume. If the temperature is raised to 36.0°C, what is the final pressure?

b) If the block is maintained at constant volume by rigid walls that can withstand a maximum pressure of 1500 atm (1.52×10^8 Pa), what is the highest temperature to which the system may be raised? Assume B and β to remain practically constant at the values 1.60×10^{11} Pa and 3.60×10^{-5} (C°)$^{-1}$, respectively.

14–22 What applied pressure is necessary to prevent a copper block from expanding when its temperature is increased from 20.0°C to 50.0°C?

Problems

14–23 An aluminum cube 0.100 m on a side is heated from 10.0°C to 50.0°C.

a) What is the change in its volume?

b) In its density?

14–24 A surveyor's 30-m steel tape is correct at a temperature of 20.0°C. The distance between two points, as measured by this tape on a day when the temperature is 5.0°C, is 25.970 m. What is the true distance between the points?

14–25 Suppose that a steel hoop could be constructed around the earth's equator, just fitting it at a temperature of 20.0°C. What would be the thickness of the space between the hoop and the earth if the temperature of the hoop were increased by 1.0 C°?

14–26 A steel ring with 3.000-in. inside diameter at 20°C is to be heated and slipped over a brass shaft measuring 3.004 in. in diameter at 20°C.

a) To what temperature should the ring be heated?

b) If the ring and shaft together are cooled by some means such as liquid air, at what temperature will the ring just slip off the shaft?

14–27 An area is measured on the surface of a solid body. If the area is A_0 at some initial temperature and then changes by ΔA when the temperature changes by ΔT, show that

$$\Delta A = (2\alpha)A_0\,\Delta T.$$

14–28 At a temperature of 20.0°C, the volume of a certain glass flask, up to a reference mark on the long stem of the flask, is exactly 100 cm^3. The flask is filled to this point with a liquid whose coefficient of volume expansion is 40.0×10^{-5} (C°)$^{-1}$, with both flask and liquid at 20.0°C. The coefficient of volume expansion of the glass is 2.00×10^{-5} (C°)$^{-1}$. The cross-sectional area of the stem is 3.00 mm^2 and can be considered constant. How far will the liquid rise or fall in the stem when the temperature is raised to 35.0°C?

14–29 A metal rod that is 40.0 cm long expands by 0.0750 cm when its temperature is raised from 0°C to 100°C. A rod of a different metal and of the same length expands by 0.0300 cm for the same rise in temperature. A third rod, also 40.0 cm long, is made up of pieces of each of the above metals placed end to end and expands 0.0650 cm between 0°C and 100°C. Find the length of each portion of the composite rod.

14–30 A heavy brass bar has projections at its ends, as in Fig. 14–10. Two fine steel wires fastened between the projections are just taut (zero tension) when the whole system is at 0°C. What is the tensile stress in the steel wires when the temperature of the system is raised to 180°C? Make any simplifying assumptions that you think are justified, but state what they are.

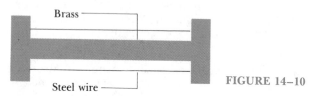

Brass

Steel wire

FIGURE 14–10

14–31 Table 14–3 lists the density of water and the volume of 1.00 g at atmospheric pressure. A hollow steel cylinder is filled with water at 10.0°C and atmospheric pressure, and the system is heated to 75.0°C. What is then the pressure in the cylinder? Assume that the steel cylinder is sufficiently rigid that its volume is not affected by the increased pressure.

14–32 Prove that if a body subjected to an applied pressure is raised in temperature but not allowed to expand, the increase in pressure is

$$\Delta p = B\beta \, \Delta T,$$

where the bulk modulus B and the average coefficient of volume expansion β are both assumed to be positive and constant.

14–33 A liquid is enclosed in a metal cylinder provided with a piston of the same metal. The system is originally at atmospheric pressure and at a temperature of 40.0°C. The piston is forced down until the pressure on the liquid is increased by 100 atm (1.013×10^7 Pa), and it is then clamped in this position. Find the new temperature at which the pressure of the liquid is again 1 atm (1.013×10^5 Pa). Assume that the cylinder is sufficiently strong that its volume is not altered by changes in pressure but only by changes in temperature.

Compressibility of liquid: $k = 7.00 \times 10^{-10}$ Pa^{-1}.

Coefficient of volume expansion of liquid:
$\beta = 60.0 \times 10^{-5}$ (C°)$^{-1}$.

Coefficient of volume expansion of metal:
$\beta = 4.50 \times 10^{-5}$ (C°)$^{-1}$.

Challenge Problems

14–34 A steel rod with a length of 0.440 m and a copper rod with a length of 0.320 m, both of the same diameter, are placed end to end between rigid supports, with no initial stress in the rods. The temperature of the rods is now raised by 50.0 C°. What is the stress in each rod?

14–35 A clock whose pendulum makes one complete oscillation in 2.00 s is correct at 25.0°C. The pendulum shaft is made of steel, and its mass may be neglected in comparison with that of the bob.

a) What is the fractional change in length of the shaft when it is cooled to 5.0°C?

b) How many seconds per day will the clock gain or lose at 5.0°C?

c) How closely must the temperature be controlled if the clock is not to gain or lose more than 1.00 s

a day? Does the answer depend on the period of the pendulum?

14–36

a) The pressure p, volume V, number of moles n, and Kelvin temperature T of an ideal gas are related by the equation $pV = nRT$, where R is a constant. Prove that the coefficient of volume expansion is equal to the reciprocal of the Kelvin temperature if the expansion occurs at constant pressure.

b) Compare the coefficients of volume expansion of copper and air at a temperature of 20°C. Assume that air may be treated as an ideal gas and that the pressure remains constant.

Quantity of Heat

In Chapter 14 we studied the concept of temperature and its relation to thermal equilibrium. When two bodies are in thermal equilibrium, they must have the same temperature. When two bodies that are *not* initially in thermal equilibrium are placed in contact, their temperatures change until they reach thermal equilibrium. In describing the interaction that takes place during the approach to thermal equilibrium, we are led to the concept of *heat*, the subject of this chapter. We define what we mean by *quantity of heat*, and we define units to measure quantity of heat. Then we study the quantities of heat exchanged during temperature changes and changes of phase of materials.

15–1
Heat Transfer

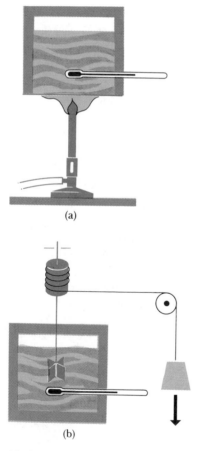

(a)

(b)

15–1
The same temperature change of the same system may be accomplished by either (a) a heat flow or (b) the performance of work.

Suppose we have two systems, A and B, with A initially at higher temperature than B. System A might be a cup of hot coffee and B a cold spoon. We place them in contact; when they have reached thermal equilibrium, A's temperature has decreased and B's has increased. What kind of interaction is taking place to cause these temperature changes? It seems plausible that during the interaction something is transferred from A to B; we call this interaction a **heat transfer** or a *heat flow* from A to B. But what *is* this "something" that flows from A to B?

The answer to this question emerged gradually during the eighteenth and nineteenth centuries. Count Rumford (1753–1814) studied the temperature rise of cannons during the drilling of their barrels. It had been thought that heat was evolved as the drill broke up bits of metal, but Rumford found that the temperature rise was even greater when the drill was too dull to cut the metal at all. Sir James Joule (1818–1889) discovered that water can be warmed by vigorous stirring with a paddle wheel and that the temperature rise is related directly to the *work* expended to turn the wheel. These and many other experimental studies have established that heat flow is *energy transfer* and that there is an equivalence between heat and work. Indeed, the relation of heat to work is at the core of the branch of physics that we call thermodynamics, the subject of the next several chapters.

Heat transfer is energy transfer that takes place solely because of a temperature difference. For example, cold water in a steam boiler is converted to steam by contact with a metal pipe kept at a high temperature by a hot flame from burning coal or gas. Steam has a greater ability to do *work* (by pushing against a turbine blade or the piston in a steam engine) than does an equal mass of cold liquid water. During its conversion to steam the water must have received *energy* by means of heat transfer from the hot flame to the cooler water. There is no transfer of matter or material particles into the water during this process.

When a material undergoes a temperature change as a result of energy exchange with its surroundings, the change can often be brought about in various ways. In Fig. 15–1a the temperature of a quantity of water is raised by a gas flame. In Fig. 15–1b the same temperature change is produced by a falling weight that turns a paddle wheel in the water. In the second case, is the change caused by heat transfer or by mechanical work? The answer depends on whether or not we consider the weight and paddle wheel to be part of our system. If our system includes only the water, there is certainly heat flow into it. But if the system also includes the weight and paddle wheel, we can say that the temperature rise results not from heat flow but from the work done on the falling weight by the earth's gravitational attraction. There's a lesson in this: When we describe energy-transfer processes, we must always be careful to specify what is and is not included in the system under discussion.

This example shows again that there has to be an equivalence between heat and mechanical work because the same change of state of a system can be produced by *either* heat flow or work. A detailed study of the relation of heat to work leads to the *first law of thermodynamics*, which we will study in detail in Chapter 18.

15–2
Quantity of Heat

Heat transfer is energy transfer brought about solely by a temperature difference. We will use the term *heat* only in reference to *transfer* of energy from one body or system to another, never in reference to the amount of energy *contained* within a particular system. We can define a unit of quantity of heat based on temperature changes of some specific material. The **calorie** (abbreviated cal) was originally defined in the eighteenth century as the amount of heat required to raise the temperature of 1 g of water by 1 C° (1 kelvin). This is somewhat ambiguous; it was later found that more heat is required to raise the temperature from, say, 90° to 91° than from 20° to 21°. The present definition of the calorie is *the amount of heat required to raise the temperature of 1 gram of water from* 14.5°C *to* 15.5°C.

A corresponding unit defined in terms of Fahrenheit degrees and British units is the **British thermal unit** (Btu). By definition, 1 Btu is the quantity of heat required to raise the temperature of 1 lb of water 1 F° from 63°F to 64°F. A third unit in common use is the kilocalorie (kcal), which is equal to 1000 cal. A food-value calorie is actually a kilocalorie. Here are some useful conversion factors:

$$1 \text{ Btu} = 252 \text{ cal} = 0.252 \text{ kcal}.$$

Because heat is energy in transit, there must be a relation between these units and the familiar mechanical energy units such as the joule. Experiments similar in concept to Joule's paddle-wheel experiment have shown that

$$1 \text{ cal} = 4.186 \text{ joules} = 4.186 \text{ J},$$
$$1 \text{ kcal} = 1000 \text{ cal} = 4186 \text{ J},$$
$$1 \text{ Btu} = 778 \text{ ft-lb} = 252 \text{ cal} = 1055 \text{ J}.$$

Figure 15–2 shows an example of this equivalence.

The International Committee on Weights and Measures no longer recognizes the calorie as a fundamental unit; it recommends use of the joule for quantity of heat as well as for all other forms of energy. The calorie is a convenient unit for problems involving water, but it is awkward when both heat and other forms of energy are involved. We will use the joule in most of the examples and problems in this chapter and the following ones. We will explore the relationship between heat and mechanical energy in Chapters 18 through 20.

15–2
Sugar cubes obtained in a restaurant in West Germany. A rough translation is "This package has 22 Calories (i.e., kilocalories), equal to 92 kilojoules" and "Get into the swing with sugar." By law, foods marketed in West Germany must show the energy content in joules; the equivalent in calories is optional.

15–3
Heat Capacity

We use the symbol Q for quantity of heat. When the quantity is associated with a small temperature change ΔT, we often call it ΔQ. The quantity of heat ΔQ required to increase the temperature of a mass m of a certain material by an amount ΔT is found to be approximately proportional to ΔT. It is also proportional to the mass m of substance. Twice as much heat is needed to warm up two cups of water to make tea than for only one cup if the temperature interval is the same. The quantity of heat needed also depends on the nature of the material; to raise the temperature of 1 kg of water by 1 C° requires over five times as much heat as to raise the temperature of 1 kg of aluminum by 1 C°.

Putting all these relationships together, we have

$$\Delta Q = mc\,\Delta T, \tag{15–1}$$

where c is a constant, different for different materials, called the **specific heat capacity** for the material. The specific heat capacity of water is approximately

$$4190 \ \text{J·kg}^{-1}\text{·(C°)}^{-1}, \qquad 4.19 \ \text{J·g}^{-1}\text{·(C°)}^{-1},$$
$$1 \ \text{cal·g}^{-1}\text{·(C°)}^{-1}, \qquad \text{or} \qquad 1 \ \text{Btu·lb}^{-1}\text{·(F°)}^{-1}.$$

For a finite temperature interval from T_1 to T_2 we will use Q for quantity of heat. If c is constant over this interval, then Eq. (15–1) becomes

$$Q = mc(T_2 - T_1). \tag{15–2}$$

Strictly speaking, c for a particular substance is not precisely constant; it depends somewhat on the initial temperature and the temperature interval. In the problems and examples in this chapter we will usually ignore this small variation.

In Eqs. (15–1) and (15–2), ΔQ and ΔT can be either positive or negative. When they are positive, heat enters the body and its temperature increases; when they are negative, heat *leaves* the body and its temperature decreases.

Example 15–1   During a bout with the flu, an 80-kg man ran a fever of 2 C° above normal, that is, a body temperature of 39.0°C or 102.2°F instead of the normal 37.0°C = 98.6°F. Assuming that the human body is mostly water, how much heat is required to raise the man's temperature by that amount?

Solution   From Eq. (15–1),

$$\Delta Q = (80 \text{ kg})(4190 \ \text{J·kg}^{-1}\text{·(C°)}^{-1})(2.0 \text{ C°})$$
$$= 6.7 \times 10^5 \text{ J},$$

or

$$\Delta Q = (8.0 \times 10^4 \text{ g})(1.00 \text{ cal·g}^{-1}\text{·(C°)}^{-1})(2.0 \text{ C°})$$
$$= 1.6 \times 10^5 \text{ cal}$$
$$= 160 \text{ kcal}   (160 \text{ food-value calories}). \qquad\blacksquare$$

Usually, we describe how much material is in a system by stating its *mass*. But sometimes it is more convenient to describe a quantity of substance by use of the number of *moles n* rather than the *mass m* of material. One mole (1 mol) of any substance is a quantity of the substance having a mass in grams numerically equal to the *molecular mass M*. For example, the molecular mass of water is 18.0 g·mol^{-1}, so 1 mol of water has a mass of 18.0 g. Molecular mass is amount of mass per mole; the mass m of material is equal to the mass per mole M times the number of moles n. That is, $m = nM$. (The quantity M is sometimes called *molecular weight*, but *molecular mass* is preferable because the quantity depends on the mass of a molecule, not its weight. A mole of any pure substance always contains the same number of molecules; we will discuss this point in detail in Chapter 20.)

Replacing the mass m in Eq. (15–1) by the product nM, we find that

$$\Delta Q = nMc\, \Delta T. \qquad (15\text{–}3)$$

The product Mc is called the **molar heat capacity** and is represented by the symbol C. With this notation we rewrite Eq. (15–3) as

$$\Delta Q = nC\, \Delta T. \qquad (15\text{–}4)$$

For example, the molar heat capacity of water is

$$C = Mc = (18.0 \text{ g·mol}^{-1})(4.19 \text{ J·g}^{-1}\text{·(C°)}^{-1})$$
$$= 75.4 \text{ J·mol}^{-1}\text{·(C°)}^{-1} = 18.0 \text{ cal·mol}^{-1}\text{·(C°)}^{-1}.$$

Specific heat capacity c, defined by Eq. (15–1), is sometimes called simply *specific heat*, and molar heat capacity C, defined by Eq. (15–4) is often called *molar specific heat*. However, we will use the terms *specific heat capacity* and *molar heat capacity* in this book. Values of specific and molar heat capacities for several substances are given in Table 15–1.

In later sections we will discuss several other physical properties of materials that involve quantity of heat. Thermal conductivity, heat of fusion, heat of vaporization, and heat of combustion are a few other examples of *thermal properties* of matter. The field of physics and physical chemistry concerned with the measurement of thermal properties is called **calorimetry.**

We conclude this section with a short sermon. It is absolutely essential for you to keep clearly in mind the distinction between the two physical quantities *temperature* and *heat*. Temperature depends on the physical state of a material and is a quantitative description of its hotness or coldness; heat is energy transferred from one body to another because of a temperature difference. We can change the temperature of a body by

TABLE 15–1   **Mean specific and molar heat capacities (constant pressure, temperature range 0°C to 100°C)**

Metal	Specific (c)		M, g·mol^{-1}	Molar (C), J·mol^{-1}·(C°)$^{-1}$
	J·kg^{-1}·(C°)$^{-1}$	cal·g^{-1}·(C°)$^{-1}$		
Aluminum	0.91×10^3	0.217	27.0	24.6
Beryllium	1.97×10^3	0.471	9.01	17.7
Copper	0.39×10^3	0.093	63.5	24.8
Ethanol	2.43×10^3	0.58	46.0	112.0
Ethylene glycol	2.39×10^3	0.57	62.0	148.0
Ice ($-25°C$ to $0°C$)	2.01×10^3	0.48	18.0	36.5
Iron	0.47×10^3	0.112	55.9	26.3
Lead	0.13×10^3	0.031	207.0	26.9
Marble ($CaCO_3$)	0.88×10^3	0.21	100.0	87.9
Mercury	0.14×10^3	0.033	201.0	27.7
Salt	0.88×10^3	0.21	58.5	51.4
Silver	0.23×10^3	0.056	108.0	25.3
Water	4.19×10^3	1.00	18.0	75.4

adding heat to it or taking heat away. If we cut a body in half, each half has the same temperature as the whole, but to raise the temperature of each half by a given interval, we add *half* as much heat as we would for the whole. The temperature of a body can be changed in other ways than by heat exchange; we will return to some of these in Chapter 18.

15–4
Measurement of Heat Capacity

To measure a heat capacity, we need to add a measured quantity of heat to a measured quantity of a material and observe the resulting temperature change. For maximum precision the measurements are often made electrically. In a typical laboratory procedure we supply heat input by passing a current through a heater wire wound around the specimen; by measuring the voltage, current, and time interval we can determine the total energy (heat) input Q. We measure the temperature change ΔT using a resistance thermometer or thermocouple embedded in the specimen, and we measure the mass m by weighing. We can then use Eq. (15–1) to determine the specific heat capacity c. This sounds simple, but great experimental skill is needed to avoid or compensate for unwanted heat transfer between the sample and its surroundings.

Figure 15–3 shows the results of specific heat capacity measurements for water. The value of c varies by about 1% in the interval between 0°C and 100°C. The quantity of heat needed to raise the temperature of 1 g of water from 14.5°C to 15.5°C is 4.186 J. We have defined this to be one calorie; this unit is sometimes called the 15° calorie. Unfortunately, two other calories are also frequently used. The *inter-

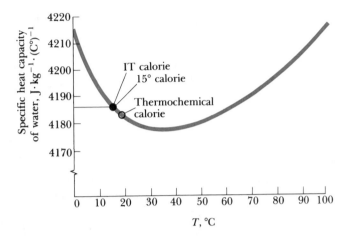

15–3
Specific heat capacity of water as a function of temperature.

national table calorie (IT cal) is defined to be precisely 3600/860 J = 4.18605 J, and the *thermochemical calorie* is defined as 4.1840 J. From Fig. 15–3 we see that this corresponds to about a 17° calorie. There are also several different definitions of the Btu, differing by as much as 0.5%. This variety of definitions is an additional argument in favor of eliminating the calorie and the Btu and adopting the joule as the fundamental unit of all forms of energy, including quantity of heat.

The heat capacity of a material also depends on the conditions imposed during the heat transfer. The two conditions of greatest practical usefulness are for the system to be kept at *constant pressure* or *constant volume*; the corresponding specific heat capacities are denoted as c_p and c_v, respectively, and the molar heat capacities as C_p and C_v, respectively. Measurements for solid materials are usually easiest at ordinary atmospheric pressure, corresponding to constant-pressure conditions. For a gas it is often easiest to keep the substance in a container with constant volume. The two heat capacities differ because if the system can expand while heat is added, there is additional energy exchange through the performance of *work* by the system on its surroundings. If the volume is held constant, the system does no work. For gases the difference between c_p and c_v is substantial. We will study heat capacities of gases in detail in Section 18–7.

Heat capacities of several metals and familiar compounds are listed in Table 15–1 (Section 15–3). All the specific heat capacities are less than that of water, and they generally decrease with increasing molecular mass. The last column is of particular interest; it shows that the molar heat capacities for most metals are approximately the same, about 25 $J \cdot mol^{-1} \cdot (C°)^{-1}$. This correlation is called the **rule of Dulong and Petit,** after its discoverers.

Although this is only an approximate rule, it forms the basis for a very important idea. The number of molecules in one mole is the same for all substances. This means that on a *per molecule* basis about the same amount of heat is required to raise the temperature of each of these metals by a given amount, even though the *masses* of the molecules are very different. A molecule of lead, for example, is nearly ten times as massive as a molecule of aluminum. The heat required for a given temperature increase depends only on *how many* molecules the sample contains and not on the mass of an individual molecule. We will study the molecular basis of heat capacities in greater detail in Chapter 20, and we will find that in some simple cases the total energy of a molecule is directly proportional to its absolute temperature.

15–5
Phase Changes

The term **phase,** as we use it here, refers to a specific state of matter, such as a solid, liquid, or gaseous state. For example, the chemical compound H_2O exists in the *solid phase* as ice, in the *liquid phase* as water, and in the *gaseous phase* as steam. All substances that do not decompose at high temperatures can exist in any of these phases under proper conditions of temperature and pressure. A transition from one phase to another is called a **phase change** or phase transition. For any given pressure, a phase change takes place at a definite temperature. Usually, a phase change is accompanied by absorption or liberation of heat and a change of volume and density.

A familiar example of a phase change is the melting of ice. When we add heat to ice at 0°C and normal atmospheric pressure, we find that the temperature of the ice *does not* increase. Instead, some of it melts to form liquid water. If the heat is added slowly, so that thermal equilibrium is maintained between the ice and liquid water, then the temperature remains at 0°C as the heat is added until all the ice is melted. The effect of adding heat to this system is not to raise its temperature but to change its *phase* from solid to liquid.

Experiment shows that to change 1 kg of ice at 0°C to 1 kg of liquid water at 0°C and normal atmospheric pressure requires the addition of 3.33×10^5 J of heat. This quantity of heat is called the **heat of fusion** of water. The term *latent* heat of fusion is sometimes used. We will not use that term, but we use the symbol L, with a subscript, for a quantity of heat (per unit mass) associated with a phase transition. The heat of fusion L_F of water, at normal atmospheric pressure, is

$$L_F = 3.33 \times 10^5 \ \text{J·kg}^{-1} = 79.6 \ \text{cal·g}^{-1} = 143 \ \text{Btu·lb}^{-1}.$$

More generally, to melt a mass m of material that has a heat of fusion L_F, we have to add a quantity of heat Q given by

$$Q = mL_F. \tag{15–5}$$

The heat of fusion is different for different materials, and it also varies somewhat with pressure.

The phase change we have just described is *reversible*. To freeze liquid water to ice at 0°C, we have to *remove* heat; the amount of heat is given again by Eq. (15–5), but in this case, Q is negative because heat is removed rather than added. At any given pressure, the freezing and melting temperatures are always the same. We also note that, at a given pressure, liquid water and ice can coexist only at one very specific temperature; we call this the *melting temperature*. The coexistence of two phases at this special temperature is called **phase equilibrium.**

TABLE 15–2   **Heats of fusion and vaporization**

Substance	Normal melting point		Heat of fusion, L_F, J·kg^{-1}	Normal boiling point		Heat of vaporization, L_V, J·kg^{-1}
	K	°C		K	°C	
Helium	3.5	−269.65	5.23×10^3	4.216	−268.93	20.9×10^3
Hydrogen	13.84	−259.31	58.6×10^3	20.26	−252.89	452×10^3
Nitrogen	63.18	−209.97	25.5×10^3	77.34	−195.81	201×10^3
Oxygen	54.36	−218.79	13.8×10^3	90.18	−182.97	213×10^3
Ethyl alcohol	159	−114	104.2×10^3	351	78	854×10^3
Mercury	234	−39	11.8×10^3	630	357	272×10^3
Water	273.15	0.00	333×10^3	373.15	100.00	2256×10^3
Sulfur	392	119	38.1×10^3	717.75	444.60	326×10^3
Lead	600.5	327.3	24.5×10^3	2023	1750	871×10^3
Antimony	903.65	630.50	165×10^3	1713	1440	561×10^3
Silver	1233.95	960.80	88.3×10^3	2466	2193	2336×10^3
Gold	1336.15	1063.00	64.5×10^3	2933	2660	1578×10^3
Copper	1356	1083	134×10^3	1460	1187	5069×10^3

We can go through this whole story again, changing the names of the characters, for *boiling* or *evaporation*, a phase transition between liquid and gaseous phases. The corresponding heat (per unit mass) is called the **heat of vaporization** L_V. Both L_V and the boiling temperature of a material depend on pressure. Water boils at a lower temperature (about 95°C) in Denver than in Pittsburgh because Denver is at a higher elevation and the average atmospheric pressure is less. The heat of vaporization is somewhat greater at this lower pressure, about 2.27×10^6 J·kg^{-1}. At normal atmospheric pressure the heat of vaporization L_V for water is

$$L_V = 2.26 \times 10^6 \text{ J·kg}^{-1} = 539 \text{ cal·g}^{-1} = 970 \text{ Btu·lb}^{-1}.$$

Note that over five times as much heat is required to vaporize a quantity of water at 100°C as to raise its temperature from 0° to 100°C.

Like melting, boiling is a *reversible* transition. When heat is removed from a gas at the boiling temperature, the gas returns to the liquid phase, or *condenses*. When it does this, it gives up to its surroundings the same quantity of heat (heat of vaporization) that was required to vaporize it. At a given pressure the boiling and condensation temperatures are always the same.

Table 15–2 lists heats of fusion and vaporization for several materials. The table also gives the melting and boiling temperatures at normal atmospheric pressure, called the *normal* melting and boiling temperatures. Very few *elements* have melting temperatures in the vicinity of ordinary room temperatures; one of the few is the metal gallium, shown in Fig. 15–4.

Under some conditions a substance can change directly from the solid to the gaseous phase without passing through the liquid phase. The transition from solid to vapor is called **sublimation,** and the solid is said to *sublime*. "Dry ice" (solid carbon dioxide) sublimes at atmospheric pressure. Liquid carbon dioxide cannot exist at a pressure lower than about

15–4
The metal gallium is one of the few *elements* that melt in the vicinity of room temperature; its melting temperature is 29.8°C; its heat of fusion is 8.04×10^4 J·kg^{-1}, or 19.2 cal·g^{-1}. A crystal of gallium is shown melting in a person's hand. (Photo by Chip Clark.)

5×10^5 Pa (about 5 atm). The material absorbs heat during sublimation and liberates it in the reverse process. The quantity of heat per unit mass is called the **heat of sublimation,** L_S. When food is freeze-dried, it is first frozen; then the pressure is reduced, and water is removed by sublimation. The heat of sublimation is often supplied by infrared or microwave radiation.

Here's an example of successive changes of state brought about by continuous addition of heat. We take crushed ice from a freezer at $-25°C$, place it in a container with a thermometer, and surround it with a heating coil that supplies heat at a constant rate. We insulate the system from its surroundings so that no other heat enters it, and we observe how its temperature varies with time. The result is shown in Fig. 15–5, a graph of temperature as a function of time. The temperature of the ice increases steadily (*a* to *b*) until it reaches 0°C. The specific heat capacity of ice is approximately

$$c = 2010 \text{ J·kg}^{-1}·(\text{C°})^{-1} = 0.48 \text{ cal·g}^{-1}·(\text{C°})^{-1}.$$

When the temperature reaches 0°C, the ice begins to *melt*, a *change of phase* from solid to liquid phase. We continue to supply heat at the same rate as before, but the temperature remains at 0°C until all the ice has melted (point *c*).

As soon as the last of the ice has melted, the temperature begins to rise again at a uniform rate (from *c* to *d*). This rate is *slower* than the rate for melting of ice because the specific heat capacity for liquid water is larger than that for ice. When the temperature reaches 100°C (point *d*), the water begins to *boil*. The temperature then remains constant at 100°C until all the water has boiled away. Another change of phase has taken place, from the liquid phase to the gaseous phase.

If we collect all the water vapor in a large container, we can continue the heating process, as from *e* to *f*. The gas is now called "superheated steam."

When heat is added slowly (to maintain thermal equilibrium) to a substance that can exist in different phases, *either* the temperature rises *or* some of the substance undergoes a phase change, but *never* both at the same time. Once the temperature for a phase change (e.g., the melting or boiling temperature) has been reached, no further temperature change occurs until *all* the substance has undergone the phase change.

15–5

The temperature remains constant during each change of phase, provided that the pressure remains constant.

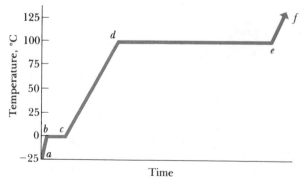

We have used water as an example, but the same type of curve as in Fig. 15–5 is obtained for many other substances. Some solids, such as glass, tar, and butter, do not have a definite melting temperature but become gradually softer as their temperature is raised. Crystalline substances, such as ice and most solid metals, melt at a definite temperature. Glass and tar are *amorphous* solids with no definite crystal structure, and their solid behavior is similar to that of very viscous liquids.

Under some conditions a material can be cooled below the normal phase-change temperature without a phase change occurring. The resulting state is unstable and is described as *supercooled*. Very pure water can be cooled several degrees below the normal freezing point under ideal conditions. When a small ice crystal is dropped in or the water is agitated, it crystallizes very quickly. Similarly, supercooled water vapor condenses quickly into fog droplets when a disturbance, such as dust particles or ionizing radiation, is introduced. This principle is used in "seeding" clouds, which often contain supercooled water vapor, to cause condensation and rain.

A liquid can sometimes be *superheated* above its normal boiling temperature. Again, any small disturbance such as agitation or the passage of a charged particle through the material causes local boiling with bubble formation. This phenomenon is used in the *bubble chamber*, historically an important instrument in high-energy physics that was used to observe tracks of high-energy particles.

Steam heating systems use a boiling–condensing process to transfer heat from the furnace to the radiators. Each kilogram of water that is turned to steam in the boiler absorbs 2.26×10^6 J (the heat of vaporization L_V of water) from the boiler and gives up this same amount when it condenses in the radiators. (If the steam pressure is appreciably greater than 1 atm, L_V is smaller.) Thus a steam-heating system does not need to circulate as much water as a hot-water heating system. If water leaves a hot-water boiler at 60°C and returns at 40°C, dropping 20 C°, about 27 kg of water must circulate to transfer the same amount of heat as 1 kg of steam. We invite you to verify this ratio.

The temperature-control mechanisms of many warm-blooded animals operate on a similar principle. As sweat (mostly water) evaporates from the surface of the body, it removes heat from the body as heat of vaporization. At the normal human body temperature (37°C) the heat of vaporization of water is 2.41×10^6 J·kg^{-1}, so each gram of sweat that evaporates carries away 2410 J of heat with it. Evaporative cooling makes it possible for humans to maintain normal body temperature in hot, dry desert climates where the air temperature may reach 55°C (about 130°F). Evaporation keeps the skin temperature as much as 20 C° cooler than the surrounding air. Adequate water intake is vital; a normal person may perspire several liters per day, and unless this lost water is replaced regularly, dehydration, heat stroke, and death result. (Old-time desert rats state that in the desert any canteen that holds less than a gallon should be viewed as a toy.)

The same principle is used in household evaporative cooling systems. Hot, dry air is pushed through wet filters. As some of the water evaporates, it takes its heat of vaporization from the air, which thus becomes cooler by as much as 20 C° in hot, dry climates. Evaporative cooling is also used to condense and recirculate "used" steam in coal-fired or nuclear-powered electric power plants. That's what is going on in the large cone-shaped concrete towers that are often seen at power-generating plants.

Definite quantities of heat are also involved in many chemical reactions. A familiar example is combustion; complete combustion of 1 g of gasoline produces about 46,000 J or about 11,000 cal, and the **heat of combustion** L_C of gasoline is

$$L_C = 46,000 \ \text{J·g}^{-1} = 46 \times 10^6 \ \text{J·kg}^{-1}.$$

Energy values of foods are defined similarly; the unit of food energy, although called a calorie, is a *kilocalorie*, equal to 1000 cal or 4186 J. When we say that 1 g of peanut butter "contains" 12 calories, we mean that, when it reacts with oxygen with the help of enzymes to convert the carbon and hydrogen completely to CO_2 and H_2O, the total energy liberated as heat is 12 kcal (12,000 cal or 50,200 J). Not all of this energy is directly useful for mechanical work; we will study the *efficiency* of utilization of energy in Chapter 19.

15–6
Examples

The basic principle in heat calculations is very simple: When heat flow occurs between two bodies, the amount of heat lost by one body must equal the amount gained by the other. Heat is energy in transit, so this is really just conservation of energy. We take each quantity of heat *added to* a body as *positive* and each quantity *leaving* a body as *negative*. Then when several bodies interact, the *algebraic sum* of the quantities of heat transferred to all the bodies must be zero. This is the basic principle of *calorimetry*, which in many ways is the simplest of all physical theories.

PROBLEM-SOLVING STRATEGY: Calorimetry Problems

1. To avoid confusion about algebraic signs when calculating quantities of heat, use Eqs. (15–1) and (15–5) consistently for each body, noting that each Q (or ΔQ) is positive when heat enters a body and negative when it leaves. Then the algebraic sum of all the Q's must be zero.

2. The temperature change for a body is $\Delta T = T_{final} - T_{initial}$, not the reverse. When you need to find an unknown temperature, represent it by an algebraic symbol such as T. Then if a body has an initial temperature of 20°C and an unknown final temperature T, $\Delta T = T - 20°C$ (*not* 20°C $- T$!).

3. In problems in which a phase change takes place, be careful with the sign of the heat of the phase change. When ice melts, the heat of fusion is positive (heat entering the material), but when water freezes, the heat of fusion is negative. You may not know in advance whether *all* the material undergoes a phase change or only part of it. You can always assume one or the other, and if the resulting calculation gives an absurd result (such as a final temperature that is higher or lower than *any* of the initial temperatures), you know that the initial assumption was wrong. Back up and try again!

Example 15–2   An ethnic restaurant down by the docks serves coffee in copper mugs. A waiter fills a cup having a mass of 0.10 kg, initially at 20°C, with 0.20 kg of coffee initially at 70°C. What is the final temperature after the coffee and the cup attain thermal equilibrium? (Assume that coffee has the same specific heat capacity as water and that there is no heat transfer with the surroundings.)

Solution   Let the final temperature be T. The (negative) heat gained by the coffee is

$$Q_{\text{coffee}} = mc_{\text{water}} \, \Delta T_{\text{coffee}}$$
$$= (0.20 \text{ kg})(4190 \text{ J·kg}^{-1} \text{·(C°)}^{-1})(T - 70°C).$$

The (positive) heat gained by the copper cup is

$$Q_{\text{copper}} = mc_{\text{copper}} \, \Delta T_{\text{copper}}$$
$$= (0.10 \text{ kg})(390 \text{ J·kg}^{-1} \text{·(C°)}^{-1})(T - 20°C).$$

We equate the sum of these two quantities of heat to zero, obtaining an algebraic equation for T: $Q_{\text{coffee}} + Q_{\text{copper}} = 0$, or

$$(0.20 \text{ kg})(4190 \text{ J·kg}^{-1} \text{·(C°)}^{-1})(T - 70°C)$$
$$+ \; (0.10 \text{ kg})(390 \text{ J·kg}^{-1} \text{·(C°)}^{-1})(T - 20°C) = 0.$$

Solution of this equation gives $T = 67.8°C$. The final temperature is much closer to the initial temperature of the coffee than to that of the cup; water has a much larger specific heat capacity than copper, and we have twice as much mass of water. We can also find the quantities of heat by substituting this value for T back into the original equations. We leave it for you to show that $Q_{\text{coffee}} = -1850$ J and $Q_{\text{copper}} = +1850$ J; Q_{coffee} is negative, as expected. ■

Example 15–3   A physics student wants to cool 0.25 kg of Omni-Cola (mostly water), initially at 20°C, by adding ice that is initially at −20°C. How much ice should she add so that the final temperature will be 0°C with all the ice melted, if the heat capacity of the container may be neglected?

Solution   The (negative) heat added to the water is

$$Q = mc_{\text{water}} \, \Delta T_{\text{water}}$$
$$= (0.25 \text{ kg})(4190 \text{ J·kg}^{-1} \text{·(C°)}^{-1})(0°C - 20°C)$$
$$= -2.09 \times 10^4 \text{ J}.$$

The specific heat capacity of ice is $2010 \text{ J·kg}^{-1} \text{·(C°)}^{-1}$. Let the mass of ice be m; then the heat needed to warm it from −20°C to 0°C is

$$Q = mc_{\text{ice}} \, \Delta T_{\text{ice}}$$
$$= m(2010 \text{ J·kg}^{-1} \text{·(C°)}^{-1})(0°C - (-20°C))$$
$$= m(4.02 \times 10^4 \text{ J·kg}^{-1}).$$

The additional heat needed to melt the ice is the heat of fusion times the mass:

$$Q = mL_F = m(3.33 \times 10^5 \text{ J·kg}^{-1}).$$

The sum of these three quantities must equal zero:

$$-2.09 \times 10^4 \text{ J} + m(4.02 \times 10^4 \text{ J·kg}^{-1}) + m(33.3 \times 10^4 \text{ J·kg}^{-1}) = 0.$$

Solving this for m, we get $m = 0.056$ kg $= 56$ g (two or three medium-size ice cubes).   ∎

Example 15–4   A gasoline lantern emits as much light as a 25-W electric light bulb. Assuming that the efficiency of converting heat into light is the same for the lantern and the bulb (which is not actually correct), how much gasoline does the lantern burn in 10 hours?

Solution   The rate of energy conversion in the lantern is 25 W, so in 10 hours (36,000 s) the total energy needed is

$$(25 \text{ J·s}^{-1})(36,000 \text{ s}) = 0.90 \times 10^6 \text{ J}.$$

As we mentioned in Section 15–5, combustion of 1 g of gasoline produces 46,000 J, so the mass of gasoline required is

$$\frac{0.90 \times 10^6 \text{ J}}{46,000 \text{ J·g}^{-1}} = 19.6 \text{ g}.$$

Actual lanterns are much less efficient than this; typical fuel consumption is of the order of 300–400 g of gasoline (roughly 1 pint) for 10 hours.   ∎

Questions

15–1 Suppose you have a thermos bottle half full of cold coffee. Can you warm it up to drinking temperature by shaking it? Is this possible *in principle*? Is it feasible in practice? Are you adding heat to the coffee?

15–2 When the oil in an automatic transmission is churned up by the turbine blades, it becomes hot, and usually an oil-cooling system is required. Is the engine adding heat to the oil?

15–3 A student asserted that a suitable unit for specific heat capacity was $1 \text{ m}^2 \cdot \text{s}^{-2} \cdot (\text{C}°)^{-1}$. Is this correct?

15–4 The specific heat capacity of water has the same numerical value when expressed in $\text{cal·g}^{-1} \cdot (\text{C}°)^{-1}$ as when expressed in $\text{Btu·lb}^{-1} \cdot (\text{F}°)^{-1}$. Is this a coincidence? Does the same relation hold for heat capacities of other materials?

15–5 A student claimed that when two bodies that are not initially in thermal equilibrium are placed in contact, the temperature rise of the cooler body must always equal the temperature drop of the warmer. Do you agree? Is there a principle of conservation of temperature or something like that?

15–6 In choosing a fluid to circulate inside a gasoline engine to cool it (such as water or antifreeze), should you choose a material with a large or a small specific heat capacity? Why? What other considerations are important?

15–7 Any heat of a phase transition has a numerical value that is 5/9 as great when expressed in calories per gram as when expressed in Btu per pound. Why is the conversion so simple?

15–8 Why do you think the heat of vaporization for water is so much larger than the heat of fusion?

15–9 Some household air conditioners used in dry climates cool air by blowing it through a water-soaked filter, evaporating some of the water. How does this work? Would such a system work well in a high-humidity climate?

15–10 Why does food cook faster in a pressure cooker than in boiling water?

15–11 How does the human body maintain a temperature of 37.0°C (98.6°F) in the desert where the temperature is 50°C (122°F)?

15–12 Desert travelers sometimes keep water in a canvas bag. Some water seeps through the bag and evaporates. How does this cool the water inside?

15–13 When water is placed in ice-cube trays in a freezer, why does the water not freeze all at once when the temperature has reached 0°C? In fact, it freezes first in a layer adjacent to the sides of the tray. Why?

15–14 When an automobile engine overheats and the radiator water begins to boil, the car can still be driven some distance before catastrophic engine damage occurs. Why? What determines the onset of really disastrous overheating?

15–15 Why do automobile manufacturers recommend that antifreeze (typically a 50% solution of ethylene glycol in water) be kept in the engine in summer as well as in winter?

15–16 When you step out of the shower, you feel cold; but as soon as you are dry, you feel warmer, even though the room temperature is the same. Why?

15–17 Suppose the heat of fusion of ice were only 10 J·g^{-1} instead of 333 J·g^{-1}. Would this change the way we make iced tea? Martinis? Lemonade?

15–18 Why is the climate of regions adjacent to large bodies of water usually more moderate than that of regions far from large bodies of water?

Exercises

Section 15–2   Quantity of Heat

15–1 A taxi driver drives an automobile with a mass of 1500 kg at a speed of 8.00 m·s^{-1}. How many joules of heat are generated in the brake mechanism when the automobile is brought to rest by applying the brakes?

15–2 A crate with a mass of 50.0 kg slides down a ramp inclined at 53.1° below the horizontal. The ramp is 12.0 m long. If the crate was at rest at the top of the incline and has a speed of 8.00 m·s^{-1} at the bottom, how much heat was generated by friction? Express your answer in joules, calories, and Btu.

Section 15–3   Heat Capacity

15–3 An engineer is working on an innovative engine design. One of the moving parts, designed to operate at 150°C, contains 1.20 kg of aluminum and 0.80 kg of iron. How much heat is required to raise its temperature from 20°C to 150°C?

15–4

a) How much heat is required to raise the temperature of 0.250 kg of water from 20°C to 30°C?

b) If this amount of heat is added to an equal mass of mercury that is initially at 20°C, what is the final temperature?

c) If this amount of heat is added to an equal volume of mercury that is initially at 20°C, what is the final temperature?

15–5 A student uses a 150-W electric immersion heater to heat 0.200 kg of water from 20.0°C to 100.0°C to make tea.

a) How much heat must be added to the water?

b) How much time is required?

15–6 A nail being driven into a board heats up. If we assume that all the kinetic energy delivered by a 2.00-kg hammer with a speed of 1.60 m·s^{-1} is converted into heat that stays in the nail, what is the temperature increase of a 10.0-g aluminum nail after it has been struck five times?

15–7 A significant mechanism for heat loss in very cold weather is energy expended in warming the air taken into the lungs with each breath. Assume that the specific heat capacity of air is $1020 \text{ J·kg}^{-1}·(\text{C}°)^{-1}$ and that 1.00 L of air has mass 1.29×10^{-3} kg.

a) On an arctic winter day when the temperature is -40.0°C, calculate the amount of heat needed to warm to body temperature (37.0°C) the 0.50 L of air exchanged with each breath.

b) How much heat is lost per hour if the respiration rate is 12 breaths per minute?

15–8 The average 70-kg student generates waste heat at a rate of 300 W while jogging. If this heat were not disposed of (by perspiration and other mechanisms) but remained in the student's body, how much would his body temperature rise after jogging for one hour? As in Example 15–1, assume that the student's specific heat capacity is $4190 \text{ J·kg}^{-1}·(\text{C}°)^{-1}$.

15–9 A technician measures the specific heat capacity of an unidentified liquid by immersing an electrical resistor in it. Electrical energy is converted to heat and transferred to the liquid for 100 s at a constant rate of 75.0 W. The mass of the liquid is 0.780 kg, and its temperature increases from 17.64°C to 20.77°C. Find the mean specific heat capacity of the liquid in this temperature range. Assume that negligible heat is transferred to the container that holds the liquid and that no heat is lost to the surroundings.

15–10 A copper cup with a mass of 0.200 kg contains 0.400 kg of water. The water is heated by a friction device that converts mechanical energy to heat, and it is observed that the temperature of the system rises at the rate of 5.00 C°·min^{-1}. Neglect heat losses to the surroundings. At what rate, in watts, is heat energy being transferred to the system?

Section 15–5   Phase Changes

15–11 An ice-cube tray of negligible mass contains 0.30 kg of water at 20.0°C. How much heat must be removed to cool the water to 0.0°C and freeze it? Express your answer in joules, calories, and Btu.

15–12 How much heat is required to convert 8.00 g of ice at −10.0°C to steam at 100.0°C?

15–13 A skin burn caused by steam at 100°C is much worse than a burn caused by water at 100°C. To see why, calculate the amount of heat input to your skin when it receives the heat released

a) by 10.0 g of steam initially at 100.0°C when it is cooled to skin temperature (34.0°C);

b) by 10.0 g of water initially at 100.0°C when it is cooled to 34.0°C.

15–14 An automobile engine whose output is 3.00 × 10^4 W (about 40 hp) uses 13.2 L (3.5 gal) of gasoline per hour. The heat of combustion is 3.2 × 10^7 J·L^{-1}. What is the efficiency of the engine? That is, what fraction of the heat of combustion is converted to mechanical work?

15–15 An open vessel contains 0.400 kg of ice at −20.0°C. The mass of the container can be neglected. Heat is supplied to the vessel at the constant rate of 420 J·min^{-1} for 500 min.

a) After how many minutes does the ice *start* to melt?

b) After how many minutes, from the time when the heating is first started, does the temperature start to rise above 0°C?

c) Plot a curve showing the elapsed time horizontally and the temperature vertically.

15–16 The nominal food-energy value of butter is about 6.00 kcal·g^{-1}. If all this energy could be converted completely to mechanical energy, how much butter would be required to power a 65.0-kg mountaineer on her journey from Lupine Meadows (elevation 2070 m) to the summit of Grand Teton (4196 m)?

15–17 What must be the initial speed of a lead bullet at a temperature of 25°C so that the heat developed when the bullet is brought to rest is just sufficient to melt it? (Assume that all of the heat developed remains in the bullet.)

15–18 Evaporation of sweat is an important mechanism for temperature control in warm-blooded animals. What mass of water must evaporate from the surface of a 70.0-kg human body to cool it 1.00 C°? The heat of vaporization of water at body temperature (37°C) is 2420 × 10^3 J·kg^{-1}. As in Example 15–1, assume that the specific heat capacity of the human body is 4.19 × 10^3 J·kg^{-1}·(C°)$^{-1}$.

15–19 The capacity of air conditioners is sometimes expressed in "tons," the number of tons of ice (1 ton = 2000 lb) that can be frozen from water at 0°C in 24 hr by the unit. Express the capacity of a one-ton air conditioner in watts and in Btu per hour.

Section 15–6   Examples

15–20 An aluminum can with a mass of 0.500 kg contains 0.140 kg of water at a temperature of 20.0°C. A 0.200-kg block of iron at 75.0°C is dropped into the can. Find the final temperature, assuming no heat loss to the surroundings.

15–21 In a physics lab experiment a student immersed 100 copper pennies (having a mass of 3.00 g each) in boiling water. After they reached thermal equilibrium, she fished them out and dropped them into 0.150 kg of water at 20.0°C in a container of negligible mass. What was the final temperature?

15–22 A laboratory technician dropped a 0.050-kg sample of unknown material, at a temperature of 100.0°C, into a calorimeter containing 0.200 kg of water initially at 20.0°C. The calorimeter is of copper, and its mass is 0.100 kg. The final temperature of the calorimeter is 23.2°C. Compute the specific heat capacity of the sample.

15–23 A 2.50-kg iron block is taken from a furnace where its temperature was 650°C and placed on a large block of ice at 0°C. Assuming that all the heat given up by the iron is used to melt the ice, how much ice is melted?

15–24 A beaker with negligible mass contains 0.500 kg of water at a temperature of 80.0°C. How many grams of ice at a temperature of −20.0°C must be dropped in the water so that the final temperature of the system is 30.0°C?

15–25 A copper calorimeter with a mass of 0.100 kg contains 0.150 kg of water and 0.012 kg of ice in thermal equilibrium at atmospheric pressure. If 0.500 kg of lead at a temperature of 200°C is dropped into the calorimeter, what is the final temperature, assuming that no heat is lost to the surroundings?

15–26 A glass vial containing a 10.0-g sample of an enzyme must be cooled in an ice bath. The bath contains water and 0.120 kg of ice. The sample has a specific heat capacity of 5450 J·kg^{-1}·(C°)$^{-1}$; the glass vial has a mass of 6.0 g and a specific heat capacity of 2800 J·kg^{-1}·(C°)$^{-1}$. How much ice melts in cooling the enzyme sample from room temperature (24.2°C) to the temperature of the ice bath?

Problems

15–27 An artificial satellite made of aluminum circles the earth at a speed of 6000 m·s^{-1}.

a) Find the ratio of its kinetic energy to the energy required to raise its temperature by 600 C°. (The melting point of aluminum is 660°C.) Assume a constant specific heat capacity of 910 J·kg^{-1}·(C°)$^{-1}$.

b) Discuss the bearing of your answer on the problem of the reentry of a satellite into the earth's atmosphere.

15–28 A piece of ice at 0°C falls from rest into a lake whose temperature is 0°C, and 1.00% of the ice melts. Compute the minimum height from which the ice falls.

15–29 Much of the energy of falling water in a waterfall is converted into heat. If all the mechanical energy decrease is converted into heat that stays in the water, how much temperature rise occurs in a 100-m waterfall?

15–30

a) The typical student, while listening quietly to a physics lecture, has a heat output of 200 W. How much heat energy does a class of 200 physics students release into a lecture hall over the course of a 50-min lecture?

b) Assume that all the heat energy in part (a) is transferred to the 3200 m^3 of air in the room. The air has a specific heat of 1020 J·kg^{-1}·(C°)$^{-1}$ and a density of 1.29 kg·m^{-3}. If none of the heat escapes and the air-conditioning system is off, how much will the temperature of the air in the room rise during the 50-min lecture?

c) If the class is taking an exam, the heat output per student rises to 350 W. What then is the temperature rise?

15–31 A capstan is a rotating drum or cylinder over which a rope or cord slides to provide a great amplification of the rope's tension while keeping both ends free (see Fig. 15–6). Since the added tension in the rope is due to friction, the capstan generates heat.

a) If the difference in tension between the two parts of the rope is 680 N and the capstan has a diameter of 14.0 cm and turns once in 1.00 s, find the

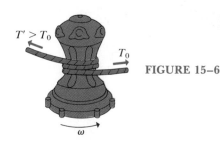

$T' > T_0$ T_0 **FIGURE 15–6**

ω

rate at which heat is being generated. Why does the number of turns not matter?

b) If the capstan is made of iron and has a mass of 5.00 kg, at what rate does its temperature rise? Assume that the temperature in the capstan is uniform.

15–32 An ice cube whose mass is 0.060 kg is taken from a freezer where its temperature was -10.0°C and dropped into a glass of water at 0.0°C. If no heat is gained or lost from outside, how much water freezes onto the cube?

15–33 In a household hot-water heating system, water is delivered to the radiators at 60.0°C (140°F) and leaves at 27.0°C (80°F). The system is to be replaced by a steam system in which steam at atmospheric pressure condenses in the radiators and the condensed steam leaves the radiators at 40.0°C (104°F). How many kilograms of steam will supply the same heat as was supplied by 1.00 kg of hot water in the first installation?

15–34 A vessel whose walls are thermally insulated contains 2.10 kg of water and 0.20 kg of ice, all at a temperature of 0.0°C. The outlet of a tube leading from a boiler in which water is boiling at atmospheric pressure is inserted into the water. How many grams of steam must condense to raise the temperature of the system to 30.0°C? Neglect the heat transferred to the container.

15–35 A thirsty farmer cools a 1.00-L bottle of a soft drink (mostly water) by pouring the contents into a large copper mug with a mass of 0.278 kg and adding 0.0580 kg of ice initially at -16.0°C. If the soft drink and mug are initially at 20.0°C, what is the final temperature of the system, assuming no heat losses?

15–36 A tube leads from a flask in which water is boiling under atmospheric pressure to a calorimeter. The mass of the calorimeter is 0.150 kg, its specific heat capacity is 420 J·kg^{-1}·(C°)$^{-1}$, and it originally contains 0.340 kg of water at 15.0°C. Steam is allowed to condense in the calorimeter until its temperature increases to 71.0°C, after which the total mass of the calorimeter and its contents is found to be 0.525 kg. Compute the heat of vaporization of water from these data.

15–37 A copper calorimeter can with a mass of 0.322 kg contains 0.050 kg of ice. The system is initially at 0.0°C. If 0.014 kg of steam at 100.0°C and 1 atm pressure are admitted into the calorimeter, what is the final temperature of the calorimeter and its contents?

15–38

a) A home owner in a cold climate has a coal-burning furnace that burns 9000 kg (about 10 tons) of coal during a winter. The heat of combustion of coal is 2.50×10^7 J·kg^{-1}. If stack losses are 20% (the amount of heat energy lost up the chimney), how many joules were actually used to heat the house?

b) The home owner proposes to install a solar heating system, heating large tanks of water by solar radiation during the summer and using the stored energy for heating during the winter. Find the required dimensions of the storage tank, assuming it to be a cube, to store a quantity of energy equal to that computed in part (a). Assume that the water is raised to 49.0°C (120°F) in the summer and cooled to 27.0°C (80°F) in the winter.

15–39 A "solar house" has storage facilities for 5.25×10^9 J (about 5 million Btu). Compare the space requirements (in cubic meters) for this storage on the assumption

a) that the heat is stored in water heated from a minimum temperature of 21.0°C (70°F) to a maximum of 49.0°C (120°F);

b) that the heat is stored in Glauber salt ($Na_2SO_4 \cdot 10H_2O$) heated in the same temperature range.

Properties of Glauber salt

Specific heat capacity	
Solid	1930 J·kg^{-1}·(C°)$^{-1}$
Liquid	2850 J·kg^{-1}·(C°)$^{-1}$
Density	1600 kg·m^{-3}
Melting point	32.0°C
Heat of fusion	2.42×10^5 J·kg^{-1}

15–40 The energy output of an animal engaged in an activity is called the basal metabolic rate (BMR) and is a measure of the conversion of food energy into other forms of energy. A simple calorimeter to measure the BMR consists of an insulated box with a thermometer to measure the temperature of the air. The air has a density of 1.29 kg·m^{-3} and a specific heat capacity of 1020 J·kg^{-1}·(C°)$^{-1}$. A 50.0-g hamster is placed in a calorimeter that contains 0.0500 m^3 of air at room temperature.

a) When the hamster is running in a wheel, the temperature of the air in the calorimeter rises 1.8 C° per hour. How much heat does the running hamster generate in an hour? (Assume that all this heat goes into the air in the calorimeter. Neglect the heat that goes into the walls of the box and into the thermometer, and assume that no heat is lost to the surroundings.)

b) Assuming that the hamster converts seed into heat with an efficiency of 10% and that hamster seed has a food energy value of 24 J·g^{-1}, how many grams of seed must the hamster eat per hour to supply this energy?

▮ *Challenge Problems*

15–41 An engineer is developing an electric water heater to provide a continuous supply of hot water. One trial design is shown in Fig. 15–7. Water is flowing at the rate of 0.300 kg·min^{-1}, the inlet thermometer registers 20.0°C, the voltmeter reads 120 V, and the ammeter reads 10.0 A (corresponding to a power input of [120 V][10.0 A] = 1200 W).

a) When a steady state is finally reached, what is the reading of the outlet thermometer?

b) Why is it unnecessary to take into account the heat capacity mc of the apparatus itself?

15–42 An engineer has designed a continuous-flow calorimeter to measure the heat of combustion of a gas-

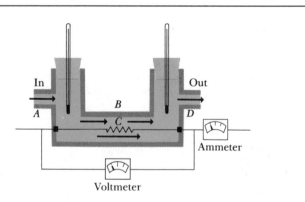

FIGURE 15–7

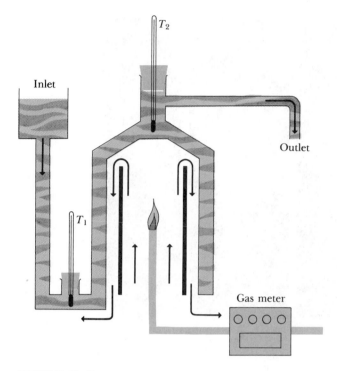

T_2

Inlet

Outlet

T_1

Gas meter

FIGURE 15–8

eous fuel. A sketch of his design is shown in Fig. 15–8. Water is supplied at the rate of 5.70 kg·min⁻¹ and natural gas at 6.50×10^{-4} m³·min⁻¹. In the steady state the inlet and outlet thermometers register 15.6°C and 24.4°C, respectively. What is the heat of combustion of natural gas in joules per cubic meter? Why should the gas flow be made as small as possible?

15–43 An aluminum rod with cross-sectional area 0.0400 cm² and length 80.00 cm at a temperature of 140.0°C is laid alongside a copper rod of cross-sectional area 0.0200 cm² and length 79.92 cm at temperature T. The two rods are laid alongside each other so that they are in thermal contact. No heat is lost to the surroundings, and after they have come to thermal equilibrium, they are observed to be the same length. Calculate the original temperature T of the copper rod and the final temperature of the rods after they come to equilibrium.

16

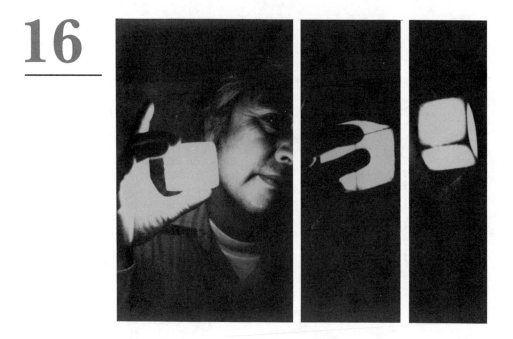

Heat Transfer

We mentioned conduction of heat in Chapter 15 in connection with the transfer of heat between two bodies at different temperatures. We did not consider the *rate* of transfer of heat from one body to another. But if you are boiling water to make tea or trying to build an energy-efficient house, you need to know how quickly or slowly heat is transferred. In this chapter we study the three mechanisms of heat transfer—conduction, convection, and radiation— and how the rate of heat transfer depends on the properties of the system. Conduction occurs within a body (such as a silver spoon in a cup of tea) or between two bodies that are in actual contact with each other. Convection depends on the motion of mass from one region of space to another, and radiation is heat transfer by electromagnetic radiation, such as sunshine, with no need for matter to be present in the space between bodies.

16–1
Conduction

If you place one end of a metal rod in a flame and hold the other end, the end that you are holding gets hotter and hotter, even though it is not in direct contact with the flame. Heat reaches the cooler end by **conduction** through the material. The same thing happens when you stick a sterling silver spoon into a cup of hot coffee.

Conduction of heat occurs only between regions that are at different temperatures, and the direction of heat flow is always from points of higher temperature to points of lower temperature. Figure 16–1 shows a rod of material with cross-sectional area A and length L. The left end of the rod is kept at a temperature T_2, and the right end at a lower temperature T_1. The direction of the flow of heat is then from left to right through the rod. We assume that the sides of the rod are covered by an insulating material, so no heat transfer occurs at the sides. This is an idealized model; all real materials, even the best thermal insulators, conduct heat to some extent.

When a quantity of heat ΔQ is transferred in a time Δt, the rate of heat flow is $\Delta Q / \Delta t$. We call this rate the **heat current** and denote it by H. That is, $H = \Delta Q / \Delta t$. Experiments show that the heat current through the rod is proportional to its cross-sectional area A, proportional to the temperature difference $(T_2 - T_1)$, and inversely proportional to the length L. We can express these proportions as an equation by introducing a constant k called the **thermal conductivity** of the material:

$$\frac{\Delta Q}{\Delta t} = H = kA\frac{T_2 - T_1}{L}. \qquad (16\text{–}1)$$

The quantity $(T_2 - T_1)/L$ is the temperature difference *per unit length* and is called the **temperature gradient.** The numerical value of k depends on the material of the rod.

We can use Eq. (16–1) to compute the heat current through a slab, or through *any* homogeneous body having a uniform cross section perpendicular to the direction of flow, provided that the flow has attained steady state conditions and the ends are kept at constant temperatures.

The units of heat current are energy per unit time; thus the SI unit of heat current is the joule per second, or watt; other units such as the calorie per second or Btu per second are also sometimes used. We can find the units of k by solving Eq. (16–1) for k. We invite you to verify that the SI units of k are $\mathrm{J \cdot (s \cdot m \cdot C°)^{-1}}$. Thermal conductivities are sometimes given in cgs units, with the calorie as the energy unit. The unit of k then is $1\ \mathrm{cal \cdot (s \cdot cm \cdot C°)^{-1}}$. The conversion is

$$1\ \mathrm{cal \cdot (s \cdot cm \cdot C°)^{-1}} = 419\ \mathrm{J \cdot (s \cdot m \cdot C°)^{-1}}.$$

Some numerical values of k at temperatures near room temperature are given in Table 16–1.

As Eq. (16–1) shows, larger thermal conductivity k results in larger heat current if other factors are equal. A good heat conductor has a large value of k, and a good insulator has a small k. A perfect insulator would

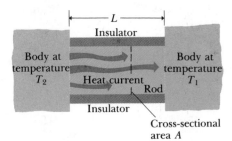

16–1
Steady-state heat flow in a uniform rod.

TABLE 16–1	Thermal conductivities (k)	
Material	$J \cdot s^{-1} \cdot m^{-1} \cdot (C°)^{-1}$	$cal \cdot s^{-1} \cdot cm^{-1} \cdot (C°)^{-1}$
Metals		
Aluminum	205.0	0.49
Brass	109.0	0.26
Copper	385.0	0.92
Lead	34.7	0.083
Mercury	8.3	0.020
Silver	406.0	0.97
Steel	50.2	0.12
Various nonmetallic solids		
(Representative values)		
Insulating brick	0.15	0.00035
Red brick	0.6	0.0015
Concrete	0.8	0.002
Cork	0.04	0.0001
Felt	0.04	0.0001
Fiberglass	0.04	0.0001
Glass	0.8	0.002
Ice	1.6	0.004
Polyurethane foam	0.02	0.00005
Rock wool	0.04	0.0001
Styrofoam	0.01	0.00002
Wood	0.12–0.04	0.0003–0.0001
Gases		
Air	0.024	0.000057
Argon	0.016	0.000039
Helium	0.14	0.00033
Hydrogen	0.14	0.00033
Oxygen	0.023	0.000056

have $k = 0$. This is an unattainable idealization, but Table 16–1 shows that thermal conductivities of materials commonly used as thermal insulators are generally much smaller than those of metals. Thermal conductivities of gases are extremely small. A wool sweater is warm because it traps air between the fibers. Figure 16–2 shows a "space-age" ceramic material that has very unusual thermal properties.

For thermal insulation in buildings, engineers use the concept of **thermal resistance,** denoted by R. The thermal resistance R of a slab of material with area A is defined so that the heat current H through the slab is given by

$$H = \frac{A(T_2 - T_1)}{R}, \tag{16–2}$$

where T_1 and T_2 are the temperatures on the two sides of the slab. Heat current H is *inversely* proportional to R, hence the term thermal resis-

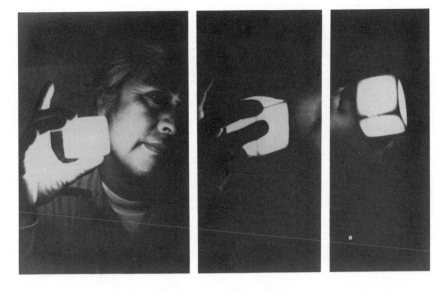

16–2
This protective tile, developed for use on the space shuttle *Columbia,* has extraordinary thermal properties. The extremely small thermal conductivity and small heat capacity of the material make it possible to hold the tile by its edges, even though it is hot enough to emit the light for these photographs. (Courtesy Lockheed Corp.)

tance. Comparing this with Eq. (16–1), we see that R is given by

$$R = \frac{L}{k}, \qquad (16\text{–}3)$$

where L is the thickness of the slab. Equation (16–3) shows that R is directly proportional to thickness L and *inversely* proportional to thermal conductivity k. In the units used for commercial insulating materials, H is expressed in Btu per hour. (A useful conversion factor is that 1 Btu·hr^{-1} = 0.293 W.) A is in square feet, and $T_2 - T_1$ in Fahrenheit degrees. The units of R are then ft^2·F°·hr·Btu^{-1}. Values of R are usually quoted without units; a 6-inch-thick layer of fiberglass has an R value of 19, a two-inch-thick slab of polyurethane foam has a value of 12, and so on. Doubling the thickness doubles the R value. Common practice in new construction in severe northern climates is to specify R values of around 30 for exterior walls and ceilings. When the insulating material is in layers, such as a plastered wall, fiberglass insulation, and wood exterior siding, the R values are additive. Do you see why? (See Problem 16–23.)

PROBLEM-SOLVING STRATEGY: *Heat Conduction*

1. Identify the direction of heat flow in the problem; in Eq. (16–1), L is always measured along this direction, and A is always an area perpendicular to this direction. Often when a box or other container has an irregular shape but uniform wall thickness, you can approximate it as a flat slab with the same thickness and total wall area.

2. In some problems the heat flows through two different materials in succession. The temperature at the interface between the two materials is then intermediate between T_1 and T_2; represent it by a symbol such as T_3. The temperature differences for the two materials are then $(T_2 - T_3)$ and $(T_3 - T_1)$. In steady-state heat flow, heat cannot accumulate

within either material. The same heat has to pass through both materials in succession, so the heat current H must be *the same* in both materials. This is like an electric circuit with the elements connected in series.

3. If there are two *parallel* heat flow paths, so that some heat flows through each, then the total H is the sum of the quantities H_1 and H_2 for the separate paths. An example is heat flow from inside to outside a house, both through the glass in a window and through the surrounding frame. In this case the temperature difference is the same for the two materials, but L, A, and k may be different for the two paths.

4. As always, it is essential to use a consistent set of units. If you use a value of k expressed in $J \cdot s^{-1} \cdot m^{-1} \cdot (C°)^{-1}$, don't use distances in centimeters, heat in calories, or T in Fahrenheit degrees.

Example 16–1   A styrofoam box used to keep drinks cold at a picnic has a total wall area (including the lid) of 0.80 m² and a wall thickness of 2.0 cm. It is filled with ice and cans of orange soda at 0°C. What is the rate of heat flow into the box if the outside temperature is 30°C? How much ice melts in one day?

Solution   We assume that the total heat flow is approximately the same as it would be through a flat slab of area 0.80 m² and thickness 2.0 cm = 0.020 m. We find k from Table 16–1. From Eq. (16–1), the heat current (rate of heat flow) is

$$H = kA \frac{T_2 - T_1}{L}$$

$$= (0.010 \; J \cdot m^{-1} \cdot s^{-1} \cdot (C°)^{-1})(0.80 \; m^2) \frac{30°C - 0°C}{0.020 \; m}$$

$$= 12 \; J \cdot s^{-1}.$$

There are 86,400 s in one day, so the total heat flow Q in one day is

$$(12 \; J \cdot s^{-1})(86,400 \; s) = 1.04 \times 10^6 \; J.$$

The heat of fusion of ice is $3.33 \times 10^5 \; J \cdot kg^{-1}$, so the quantity of ice melted by this quantity of heat is

$$m = \frac{Q}{L_F} = \frac{1.04 \times 10^6 \; J}{3.33 \times 10^5 \; J \cdot kg^{-1}} = 3.1 \; kg. \qquad \blacksquare$$

Example 16–2   A steel bar 10.0 cm long is welded end to end to a copper bar 20.0 cm long. Each bar has a square cross section, 2.00 cm on a side. The free end of the steel bar is in contact with steam at 100°C, and the free end of the copper bar is in contact with ice at 0°C. Find the temperature at the junction of the two bars and the total rate of heat flow.

Solution   The key to the solution is the fact that the heat currents in the two bars must be equal; otherwise, some sections would have more heat flowing in than out, or the reverse, and steady-state conditions could not exist. Let T be the unknown junction temperature; we use Eq. (16–1) for each bar and equate the two expressions:

$$\frac{k_s A(100°C - T)}{L_s} = \frac{k_c A(T - 0°C)}{L_c}.$$

The areas A are equal and may be divided out. Substituting numerical values, we find

$$\frac{(50.2 \text{ J·s}^{-1}\text{·m}^{-1}\text{·(C°)}^{-1})(100°C - T)}{0.100 \text{ m}} =$$

$$\frac{(385 \text{ J·s}^{-1}\text{·m}^{-1}\text{·(C°)}^{-1})(T - 0°C)}{0.200 \text{ m}}.$$

Rearranging and solving for T, we find

$$T = 20.7°C.$$

Even though the steel bar is shorter, the temperature drop across it is much greater than that across the copper bar because steel is a much poorer conductor.

We can find the total heat current by substituting this value for T back into either of the above expressions:

$$H = \frac{(50.2 \text{ J·s}^{-1}\text{·m}^{-1}\text{·(C°)}^{-1})(0.0200 \text{ m})^2(100°C - 20.7°C)}{0.100 \text{ m}}$$

$$= 15.9 \text{ J·s}^{-1} = 15.9 \text{ W},$$

or

$$H = \frac{(385 \text{ J·s}^{-1}\text{·m}^{-1}\text{·(C°)}^{-1})(0.0200 \text{ m})^2(20.7°C - 0°C)}{0.200 \text{ m}}$$

$$= 15.9 \text{ J·s}^{-1} = 15.9 \text{ W}. \qquad \blacksquare$$

Example 16–3   In Example 16–2, suppose the two bars are separated; one end of each bar is placed in contact with steam at 100°C, and the other end of each bar contacts ice at 0°C. What is the *total* rate of heat flow in the two bars?

Solution   In this case the bars are in parallel rather than in series. The total heat current is now the *sum* of the currents in the two bars, and for each bar, $T_2 - T_1 = 100°C - 0°C = 100 \text{ C°}$:

$$H = \frac{(50.2 \text{ J·s}^{-1}\text{·m}^{-1}\text{·(C°)}^{-1})(0.0200 \text{ m})^2(100 \text{ C°})}{0.100 \text{ m}}$$

$$+ \frac{(385 \text{ J·s}^{-1}\text{·m}^{-1}\text{·(C°)}^{-1})(0.0200 \text{ m})^2(100 \text{ C°})}{0.200 \text{ m}}$$

$$= 20.1 \text{ J·s}^{-1} + 77.0 \text{ J·s}^{-1} = 97.1 \text{ J·s}^{-1} = 97.1 \text{ W}.$$

The heat flow in the copper bar is much greater than that in the steel bar, even though the copper bar is longer, because its thermal conductivity is much larger. The total heat flow is much larger than that in Example 16–2, partly because the cross section for heat flow is greater and partly because the full 100 C° temperature difference appears across each bar.   ■

To conclude our discussion of heat conduction, let's look briefly at what is happening at the molecular level. The kinetic and potential energies of molecular motion increase with temperature. The energetic molecules in a hot region of a material interact with their more slowly moving neighbors in cooler regions; they share some of their energy with these neighbors, which in turn pass it on to those in still cooler regions. Energy of molecular motion is passed along from molecule to molecule, from the hotter region to the cooler, while each individual molecule remains at its original position.

Most metals are good conductors of electricity and also good conductors of heat. The ability of a metal to conduct an electric current is due to the fact that some electrons in the material have become detached from their parent molecules. These "free" electrons also provide an effective mechanism for heat transfer from the hotter to the cooler portions of the metal. The best thermal conductors (silver, copper, aluminum, and gold) are also the best electrical conductors.

16–2
Convection

In heat conduction, energy is transferred by molecular vibrations and electron motion, but there is no overall bulk motion of the material. In contrast, **convection** is transfer of heat by actual motion of a fluid from one region of space to another. The hot-air furnace, the hot-water heating system, the cooling system of an automobile engine, and the flow of blood in the body are examples. If the fluid is circulated by a blower or pump, the process is called *forced convection*; if the flow is caused by differences in density due to thermal expansion, the process is called *natural* or *free convection*. The difference is like stirring your coffee versus letting it cool by itself.

A simple example of natural convection is shown in Fig. 16–3. In (Fig. 16–3a) the water is at the same temperature throughout, so the levels are the same in the two sides of the U-tube. In (Fig. 16–3b) we warm the right side; the water expands, becoming less dense, and a taller column is needed to balance the pressure of the left-hand side. When we open the valve, water flows from the top of the warm column into the cooler column. If we supply heat continuously to the hot side and remove it from the cold side, this circulation continues indefinitely. The net result is a continuous heat transfer from the hot to the cold side. In hot-water heating systems the cold side corresponds to the radiators and the hot side to the boiler.

In Section 14–5 we discussed the anomalous thermal expansion of water and its ecological importance for lakes. When the air temperature

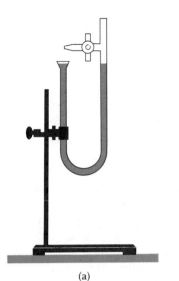

(a)

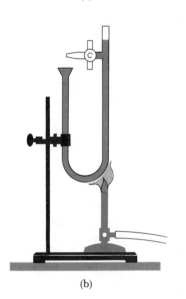

(b)

16–3
Free convection is caused by density differences due to thermal expansion. In (b) the level in the right side is higher than that in the left side because the liquid on the right is warmer and therefore less dense.

is below freezing, the lake cools at the surface; convection currents carry the cooler and more dense water to the bottom of the lake. But when the water temperature reaches 4°C, the temperature of maximum density, convection stops. Further cooling occurs only by conduction; water is a relatively poor conductor of heat, so this is a much slower process. When the surface begins to freeze, the ice floats above the liquid. The absence of convective heat transfer below 4°C saves many lakes from freezing solid in winter, which they would do if it were not for this anomalous expansion behavior.

Convective heat transfer is a very complex process, and there is no simple equation to describe it. Convective heat transfer between a surface at one temperature and a fluid at a different temperature depends on the shape and orientation of the surface, the properties of the fluid, and the nature of the fluid flow. Its dependence on the temperature difference ΔT between the surface and the main body of the fluid is not a direct proportion. In air the rate of convective heat transfer is approximately proportional to $(\Delta T)^{5/4}$. A rough, approximate formula for the heat current H in convective heat transfer is

$$H = hA(\Delta T)^{5/4}, \tag{16–4}$$

where A is the surface area and h is a constant determined by experiment that depends on the properties of the fluid and the shape and orientation of the surface. We invite you to verify that the SI units of h are $W \cdot m^{-2} \cdot (C°)^{-5/4}$. For air in contact with solid surfaces, typical values of h are 1.5–2.5 $W \cdot m^{-2} \cdot (C°)^{-5/4}$.

Example 16–4   The air inside a warm room is at 25°C, and the outside air is at −15°C. How much heat is transferred through 1.00 m² of a glass windowpane with a thermal conductivity of 0.80 $J \cdot m^{-1} \cdot s^{-1} \cdot (C°)^{-1}$ and a thickness of 2.00 mm if $h = 2.0$ $W \cdot m^{-2} \cdot (C°)^{-5/4}$?

Solution   It would be wrong to assume that the inner surface of the glass is at 25°C and the outer surface is at −15°C; you can confirm that by touching the inner surface of a glass windowpane on a cold day. Instead, we should expect a much *smaller* temperature difference across the windowpane, so that in the steady state the rates of heat transfer (1) by convection in the room, (2) by conduction through the glass, and (3) by convection in the outside air are all equal.

As a first approximation in the solution of this problem, let us assume that the glass is at a uniform temperature T. If $T = 5°C$, then the temperature difference between the inside air and the glass is the same as that between the glass and the outside air, 20 C° for each. Then from Eq. (16–4) the convective heat current at each surface is

$$H = hA(\Delta T)^{5/4}$$
$$= (2.0 \ W \cdot m^{-2} \cdot (C°)^{-5/4})(1.00 \ m^2)(20 \ C°)^{5/4}$$
$$= 85 \ W.$$

The glass can't *really* be at uniform temperature; there has to be a temperature gradient just large enough that the *conductive* heat current through it is 85 W. We can find the corresponding temperature difference $T_2 - T_1$ from Eq. (16–1):

$$T_2 - T_1 = \frac{LH}{kA} = \frac{(0.00200 \text{ m})(85 \text{ W})}{(0.80 \text{ J·m}^{-1}\text{·s}^{-1}\text{·(C}°)^{-1})(1.00 \text{ m}^2)} = 0.21 \text{ C}°.$$

Thus the inner surface is at about 5.1°C, and the outer at 4.9°C. ∎

Heat transfer in the human body involves a combination of mechanisms that together maintain a remarkably constant and uniform temperature despite large changes in environmental conditions. As we mentioned above, the most important *internal* mechanism is forced convection; the circulating fluid is blood, and the pump is the heart. Heat transfer between the body and its surroundings involves conduction, convection, and radiation; the proportions depend on circumstances. The total rate of heat loss from the body is of the order of 100 to 200 W (2000 to 4000 kcal per day). A dry, unclothed body in still air loses about half this heat by radiation, but during vigorous exercise and copious perspiration, evaporative cooling is the dominant mechanism. We will discuss radiation next.

16–3
Radiation

Heat transfer by **radiation** depends on electromagnetic waves such as visible light, infrared, and ultraviolet radiation. Everyone has felt the warmth of the sun's radiation and the intense heat from a charcoal grill or the glowing coals in a fireplace. Heat from these very hot bodies reaches you not by conduction or convection in the intervening air but by *radiation*. This heat transfer would occur even if there were nothing but vacuum between you and the source of heat.

It turns out that *every* body, even if its temperature is not elevated, emits electromagnetic radiation with its associated *radiant energy*. This radiation contains a mixture of different wavelengths. At ordinary temperatures, say 20°C, nearly all the energy is carried by infrared waves with wavelengths much longer than those of visible light. As the temperature rises, the wavelengths shift to shorter values. At 800°C a body emits enough visible radiation to be self-luminous and appears "red-hot," although even at this temperature most of the energy is carried by infrared waves. At 3000°C, the temperature of an incandescent lamp filament, the radiation has enough visible light that the body appears "white-hot."

We can study infrared radiation emitted by a body using a camera with infrared-sensitive film or with a device similar to a television camera that is sensitive to infrared radiation. The resulting picture is called a *thermograph*. The rate of emission of energy depends strongly on temperature, so thermography permits detailed study of temperature distributions, with a precision as great as 0.1 C°. Thermography is used to study energy losses in heated buildings, and it has several important medical applications. Various tumors, such as breast cancer, cause local temperature variations, and growths as small as 1 cm can be detected. Circulatory disorders that cause local temperature anomalies can be studied, and thermography has many other applications.

The total rate of radiation of energy from a surface increases very rapidly with temperature in proportion to the *fourth power* of the absolute (Kelvin) temperature. For example, a copper block at a temperature of 100°C (373 K or 212°F) radiates about 0.03 J·s^{-1} or 0.03 W from each square centimeter of its surface. At 500°C (773 K or 932°F) it radiates about 0.54 W from each square centimeter, and at 1000°C (1273 K or 1832°F) it radiates 4 W per square centimeter, 130 times as much as it radiates at 100°C.

Experimental studies show that the rate of radiation of energy from a surface is proportional to the surface area A. It also depends on the nature of the surface; this dependence is described by a quantity e called the **emissivity**; it is a dimensionless number between 0 and 1, representing the ratio of the rate of radiation from a particular surface to that of an equal area of an ideal radiating surface at the same temperature. The heat current $H = \Delta Q / \Delta t$ due to radiation from a surface area A with emissivity e at absolute temperature T can be expressed as

$$H = Ae\sigma T^4, \tag{16–5}$$

where σ is a fundamental physical constant called the **Stefan–Boltzmann constant.** This relation is called the **Stefan–Boltzmann law** in honor of its late nineteenth century discoverers.

In Eq. (16–5), as in other heat-transfer equations, H has units of power (energy per unit time). Thus in SI units, σ has the units W·m^{-2}·K^{-4}. The numerical value is found experimentally to be

$$\sigma = 5.6699 \times 10^{-8} \text{ W·m}^{-2}\text{·K}^{-4}.$$

Emissivity (e) is usually larger for dark, rough surfaces than for light, smooth ones. The emissivity of a smooth copper surface is about 0.3, but e for a dull black surface can be close to unity.

Example 16–5   A thin, square steel plate, 10 cm on a side, is heated in a blacksmith's forge to a temperature of 800°C. If the emissivity is unity, what is the total rate of radiation of energy?

Solution   The total surface area, including both sides, is $2(0.10 \text{ m})^2 = 0.020 \text{ m}^2$. The temperature in Eq. (16–5) must be *absolute* (Kelvin) temperature; 800°C = 1073 K. Then Eq. (16–5) gives

$$H = (0.020 \text{ m}^2)(1)(5.67 \times 10^{-8} \text{ W·m}^{-2}\text{·K}^{-4})(1073 \text{ K})^4$$
$$= 1.5 \times 10^3 \text{ W} = 1.5 \text{ kW}.$$

If the plate were heated by an electric heater instead, an electric power input of 1.5 kW would be required to maintain it at constant temperature. ■

Now here's a puzzle: If all bodies emit radiant energy continuously according to Eq. (16–5), then why don't they eventually radiate away *all* their energy and cool down to absolute zero? The answer is that they *would* do so if energy were not supplied to them in some way. In the coils of an electric heater element or a light-bulb filament, energy is supplied electrically to replace the energy radiated and keep the coils at constant temperature. When this energy supply is cut off, these bodies *do* cool down very quickly to the temperature of their surroundings.

But why don't they continue to radiate and cool still more? The reason is that their surroundings are *also* radiating. Some of this radiated energy is intercepted and absorbed. The rate at which a body *radiates* energy is determined by the temperature of the *body*, but the rate at which it *absorbs* energy by radiation depends on the temperature of its *surroundings*. When a body is hotter than its surroundings, the rate of emission is greater than the rate of absorption; there is a net loss of energy, and the body cools down unless its temperature is maintained by some other means. When a body is colder than its surroundings, the rate of absorption is greater than the rate of emission, and the body's temperature rises. At thermal equilibrium the two rates must be equal.

Thus when a body at temperature T is surrounded by walls that are also at temperature T, maintenance of thermal equilibrium requires that the body's rate of *absorption* of radiant energy from the walls be equal to the rate of radiation from its surface, which is $H = Ae\sigma T^4$. When a body at temperature T_1 is surrounded by walls at temperature T_2, the *net* rate of loss (or gain) of energy per unit area by radiation is

$$H_{\text{net}} = Ae\sigma T_1^4 - Ae\sigma T_2^4 = Ae\sigma(T_1^4 - T_2^4). \qquad (16-6)$$

In this equation a positive value of H means a net heat flow *out of* the body.

Example 16–6   If the total surface of the human body is 1.2 m^2 and the surface temperature is 30°C = 303 K, find the total rate of radiation of energy from the body. If the surroundings are at a temperature of 20°C, what is the *net* rate of heat loss from the body by radiation?

Solution   The emissivity of the body is very close to unity, irrespective of skin pigmentation. The rate of radiation of energy per unit area is given by Eq. (16–5). Taking $e = 1$, we find

$$H = Ae\sigma T^4$$
$$= (1.2 \text{ m}^2)(1)(5.67 \times 10^{-8} \text{ W·m}^{-2}\text{·K}^{-4})(303 \text{ K})^4 = 574 \text{ W}.$$

This loss is partly offset by *absorption* of radiation, which depends on the temperature of the surroundings. The *net* rate of radiative energy transfer is given by Eq. (16–6):

$$H = Ae\sigma(T_1^4 - T_2^4)$$
$$= (1.2 \text{ m}^2)(1)(5.67 \times 10^{-8} \text{ W·m}^{-2}\text{·K}^{-4})[(303 \text{ K})^4 - (293 \text{ K})^4]$$
$$= 72 \text{ W}. \qquad \blacksquare$$

From the above discussion we see that a body that is a good absorber must also be a good emitter. An ideal radiator, with an emissivity of unity, is also an ideal absorber, absorbing *all* of the radiation that strikes it. Such an ideal surface is called an ideal black body or simply a **blackbody.** Conversely, an ideal *reflector*, which absorbs *no* radiation at all, is also a very ineffective radiator.

This is the reason for the silver coatings on vacuum (thermos) bottles. A vacuum bottle has double glass walls. The air is pumped out of the spaces between the walls; this eliminates nearly all heat transfer by conduction and convection. The silver coating on the walls reflects most of the radiation from the contents back into the container, and the wall itself is a very poor emitter. Thus a vacuum bottle can keep coffee or soup hot for several hours. The Dewar flask, used to store liquefied gases, is exactly the same in principle.

Heat transfer by radiation is important in some surprising places. A premature baby in an incubator can be cooled dangerously by radiation if the walls of the incubator happen to be cold, even when the *air* in the incubator is warm. Some incubators regulate the air temperature by measuring the baby's skin temperature.

*16–4
Solar Energy and Resource Conservation

The principles of heat transfer that we have studied in this chapter have many very practical applications in a civilization such as ours, with growing energy consumption and dwindling energy resources. A substantial fraction of all energy consumption in the United States is used for heating and cooling of homes and other buildings, to maintain comfortable temperature and humidity inside when the outside temperature is much hotter or much colder.

For space heating the objective is to prevent as much heat flow as possible from inside to outside; heating units replace the inevitable loss of heat. Walls insulated with material of low thermal conductivity, storm windows, and multiple-layer glass windows all help to reduce heat loss. It has been estimated that if all buildings used such materials, the total energy needed for space heating would be reduced by at least one third.

Air conditioning in summer poses the reverse problem; heat flows from outside to inside, and energy must be expended in refrigeration units to remove it. Again, appropriate insulation can decrease this energy cost considerably.

Direct conversion of solar energy is a promising development in energy technology. Near the earth the rate of energy transfer due to solar radiation is about 1400 W for each square meter of surface area. Not all of this energy reaches the earth's surface; even on a clear day, about one fourth of this energy is absorbed by the earth's atmosphere. In a typical household solar heating system, large black plates facing the sun are backed with pipes through which water circulates. The black surface absorbs most of the sun's radiation; the heat is transferred by conduction to the water and then by forced convection to radiators inside the house.

Heat loss by convection of air near the solar collecting panels is reduced by covering them with glass, with a thin air space. An insulated heat reservoir provides for storage of collected energy for use at night and on cloudy days. Many larger-scale solar-energy conversion systems are also currently under study; a few examples are discussed in Section 19–9.

From an environmental standpoint, solar energy has multiple advantages over the use of fossil fuels (burning of coal or oil) or nuclear power. Fossil fuels are being used up; solar power continues indefinitely. Obtaining fossil fuels may involve strip mining, with its associated destruction of landscape and elimination of other useful land functions, such as farming or timber. Offshore oil drilling is a source of ocean water pollution. Air pollution from combustion products is a familiar problem, as is acid rain, which is directly attributable in many cases to coal smoke. The long-range effects on our climate of excess atmospheric carbon dioxide produced by combustion are unknown, but some scientists believe that the results of the so-called "greenhouse effect" may be serious or even catastrophic. With nuclear power there are radiation hazards and the problem of disposal of radioactive waste material. Solar power avoids all these problems. Some practical problems need to be worked out, including high installation costs and the need for energy storage facilities for night and cloudy days.

Intelligent consideration of the effects of solar radiation in the design of buildings can also reduce energy consumption in heating and cooling. An example is the use of moveable shades on the outsides of buildings, permitting the sun to enter windows in winter but keeping it out in summer. Architects have unfortunately tended to ignore such solutions, but there has been some growth of awareness of the need to design buildings with energy costs in mind. Even though fuel costs are somewhat lower in the late 1980s than they were a decade ago, the need to conserve is still pressing and will undoubtedly become more so.

Questions

16–1 Why does a marble floor feel cooler to the feet than a carpet at the same temperature?

16–2 A beaker of boiling water can be picked up with bare fingers without burning if it is grasped only at the thin turned-out rim at the top. Why?

16–3 Old-time kitchen lore suggests that things cook better (evenly and without burning) in heavy cast-iron pots. What desirable characteristics would such pots have?

16–4 If you have wet hands and pick up a piece of metal that is below freezing, you may stick to it. This doesn't happen with wood. Why not?

16–5 A cold block of metal feels colder than a block of wood at the same temperature, but a hot block of metal feels hotter than a block of wood at the same temperature. Is there any temperature at which they feel equally hot or cold?

16–6 A person pours a cup of hot coffee, intending to drink it five minutes later. To keep it as hot as possible, should he put cream in it now or wait until just before he drinks it?

16–7 In late afternoon when the sun is about to set, swarms of insects such as mosquitoes are sometimes seen in vertical "plumes" above a tree or above the hood of a car with a hot engine. Why?

16–8 Mountaineers caught in a storm sometimes survive by digging a cave in snow or ice. How in the world can you keep warm in an ice cave?

16–9 Old-time pioneers sometimes kept themselves warm on cold winter nights by heating bricks in the fire, wrapping them in thick layers of cloth, and taking them to bed. Discuss the roles of conduction, convection, and radiation in this technique.

16–10 It is well known that a potato bakes faster if a

large nail is stuck through it. Why? Is aluminum better than steel? There is also a gadget on the market to hasten roasting of meat, consisting of a hollow metal tube containing a wick and some water; this is claimed to be much better than a solid metal rod. How does this work?

16–11 The temperature in outer space, far from any solid body, is believed to be about 3 K. If you leave a spaceship and go for a space walk, do you get cold very quickly?

16–12 Aluminum foil used for food cooking and storage sometimes has one shiny surface and one dull surface. When food is wrapped for baking, should the shiny side be in or out? Which side should be out when it is to be frozen?

16–13 Some cooks claim that the bottom crust of a pie gets browner if the pie pan is glass than if it is metal. Why should this be?

16–14 Glider pilots in the midwest know that thermal updrafts are likely to occur above freshly plowed fields. Why?

16–15 We're lucky the earth isn't in thermal equilibrium with the sun. But why isn't it?

16–16 On a chilly fall morning the grass is covered with frost, but the concrete sidewalk isn't. Why?

16–17 Why can a microwave oven cook massive objects such as potatoes and beef roasts much faster than a conventional oven? What disadvantages are associated with the reasons for this greater speed?

16–18 Some folks claim that ice cubes freeze faster if the trays are filled with hot water because hot water cools off faster than cold water. What do you think?

▮ *Exercises*

Section 16–1   Conduction

16–1 A slab of a thermal insulator with a cross-sectional area of 100 cm^2 is 3.00 cm thick. Its thermal conductivity is 0.075 J·s^{-1}·m^{-1}·(C°)$^{-1}$. If the temperature difference between opposite faces is 80 C°, how much heat flows through the slab in one day?

16–2 Use Eq. (16–1) to show that the SI units of thermal conductivity are J·(s·m·C°)$^{-1}$.

16–3 A boiler with a steel bottom 1.50 cm thick rests on a hot stove. The area of the bottom of the boiler is 0.150 m^2. The water inside the boiler is at 100.0°C, and 0.900 kg are evaporated every 5.00 min. Find the temperature of the lower surface of the boiler, which is in contact with the stove.

16–4 The electric oven in a kitchen range has a total wall area of 1.20 m^2 and is insulated with a layer of fiberglass 4.0 cm thick. The inside surface has a temperature of 200°C, and the outside surface is at room temperature, 20°C. The fiberglass has a thermal conductivity of 0.040 J·(s·m·C°)$^{-1}$.

a) What is the heat current through the insulation, assuming that it may be treated as a flat slab with an area of 1.20 m^2?

b) What electric-power input to the heating element is required to maintain this temperature?

16–5 A carpenter builds an outer house wall with a layer of wood 3.0 cm thick on the outside and a layer of styrofoam insulation 3.0 cm thick as the inside wall surface. The wood has $k = 0.080$ J·s^{-1}·m^{-1}·(C°)$^{-1}$, and the styrofoam has $k = 0.010$ J·s^{-1}·m^{-1}·(C°)$^{-1}$.

The interior surface temperature is 20.0°C, and the exterior surface temperature is −10.0°C.

a) What is the temperature at the plane where the wood meets the styrofoam?

b) What is the rate of heat flow per square meter through this wall?

16–6 Suppose that the rod in Fig. 16–1 is made of copper, has a length of 25.0 cm, and has a cross-sectional area of 1.50 cm^2. Let $T_2 = 100.0$°C and $T_1 = 0.0$°C.

a) What is the final steady-state temperature gradient along the rod?

b) What is the heat current in the rod in the final steady state?

c) What is the final steady-state temperature at a point in the rod 2.00 cm from its left end?

16–7 The ceiling of a room has an area of 200 ft^2. The ceiling is insulated to an R-value of 30.0 (in commercial units of ft^2·F°·hr·Btu^{-1}). The surface in the room is maintained at 72°F, and the surface in the attic has a temperature of 105°F. How many Btu of heat flow through the ceiling into the room in 6.0 hr? Also express your answer in joules.

16–8 One end of an insulated metal rod is maintained at 100°C, and the other one is placed in an ice–water mixture. The bar has a length of 50.0 cm and a cross-sectional area of 0.800 cm^2. The heat conducted by the rod melts 4.00 g of ice in 5.00 min. Calculate the thermal conductivity k of the metal. Express your answer in J·s^{-1}·m^{-1}·(C°)$^{-1}$.

16–9 A long rod, insulated to prevent heat losses, has one end immersed in boiling water (at atmospheric pressure) and the other end in a water–ice mixture. The rod consists of a 1.00-m section of copper (one end in steam) joined end-to-end to a length L_2 of steel (one end in ice). Both sections of the rod have cross-sectional areas of 5.00 cm². The temperature of the copper–steel junction is 70.0°C after a steady state has been set up.

a) How much heat per second flows from the steam bath to the ice–water mixture?

b) What is the length L_2 of the steel section?

Section 16–2   Convection

16–10

a) What is the difference in height between the columns in the U-tube in Fig. 16–3 if the liquid is water and the left arm is 0.500 m high at 4°C while the other is at 75°C? (Recall that the density of water at various temperatures is given in Table 14–3.)

b) What is the difference between the pressures at the bottoms of two columns of water each 2.00 m high if the temperature of one is 4°C and that of the other is 75°C?

16–11 A flat vertical plate is maintained at a constant temperature of 100.0°C, and the air on both sides is at 20.0°C. How much heat is lost by natural convection from 1.00 m² of the plate (both sides) per hour if $h = 1.80$ W·m⁻²·(C°)⁻⁵ᐟ⁴?

16–12 A vertical steam pipe with an outside diameter of 7.50 cm and a length of 5.00 m has its outer surface at the constant temperature of 95.0°C. The surrounding air is at 20.0°C. How much heat is delivered per hour to the air by natural convection if $h = 2.50$ W·m⁻²·(C°)⁻⁵ᐟ⁴?

16–13 The air inside an air-conditioned room is at 20°C, and the outside air is a warm 36°C. A glass windowpane in the wall of the room has an area of 0.50 m², a thermal conductivity of 0.80 J·m⁻¹·s⁻¹·(C°)⁻¹, and a thickness of 3.0 mm.

a) If the convective heat transfer constant is $h = 2.0$ W·m⁻²·(C°)⁻⁵ᐟ⁴ and the approximate temperature of the glass is 28°C, what is the convective heat current on each side of the glass?

b) What is the conductive heat current through the glass?

c) What is the temperature difference $T_2 - T_1$ between the outer and inner surfaces of the glass?

Section 16–3   Radiation

16–14 What is the rate of energy radiation per unit area of a blackbody at a temperature of

a) 400 K?   b) 4000 K?

16–15 In Example 16–6, what is the net rate of heat loss by radiation if the temperature of the surroundings is 5.0°C?

16–16 The emissivity of tungsten is 0.350. A tungsten sphere with a radius of 1.50 cm is suspended within a large evacuated enclosure whose walls are at 300 K. What power input is required to maintain the sphere at a temperature of 3000 K if heat conduction along the supports is neglected?

Section 16–4   Solar Energy and Resource Conservation

16–17 A well-insulated house of moderate size in a temperate climate requires a maximum heat input rate of 20.0 kW. If this heat is to be supplied by a solar collector with an average (night and day) energy input of 300 W·m⁻² and a collection efficiency of 60.0%, what area of solar collector is required?

16–18 In Exercise 16–17, suppose that a heat reservoir is required that can store enough energy for a week of cloudy days by means of a large tank of water that is heated to 90.0°C by solar energy and cooled to 40.0°C as it circulates through the house. What volume of water is required?

16–19 A solar water heater for domestic hot-water supply uses solar collecting panels with a collection efficiency of 50% in a location where the average solar-energy input is 200 W·m⁻². If the water comes into the house at 15.0°C and is to be heated to 60.0°C, what volume of water can be heated per hour if the collector area is 30.0 m²?

16–20 The average rate of energy consumption of all forms in the United States is of the order of 3×10^{11} W. Suppose this energy were to be supplied by solar collectors in the desert. Assume an average solar-energy input of 500 W·m⁻² for 12 hours each day and a collection efficiency of 50%. What total collector area would be required? Express your result in square kilometers and square miles.

16–21

a) Calculate the heat conducted per hour through an uninsulated brick wall 0.10 m thick and with an area of 35 m² if the inside surface of the wall is at a temperature of 25°C and the outside surface is at 0°C. The thermal conductivity of the brick is 0.60 J·m⁻¹·s⁻¹·(C°)⁻¹.

b) What is the heat conducted per hour through the wall if it is insulated with styrofoam 0.050 m thick having a thermal conductivity of 0.10 J·m⁻¹·s⁻¹·(C°)⁻¹?

Problems

16–22 Ninety-five percent of the electrical energy consumed by a 60-W incandescent light bulb is converted to heat. The spherical glass envelope of the bulb has a radius of 2.5 cm, and it is 0.50 mm thick. The thermal conductivity of the glass is 0.80 J·m^{-1}·s^{-1}·(C°)$^{-1}$. What is the temperature difference between the inside and outside surfaces of the glass?

16–23 A wood ceiling with thermal resistance R_1 is covered with a layer of insulation with thermal resistance R_2. Prove that the effective thermal resistance of the combination is given by $R = R_1 + R_2$.

16–24 A carpenter builds a solid wood door with dimensions 2.00 m × 0.80 m × 4.0 cm. Its thermal conductivity is $k = 0.0600$ J·s^{-1}·m^{-1}·(C°)$^{-1}$. The inside air temperature is 20.0°C, and the outside air temperature is −10.0°C.

a) What is the rate of heat flow through the door, assuming that the surface temperatures are those of the surrounding air?

b) By what factor is the heat flow increased if a square window 0.50 m on a side is inserted, assuming that the glass is 0.40 cm thick and the surface temperatures are again those of the surrounding air? The glass has a thermal conductivity of 0.80 J·m^{-1}·s^{-1}·(C°)$^{-1}$.

16–25 One experimental method of measuring the thermal conductivity of an insulating material is to construct a box out of the material and measure the power input to an electric heater inside the box that maintains the interior at a measured temperature above the outside surface. Suppose that in such an apparatus a power input of 120 W is required to keep the interior surface of the box 65.0 C° (about 120 F°) above the temperature of the outer surface. The total area of the box is 2.60 m^2, and the wall thickness is 3.8 cm. Find the thermal conductivity of the material in SI units.

16–26 Two metal bars with the same length L and cross-sectional area A are laid side by side, in good thermal contact, as shown in Fig. 16–4. If the bars have thermal conductivities k_1 and k_2, respectively, calculate the total heat current carried by the bars and, from this, deduce the effective thermal conductivity of the two combined bars. (The effective thermal conductivity is the thermal conductivity of a *single* bar of length L and cross-sectional area $2A$ and with temperature dif-

ference $T_2 - T_1$ between its ends that has the same heat current as the total heat current in the two bars.) Does your result make sense in the special case in which $k_1 = k_2$?

16–27 Compute the ratio of the rate of heat loss through a single-pane window with an area of 0.10 m^2 to that for a double-pane window with the same area. The glass of each pane is 2.5 mm thick, and the air space between the two panes of the double-pane window is 5.0 mm thick. The glass has a thermal conductivity of 0.80 J·m^{-1}·s^{-1}·(C°)$^{-1}$.

16–28 An engineer designs a camping icebox having a wall area of 2.00 m^2 and a thickness of 3.00 cm, using insulating material having a thermal conductivity of 0.050 J·s^{-1}·m^{-1}·(C°)$^{-1}$. The temperature of the outside surface of the icebox is 20.0°C, and the inside wall of the box is maintained at 5.0°C by ice. The melted ice drains from the box at a temperature of 2.5°C. If ice costs 25 cents per kilogram, what is the cost per hour to run the icebox?

16–29 Three rods with equal length and cross-sectional area are placed end-to-end. The rods are copper, aluminum, and steel, in that order. The free end of the copper rod is in contact with ice water at 0.0°C, and the free end of the steel rod is in contact with steam at 100.0°C. If no heat transfer occurs at the sides of the rods, find the temperature at each junction. (*Note:* The concept of thermal resistance R can be used here to reduce the algebra. See Problem 16–23.)

16–30 A layer of ice 5.0 cm thick has formed on the surface of a lake, where the temperature is −10.0°C. The water under the slab is at 0.0°C. At what rate does the thickness of the slab increase if the heat of fusion of water freezing on the underside of the slab is conducted through the slab? Express your answer in units of centimeters per hour. Assume that the top surface of the ice has the same temperature as the air, −10.0°C.

16–31 If the solar radiation energy incident per second on the frozen surface of a lake is 600 W·m^{-2} and 70% of this energy is absorbed by the ice, how much time will it take for a 1.40-cm-thick layer of ice to melt? The ice is at a temperature of 0°C.

16–32 A compound bar 1.20 m long is constructed of a solid steel core 1.50 cm in diameter surrounded by a copper casing whose outside diameter is 2.00 cm. The outer surface of the bar is thermally insulated. One end is maintained at 100°C, and the other at 0°C.

a) Find the total heat current in the bar.

b) What fraction of this total is carried by each material?

T_1 k_1 T_2

k_2

FIGURE 16–4

16–33 Rods of copper, brass, and steel are welded together to form a Y-shaped figure. The cross-sectional area of each rod is 2.00 cm². The free end of the copper rod is maintained at 100.0°C, and the free ends of the brass and steel rods at 0.0°C. Assume there is no heat loss from the surfaces of the rods. The lengths of the rods are: copper, 46.0 cm; brass, 24.0 cm; steel, 18.0 cm.

a) What is the temperature of the junction point?

b) What is the heat current in each of the three rods?

16–34 The operating temperature of a tungsten filament in an incandescent lamp is 2450 K, and its emissivity is 0.300. Find the surface area of the filament of a 60-W lamp.

16–35 A rod is initially at a uniform temperature of 0°C throughout. One end is kept at 0°C, and the other is brought into contact with a steam bath at 100°C. The surface of the rod is insulated so that heat can flow only lengthwise along the rod. The cross-sectional area of the rod is 2.00 cm², its length is 100 cm, its thermal conductivity is 335 $J \cdot s^{-1} \cdot m^{-1} \cdot (C°)^{-1}$, its density is 1.00×10^4 $kg \cdot m^{-3}$, and its specific heat capacity is 419 $J \cdot kg^{-1} \cdot (C°)^{-1}$. Consider a short cylindrical element of the rod 1.00 cm in length.

a) If the temperature gradient at the cooler end of this element is 150 $C° \cdot m^{-1}$, how many joules of heat energy flow across this end per second?

b) If the average temperature of the element is increasing at the rate of 0.200 $C° \cdot s^{-1}$, what is the temperature gradient at the other end of the element?

16–36 A physicist uses a cylindrical metal can 0.100 m high and 0.070 m in diameter to store liquid helium at 4.22 K. At this temperature the heat of vaporization of liquid helium is 2.09×10^4 $J \cdot kg^{-1}$. Completely surrounding the can are walls maintained at the temperature of liquid nitrogen, 77.3 K. The intervening space is evacuated. What mass of helium is lost per hour? Assume that the emissivity of the can is 0.200.

16–37 An electrician installs an electric transformer in a cylindrical tank 0.600 m in diameter and 1.00 m high, with flat top and bottom. The convective heat transfer constants are $h = 2.50$ $W \cdot m^{-2} \cdot (C°)^{-5/4}$ for the flat top, $h = 1.30$ $W \cdot m^{-2} \cdot (C°)^{-5/4}$ for the flat bottom, and $h = 1.50$ $W \cdot m^{-2} \cdot (C°)^{-5/4}$ for the curved sides of the tank. If the tank transfers heat to the air only by natural convection and electrical losses are to be dissipated at the rate of 0.500 kW, how many degrees will the tank surface rise above room temperature?

Challenge Problems

16–38 The rate at which radiant energy reaches the surface of the earth from the sun is 1.40 $kW \cdot m^{-2}$. The distance from earth to sun is 1.49×10^{11} m, and the radius of the sun is 6.95×10^8 m.

a) What is the rate of radiation of energy per unit area from the sun's surface?

b) If the sun radiates as an ideal blackbody, what is the temperature of its surface?

16–39 A solid cylindrical copper rod 0.100 m long has one end maintained at a temperature of 20.00 K. The other end is blackened and exposed to thermal radiation from surrounding walls at 400 K. The sides of the rod are insulated, so no energy is lost or gained except at the ends of the rod. When equilibrium is reached, what is the temperature of the blackened end? (*Hint:* Since copper is a very good conductor of heat at low temperature, $k = 1670$ $J \cdot s^{-1} \cdot m^{-1} \cdot (C°)^{-1}$, the temperature of the blackened end is only slightly greater than 20.00 K.)

Thermal Properties of Matter

In previous chapters we have discussed several properties of materials, including elasticity, thermal expansion, specific heat capacity, and thermal conductivity. All these properties describe how a material behaves when some aspect of its environment changes, such as temperature or pressure. We have used physical quantities such as total mass m, number of moles n, pressure p, volume V, and temperature T to describe the quantity and condition of the material. We now want to pull several relationships together into a more general formulation of the behavior of materials. A central concept in this synthesis is the *equation of state* of a material. We also look in greater detail at the conditions that determine the *phase* of a material (e.g., solid, liquid, or gas) and the conditions under which *phase transitions* occur. This discussion provides some of the language we need for our study of *thermodynamics*, the relation of heat to other forms of energy, in the following chapters.

17–1
Equations of State

Physical quantities such as pressure, volume, temperature, and amount of substance describe the conditions in which a particular material exists. They describe the *state* of the material, and they are called *state variables* or **state coordinates.** For some physical phenomena we need additional state variables such as magnetization or electric polarization, but those named above are sufficient for our present discussion.

The state variables are interrelated; ordinarily, we cannot change one without also causing a change in one or more of the others. For example, when we heat a gas such as oxygen or hydrogen in a closed container with constant volume, the pressure *must* increase as the temperature increases. If the temperature goes high enough, the pressure may cause the container, such as a boiler, to explode. The volume V of a substance is determined by its pressure p, temperature T, and amount of substance, m or n.

In some cases the relationship among p, V, and T is simple enough that we can express it in the form of an equation called the **equation of state.** We can construct a simple (though approximate) equation of state for a solid material. The temperature coefficient of volume expansion β is the fractional volume change per unit temperature change, and the isothermal compressibility k is the fractional volume change per unit pressure change. Thus if a specimen of material has volume V_0 when the pressure is p_0 and the temperature is T_0, the volume V at slightly differing pressure p and temperature T is given approximately by

$$V = V_0[1 + \beta(T - T_0) - k(p - p_0)], \qquad (17\text{--}1)$$

provided that the temperature and pressure changes are not too great. Equation (17–1) is called an *equation of state* for the material.

Another simple equation of state is the one for an *ideal gas*, which we will discuss in Section 17–2. In many cases the relationship among p, V, and T is so complex that it cannot be expressed in a simple equation; we then have to resort to graphs or tables of numerical values. But even then the relationship among the variables still *exists*; we call this relationship an equation of state even when we don't know the actual equation.

In this chapter we will consider only **equilibrium states,** that is, states in which the system is in mechanical and thermal equilibrium. In an equilibrium state the temperature and pressure are uniform throughout the system. When a system changes from one state to another, *non-equilibrium* states must occur during the transition. For example, when a material expands or is compressed, there must be mass in motion; this requires acceleration and non-uniform pressure. After the system has returned to mechanical equilibrium, the pressure is again the same throughout the system. When heat conduction occurs within a system, different regions must have different temperatures. Only in thermal equilibrium is the temperature the same throughout.

17–2
Ideal Gases

Gases at low pressures have particularly simple equations of state. Figure 17–1 shows an experimental setup to study the relationships among pressure, volume, temperature, and quantity of substance for a gas. The cylinder has a movable piston and is equipped with a pressure gauge and a thermometer. We can vary the pressure, volume, and temperature and pump any desired mass of any gas into the cylinder. It is often convenient to measure the amount of gas in terms of the number of *moles n*, rather than the mass m. We did this when we defined molar heat capacity in Section 15–3; you may want to review that section. Molecular mass M is mass per mole, and the total mass m is given by

$$m = nM. \tag{17–2}$$

Equation (17–2) says that the total mass m of material is the mass of one mole M multiplied by the number of moles n.

Several conclusions emerge from measurements of the behavior of various gases. First, the volume V is proportional to the number of moles n. If we double the number of moles, keeping pressure and temperature constant, the volume doubles. Second, the volume varies *inversely* with pressure p; if we double the pressure, holding the temperature T and quantity of material n constant, the gas is compressed to one half of its initial volume. Thus

$$pV = \text{constant} \quad (T \text{ constant}), \tag{17–3}$$

or, if p_1 and V_1 are the pressure and volume in the initial state and p_2 and V_2 those of the final state, then

$$p_1V_1 = p_2V_2 \quad (T \text{ constant}). \tag{17–4}$$

This relation is called Boyle's law, after Robert Boyle (1627–1691), a contemporary of Newton.

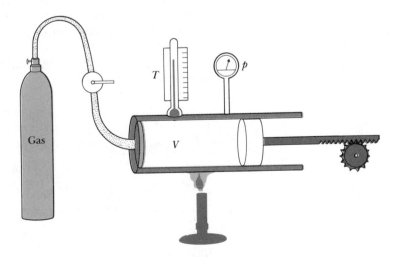

17–1
A hypothetical setup for studying the behavior of gases. The pressure, volume, temperature, and number of moles of gas can be controlled and measured.

Third, the pressure is proportional to the absolute temperature. If we double the absolute temperature, keeping the volume and quantity of material constant, the pressure doubles. Thus

$$p = (\text{constant})T \quad (V \text{ constant}), \tag{17–5}$$

or, if p_1 and T_1 are the pressure and absolute temperature in the initial state and p_2 and T_2 those of the final state, then

$$\frac{p_1}{T_1} = \frac{p_2}{T_2}. \tag{17–6}$$

This is called Charles' law, after Jacques Charles (1746–1823).

These three relationships can be combined neatly into a single equation of state:

$$pV = nRT. \tag{17–7}$$

We might expect that the constant of proportionality R would have different values for different gases, but instead it turns out to have the same value for *all* gases, at least at sufficiently high temperature and low pressure. This constant R is called the **ideal gas constant.** Its numerical value depends on the units of p, V, and T, of course. In SI units, in which the unit of p is the pascal or newton per square meter and the unit of V is the cubic meter, the numerical value of R is found to be

$$R = 8.314 \ (\text{N·m}^{-2})\cdot\text{m}^3\cdot\text{mol}^{-1}\cdot\text{K}^{-1} = 8.314 \ \text{J·mol}^{-1}\cdot\text{K}^{-1}.$$

The units of pressure times volume are the same as units of energy, so in *all* systems of units, R has units of energy per mole per unit of absolute temperature. If we use the calorie as our energy unit,

$$R = 1.99 \ \text{cal·mol}^{-1}\cdot\text{K}^{-1}.$$

In chemical calculations, volumes are commonly expressed in liters (L) and pressures in atmospheres. In this system,

$$R = 0.08207 \ \text{L·atm·mol}^{-1}\cdot\text{K}^{-1}.$$

We define an **ideal gas** as one for which Eq. (17–7) holds precisely for *all* pressures and temperatures. As the term suggests, an ideal gas is an idealized model. It represents the behavior of gases very well in some circumstances and less well in others. Generally, gas behavior approximates the ideal-gas model most closely at very low pressures, when the gas molecules are far apart. However, the deviations are not very great at moderate pressures (e.g., 1 atm) and at temperatures not too near those at which the gas liquefies.

For a *constant mass* (or constant number of moles) of an ideal gas the product nR is constant, so the quantity pV/T is also constant. If the subscripts 1 and 2 refer to two states of the same mass of a gas, but at different pressures, volumes, and temperatures,

$$\frac{p_1 V_1}{T_1} = \frac{p_2 V_2}{T_2} = \text{constant}. \tag{17–8}$$

If the temperatures T_1 and T_2 are the same, then

$$p_1 V_1 = p_2 V_2 = \text{constant},$$

which is again Boyle's law, Eq. (17–4).

Now let's think back to our definition of *temperature* in Chapter 14. Our best definition was stated in terms of the constant-volume gas thermometer, for which pressure is proportional to absolute temperature. Hence the proportionality of pressure to absolute temperature, as expressed by Eqs. (17–5) and (17–6), is not at all surprising; indeed, it is inevitable! You may now have the feeling that we have been treating as a *natural law* a relationship that is really only a matter of *definition*.

To this charge we plead guilty, but with mitigating circumstances. Toward the end of Chapter 19 we will arrive at a definition of temperature that really *is* independent of the properties of any particular material (including ideal gases). The temperature scale based on the gas thermometer will then emerge as a very close approximation of this truly absolute scale. Until then, consider Charles' law and the ideal-gas equation of state as based on this genuinely material-independent temperature scale, even though we haven't actually defined it yet.

PROBLEM-SOLVING STRATEGY: *Ideal Gases*

1. In some problems you will be concerned with only one state of the system; some of the quantities in Eq. (17–7) will be known, some unknown. Make a list of what you know and what you have to find. For example, $p = 1.0 \times 10^6$ Pa, $V = 4$ m^3, $T = ?$, $n = 2$ mol, or something comparable.

2. In other problems there will be two different states of the same quantity of gas. Decide which is state 1 and which is state 2, and make a list of the quantities for each: p_1, p_2, V_1, V_2, T_1, T_2. If all but one of these quantities are known, you can use Eq. (17–8). Otherwise, you have to use Eq. (17–7). For example, if p_1, V_1, and n are given, you can't use Eq. (17–8) because you don't know T_1.

3. As always, be sure to use a consistent set of units. First decide which value of the gas constant R you are going to use, and then convert the units of the other quantities accordingly. You may have to convert atmospheres to pascals or liters to cubic meters. Sometimes the problem statement will make one system of units clearly more convenient than others. Decide on your system, and stick to it.

4. Don't forget that T must always be an *absolute* temperature. If you are given temperatures in degrees Celsius, be sure to add 273 to convert to kelvins.

5. You may sometimes have to convert between mass m and number of moles n. The relationship is $m = Mn$, where M is the molecular mass. Here's a tricky point: If you replace n in Eq. (17–7) by (m/M), you *must* use the same mass units for m and M. So if M is in grams per mole (the usual units for molecular mass), then m must also be in grams. If you want to use m in kilograms, then you must convert M to kilograms per mole. For example, the molecular mass of oxygen is 32 g·mol^{-1} or 32×10^{-3} kg·mol^{-1}. Be careful!

Example 17–1   The condition called **standard temperature and pressure (STP)** for a gas is defined to be a temperature of 0°C = 273 K and a pressure of 1 atm = 1.013×10^5 Pa. Find the volume of 1 mol of any gas at STP.

Solution   From Eq. (17–7), using R in J·mol^{-1}·K^{-1},

$$V = \frac{nRT}{p} = \frac{(1 \text{ mol})(8.314 \text{ J·mol}^{-1}\text{·K}^{-1})(273 \text{ K})}{1.013 \times 10^5 \text{ Pa}} = 0.0224 \text{ m}^3 = 22.4 \text{ L}.$$

Alternatively, using R in $L \cdot atm \cdot mol^{-1} \cdot K^{-1}$,

$$V = \frac{nRT}{p} = \frac{(1 \text{ mol})(0.0821 \text{ L} \cdot \text{atm} \cdot \text{mol}^{-1} \cdot \text{K}^{-1})(273 \text{ K})}{1.00 \text{ atm}}$$

$$= 22.4 \text{ L.}$$

Example 17–2   A tank attached to an air compressor contains 20.0 L of air at a temperature of 30°C and a gauge pressure of 4.00×10^5 Pa (about 60 psi). What is the mass of air, and what volume would it occupy at STP (1 atm and 0°C)? Air is a mixture of gases, consisting of about 78% nitrogen and 21% oxygen, with small percentages of other gases. The *average* molecular mass is $M = 28.8 \text{ g} \cdot \text{mol}^{-1}$.

Solution   Call the initial conditions state 1 and STP state 2. Gauge pressure is the amount in excess of atmospheric pressure (1.01×10^5 Pa), so the total initial pressure is

$$p_1 = 4.00 \times 10^5 \text{ Pa} + 1.01 \times 10^5 \text{ Pa} = 5.01 \times 10^5 \text{ Pa.}$$

We express the temperatures in kelvins: $T_1 = 30°C = 303 \text{ K}$, $T_2 = 0°C = 273 \text{ K}$.

To find the mass of gas, we first use Eq. (17–7) to find n, the number of moles, and then use Eq. (17–2) to find the mass m:

$$n = \frac{p_1 V_1}{RT_1} = \frac{(5.01 \times 10^5 \text{ Pa})(20 \times 10^{-3} \text{ m}^3)}{(8.314 \text{ J} \cdot \text{mol}^{-1} \cdot \text{K}^{-1})(303 \text{ K})} = 3.98 \text{ mol;}$$

$$m = nM = (3.98 \text{ mol})(28.8 \text{ g} \cdot \text{mol}^{-1}) = 115 \text{ g} = 0.115 \text{ kg.}$$

The volume V_2 at 1 atm and 0°C (273 K) is

$$V_2 = \frac{nRT_2}{p_2} = \frac{(3.98 \text{ mol})(8.314 \text{ J} \cdot \text{mol}^{-1} \cdot \text{K}^{-1})(273 \text{ K})}{1.01 \times 10^5 \text{ Pa}}$$

$$= 89.4 \times 10^{-3} \text{ m}^3 = 89.4 \text{ L.}$$

Alternatively, we can find V_2 from Eq. (17–8), where everything except V_2 is known. Solving for V_2 and substituting the known quantities, we find

$$V_2 = \frac{p_1 T_2}{p_2 T_1} V_1 = \frac{(5.01 \times 10^5 \text{ Pa})(273 \text{ K})}{(1.01 \times 10^5 \text{ Pa})(303 \text{ K})} (20 \times 10^{-3} \text{ m}^3)$$

$$= 89.4 \times 10^{-3} \text{ m}^3.$$

When we deal with mixtures of ideal gases, the concept of **partial pressure** is useful. In a mixture the partial pressure of each gas is the pressure that gas would exert if it occupied the entire volume by itself and the other gases were not present. It turns out that the actual total pressure of the mixture is the sum of the partial pressures of the components, provided that each component behaves as an ideal gas. In air at normal atmospheric pressure, the partial pressure of nitrogen is about 0.8 atm or 0.8×10^5 Pa, and the partial pressure of oxygen is about 0.2 atm or 0.2×10^5 Pa.

The ability of the human body to absorb oxygen from the atmosphere depends critically on the partial pressure of oxygen. Absorption drops sharply when the partial pressure of oxygen is less than about 0.13×10^5 Pa, corresponding to an elevation above sea level of about 4700 m (15,000 ft). At partial pressures less than 0.11×10^5 Pa, oxygen absorption is not sufficient to maintain life. There is no permanently maintained human habitation on earth above 16,000 ft, although survival for short periods of time is possible at higher elevations. At the summit of Mount Everest (elevation 8882 m or 29,141 ft) the partial pressure of oxygen is only about 0.07×10^5 Pa, and climbers nearly always carry oxygen tanks. For similar reasons, jet airplanes, which typically fly at altitudes of 8,000 to 12,000 m, *must* have pressurized cabins for passenger comfort and health.

*17–3
pV-Diagrams

For a given quantity of a material the equation of state is a relation among the three state coordinates pressure p, volume V, and temperature T. We could in principle represent this relationship graphically as a *surface* in a three-dimensional space with coordinates p, V, and T. This representation sometimes helps in grasping the overall behavior of the material, but ordinary two-dimensional graphs are usually more convenient. One of the most useful of these is a set of graphs in which each curve is a graph of pressure as a function of volume for a particular temperature. Such a diagram is called a *pV*-**diagram.** Each curve, representing a specific constant temperature, is called an **isotherm,** or a *pV*-*isotherm.*

A *pV*-diagram for an ideal gas is shown in Fig. 17–2. Each curve is an isotherm, showing the relation of pressure to volume at a certain constant temperature. The highest temperature is T_4; the lowest is T_1. We can think of this as a set of graphs of Boyle's law, Eq. (17–3), for each of several temperatures. It is also a graphical representation of the ideal-gas equation of state; from these curves we can read off the volume V corresponding to any given pressure p and temperature T.

Figure 17–3 shows a *pV*-diagram for a material that *does not* obey the ideal-gas equation. At a high enough temperature, say T_4, the curves resemble the ideal-gas curves of Fig. 17–2, but at lower temperatures the behavior is rather different. At temperatures below a certain critical temperature T_c the isotherms develop flat parts. If we follow such an isotherm, compressing the material and keeping the temperature constant, the pressure increases at first. But after we reach the flat part of the isotherm, there is no further pressure increase until we reach the end of the flat part. At that point the pressure begins to increase very rapidly with a further decrease of volume.

When we look at the material during this constant-pressure compression, we see that it is *condensing* from the vapor (gas) to the liquid phase. The flat part of the isotherm represents a condition of *phase equilibrium.* As the volume decreases along this flat part, more and

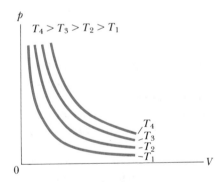

17–2
A *pV*-diagram for an ideal gas. Each curve represents the relation between pressure and volume at the indicated constant temperature. This is a graphical representation of Boyle's law; for each curve the product pV is constant; the value of that constant is different for different temperatures, increasing with increasing temperature. These curves are called *pV*-isotherms for the substance.

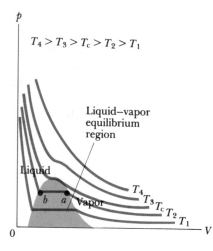

17–3

A pV-diagram for a nonideal gas, showing pV-isotherms for temperatures above and below the critical temperature T_c. The liquid–vapor equilibrium region is shown as a shaded area. At a still lower temperature the material might undergo a phase transition from liquid to solid or from gas to solid; these are not shown on this diagram.

more material goes from vapor to liquid, but the pressure does not change. During this process we have to remove heat to keep the temperature constant; this is heat of vaporization, which we discussed in Section 15–5.

When we compress a real (non-ideal) gas at a constant temperature less than T_c, such as T_2 in Fig. 17–3, it remains in the gaseous phase until point a in the diagram is reached. At a it begins to liquefy; as the volume decreases further, more material liquefies, with *both* pressure and temperature remaining constant. At point b, *all* the material is in the liquid state. After this, any further compression results in a rapid rise of pressure because in general liquids are much less compressible than gases. At a lower constant temperature T_1, similar behavior occurs, but the onset of condensation occurs at lower pressure and greater volume than at the constant temperature T_2.

The shaded area in Fig. 17–3 is the region of liquid–vapor *phase equilibrium* for this material. At temperatures greater than T_c, no phase transition occurs as the material is compressed. The temperature T_c is called the *critical temperature* for this material. We will explore its significance in greater detail in the next section.

We will find many uses for pV-diagrams in the next two chapters in connection with energy calculations. We will find that the *area* under a pV-curve, whether or not it is an isotherm, represents the *work* done by the system during a volume change. This work, in turn, is directly related to heat transfer and changes in the *internal energy* of the system, which we will study in detail in Chapter 18.

*17–4

Phase Diagrams, Triple Point, Critical Point

We have discussed the usefulness of pV-diagrams for describing the behavior of materials, including the equation of state. Another useful diagram, especially for describing phases of matter and phase transitions, is a graph with axes p and T, called a **phase diagram.**

In our discussion of phases of matter in Section 15–5 we found that each phase is stable only in certain ranges of temperature and pressure. A transition from one phase to another takes place ordinarily under conditions of **phase equilibrium** between the two phases, and for a given pressure this occurs at only one specific temperature. A phase diagram shows what phase occurs for each possible combination of temperature and pressure. A typical example is shown in Fig. 17–4. Each point on the diagram represents a pair of values of p and T. At each point, only a single phase can exist, except for points on the color curves, where two phases can coexist in phase equilibrium. Each area on the diagram corresponds to a single phase, and each point on a line separating two areas represents a set of conditions under which phase changes between the two phases can occur. The fusion curve separates the solid and liquid areas, the vaporization curve separates the liquid and vapor areas, and the sublimation curve separates the solid and vapor areas.

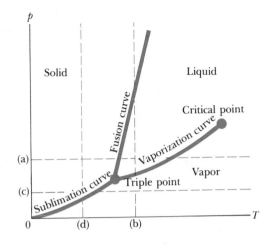

17–4
A pT phase diagram, showing regions of temperature and pressure at which the various phases exist and where phase changes occur.

If we increase the temperature of a substance, keeping the pressure constant, it passes through a sequence of states represented by points on a horizontal line such as line (a) in the figure. The melting and boiling temperatures at this pressure are the temperatures at which this line intersects the fusion and vaporization curves, respectively. If we *compress* a material by increasing the pressure while we hold the temperature constant, as represented by a vertical line such as line (b), the material passes from vapor to liquid and then to solid at the points where the line crosses the vaporization curve and fusion curve, respectively.

When the pressure is low enough, constant-pressure heating can transform a substance from solid directly to vapor, as shown by line (c). This process is called *sublimation*; it occurs at a pressure and temperature corresponding to the intersection of the line and the sublimation curve. At atmospheric pressure, solid carbon dioxide undergoes sublimation; no liquid phase can exist at this pressure. When a substance with an initial temperature lower than the temperature at the point labeled "triple point" is compressed by increasing its pressure, it goes directly from the vapor to the solid phase, as shown by line (d).

Figure 17–4 is characteristic of materials that expand on melting. A few materials *contract* on melting. A familiar example is water, and the metal antimony also has this property. For such a substance the fusion curve always slopes upward to the left, rather than to the right. The melting temperature decreases when the pressure increases, so these solid materials can be melted by an increase of pressure. This is part of the reason that ice cubes stick together.

The intersection point of the equilibrium curves in Fig. 17–4 is called the **triple point.** For any substance this point represents the unique pressure–temperature combination at which *all three* phases can coexist. We call these the triple-point pressure and temperature. Triple-point data for a few substances are given in Table 17–1. In Section 14–4 we used the triple-point temperature of water to define a temperature scale.

We saw in the pV-diagram of Fig. 17–3 that a liquid–vapor phase transition occurs only when the temperature and pressure are less than those at the point lying at the top of the tongue-shaped area labeled

TABLE 17–1	Triple-point data	
Substance	**Temperature, K**	**Pressure, Pa**
Hydrogen	13.84	0.0704×10^5
Deuterium	18.63	0.171×10^5
Neon	24.57	0.432×10^5
Nitrogen	63.18	0.125×10^5
Oxygen	54.36	0.00152×10^5
Ammonia	195.40	0.0607×10^5
Carbon dioxide	216.55	5.17×10^5
Sulfur dioxide	197.68	0.00167×10^5
Water	273.16	0.00610×10^5

"liquid–vapor equilibrium region." This point corresponds to the end-point at the top of the vaporization curve in Fig. 17–4. It is called the **critical point,** and the corresponding values of p and T are called the critical pressure and temperature, p_c and T_c. A gas at a temperature *above* the critical temperature does not separate into two phases when it is compressed isothermally (along a vertical line to the right of the critical point in Fig. 17–4). Instead, its properties change gradually and continuously from those we ordinarily associate with a gas (low density, large compressibility) to those of a liquid (high density, small compressibility) *without a phase transition*. Similarly, when a material is heated at a constant pressure greater than the critical-point pressure (a horizontal line above the critical point in Fig. 17–4), its properties change gradually from liquidlike to gaslike.

If this stretches credibility, here is another point of view. Look at liquid–phase transitions at successively higher points on the vaporization curve. As we approach the critical point, the *differences* in physical properties such as density, bulk modulus, index of refraction, and viscosity, between the liquid and vapor phases, become smaller and smaller. Exactly *at* the critical point they all become zero, and at this point the distinction between liquid and vapor disappears. The heat of vaporization also grows smaller and smaller as we approach the critical point, and it too becomes zero at the critical point.

Table 17–2 lists critical constants for a few substances. The very low critical temperatures of hydrogen and helium show why these gases defied attempts to liquefy them for many years.

Figure 17–5 shows pT phase diagrams for water and carbon dioxide. In Fig. 17–5a the horizontal line at 1 atm intersects the fusion curve at 0°C and the vaporization curve at 100°C. These are the normal melting and boiling points at this pressure. The boiling point increases with increasing pressure up to the critical temperature of 374°C. Solid, liquid, and vapor can remain in equilibrium only at the triple point, at which the vapor pressure is 0.006 atm and the temperature is 0.01°C.

For carbon dioxide the triple-point temperature is −56.6°C, and the corresponding pressure is 5.11 atm. At atmospheric pressure, CO_2 can exist only as a solid or vapor; hence the name "dry ice." Liquid CO_2 can exist only at a pressure greater than 5.11 atm.

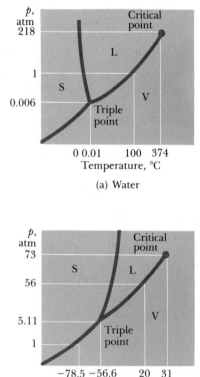

(a) Water

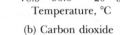

(b) Carbon dioxide

17–5

Pressure–temperature diagrams (not to a uniform scale).

TABLE 17–2	**Critical constants**			
Substance	Critical temperature, K	Critical pressure, Pa	Critical volume, $m^3 \cdot mol^{-1}$	Critical density, $kg \cdot m^{-3}$
Helium (4)	5.3	2.29×10^5	57.8×10^{-6}	69.3
Helium (3)	3.34	1.17×10^5	72.6×10^{-6}	41.3
Hydrogen (normal)	33.3	13.0×10^5	65.0×10^{-6}	31.0
Deuterium (normal)	38.4	16.6×10^5	60.3×10^{-6}	66.3
Nitrogen	126.2	33.9×10^5	90.1×10^{-6}	311
Oxygen	154.8	50.8×10^5	78×10^{-6}	410
Ammonia	405.5	112.8×10^5	72.5×10^{-6}	235
Freon 12	384.7	40.1×10^5	218×10^{-6}	555
Carbon dioxide	304.2	73.9×10^5	94.0×10^{-6}	468
Sulfur dioxide	430.7	78.8×10^5	122×10^{-6}	524
Water	647.4	221.2×10^5	56×10^{-6}	320
Carbon disulfide	552.0	79.0×10^5	170×10^{-6}	440

The information presented by the pT phase diagram is also contained in the pV-diagram. In Fig. 17–3, for example, we can read off for each temperature the pressure at which liquid and vapor are in equilibrium. Then we can use this set of pairs of values of p and T to plot the vaporization curve of Fig. 17–4, and we can also obtain the critical-point temperature and pressure.

Many substances can exist in more than one solid phase. A familiar example is carbon, which exists as noncrystalline lampblack and crystalline graphite and diamond. Water is another example; at least eight types of ice, differing in crystal structure and physical properties, have been observed at very high pressures.

We remarked at the beginning of Section 17–3 that the equation of state of any material can be represented graphically as a surface in a three-dimensional space with coordinates p, V, and T. Such a surface is seldom useful in representing detailed quantitative information, but it can add to our general understanding of the behavior of materials at various temperatures and pressure. Figure 17–6 shows a typical pVT-surface. The thin black lines represent pV-isotherms, and we see that their projections on the pV-plane give a diagram similar to Fig. 17–3. The pV-isotherms represent contour lines on the pVT-surface, just as contour lines on a topographic map represent the elevation (the third dimension) at each point. The projections of the edges of the surface onto the pT-plane gives the pT phase diagram of Fig. 17–5b.

Three lines on the surface show specific processes. Line *abcdef* shows constant-pressure heating, with melting at *bc* and vaporization at *de*. Note the volume changes that occur as T increases along this line. Line *ghjklm* is an isothermal (constant temperature) compression; *hj* shows liquefaction, and *kl* shows solidification. Between these, sections *gh* and *jk* represent isothermal compression with increase in pressure; the pressure increases are much greater in the liquid region *jk* and the solid

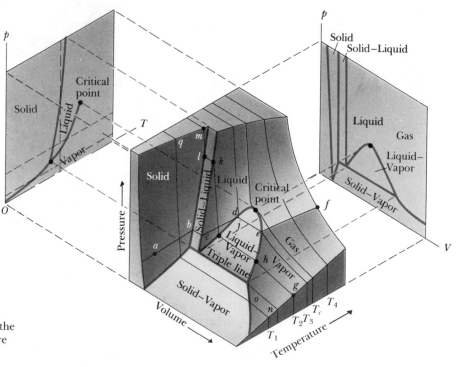

17–6

pVT-surface for a substance that
expands on melting. Projections of the
surface on the *pT*- and *pV*-planes are
also shown.

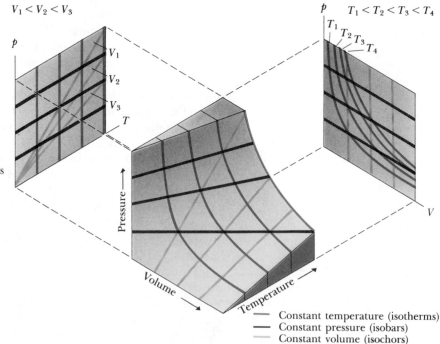

17–7

pVT-surface for an ideal gas. At the
left, each light color line corresponds
to a certain constant volume; at the
right, each dark color line corresponds
to a certain constant temperature.

——— Constant temperature (isotherms)
——— Constant pressure (isobars)
——— Constant volume (isochors)

region *lm* than in the vapor region *gh*. Finally, *nopq* represents isothermal solidification directly from the vapor phase; this is the process that is involved in epitaxial growth of crystals directly from vapor, as in the formation of snowflakes. These three lines on the *pVT*-surface are worth careful study.

For contrast, Fig. 17–7 shows the much simpler *pVT*-surface for a substance that obeys the ideal-gas equation of state under all conditions. The projections of the constant-temperature curves onto the *pV*-plane correspond to the curves of Fig. 17–2, and the projections of the constant-volume curves onto the *pT*-plane show the direct proportionality of pressure to absolute temperature (Charles' law).

*17–5
Vapor Pressure and Humidity

When the vapor phase of any substance is in equilibrium with the liquid or solid phase of the same substance, at any temperature, the pressure is called the **vapor pressure** of the substance at that temperature. For any given substance the vapor pressure depends only on temperature, not on volume or amount of substance. For example, suppose we have a container with liquid water and water vapor, and we keep the container at constant temperature. We try to increase the pressure by decreasing the volume. If the temperature is constant, what happens instead is that some of the vapor condenses, and the pressure of vapor does not change. Heat of vaporization has to be removed to keep the temperature constant.

The vapor pressure of a substance at a particular temperature is independent of other gases that may be present. For example, liquid water may be in equilibrium with air containing water vapor. At 60°C the vapor pressure of water is about 0.2×10^5 Pa, or about 0.2 atm. If liquid water and water vapor are in equilibrium, and the total pressure is 1.0 atm, then the partial pressure of water vapor is 0.2 atm, and the partial pressure of air (the sum of the partial pressures of its constituents) is about 0.8 atm. Table 17–3 shows the vapor pressure of water at various temperatures.

The vapor pressure of a substance always increases rapidly with temperature. The *boiling* temperature at any given total atmospheric pressure is the temperature at which vapor pressure is equal to atmospheric pressure. When water boils in a teakettle, bubbles of steam form on the bottom (where the heat is being added) and rise to the surface. If the vapor pressure inside the bubbles is not as great as atmospheric pressure, then the atmospheric pressure collapses the bubbles, or rather prevents them from forming at all.

Water boils at lower temperatures at higher elevations because of the smaller atmospheric pressure. For example, Denver is about 1600 m above sea level; atmospheric pressure there is about 0.82 atm, and the boiling temperature of water is about 95°C. At the summit of Mount

TABLE 17–3 Vapor pressure of water	
T, °C	**Vapor pressure, Pa**
0	0.00610×10^5
5	0.00868×10^5
10	0.0119×10^5
15	0.0169×10^5
20	0.0233×10^5
40	0.0734×10^5
60	0.199×10^5
80	0.473×10^5
100	$\mathbf{1.01 \times 10^5}$
120	1.99×10^5
140	3.61×10^5
160	6.17×10^5
180	10.0×10^5
200	15.5×10^5
220	23.2×10^5

Everest, 8882 m above sea level, atmospheric pressure is about 0.33 atm, and the boiling temperature is about 72°C. Any food-cooking process that involves boiling water takes longer at higher elevations because of the reduced temperatures. Moutaineering expeditions sometimes carry lightweight pressure cookers to permit cooking at pressures of up to 2 atm or so, with corresponding boiling temperature of 120°C (248°F). The extra weight of the cooker is offset by the reduced fuel needs.

Humidity is water vapor in the atmosphere. The mass of water vapor per unit volume of air is called the **absolute humidity.** Water-vapor content can also be described in terms of its partial pressure. As we mentioned at the end of Section 17–2, the total pressure of the atmosphere (or any mixture of ideal gases) is the sum of the partial pressures of the component gases. The partial pressure of atmospheric water vapor usually ranges from about 0.002 to 0.05×10^5 Pa, or about 0.002 to 0.05 atm.

This partial pressure, at any given air temperature, can never exceed the vapor pressure of water at that temperature. From Table 17–3 the partial pressure at 10°C (50°F) cannot exceed 0.0119×10^5 Pa, and at 40°C (104°F) it cannot exceed 0.0734×10^5 Pa. If there is enough water vapor that its partial pressure is *equal* to the vapor pressure, the vapor is *saturated*. The ratio of the partial pressure to the vapor pressure at the same temperature is called the **relative humidity;** it is usually expressed as a percentage:

$$\text{Relative humidity (\%)} = (100\%) \; \frac{\text{partial pressure of water vapor}}{\text{vapor pressure at same temperature}}.$$

The relative humidity is 100% if the vapor is saturated and zero if no water vapor at all is present. Saturation can be brought about either by increasing the water vapor content or by lowering the temperature.

Example 17–3 Suppose the partial pressure of water vapor in the atmosphere is 0.010×10^5 Pa and the temperature is 20°C. Find the relative humidity.

Solution From Table 17–3 the vapor pressure at 20°C is 0.0233×10^5 Pa, so

$$\text{Relative humidity} = \frac{0.010 \times 10^5 \text{ Pa}}{0.0233 \times 10^5 \text{ Pa}} \; (100\%) = 43\%. \qquad \blacksquare$$

Example 17–4 In Example 17–3, at what temperature does saturation (or 100% relative humidity) occur?

Solution At the temperature asked for, the vapor pressure of water is 0.010×10^5 Pa. By interpolating in Table 17–3 we find that this occurs at about 7°C.

$\qquad\qquad\qquad\qquad\qquad\qquad\qquad\qquad\qquad\qquad\qquad\qquad\qquad$ $\blacksquare$

The temperature at which water vapor becomes saturated is called the **dew point.** In Example 17–4, if we lower the temperature *below* 7°C, the vapor pressure is less than 0.01×10^5 Pa. The partial pressure is then higher than the vapor pressure, and vapor condenses until the partial pressure is equal to the vapor pressure at the lower temperature. This process causes the formation of clouds, fog, and rain. At night, when the earth's surface is cooled by radiation, the condensed moisture is called *dew*. If the partial pressure is so low that the temperature must fall below 0°C before condensation occurs, the vapor condenses directly into ice crystals in the form of frost or snow, the opposite of sublimation.

A simple procedure for determining relative humidity uses two liquid-filled thermometers. The bulb of one is dry, and the bulb of the other is kept wet by means of a wick dipping in water. The wet bulb cools by evaporation, and its final temperature is the temperature at which the water vapor in the surrounding air becomes saturated. In practice the relative humidity corresponding to any pair of wet- and dry-bulb temperatures is read from a table. In very low humidity the wet-bulb temperature may be as much as 20 C° below that of the dry bulb. The principle is the same as that of evaporative cooling, discussed in Section 15–5.

The *rate* of evaporation of water from a water–air surface depends on the relative humidity; evaporation is fastest with low humidity. At 100% relative humidity, *no* evaporation can take place. The added discomfort that high relative humidity brings to a hot summer day is familiar. "It's not the heat; it's the humidity!" At high relative humidity the effectiveness of evaporative cooling of the body is reduced. But in hot dry desert climates, evaporative cooling makes it possible to maintain normal body temperature (37°C or 98.6°F) even when the air temperature may reach 55°C (about 130°F). As we mentioned in Section 15–5, you can sweat as much as 2 gallons a day in such climates, and you have to drink lots of water to stay alive.

Questions

17–1 If the ideal-gas model were perfectly valid at all temperatures, what would be the volume of a gas when the temperature is absolute zero?

17–2 In the ideal-gas equation of state, could Celsius temperature be used instead of Kelvin if an appropriate numerical value of the gas constant R were used?

17–3 Comment on this statement:

Equal masses of two different gases, placed in containers of equal volume at equal temperature, must exert equal pressures.

17–4 When a car is driven some distance, the air pressure in the tires increases. Why? Should you let some air out to reduce the pressure?

17–5 Section 17–1 states that pressure, volume, and temperature cannot change individually without one affecting the others. Yet when a liquid evaporates, its volume changes, even though its pressure and temperature are constant. Is this inconsistent?

17–6 At low pressure or high temperature, gas behavior deviates from the ideal-gas model. One reason is the finite size of gas molecules. From these deviations, how could we estimate what fraction of the total volume in a gas is occupied by the molecules themselves?

17–7 Radiator caps in automobile engines release coolant when the pressure reaches a certain value, typically 15 psi or so. Why is it desirable to have the coolant under pressure? Why not just seal the system completely?

17–8 People speak of being angry enough to make

their blood boil. Could your blood boil if you went to a high enough altitude? Is the pressure of your blood the same as atmospheric pressure? Does this matter?

17–9 Can it be too cold for good ice skating? What about skiing? Does a thin layer of ice under the skis melt?

17–10 Why does the air cool off more on a clear night than on a cloudy night? Desert areas often have exceptionally large day–night temperature variations. Why?

17–11 On a chilly evening you can "see your breath." Can you really? What are you really seeing? Does this phenomenon depend on the temperature of the air, the humidity, or both?

17–12 Why do frozen water pipes burst? Would a mercury thermometer break if the temperature went below the freezing temperature of mercury?

17–13 Why does moisture condense on the insides of windows on cold days? If it is cold enough outside, frost will form, but only when the outside temperature is far below freezing. Why is this so? Why are the bottoms frostier than the tops? How do storm windows change the situation?

17–14 "It's not the heat; it's the humidity!" Why are you more uncomfortable on a hot day when the humidity is high than when it is low?

17–15 Why does a shower room get steamy or foggy when the hot water runs for a long time?

17–16 The critical volumes of several substances are listed in Table 17–2, and with a few exceptions they are all in the range of 50 to 100×10^{-6} m³·mol⁻¹. Why is there not more variation?

17–17 Why do flames from a fire always go up rather than down?

17–18 Unwrapped food placed in a freezer experiences dehydration, known as "freezer burn." Why? The same process, carried out intentionally, is called "freeze-drying." For freeze-drying, the food is usually frozen first and then placed in a partial vacuum. Why? What advantages might freeze-drying have in comparison to ordinary drying?

17–19 An old or burned-out incandescent light bulb usually has a dark gray area on part of the inside of the bulb. What is this? Why is it not a uniform deposit all over the inside of the bulb?

17–20 Why do glasses containing cold liquids sweat in warm weather? Glasses containing alcoholic drinks sometimes form frost on the outside. How can this happen?

17–21 Why does a person perspire more when working hard than when resting?

17–22 Hiking down a steep trail ought to be much easier than hiking up, yet people perspire a lot when descending a steep trail. Why?

17–23 In a hot desert climate a person can survive a lot longer without food than without water. Why?

Exercises

Section 17–2   Ideal Gases

17–1 A cylindrical tank has a tight-fitting piston that allows the volume of the tank to be changed. The tank originally contains 0.120 m³ of air at a pressure of 1.00 atm. The piston is slowly pushed in until the volume of the gas is decreased to 0.0300 m³. If the temperature remains constant, what is the final value of the pressure?

17–2 Helium gas with a volume of 1.40 L, under a pressure of 3.00 atm and at a temperature of 57.0°C, is heated until both pressure and volume are doubled.

  a) What is the final temperature?

  b) How many grams of helium are there? The atomic mass of helium is 4.00 g·mol⁻¹.

17–3 A 2.00-L tank contains air at 1.00 atm and 20.0°C. The tank is sealed and heated until the pressure is 4.00 atm.

  a) What is the temperature now in degrees Celsius? Assume that the volume of the tank is constant.

  b) If the temperature is kept at the value found in part (a) and the gas is permitted to expand, what is the volume when the pressure again becomes 1.00 atm?

17–4 A 20.0-L tank contains 0.360 kg of helium at 27.0°C.

  a) What is the number of moles of helium? The atomic mass of helium is 4.00 g·mol⁻¹.

  b) What is the pressure in pascals? In atmospheres?

17–5 A room with dimensions 5.00 m × 6.00 m × 3.00 m is filled with pure oxygen at 20.0°C and 1.00 atm.

  a) What is the number of moles of oxygen?

  b) What is the mass of oxygen in kilograms? The molecular mass of oxygen is 32.0 g·mol⁻¹.

17–6 A tank contains 0.460 kg of nitrogen gas at a pressure of 50.0 atm. What mass of oxygen would an identical tank contain, also at 50.0 atm and at the same temperature? The molecular mass of nitrogen (N_2) is 28.0 g·mol^{-1}, and that of oxygen (O_2) is 32.0 g·mol^{-1}.

17–7 A large cylindrical tank with a tight-fitting piston that allows the volume to be changed contains 0.500 m^3 of nitrogen at 27°C and 1.50×10^5 Pa (absolute pressure). What is the pressure if the volume is increased to 3.00 m^3 and the temperature is increased to 327°C?

17–8 A tank with a volume of 2.50 L will burst if the absolute pressure of the gas it contains exceeds 100 atm. If 6.0 moles of an ideal gas is put into the tank at a temperature of 23.0°C, to what temperature can the gas be heated before the tank ruptures? Neglect the thermal expansion of the tank.

17–9 The total lung volume for a typical physics student is 6.0 L. A physics student fills her lungs with air at an absolute pressure of 1.0 atm. Then, holding her breath, she compresses her chest cavity, decreasing her lung volume to 5.5 L. What is then the pressure of the air in her lungs? Assume that the temperature of the air remains constant.

17–10 At the beginning of the compression stroke a cylinder of a diesel engine contains 800 cm^3 of air at atmospheric pressure (1.01×10^5 Pa) and a temperature of 27.0°C. At the end of the stroke the air has been compressed to a volume of 75.0 cm^3, and the gauge pressure has increased to 2.78×10^6 Pa. Compute the final temperature.

17–11 A diver observes a bubble of air rising from the bottom of a lake, where the pressure is 3.50 atm, to the surface, where the pressure is 1.00 atm. The temperature at the bottom is 7.0°C, and the temperature at the surface is 27.0°C. What is the ratio of the volume of the bubble as it reaches the surface to its volume at the bottom?

17–12

a) Derive from the equation of state of an ideal gas an equation for the density of an ideal gas in terms of pressure, temperature, and appropriate constants.

b) What is the density of air in kilograms per cubic meter at 1.00 atm and 27.0°C? The average molecular mass of air is 28.8 g·mol^{-1}.

17–13 The gas inside a balloon will always have a pressure equal to atmospheric pressure, since that is the pressure applied to the outside of the balloon. You fill a balloon with an ideal gas to a volume of 1.00 L at a temperature of 27.0°C. What is the volume of the balloon if you cool it to the boiling point of liquid nitrogen (77.3 K)?

Section 17–4   Phase Diagrams, Triple Point, Critical Point

17–14 Solid nitrogen is slowly heated from a very low

temperature.

a) What minimum external pressure p_1 must be applied to the solid if a melting phase transition is to be observed? Describe the sequence of phase transitions that occur if the applied pressure p is such that $p < p_1$.

b) Above a certain maximum pressure p_2, no liquid-to-vapor (boiling) transition is observed. What is the pressure? Describe the sequence of phase transitions that occur as the nitrogen is heated if $p_1 < p < p_2$.

17–15 Calculate the volume of 1.00 mol of liquid water at a temperature of 20°C (use Table 14–3), and compare this to the volume occupied by 1.00 mol of water at the critical point. Water has a molecular mass of 18.0 g·mol^{-1}.

17–16 A physicist places a piece of ice at 0.00°C alongside a beaker of water at 0.00°C in a glass vessel, from which all the air is then removed. If the ice, water, and vessel are all maintained at a temperature of 0.00°C by a suitable thermostat, describe the final equilibrium state inside the vessel.

Section 17–5   Vapor Pressure and Humidity

17–17

a) What is the relative humidity on a day when the temperature is 20°C and the dew point is 10°C?

b) What is the partial pressure of water vapor in the atmosphere?

c) What is the absolute humidity in kilograms per cubic meter? The molecular mass of water is 18.0 g·mol^{-1}. Use the expression derived in Exercise 17–12a.

17–18 On a cool day the temperature is 15°C, and the partial pressure of water vapor in the atmosphere is 0.0119×10^5 Pa.

a) What is the relative humidity?

b) What is the dew-point temperature?

17–19 The temperature in a room is 40°C. A meteorologist cools a metal can by gradually adding cold water. At 15°C the surface of the can clouds over. What is the relative humidity in the room?

17–20

a) What is the dew-point temperature on a day when the air temperature is 20°C and the relative humidity is 37.3%?

b) What is the absolute humidity, expressed in grams per cubic meter? The molecular mass of water is 18.0 g·mol^{-1}. Use the expression derived in Exercise 17–12a.

Problems

17–21 A glassblower makes a barometer from a tube 0.900 m long with a cross-sectional area of 0.450 cm². Mercury stands in this tube to a height of 0.750 m. The room temperature is 27.0°C. A small amount of nitrogen is introduced into the evacuated space above the mercury, and the column drops to a height of 0.700 m. How many grams of nitrogen were introduced? The molecular mass of nitrogen (N_2) is 28.0 g·mol⁻¹.

17–22 Partial vacuums in which the residual gas pressure is about 1.00×10^{-10} atm are not difficult to obtain with modern technology. Calculate the mass of nitrogen present in a volume of 3000 cm³ at this pressure if the temperature of the gas is 27.0°C. The molecular mass of nitrogen (N_2) is 28.0 g·mol⁻¹.

17–23 A bicyclist uses a tire pump whose cylinder is initially full of air at an absolute pressure of 1.01×10^5 Pa. The length of stroke of the pump (the length of the cylinder) is 36.0 cm. At what part of the stroke (i.e., what length of the air column) does air begin to enter a tire in which the gauge pressure is 2.76×10^5 Pa? Assume that the temperature remains constant during the compression.

17–24 An automobile tire has a volume of 0.0150 m³ on a cold day when the temperature of the air in the tire is 0.0°C and atmospheric pressure is 1.03 atm. Under these conditions the gauge pressure is measured to be 2.45 atm (about 36.0 lb·in⁻²). After the car has been driven on the highway for 30 min, the temperature of the air in the tires has risen to 47.0°C and the volume to 0.0160 m³. What then is the gauge pressure? Neglect the thermal expansion of the tire.

17–25 A welder using a tank having a volume of 0.0600 m³ fills it with oxygen (whose molecular mass is 32.0 g·mol⁻¹) at a gauge pressure of 4.00×10^5 Pa and a temperature of 47.0°C. The tank has a small leak, and in time some of the gas leaks out. On a day when the temperature is 27.0°C the gauge pressure of the gas in the tank is 3.00×10^5 Pa. Find

a) the initial mass of oxygen;

b) the mass that has leaked out.

17–26 The submarine *Squalus* sank at a point where the depth of water is 73.0 m. The temperature at the surface is 27.0°C, and at the bottom it is 7.0°C. The density of seawater is 1030 kg·m⁻³.

a) If a diving bell in the form of a circular cylinder 2.80 m high, open at the bottom and closed at the top, is lowered to this depth, to what height will water rise within the diving bell when it reaches the bottom?

b) At what gauge pressure must compressed air be

supplied to the bell while it is on the bottom to expel all the water from it?

17–27 A flask of volume 1.60 L, provided with a stopcock, contains oxygen (whose molecular mass is 32.0 g·mol⁻¹) at 300 K and atmospheric pressure (1.013×10^5 Pa). The system is heated to a temperature of 400 K, with the stopcock open to the atmosphere. The stopcock is then closed, and the flask cooled to its original temperature.

a) What is the final pressure of the oxygen in the flask?

b) How many grams of oxygen remain in the flask?

17–28 A hot-air balloon makes use of the fact that hot air at atmospheric pressure is less dense than cooler air at the same pressure; the buoyant force is calculated as discussed in Chapter 13. If the volume of the balloon is 500 m³ and the surrounding air is at 0°C, what must be the temperature of the air in the balloon for it to lift a total load of 300 kg (in addition to the mass of the hot air)? The density of air at 0°C and atmospheric pressure is 1.29 kg·m⁻³.

17–29 A balloon whose volume is 500 m³ is to be filled with hydrogen at atmospheric pressure (1.01×10^5 Pa).

a) If the hydrogen is stored in cylinders of volume 2.50 m³ at an absolute pressure of 35.0×10^5 Pa, how many cylinders are required? Assume that the temperature of the hydrogen remains constant.

b) What is the total weight (in addition to the weight of the gas) that can be supported by the balloon if the gas in the balloon and the surrounding air are both at 0°C? The molecular mass of hydrogen (H_2) is 2.02 g·mol⁻¹. The density of air at 0°C and atmospheric pressure is 1.29 kg·m⁻³.

c) What weight could be supported if the balloon were filled with helium (with an atomic mass of 4.00 g·mol⁻¹) instead of hydrogen, again at 0°C?

17–30 The volume of a closed hospital room, kept at a constant temperature of 20°C, is 32.0 m³. The relative humidity in the room is initially 10.0%. If a nurse brings a large pan of water into the room, how many kilograms of water must evaporate to raise the relative humidity to 30.0%? The molecular mass of water is 18.0 g·mol⁻¹.

17–31 An engineer was hired to design an air-conditioning system to increase the relative humidity of 0.400 m³ of air per second from 30.0% to 65.0%. The air temperature is 20°C. How many kilograms of water are needed by the system per hour? The molecular mass of water is 18.0 g·mol⁻¹.

Challenge Problems

17–32 A vertical cylindrical tank 0.900 m high has its top end closed by a tightly fitting frictionless piston of negligible weight. The air inside the cylinder is at an absolute pressure of 1.00 atm. The piston is depressed by pouring mercury on it slowly. How far will the piston descend before mercury spills over the top of the cylinder? The temperature of the air is maintained constant.

17–33 A large tank of water has a hose connected to it, as shown in Fig. 17–8. The tank is sealed at the top and has compressed air between the water surface and the top. When the water height h_2 has the value 3.00 m, the absolute pressure p_1 is 2.50×10^5 Pa. Assume that the air above the water expands isothermally (i.e., at constant T). Take the atmospheric pressure to be 1.00×10^5 Pa.

a) What is the speed of flow out of the hose when $h_2 = 3.00$ m?

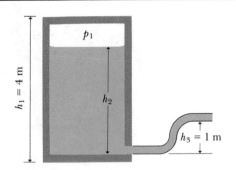

FIGURE 17–8

b) As water flows out of the tank, h_2 decreases. Calculate the speed of flow for $h_2 = 2.00$ m and $h_2 = 1.60$ m.

c) At what value of h_2 does the flow stop?

18

The First Law
of Thermodynamics

Energy relationships are of central importance in the study of energy-conversion devices such as engines, batteries, and refrigerators and also in the functioning of living organisms. *Thermodynamics* is the study of energy relationships that involve heat, mechanical work, and other aspects of energy and energy transfer. The first law of thermodynamics is an extension of the principle of conservation of energy to include both heat and mechanical energy.

Conservation of energy plays a vital role in every area of physical science, and the first law has an extremely broad area of usefulness. To state energy relationships precisely, we use the concept of a *thermodynamic system*, and we discuss *heat* and *work* as two means of transferring energy into or out of such a system. Emerging from this discussion is the concept of *internal energy* of a system.

18–1
Energy, Heat, and Work

We have studied energy transfer through mechanical work (Chapter 7) and through heat transfer (Chapters 15 and 16); now we are ready to combine and generalize these principles. Our formulation will always refer to some specific system, usually a specified quantity of material, a particular device, or an organism. A **thermodynamic system** is a system that can interact with its surroundings in at least two ways, one of which must be heat transfer. A familiar example is a quantity of a gas confined in a cylinder with a piston. Energy can be added to the system by conduction of heat, and the system can also do *work* as the gas exerts a force on the piston and moves it through a displacement.

The concept of a system is familiar. In Chapters 4, 5, and 9 we used free-body diagrams to help identify the forces acting on a particular mechanical system. In Chapter 8 we studied the principle of conservation of momentum for an isolated mechanical system. In both of these examples it is essential to define clearly at the outset precisely what is and is not included in the system. This is also true of thermodynamic systems; we must always be careful to specify clearly what is and is not included in the system we are considering and to describe unambiguously the energy transfers into and out of that system.

As we have mentioned, thermodynamics has its roots in practical problems. The engine in an automobile and the jet engines in an airplane use the heat of combustion of their fuel to perform mechanical work in propelling the vehicle. Muscle tissue in living organisms metabolizes chemical energy in food and performs mechanical work on the surroundings of the organism. A steam engine or steam turbine uses the heat of combustion of coal or other fuel to perform mechanical work such as driving an electric generator, pulling a train, or performing some other useful function.

In all these situations we will describe the energy relations in terms of the quantity of heat Q added *to* the system and the work W done *by* the system. Both Q and W may be positive or negative. A positive value of Q represents heat flow *into* the system, with a corresponding input of energy to it; negative Q represents heat flow *out of* the system. A positive value of W represents work done *by* the system against its surroundings, such as an expanding gas, and hence corresponds to energy leaving the system. Negative W, such as compression of a gas in which work is done *on it* by its surroundings, represents energy entering the system. We will use these conventions consistently in the examples in this chapter and the next.

Heat can also be understood on the basis of *microscopic* mechanical energy, that is, the kinetic and potential energies of individual molecules in a material; and it is possible to develop the principles of thermodynamics from a microscopic viewpoint. In this chapter we deliberately avoid that development. There's a good reason for this; it is important to emphasize that the central principles and concepts of thermodynamics can be treated in a completely *macroscopic* way, without reference to microscopic models. Indeed, part of the great power and generality of thermodynamics springs from the fact that it *does not* depend on details of the structure of matter. However, in Chapter 20 we will return to microscopic considerations and will look at their relation to the principles of thermodynamics.

18–2
Work Done during Volume Changes

A gas in a cylinder with a movable piston is a simple example of a thermodynamic system. In the next several sections we will use this system as an example as we explore several kinds of processes that involve energy considerations. Let's look first at the *work* done by the system during a volume change. When a gas expands, it pushes out on its boundary surfaces as they move outward; an expanding gas always does positive work. The same thing is true of any solid or fluid material confined under pressure. Figure 18–1 shows a solid or fluid in a cylinder with a moveable piston. Suppose that the cylinder has cross-sectional area A and that the pressure exerted by the system at the piston face is p. The force F exerted on the piston by the system is therefore $F = pA$. When the piston moves out a small distance Δx, the work ΔW done by this force is

$$\Delta W = F \, \Delta x = pA \, \Delta x.$$

But

$$A \, \Delta x = \Delta V,$$

where ΔV is the change of volume of the system. Thus we can express the work done by the system as

$$\Delta W = p \, \Delta V. \tag{18–1}$$

If the pressure remains constant while the volume changes by a finite amount, say from V_1 to V_2, the total work W done by the system is

$$W = p(V_2 - V_1) \quad \text{(constant pressure only).} \tag{18–2}$$

But what if the pressure is *not* constant during the expansion? Suppose, for example, that we let an ideal gas expand, keeping its temperature constant. The product pV is constant, so as the volume V increases, the pressure p must decrease. This problem is very similar to the work done by a varying force, which we studied in Section 7–3, and we can handle it in the same way. We divide the total volume change into many small changes $\Delta V_1, \Delta V_2, \ldots$, each so small that we can consider the pressure to be constant within each one. Calling the various pressures $p_1, p_2, \ldots$, we represent the total work as

$$W = p_1 \, \Delta V_1 + p_2 \, \Delta V_2 + \cdots.$$

As we take the ΔV's smaller and smaller, this approximation becomes more and more precise.

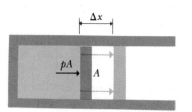

18–1
Force exerted *by* a system during a small expansion. The force on the piston is pA, and the work done by the system is $(pA) \, \Delta x = p \, \Delta V$.

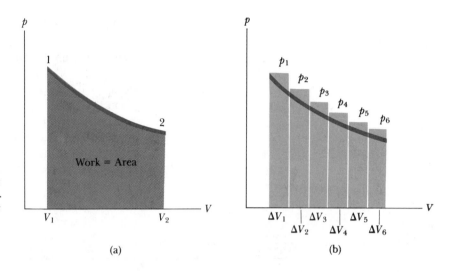

18–2
(a) The work done when a substance changes its volume and pressure is the area under the curve on a pV-diagram. (b) The total area is approximately the sum of the rectangular areas $p_1 \, \Delta V_1$, $p_2 \, \Delta V_2$, and so on.

Let's also draw a graph showing the variation of p with V, as in Fig. 18–2, with pressure p on the vertical axis and volume V on the horizontal axis. Then each product $p_1 \, \Delta V_1$, $p_2 \, \Delta V_2$, and so on corresponds to the area of one of the rectangles in Fig. 18–2b, and the sum of these areas is approximately equal to the total area under the curve between V_1 and V_2. As the ΔV's become smaller and smaller, the approximation gets better and better. So we have the general result that

$$W = \text{Area under a curve on a } pV\text{-diagram.} \qquad (18\text{–}3)$$

According to the sign rule that we stated in Section 18–1, W is always the work done *by* the system, and it is always *positive* when a system *expands*. When a system expands from state 1 to state 2 in Fig. 18–2, the area is positive. In a *compression* from 2 to 1, all the ΔV's are negative, and the total work done by the system on the piston is negative. This corresponds to a *negative* area; when a system is compressed, its volume decreases, and it does *negative* work on its surroundings.

When a system undergoes a change of state from an initial state to a final state, the system passes through a series of intermediate states; we call this series of states a **path.** There are always infinitely many different possibilities for these intermediate states. When they are all equilibrium states, the path can be plotted on a pV-diagram, as in Fig. 18–3. Points 1 and 2 represent an initial state (1) with pressure p_1 and volume V_1 and a final state (2) with pressure p_2 and volume V_2. For example, we can keep the pressure constant at p_1 while the system expands to volume V_2 (point 3 on the diagram) and then reduce the pressure to p_2 (probably by decreasing the temperature) while keeping the volume constant at V_2 (to point 2 on the diagram). The work done by the system during this process is the area under the line $1 \rightarrow 3$; it does no work during the constant-volume process $3 \rightarrow 2$. Or the system might traverse the path $1 \rightarrow 4 \rightarrow 2$; in that case the work is the area under the line $4 \rightarrow 2$. The wiggly line and the smooth curve from 1 to 2 are two other possibilities, and the work is different for each one.

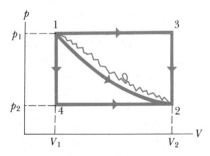

18–3
Several paths from state 1 to state 2 shown on a pV-diagram. The work is different for each path.

We conclude that *the work done by the system depends not only on the initial and final states but also on the intermediate states, that is, on the path.* Furthermore, we can take the system through a series of states forming a closed loop, such as $1 \rightarrow 3 \rightarrow 2 \rightarrow 4 \rightarrow 1$. In this case the final state is the same as the initial state, but the total work done by the system is *not* zero. (In fact, it is represented on the graph by the *area* enclosed by the loop; can you prove that? See Problem 18–4.) It follows that it doesn't make sense to talk about the amount of work contained in a system in a particular state; such a concept has no meaning. In this respect the character of work is very different from that of the state coordinates p, V, and T.

18–3
Heat Transfer during Volume Changes

We have learned that *heat* is energy that is transferred into or out of a system when there is a temperature difference between the system and its surroundings. Heat transfer and work (discussed in Section 18–2) are two means by which the energy of a thermodynamic system may increase or decrease.

The discussion of Section 18–2 showed that when a thermodynamic system undergoes a change of state, the *work* done by the system depends not only on the initial and final states but also on the series of intermediate states through which it passes, that is, on the *path* from the initial state to the final state. We will now show that the *heat* added to the system in such a process also depends on the path.

Here is an example. We want to change the volume of a certain quantity of an ideal gas from 2.0 L to 5.0 L while keeping the temperature constant at $T = 300$ K. Figure 18–4 shows two different ways in which we can do this. In Fig. 18–4a the gas is contained in a cylinder with a piston, with an initial volume of 2.0 L. We let the gas expand slowly, supplying heat from the electric heater to keep the temperature at 300 K. After expanding in this slow, controlled, isothermal manner the gas reaches its final volume of 5.0 L, having absorbed a definite amount of heat in the process.

Figure 18–4b shows a different process leading to the same final state. The container is surrounded by insulating walls and is divided by a thin, breakable partition into two compartments. The lower part has a volume of 2.0 L, and the upper part has a volume of 3.0 L. In the lower compartment we place the same amount of the same gas as in Fig. 18–4a, again at $T = 300$ K. The initial state is the same as before. Now we break the partition; the gas undergoes a rapid, uncontrolled expansion, with no heat passing through the insulating walls. The final volume is 5.0 L, the same as in Fig. 18–4a. This uncontrolled expansion of a gas into vacuum is called a **free expansion;** we will discuss it further in Section 18–6. Experiments have shown that when an ideal gas undergoes a free expansion, there is no temperature change. Therefore the final state of the gas is the same as in Fig. 18–4a. The intermediate states (pressures and volumes) during the transition from state 1 to state 2 are

Gas at 300 K

Electric stove at 300 K

(a)

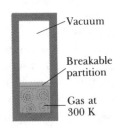

Vacuum

Breakable partition

Gas at 300 K

(b)

18–4
(a) Slow, controlled isothermal expansion of a gas from an initial state 1 to a final state 2. (b) Rapid, uncontrolled expansion of the same gas starting at the same state 1 and ending at the same state 2.

entirely different in the two cases; Figs. 18–4a and 18–4b represent *two different paths* connecting the *same states* 1 and 2. For the path in Fig. 18–4b, *no* heat is transferred into the system, and it does no work. Like work, *heat depends not only on the initial and final states but also on the path*.

Because of this path dependence, it would not make sense to say that a system "contains" a certain quantity of heat. Look what happens if we try to develop such an idea. Suppose we assign an arbitrary value to "the heat in a body" in some standard reference state. Then presumably the "heat in the body" in some other state would equal the heat in the reference state plus the heat added when the body goes to the second state. But that's ambiguous, as we have just seen; the heat added depends on the *path* we take from the reference state to the second state. We are forced to conclude that there is no consistent way to define "heat in a body"; it is not a useful concept. It *does* make sense, however, to speak of the amount of *internal energy* in a body; this important concept is our next topic.

18–4
Internal Energy and the First Law

The concept of internal energy is one of the most important concepts in thermodynamics. We can look at it in various ways, some simple, some subtle. Let's start with the simple. Matter consists of atoms and molecules, and these are made up of particles having kinetic and potential energies. We tentatively define the **internal energy** of a system as the sum of all the kinetic and potential energies of its constituent particles. We use the symbol U for internal energy. During a change of state of the system the internal energy may change from an initial value U_1 to a final value U_2; we denote the change in internal energy as $\Delta U = U_2 - U_1$.

We also know that heat transfer is energy transfer. When we add a quantity of heat Q to a system and it does no work during the process, the internal energy should increase by an amount equal to Q; that is, $\Delta U = Q$. When a system does work W by expanding against its surroundings and no heat is added during the process, energy leaves the system, and the internal energy decreases. That is, when W is positive, ΔU is negative, and conversely, so $\Delta U = -W$. When *both* heat transfer and work occur, the *total* change in internal energy is

$$U_2 - U_1 = \Delta U = Q - W. \tag{18–4}$$

We can rearrange this into the form

$$Q = \Delta U + W. \tag{18–5}$$

Translation: When heat Q is added to a system, some of this added energy remains within the system, increasing its internal energy by an amount ΔU; the remainder leaves the system again as it does work W against its surroundings. Because W and Q may be either positive or negative, we also expect ΔU to be positive for some processes and negative for others.

Equation (18–4) or (18–5) is the **first law of thermodynamics.** It represents a generalization of the principle of conservation of energy to include energy transfer through heat as well as mechanical work. We studied conservation of energy in Chapter 7 in a purely *mechanical* context, and it seems reasonable that it should have this more general validity. Nevertheless, it is worth a somewhat closer look.

One problem is that defining internal energy in terms of microscopic kinetic and potential energies isn't entirely convincing. Actually *calculating* this total energy for any real system would be hopelessly complicated. We can't use this as an *operational* definition because it doesn't describe how to determine internal energy from physical quantities that we can measure directly. So we need to backtrack a little to show clearly the empirical and experimental basis of the first law of thermodynamics.

Starting over, we *define* the internal energy change ΔU in any change of a system as the quantity given by Eq. (18–4). This *is* an operational definition because we can measure Q and W. It does not define U itself, only ΔU. This is not a serious shortcoming; we can *define* the internal energy of a system to have a specified value in some reference state and then use Eq. (18–4) to define the internal energy in any other state. This is analogous to our treatment of potential energy in Chapter 7, in which we arbitrarily defined the potential energy of a mechanical system to be zero at a certain position.

This new definition trades one difficulty for another. If we define ΔU via Eq. (18–4), then we have to ask the following question: If the system goes from some initial state to some final state, by two different paths, is ΔU necessarily the same for the two paths? We have already seen that in such a case, Q and W are in general *not* the same for different paths. If ΔU, which equals $Q - W$, is also path-dependent, then ΔU is ambiguous. In that case the concept of internal energy in a system is subject to the same criticism as the erroneous concept of quantity of heat in a system, as we discussed at the end of Section 18–3.

The only way to answer this question is through *experiment*. We study the properties of various materials; in particular, we measure Q and W for various changes of state and various paths in order to learn whether ΔU is or is not path-dependent. The results of many such investigations are clear and unambiguous: ΔU *is independent of path*. The change in internal energy of a system during any thermodynamic process depends only on the initial and final states, *not* on the path leading from one to the other.

Experiment, then, is the ultimate justification for believing that in any state a thermodynamic system has a unique internal energy that depends only on the state the system is in. An equivalent statement is that the internal energy U of a system is a function of the state coordinates p, V, and T (or actually of any two of these, since the three variables are related by the equation of state).

Now let's return to the first law of thermodynamics. To say that the first law, given by Eq. (18–4) or (18–5), represents conservation of energy for thermodynamic processes is correct, as far as it goes. But there is an important *additional* part of the content of the first law, namely, the fact that internal energy depends only on the state of a system. In changes of state, the change in internal energy is path-independent.

All this may seem a little abstract if you are satisfied to think of internal energy as microscopic mechanical energy. There is nothing wrong with that view. But in the interest of precise *operational* definitions, internal energy, like heat, can and must be defined in a way that is independent of the detailed microscopic structure of the material.

If we take a system through a process that eventually returns it to its initial state (a *cyclic* process), the *total* internal energy change must be zero. Then

$$U_2 = U_1 \quad \text{and} \quad Q = W.$$

If a net quantity of work W is done by the system during this process, an equal amount of energy must have flowed into the system as heat Q. But there is no reason why either Q or W individually has to be zero.

An *isolated* system is one that does no work on its surroundings and has no heat flow. For any process taking place in an isolated system,

$$W = Q = 0 \quad \text{and} \quad U_2 - U_1 = \Delta U = 0.$$

In other words, *the internal energy of an isolated system is constant.*

PROBLEM-SOLVING STRATEGY: First Law of Thermodynamics

1. The internal energy change ΔU in any thermodynamic process or series of processes is independent of the path, no matter whether the substance is an ideal gas or not. This is of the utmost importance in the problems in this chapter and the next. Sometimes you will be given enough information about one path between given initial and final states to calculate ΔU for that path. Then you can use the fact that ΔU is the same for every other path between the same two states to relate the various energy quantities for other paths.

2. As usual, consistent units are essential. If p is in pascals and V is in cubic meters, then W is in joules. Otherwise, you may want to convert the pressure and volume units into pascals and cubic meters. If a heat capacity is given in terms of calories, the simplest procedure is usually to convert it to joules. Be especially careful with moles. When you use $n = m/M$ to convert between mass and number of moles, remember that if m is in kilograms, M must be in *kilograms* per mole. The usual units for M are *grams* per mole; be careful!

3. When a process consists of several distinct steps, it often helps to make a chart showing Q, W, and ΔU for each step. Put these quantities for each step on a different line, and arrange them so that the Q's, W's, and ΔU's form columns. Then you can apply the first law to each line; in addition, you can add each column and apply the first law to the sums. Do you see why?

Example 18–1   A particular thermodynamic process is shown in the pV-diagram of Fig. 18–5. In process ab, 600 J of heat are added to the system, and in process bd, 200 J of heat are added. Find (a) the internal energy change in process ab, (b) the internal energy change in process abd, and (c) the total heat added in process acd.

Solution

a) There is no volume change during process ab, so $W = 0$ and
   $$\Delta U = Q = 600 \text{ J.}$$

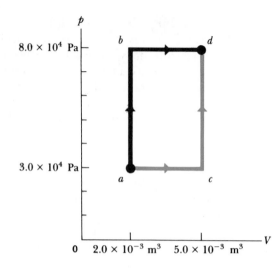

18–5
A pV-diagram for Example 18–1, showing the various thermodynamic processes.

b) Process bd occurs at constant pressure, so the work done by the system during this expansion is

$$W = p(V_2 - V_1)$$
$$= (8.0 \times 10^4 \text{ Pa})(5.0 \times 10^{-3} \text{ m}^3 - 2.0 \times 10^{-3} \text{ m}^3)$$
$$= 240 \text{ J.}$$

The total work for abd is $W = 240$ J, and the total heat is $Q = 800$ J. Applying Eq. (18–4) to abd, we find

$$\Delta U = Q - W = 800 \text{ J} - 240 \text{ J} = 560 \text{ J.}$$

c) Because ΔU is independent of path, the internal energy change is the same for path acd as for abd, that is, 560 J. The total work for the path acd is

$$W = p(V_2 - V_1)$$
$$= (3.0 \times 10^4 \text{ Pa})(5.0 \times 10^{-3} \text{ m}^3 - 2.0 \times 10^{-3} \text{ m}^3)$$
$$= 90 \text{ J.}$$

Now we apply Eq. (18–5) to process acd:

$$Q = \Delta U + W = 560 \text{ J} + 90 \text{ J} = 650 \text{ J.}$$

We see that although ΔU is the same for abd and acd, W and Q are quite different for the two processes. Here is a tabulation of the various quantities:

Process	Q	W	$\Delta U = Q - W$
ab	600 J	0	600 J
bd	200 J	240 J	−40 J
abd	800 J	240 J	560 J
acd	650 J	90 J	560 J

Example 18–2   One gram of water (1 cm^3) becomes 1671 cm^3 of steam when boiled at a constant pressure of 1 atm. The heat of vaporization at this pressure is 2256 J·g^{-1}. Compute (a) the work done by the water when it vaporizes and (b) its increase in internal energy.

Solution

a) For a constant-pressure process we may use Eq. (18–2) to compute the work done by the vaporizing water:

$$W = p(V_2 - V_1)$$
$$= (1.013 \times 10^5 \text{ Pa})(1671 \times 10^{-6} \text{ m}^3 - 1 \times 10^{-6} \text{ m}^3)$$
$$= 169 \text{ J}.$$

b) The heat added is the heat of vaporization:

$$Q = mL_V$$
$$= (1 \text{ g})(2256 \text{ J·g}^{-1}) = 2256 \text{ J}.$$

From the first law of thermodynamics, Eq. (18–4), the change in internal energy is

$$\Delta U = Q - W = 2256 \text{ J} - 169 \text{ J} = 2087 \text{ J}.$$

When 1 g of water vaporizes, 2256 J of heat are added. Most of this added energy, 2087 J, remains in the system as an increase in internal energy. The remaining 169 J leaves the system again as it does work against the surroundings while expanding from liquid to vapor. The increase in internal energy is associated with the intermolecular forces that hold the molecules together in the liquid state. Because the forces are attractive, the associated potential energies are greater when the molecules have been pulled apart to form the vapor state.   ■

18–5
Thermodynamic Processes

Here are four specific kinds of thermodynamic processes that occur often enough in practical problems to be worth special mention. With each process we can use a simplified form of the first law of thermodynamics, at least in some cases. Their characteristics can be summarized briefly as "no heat transfer," "constant volume," "constant pressure," and "constant temperature," respectively.

1. Adiabatic Process

An **adiabatic process** is one in which there is no heat transfer into or out of a system; in other words, $Q = 0$. We can prevent heat flow either by surrounding the system with thermally insulating material or by carrying out the process so quickly that there is not enough time for appreciable heat flow. From the first law we find that for every adiabatic process

$$U_2 - U_1 = \Delta U = -W \quad \text{(adiabatic process).} \qquad (18\text{–}6)$$

When a system expands under adiabatic conditions, W is positive, ΔU is negative, and the internal energy decreases. When a system is *compressed* adiabatically, W is negative and U increases. An increase of internal energy is often, though not always, accompanied by a rise in temperature.

The compression stroke in an internal-combustion engine is an example of a process that is approximately adiabatic. The temperature rises as the air–fuel mixture in the cylinder is compressed. Similarly, the expansion of the burned fuel during the power stroke is an approximately adiabatic expansion with a drop in temperature.

2. Isochoric Process

Isochoric means *constant-volume*. When the volume of a thermodynamic system is constant, it does no work on its surroundings. Then $W = 0$, and

$$U_2 - U_1 = \Delta U = Q \quad \text{(isochoric process).} \qquad (18\text{–}7)$$

In an isochoric process, all the heat added remains in the system as an increase in internal energy. Heating a gas in a closed constant-volume container is an example of an isochoric process.

3. Isobaric Process

Isobaric means *constant-pressure*. In general, *none* of the three quantities ΔU, Q, and W in the first law is zero, but calculating W is easy, as we saw in Section 18–2. For an isobaric process,

$$W = p(V_2 - V_1) \quad \text{(isobaric process).} \qquad (18\text{–}8)$$

Example 18–2 (Section 18–4) is an example of an isobaric process.

4. Isothermal Process

Isothermal means *constant-temperature*. For a process to be isothermal the system must remain in thermal equilibrium; this means that any heat flow into or out of the system must occur slowly enough to maintain thermal equilibrium. In general, *none* of the quantities ΔU, Q, and W is zero. Example 18–2 (Section 18–4) is an example of an isothermal process.

There are a few special cases, which we will consider later in this chapter, in which the internal energy of a system depends *only* on its temperature, not on its pressure or volume. The most familiar system having this property is an ideal gas. For these special systems, if the temperature is constant, the internal energy is also constant; $\Delta U = 0$ and $Q = W$. That is, any energy entering the system as heat Q must leave it again as work W done by the system. This does *not* hold for most systems other than ideal gases because in general the internal energy of a system depends on pressure as well as temperature, and it may vary even when T is constant.

18–6
Internal Energy of an Ideal Gas

We mentioned in Section 18–5 that for an ideal gas the internal energy U depends only on temperature, not on pressure or volume. To explore this special property in more detail, let's imagine a thermally insulated container with rigid walls, divided into two compartments by a partition, as in Fig. 18–4b. Suppose one compartment has a quantity of an ideal gas and the other contains only vacuum. When the partition is removed or broken, the gas expands to fill both parts of the container. This process is called a *free expansion*; the gas does no work on its surroundings because it does not have to push against moving walls of a container as it expands. From the first law, since both Q and W are zero, it follows that *during a free expansion the internal energy is constant*. This is true of any substance, whether it is an ideal gas or not.

Whether or not the *temperature* of a gas changes during a free expansion is an important question. Suppose the temperature *does* change while the internal energy stays the same; then we have to conclude that the internal energy depends on both the temperature and the volume, or on both the temperature and the pressure, but certainly not on the temperature alone. But if T is constant during a free expansion, when we know U is constant but both p and V change, then we have to conclude that U depends only on T not on p or V.

Many experiments have shown that when an ideal gas undergoes a free expansion, its temperature does not change. We conclude from this that *the internal energy of an ideal gas depends only on its temperature, not on its pressure or volume*. This property, in addition to the ideal-gas equation of state, is part of the ideal-gas model. We will use this property several times in the following sections.

For real gases that do not precisely obey the ideal-gas equation, experiments have shown that there is some temperature change during free expansions. For such gases the internal energy depends on the pressure as well as the temperature. From a microscopic viewpoint this is not surprising. Non-ideal gases usually have attractive intermolecular forces. When molecules move farther apart, the associated potential energies increase, and the kinetic energies decrease. Temperature is directly related to molecular kinetic energy, as we will see in Chapter 20. For such a gas a free expansion is accompanied by a drop in temperature.

18–7
Heat Capacities of an Ideal Gas

We defined specific heat capacity and molar heat capacity of a substance in Section 15–3 in terms of the quantity of heat needed to increase the temperature of a specified amount of the substance by a specified amount. You may want to review these definitions before proceeding with this section. We also remarked briefly in Section 15–4 that the specific or molar heat capacity of a substance depends on the conditions under which the heat is added. For example, the volume of the substance may be kept constant, or the pressure applied to it may be constant, or both pressure and volume may change in various ways. So a substance has *many different* heat capacities, depending on the conditions under which the heat is added or removed.

For solid and liquid materials the transfer of heat is most often carried out under constant-pressure conditions; for example, we put a cold spoon into hot coffee under normal atmospheric pressure. In such problems we nearly always want to use the heat capacities for *constant-pressure* conditions, and other possible heat capacities are of little practical importance.

For gases the situation is quite different; several different kinds of heat capacity are of practical importance. Two conditions occur particularly often. One is raising the temperature of a gas at *constant volume*, as in a rigid container whose volume doesn't change appreciably with increasing temperature or pressure. The other is *constant pressure*, in which the gas is allowed to expand just enough to keep the pressure constant. The two corresponding molar heat capacities are called the **molar heat capacity at constant volume,** denoted as C_v, and the **molar heat capacity at constant pressure,** denoted as C_p.

Why should these two molar heat capacities be different? The answer lies in the first law of thermodynamics. In a constant-volume temperature change, the system does no work, and the change in internal energy ΔU equals the heat added ΔQ. In a constant-pressure temperature change, on the other hand, the volume *must* increase; otherwise, the pressure could not remain constant. As the material expands, it does an amount of work ΔW. According to the first law,

$$\Delta Q = \Delta U + \Delta W. \tag{18-9}$$

For a given temperature change, the heat input for a constant-pressure process must be *greater* than for a constant-volume process because additional energy must be supplied to account for the work ΔW done during the expansion. For air, for example, the heat capacity at constant pressure is 40% greater than at constant volume. If the volume were to *decrease* during heating, ΔW would be negative, and the heat input would be *less* than in the constant-volume case.

This discussion shows that ordinarily C_p is larger than C_v. For the special case of an ideal gas there is a simple relation between these two quantities; our next project is to derive that relation. First consider the constant-*volume* process. We place n moles of an ideal gas at temperature T in a constant-volume container. We place it in thermal contact with a hotter body; a quantity of heat ΔQ flows into the gas, and its temperature increases by an amount ΔT. By definition of C_v, the molar heat capacity at constant volume,

$$\Delta Q = nC_v\,\Delta T. \tag{18-10}$$

The pressure increases during this process, but the gas does no *work* ($\Delta W = 0$) because the volume is constant. From the first law, when

$\Delta W = 0$, $\Delta Q = \Delta U$, so we also have

$$\Delta U = nC_v\,\Delta T. \tag{18–11}$$

Next we consider a constant-*pressure* process. We place the same gas in a cylinder with a piston that we can allow to move just enough to maintain constant pressure. Again we bring the system into contact with a hotter body. As heat flows into the gas, it expands at constant pressure and does work. By definition of C_p, the molar heat capacity at constant pressure, the amount of heat ΔQ entering the gas is

$$\Delta Q = nC_p\,\Delta T. \tag{18–12}$$

The work ΔW done by the gas in this constant-pressure process is

$$\Delta W = p\,\Delta V.$$

We can also express ΔW in terms of the temperature change ΔT by using the ideal-gas equation of state $pV = nRT$. Because p is constant, the change in V is proportional to the change in T:

$$p\,\Delta V = nR\,\Delta T$$

and

$$\Delta W = nR\,\Delta T. \tag{18–13}$$

When we substitute Eqs. (18–12) and (18–13) into the first law ($\Delta Q = \Delta U + \Delta W$), we obtain

$$nC_p\,\Delta T = \Delta U + nR\,\Delta T. \tag{18–14}$$

Now, here comes the crux of the calculation. The internal energy change ΔU is again given by Eq. (18–11), that is, $\Delta U = nC_v\,\Delta T$, *even though now the volume is not constant.* Why is this so? Recall the discussion in Section 18–6; one of the special properties of an ideal gas is that its internal energy depends *only* on temperature. Thus the *change* in internal energy during any process must be determined only by the temperature change. If Eq. (18–11) is valid for an ideal gas for one particular kind of process, it must be valid for an ideal gas for *every* kind of process.

To complete our derivation, we replace ΔU in Eq. (18–14) by $nC_v\,\Delta T$ to obtain

$$nC_p\,\Delta T = nC_v\,\Delta T + nR\,\Delta T.$$

Then we divide each term by the common factor $n\,\Delta T$; the final result is

$$C_p = C_v + R. \tag{18–15}$$

As we predicted, the molar heat capacity of an ideal gas at constant pressure is *greater* than the molar heat capacity at constant volume; the difference is the gas constant R. Of course, R must be expressed in the same units as C_p and C_v, such as $J \cdot mol^{-1} \cdot K^{-1}$.

We used the ideal-gas equation to derive Eq. (18–15), but it turns out to be obeyed quite well also for many real gases at moderate pressures. Measured values of C_p and C_v are given in Table 18–1 for some real gases at low pressures; the difference in most cases is approximately $8.31\ J \cdot mol^{-1} \cdot K^{-1}$.

TABLE 18–1		Molar heat capacities of gases at low pressure			
Type of gas	Gas	C_p, J·mol^{-1}·K^{-1}	C_v, J·mol^{-1}·K^{-1}	$C_p - C_v$	$\gamma = \dfrac{C_p}{C_v}$
Monatomic	He	20.78	12.47	8.31	1.67
	A	20.78	12.47	8.31	1.67
Diatomic	H_2	28.74	20.42	8.32	1.41
	N_2	29.07	20.76	8.31	1.40
	O_2	29.41	21.10	8.31	1.40
	CO	29.16	20.85	8.31	1.40
Polyatomic	CO_2	36.94	28.46	8.48	1.30
	SO_2	40.37	31.39	8.98	1.29
	H_2S	34.60	25.95	8.65	1.33

Table 18–1 also shows that the molar heat capacity of a gas is related to its molecular structure. All the *monatomic* gases have approximately equal values of C_v, and all the *diatomic* gases have about equal values. This is not an accident; in Chapter 20 we will take a more detailed look at the molecular basis of heat capacities of gases.

The last column of Table 18–1 lists the values of the ratio C_p/C_v, denoted by the Greek letter γ (gamma):

$$\gamma = \frac{C_p}{C_v}. \tag{18–16}$$

The quantity γ plays an important role in *adiabatic* processes for an ideal gas, which we will study in the next section. We see from Table 18–1 that γ is 1.67 for monatomic gases and about 1.40 for diatomic gases.

Here's a final reminder: For an ideal gas the internal energy change in *any* process is given by $\Delta U = nC_v \, \Delta T$, *whether the volume is constant or not*. This relation holds for other substances *only* when the volume is constant.

Our discussion of molar heat capacities of an ideal gas can be represented graphically by using isotherms on a pV-diagram. Figure 18–6 shows two isotherms for an ideal gas, one for temperature T and the other for $T + \Delta T$. The internal energy U of an ideal gas depends only on the temperature T, so U is constant if T is constant. This means that an isotherm is also a curve of *constant internal energy*. The internal energy has a constant value U at every point on the isotherm at temperature T and a constant value $U + \Delta U$ at every point on the isotherm at $T + \Delta T$. The *change* in internal energy, ΔU, is the same in every process in which the gas is taken from *any* point on one isotherm to *any* point on the other. In Fig. 18–6, ΔU is the same for processes ab, ac, ad, and ef. In particular, ab represents a constant-volume process from temperature T to $T + \Delta T$, and ad is a constant-pressure process through the same temperature interval. No work is done in process ab; the work in process ad is the area under the horizontal line ad.

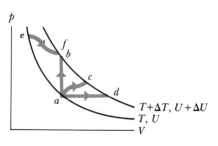

18–6
The change in internal energy of an ideal gas is the same in all processes between two given temperatures.

18–8
Adiabatic Processes for an Ideal Gas

We defined an adiabatic process in Section 18–5 as a process in which no heat transfer takes place between a system and its surroundings. Zero heat transfer is an idealization, but a process is *approximately* adiabatic if the system is well insulated or if the process takes place so quickly that there is not enough time for appreciable heat flow to occur.

An **adiabatic process for an ideal gas** is shown on the pV-diagram of Fig. 18–7. As the gas expands from volume V_a to V_b, its temperature drops because the internal energy decreases. If point a, representing the initial state, lies on an isotherm at temperature $T + \Delta T$, then point b for the final state is on a different isotherm at a lower temperature T. An adiabatic curve at any point is always steeper than the isotherm passing through the same point. For an adiabatic *compression* from V_b to V_a the situation is reversed, and the temperature rises.

The air in the output pipe of an air compressor, as used in gasoline stations and paint-spraying equipment, is always warmer than the air entering the compressor, a result of the approximately adiabatic compression. When air is compressed in the cylinders of a diesel engine, during the compression stroke, it becomes so hot that, when fuel is injected into the cylinders during the power stroke, the fuel ignites spontaneously.

We can derive a relation between volume and temperature changes for an adiabatic process in which the volume changes by a small amount ΔV and the temperature by ΔT. Equation (18–11) gives the internal energy change for *any* process for an ideal gas, adiabatic or not, so we have $\Delta U = nC_v\,\Delta T$. If we assume that ΔV is small enough that the pressure p doesn't change appreciably, then the work done by the gas during the process is given by $\Delta W = p\,\Delta V$. For an adiabatic process, $\Delta Q = 0$, so from the first law, $\Delta U = -\Delta W$, or

$$nC_v\,\Delta T = -p\,\Delta V. \qquad (18\text{–}17)$$

To obtain a relation containing only volume V and temperature T, we eliminate p using the ideal-gas equation in the form $p = nRT/V$. Substituting this into Eq. (18–17) and rearranging, we obtain

$$\frac{\Delta T}{T} = -\frac{R}{C_v}\frac{\Delta V}{V}.$$

The coefficient R/C_v can be expressed in terms of γ. We have $R/C_v = (C_p - C_v)/C_v = C_p/C_v - 1 = \gamma - 1$ and

$$\frac{\Delta T}{T} = -(\gamma - 1)\frac{\Delta V}{V}. \qquad (18\text{–}18)$$

Because γ is always greater than unity, $(\gamma - 1)$ is always positive. This means that in Eq. (18–18), ΔV and ΔT always have opposite signs. An adiabatic *expansion* always occurs with a *drop* in temperature and an adiabatic *compression* with a *rise* in temperature, confirming our earlier discussion.

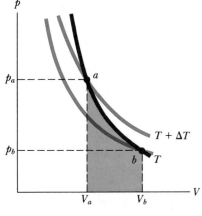

18–7
A pV-diagram for an adiabatic process for an ideal gas. As the gas expands from V_a to V_b, its temperature drops from $T + \Delta T$ to T, corresponding to the decrease in internal energy due to the work done by the gas (indicated by shaded area). For an ideal gas, when an isotherm and an adiabatic curve pass through the same point, the adiabatic curve is always steeper.

Equation (18–18) is valid only when ΔV and ΔT are infinitesimally small because when ΔV is finite, the pressure varies appreciably during the process, and the work is no longer given precisely by $\Delta W = p\,\Delta V$. Deriving the relation between volume and temperature for a *finite* volume change requires the use of calculus, but the result is simple enough that we can quote it and use it even without a detailed derivation. The result is

$$TV^{\gamma-1} = \text{constant.} \qquad (18\text{--}19)$$

For an initial state (T_1, V_1) and a final state (T_2, V_2),

$$T_1 V_1{}^{\gamma-1} = T_2 V_2{}^{\gamma-1}. \qquad (18\text{--}20)$$

Because we have used the ideal-gas equation in deriving Eqs. (18–19) and (18–20), the T's must always be *absolute* (Kelvin) temperatures; keep this in mind when you use these equations.

We can also convert Eq. (18–19) into a relation between pressure and volume by eliminating T, using the ideal-gas equation in the form $T = pV/nR$. Substituting this into Eq. (18–19), we find

$$\frac{pV}{nR} V^{\gamma-1} = \text{constant,}$$

or, because n and R are constants,

$$pV^{\gamma} = \text{constant.} \qquad (18\text{--}21)$$

For an initial state (p_1, V_1) and a final state (p_2, V_2),

$$p_1 V_1{}^{\gamma} = p_2 V_2{}^{\gamma}. \qquad (18\text{--}22)$$

These equations show that in an adiabatic process p is inversely proportional not to V, as in an isothermal process, but rather to V to the power γ, a more rapid variation of p with V.

We can calculate the *work* done by an ideal gas during an adiabatic process. We know that $\Delta Q = 0$ and $W = -\Delta U$ for any adiabatic process. For an ideal gas, $\Delta U = nC_v\,\Delta T = nC_v(T_2 - T_1)$. If the number of moles n and the initial and final temperatures T_1 and T_2 are known, we have simply

$$W = nC_v(T_1 - T_2). \qquad (18\text{--}23)$$

We may also use $pV = nRT$ in Eq. (18–23) to obtain

$$W = \frac{C_v}{R}(p_1 V_1 - p_2 V_2) = \frac{1}{\gamma - 1}(p_1 V_1 - p_2 V_2). \qquad (18\text{--}24)$$

If the process is an expansion, the temperature drops, T_1 is greater than T_2, $p_1 V_1$ is greater than $p_2 V_2$, and the work done by the gas is *positive*, as we should expect. If it is a compression, the work is negative.

Example 18–3   The compression ratio of a certain diesel engine is 15. This means that air in the cylinders is compressed to 1/15 of its initial volume. If the initial pressure is 1.0×10^5 Pa and the initial temperature is 27°C (= 300 K), find the final pressure and the temperature after compression. Air is mostly a mixture of oxygen and nitrogen, and $\gamma = 1.40$.

Solution   From Eq. (18–20),

$$T_2 = T_1\left(\frac{V_1}{V_2}\right)^{\gamma-1} = (300 \text{ K})(15)^{0.40} = 886 \text{ K} = 613°\text{C}.$$

From Eq. (18–22),

$$p_2 = p_1\left(\frac{V_1}{V_2}\right)^{\gamma} = (1.0 \times 10^5 \text{ Pa})(15)^{1.40} = 44.3 \times 10^5 \text{ Pa} = 44 \text{ atm}.$$

If the compression had been isothermal, the final pressure would have been 15 atm, but because the temperature also increases during an adiabatic compression, the final pressure is much greater. The high temperature attained during compression causes the fuel to ignite spontaneously without the need for spark plugs when the fuel is injected into the cylinders at the end of the compression stroke.   ■

Example 18–4   In Example 18–3, how much work does the gas do during the compression if the initial volume of the cylinder is 1.0 L = 1.0×10^{-3} m³?

Solution   We may determine the number of moles and then use Eq. (18–23), or we may use Eq. (18–24). With the first method we have

$$n = \frac{p_1V_1}{RT_1} = \frac{(1.0 \times 10^5 \text{ Pa})(1.0 \times 10^{-3} \text{ m}^3)}{(8.314 \text{ J·mol}^{-1}\text{·K}^{-1})(300 \text{ K})} = 0.040 \text{ mol}.$$

C_v for air is 20.8 J·mol⁻¹·K⁻¹; so

$$\begin{aligned} W &= nC_v(T_1 - T_2) \\ &= (0.040 \text{ mol})(20.8 \text{ J·mol·K}^{-1})(300 \text{ K} - 886 \text{ K}) \\ &= -488 \text{ J}. \end{aligned}$$

With the second method,

$$\begin{aligned} W = \frac{1}{1.40 - 1}\Big[&(1.0 \times 10^5 \text{ Pa})(1.0 \times 10^{-3} \text{ m}^3) \\ &- (44.3 \times 10^5 \text{ Pa})\left(\frac{1.0}{15} \times 10^{-3} \text{ m}^3\right)\Big] \\ = -488 \text{ J}.& \end{aligned}$$

The work is negative because the gas is compressed.   ■

Throughout this analysis we have used the ideal-gas equation of state; this equation holds only when the state of the gas changes slowly enough that the pressure and temperature are *uniform* throughout the gas at every instant. Thus the validity of our results is limited to situations in which the process is fast enough to prevent appreciable heat exchange with the surroundings, yet slow enough that the system does not depart very much from thermal and mechanical equilibrium.

Questions

18–1 It is not correct to say that a body contains a certain amount of heat, yet a body can transfer heat to another body. How can a body give away something it does not have in the first place?

18–2 Discuss the application of the first law of thermodynamics to a mountaineer who eats food, gets warm and sweats a lot during the climb, and does a lot of mechanical work in raising himself to the summit. What about the descent? One also gets warm during the descent. Is the source of this energy the same as the source during the ascent?

18–3 How can you cool a room (i.e., take heat out of it) by adding energy to it in the form of electric energy supplied to an air conditioner?

18–4 If you are told the initial and final states of a system and the associated change in internal energy, can you determine whether the internal energy change was due to work or to heat transfer?

18–5 Household refrigerators always have arrays or coils of tubing on the outside, usually at the back or bottom. When the refrigerator is running, the tubing becomes quite hot. Where does the heat come from?

18–6 There are a few materials that contract when heated, such as water between 0°C and 4°C. Would you expect C_p for such a material to be greater or less than C_v?

18–7 When ice melts (decreasing its volume), is the internal energy change greater or less than the heat added?

18–8 When one drives a car in cool, foggy weather, ice sometimes forms in the throat of the carburetor, even though the outside air temperature is above freezing. Why?

18–9 On a warm summer day a large cylinder of compressed gas (propane or butane) was used to supply several large gas burners at a cookout. After a while, frost formed on the outside of the tank. Why?

18–10 Air escaping from an air hose at a gas station always feels cold. Why?

18–11 The prevailing winds blow across the central valley of California and up the western slopes of the Sierra Nevada. They cool as they reach the slopes, and the precipitation there is much greater than in the valley. But what makes them cool?

18–12 Applying the same considerations as in Question 18–11, can you explain why Death Valley, on the opposite side of the Sierra from the central valley, is so hot and dry?

18–13 In the situation of Question 18–11, during certain seasons the wind blows in the opposite direction. Although the mountains are cool, the wind in the valley (called the "Santa Ana," after the notorious Mexican general) is always very hot. What heats it? A similar phenomenon in the Alps is called the "Foehn"; by local legend it is blamed for irrational behavior in humans and animals and has even been used as a defense in murder trials.

18–14 When a gas expands adiabatically, it does work on its surroundings. But if there is no heat input to the gas, where does the energy come from?

18–15 In a constant-volume process, $\Delta U = nC_v \Delta T$, but in a constant-pressure process it is *not* true that $\Delta U = nC_p \Delta T$. Why not?

18–16 Since C_v is defined with specific reference to a constant-volume process, how can it be correct that for an ideal gas, $\Delta U = nC_v \Delta T$ even when the volume is not constant?

Exercises

Section 18–2   Work Done during Volume Changes

18–1 Two moles of oxygen are in a container with rigid walls. The gas is heated until the pressure doubles. Neglect the thermal expansion of the container. Calculate the work done by the gas.

18–2 A gas under a constant pressure of 2.50×10^5 Pa and with an initial volume of 0.0500 m^3 is cooled until its volume becomes 0.0400 m^3. Calculate the work done by the gas.

18–3 Four moles of an ideal gas are heated at constant pressure from $T = 27°C$ to $127°C$. Calculate the work done by the gas.

18–4

a) In Fig. 18–3, consider the closed loop $1 \to 3 \to 2 \to 4 \to 1$. Prove that the total work done by the system is equal to the area enclosed by the loop.

b) How is the work done for the process in part (a) related to the work done if the loop is traversed in the opposite direction, $1 \to 4 \to 2 \to 3 \to 1$?

Section 18–4   Internal Energy and the First Law

18–5 A student performs a combustion experiment by burning a mixture of fuel and oxygen in a constant-volume metal can surrounded by a water bath. During the experiment the temperature of the water is observed to rise. Regarding the mixture of fuel and oxygen as the system,

a) has heat been transferred?

b) has work been done?

c) what is the sign of ΔU?

18–6 A liquid is irregularly stirred in a well-insulated container and thereby undergoes a rise in temperature. Regarding the liquid as the system,

a) has heat been transferred?

b) has work been done?

c) what is the sign of ΔU?

18–7 In a certain chemical process a lab technician supplies 180 J of heat to a system, and at the same time, 100 J of work are done on the system by its surroundings. What is the increase in the internal energy of the system?

18–8 When a system is taken from state a to state b in Fig. 18–8 along the path acb, 90.0 J of heat flow into the system, and 70.0 J of work are done by the system.

a) How much heat flows into the system along path adb if the work done by the system is 10.0 J?

b) When the system is returned from b to a along the curved path, the magnitude of the work is 45.0 J. Does the system absorb or liberate heat; and how much?

c) If $U_a = 0$ and $U_d = 6.0$ J, find the heat absorbed or liberated by the system in the processes ad and db.

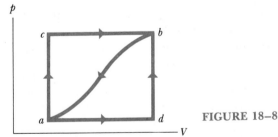

FIGURE 18–8

18–9 When water is boiled under a pressure of 2.00 atm, the heat of vaporization is 2.20×10^6 J·kg^{-1}, and the boiling point is 120°C. At this pressure, 1.00 kg of water has a volume of 1.00×10^{-3} m³, and 1.00 kg of steam has a volume of 0.824 m³.

a) Compute the work done by the water when 1.00 kg of steam is formed at this temperature.

b) Compute the increase in internal energy of the water.

18–10 A gas in a cylinder expands from a volume of 0.400 m³ to 0.700 m³. Heat is added just rapidly enough to keep the pressure constant at 2.00×10^5 Pa during the expansion. The total heat added is 1.40×10^5 J.

a) Find the work done by the gas.

b) Find the change in internal energy of the gas.

c) Does it matter whether or not the gas is ideal?

18–11 A gas in a cylinder is cooled and compressed at a constant pressure of 2.00×10^5 Pa, from 1.20 m³ to 0.80 m³. A quantity of heat of magnitude 3.20×10^5 J is removed from the gas.

a) Find the work done by the gas.

b) Find the change in internal energy of the gas.

c) Does it matter whether or not the gas is ideal?

Section 18–6   Internal Energy of an Ideal Gas

Section 18–7   Heat Capacities of an Ideal Gas

18–12 During an isothermal compression of an ideal gas, 185 J of heat must be removed from the gas to maintain constant temperature. How much work is done by the gas during the process?

18–13 A cylinder contains 2.00 mol of oxygen gas at a temperature of 27°C. The cylinder is provided with a frictionless piston, which maintains a constant pressure of 1.00 atm on the gas. The gas is heated until its temperature increases to 127°C. Assume that the oxygen can be treated as an ideal gas.

a) Draw a pV-diagram representing the process.

b) How much work is done by the gas in this process?

c) On what is this work done?

d) What is the change in internal energy of the gas?

e) How much heat was supplied to the gas?

f) How much work would the gas have done if the pressure had been 0.500 atm?

18–14 A certain ideal gas has $\gamma = 1.33$. Determine the molar heat capacities at constant volume and at constant pressure.

Section 18–8   Adiabatic Processes for an Ideal Gas

18–15 An ideal gas initially at 8.00 atm and 300 K is permitted to expand adiabatically until its volume doubles. Find the final pressure and temperature if the gas is

a) monatomic;   b) diatomic.

18–16 A gasoline engine takes in air at 20.0°C and 1.00 atm and compresses it adiabatically to one fifth of the original volume. Find the final temperature and pressure.

18-17 An engineer is designing an engine that runs on compressed air. Air enters the engine at a pressure of 2.00×10^6 Pa and leaves at a pressure of 4.00×10^5 Pa. What must be the temperature of the compressed air in order that there may be no possibility of frost forming in the exhaust ports of the engine? Assume the expansion to be adiabatic. (*Note:* Frost frequently forms in the exhaust ports of an air-driven engine. This happens when the moist air is cooled below 0°C by the expansion that takes place in the engine.)

18-18 A monatomic ideal gas initially at a pressure of 5.00×10^5 Pa and with a volume of 0.0800 m³ is compressed adiabatically to a volume of 0.0300 m³.

a) What is the final pressure?

b) How much work is done by the gas?

18-19 During an adiabatic expansion the temperature of 0.400 mol of oxygen drops from 30.0°C to 10.0°C.

a) How much work does the gas do?

b) How much heat is added to the gas?

Problems

18-20 In a certain process, 3.20×10^5 J of heat energy are supplied to a system, and at the same time the system expands against a constant external pressure of 6.90×10^5 Pa. The internal energy of the system is the same at the beginning and end of the process. Find the increase in volume of the system.

18-21 Nitrogen gas in an expandable container is raised from 0.0°C to 50.0°C, with the pressure held constant at 4.00×10^5 Pa. The total heat added is 5.00×10^4 J.

a) Find the number of moles of gas.

b) Find the change in internal energy of the gas.

c) Find the work done by the gas.

d) How much heat would be needed to cause the same temperature change if the volume were constant?

18-22 A chemical engineer studying the properties of glycerin uses a steel cylinder of cross-sectional area 0.0300 m² that contains 1.50×10^{-2} m³ of glycerin. The cylinder is equipped with a tightly fitting piston that supports a load of 3.00×10^4 N. The temperature of the system is increased from 20.0°C to 70.0°C. The coefficient of volume expansion of glycerin is given in Table 14-2, and the density in Table 13-1. Neglect the expansion of the steel cylinder. Find

a) the increase in volume of the glycerin;

b) the mechanical work done by the 3.00×10^4 N force;

c) the amount of heat added to the glycerin [c_p for glycerin is 2.43×10^3 J·kg⁻¹·(C°)⁻¹];

d) the change in internal energy of the glycerin.

18-23 An ideal gas expands slowly to twice its original volume, doing 800 J of work in the process. Find the heat added to the gas and its change in internal energy if the process is

a) isothermal;

b) adiabatic.

18-24 Initially at a temperature of 80.0°C, 0.28 m³ of air expands at a constant gauge pressure of 1.38×10^5 Pa to a volume of 1.42 m³ and then expands further adiabatically to a final volume of 2.27 m³ and a final gauge pressure of 2.29×10^4 Pa. Draw a pV-diagram for this sequence of processes, and compute the total work done by the air. (Take atmospheric pressure to be 1.01×10^5 Pa. C_v for air is 20.8 J·mol⁻¹·K⁻¹.)

18-25 In a cylinder, 4.00 mol of an ideal monatomic gas initially at 1.00×10^6 Pa and 300 K expands until its volume doubles. Compute the work done by the gas if the expansion is

a) isobaric;

b) adiabatic.

c) Show each process on a pV-diagram. In which case is the magnitude of the work done by the gas the greatest?

d) In which case is the magnitude of the heat transfer greatest?

e) In which case is the magnitude of the internal energy change greatest?

18-26 Two moles of helium are initially at a temperature of 27.0°C and occupy a volume of 0.0300 m³. The helium first expands at constant pressure until the volume has doubled. Then it expands adiabatically until the temperature returns to its initial value. Assume that the helium can be treated as an ideal gas.

a) Draw a diagram of the process in the pV-plane.

b) What is the total heat supplied to the helium in the process?

c) What is the total change in internal energy of the helium?

d) What is the total work done by the helium?

e) What is the final volume?

18-27 A cylinder with a piston contains 0.500 mol of oxygen at 4.00×10^5 Pa and 300 K. The oxygen may be treated as an ideal gas. The gas first expands at constant pressure to twice its original volume. It is then compressed isothermally back to its original volume, and finally it is cooled at constant volume to its original pressure.

a) Show the series of processes on a pV-diagram.

b) Compute the temperature during the isothermal compression.

c) Compute the maximum pressure.

18–28 Use the conditions and processes of Problem 18–27 to compute

a) the work done by the gas, the heat added to it, and its internal-energy change during the initial expansion;

b) the work done, the heat added, and the internal-energy change during the final cooling;

c) the internal-energy change during the isothermal compression.

Challenge Problem

18–29 A pump compressing air from atmospheric pressure (1.01×10^5 Pa) into a very large tank at 4.80×10^5 Pa gauge pressure has a cylinder 0.255 m long. C_v for air is 20.8 J·mol^{-1}·K^{-1}.

a) At what position in the stroke will air begin to enter the tank? Assume that the compression is adiabatic. (You are being asked to calculate the distance the piston has moved in the cylinder.)

b) If the air is taken into the pump at 27.0°C, what is the temperature of the compressed air?

c) How much work does the pump do in putting 30.0 mol of air into the tank?

19

The Second Law of Thermodynamics

The *first* law of thermodynamics expresses conservation of energy in thermodynamic processes. But there is a whole category of questions that the first law *cannot* answer, having to do with the *directions* of thermodynamic processes. A study of inherently one-way processes, such as the flow of heat from hotter to colder regions and the irreversible conversion of work into heat by friction, leads to the *second law of thermodynamics*. This law places fundamental limitations on the efficiency with which an engine can convert heat into useful mechanical work; it also places limitations on the minimum energy input needed to operate a refrigerator. Hence the second law is directly relevant for many important practical problems. We can also use the second law to define a temperature scale that is independent of the properties of any specific material. Finally, we restate the second law in terms of the concept of *entropy*, a quantitative measure of the degree of disorder or randomness of a system.

19–1
Directions of Thermodynamic Processes

Many thermodynamic processes proceed naturally in one direction but not the opposite. For example, heat always flows from a hot body to a cooler body, never the reverse. Heat flow from a cool body to a hot body, making the cool body cooler and the hot one hotter, would not violate the first law, but such flow does not occur in nature. Or suppose that all the air in a box were to rush to one side, leaving vacuum in the other side, the reverse of the free expansion described in Section 18–3. This does not occur in nature either, although the first law does not forbid it. It is easy to convert mechanical energy completely into heat; we do this every time we use a car's brakes to stop it. It is not so easy to convert heat into mechanical energy. Many would-be inventors have proposed to cool the air a little, extracting heat from it, and convert that heat to mechanical energy to propel a car or an airplane. None has ever succeeded; no one has ever built a machine that converts heat *completely* into mechanical energy.

What these examples have in common is a preferred *direction*. In each case a process proceeds spontaneously in one direction but not in the other. The physical law that determines what the preferred direction is for a given process is the *second law of thermodynamics*, the principal topic of this chapter.

Despite this preferred direction for every natural process, we can think of a class of idealized processes that are *reversible*. We say that a process is *reversible* if it involves a system that is always very close to being in thermodynamic equilibrium, within itself and with its surroundings. When this is the case, any change of state that takes place can be reversed (i.e., made to go the other way) by making only an infinitesimal change in the conditions of the system. For example, heat flow between two bodies whose temperatures differ only infinitesimally can be reversed by making only a very small change in one temperature or the other. A gas that is expanding slowly and adiabatically can be compressed slowly by an infinitesimal increase in pressure.

Reversible processes are thus **equilibrium processes.** By contrast, heat flow with finite temperature difference, free expansion of a gas, and conversion of work to heat by friction are all **irreversible processes;** no small change in conditions could make any of them go the other way. They are also all *non-equilibrium* processes.

You may notice an apparent contradiction in this discussion. If a system is *really* in thermodynamic equilibrium, how can any change of state at all take place? How can heat flow into or out of a system if the temperature is uniform throughout? How can the system start to move in order to expand and do work against its surroundings if it is in mechanical equilibrium?

The answer to all these questions is that a reversible process is an idealization that can never be precisely attained in the real world. But by making the temperature gradients and the pressure differences in the substance very small, we can come very close to the goal of keeping the system in equilibrium states. The term *quasi-equilibrium process* is sometimes used to emphasize the idealized nature of a reversible process.

Finally, we will find that there is a relationship between the direction of a process and the *disorder* or *randomness* of the resulting state. For example, imagine a tedious sorting job, such as alphabetizing a thousand book titles written on file cards. If you throw the alphabetized stack of cards into the air, do they come down in alphabetical order? No; the tendency is for them to come down in a random or disordered state. In the free expansion example the air is more disordered after it has expanded into the entire box than it was when it was confined in one side because the molecules are scattered over more space.

Similarly, macroscopic kinetic energy is energy associated with organized, coordinated motions of many molecules, while energy associated with heat is random, disordered molecular motion. Therefore conversion of mechanical energy into heat involves an increase of randomness or disorder.

In the following sections we will introduce the second law of thermodynamics by considering two broad classes of devices: *heat engines*, which are partly successful in converting heat into work, and *refrigerators*, which are partly successful in transporting heat from cooler to hotter bodies.

19–2
Heat Engines

An essential characteristic of a technological society is its ability to use sources of energy other than muscle power. Sometimes, as with water power, mechanical energy is directly available. Most of our energy, however, comes from the burning of fossil fuels (coal, oil, and gas) and from nuclear reactions; both of these supply energy that is transferred as *heat*. Some heat can be used directly for heating buildings, for cooking, and for chemical and metallurgical processing, but to operate a machine or propel a vehicle, we need *mechanical* energy.

Thus a problem of the utmost practical importance is how to take heat from a source and convert as much of it as possible into mechanical energy or work. This is exactly what happens in gasoline engines in automobiles, jet engines in airplanes, steam turbines in electric power plants, and many other systems. Closely related processes occur in the animal kingdom, in which food energy is "burned" (i.e., carbohydrates combine with oxygen to yield water, carbon dioxide, and energy) and partly converted to mechanical energy as the animal's muscles do work on their surroundings.

Any device that transforms heat into work or mechanical energy is called a **heat engine.** Usually, a quantity of matter inside the engine undergoes addition and subtraction of heat, expansion and compression, and sometimes change of phase. We call this matter the **working substance** of the engine. In internal-combustion engines the working substance is a mixture of air and burnt fuel; in a steam turbine it is water.

The simplest kind of engine to discuss is one in which the working substance undergoes a **cyclic process,** that is, a sequence of processes that eventually leaves the substance in the same state in which it started. In a steam turbine the water is recycled and used over and over. Internal-combustion engines do not use the same air over and over, but we can still analyze them in terms of cyclic processes that approximate their actual operation. (In principle, we *could* take the air from the exhaust and recycle it, but this is not practical.)

All the heat engines mentioned absorb heat from a source at a relatively high temperature, perform some mechanical work, and discard some heat at a lower temperature. As far as the engine is concerned, the discarded heat is wasted. In internal-combustion engines the waste heat is discarded in the hot exhaust gases and the cooling system; in a steam turbine it is heat that must be taken from the used steam to condense and recycle it.

When a system is carried through a cyclic process, its initial and final internal energies are equal. For any cyclic process the first law of thermodynamics requires that

$$U_2 - U_1 = 0 = Q - W \quad \text{and} \quad Q = W.$$

In other words, the net heat flowing into the engine in a cyclic process equals the net work done by the engine.

In the analysis of heat engines it is useful to think of two bodies with which the working substance of the engine can interact. One of these, called the *hot reservoir*, can give the working substance large amounts of heat without appreciably changing its own temperature. The other body, called the *cold reservoir*, can absorb large amounts of discarded heat from the engine. Thus in a steam-turbine system the flames and hot gases in the boiler are the hot reservoir, and the cold water and air used to condense and cool the used steam are the cold reservoir.

We denote the quantities of heat transferred from the hot and cold reservoirs as Q_H and Q_C, respectively. Each Q is positive when heat is transferred *from* a reservoir *into* the working substance and negative when the reverse happens. Thus in a heat engine, Q_H is positive but Q_C is negative, representing heat *leaving* the working substance. This sign convention is consistent with our usage in preceding chapters, and we will continue to use it consistently here.

We can represent the energy transformations in a heat engine by the *flow diagram* of Fig. 19–1. The engine itself is represented by the circle. The amount of heat Q_H supplied to the engine by the hot reservoir is proportional to the cross section of the incoming pipeline at the top of the diagram. The cross section of the outgoing pipeline at the bottom is proportional to the magnitude $|Q_C|$ of the heat discarded in the exhaust. The branch line to the right represents that portion of the heat supplied that the engine converts to mechanical work, W.

When an engine repeats the same cycle over and over, Q_H and Q_C represent the quantities of heat absorbed and rejected by the engine *during one cycle*. The *net* heat absorbed per cycle is

$$Q = Q_H + Q_C = Q_H - |Q_C|, \tag{19–1}$$

where Q_C is a negative number. The useful output of the engine is the net work W done by the working substance; from the first law,

$$W = Q = Q_H + Q_C. \tag{19–2}$$

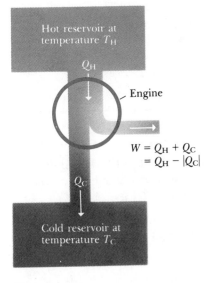

19–1
Schematic flow diagram of a heat engine.

Hot reservoir at temperature T_H

Q_H

Engine

$W = Q_H + Q_C$
$= Q_H - |Q_C|$

Q_C

Cold reservoir at temperature T_C

Ideally, we would like to convert *all* the heat Q_H into work; in that case we would have $Q_H = W$ and $Q_C = 0$. Experience shows that this is impossible; there is always some heat wasted, and Q_C is never zero. We define the **thermal efficiency** of an engine, denoted by e, as the quotient

$$e = \frac{W}{Q_H}. \tag{19-3}$$

The thermal efficiency e represents the fraction of Q_H that *is* converted to work. To put it another way, e is what you get divided by what you pay for. This is always less than unity, an all-too-familiar experience! In terms of the flow diagram of Fig. 19–1 the most efficient engine is the one for which the branch pipeline representing the work output is as *large* as possible and the exhaust pipeline representing the heat thrown away is as small as possible.

Using Eq. (19–2) and keeping in mind the signs of Q_H and Q_C, we can write the following equivalent expressions:

$$e = \frac{W}{Q_H} = \frac{Q_H + Q_C}{Q_H} = 1 + \frac{Q_C}{Q_H} = 1 - \left| \frac{Q_C}{Q_H} \right|. \tag{19-4}$$

We note that e is a quotient of two energy quantities and thus is a pure number, without units. Of course, we must always express W and Q_H in the same units.

PROBLEM-SOLVING STRATEGY: *Heat Engines*

We recommend that you reread the strategy in Section 18–4; those suggestions are equally useful throughout the present chapter. The following points may need additional emphasis.

1. Be very careful with the sign conventions for W and the various Q's. W is positive when the system expands and does work, negative when it is compressed. Each Q is positive if it represents heat entering the working substance of the engine or other system, negative when heat leaves the system. When in doubt, use the first law when possible, to check consistency.

2. Some problems deal with power rather than energy quantities. Power is work per unit time ($P = W/t$), and rate of heat transfer (heat current) H is heat transfer per unit time ($H = Q/t$). Sometimes it helps to ask, "What is W or Q in one second (or one hour)?"

Example 19–1   A gasoline engine takes in 2500 J of heat and delivers 500 J of mechanical work per cycle. The heat is obtained by burning gasoline with heat of combustion $L_C = 5.0 \times 10^4$ J·g^{-1}.

a) What is the thermal efficiency of this engine?

b) How much heat is discarded in each cycle?

c) How much gasoline is burned in each cycle?

d) If the engine goes through 100 cycles per second, what is its power output in watts? In horsepower?

e) How much gasoline is burned per second? Per hour?

Solution   We have $Q_H = 2500$ J and $W = 500$ J.

a) From Eq. (19–3) the thermal efficiency is

$$e = \frac{W}{Q_H} = \frac{500 \text{ J}}{2500 \text{ J}} = 0.20 = 20\%.$$

b) From Eq. (19–2),

$$W = Q_H + Q_C, \qquad 500 \text{ J} = 2500 \text{ J} + Q_C, \qquad Q_C = -2000 \text{ J}.$$

That is, 2000 J of heat leave the engine during each cycle.

c) Let m be the mass of gasoline burned; then

$$Q_H = mL_C, \qquad 2500 \text{ J} = m(5.0 \times 10^4 \text{ J} \cdot \text{g}^{-1}), \qquad m = 0.050 \text{ g}.$$

d) The rate of doing work P is the work per cycle multiplied by the number of cycles per second:

$$P = (500 \text{ J})(100 \text{ s}^{-1}) = 50{,}000 \text{ W} = 50 \text{ kW}$$

$$= (50{,}000 \text{ W})\frac{1 \text{ hp}}{746 \text{ W}} = 67 \text{ hp}.$$

e) The mass of gasoline burned per second is the mass per cycle multiplied by the number of cycles per second:

$$(0.050 \text{ g})(100 \text{ s}^{-1}) = 5.0 \text{ g} \cdot \text{s}^{-1}.$$

The mass burned per hour is

$$(5.0 \text{ g} \cdot \text{s}^{-1})\frac{3600 \text{ s}}{1 \text{ hr}} = 18{,}000 \text{ g} \cdot \text{hr}^{-1} = 18 \text{ kg} \cdot \text{hr}^{-1}$$

The density of gasoline is about 0.70 $\text{g} \cdot \text{cm}^{-3}$, so this is about 25,700 cm^3, 25.7 L, or 6.8 gal of gasoline per hour.   ∎

19–3
Internal-Combustion Engines

As an example of a heat engine and a calculation of thermal efficiency, let's consider the common gasoline engine found in automobiles and many other types of machinery. Figure 19–2 shows the sequence of processes. First, a mixture of air and gasoline vapor flows into a cylinder through an open intake valve while the piston descends, increasing the volume of the cylinder from a minimum of V (when the piston is all the way up) to a maximum of rV (when it is all the way down). The quantity r is called the **compression ratio;** for present-day automobile engines it is typically about 8. At the end of this *intake stroke* the intake valve closes, and the mixture is compressed, approximately adiabatically, to volume V during the *compression stroke*. The mixture is then ignited by the spark plug, and the heated gas expands, approximately adiabatically, back to volume rV, pushing on the piston and doing work; this is the *power stroke*. Finally, the exhaust valve opens, and the combustion products are

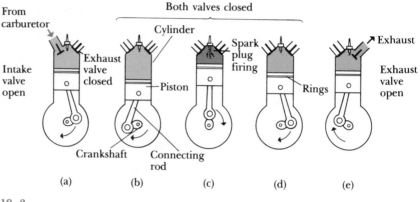

(a)   (b)   (c)   (d)   (e)

19–2
Cycle of a four-stroke internal-combustion engine. (a) Intake stroke: piston moves down, causing a partial vacuum in cylinder; gasoline and air are mixed in carburetor and flow through open intake valve into cylinder. (b) Compression stroke: intake valve closes, and mixture is compressed as piston moves up. (c) Ignition: spark plug ignites mixture. (d) Power stroke: hot burned mixture pushes piston down, doing work. (e) Exhaust stroke: exhaust valve opens and piston moves up, pushing burned mixture out of cylinder. Engine is now ready for next intake stroke, and the cycle repeats.

pushed out (during the *exhaust stroke*) to prepare the cylinder for the next intake stroke.

Figure 19–3 is a pV-diagram showing an idealized model of the corresponding thermodynamic processes. This model is called the **Otto cycle.** At point a the gasoline–air mixture has entered the cylinder. The mixture is compressed adiabatically along line ab and is then ignited. Heat Q_H is added to the system by the burning gasoline (line bc), and the power stroke is the adiabatic expansion cd. The gas is cooled to the temperature of the outside air (da); during this process, heat Q_C is released. In practice, of course, this same air does not enter the engine again, but since an equivalent amount does enter, we may consider the process to be cyclic.

We can calculate the efficiency of this idealized cycle. Processes bc and da are constant-volume, so the heats Q_H and Q_C are related simply to the temperatures:

$$Q_H = nC_v(T_c - T_b), \qquad Q_C = nC_v(T_a - T_d).$$

The thermal efficiency is given by Eq. (19–4); inserting the above expressions and cancelling out the common factor nC_v, we find

$$e = \frac{T_c - T_b + T_a - T_d}{T_c - T_b}. \qquad (19–5)$$

To simplify this further, we use the temperature–volume relation for adiabatic processes, Eq. (18–20). For the two adiabatic processes ab and cd we find

$$T_a(rV)^{\gamma-1} = T_bV^{\gamma-1}, \qquad T_d(rV)^{\gamma-1} = T_cV^{\gamma-1}.$$

We divide this equation by the common factor $V^{\gamma-1}$ and substitute the

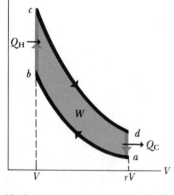

19–3
pV-diagram for the Otto cycle, an idealized model of the thermodynamic process in a gasoline engine.

resulting expressions for T_b and T_c back into Eq. (19–5). The result is

$$e = \frac{T_d r^{\gamma-1} - T_a r^{\gamma-1} + T_a - T_d}{T_d r^{\gamma-1} - T_a r^{\gamma-1}} = \frac{(T_d - T_a)(r^{\gamma-1} - 1)}{(T_d - T_a) r^{\gamma-1}}.$$

Finally, we divide this by the common factor $(T_d - T_a)$, obtaining the simple result

$$e = 1 - \frac{1}{r^{\gamma-1}}. \tag{19–6}$$

The thermal efficiency given by Eq. (19–6) is always less than unity, even for this idealized model. Using $r = 8$ and $\gamma = 1.4$ (the value for air), we find $e = 0.56$ or 56%. The efficiency can be increased by increasing r. However, this also increases the temperature at the end of the adiabatic compression of the air–fuel mixture. If the temperature is too high, the mixture explodes spontaneously during compression instead of burning evenly after the spark plug ignites it. This is called *pre-ignition* or *detonation*; it causes a knocking sound and can damage the engine. The maximum practical compression ratio for ordinary gasoline is about 10. Higher ratios can be used with more exotic fuels.

The Otto cycle, which we have just described, is a highly idealized model. It assumes that the mixture behaves as an ideal gas; it neglects friction, turbulence, loss of heat to cylinder walls, and many other effects that combine to reduce the efficiency of a real engine. Another source of inefficiency is incomplete combustion. A mixture of gasoline vapor with just enough air for complete combustion of the hydrocarbons to H_2O and CO_2 does not ignite readily. Reliable ignition requires a mixture that is "richer" in gasoline; the resulting incomplete combustion leads to CO and unburned hydrocarbons in the exhaust. The heat obtained from the gasoline is then less than the total heat of combustion; the difference is wasted, and the exhaust products contribute to air pollution. Efficiencies of real gasoline engines are typically around 20%.

The operation of the Diesel engine is similar to that of the gasoline engine. The most important difference is that there is no fuel in the cylinder during compression. At the beginning of the power stroke, fuel is injected directly into the cylinder just rapidly enough to keep the pressure approximately constant during the first part of the power stroke. Because of the high temperature developed during the adiabatic compression, the fuel ignites spontaneously as it is injected; no spark plugs are needed.

The idealized **Diesel cycle** is shown in Fig. 19–4. Starting at point a, air is compressed adiabatically to point b, heated at constant pressure to point c, expanded adiabatically to point d, and cooled at constant volume to point a. Because there is no fuel in the cylinder during the compression stroke, pre-ignition cannot occur, and the compression ratio r may be much higher than that for a gasoline engine. Values of 15 to 20 are typical; with these values and $\gamma = 1.4$ the efficiency of the idealized Diesel cycle is about 0.65 to 0.70. As with the Otto cycle, the efficiency of any actual engine is substantially less than this. Diesel engines are usually more efficient than gasoline engines. They are also heavier

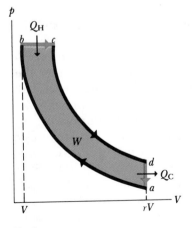

19–4
A pV-diagram of the Diesel cycle.

(per unit power output) and often harder to start. Diesel engines need no carburetor or ignition system, but the fuel-injection system requires expensive high-precision machining.

19–4
Refrigerators

We can think of a **refrigerator** as a heat engine operating in reverse. A heat engine takes heat from a hot place and gives off heat to a colder place. A refrigerator does the opposite; it takes heat from a cold place (the inside of the refrigerator) and gives it off to a warmer place (usually the air in the room where the refrigerator is located). A heat engine has a net *output* of mechanical work; the refrigerator requires a net *input* of mechanical work. With the symbols we used in Section 19–2, Q_C is positive for a refrigerator, but both W and Q_H are negative.

A flow diagram for a refrigerator is shown in Fig. 19–5. From the first law for a cyclic process,

$$Q_H + Q_C - W = 0, \qquad \text{or} \qquad -Q_H = Q_C - W,$$

or, since both Q_H and W are negative,

$$|Q_H| = Q_C + |W|. \qquad (19\text{–}7)$$

Thus, as the diagram shows, the heat Q_H leaving the working substance of the engine and given to the hot reservoir is always *greater* than the heat Q_C taken from the cold reservoir.

From an economic point of view the best refrigeration cycle is one that removes the greatest amount of heat Q_C from the refrigerator for the least expenditure of mechanical work, W. The relevant ratio is therefore $|Q_C/W| = -Q_C/W$. We call this the **performance coefficient,** denoted by K. Also, we have $W = Q_H + Q_C$, so

$$K = -\frac{Q_C}{W} = -\frac{Q_C}{Q_H + Q_C}. \qquad (19\text{–}8)$$

As always, we measure Q_H, Q_C, and W all in the same energy units; K is then a dimensionless number.

The principles of the common refrigeration cycle are shown schematically in Fig. 19–6. The fluid "circuit" contains a refrigerant fluid (the working substance), typically CCl_2F_2 or another member of the "Freon" family. The left side is at low temperature and low pressure, and the right side is at high temperature and high pressure. Ordinarily, both sides contain liquid and vapor in phase equilibrium. The compressor takes in fluid, compresses it adiabatically, and delivers it to the condenser coil at high pressure. The fluid temperature is then higher than that of the air surrounding the condenser, so the refrigerant gives off heat (Q_H) and partially condenses to liquid. When the expansion valve opens, fluid expands adiabatically into the evaporator. As it does so, it cools considerably, enough that the fluid in the evaporator coil is colder than its surroundings. The fluid absorbs heat (Q_C) from its surroundings, cooling them and partially vaporizing. The fluid then enters the compressor to

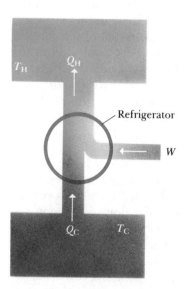

19–5
Schematic flow diagram of a refrigerator.

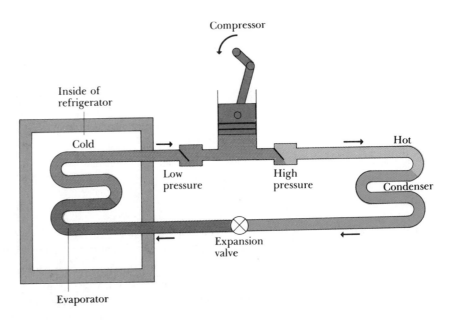

19–6
Principle of the mechanical refrigeration cycle.

begin another cycle. The compressor, usually driven by an electric motor, requires energy input and does work $|W|$ *on* the working substance during each cycle.

An air conditioner operates on exactly the same principle. In this case the refrigerator box becomes a room or an entire building. The evaporator coils are inside, the condenser is outside, and fans are used to circulate air through these. In large installations the condenser coils are often cooled by water. For air conditioners the quantities of greatest practical importance are the *rate* of heat removal (the heat current H from the region being cooled) and the *power* input $P = |W|/t$ to the compressor. If heat Q_C is removed in time t, then $H = Q_C/t$. Then we can express the performance coefficient as

$$K = -\frac{Q_C}{W} = \frac{Ht}{Pt} = \frac{H}{P}.$$

Typical room air conditioners have heat removal rates H of 5,000 to 10,000 Btu·hr^{-1}, or about 1500 to 3000 W, and require electric power input of about 600 to 1200 W. Typical performance coefficients are about 2.5, with somewhat larger values for larger-capacity units.

Unfortunately, K is usually expressed commercially in mixed units, with H in Btu per hour and P in watts. In these units, H/P is called the **energy efficiency rating** (EER); for room air conditioners the EER typically has a numerical value of 7–10. The units, which are customarily omitted, are Btu·hr^{-1}·W^{-1}.

A variation on this theme is the **heat pump,** which is used to heat buildings by cooling the outside air. It functions like a refrigerator turned inside out. The evaporator coils are outside, where they take heat from cold air, and the condenser coils are inside, where they give off heat to the warmer air. With proper design the heat Q_H delivered to the inside per cycle can be considerably greater than the work W required to get it there.

Work is *always* needed to transfer heat from a colder to a hotter body. Heat flows spontaneously from hotter to colder, and reversing this flow requires the addition of work from the outside. Experience shows that it is impossible to make a refrigerator that transports heat from a cold body to a hotter body without the addition of work. If no work were needed, the performance coefficient would be infinite. We call such a device a *workless refrigerator*; it is a mythical beast, like the unicorn and the free lunch.

19–5
The Second Law of Thermodynamics

Experimental evidence suggests strongly that it is *impossible* to build a heat engine that converts heat completely to work, that is, an engine with 100% thermal efficiency. This impossibility forms the basis of one form of the **second law of thermodynamics,** as follows:

It is impossible for any system to undergo a process in which it absorbs heat from a reservoir at a single temperature and converts it completely into mechanical work while ending in the same state in which it began.

In other words, it is impossible *in principle* for any heat engine to have a thermal efficiency of 100%.

The basis of the second law of thermodynamics lies in the difference between the nature of internal energy and that of macroscopic mechanical energy. In a moving body the molecules have random motion, but superimposed on this is a coordinated motion of every molecule in the direction of the velocity of the body. The kinetic energy associated with this coordinated macroscopic motion is what we call the kinetic energy of the moving body. The kinetic and potential energies associated with the *random* motion constitute the internal energy.

When a moving body makes an inelastic collision or comes to rest as a result of friction, the organized part of the motion is converted to random motion. Since we cannot control the motions of individual molecules, we cannot convert this random motion completely back to organized motion. We can convert *part* of it, and this is what a heat engine does.

Think what we could do if the second law were *not* true. We could power an automobile or run a power plant by extracting heat from the surrounding air. Neither of these impossibilities violates the *first* law of thermodynamics. The second law, therefore, is not a deduction from the first but stands by itself as a separate law of nature. The first law denies the possibility of creating or destroying energy; the second law limits the ways in which energy can be used and converted.

Our analysis of refrigerators in Section 19–4 forms the basis for an alternative statement of the second law of thermodynamics. Heat flows spontaneously from hotter to colder bodies, never the reverse. A refrigerator does take heat from a colder to a hotter body, but its operation

19–7
Energy-flow diagrams for equivalent forms of the second law. (a) A workless refrigerator (left), if it existed, could be used in combination with an ordinary heat engine (right) to form a composite device that functions as an engine with 100% efficiency, converting heat $Q_H - |Q_C|$ completely to work. (b) An engine with 100% efficiency (left), if it existed, could be used in combination with an ordinary refrigerator (right) to form a workless refrigerator, transferring heat Q_C from the cold reservoir to the hot with no net input of work. Thus if either of these is impossible, the other must be also.

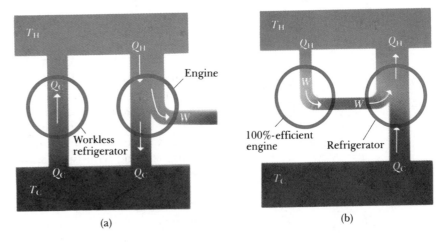

(a)   (b)

depends on input of mechanical energy or work. Generalizing this observation, we state:

> *It is impossible for any process to have as its sole result the transfer of heat from a cooler to a hotter body.*

This statement may not seem to be very closely related to the previous statement about heat engines. In fact, though, the two statements are completely equivalent. For example, if we could build a workless refrigerator, violating the second or "refrigerator" statement of the second law, we could use it in conjunction with a heat engine, pumping the heat rejected by the engine back to the hot reservoir to be reused. The composite machine (Fig. 19–7a) would violate the "engine" statement of the second law because its net effect would be to take a net quantity of heat $Q_H - |Q_C|$ from the hot reservoir and convert it completely to work W.

Alternatively, if we could make an engine with 100% thermal efficiency, in violation of the first statement, we could run it using heat from the hot reservoir and use the work output to drive a refrigerator that pumps heat from the cold reservoir to the hot reservoir (Fig. 19–7b). This composite device would violate the "refrigerator" statement because its net effect would be to take heat Q_C from the cold reservoir and deliver it to the hot reservoir without requiring any input of work. Thus any device that violates one form of the second law can also be used to make a device that violates the other form. If violations of the first form are impossible, so are violations of the second.

The conversion of work to heat, as in friction or viscous fluid flow, and heat flow from hot to cold across a finite temperature gradient, are *irreversible* processes. The "engine" and "refrigerator" statements of the second law state that these processes can be only partially reversed. We could cite other examples. Gases always seep through an opening spontaneously from a region of high pressure to a region of low pressure; gases and liquids left by themselves always tend to mix, not to unmix. The second law of thermodynamics is an expression of the inherent one-way aspect of these and many other irreversible processes that take place naturally in only one direction.

19–6
The Carnot Cycle

According to the second law, no heat engine can have a thermal efficiency of 100%. But how great an efficiency *can* an engine have, given two heat reservoirs at temperatures T_H and T_C? This question was answered in 1824 by the French engineer Sadi Carnot (1796–1832), who developed a hypothetical, idealized heat engine that has the maximum possible efficiency consistent with the second law. The cycle of this engine is called the **Carnot cycle.**

To understand the rationale of the Carnot cycle, we return to a theme that has recurred several times in this chapter: the concept of reversibility and its relationship to natural directions of thermodynamic processes. Conversion of work to heat is an irreversible process; the purpose of a heat engine is a *partial* reversal of this process, the conversion of heat to work with as great efficiency as possible. For maximum heat-engine efficiency, therefore, we must *avoid* all irreversible processes. This requirement turns out to be enough to determine the basic sequence of steps in the Carnot cycle, as we will show next.

Heat flow through a finite temperature drop is an irreversible process. Therefore during heat transfer in the Carnot cycle there must be *no* finite temperature difference. This means that when the engine takes heat from the hot reservoir at temperature T_H, the engine itself must also be at T_H; otherwise, irreversible heat flow would occur. Similarly, when the engine discards heat to the cold reservoir at temperature T_C, the engine itself must be at T_C. So every process that involves heat transfer must be *isothermal* at either T_H or T_C.

Conversely, in any process in which the temperature of the working substance of the engine is intermediate between T_H and T_C, there must be *no* heat transfer between the engine and either reservoir. Heat transfer between a constant-temperature reservoir and a working substance whose temperature is different from that of the reservoir could not be reversible. The bottom line is that *every process* in our idealized cycle must be either *isothermal* or *adiabatic*. In addition, both thermal and mechanical equilibrium must be maintained at all times so that each process is completely reversible.

The Carnot cycle includes two isothermal and two adiabatic processes. A Carnot cycle using an ideal gas as the working substance is shown on a pV-diagram in Fig. 19–8. It consists of the following steps:

1. The gas expands isothermally at temperature T_H, absorbing heat Q_H from the hot reservoir (curve *ab* on the diagram).
2. The gas expands adiabatically until its temperature drops to T_C (curve *bc* on the diagram).
3. The gas is compressed isothermally at T_C, discarding heat Q_C to the cold reservoir (curve *cd*).
4. The gas is compressed adiabatically back to its initial state at temperature T_H (curve *da*).

When the working substance in a Carnot engine is an ideal gas, it is a straightforward calculation to find the heat and work for each step.

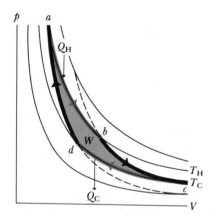

19–8
The Carnot cycle for an ideal gas. Color lines are isothermals; black lines are adiabatic curves.

From these quantities the thermal efficiency can be obtained. The details of these calculations are a little involved, and we will state the results here, without derivation. The ratio Q_C/Q_H of the two quantities of heat turns out to be equal (apart from a negative sign) to the ratio of the absolute temperatures of the reservoirs:

$$\frac{Q_C}{Q_H} = -\frac{T_C}{T_H}. \qquad (19\text{–}9)$$

Combining this with the general expression for the thermal efficiency of *any* heat engine, Eq. (19–4), we find that the thermal efficiency of the Carnot engine is

$$e_{\text{Carnot}} = 1 - \frac{T_C}{T_H}. \qquad (19\text{–}10)$$

This surprisingly simple result says that the thermal efficiency of the Carnot engine depends only on the ratio T_C/T_H of the absolute temperatures of the two heat reservoirs. The efficiency is large when the temperature *difference* is large, and it is very small when the temperatures are nearly equal. The efficiency can never be exactly unity unless $T_C = 0$. As we shall see later, this too is impossible.

Example 19–2   A Carnot engine takes 2000 J of heat from a reservoir at 500 K, does some work, and discards some heat to a reservoir at 350 K. How much work does the engine do, how much heat is discarded, and what is the efficiency?

Solution   From Eq. (19–9),

$$Q_C = -Q_H \frac{T_C}{T_H} = -(2000 \text{ J})\frac{350 \text{ K}}{500 \text{ K}} = -1400 \text{ J}.$$

Then from the first law,

$$W = Q_H + Q_C = 2000 \text{ J} + (-1400 \text{ J}) = 600 \text{ J}.$$

From Eq. (19–10) the thermal efficiency is

$$e = 1 - \frac{350 \text{ K}}{500 \text{ K}} = 0.30 = 30\%.$$

Alternatively, from the basic definition of thermal efficiency,

$$e = \frac{W}{Q_H} = \frac{600 \text{ J}}{2000 \text{ J}} = 0.30 = 30\%. \qquad \blacksquare$$

Because each step in the Carnot cycle is reversible, the *entire cycle* may be reversed, converting the engine into a refrigerator. We can derive an expression for the performance coefficient K of a Carnot refrigerator by combining the general definition of K, Eq. (19–8), with Eq.

(19–9) for the Carnot cycle. We first rewrite Eq. (19–8) as

$$K = -\frac{Q_C}{Q_H + Q_C} = -\frac{Q_C/Q_H}{1 + (Q_C/Q_H)}.$$

Then we substitute Eq. (19–9) into this. We leave the details for you to work out; the result is

$$K_{\text{Carnot}} = \frac{T_C}{T_H - T_C}. \tag{19–11}$$

When the temperature difference is small, K is much larger than unity. In this case a lot of heat can be "pumped" from the lower to the higher temperature with only a little expenditure of work. But the greater the temperature difference, the smaller is K, and the more work is required to transfer a given quantity of heat.

Example 19–3 If the cycle described in Example 19–2 is run backward as a refrigerator, what is the performance coefficient?

Solution The performance coefficient is given by Eq. (19–8):

$$K = -\frac{Q_C}{W} = -\frac{1400 \text{ J}}{-600 \text{ J}} = 2.33.$$

Because the cycle is a Carnot cycle, we may also use Eq. (19–11):

$$K = \frac{T_C}{T_H - T_C} = \frac{350 \text{ K}}{500 \text{ K} - 350 \text{ K}} = 2.33.$$

For a Carnot cycle, e and K depend only on the temperatures, as shown by Eqs. (19–10) and (19–11), and it is not necessary to calculate Q and W. For cycles containing irreversible processes, however, these equations are not valid, and more detailed calculations are necessary. ∎

It is easy to prove that:

No engine can be more efficient than a Carnot engine operating between the same two temperatures.

The key to the proof is the above observation that since each step in the Carnot cycle is reversible, the *entire cycle* may be reversed. Run backward, the engine becomes a refrigerator. Suppose we have an engine that is more efficient than a Carnot engine. Let Q_H' be the heat input it requires for a certain work output W. The Carnot engine, being less efficient, would require a greater amount of heat input Q_H for the same work output. The heat $|Q_C'|$ that this superefficient engine discards to the cold reservoir is also less than the quantity $|Q_C|$ for the Carnot engine with the same work output. Thus when we use the work W from the super-efficient engine to drive the Carnot engine backward, a net amount of heat $Q_C - Q_C'$ is removed from the cold reservoir, and a net amount of heat $Q_H - Q_H'$ is delivered to the hot reservoir, without any net input of work to the composite device. This violates the refrigerator statement of the second law. Thus the above statement is still another equivalent statement of the second law of thermodynamics. It also follows directly that:

All Carnot engines operating between the same two temperatures have the same efficiency, irrespective of the nature of the working substance.

That is, Eqs. (19–9), (19–10), and (19–11) are not restricted to a Carnot engine using an ideal gas; they are valid for *any* Carnot engine, no matter what its working substance. Finally, it is easy to show that no refrigerator can have a greater performance coefficient than a Carnot refrigerator for two given reservoir temperatures.

Equation (19–10) shows that to attain the maximum possible efficiency for a real engine, we should make T_H as high as possible and T_C as low as possible. For a steam turbine in an electric power plant, T_H is the temperature of the steam from the boiler. The vapor pressures of all liquids increase rapidly with increasing temperature, so the mechanical strength of the boiler sets a limit on the boiler temperature. At 500°C the vapor pressure of water is about 240×10^5 Pa, 235 atm, or 3450 psi, and this is about the maximum practical pressure in large present-day steam boilers.

The temperature of the condensed steam, T_C, from the turbine must be as low as possible. But T_C cannot be lower than the lowest temperature available for cooling and condensing the used steam. This is usually the temperature of the air, or perhaps of river or lake water if this is available at the plant. The unavoidable discarded heat in electric power plants creates a serious environmental problem. When a river or lake is used for cooling, the temperature of the body of water may be raised several degrees. Relatively small temperature changes can have significant effects on metabolic rates in plants and animals, so this can cause serious disruption of the overall ecological balance. This effect is called **thermal pollution,** and it is an inevitable consequence of the second law of thermodynamics. The sites of new power plants must be planned very carefully to minimize their ecological impact.

*19–7
Entropy

The second law of thermodynamics, as we have stated it, is a rather strange beast compared with many familiar physical laws. It is not an equation or a quantitative relationship but rather a statement of *impossibility.* But we can also state the second law as a quantitative relation, using the concept of **entropy,** the subject of this section.

We have discussed several processes that proceed naturally in the direction of increasing *disorder.* Irreversible heat flow increases disorder because the molecules are initially sorted into hotter and cooler regions; this sorting is lost when the system comes to thermal equilibrium. Adding heat to a body increases its disorder because it increases average molecular speeds and therefore the randomness of molecular motion.

Free expansion of a gas increases its disorder because the molecules have greater randomness of position after the expansion than before.

Entropy provides a *quantitative* measure of disorder. To introduce the concept, let's consider an isothermal expansion of an ideal gas. We add heat Q and let the gas expand just enough that the temperature remains constant. Because the internal energy of an ideal gas depends only on its temperature, the internal energy is also constant, so from the first law the work W done by the gas during this expansion is equal to the heat Q added to it. That is,

$$Q = W = p \, \Delta V = \frac{nRT}{V} \, \Delta V.$$

The gas is in a more disordered state after the expansion than before because the molecules are moving in a larger volume and have more randomness of position. Thus ΔV is a measure of the increase in disorder, and we see that it is proportional to the quantity Q/T. We introduce the symbol S, called the *entropy* of the system, and we define the entropy change ΔS during a reversible isothermal process as

$$\Delta S = \frac{Q}{T} \quad \text{(reversible isothermal process).} \qquad (19\text{--}12)$$

Note that T must be the *absolute* (Kelvin) temperature of the substance.

We can extend this definition to situations in which the temperature changes during the heat transfer. We think of the process as a series of small steps in which a small quantity of heat ΔQ_1 is added at temperature T_1, a quantity ΔQ_2 at temperature T_2, and so on, and add all the $\Delta Q/T$ quantities to find the total entropy change. Working out the details of such calculations often requires the use of integral calculus. In such a process we can again see the relation of the entropy increase to the increase in disorder. Higher temperature means greater average molecular speeds and therefore more randomness of motion. The increase in randomness is greater, relatively speaking, when the substance is initially cold, with little molecular motion, than when it is already hot, when we add relatively little to the molecular motion already present. Thus again the quotient Q/T, where T is *absolute* temperature, is an appropriate characterization of the increase in randomness or disorder.

Because entropy is a measure of the disorder of a system in any specific state, we expect it to depend only on the current *state* of the system, not on its past history. It can be shown by using the second law that this is indeed the case. Then when a system proceeds from an initial state with entropy S_1 to a final state with entropy S_2, the change in entropy $\Delta S = S_2 - S_1$ defined by Eq. (19–12) does not depend on the path leading from the initial to the final state but is the same for *all possible* processes leading from state 1 to state 2. We recall that *internal energy*, introduced in Chapter 18, also has this property, although entropy and internal energy are very different quantities. The units of entropy are energy divided by temperature, such as joules per kelvin $(\text{J}\cdot\text{K}^{-1})$ or calories per kelvin $(\text{cal}\cdot\text{K}^{-1})$.

The fact that entropy is a function only of the state of a system shows us how to compute entropy changes in *irreversible* (nonequilibrium) processes, in which Eq. (19–12) is not applicable. We simply invent a path connecting the given initial and final states that *does* consist entirely of reversible, equilibrium processes and compute the total entropy change for that path. It is not the actual path, but the entropy change must be the same as that for the actual path.

As with internal energy, the above discussion does not define entropy itself, but only the change in entropy in any given process. To complete the definition, we may arbitrarily assign a value to the entropy of a system in a specified reference state and then calculate the entropy of any other state with reference to this.

Example 19–4   One kilogram of ice at 0°C is melted and converted to water at 0°C. Compute its change in entropy.

Solution   The temperature T is constant at 273 K, and Q is the heat of fusion needed to melt the ice, 333×10^3 J. From Eq. (19–12) the increase in entropy of the system is

$$\Delta S = \frac{Q}{T} = \frac{3.33 \times 10^5 \text{ J}}{273 \text{ K}} = 1220 \text{ J} \cdot \text{K}^{-1},$$

In any *isothermal* reversible process the entropy change equals the heat added divided by the absolute temperature.   ■

Example 19–5   A gas expands adiabatically and reversibly. What is its change in entropy?

Solution   In an adiabatic process, no heat enters or leaves the system. Hence $Q = 0$, and there is *no* change in entropy; $\Delta S = 0$. Every *reversible* adiabatic process is a constant-entropy process. The increase in disorder resulting from the gas occupying a greater volume after the expansion is exactly balanced by the decrease in disorder associated with the lowered temperature and reduced molecular speeds.   ■

Example 19–6   For the Carnot engine in Example 19–2 (Section 19–6), find the total entropy change in the engine during one cycle.

Solution   During the isothermal expansion at 500 K the engine takes in 2000 J, and its entropy change is

$$\Delta S = \frac{Q}{T} = \frac{2000 \text{ J}}{500 \text{ K}} = 4.0 \text{ J} \cdot \text{K}^{-1}.$$

During the isothermal compression at 350 K the engine gives off 1400 J of heat, and its entropy change is

$$\Delta S = \frac{-1400 \text{ J}}{350 \text{ K}} = -4.0 \text{ J} \cdot \text{K}^{-1}.$$

Thus the total entropy change is $4.0 \text{ J} \cdot \text{K}^{-1} - 4.0 \text{ J} \cdot \text{K}^{-1} = 0$. This is to be expected because the final state is the same as the initial state. Each heat reservoir has an entropy change, but the total entropy change of the two reservoirs is zero. This cycle contains no irreversible processes, and the total entropy change is zero. This fact can be used for a very simple derivation of Eq. (19–9); because the total entropy change is zero, we have $Q_H/T_H + Q_C/T_C = 0$. ∎

Unlike energy, entropy is *not* a conserved quantity. In fact, the reverse is true; the entropy of an isolated system *can* change, but as we will see, it can never decrease. An entropy increase occurs in every natural process if all systems taking part in the process are included. In an idealized, completely reversible process involving only equilibrium states, no entropy change occurs, but all natural (i.e., irreversible) processes take place with an increase in entropy.

Example 19–7   Suppose that 1 kg of water at 100°C is placed in thermal contact with 1 kg of water at 0°C. What is the total change in entropy of the system when the hot water has cooled to 99°C and the cold water has warmed to 1°C?

Solution   This process involves irreversible heat flow. We assume the specific heat capacity of water is constant ($c = 4186\ \text{J·kg}^{-1}\text{·(C}^{\circ-1}\text{)}$) in this temperature range. The specified temperature changes require the transfer of 4186 J of heat. The total change of entropy is approximately

$$\Delta S = -\frac{4186\ \text{J}}{373\ \text{K}} + \frac{4186\ \text{J}}{273\ \text{K}} = 4.1\ \text{J·K}^{-1}.$$

Further increases in entropy occur as the system approaches thermal equilibrium at 50°C. To calculate the *total* increase in entropy requires calculus; the result turns out to be 102 J·K^{-1}.

An irreversible heat flow in an isolated system is accompanied by an increase in entropy. We could have reached the same end state by simply mixing the two quantities of water. This too is an irreversible process, and since entropy depends only on the state of the system, the total entropy change would be the same, 102 J·K^{-1}. ∎

In all these examples of irreversible processes, such as the mixing of substances at different temperatures or heat flow from a higher to a lower temperature, the net entropy change is always positive. In the special case of a *reversible* process the increases and decreases are equal, and the net change is zero. Generalizing from these examples, we can state that *in any thermodynamic process the total entropy of all systems taking part in the process either remains constant or increases.* Alternatively, *the entropy of an isolated system can never decrease.* This is yet another alternative statement of the second law of thermodynamics, in terms of entropy. It can be shown that this statement is logically equivalent to the "engine" and "refrigerator" statements that we discussed earlier.

The increase of entropy that accompanies every natural (irreversible) process measures the increase of disorder or randomness in the universe during that process. Consider again the mixing of hot and cold water. We *might* have used the hot and cold water as the high- and low-temperature reservoirs of a heat engine. While removing heat from the hot water and giving heat to the cold water, we could have obtained some mechanical work. But once the hot and cold water have been mixed and have come to a uniform temperature, this opportunity for converting heat to mechanical work is irretrievably lost. The warm water will never *unmix* itself and separate into hotter and colder parts. There is no loss of *energy* when the hot and cold water are mixed; what has been lost is *opportunity*—the opportunity to convert part of the heat from the hot water into mechanical work. When entropy increases, energy becomes less *available*, and the universe has become more random, disordered, or "run down."

*19–8
The Kelvin Temperature Scale

When we studied temperature scales in Chapter 14, we expressed the wish for a temperature scale that is independent of the properties or behavior of any particular material. We can now use the Carnot cycle to define such a scale. As we have seen, the efficiency of a Carnot engine operating between two heat reservoirs at temperatures T_H and T_C is independent of the nature of the working substance and depends only on the temperatures. If several Carnot engines with different working substances operate between the same two heat reservoirs, their thermal efficiencies are all the same:

$$e = \frac{Q_H + Q_C}{Q_H} = 1 + \frac{Q_C}{Q_H}.$$

Therefore the ratio Q_C/Q_H is the same for *all* Carnot engines operating between two given temperatures T_H and T_C. Kelvin proposed that we *define* the ratio of the reservoir temperatures, T_C/T_H, to be equal to the magnitude of this constant ratio Q_C/Q_H of the quantities of heat absorbed and rejected:

$$\frac{T_C}{T_H} = \frac{|Q_C|}{|Q_H|} = -\frac{Q_C}{Q_H}. \qquad (19\text{–}13)$$

Equation (19–13) appears to be identical to Eq. (19–9), but there is a subtle and crucial difference. The temperatures in Eq. (19–9) are based on an ideal-gas thermometer, as defined in Sections 14–2 and 14–4, while Eq. (19–13) *defines* a temperature scale, based on the Carnot cycle and the second law of thermodynamics, that is independent of the behavior of any particular substance. Thus the **Kelvin temperature scale** is truly *absolute*. To complete the definition of the Kelvin scale, we proceed, as in Chapter 14, to assign the arbitrary value of 273.16 K to the temperature of the triple point of water. When a substance is taken around a

Carnot cycle, the ratio of the heats absorbed and rejected, $|Q_H|/|Q_C|$, is equal to the ratio of the temperatures of the reservoirs *as expressed on the gas scale* defined in Chapter 14. Since in both scales the triple point of water is chosen to be 273.16 K, it follows that *the Kelvin and the ideal gas scales are identical.*

The zero point on the Kelvin scale is called **absolute zero.** There are theoretical reasons for believing that absolute zero cannot be attained experimentally, although temperatures as low as 10^{-6} K have been achieved. The more closely we approach absolute zero, the more difficult it is to get closer. Absolute zero can also be interpreted on a molecular level, although this must be done with some care. Because of quantum effects, it would *not* be correct to say that all molecular motion ceases at $T = 0$. At absolute zero the system has its *minimum* possible total energy (kinetic plus potential).

*19–9
Energy Conversion

The laws of thermodynamics place very general limitations on conversion of energy from one form to another. In this time of increasing energy demand and diminishing resources these matters are of the utmost practical importance. We conclude this chapter with a brief discussion of a few energy-conversion systems, present and proposed.

Over half of the electric power generated in the United States is obtained from coal-fired steam-turbine generating plants. Modern boilers can transfer about 80 to 90% of the heat of combustion of coal into steam. The theoretical maximum thermal efficiency of the turbine, given by Eq. (19–10), is usually limited to about 0.55, and the actual efficiency is typically 90% of this value, or about 0.50. The efficiency of large electrical generators in converting mechanical power to electrical is very large, typically 99%. Thus the overall thermal efficiency of such a plant is roughly (0.85)(0.50)(0.99), or about 40%.

In 1970 a generator with a capacity of about 1 GW (= 1000 MW = 10^9 W) went into operation at the Tennessee Valley Authority's Paradise power plant. The steam is heated to 540°C (1003°F) at a pressure of 248 atm (2.51×10^7 Pa or 3650 psi). The plant burns 10,500 tons of coal per day, and the overall thermal efficiency is 39.3%.

In a nuclear power plant the heat to generate steam is supplied by a nuclear reaction rather than the chemical reaction of burning coal. The steam turbines in nuclear power plants have the same theoretical efficiency limit as those in coal-fired plants. At present it is not practical to run nuclear reactors at temperatures and pressures as high as those in coal boilers, so the thermal efficiency of a nuclear plant is somewhat lower, typically 30%.

In both coal-fired and nuclear plants the energy that is not converted to electrical energy is wasted and must be disposed of. A common practice is to locate such a plant near a lake or river and to use the water for disposal of excess heat. This can raise the water temperature by several degrees, often with serious ecological consequences.

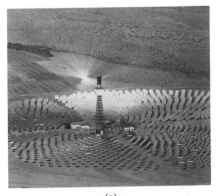

(a)

(b)

19–9

(a) A solar-energy installation in the Mojave Desert near Barstow, California. An array of mirrors concentrates the sun's energy on a boiler (central tower) to generate steam for turbines. The mirrors move continuously, controlled by a computer, to track the sun's motion. (b) An array of photovoltaic cells for direct conversion of sun power to electric power. Such an array supplies the electrical needs of the Headquarters and Visitors Center of Natural Bridges National Monument, Utah. (Photos by Dan McCoy/Rainbow.)

Solar energy is an inviting possibility. The power in the sun's radiation (before it passes through the earth's atmosphere) is about 1.4 kW per square meter. A maximum of about 1.0 kW·m^{-2} reaches the surface of the earth on a clear day, and the time average, over a 24-hour period, is about 0.2 kW·m^{-2}. This radiation can be collected and focused with mirrors and used to generate steam for a heat engine, as in Fig. 19–9a. A different scheme is to use large banks of photocells, as in Fig. 19–9b, for direct conversion of solar energy to electricity. Such a process is not a heat engine in the usual sense and is not limited by the Carnot efficiency. There are other fundamental limitations on photocell efficiency, but 50% seems attainable in multilayer semiconductor photocells. The energy of wind, which is fundamentally solar in origin, can be gathered and converted by "forests" of windmills, as shown in Fig. 19–10. At present, the capital costs of energy-collection systems such as these are usually considerably higher than costs for coal-fired generating plants of equal capacity.

An indirect scheme for collection and conversion of solar energy would use the temperature gradient in the ocean. In the Caribbean, for example, the water temperature near the surface is about 25°C, while at a depth of a few hundred meters it is about 10°C. The second law of thermodynamics forbids taking heat from the ocean and converting it completely into work, but there is nothing to forbid running a heat engine between these two temperatures. The thermodynamic efficiency would be very low (about 0.05), but a vast supply of energy would be available.

The present level of activity in energy-conversion research is rather low in comparison to the level in the 1970s, when we experienced a real and serious energy shortage. Fossil fuel prices have dropped, and there is less sense of urgency for this research. However, as we use up available fossil-fuel resources, we will certainly have to develop alternative energy sources, and the principles of thermodynamics will play a central role in their development.

19–10

An array of windmills to collect and convert wind energy. The propellerlike blades turn electric generators, converting the kinetic energy of moving air into electrical energy. (Photo by Paul Gipe.)

Questions

19–1 Suppose you want to increase the efficiency of a heat engine. Would it be better to increase T_H or to decrease T_C by an equal amount?

19–2 If an energy-conversion process involves two steps, each with its own efficiency, such as heat to work and work to electric energy, is the efficiency of the composite process equal to the product of the two efficiencies, or the sum, or the difference, or what?

19–3 In some climates it is practical to heat a house by using a heat pump, which acts as an air conditioner in reverse, cooling the outside air and heating the inside air. Can the heat delivered to the house ever exceed the electric-energy input to the pump?

19–4 What irreversible processes occur in a gasoline engine?

19–5 A housewife tries to cool her kitchen on a hot day by leaving the refrigerator door open. What happens? Would the result be different if an old-fashioned icebox were used?

19–6 Is it a violation of the second law to convert mechanical energy completely into heat? To convert heat completely into work?

19–7 A growing plant creates a highly complex and organized structure out of simple materials such as air, water, and trace minerals. Does this violate the second law of thermodynamics? What is the plant's ultimate source of energy?

19–8 An electric motor has its shaft coupled to that of a generator. The motor drives the generator, and the current from the generator is used to run the motor. The excess current is used to power a television set. What is wrong with this scheme?

19–9 Think of some reversible and some irreversible processes in purely mechanical systems, such as blocks sliding on planes, springs, pulleys, and strings.

19–10 Why must a room air conditioner be placed in a window? Why can't it just be set on the floor and plugged in?

19–11 Discuss the following examples of increasing disorder or randomness: mixing of hot and cold water, free expansion of a gas, irreversible heat flow, and development of heat through mechanical friction. Are entropy increases involved in all these?

19–12 When the sun shines on a glass-roofed greenhouse, the temperature becomes higher inside than outside. Does this phenomenon violate the second law?

19–13 When a wet cloth is hung up in a hot wind in the desert, the cloth is cooled by evaporation to a temperature that may be 20 C° or so below that of the air. Discuss this process in light of the second law.

19–14 Are the earth and sun in thermal equilibrium? Are there entropy changes associated with the transmission of energy from sun to earth? Does radiation differ from other modes of heat transfer with respect to entropy changes?

19–15 Discuss the entropy changes involved in the preparation and consumption of a hot-fudge sundae.

Exercises

Section 19–2 Heat Engines

19–1 A large Diesel engine takes in 9000 J of heat and delivers 3000 J of work per cycle. The heat is obtained by burning Diesel fuel with a heat of combustion of 5.00×10^4 J·g^{-1}.

a) What is the thermal efficiency?

b) How much heat is discarded in each cycle?

c) What mass of fuel is burned in each cycle?

d) If the engine goes through 50.0 cycles per second, what is its power output in watts? In horsepower?

19–2 A gasoline engine has a power output of 20.0 kW (about 27 hp). Its thermal efficiency is 25.0%.

a) How much heat must be supplied to the engine per second?

b) How much heat is discarded by the engine per second?

19–3 A nuclear-power plant has a mechanical-power output (used to drive an electric generator) of 200 MW. Its rate of heat input from the nuclear reactor is 500 MW.

a) What is the thermal efficiency of the system?

b) At what rate is heat discarded by the system?

19–4 An engine takes in 7000 J of heat and discards 5000 J during each cycle.

a) What is the mechanical work output of the engine during one cycle?

b) What is the thermal efficiency of the engine?

19–5 A gasoline engine performs 8000 J of mechanical work and discards 6000 J of heat each cycle.

a) How much heat must be supplied to the engine in each cycle?

b) What is the thermal efficiency of the engine?

Section 19–3   Internal-Combustion Engines

19–6 For a gas with $\gamma = 1.40$, what compression ratio r must an Otto cycle have to achieve an ideal efficiency of 60.0%?

19–7 For an Otto cycle with $\gamma = 1.40$ and $r = 6$ the temperature of the gasoline–air mixture when it enters the cylinder is 22.0°C (point a of Fig. 19–3). What is the temperature at the end of the compression stroke (point b)?

Section 19–4   Refrigerators

19–8 A window air-conditioning unit absorbs 5.00×10^4 J of heat per minute from the room being cooled and in the same time period deposits 7.00×10^4 J of heat into the outside air.

a) What is the power consumption of the unit in watts?

b) What is the performance coefficient of the unit?

19–9 A refrigerator has a performance coefficient of 2.00. During each cycle it absorbs 1.50×10^4 J of heat from the cold reservoir.

a) How much mechanical energy is required each cycle to operate the refrigerator?

b) Each cycle how much heat is discarded to the high-temperature reservoir?

19–10 A freezer has a performance coefficient $K = 3.00$. The freezer is to convert 0.800 kg of water at $T = 20.0°C$ into 0.800 kg of ice at $T = -10.0°C$ in 1 hr.

a) What amount of heat must be removed from the water at 20.0°C to convert it to ice at $-10.0°C$?

b) How much electrical energy is consumed by the freezer during this hour?

c) How much wasted heat is rejected to the room in which the freezer sits?

Section 19–6   The Carnot Cycle

19–11 Fill in the details of the derivation of Eq. (19–11).

19–12 Show that the efficiency e of a Carnot engine and the performance coefficient K of a Carnot refrigerator are related by $K = (1 - e)/e$. The engine and refrigerator operate between the same hot and cold reservoirs.

19–13 A Carnot engine whose high-temperature reservoir is at 400 K takes in 520 J of heat at this temperature in each cycle and gives up 335 J to the low-temperature reservoir.

a) What is the temperature of the low-temperature reservoir?

b) What is the thermal efficiency of the cycle?

c) How much mechanical work does the engine perform during each cycle?

19–14 An ice-making machine operates in a Carnot cycle; it takes heat from water at 0.0°C and rejects heat to a room at 27.0°C. Suppose that 30.0 kg of water at 0°C are converted to ice at 0°C.

a) How much heat is rejected to the room?

b) How much energy must be supplied to the refrigerator?

19–15 A Carnot engine is operated between two heat reservoirs at temperatures of 400 K and 300 K.

a) If the engine receives 5000 J of heat energy from the reservoir at 400 K in each cycle, how many joules per cycle does it reject to the reservoir at 300 K?

b) How much mechanical work is performed by the engine during each cycle?

c) What is the thermal efficiency of the engine?

19–16 A Carnot refrigerator is operated between two heat reservoirs at temperatures of 350 K and 250 K.

a) If in each cycle the refrigerator receives 400 J of heat energy from the reservoir at 250 K, how many joules of heat energy does it deliver to the reservoir at 350 K?

b) If the refrigerator goes through 3.0 cycles each second, what mechanical power input is required to operate the refrigerator?

c) What is the performance coefficient of the refrigerator?

Section 19–7   Entropy

19–17 A sophomore with nothing better to do adds heat to 0.40 kg of ice at 0°C until it is all melted.

a) What is the change in entropy of the water?

b) If the source of heat is a very massive body at a temperature of 20°C, what is the change in entropy of this body?

c) What is the total change in entropy of the water and the heat source?

19–18 Two moles of an ideal gas undergo a reversible isothermal expansion at a temperature of 300 K. During this expansion the gas does 2500 J of work. What is the change of entropy of the gas?

19–19 What is the entropy change of 0.500 kg of steam at 1.00 atm pressure and 100°C when it condenses to 0.500 kg of water at 100°C?

Section 19–9   Energy Conversion

19–20 A solar-power plant is to be built with a power output capacity of 2500 MW. What land area must the solar energy collectors occupy if they are:

a) photocells with 60.0% efficiency?

b) mirrors that generate steam for a turbine-generator unit with an overall efficiency of 30.0%?

Take the average power from the sun's radiation to be 200 W·m^{-2} at the earth's surface. Express your answers in square kilometers and square miles.

19–21 An engine is to be built to extract power from the temperature gradient of the ocean. If the surface and deep-water temperatures are 25.0°C and 8.0°C, respectively, what is the maximum theoretical efficiency of such an engine?

Problems

19–22 A coal-fired steam-turbine power plant has a mechanical-power output of 600 MW and a thermal efficiency of 40.0%.

a) At what rate must heat be supplied by burning coal?

b) If the heat of combustion of coal is 2.50×10^4 J·g^{-1}, what mass of coal is burned per second? Per day?

c) At what rate is heat discarded by the system?

d) If the discarded heat is given to water in a river, and its temperature is to rise by 5.00 C°, what volume of water is needed per second?

e) In part (d), if the river is 100 m wide and 5.0 m deep, what must be the speed of flow of the water?

19–23 A heat engine takes 0.400 mol of an ideal gas around the cycle shown in the pV-diagram of Fig. 19–11. Process 1 → 2 is at constant volume, process 2 → 3 is adiabatic, and process 3 → 1 is at a constant pressure of 1.00 atm. The value of γ for this gas is 1.67.

a) Find the pressure and volume at points 1, 2, and 3.

b) Calculate Q, W, and ΔU for each of the three processes.

c) Find the net work done by the gas in the cycle.

d) Find the net heat flow into the engine in one cycle.

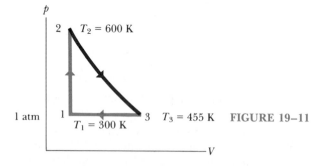

1 atm

$T_1 = 300$ K   3 $T_3 = 455$ K   **FIGURE 19–11**

19–24 A cylinder contains oxygen at a pressure of 3.00 atm. The volume is 2.00 L, and the temperature is 300 K. The oxygen is carried through the following

processes:

1. Heated at constant pressure from the initial state, state 1, to state 2, which has $T = 500$ K.

2. Cooled at constant volume to 250 K (state 3).

3. Cooled at constant pressure to 150 K (state 4).

4. Heated at constant volume to 300 K, which takes the system back to state 1.

a) Show these four processes in a pV-diagram, giving the numerical values of p and V in each of the four states.

b) Calculate Q and W for each of the four processes.

c) Calculate the net work done by the oxygen.

d) What is the efficiency of this device as a heat engine?

19–25 What is the thermal efficiency of an engine that operates by taking n moles of an ideal gas through the following cycle?

1. Start with n moles at p_0, V_0, T_0.

2. Change to $2p_0$, V_0 at constant volume.

3. Change to $2p_0$, $2V_0$ at constant pressure.

4. Change to p_0, $2V_0$ at constant volume.

5. Change to p_0, V_0 at constant pressure.

Let $C_v = 20.5$ J·mol^{-1}·K^{-1}.

19–26 A Carnot engine whose low-temperature reservoir is at 240 K has an efficiency of 40.0%. An engineer is assigned the problem of increasing this to 50.0%.

a) By how many degrees must the temperature of the high-temperature reservoir be increased if the temperature of the low-temperature reservoir remains constant?

b) By how many degrees must the temperature of the low-temperature reservoir be decreased if that of the high-temperature reservoir remains constant?

19–27 A physics student performing a heat-conduction experiment immerses one end of a copper rod in boiling water at 100°C and the other end in an ice–water mixture at 0°C. The sides of the rod are insulated. After steady-state conditions have been achieved in the rod, 0.200 kg of ice melts in a certain time interval. Find

a) the entropy change of the boiling water;

b) the entropy change of the ice–water mixture;

c) the entropy change of the copper rod;

d) the total entropy change of the entire system.

19–28 A Carnot engine operates between two heat reservoirs at temperatures T_H and T_C. An inventor proposes to increase the efficiency by running one engine between T_H and an intermediate temperature T' and a second engine between T' and T_C, using the heat expelled by the first engine. Compute the efficiency of this composite system, and compare it to that of the original engine.

Challenge Problems

19–29 Consider a Diesel cycle that starts (point a in Fig. 19–4) with 1.20 L of air at a temperature of 300 K and a pressure of 1.00×10^5 Pa. If the temperature at point c is $T_c = 1200$ K, derive an expression for the efficiency of the cycle in terms of the compression ratio r. What is the efficiency when $r = 15.0$?

19–30

a) Draw a graph of a Carnot cycle, plotting Kelvin temperature vertically and entropy horizontally (a temperature–entropy or TS diagram).

b) Show that the area under any curve in a temperature–entropy diagram represents the heat absorbed by the system.

c) Derive from your diagram the expression for the thermal efficiency of a Carnot cycle.

20

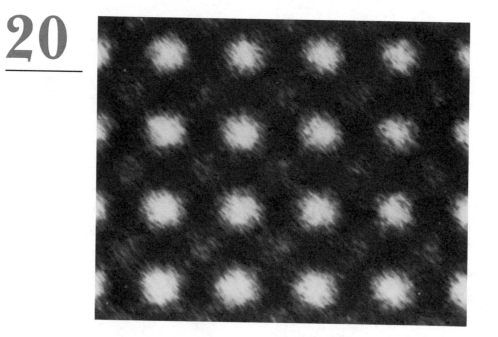

Molecular Properties of Matter

In preceding chapters we have studied several properties of matter in bulk, including elasticity, density, surface tension, equations of state, heat capacities, phase changes, internal energy, entropy, and others. We have mentioned the relationships of these properties to molecular structure, but we have deliberately avoided any detailed discussion of these relationships. There's a good reason for this; we can use all of these macroscopic (bulk) properties in problems without having to understand their microscopic (molecular) basis. Quantities such as heat, internal energy, and entropy can be defined independently of the details of molecular structure. Indeed, much of the power and usefulness of thermodynamics lies in its lack of dependence on microscopic models.

Nevertheless, we can gain a lot of additional insight into the behavior of matter by looking at the relationship of bulk behavior to microscopic structure. We begin with a general discussion of the molecular structure of matter. Then we develop the kinetic–molecular model of an ideal gas, deriving the equation of state and heat capacity from a molecular model. Next we look at the heat capacities of solids and their relation to molecular structure. Finally, we discuss the phenomena of diffusion and osmosis.

20–1
Molecular Structure of Matter

It has been established beyond doubt that all matter is made up of particles called **molecules.** For any specific chemical compound, all the molecules are identical. The smallest molecules are of the order of 10^{-10} m in size; the largest are at least 10,000 times as large as this. In liquids and solids, molecules are held together by intermolecular forces that are *electrical* in nature, arising from interactions of the electrically charged fundamental particles that make up the molecules. *Gravitational* forces between molecules are negligible in comparison with electrical forces.

The interaction of two *point* electric charges is described by a force (repulsive for like charges, attractive for unlike charges) with a magnitude proportional to $1/r^2$, where r is the distance between the points. This relationship is called *Coulomb's law*; we will study it in detail in Chapter 24. Forces between *molecules*, however, are not this simple. Molecules are not point charges but complex structures containing both positive and negative charge, and their interactions are correspondingly complex. When molecules are far apart, as in a gas, the intermolecular forces are very small and usually attractive. As a gas is compressed and its molecules are brought closer together, the forces increase. In liquids and solids, relatively large pressures are needed to compress the substance appreciably. This shows that at molecular distances slightly *less* than the normal spacing, the forces become *repulsive* and relatively large.

Thus the intermolecular force must vary with the distance r between molecules somewhat as shown in Fig. 20–1, where a positive F corresponds to a repulsive force and a negative F to an attractive force. At large distances the force is small and attractive. As the molecules come closer together, it becomes larger in magnitude (more negative), passes through a greatest negative value, and then goes to zero at an equilibrium separation r_0. When the distance is less than r_0, the force becomes repulsive and increases quite rapidly. Figure 20–1 also shows the potential energy as a function of r. This function has a *minimum* at r_0, where the force is zero. Such a potential-energy function is often called a **potential well.**

In view of these attractive intermolecular forces, why don't all molecules eventually coalesce into matter in the liquid or solid phase? The answer is that molecules are always in *motion*. The kinetic energy associated with this motion increases with temperature. At very low temperatures the average kinetic energy of a molecule may be much *less* than the maximum magnitude of potential energy, which is the "depth" of the potential well in Fig. 20–1. The molecules then condense into the liquid or solid phase with average intermolecular spacings of about r_0. But at higher temperatures the average kinetic energy becomes larger than the depth of the potential well; molecules can then escape the intermolecular force and become free to move independently, as in the gaseous phase of matter.

In *solids*, molecules vibrate about more or less fixed centers. The potential well is usually approximately parabolic in shape near its minimum, and the motion is then approximately simple harmonic. The

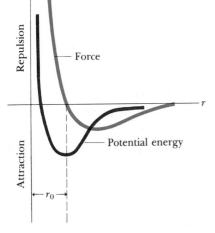

20–1
The force between two molecules (color curve) changes from an attraction when the separation is large to a repulsion when the separation is small. The potential energy (black curve) is minimum at r_0, where the force is zero.

20-2
Crystal of necrosis virus protein. The actual size of the entire crystal is about two thousandths of a millimeter (0.002 mm). (Courtesy of Ralph W. G. Wyckoff.)

amplitudes of the vibratory motions are relatively small, and the fixed centers form a space lattice, corresponding to the repeated spatial patterns and symmetry of *crystals*. A photograph of the individual, very large molecules of necrosis virus protein is shown in Fig. 20–2. It was taken with an electron microscope with a magnification of about 80,000. The molecules look like neatly stacked oranges. Each molecule is about 1.2×10^{-8} m in diameter.

In a *liquid* the intermolecular distances are usually only slightly greater than in the solid phase of the same substance. When a solid melts, the volume usually increases only a little, but the molecules have much greater freedom of movement. Liquids show regularity of structure only in the immediate neighborhood of a few molecules. This is called **short-range order,** in contrast with the **long-range order** of a solid crystal.

The molecules of a *gas* are usually widely separated and have only very small attractive forces. A gas molecule moves in a straight line until it collides with another molecule or with a wall of the container. In molecular terms an *ideal gas* is a gas whose molecules exert *no* attractive forces on each other and therefore have no *potential* energy. In Section 20–3 we will derive the ideal-gas equation of state from this simple molecular picture. This is a simple example of the *kinetic-molecular theory of gases*.

At low temperatures, most common substances are in the solid phase. As the temperature rises, a substance melts and then vaporizes. From a *macroscopic* point of view the transitions from solid to liquid to gas are in the direction of increasing temperature. From a *molecular* point of view these transitions are in the direction of increasing molecular kinetic energy. So we see that temperature and molecular kinetic energy are closely related.

20-2
Avogadro's Number

One **mole** of any pure chemical element or compound contains a definite number of molecules, the same number for all elements and compounds. According to the official SI definition of the mole,

The mole is the amount of substance that contains as many elementary entities as there are atoms in 0.012 kilograms of carbon 12.

In our discussion the "elementary entities" are atoms or molecules.

The number of atoms or molecules in a mole is called **Avogadro's number,** denoted by N_A. The numerical value of N_A, determined by using X-rays to measure the distance between layers of molecules in a crystal, is known with an uncertainty of less than six parts per million. To four significant figures it is

$$N_A = 6.022 \times 10^{23} \text{ molecules} \cdot \text{mol}^{-1}.$$

The **molecular mass** M of a compound is the mass of one mole; this is equal to the mass m of a single molecule, multiplied by Avogadro's number:

$$M = N_A m. \tag{20-1}$$

When the molecule consists of a single atom, the term *atomic mass* is often used.

We can use Eq. (20–1) to compute the mass of a molecule. For example, the mass of 1 mol of atomic hydrogen (i.e., the atomic mass) is 1.008 g. Therefore the mass m_H of a single hydrogen atom is

$$m_H = \frac{1.008 \text{ g·mol}^{-1}}{6.022 \times 10^{23} \text{ molecules·mol}^{-1}}$$

$$= 1.674 \times 10^{-24} \text{ g·molecule}^{-1}.$$

The molecular mass of oxygen, with diatomic molecules, is 32.0 g·mol^{-1}; the mass of a single molecule of O_2 is

$$m_{O_2} = \frac{32.0 \text{ g·mol}^{-1}}{6.022 \times 10^{23} \text{ molecules·mol}^{-1}}$$

$$= 53.1 \times 10^{-24} \text{ g·molecule}^{-1}.$$

Figure 20–3 shows one mole of each of several familiar materials.

20–3
How much is one mole? The photograph shows one mole each of sucrose (ordinary sugar, rear pile), iodine (metallic-looking chips), water, mercury, iron (cube), acetylsalicylic acid (aspirin tablets), and sodium chloride (ordinary salt, front pile). (Photo by Chip Clark.)

20–3
Kinetic-Molecular Theory of an Ideal Gas

The goal of any molecular theory of matter is to understand the *macroscopic* (bulk) properties of matter on the basis of its molecular structure and behavior. This kind of molecular-level analysis has led to the development of new materials with specific desirable properties, including high-strength steels, glasses with special optical properties, semiconductor materials for solid-state electronic devices, superconducting alloys, and countless other materials that are essential to contemporary technology.

One of the simplest examples of a molecular theory is the kinetic-molecular model of an ideal gas. With the help of this model we can understand how ideal-gas behavior, including the ideal-gas equation of state (Section 17–2), is related to Newton's laws. The following development has several steps, and you may need to go over it several times to grasp how it all goes together.

Consider a container with volume V, containing N identical molecules, each with mass m. The molecules are in constant motion; each molecule collides occasionally with a wall of the container. During collisions the molecules exert *forces* on the walls; this is the origin of the *pressure* the gas exerts on the walls of the container. We assume that the collisions are *perfectly elastic*, as shown in Fig. 20–4. During each collision the velocity component v_y parallel to the wall is unchanged, and the component v_x perpendicular to the wall changes direction.

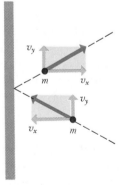

20–4
Elastic collision of a molecule with container wall. The component v_y parallel to the wall does not change; the component v_x perpendicular to the wall reverses direction. The speed v does not change.

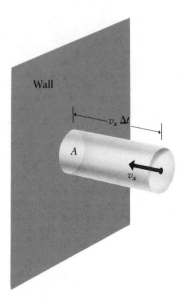

20–5
A molecule moving toward the wall with speed v_x collides with the area A during the time interval Δt only if it is within a distance $v_x \Delta t$ of the wall at the beginning of the interval. All such molecules are contained within a volume $A v_x \Delta t$.

Here is our program. First we determine the *number* of collisions per unit time for a certain wall area A. Then we find the total momentum change associated with these collisions and the *force* needed to cause this momentum change. Then we can determine the pressure, which is force per unit area. We let v_x be the *magnitude* of the x-component of velocity of a molecule. For now we assume that all molecules have the same v_x. This isn't right, but making this temporary assumption helps to clarify the basic ideas. We will show soon that it is easy to make our model more realistic and avoid the need for this assumption.

For each collision the change in the x-component of momentum is $2mv_x$. If a molecule is going to collide with a given wall area A during a time interval Δt, then at the beginning of Δt it must be within a distance $v_x \Delta t$ from the wall, as shown in Fig. 20–5, and it must be headed toward the wall. So the number of molecules that collide with A during Δt is equal to the number of molecules that are within a cylinder with base area A and length $v_x \Delta t$ and have their v_x aimed toward the wall. The volume of such a cylinder is $A v_x \Delta t$.

Assuming that the number of molecules per unit volume (N/V) is uniform, the *number* of molecules in this cylinder is $(N/V)(A v_x \Delta t)$. On the average, half of these molecules are moving *toward* the wall and half *away from* it. So the number of collisions with A during Δt is

$$\frac{1}{2}\frac{N}{V}(A v_x \Delta t). \tag{20–2}$$

The total momentum change ΔP_x due to all these collisions is $2mv_x$ times the *number* of collisions. (We are using capital P for momentum and small p for pressure; be careful!)

$$\Delta P_x = \frac{1}{2}\left(\frac{N}{V}\right)(A v_x \Delta t)(2mv_x) = \frac{NAmv_x^2 \Delta t}{V}, \tag{20–3}$$

and the *rate* of change of momentum is

$$\frac{\Delta P_x}{\Delta t} = \frac{NAmv_x^2}{V}. \tag{20–4}$$

According to Newton's second law, this rate of change of momentum equals the average force exerted by the wall area A on the molecules. From Newton's *third* law this is the negative of the force exerted *on* the wall *by* the molecules. Finally, pressure p is force per unit area, and we obtain

$$p = \frac{F}{A} = \frac{Nmv_x^2}{V}. \tag{20–5}$$

We have mentioned that v_x is *not* really the same for all the molecules. But we could have sorted the molecules into groups having the same v_x within each group and added up the resulting contributions to the pressure. The net effect of all this is just to replace v_x^2 in Eq. (20–5) by the *average* value of v_x^2, which we denote by $(v_x^2)_{av}$. Furthermore, $(v_x^2)_{av}$ is related simply to the *speeds* of the molecules. The speed v (magnitude of velocity) of any molecule is related to the velocity components v_x, v_y, and v_z by

$$v^2 = v_x^2 + v_y^2 + v_z^2.$$

We can average this relation over all molecules:

$$(v^2)_{av} = (v_x{}^2)_{av} + (v_y{}^2)_{av} + (v_z{}^2)_{av}.$$

But since the x-, y-, and z-directions are all equivalent,

$$(v_x{}^2)_{av} = (v_y{}^2)_{av} = (v_z{}^2)_{av}.$$

So finally,

$$(v_x{}^2)_{av} = \frac{1}{3}(v^2)_{av},$$

and Eq. (20–5) becomes

$$pV = \frac{1}{3}Nm(v^2)_{av} = \frac{2}{3}N\left(\frac{1}{2}m(v^2)_{av}\right). \qquad (20\text{–}6)$$

We notice that $\frac{1}{2}m(v^2)_{av}$ is the average kinetic energy of a single molecule. The product of this and the total number of molecules N equals the total random kinetic energy, which is equal to the total internal energy U. (The molecules of an ideal gas have no *potential* energy.) Hence the product pV equals two thirds of the internal energy:

$$pV = \frac{2}{3}U. \qquad (20\text{–}7)$$

Let's compare this with the ideal-gas equation,

$$pV = nRT,$$

which is based on experimental studies of gas behavior. For the two equations to agree we must have

$$U = \frac{3}{2}nRT. \qquad (20\text{–}8)$$

This is not completely unexpected; we have already learned that the internal energy U of an ideal gas depends only on its absolute temperature T. Equation (20–8) shows that in fact U is *directly proportional* to T. Alternatively, if we begin by *assuming* that U is directly proportional to T, then we can view the above development as a derivation of the ideal-gas equation. In any case our analysis shows directly the relation between internal energy and temperature, and it also helps us to understand the molecular basis of ideal-gas behavior.

The average kinetic energy of a single molecule is the total kinetic energy U of all molecules, divided by the number N of molecules:

$$\frac{U}{N} = \frac{1}{2}m(v^2)_{av} = \frac{3nRT}{2N}.$$

Also, the number of moles, n, equals the total number of molecules, N, divided by Avogadro's number N_A:

$$n = \frac{N}{N_A}, \qquad \frac{n}{N} = \frac{1}{N_A}.$$

So

$$\frac{1}{2}m(v^2)_{av} = \frac{3}{2}\frac{R}{N_A}T. \qquad (20\text{–}9)$$

The ratio R/N_A occurs frequently in molecular theory. It is called the **Boltzmann constant**, k:

$$k = \frac{R}{N_A} = \frac{8.314 \text{ J·mol}^{-1} \cdot \text{K}^{-1}}{6.022 \times 10^{23} \text{ molecules·mol}^{-1}}$$
$$= 1.381 \times 10^{-23} \text{ J·molecule}^{-1} \cdot \text{K}^{-1}.$$

In terms of k we can rewrite Eq. (20–9) as

$$\frac{1}{2} m(v^2)_{\text{av}} = \frac{3}{2} kT. \tag{20–10}$$

Thus the average kinetic energy *per molecule* depends only on the temperature, not on the pressure, volume, or kind of molecule. We can obtain an equivalent statement from Eq. (20–9) by using the relation $M = N_A m$:

$$N_A \frac{1}{2} m(v^2)_{\text{av}} = \frac{1}{2} M(v^2)_{\text{av}} = \frac{3}{2} RT. \tag{20–11}$$

That is, the kinetic energy of a *mole* of molecules depends only on T.

From Eqs. (20–10) and (20–11) we can obtain expressions for the square root of $(v^2)_{\text{av}}$, called the *root-mean-square speed* v_{rms}:

$$v_{\text{rms}} = \sqrt{(v^2)_{\text{av}}} = \sqrt{\frac{3kT}{m}} = \sqrt{\frac{3RT}{M}}. \tag{20–12}$$

It might seem more natural to characterize molecular speeds by their *average* value rather than with v_{rms}, but we see that v_{rms} evolves more simply from our analysis.

Finally, it is sometimes convenient to rewrite the ideal-gas equation on a molecular basis. We use $N = N_A n$ and $R = N_A k$ to obtain the alternative form of the ideal-gas equation:

$$pV = NkT. \tag{20–13}$$

This shows that we can think of k as a gas constant on a "per molecule" basis instead of the usual "per mole" basis for R.

PROBLEM-SOLVING STRATEGY: *Kinetic-Molecular Theory*

1. As usual, using a consistent set of units is essential. Following are several places where caution is needed.

2. The usual units for molecular mass M are grams per mole; the molecular mass of oxygen is 32 g·mol^{-1}, for example. These units are often omitted in tables. In equations such as Eq. (20–12), when you use SI units, you *must* express M in kilograms per mole by dividing by 10^3. Thus in SI units $M = 32 \times 10^{-3}$ kg·mol^{-1} for oxygen.

3. Are you working on a "per molecule" basis or a "per mole" basis? Remember that m is the mass

of a molecule and M is the mass of a mole. N is the number of molecules, and n is the number of moles; k is the gas constant per molecule, and R is the gas constant per mole. Although N, the number of molecules, is in one sense a dimensionless number, you can do a complete unit check if you think of N as having the unit "molecules"; then m has the unit "mass per molecule," and k has the unit "joules per molecule per kelvin."

4. Remember that T is always *absolute* (Kelvin) temperature.

Example 20–1 What is the average kinetic energy of a molecule of a gas at a temperature of 300 K?

Solution From Eq. (20–10),

$$\frac{1}{2}m(v^2)_{av} = \frac{3}{2}kT = \frac{3}{2}(1.38 \times 10^{-23} \text{ J·K}^{-1})(300 \text{ K})$$

$$= 6.21 \times 10^{-21} \text{ J.} \qquad \blacksquare$$

Example 20–2 What is the total random kinetic energy of the molecules in 1 mol of a gas at a temperature of 300 K?

Solution From Eq. (20–8),

$$U = \frac{3}{2}nRT = \frac{3}{2}(1 \text{ mol})(8.314 \text{ J·mol}^{-1}\text{·K}^{-1})(300 \text{ K})$$

$$= 3741 \text{ J} = 894 \text{ cal.} \qquad \blacksquare$$

Example 20–3 What is the root-mean-square speed of a hydrogen molecule at 300 K?

Solution The mass of a hydrogen molecule (see Section 20–2) is

$$m_{H_2} = (2)(1.674 \times 10^{-27} \text{ kg}) = 3.348 \times 10^{-27} \text{ kg.}$$

From Eq. (20–12),

$$v_{rms} = \sqrt{\frac{3kT}{m}} = \sqrt{\frac{3(1.381 \times 10^{-23} \text{ J·K}^{-1})(300 \text{ K})}{3.348 \times 10^{-27} \text{ kg}}}$$

$$= 1927 \text{ m·s}^{-1}.$$

Alternatively,

$$v_{rms} = \sqrt{\frac{3RT}{M}} = \sqrt{\frac{3(8.314 \text{ J·mol}^{-1}\text{·K}^{-1})(300 \text{ K})}{2(1.008 \times 10^{-3} \text{ kg·mol}^{-1})}}$$

$$= 1927 \text{ m·s}^{-1}.$$

Note that when we use Eq. (20–12) with R in SI units, we have to express M in *kilograms* per mole, not grams per mole. In this example, $M = 2.016 \times 10^{-3}$ kg·mol^{-1}, not 2.016 g·mol^{-1}. $\qquad \blacksquare$

Example 20–4 Five gas molecules chosen at random are found to have speeds of 500, 600, 700, 800, and 900 m·s^{-1}. Find the rms speed; is it the same as the *average* speed?

Solution The average value of v^2 for the five molecules is

$$(v^2)_{av} = \frac{(500 \text{ m·s}^{-1})^2 + (600 \text{ m·s}^{-1})^2 + (700 \text{ m·s}^{-1})^2 + (800 \text{ m·s}^{-1})^2 + (900 \text{ m·s}^{-1})^2}{5}$$

$$= 510{,}000 \text{ m}^2\text{·s}^{-2},$$

and v_{rms} is the square root of this:

$$v_{rms} = 714 \text{ m·s}^{-1}.$$

The *average* speed v_{av} is given by

$$v_{av} = \frac{500 \text{ m·s}^{-1} + 600 \text{ m·s}^{-1} + 700 \text{ m·s}^{-1} + 800 \text{ m·s}^{-1} + 900 \text{ m·s}^{-1}}{5}$$

$$= 700 \text{ m·s}^{-1}.$$

This illustrates the point that in general v_{rms} and v_{av} are not the same. Roughly speaking, v_{rms} gives greater weight to the larger speeds than does v_{av}. ∎

Example 20–5   Find the number of molecules and the number of moles in 1 m^3 of air at atmospheric pressure and 0°C.

Solution   From Eq. (20–13),

$$N = \frac{pV}{kT} = \frac{(1.013 \times 10^5 \text{ Pa})(1 \text{ m}^3)}{(1.38 \times 10^{-23} \text{ J·K}^{-1})(273 \text{ K})} = 2.69 \times 10^{25}.$$

The number of moles n is given by

$$n = \frac{N}{N_A} = \frac{2.69 \times 10^{25} \text{ molecules}}{6.022 \times 10^{23} \text{ molecules·mol}^{-1}} = 44.7 \text{ mol}.$$

The total volume is 1.00 m^3, so the volume of 1 mol is

$$\frac{1.00 \text{ m}^3}{44.7 \text{ mol}} = 0.0224 \text{ m}^3\text{·mol}^{-1} = 22.4 \text{ L·mol}^{-1}.$$

This is the same result that we obtained in Example 17–1 (Section 17–2). ∎

When a gas expands against a moving piston, it does work and its internal energy decreases. When a gas is compressed, its internal energy increases. But if the collisions with the walls are perfectly elastic, as we have assumed, how can a molecule gain or lose energy when it collides with a piston? To answer this question, consider the collision of a molecule with a *moving* wall. When a molecule collides with a *stationary* wall, it exerts a momentary force on the wall but does no work because the wall does not move. But if the wall is in motion, the molecule *does* do work on the wall during the collision. If the wall in Fig. 20–4 is moving to the left, the molecules that strike it do work; their speeds and kinetic energies after colliding are smaller than they were before. If the piston is moving toward the right, the kinetic energy of a colliding molecule *increases* by an amount equal to the work done on the molecule.

The assumption that individual molecules undergo elastic collisions with the container wall is actually a little too simple. More detailed investigation has shown that in most cases, molecules actually adhere to the wall for a short time and then leave again with speeds characteristic of the temperature *of the wall.* However, the gas and the wall are ordinarily in thermal equilibrium, and this discovery does not alter the validity of our conclusions.

20–4
Molar Heat Capacity of a Gas

We discussed heat capacities of gases in Section 18–7; you may want to review that discussion before reading on. We noted the correlation of values of C_v, the molar heat capacity at constant volume, with molecular structure. We can now analyze that correlation on the basis of the molecular picture of an ideal gas that we developed in Section 20–3. When we add heat to a gas while keeping the volume constant, the gas does no work. According to the first law, then, the heat added is equal to the internal energy change: $\Delta U = \Delta Q$. From the *molecular* viewpoint the internal energy is the sum of the kinetic and potential energies of the molecules. If we know how this total internal energy depends on temperature, then from its rate of change with temperature we can make a theoretical prediction of the molar heat capacity of the system.

The simplest system is a *monatomic* ideal gas. We represent each molecule (a single atom) as a point particle. There is no potential energy of interaction of the molecules, and the only energy is the translational kinetic energy of random motion. For n moles of gas at absolute temperature T this is given by Eq. (20–8):

$$\text{Kinetic energy} = U = \frac{3}{2}nRT.$$

When the temperature increases by ΔT, the kinetic energy increases by

$$\Delta U = \frac{3}{2}nR\,\Delta T.$$

But by definition of C_v and the fact that $\Delta U = \Delta Q$,

$$\Delta Q = nC_v\,\Delta T = \Delta U.$$

Comparing these two expressions for ΔU, we find that

$$C_v = \frac{3}{2}R. \tag{20–14}$$

In SI units,

$$C_v = \frac{3}{2}(8.314\ \text{J·mol}^{-1}\text{·K}^{-1}) = 12.47\ \text{J·mol}^{-1}\text{·K}^{-1}.$$

The experimental values of C_v listed in Table 18–1 for monatomic gases are very close to this value and thus tend to confirm the validity of our analysis.

We also know from Section 18–7 that for any ideal gas $C_p = C_v + R$, so we predict that γ, the ratio of molar heat capacities for a monatomic ideal gas, is

$$\frac{C_p}{C_v} = \gamma = \frac{\frac{3}{2}R + R}{\frac{3}{2}R} = \frac{5}{3} = 1.67.$$

This also agrees with the experimental values in Table 18–1.

Thus far we have treated each molecule as a point particle. For a *polyatomic* gas, whose molecules have two or more atoms each, the problem is more complicated. For example, we can picture a diatomic molecule as *two* point masses with an interaction force of the kind shown in Fig. 20–1, like a little elastic dumbbell. Such a molecule can have additional kinetic energy associated with *rotation* about an axis through its center of mass, and the atoms may also have a back-and-forth *vibrating* motion along the line joining them, with additional kinetic and potential energies.

Equation (20–10) shows that the *temperature* of a gas is determined by the average random *translational* kinetic energy of its molecules. When heat flows into a *monatomic* gas at constant volume, all of this energy goes into an increase in random *translational* molecular kinetic energy. But when heat is added to a *diatomic* or *polyatomic* gas, part of the energy goes into increasing rotational and vibrational motion. So a greater total amount of energy is required for a given temperature change in order to increase the rotational and vibrational as well as translational energy. Thus polyatomic gases have *larger* molar heat capacities than do monatomic gases. The experimental values in Table 18–1 show this effect.

To proceed further in our analysis of heat capacities, we need some principle that will tell us *how much* energy is associated with each additional kind of motion of a complex molecule compared to the translational kinetic energy we have already discussed. The necessary principle goes by the fancy name **principle of equipartition of energy.** This principle can be derived from sophisticated statistical-mechanics considerations; that derivation is beyond our scope, and we will treat the principle as an axiom.

The principle of equipartition of energy states that each velocity component (either linear or angular) has, on the average, an associated kinetic energy per molecule of $\frac{1}{2}kT$. The number of velocity components needed to describe the motion of a molecule completely is called the number of **degrees of freedom.** For a monatomic gas the number is three. For a diatomic molecule there are two possible axes of rotation, perpendicular to each other and to the molecule's axis. (Rotation about the molecule's own axis is not counted because in ordinary collisions there is no way for this rotational motion to change.) If we assign five degrees of freedom to a diatomic molecule, the average total kinetic energy per molecule is $\frac{5}{2}kT$ instead of $\frac{3}{2}kT$. The total internal energy of n moles is $U = \frac{5}{2}nRT$, and the molar heat capacity (at constant volume) is

$$C_v = \frac{5}{2}R. \qquad (20\text{--}15)$$

In SI units,

$$C_v = \frac{5}{2}(8.314 \text{ J·mol}^{-1}\text{·K}^{-1}) = 20.78 \text{ J·mol}^{-1}\text{·K}^{-1}.$$

Reference to Table 18–1 shows that this agrees with measured values for diatomic gases, within a few percent. The corresponding value of γ is

$$\gamma = \frac{C_p}{C_v} = \frac{\frac{5}{2}R + R}{\frac{5}{2}R} = \frac{7}{5} = 1.40,$$

which also agrees well with experimental values.

Vibrational motion can also contribute to the heat capacities of gases. The molecular bonds are not rigid; they can stretch and bend, and the resulting vibrations lead to additional degrees of freedom and additional energies. For most diatomic gases, however, vibrational motion does *not* contribute appreciably to heat capacity. The reason for this is a little subtle and involves some concepts of quantum mechanics. Briefly, vibrational energy can change only in finite steps. If the energy change of the first step is much *larger* than the energy possessed by most molecules, then nearly all the molecules remain in the minimum-energy state of motion. In that case, changing the temperature does not change their average vibrational energy appreciably, and the vibrational degrees of freedom are said to be "frozen out." In more complex molecules the gaps between permitted energy levels are sometimes much smaller, and then vibration *does* contribute to heat capacity. In Table 18–1 the large values of C_v for some polyatomic molecules show the contributions of vibrational energy. In addition, a molecule with three or more atoms that are not in a straight line has three, not two, rotational degrees of freedom.

*20–5
Distribution of Molecular Speeds

We mentioned in Section 20–3 that the molecules in a gas do not all have the same speed. Direct measurements of the distribution of molecular speeds can be made; one experimental scheme is shown in Fig. 20–6. A substance is vaporized in a hot oven; molecules of the vapor escape through an aperture in the oven wall and into a vacuum chamber. A series of slits blocks all molecules except those in a narrow beam; the beam is aimed at a pair of rotating disks. A molecule passing through the slit in the first disk arrives at the second disk just as *its* slit is lined up with the beam only if the molecule has a certain speed. The setup thus functions as a speed selector that allows only molecules with a certain narrow range of speeds to pass. This speed can be varied by changing the disk speed, and we can measure how many molecules have each of various speeds.

The results of such measurements can be represented graphically as shown in Fig. 20–7. The function $f(v)$ is called a *distribution function*; it shows the relative numbers of molecules having various speeds v. The figure shows distribution functions for three different temperatures; at each temperature the height of the curve for any value of v is proportional to the number of molecules with speeds near v. The peak of each

20–6
Apparatus for producing a molecular beam and observing the distribution of molecular speeds in the beam.

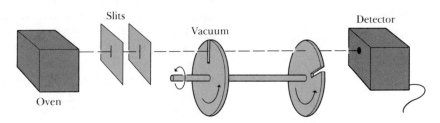

Oven   Slits   Vacuum   Detector

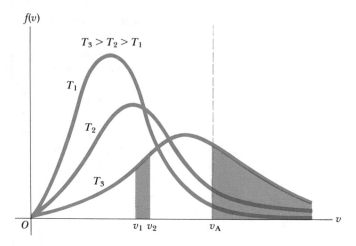

20–7
Maxwell–Boltzmann distribution curves for various temperatures. As the temperature increases, the curve becomes flatter, and its maximum shifts to higher temperature. At temperature T_3 the number of molecules having speeds in the range v_1 to v_2 and the number having speeds greater than v_A are shown by the shaded areas under the T_3 curve.

curve represents the *most probable speed* for the corresponding temperature. Much larger and much smaller values of v occur rarely. As the temperature increases, the peak shifts to higher and higher speeds, corresponding to the increase in average molecular kinetic energy with temperature. These experimental curves agree well with a theoretical prediction of molecular speed distributions, called the *Maxwell–Boltzmann distribution*.

The distribution of molecular speeds in liquids is similar, although not identical, to that for gases. We can understand the vapor pressure of a liquid and the phenomenon of boiling on this basis. Suppose a molecule must have a speed at least as great as v_A in Fig. 20–7 to escape from the surface of a liquid into the adjacent vapor. The total number of such molecules, represented by the area under each curve to the right of v_A, increases rapidly with temperature. Thus the rate at which molecules can escape is strongly temperature-dependent. This process is balanced by another one in which molecules in the vapor phase collide inelastically with the surface and are trapped back into the liquid phase. The number of molecules suffering this fate per unit time is proportional to the pressure in the vapor phase. Phase equilibrium between liquid and vapor occurs when these two competing processes proceed at exactly the same rate. Hence if we have an accurate collection of curves such as Fig. 20–7 for a variety of temperatures, we can make a theoretical prediction of the vapor pressure of a substance as a function of temperature.

Rates of chemical reactions are often strongly temperature-dependent, and the Maxwell–Boltzmann distribution contains the reason for this dependence. When two reacting molecules collide, the reaction can occur only when the molecules are close enough for the electric-charge distributions of their electrons to interact strongly. This requires a minimum energy, called the *activation energy*, and thus a certain minimum speed. The curves in Fig. 20–7 show that the number of molecules that have speeds greater than some specified value, such as v_A, increases rapidly with temperature. Thus we expect the rate of any reaction that depends on an activation energy to increase rapidly with temperature. Similarly, many plant growth processes proceed at rates that are strongly temperature-dependent.

20–6
Heat Capacity of Crystals

In Section 20–4 we analyzed the heat capacities of ideal gases on the basis of a kinetic-molecular model. We can carry out a similar analysis for a crystalline solid. Consider a crystal consisting of N identical atoms. Each atom is bound to an equilibrium position by interatomic forces. The macroscopic elasticity of solid materials shows us that these forces must permit stretching and bending of the bonds. We can think of a crystal lattice as an array of atoms connected by little springs, as shown in Fig. 20–8. Thus each atom can *vibrate* about its equilibrium position.

Each atom has three degrees of freedom, corresponding to the three components of velocity needed to describe its vibrational motion. According to the equipartition principle, which we introduced in Section 20–4, each atom should have an average kinetic energy of $\frac{1}{2}kT$ for each of its three degrees of freedom (corresponding to the three components of velocity). In addition, each atom has on the average some *potential* energy associated with the elastic deformation. Now, for a simple harmonic oscillator (discussed in Chapter 11), it is not hard to show that the average kinetic energy of an atom is *equal* to its average potential energy. In our crystal lattice model, each atom is essentially a three-dimensional harmonic oscillator; and it can be shown that the equality of average kinetic and potential energies also holds here, provided that the "spring" forces are proportional to the displacement from the equilibrium position.

Thus we expect each atom to have an average kinetic energy $\frac{3}{2}kT$ and an average potential energy $\frac{3}{2}kT$, or an average total energy $3kT$. If the

20–8
The forces between neighboring particles in a crystal may be visualized by imagining every particle to be connected to its neighbors by springs.

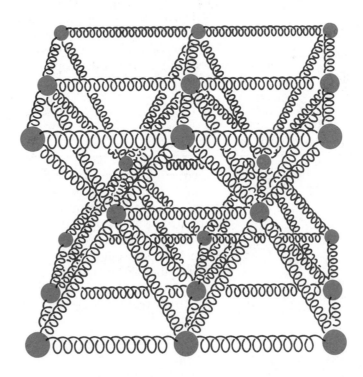

crystal contains N atoms or n moles, its total energy is

$$U = 3NkT, \tag{20-16}$$

or, in molar terms,

$$U = 3nRT. \tag{20-17}$$

From this we conclude that the molar heat capacity of a crystal should be

$$C = 3R. \tag{20-18}$$

In SI units,

$$C = (3)(8.314 \text{ J·mol}^{-1}\text{·K}^{-1}) = 24.9 \text{ J·mol}^{-1}\text{·K}^{-1}.$$

But this is just the **rule of Dulong and Petit,** which we encountered in Section 15–4. There we regarded it as an *empirical* rule, but now we have *derived* it from kinetic theory. The agreement is only approximate, to be sure; but considering the very simple nature of our model, it is quite significant.

At low temperatures the heat capacities of most solids *decrease* with decreasing temperature. As with vibrational energy of molecules, this phenomenon requires quantum-mechanical concepts for its understanding. The vibrating atoms in the crystal lattice can gain or lose energy only in certain finite increments. At very low temperatures the quantity kT is much *smaller* than the smallest energy increment the vibrating atoms can accommodate. As a result, at low T, most of the atoms remain in their lowest energy states because the next higher energy level is out of reach. Thus at low temperatures the average vibrational energy per atom is *less* than kT, and the heat capacity per molecule is correspondingly *less* than k. But in the other limit, where kT is *large* in comparison to the minimum energy increment, the classical equipartition theorem holds, and the total heat capacity is $3k$ per molecule, or $3R$ per mole, as the Dulong and Petit relation predicts. Quantitative understanding of the temperature variation of heat capacities was one of the triumphs of quantum mechanics during its initial development, early in the twentieth century.

*20–7
Diffusion and Osmosis

When you add a drop of ink to a glass of water, the color eventually permeates all the water uniformly, even if the water is not stirred. Similarly, perfume sprayed into the air at one end of a room can be detected after a while at the opposite end, even when there is no air circulation. These are two familiar examples of **diffusion,** the migration of one kind of molecules through a material consisting of another kind caused entirely by the random motions of the molecules. In each example, minority molecules are introduced into a specific region of a material, and they move from regions of greater concentration to those of smaller concentration.

Kinetic theory provides the key to understanding diffusion. In Fig. 20–9 the concentration of perfume molecules (represented by colored

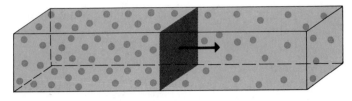

20–9
The concentration of minority molecules, shown by colored dots, is greater on the left side, and more molecules from the left pass through the imaginary surface in the middle than from the right. Thus there is a net diffusion of molecules from left to right.

dots) is greater in the left side of the box than in the right. In the center is an imaginary surface (not a real physical barrier) dividing the box into two halves. In any specific time interval, more molecules cross over this surface from left to right than from right to left because the concentration is greater on the left. Thus there is a net drift from left to right; this apparent flow stops only when the concentration becomes uniform and the left-to-right and right-to-left drifts become equal.

More detailed analysis shows that the rate of diffusion across any given area A is directly proportional to the change in concentration per unit distance. Concentration, denoted by C, is usually measured in moles per unit volume; thus the SI unit of concentration is 1 mol·m^{-3}. The rate of diffusion of matter, denoted by Q, is measured in amount of substance per unit time; hence in SI units, Q is in moles per second. Specifically, the rate of diffusion Q across any area A between two regions a distance L apart, where the concentrations are C_1 and C_2, is given by

$$Q = \frac{DA(C_2 - C_1)}{L}, \tag{20-19}$$

where D is a proportionality constant, different for different combinations of materials, called the *diffusion constant*. We invite you to verify that for unit consistency, D must have the unit square meters per second.

Equation (20–19) is called the *diffusion equation* or *Fick's law*. Its similarity in form to the heat-flow equation, Eq. (16–1), is striking; heat flow can be considered as a kind of diffusion phenomenon, and both relations can be derived from kinetic-theory considerations in similar ways. The quantity $(C_2 - C_1)/L$, the change in concentration per unit length, is called the **concentration gradient;** it is analogous to the temperature gradient in heat flow. We invite you to verify that the SI unit of concentration gradient is 1 mol·m^{-4}.

Example 20–6   A hydrogen storage tank is fitted with a horizontal pipe that is 2.0 m long and 5.0 cm² in cross-sectional area. There is a shutoff valve close to the tank, and the other end of the pipe is open to the atmosphere. The valve is slightly leaky, and the concentration of hydrogen in the pipe near the valve is 0.50 mol·m^{-3}. The diffusion constant for hydrogen in air at one atmosphere and 273 K is $D = 6.3 \times 10^{-5} \text{ m}^2 \cdot \text{s}^{-1}$. If the concentration of hydrogen in the outside atmosphere is negligible, what is the rate of diffusion of hydrogen out of the pipe?

Solution   From Eq. (20–19) the diffusion rate is

$$Q = \frac{(6.3 \times 10^{-5} \text{ m}^2\cdot\text{s}^{-1})(5.0 \times 10^{-4} \text{ m}^2)(0.50 \text{ mol}\cdot\text{m}^{-3} - 0)}{2.0 \text{ m}}$$

$$= 7.9 \times 10^{-9} \text{ mol}\cdot\text{s}^{-1}.$$

The number of *molecules* per second is this number multiplied by Avogadro's number, or about 4.7×10^{15} molecules·s^{-1}. We note that the hydrogen concentrations are much smaller than the concentration of air molecules; at STP, 1 mol of an ideal gas occupies a volume of 22.4 L or 0.0224 m^3, so the concentration of air molecules is $(1/0.0224)$ mol·m^{-3} = 44.6 mol·m^{-3}, about 90 times the concentration of hydrogen near the valve. ∎

The diffusion constant D depends on the substances involved and also on temperature. It is generally much smaller for diffusion in liquids and solids than in gases because in condensed matter the diffusing molecules collide with other molecules much more frequently and travel, on the average, much shorter distances between collisions. Diffusion constants usually increase with increasing temperature because average speeds of random molecular motion increase with temperature.

Diffusion plays an essential role in many life processes. The exchange of oxygen from air to blood in the lungs and from blood to cells in muscle tissue are diffusion processes. (See the remarks at the end of Section 17–2.) Diffusion is also the mechanism by which plants exchange oxygen and carbon dioxide with the atmosphere.

Diffusion phenomena in which fluid molecules pass through a semipermeable membrane are called **osmosis;** these too are of central importance in many biological processes. The structure or chemical makeup of a membrane may be such that small or special molecules can pass through nearly unimpeded while larger or chemically different ones are blocked. This can result in pressure differences across the membrane as well as other interesting phenomena.

A simple example of osmosis is shown in Fig. 20–10. The left side of the U-tube contains a sugar solution, and the right side contains pure

20–10
The concentration of water molecules on the right side of the membrane is greater than on the left, and water molecules diffuse from right to left. The large sugar molecules (color dots) are blocked by the membrane.
(b) Equilibrium is reached when the diffusion of water molecules is the same on the two sides of the membrane. In this case the difference of hydrostatic pressure $\rho g h$ is equal to the osmotic pressure Π.

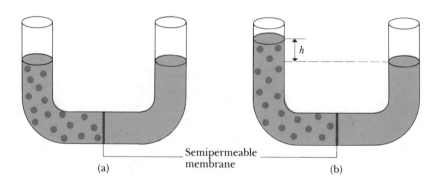

(a)   Semipermeable
                       membrane   (b)

water. The two sides are separated by a **semipermeable membrane,** permeable to the relatively small water molecules but impermeable to the much larger sugar molecules. Because on the left side the sugar molecules occupy some of the space that would otherwise contain water molecules, the concentration of water molecules is less on the left side than on the right. Thus there is a net diffusion of water from right to left through the membrane. The sugar molecules on the left would like to diffuse into the right side, but the membrane stops them. Thus the fluid level rises in the left side of the tube and drops in the right side.

The total pressure on each side of the membrane can be represented as the sum of partial pressures due to water molecules and to sugar molecules. The diffusion of water from right to left continues until the partial pressures of water are the same on the two sides of the membrane. But then the *total* pressure on the left is greater than on the right because it includes also the pressure due to sugar molecules. It turns out that when equilibrium has been reached, the pressure difference is approximately proportional to the concentration C of the dissolved substance. The equilibrium pressure difference, equal to the partial pressure of the dissolved substance, is called the **osmotic pressure,** denoted by Π. Specifically, it is found that

$$\Pi = CRT, \tag{20-20}$$

where R is the ideal gas constant and T is the absolute temperature. Because C is the number of moles n of solute per unit volume V of solution (i.e., $C = n/V$), we can also express this as

$$\Pi = \frac{nRT}{V}. \tag{20-21}$$

This somewhat surprising result states that the partial pressure of the dissolved substance is the same as though it were an ideal gas! Although the large molecules collide continually with water molecules, they rarely encounter each other. In this respect they act like noninteracting particles, the basic assumption of an ideal gas.

Example 20-7 The left side of the U-tube in Fig. 20-10 contains a sugar solution prepared by dissolving 15.0 g of table sugar in 1.0 L of water. At equilibrium, at $T = 20°C$, what is the difference in height of fluid on the two sides of the U-tube? Table sugar is sucrose, $C_{12}H_{22}O_{11}$; its molecular mass is $M = 342$ g·mol^{-1}.

Solution We first find the concentration of the solution. The number of moles of sugar is (15.0 g)/(342 g·mol^{-1}) = 0.0439 mol. This is dissolved in 1.0×10^{-3} m^3 of water, so the concentration is

$$C = \frac{0.0439 \text{ mol}}{1.0 \times 10^{-3} \text{ m}^3} = 43.9 \text{ mol·m}^{-3}.$$

The osmotic pressure is then given by Eq. (20-20):

$$\Pi = CRT = (43.9 \text{ mol·m}^{-3})(8.314 \text{ J·mol}^{-1}\text{·K}^{-1})(293 \text{ K})$$
$$= 1.07 \times 10^5 \text{ Pa} = 1.06 \text{ atm}.$$

The difference in height h of the other two columns is then given by $\Pi = \rho g h$, where ρ is the density of the liquid and g is the acceleration due to gravity:

$$h = \frac{\Pi}{\rho g} = \frac{1.07 \times 10^5 \text{ Pa}}{(1.0 \times 10^3 \text{ kg·m}^{-3})(9.8 \text{ m·s}^{-2})} = 10.9 \text{ m.}$$

(We have ignored the small difference in density of pure water and the sugar solution.) This is a surprisingly great height difference for a rather modest concentration of sugar. ∎

Osmotic pressure in the roots of maple trees causes the rising of sap in the trees in spring. Pure water diffuses through semipermeable membranes in the roots, pushing the dilute sugar solution inside the roots up into the tree.

The direction of diffusion in Fig. 20–10a can be reversed by applying a pressure to the surface of the liquid on the left side that exceeds the pressure on the right by more than the osmotic pressure. Pure water then diffuses through the membrane from left to right, leaving the solute molecules behind. This process, called *reverse osmosis*, has been explored as a process for desalinizing seawater. The required pressure turns out to be about 25 atm, and the principal practical difficulty is finding efficient yet durable membranes that can withstand this pressure differential.

Osmosis is important in many biological processes. Cell walls are semipermeable membranes. The diffusion of water into or out of a cell depends on the concentrations of dissolved substances on the two sides of the cell wall. When fluids are administered intravenously, the concentrations of salt and glucose are adjusted to balance the osmotic pressures across the cell walls. Such a solution is said to be *isotonic*.

Osmotic pressure in plant cells is important in maintaining the rigidity of the plant's structure, just as an inflated balloon has a definite shape but a deflated balloon collapses. When the water supply is insufficient, the plant wilts and droops, or, in the case of cacti and other succulents, looks shriveled and emaciated. Addition of water, either through the roots or by diffusion through the semipermeable membranes forming the plant surfaces, restores the osmotic pressure needed for normal firmness of structure.

A semipermeable membrane that blocks large molecules *completely* is an idealization. Real membranes permit some passage of large molecules, although more slowly than smaller molecules. A more precise term is *differentially permeable membrane*.

Questions

20–1 Which has more atoms, a kilogram of hydrogen or a kilogram of lead? Which has more mass?

20–2 Chlorine is a mixture of two isotopes, one having a molecular mass of 35 g·mol^{-1}, the other 37 g·mol^{-1}. Which molecules move faster on the average?

20–3 The proportion of various gases in the earth's atmosphere changes somewhat with altitude. Would you expect the proportion of oxygen at high altitude to be greater or less than that at sea level?

20–4 *Comment on this statement:* When two gases are

mixed, if they are to be in thermal equilibrium, they must have the same average molecular speed.

20–5 In deriving the ideal-gas equation from the kinetic-molecular model, we ignored potential energy due to the earth's gravity. Is this omission justified?

20–6 In deriving the ideal-gas equation we assumed the number of molecules to be very large so that we could compute the average force due to many collisions; however, the ideal-gas equation holds accurately only at low pressures, where the molecules are few and far between. Is this inconsistent?

20–7 Some elements of solid crystalline form have molar heat capacities *larger* than $3R$. What effects could account for this?

20–8 Considering molecular speeds, is v_{rms} equal to the *most probable* speed, as indicated by the peak on one of the curves in Fig. 20–7?

20–9 A gas storage tank has a small leak. The pressure in the tank drops more quickly if the gas is hydrogen or helium than if it is oxygen. Why?

20–10 Consider two specimens of gas at the same temperature, both having the same total mass but different molecular masses. Which has the greater internal energy? Does your answer depend on the molecular structure of the gases?

20–11 A process called *gaseous diffusion* is sometimes used to separate isotopes of uranium, i.e., atoms of the element having different masses, such as ^{235}U and ^{238}U. Can you speculate on how this might work?

20–12 When food is preserved by freeze-drying, it is first quick-frozen, then placed in a vacuum chamber and irradiated with infrared radiation. What is the purpose of the vacuum? Of the radiation?

Exercises

Section 20–2   Avogadro's Number

20–1 How many moles are there in a glass of water (0.300 kg)? How many molecules? The molecular mass of water is 18.0 g·mol^{-1}.

20–2 Consider 1.00 mol of liquid water.
a) What volume is occupied by this amount of water? The molecular mass of water is 18.0 g·mol^{-1}.
b) Imagine each molecule to be, on the average, at the center of a small cube. What is the length of an edge of this small cube?
c) How does this distance compare with the diameter of a molecule?

20–3 Consider an ideal gas at 0°C and 1.00 atm pressure. Imagine each molecule to be, on the average, at the center of a small cube.
a) What is the length of an edge of this small cube?
b) How does this distance compare with the diameter of a molecule?

20–4 What is the length of the side of a cube, in a gas at standard conditions, that contains a number of molecules equal to the population of the United States (about 240 million)?

Section 20–3   Kinetic-Molecular Theory of an Ideal Gas

20–5 At what temperature is the root-mean-square speed of nitrogen molecules equal to the root-mean-square speed of hydrogen molecules at 0.0°C? The molecular mass of hydrogen (H_2) is 2.02 g·mol^{-1}, and that of nitrogen (N_2) is 28.01 g·mol^{-1}.

20–6 A flask contains a mixture of krypton, neon, and helium gases. Compare
a) the average kinetic energies of the three types of atoms;
b) the root-mean-square speeds.

The atomic masses are: helium, 4.00 g·mol^{-1}; neon, 20.18 g·mol^{-1}; krypton, 83.80 g·mol^{-1}.

20–7 Isotopes of uranium are sometimes separated by gaseous diffusion, using the fact that the root-mean-square speeds of the molecules in vapor are slightly different, and hence the vapors diffuse at slightly different rates. Assuming that the atomic masses for ^{235}U and ^{238}U are 0.235 kg·mol^{-1} and 0.238 kg·mol^{-1}, respectively, what is the ratio of the root-mean-square speed of the ^{235}U atoms in the vapor to that of the ^{238}U atoms if the temperature is uniform?

20–8
a) What is the average translational kinetic energy of a helium atom (with an atomic mass of 4.00 g·mol^{-1}) at a temperature of 300 K?
b) What is the average value of the square of its speed?
c) What is the root-mean-square speed?
d) What is the momentum of a helium atom traveling at this speed?
e) Suppose an atom traveling at this speed bounces back and forth between opposite sides of a cubical vessel 0.100 m on a side. What is the average force it exerts on one of the walls of the container? (Assume that the atom's velocity is perpendicular to the two sides that it strikes.)

f) What is the average force per unit area?

g) How many atoms traveling at this speed are necessary to produce an average pressure of 1.00 atm?

h) Compute the number of helium atoms actually contained in a vessel of this size at 300 K and atmospheric pressure.

i) Your answer for part (h) should be three times as large as the answer for part (g). Where does this discrepancy arise?

20–9 Smoke particles in the air typically have masses of the order of 10^{-16} kg. The Brownian motion of these particles resulting from collisions with air molecules can be observed with a microscope.

a) Find the root-mean-square speed of Brownian motion for a particle of mass 1.00×10^{-16} kg in air at 293 K.

b) Would the speed be different if the particle were in hydrogen gas at the same temperature? Explain.

Section 20–4   Molar Heat Capacity of a Gas

20–10 Calculate the molar heat capacity at constant volume of water vapor, assuming that the nonlinear triatomic molecule has three translational and three rotational degrees of freedom and that vibrational motion does not contribute. The actual specific heat capacity of water vapor at low pressures is about 2000 $J \cdot kg^{-1} \cdot K^{-1}$. Compare this with your calculation, and comment on the actual role of vibrational motion. The molecular mass of water is 18.0 $g \cdot mol^{-1}$.

20–11 Compute the specific heat capacity at constant volume of hydrogen gas, and compare with the specific heat capacity of liquid water. The molecular mass of hydrogen (H_2) is 2.02 $g \cdot mol^{-1}$.

20–12

a) How much heat does it take to increase the temperature of two moles of a diatomic ideal gas by 25.0 K if the gas is held at constant volume? If it is held at constant pressure?

b) What are the answers to the two questions in part (a) if the gas is monatomic rather than diatomic?

Section 20–7   Diffusion and Osmosis

20–13

a) Use Eq. (20–19) to determine the SI unit of the diffusion constant D.

b) Show that the SI unit of concentration gradient is $mol \cdot m^{-4}$.

20–14 What is the concentration in moles per cubic meter of

a) pure water (whose molecular mass is 18.0 $g \cdot mol^{-1}$) at 20.0°C and 1.00 atm (density given in Table 14–3);

b) pure nitrogen gas (whose molecular mass is 28.0 $g \cdot mol^{-1}$) at 20.0°C and 1.00 atm. Assume that the nitrogen can be treated as an ideal gas.

20–15 A horizontal glass tube is filled with water, and a lump of sucrose is inserted at one end. The tube is 0.400 m long and 1.20 cm in diameter. The concentration of sucrose near the lump is found to be 300 $mol \cdot m^{-3}$. The diffusion constant for sucrose in water is 0.520×10^{-9} $m^2 \cdot s^{-1}$. What is the initial diffusion rate of sucrose from one end of the tube to the other?

20–16 What is the concentration in moles per cubic meter of Na^+ sodium ions in a solution made by dissolving 25.0 g of table salt (NaCl) in 1.50 L of water? The atomic mass of sodium is 23.0 $g \cdot mol^{-1}$, and that of chlorine is 35.5 $g \cdot mol^{-1}$. In the solution the NaCl molecules are fully dissociated into Na^+ and Cl^- ions.

20–17 What minimum concentration of sucrose in maple sap would be needed for the osmotic pressure in the roots to push the sap to a height of 5.00 m at a temperature of 10.0°C? (Assume that the density of sap is the same as that of water.)

20–18 A ripe cherry is immersed in water at 20.0°C. The osmotic pressure is found to be 4.00 atm. If the interior of the cherry is principally a solution of glucose in water, what is the concentration of the solution?

▇ *Problems*

20–19 Estimate the number of atoms in the body of a 60-kg physics student. Base the estimate on the fact that the human body is mostly water. The molecular mass of water (H_2O) is 18.0 $g \cdot mol^{-1}$, and each water molecule contains three atoms.

20–20 The lowest pressures readily attainable in the laboratory are of the order of 10^{-13} atm. At a pressure of 1.00×10^{-13} atm and ordinary temperature (say, $T = 300$ K), how many molecules are present in a volume of 1.00 cm^3?

20–21 Experiment shows that the size of an oxygen molecule is of the order of 2×10^{-10} m. Make a rough estimate of the pressure at which the finite volume of the molecules should cause noticeable deviations from ideal-gas behavior at ordinary temperatures ($T = 300$ K).

20–22 The speed of propagation of a sound wave in air at 27.0°C is about 350 m·s^{-1}. Calculate, for comparison,

a) v_{rms} for nitrogen molecules;

b) the root-mean-square value of v_x at this temperature.

(The molecular mass of nitrogen (N_2) is 28.0 g·mol^{-1}. If sound propagation were an isothermal process, which it ordinarily is not, the speed of sound would be equal to $(v_x)_{rms}$. See Section 21–5.)

20–23

a) Compute the increase in gravitational potential energy of a nitrogen molecule (molecular mass 28.0 g·mol^{-1}) for an increase in elevation of 100 m near the earth's surface.

b) At what temperature is this equal to the average translational kinetic energy of nitrogen molecules?

20–24

a) For what mass of molecule or particle is v_{rms} equal to 0.100 m·s^{-1} at a temperature of 300 K?

b) If the particle is a piece of ice, how many molecules does it contain? (The molecular mass of water is 18.0 g·mol^{-1}.)

c) Calculate the diameter of the particle if it is a spherical piece of ice. Would it be visible to the naked eye?

20–25 The surface of the sun has a temperature of about 6000 K and consists largely of hydrogen atoms. (In fact, most of the atoms are ionized, so the hydrogen "atom" is actually a proton.)

a) Find the rms speed of a hydrogen atom at this temperature. (The mass of a single hydrogen atom is 1.67×10^{-27} kg.)

b) The escape speed for a particle to leave the gravitational influence of the sun is given by $(2GM/R)^{1/2}$, where M is the sun's mass, R its radius, and G the gravitational constant (Example 7–9). Use the data in Appendix F to calculate this escape speed.

c) Can appreciable quantities of hydrogen escape from the sun's gravitational field?

20–26

a) Show that a projectile of mass m can "escape" from the earth's gravitational field if it is launched vertically upward with a kinetic energy greater than mgR, where g is the acceleration due to gravity at the earth's surface and R is the earth's radius. (See the preceding problem.)

b) At what temperature would the average translational kinetic energy of an oxygen molecule equal that required for escape? Of a hydrogen molecule?

(The molecular mass of oxygen (O_2) is 32.0 g·mol^{-1}, and that of hydrogen (H_2) is 2.02 g·mol^{-1}.)

20–27

a) What is the total random translational kinetic energy of 12.0 L of helium gas with pressure 1.01×10^5 Pa and temperature 300 K?

b) If the tank containing the gas is moved with a speed of 10.0 m·s^{-1}, by what percentage is the total kinetic energy of the gas increased? The atomic mass of helium is 4.00 g·mol^{-1}.

20–28 For each of the triatomic gases in Table 18–1, compute the value of C_v on the assumption that there is no vibrational energy. Compare with the measured values in the table, and compute the percentage of the total heat capacity that is due to vibration for each of the three gases. (*Note:* The CO_2 molecule is linear; SO_2 and H_2S are not. Recall that a linear polyatomic molecule has two rotational degrees of freedom, whereas a nonlinear molecule has three.)

20–29 Seawater contains about 30.0 kg per cubic meter of salt. Salt is sodium chloride (NaCl), with a molecular mass $M = 58.5$ g·mol^{-1}. The molecules are fully dissociated into Na^+ and Cl^- ions, so the total ion concentration is twice the number of moles of NaCl per cubic meter. (See Exercise 20–16.)

a) What is the total concentration of ions in moles per cubic meter?

b) What is the osmotic pressure across a semipermeable membrane with fresh water on one side and seawater on the other at a temperature of 20°C?

c) What minimum pressure would be needed for reverse osmosis, that is, diffusion of water from the salty side to the pure side, leaving the salt ions behind?

20–30 The diffusion constant for water vapor in air at 20°C is 0.240×10^{-4} m^2·s^{-1}. A horizontal glass tube 0.150 m long and 3.00 cm^2 in cross-sectional area is stoppered at one end with a wet sponge; the other end is open to dry air. The temperature is 20°C.

a) If the air in the tube near the sponge is saturated with water vapor, what is the concentration of water vapor there in moles per cubic meter?

b) At what rate does water vapor diffuse out of the open end of the tube?

c) If the sponge initially contains 2.00 g of water, how much time is required for it to become completely dry? (The molecular mass of water is 18.0 g·mol^{-1}.)

d) What is the diffusion rate if the air outside is not perfectly dry but has 60.0% relative humidity?

Challenge Problems

20–31 The position and velocity of a simple harmonic oscillator are given by Eqs. (11–18) and (11–19). For simplicity, assume that the initial position and velocity make the phase angle ϕ_0 equal to zero. Use these equations to show that the potential energy of the oscillator averaged over one period of the motion is equal to the kinetic energy averaged over one period. This result was used in Section 20–6. (*Hint:* Use the trigonometric identities $\cos^2(\theta) = (1 + \cos(2\theta))/2$ and $\sin^2(\theta) = (1 - \sin(2\theta))/2$. What is the average value of $\sin(2\omega t)$ and of $\cos(2\omega t)$ averaged over one period?)

20–32 In Example 20–4 we saw that $v_{rms} > v_{av}$. It is not difficult to show that this is *always* the case. (Unless all the particles have the same speed, in which case $v_{rms} = v_{av}$.)

a) For two particles with speeds v_1 and v_2, show that $v_{rms} \geq v_{av}$, regardless of the numerical values of v_1 and v_2. Then show that $v_{rms} > v_{av}$ if $v_1 \neq v_2$.

Suppose that for a collection of N particles you know that $v_{rms} > v_{av}$. Another particle, with speed u, is added to the collection of particles.

b) If the new root-mean-square and average speeds are denoted as v'_{rms} and v'_{av}, show that

$$v'_{rms} = \sqrt{\frac{N v_{rms}^2 + u^2}{N + 1}}, \qquad v'_{av} = \frac{N v_{av} + u}{N + 1}.$$

c) Use the expressions in part (b) to show that $v'_{rms} > v'_{av}$, regardless of the numerical value of u.

d) Explain why your results in parts (a) and (c) together show that $v_{rms} > v_{av}$ for any collection of particles if the particles do not all have the same speed.

Mechanical Waves

Ripples on a pond, musical sounds, the wiggles of a Slinky stretched out on the floor, a row of dominoes successively falling over—all these are *wave* phenomena. Waves can occur whenever a system has an equilibrium position and when a disturbance from that position can travel or *propagate* from one region of the system to another. Sound, light, ocean waves, radio and television transmission, and earthquakes are all wave phenomena. The photograph above (Fig. 21–1) shows a familiar wave pattern that is produced when a small ball is dropped vertically into water. The wave pattern moves radially outward from the source of the wave. The wave crests and troughs are concentric circles. (Photo by Fundamental Photographs, New York.) Wave phenomena occur in all branches of physical and biological sci-

ence, and the concept of waves is one of the most important unifying threads running through the entire fabric of the natural sciences.

In this chapter and the next two we consider **mechanical waves.** These waves always travel within some material substance that we call a **medium.** The speed of travel of a wave depends on the mechanical properties of the medium. Some waves are **periodic;** in these the particles of the medium undergo back-and-forth periodic motions during wave propagation. If the motions are simple harmonic (sinusoidal), the wave is called a **sinusoidal wave.** The concepts of this chapter form a foundation for the study of other kinds of waves, including electromagnetic waves, later in this book.

21–1
Mechanical Wave Phenomena

Every type of mechanical wave is associated with some material or substance called the *medium* for that type. As the wave travels through the medium, the particles that make up the medium undergo displacements of various kinds, depending on the nature of the wave.

Here are a few examples of mechanical waves. In Fig. 21–2a the medium is a long spring or Slinky, or even just a wire or rope under tension. If we give the left end a small sideways shake or wriggle, the wriggle travels down the length of the spring. Successive sections of spring go through the same sideways motion that we gave to the end, but at successively later times. Because the displacements of the medium are perpendicular (transverse) to the direction of travel of the wave along the medium, this is called a **transverse wave.**

In Fig. 21–2b the medium is a liquid or a gas in a tube with a rigid wall at the right end and a moveable piston at the left end. If we give the piston a back-and-forth motion, a displacement and a pressure fluctuation travel down the length of the medium. This time the motions of the particles of the medium are back and forth along the *same* direction as the travel of the wave, and we call this a **longitudinal wave.**

In Fig. 21–2c the medium is water in a trough such as an irrigation ditch or canal. When we move the flat board at the left end back and forth, a disturbance travels down the length of the trough. Careful observation shows that in this case the displacements of the water have *both* longitudinal and transverse components.

In each of these situations there is an equilibrium state. For the Slinky or stretched rope, it is the state in which the system is at rest, stretched out along a straight line. For the fluid in a tube it is a state of rest with uniform pressure, and for the water in a trough it is a smooth level water surface. In each case the wave motion is a disturbance from the equilibrium state that travels from one region of the medium to another. In each case there are forces that tend to restore the system to its equilibrium position when it is displaced, just as the force of gravity tends to pull a pendulum toward its straight-down equilibrium position when it is displaced.

These examples have three things in common. First, the medium itself does not travel through space; its individual particles undergo

(a) Transverse displacement

(b) Longitudinal displacement

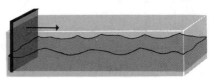

(c) Longitudinal and transverse displacement

21–2
Propagation of disturbances.

back-and-forth motions around their equilibrium positions. What *does* travel is the pattern of the wave disturbance. Second, to set any of these systems in motion, we have to put in energy by doing mechanical work on the system. The wave motion transports this energy from one region of the medium to another. Waves transport energy, but not matter, from one region to another. Third, in each case the disturbance is found to travel or *propagate* with a definite speed through the medium. This speed is called the speed of propagation or simply the **wave speed.** It is determined in each case by the mechanical properties of the medium. We will use the symbol c for wave speed.

Not all waves are mechanical in nature. Another broad class is *electromagnetic* waves, which include light, radio waves, infrared, ultraviolet, X-rays, and gamma rays. There is *no* medium for electromagnetic waves; they can travel through empty space. Yet another class of wave phenomena is the wavelike behavior of fundamental particles. This behavior forms part of the foundation of quantum mechanics, the basic theory used for the analysis of atomic and molecular structure. We will return to electromagnetic waves in Chapter 35 and to the wave nature of particles in Chapter 42. Meanwhile, we can learn the essential language of waves in the context of mechanical waves.

21–2
Periodic Waves

One of the easiest kinds of wave to demonstrate is a transverse wave on a stretched rope. Suppose we tie one end of a long, flexible rope to a stationary object and pull on the other end, stretching the rope tight. We then give this end a sideways shake, exerting a transverse force on it as we do so. The result is a "wiggle," or *wave pulse*, that travels down the length of the rope. The tension in the rope restores the rope's straight-line shape once the wiggle has passed.

A more interesting situation develops when we give the free end of the rope a repetitive or *periodic* motion. (We studied periodic motion in Chapter 11, and we suggest that you review that discussion now.) In particular, suppose we move it back and forth with *simple harmonic motion* with amplitude A, frequency f, and period τ. As usual, $f = 1/\tau$. A possible experimental setup is shown in Fig. 21–3.

21–3
The mass–spring system undergoes simple harmonic motion, producing a sinusoidal wave that travels to the right on the rope. In a real-life system a driving force would have to be applied to the mass m to replace the energy carried away by the wave.

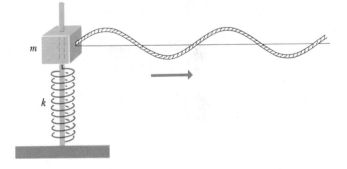

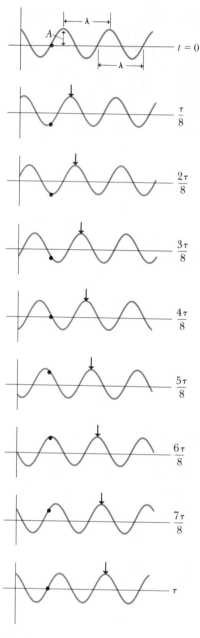

A *continuous succession* of transverse sinusoidal waves then advances along the rope. Figure 21–4 shows the shape of a part of the rope near the left end, at intervals of one eighth of a period, for a total time of one period. The waveform advances steadily toward the right, as indicated by the short vertical arrow pointing to a particular wave crest, while any one point on the rope (the black dot, for example) oscillates back and forth about its equilibrium position with simple harmonic motion. Be very careful to distinguish between the motion of a *waveform*, which moves with constant speed c *along* the rope, and the motion of *a particle of the rope*, which is simple harmonic and *transverse* (perpendicular) to the length of the rope.

The shape of the rope at any instant is a repeating pattern, a series of identical shapes. For a periodic wave the distance between two successive maxima, or between any two points at corresponding positions on successive repetitions in the wave shape, is the **wavelength** of the wave, denoted by λ. The waveform travels with constant speed c and advances a distance of one wavelength λ in a time interval of one period τ, so the wave speed c is given by $c = \lambda/\tau$, or, because $f = 1/\tau$,

$$c = \lambda f. \tag{21–1}$$

The speed of propagation equals the product of wavelength and frequency.

To understand the mechanics of a *longitudinal* wave, we consider a long tube filled with a fluid, with a plunger at the left end, as shown in Fig. 21–5. If we push the plunger in, we compress the fluid near the plunger, increasing the pressure in this region. This region then pushes against the neighboring region of fluid, and so on, as a wave pulse moves

21–4

A sinusoidal transverse wave traveling toward the right. The shape of the rope is shown at intervals of one eighth of a period. The vertical scale is exaggerated.

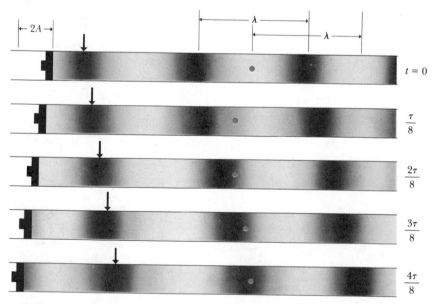

21–5

A sinusoidal longitudinal wave traveling toward the right, shown at intervals of one eighth of a period.

along the tube. The pressure fluctuations play the role of the restoring force, trying to restore the fluid to equilibrium and uniform pressure.

Now suppose we move the plunger back and forth with simple harmonic motion along a line parallel to the direction of the tube. This motion forms regions where the pressure and density are greater and less than the equilibrium values. We call a region of increased pressure a *compression*. In the figure, compressions are represented by darkly shaded areas. A region of reduced pressure is an *expansion*; in the figure, expansions are represented by lightly shaded areas. The compressions and expansions move to the right with constant speed c, as indicated by successive positions of the small vertical arrow. The speed of longitudinal waves in air (i.e., sound) depends on temperature. At 20°C it is 344 m·s^{-1} or 1130 ft·s^{-1}. The motion of a single particle of the medium, shown by a colored dot, is simple harmonic, parallel to the direction of propagation.

The wavelength is the distance between two successive compressions or two successive expansions. The same fundamental equation, $c = \lambda f$, holds in this example as in the case of transverse waves and indeed *all* types of periodic waves.

Example 21–1   What is the wavelength of a sound wave in air at 20°C if the frequency is $f = 262$ Hz (the approximate frequency of the note "middle C" on the piano)?

Solution   At 20°C the speed of sound in air is $c = 344$ m·s^{-1}, as was mentioned above. From Eq. (21–1),

$$\lambda = \frac{c}{f} = \frac{344 \text{ m·s}^{-1}}{262 \text{ s}^{-1}} = 1.31 \text{ m.}$$

The "high C" sung by coloratura sopranos is two octaves above middle C. The corresponding frequency is four times as large, $f = 4(262 \text{ Hz}) = 1048$ Hz, and the wavelength is one fourth as large, $\lambda = (1.31 \text{ m})/4 = 0.328$ m.   ∎

21–3
Speed of a Transverse Wave

How is the speed of propagation c of a transverse wave on a rope related to the *mechanical* properties of the system? The relevant physical quantities are the *tension* in the rope and its *mass per unit length*. We might guess that increasing the tension should increase the restoring forces that tend to straighten the rope when it is disturbed, thus increasing the wave speed. We might also guess that increasing the mass should make the motion more sluggish and decrease the speed. Both these guesses turn out to be correct. We now develop the exact relationship by analyzing a particularly simple type of wave motion.

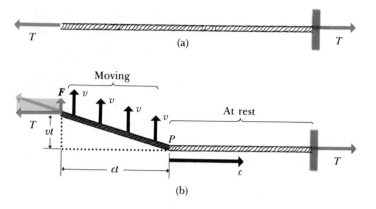

21–6
Propagation of a transverse disturbance in a rope.

We consider a perfectly flexible rope, as shown in Fig. 21–6, with linear mass density (mass per unit length) μ, stretched with a tension T. In Fig. 21–6a the rope is at rest. Starting at time $t = 0$, we apply a constant transverse force $\boldsymbol{F}$ at the left end of the rope. We might expect that the end would move with constant acceleration; this is certainly what would happen if the force were applied to a *point* mass. But here the effect of the force $\boldsymbol{F}$ is to set successively more and more mass into motion. The wave travels with constant speed, so the division point between moving and nonmoving portions also travels with definite speed. The total mass in motion is proportional to the time the force has been acting and thus to the *impulse* of the force. This in turn is equal to the total transverse component of momentum mv of the moving part of the rope. The total momentum thus must increase proportionately with time, so the *change* of momentum must be associated entirely with the increasing amount of mass in motion, not with an increasing velocity of an individual mass element. Force is rate of change of momentum mv. In this case, mv changes because m changes, not v. Hence the end of the rope moves upward with constant *velocity* v.

Figure 21–6b shows the shape of the rope at time t. All particles of the rope to the left of point P are moving upward with speed v, and all particles to the right of P are still at rest. The boundary point P between the moving and stationary portions is traveling to the right along the rope with a speed equal to the speed of propagation or *wave speed* c. At time t the left end of the rope has moved up a distance vt, and the boundary point P has advanced a distance ct.

The total force at the left end of the rope is the vector sum of the forces $\boldsymbol{T}$ and $\boldsymbol{F}$. Because there is no motion in the direction along the length of the rope, there is no unbalanced horizontal force. This shows that T, the magnitude of the horizontal component, does not change when the rope is displaced. Because of the increased total force, the rope stretches somewhat.

We can derive an expression for the speed of propagation c (the wave speed) by applying the impulse–momentum relation to the portion of the rope in motion at time t; that is, the darkly shaded portion in Fig. 21–6b. We set the transverse *impulse* (transverse force × time) equal to

the change of transverse *momentum* of the moving portion (mass ×
transverse component of velocity). The impulse of the transverse force F
in time t is Ft. By similar triangles,

$$\frac{F}{T} = \frac{vt}{ct}, \qquad F = T\frac{v}{c},$$

and

$$\text{Transverse impulse} = Ft = T\frac{v}{c}t.$$

The mass of the moving portion of the rope is the product of the mass
per unit length μ and the length ct, or μct. The transverse momentum is
the product of this mass and the transverse velocity v:

$$\text{Transverse momentum} = \mu ctv.$$

We note again that the momentum increases with time *not* because mass
is moving faster, as was usually the case in Chapter 8, but because *more
mass* is brought into motion. But the impulse of the force F is still equal to
the total change in momentum of the system. Applying this relation, we
obtain

$$T\frac{v}{c}t = \mu ctv.$$

Solving this for c, we find

$$c = \sqrt{\frac{T}{\mu}} \quad \text{(transverse wave)}. \tag{21–2}$$

This confirms our prediction that the wave speed c should increase when
the tension T increases but decrease when the mass per unit length μ
increases.

Our calculation considered only a very special kind of pulse, but we
can consider *any* shape of wave disturbance as a series of pulses with
different rates of transverse displacement. Even though we derived Eq.
(21–2) for a special case, it is valid for *any* transverse wave motion on a
rope, including in particular the sinusoidal and other periodic waves we
discussed in Section 21–2.

Example 21–2   One end of a nylon mountaineering rope is tied to a
stationary support. The rope is stretched out horizontally; the other end
passes over a pulley that is 8.0 m from the support, and a body with a
mass of 2.0 kg is tied to this end. The mass of rope between the support
and the pulley is 0.60 kg.

a) What is the speed of a transverse wave on the rope?

b) If a point on the rope is given a transverse simple harmonic
   motion with a frequency of 20 Hz, what is the wavelength of the
   wave?

Solution

a) The tension in the rope is the weight of the 2.0-kg load:

$$T = (2.0 \text{ kg})(9.8 \text{ m·s}^{-2}) = 19.6 \text{ N}.$$

The mass per unit length is

$$\mu = \frac{m}{L} = \frac{0.60 \text{ kg}}{8.0 \text{ m}} = 0.075 \text{ kg·m}^{-1}.$$

The speed of propagation is given by Eq. (21–2):

$$c = \sqrt{\frac{T}{\mu}} = \sqrt{\frac{19.6 \text{ N}}{0.075 \text{ kg·m}^{-1}}} = 16.2 \text{ m·s}^{-1}.$$

b) From Eq. (21–1),

$$\lambda = \frac{c}{f} = \frac{16.2 \text{ m·s}^{-1}}{20 \text{ s}^{-1}} = 0.81 \text{ m}. \qquad \blacksquare$$

A transverse wave traveling along a rope carries *energy* from one region of the rope to another. Suppose we look at a particular point on the rope; if the wave is traveling from left to right, then the part of the rope to the left exerts a transverse force on the part to the right as the point undergoes vertical displacements. Thus the left part does *work* on the right part and transfers energy to it. A detailed calculation of the rate of doing work (power) shows that for a sinusoidal wave with amplitude *A* and frequency *f* the rate of energy transfer is proportional to the *square* of the amplitude and to the square of the frequency.

Another important property of transverse waves is **polarization.** When we produce a transverse wave on a horizontal rope, we have a choice of moving the end either up and down or sideways; in either case the wave displacements are perpendicular or *transverse* to the length of the rope. If the end moves up and down, the motion of the entire rope is confined to a vertical plane; if the end moves sideways, the wave moves in a horizontal plane. In either case the wave is said to be *linearly polarized* because the individual particles move back and forth along straight lines perpendicular to the rope.

The motion may also be more complex, containing both vertical and horizontal components. If we combine two perpendicular sinusoidal motions that have equal amplitude but are out of step by a quarter-cycle, the result is a wave in which each particle moves in a *circular* path perpendicular to the rope. Such a wave is said to be *circularly polarized*.

We can make a device to separate the various components of motion. We cut a thin slot in a flat board, thread the rope through it, and orient the board with its plane perpendicular to the rope. Then any transverse motion parallel to the slot passes through unimpeded, while any motion perpendicular to the slot is blocked. Such a device is called a *polarizing filter*. Analogous optical devices for polarized light form the basis of some kinds of sunglasses and also of polarizing filters used in photography. We will discuss polarization of light waves in Chapter 36.

21–4
Speed of a Longitudinal Wave

Propagation speeds of longitudinal as well as transverse waves are determined by the mechanical properties of the medium. We can derive relations for longitudinal waves that are analogous to Eq. (21–2) for transverse waves on a rope. Here is a derivation for longitudinal waves in a fluid in a pipe. Our analysis will be similar to the derivation of Eq. (21–2), and we invite you to compare the two developments.

Figure 21–7 shows a fluid (either liquid or gas) with density ρ in a pipe with cross-sectional area A. In the equilibrium state the fluid is under a uniform pressure p. In Fig. 21–7a the fluid is at rest. At time $t = 0$ we start the piston at the left end moving toward the right with constant speed v. This initiates a wave motion that travels to the right along the length of the pipe, in which successive sections of fluid begin to move and become compressed at successively later times.

Figure 21–7b shows the fluid at time t. All portions of fluid to the left of point P are moving with speed v, and all portions to the right of P are still at rest. The boundary between the moving and stationary portions travels to the right with a speed equal to the speed of propagation or wave speed c. At time t the piston has moved a distance vt, and the boundary has advanced a distance ct. As with a transverse disturbance in a rope, we can compute the speed of propagation from the impulse–momentum theorem.

The quantity of fluid set in motion in time t is the amount that originally occupied a section of the cylinder with length ct, cross-sectional area A, and volume ctA. The mass of this fluid is ρctA, and its longitudinal momentum is

$$\text{Longitudinal momentum} = \rho ctAv.$$

Next we compute the increase of pressure, Δp, in the moving fluid. The original volume of the moving fluid, Act, has decreased by an amount Avt. From the definition of the bulk modulus B (Section 12–2),

$$B = \frac{\text{pressure change}}{\text{fractional volume change}} = \frac{\Delta p}{Avt/Act},$$

and

$$\Delta p = B\frac{v}{c}.$$

The pressure in the moving fluid is $p + \Delta p$, and the force exerted on it by the piston is $(p + \Delta p)A$. The net force on the moving fluid (see Fig. 21–7b) is $\Delta p A$, and the longitudinal impulse is

$$\text{Longitudinal impulse} = \Delta p\, At = B\frac{v}{c}At.$$

Applying the impulse–momentum theorem, we find

$$B\frac{v}{c}At = \rho ctAv. \tag{21–3}$$

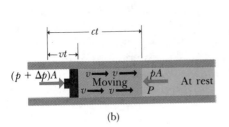

21–7
Propagation of a longitudinal disturbance in a fluid confined in a pipe.

When we solve this for c, we obtain

$$c = \sqrt{\frac{B}{\rho}} \quad \text{(longitudinal wave).} \qquad (21-4)$$

The speed of propagation of a longitudinal pulse in a fluid depends only on the bulk modulus B and the density ρ of the medium. The form of this relation is similar to that of Eq. (21-2); in both cases the numerator is a quantity characterizing the strength of the restoring force, and the denominator is a quantity describing the *inertial* properties of the medium.

When a longitudinal wave propagates in a *solid* bar, the situation is somewhat different; the bar expands sidewise slightly when it is compressed longitudinally, while a fluid in a pipe with constant cross section cannot move sideways. Using the same kind of reasoning that led us to Eq. (21-4), we can show that the speed of a longitudinal pulse in the bar is given by

$$c = \sqrt{\frac{Y}{\rho}} \quad \text{(longitudinal wave),} \qquad (21-5)$$

where Y is Young's modulus, defined in Chapter 12.

The speed of longitudinal waves in a bulk material, either solid or fluid, is given by Eq. (21-4), not Eq. (21-5). In that case the material cannot expand and contract sideways as a rod can. When the frequency of a longitudinal wave is within the range of human hearing, we call it **sound.** Thus the speed of sound in air or water is determined by Eq. (21-4).

As with the derivation for a transverse wave on a rope, Eqs. (21-4) and (21-5) are valid for sinusoidal and other periodic waves, not just for the special case discussed here.

Longitudinal waves, unlike transverse waves, *do not* have polarization. This concept has no meaning for a longitudinal wave.

Visualizing the relation between particle motion and wave motion is not as easy for longitudinal waves as for transverse waves on a rope. Figure 21-8 will help you understand these motions. To use this figure, tape two index cards together, edge to edge, with a gap of 1 mm or so between them, forming a thin slit. Place the cards over the figure with the slit horizontal at the top of the diagram, and move them downward with constant speed. The portions of the sine curves that are visible through the slit correspond to a row of particles in a medium in which a longitudinal sinusoidal wave is traveling. Each particle undergoes simple harmonic motion about its equilibrium position, with delays or phase shifts that increase continuously along the slit. The regions of maximum compression and expansion move from left to right with constant speed. Moving the card upward simulates a wave traveling from right to left.

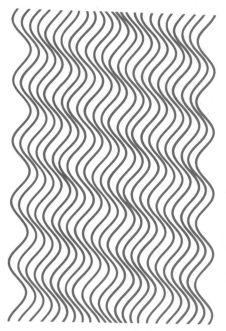

21-8
Diagram for illustrating longitudinal traveling waves.

Example 21-3   Determine the speed of sound waves in water, and find the wavelength of a wave having a frequency of 262 Hz.

Solution   We use Eq. (21–4) to find the wave speed. From Table 12–2 we find that the compressibility of water, which is the reciprocal of the bulk modulus, is $k = 45.8 \times 10^{-11}$ Pa^{-1}. Thus $B = (1/45.8) \times 10^{11}$ Pa. The density of water is $\rho = 1.00 \times 10^3$ kg·m^{-3}. We obtain

$$c = \sqrt{\frac{B}{\rho}} = \sqrt{\frac{(1/45.8) \times 10^{11} \text{ Pa}}{1.00 \times 10^3 \text{ kg·m}^{-3}}} = 1480 \text{ m·s}^{-1}.$$

This is over four times the speed of sound in air at ordinary temperatures. The wavelength is given by

$$\lambda = \frac{c}{f} = \frac{1480 \text{ m·s}^{-1}}{262 \text{ s}^{-1}} = 5.64 \text{ m}.$$

A wave of this frequency in air has a wavelength of 1.31 m, as we found in Example 21–1 (Section 21–2).

Dolphins emit high-frequency sound waves (typically 100,000 Hz) and use the echoes for guidance and for hunting. The corresponding wavelength is 1.48 cm. With this high-frequency "sonar" system they can sense objects of about the size of the wavelength, but not much smaller. ∎

Example 21–4   What is the speed of longitudinal sound waves in a steel rod?

Solution   We use Eq. (21–5). From Table 12–1, $Y = 2.0 \times 10^{11}$ Pa, and from Table 13–1, $\rho = 7.8 \times 10^3$ kg·m^{-3}. We find

$$c = \sqrt{\frac{Y}{\rho}} = \sqrt{\frac{2.0 \times 10^{11} \text{ Pa}}{7.8 \times 10^3 \text{ kg·m}^{-3}}} = 5064 \text{ m·s}^{-1}. \qquad ∎$$

21–5
Sound Waves in Gases

In Section 21–4 we derived an expression for the speed of longitudinal waves in a fluid, in terms of its density ρ and bulk modulus B. We can use this to predict the speed of sound in air and other gases, but we need to know what to use for B. The bulk modulus is defined in general by Eq. (12–7), and for any specific material it is determined by the relation of pressure p to volume V during an expansion or compression. If the temperature of the gas is constant, then Boyle's law, Eq. (17–3), tells us that p is inversely proportional to V. From that equation it can be shown that the bulk modulus of an ideal gas, when it is compressed under constant-temperature conditions, is simply equal to its pressure p. We call this the *isothermal* bulk modulus B_{iso}, and $B_{iso} = p$. The greater the pressure, the greater the increment of pressure Δp needed to cause a given fractional volume change $\Delta V/V$.

But suppose the expansions and compressions occur so rapidly that there isn't enough time for the heat conduction needed to maintain thermal equilibrium. Then it would be better to assume that the process is *adiabatic* rather than isothermal. We learned in Section 18–8 that when a gas is compressed adiabatically, its temperature rises, and when it expands adiabatically, its temperature drops. In this case, p is inversely proportional not just to V but to V^γ, where γ is the ratio of heat capacities from Section 18–7. The pressure changes more rapidly with volume than in the isothermal case, and the bulk modulus is correspondingly larger. It turns out that the **adiabatic bulk modulus** is given by

$$B_{ad} = \gamma p.$$

That is, the adiabatic bulk modulus is larger than the isothermal bulk modulus by a factor of γ.

Which of these is the right one to use? Experiments show that for ordinary sound frequencies, say 20 to 20,000 Hz, the thermal conductivity of gases is so small that the propagation of sound is very nearly *adiabatic*. So in applying Eq. (21–4) we should use the adiabatic bulk modulus $B_{ad} = \gamma p$. Then Eq. (21–4) becomes

$$c = \sqrt{\frac{\gamma p}{\rho}} \quad \text{(ideal gas).} \tag{21-6}$$

We can obtain an alternative form by working out an expression for the density ρ of an ideal gas in terms of its molecular mass M and absolute temperature T. Density is mass per unit volume; the total mass of gas is nM (the molecular mass M multiplied by the number of moles n). So the density is given by $\rho = nM/V$. Also, from the ideal-gas equation ($pV = nRT$) we find $n/V = p/RT$. Combining these, we find

$$\rho = \frac{pM}{RT}. \tag{21-7}$$

When we combine this with Eq. (21–6), we obtain

$$c = \sqrt{\frac{\gamma RT}{M}} \quad \text{(ideal gas).} \tag{21-8}$$

For any particular gas, γ, R, and M are constants, and the wave speed is proportional to the square root of the absolute temperature. It is interesting to compare this result with Eq. (20–12), which gives the rms speed of molecules in an ideal gas. The two expressions are identical except for the numerical factor of 3 in one and γ in the other. It isn't surprising that the wave speed in a gas should be related directly to the speeds of its molecules.

Example 21–5   Compute the speed of longitudinal waves (sound) in air.

Solution   From Example 17–2 (Section 17–2) the mean molecular mass of air is

$$M = 28.8 \ \text{g·mol}^{-1} = 28.8 \times 10^{-3} \ \text{kg·mol}^{-1}.$$

Also, $\gamma = 1.40$ for air, and $R = 8.314$ J·mol^{-1}·K^{-1}. At $T = 300$ K we obtain

$$c = \sqrt{\frac{(1.40)(8.314 \text{ J·mol}^{-1}\text{·K}^{-1})(300 \text{ K})}{28.8 \times 10^{-3} \text{ kg·mol}^{-1}}} = 348 \text{ m·s}^{-1}.$$

This agrees with the measured speed of sound at this temperature to within 0.3%. ∎

The human ear is sensitive to a range of sound frequencies from about 20 Hz to about 20,000 Hz. From the relation $c = \lambda f$ the corresponding wavelength range is from about 17 m, corresponding to a 20-Hz note, to about 1.7 cm, corresponding to 20,000 Hz.

Bats can hear much higher frequencies. Like dolphins, bats use high-frequency sound waves for navigation. A typical frequency is 100,000 Hz; the corresponding wavelength is about 3.5 mm, small enough for them to detect the flying insects they eat.

In this discussion we have ignored the *molecular* nature of a gas and have treated it as a continuous medium. We know that a gas is actually composed of molecules in random motion, separated by distances that are large in comparison with their diameters. The vibrations that constitute a wave in a gas are superposed on the random thermal motion. At atmospheric pressure a molecule travels an average distance of about 10^{-5} cm between collisions, while the displacement amplitude of a faint sound may be less than a thousandth of this distance. We can think of a gas with a sound wave passing through as comparable to a swarm of bees; the swarm as a whole oscillates slightly while individual insects move about through the swarm, apparently at random.

21–6
Mathematical Description of a Wave

We have described the characteristics of waves using the concepts of wave speed, period, frequency, wavelength, and amplitude. Sometimes, though, we need a more detailed description of the positions and motions of individual particles of the medium at particular times during wave propagation. For this description we need the concept of a *wave function,* a function that describes the position of any particle in the medium at any time. We will concentrate on *sinusoidal* waves, in which each particle undergoes *simple harmonic motion* about its equilibrium position.

As a specific example, let's look at waves on a stretched rope. If we ignore the sag of the rope due to gravity, the equilibrium position of the rope is along a straight line. We take this to be the x-axis of a coordinate system. Waves on a rope are *transverse;* during wave motion a particle with equilibrium position x is displaced some distance y in the direction perpendicular to the x-axis. The value of y depends on which particle we are talking about (that is, on x) and also on the time t when we look at it. Thus y is a *function* of x and t; $y = f(x, t)$. If we know this function for a particular wave motion, we can use it to predict the position of any particle at any time. From this we can find the velocity and acceleration of any particle, the shape of the rope, and in fact anything we want to know about the position and motion of the rope at any time.

Now let's think about what a wave function for a sinusoidal wave might look like. Suppose a wave travels from left to right (the direction of increasing x) along the rope. We can compare the motion of any one particle of the rope with the motion of a second particle to the right of the first. We find that the second particle has the same motion as the first, but after a *time lag* that is proportional to the distance between the particles. If one end of a stretched rope oscillates with simple harmonic motion, every other point also oscillates with simple harmonic motion with the same amplitude and frequency.

But the cyclic motions of various points are out of step with each other by various fractions of a cycle. We call these differences *phase differences*, and we say that the **phase** of the motion is different for different points. For example, if one point has its maximum positive displacement at the same time that another has its maximum negative displacement, the two are a half-cycle out of phase.

Suppose the displacement of a particle at the left end (at $x = 0$), where the motion originates, is given by

$$y = A \sin \omega t = A \sin 2\pi f t. \tag{21-9}$$

The wave disturbance travels from $x = 0$ to some point x to the right of the origin in an amount of time given by x/c, where c is the wave speed. So the motion of point x at time t is the same as the motion of point $x = 0$ at the earlier time $(t - x/c)$, and we can find the displacement of point x at time t by simply replacing t in Eq. (21-9) by $(t - x/c)$. When we do that, we find

$$y(x, t) = A \sin \omega\left(t - \frac{x}{c}\right) = A \sin 2\pi f\left(t - \frac{x}{c}\right). \tag{21-10}$$

The notation $y(x, t)$ is a reminder that the displacement y is a function of both the location x of the point and the time t.

We can rewrite Eq. (21-10) in several other useful forms, conveying the same information in different ways. We can express it in terms of the period $\tau = 1/f$ and the wavelength $\lambda = c/f$:

$$y(x, t) = A \sin 2\pi\left(\frac{t}{\tau} - \frac{x}{\lambda}\right). \tag{21-11}$$

We get another convenient form if we define a quantity k, called the **wave number** or the **propagation constant**:

$$k = \frac{2\pi}{\lambda}. \tag{21-12}$$

In terms of k and the angular frequency ω, the wavelength–frequency

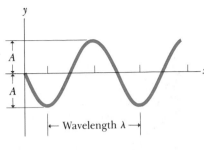

A

A

← Wavelength λ →

21–9
Waveform at $t = 0$.

relation $c = \lambda f$ becomes

$$\omega = ck, \tag{21–13}$$

and we can rewrite Eq. (21–11) as

$$y(x, t) = A \sin (\omega t - kx). \tag{21–14}$$

In a specific problem, the choice of which of these various forms to use is a matter of convenience; they all say the same thing, but they express it in terms of different quantities. We should mention in passing that a few authors define the wave number as $1/\lambda$ rather than $2\pi/\lambda$. In that case our k is still called the propagation constant.

At any specific *time t*, Eq. (21–10), (21–11), or (21–14) gives the displacement y of a particle from its equilibrium position, as a function of the *coordinate x* of the particle. If the wave is a transverse wave on a rope, the equation represents the *shape* of the rope at that instant, as if we had taken a photograph of the rope. Thus at time $t = 0$,

$$y = A \sin (-kx) = -A \sin kx = -A \sin 2\pi\frac{x}{\lambda}.$$

This curve is plotted in Fig. 21–9.

At any given *coordinate x*, Eq. (21–10), (21–11), or (21–14) gives the displacement y of the particle at that coordinate as a function of *time*. That is, it describes the motion of that particle. Thus at the position $x = 0$,

$$y = A \sin \omega t = A \sin 2\pi\frac{t}{\tau}.$$

This curve is plotted in Fig. 21–10. Note that this is *not* a picture of the shape of the rope but a graph of the position y of a particle as a function of time.

We can also modify these formulas to represent a wave traveling in the *negative x*-direction. In this case the displacement of point x at time t is the same as the motion of point $x = 0$ at the *later* time $(t + x/c)$, so in Eq. (21–9) we replace t by $(t + x/c)$. For a wave traveling in the negative x-direction,

$$y = A \sin 2\pi f\left(t + \frac{x}{c}\right) = A \sin 2\pi\left(\frac{t}{\tau} + \frac{x}{\lambda}\right)$$

$$= A \sin (\omega t + kx). \tag{21–15}$$

We have introduced the concept of wave function with reference to transverse waves on a rope, but the concept is equally useful with *longitudinal* waves. The quantity y still measures the displacement of a particle of the medium from its equilibrium position; the difference is that for a longitudinal wave this displacement is *parallel* to the x-axis instead of perpendicular to it. Thus the distance y is measured parallel to the x-axis, and x and y no longer represent distances measured in perpendicular directions, as in the usual xy-coordinate system. If this sounds confusing, don't panic! It will become clear as we work out more problems with longitudinal waves in this chapter and in the next.

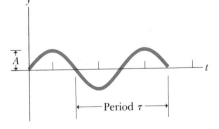

A

← Period τ →

21–10
Motion of point at $x = 0$.

PROBLEM-SOLVING STRATEGY: *Mechanical Waves*

1. It helps to make a distinction between *kinematics* problems and *dynamics* problems. In kinematics problems we are concerned only with *describing* motion; the relevant quantities are wave speed, wavelength (or wave number), frequency (or angular frequency), amplitude, and the position, velocity, and acceleration of individual particles. In dynamics problems, concepts such as force and mass enter; the relation of wave speed to the mechanical properties of a system is an example.

2. If f is given, it is easy to find τ, and vice versa. If λ is given, it is easy to find k, and vice versa. If any two of the quantities c, λ, and f are known, it is easy to find the third. In some problems that is all you need. To determine the wave function

completely, you need to know A and any two of c, λ, and f. Once this information is known, you can use it in Eq. (21–10), (21–11), or (21–14) to get the specific wave function for the problem at hand. Once you have that, you can find the value of y at any point (value of x) and at any time, by substituting into the wave function.

3. The wave speed c, the tension T, and the mass per unit length μ are related by Eq. (21–2). If you know any two of these, it is easy to find the third. Look to see what you are given in the problem statement. For longitudinal waves, use the corresponding relations in Sections 21–4 and 21–5, Eq. (21–4), (21–5), or (21–8).

Example 21–6 A clothesline has a linear mass density $\mu = 0.25$ kg·m^{-1} and is stretched with a tension $T = 25$ N. One end is given a sinusoidal motion with a frequency of 5.0 Hz and an amplitude of 0.010 m. At time $t = 0$ the end has zero displacement and is moving in the $+y$-direction.

a) Find the wave speed, amplitude, angular frequency, period, wavelength, and wave number.

b) Write a wave function describing the wave.

c) Find the position of the point at $x = 0.25$ m at time $t = 0.10$ s.

Solution

a) From Eq. (21–2) the wave speed is

$$c = \sqrt{\frac{T}{\mu}} = \sqrt{\frac{25 \text{ N}}{0.25 \text{ kg·m}^{-1}}} = 10 \text{ m·s}^{-1}.$$

The amplitude A is just the amplitude of the motion of the endpoint, $A = 0.010$ m. The angular frequency is

$$\omega = 2\pi f = 2\pi(5.0 \text{ s}^{-1}) = 31.4 \text{ s}^{-1}.$$

The period is $\tau = 1/f = 0.20$ s. We get the wavelength from Eq. (21–1):

$$\lambda = \frac{c}{f} = \frac{10 \text{ m·s}^{-1}}{5.0 \text{ s}^{-1}} = 2.0 \text{ m}.$$

We find the wave number from Eq. (21–12) or Eq. (21–13):

$$k = \frac{2\pi}{\lambda} = \frac{2\pi}{2.0 \text{ m}} = 3.14 \text{ m}^{-1},$$

or

$$k = \frac{\omega}{c} = \frac{31.4 \text{ s}^{-1}}{10 \text{ m·s}^{-1}} = 3.14 \text{ m}^{-1}.$$

b) The wave function, using the form of Eq. (21–11), is

$$y = (0.010 \text{ m}) \sin 2\pi\left(\frac{t}{0.20 \text{ s}} - \frac{x}{2.0 \text{ m}}\right)$$

$$= (0.010 \text{ m}) \sin [(31.4 \text{ s}^{-1})t - (3.14 \text{ m}^{-1})x].$$

We can also get this same equation from Eq. (21–14), using the values of ω and k obtained above.

c) We find the displacement of the point $x = 0.25$ m at time $t = 0.10$ s by substituting these values into either of the above wave equations:

$$y = (0.010 \text{ m}) \sin 2\pi\left(\frac{0.10 \text{ s}}{0.20 \text{ s}} - \frac{0.25 \text{ m}}{2.0 \text{ m}}\right)$$

$$= (0.010 \text{ m}) \sin 2\pi(0.375) = 0.0071 \text{ m.} \quad \blacksquare$$

Questions

21–1 The term *wave* has a variety of meanings in ordinary language. Think of several, and discuss their relation to the precise physical sense in which the term is used in this chapter.

21–2 What kinds of energy are associated with waves on a stretched string? How could such energy be detected experimentally?

21–3 Is it possible to have a longitudinal wave on a stretched string? A transverse wave on a steel rod?

21–4 The speed of sound waves in air depends on temperature, but the speed of light waves does not. Why?

21–5 For the wave motions discussed in this chapter, does the speed of propagation depend on the amplitude?

21–6 Children make toy telephones by sticking each end of a long string through a hole in the bottom of a paper cup and knotting it so that it will not pull out. When the string is pulled taut, sound can be transmitted from one cup to the other. How does this work? Why is the transmitted sound louder than the sound traveling through air for the same distance?

21–7 An echo is sound reflected from a distant object, such as a wall or a cliff. Explain how you can determine how far away the object is by timing the echo.

21–8 Why do you see lightning before you hear the thunder? A familiar rule of thumb is to start counting slowly, once per second, when you see the lightning;

when you hear thunder, divide the number you have reached by 5 to obtain your distance (in miles) from the lightning. Why does this work? Or does it?

21–9 When ocean waves approach a beach, the crests are always nearly parallel to the shore, despite the fact that they must come from various directions. Why?

21–10 The amplitudes of ocean waves increase as they approach the shore, and often the crests bend over and "break." Why?

21–11 When a rock is thrown into a pond and the resulting ripples spread in ever-widening circles, the amplitude decreases with increasing distance from the center. Why?

21–12 In speaker systems designed for high-fidelity music reproduction the "tweeters" that reproduce the high frequencies are always much smaller than the "woofers" used for low frequencies. Why?

21–13 When sound travels from air into water, does the frequency of the wave change? The wavelength? The speed?

21–14 Which of the quantities describing a sinusoidal wave is most closely related to musical pitch? To loudness?

21–15 Musical notes produced by different instruments (such as a flute and an oboe) may have the same pitch and loudness and yet sound different. What is the difference in physical terms?

Exercises

Section 21–2   Periodic Waves

21–1 The speed of sound in air at 20°C is 344 m·s^{-1}.

a) What is the wavelength of a sound wave with a frequency of 32.0 Hz, corresponding to the lowest pedal note on medium-size pipe organs?

b) What is the frequency of a wave with a wavelength of 1.22 m (4 ft), corresponding approximately to the note D above middle C on the piano?

21–2 The speed of radio waves in vacuum (equal to the speed of light) is 3.00×10^8 m·s^{-1}. Find the wavelength for

a) an AM radio station with a frequency of 1240 kHz;

b) an FM radio station with a frequency of 90.9 MHz.

21–3 Provided that the amplitude is sufficiently great, the human ear can respond to longitudinal waves over a range of frequencies from about 20.0 Hz to about 20,000 Hz. Compute the wavelengths corresponding to these frequencies

a) for waves in air ($c = 344$ m·s^{-1});

b) for waves in water ($c = 1480$ m·s^{-1}).

21–4 The sound waves from a loudspeaker spread out nearly uniformly in all directions when their wavelengths are large in comparison with the diameter of the speaker. When the wavelength is small in comparison with the diameter of the speaker, much of the sound energy is concentrated forward. For a speaker of diameter 15.0 cm, compute the frequency for which the wavelength of the sound waves in air ($c = 344$ m·s^{-1}) is

a) 10 times the diameter of the speaker;

b) equal to the diameter of the speaker;

c) 1/10 the diameter of the speaker.

21–5 A fisherman notices that his boat is moving up and down in a periodic way because of waves on the surface of the water. It takes 4.0 s for the boat to travel from its highest point to its lowest, a total distance of 3.0 m. The fisherman sees that the wave crests are spaced 8.0 m apart.

a) How fast are the waves traveling?

b) What is the amplitude of the wave?

Section 21–3   Speed of a Transverse Wave

21–6 A steel wire 4.00 m long has a mass of 0.0600 kg and is stretched with a tension of 1000 N. What is the speed of propagation of a transverse wave on the wire?

21–7 With what tension must a rope of length 5.00 m and mass 0.160 kg be stretched for transverse waves of frequency 60.0 Hz to have a wavelength of 0.800 m?

21–8 One end of a horizontal string is attached to a prong of an electrically driven tuning fork whose frequency of vibration is 240 Hz. The other end passes over a pulley and supports a 5.00-kg mass. The linear mass density of the string is 0.0120 kg·m^{-1}.

a) What is the speed of a transverse wave on the string?

b) What is the wavelength?

Section 21–4   Speed of a Longitudinal Wave

Section 21–5   Sound Waves in Gases

21–9 Longitudinal waves with a frequency of 200 Hz in a liquid with a density of 800 kg·m^{-3} are found to have a wavelength of 5.00 m. Calculate the bulk modulus of the liquid.

21–10 A metal bar with a length of 20.0 m has a density of 4000 kg·m^{-3}. Longitudinal sound waves take 5.00×10^{-3} s to travel from one end of the bar to the other. What is Young's modulus for this metal?

21–11 A scuba diver below the surface of a lake hears the sound of a horn of a boat on the surface directly above her. At the same time a friend standing on dry land 14.0 m from the boat hears the horn. At what depth is the diver?

21–12 A steel pipe 150 m long is struck at one end. A person at the other end hears two sounds as a result of two longitudinal waves, one traveling in the metal pipe and the other traveling in the air. What is the time interval between the two sounds? Take Young's modulus for steel to be 2.00×10^{11} Pa, the density of steel to be 7800 kg·m^{-3}, and the speed of sound in air to be 344 m·s^{-1}.

21–13 At a temperature of 27.0°C, what is the speed of longitudinal waves in

a) argon (atomic mass 39.9 g·mol^{-1})?

b) hydrogen (molecular mass 2.02 g·mol^{-1})?

c) Compare your answers to parts (a) and (b) with the speed in air at the same temperature.

21–14 What is the difference between the speeds of longitudinal waves in air at −3.0°C and at 57.0°C?

Section 21–6   Mathematical Description of a Wave

21–15 Show that Eq. (21–11) may be written

$$y = -A \sin \frac{2\pi}{\lambda}(x - ct).$$

21–16 The equation of a certain traveling transverse

wave is

$$y = (2.50 \text{ cm}) \sin 2\pi\left(\frac{t}{0.0100 \text{ s}} - \frac{x}{30.0 \text{ cm}}\right).$$

Determine the wave's

a) amplitude,

b) wavelength,

c) frequency, and

d) speed of propagation.

21–17 Transverse waves on a string have a wave speed of 15.0 m·s^{-1}, an amplitude of 0.0800 m, and a wavelength of 0.600 m. The waves travel in the +x-direction, and at $t = 0$ the $x = 0$ end of the string is at $y = 0$ and moving downward.

a) Find the frequency, period, and wave number of these waves.

b) Write a wave function describing the wave.

c) Find the transverse displacement of a point at $x = 0.400$ m at time $t = 0.200$ s.

21–18 A traveling transverse wave on a string is represented by the equation in Exercise 21–15. Let $A = 8.0$ cm, $\lambda = 12.0$ cm, and $c = 2.0$ cm·s^{-1}.

a) At time $t = 0$, compute the transverse displacement y at 2-cm intervals of x (that is, at $x = 0$, $x = 2$ cm, $x = 4$ cm, etc.) from $x = 0$ to $x = 24$ cm. Show the results in a graph. This is the shape of the string at time $t = 0$.

b) Repeat the calculations, for the same values of x, at times $t = 2$ s and $t = 4$ s. Show on the same graph the shape of the string at these instants. In what direction is the wave traveling?

Problems

21–19 One end of a stretched rope is given a periodic transverse motion with a frequency of 10.0 Hz. The rope is 20.0 m long, has a total mass of 0.500 kg, and is stretched with a tension of 400 N.

a) Find the wave speed and the wavelength.

b) If the tension is doubled, how must the frequency be changed to maintain the same wavelength?

21–20 One end of a rubber tube 20.0 m long, with a total mass of 1.40 kg, is fastened to a fixed support. A cord attached to the other end passes over a pulley and supports a body with a mass of 12.0 kg. The tube is struck a transverse blow at one end. Find the time required for the pulse to reach the other end.

21–21 What is the ratio of the speed of sound in a diatomic gas at some temperature to the rms speed of gas molecules at the same temperature?

21–22

a) If the propagation of sound waves in gases were characterized by isothermal rather than adiabatic expansions and compressions, and assuming that the gas behaves as an ideal gas, show that the speed of sound would be given by $(RT/M)^{1/2}$.

b) What would be the speed of sound in air at 27.0°C in this case?

c) Under what circumstances might the wave propagation be expected to be isothermal?

21–23 What must be the stress in a stretched wire of a material whose Young's modulus is Y for the speed of longitudinal waves to equal 20 times the speed of transverse waves?

21–24 The equation of a transverse traveling wave on a string is $y(x, t) = (1.75 \text{ cm}) \sin \pi([250 \text{ s}^{-1}]t + [0.400 \text{ cm}^{-1}]x)$.

a) Find the amplitude, wavelength, frequency, period, and speed of propagation.

b) Sketch the shape of the string at the following values of t: 0, 0.0020 s, and 0.0040 s.

c) Is the wave traveling in the positive or negative x-direction?

d) If the mass per unit length of the string is 0.50 kg·m^{-1}, find the tension.

21–25 A transverse sine wave with an amplitude of 0.120 m and a wavelength of 1.60 m travels from left to right along a long horizontal stretched string with a speed of 1.00 m·s^{-1}. Take the origin at the left end of the undisturbed string. At time $t = 0$ the left end of the string is at the origin and is moving downward.

a) What are the frequency, angular frequency, and propagation constant of the wave?

b) What is the equation of the wave?

c) What is the equation of motion of the left end of the string?

d) What is the equation of motion of a particle 1.20 m to the right of the origin?

e) What is the maximum magnitude of transverse velocity of any particle of the string?

f) Find the transverse displacement of a particle 1.20 m to the right of the origin at time $t = 2.40$ s.

Challenge Problems

21–26 A metal wire, with a density of 4.00×10^3 kg·m^{-3} and Young's modulus 2.00×10^{11} Pa, is stretched between rigid supports. At one temperature the speed of a transverse wave is found to be 200 m·s^{-1}. When the temperature is raised 25.0 C°, the speed decreases to 160 m·s^{-1}. Determine the coefficient of linear expansion.

21–27 A student who couldn't get tickets to a Red Sox–Yankees baseball game at Fenway Park is listening to the radio broadcast of the game in her dorm room while doing her physics homework. In the bottom of the fourth inning, a thunderstorm approaching from a generally westward direction makes its presence known in three ways: (1) The student sees a lightning flash (and hears the electromagnetic pulse on her radio receiver); (2) 3.00 s later, she hears the thunder over the radio; (3) 4.43 s after the lightning flash, the thunder rattles her window. By a previous careful measurement she knows that she is 1.12 km due north of the broadcast booth at the ballpark and that the speed of sound is 344 m·s^{-1}. Where did the lightning flash occur in relation to the ballpark?

Reflections and Normal Modes

In our study of mechanical waves in Chapter 21 we weren't concerned with what happens when a wave arrives at an end or boundary of its medium. But there are many wave phenomena in which boundaries play a significant role. When you yell at a flat wall some distance away, the sound wave is reflected from the rigid surface, and an echo comes back. When you send a wave pulse down a rope or string whose far end is tied to a rigid support, a reflected pulse comes back to you. In both cases the initial and reflected waves overlap in the same region of the medium. When there are *two* boundary points or surfaces we get repeated reflections. In such situations we find that sinusoidal waves can occur only for certain particular frequencies. These special frequencies and their associated wave patterns are called *normal modes*. The pitches of most musical instruments are determined by normal-mode frequencies, and many other mechanical vibrations involve normal-mode motion. This concept will also reappear later in some unexpected places such as the energy levels of atoms.

22–1
Boundary Conditions for a String

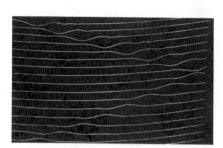

22–1
A pulse starts at the left in the top image, travels to the right, and is reflected from the stationary end of the string at the right.

As a simple example of reflections and the role of the boundary of a wave medium, let's look again at transverse waves on a stretched rope or string. What happens when a wave pulse or a sinusoidal wave arrives at the end of the string? If the end is fastened to a rigid support, it cannot move. The arriving wave exerts a force on the support; the reaction to this force, exerted *by* the support *on* the string, "kicks back" on the string and sets up a *reflected* pulse or wave traveling in the reverse direction.

At the opposite extreme from an end that is held stationary is one that is perfectly free to move in the direction transverse to the length of the string. For example, the string might be tied to a light ring that slides on a smooth rod perpendicular to the length of the string. The ring and rod maintain the tension but exert no transverse force. When a wave arrives at a free end where there is no transverse force, the end "overshoots," and again a reflected wave is set up. The conditions at the end of the string, such as a rigid support or the complete absence of transverse force, are called **boundary conditions.**

Figure 22–1 is a multiflash photograph showing the reflection of a pulse at a stationary end of a string. (The camera was moved vertically while the photographs were taken, so successive images are spread out.) Both the displacement and the direction of propagation of the reflected pulse are opposite to the initial pulse. When reflection takes place at a *free* end (not shown in Fig. 22–1), the direction of propagation is again reversed, but the direction of the displacement is the same as for the initial pulse.

Here's a useful way to picture the process of reflection. Imagine that the string extends beyond its actual end and that the pulse continues on into the imaginary portion as though the support were not there. At the same time a pulse traveling in the opposite direction in the imaginary portion moves into the real portion of the string and forms the reflected pulse. The reflected pulse is inverted if the end is held but not if the end is free. The two cases are shown in Fig. 22–2.

22–2
Description of the reflection of a pulse (a) at a stationary end of a string and (b) at a free end, in terms of a reflected pulse originating in an imaginary portion of the string.

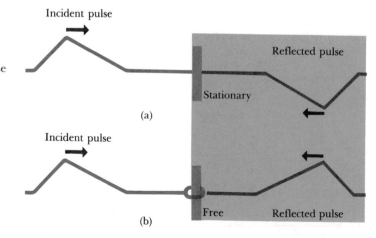

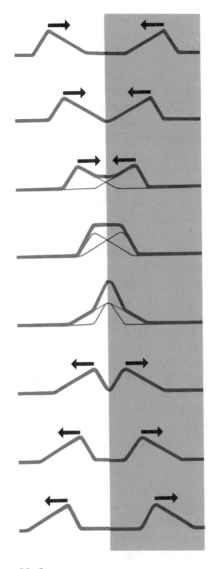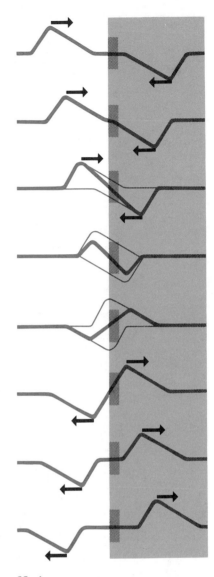

22–3
Reflection at a free end.

22–4
Reflection at a stationary end.

At any point where the initial and reflected pulses overlap, the actual displacement of the string is the *algebraic sum* of the displacements in the individual pulses. Figures 22–3 and 22–4 show the shape of the region near the end of the string for both types of reflected pulses, Fig. 22–3 for a free end and Fig. 22–4 for a stationary end. If the end is stationary, the incident and reflected pulses must combine in such a way that the total displacement at the end of the string is *always* zero. This process of combining the displacements of the separate pulses at each point to obtain the actual displacement is an example of the *principle of superposition*, which plays a central role in most of this chapter.

22–2
Superposition and Standing Waves

When a sinusoidal wave on a rope or string arrives at a boundary point (either a stationary point or an end that is free to move transversely), a reflected wave originates at this point and travels in the opposite direction. The resulting motion of the string is determined by the **principle of superposition.** This principle states that when two waves overlap, the actual displacement of any point on the string, at any time, is obtained by adding two displacements: the displacement the point would have if only the first wave were present and the displacement it would have with only the second wave.

The principle of superposition is of central importance in all types of wave motion. It applies not only to waves on a string, but also to sound waves, electromagnetic waves (such as light), and many other wave phenomena. The general term **interference** is used to describe phenomena that result from two or more waves passing through the same region at the same time.

Now let's look in more detail at what happens when a *sinusoidal* wave is reflected by a stationary point on a string. When the two waves combine, the resulting motion no longer looks like two waves traveling in opposite directions. If the frequency is great enough that the eye cannot follow the motion, the string appears to be subdivided into a number of segments, as in the time-exposure photograph of Fig. 22–5a. A multiflash photograph of the same string, in Fig. 22–5b, shows a few instantaneous shapes of the string at particular times. The behavior is quite different from the traveling waves we have been studying. In a traveling wave the amplitude remains constant while the waveform moves with a speed equal to the wave speed. Here, instead, the waveform remains in the same position along the string while its amplitude fluctuates. There are particular points, called **nodes,** that do not move at all. Midway between the nodes are points called *loops* or **antinodes,** where the amplitude of motion is greatest. Because the wave pattern doesn't appear to be moving in either direction along the string, it is called a **standing wave.**

Figure 22–6 shows how we can use the superposition principle to understand the formation of a standing wave. The figure shows the separate graphs of the waveforms at four instants, one tenth of a period

22–5
(a) Standing waves in a stretched string (time exposure). (b) Multiflash photograph of a standing wave, with nodes at the center and at the ends.

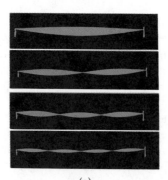

(a)   (b)

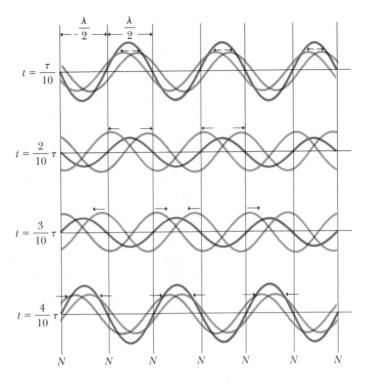

22–6
The formation of a standing wave.
A wave traveling to the right (gray
curves) combines with a wave traveling
to the left (light color curves) to form a
standing wave (dark color curves). The
thin horizontal line in each part shows
the equilibrium position of the string.

apart. The gray curves show a wave traveling to the right. The light color
curves show a wave with the same propagation speed, wavelength, and
amplitude traveling to the *left*. The dark color curves are the resultant
waveform; we obtain it by applying the principle of superposition, that
is, by adding the displacements (the values of y) for the two separate
waves at each point. At those places marked N at the bottom of Fig. 22–6
the resultant displacements are *always* zero. These are the *nodes*. Midway
between the nodes are the points of *greatest* amplitude; these are the
antinodes. We can see from the figure that *the distance between successive
nodes or between successive antinodes is one-half wavelength,* $\lambda/2$.

We can derive a wave function for the standing wave of Fig. 22–6 by
adding the wave functions for two waves with equal amplitude, period,
and wavelength traveling in opposite directions. Call these two wave
functions y_1 and y_2:

$$y_1 = A \sin (\omega t - kx) \quad \text{(traveling to the right),}$$

$$y_2 = -A \sin (\omega t + kx) \quad \text{(traveling to the left).}$$

The wave function for the standing wave is the sum of these:

$$y_1 + y_2 = A[\sin (\omega t - kx) - \sin (\omega t + kx)].$$

We can rearrange this in an illuminating way by using the identities for
the sine of the sum and difference of two angles: $\sin (a \pm b) = \sin a \cos
b \pm \cos a \sin b$. Using these and combining terms, we obtain

$$y_1 + y_2 = [-2A \cos \omega t] \sin kx. \qquad (22\text{--}1)$$

This expression has two factors, a function of t multiplied by a function of x. The factor $\sin kx$ shows that at each instant the shape of the

string is a sine curve. The amplitude is the expression in the square brackets, and it varies sinusoidally with time from $-2A$ to $2A$ and back. The wave shape does not move along the string; it stays in the same position, but the amplitude grows larger and smaller with time. This behavior is shown graphically in Fig. 22–6. Each point in the string still undergoes simple harmonic motion, but all the points between any successive pair of nodes move *in phase*. This is in contrast to the successive phase differences between motions of adjacent points that we see with a wave traveling in one direction.

We can use Eq. (22–1) to find the positions of the nodes. At any point for which $\sin kx = 0$ the displacement is *always* zero. This occurs when $kx = 0, \pi, 2\pi, 3\pi, \ldots$, or

$$x = 0, \; \pi/k, \; 2\pi/k, \; 3\pi/k, \ldots \; = \; 0, \; \lambda/2, \; \lambda, \; 3\lambda/2, \ldots . \quad (22\text{–}2)$$

In particular, there is a node at $x = 0$; this standing wave could correspond to a wave traveling in the $-x$-direction, reflected from a stationary point at $x = 0$. The reflected wave is inverted; that's why we chose the two wave functions y_1 and y_2 to have opposite amplitudes A and $-A$.

22–3
Normal Modes of a String

We have mentioned the reflection or echo of a sound wave from a rigid wall. Now suppose we have two parallel walls. If we produce a sharp sound pulse, such as a hand clap, at some point between the walls, the result is a series of regularly spaced echoes caused by repeated back-and-forth reflection between the walls. In room acoustics this phenomenon is called "flutter echo"; it is the bane of acoustical engineers.

The analogous situation with transverse waves on a string is a string with some definite length L, rigidly held at *both* ends. If we produce a sinusoidal wave on such a string, the wave is reflected and re-reflected from the ends. Because the string is held at both ends, both ends must be nodes. Because adjacent nodes are one-half wavelength ($\lambda/2$) apart, the length of the string has to be ($\lambda/2$), $2(\lambda/2)$, $3(\lambda/2)$, or in general some integer number of half-wavelengths:

$$L = n\frac{\lambda}{2} \qquad (n = 1, 2, 3, \ldots). \qquad (22\text{–}3)$$

That is, a standing wave can exist in a string with length L, held at both ends, only when its wavelength satisfies Eq. (22–3). Solving this equation for λ, we find

$$\lambda = \frac{2L}{n} \qquad (n = 1, 2, 3, \ldots). \qquad (22\text{–}4)$$

When the wavelength is *not* equal to one of these values, no standing wave is possible.

Corresponding to this series of possible wavelengths is a series of possible frequencies, each related to its corresponding wavelength by

$f = c/\lambda$. Labeling these frequencies f_1, f_2, and so on, we find

$$f_1 = \frac{c}{2L}, \qquad f_2 = 2\frac{c}{2L}, \qquad f_3 = 3\frac{c}{2L}, \cdots,$$

or, in general,

$$f_n = \frac{nc}{2L} \qquad (n = 1, 2, 3, \ldots). \tag{22–5}$$

The smallest possible frequency, $f_1 = c/2L$, is called the **fundamental frequency.** All the other possible frequencies are integer multiples of f_1, such as $2f_1$, $3f_1$, $4f_1$, and so on. Thus we can rewrite Eq. (22–5) as

$$f_n = n\frac{c}{2L} = nf_1 \qquad (n = 1, 2, 3, \ldots). \tag{22–6}$$

These frequencies, all integer multiples of f_1, are called **harmonics,** and the series is called a **harmonic series.** Musicians sometimes call f_2, f_3, and so on **overtones;** f_2 is the second harmonic or the first overtone, f_3 is the third harmonic or the second overtone, and so on.

As we mentioned in the chapter introduction, a **normal mode** is a motion in which all particles of the string move sinusoidally with the same frequency. Each of the frequencies given by Eq. (22–5) corresponds to a possible normal mode. There are infinitely many normal modes, each with its characteristic frequency and vibration pattern. We can contrast this with a simpler vibrating system, the harmonic oscillator, which has only one normal mode and one characteristic frequency.

If we displace a string so that its shape is the same as one of the normal-mode patterns, then when we release it, it vibrates with the frequency of that mode. But when a piano string is struck or a guitar string is plucked, not only the fundamental but many of the overtones are present in the resulting vibration. This motion is therefore a combination or *superposition* of many normal modes. Several frequencies and motions are present simultaneously, and the displacement of any point on the string is the sum (or superposition) of displacements associated with the individual modes. Indeed, it is possible to represent *every possible* motion of the string as some superposition of normal-mode motions. Finding this representation for a given vibration pattern is called *harmonic analysis*.

As we have seen, the fundamental frequency of a vibrating string is $f_1 = c/2L$. The wave speed c is determined by Eq. (21–2), $c = \sqrt{T/\mu}$. Combining these, we find

$$f_1 = \frac{1}{2L}\sqrt{\frac{T}{\mu}}. \tag{22–7}$$

This equation is the basis of tuning of stringed instruments. All such instruments are "tuned" by varying the tension T. An increase of tension increases the wave speed c and thus increases the frequency (and the pitch) for a string of any fixed length L. The inverse dependence of frequency on length L is illustrated by the long strings of the bass (low-frequency) section of the piano or the bass viol compared with the shorter strings on the piano treble or the violin. One reason for winding the bass strings of a piano with wire is to increase the mass per unit length μ so as to obtain the desired low frequency without resorting to a string that is inconveniently long. In playing the violin or guitar the usual means of varying the pitch is to press the strings against the fingerboard with the fingers to change the length L of the vibrating portion of the string. As Eq. (22–7) shows, decreasing L increases f_1.

PROBLEM-SOLVING STRATEGY: *Standing Waves*

1. As with the problems in Chapter 21, it is useful to distinguish between the purely kinematic quantities, such as wave speed c, wavelength λ, and frequency f, and the dynamic quantities involving the properties of the medium, including T, μ, and (in the next section) B and ρ. The latter determine the wave speed c. Try to determine, in the problem at hand, whether the properties of the medium are involved or whether the problem is only kinematic in nature.

2. In visualizing nodes and antinodes in standing waves it is always helpful to draw diagrams. For a string you can draw the shape at one instant and label the nodes N and antinodes A. For longitudinal waves (discussed in the next section) it is not so easy to draw the shape, but you can still label the nodes and antinodes. The distance between two adjacent nodes or two adjacent antinodes is always $\lambda/2$, and the distance between a node and the adjacent antinode is always $\lambda/4$.

22–4
Longitudinal Standing Waves

When longitudinal waves propagate in a fluid in a pipe with finite length, the waves are reflected from the ends in the same way that transverse waves on a string are reflected at its ends. The superposition of the waves traveling in opposite directions again forms a standing wave.

When reflection takes place at a *closed* end (that is, an end with a rigid barrier or plug), the displacement of the particles at this end must always be zero. This situation is analogous to a stationary end of a string; in both cases there is no displacement at the end, and the end is a *node*. In the following discussion we will call a closed end of a pipe a *displacement node*. If the end of the pipe is open and the pipe is narrow in comparison with the wavelength (which is true for most musical instruments), the open end is a *displacement antinode*. We will explain below why this is the case. (A *free* end of a stretched string, as discussed in Section 22–1, is also a displacement antinode.) Thus longitudinal waves in a column of fluid are reflected at the closed and open ends of a pipe in the same way that transverse waves in a string are reflected at stationary and free ends, respectively.

We can demonstrate longitudinal standing waves in a column of gas and also measure the wave speed, using the apparatus called Kundt's tube, shown in Fig. 22–7. A horizontal glass tube a meter or so long is closed at one end and has a flexible diaphragm at the other end that can transmit vibrations. We use as our sound source a small loudspeaker

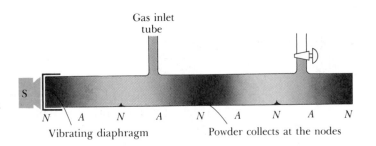

Gas inlet
tube

22–7
Kundt's tube for determining the speed of sound in a gas. The shading represents the density of the gas molecules at an instant when the pressure at the displacement nodes is a maximum or a minimum.

$N \quad A \quad N \quad A \quad N \quad A \quad N \quad A \quad N$

Vibrating diaphragm   Powder collects at the nodes

driven by an audio oscillator and amplifier to vibrate the diaphragm sinusoidally with a frequency that we can vary. We place a small amount of light powder or cork dust inside the pipe and distribute it uniformly along the bottom side of the pipe.

As we vary the frequency of the sound, we pass through frequencies at which the amplitude of the standing waves becomes large enough for the moving gas to sweep the cork dust along the pipe at all points where the gas is in motion. The powder therefore collects at the displacement nodes (where the gas is not moving). Adjacent nodes are separated by a distance equal to $\lambda/2$, and we can measure this distance. We read the frequency f from the oscillator dial, and we can then calculate the speed c of the waves from the relation $c = \lambda f$.

Figure 22–8 will help you to visualize longitudinal standing waves; it is analogous to Fig. 21–8 for longitudinal traveling waves. Again tape two index cards together, edge to edge, with a gap of a millimeter or two, forming a thin slit. Place the card over the diagram with the slit horizontal and move it vertically with constant velocity. The portions of the sine curves that appear in the slit correspond to the oscillations of the particles in a longitudinal standing wave. Each particle moves with longitudinal simple harmonic motion about its equilibrium positions. The particles at the nodes do not move, and the nodes are regions of maximum compression and expansion. Midway between the nodes are the antinodes, regions of maximum displacement but zero compression and expansion.

At a displacement node the pressure variations above and below the average have their *maximum* value, while at a displacement antinode the pressure does not vary. To understand this, note that points on opposite sides of a displacement *node* vibrate in *opposite phase*. When the points approach each other, the gas between them is compressed and the pressure rises; when they recede from each other, the pressure drops. But two points on opposite sides of a displacement *antinode* vibrate *in phase*; the distance between them is nearly constant, and there is *no* pressure variation at the antinode.

We can describe this relationship in terms of **pressure nodes,** points where the pressure does not vary, and **pressure antinodes,** points where the pressure variation is greatest. *A pressure node is always a displacement antinode, and a pressure antinode is always a displacement node.* An *open* end of a narrow tube or pipe is a pressure node because it is open to the atmosphere, where the pressure is constant. Because of this, an open end is always a displacement *antinode.*

22–8
Diagram for illustrating longitudinal standing waves.

22–5
Normal Modes of Organ Pipes

Organ pipes provide us with a good example of longitudinal standing waves and normal modes in vibrating air columns. Air is supplied by a blower, at a gauge pressure typically of the order of 10^3 Pa or 10^{-2} atm, to the left ends of the pipes in Figs. 22–9 and 22–10. A stream of air emerges from the narrow opening formed by the vertical surface and is directed against the right edge of the opening in the top surface of the pipe, called the *mouth* of the pipe. The column of air in the pipe is set into vibration; just as in the case of the stretched string, there is a series of possible normal modes.

The mouth (the left end) always acts as an open end; thus it is a pressure node and a displacement antinode. In Fig. 22–9 the right end is also open and thus is also a pressure node and a displacement antinode. For this pipe, called an *open pipe*, the fundamental frequency f_1 corresponds to a standing-wave pattern with a displacement antinode at each end and a displacement node in the middle, as shown in Fig. 22–9a. The distance between adjacent nodes is always equal to one-half wavelength, and in this case this is equal to the length L of the pipe; $\lambda/2 = L$. The corresponding frequency, obtained from the relation $f = c/\lambda$, is $f_1 = c/2L$.

The other two parts of Fig. 22–9 show the second and third harmonics; their vibration patterns have two and three displacement nodes, respectively. For these a half-wavelength is equal to $L/2$ and $L/3$, respectively, and the frequencies are twice and three times the fundamental, respectively. That is, $f_2 = 2f_1$ and $f_3 = 3f_1$. All the normal-mode frequencies for an open pipe are given by the equation

$$f_n = \frac{nc}{2L} \qquad (n = 1, 2, 3, \ldots). \qquad (22\text{–}8)$$

The value $n = 1$ corresponds to the fundamental frequency, $n = 2$ to the second harmonic (or first overtone), and so on.

Figure 22–10 shows a pipe that is open at the left (mouth) end but closed at the right end. We call this a *stopped pipe*. The left (open) end is a displacement antinode (pressure node), but the right (closed) end is a

22–9

Modes of vibration of an open organ pipe.

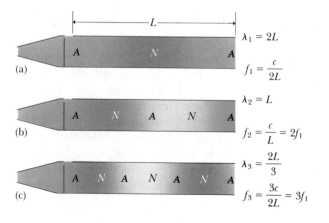

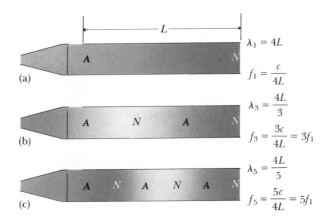

22–10
Modes of vibration of a stopped organ pipe.

displacement node (pressure antinode). The distance between a node and the adjacent antinode is always one-quarter wavelength. Figure 22–10a shows the lowest frequency mode; the length of the pipe is a quarter-wavelength ($L = \lambda/4$). The fundamental frequency is $f_1 = c/\lambda = c/4L$, which is one-half the fundamental frequency for an *open* pipe of the same length. In musical language the *pitch* of a closed pipe is one octave lower (a factor of two in frequency) than that of an open pipe of the same length. Figure 22–10b shows the next mode, for which the length of the pipe is *three quarters* of a wavelength, corresponding to a frequency $3f_1$. For Fig. 22–10c, $L = 5\lambda/4$ and the frequency is $5f_1$. The second, fourth, and all *even* harmonics are missing. Thus in a stopped pipe the fundamental frequency is $f_1 = c/4L$, and only the odd harmonics in the series ($3f_1, 5f_1, \ldots$) are possible. The normal-mode frequencies for a stopped pipe are given by

$$f_n = \frac{nc}{4L} \qquad (n = 1, 3, 5, \ldots). \qquad (22–9)$$

In an organ pipe in actual use, several modes are usually present at once. This situation is analogous to a string that is struck or plucked, producing several modes at the same time. In each case the motion is a *superposition* of various modes. The extent to which modes higher than the fundamental are present depends on the cross section of the pipe, the proportion of length to width, the shape of the mouth, and other more subtle factors. The harmonic content of the tone is an important factor in determining the tone quality or timbre. A very narrow pipe produces a tone that is rich in higher harmonics, which we hear as a thin, "stringy" tone; a fatter pipe produces mostly the fundamental mode, heard as a softer, more flutelike tone.

We have talked about organ pipes, but this discussion is also applicable to other wind instruments. The flute and the recorder are directly analogous. The most significant difference is that those instruments have holes along the pipe. Opening and closing the holes with the fingers changes the effective length L of the air column and thus changes the pitch. Any individual organ pipe, by comparison, plays only a single note. The flute and recorder behave as *open* pipes, while the clarinet acts as a *closed* pipe (closed at the reed end, open at the bell).

Equations (22–8) and (22–9) show that the frequencies of any such instrument are proportional to the speed of sound c in the air column inside the instrument. As Eq. (21–8) shows, c depends on temperature; it increases when temperature increases. Thus the pitch of all wind instruments rises with increasing temperature. An organ that has some of its pipes at one temperature and others at a different temperature is bound to sound out of tune.

22–6
Interference of Waves

Wave phenomena that occur when two or more waves overlap in the same region of space are grouped under the heading **interference.** As we have seen, standing waves are a simple example of an interference effect. Two waves traveling in opposite directions in a medium combine to produce a standing wave pattern with nodes and antinodes that do not move.

Figure 22–11 shows another example of an interference phenomenon. Two speakers, driven by the same amplifier, emit identical sinusoidal sound waves with the same constant frequency. We place a microphone at point A in the figure, equidistant from the speakers. Wave crests emitted from the two speakers at the same time travel equal distances and arrive at point A at the same time. The amplitudes add, according to the principle of superposition. The total wave amplitude at A is twice the amplitude from each individual wave, and we can measure this combined amplitude with the microphone.

Now we move the microphone to point B, where the distances from the two speakers to the microphone differ by a half-wavelength. Then the two waves arrive a half-cycle out of step or *out of phase*; a positive crest from one speaker arrives at the same time as a negative crest from the other, and the amplitude measured by the microphone is much *smaller* than when only one speaker is present. If the amplitudes from the two speakers are equal, the two waves cancel each other out completely at point B, and the total amplitude there is zero.

Experiments closely analogous to this one, but using light, have provided strong evidence for the wave nature of light and a means of measuring its wavelengths. We will discuss these experiments in detail in Chapter 39.

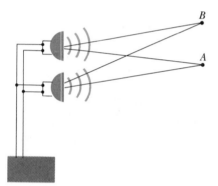

Amplifier

22–11
Two speakers driven by the same amplifier. The waves emitted by the speakers are in phase; they arrive at point A in phase because the two path lengths are the same. They arrive at point B a half-cycle out of phase because the path lengths differ by $\lambda/2$.

22–7
Resonance

We have discussed several examples of mechanical systems that have normal modes of oscillation. In each mode, every particle of the system oscillates with simple harmonic motion with the same frequency as the frequency of this mode. The systems we have discussed have an infinite series of normal modes, but the basic concept is closely related to the simple harmonic oscillator, discussed in Chapter 11, which has only a single normal mode.

Now suppose we apply a periodically varying force to a system that has normal modes. The system is then forced to vibrate with a frequency equal to the frequency of the *force*. This motion is called a **forced oscillation.** In general, the amplitude of this motion is relatively small, but if the frequency of the force is close to one of the normal-mode frequencies, the amplitude can become quite large. We talked about forced oscillations of the harmonic oscillator in Section 11–7, and we suggest that you review that discussion now.

If the frequency of the force were precisely *equal* to a normal-mode frequency and if there were no friction or other energy-dissipating mechanism, then the force would continue to add energy to the system, and the amplitude would increase indefinitely. In any real system there is always some dissipation of energy, or damping, as we discussed in Section 11–7. Even so, the "response" of the system (that is, the amplitude of the forced oscillation) is greatest when the force frequency is equal to one of the normal-mode frequencies. This behavior is called **resonance.**

In Section 11–7 we mentioned pushing a child's swing as a familiar example of mechanical resonance. The swing is a pendulum; it has only a single natural frequency, determined by its length. If we give the swing a series of regularly spaced pushes, with a frequency that is equal to the natural frequency of the swing, we can build up the motion to quite a large amplitude. But if we push with a frequency that is very different from the natural frequency of the swing, or if we push at irregular intervals, the swing hardly moves at all. The same principle applies to "pumping up," in which the person on the swing builds up amplitude by shifting his or her weight in phase with the back-and-forth oscillations.

Unlike a simple pendulum, which has only one natural frequency, a stretched string (along with the other systems discussed in this chapter) has an infinite number of natural frequencies. Suppose that one end of a stretched string is held stationary while the other is given a transverse sinusoidal motion, setting up standing waves. The amplitude at the driven end is determined by the driving mechanism. If the frequency of the driving mechanism is *not* equal to one of the natural frequencies of the string, the amplitude at the antinodes is fairly small.

However, if the frequency is equal to any one of the natural frequencies, the string is in resonance, and the amplitude at the antinodes is very much *larger* than that at the driven end. In other words, although the driven end is not a node, it lies much closer to a node than to an antinode when the string is in resonance. In Fig. 22–5a the right end of the string was held stationary, and the left end was forced to oscillate vertically with small amplitude. The photographs show the standing waves of relatively large amplitude that resulted when the frequency of oscillation of the left end was equal either to the fundamental frequency or to one of the first three overtones.

A steel bridge, like any elastic structure, has normal modes and can vibrate with certain natural frequencies. If the regular footsteps of a marching band have a frequency equal to one of the natural frequencies of a bridge that the band is crossing, a vibration of dangerously large amplitude may result. Therefore when crossing a bridge, a marching group should always "break step." Similarly, an unbalanced wheel on a car can cause large-amplitude vibrations of parts of the suspension system at certain speeds. There have been cases in which vibrations of aircraft engines happened to coincide with normal-mode frequencies of an airplane frame, resulting in catastrophic resonance-induced vibrations.

We can demonstrate resonance with two identical tuning forks. We place them some distance apart and strike one to start it vibrating. The resulting sound waves have just the right frequency to start the other fork vibrating, and we can hear its vibration if we suddenly stop the first fork. If we place a small piece of wax or modeling clay on one of the forks, the natural frequency of that fork is shifted enough to destroy the resonance.

We can do something similar with a piano. Try this: Push down the damper pedal (the right-hand pedal), so that the dampers are lifted and the strings are free to vibrate, and then sing a steady tone into the piano. When you stop singing, the piano seems to continue to sing the same note. The sound waves from your voice excite vibrations in the strings that have natural frequencies close to the frequencies (fundamental and harmonics) that are present in the note you sang.

Resonance is a very important concept, not only in mechanical systems but in all areas of physics. Later we will see examples of resonance in electric circuits (Chapter 34) and in atomic systems (Chapter 42).

Questions

22–1 When you inhale helium, your voice becomes high and squeaky. Why? (Don't try this with hydrogen; you might explode like the Hindenburg.) What happens when you inhale carbon dioxide?

22–2 A musical interval of an octave corresponds to a factor of two in frequency. By what factor must the tension in a piano or violin string be increased to raise its pitch one octave?

22–3 The pitch (or frequency) of an organ pipe changes with temperature. Does it increase or decrease with increasing temperature? Why?

22–4 By touching a string lightly at its center while bowing, a violinist can produce a note exactly one octave above the note to which the string is tuned, that is, a note with exactly twice the frequency. Why is this possible?

22–5 In most modern wind instruments the pitch is changed by changing the length of the vibrating air column with keys or valves. The bugle, however, has no valves or keys, yet it can play many notes. How? Are there restrictions on what notes it can play?

22–6 Kettledrums (tympani) have a pitch determined by the frequencies of the normal modes. How can a kettledrum be tuned?

22–7 Energy can be transferred along a string by wave motion. However, in a standing wave, no energy can ever be transferred past a node. Why?

22–8 Can a standing wave be produced on a string by superposing two waves with the same frequency but different amplitudes, traveling in opposite directions?

22–9 In discussing standing longitudinal waves in an organ pipe we spoke of pressure nodes and antinodes. What physical quantity is analogous to pressure for standing transverse waves on a stretched string?

22–10 A glass of water sits on a kitchen counter just above a dishwasher that is running. The surface of the water has a set of concentric stationary circular ripples. What is happening?

22–11 Consider the peculiar sound of a large bell. Do you think the overtones are harmonic?

22–12 What is the difference between music and noise?

22–13 Is the mass per unit length the same for all strings on a piano? On a guitar? Why?

22–14 When a heavy truck drives up a steep hill, the windows in nearby houses sometimes vibrate. Why?

22–15 A popular children's pastime is lining up a row of dominoes, standing on edge, so that when the first one is pushed over, the whole row falls, one after another. Is this a wave motion? In what respects is it similar to waves on a stretched string? In what respects is it different?

22–16 A series of traffic lights along a street is timed so that a car going at the right speed can hit a succession of green lights and not have to stop. If several cars are on the same street, does this situation have wavelike properties?

22–17 Some opera singers are reputed to be able to break a glass by singing the appropriate note. What physical phenomenon could account for this?

22–18 A pipe organ in a church is tuned when the temperature is 20°C. On a cold winter day when the temperature in the room is 10°C, the organ still sounds "in tune," despite the phenomenon mentioned in Question 22–3. Why?

Exercises

Unless otherwise indicated, assume the speed of sound in air to be $c = 344$ m·s^{-1}.

Section 22–2   Superposition and Standing Waves

22–1 Standing waves on a string with a length of 2.40 m are described by Eq. (22–1), with $A = 3.00$ cm, $\omega = 314$ s^{-1}, $k = 1.67\pi$ m^{-1} and with the left-hand end of the string at $x = 0$. At what distances from the left-hand end are

a) the nodes of the standing wave?

b) the antinodes of the standing wave?

22–2 Fill in the details of the derivation of Eq. (22–1) from $y_1 + y_2 = A[\sin(\omega t - kx) - \sin(\omega t + kx)]$.

Section 22–3   Normal Modes of a String

22–3 A piano tuner stretches a steel piano string with a tension of 400 N. The steel string is 0.500 m long and has a mass of 4.00 g.

a) What is the frequency of its fundamental mode of vibration?

b) What is the number of the highest harmonic that could be heard by a person who is capable of hearing frequencies up to 10,000 Hz?

22–4 A rope with a length of 1.60 m is stretched between two supports with a tension that makes the speed of transverse waves 50.0 m·s^{-1}. What are the wavelength and frequency of

a) the fundamental?

b) the first overtone?

c) the third harmonic?

22–5 A physics student observes that a stretched string vibrates with a frequency of 45.0 Hz in its fundamental mode when the supports to which the ends of the string are tied are 0.600 m apart. The amplitude at the antinode is 3.00 cm. The string has a mass of 0.0300 kg.

a) What is the speed of propagation of a transverse wave in the string?

b) Compute the tension in the string.

22–6 The portion of a violin string between the bridge and upper end of the finger board (that part of the string that is free to vibrate) is 50.0 cm long, and this length of the string has a mass of 2.00 g. The string sounds an A note (440 Hz) when played.

a) Where must the violinist put a finger (how far from the upper end of the finger board) to play a C note (528 Hz)? For both the A and C notes the string vibrates in its fundamental mode.

b) Without retuning, is it possible to play a D note (294 Hz) on this string? Why or why not?

Section 22–4   Longitudinal Standing Waves

Section 22–5   Normal Modes of Organ Pipes

22–7 Standing sound waves are produced in a pipe that is 2.40 m long, open at one end, and closed at the other. For the fundamental and first two overtones, where along the pipe (measured from the closed end) are the

a) displacement antinodes?

b) pressure antinodes?

22–8 Standing sound waves are produced in a pipe that is 2.40 m long and open at both ends. For the fundamental and first two overtones, where along the pipe (measured from one end) are the

a) displacement nodes?

b) pressure nodes?

22–9 Find the fundamental frequency and the frequencies of the first three overtones of a 36.0-cm pipe

a) if the pipe is open at both ends;

b) if the pipe is closed at one end.

c) What is the number of the highest harmonic that may be heard by a person having normal hearing for each of the above cases? (A person with normal hearing can hear frequencies in the range 20 to 20,000 Hz.)

22–10 The longest pipe found in most medium-size pipe organs is 4.88 m (16 ft) long. What is the frequency of the note corresponding to the fundamental mode if the pipe is

a) open at both ends?

b) open at one end and closed at the other?

22–11 A certain pipe produces a frequency of 520 Hz in air. If the pipe is filled with helium at the same temperature, what frequency does it produce? (The molecular mass of air is 28.8 g·mol^{-1}, and the atomic mass of helium is 4.00 g·mol^{-1}.)

◼ Problems

22–12

a) A string with both ends held stationary is vibrating in its fundamental mode. The waves have a speed of 3.20 m·s^{-1} and a frequency of 20.0 Hz. The amplitude of the standing wave at its antinode is 12.0 cm. Calculate the amplitude of the motion of points on the string a distance of

   i) 8.0 cm,   ii) 4.0 cm,   iii) 2.0 cm

   from the left-hand end of the string.

b) At each of the points in part (a), how much time does it take the string to go from its largest upward displacement to its largest downward displacement?

22–13 A standing wave with a frequency of 1100 Hz in a column of methane (CH_4) at 20.0°C produces nodes that are 0.200 m apart. What is the ratio γ of the molar heat capacity at constant pressure to that at constant volume for methane? The molecular mass of methane is 16.0 g·mol^{-1}.

22–14 A steel wire with length $L = 1.00$ m and density $\rho = 7800$ kg·m^{-3} is stretched tightly between two rigid supports. When the wire vibrates in its fundamental mode, the frequency is $f = 300$ Hz.

a) What is the speed of transverse waves on this wire?

b) What is the longitudinal stress (force per unit area) in the wire?

c) If the maximum acceleration at the midpoint of the wire is 3600 m·s^{-2}, what is the amplitude of vibration at the midpoint?

22–15 A wooden plank is placed over a pit that is 10.0 m wide. A physics student stands in the middle of the plank and begins to jump up and down such that she jumps upward from the plank two times each second. The plank oscillates with a large amplitude, with maximum amplitude at its center.

a) What is the speed of transverse waves on the plank?

b) At what rate does the student have to jump to produce large-amplitude oscillations if she is standing 2.5 m from the edge of the pit? (*Note:* The transverse standing waves of the plank have nodes at the two ends that rest on the ground on either side of the pit.)

22–16 A solid aluminum sculpture is hung from a steel wire. The fundamental frequency for transverse standing waves on the wire is 240 Hz. The sculpture is then immersed in water so that one half of its volume is submerged. What is the new fundamental frequency?

22–17 A cellist tunes the A-string of her instrument to a fundamental frequency of 220 Hz. The vibrating portion of the string is 0.680 m long and has a mass of 1.52 g.

a) With what tension must it be stretched?

b) What percent increase in tension is needed to increase the frequency from 220 Hz to 233 Hz, corresponding to a rise in pitch from A to A-sharp?

22–18 A long tube contains air at a pressure of 1.00 atm and a temperature of 77.0°C. The tube is open at one end and closed at the other by a moveable piston. A tuning fork near the open end is vibrating with a frequency of 500 Hz. Resonance is produced when the piston is at distances 18.0, 55.5, and 93.0 cm from the open end.

a) From these measurements, what is the speed of sound in air at 77.0°C?

b) From the above result, what is the ratio of the specific heat capacities at constant pressure and constant volume (γ) for air at this temperature? (The molecular mass of air is 28.8 g·mol^{-1}.)

22–19 The atomic mass for iodine atoms is 127 g·mol^{-1}. A standing wave in iodine vapor at 400 K produces nodes that are 6.77 cm apart when the frequency is 1000 Hz. Is iodine vapor monatomic or diatomic?

22–20 Your physics professor has invented a musical instrument. It consists of a metal can with length L and diameter L. The top of the can is cut out, and a string is stretched across this open end of the can.

a) The tension in the string is adjusted so that the fundamental frequency for longitudinal sound waves in the air column in the can equals the frequency of the third harmonic for transverse waves on the string. What is the relationship between the speed v_t of transverse waves on the string and the speed v_a of sound waves in the air?

b) What happens to the sound produced by the instrument if the tension in the string is increased by a factor of four?

22–21 An organ pipe open at both ends has two successive harmonics with frequencies 240 and 280 Hz.

a) What is the length of the pipe?

b) What two harmonics are these?

22–22 The steel B string of an acoustic guitar is 63.5 cm long and has a diameter of 0.406 mm (16 gauge).

a) Under what tension must the string be placed to give a frequency for transverse waves of 247.5 Hz? The density of steel is 7.80 g·cm^{-3}. Assume that the string vibrates in its fundamental mode.

b) If the tension is changed by a small amount ΔT, the frequency changes by Δf. Show that

$$\frac{\Delta f}{f} = \frac{1}{2}\frac{\Delta T}{T}.$$

c) If the string is tuned indoors as in part (a), where the temperature is 22.0°C, and the guitar then taken to an outdoor stage where the temperature is 11.0°C, the frequency will change, with unpleasant results. Find Δf if the Young's modulus Y of the steel string is 2.00×10^{11} Pa and the coefficient of linear expansion α is 1.20×10^{-5}(C°)$^{-1}$. Will the pitch be raised or lowered?

22–23 The frequency of middle C is 262 Hz.

a) If an organ pipe is open at both ends, what length must it have for its fundamental mode to produce this note at 20.0°C?

b) At what temperature will the frequency be 6.00% higher, corresponding to a rise in pitch from C to C-sharp?

Challenge Problems

22–24 A simple example of resonance in a mechanical system is as follows. A mass m is attached to one end of a massless spring with force constant k and unstretched length l_0. The other end of the spring is free to turn about a nail driven into a horizontal frictionless surface (Fig. 22–12). The mass is then made to revolve in a circle with an angular frequency of revolution ω'.

a) Calculate the length l of the spring as a function of ω'.

b) What happens to the result in part (a) when ω' approaches the natural frequency $\omega = \sqrt{k/m}$ of the mass–spring system? (If your result bothers you, remember that massless springs and frictionless

surfaces don't precisely exist but can only be approximated. Also, Hooke's law is itself only an approximation to the way real springs behave; the greater the elongation of the spring, the greater the deviation from Hooke's law.)

22–25 Two identical loudspeakers are located at points A and B, 2.00 m apart. The loudspeakers are driven by the same amplifier and produce sound waves of frequency 520 Hz. Take the speed of sound in air to be 344 m·s^{-1}. A small microphone is moved out from point B along a line perpendicular to the line connecting A and B (line BC in Fig. 22–13). At what distances from B will there be *destructive* interference?

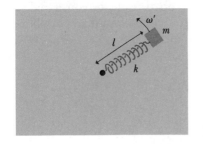

FIGURE 22–12

FIGURE 22–13

23

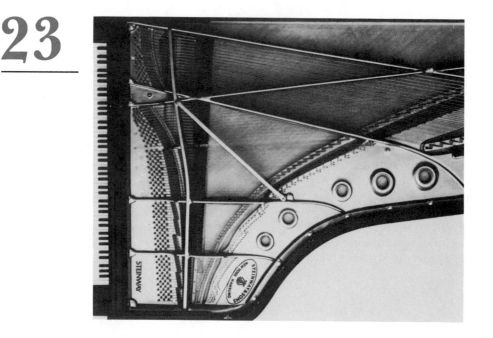

Sound

Sound consists of longitudinal waves in air. The human ear is sensitive to sound waves in the frequency range from about 20 to 20,000 Hz, but we sometimes use the term *sound* for similar waves with frequencies outside this range. Among the important properties of sound waves are frequency, amplitude, and intensity. These are related to the various perceived qualities of musical tones such as pitch, loudness, and timbre (or tone quality). We will look at the relationships between the physical quantities and the perceptions. Interference of two sound waves differing in frequency by a few hertz causes a wavering sound called a *beat*; an out-of-tune piano is an all-too-familiar example. When the source of sound or the observer, or both, are in motion relative to the air, frequency shifts known as the Doppler effect are observed. That is what makes the pitch of a car horn seem to drop as it passes you. Finally, we take a brief look at sources of sound and applications of acoustic phenomena.

23–1
Sound Waves

The simplest sound waves are *sinusoidal* waves with definite frequency, amplitude, and wavelength. When a sound wave arrives at the ear, the air particles at the eardrum vibrate with definite frequency and amplitude. We can also describe this vibration in terms of variations of *air pressure*. The pressure fluctuates sinusoidally above and below atmospheric pressure with the same frequency as the motions of the air particles.

In Section 21–6 we discussed wave functions that describe the *displacements* in a wave medium during wave propagation; one of the forms we used was

$$y(x, t) = A \sin (\omega t - kx), \qquad (23\text{–}1)$$

where the amplitude A is the maximum displacement of a particle of the medium from its equilibrium position. For sound waves it is nearly always easier to measure the *pressure* variations than the displacements. It can be shown that for the sinusoidal wave described by Eq. (23–1) the pressure variation at any point is given by

$$p = BkA \cos (\omega t - kx), \qquad (23\text{–}2)$$

where B is the bulk modulus for the medium and k is the wave number ($k = 2\pi/\lambda$) defined in Section 21–6. This expression shows that the quantity BkA represents the *maximum* pressure variation from the equilibrium value. We call this the **pressure amplitude** and denote it by p_{max}:

$$p_{max} = BkA. \qquad (23\text{–}3)$$

The pressure amplitude is directly proportional to the displacement amplitude A, as we might expect, and it also depends on wavelength. Waves of shorter wavelength (larger k) have greater pressure variations for a given amplitude because the maxima and minima are squeezed closer together. Media having large values of B require comparatively greater pressures for a given displacement because large B means a greater pressure change needed for a given volume change.

Example 23–1   Measurements of sound waves show that in the loudest sounds that the human ear can tolerate without pain, the maximum pressure variations are of the order of 30 Pa (above and below atmospheric pressure, which is about 100,000 Pa). Find the corresponding maximum displacement if the frequency is 1000 Hz and $c = 344$ m·s^{-1}.

Solution   We have $\omega = (2\pi)(1000$ Hz$) = 6283$ s^{-1} and

$$k = \frac{\omega}{c} = \frac{6283 \text{ s}^{-1}}{344 \text{ m·s}^{-1}} = 18.3 \text{ m}^{-1}.$$

The adiabatic bulk modulus for air at normal atmospheric pressure is

$$B = \gamma p = (1.4)(1.013 \times 10^5 \text{ Pa}) = 1.42 \times 10^5 \text{ Pa}.$$

From Eq. (23–3) we find

$$A = \frac{p_{\max}}{Bk} = \frac{30 \text{ Pa}}{(1.42 \times 10^5 \text{ Pa})(18.3 \text{ m}^{-1})}$$
$$= 1.2 \times 10^{-5} \text{ m} = 0.012 \text{ mm}.$$

This shows that the displacement amplitude of even the loudest sound is *extremely* small. The maximum pressure variation in the *faintest* audible sound of frequency 1000 Hz is only about 3×10^{-5} Pa. The corresponding displacement amplitude is about 10^{-11} m. For comparison the diameter of an atom is about 10^{-10} m!   ∎

Like all other waves, sound waves transfer energy from one region to another. We define the **intensity** of a wave, denoted by I, as *the time average rate at which energy is transported by the wave, per unit area*, across a surface perpendicular to the direction of propagation. That is, intensity I is the average *power* transported per unit area.

Our study of power in Section 7–8 showed that the power developed by a force equals the product of force and velocity, Eq. (7–26). So the power *per unit area* in a sound wave equals the product of the excess pressure p (force per unit area) and the velocity v of a particle in the medium. The *maximum* power per unit area is the product of the pressure amplitude $p_{\max}$ and the maximum velocity, which we denote by V. From our study of simple harmonic motion in Chapter 11 we know that V is related to the amplitude A by $V = \omega A$. Combining this with Eq. (23–3), we find that the maximum power per unit area is given by

$$p_{\max}V = (BkA)(\omega A) = B\omega k A^2.$$

Of course, the *average* value of the product pv is less than this because each quantity is a sinusoidal function. It turns out that the average value is exactly *one half* the maximum value. This simple result stems from the fact that the average value of $\sin^2 x$ or $\cos^2 x$ over a complete cycle is $1/2$. So the intensity, or *average* power per unit area is given by

$$I = \tfrac{1}{2}B\omega k A^2. \qquad (23\text{–}4)$$

It is usually more useful to express I in terms of the pressure amplitude $p_{\max}$. Using Eq. (23–3), the relation $\omega = ck$, and the wave-speed relation $c^2 = B/\rho$, we obtain the alternative forms

$$I = \frac{p_{\max}{}^2}{2\rho c} = \frac{p_{\max}{}^2}{2\sqrt{\rho B}}. \qquad (23\text{–}5)$$

We invite you to derive these expressions.

Example 23–2   Find the intensity of the loud sound wave in Example 23–1, with $p_{\max} = 30$ Pa, if the temperature is 20°C.

Solution   At 20°C the density of air, from Eq. (21–7), is $\rho = 1.20$ kg·m^{-3}, and the speed of sound is $c = 344$ m·s^{-1}. From Eq. (23–5),

$$I = \frac{(30 \text{ Pa})^2}{2(1.20 \text{ kg·m}^{-3})(344 \text{ m·s}^{-1})}$$
$$= 1.1 \text{ J·s}^{-1}\text{·m}^{-2} = 1.1 \text{ W·m}^{-2}.$$

The pressure amplitude of the *faintest* sound wave that can be heard is about 3×10^{-5} Pa, and the corresponding intensity is about 10^{-12} W·m^{-2}, or 10^{-16} W·cm^{-2}. We invite you to verify this number. ■

The average *total* power carried across a surface by a sound wave equals the product of the intensity (power per unit area) at the surface and the surface area if the intensity over the surface is uniform. The average total sound power emitted by a person speaking in an ordinary conversational tone is about 10^{-5} W, and a loud shout corresponds to about 3×10^{-2} W. If all the residents of New York City were to talk at the same time, the total sound power would be about 100 W, equivalent to the electric power requirement of a medium-sized light bulb! On the other hand, the power required to fill a large auditorium with loud sound is considerable. Suppose you want the sound intensity over the surface of a hemisphere 20 m in radius to be 1 W·m^{-2}. The area of the surface is about 2500 m^2. Hence the acoustic power output of a speaker at the center of the sphere would have to be

$$(1 \text{ W·m}^{-2})(2500 \text{ m}^2) = 2500 \text{ W},$$

or 2.5 kW. The efficiency of loudspeakers in converting electrical energy into sound is not very great, so the electrical power input to the speaker would need to be considerably larger than this.

Because the ear is sensitive over such a broad range of intensities, a *logarithmic* intensity scale is usually used. The **intensity level β** of a sound wave is defined by the equation

$$\beta = 10 \log \frac{I}{I_0}. \tag{23–6}$$

In this equation, I_0 is a reference intensity, chosen arbitrarily to be 10^{-12} W·m^{-2}. This corresponds roughly to the faintest sound that can be heard by a person with normal hearing, although this depends on the frequency of the sound. The units of β are **decibels,** abbreviated dB. A decibel is 1/10 of a *bel*, a unit named for Alexander Graham Bell. The bel is inconveniently large for most purposes, and the decibel is the usual unit of sound intensity level.

A sound wave with an intensity equal to I_0 or 10^{-12} W·m^{-2} has an intensity level of 0 dB. The intensity at the pain threshold, about 1 W·m^{-2}, corresponds to an intensity level of 120 dB. Table 23–1 gives the intensity levels in decibels of several familiar noises. It is taken from a survey made by the New York City Noise Abatement Commission.

TABLE 23–1 Noise levels due to various sources (representative values)

Source or description of noise	Noise level, dB	Intensity, $W \cdot m^{-2}$
Threshold of pain	120	1
Riveter	95	3.2×10^{-3}
Elevated train	90	10^{-3}
Busy street traffic	70	10^{-5}
Ordinary conversation	65	3.2×10^{-6}
Quiet automobile	50	10^{-7}
Quiet radio in home	40	10^{-8}
Average whisper	20	10^{-10}
Rustle of leaves	10	10^{-11}
Threshold of hearing	0	10^{-12}

PROBLEM-SOLVING STRATEGY: Sound Waves

1. Quite a few quantities are involved in characterizing the amplitude and intensity of a sound wave, and it is easy to get lost in the maze of relationships. It helps to put them in categories: the amplitude is described by A or p_{max}, and the frequency by f, ω, k, or λ. These quantities are related through the wave speed c, which in turn is determined by the properties of the medium, B and ρ. Take a hard look at the problem at hand, identify which of these quantities are given and which you have to find; then start looking for relationships that take you where you want to go.

2. In using Eq. (23–6) for the sound intensity level, remember that I and I_0 must be in the same units, usually $W \cdot m^{-2}$. If they aren't, convert!

*23–2
Hearing and Musical Tones

In this section we look at the ways in which our ears respond to sound waves. We represent the range of frequencies and intensities to which the ear is sensitive with the diagram shown in Fig. 23–1. The height of the lower colored curve at any frequency represents the intensity level β of the faintest pure (sinusoidal) tone of that frequency that can be heard by a person with normal hearing. This is called the **threshold of hearing.** The diagram shows that the human ear is most sensitive to frequencies between 2000 and 3000 Hz, at which the threshold of hearing is about −5 dB. The upper colored curve shows the intensity level, for each frequency, at which the sound becomes painful. This is called the **threshold of pain.** The height of this curve is approximately constant at about 120 dB for all frequencies between 20 and 20,000 Hz.

Here are some examples of the meaning of Fig. 23–1; we invite you to verify the numbers. For a loud tone of intensity level 80 dB, the range of audibility is from 20 to 20,000 Hz, but at a level of 20 dB it is only

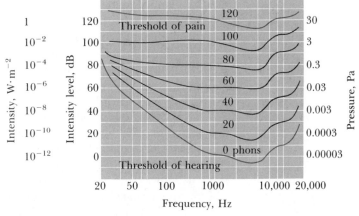

23–1

Thresholds of hearing and pain (color curves) and contours of constant loudness (black curves). All sinusoidal tones on a contour sound equally loud. (Courtesy of Dr. Harvey Fletcher.)

from 200 to 15,000 Hz. At 1000 Hz the threshold of hearing is at 0 dB, but at 100 Hz it is 30 dB.

The term *loudness* refers to a listener's subjective perception of a sound sensation. Loudness increases with intensity, but because of the varying sensitivity of the ear, it also depends on frequency. To establish the relationship of loudness to intensity and frequency, experiments with human subjects are needed. The results of many such experiments are summarized in the black curves of Fig. 23–1. The **loudness level** of a pure tone with *any* frequency is defined to be the intensity level of a 1000-Hz tone that *sounds* equally loud. Each curve in Fig. 23–1 is drawn through points representing pure (sinusoidal) tones having equal perceived loudness. For example, a 100-Hz tone at 52 dB, a 1000-Hz tone at 40 dB, and a 10,000-Hz tone at 52 dB all sound equally loud, and all these tones have the same loudness level. The unit of loudness level is the **phon.** Each of these tones has a loudness level of 40 phons; they all sound as loud as a 40-dB tone at 1000 Hz. Similarly, the other curves show loudness levels of 0, 20, 60, 80, 100, and 120 phons.

Going one step further, we can define a **loudness** scale having the property that a sound with a loudness of 2 units on this scale sounds twice as loud as a sound with a loudness of 1 unit. Again, experiments with human subjects are needed to define this scale. The unit of perceived loudness is the **sone;** by definition, 1 sone is the loudness, for an average listener with normal hearing, of a 1000-Hz tone at 40 dB heard by both ears. As the above discussion shows, a 100-Hz tone at 52 dB and a 10,000-Hz at 52 dB also have a loudness of 1 sone. Then a 2-sone tone is defined to be a tone judged by human subjects to sound twice as loud as a 1-sone tone. The experimentally determined correlation between loudness level (in phons) and loudness (in sones) is shown in Fig. 23–2. For example, a loudness of 6 sones corresponds to a loudness level of 60 phons. Referring to Fig. 23–1, we find that this might be a 1000-Hz tone at 60 dB, a 100-Hz tone at 67 dB, a 10,000-Hz tone at 73 dB, and so on. All these have the same loudness level and the same loudness, and the average listener would judge any of them to be six times as loud as a 1000-Hz tone at 40 dB.

The **pitch** of a musical tone is the quality that lets us classify it as "high" or "low." It is determined primarily by frequency; middle C on

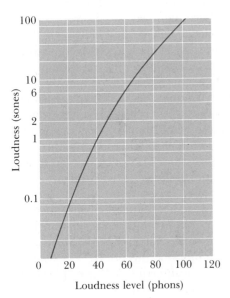

23–2

Graph showing the relation between loudness (in sones) and loudness level (in phons). The loudness level of any tone is equal to the sound intensity level (in dB) of a 1000-Hz tone having the same perceived loudness as that tone.

the piano has a frequency of 262 Hz. The musical interval of an *octave* corresponds to a factor of two in frequency. The "high C" sung by coloratura sopranos, two octaves above middle C, has a frequency of 4 × 262 Hz, or 1048 Hz. There are some subjective elements in pitch perception; when a listener compares two sinusoidal tones with the same frequency but different intensities, the louder one usually seems to be slightly lower in pitch.

Musical tones usually contain many frequencies. A string that has been plucked, bowed, or struck or the column of air in a wind instrument vibrates with many frequencies, the fundamental and many harmonics, at the same time. One tone might include a fundamental of 200 Hz and harmonics 2, 3, 4, and 5 (frequencies 400, 600, 800, and 1000 Hz, respectively), each with a different intensity. Another tone might have the same frequencies but with different intensities. The two tones sound different; the difference is described as *tone color*, *quality*, or **timbre.** We describe timbre with subjective terms such as reedy, golden, round, mellow, and tinny. The quality of a tone is determined in part by the relative intensities of the various harmonics. A tone that is rich in harmonics usually sounds thin and "stringy" or "reedy," while a tone containing mostly fundamental is more mellow and flutelike.

The harmonic spectrum of an instrument often changes considerably with loudness. A French horn played very softly produces mostly the fundamental frequency, with rather little harmonic content. As the tone grows louder, it also becomes much richer in harmonics. This effect is inherent in the instrument, and the player has only limited control over it. The sound spectra of *percussion* instruments (including the piano) vary with time as the various harmonics die away at different rates.

Another factor in determining tone quality is the behavior at the beginning and end of a tone. A piano tone begins percussively with a thump and then dies away gradually. A harpsichord tone, in addition to having a different harmonic content, begins much more quickly and incisively with a click, and the higher harmonics begin before the lower ones. The ending of the tone, when the key is released, is also much more incisive on the harpsichord than the piano. Similar effects are present in other musical instruments; with wind and string instruments the player has considerable control over the attack and decay of the tone, and these characteristics help to define the unique characteristics of each instrument.

When combinations of musical tones are heard together or in succession, even a listener with no musical training recognizes a relationship among them; they sound comfortable together, or they clash. Musicians use the terms *consonant* and *dissonant* to describe this effect. A *consonant interval* is a combination of two tones that sound comfortable or pleasing together. The most consonant interval is the *octave*; it consists of two tones with a frequency ratio of 2 to 1. An example is middle C on the piano and the next C above it. Another set of consonant tones is obtained by playing C, E, and G. These form what is called a *major triad*, and the frequencies are in the ratios 4:5:6. The interval from C to G, with a frequency ratio of 3:2, is a perfect fifth; C to E, with 5:4, is a major third, and so on. These combinations sound good together because they have many harmonics in common. For example, for the interval of the octave, every harmonic in the harmonic series of the lower-frequency tone is also present in the harmonic series of the upper tone. For other intervals the overlap of harmonics is only partial, but it is there.

If we want to be able to play 4:5:6 major triads starting on various tones on a keyboard instrument such as the piano or organ, complications arise. Either we add a lot of extra keys in each octave to get the exact frequencies we need, or else we compromise a little on the frequencies. The most common compromise in piano tuning is called *equal temperament*, in which every pair of adjacent keys is tuned to the same frequency ratio of $2^{1/12}$. This interval is called a *semitone* or a *halftone*; a succession of twelve of these intervals then forms an exact 2:1 octave. The perfect fifth is seven semitones; the corresponding frequency ratio is $2^{7/12} = 1.4983$. This is close to the ideal ratio of $3/2 = 1.5000$, but a sensitive ear can hear the difference.

Thus a piano tuned in equal temperament is not quite in tune, in terms of the ideal ratios, in *any* key, but it is equally good (or bad) in all keys. An alternative would be to tune the white keys to form ideal intervals. This would sound better for music in the key of C, but music in some other keys would sound worse in comparison to how they would sound in equal temperament. So an instrument that is intended to be used for compositions in all keys is usually tuned to equal temperament.

In the Baroque period, however, keys with more than three sharps or flats were seldom used, and various compromise temperaments were invented to favor the commonly used keys. Organs and harpsichords that are intended primarily for music of this period are often tuned to one of these unequal temperaments. The great J. S. Bach favored these rather than equal temperament. His composition "The Well-Tempered Clavier" contains preludes and fugues in all the major and minor keys, but it is important not to misconstrue *well-tempered* as meaning *equally tempered*!

23–3
Beats

In Section 22–6 we talked about *interference* effects that occur when two different waves with the same frequency overlap in the same region of space. Now let's look at what happens when we have two waves with equal amplitude but slightly different frequencies. This occurs, for example, when two tuning forks with slightly different frequencies are sounded together or when two organ pipes that are supposed to have exactly the same frequency are slightly "out of tune."

Consider a particular point in space where the two waves overlap. The displacements of the individual waves at this point are plotted as functions of time in Fig. 23–3a. The total length of the time axis represents about 1 s, and the frequencies are 16 Hz and 18 Hz. Applying the principle of superposition, we add the two displacements at each instant of time to find the total displacement at that time, obtaining the graph in Fig. 23–3b. At certain times the two waves are in phase; their maxima coincide, and their amplitudes add. But as time goes on, they become

23-3
Beats are fluctuations in amplitude produced by two sound waves of slightly different frequency. (a) Individual waves. (b) Pattern formed by superposition of the two waves.

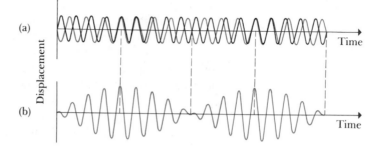

more and more out of phase because of their slightly different frequencies. Eventually, a maximum of one wave coincides with a maximum in the opposite direction for the other wave. The two waves then cancel each other, and the total amplitude is zero.

The resulting wave looks like a single sinusoidal wave with a varying amplitude that goes from a maximum to zero and back, as Fig. 23-3b shows. In this example the amplitude goes through two maxima and two minima in 1 s, and thus the frequency of this amplitude variation is 2 Hz. The amplitude variation causes variations of loudness called **beats,** and the frequency with which the amplitude varies is called the **beat frequency.** In this example the beat frequency is the *difference* of the two frequencies. If the beat frequency is a few hertz, we hear it as a waver or pulsation in the tone.

We can prove that the beat frequency is *always* the difference of the two frequencies f_1 and f_2. Suppose f_1 is larger than f_2; the corresponding periods are τ_1 and τ_2, with $\tau_1 < \tau_2$. If the two waves start out in phase at time $t = 0$, they will again be in phase at a time T such that the first wave has gone through exactly one more cycle than the second. Let n be the number of cycles of the first wave in time T; then the number of cycles of the second wave in the same time is $(n - 1)$, and we have the relations

$$T = n\tau_1 = (n - 1)\tau_2.$$

We solve the second equation for n and substitute the result back into the first equation, obtaining

$$T = \frac{\tau_1\tau_2}{\tau_2 - \tau_1}.$$

Now T is just the *period* of the beat, and its reciprocal is the beat *frequency,* $f_\text{beat} = 1/T$, so

$$f_\text{beat} = \frac{\tau_2 - \tau_1}{\tau_1\tau_2} = \frac{1}{\tau_1} - \frac{1}{\tau_2},$$

and finally

$$f_\text{beat} = f_1 - f_2. \tag{23-7}$$

Beats between two tones can be heard up to a beat frequency of 6 or 7 Hz. Two piano strings or two organ pipes differing in frequency by 2 or 3 Hz sound wavery and "out of tune," although some organ stops contain two sets of pipes deliberately tuned to beat frequencies of about

1 to 2 Hz for a gently undulating effect. Listening for beats is an important technique in tuning all musical instruments.

At higher frequency differences we no longer hear individual beats, and the sensation merges into one of *consonance* or *dissonance*, depending on the frequency ratio of the two tones. In some cases the ear perceives a tone called a *difference tone*, with a pitch equal to the beat frequency of the two tones.

23–4
The Doppler Effect

When a source of sound or a listener or both are in motion relative to the air, the pitch of the sound heard by the listener is not the same as when source and listener are at rest. This phenomenon is called the **Doppler effect.** A common example is the sudden drop in pitch of the horn of a passing automobile or locomotive.

To keep things simple, we will consider only the special case in whi the velocities of both source and listener lie along the line joining them. Let v_S and v_L be the velocities of source and listener relative to the air. We will consider each velocity as positive when it points in the direction from the listener L toward the source S and negative when the opposite is true. The speed of sound c is always considered positive.

Let's think first about a listener L moving with velocity v_L toward a stationary source S, as in Fig. 23–4. The source emits a wave with frequency f_S and wavelength $\lambda = c/f_S$. The figure shows several wave crests, separated by equal distances λ. The waves approaching the moving listener have a speed of propagation *relative to the listener* of $(c + v_L)$, so the

23–4
A listener moving toward a stationary source hears a frequency higher than the source frequency because the relative velocity of listener and wave is greater than c.

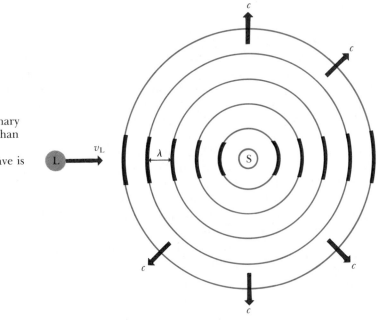

23–5
Wave surfaces emitted by a moving source are crowded together in front of the source and stretched out behind it.

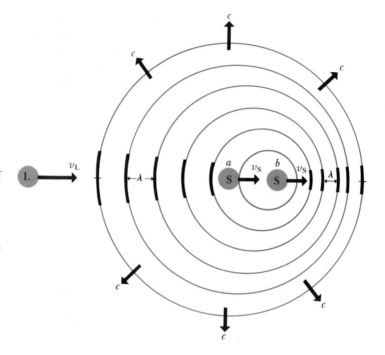

frequency f_L with which the wave crests arrive at the listener's position (i.e., the frequency he or she hears) is

$$f_L = \frac{c + v_L}{\lambda} = \frac{c + v_L}{c/f_S}, \tag{23-8}$$

or

$$f_L = f_S\left(\frac{c + v_L}{c}\right) = f_S\left(1 + \frac{v_L}{c}\right). \tag{23-9}$$

Therefore a listener moving *toward* a source ($v_L > 0$) hears a larger frequency and a higher pitch than a stationary listener. A listener moving *away from* the source ($v_L < 0$) hears a lower pitch.

Now suppose the source is also moving, with velocity v_S, as in Fig. 23–5. The wave speed relative to the air is still c; it is determined by the properties of the wave medium and is not changed by the motion of the source. But the wavelength is no longer equal to c/f_S. Here's why: The time for emission of one cycle of the wave is the period $\tau = 1/f_S$. During this time the wave travels a distance $c\tau = c/f_S$, and the source moves a distance $v_S\tau = v_S/f_S$. The wavelength is the distance between successive wave crests, and this is determined by the *relative* displacement of source and wave. As Fig. 23–5 shows, this is different in front of and behind the source. In the region to the right of the source in Fig. 23–5 the wavelength is

$$\lambda = \frac{c}{f_S} - \frac{v_S}{f_S} = \frac{c - v_S}{f_S}, \tag{23-10}$$

and in the region to the left it is

$$\lambda = \frac{c + v_S}{f_S}. \tag{23–11}$$

The waves are compressed and stretched out, respectively, by the motion of the source.

To find the frequency measured by the listener, we substitute Eq. (23–11) into the first form of Eq. (23–8):

$$f_L = \frac{c + v_L}{\lambda} = \frac{c + v_L}{(c + v_S)/f_S},$$

or

$$\frac{f_L}{c + v_L} = \frac{f_S}{c + v_S}. \tag{23–12}$$

This expresses the frequency f_L heard by the listener in terms of the frequency f_S of the source.

Equation (23–12) includes all possibilities for motion of source and listener (relative to the medium) along the line joining them. If the listener happens to be at rest in the medium, v_L is zero. When both source and listener are at rest or have the same velocity relative to the medium, then $v_L = v_S$ and $f_L = f_S$. Whenever the direction of the source or listener velocity is opposite to the direction from listener toward source (which we have defined as positive), the corresponding velocity to be used in Eq. (23–12) is negative.

PROBLEM-SOLVING STRATEGY: Doppler Effect

1. Establish a coordinate system, decide which direction is positive, and make sure you know the signs of all the relevant velocities. A velocity in the direction from listener toward source is positive; a velocity in the opposite direction is negative. Also, the velocities must all be measured with respect to the air in which the sound is traveling.

2. Use consistent notation to identify the various quantities: subscript S for source, L for listener.

3. When a wave is reflected from a surface, either stationary or moving, the analysis can be carried out in two steps. In the first the surface plays the role of listener; the frequency with which the wave crests arrive at the surface is f_L. Then think of the surface as a new source, emitting waves with this same frequency f_L. Finally, determine what frequency is heard by a listener detecting this new wave.

Example 23–3   To keep the arithmetic simple, suppose that $f_S = 300$ Hz and $c = 300$ m·s^{-1}. The wavelength of the waves emitted by a stationary source is then $c/f_S = 1.00$ m.

a) What are the wavelengths ahead of and behind the moving source in Fig. 23–5 if its velocity is 30 m·s^{-1}?

We use Eqs. (23–10) and (23–11). In front of the source,

$$\lambda = \frac{c - v_S}{f_S} = \frac{300 \text{ m·s}^{-1} - 30 \text{ m·s}^{-1}}{300 \text{ Hz}} = 0.90 \text{ m}.$$

Behind the source,

$$\lambda = \frac{c + v_S}{f_S} = \frac{300 \text{ m·s}^{-1} + 30 \text{ m·s}^{-1}}{300 \text{ Hz}} = 1.10 \text{ m}.$$

b) If the listener L in Fig. 23–5 is at rest and the source is moving away from L at 30 m·s^{-1}, what frequency does the listener hear?

We have $v_L = 0$ and $v_S = 30$ m·s^{-1}. (The source velocity v_S is positive because the source is moving in the same direction as the direction from listener to source.) From Eq. (23–12),

$$f_L = f_S \frac{c}{c + v_S} = 300 \text{ Hz}\left(\frac{300 \text{ m·s}^{-1}}{300 \text{ m·s}^{-1} + 30 \text{ m·s}^{-1}}\right) = 273 \text{ Hz}.$$

c) If the source in Fig. 23–5 is at rest and the listener is moving toward the left at 30 m·s^{-1}, what frequency does the listener hear?

The positive direction (from listener to source) is still from left to right, so $v_L = -30$ m·s^{-1}, $v_S = 0$, and

$$f_L = f_S \frac{c + v_L}{c} = 300 \text{ Hz}\left(\frac{300 \text{ m·s}^{-1} - 30 \text{ m·s}^{-1}}{300 \text{ m·s}^{-1}}\right) = 270 \text{ Hz}.$$

d) If the source in Fig. 23–5 is moving away from the listener with a speed of 45 m·s^{-1} relative to the air and the listener is moving toward the source with a speed of 15 m·s^{-1} relative to the air, what frequency does the listener hear?

In this case, $v_L = 15$ m·s^{-1}, and $v_S = 45$ m·s^{-1}. (Both velocities are positive because both velocity vectors point in the same direction as the direction from the listener to the source.) From Eq. (23–12),

$$f_L = f_S \frac{c + v_L}{c + v_S} = 300 \text{ Hz}\left(\frac{300 \text{ m·s}^{-1} + 15 \text{ m·s}^{-1}}{300 \text{ m·s}^{-1} + 45 \text{ m·s}^{-1}}\right) = 274 \text{ Hz}.$$

In cases (b) through (d) the source and listener are moving farther apart, and the frequency f_L heard by the listener is *less than* the source frequency f_S. The *relative velocity* of source and listener is the same in these three cases, but the frequency shift is different in all three. ∎

In this entire discussion the velocities v_L, v_S, and c are all measured *with respect to the air* or whatever medium we are considering. There is also a Doppler effect for electromagnetic waves in empty space, such as light waves or radio waves. In this case there is no medium that we can use as a reference to measure velocities, and the only velocity we can talk about is the *relative* velocity v of source and receiver.

To derive the expression for the Doppler frequency shift for light, we have to use relativistic kinematic relations. We will derive these in Chapter 40, but meanwhile we quote the result without derivation. The

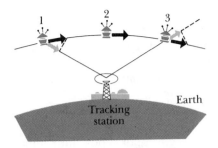

23–6
Change of velocity component along the line of sight of a satellite passing a tracking station.

wave speed c is the speed of light and is the same for both source and listener. In the frame of reference in which the listener is at rest, the source is moving away from the listener with velocity v. (If the source is *approaching* the listener, v is negative.) The source frequency is again f_S. The frequency f_L measured by the listener (i.e., the frequency of arrival of the waves at L) is then given by

$$f_L = \sqrt{\frac{c - v}{c + v}} f_S. \qquad (23\text{–}13)$$

When v is positive, the source moves *away* from the listener and f_L is always less than f_S; when v is negative, the source moves *toward* the listener and f_L is *greater* than f_S. The qualitative effect is the same as for sound, but the quantitative relationship is different.

A familiar application of the Doppler effect with radio waves is the radar device mounted on the side window of a police car to check other cars' speeds. The electromagnetic wave emitted by the device is reflected from a moving car, which acts as a moving source, and the wave reflected back to the device is Doppler-shifted in frequency. The transmitted and reflected signals are combined to produce beats, and the speed can be computed from the frequency of the beats.

The Doppler effect is also used to track satellites. In Fig. 23–6 a satellite emits a radio signal with constant frequency f_S. Initially, the source has a component of velocity toward the listener, but after it passes overhead, it has a component of velocity away from the listener. The frequency f_L of the signal received on earth decreases as the satellite passes overhead. The Doppler frequency shift can be measured by using beats, as with police radar, and the satellite's speed can be determined.

The Doppler effect for *light* is important in astronomy. Light emitted by elements in distant stars shows shifts toward longer wavelength and smaller frequency, compared to light from the same elements on earth. These are Doppler shifts caused by receding motion of the stars. Because the shift is nearly always toward the longer wavelength or red end of the spectrum, it is called the *red shift*. These observations have provided much of the evidence for the "big bang" cosmological theories, which represent the universe as having evolved from a great explosion several billion years ago in a relatively small region of space.

*23–5
Sources of Sound

To produce sound, we have to make air molecules move back and forth; we can do this either with acoustic vibrations in an enclosed space or with vibration of a solid body that sets the adjacent air molecules into motion.

The acoustic-vibration category includes organ pipes (Section 22–5) and the flute and recorder families of instruments. None of these has any moving parts in the usual sense; a steady stream of air causes vibrating air motion within the device, and some of this motion is transmitted through openings to the outside. The pitch is determined by the frequencies of the normal modes, which depend on the dimensions of the

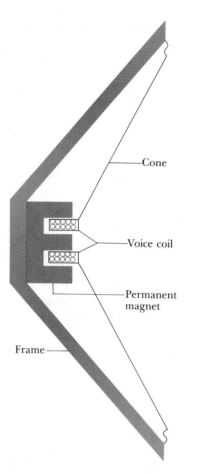

Cone

Voice coil

Permanent magnet

Frame

23–7
Cross section of a loudspeaker. The folds at the outer edge of the paper cone permit the voice coil to move freely into and out of the magnet. When a fluctuating current passes through the voice coil, the magnetic forces exerted by the field of the permanent magnet cause the coil, and with it the cone, to vibrate back and forth from left to right. For low-frequency sound reproduction the cone is typically 20 cm to 30 cm in diameter. For high-frequency reproduction the cone is often replaced by a rigid dome a few centimeters in diameter, with a flexible mounting at its edge. High-quality speaker systems often use several speakers for optimum reproduction of the entire audible frequency range.

pipe and the speed of sound. Each pipe in a pipe organ produces only a single note, but flutes and recorders have series of holes that are opened and closed by the player's fingers, sometimes with the help of mechanical linkage, to provide a variety of pitches. Producing a musical note by blowing into a beer bottle or a jug is the same idea; entire bands have been built on this principle!

The other wind instruments of the orchestra combine acoustic vibrations in an air column with a reed that vibrates in response to air blown through or past it. In the clarinet, oboe, reed organ pipes, and similar instruments the reed is part of the instrument. In brass instruments, such as the trumpet, trombone, and tuba, the player's lips in the mouthpiece serve as the reed. The human voice is similar, the vocal cords serving as the reed.

We don't usually think of an internal-combustion engine as a musical instrument, but it does produce a periodic sound wave in its exhaust noise. Hot gases under high pressure are released suddenly by the opening of the exhaust valves, which perform the function of the reed in this instrument. The pitch is determined by the frequency of opening and closing of the exhaust valves, which is proportional to engine speed.

Instruments in the string and percussion families make use of vibrations of solid bodies. In string instruments such as the violin family, the guitar, banjo, and the piano, a string or several strings are set into vibration by bowing, plucking, or striking with hammers. They vibrate with their normal-mode frequencies, as we discussed in Section 22–3. The strings are thin and not very effective in transmitting their vibration to the surrounding air, so this vibration is coupled to a solid body with a larger surface area for more effective acoustic coupling. In the violin family the string motion is transmitted through the bridge to the body of the instrument, which vibrates with the same frequency as the string. The sounding board on a piano or harpsichord serves the same function. A piano without a sounding board has a tinny, weak, and unsatisfying sound.

In sound reproduction and amplification systems the source of sound is the familiar loudspeaker. The structure of a common type of loudspeaker is shown in Fig. 23–7. The stiff cone has flexible folds at its outer edge. Attached to its center is a coil of wire (the voice coil) that moves within the field of a permanent magnet. Fluctuating current in the voice coil causes the magnetic field to exert fluctuating forces on the coil, and the mechanical vibration of the speaker cone reproduces the electrical vibration of the current in the voice coil.

Microphones have the opposite function, the conversion of sound waves to electrical waves. In principle the speaker in Fig. 23–7 could also be used as a microphone, but actual microphones can be made much more compact. In a sound-amplification system, sound is converted to electrical vibrations, amplified electronically, and then converted back to sound by means of loudspeakers.

In recording and reproducing sound there are at least two additional steps, which are associated with storing and retrieving the signal. In the familiar phonograph record the amplified electrical signal from the microphone is fed to a device that is similar in principle to a speaker but equipped with a stylus that scratches a wavy spiral line in a rotating disk.

The signal is thus stored mechanically; in playback it is traced by another stylus attached to a device that plays the role of a microphone, converting the mechanical vibrations once again to an electrical signal for amplification and final conversion to sound in the speaker. In magnetic tape recording the record is replaced by a moving tape that can be permanently magnetized; the signal is then stored in the form of a series of regions of greater and lesser magnetization. In compact disks the amplitude of the waveform to be recorded is measured 40,000 times each second; these amplitudes are converted to digital form and stored on the disk as a series of pits and flat spots, corresponding to a series of binary digits. In reproduction they are read off the disk by reflection of a laser beam and then converted back to the original sound wave. There is no surface noise or tape hiss in compact disks, and the playback is not affected by variations in disk speed.

Interference effects play an important role in loudspeakers. Each element of the speaker cone acts as a source of sound. The sounds from these individual sources are at different distances from the listener; they do not all arrive in phase, and there are interference effects. If the wavelength of the sound is long in comparison to the dimensions of the cone, this doesn't matter, but at shorter wavelengths and higher frequencies, interference effects become significant. One noticeable effect is that the higher frequencies tend to be focused in a narrow cone along the speaker axis. When broad dispersion of high-frequency sound is required, very small speakers are used; the cones are often convex or are fitted with cellular horns to help disperse the sound. For *low* frequencies, large cones are required to provide enough surface area for effective coupling to the air.

*23-6
Applications of Acoustic Phenomena

The importance of acoustic principles goes far beyond human hearing. Here are some examples.

Several animals use sound for navigation. Bats depend primarily on sound rather than sight for guidance during flight. That's how they can fly in the total darkness of a cave. They emit short pulses of ultrasonic sound, typically 30 to 150 kHz; the returning echoes give information about the location and size of obstacles and potential prey such as flying insects.

Dolphins use an analogous system for underwater navigation, as we mentioned in Example 21-3 (Section 21-4). The frequencies are again ultrasonic, about 100 kHz. With such a system the animal can sense objects of about the size of the wavelength of the sound (1.4 cm) or larger. The corresponding manufactured systems, used for submarine navigation, depth measurements, location of fish or wrecked ships, and so on, are called **sonar.** Sonar systems using the Doppler effect can measure the motion as well as position of submerged objects.

Analysis of elastic waves in the earth provides important information about its structure. The interior of the earth may be pictured crudely as

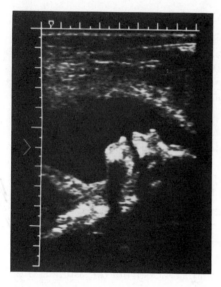

23–8
Sonogram of a human fetus in the womb showing the facial profile of a 19-week fetus. (Courtesy of Acuson Computed Sonography.)

being made of concentric spherical shells around a fluid core. The mechanical properties such as density and elastic moduli are different in different shells. Waves produced by explosions or earthquakes are reflected and refracted at the interfaces between these shells, and analysis of these waves helps geologists to measure the dimensions and properties of the shells. Local anomalies such as oil deposits can also be detected by study of wave propagation.

Some of the most interesting recent applications of acoustics lie in the field of medicine. Reflection of ultrasonic waves from regions in the interior of the body can be used for prenatal examinations, to detect anomalous conditions such as tumors, and to study heart-valve action, to name a few possibilities. Ultrasound is more sensitive than X-rays in distinguishing various kinds of tissues, and it does not have the radiation hazards associated with X-rays. At much higher power levels, ultrasound is used to pulverize gallstones and kidney stones, and it appears to have promise as a selective destroyer of pathological tissue in the treatment of arthritis and certain cancers.

Medical and other applications of ultrasonics use a variety of electronic instrumentation. The sound is always produced by first generating an electrical wave, then using this to drive a loudspeakerlike device called a **transducer** that converts electrical waves to sound. The detecting instruments include transducers (functioning as microphones) as well as amplifiers and devices for displaying reflected signals. Techniques have been developed in which transducers move over or *scan* the region of interest and a computer-reconstructed image is produced. An example of such techniques is shown in Fig. 23–8.

The applications of acoustic principles to environmental problems are obvious. Noise is a very important aspect of environmental degradation. The design of quiet mass-transit vehicles, for example, involves detailed study of sound generation and propagation in the motors, wheels, and supporting structures of vehicles. Excessive noise levels can lead to permanent hearing impairment; studies have shown that many young rock musicians have suffered hearing losses typical of persons 65 years of age. Prolonged listening to high-level rock music (100 to 120 dB) can lead to permanent hearing loss. Stereo headsets used at high volume levels pose similar threats to hearing. Be careful!

Questions

23–1 Ultrasonic cleaners use ultrasonic waves of high intensity in water or a solvent to clean dirt from dishes, engine parts, and so on. How do they work? What advantages and disadvantages does this process have in comparison with other cleaning methods?

23–2 Lane dividers on highways sometimes have regularly spaced ridges or ripples. When the tires of a moving car roll along such a divider, a musical note is produced. Why? Could this phenomenon be used to measure the car's speed? How?

23–3 Two tuning forks have identical frequencies, but one is stationary while the other is mounted on a rotating record turntable. What does a listener hear?

23–4 The organist in a cathedral plays a loud chord and then releases it. The sound persists for a few seconds and gradually dies away. Why does it persist? What happens to the energy when it dies away?

23–5 Why do foghorns always have very low pitches?

23–6 Some stereo amplifiers intended for home use have a maximum power output of 600 W or more. What would happen if you had 600 W of actual sound power in a moderate-sized room?

23–7 Why does your voice sound different over the telephone than in person?

23–8 Why does a guitar have a sharper, more metallic sound when it is played with a hard pick than when it is plucked with the bare fingertips?

23–9 When a record is being played with the volume control turned down all the way, a faint sound can be heard coming directly from the stylus. It seems to be all treble and no bass. How is the sound produced, and why are the frequencies so unbalanced?

23–10 The tone quality of a violin is different when the bow is near the bridge (the ends of the strings) than when it is nearer the centers of the strings. Why?

23–11 An engineer who likes to express everything in technical terms remarked that the price of gasoline fell by 2 dB in 1988. What do you think he meant?

23–12 When you are shouting at someone a fair distance away, it is easier for the person to hear you if the wind is blowing from you to him or her than if it is in

the opposite direction. What is the physical basis for this difference?

23–13 Two notes an octave apart on a piano have a frequency ratio of 2:1. When one is slightly out of tune, beats are heard. How are they produced?

23–14 A large church has part of the organ in front and part in back. When both divisions are playing at once and a person walks rapidly down the center aisle, the two divisions sound out of tune. Why?

23–15 Can you think of circumstances in which a Doppler effect would be observed for surface waves in water? For elastic waves propagating in a body of water?

23–16 How does a person perceive the direction from which a sound comes? Is our directional perception more acute for some frequency ranges than for others? Why?

23–17 A sound source and a listener are both at rest on the earth, but a strong wind is blowing. Is there a Doppler effect?

Exercises

Unless indicated otherwise, assume that the speed of sound in air is $c = 344$ m·s^{-1} and that atmospheric pressure is 1.01×10^5 Pa.

Section 23–1   Sound Waves

23–1

a) If the pressure amplitude in a sound wave is doubled, by what factor does the intensity of the wave increase?

b) By what factor must the pressure amplitude of a sound wave be increased in order to increase the intensity by a factor of 9?

23–2

a) Two sound waves of the same frequency, one in air and one in water, are equal in intensity. What is the ratio of the pressure amplitude of the wave in water to that of the wave in air? The temperature of the air is 20°C.

b) If the pressure amplitudes of the waves are equal, what is the ratio of the intensity of the wave in water to that of the wave in air?

23–3 Consider a sound wave in air that has displacement amplitude 0.0140 mm. Calculate the pressure amplitude for frequencies of

a) 500 Hz;

b) 20,000 Hz (barely audible).

In each case, compare the results to the pain threshold given in Example 23–1.

23–4 Derive Eq. (23–5) from the preceding equations.

23–5

a) Relative to the arbitrary reference intensity of 1.00×10^{-12} W·m^{-2}, what is the intensity level in decibels of a sound wave whose intensity is 1.00×10^{-8} W·m^{-2}?

b) What is the intensity level of a sound wave in air at 20°C whose pressure amplitude is 0.340 Pa?

23–6 A sound wave in air has a frequency of 400 Hz, a wave speed of 344 m·s^{-1}, and a displacement amplitude of 0.00750 mm. Calculate the intensity (in watts per square meter) and intensity level (in decibels) for this sound wave.

Section 23–3   Beats

23–7 A trumpet player is tuning his instrument by playing an A note simultaneously with the first-chair trumpeter, who has perfect pitch. The first-chair player's note is exactly 440 Hz, and 2.8 beats per second are heard. What are the two possible frequencies of the other player's note?

23–8 Two identical piano strings, when stretched with the same tension, have a fundamental frequency of 440 Hz. By what fractional amount must the tension in one string be increased so that 3.5 beats per second will occur when both strings vibrate simultaneously?

Section 23–4   The Doppler Effect

23–9 A railroad train is traveling at 30.0 m·s^{-1} in still air. The frequency of the note emitted by the locomotive whistle is 440 Hz. What is the wavelength of the sound waves

a) in front of the locomotive?

b) behind the locomotive?

What is the frequency of the sound heard by a stationary listener

c) in front of the locomotive?

d) behind the locomotive?

What frequency is heard by a passenger on a train moving in the opposite direction to the first at 15.0 m·s^{-1} and

e) approaching the first?   f) receding from the first?

23–10 On the planet Vulcan a male Nameloc is flying toward its mate at 0.250 m·s^{-1} while singing at a frequency of 1200 Hz. If the stationary female hears a tone of 1600 Hz, what is the speed of sound in the atmosphere of Vulcan?

23–11 Two whistles, A and B, each have frequency 440 Hz. A is stationary, and B is moving toward the right (away from A) at a speed of 50.0 m·s^{-1}. An observer is between the two whistles, moving toward the right with a speed of 25.0 m·s^{-1}. No wind is blowing.

a) What is the frequency from A as heard by the observer?

b) What is the frequency from B as heard by the observer?

c) What is the beat frequency detected by the observer?

Problems

23–12 A very noisy chain saw operated by a tree surgeon emits a total acoustic power of 20.0 W uniformly in all directions. At what distance from the source is the sound level

a) 100 dB?

b) 60 dB?

23–13 A certain sound source radiates uniformly in all directions in air at 20°C. At a distance of 8.00 m from the source the sound level is 80.0 dB. The frequency is 440 Hz.

a) What is the pressure amplitude at this distance?

b) What is the displacement amplitude?

c) At what distance is the sound level 60.0 dB?

23–14 A window whose area is 0.80 m^2 opens on a street where the street noises result in an intensity level, at the window, of 60 dB. How much "acoustic power" enters the window via the sound waves?

23–15

a) Show that if β_1 and β_2 are the intensity levels in decibels of sounds of intensities I_1 and I_2, respectively, the difference in intensity levels of the sounds is

$$\beta_2 - \beta_1 = 10 \log \frac{I_2}{I_1}.$$

b) When a physics professor lectures, she produces sound with an intensity 500 times greater than when she whispers. What is the difference in intensity levels, in decibels?

23–16

a) Show that if $(p_{max})_1$ and $(p_{max})_2$ are the pressure amplitudes of two sound waves, the difference in intensity levels of the waves is

$$\beta_2 - \beta_1 = 20 \log \frac{(p_{max})_2}{(p_{max})_1}.$$

b) Show that if the reference level of intensity is $I_0 = 1.00 \times 10^{-12}$ W·m^{-2}, the intensity level of a sound of intensity I (in W·m^{-2}) is

$$\beta = 120 + 10 \log I.$$

23–17 What is the difference in intensity level of a baby's cry heard by the father if the baby's mouth is 40 cm from his ear compared to the intensity level heard by the baby's mother, who is 3.00 m away from the baby? (Use the expression derived in part (a) of Problem 23–15.)

23–18 The intensity due to a number of independent sound sources is the sum of the individual intensities.

a) How many decibels greater is the intensity level when all four quadruplets cry simultaneously than when a single one cries?

b) How many more crying babies are required to produce a further increase in the intensity level of an equal number of decibels?

(Use the expression derived in part (a) of Problem 23–15.)

23–19 The frequency ratio of a half-tone interval on the equally tempered scale is 1.059. Find the speed of an automobile passing a listener at rest in still air if the pitch of the car's horn drops a half-tone between the times when the car is coming directly toward him and when it is moving directly away from him.

23–20 How would each of the answers in Exercise 23–9 be altered if a wind speed of 10.0 m·s^{-1} is blowing in the same direction as that in which the first locomotive is traveling?

23–21 A swimming duck paddles the water with its feet once every 2 s, producing surface waves with this frequency. The duck is moving at constant speed in a pond where the speed of surface waves is 0.50 m·s^{-1}, and the crests of the waves ahead of the duck are spaced 0.20 m apart.

a) What is the speed of the duck?

b) How far apart are the crests behind the duck?

23–22 A sound wave of frequency f_0 and wavelength λ_0 travels horizontally toward the right. It strikes and is reflected from a large, rigid, vertical plane surface that is perpendicular to the direction of propagation of the wave and moving toward the left with a speed v.

a) How many positive wave crests strike the surface in a time interval t?

b) At the end of this time interval, how far to the left of the surface is the wave that was reflected at the beginning of the time interval?

c) What is the wavelength of the reflected waves, in terms of λ_0?

d) What is the frequency in terms of f_0?

e) A listener is at rest at the left of the moving surface. How many beats per second does she detect as a result of the combined effect of the incident and reflected waves?

23–23 The sound source of a sonar system operates at a frequency of 40,000 Hz. The speed of sound in water is 1480 m·s^{-1}.

a) What is the wavelength of the waves emitted by the source?

b) What is the difference in frequency between the directly radiated waves and the waves reflected from a whale traveling directly away from the ship at 6.4 m·s^{-1}? The ship is at rest in the water. A situation similar to this one is analyzed in detail in Problem 23–22.

23–24 To see how ultrasonics can be used in medicine, consider the following. A 2.00-MHz sound wave travels through the mother's abdomen and is reflected from the fetal heart wall of her unborn baby, which is moving toward the sound receiver as the heart beats. The reflected sound is then mixed with the transmitted sound, and 200 beats per second are detected. The speed of sound in body tissue is 1500 m·s^{-1}. Calculate the speed of the fetal heart wall at the instant this measurement is made. (This situation is considered in detail in Problem 23–22.)

23–25

a) Show that Eq. (23–13) can be written
$$f_L = f_S\left(1 - \frac{v}{c}\right)^{1/2}\left(1 + \frac{v}{c}\right)^{-1/2}.$$

b) Use the bionomial theorem to show that if $v \ll c$, this expression is approximately equal to
$$f_L = f_S\left(1 - \frac{v}{c}\right).$$

c) An earth satellite emits a radio signal with a frequency of 1.00×10^8 Hz. An observer on the ground detects beats between the received signal and a local signal also of frequency 1.00×10^8 Hz. At a particular moment the beat frequency is 1600 Hz. What is the component of the satellite's velocity directed toward the earth at this moment? (The speed of light is 3.00×10^8 m·s^{-1}.)

23–26 A man stands at rest in front of a large, smooth wall. Directly in front of him, between him and the wall, he holds a vibrating tuning fork of frequency f_0. He now runs toward the wall with a speed v. How many beats per second will he detect between the sound waves reaching him directly from the fork and those reaching him after being reflected from the wall? (Note: If the beat frequency is too large, the man may have to use some instrumentation other than his ears to detect and count the beats.)

Challenge Problems

23–27 A source of sound waves, S, emitting waves of frequency f_0, is traveling toward the right in still air with a speed v_1. At the right of the source is a large, smooth, reflecting surface moving toward the left with a speed v_2. The speed of the sound waves is c.

a) How far does an emitted wave travel in time t?

b) What is the wavelength of the emitted waves in front of (i.e., at the right of) the source?

c) How many waves strike the reflecting surface in time t?

d) What is the speed of the reflected waves?

e) What is the wavelength of the reflected waves?

f) What is the frequency of the reflected waves as heard by a stationary listener?

g) Calculate a numerical value for the frequency in part (f) for $c = 344$ m·s^{-1}, $v_1 = 20.0$ m·s^{-1}, $v_2 = 50.0$ m·s^{-1}, and $f_0 = 1000$ Hz.

23–28 This problem asks you to perform an alternative derivation of the phenomenon of beats.

a) Consider two sound waves of the same amplitude but different frequencies f_1 and f_2. The displacements of the air as a function of time produced by the individual waves are $y_1 = A \sin (2\pi f_1 t)$ and $y_2 = A \sin (2\pi f_2 t)$. (For convenience we take $x = 0$ in Eq. (23–1).) Apply the principle of superposition and the appropriate trigonometric identities to show that the resultant displacement produced by the two simultaneous waves is

$$y = \left[2A \cos 2\pi \left(\frac{f_1 - f_2}{2} \right) t \right] \sin 2\pi \left(\frac{f_1 + f_2}{2} \right) t.$$

b) From the result in part (a), show that for f_1 and f_2 that are not too different, one will hear beats with a frequency of occurrence given by Eq. (23–7).

23–29 Two loudspeakers, A and B, radiate sound uniformly in all directions in air at 20°C. The output of acoustic power from A is 9.00×10^{-4} W, and from B it is 12.0×10^{-4} W. Both loudspeakers are vibrating in phase at a frequency of 172 Hz.

a) Determine the difference in phase of the two signals at a point C along the line joining A and B, 3.00 m from B and 4.00 m from A.

b) Determine the intensity and intensity level at C from speaker A if speaker B is turned off.

c) Determine the intensity and intensity level at C from speaker B if speaker A is turned off.

d) With both speakers on, what are the intensity and intensity level at C?

Coulomb's Law

Evidence of electric charges and their interactions are all around us—lightning, the infamous "static cling" of TV fame, the sparks you get when you scuff your shoes across the carpet. Interactions between electrically charged bodies are one of the four fundamental classes of interactions found in nature, as we mentioned at the beginning of Chapter 5. In this chapter we study interactions of electric charges at rest; we call these **electrostatic** interactions. The basic force law for interaction of electric charges at rest is called *Coulomb's law*. In this chapter we look at a variety of electrostatic phenomena and work out several applications of Coulomb's law.

24–1
Electric Charge

The ancient Greeks discovered as early as 600 B.C. that when they rubbed amber with wool, it became able to attract other objects. Today we say that the amber has acquired an **electric charge** or is *electrified*. Indeed, these terms are derived from the Greek word *elektron*, meaning amber. When you scuff your shoes across a nylon carpet, you become electrified, and you can electrify a comb by passing it through dry hair.

Plastic rods and fur are particularly good for demonstrating electric-charge interactions. Suppose we electrify a plastic rod by rubbing it with fur and then touch the rod to two small, light balls of cork or styrofoam that are suspended from thin silk or nylon threads. We find that the rod then *repels* the balls and that they also repel each other.

We get the same results when we rub a glass rod with silk. However, when a cork ball that has been in contact with electrified plastic is placed near one that has been in contact with electrified glass, the cork balls *attract* each other. These experiments show that there are two kinds of electric charge, the kind on the plastic rod rubbed with fur and the kind on the glass rod rubbed with silk. Benjamin Franklin suggested calling these charges *negative* and *positive*, respectively, and these names are still used. Two positive charges or two negative charges repel each other, and a positive and a negative charge attract each other.

Here is another fundamental experiment. We rub a plastic rod with fur and then touch it to a suspended cork ball. Both the rod and the ball then have negative charge. If we now bring the *fur* near the cork ball, the ball is *attracted*, showing that the fur is *positively* charged. This shows that when plastic is rubbed with fur, *opposite* charges appear on the two materials. The same thing happens with glass and silk. These experiments suggest that electric charge is not *created* but is *transferred* from one body to another. We now know that the plastic rod acquires extra electrons, which have negative charge. These electrons are taken from the fur, which is left with a net positive charge. The *total* electric charge on both bodies does not change. This is an example of *conservation of charge*; we'll come back to this important principle later in the chapter.

24–2
Atomic Structure

The interactions responsible for the structure and properties of atoms and molecules, and indeed of all ordinary matter, are primarily *electrical* interactions between electrically charged particles. The fundamental building blocks of ordinary matter are three particles, the negatively charged **electron,** the positively charged **proton,** and the uncharged **neutron.** The negative charge of the electron has the same magnitude as the positive charge of the proton; the charge of a proton or an electron is the fundamental natural unit of charge. In the currently accepted theory of fundamental particles the proton and neutron are combinations of other entities called *quarks*, which have charges of $\pm\frac{1}{3}$ and $\pm\frac{2}{3}$ times the electron charge. We will look at the quark model of fundamental particles in Chapter 44.

The protons and neutrons in an atom always form a closely packed, dense, positively charged cluster called the **nucleus.** The size of the nucleus is of the order of 10^{-14} m. (The forces that hold these particles together, despite the repulsion of the protons, will be discussed in Chapter 44.) Outside the nucleus are the electrons. The size of the electron charge distribution, which determines the overall size of the atom, is of the order of 10^{-10} m, or roughly 10^4 times as great as the size of the nucleus. The structure of the atom is analogous to a miniature solar system, with electrical forces taking the place of gravitational forces. The massive, positively charged central nucleus corresponds to the sun, and the electrons correspond to the planets.

In a neutral atom, the number of electrons equals the number of protons in the nucleus, and the net electrical charge (the algebraic sum of all the charges) is zero. If one or more electrons are removed, the remaining positively charged structure is called a **positive ion.** A **negative ion** is an atom that has *gained* one or more electrons. This gaining or losing of electrons is called *ionization*.

The masses of the individual particles, to the precision that they are presently known, are

$$\text{Mass of electron} = m_e = 9.1093897(54) \times 10^{-31} \text{ kg,}$$

$$\text{Mass of proton} = m_p = 1.6726231(10) \times 10^{-27} \text{ kg,}$$

$$\text{Mass of neutron} = m_n = 1.6749286(10) \times 10^{-27} \text{ kg.}$$

The numbers in parentheses are the uncertainties in the last two digits. For example, the last two digits in the neutron mass are 86 ± 10. Note that the masses of the proton and neutron are nearly equal and that the mass of the proton is about 1836 times that of the electron. This shows that nearly all the mass of any atom is concentrated in its nucleus.

The simplest atom, hydrogen, has one electron and a nucleus consisting of a single proton. One mole of monatomic hydrogen contains 6.022×10^{23} particles (Avogadro's number), and its mass (the atomic mass) is 1.008 g. The mass of a single hydrogen atom, the sum of the proton and electron masses, is

$$m_H = \frac{1.008 \text{ g}}{6.022 \times 10^{23}} = 1.674 \times 10^{-24} \text{ g} = 1.674 \times 10^{-27} \text{ kg.}$$

After hydrogen the atom with the next simplest structure is helium. It has two electrons and a nucleus consisting of two protons and two neutrons. The helium nucleus itself, with the two electrons removed, is called an *alpha particle*, or α particle. The next element, lithium, has three electrons and a nucleus containing three protons and three or four neutrons. Each element has a different number of protons in its nucleus; this number is called the **atomic number.** In the *periodic table of elements* (Appendix D), each element occupies a box labeled with its atomic number.

Every material body contains a tremendous number of charged particles, positively charged protons in the nuclei of its atoms and negatively charged electrons outside the nuclei. When the total number of protons equals the total number of electrons, the body as a whole is electrically neutral. To give a body an excess negative charge, we may either *add negative* charges to a neutral body or *remove positive* charges. Similarly, we can create an excess positive charge by either *adding positive* charge or *removing negative* charge. In most cases it is negative charge (electrons) that is added or removed, and a "positively charged body" is one that has lost some of its normal complement of electrons. When we speak of the charge of a body, we always mean its *net* charge. The net charge is always a very small fraction of the total positive or negative charge in the body.

Implicit in these statements is the principle of **conservation of charge.** This principle states that *the algebraic sum of all the electric charges in any closed system is constant.* Charge can be transferred from one body to another, but it cannot be created or destroyed. Conservation of charge is believed to be a *universal* conservation law; there is no experimental evidence for any violation of this principle.

Electrical interactions play a central and dominant role in most aspects of the structure of matter. The forces that hold atoms together in a molecule or in a solid crystal lattice, the adhesive force of glue, the forces associated with surface tension—all of these are *electrical* in nature, arising from the electrical forces between the charged particles in the interacting atoms.

Electrical interactions alone are *not* sufficient to understand the structure of atomic *nuclei,* however. A nucleus consists of protons, which repel each other, and neutrons, which have no electrical charge. For nuclei to be stable there must be additional forces, attractive in nature, that hold the nucleus together despite the electrical repulsion. This additional interaction is called the *nuclear force;* it is an example of the *strong interaction* we mentioned in Section 5–1. The nuclear force has a short range, of the order of nuclear dimensions, and its effects do not extend far beyond the nucleus. In analyzing the structure of atoms we don't have to worry about the details of nuclear structure; we can consider the nucleus as a rigid structure and concentrate on the electrical interactions.

But when the structure of the nucleus itself is the subject of our study, we do need to consider the strong interactions. The stability or instability of a nucleus is determined by the competition between the repulsive electrical forces and the attractive nuclear forces. We will study nuclear stability in Chapter 44.

24–3
Electrical Conductors and Insulators

Some materials permit electric charge to move from one region of the material to another, while others do not. For example, suppose you touch one end of a copper wire to an electrified plastic rod and the other end to a metal ball that is initially uncharged, as in Fig. 24–1. You then bring another charged body up close to the ball; the ball is attracted or repelled, showing that it has become electrically charged. Electric charge has traveled from the plastic rod through the copper wire and onto the ball. The wire is called a **conductor** of electricity. If you repeat the experiment using a rubber band or nylon thread in place of the wire, you find

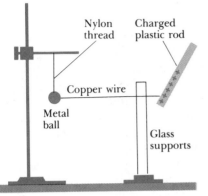

24–1
Copper is a conductor of electricity. Charge can move from the plastic rod through the wire to the metal ball.

that *no* charge is transferred to the ball. Materials like rubber and nylon are called **insulators.** Conductors permit the movement of charge through them; insulators do not.

Most *metals* are good conductors, while most *nonmetals* are insulators. An atom of a metal can easily lose one or two of its outermost electrons. Metallic elements form positive ions in solutions, and they form electrovalent bonds in which they give up one or two electrons. Within a solid metal, such as a copper wire, one or two outer electrons become detached from each atom. These electrons can then move freely throughout the material, in much the same way that the molecules of a gas move freely through the spaces between grains of sand in a sand-filled container. In fact, these free electrons are sometimes described as an "electron gas." The positive nuclei and the other electrons remain bound in fixed positions within the material. In an insulator, on the other hand, there are no free electrons, or at most very few, and electric charge cannot move freely from one region of the material to another.

*24–4
Charging by Induction

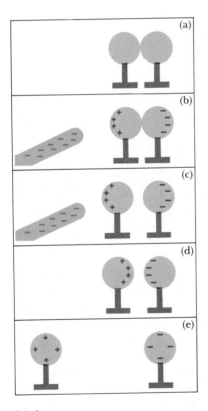

24–2
Two metal spheres are oppositely charged by induction.

When you charge a metal ball by touching it with an electrified (electrically charged) plastic rod, some of the extra electrons on the plastic are transferred to the ball, leaving the plastic with a smaller negative charge. However, there is a different technique in which the plastic rod can give another body a charge of *opposite* sign without losing any of its own charge. This process is called charging by **induction.**

Here's how it works. In Fig. 24–2a, two neutral metal spheres are in contact, each supported on an insulating stand. When you bring a negatively charged rod near one of the spheres, without actually touching it, as in Fig. 24–2b, the free electrons in the metal spheres are repelled by the excess electrons on the rod, and they shift slightly toward the right, away from the rod. The electrons cannot escape from the spheres because the supporting stands and the surrounding air are insulators. So there is an accumulation of excess negative charge at the right surface of the right sphere and a deficiency of negative charge (i.e., a net positive charge) at the left surface of the left sphere. These excess charges are called **induced charges.**

Of course, not *all* of the free electrons are forced to the surface of the right sphere. As soon as any induced charge develops, it also exerts forces on the other free electrons. This force is toward the left; it consists of a repulsion by the negative induced charge on the right and an attraction toward the positive induced charge on the left. Thus the system reaches an equilibrium state in which the force toward the right on an electron, due to the charged rod, is just balanced by the force toward the left due to the induced charge. When the charged rod is removed, the free electrons shift back to the left, and the original neutral condition returns.

What happens if you separate the two spheres slightly, as shown in Fig. 24–2c, while the plastic rod is nearby? If you now remove the rod, as

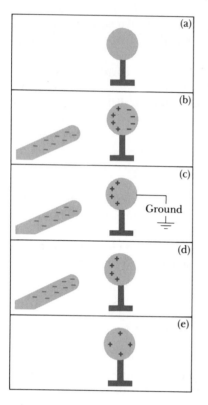

24–3
Charging a single metal sphere by induction.

in Fig. 24–2d, you are left with two oppositely charged metal spheres whose charges attract each other. When you separate the two spheres farther, as in Fig. 24–2e, each of the two charges becomes uniformly distributed over its sphere. Note that the charge on the negatively charged rod has not changed during this process.

Figure 24–3 shows a variation of this technique in which a single metal sphere on an insulating stand is charged by induction. The symbol labeled "ground" in Fig. 24–3c simply means that the sphere is connected to the earth (a conductor). The earth takes the place of the second sphere in Fig. 24–2. In Fig. 24–3c, electrons are repelled to ground, either through a conducting wire or along the moist skin of a person who touches the sphere and provides a conducting path. The earth thus acquires a negative charge equal to the induced positive charge remaining on the sphere.

Charging by induction, as shown in Figs. 24–2 and 24–3, would work just as well if the mobile charges in the spheres were positive charges instead of (negatively charged) electrons, or even if both positive and negative mobile charges were present. In a metallic conductor the mobile charges are always negative electrons; in spite of this, it is often convenient to describe a process *as though* the moving charges were positive. In ionic solutions and some semiconductors, both positive and negative charges participate in the conduction process.

24–5
Coulomb's Law

We describe the electrical interaction between two charged particles in terms of the *forces* they exert on each other. Charles Augustin de Coulomb (1736–1806) studied this interaction in detail in 1784, using a torsion balance similar to that used 13 years later by Henry Cavendish to study the (much weaker) gravitational interaction, as we discussed in Section 6–3.

Coulomb studied the force of attraction or repulsion between two "point charges," that is, charged bodies that are very small in comparison with the distance between them. He found that the force grows weaker with increasing separation between the bodies. When the distance doubles, the force decreases to 1/4 of its initial value. That is, it varies inversely with the square of the distance. If the distance between the particles is r, then the force is proportional to $1/r^2$.

The force also depends on the quantity of charge on each body, which we will denote by q or Q. To explore this dependence, Coulomb divided a charge into two equal parts by placing a charged spherical conductor into contact with an identical but uncharged sphere; by symmetry the charge is shared equally between the two spheres. Thus he could obtain one half, one quarter, and so on, of any initial charge. He found that the force that each of two point charges q_1 and q_2 exerts on the other is proportional to each charge and therefore is proportional to the *product* q_1q_2 of the two charges.

The magnitude F of the force that each of two point charges q_1 and q_2 a distance r apart exerts on the other can be expressed as

$$F = k\frac{|q_1q_2|}{r^2}, \tag{24–1}$$

where k is a proportionality constant. The numerical value of k depends on the units we use for F, q_1, q_2, and r. Equation (24–1) is the mathematical statement of what we now call **Coulomb's law:**

The magnitude of the force of interaction between two point charges is directly proportional to the product of the charges and inversely proportional to the square of the distance between them.

The forces that the two charges exert on each other always act along the line joining them; they are always equal in magnitude and opposite in direction, even when the charges are not equal. That is, *the forces obey Newton's third law.*

There are positive charges and negative charges, so q_1 and q_2 can be either positive or negative quantities. When the charges have the same sign (both positive or both negative), the forces are repulsive; when they are unlike, the forces are attractive. We need the "absolute value" bars in Eq. (24–1) because F is the magnitude of a vector quantity and by definition is always positive, while the product q_1q_2 is negative whenever the two charges have opposite signs.

The proportionality of the electrical force to $1/r^2$ has been verified with great precision. There is no reason to suspect, for example, that the electrical force might be proportional to $1/r^{2.0001}$.

The form of Eq. (24–1) is the same as that of the law of gravitation, discussed in Section 6–3, but electrical and gravitational interactions are two distinct classes of phenomena. Electrical interactions depend on electric charges and can be either attractive or repulsive, while gravitational interactions depend on mass and are always attractive.

When two charges exert forces simultaneously on a third charge, the total force acting on that charge is the *vector sum* of the forces that the two charges would exert individually. This important property, called the **principle of superposition,** holds for any number of charges. We can use it to apply Coulomb's law to any collection of charge, although the computational problems can be considerable. Examples 24–1, 24–4, and 24–5 (Section 24–6) show applications of the superposition principle.

If matter is present in the space between the charges, the net force acting on each charge is altered because charges are induced in the molecules of the intervening material. We will describe this effect later. Strictly speaking, Coulomb's law as we have stated it should be used only for point charges *in vacuum.* As a practical matter, though, we can use it also for point charges in air; at normal atmospheric pressure the effect of the air changes the electrical force from its vacuum value by only about one part in 2000.

In the first half of this book we usually used the SI mechanical units, including the meter, the kilogram, and the second. In the chapters on electricity and magnetism we will use SI units exclusively. The SI electrical units include most of the common electrical units such as the volt, the ampere, the ohm, and the watt. (There is *no* British system of electrical units.) To the three basic SI units (the meter, the kilogram, and the second) we add a fourth: the unit of electric charge. This unit is called one **coulomb** (1 C). In this system the constant k in Eq. (24–1) is

$$k = 8.987551787 \times 10^9 \text{ N·m}^2\text{·C}^{-2} \cong 8.988 \times 10^9 \text{ N·m}^2\text{·C}^{-2}.$$

In principle we can measure the interaction force F between two equal charges q at a measured distance r and use Coulomb's law to determine the charge. Thus we can regard this value of k as an operational definition of the coulomb. For reasons of experimental precision it is better to define the coulomb instead in terms of a unit of electric *current* (charge per unit time), the *ampere*. We will return to this definition in Chapter 31.

When we study electromagnetic radiation in Chapter 35, we will show that the numerical value of k is closely related to the *speed of light*. As we discussed in Section 1–3, this is *defined* to be precisely

$$c = 2.99792458 \times 10^8 \text{ m·s}^{-1} \cong 2.998 \times 10^8 \text{ m·s}^{-1}.$$

The numerical value of k is defined to be precisely

$$k = 10^{-7}c^2.$$

That's why it is known to such a large number of significant figures.

In the cgs system of electrical units (not used in this book) the constant k is defined to be unity, without units. This defines a different unit of electric charge called the *statcoulomb* or the *esu* (electrostatic unit). The conversion factor is, to four significant figures,

$$1 \text{ C} = 2.998 \times 10^9 \text{ esu}.$$

In SI units the constant k in Eq. (24–1) is usually written not as k but as $1/4\pi\epsilon_0$, where ϵ_0 is another constant. This appears to complicate matters, but it actually simplifies many formulas to be encountered later. From now on, we will usually write Coulomb's law as

$$F = \frac{1}{4\pi\epsilon_0} \frac{|q_1 q_2|}{r^2}. \tag{24–2}$$

To four significant figures, the constants in Eq. (24–2) are

$$\frac{1}{4\pi\epsilon_0} = 8.988 \times 10^9 \text{ N·m}^2\text{·C}^{-2}$$

and

$$\epsilon_0 = 8.854 \times 10^{-12} \text{ C}^2\text{·N}^{-1}\text{·m}^{-2}.$$

In examples and problems we sometimes use the approximate value

$$\frac{1}{4\pi\epsilon_0} = 9.0 \times 10^9 \text{ N·m}^2\text{·C}^{-2},$$

which is within about 0.1% of the correct value.

As we mentioned in Section 24–2, the most fundamental unit of charge is the magnitude of the charge of an electron or a proton. This quantity is denoted by e; the most precise value available, as of 1990, is

$$e = 1.60217733(49) \times 10^{-19} \text{ C.}$$

We see that 1 coulomb represents the negative of the total charge carried by about 6×10^{18} electrons. For comparison, the population of the earth is about 5×10^{9} persons, and a cube of copper 1 cm on a side contains about 2.4×10^{24} electrons.

In electrostatics problems, charges as large as 1 coulomb are very unusual. Two charges with magnitude 1 C, at a distance 1 m apart, would exert forces of magnitude 9×10^{9} N (about a million tons) on each other! A more typical range of magnitude is 10^{-9} to 10^{-6} C. The micro-coulomb (1 μC = 10^{-6} C) is often used as a practical unit of charge.

24–6
Applications of Coulomb's Law

Here are several examples of problems using Coulomb's law. There are no new principles in this section, but the problem-solving methods will help you here and in the next several chapters.

PROBLEM-SOLVING STRATEGY: *Coulomb's Law*

1. As always, consistent units are essential. With the value of $k = 1/4\pi\epsilon_0$ given in Section 24–5, distances *must* be in meters, charge in coulombs, and force in newtons. If you are given distances in centimeters, inches, or furlongs, don't forget to convert! When a charge is given in microcoulombs, remember that 1 μC = 10^{-6} C.

2. When the forces acting on a charge are caused by two or more other charges, the total force on the charge is the *vector sum* of the individual forces. Don't forget what you have learned about vector addition; you may want to go back and review the vector algebra in Sections 1–7 and 1–8. It is often useful to use components in an xy-coordinate system. Be sure to use correct vector notation; if a symbol represents a vector quantity, underline it or put an arrow over it. If you get sloppy with your notation, you will also get sloppy with your thinking. It is absolutely essential to distinguish between vector quantities and scalar quantities and to treat vectors as vectors.

3. Some of the examples and problems in this and later chapters involve a continuous distribution of charge along a line or over a surface. In these cases you can sometimes carry out the vector sum described above by dividing the total charge distribution into infinitesimal pieces, using Coulomb's law for each piece, and finding the vector sum. Sometimes this requires calculus, but not always. Study Example 24–5 in this section carefully.

Example 24–1   Two charges are located on the positive x-axis of a coordinate system, as shown in Fig. 24–4. Charge $q_1 = 2.0 \times 10^{-9}$ C is 2.0 cm from the origin, and charge $q_2 = -3.0 \times 10^{-9}$ C is 4.0 cm from the origin. What is the total force exerted by these two charges on a charge $q_3 = 5.0 \times 10^{-9}$ C located at the origin?

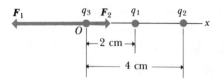

24–4
Forces on charge q_3 caused by charges q_1 and q_2. The total force is the vector sum of $\mathbf{F}_1$ and $\mathbf{F}_2$.

Solution   The total force on q_3 is the vector sum of the forces due to q_1 and q_2 individually. Converting distance to meters, we use Eq. (24–2) to find the magnitude F_1 of the force on q_3 due to q_1:

$$F_1 = \frac{(9.0 \times 10^9 \text{ N·m}^2\text{·C}^{-2})(2.0 \times 10^{-9} \text{ C})(5.0 \times 10^{-9} \text{ C})}{(0.020 \text{ m})^2}$$

$$= 2.25 \times 10^{-4} \text{ N}.$$

This force has a negative x-component because q_3 is repelled (i.e., pushed in the negative x-direction) by q_1, which has the same sign. Similarly, the magnitude F_2 of the force due to q_2 is

$$F_2 = \frac{(9.0 \times 10^9 \text{ N·m}^2\text{·C}^{-2})(3.0 \times 10^{-9} \text{ C})(5.0 \times 10^{-9} \text{ C})}{(0.040 \text{ m})^2}$$

$$= 0.84 \times 10^{-4} \text{ N}.$$

This force has a positive x-component because q_3 is attracted (i.e., pulled in the positive x-direction) by the opposite charge q_2. The sum of the x-components is

$$\sum F_x = -2.25 \times 10^{-4} \text{ N} + 0.84 \times 10^{-4} \text{ N} = -1.41 \times 10^{-4} \text{ N}.$$

There are no y- or z-components. Thus the total force on q_3 is directed to the left, with magnitude 1.41×10^{-4} N.   ∎

Example 24–2   An α particle is a nucleus of a helium atom. It has a mass m of 6.64×10^{-27} kg and a charge q of $+2e$ or 3.2×10^{-19} C. Compare the force of the electrostatic repulsion between two α particles with the force of gravitational attraction between them.

Solution   The magnitude F_e of the electrostatic force is

$$F_e = \frac{1}{4\pi\epsilon_0} \frac{q^2}{r^2},$$

and the magnitude F_g of the gravitational force is

$$F_g = G \frac{m^2}{r^2}.$$

The ratio of the two magnitudes is

$$\frac{F_e}{F_g} = \frac{1}{4\pi\epsilon_0 G} \frac{q^2}{m^2} = \frac{(9.0 \times 10^9 \text{ N·m}^2\text{·C}^{-2})}{(6.67 \times 10^{-11} \text{ N·m}^2\text{·kg}^{-2})} \frac{(3.2 \times 10^{-19} \text{ C})^2}{(6.64 \times 10^{-27} \text{ kg})^2}$$

$$= 3.1 \times 10^{35}.$$

Thus the gravitational force is negligible in comparison to the electrostatic force. This is always true for interactions of atomic and subatomic particles. But for objects the size of the earth the positive and negative charges are nearly equal, and the net electrical interactions are usually much smaller than the gravitational interactions.   ∎

Example 24–3   In the Bohr model of the hydrogen atom (discussed in detail in Section 41–5) a single electron with mass m and charge $-e$ revolves in a circular orbit with radius r around a single proton of charge

$+e$. The electrostatic force of attraction between electron and proton provides the centripetal force that retains the electron in its orbit. If v is the orbital speed, the centripetal acceleration is v^2/r, and Newton's second law ($\Sigma \mathbf{F} = m\mathbf{a}$) gives

$$\frac{1}{4\pi\epsilon_0} \frac{e^2}{r^2} = m\frac{v^2}{r}. \tag{24–3}$$

This motion is analogous to the motion of a satellite around the earth, which we discussed in Section 6–5.

In Bohr's theory, only certain particular orbit radii are allowed. The smallest orbit is one for which the angular momentum L of the electron is equal to $h/2\pi$, where h is a universal constant called *Planck's constant*, equal to 6.625×10^{-34} J·s. That is,

$$L = mvr = \frac{h}{2\pi}. \tag{24–4}$$

We solve this for v and substitute the result into Eq. (24–3) to eliminate v; then we solve for r:

$$r = \frac{\epsilon_0 h^2}{\pi m e^2}. \tag{24–5}$$

Inserting appropriate numerical values, we find that the radius of the orbit is

$$r = 5.29 \times 10^{-11} \text{ m} = 0.529 \times 10^{-8} \text{ cm}.$$

This result corresponds roughly with other estimates of the "size" of a hydrogen atom obtained from deviations from ideal gas behavior, the density of hydrogen in the liquid and solid states, and other observations. ∎

Example 24–4   In Fig. 24–5, two equal positive charges $q = 2.0 \times 10^{-6}$ C interact with a third charge $Q = 4.0 \times 10^{-6}$ C. Find the magnitude and direction of the total (resultant) force on Q.

Solution   The key word is *total*; we have to compute the force each charge exerts on Q and then find the *vector sum* of the forces. The easiest way to do this is to use components. The figure shows the force on Q due to the upper charge q. From Coulomb's law the magnitude F of this force is

$$F = (9.0 \times 10^9 \text{ N·m}^2\text{·C}^{-2})\frac{(4.0 \times 10^{-6} \text{ C})(2.0 \times 10^{-6} \text{ C})}{(0.50 \text{ m})^2}$$

$$= 0.29 \text{ N}.$$

The components of this force are given by

$$F_x = F \cos \theta = (0.29 \text{ N})\frac{0.40 \text{ m}}{0.50 \text{ m}} = 0.23 \text{ N},$$

$$F_y = -F \sin \theta = -(0.29 \text{ N})\frac{0.30 \text{ m}}{0.50 \text{ m}} = -0.17 \text{ N}.$$

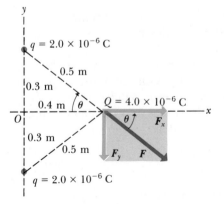

24–5
$\mathbf{F}$ is the force on Q due to the upper charge q.

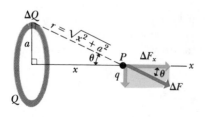

24–6
A charged ring with radius a and total charge Q exerts a force on charge q. The components of force caused by an element of charge ΔQ are shown.

The lower charge q exerts a force with the same magnitude but a different direction. From symmetry we see that its x-component is the same as that due to the upper charge, but its y-component has the opposite direction. So we find

$$\sum F_x = 2(0.23 \text{ N}) = 0.46 \text{ N}, \qquad \sum F_y = 0.$$

The total force on Q is horizontal, with a magnitude of 0.46 N. How would this solution differ if the lower charge were *negative*? ∎

Example 24–5 A ring-shaped conductor with radius a carries a total charge Q, uniformly distributed around it, as shown in Fig. 24–6. A charge q is placed at point P, at a distance x from the center of the ring, along the line perpendicular to the plane of the ring at its center. Find the force exerted on charge q by the ring.

Solution First, notice the close resemblance of this problem to the gravitational-field calculation in Example 6–10 (Section 6–4). We imagine the total charge of the ring as being divided into small charges; let's call a typical small piece ΔQ. The square of the distance from this piece to charge q is $x^2 + a^2$, so Coulomb's law gives the magnitude of the force on q due to ΔQ as

$$\Delta F = \frac{1}{4\pi\epsilon_0} \frac{q\,\Delta Q}{x^2 + a^2}.$$

The component ΔF_x of this force along the x-axis is

$$\Delta F_x = \Delta F \cos\theta = \frac{1}{4\pi\epsilon_0} \frac{q\,\Delta Q}{x^2 + a^2} \frac{x}{\sqrt{x^2 + a^2}} = \frac{1}{4\pi\epsilon_0} \frac{q\,\Delta Q\, x}{(x^2 + a^2)^{3/2}}.$$

We have to compute the *vector sum* of the ΔF_x's from all the pieces of charge ΔQ on the ring. All the pieces are at the same distance from point P, so the above equation is the same for every ΔQ. To get the *total* x-component of force, we simply replace ΔQ in this expression by the total charge Q:

$$F_x = \frac{1}{4\pi\epsilon_0} \frac{qQx}{(x^2 + a^2)^{3/2}}. \tag{24–6}$$

We can see from symmetry that there can't be any component of force *perpendicular* to the x-axis, so the force on q is described completely by this expression for its x-component.

Equation (24–6) shows that at the center of the ring ($x = 0$) the force is zero. This is what you should expect; charges on opposite sides push in opposite directions, and the forces add to zero. When x is much *larger* than a, the denominator of Eq. (24–6) becomes approximately equal to x^3, and the expression becomes approximately

$$F_x = \frac{1}{4\pi\epsilon_0} \frac{qQ}{x^2}.$$

This means that when we are so far from the ring that its size a is negligible in comparison to the distance x, it looks like a point charge. Again, just what you should expect! ∎

Questions

24–1 Plastic food wrap can be used to cover a container by simply stretching the material across the top and pressing the overhanging material against the sides. What makes it stick? Does it stick to itself with equal tenacity? Why? Does it matter whether the container is metallic?

24–2 Bits of paper are attracted to an electrified comb or rod even though they have no net charge. How is this possible?

24–3 How do we know that the magnitudes of electron and proton charge are *exactly* equal? With what precision is this really known?

24–4 When you walk across a nylon rug and then touch a large metal object, you may get a spark and a shock. Why does this tend to happen more in the winter than the summer? Why do you not get a spark when you touch a *small* metal object?

24–5 The free electrons in a metal have mass and therefore weight and are gravitationally attracted toward the earth. Why, then, do they not all settle to the bottom of the conductor, as sediment settles to the bottom of a river?

24–6 Simple electrostatics experiments, such as picking up bits of paper with an electrified comb, never work as well on rainy days as on dry days. Why?

24–7 High-speed printing presses sometimes use gas flames to reduce electric charge buildup on the paper passing through the press. Why does this help? (An added benefit is rapid drying of the ink.)

24–8 What similarities do electrical forces have to gravitational forces? What are the most significant differences?

24–9 Given two identical metal objects mounted on insulating stands, describe a procedure for placing charges of equal magnitude and opposite sign on the two objects.

24–10 How do we know that protons have positive charge and electrons have negative charge, rather than the reverse?

24–11 Gasoline transport trucks sometimes have chains that hang down and drag on the ground at the rear end. What are these for?

24–12 When a nylon sleeping bag is dragged across a rubberized-cloth air mattress in a dark tent, small sparks are sometimes seen. What causes them?

24–13 Atomic nuclei are made of protons and neutrons. This fact by itself shows that there must be another kind of interaction in addition to the electrical forces. Explain.

24–14 When transparent plastic tape is pulled off a roll and one tries to position it precisely on a piece of paper, the tape often jumps over and sticks where it is not wanted. Why does it do this?

24–15 When a thunderstorm is approaching, sailors at sea sometimes observe a phenomenon called "St. Elmo's fire," a bluish flickering light at the tips of masts and along wet rigging. What causes this?

Exercises

Section 24–2   Atomic Structure

24–1 What is the total negative charge, in coulombs, of all the electrons in 20 g of aluminum? The atomic mass of aluminum is 27.0 $g \cdot mol^{-1}$, and its atomic number is 13.

24–2 What is the total positive charge, in coulombs, of all the protons in 2.5 moles of hydrogen atoms?

Section 24–5   Coulomb's Law

Section 24–6   Applications of Coulomb's Law

24–3 Two equal point charges of $+3.00 \times 10^{-6}$ C are placed 0.200 m apart. What is the magnitude of the force each exerts on the other? What are the directions of the forces?

24–4 A negative charge -0.500×10^{-6} C exerts an attractive force of magnitude 0.600 N on an unknown charge 0.200 m away.

a) What is the unknown charge (magnitude and sign)?

b) What force does this charge exert on the -0.500×10^{-6} C charge?

24–5 At what distance would the repulsive force between two electrons have a magnitude of 2.00 N? Between two protons?

24–6 Two small plastic balls are given positive electric charges. When they are 25.0 cm apart, the repulsive forces between them have magnitude 0.180 N. What is the charge on each ball

a) if the two charges are equal?

b) if one ball has twice the charge of the other?

24–7 How many excess electrons must be placed on each of two small spheres spaced 15.0 cm apart if the spheres are to have equal charge and if the magnitude of the force of repulsion between them is to be 5.00×10^{-19} N?

24–8 How far would the electron of a hydrogen atom have to be removed from the nucleus for the force of attraction to equal the weight of the atom?

24–9 Two copper spheres, each having a mass of 0.400 kg, are separated by 2.00 m.

a) How many electrons does each sphere contain? The atomic mass of copper is 63.5 g·mol^{-1}, and its atomic number is 29.

b) How many electrons would have to be removed from one sphere and added to the other to cause an attractive force of 1.00×10^4 N (roughly 1 ton)?

c) What fraction of all the electrons on a sphere does this represent?

24–10 Use the Bohr model to calculate the speed of the electron in a hydrogen atom when the electron is in the orbit of smallest radius.

24–11 Two point charges are located on the y-axis as follows: charge $q_1 = +3.80 \times 10^{-9}$ C at y = 0.600 m and charge $q_2 = -2.50 \times 10^{-9}$ C at the origin (y = 0). What is the total force (magnitude and direction) exerted by these two charges on a third charge $q_3 = +6.00 \times 10^{-9}$ C located at y = −0.400 m?

24–12 Two point charges are placed on the x-axis as follows. Point charge $q_1 = +3.00 \times 10^{-9}$ C is located at x = 0.400 m, and point charge $q_2 = +5.00 \times 10^{-9}$ C is at x = −0.200 m. What are the magnitude and direction of the total force exerted by these two charges on a negative point charge $q_3 = -2.00 \times 10^{-9}$ C that is placed at the origin?

24–13 A ring-shaped conductor with radius a = 0.250 m carries a total positive charge Q = +8.40 μC, uniformly distributed around it, as shown in Fig. 24–6. The center of the ring is at the origin of coordinates. A point charge q = −1.20 μC is located at point P, which is at x = 0.500 m. What are the magnitude and direction of the force exerted by the charge q on the ring?

24–14 Two positive point charges, each of magnitude q, are located on the y-axis at points y = +a and y = −a. A third positive charge of the same magnitude is located at some point on the x-axis.

a) What is the net force exerted on the third charge when it is at the origin?

b) What are the magnitude and direction of the net force on the third charge when its coordinate is x?

c) Sketch a graph of the x-component of the net force on the third charge as a function of x for values of x between +4a and −4a. Plot forces to the right upward and forces to the left downward.

d) How does the net force on the third charge vary with x when x is very large?

24–15 A negative point charge of magnitude q is located on the y-axis at the point y = +a, and a positive charge of the same magnitude is located at y = −a. A third charge that is positive and of the same magnitude q is located at some point on the x-axis.

a) What are the magnitude and direction of the net force exerted on the third charge when it is at the origin?

b) What are the magnitude and direction of the net force on the third charge when its coordinate is x?

c) Sketch a graph of the nonzero component of the net force on the third charge as a function of x for values of x between +4a and −4a.

Problems

24–16 Point charge $q_1 = 6.00 \times 10^{-9}$ C is located at x = 0.300 m, and point charge $q_2 = -4.00 \times 10^{-9}$ C is at x = −0.200 m. A positive point charge q_3 is located at the origin.

a) What must be the magnitude of q_3 for the resultant force on it to have magnitude 5.00×10^{-4} N?

b) What is the direction of the resultant force on q_3?

24–17

a) Suppose all the electrons in 10.0 g of hydrogen atoms could be located at the north pole of the earth and all the protons at the south pole. What would be the magnitude of the total force of attrac-

tion exerted on each group of charges by the other?

b) What would be the magnitude and direction of the force exerted by the charges in part (a) on a third charge that is positive, equal in magnitude to the total charge at one of the poles, and located at a point on the surface of the earth at the equator? Draw a diagram.

24–18 Each of two small spheres is positively charged; the combined charge totals 6.00×10^{-8} C. What is the charge on each sphere if the spheres are repelled with a force of magnitude 2.70×10^{-4} N when placed 0.100 m apart?

24–19 Two point charges are located in the xy-plane, as follows: A charge 2.00×10^{-9} C is at the point $x = 0$, $y = 4.00$ cm, and a charge -3.00×10^{-9} C is at the point $x = 3.00$ cm, $y = 4.00$ cm.

a) If a third charge of 5.00×10^{-9} C is placed at the origin, find the x- and y-components of the total force on this third charge.

b) Find the magnitude and direction of this force.

24–20 A charge -3.00×10^{-9} C is placed at the origin of an xy-coordinate system, and a charge 2.00×10^{-9} C is placed on the positive y-axis at $y = 4.00$ cm.

a) If a third charge 5.00×10^{-9} C is now placed at the point $x = 3.00$ cm, $y = 4.00$ cm, find the x- and y-components of the total force exerted on this charge by the other two.

b) Find the magnitude and direction of this force.

24–21 The pair of equal and opposite charges in Exercise 24–15 is called an *electric dipole*.

a) Show that when the x-coordinate of the third charge in Exercise 24–15 is large in comparison with the distance a, the net force on it is inversely proportional to the *cube* of its distance from the midpoint of the dipole. What is the direction of this force?

b) Show that if the third charge is located on the y-axis, at a y-coordinate that is large in comparison with the distance a, the net force on it is also in-versely proportional to the cube of its distance from the midpoint of the dipole. What is the direc-tion of this force?

24–22 Point charges of 3.00×10^{-9} C are situated at each of three corners of a square whose side is 0.200 m. What are the magnitude and direction of the resultant force on a point charge of -1.00×10^{-9} C if it is placed

a) at the center of the square?

b) at the vacant corner of the square?

24–23 According to the Bohr theory of the hydrogen atom (see Example 24–3), the electron orbits the hydro-gen nucleus (a proton) in a circular path of radius 0.529×10^{-10} m when in the orbit of smallest radius. Consider an atom whose constituents are an electron and a positron (positronium). The positron is the anti-particle of the electron and has the same mass as the electron and a charge that is the same in magnitude but opposite in sign. The electron and positron follow circular orbits about the center of mass of the system. If such a system conforms to the Bohr theory, the orbital angular momentum of the electron–positron system about the center of mass of the system must equal $h/2\pi$ for the orbit of smallest radius. Calculate

a) the distance between the particles;

b) the magnitude of the velocity of each particle with respect to the center of mass.

Challenge Problems

24–24 Three charges are placed as shown in Fig. 24–7. It is known that the magnitude of q_1 is 4.00×10^{-6} C, but its sign and the value of the charge q_2 are not known. The charge q_3 equals $+2.00 \times 10^{-6}$ C, and the resultant force F on q_3 is measured to be entirely in the negative x-direction.

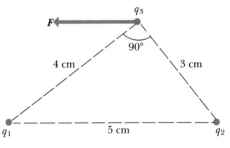

FIGURE 24–7

a) Considering the different possible signs of q_1 and q_2, there are four possible force diagrams repre-senting the forces F_1 and F_2 that q_1 and q_2 exert on q_3. Sketch these four possible force configurations.

b) Using the sketches from part (a) and the fact that the net force on q_3 has no y-component and a neg-ative x-component, deduce the signs of the charges q_1 and q_2.

c) Calculate the magnitude of q_2.

d) Determine F, the magnitude of the resultant force on q_3.

24–25 Two small balls, each with a mass of 25.0 g, are attached to silk threads 1.00 m long and hung from a common point. When the balls are given equal quanti-ties of negative charge, each thread makes an angle of 20.0° with the vertical.

a) Draw a diagram showing all of the forces on each ball.

b) Find the magnitude of the charge on each ball.

c) The two threads are now shortened to length $l = 0.500$ m, while the charge on each ball is held fixed. What will be the new angle that the threads each make with the vertical? (*Hint:* This part of the problem can be solved numerically by using trial values for θ and adjusting the values of θ until a self-consistent answer is obtained.)

24–26 Two identical 4.00-g styrofoam balls are each attached to insulating threads of length $l = 0.500$ m and hung from a common point. One ball is given charge q_1, and the other is given a different charge q_2, which causes the balls to separate such that each thread makes an angle of 30.0° with the vertical. A small wire is then connected between the styrofoam balls, allowing charge to be transferred from one ball to the other until the two balls have equal charges. The wire is removed, and the threads from which the balls are hanging now each make an angle of 40.0° with the vertical.

a) Determine the magnitude of the electrostatic force **F** between the balls before the equalization of the charges.

b) Determine the product $q_1 q_2$ of the charges before equalization of the charges.

c) Determine the magnitude of the electrostatic force **F'** between the balls after equalization of the charges.

d) Determine the original charges q_1 and q_2. (*Hint:* The total charge on the pair of balls is conserved.)

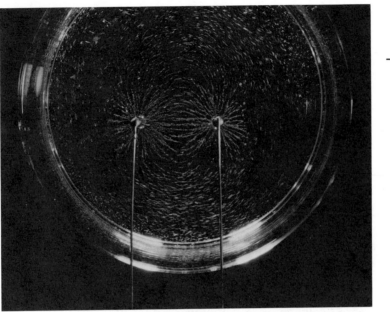

The Electric Field

When two electrically charged particles in empty space interact, how does each one know that the other one is there? What goes on in the space between them to communicate the effect of each one to the other? We can begin to answer these questions, and at the same time reformulate Coulomb's law in a very useful way, using the concept of *electric field*. We think of an electric charge as creating an electric field in the region of space surrounding it. That is, the properties of space itself are modified by the presence of an electric charge. The electric field in turn exerts a force on any other charge that happens to be in the neighborhood. In this chapter you will learn how to calculate electric fields caused by various arrangements of charge. When a charge distribution is symmetric, you can often use the symmetry to simplify the electric field calculations, using a principle called *Gauss's law*. This law is also useful in exploring several general properties of electric fields.

25–1
Electric Field and Electrical Forces

To introduce the concept of electric field, let's look at the mutual repulsion of two positively charged bodies A and B, as shown in Fig. 25–1a. In particular, consider the force on B, labeled F in the figure. This force can act across empty space; we don't need any matter in the intervening space to transmit the force.

Now think of body A as having the effect of somehow modifying the properties of the space around it. We remove body B and label its former position as point P (Fig. 25–1b). We say that the charged body A produces or causes an **electric field** at point P (and at all other points in the neighborhood). Then when body B is placed at point P and experiences the force F, we take the point of view that the force is exerted on B *by the field* at P. Because B would experience a force at *any* point in the neighborhood of A, the electric field exists at all points in the region around A. (We can also say that body B sets up an electric field, which in turn exerts a force on body A.)

The concept of electric field is directly analogous to the concept of *gravitational* field, which we introduced in Section 6–4. Reviewing that section now will help you to understand what comes next.

To find out experimentally whether there is an electric field at a particular point, all we have to do is to place a charged body, which we call a **test charge,** at the point. If the test charge experiences a force of electrical origin, then there is an electric field at that point.

Force is a vector quantity, so electric field is also a vector quantity. (Note the use of boldface letters and $+$, $-$, and $=$ signs in the following discussion.) To define the *electric field* E at any point, we place a test charge q' at the point and measure the electrical force F on it, as in Fig. 25–1c. We define E at this point to be equal to F divided by q':

$$E = \frac{F}{q'} \qquad \text{or} \qquad F = q'E. \qquad (25-1)$$

If q' is positive, the direction of E is the direction of F. The force on a *negative* charge, such as an electron, is *opposite* to the direction of the electric field.

Electric field is sometimes called *electric intensity* or *electric field intensity*. In SI units, in which the unit of force is 1 N and the unit of charge is 1 C, the unit of electric field magnitude is 1 newton per coulomb (1 N·C^{-1}).

The force experienced by the test charge q' varies from point to point, so the electric field is also different at different points. Be sure you understand that E is not a single vector quantity but an infinite set of vector quantities, one associated with each point in space. This is an example of a **vector field.** Another example of a vector field is the motion of a flowing fluid. Different points in the fluid have different velocities, so the velocity of the fluid is a vector field. If we use a rectangular (xyz) coordinate system, each component of E at a point with coordinates (x, y, z) is a function of these coordinates. Vector fields are an important part of the language of physics, particularly in electricity and magnetism.

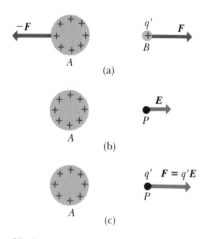

25–1
A charged body creates an electric field in the space around it.

Here's a slight difficulty with our definition of electric field: In Fig. 25–1 the force exerted by the test charge q' on the charge distribution A may cause this distribution to shift around, especially if the body is a conductor, where charge is free to move. The electric field around A when q' is present is not the same as when q' is absent. But if q' is very small, the redistribution of charge on body A is also very small. So we refine our definition of electric field by imagining that the test charge q' grows smaller and smaller until its disturbing effect on the charge distribution is negligible. In mathematical language we call this the *limit* of F/q' as q' approaches zero. Symbolically,

$$E = \lim_{q' \to 0} \frac{F}{q'}. \qquad (25\text{–}2)$$

If there is an electric field within a *conductor*, the field exerts a force on every charge in the conductor, causing the free charges to move. This motion is called a *current*. Thus if there is *no* current in a conductor (no motion of its free charges), *the electric field at every point inside the conductor must be zero.*

In general the magnitude and direction of an electric field can vary from point to point. If in a particular situation the magnitude and direction are the same at every point throughout a certain region, we say that the field is *uniform* in this region.

PROBLEM-SOLVING STRATEGY: *Electric-Field Forces*

1. One way to calculate the electric field at a point is to use Coulomb's law to find the total force F on a test charge q' placed at the point. Then divide F by q' to obtain E. Assuming that q' is positive, F and E have the same direction, and the magnitude of E is the magnitude of F divided by q'.

2. To analyze the motion of a particle with charge q in an electric field, you will need to use Newton's second law, $F = ma$, with F caused by the electric field, $F = qE$. If the field is uniform, the acceleration is constant. Find its components and then use the kinematic language we developed back in Chapters 2 and 3. It wouldn't hurt to review those chapters now.

Example 25–1   What is the electric field 30 cm from a charge $q = 4.0 \times 10^{-9}$ C?

Solution   From Coulomb's law the force on a test charge q' 30 cm from q has magnitude F given by

$$F = \frac{1}{4\pi\epsilon_0} \frac{|qq'|}{r^2}$$

$$= \frac{(9.0 \times 10^9 \text{ N·m}^2\text{·C}^{-2})(4.0 \times 10^{-9} \text{ C})(q')}{(0.30 \text{ m})^2}.$$

Then from Eq. (25–1) the magnitude of E is

$$E = \left| \frac{F}{q'} \right| = 400 \text{ N·C}^{-1}.$$

The *direction* of E at this point is along the line from q toward q'. The sign of q' doesn't matter. Do you see why? ∎

Example 25–2   When the terminals of a 100-V battery are connected to two large parallel horizontal plates 1.0 cm apart, the electric field E in the region between the plates is very nearly uniform, with magnitude $E = 10^4$ N·C^{-1}. Suppose the direction of E is vertically upward. Compute the force on an electron in this field and compare it with the weight of the electron.

Solution   We need the following data, found in Appendix F:

Magnitude of electron charge $e = 1.60 \times 10^{-19}$ C,

Electron mass $m = 9.11 \times 10^{-31}$ kg.

From Eq. (25–1),

$$F_{\text{elec}} = eE = (1.60 \times 10^{-19} \text{ C})(10^4 \text{ N·C}^{-1}) = 1.60 \times 10^{-15} \text{ N};$$

$$F_{\text{grav}} = mg = (9.11 \times 10^{-31} \text{ kg})(9.8 \text{ m·s}^{-2}) = 8.93 \times 10^{-30} \text{ N}.$$

The ratio of the electrical to the gravitational force is

$$\frac{F_{\text{elec}}}{F_{\text{grav}}} = \frac{1.60 \times 10^{-15} \text{ N}}{8.93 \times 10^{-30} \text{ N}} = 1.8 \times 10^{14}.$$

The gravitational force is negligibly small in comparison to the electrical force. ∎

Example 25–3   If the electron of Example 25–2 is released from rest at the upper plate, what speed does it acquire while traveling 1.0 cm? What is its kinetic energy after 1.0 cm? How much time is required for it to travel this distance?

Solution   Note that E is upward but F is downward because the charge is negative. The force is constant, so the electron moves with constant acceleration a given by

$$a = \frac{F}{m} = \frac{eE}{m} = \frac{1.60 \times 10^{-15} \text{ N}}{9.11 \times 10^{-31} \text{ kg}} = 1.76 \times 10^{15} \text{ m·s}^{-2}.$$

We can find its speed at any position from one of the constant-acceleration formulas, Eq. (2–13): $v^2 = v_0{}^2 + 2a(x - x_0)$. In our case, $v_0 = 0$ and $x_0 = 0$, so the speed v when $x = 1.0$ cm ($= 1.0 \times 10^{-2}$ m) is given by

$$v = \sqrt{2ax} = \sqrt{2(1.76 \times 10^{15} \text{ m·s}^{-2})(1.0 \times 10^{-2} \text{ m})}$$
$$= 5.9 \times 10^6 \text{ m·s}^{-1}.$$

Its kinetic energy is

$$\tfrac{1}{2}mv^2 = \tfrac{1}{2}(9.11 \times 10^{-31} \text{ kg})(5.9 \times 10^6 \text{ m·s}^{-1})^2 = 1.6 \times 10^{-17} \text{ J}.$$

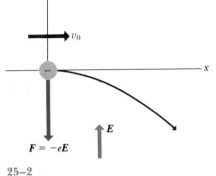

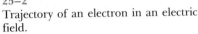

$F = -eE$

25–2
Trajectory of an electron in an electric field.

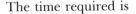

The time required is

$$t = \frac{v}{a} = \frac{5.9 \times 10^6 \text{ m·s}^{-1}}{1.76 \times 10^{15} \text{ m·s}^{-2}} = 3.4 \times 10^{-9} \text{ s.} \quad\blacksquare$$

Example 25–4   If we launch the electron of Example 25–2 into the electric field with an initial horizontal velocity v_0, as in Fig. 25–2, find the equation of its trajectory.

Solution   The direction of the field is upward in Fig. 25–2, so the force on the (negatively charged) electron is downward. We take the positive x-direction to be the direction of the initial velocity. The x-acceleration is zero, the y-acceleration is $-(eE/m)$. At time t,

$$x = v_0 t,$$

$$y = \frac{1}{2}a_y t^2 = -\frac{1}{2}\frac{eE}{m}t^2.$$

Eliminating t in these equations, we get

$$y = -\frac{1}{2}\frac{eE}{mv_0{}^2}x^2,$$

which is the equation of a parabola. The motion is the same as that of a body projected horizontally in the earth's gravitational field (Section 3–4). In Section 26–7 we will see how electric fields are used to control electron beams in TV picture tubes, cathode-ray oscilloscopes, and CRT computer monitors. $\blacksquare$

25–2
Electric-Field Calculations

We can calculate the electric field at any point if we know the magnitudes and positions of all the charges that contribute to the field at that point. First we determine the electric field E at a point P caused by a single point charge q at a distance r from P. To do this, we imagine a test charge q' at P. According to Coulomb's law, the force F on the test charge has magnitude

$$F = \frac{1}{4\pi\epsilon_0}\frac{|qq'|}{r^2},$$

so the electric field at P has magnitude

$$E = \left|\frac{F}{q'}\right| = \frac{1}{4\pi\epsilon_0}\frac{|q|}{r^2}. \quad (25\text{--}3)$$

We call the location of charge q the *source point* and P the *field point*. When q is positive, the field at every point is in the direction from q to point P, that is, away from the source point and toward the field point. When q is negative, the field is directed toward q.

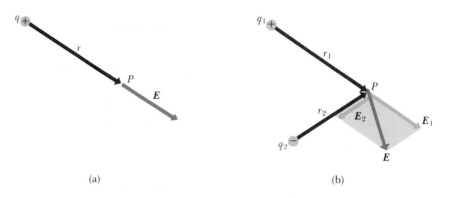

25–3
(a) The electric field E is in the same direction as the vector r when q is positive. (b) The resultant electric field at point P is the vector sum of E_1 and E_2.

(a)   (b)

Now suppose the field at point P is caused by several point charges q_1, q_2, q_3, . . ., at distances r_1, r_2, r_3, ... From the principle of superposition (Section 24–5) it follows that the *total* electric field at P is the *vector sum* of the fields E_1, E_2, and so on, caused by the individual charges. That is,

$$E = E_1 + E_2 + E_3 + \cdots.$$

An example with two charges, one positive and one negative, is shown in Fig. 25–3.

■ PROBLEM-SOLVING STRATEGY: *Electric-Field Calculations*

The strategy outlined in Section 24–6 is directly relevant here, too. We suggest that you review it now. Briefly, the key points are:

1. Be sure to use a consistent set of units.

2. Use proper vector notation; distinguish carefully between scalars, vectors, and components of vectors. Indicate your coordinate axes clearly on your diagram, and be certain that the components are consistent with your choice of axes. Use the methods for finding vector sums that you learned in Chapter 1.

3. Occasionally, you will have a continuous distribution of charge along a line, over a surface, or through a volume. Then you will have to define a small element of charge that can be considered as a point, find its electric field, and then find a way to add the fields of all the charge elements. Usually, it is easiest to do this for each component of E separately.

Example 25–5   Point charges q_1 and q_2 of $+12 \times 10^{-9}$ C and -12×10^{-9} C, respectively, are placed 0.10 m apart, as in Fig. 25–4. This combination, two charges with equal magnitude and opposite sign, is called an **electric dipole.** Compute the electric fields caused by these charges at points a, b, and c.

Solution   At point a the field caused by the positive charge q_1 is directed toward the right; its magnitude is

$$E_1 = (9.0 \times 10^9 \text{ N·m}^2\text{·C}^{-2})\frac{12 \times 10^{-9} \text{ C}}{(0.060 \text{ m})^2} = 3.0 \times 10^4 \text{ N·C}^{-1}.$$

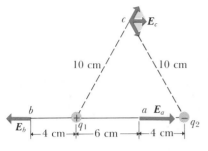

25–4
Electric field at three points, a, b, and c in the field set up by charges q_1 and q_2.

The field caused by the negative charge q_2 is also directed toward the right; its magnitude is

$$E_2 = (9.0 \times 10^9 \text{ N·m}^2\text{·C}^{-2})\frac{12 \times 10^{-9} \text{ C}}{(0.040 \text{ m})^2} = 6.8 \times 10^4 \text{ N·C}^{-1}.$$

So at point a,

$$E_a = (3.0 + 6.8) \times 10^4 \text{ N·C}^{-1}$$
$$= 9.8 \times 10^4 \text{ N·C}^{-1} \qquad \text{toward the right.}$$

At point b the field due to q_1 is directed toward the left, with magnitude

$$E_1 = (9.0 \times 10^9 \text{ N·m}^2\text{·C}^{-2})\frac{12 \times 10^{-9} \text{ C}}{(0.040 \text{ m})^2} = 6.8 \times 10^4 \text{ N·C}^{-1}.$$

The field due to q_2 is directed toward the right; its magnitude is

$$E_2 = (9.0 \times 10^9 \text{ N·m}^2\text{·C}^{-2})\frac{12 \times 10^{-9} \text{ C}}{(0.140 \text{ m})^2} = 0.55 \times 10^4 \text{ N·C}^{-1}.$$

At point b,

$$E_b = (6.8 - 0.55) \times 10^4 \text{ N·C}^{-1}$$
$$= 6.2 \times 10^4 \text{ N·C}^{-1} \qquad \text{toward the left.}$$

At point c the magnitude of each vector is

$$E = (9.0 \times 10^9 \text{ N·m}^2\text{·C}^{-2})\frac{12 \times 10^{-9} \text{ C}}{(0.100 \text{ m})^2} = 1.1 \times 10^4 \text{ N·C}^{-1}.$$

The directions of these vectors are shown in Fig. 25–4. The triangle representing their vector sum is equilateral, and the magnitude E of the resultant $\mathbf{E}$ field is

$$E_c = 1.1 \times 10^4 \text{ N·C}^{-1}.$$

As the diagram shows, the direction is toward the right.

The total $\mathbf{E}$ field at point c can also be obtained by using components to add the fields. The field from each charge makes an angle of 60° with the horizontal axis, and the magnitudes of the two fields are both equal to $1.1 \times 10^4 \text{ N·C}^{-1}$. The vertical components add to zero, and the sum of the horizontal components is

$$E_c = 2 \ (1.1 \times 10^4 \text{ N·C}^{-1}) \cos 60°$$
$$= 1.1 \times 10^4 \text{ N·C}^{-1}. \qquad \blacksquare$$

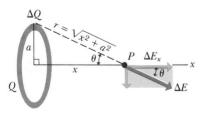

25–5
Electric field due to ring of charge.

Example 25–6   A ring-shaped conductor with radius a carries a total charge Q, uniformly distributed around it, as shown in Fig. 25–5. Find the electric field at a point P, a distance x from the center of the ring, along the line perpendicular to the plane of the ring at its center.

Solution   We have seen this situation before, in Example 24–5 (Section 24–6). In that example the charge q plays the role of the test charge, so we see immediately that the x-component of electric field at point P is given by

$$E_x = \frac{F_x}{q} = \frac{1}{4\pi\epsilon_0}\frac{Qx}{(x^2 + a^2)^{3/2}}.$$

All the comments at the end of Example 24–5 are equally applicable here. At the center of the ring ($x = 0$) the field is zero. At a distance x much greater than the ring's radius a, it looks like a point charge Q at a distance x, we can neglect the a in the denominator, and the field is approximately $E = Q/4\pi\epsilon_0 x^2$. ∎

Example 25–7   A charge $q_1 = +5.0 \times 10^{-9}$ C is located at the origin of an xy-coordinate system, and a charge $q_2 = -2.0 \times 10^{-9}$ C is located on the y-axis, at $y = 0.30$ m. Find the components of the electric field and its magnitude and direction at a point P with coordinates (0.40 m, 0.30 m), as shown in Fig. 25–6.

Solution   At point P the magnitude E_1 of the field caused by charge q_1 is

$$E_1 = (9.0 \times 10^9 \text{ N·m}^2\text{·C}^{-2})\frac{5.0 \times 10^{-9} \text{ C}}{(0.50 \text{ m})^2} = 180 \text{ N·C}^{-1}.$$

The components of this field are

$$E_{1x} = E_1 \cos\theta = (180 \text{ N·C}^{-1})\frac{0.40 \text{ m}}{0.50 \text{ m}} = 144 \text{ N·C}^{-1},$$

$$E_{1y} = E_1 \sin\theta = (180 \text{ N·C}^{-1})\frac{0.30 \text{ m}}{0.50 \text{ m}} = 108 \text{ N·C}^{-1}.$$

The magnitude of the field E_2 caused by charge q_2 is

$$E_2 = (9.0 \times 10^9 \text{ N·m}^2\text{·C}^{-2})\frac{|-2.0 \times 10^{-9} \text{ C}|}{(0.40 \text{ m})^2} = 112 \text{ N·C}^{-1}.$$

Its components are

$$E_{2x} = -E_2 = -112 \text{ N·C}^{-1},$$

$$E_{2y} = 0.$$

The components E_x and E_y of the total field E at point P are

$$E_x = E_{1x} + E_{2x} = 144 \text{ N·C}^{-1} + (-112 \text{ N·C}^{-1}) = 32 \text{ N·C}^{-1},$$

$$E_y = E_{1y} + E_{2y} = 108 \text{ N·C}^{-1} + 0 = 108 \text{ N·C}^{-1}.$$

The magnitude E of the electric field E at point P is

$$E = \sqrt{E_x^2 + E_y^2} = \sqrt{(32 \text{ N·C}^{-1})^2 + (108 \text{ N·C}^{-1})^2} = 113 \text{ N·C}^{-1}.$$

The angle α describing the direction of E in the figure is given by

$$\alpha = \arctan\frac{108 \text{ N·C}^{-1}}{32 \text{ N·C}^{-1}} = 73.5°. \quad ∎$$

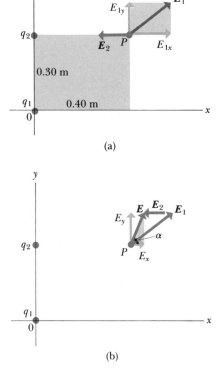

(a)

(b)

25–6
(a) The electric fields E_1 and E_2 at point P caused by charges q_1 and q_2.
(b) The total electric field E at point P is the vector sum of E_1 and E_2. The components of E are shown.

25–3
Field Lines

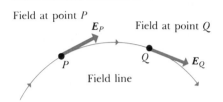

Field at point P

E_P

Field at point Q

P

Q

E_Q

Field line

25–7
The direction of the electric field at any point is tangent to the field line through that point.

The concept of an electric field can be a little elusive because you can't directly see (or feel or taste) an electric field. Field lines can be a big help for visualizing electric fields and making them seem more real. A **field line** is an imaginary line drawn through a region of space so that at every point it is tangent to the direction of the electric-field vector at that point. The basic idea is shown in Fig. 25–7. Michael Faraday (1791–1867) first introduced the concept of field lines. He called them "lines of force," but the term "field lines" is preferable.

Field lines show the direction of E at each point, and their spacing gives a general idea of the *magnitude* of E at each point. Where the lines are bunched closely together, E is strong; where they are farther apart, E is weaker. In fact, we will show later that for a small area A perpendicular to the direction of E at any point, the number of field lines passing through the area is *directly proportional* to the magnitude of the field at that point.

Figure 25–8 shows some of the field lines in two planes containing (a) a single positive charge; (b) two equal charges, one positive and one negative; and (c) two equal positive charges. The direction of the resultant field at every point in each diagram is along the tangent to the field line passing through the point. Arrowheads on the field lines indicate the sense of the E-field vector along each line.

Every field line in an *electrostatic* field is a continuous curve with a positive charge at one end and a negative charge at the other. Field lines never begin or end in the space surrounding a charge. We sometimes speak of an "isolated" charge and draw its field as in Fig. 25–8a, but this means that the charges where the lines end are far away from the charge under consideration. For example, if the charged body in Fig. 25–8a is a small positively charged sphere suspended by a thread from the laboratory ceiling, the negative charges where its field lines end would be found on the walls, floor, and ceiling and on other objects in the laboratory.

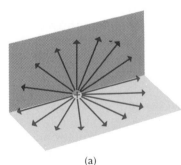

(a)

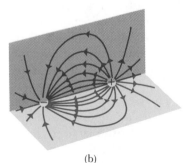

(b)

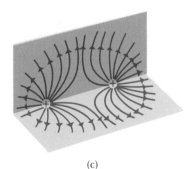

(c)

25–8
The mapping of an electric field with the aid of field lines.

At any particular point the electric field has a unique direction, so only one field line can pass through each point of the field. In other words, *field lines never intersect.*

If we were to draw a field line through *every* point in an electric field, the whole space would be filled with lines, and we wouldn't be able to distinguish them. By limiting the number of lines, we can use them to show the *magnitude* of a field as well as its *direction*. In regions where the field magnitude is large, such as the space between the positive and negative charges in Fig. 25–8b, the field lines are closely spaced. In regions where it is small, such as between the two positive charges in Fig. 25–8c, the lines are widely separated. In a *uniform* field the field lines are straight, parallel, and uniformly spaced.

25–4
Gauss's Law

Gauss's law is an alternative formulation of the relationship between electric charge and electric field. It is logically equivalent to Coulomb's law, but it is sometimes much easier to use, particularly for finding the electric field produced by a spread-out symmetric charge distribution. It was formulated by Karl Friedrich Gauss (1777–1855), one of the greatest mathematical geniuses of all time. Many areas of mathematics, from number theory and geometry to the theory of differential equations, bear the mark of his influence, and he made equally significant contributions to theoretical physics. We will derive Gauss's law in this section, and in the next section we will use it to find the electric fields caused by several different charge distributions.

Gauss's law is related very directly to field lines, which we discussed in Section 25–3. The field of an isolated positive point charge q is represented by lines radiating out in all directions. Let's imagine that we surround this charge with a spherical surface of radius R, with the charge at its center. The surface area of this sphere is $4\pi R^2$. If the *total* number of field lines radiating out from q is N, then the number of lines *per unit area* on the surface is $N/4\pi R^2$. Now imagine a second sphere, concentric with the first but with radius $2R$. Its area is $4\pi(2R)^2 = 16\pi R^2$, and the number of lines per unit area on this sphere is $N/16\pi R^2$, one fourth the number for the first sphere. We know from Coulomb's law that at distance $2R$ the field has only one fourth the magnitude it has at distance R. So this result confirms our claim in Section 25–3 that the number of lines per unit area is proportional to the magnitude of the field.

The fact that the *total* number of lines at distance $2R$ is the same as that at R can be expressed another way. The field magnitude E is inversely proportional to R^2, but the *area A* of the sphere is proportional to R^2. Thus the *product* of the two, EA, is independent of R. For a sphere of any radius r the magnitude of E on the surface is

$$E = \frac{1}{4\pi\epsilon_0}\frac{q}{r^2},$$

the surface area is

$$A = 4\pi r^2,$$

and the product of the two is

$$EA = \frac{q}{\epsilon_0}. \tag{25–4}$$

This product is independent of r; it depends *only* on the charge q. This result is the key to the development of Gauss's law.

We have derived Eq. (25–4) only for spherical surfaces, but we can generalize it for *any* closed surface surrounding an electric charge. We imagine the surface as being divided into small elements of area ΔA. If the electric field E is perpendicular to a particular element of area, then the number of field lines passing through that area is proportional to $E \Delta A$. If not, we take the component of E perpendicular to ΔA; we call this component $E_\perp$. Then the number of lines passing through ΔA is proportional to $E_\perp \Delta A$. (We don't consider the component of E *parallel* to the surface because it doesn't correspond to any lines passing *through* the surface.)

To get the *total* number of field lines passing through the surface, we add up all the products $E_\perp \Delta A$ for all the surface elements that together make up the whole surface. The total number of field lines passing through this surface is the same as that for the spherical surfaces we have discussed. Therefore this sum is again equal to q/ϵ_0, just as in Eq. (25–4), and our generalized relation is

$$\sum E_\perp \Delta A = \frac{q}{\epsilon_0}. \tag{25–5}$$

One further detail: We have to keep track of which lines point *into* the surface and which ones point *out*; we may have both types in some problems. Let's agree that $E_\perp$ is positive when the vector E has a component pointing *out of* the surface and negative when the component points *into* the surface.

Here's a further generalization. Suppose the surface encloses not just one point charge q but several charges q_1, q_2, q_3, ... The total (resultant) electric field E at any point is the vector sum of the E fields of the individual charges. Let Q be the *total* charge enclosed by the surface: $Q = q_1 + q_2 + q_3 + \cdots$, and let $E_\perp$ be the component of the *total* field perpendicular to ΔA. Then the general statement of Gauss's law is

$$\sum E_\perp \Delta A = \frac{Q}{\epsilon_0}. \tag{25–6}$$

The quantity $\Sigma E_\perp \Delta A$ is also called the **electric flux** through the surface; we denote it by Ψ:

$$\sum E_\perp \Delta A = \Psi. \tag{25–7}$$

The total electric flux out of a closed surface is proportional to the total number of lines crossing the surface in the outward direction minus the number crossing in the inward direction. The net charge (that is, the

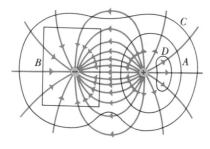

25–9
The net number of field lines leaving a closed surface is proportional to the total charge enclosed.

algebraic sum of all the charges) enclosed by the surface is proportional to this number of lines.

It may look as though evaluating the sum in Eq. (25–6) is a hopeless task. If that's what you think, then you have a pleasant surprise coming. In the next section we'll work out several examples of charge distributions for which it is quite easy to use this relation. First, though, let's think a bit more about the general relation. What happens if a point charge lies *outside* a closed surface? You can draw your own diagram. Then at some points on the surface the electric-field vector points *into* the surface, and at others it points *out of* the surface. Every field line radiating from the charge that enters the surface on one side must come out the other side, and the net number of lines coming out of the surface is zero. Equation (25–6) is still valid; there is no charge enclosed, so Q is zero, and the positive and negative contributions to the sum exactly cancel each other. Also, if the surface encloses a negative charge, then both Q and $E_\perp$ are negative, and Eq. (25–6) is still valid.

Here is an example. Figure 25–9 shows the field produced by two equal and opposite point charges (an electric dipole). Surface A encloses only the positive charge, and 18 lines cross it in an outward direction. Surface B encloses only the negative charge; it is also crossed by 18 lines, but in an inward direction. Surface C enclosed *both* charges. It is intersected by lines at 16 points; at eight intersections the lines are outward, and at eight they are inward. The *net* number of lines crossing in an outward direction is zero, and the net charge inside the surface is also zero. Surface D is intersected at six points; at three the lines are outward, and at the other three they are inward. The net number of lines crossing in an outward direction and the total charge enclosed are both zero. Note that there are points on the surfaces where E is not perpendicular to the surface, but this does not affect the counting of the field lines.

25–5
Applications of Gauss's Law

In this section we offer some strategy for applying Gauss's law and several examples leading to useful relations between charge distributions and the fields they produce.

PROBLEM-SOLVING STRATEGY: *Gauss's Law*

1. The first step is to select the surface (which we will often call a *Gaussian surface*) that you are going to use with Gauss's law. If you are trying to find the field at a particular point, then that point must lie on your Gaussian surface.

2. The Gaussian surface does not have to be a real physical surface, such as a surface of a solid body. Often you will use an imaginary geometric surface; it may be in empty space, embedded in a solid body, or partly both.

3. The Gaussian surface must have enough *symmetry* that it is possible actually to evaluate the sum in Gauss's law. If the problem itself has cylindrical or spherical symmetry, the Gaussian

surface will usually be a cylinder or a sphere, respectively.

4. Often you can think of the surface as several separate areas, such as the sides and ends of a cylinder. The sum of $E_\perp \, \Delta A$ over the whole surface is always equal to the total of the sums over the separate areas. Some of these may be zero, as in items 6 and 7 below.

5. If E is perpendicular to a surface A at every point, and if it also has the same *magnitude* at every point on the surface, then $E_\perp = E = $ constant, and $\Sigma E_\perp \, \Delta A$ over that surface is equal simply to EA.

6. If E is *parallel* to a surface at every point, then $E_\perp = 0$, and the sum over that surface is zero.

7. If $E = 0$ at every point on a surface, the sum is zero.

8. Finally, in the sum $\Sigma E_\perp \, \Delta A$, $E_\perp$ is always the perpendicular component of the *total* electric field at each point on the surface. In general, this field is caused partly by charges within the volume and partly by charges outside. Even when there is *no* charge within the volume, the field at points on the surface is not necessarily zero. In that case, however, the sum over the surface is always zero.

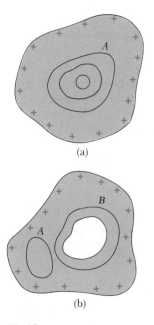

(a)

(b)

25–10
Excess charge on a conductor resides entirely on its outer surface.

Example 25–8   *Location of excess charge on a conductor.* We assert that when excess charge is placed on a conductor, it resides entirely on the *surface*, not in the interior of the material. Here's the proof. We know from the discussion in Section 25–1 that in any electrostatic situation (charges at rest) the electric field E at every point in the interior of a conducting material is zero. If E were *not* zero, the charges would move. Suppose we construct a Gaussian surface inside the conductor, such as surface A in Fig. 25–10a. Because $E = 0$ everywhere on this surface, Gauss's law requires that the net charge inside the surface is zero. Now imagine shrinking the surface down like a collapsing balloon until it encloses a region so small that we may consider it as a point; then the charge at that point must be zero. We can do this anywhere inside the conductor, so *there can be no net charge at any point within the conductor.* Thus any excess charge on the conductor must be located only on its surface, as shown.

If there is a cavity inside the conductor, as in Fig. 25–10b, the situation is somewhat different. We'll come back to that case in Section 25–6. ∎

Example 25–9   *Field of a charged conducting sphere.* We place a charge q on a solid conducting sphere with radius R. Find the electric field at any point outside the sphere.

Solution   From Example 25–8 we know that all the charge is on the surface of the sphere, and from symmetry we know that it is distributed *uniformly* over the surface. We can also conclude from the spherical symmetry that the field is radial everywhere and that its magnitude depends only on the distance r from the center. Thus the magnitude E is uniform over a spherical surface with any radius r, concentric with the conductor. So we take as our Gaussian surface an imaginary sphere with radius r greater than the radius R of the conducting sphere. The area of the Gaussian sphere is $4\pi r^2$, and because E is uniform over the sphere, the sum in Gauss's law is just $E(4\pi r^2)$. Equation (25–6) then gives

$$4\pi r^2 E = \frac{q}{\epsilon_0} \quad \text{and} \quad E = \frac{1}{4\pi\epsilon_0}\frac{q}{r^2}. \qquad (25\text{–}8)$$

This shows that the field at any point *outside* the sphere is the same as though the entire charge were concentrated at its center. Just outside the surface of the sphere, where $r = R$,

$$E = \frac{1}{4\pi\epsilon_0}\frac{q}{R^2}.$$

Inside the sphere, as with any conductor when the charges are at rest, the field is zero. Thus when r is less than R, $E = 0$.

Because gravitational forces also have a $1/r^2$ dependence, there is a Gauss's law for gravitation. Reasoning similar to this discussion can be used to prove our assertion in Section 6–3 that the *gravitational* field of any spherically symmetric mass distribution, at any point outside the distribution, is the same as though all the mass were concentrated at the center. This is why we can treat spherical bodies as points when we calculate gravitational interactions.

We can also use this method for a conducting, hollow, spherical *shell* (a spherical conductor with a concentric spherical hole in the center) if there is no charge inside the hole. We take a spherical Gaussian surface with radius r less than the radius of the hole. If there *is* a field inside the hole, it must be spherically symmetric (radial) as before, so again $E = q/4\pi\epsilon_0 r^2$. But this time $q = 0$, so E must also be zero.

Can you use this same technique to find the electric field in the interspace between a charged sphere and a concentric hollow conducting sphere that surrounds it?   ■

Example 25–10   *Field of a line charge.* Electric charge is distributed uniformly along a long thin wire; the charge *per unit length* is λ. What is the electric field?

Solution   If the wire is very long and we are not too near either end, then from symmetry the field lines outside the wire are *radial* and lie in planes perpendicular to the wire. Also from symmetry the field magnitude depends only on the radial distance from the wire. This suggests that we use as a Gaussian surface a *cylinder* with arbitrary radius r and arbitrary length l, with its ends perpendicular to the wire, as in Fig. 25–11. The total charge within the Gaussian surface is λl. Because **E** is at right angles to the wire, the component of **E** normal to the end faces is zero. Thus the end faces make no contribution to the sum in Gauss's law. From symmetry, E has the same magnitude everywhere on the curved surface and is equal to $E_\perp$. The area of this surface is $2\pi rl$, so from Eq. (25–6) we find

$$(E)(2\pi rl) = \frac{\lambda l}{\epsilon_0} \quad \text{and} \quad E = \frac{1}{2\pi\epsilon_0}\frac{\lambda}{r}. \qquad (25\text{–}9)$$

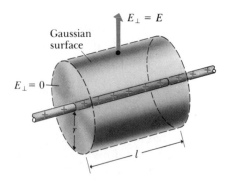

25–11
Cylindrical Gaussian surface for calculating the electric field due to a long charged wire.

Note that although the *entire* charge on the wire contributes to the field **E**, only the part of the total charge that is within the Gaussian surface is used when we apply Gauss's law. This may seem strange; it looks as though we have somehow obtained the right answer by ignoring part of the charge and that the field of a *short* wire of length *l* would be the same as that of a very long wire. But we do include the entire charge on the wire, although indirectly, when we make use of the *symmetry* of the problem. If the wire is short, the field is no longer uniform in magnitude over our Gaussian surface, and the problem is more complicated.

Can you use this method to show that the field at points outside a long uniformly charged cylinder is the same as though all the charge were concentrated on a line along its axis and to calculate the electric field in the interspace between a charged cylinder and a coaxial hollow conducting cylinder surrounding it? ■

Example 25–11   *Field of an infinite plane sheet of charge.* Find the electric field caused by a large, flat sheet of charge if the charge per unit area is σ.

25–12
Gaussian surface in the form of a cylinder for finding the field of an infinite plane sheet of charge.

Solution   We use the Gaussian surface shown by the shaded area in Fig. 25–12, a cylinder with its axis perpendicular to the sheet of charge, with ends of area A. From symmetry the electric field E has the same magnitude E on both sides of the surface, is uniform, and is directed normally away from the sheet of charge. No field lines cross the *side* walls of the cylinder, so $E_\perp$ at these walls is zero. At each end of the cylinder, $E_\perp$ is equal to E. The sum in Gauss's law therefore reduces to $2EA$. The net charge within the Gaussian surface is σA; Gauss's law, Eq. (25–6), gives

and

$$2AE = \frac{\sigma A}{\epsilon_0}$$

$$E = \frac{\sigma}{2\epsilon_0}. \qquad (25\text{–}10)$$

The field is uniform and perpendicular to the plane. Its magnitude is *independent* of the distance from the sheet. The field lines are straight, parallel, and uniformly spaced. This is because we have assumed the sheet to be infinitely large and to have zero thickness. These are idealizations; nothing in nature is really infinitely large or thin. But Eq. (25–10) is a good approximation to the electric field caused by a thin plane sheet of charge for points that are close to it and not too near its edges compared to its dimensions. In these regions the field is nearly uniform and perpendicular to the plane.

If the sheet of charge in this example is created by adding charge to a flat conducting sheet with finite thickness and with a total charge per unit area σ, and if there are no other charges around, the charge distributes itself symmetrically on the two surfaces of the conductor, with a charge per unit area of $\sigma/2$ on each surface. The field outside the conductor, near each surface, again has magnitude $\sigma/2\epsilon_0$. ■

Example 25–12   *Field between oppositely charged parallel conducting plates.* Two large plane parallel conducting plates are given equal and opposite charges; the charge per unit area is σ for one and $-\sigma$ for the other. Find the electric field in the region between the plates.

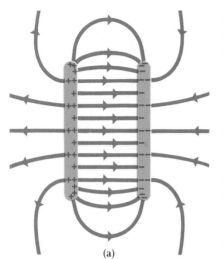

(a)

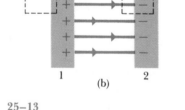

(b)

25–13
Electric field between oppositely charged parallel plates.

Solution The field between and around the plates is approximately as shown in Fig. 25–13a. Most of the charge accumulates at the opposing faces of the plates, and the field is nearly uniform in the space between them. A small amount of charge resides on the *outer* surfaces of the plates, and there is some spreading or "fringing" of the field at the edges. If the plates are very large in comparison to the distance between them, the fringing becomes negligible. In this case we can assume that the field is uniform, as in Fig. 25–13b, and that the charges are distributed uniformly over the opposing surfaces.

We can use Eq. (25–10) for each plate. The electric field at any point is the resultant of the fields due to two sheets of charge with opposite sign. At points a and c in Fig. 25–13b, each of the components $\mathbf{E}_1$ and $\mathbf{E}_2$ has magnitude $\sigma/2\epsilon_0$, but they have opposite directions, and their resultant is zero. At any point b between the plates the components are in the same direction; their resultant is

$$E = \frac{\sigma}{\epsilon_0}. \qquad (25\text{–}11)$$

We can also get this result by applying Gauss's law to the surfaces shown by broken lines. We leave this as a problem. ■

Example 25–13 Electric charge is distributed uniformly throughout the volume of a sphere of radius R; the total charge is Q. Find the electric-field magnitude at a point P inside the sphere at a distance r from the center.

Solution We choose as our Gaussian surface a sphere of radius r, concentric with the charge distribution. The charge per unit volume, which we may call the volume charge density ρ, is given by

$$\rho = \frac{Q}{4\pi R^3/3}.$$

The volume V' enclosed by the Gaussian surface is $\frac{4}{3}\pi r^3$, so the total charge q enclosed by that surface is

$$q = \rho V' = \frac{Q}{4\pi R^3/3}\left(\frac{4}{3}\pi r^3\right) = Q\frac{r^3}{R^3}.$$

From symmetry the electric-field magnitude has the same value E at every point on the Gaussian surface, and its direction at every point is radially outward. The total area of the surface is $4\pi r^2$, so the value of the sum in Gauss's law is simply $4\pi r^2 E$. We equate this to q/ϵ_0, with q given by the above equation. We find

$$4\pi r^2 E = \frac{Qr^3}{\epsilon_0 R^3} \quad \text{or} \quad E = \frac{1}{4\pi\epsilon_0}\frac{Qr}{R^3}. \qquad (25\text{–}12)$$

The field magnitude is proportional to the distance r of the field point from the center of the sphere. At the center ($r = 0$), $E = 0$, as we should expect from symmetry. At the surface of the sphere ($r = R$), the field

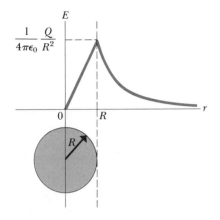

25–14
The electric field due to a solid sphere of charge with radius R is zero at the center, proportional to r inside the sphere, greatest at the surface where $r = R$, and proportional to $1/r^2$ outside the sphere.

magnitude is

$$E = \frac{1}{4\pi\epsilon_0} \frac{Q}{R^2}.$$

This shows that at the surface the field has the same magnitude as though all the charge were concentrated at the center. As we have learned, this is also the case at any field point farther from the center than R.

Figure 25–14 is a graph of E as a function of r for this problem. For $r < R$, E is directly proportional to r, and for $r > R$, E varies as $1/r^2$. We remarked earlier that there is a Gauss's law for gravitational interactions. The result of this example is directly applicable to the gravitational field inside the earth. If we could drill a hole through the earth to its center, and if the density were uniform, we would find that the gravitational field varies with r in the same way as the $\boldsymbol{E}$ field in Fig. 25–14. The *direction* of the gravitational field is toward the center; gravitational forces are always attractive.

Table 25–1 summarizes the electric fields caused by several simple charge distributions.

TABLE 25–1	Electric fields for simple charge distributions	
Charge distribution	**Point in electric field**	**Electric-field magnitude**
Single point charge q	Distance r from q	$E = \dfrac{1}{4\pi\epsilon_0} \dfrac{q}{r^2}$
Charge q on surface of conducting sphere with radius R	Outside sphere, $r > R$	$E = \dfrac{1}{4\pi\epsilon_0} \dfrac{q}{r^2}$
	Inside sphere, $r < R$	$E = 0$
Long wire, charge per unit length λ	Distance r from wire	$E = \dfrac{1}{2\pi\epsilon_0} \dfrac{\lambda}{r}$
Long conducting cylinder with radius R, charge per unit length λ	Outside cylinder, $r > R$	$E = \dfrac{1}{2\pi\epsilon_0} \dfrac{\lambda}{r}$
	Inside cylinder, $r < R$	$E = 0$
Solid sphere, charge Q distributed uniformly through volume	Outside sphere, $r > R$	$E = \dfrac{1}{4\pi\epsilon_0} \dfrac{Q}{r^2}$
	Inside sphere, $r < R$	$E = \dfrac{1}{4\pi\epsilon_0} \dfrac{Qr}{R^3}$
Two oppositely charged conducting plates, with surface charge densities σ and $-\sigma$	Any point between plates	$E = \dfrac{\sigma}{\epsilon_0}$

Charges on Conductors

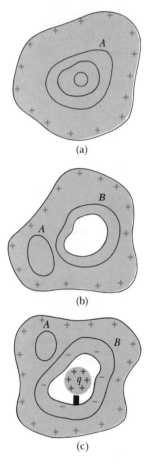

25–15

(a) Charge on a solid conductor resides entirely on its outer surface. (b) If there is no charge inside the cavity, the net charge on the surface of the cavity is zero. (c) If there is a charge q inside the cavity, the total charge on the cavity surface is $-q$.

We have learned that in any electrostatic problem (i.e., one with no moving charges) the electric field at every point within a conductor is zero and that charge on a solid conductor is located entirely on its surface, as shown in Fig. 25–15a. But what if there is a cavity inside the conductor, as in Fig. 25–15b? If there is no charge in the cavity, we can use a Gaussian surface such as B to show that the net charge on the surface *of the cavity* must be zero because $E = 0$ everywhere on the Gaussian surface. In fact, we can prove that in this situation no charge is present *anywhere* on the cavity surface, but we will postpone detailed proof of that statement until Chapter 26.

Now suppose we place a small conductor with a charge q inside the cavity, as in Fig. 25–15c. Again $E = 0$ everywhere on surface B, so according to Gauss's law the *total* charge inside this surface must be zero. Therefore there must be a total charge $-q$ on the cavity surface. The *total* charge on the outer conductor cannot change, so a charge $+q$ must appear on its outer surface. If the outer surface originally had a charge q', then the total charge on the outer surface after the charge q is inserted into the cavity must be $q + q'$.

With this prelude we are ready to consider a historic experiment, shown in Fig. 25–16. We mount a conducting container, such as a tin can with a lid, on an insulating stand. The container is initially uncharged. Then we hang a charged metal ball from an insulating thread, lower it into the can, and put the lid on, as in Fig. 25–16b. Charges are induced on the walls of the container, as shown. But now we let the ball *touch* the inner wall, as in Fig. 25–16c. The surface of the ball becomes, in effect, part of the cavity surface. The situation is now the same as Fig. 25–15b; if Gauss's law is correct, the net charge on this surface must be zero. Thus the ball must lose all its charge. Finally, we pull the ball out; we find that it has indeed lost all its charge.

This experiment was first performed by Faraday, using a metal icepail with a lid, and it is called **Faraday's icepail experiment.** The result confirms the validity of Gauss's law and therefore of Coulomb's law. Faraday's result was particularly significant because Coulomb's experimental method, using a torsion balance and dividing of charges, was not very precise. It is very difficult to confirm the $1/r^2$ dependence of the electrostatic force with great precision by direct force measurements. Faraday's experiment tests the validity of Gauss's law and therefore of Coulomb's law with potentially much greater precision.

A contemporary version of this experiment is shown in Fig. 25–17. The details of the box labeled "power supply" aren't important; its job is to place charge on the outer sphere and remove it, on demand. The inner box with a dial is a sensitive electrometer, an instrument that can detect motion of extremely small amounts of charge between the outer and inner spheres. If Gauss's law is correct, there can never be any charge on the inner surface of the outer sphere. If so, there should be no flow of charge through the electrometer while the outer sphere is being charged and discharged. The fact that no flow is actually observed is a

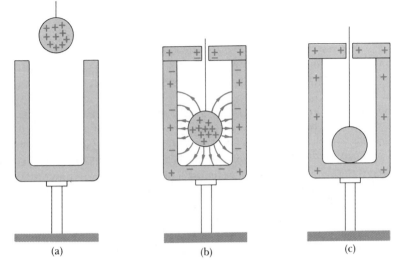

25–16
(a) A charged conducting ball suspended by an insulating thread outside a conducting container on an insulating stand. (b) The ball is lowered into the container, and the lid is put on. Charges are induced on the walls of the container. (c) When the ball is touched to the inner surface of the container, all its charge is transferred to the container and appears on its outer surface.

(a)   (b)   (c)

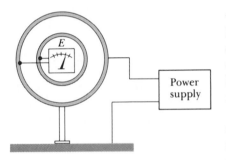

25–17
The outer surface can be alternately charged and discharged by the power supply to which it is connected. If there is any flow of charge between the inner and outer surfaces, it is detected by the electrometer inside the inner surface.

very sensitive confirmation of Gauss's law and therefore of Coulomb's law. The precision of the experiment is limited mainly by the sensitivity of the electrometer, which can be astonishing. The most recent (1971) experiments have shown that the exponent 2 in the $1/r^2$ of Coulomb's law does not differ from precisely 2 by more than 10^{-15}. So there is no reason to suspect that it is anything other than exactly 2.

This discussion also forms the basis for **electrostatic shielding,** shown in Fig. 25–18. Suppose we have a very sensitive electronic instrument that we want to protect from stray electric fields that might cause erroneous measurements. We surround the instrument with a conducting box, or we line the walls, floor, and ceiling of the room with a conducting material such as sheet copper. The external electric field redistributes the free electrons in the conductor, leaving a net positive charge on the outer surface in some regions and a net negative charge in others, as shown in Fig. 25–18. This charge distribution causes an additional electric field such that the *total* field at every point inside the box is zero, as Gauss's law says it must be. The charge distribution on the box also alters the shapes of the field lines near the box, as the figure shows.

25–18
A conducting box in a uniform electric field. The field pushes electrons toward the left, leaving a net negative charge on the left side and a net positive charge on the right. The total electric field at every point inside the box is zero; the shapes of the exterior field lines near the box are somewhat changed.

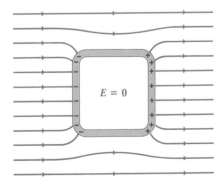

Questions

25–1 It was shown in the text that the electric field inside a spherical hole in a conductor is zero. Is this also true for a cubical hole? Can the same argument be used?

25–2 Coulomb's law and Newton's law of gravitation have the same *form*. Can Gauss's law be applied to gravitational fields as well as electric fields? Is so, what modifications are needed?

25–3 By considering how the field lines must look near a conducting surface, can you see why the charge density and electric-field magnitude at the surface of an irregularly shaped solid conductor must be greatest in regions where the surface curves most sharply and least in flat regions?

25–4 The electric field and the velocity field in a moving fluid are two examples of vector fields. Think of several other examples. There are also *scalar* fields, which associate a single number with each point in space. Temperature is an example; think of several others.

25–5 Consider the electric field caused by two point charges separated by some distance. Suppose there is a point where the field is zero. What does this tell you about the *signs* of the charges?

25–6 Does an electric charge experience a force due to the field that the charge itself produces?

25–7 A particle having electric charge and mass moves in an electric field. If it starts from rest, does it always move along the field line that passes through its starting point? Explain.

25–8 If the exponent 2 in the r^2 of Coulomb's law were 3 instead, would Gauss's law still be valid?

25–9 A student claimed that an appropriate unit for electric field magnitude is $1 \ \mathrm{J \cdot C^{-1} \cdot m^{-1}}$. Is this correct?

25–10 A certain region of space bounded by an imaginary closed surface contains no charge. Is the electric field always zero everywhere on the surface? If not,

under what circumstances is it zero on the surface?

25–11 A student claimed that the electric field produced by a dipole is represented by field lines that cross each other. Is this correct? Is there any simple rule governing field lines for a superposition of fields due to point charges if the field lines due to the separate charges are known? Do field lines *ever* cross?

25–12 Nineteenth-century physicists liked to give everything mechanical attributes. Faraday and his contemporaries thought of field lines as elastic strings that repelled each other and arranged themselves in equilibrium under the action of their elastic tension and mutual repulsion. Try this picture on several examples and decide whether it makes any sense. (These mechanical properties are of course now known to be completely fictitious.)

25–13 Are Coulomb's law and Gauss's law *completely* equivalent? Are there any situations in electrostatics in which one is valid and the other is not?

25–14 The text states that, in an electrostatic field, every field line must start on a positive charge and terminate on a negative charge. But suppose the field is that of a single positive point charge. Then what?

25–15 Is the total (net) electric charge in the universe positive, negative, or zero?

25–16 A lightning rod is a pointed copper rod mounted on top of a building and welded to a heavy copper cable running down into the ground. Lightning rods are used in prairie country to protect houses and barns from lightning; the lightning current runs through the copper rather than through the barn. Why? Why should the end of the rod be pointed? (The answer to Question 25–3 may be helpful.)

25–17 When a high-voltage power line falls on your car, you are safe as long as you stay in the car; but when you step out, you could be electrocuted. Why? What about a car as a safe place in a thunderstorm?

Exercises

Section 25–1   *Electric Field and Electrical Forces*

25–1 Find the magnitude and direction of the electric field at a point 0.500 m directly above a particle having an electric charge of $+3.00 \times 10^{-6}$ C.

25–2 The electric field caused by a certain point charge has a magnitude of $6.50 \times 10^3 \ \mathrm{N \cdot C^{-1}}$ at a distance 0.100 m from the charge. What is the magnitude of the charge?

25–3 At what distance from a particle with a charge of 5.00×10^{-9} C does the electric field of that charge have a magnitude of $4.00 \ \mathrm{N \cdot C^{-1}}$?

25–4

a) What is the electric field of a gold nucleus at a distance of 3.00×10^{-14} m from the nucleus? The atomic number of gold is 79.

b) What is the electric field of a proton at a distance of 5.28×10^{-11} m from the proton?

25–5 A small object carrying a charge of -8.00×10^{-9} C experiences a downward force of 20.0×10^{-9} N when placed at a certain point in an electric field.

a) What is the electric field at the point in magnitude and direction?

b) What would be the magnitude and direction of the force acting on a proton placed at this same point in the electric field?

25–6 What must be the charge (sign and magnitude) on a particle with a mass of 8.40 g for it to remain stationary in the laboratory when placed in a downward-directed electric field of magnitude 5000 N·C^{-1}?

25–7 What is the magnitude of an electric field in which the Coulomb force on an electron is equal in magnitude to the weight of the electron?

25–8 A uniform electric field exists in the region between two oppositely charged plane parallel plates. An electron is released from rest at the surface of the negatively charged plate and strikes the surface of the opposite plate, 3.20 cm distant from the first, in a time interval of 1.50×10^{-8} s.

a) Find the electric field magnitude.

b) Find the speed of the electron when it strikes the second plate.

25–9 An electron is projected with an initial speed $v_0 = 5.00 \times 10^6$ m·s^{-1} into the uniform field between the parallel plates in Fig. 25–19. The direction of the field is vertically downward, and the field is zero except in the space between the two plates. The electron enters the field at a point midway between the plates. If the electron just misses the upper plate as it emerges from the field, find the magnitude of the electric field.

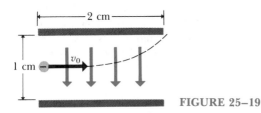

FIGURE 25–19

Section 25–2   Electric-Field Calculations

25–10 Two particles having charges $q_1 = 1.00 \times 10^{-9}$ C and $q_2 = 2.00 \times 10^{-9}$ C are separated by a distance of 1.60 m. At what point along the line passing through the charges is the total electric field due to the two charges equal to zero?

25–11 A point charge $q_1 = -4.00 \times 10^{-9}$ C is at the origin, and a second point charge $q_2 = +6.00 \times 10^{-9}$ C is on the x-axis at $x = 0.800$ m. Find the electric field

(magnitude and direction) at each of the following points on the x-axis:

a) $x = 0.200$ m;

b) $x = 1.20$ m;

c) $x = -0.200$ m.

25–12 In a rectangular coordinate system a charge of 60.0×10^{-9} C is placed at the origin of coordinates, and a charge of -60.0×10^{-9} C is placed at the point $x = 6.00$ m, $y = 0$. What are the magnitude and direction of the electric field at

a) $x = 3.00$ m, $y = 0$?

b) $x = 3.00$ m, $y = 4.00$ m?

25–13 A point charge $q_1 = +6.00 \times 10^{-9}$ C is at the point $x = 0.800$ m, $y = 0.600$ m, and a second point charge $q_2 = -2.00 \times 10^{-9}$ C is at the point $x = 0.800$ m, $y = 0$. Calculate the magnitude and direction of the resultant electric field at the origin due to these two point charges.

25–14 In a rectangular coordinate system a positive point charge with a magnitude of 2.50×10^{-8} C is placed at the point $x = +0.100$ m, $y = 0$, and an identical point charge is placed at $x = -0.100$ m, $y = 0$. Find the magnitude and direction of the electric field at the following points:

a) the origin;

b) $x = 0.200$ m, $y = 0$;

c) $x = 0.100$ m, $y = 0.150$ m;

d) $x = 0$, $y = 0.100$ m.

25–15 Repeat Exercise 25–14, for the case where the point charge at $x = +0.100$ m, $y = 0$ is positive and the other is negative.

Section 25–4   Gauss's Law

25–16 The electric flux through a closed surface is found to be 1.40 N·m^2·C^{-1}. What quantity of charge is enclosed by the surface?

25–17 A closed surface encloses a net charge of 2.50×10^{-6} C. What is the net electric flux through the surface?

25–18 A point charge $q = 8.00 \times 10^{-9}$ C is at the center of a cube with sides of length 0.200 m. What is the electric flux through one of the six faces of the cube?

Section 25–5   Applications of Gauss's Law

Section 25–6   Charges on Conductors

25–19 What is the charge per unit area, in coulombs per square meter, of an infinite plane sheet of charge if the electric field produced by the sheet of charge has a magnitude of 4.50 N·C^{-1}?

25–20 How many excess electrons must be added to an isolated spherical conductor 0.100 m in diameter to produce an electric field of 1800 N·C^{-1} just outside the surface?

25–21 The electric field in the region between a pair of oppositely charged plane parallel conducting plates, each 100 cm^2 in area, is 7.20×10^3 N·C^{-1}. What is the charge on each plate? Neglect edge effects.

25–22 A long, straight wire has a charge per unit length of 3.00×10^{-12} C·m^{-1}. At what distance from the wire is the electric field equal to 0.600 N·C^{-1}?

25–23 Prove that the electric field outside an infinitely long cylindrical conductor with a uniform surface charge is the same as if all the charge were on the axis.

25–24 Apply Gauss's law to each of the four dotted Gaussian surfaces in Fig. 25–13b to calculate the electric field between and outside the plates.

25–25 A conducting sphere carrying charge q has radius a. It is inside a concentric hollow conducting sphere of inner radius b and outer radius c. The hollow sphere has no net charge. Calculate the electric field for

a) $r < a$,

b) $a < r < b$,

c) $b < r < c$,

d) $r > c$.

e) What is the charge on the inner surface of the hollow sphere?

f) What is the charge on the outer surface?

Problems

25–26 The earth has a net electric charge that causes a field at points near its surface of the order of 100 N·C^{-1}.

a) If the earth is regarded as a conducting sphere of radius 6.38×10^6 m, what is the magnitude of its charge?

b) How much charge would a 60.0-kg human have to acquire to overcome his or her weight by repulsion by the earth's charge? Is electrostatic repulsion a feasible means of flight?

25–27 A small sphere whose mass is 0.600 g carries a charge of 3.00×10^{-9} C and is attached to one end of a silk fiber 8.00 cm long. The other end of the fiber is attached to a large vertical conducting plate, which has a surface charge of 25.0×10^{-6} C·m^{-2} on each side. Find the angle the fiber makes with the vertical plate when the sphere is in equilibrium.

25–28 A negative point charge $q_1 = -5.00 \times 10^{-9}$ C is on the x-axis at $x = 1.20$ m. A second point charge q_2 is on the x-axis at $x = -0.60$ m. What must be the sign and magnitude of q_2 for the resultant electric field at the origin to be

a) 45.0 N·C^{-1} in the +x-direction?

b) 45.0 N·C^{-1} in the −x-direction?

25–29 An electron is projected into a uniform electric field that has a magnitude of 500 N·C^{-1}. The direction of the field is vertically upward. The initial velocity of the electron has a magnitude of 6.00×10^6 m·s^{-1}, and its direction is at an angle of 30.0° above the horizontal.

a) Find the maximum distance the electron rises vertically above its initial elevation.

b) After what horizontal distance does the electron return to its original elevation?

c) Sketch the trajectory of the electron.

25–30 A point charge $q_1 = 2.50 \times 10^{-9}$ C is located at the origin, and a second point charge $q_2 = 5.00 \times 10^{-9}$ C is on the x-axis at $x = 1.00$ m. What is the total electric flux due to these two point charges through a spherical surface with a radius of 0.500 m, centered at the origin?

25–31 A charge of 16.0×10^{-9} C is placed at the origin of coordinates; a second charge of unknown magnitude is at $x = 3.00$ m, $y = 0$; and a third charge of 12.0×10^{-9} C is at $x = 6.00$ m, $y = 0$. What are the sign and magnitude of the unknown charge if the resultant field at $x = 8.00$ m, $y = 0$ has a magnitude of 18.0 N·C^{-1} and is directed to the right?

25–32 The electric field E in Fig. 25–20 is everywhere parallel to the x-axis. The field has the same magnitude at all points in any given plane perpendicular to the x-axis (parallel to the yz-plane), but the magnitude is different for various planes. That is, E_x depends on x but not on y and z, and E_y and E_z are zero. At points *in*

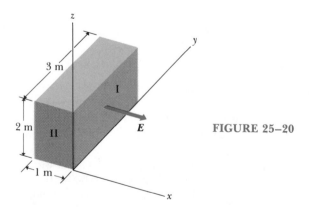

FIGURE 25–20

the yz-plane, $E_x = 300$ N·C^{-1}. (The volume shown could be a section of a large insulating slab 1 m thick, with its faces parallel to the yz-plane and with a uniform volume charge distribution imbedded in it.)

a) What is the electric flux through surface I in Fig. 25–20?

b) What is the electric flux through surface II?

c) If there is a total positive charge of 26.6×10^{-9} C within the volume, what are the magnitude and direction of $\mathbf{E}$ at the face opposite I?

25–33 A uniform electric field $\mathbf{E}_1$ is directed out of one face of a parallelopiped, and another uniform electric field $\mathbf{E}_2$ is directed into the opposite face, as shown in Fig. 25–21. $\mathbf{E}_1$ has a magnitude of 3.00×10^4 N·C^{-1}, and $\mathbf{E}_2$ has a magnitude of 5.00×10^4 N·C^{-1}. Assuming that there are no other electric-field lines crossing the surfaces of the parallelopiped, determine the net charge contained within.

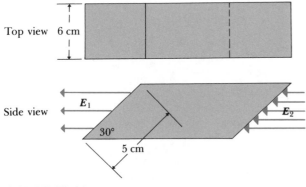

FIGURE 25–21

25–34 A long coaxial cable consists of an inner cylindrical conductor with radius a and an outer coaxial cylinder with inner radius b and outer radius c. The outer cylinder is mounted on insulating supports and has no net charge. The inner cylinder has a uniform positive charge λ per unit length. Calculate the electric field

a) at any point between the cylinders, a distance r from the axis;

b) at any point outside the outer cylinder.

c) Sketch a graph of the magnitude of the electric field as a function of the distance r from the axis of the cable, from $r = 0$ to $r = 2c$.

d) Find the charge per unit length on the inner surface of the outer cylinder and on the outer surface.

25–35 A conducting spherical shell with inner radius a and outer radius b has a positive point charge Q located at its center. The total charge on the shell is $-4Q$, and it is insulated from its surroundings.

a) Derive expressions for the electric-field magnitude in terms of the distance r from the center for the regions $r < a$, $a < r < b$, and $r > b$.

b) What is the surface charge density on the inner surface of the conducting shell?

c) What is the surface charge density on the outer surface of the conducting shell?

d) Draw a sketch showing electric-field lines and the location of all charges.

e) Draw a graph of the electric field as a function of r.

25–36 Suppose that positive charge is uniformly distributed through a very long cylindrical volume of radius R with charge per unit volume ρ.

a) Derive the expression for the electric field inside the volume at a distance r from the axis of the cylinder in terms of the charge density ρ.

b) What is the electric field at a point outside the volume in terms of the charge per unit length λ in the cylinder?

c) Compare the answers to parts (a) and (b) when $r = R$.

d) Sketch a graph of the magnitude of the electric field as a function of r from $r = 0$ to $r = 3R$.

Challenge Problems

25–37 Two charges are placed as shown in Fig. 25–22. It is known that the magnitude of q_1 is 8.00×10^{-9} C, but its sign and the value of the other charge, q_2, are not known. The direction of the resultant electric field $\mathbf{E}$ at point P is in the negative y-direction.

a) Considering the different possible signs of q_1 and q_2, there are four possible diagrams that could represent the electric fields $\mathbf{E}_1$ and $\mathbf{E}_2$ produced by q_1 and q_2. Sketch the four possible electric field configurations.

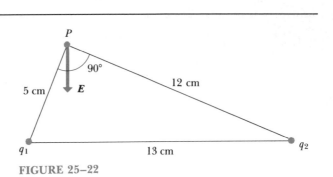

FIGURE 25–22

b) Using the sketches from part (a) and the fact that the net electric field at P has no x-component and a negative y-component, deduce the signs of q_1 and q_2.

c) Determine the magnitude of the resultant field $\boldsymbol{E}$.

25–38 Positive charge Q is distributed uniformly over each of two spherical volumes of radius R. One sphere of charge is centered at the origin and the other at $x = 2R$, as shown in Fig. 25–23. Find the magnitude and direction of the resultant electric field due to these two distributions of charge at the following points on the x-axis:

a) $x = 0$;

b) $x = R/2$;

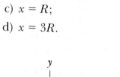

c) $x = R$;

d) $x = 3R$.

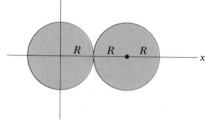

FIGURE 25–23

Electrical Potential

The concept of *potential* is directly tied to potential energies associated with electrical interactions. We can use this concept in a wide variety of problems, including electric circuits, deflection of electron beams in TV picture tubes, high-energy particle accelerators, and many others. The concepts of *work* and *energy* (Chapter 7) gave us an important analytical method for mechanics problems, and energy concepts are just as important in electricity and mag-

netism. In this chapter we apply work and energy considerations to the electric field. When a charged particle moves in an electric field, the electric-field force does *work* on the particle. This work can always be expressed in terms of a potential energy, which in turn is associated with a new concept called *electrical potential* or simply *potential*. We will work out several examples of calculations of potential and practical applications of this concept.

26–1
Electrical Potential Energy

The opening sections of this chapter are about work, potential energy, and conservation of energy. It would be a good idea to review Chapter 7 now to make sure the basic concepts are clearly in mind. Two points need special emphasis.

First, potential energy is always associated with *work* done by a force acting on a particle. When a particle moves from a point where its potential energy is U_1 to a point where it is U_2, the force does an amount of work given by

$$W_{1 \to 2} = U_1 - U_2. \tag{26–1}$$

This may look backward, but it isn't. When the work is positive, the potential energy *decreases*. That's what happens when a body falls from a high point (1) to a lower point (2) under the action of the earth's gravity. The force of gravity does positive work, and the potential energy decreases.

Second, the work–energy theorem says that the change in kinetic energy $(K_2 - K_1)$ during any displacement is equal to the total work done on the particle during this displacement. So if Eq. (26–1) gives the *total* work done on the particle, then $K_2 - K_1 = U_1 - U_2$, which we usually write as

$$K_1 + U_1 = K_2 + U_2. \tag{26–2}$$

This is the principle of conservation of energy. It is valid whenever the *total* work done on the particle is given by Eq. (26–1), that is, when W_{other}, as defined in Sections 7–5 and 7–6, is zero.

Let's look at an electrical example of these basic concepts. When a charged particle moves in an electric field, the field exerts a force on the particle and does *work* on it. In Fig. 26–1 a pair of charged parallel metal plates sets up a uniform electric field of magnitude E, and the force on a test charge q' has magnitude $F = q'E$. When the charge moves from point a to point b, the work done by this force on the test charge is

$$W_{a \to b} = Fd = q'Ed. \tag{26–3}$$

We can represent this work with a **potential-energy** function U, just as we did for gravitational potential energy in Section 7–5. If we take the potential energy to be zero at point b (i.e., $U_b = 0$), then at point a it has the value $U_a = q'Ed$, and we may say

$$W_{a \to b} = U_a - U_b. \tag{26–4}$$

More generally, the potential energy at any point at a distance y above the bottom plate is given by

$$U(y) = q'Ey, \tag{26–5}$$

and when the test charge moves from height y_1 to height y_2, the work done on the charge by the field is given by

$$W_{1 \to 2} = U(y_1) - U(y_2) = q'Ey_1 - q'Ey_2. \tag{26–6}$$

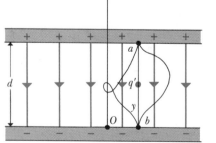

26–1
A test charge q' moving from a to b experiences a force of magnitude $q'E$; the work done by this force is $W_{a \to b} = q'Ed$ and is independent of the particle's path.

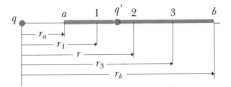

26–2
Charge q' moves along a straight line extending radially from charge q. As it moves from a to b, the distance varies from r_a to r_b.

When y_1 is greater than y_2, U decreases, and the field does positive work; when y_1 is less than y_2, U increases, and the field does negative work. If the particle has speed v_1 at height y_1 and speed v_2 at height y_2, then conservation of energy, Eq. (26–2), gives the relation

$$\tfrac{1}{2}mv_1^2 + q'Ey_1 = \tfrac{1}{2}mv_2^2 + q'Ey_2.$$

This whole situation is directly analogous to the motion of a particle in a uniform gravitational field, with its associated work and potential energy.

The work done by the electric-field force depends only on the change in the coordinate y and is independent of the *path* of the particle. We call such a force field a **conservative force field;** we defined this term in Section 7–7. In fact, we are about to prove that *every* electric field produced by charges at rest is a conservative force field and has an associated potential energy.

Let's think next about the work done on a test charge q' moving in the electric field caused by a single stationary point charge q. (We will assume that both q and q' are positive.) This force field is *not* uniform, and we can't calculate work by simply multiplying force times distance. Let's first calculate the work done on q' during a displacement along the *radial* line in Fig. 26–2, from point a to point b through points 1, 2, and 3. The magnitude F of the force acting on charge q' is given by Coulomb's law:

$$F = \frac{1}{4\pi\epsilon_0}\frac{qq'}{r^2}.$$

In the first displacement, from r_a to r_1, the force varies from $qq'/4\pi\epsilon_0 r_a^2$ to $qq'/4\pi\epsilon_0 r_1^2$; an approximate average force for the interval is $qq'/4\pi\epsilon_0 r_a r_1$. (For example, if $r_a = 1.00$ m and $r_1 = 1.10$ m, then $1/r_a^2 = 1.00$ m^{-2}, $1/r_1^2 = 0.823$ m^{-2}, and $1/r_a r_1 = 0.909$ m^{-2}.) Then the work done during this first displacement is approximately

$$W_{a\to1} = F_{av}\,\Delta s = \frac{qq'}{4\pi\epsilon_0 r_a r_1}(r_1 - r_a),$$

which we can rearrange to be

$$W_{a\to1} = \frac{qq'}{4\pi\epsilon_0}\left(\frac{1}{r_a} - \frac{1}{r_1}\right). \tag{26–7}$$

We can write similar expressions for the work in each of the other intervals:

$$W_{1\to2} = \frac{qq'}{4\pi\epsilon_0}\left(\frac{1}{r_1} - \frac{1}{r_2}\right),$$

$$W_{2\to3} = \frac{qq'}{4\pi\epsilon_0}\left(\frac{1}{r_2} - \frac{1}{r_3}\right),$$

$$W_{3\to b} = \frac{qq'}{4\pi\epsilon_0}\left(\frac{1}{r_3} - \frac{1}{r_b}\right).$$

The total work $W_{a\to b}$ done on q' is approximately equal to the sum of all these contributions:

$$W_{a\to b} = W_{a\to1} + W_{1\to2} + W_{2\to3} + W_{3\to b}.$$

When we add these, all the terms containing r_1, r_2, and r_3 drop out, leaving

$$W_{a \to b} = \frac{qq'}{4\pi\epsilon_0}\left(\frac{1}{r_a} - \frac{1}{r_b}\right). \qquad (26\text{-}8)$$

This result may seem to be only an approximation because we have used an *average* force in each interval. But we could just as well divide the interval from a to b into ten or a million intervals, and then the force would change very little in each interval. The same cancellation would occur in the calculations. In the limit, when we take a very large number of intervals, the error disappears completely. We conclude that Eq. (26–8) is in fact *exactly* correct. This conclusion can be confirmed easily by methods of integral calculus that we won't discuss here.

The work for this particular path depends only on the distances r_a and r_b. We have not yet proved that the work is the same for *all possible* paths from a to b, but it is! To prove this, we consider the more general displacement shown in Fig. 26–3, where a and b *do not* lie on the same radial line. Again we divide the path into segments; call a typical one Δs. The work done on q' in this interval is now given by Eq. (7–2): $W = F \Delta s \cos \theta$. But the figure shows that $\Delta s \cos \theta$ is equal to $\Delta r = r_1 - r_a$ for the first segment, so Eq. (26–7) still gives the work for this segment. The same thing is true for every other segment, and when we add up the quantities of work for all the segments, the same cancellation occurs as before. The final result is that Eq. (26–8) gives the total work done by the field during *any* displacement from an initial distance r_a to a final distance r_b, whether the path is along a radial line or not.

This result also proves that this force field is *conservative*. The work done on q' by the *E* field produced by q depends only on r_a and r_b, not on

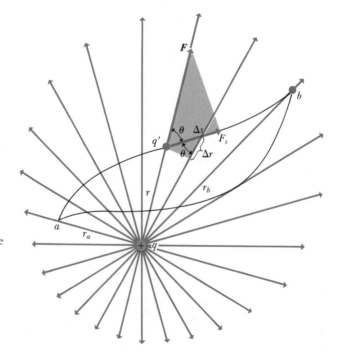

26–3

The work done by the electric-field force on charge q' depends only on the distances r_a and r_b.

the details of the path. Also, if q' returns to its starting point a by a different path, the total work done in the round-trip displacement is zero. These are the needed characteristics for a conservative force field, as we defined it in Section 7–7.

Comparing Eqs. (26–4) and (26–8), we see that the term $qq'/4\pi\epsilon_0 r_a$ is the potential energy U_a when q' is at point a, at distance r_a from q, and $qq'/4\pi\epsilon_0 r_b$ is the potential energy U_b when it is at point b, at distance r_b from q. Thus the potential energy U of the test charge q' at *any* distance r from charge q is given by

$$U = \frac{1}{4\pi\epsilon_0} \frac{qq'}{r}. \tag{26–9}$$

This is correct whether the product qq' is positive or negative.

Example 26–1   A small plastic ball with a mass of 2.0 g and an electric charge of $+0.10\ \mu C$ moves in the vicinity of a stationary metal ball with a charge of $+2.0\ \mu C$. When the plastic ball is 0.10 m from the metal one, the plastic ball is moving directly away from the metal ball with a speed of $5.0\ \text{m·s}^{-1}$.

a) What is the speed of the plastic ball when the two balls are 0.20 m apart?

b) How would the situation change if the plastic ball had a charge of $-0.10\ \mu C$?

Solution

a) The force is conservative, so energy (kinetic plus potential) is conserved. Recalling the problem-solving strategy of Section 7–5, we list the initial and final kinetic and potential energies, K_1, K_2, U_1, and U_2:

$$K_1 = \tfrac{1}{2}mv_1^2 = \tfrac{1}{2}(2.0 \times 10^{-3}\ \text{kg})(5.0\ \text{m·s}^{-1})^2 = 0.025\ \text{J},$$

$$K_2 = \tfrac{1}{2}mv_2^2 = \tfrac{1}{2}(2.0 \times 10^{-3}\ \text{kg})v_2^2,$$

$$U_1 = \frac{1}{4\pi\epsilon_0} \frac{q_1 q_2}{r_1}$$

$$= (9.0 \times 10^9\ \text{N·m}^2\text{·C}^{-2})\frac{(0.10 \times 10^{-6}\ \text{C})(2.0 \times 10^{-6}\ \text{C})}{0.10\ \text{m}}$$

$$= 0.0180\ \text{J},$$

$$U_2 = (9.0 \times 10^9\ \text{N·m}^2\text{·C}^{-2})\frac{(0.10 \times 10^{-6}\ \text{C})(2.0 \times 10^{-6}\ \text{C})}{0.20\ \text{m}}$$

$$= 0.0090\ \text{J}.$$

From conservation of energy we have

$$K_1 + U_1 = K_2 + U_2,$$

$$0.025\ \text{J} + 0.0180\ \text{J} = \tfrac{1}{2}(2.0 \times 10^{-3}\ \text{kg})v_2^2 + 0.0090\ \text{J},$$

and finally

$$v_2 = 5.8 \text{ m·s}^{-1}.$$

The force is repulsive, and the plastic ball speeds up as it moves away from the stationary charge.

b) If the moving charge is negative, the force on it is attractive rather than repulsive, and we expect the plastic ball to slow down rather than speed up. The only difference in the above calculations is that both potential-energy quantities are negative. The conservation-of-energy equation is

$$0.025 \text{ J} - 0.0180 \text{ J} = \tfrac{1}{2}(2.0 \times 10^{-3} \text{ kg})v_2{}^2 - 0.0090 \text{ J},$$

and

$$v_2 = 4.0 \text{ m·s}^{-1}.$$ ∎

It is easy to generalize Eq. (26–9) for situations where the field in which charge q' moves is caused by *several* point charges $q_1, q_2, q_3, \ldots$, at distances $r_1, r_2, r_3, \ldots$ from q'. The total electric field at each point is the *vector sum* of the fields due to the individual charges, and the total work done on q' during any displacement is the sum of the contributions from the individual charges. We conclude that the potential energy of a test charge q' at point a in Fig. 26–4, due to a collection of charges q_1, $q_2, q_3, \ldots$, at distances $r_1, r_2, r_3, \ldots$ from the test charge q' at point a, is given by

$$U = \frac{q'}{4\pi\epsilon_0}\left(\frac{q_1}{r_1} + \frac{q_2}{r_2} + \frac{q_3}{r_3} + \cdots\right) = \frac{q'}{4\pi\epsilon_0}\sum\frac{q_i}{r_i}. \qquad (26\text{–}10)$$

At a different point b the potential energy of q' is given by the same expression, but $r_1, r_2, \ldots$ are the distances from $q_1, q_2, \ldots$ to point b. The work done on charge q' when it moves from a to b along any path is equal to the difference $U_a - U_b$ between its potential energies at a and at b.

We can represent *any* charge distribution as a collection of point charges, so Eq. (26–10) shows that we can always find a potential-energy function for *any* static electric field. It follows that *every electric field due to a static charge distribution is a conservative force field.*

We mentioned in Chapter 7 that we can always add an arbitrary constant to a potential-energy function U in order to make U zero at some convenient reference position. For example, when a body moves in a uniform gravitational field, we can choose U to be zero at the surface of the earth. In Eqs. (26–9) and (26–10), U is zero when all the distances r_1, $r_2, \ldots$ are *infinite*, that is, when the test charge q' is very far away from all the charges that produce the field. Making $U = 0$ at infinity is the most convenient reference level for many electrostatic problems, but it is not the only possibility. In analysis of electric circuits, other reference levels are often more convenient.

Here's a final comment about our treatment of electrical potential energy. We have spoken consistently about the work done *by the electric-field force* on the charged particle moving in the field. In a displacement of the particle from point a to point b this work is always given by

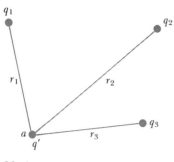

26–4
Potential energy of a charge q' at point a depends on charges q_1, q_2, and q_3 and on their distances r_1, r_2, and r_3 from point a.

$W_{a \to b} = U_a - U_b$. When U_a is greater than U_b, the field does positive work on the particle as it "falls" from a point of higher potential energy to a point of lower potential energy. This viewpoint is consistent with Chapter 7, in which we always talked about the work done on a particle by a gravitational field or by an elastic force.

An alternative viewpoint used in some books is that to "raise" a particle from a point b where the potential energy has the value U_b to a point a where it has a greater value U_a (pushing two positive charges closer together, for example), we would need to apply an additional force that *opposes* the electric-field force and does positive work. The potential-energy difference $U_a - U_b$ would then be defined as the work done *by that additional force* during the reverse displacement from b to a.

Our viewpoint, using gravitation as an example, is that the potential energy of a particle at tabletop height is greater than when it is on the floor because gravity does positive work on the particle as it falls from the table to the floor. The alternative view is that the particle has greater potential energy at tabletop level because somebody had to do work on it to lift it from the floor to the table. This alternative viewpoint is not wrong, but in our view it is sometimes confusing. We prefer to deal always with the work done *by the electric-field force* without introducing any hypothetical additional forces that may or may not be present in a particular problem. If you use other books for reference, beware of the possible confusion about these two alternative viewpoints.

26–2
Potential

In the first section we looked at the potential energy U of a test charge q' in an electric field. Just as the electric field describes the force on q' in a way that is independent of the magnitude of q', it is also useful to describe the potential energy independently of the test charge. To do this, we introduce the concept of *potential energy per unit charge*. This quantity is called **potential.** We define the potential at any point in an electric field as *the potential energy per unit charge* for a test charge q' at that point. We use the symbol V for potential:

$$V = \frac{U}{q'} \qquad \text{or} \qquad U = q'V. \qquad (26\text{--}11)$$

Potential energy and charge are both scalars, so potential is a scalar quantity. Its SI unit is 1 *joule per coulomb* (1 $J \cdot C^{-1}$). A potential of 1 $J \cdot C^{-1}$ is called 1 **volt** (1 V), in honor of the Italian scientist Alessandro Volta (1745–1827):

$$1 \text{ V} = 1 \text{ J} \cdot C^{-1}.$$

To put Eq. (26–4) on a "work per unit charge" basis, we divide both sides by q', obtaining

$$\frac{W_{a \to b}}{q'} = \frac{U_a}{q'} - \frac{U_b}{q'} = V_a - V_b, \qquad (26\text{--}12)$$

where $V_a = U_a/q'$ is the potential energy per unit charge at point a, and similarly for V_b. We call V_a and V_b the *potential at point a* and *potential at point b*, respectively. To find the potential V at a point due to any collection of point charges, we divide Eq. (26–10) by q':

$$V = \frac{U}{q'} = \frac{1}{4\pi\epsilon_0} \sum \frac{q_i}{r_i}. \qquad (26\text{–}13)$$

When we are given a collection of point charges, Eq. (26–13) is usually the easiest way to calculate the potential. But in some problems in which the E field is known or can be found easily, it is easier to work directly with the field. The force F on the test charge q' can be written as $F = q'E$. If we can calculate the work $W_{a \to b}$ done on q' when it moves from point a to point b, we can use Eq. (26–12) to find the difference in potential $V_a - V_b$. If we define V to be zero at a particular point, we can find V at any other point. At every point the direction of E is always the direction of most rapid *decrease* of V.

The difference $V_a - V_b$ is called the *potential of a with respect to b*; we sometimes abbreviate this difference as $V_{ab} = V_a - V_b$. Note that potential, like electric field, is independent of the test charge q' we use to define it. When a positive test charge moves from a region of high potential to one of lower potential (that is, $V_b < V_a$), the electric field does positive work on it. A positive charge tends to "fall" from a high-potential region to a lower-potential one. The opposite is true for a negative charge.

An instrument that measures the difference of potential between two points is called a *voltmeter*. The principle of the common type of moving-coil voltmeter will be described later. There are also much more sensitive potential-measuring devices that use electronic amplification. Instruments that can measure a potential difference of 1 μV are common, and sensitivities down to 10^{-12} V can be attained.

PROBLEM-SOLVING STRATEGY: *Potential Calculations*

1. Remember that potential is simply *potential energy per unit charge*. Understanding this simple statement can get you a long way.

2. To find the potential due to a collection of point charges, use Eq. (26–13). If you are given a continuous charge distribution, you have to divide it into small elements that you can consider as points and try to find a way to carry out the sum in Eq. (26–13). Sometimes this is easy; sometimes integral calculus is needed, although not for the problems in this book.

3. If you are given the electric field or if you can find it using any of the methods of Chapter 25, it may be easier to calculate the work done on a test charge, during a displacement from point a to point b, and then use Eq. (26–12). When it is appropriate, make use of your freedom to define V to be zero at some convenient place. For point charges this will usually be at infinity, but for other distributions of charge (especially those that extend to infinity themselves) it may be convenient or necessary to define V to be zero at some finite distance from the charge distribution, say at point b. Then the potential at any other point, say a, can be found from Eq. (26–12), with $V_b = 0$.

4. Remember that potential is a *scalar* quantity, not a *vector*. Don't get carried away and try to use components. A scalar quantity doesn't have components, and it would be wrong to try to use components.

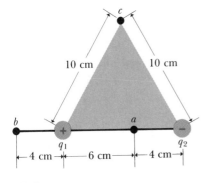

26–5
Charge distribution for Examples 26–2
and 26–3.

Example 26–2   Point charges of $+12 \times 10^{-9}$ C and -12×10^{-9} C are placed 10 cm apart, as in Fig. 26–5. Compute the potentials at points a, b, and c.

Solution   This is the same arrangement of charges as in Example 25–5. This time we have to evaluate the *algebraic* sum

$$\frac{1}{4\pi\epsilon_0} \sum \frac{q_i}{r_i}$$

at each point. At point a the potential due to the positive charge is

$$(9.0 \times 10^9 \text{ N·m}^2\text{·C}^{-2})\frac{12 \times 10^{-9} \text{ C}}{0.060 \text{ m}} = 1800 \text{ N·m·C}^{-1}$$

$$= 1800 \text{ J·C}^{-1} = 1800 \text{ V},$$

and the potential due to the negative charge is

$$(9.0 \times 10^9 \text{ N·m}^2\text{·C}^{-2})\frac{-12 \times 10^{-9} \text{ C}}{0.040 \text{ m}} = -2700 \text{ N·m·C}^{-1}$$

$$= -2700 \text{ J·C}^{-1} = -2700 \text{ V}.$$

V_a is the sum of these:

$$V_a = 1800 \text{ V} + (-2700 \text{ V}) = -900 \text{ V} = -900 \text{ J·C}^{-1}.$$

At point b the potential due to the positive charge is $+2700$ V, the potential due to the negative charge is -770 V, and

$$V_b = 2700 \text{ V} + (-770 \text{ V}) = 1930 \text{ V} = 1930 \text{ J·C}^{-1}.$$

At point c the potential is

$$V_c = 1080 \text{ V} + (-1080 \text{ V}) = 0. \qquad \blacksquare$$

Example 26–3   Compute the potential energy of a point charge of $+4.0 \times 10^{-9}$ C if it is placed at points a, b, and c in Fig. 26–5.

Solution   For any point charge q, $U = qV$. At point a,

$$U = qV_a = (4.0 \times 10^{-9} \text{ C})(-900 \text{ J·C}^{-1})$$

$$= -3.6 \times 10^{-6} \text{ J}.$$

At point b,

$$U = qV_b = (4.0 \times 10^{-9} \text{ C})(1930 \text{ J·C}^{-1}) = 7.7 \times 10^{-6} \text{ J}.$$

At point c,

$$U = qV_c = 0.$$

(All these values correspond to U and V being zero at infinity.) $\blacksquare$

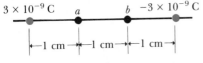

26–6
Charge distribution for Example 26–4.

Example 26–4   In Fig. 26–6 a particle with mass $m = 5.0$ g and charge $q' = 2.0 \times 10^{-9}$ C starts from rest at point a and moves in a straight line to point b. What is its speed v at point b?

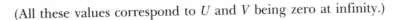

Solution   From conservation of energy,

$$K_a + U_a = K_b + U_b.$$

For this situation, $K_a = 0$ and $K_b = \frac{1}{2}mv^2$. The potential energies are given in terms of the potentials by Eq. (26–11): $U_a = q'V_a$ and $U_b = q'V_b$, and we can rewrite the energy equation as

$$0 + q'V_a = \tfrac{1}{2}mv^2 + q'V_b.$$

Solving this for v, we find

$$v = \sqrt{\frac{2q'(V_a - V_b)}{m}}.$$

We obtain the potentials just as we did in the preceding examples:

$$V_a = (9.0 \times 10^9 \ \text{N·m}^2\text{·C}^{-2})\left(\frac{3 \times 10^{-9} \ \text{C}}{0.010 \ \text{m}} + \frac{-3 \times 10^{-9} \ \text{C}}{0.020 \ \text{m}}\right) = 1350 \ \text{V},$$

$$V_b = (9.0 \times 10^9 \ \text{N·m}^2\text{·C}^{-2})\left(\frac{3 \times 10^{-9} \ \text{C}}{0.020 \ \text{m}} + \frac{-3 \times 10^{-9} \ \text{C}}{0.010 \ \text{m}}\right) = -1350 \ \text{V}.$$

Finally,

$$V_a - V_b = (1350 \ \text{V}) - (-1350 \ \text{V}) = 2700 \ \text{V},$$

and

$$v = \sqrt{\frac{2(2.0 \times 10^{-9} \ \text{C})(2700 \ \text{V})}{5.0 \times 10^{-3} \ \text{kg}}} = 4.65 \times 10^{-2} \ \text{m·s}^{-1} = 4.65 \ \text{cm·s}^{-1}.$$

We can check unit consistency by noting that $1 \ \text{V} = 1 \ \text{J·C}^{-1}$, so the numerator under the radical has units of joules or $\text{kg·m}^2\text{·s}^{-2}$.   ∎

Example 26–5   A particle with a charge $q = 3.0 \times 10^{-9}$ C moves from point a to point b along a straight line, a total distance $d = 0.50$ m. The electric field is uniform along this line, in the direction from a to b, with magnitude $E = 200 \ \text{N·C}^{-1}$. Determine (a) the force on q, (b) the work done on it by the field, and (c) the potential difference $V_a - V_b$.

Solution

a) The force is in the same direction as the electric field, and its magnitude is given by

$$F = qE = (3.0 \times 10^{-9} \ \text{C})(200 \ \text{N·C}^{-1}) = 6.0 \times 10^{-7} \ \text{N}.$$

b) The work done by this force is

$$W = Fd = (6.0 \times 10^{-7} \ \text{N})(0.5 \ \text{m}) = 3.0 \times 10^{-7} \ \text{J}.$$

c) The potential difference is the work per unit charge, which is

$$V_a - V_b = \frac{W}{q} = \frac{3.0 \times 10^{-7} \ \text{J}}{3.0 \times 10^{-9} \ \text{C}} = 100 \ \text{J·C}^{-1} = 100 \ \text{V}.$$

Alternatively, E is force per unit charge, and we can obtain the work per unit charge by multiplying E by the distance d:

$$V_a - V_b = Ed = (200 \ \text{N·C}^{-1})(0.5 \ \text{m}) = 100 \ \text{J·C}^{-1} = 100 \ \text{V}.$$ ∎

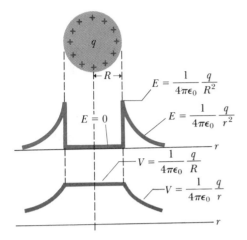

26–7
Electric-field magnitude E and potential V at points inside and outside a charged spherical conductor.

Example 26–6   A solid conducting sphere with radius R has a total charge q. Find the potential everywhere, both outside and inside the sphere.

Solution   We used Gauss's law in Example 25–9 (Section 25–5) to show that at all points *outside* the sphere, the field is the same as that of a point charge q at the center of the sphere. *Inside* the sphere the field is zero everywhere; otherwise, charge would move within the sphere. If we take $V = 0$ at infinity as we did for a point charge, then for a point outside the sphere, at a distance r from its center, the potential is the same as that for a point charge q at the center, namely,

$$V = \frac{1}{4\pi\epsilon_0} \frac{q}{r}.$$

The potential at the surface of the sphere is

$$V = \frac{1}{4\pi\epsilon_0} \frac{q}{R}. \tag{26–14}$$

Inside the sphere the field is zero everywhere, and no work is done on a test charge that moves from any point to any other point in this region. Thus the potential is the same at every point inside the sphere and is equal to its value $q/4\pi\epsilon_0 R$ at the surface. The field and potential are shown as functions of r in Fig. 26–7. The electric field $\mathbf{E}$ at the surface has magnitude

$$E = \frac{1}{4\pi\epsilon_0} \frac{q}{R^2}. \tag{26–15}$$

Here is a practical application of these results. The maximum potential to which a conductor in air can be raised is limited by the fact that air molecules become *ionized*, and air becomes a conductor, at an electric field magnitude of about 0.8×10^6 N·C^{-1}. Comparing Eqs. (26–14) and (26–15), we note that at the surface of a conducting sphere the field and potential are related by $V = ER$. Thus if E_m represents electric field magnitude at which air becomes conductive (known as the *dielectric strength* of air), the maximum potential to which a spherical conductor can be raised is

$$V_m = RE_m.$$

For a sphere 1 cm in radius, in air,

$$V_m = (10^{-2} \text{ m})(0.8 \times 10^6 \text{ N·C}^{-1}) = 8000 \text{ V},$$

and no amount of "charging" could raise the potential of a sphere of this size, in air, higher than about 8000 V. This is the reason that large spherical terminals are used on high-voltage machines such as Van de Graaff generators. If we make $R = 2$ m, then

$$V_m = (2 \text{ m})(0.8 \times 10^6 \text{ N·C}^{-1}) = 1.6 \times 10^6 \text{ V} = 1.6 \text{ MV}.$$

At the other extreme is the effect produced by a surface of very *small* radius of curvature, such as a sharp point. Since the maximum potential is proportional to the radius, even relatively small potentials applied to sharp points in air will produce sufficiently high fields just outside the point to result in ionization of the surrounding air. Sharply pointed lightning rods are used on barns in the Midwest; they are connected to ground by heavy conductors so that the lightning will strike the rod and pass harmlessly to ground, rather than striking and igniting the barn. ∎

Example 26–7   Find the potential at any height y between the two parallel plates discussed at the beginning of Section 26–1 (Fig. 26–1).

Solution   To obtain $V_y - V_b$, which we call the potential of y with respect to b, we use Eq. (26–12). The force on a test charge q' is $q'E$. The work done on the charge by the field during a displacement from y to b is

$$W_{y \to b} = q'Ey. \tag{26–16}$$

The potential difference, or work per unit charge, is

$$V_y - V_b = Ey. \tag{26–17}$$

The potential thus decreases linearly with y as we move from the upper to the lower plate. At point a, where $y = d$ and $V_y = V_a$,

$$V_a - V_b = Ed,$$

and

$$E = \frac{V_a - V_b}{d} = \frac{V_{ab}}{d}. \tag{26–18}$$

That is, *the electric field equals the potential difference between the plates divided by the distance between them.*

   In Section 25–5 we derived the expression $E = \sigma/\epsilon_0$ for the electric field E between two conducting plates, in terms of the surface charge density σ on a plate. Equation (26–18) is more generally useful than this because the potential difference V_{ab} can be measured easily with a voltmeter, while there are no instruments that read surface charge density directly.

   Equation (26–18) also shows that the unit of electric field can be expressed as 1 *volt per meter* (1 V·m^{-1}), as well as 1 N·C^{-1}:

$$1 \text{ V·m}^{-1} = 1 \text{ N·C}^{-1}.$$

In practice the volt per meter is the usual unit of E. ∎

Example 26–8   Electric charge is distributed uniformly around a thin ring of radius a, with total charge Q, as shown in Fig. 26–8. Find the potential at a point along the line perpendicular to the plane of the ring, through its center, at a point P, a distance x from the center of the ring.

Solution   We have seen this ring several times before, most recently in Section 25–2 (Example 25–6). Referring to that example, we note that the entire charge is at a distance $r = (x^2 + a^2)^{1/2}$ from point P. We conclude immediately that the potential at point P, which is a function of x,

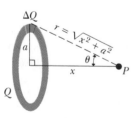

26–8
Potential at point P due to a ring of charge.

is given by

$$V(x) = \frac{1}{4\pi\epsilon_0} \frac{Q}{\sqrt{x^2 + a^2}}. \qquad (26\text{–}19)$$

Potential is a *scalar* quantity; there is no need to consider components of vectors in this calculation, as we had to do when we found the electric field at P, and the potential calculation is simpler than the field calculation. When x is much larger than a, Eq. (26–19) becomes approximately equal to

$$V(x) = \frac{1}{4\pi\epsilon_0} \frac{Q}{x},$$

corresponding to the potential of a point charge Q at distance x. When we are very far away from a charged ring, it looks like a point charge. ∎

26–3
Equipotential Surfaces

Field lines (Section 25–3) help us to visualize electric fields. In a similar way the potential at various points in an electric field can be represented graphically by **equipotential surfaces.** An equipotential surface is a surface such that every point on the surface has the same potential. We can construct an equipotential surface through any point of an electric field; in diagrams we usually show only a few representative equipotentials.

The potential energy of a charged body is the same at every point on a given equipotential surface. It follows that the E field does no work on a charged body when it moves over such a surface. For this to be true the equipotential surface through any point must be perpendicular to the direction of the field at that point. If this were not so, the field would have a component *tangent* to the surface, and the electric-field force would do work when a charge moved along the surface. We conclude that field lines and equipotential surfaces are always mutually perpendicular. In general, the field lines are curves, and the equipotentials are curved surfaces. For the special case of a *uniform* field, in which the field lines are straight, parallel, and equally spaced, the equipotentials are parallel *planes* perpendicular to the field lines.

Figure 26–9 shows several arrangements of charges. The field lines are represented by colored lines, and *cross sections* of the equipotential surfaces are shown as black lines. The actual field is, of course, three-dimensional. At each crossing of an equipotential and a field line the two are perpendicular.

When all charges are at rest, the surface of a conductor is always an equipotential surface. If different points were at different potentials, there would have to be an electric field inside the conductor, but we have proved that the field inside a conductor must be zero. From this and the preceding discussion it follows that when charges at rest reside on the

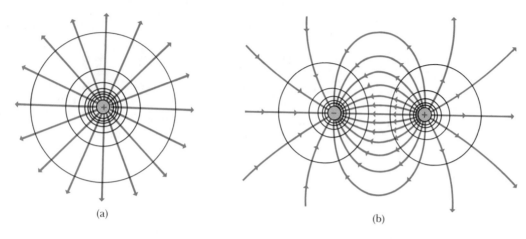

(a)

(b)

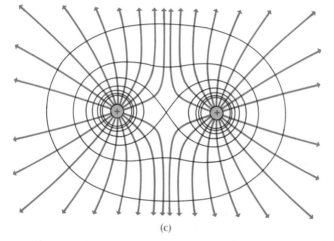

(c)

26–9
Equipotential surfaces (black lines) and field lines (colored lines) in the neighborhood of point charges.

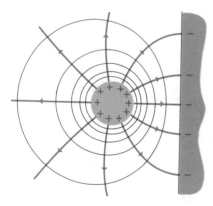

26–10
Field lines always meet charged conducting surfaces at right angles.

surface of a conductor, the electric field just outside the conductor must be *perpendicular* to the surface at every point. At the surface there can never be a component of **E** *parallel* to the surface. Figure 26–10 shows this characteristic of field lines near a conducting surface.

Finally, we can now prove a theorem that we quoted without proof in Section 25–6. The theorem is as follows: In an electrostatic situation, if a conductor contains a cavity, and if no charge is present inside the cavity, then there can be no net charge *anywhere* on the surface of the cavity. To prove this theorem, we first prove that *every point in the cavity is at the same potential*. In Fig. 26–11 the surface A of the cavity is an equipotential surface, as we have just proved. Suppose point P in the cavity is at a different potential; then we can construct a different equipotential surface B including point P.

Now consider a Gaussian surface, shown as a broken line in Fig. 26–11, between the two equipotential surfaces. Because of the relation

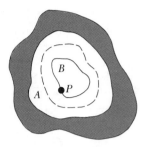

26–11
A cavity in a conductor. If the cavity contains no charge, every point in the cavity is at the same potential, the electric field is zero everywhere, and there is no charge on the surface of the cavity.

between E and the equipotentials, we know that the field at every point between the equipotentials is from A toward B, or else at every point it is from B toward A, depending on which equipotential surface is at higher potential. In either case the flux through this Gaussian surface is certainly not zero. But then Gauss's law says that the charge enclosed by the Gaussian surface cannot be zero. This contradicts our initial assumption that there is *no* charge in the cavity. So the potential at P *cannot* be different from that at the cavity wall.

The entire region of the cavity must therefore be at the same potential. But for this to be true, the electric field inside the cavity must be zero everywhere. Finally, Gauss's law shows that the electric field at any point on the surface of a conductor is proportional to the surface charge density σ at that point, so we conclude that *the surface charge density on the wall of the cavity is zero at every point.* This chain of reasoning may seem tortuous, but it is worth careful study.

26–4
Potential Gradient

Electric field and potential are closely related. Equation (26–12) expresses one aspect of that relationship; if we know E at various points, we can use Eq. (26–12) to calculate potential differences. We should be able to turn this around; if we know the potential V at various points, we ought to be able to use it to determine E, and in fact we can.

Here's how we do it. Suppose we have mapped a particular electric field by drawing its network of field lines and equipotential surfaces, with the potential difference between adjacent equipotentials equal to some constant value ΔV such as 1 V or 100 V. Let Δs be the perpendicular distance between two equipotentials near a certain point. Potential difference is work per unit charge, and electric field is force per unit charge, so for a displacement Δs perpendicular to the equipotentials from one to the next, the work W done on a test charge q' is $W = F \Delta s = (q'E) \Delta s$. The difference in potential ΔV is equal to the work per unit charge, W/q', so we find

$$\Delta V = \frac{W}{q'} = \frac{q'E \, \Delta s}{q'} = E \, \Delta s. \qquad (26\text{–}20)$$

The greater the electric-field magnitude E, the smaller the distance Δs between adjacent equipotentials. That is, in a strong field the equipotentials are crowded together closely, and in a weak field they are farther apart.

Another way to express this relationship is

$$E = \frac{\Delta V}{\Delta s} \qquad (26\text{–}21)$$

Thus the magnitude of the electric field is proportional to the *rate of change* of potential with distance, in a direction perpendicular to the equipotentials. The ratio $\Delta V/\Delta s$ is also called the **potential gradient,** just as the rate of change of temperature with distance is called the temperature gradient.

The units of potential gradient (volts per meter, $V \cdot m^{-1}$) must be the same as those of electric field (newtons per coulomb, $N \cdot C^{-1}$). We have already seen this relationship in Example 26–7. To verify it directly, we recall that potential is potential energy per unit charge and $1 \; V = 1 \; J \cdot C^{-1}$. Then

$$1 \; V \cdot m^{-1} = 1 \; J \cdot C^{-1} \cdot m^{-1} = 1 \; N \cdot m \cdot C^{-1} \cdot m^{-1} = 1 \; N \cdot C^{-1}.$$

One final point about potential gradient is the relation of the *direction* of **E** to the behavior of V. Specifically, **E** always points in the direction in which V *decreases* most rapidly. As we move away from a distribution of positive charge, the potential decreases, and the electric field points away from the charge. If the charge is negative, the potential increases algebraically (becoming less negative) as we move away from the charge, and **E** points *toward* the charge. The situation is completely analogous to gravitational potential energy, which we studied in Section 7–5. Near the surface of the earth, for example, the gravitational field points down, the direction of most rapid decrease of gravitational potential energy.

26–5
The Millikan Oil-Drop Experiment

Have you ever wondered how the charge on an individual electron can be measured? The first solution to this formidable experimental problem was the **Millikan oil-drop experiment,** a brilliant piece of work carried out at the University of Chicago during the years 1909–1913 by Robert Andrews Millikan (1868–1953).

Millikan's apparatus is shown schematically in Fig. 26–12a. Two parallel horizontal metal plates, A and B, are insulated from each other and separated by a few millimeters. Oil is sprayed in very fine drops (around 10^{-5} cm diameter) from an atomizer above the upper plate, and a few drops are allowed to fall through a small hole in this plate. A beam of light is directed horizontally between the plates, and a telescope is set up with its axis at right angles to the light beam. The oil drops, illuminated by the light beam and viewed through the telescope, look like tiny bright stars. A scale in the telescope permits precise measurements of the vertical positions of the drops, so their speeds can also be measured.

Some of the oil drops are electrically charged because of frictional effects or because of ionization of the surrounding air by X-rays or radioactivity. The drops are usually negatively charged, but one with a positive charge is occasionally found.

Here's how we can measure the charge on a drop: Suppose a drop has a negative charge and the plates are maintained at a potential difference such that there is a downward electric field with magnitude E between them. The forces on the drop are then its weight mg and the upward force qE. By adjusting the field E we can make qE equal to mg, as

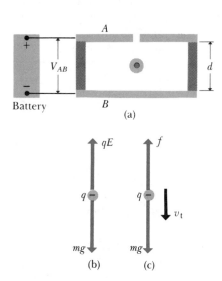

26–12
(a) Schematic diagram of Millikan apparatus. (b) Forces on a drop at rest. (c) Forces on a drop falling with its terminal velocity v_t.

in Fig. 26–12b. The drop is then in static equilibrium, and

$$q = \frac{mg}{E}. \tag{26-22}$$

The electric-field magnitude E is the potential difference V_{AB} divided by the distance d between the plates, as we found in Example 26–7. We can find the mass m of the drop if we know its radius r because the mass equals the product of the density ρ and the volume, $4\pi r^3/3$. So we can rewrite Eq. (26–22) as

$$q = \frac{4\pi}{3} \frac{\rho r^3 gd}{V_{AB}}. \tag{26-23}$$

Everything on the right side of Eq. (26–23) is easy to measure except for the drop radius r, which is much too small to measure directly with any degree of precision. But here comes an example of Millikan's genius. He determined the drop's radius by cutting off the electric field and measuring the *terminal speed* v_t of the drop as it fell. You may want to review the concept of terminal speed in Section 5–4 (Example 5–17).

Here's how Millikan found the drop's radius from v_t: At terminal speed the weight mg is just balanced by the viscous air-resistance force f. The viscous force on a sphere of radius r moving with speed v through a fluid with viscosity η is given by Stokes' law; we discussed this in Section 13–8, Eq. (13–25): $f = 6\pi\eta rv$. At terminal speed, $f = mg$. Using Stokes' law for f and expressing the mass m of the drop in terms of its density ρ and radius r, we find

$$\frac{4}{3}\pi r^3 \rho g = 6\pi\eta rv_t,$$

and

$$r = 3\sqrt{\frac{\eta v_t}{2\rho g}}. \tag{26-24}$$

Combining this expression for r with Eq. (26–23), we find

$$q = 18\pi\frac{d}{V_{AB}}\sqrt{\frac{\eta^3 v_t^3}{2\rho g}}. \tag{26-25}$$

This expresses the charge q in terms of quantities we can measure.

The actual experiment was a little more complicated. Millikan had to correct for the buoyant force of air on the falling drop by replacing the density ρ of the oil by $(\rho - \rho_{air})$. He also had to use a more elaborate version of Stokes' law that takes into account the molecular nature of air because the intermolecular distances turn out to be in the same range as the sizes of the drops.

Millikan and his co-workers measured the charges of thousands of drops. Within the limits of their experimental error, every drop had a charge equal to some small integer multiple of a basic charge e. That is, they found drops with charges of $4e$, $7e$, $12e$, and so on, but never with values such as $0.76e$ or $2.49e$. A drop with charge e has acquired one extra electron; if its charge is $2e$, it has acquired two extra electrons, and so on.

As we stated in Section 24–5, the best experimental value of the magnitude e of the electron charge is

$$e = 1.60217733(49) \times 10^{-19} \text{ C,}$$

where the (49) indicates the uncertainty in the last two digits (33).

In the quark model of fundamental particle structure, which we will study in Section 44–10, there are particles called *quarks*, with fractional charges $\pm e/3$ and $\pm 2e/3$. But quarks always appear in combinations of two or three, and the charge of a single quark is probably not observable.

26–6
The Electronvolt

The magnitude e of the electron charge can be used to define a new unit of energy, the *electronvolt*, that is useful in many calculations with atomic and nuclear systems. We know that when a particle with charge q moves from a point where the potential is V_a to a point where it is V_b, the change ΔU in the potential energy U of the charge is

$$\Delta U = q(V_b - V_a) = qV_{ba}.$$

If the charge q equals the electron charge $e = 1.602 \times 10^{-19}$ C, and the potential difference is $V_{ba} = 1$ V, the change in energy is

$$\Delta U = (1.602 \times 10^{-19} \text{ C})(1 \text{ V}) = 1.602 \times 10^{-19} \text{ J.}$$

This quantity of energy is defined to be 1 **electronvolt** (1 eV):

$$1 \text{ eV} = 1.602 \times 10^{-19} \text{ J.}$$

Other commonly used multiples are

$$1 \text{ keV} = 10^3 \text{ eV,} \qquad 1 \text{ MeV} = 10^6 \text{ eV,}$$
$$1 \text{ GeV} = 10^9 \text{ eV,} \qquad 1 \text{ meV} = 10^{-3} \text{ eV.}$$

For a particle with charge e the change in potential *energy* between two points along the path of the particle, when expressed in electronvolts, is *numerically* equal to the potential difference between the points, in volts. If the charge is some multiple of e, say Ne, the change in potential energy in electronvolts is, numerically, N times the potential difference in volts. For example, when a particle with charge $2e$ moves between two points with a potential difference of 1000 V, the change in its potential energy is

$$\Delta U = qV_{ba} = (2)(1.602 \times 10^{-19} \text{ C})(1000 \text{ V})$$
$$= 3.204 \times 10^{-16} \text{ J} = 2000 \text{ eV.}$$

We have defined the electronvolt in terms of *potential* energy, but we can use this unit for energy of *any* form, such as the kinetic energy of a moving particle. When we speak of a "one-million-volt electron," we mean an electron with a kinetic energy of one million electronvolts (1 MeV), equal to $(10^6)(1.602 \times 10^{-19} \text{ J}) = 1.602 \times 10^{-13}$ J.

One of the principles of the special theory of relativity, to be developed in Chapter 40, is that the rest mass m of a particle is equivalent to a quantity of energy $E_0 = mc^2$, where c is the speed of light. The rest mass of an electron is 9.109×10^{-31} kg; the energy equivalent of this is

$$E_0 = mc^2 = (9.109 \times 10^{-31} \text{ kg})(2.998 \times 10^8 \text{ m·s}^{-1})^2$$
$$= 81.87 \times 10^{-15} \text{ J} = 511{,}000 \text{ eV} = 0.511 \text{ MeV}.$$

When the kinetic energy of a particle becomes comparable in magnitude to its rest energy, Newton's laws of motion are no longer valid; they must be replaced by the more general relations of relativistic mechanics, which we will develop in detail in Chapter 40. For example, an electron accelerated through a potential difference of 500 kV acquires a kinetic energy of 500 keV, approximately *equal* to its rest energy. A correct analysis of the motion of the particle requires the use of relativistic mechanics.

26–7
The Cathode-Ray Tube

To conclude this chapter, let's look at applications of the concept of potential to a class of devices called **cathode-ray tubes.** Such devices are found in oscilloscopes and computer terminal displays, and the principle of the TV picture tube is similar. Figure 26–13 is a schematic diagram of the principal elements of a cathode-ray tube. The name dates from the turn of the century. Cathode-ray tubes use an electron beam; such a beam was called a cathode ray before its basic nature was understood. We now know that "cathode rays" are beams of electrons.

The interior of the tube has a high vacuum, with a residual pressure of around 0.01 Pa (10^{-7} atm) or less. At any greater pressure, collisions of electrons with air molecules would scatter the electron beam excessively. The *cathode* at the left end is raised to a high temperature by the *heater*, and electrons evaporate from the surface of the cathode. The *accelerating anode*, with a small hole at its center, is maintained at a high positive potential V_1, of the order of 1 to 20 kV, relative to the cathode. This potential causes an electric field, directed from right to left, in the

26–13
Basic elements of a cathode-ray tube.

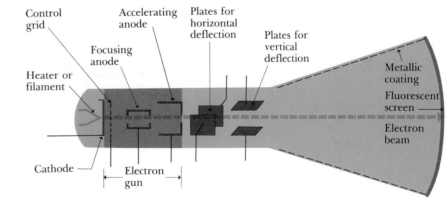

Control grid
Accelerating anode
Plates for horizontal deflection
Focusing anode
Plates for vertical deflection
Heater or filament
Metallic coating
Fluorescent screen
Electron beam
Cathode
Electron gun

region between the accelerating anode and the cathode. Electrons passing through the hole in the anode form a narrow beam and travel with constant horizontal velocity from the anode to the *fluorescent screen*. The area where the electrons strike the screen glows brightly.

The function of the *control grid* is to regulate the number of electrons that reach the anode and hence the brightness of the spot on the screen. The *focusing anode* ensures that electrons leaving the cathode in slightly different directions are focused down to a narrow beam and all arrive at the same spot on the screen. We won't need to worry about these two electrodes in the following analysis. The assembly of cathode, control grid, focusing anode, and accelerating electrode is called the *electron gun*.

The beam of electrons passes between two pairs of *deflecting plates*. An electric field between the first pair of plates deflects the electrons horizontally, and an electric field between the second pair deflects them vertically. If no deflecting fields are present, the electrons travel in a straight line from the hole in the accelerating anode to the center of the screen, where they produce a bright spot.

To analyze the electron motion, let's first calculate the speed v of the electrons as they leave the electron gun. We can use the same method as in Example 26–4 (Section 26–2). The initial speeds of the electrons as they are emitted from the cathode are very small in comparison to their final speeds, so we assume that the initial speeds are zero. Then the speed v_x of the electrons as they leave the electron gun is given by

$$v_x = \sqrt{\frac{2eV_1}{m}}. \tag{26–26}$$

As a numerical example, if $V_1 = 2000$ V,

$$v_x = \sqrt{\frac{2(1.60 \times 10^{-19} \text{ C})(2.00 \times 10^3 \text{ V})}{9.11 \times 10^{-31} \text{ kg}}} = 2.65 \times 10^7 \text{ m·s}^{-1}.$$

The kinetic energy of an electron leaving the anode depends only on the *potential difference* between anode and cathode, not on the details of the fields or the electron trajectories within the electron gun.

If there is no electric field between the horizontal deflection plates, the electrons enter the region between the vertical deflection plates, shown in Fig. 26–14, with speed v_x. If there is a potential difference V_2 between these plates, with the upper plate positive (i.e., at higher poten-

26–14
Electrostatic deflection of an electron beam in a cathode-ray tube.

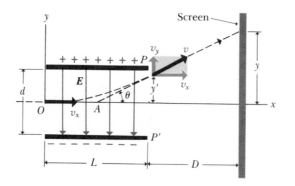

tial), there is a *downward* electric field with magnitude $E = V_2/d$ between the plates. A constant upward force eE then acts on the electrons, and their upward (y-component) acceleration is

$$a_y = \frac{eE}{m} = \frac{eV_2}{md}. \tag{26–27}$$

The *horizontal* component of velocity v_x is constant. The path of the electrons in the region between the plates is a parabolic trajectory, just as in Example 25–4 (Section 25–1) and the ballistic trajectories of Section 3–4. In all these cases the particle moves with constant x-velocity and constant y-acceleration. After the electrons emerge from this region, their paths again become straight lines, and they strike the screen S at a point a distance y above its center. We are going to prove that this distance is *directly proportional* to the deflecting potential V_2.

Proceeding one step at a time, we first note that the time t required for the electrons to travel the length L of the plates is

$$t = \frac{L}{v_x}. \tag{26–28}$$

During this time they acquire an upward velocity component v_y given by

$$v_y = a_y t, \tag{26–29}$$

Combining this with Eqs. (26–27) and (26–28), we find that

$$v_y = \frac{eV_2}{md}\frac{L}{v_x}. \tag{26–30}$$

When the electrons emerge from the deflecting field, their velocity v makes an angle θ with the x-axis given by

$$\tan \theta = \frac{v_y}{v_x}. \tag{26–31}$$

Ordinarily, the length L of the deflection plates is much smaller than the distance D from the plates to the screen. In this case the angle θ is also given approximately by $\tan \theta = y/D$. Combining this with Eq. (26–31), we find

$$\frac{y}{D} = \frac{v_y}{v_x}, \tag{26–32}$$

or, using Eq. (26–30) to eliminate v_y,

$$y = \frac{DeV_2L}{mdv_x^2}. \tag{26–33}$$

Finally, we substitute the expression for v_x given by Eq. (26–26) into Eq. (26–33); the result is

$$y = \left(\frac{LD}{2d}\right)\frac{V_2}{V_1}. \tag{26–34}$$

The factor in parentheses depends only on the dimensions of the system, which are all constants. So we have proved that the deflection y is proportional to the deflecting voltage V_2, as claimed. It is also *inversely* proportional to the accelerating voltage V_1. This isn't surprising; the faster the electrons are going, the less they are deflected by the deflecting voltage.

If there is also a field between the *horizontal* deflecting plates, the beam is also deflected in the horizontal direction, perpendicular to the plane of Fig. 26–14. The coordinates of the luminous spot on the screen are then proportional to the horizontal and vertical deflecting voltages, respectively. This is the principle of the *cathode-ray oscilloscope*. If the horizontal deflection voltage sweeps the beam from left to right at a uniform rate, the beam traces out a graph of the vertical voltage as a function of time. Oscilloscopes are extremely useful laboratory instruments in many areas of pure and applied science.

The picture tube in a television set is similar, but the beam is deflected by *magnetic* fields (to be discussed in later chapters) rather than electric fields. The electron beam traces out the area of the picture 30 times per second in an array of 525 horizontal lines, as the intensity of the beam is varied to make bright and dark areas on the screen. (In a color TV set the screen is an array of dots of phosphors with three different colors.) The accelerating voltage in TV picture tubes (V_1 in the above discussion) is typically about 20 kV. Computer terminal displays and monitors operate on the same principle, using a magnetically deflected electron beam to trace out images on a fluorescent screen. In this context the device is called a CRT (cathode-ray tube) display or a VDT (video display terminal).

Questions

26–1 Are there cases in electrostatics in which a conducting surface is *not* an equipotential surface? If so, give an example.

26–2 If the electrical potential at a single point is known, can the electric field at that point be determined?

26–3 If two points are at the same potential, is the electric field necessarily zero everywhere between them?

26–4 If the electric field is zero throughout a certain region of space, is the potential also zero in this region? If not, what *can* be said about the potential?

26–5 A student said: "Since electrical potential is always proportional to potential energy, why bother with the concept of potential at all?" How would you respond?

26–6 Is potential gradient a scalar quantity or a vector quantity?

26–7 A conducting sphere is to be charged by bringing in positive charge, a little at a time, until the total charge is Q. The total work required for this process is alleged to be proportional to Q^2. Is this correct? Why or why not?

26–8 The potential (relative to a point at infinity) midway between two charges of equal magnitude and opposite sign is zero. Can you think of a way to bring a test charge from infinity to this midpoint in such a way that no work is done in any part of the displacement?

26–9 A high-voltage dc power line falls on a car, so the entire metal body of the car is at a potential of 10,000 V with respect to the ground. What happens to the occupants

a) when they are sitting in the car?

b) when they step out of the car?

26–10 In electronics it is customary to define the potential of ground (thinking of the earth as a large conductor) as zero. Is this consistent with the fact that the earth has a net electric charge that is not zero? (Cf. Problem 25–26.)

26–11 A positive point charge is placed near a very large conducting plane. A professor of physics asserted that the field caused by this configuration is the same as would be obtained by removing the plane and placing a negative point charge of equal magnitude in the mirror-image position behind the initial position of the plane. Is this correct?

26–12 It is easy to produce a potential of several thousand volts on your body by scuffing your shoes across a nylon carpet; yet contact with a power line of comparable voltage would probably be fatal. What is the difference?

Exercises

Section 26–1   Electrical Potential Energy

26–1 A point charge $q_1 = +2.80$ μC is held stationary at the origin. How far away must a second point charge $q_2 = +5.20$ μC be placed for the electrical potential energy U of the pair of charges to be 0.600 J? Take U to be zero when the charges have an infinite separation.

26–2 A point charge q_1 is held stationary at the origin. A second charge q_2 is placed at point a, and the electrical potential energy of the pair of charges is -5.60×10^{-8} J. When the second charge is moved to point b, the electrical force on the charge does 2.40×10^{-8} J of work. What is the electrical potential energy of the pair of charges when the second charge is at point b?

26–3 A point charge $q_1 = -5.00$ μC is held stationary at the origin. A second point charge $q_2 = +4.00$ μC moves from the point $x = 0.16$ m, $y = 0$ to the point $x = 0.28$ m, $y = 0$. How much work is done by the electrical force on q_2?

26–4 A point charge with charge $Q = +6.00$ μC is held at the origin.

a) A second point charge with a charge of $q = -0.50$ μC and a mass of 3.00×10^{-4} kg is placed on the x-axis, 0.800 m from the origin. What is the electrical potential energy of the pair of charges? (Take the potential energy to be zero when the charges have infinite separation.)

b) The second point charge is released at rest. What is its speed when it is 0.200 m from the origin?

26–5 A small, charged metal sphere, carrying a net charge of $q_1 = +6.00$ μC, is held in a stationary position by insulating supports. A second small metal sphere, with a net charge of $q_2 = +2.50$ μC and a mass of 2.00 g, is projected toward q_1. When the two spheres are 0.800 m apart, q_2 is moving toward q_1 with a speed of 18.0 m·s^{-1}. Assume that the two spheres can be treated as point charges.

a) What is the speed of q_2 when the spheres are 0.500 m apart? (Neglect the effects of gravity.)

b) How close does q_2 get to q_1?

Section 26–2   Potential

26–6 The potential at a distance of 0.600 m from a very small charged sphere is 36.0 V. If the sphere is treated as a point charge, what is its charge?

26–7 A point charge has a charge of 8.00×10^{-11} C. At what distance from the point charge is the electrical potential

a) 12.0 V?   b) 24.0 V?

26–8 A uniform electric field has magnitude E and is directed in the positive x-direction. Consider point a at $x = 0.80$ m and point b at $x = 1.20$ m. The potential difference between these two points is 400 V.

a) Which point, a or b, is at the higher potential?

b) Calculate the magnitude E of the electric field.

c) A negative point charge $q = -0.200$ μC moves from b to a. Calculate the work done on the point charge by the electric field.

26–9 Two point charges $q_1 = +5.00 \times 10^{-9}$ C and $q_2 = -3.00 \times 10^{-9}$ C are 10.0 cm apart. Point A is midway between them; point B is 8.00 cm from q_1 and 2.00 cm from q_2. Find

a) the potential at point A;

b) the potential at point B;

c) the work done by the electric field on a charge of 2.50×10^{-9} C that moves from point B to point A.

26–10 Two stationary point charges, $+2.40 \times 10^{-10}$ C and -1.20×10^{-10} C, are separated by a distance of 5.00 cm. An electron is released from rest between the two charges, 1.00 cm from the negative charge, and moves along the line connecting the two charges. What is its speed when it is 1.00 cm from the positive charge?

26–11 Two positive point charges, each of magnitude q, are fixed on the y-axis at the points $y = +a$ and $y = -a$.

a) Draw a diagram showing the positions of the charges.

b) What is the potential V_0 at the origin?

c) Show that the potential at any point on the
   x-axis is

$$V = \frac{1}{4\pi\epsilon_0} \frac{2q}{\sqrt{a^2 + x^2}}.$$

d) Sketch a graph of the potential on the x-axis as a
   function of x over the range from $x = -4a$ to
   $x = +4a$.

e) At what value of x is the potential one-half that at
   the origin?

26–12 A positive charge $+q$ is located at the point
$(x = 0, y = -a)$, and an equal negative charge $-q$ is
located at the point $(x = 0, y = +a)$.

a) Draw a diagram showing the positions of the
   charges.

b) What is the potential at a point on the x-axis, a distance x from the origin?

c) Derive an expression for the potential at a point on
   the y-axis, a distance y from the origin.

d) Sketch a graph of the potential at points on the
   y-axis as a function of y in the range from $y = -4a$
   to $y = +4a$. Plot positive potentials upward and
   negative potentials downward.

26–13 A charge of 4.50×10^{-8} C is placed in a uniform electric field that is directed vertically upward and
that has magnitude 5.00×10^4 N·C^{-1}. What work is
done by the electrical force when the charge moves

a) 0.450 m to the right?

b) 0.800 m downward?

c) 2.60 m at an angle of 45.0° upward from the horizontal?

26–14 A simple type of vacuum tube known as a *diode*
consists essentially of two electrodes within a highly
evacuated enclosure. One electrode, the *cathode*, is
maintained at a high temperature and emits electrons
from its surface. A potential difference of a few hundred volts is maintained between the cathode and the
other electrode, known as the *anode*, with the anode at
the higher potential. Suppose that a diode consists of a
cylindrical cathode of radius 0.0500 cm, mounted coaxi-
ally within a cylindrical anode 0.450 cm in radius. The
potential of the anode is 250 V higher than that of the
cathode. An electron leaves the surface of the cathode
with zero initial speed. Find its speed when it strikes
the anode.

26–15 Two large parallel metal sheets carrying equal
and opposite electric charges are separated by a distance of 0.0500 m. The electric field between them is
uniform and has magnitude 400 V·m^{-1}.

a) What is the potential difference between the sheets?

b) Which sheet is at the higher potential, the one with
   positive charge or the one with negative charge?

26–16 Two large parallel metal plates carry opposite
charges. They are separated by 0.0600 m, and the potential difference between them is 500 V.

a) What is the magnitude of the electric field (assumed to be uniform) in the region between the
   plates?

b) What is the magnitude of the force this field exerts
   on a particle with charge $+2.00 \times 10^{-9}$ C?

c) Use the results of part (b) to compute the work
   done by the field on the particle as it moves from
   the higher-potential plate to the lower.

d) Compare the result of part (c) to the change of
   electrical potential energy of the same particle,
   computed from the electrical potential.

26–17 A potential difference of 1400 V is established
between parallel plates in air. If the air becomes electrically conducting when the electric field exceeds $0.800 \times
10^6$ N·C^{-1}, what is the minimum separation of the
plates?

26–18 A particle with a charge of $+2.20 \times 10^{-9}$ C is in
a uniform electric field directed to the left. It is released from rest and moves a distance of 5.00 cm; after
this its kinetic energy is $+4.50 \times 10^{-6}$ J.

a) What work was done by the electrical force?

b) What is the potential of the starting point with respect to the endpoint?

c) What is the magnitude of the electric field?

26–19 A total electric charge of 3.50×10^{-9} C is distributed uniformly over the surface of a metal sphere
with a radius of 0.200 m. If the potential is zero at a
point at infinity, what is the value of the potential

a) at a point on the surface of the sphere?

b) at a point inside the sphere, 0.100 m from its
   center?

Section 26–5   The Millikan Oil-Drop Experiment

26–20 In an apparatus for measuring the electronic
charge e by Millikan's method, an electric field of
5.26×10^4 V·m^{-1} is required to maintain a certain
charged oil drop at rest. If the plates are 1.50 cm apart,
what potential difference between them is required?

26–21 An oil droplet of mass 3.00×10^{-14} kg and of
radius 2.00×10^{-6} m carries six excess electrons. What
is its terminal speed

a) when falling in a region in which there is no electric field?

b) when falling in an electric field of magnitude
   3.00×10^5 N·C^{-1} directed downward?

(The viscosity of air is 180×10^{-7} N·s·m^{-2}. Neglect the
buoyant force of the air.)

Section 26–6 The Electronvolt

26–22 Find the potential energy of the interaction of two protons at a distance of 1.00×10^{-15} m, typical of the dimensions of atomic nuclei. Express your result in MeV.

26–23 Use the relation $E_0 = mc^2$ to find the energy equivalent of the rest mass of the proton. Express your result in MeV.

26–24

a) Prove that when a charged particle is accelerated from rest in an electric field, its final speed is proportional to the square root of the potential difference through which it is accelerated.

b) What is the final speed of an electron accelerated through a potential difference of 1136 V if it has an initial speed of 4.00×10^5 m·s^{-1}?

26–25

a) What is the maximum potential difference through which an electron can be accelerated from rest if its kinetic energy is not to exceed 1% of the rest energy?

b) What is the speed of such an electron expressed as a fraction of the speed of light, c?

c) Make the same calculations for a *proton*.

Section 26–7 The Cathode-Ray Tube

26–26 The electric field in the region between the deflecting plates of a certain cathode-ray oscilloscope is 1.80×10^4 N·C^{-1}.

a) What is the magnitude of the force on an electron in this region?

b) What is the magnitude of the acceleration of an electron when acted on by this force?

26–27 In Fig. 26–15, an electron is projected along the axis midway between the deflection plates of a cathode-ray tube with an initial speed of 8.00×10^6 m·s^{-1}. The uniform electric field between the plates has a magnitude of 6.00×10^3 N·C^{-1} and is upward.

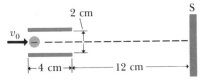

FIGURE 26–15

a) How far below the axis has the electron moved when it reaches the end of the plates?

b) At what angle with the axis is it moving as it leaves the plates?

c) How far below the axis will it strike the fluorescent screen S?

Problems

26–28 Three equal point charges of 5.00×10^{-7} C are placed at the corners of an equilateral triangle whose side is 1.00 m. What is the electrical potential energy of the system? Take as zero potential the energy of the three charges when they are infinitely far apart.

26–29 In Exercise 26–18, suppose that another force in addition to the electrical force acts on the particle so that when it is released from rest it moves to the right. After it has moved 5.00 cm, the additional force has done 9.00×10^{-5} J of work, and the particle has 6.00×10^{-5} J of kinetic energy.

a) What work was done by the electrical force?

b) What is the potential of the starting point with respect to the endpoint?

c) What is the magnitude of the electric field?

26–30 A small sphere of mass 4.00 g hangs by a thread between two parallel vertical plates 5.00 cm apart. The charge on the sphere is 6.00×10^{-6} C. What potential difference between the plates will cause the thread to assume an angle of 30.0° with the vertical?

26–31 Consider the same distribution of charge as in Exercise 26–12. Show that the potential at a point on the y-axis is given by

$$V = -\frac{2qa}{4\pi\epsilon_0 y^2},$$

when $y \gg a$.

26–32 Consider the same distribution of charges as in Exercise 26–11.

a) Find the potential at a point on the y-axis, a distance y from the origin. Use your result to sketch a graph of the potential on the y-axis as a function of y over the range from $y = -4a$ to $y = +4a$.

b) Discuss the physical meaning of the graph at the points $+a$ and $-a$.

c) At what point or points on the y-axis is the potential equal to its value at the origin?

d) Show that the potential is given by

$$V = \frac{2q}{4\pi\epsilon_0 y}$$

when $y \gg a$.

26–33 Consider the same distribution of charges as in Exercise 26–11.

a) Suppose a positively charged particle of charge q' and mass m is placed precisely at the origin and released from rest. What happens?

b) What will happen if the charge in part (a) is constrained to move along the y-axis and is displaced slightly along the +y-axis and then released?

c) What will happen if the charge is instead constrained to move along the x-axis and is displaced slightly in the direction of the +x-axis and then released?

26–34 Again consider the charge distribution of Exercise 26–11. Suppose a positively charged particle of charge q' and mass m is displaced slightly from the origin in the direction of the x-axis and is constrained to stay on the x-axis. Its initial speed is zero.

a) Determine the speed of the particle as a function of its distance x from the origin. Sketch a graph of the speed of the particle as a function of x.

b) What is its speed at infinity?

c) If the particle is projected toward the left along the x-axis from a point at a large distance to the right of the origin, with a speed half that acquired in part (b), at what distance from the origin does it come to rest?

d) If a negatively charged particle, of charge $-q'$ and mass m, is released from rest on the x-axis, at a very large distance to the left of the origin, what is its speed as it passes the origin?

26–35 The potential at a certain distance from a point charge is 800 V, and the electric field is 200 N·C^{-1}.

a) What is the distance to the point charge?

b) What is the magnitude of the charge?

26–36 A metal sphere of radius r_a is supported on an insulating stand at the center of a hollow metal sphere of inner radius r_b. There is a charge $+q$ on the inner sphere and a charge $-q$ on the outer.

a) Calculate the potential $V(r)$ for

   i) $r > r_b$,   ii) $r_a < r < r_b$,   iii) $r < r_a$.

   Use the fact that the net potential is the sum of the potentials due to the individual spheres. Take $V(r)$ to be zero when r is infinite.

b) Show that the potential of the inner sphere with respect to the outer is

$$V_{ab} = \frac{q}{4\pi\epsilon_0}\left(\frac{1}{r_a} - \frac{1}{r_b}\right).$$

26–37 Some cell walls in the human body have a double layer of surface charge, with a layer of negative charge inside and a layer of positive charge of equal magnitude on the outside. Consider a model for such a cell in which the surface charge densities are $\pm 0.50 \times 10^{-3}$ C·m^{-2} and the cell wall is 5.0×10^{-9} m thick. Find

a) the electric field magnitude in the wall, between the two charge layers;

b) the potential difference between inside and outside the cell. Which is at higher potential?

26–38 A potential difference of 800 V is established between two parallel plates 3.00 cm apart. An electron is released from the negative plate at the same instant that a proton is released from the positive plate.

a) How far from the positive plate will they pass each other?

b) What is the ratio of their speeds when they strike the opposite plates?

c) What is the ratio of their kinetic energies when they strike the opposite plates?

26–39 An alpha particle with a kinetic energy of 10.0 MeV makes a head-on collision with a gold nucleus at rest. What is the distance of closest approach of the two particles? (Assume that the gold nucleus remains stationary and that it may be treated as a point charge. The atomic number of gold is 79. An alpha particle is a helium nucleus, with atomic number 2.)

26–40 In the Bohr model of the hydrogen atom a single electron revolves around a single proton in a circle of radius r. Assume that the proton remains at rest.

a) By equating the electrical force to the electron mass times its acceleration, derive an expression for the electron's speed.

b) Obtain an expression for the electron's kinetic energy, and show that its magnitude is just half that of the electrical potential energy.

c) Obtain an expression for the total energy, and evaluate it using $r = 5.29 \times 10^{-11}$ m. Give your numerical result in joules and in electronvolts.

26–41 Refer to Problem 24–20.

a) Calculate the potential at the point $x = 3.00$ cm, $y = 0$ and at the point $x = 3.00$ cm, $y = 4.00$ cm due to the first two charges.

b) If the third charge moves from the point $x = 3.00$ cm, $y = 0$ to the point $x = 3.00$ cm, $y = 4.00$ cm, calculate the work done on it by the field of the first two charges. Comment on the *sign* of this work. Is your result reasonable?

26–42 Refer to Problem 24–19.

a) Calculate the potential at the origin and at the point $x = 3.00$ cm, $y = 0$ due to the first two point charges.

b) Calculate the work the electric field does on the third charge when it moves from the origin to the point $x = 3.00$ cm, $y = 0$.

26–43 Electric charge Q is distributed uniformly along a semicircle of radius a. Calculate the potential at the center of curvature if the potential is assumed to be zero at infinity.

26–44 A charged oil drop in a Millikan oil-drop apparatus is observed to fall at constant speed 1.00 mm in a time of 27.4 s in the absence of any external field. The same drop can be held stationary in a field of 1.58×10^4 N·C^{-1}. How many excess electrons has the drop acquired? The viscosity of air is 180×10^{-7} N·s·m^{-2}. The density of the oil is 824 kg·m^{-3}, and the density of air is 1.29 kg·m^{-3}.

26–45 Two metal spheres of different sizes are charged such that the electrical potential is the same at the surface of each. Sphere A has a radius three times that of sphere B. Let Q_A and Q_B be the charges on each sphere, and let E_A and E_B be the electric-field magnitudes at the surface of each sphere. What is

a) the ratio Q_B/Q_A?

b) the ratio E_B/E_A?

Challenge Problems

26–46 A metal sphere of radius $R_1 = 0.160$ m has a charge $Q_1 = 2.40 \times 10^{-8}$ C.

a) What are the electric field and electrical potential at the surface of the sphere?

This sphere is now connected by a long, thin conducting wire to another sphere, of radius $R_2 = 0.040$ m, that is several meters' distance from the first sphere. Before the connection is made, this second sphere is uncharged. After electrostatic equilibrium has been reached, what is

b) the total charge on each sphere?

c) the electrical potential at the surface of each sphere?

d) the electric field at the surface of each sphere?

Assume that the amount of charge on the wire is much less than the charge on each sphere.

26–47 Two point charges are moving toward the right along the x-axis. Point charge 1 has charge $q_1 = 2.00$ μC, mass $m_1 = 6.00 \times 10^{-5}$ kg, and speed v_1. Point charge 2 is to the right of q_1 and has charge $q_2 = -5.00$ μC, mass $m_2 = 3.00 \times 10^{-5}$ kg, and speed v_2. At a particular instant the charges are separated by a distance of 9.00 mm and have speeds $v_1 = 400$ m·s^{-1} and $v_2 = 1200$ m·s^{-1}. The only forces on the particles are the forces they exert on each other.

a) Determine the speed v_{cm} of the center of mass of the system.

b) The "relative energy" E_r of the system is defined as the total energy minus the kinetic energy contributed by the motion of the center of mass:

$$E_r = E - \tfrac{1}{2}(m_1 + m_2)v_{cm}^2,$$

where $E = \tfrac{1}{2}m_1v_1^2 + \tfrac{1}{2}m_2v_2^2 + q_1q_2/4\pi\epsilon_0 r$ is the total energy of the system and r is the distance between the charges. Show that $E_r = \tfrac{1}{2}\mu v^2 + q_1q_2/4\pi\epsilon_0 r$, where μ is called the *reduced mass* of the system and is equal to $m_1m_2/(m_1 + m_2)$ and $v = v_2 - v_1$ is the relative speed of the moving particles.

c) For the numerical values given above, calculate the numerical value of E_r.

d) The value of E_r can be used to determine whether or not the particles will "escape" from one another. For the conditions given above, will the particles escape from one another? Explain.

e) If the particles do escape, what will be their final relative speed? That is, what will their relative speed be when $r \to \infty$? If the particles do not escape, what will be their distance of maximum separation? That is, what will be the value of r when $v = 0$?

f) Repeat parts (c) through (e) for $v_1 = 400$ m·s^{-1} and $v_2 = 1800$ m·s^{-1} when the separation is 9.00 mm.

27

Capacitance and Dielectrics

Capacitors are among the indispensable elements of modern electronic devices, including communication equipment, photoflash units, high-energy accelerators, and many others. In principle, a capacitor is a simple device consisting of two conductors separated by vacuum or an insulating material. When charges of equal magnitude and opposite sign are placed on the conductors, there is a potential difference between them and an electric field in the region between them. For a given capacitor the ratio of charge to potential difference is a constant, called the *capacitance*. A charged capacitor has stored energy, analogous to mechanical potential energy, that it can deliver to a circuit when it discharges. This energy is directly related to the electric field between the conductors. When an insulating material (a *dielectric*) is present, the capacitance is increased because of redistribution of charge, called *polarization*, within the material.

27–1
Capacitors

Any two conductors separated by an insulator form a **capacitor.** In most practical applications the conductors have charges with equal magnitude and opposite sign, and the *net* charge on the capacitor as a whole is zero. The electric field in the region between the conductors is proportional to the magnitude Q of charge on each conductor, so the *potential difference* V_{ab} between the conductors is also proportional to Q. If we double the magnitude of charge on each conductor, the charge density at each point doubles, the electric field at each point doubles, the potential difference between conductors doubles, and the *ratio* of charge to potential difference does not change. (In older literature a capacitor is sometimes called a *condenser*; this term is generally regarded as obsolete.)

When we say a capacitor has charge Q, we mean that the conductor at higher potential has a charge Q and the conductor at lower potential has a charge $-Q$ (assuming that Q is positive). Keep this in mind in the following discussion and examples.

We define the **capacitance C** of a capacitor as the ratio of the magnitude of the charge Q on *either* conductor to the magnitude of the potential difference V_{ab} between the conductors:

$$C = \frac{Q}{V_{ab}}. \tag{27–1}$$

From this definition the unit of capacitance is 1 *coulomb per volt* (1 C·V^{-1}). A capacitance of one coulomb per volt is called 1 **farad** (1 F), in honor of Michael Faraday:

$$1\ \text{F} = 1\ \text{C·V}^{-1}.$$

In circuit diagrams a capacitor is represented by the symbol

Capacitors have thousands of practical uses, and contemporary electronics could not exist without them. They are an essential element in tuning circuits in radio transmitters and receivers, in circuits that smooth and regulate the output of electronic power supplies, in flash units for cameras, and in many other areas. The study of capacitors also helps us to develop insight into the behavior of electric fields and their interactions with matter. So there are many reasons to study capacitors!

27–2
The Parallel-Plate Capacitor

The most common form of capacitor, and one that is easy to analyze, consists of two parallel conducting plates, as shown in Fig. 27–1, separated by a distance that is small in comparison with their dimensions. Nearly all the field of such a capacitor is localized in the region between

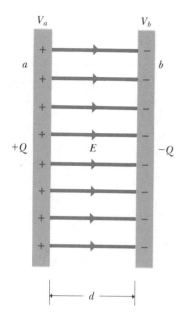

27–1
Parallel-plate capacitor.

the plates, as shown. There is some "fringing" of the field at the edges, but if the spacing is small in comparison to their size, we can neglect this. The field between the plates is then *uniform*, and the charges on the plates are uniformly distributed over their opposing surfaces. We call this arrangement a **parallel-plate capacitor.**

We worked out the electric-field magnitude for this arrangement in Example 25–12 (Section 25–5), and it would be a good idea to review this discussion. The total charge Q on each plate is the surface charge density σ multiplied by the area A of the plate, and the electric field E can be expressed as

$$E = \frac{\sigma}{\epsilon_0} = \frac{Q}{\epsilon_0 A},$$

The field is uniform; if the distance between the plates is d, then the potential difference ("voltage") between them is

$$V_{ab} = Ed = \frac{1}{\epsilon_0}\frac{Qd}{A}.$$

From this we see that the capacitance C of the parallel-plate capacitor is

$$C = \frac{Q}{V_{ab}} = \epsilon_0 \frac{A}{d}. \qquad (27\text{--}2)$$

The quantities ϵ_0, A, and d are constants for a given capacitor. The capacitance C is therefore a constant independent of the charge on the capacitor. It is directly proportional to the area A of each plate and inversely proportional to their separation d.

In Eq. (27–2), if A is in square meters and d in meters, C is in farads. The units of ϵ_0 are $C^2 \cdot N^{-1} \cdot m^{-2}$, so we see that

$$1\text{ F} = 1\text{ C}^2 \cdot N^{-1} \cdot m^{-1}.$$

Using the fact that $1\text{ N} \cdot m = 1\text{ J}$ and $1\text{ V} = 1\text{ J} \cdot C^{-1}$, we see that these units are equivalent to

$$1\text{ F} = 1\text{ C} \cdot V^{-1},$$

as we mentioned in Section 27–1.

In this analysis we have assumed that there is only vacuum in the space between the plates. When matter is present, things are somewhat different. We will return to this topic in Section 27–5. Meanwhile, we remark that if the space contains air at atmospheric pressure instead of vacuum, the capacitance differs from the prediction of Eq. (27–2) by less than 0.1%.

Example 27–1   A parallel-plate capacitor has a capacitance of 1.0 F, and the plates are 1.0 mm apart. What is the area of the plates?

Solution   From Eq. (27–2),

$$A = \frac{Cd}{\epsilon_0} = \frac{(1.0\text{ F})(1.0 \times 10^{-3}\text{ m})}{8.85 \times 10^{-12}\text{ C}^2 \cdot N^{-1} \cdot m^{-2}} = 1.1 \times 10^8\text{ m}^2.$$

This corresponds to a square about 10 km or about 6 miles on a side! ∎

Because the farad is such a large unit of capacitance, the most commonly used units are the *microfarad* ($1 \ \mu F = 10^{-6}$ F) and the *picofarad* ($1 \ pF = 10^{-12}$ F). For example, the power supply of an ac-powered AM radio contains several capacitors with capacitances of the order of 10 or more μF, and the capacitances in the tuning circuits are of the order of 10 to 100 pF.

Example 27–2   The plates of a parallel-plate capacitor are 5.00 mm apart and 2.00 m^2 in area. A potential difference of 10,000 V (= 10.0 kV) is applied across the capacitor. Compute (a) the capacitance, (b) the charge on each plate, and (c) the magnitude of electric field in the space between them.

Solution

a) From Eq. (27–2),

$$C = \epsilon_0 \frac{A}{d} = \frac{(8.85 \times 10^{-12} \ C^2 \cdot N^{-1} \cdot m^{-2})(2.00 \ m^2)}{5.00 \times 10^{-3} \ m}$$

$$= 3.54 \times 10^{-9} \ F = 0.00354 \ \mu F.$$

b) The charge on the capacitor is

$$Q = C V_{ab} = (3.54 \times 10^{-9} \ C \cdot V^{-1})(1.00 \times 10^4 V)$$

$$= 3.54 \times 10^{-5} \ C = 35.4 \ \mu C.$$

That is, the plate at higher potential has a charge of $+35.4 \ \mu C$, and the other plate has a charge of $-35.4 \ \mu C$.

c) The electric field is

$$E = \frac{\sigma}{\epsilon_0} = \frac{Q}{\epsilon_0 A} = \frac{3.54 \times 10^{-5} \ C}{(8.85 \times 10^{-12} \ C^2 \cdot N^{-1} \cdot m^{-2})(2.00 \ m^2)}$$

$$= 2.00 \times 10^6 \ N \cdot C^{-1};$$

or, because the electric field equals the potential gradient,

$$E = \frac{V_{ab}}{d} = \frac{1.00 \times 10^4 \ V}{5.00 \times 10^{-3} \ m} = 2.00 \times 10^6 \ V \cdot m^{-1}.$$

(Remember that the newton per coulomb and the volt per meter are equivalent units.) ∎

For more complex conductor shapes the relation of capacitance to the shapes and dimensions of the conductors is more complex than Eq. (27–2). In all cases, though, the capacitance of any pair of conductors is always determined completely by their geometric properties. When there is a material in the space between conductors, its properties also play a role, as we will see in Section 27–5.

27–3
Capacitors in Series and Parallel

The arrangement shown in Fig. 27–2a is called a **series** connection. Two capacitors are connected in series between points a and b, and a constant potential difference V_{ab} is maintained. The capacitors are both initially uncharged. In this connection, both capacitors always have the same charge Q. The total charge on the lower plate of C_1, and the upper plate of C_2 must be zero because these plates aren't connected to anything except each other. Also, the magnitudes of these charges must be the same as those on the remaining two plates. If they weren't, the net charge on each capacitor would not be zero, and the resulting electric fields in the connecting conductors would cause charge to flow until the total charge on each capacitor was zero. *In a series connection the magnitude of charge on all plates is the same.*

Referring again to Fig. 27–2a, we have

$$V_{ac} = V_1 = \frac{Q}{C_1}, \qquad V_{cb} = V_2 = \frac{Q}{C_2},$$

$$V_{ab} = V = V_1 + V_2 = Q\left(\frac{1}{C_1} + \frac{1}{C_2}\right),$$

and

$$\frac{V}{Q} = \frac{1}{C_1} + \frac{1}{C_2}. \qquad (27\text{--}3)$$

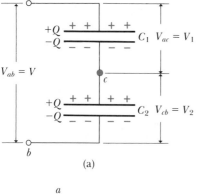

The **equivalent capacitance** C of the series combination is defined as the capacitance of a *single* capacitor for which the charge Q is the same as for the combination, when the potential difference V is the same. For such a capacitor, shown in Fig. 27–2b,

$$Q = CV, \qquad \frac{V}{Q} = \frac{1}{C}. \qquad (27\text{--}4)$$

Combining Eqs. (27–3) and (27–4), we find

$$\frac{1}{C} = \frac{1}{C_1} + \frac{1}{C_2}.$$

We can extend this analysis to any number of capacitors in series; we find

$$\frac{1}{C} = \frac{1}{C_1} + \frac{1}{C_2} + \frac{1}{C_3} + \cdots. \qquad (27\text{--}5)$$

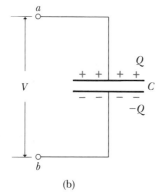

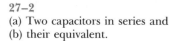

27–2
(a) Two capacitors in series and (b) their equivalent.

The reciprocal of the equivalent capacitance of a series combination equals the sum of the reciprocals of the individual capacitances.

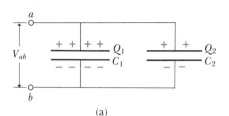

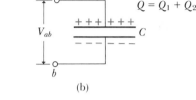

27–3
(a) Two capacitors in parallel and
(b) their equivalent.

The arrangement shown in Fig. 27–3a is called a **parallel** connection. Two capacitors are connected in parallel between points a and b. In this case the upper plates of the two capacitors are connected together to form an equipotential surface, and the lower plates form another. The potential difference is the same for both capacitors and is equal to $V_{ab} = V$. The charges Q_1 and Q_2, which are not necessarily equal, are given by

$$Q_1 = C_1 V, \qquad Q_2 = C_2 V.$$

The *total* charge Q of the combination is

$$Q = Q_1 + Q_2 = V(C_1 + C_2),$$

so

$$\frac{Q}{V} = C_1 + C_2. \tag{27–6}$$

The *equivalent* capacitance C of the parallel combination is defined as that of a single capacitor, shown in Fig. 27–3b, for which the total charge is the same as in Fig. 27–3a. For this capacitor, $Q/V = C$, and so

$$C = C_1 + C_2.$$

In the same way we can show that for any number of capacitors in parallel,

$$C = C_1 + C_2 + C_3 + \cdots. \tag{27–7}$$

The equivalent capacitance of a parallel combination equals the *sum* of the individual capacitances.

PROBLEM-SOLVING STRATEGY: *Equivalent Capacitance*

1. Keep in mind that when we say that a capacitor has a charge Q, we always mean that one plate has a charge Q and the other plate has a charge $-Q$.

2. When two capacitors are connected in series, as in Fig. 27–2a, they always have the same charge, assuming that they were uncharged before they were connected. The potential differences are *not* equal unless the capacitances are equal. The total potential difference across the combination is the sum of the individual potential differences.

3. When two capacitors are connected in parallel, as in Fig. 27–3a, the potential difference V is always the same for both. The charges on the two are *not* equal unless the capacitances are equal; the total charge on the combination is the sum of the individual charges.

Example 27–3   In Figs. 27–2 and 27–3, let $C_1 = 6.0 \ \mu F$, $C_2 = 3.0 \ \mu F$, and $V_{ab} = 18$ V. Find the equivalent capacitance, and find the charge and potential difference for each capacitor when the two capacitors are connected in (a) series and (b) parallel.

Solution

a) The equivalent capacitance of the series combination (Fig. 27–2a) is given by Eq. (27–5):

$$\frac{1}{C} = \frac{1}{6.0 \ \mu\text{F}} + \frac{1}{3.0 \ \mu\text{F}}, \qquad C = 2.0 \ \mu\text{F}.$$

The charge Q is

$$Q = CV = (2.0 \ \mu\text{F})(18 \ \text{V}) = 36 \ \mu\text{C}.$$

The potential differences across the capacitors are

$$V_{ac} = V_1 = \frac{Q}{C_1} = \frac{36 \ \mu\text{C}}{6.0 \ \mu\text{F}} = 6.0 \ \text{V},$$

$$V_{cb} = V_2 = \frac{Q}{C_2} = \frac{36 \ \mu\text{C}}{3.0 \ \mu\text{F}} = 12 \ \text{V}.$$

The *larger* potential difference appears across the *smaller* capacitor.

b) The equivalent capacitance of the parallel combination (Fig. 27–3a) is given by Eq. (27–7):

$$C = C_1 + C_2 = 6.0 \ \mu\text{F} + 3.0 \ \mu\text{F} = 9.0 \ \mu\text{F}.$$

The charges Q_1 and Q_2 are

$$Q_1 = C_1V = (6.0 \ \mu\text{F})(18 \ \text{V}) = 108 \ \mu\text{C},$$

$$Q_2 = C_2V = (3.0 \ \mu\text{F})(18 \ \text{V}) = 54 \ \mu\text{C}.$$

The potential difference across each capacitor is 18 V. ∎

27–4
Energy of a Charged Capacitor

A charged capacitor has electrical potential energy. The opposite charges on the plates, separated and attracted toward each other, are analogous to a stretched spring. Imagine detaching a small amount of charge ΔQ from the positively charged plate and letting it move to the negatively charged plate. If the potential difference is V, then it loses an amount of potential energy equal to V (the potential energy per unit charge) multiplied by ΔQ. This is also equal to the work done on ΔQ by the electric field between the plates.

The total potential energy isn't just QV, though, because the potential is proportional to the remaining charge. When we transfer a little charge from the positive to the negative plate, the potential decreases proportionally. If we transfer *all* the charge, a little at a time, to discharge the capacitor completely, the total decrease of potential energy is the *average* potential during the process, which is $V/2$, multiplied by the total charge Q. We conclude that the initial potential energy U, when the charge is Q and the potential difference is V, is

$$U = \frac{1}{2}QV.$$

Using the relation $Q = CV$, we can also write this as

$$U = \frac{1}{2}QV = \frac{1}{2}CV^2 = \frac{Q^2}{2C}. \tag{27–8}$$

A charged capacitor is the electrical analog of a stretched spring with elastic potential energy $U = \frac{1}{2}kx^2$. The charge Q is analogous to the elongation x, and the *reciprocal* of the capacitance, $1/C$, is analogous to the force constant k. The energy supplied to a capacitor in the charging process is analogous to the work done in stretching the spring.

There is a very direct relationship between the energy stored in a capacitor and the electric field between the capacitor plates. Indeed, we can think of the energy as stored *in the field*. To develop this relationship, let's find the energy *per unit volume* in the space between the plates. We call this the **energy density** and denote it by u. From Eq. (27–8) the total energy is $\frac{1}{2}CV^2$, and the volume between the plates is just Ad. The energy density is

$$u = \text{energy density} = \frac{\frac{1}{2}CV^2}{Ad}. \tag{27–9}$$

The capacitance C is given by Eq. (27–2): $C = \epsilon_0 A/d$, and the electric field magnitude E is equal to V/d. Using these in Eq. (27–9), we find

$$u = \frac{1}{2}\epsilon_0 E^2. \tag{27–10}$$

Although we have derived Eq. (27–10) only for one specific situation, it turns out to be valid in general. That is, the energy per unit volume associated with *any* electric-field configuration is given by Eq. (27–10). We will use this result in Chapter 35 in connection with the energy transported by electromagnetic waves.

Example 27–4   In Fig. 27–4 we charge a capacitor C_1 by connecting it to a source of potential difference V_0 (not shown in the figure). Let $C_1 = 8.0 \ \mu F$ and $V_0 = 120$ V. The charge Q_0 is

$$Q_0 = C_1 V_0 = 960 \ \mu C,$$

and the energy of the capacitor is

$$U = \tfrac{1}{2}Q_0 V_0 = \tfrac{1}{2}(960 \times 10^{-6} \ \text{C})(120 \ \text{V}) = 0.058 \ \text{J}.$$

After we close the switch S, the positive charge Q_0 is distributed over the upper plates of both capacitors, and the negative charge $-Q_0$ is distributed over the lower plates of both. Let Q_1 and Q_2 be the magnitudes of the final charges on the two capacitors. Then

$$Q_1 + Q_2 = Q_0.$$

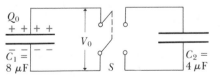

27–4
When the switch S is closed, the charged capacitor C_1 is connected to an uncharged capacitor C_2.

In the final state, both upper plates are at the same potential; they are connected by a wire and so form a single equipotential surface. Both lower plates are at the same potential, different from that of the upper plates. The final potential difference between the plates, V, is therefore the same for both capacitors, and

$$Q_1 = C_1 V, \qquad Q_2 = C_2 V.$$

When we combine this with the preceding equation, we find

$$V = \frac{Q_0}{C_1 + C_2} = \frac{960 \ \mu C}{12 \ \mu F} = 80 \ V,$$

$$Q_1 = 640 \ \mu C, \qquad Q_2 = 320 \ \mu C.$$

The final energy of the system is

$$\tfrac{1}{2}Q_1 V + \tfrac{1}{2}Q_2 V = \tfrac{1}{2}Q_0 V = \tfrac{1}{2}(960 \times 10^{-6} \ C)(80 \ V) = 0.038 \ J.$$

This is less than the original energy of 0.058 J; the difference has been converted to energy of some other form. The conductors become a little warmer, and some energy is radiated as electromagnetic waves.

This process is analogous to the mechanical process of an inelastic collision of a moving car with a stationary car. In the electrical case the charge $Q = CV$ is conserved; in the mechanical case the momentum $p = mv$ is conserved. The electrical energy $\tfrac{1}{2}CV^2$ is *not* conserved, and the mechanical energy $\tfrac{1}{2}mv^2$ is *not* conserved. ∎

27–5
Effect of a Dielectric

Most capacitors have a solid, nonconducting material or **dielectric** between their plates. A common type of capacitor uses long strips of metal foil, forming the plates, separated by strips of plastic sheet such as Mylar. A sandwich of these materials is rolled up, forming a compact unit that can provide a capacitance of several microfarads in a compact package.

Placing a solid dielectric between the plates of a capacitor serves three functions. First, it solves the mechanical problem of maintaining two large metal sheets at a very small separation without actual contact.

Second, any dielectric material, when subjected to a sufficiently large electric field, experiences **dielectric breakdown,** a partial ionization that permits conduction through a material that is supposed to insulate. Many insulating materials can tolerate stronger electric fields without breakdown than can air.

Third, the capacitance of a capacitor of given dimensions is *greater* when there is a dielectric material between the plates than in air or vacuum. We can demonstrate this effect with the aid of a sensitive electrometer, a device that measures the potential difference between two conductors without letting any charge flow from one to the other. Figure 27–5a shows a charged capacitor, with magnitude of charge Q on each plate and potential difference V_0. When we insert a sheet of

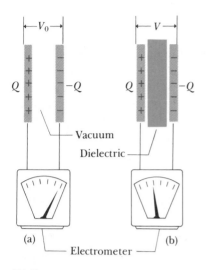

Vacuum

Dielectric

(a)

(b)

Electrometer

27–5
Effect of a dielectric between the plates of a parallel-plate capacitor. The electrometer measures potential difference. (a) With a given charge the potential difference is V_0. (b) With the same charge the potential difference V is smaller than V_0, and the capacitance C is greater than its vacuum value C_0 by the same factor.

dielectric, such as glass, paraffin, or polystyrene, between the plates, the potential difference *decreases* to a smaller value V, as shown in Fig. 27–5b. When we remove the dielectric, the potential difference returns to its original value V_0, showing that the original charges on the plates have not changed.

The original capacitance C_0 is given by $C_0 = Q/V_0$, and the capacitance C with the dielectric present is $C = Q/V$. The charge Q is the same in both cases, and V is less than V_0, so we conclude that the capacitance C with the dielectric present is *greater* than C_0. The ratio of C to C_0, equal to the ratio of V_0 to V, is called the **dielectric constant** of the material, K:

$$K = \frac{C}{C_0}. \tag{27–11}$$

The potential is *reduced* by a factor K:

$$K = \frac{V_0}{V}. \tag{27–12}$$

The dielectric constant K is a pure number. Because C is always greater than C_0, K is always greater than unity. A few representative values of K are given in Table 27–1. For vacuum, $K = 1$ by definition; for air, K is so nearly equal to 1 that for most purposes an air capacitor is equivalent to one in vacuum.

Because the potential difference between the plates is reduced by a factor K when a dielectric material is present, the electric field between the plates is reduced by the same factor. If E_0 is the vacuum value and E the value with the dielectric, then

$$E = \frac{E_0}{K}. \tag{27–13}$$

The fact that E is smaller when the dielectric is present means that the surface charge density is smaller. The surface charge on the conducting plates does not change, but an *induced* charge of the opposite sign appears on each surface of the dielectric, as shown in Fig. 27–6. These induced surface charges are a result of redistribution of charge within the dielectric material, a phenomenon called **polarization.**

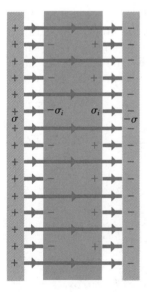

27–6
Induced charges on the faces of a dielectric in an external field.

TABLE 27–1	**Dielectric constant K at 20°C**		
Material	**K**	**Material**	**K**
Vacuum	1	Germanium	16
Glass	5–10	Strontium titanate	310
Mica	3–6	Water	80.4
Mylar	3.1	Glycerin	42.5
Neoprene	6.70	Benzene	2.28
Plexiglas	3.40	Air (1 atm)	1.00059
Polyethylene	2.25	Air (100 atm)	1.0548
Polyvinyl chloride	3.18		
Teflon	2.1		

We can derive a relation between this induced surface charge and the charge on the plates. Let's denote the magnitude of the induced charge per unit area (surface charge density) on the surfaces of the dielectric by σ_i. The magnitude of the surface charge density on the capacitor plates is σ, as usual. Then the *net* surface charge on each side of the capacitor has magnitude $(\sigma - \sigma_i)$. The field between the plates is related to the net surface charge density by Eq. (25–11). Without and with the dielectric, respectively, we have

$$E_0 = \frac{\sigma}{\epsilon_0}, \qquad E = \frac{\sigma - \sigma_i}{\epsilon_0}.$$

When we use these expressions in Eq. (27–13) and rearrange the result, we find

$$\sigma_i = \sigma\left(1 - \frac{1}{K}\right). \tag{27–14}$$

This equation shows that when K is very large, σ_i is nearly as large as σ, and the field and potential difference are very much smaller than their vacuum values.

The product $K\epsilon_0$ is called the **permittivity** of the dielectric; we denote it by ϵ:

$$\epsilon = K\epsilon_0. \tag{27–15}$$

In terms of ϵ we can express the electric field within the dielectric as

$$E = \frac{\sigma}{\epsilon}. \tag{27–16}$$

The capacitance when the dielectric is present is given by

$$C = KC_0 = K\epsilon_0\frac{A}{d} = \epsilon\frac{A}{d}. \tag{27–17}$$

In empty space, where $K = 1$, $\epsilon = \epsilon_0$. For this reason, ϵ_0 is sometimes called the "permittivity of empty space" or the "permittivity of vacuum." Because K is a pure number, ϵ and ϵ_0 have the same units, $C^2 \cdot N^{-1} \cdot m^{-2}$.

We can repeat the derivation of Eq. (27–10) for the energy density u in an electric field, for the case in which a dielectric is present. The result is

$$u = \tfrac{1}{2}K\epsilon_0 E^2 = \tfrac{1}{2}\epsilon E^2. \tag{27–18}$$

PROBLEM-SOLVING STRATEGY: *Dielectrics*

1. As usual, be careful with units. Distances must be in meters; remember that a microfarad is 10^{-6} F, and so on. Don't confuse the numerical value of ϵ_0 with that of $1/4\pi\epsilon_0$. There are several alternative sets of units for electric field magnitude, including newton per coulomb and volt per meter.

Always check for consistency of units; it's a bit more of a nuisance with electrical quantities than it was in mechanics, but it's worth it!

2. In problems such as the following example, it is easy to get lost in a blizzard of formulas. Ask

yourself at each step what kind of quantity each symbol represents. For example, distinguish clearly between charges and charge densities and between electric fields and potentials. When you check numerical values, remember that the capacitance with a dielectric present is always greater than without and that the induced surface charge density σ_i on the dielectric is always less than the charge density σ on the capacitor plates. With a given charge on a capacitor the electric field and potential difference are less with a dielectric present than without it.

Example 27–5 The parallel plates in Fig. 27–6 have an area of 2000 cm^2 (= 2.00×10^{-1} m^2) and are 1.00 cm (= 1.00×10^{-2} m) apart. The original potential difference between them, V_0, is 3000 V (= 3.00 kV), and it decreases to 1000 V when a sheet of dielectric is inserted between the plates. Compute

a) the original capacitance C_0;

b) the magnitude of charge Q on each plate;

c) the capacitance C after the dielectric is inserted;

d) the dielectric constant K of the dielectric;

e) the permittivity ϵ of the dielectric;

f) the magnitude of induced charge Q_i on each face of the dielectric;

g) the original electric field E_0 between the plates; and

h) the electric field E after the dielectric is inserted.

Solution Most of these quantities can be obtained in several different ways. Here is a representative sample; try to think of others and compare them.

a) $C_0 = \epsilon_0 \dfrac{A}{d} = (8.85 \times 10^{-12} \text{ C}^2 \cdot \text{N}^{-1} \cdot \text{m}^{-2}) \dfrac{2.00 \times 10^{-1} \text{ m}^2}{1.00 \times 10^{-2} \text{ m}}$

$$= 17.7 \times 10^{-11} \text{ F} = 177 \text{ pF}.$$

b) $Q = C_0 V_0 = (17.7 \times 10^{-11} \text{ F})(3.00 \times 10^3 \text{ V}) = 53.1 \times 10^{-8} \text{ C}.$

c) $C = \dfrac{Q}{V} = \dfrac{53.1 \times 10^{-8} \text{ C}}{1.00 \times 10^3 \text{ V}} = 53.1 \times 10^{-11} \text{ F} = 531 \text{ pF}.$

d) $K = \dfrac{C}{C_0} = \dfrac{53.1 \times 10^{-11} \text{ F}}{17.7 \times 10^{-11} \text{ F}} = 3.00.$

Or, from Eq. (27–12),

$$K = \frac{V_0}{V} = \frac{3000 \text{ V}}{1000 \text{ V}} = 3.00.$$

e) $\epsilon = K\epsilon_0 = (3.00)(8.85 \times 10^{-12} \text{ C}^2 \cdot \text{N}^{-1} \cdot \text{m}^{-2})$

$$= 26.6 \times 10^{-12} \text{ C}^2 \cdot \text{N}^{-1} \cdot \text{m}^{-2}.$$

f) From Eq. (27–14),

$$Q_i = Q\left(1 - \frac{1}{K}\right) = (53.1 \times 10^{-8} \text{ C})\left(1 - \frac{1}{3.00}\right)$$

$$= 35.4 \times 10^{-8} \text{ C}.$$

g)
$$E_0 = \frac{V_0}{d} = \frac{3000 \text{ V}}{1.00 \times 10^{-2} \text{ m}} = 3.00 \times 10^5 \text{ V·m}^{-1}.$$

h)
$$E = \frac{V}{d} = \frac{1000 \text{ V}}{1.00 \times 10^{-2} \text{ m}} = 1.00 \times 10^5 \text{ V·m}^{-1};$$

or

$$E = \frac{\sigma}{\epsilon} = \frac{Q}{A\epsilon} = \frac{53.1 \times 10^{-8} \text{ C}}{(2.00 \times 10^{-1} \text{ m}^2)(26.6 \times 10^{-12} \text{ C}^2\text{·N}^{-1}\text{·m}^{-2})}$$

$$= 1.00 \times 10^5 \text{ V·m}^{-1};$$

or

$$E = \frac{\sigma - \sigma_i}{\epsilon_0} = \frac{Q - Q_i}{A\epsilon_0}$$

$$= \frac{(53.1 - 35.4) \times 10^{-8} \text{ C}}{(2.00 \times 10^{-1} \text{ m}^2)(8.85 \times 10^{-12} \text{ C}^2\text{·N}^{-1}\text{·m}^{-2})}$$

$$= 1.00 \times 10^5 \text{ V·m}^{-1};$$

or, from Eq. (27–13),

$$E = \frac{E_0}{K} = \frac{3.00 \times 10^5 \text{ V·m}^{-1}}{3.00} = 1.00 \times 10^5 \text{ V·m}^{-1}. \quad \blacksquare$$

We mentioned earlier that when any dielectric material is subjected to a sufficiently strong electric field, it becomes a conductor. This phenomenon is called dielectric breakdown. The onset of conduction, associated with cumulative ionization of molecules of the material, is often quite sudden and may be characterized by spark or arc discharges. Capacitors always have maximum voltage ratings. When a capacitor is subjected to excessive voltage, an arc may form through a layer of dielectric, burning or melting a hole in it. This permits the two metal foils to come into contact, creating a short circuit and rendering the device permanently useless as a capacitor.

The maximum electric field a material can withstand without the occurrence of breakdown is called its **dielectric strength.** This quantity is affected significantly by impurities in the material, small irregularities in the metal electrodes, and other factors that are difficult to control. For this reason we can give only approximate figures for dielectric strengths. The dielectric strength of dry air is about 0.8×10^6 V·m^{-1}. Typical values for the plastic and ceramic materials that are commonly used to insulate capacitors and current-carrying wires are of the order of 10^7 V·m^{-1}. For example, a layer of such a material, 10^{-4} m in thickness, could withstand a maximum voltage of 1000 V, since 1000 V/10^{-4} m = 10^7 V·m^{-1}. Figure 27–7 shows a spectacular example of dielectric breakdown.

27–7
Dendritic pattern formed in a Plexiglas block by dielectric breakdown under the action of a very strong electric field. (Courtesy of High Voltage Research Laboratory, M.I.T.)

*27–6
Molecular Model of Induced Charge

In the preceding section we discussed induced surface charges on a dielectric in an electric field. Now let's look at how these surface charges can come about. If the material were a *conductor*, the answer would be simple. Conductors contain charge that is free to move, and when an electric field is present, some of the charge redistributes itself on the surface so that there is no electric field inside the conductor. But dielectrics have no charges that are free to move, so how can a surface charge occur?

To understand this, we have to look at rearrangement of charge at the *molecular* level. First, some molecules, such as H_2O and N_2O, have equal amounts of positive and negative charge but a lopsided distribution, with excess positive charge concentrated on one side of the molecule and negative charge on the other. This arrangement is called an *electric dipole*, and the molecule is called a *polar molecule*. When no electric field is present, the molecules are oriented randomly. When they are placed in an electric field, however, they tend to orient themselves as in Fig. 27–8 as a result of the electric-field forces.

Even a molecule that is *not* ordinarily polar becomes a dipole when it is placed in an electric field because the field forces cause some redistribution of charge within the molecule, as shown in Fig. 27–9. Such dipoles are called *induced* dipoles. With either polar or nonpolar molecules an external field causes the formation of a layer of charge on each surface of the dielectric material, as shown in Fig. 27–10. These layers are

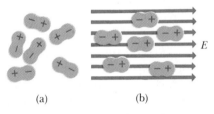

27–8
Behavior of polar molecules (a) in the absence and (b) in the presence of an electric field.

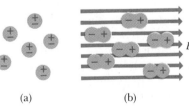

27–9
Behavior of nonpolar molecules (a) in the absence and (b) in the presence of an electric field.

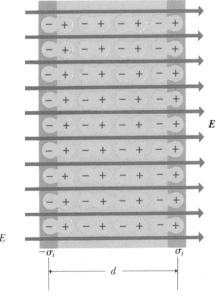

27–10
Polarization of a dielectric in an electric field gives rise to thin layers of bound charges on the surfaces.

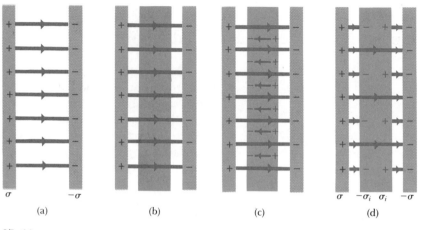

27–11
(a) Electric field between two charged plates. (b) Introduction of a dielectric.
(c) Induced surface charges and their field. (d) Resultant field when a dielectric is
between charged plates.

the surface charges described in Section 27–5; their surface charge density is denoted by σ_i. The charges are not free to move indefinitely, as they would be in a conductor, because each charge is bound to a molecule. They are in fact called **bound charges** to distinguish them from the **free charges** that are added to and removed from the conducting capacitor plates. In the interior of the material the net charge per unit volume remains zero. We say that in this state the material is *polarized*.

The four parts of Fig. 27–11 show the behavior of a slab of dielectric when it is inserted into the field between a pair of oppositely charged capacitor plates. Figure 27–11a shows the original field. Figure 27–11b is the situation after the dielectric has been inserted but before any rearrangement of charges has occurred. Figure 27–11c shows by thinner lines the additional field set up in the dielectric by its induced surface charges. This field is *opposite* to the original field, but it is not great enough to cancel the original field completely because the charges in the dielectric are not free to move indefinitely. The field in the dielectric is therefore decreased in magnitude. The resultant field is shown in Fig. 27–11d. Some of the field lines leaving the positive plate penetrate the dielectric; others terminate on the induced charges on the faces of the dielectric.

Induced charge is also the reason a charged body such as an electrified plastic rod can exert a force on an *uncharged* body such as a cork ball or bit of paper. Figure 27–12 shows an uncharged dielectric sphere B in the radial field of a positive charge A. The induced positive charges on B experience a force toward the right, while the force on the negative charges is toward the left. The negative charges are closer to A and in a stronger field than are the positive charges. The force toward the left is stronger than that toward the right, and B is attracted toward A, even though its net charge is zero. The sign of A's charge does not matter. Furthermore, the effect is not limited to dielectrics; an uncharged conducting body would be attracted the same way.

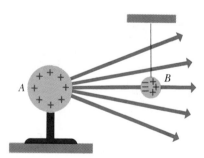
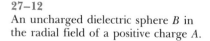

27–12
An uncharged dielectric sphere B in the radial field of a positive charge A.

Questions

27–1 A student claimed that two capacitors connected in parallel always have an effective capacitance *greater* than that of either capacitor, but when they are in series the effective capacitance is always *less* than that of either capacitor. Confirm or refute these claims.

27–2 Could one define a capacitance for a single conductor? What would be a reasonable definition?

27–3 Suppose the two plates of a capacitor have different areas. When the capacitor is charged by connecting it to a battery, do the charges on the two plates have equal magnitude, or may they be different?

27–4 Can you think of a situation in which the two plates of a capacitor *do not* have equal magnitudes of charge?

27–5 A capacitor is charged by being connected to a battery and is then disconnected from the charging agency. The plates are then pulled apart a little. How does the electric field change? The potential difference? The total energy?

27–6 According to the text, one can consider the energy in a charged capacitor to be located in the field between the plates. But suppose there is vacuum between the plates; can there be energy in vacuum?

27–7 The charged plates of a capacitor attract each other. To pull the plates farther apart therefore requires work by some external force. What becomes of the energy added by this work?

27–8 A solid slab of metal is placed between the plates of a capacitor without touching either plate. Does the capacitance increase, decrease, or remain the same?

27–9 The two plates of a capacitor are given charges $\pm Q$, and then they are immersed in a tank of oil. Does the electric field between them increase, decrease, or remain the same? How may this field be measured?

27–10 Is dielectric strength the same thing as dielectric constant?

27–11 Liquid dielectrics having polar molecules (such as water) always have dielectric constants that decrease with increasing temperature. Why?

27–12 A capacitor made of aluminum foil strips separated by Mylar film was subjected to excessive voltage, and the resulting dielectric breakdown melted holes in the Mylar. After this the capacitance was found to be about the same as before, but the breakdown voltage was much less. Why?

27–13 Two capacitors have equal capacitance, but one has a higher maximum voltage rating than the other. Which one is likely to be bulkier? Why?

27–14 A capacitor is made by rolling a sandwich of aluminum foil and Mylar, as described in Section 27–5. A student claimed that the capacitance when the sandwich is rolled up is twice the value when it is flat. Discuss this allegation.

Exercises

Section 27–2   The Parallel-Plate Capacitor

27–1 Show that the two definitions for the farad, $1\ \mathrm{F} = 1\ \mathrm{C \cdot V^{-1}}$ and $1\ \mathrm{F} = 1\ \mathrm{C^2 \cdot N^{-1} \cdot m^{-1}}$, are equivalent.

27–2 The plates of a parallel-plate capacitor are 2.50 mm apart, and each carries a charge of magnitude 8.00×10^{-8} C. The plates are in vacuum. The electric field between the plates has a magnitude of $4.00 \times 10^6\ \mathrm{V \cdot m^{-1}}$.

a) What is the potential difference between the plates?

b) What is the area of each plate?

c) What is the capacitance?

27–3 A parallel-plate air capacitor has a capacitance of 500 pF and a charge of magnitude 0.200 μC on each plate. The plates are 0.600 mm apart.

a) What is the potential difference between the plates?

b) What is the area of each plate?

c) What is the electric-field magnitude between the plates?

d) What is the surface charge density on each plate?

27–4 A capacitor has a capacitance of 7.20 μF. How much charge must be removed to decrease the potential difference of its plates by 50.0 V?

Section 27–3   Capacitors in Series and Parallel

27–5 In Fig. 27–2a, let $C_1 = 4.00\ \mu$F, $C_2 = 6.00\ \mu$F, and $V_{ab} = 48.0$ V. Calculate

a) the charge on each capacitor;

b) the potential difference across each capacitor.

27–6 In Fig. 27–3a, let $C_1 = 4.00$ μF, $C_2 = 6.00$ μF, and $V_{ab} = 48.0$ V. Calculate

a) the charge on each capacitor;

b) the potential difference across each capacitor.

27–7 In the circuit shown in Fig. 27–13, $C_1 = 2.00$ μF, $C_2 = 4.00$ μF, and $C_3 = 9.00$ μF. The applied potential is $V_{ab} = +36.0$ V. Calculate

a) the charge on each capacitor;

b) the potential difference across each capacitor;

c) the potential difference between points a and d.

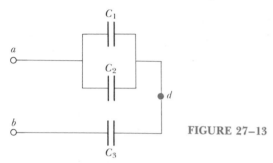

FIGURE 27–13

27–8 In Fig. 27–14, each capacitor has $C = 2.00$ μF and $V_{ab} = +24.0$ V. Calculate

a) the charge on each capacitor;

b) the potential difference across each capacitor;

c) the potential difference between points a and d.

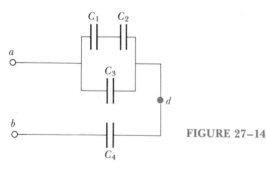

FIGURE 27–14

Section 27–4   Energy of a Charged Capacitor

27–9 A 300-μF capacitor is charged to 120 V. Then a wire is connected between the plates. How many joules of heat are produced as the capacitor discharges if all of the energy that was stored goes into heating the wire?

27–10 A 8.00-μF parallel-plate capacitor has a plate separation of 4.00 mm and is charged to a potential difference of 250 V. Calculate the energy density in the region between the plates, in units of J·m^{-3}.

27–11 An air capacitor is made from two flat parallel plates 1.75 mm apart. The magnitude of charge on each plate is 0.0150 μC when the potential difference is 200 V.

a) What is the capacitance?

b) What is the area of each plate?

c) What total energy is stored?

d) What maximum voltage can be applied without dielectric breakdown? (Dielectric breakdown for air occurs at an electric-field strength of 8.00×10^5 V·m^{-1}.)

27–12 A parallel-plate air capacitor has a capacitance of 3.50×10^{-11} F.

a) What potential difference is required for a charge of magnitude 0.500×10^{-8} C on each plate?

b) In part (a), what is the total stored energy?

c) If the plates are 3.00 mm apart, what is the area of each plate?

d) What potential difference is required for dielectric breakdown? (See Exercise 27–11d.)

27–13 An air capacitor consisting of two closely spaced parallel plates has a capacitance of 1000 pF. The magnitude of the charge on each plate is 4.00 μC.

a) What is the potential difference between the plates?

b) If the charge is kept constant, what will be the potential difference between the plates when the separation is doubled?

c) How much work is required to double the separation?

27–14 A 20.0-μF capacitor is charged to a potential difference of 800 V. The terminals of the charged capacitor are then connected to those of an uncharged 10.0-μF capacitor. Compute

a) the original charge of the system;

b) the final potential difference across each capacitor;

c) the final energy of the system;

d) the decrease in energy when the capacitors are connected.

Section 27–5   Effect of a Dielectric

27–15 Show that Eq. (27–18) holds for a parallel-plate capacitor with a dielectric material between the plates; use a derivation analogous to that used for Eq. (27–10).

27–16 A parallel-plate capacitor is to be constructed by using, as a dielectric, rubber with a dielectric constant of 3.20 and a dielectric strength of 2.00×10^7 V·m^{-1}. The capacitor is to have a capacitance of 1.50×10^{-9} F and must be able to withstand a maximum potential difference of 4000 V. What is the minimum area the plates of the capacitor can have?

27–17 The paper dielectric in a paper-and-foil capacitor is 0.0800 mm thick. Its dielectric constant is 2.50, and its dielectric strength is 50.0×10^6 V·m^{-1}. Assume that the geometry is that of a parallel-plate capacitor, with the metal foil serving as the plates.

  a) What area of each plate is required for a 0.200-μF capacitor?

  b) If the electric field in the paper is not to exceed one-half the dielectric strength, what is the maximum potential difference that can be applied across the capacitor?

27–18 Two parallel plates have equal and opposite charges. When the space between the plates is evacuated, the electric field is 2.80×10^5 V·m^{-1}. When the space is filled with a dielectric material, the electric field is 1.20×10^5 V·m^{-1}.

  a) What is the charge density on the surface of the dielectric?

  b) What is the dielectric constant?

27–19 Two oppositely charged conducting plates, with equal magnitude of charge per unit area, are separated by a dielectric 3.00 mm thick, with a dielectric constant of 4.50. The resultant electric field in the dielectric is 2.80×10^6 V·m^{-1}. Compute

  a) the charge per unit area on the conducting plates;

  b) the charge per unit area on the surfaces of the dielectric.

27–20 Two parallel plates, each with an area of 100 cm^2, are given equal and opposite charges of magnitude 1.80×10^{-7} C. The space between the plates is filled with a dielectric material, and the electric field within the dielectric is 3.30×10^5 V·m^{-1}.

  a) What is the dielectric constant of the dielectric?

  b) What is the total induced charge on either face of the dielectric?

Problems

27–21 A parallel-plate air capacitor is made from two plates 0.200 m square, spaced 0.800 cm apart. It is connected to a 120-V battery.

  a) What is the capacitance?

  b) What is the charge on each plate?

  c) What is the electric field between the plates?

  d) What is the energy stored in the capacitor?

  e) If the battery is disconnected and then the plates are pulled apart to a separation of 1.60 cm, what are the answers to parts (a), (b), (c), and (d)?

27–22 In Problem 27–21, suppose the battery remains connected while the plates are pulled apart. What are the answers then to parts (a), (b), (c), and (d) after the plates have been pulled apart?

27–23 A parallel-plate capacitor with plate area A and separation x is charged, with a charge of magnitude q on each plate.

  a) What is the total energy stored in the capacitor?

  b) The plates are now pulled apart a small additional distance Δx; now what is the total energy?

  c) If F is the magnitude of the force with which the plates attract each other, then the difference in the two energies above must equal the work $\Delta W = F \, \Delta x$ done in pulling the plates apart. Show that $F = q^2/2\epsilon_0 A$.

  d) Explain why F is not equal to qE, where E is the electric field between the plates.

27–24 Several 0.500-μF capacitors are available. The voltage across each is not to exceed 350 V. We need to make a capacitor with capacitance 0.500 μF, to be connected across a potential difference of 600 V.

  a) Show in a diagram how an equivalent capacitor having the desired properties can be obtained.

  b) No dielectric is a perfect insulator with infinite resistance. Suppose that the dielectric in one of the capacitors in your diagram is a moderately good conductor. What will happen?

27–25 In Fig. 27–15, each capacitance C_3 is 6.00 μF, and each capacitance C_2 is 4.00 μF.

  a) Compute the equivalent capacitance of the network between points a and b.

  b) Compute the charge on each of three capacitors nearest a and b when $V_{ab} = 900$ V.

  c) With 900 V across a and b, compute V_{cd}.

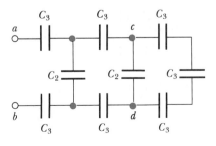

FIGURE 27–15

27–26 A 2.00-μF capacitor and a 3.00-μF capacitor are connected in parallel across a 1200-V supply line.

a) Find the charge on each capacitor and the voltage across each.

b) The charged capacitors are disconnected from the line and from each other and then reconnected, with terminals of unlike sign together. Find the final charge on each and the voltage across each.

27–27 A 2.00-μF capacitor and a 3.00-μF capacitor are connected in series across a 1200-V supply line.

a) Find the charge on each capacitor and the voltage across each.

b) The charged capacitors are disconnected from the line and from each other and then reconnected, with terminals of like sign together. Find the final charge on each and the voltage across each.

27–28 Three capacitors having capacitances of 8.00, 8.00, and 4.00 μF are connected in series across a 48.0-V line.

a) What is the charge on the 4.00-μF capacitor?

b) What is the total energy of all three capacitors?

c) The capacitors are disconnected from the line and reconnected in parallel with each other, with the positively charged plates connected together. What is the voltage across the parallel combination?

d) What is the total energy now stored in the capacitors?

27–29 In Fig. 27–3a, let $C_1 = 6.00$ μF, $C_2 = 3.00$ μF, and $V_{ab} = 24.0$ V. Suppose that the charged capacitors are disconnected from the source and from each other and reconnected to each other, with plates of *opposite* sign together. By how much does the energy of the system decrease?

27–30 A spherical capacitor consists of an inner metal sphere of radius r_a supported on an insulating stand at the center of a hollow metal sphere of inner radius r_b; there is a charge $+Q$ on the inner sphere and a charge $-Q$ on the outer. (See Problem 26–36.)

a) What is the potential difference V_{ab} between the spheres?

b) Prove that the capacitance is

$$C = 4\pi\epsilon_0 \cdot \frac{r_a r_b}{r_b - r_a}.$$

c) If $r_b - r_a = d$, show that the equation obtained in part (b) reduces to Eq. (27–2) when $d \ll r_a$, with A equal to the surface area of each sphere.

27–31 An air capacitor is made by using two flat plates, each with area A, separated by a distance d. Then a metal slab having thickness a (less than d) and the same shape and size as the plates is inserted between them, parallel to the plates and not touching either plate.

a) What is the capacitance of this arrangement?

b) Express the capacitance as a multiple of the capacitance C_0 when the metal slab is not present.

27–32 A capacitor consists of two parallel plates, each with an area of 16.0 cm^2, separated by a distance of 0.200 cm. The material that fills the volume between the plates has a dielectric constant of 5.00. The plates of the capacitor are connected to a 300-V battery.

a) What is the capacitance of the capacitor?

b) What is the charge on either plate?

c) What is the energy stored in the charged capacitor?

d) What is the energy density in the dielectric?

27–33 A parallel-plate capacitor has the space between the plates filled with two slabs of dielectric, one with constant K_1 and one with constant K_2. Each slab has thickness $d/2$, where d is the plate separation. Show that the capacitance is

$$C = \frac{2\epsilon_0 A}{d}\left(\frac{K_1 K_2}{K_1 + K_2}\right).$$

▇ *Challenge Problems*

27–34 The capacitors in Fig. 27–16 are initially uncharged and are connected as in the diagram with switch S open. The applied potential difference is 200 V.

a) What is the potential difference V_{ab}?

b) What is the potential difference across each capacitor after switch S is closed?

c) How much charge flowed through the switch when it was closed?

27–35 Three square metal plates A, B, and C, each 8.00 cm on a side and 3.00 mm thick, are arranged as in Fig. 27–17. The plates are separated by sheets of paper 0.600 mm thick and with dielectric constant 5.00. The outer plates are connected together and connected to point b. The inner plate is connected to point a.

a) Copy the diagram and show by + and − signs the charge distribution on the plates when point a is maintained at a positive potential relative to point b.

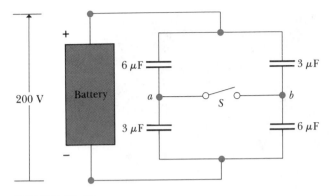

FIGURE 27–16

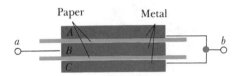

FIGURE 27–17

b) What is the capacitance between points a and b?

27–36 A fuel gauge uses a capacitor to determine the height of the fuel in a tank. The effective dielectric constant K_{eff} changes from a value of 1 when the tank is empty to a value of K, the dielectric constant of the fuel, when the tank is full. The appropriate electronic circuitry can determine the effective dielectric constant of the combined air and fuel between the capacitor plates. Each of the two rectangular plates has a width w (not shown) and a length l. (See Fig. 27–18.) The height of the fuel between the plates is h. Neglect any fringing effects.

a) Derive an expression for K_{eff} as a function of h.

b) What is the effective dielectric constant for a tank one-quarter full, one-half full, and three-quarters full if the fuel is gasoline ($K = 1.95$)?

c) Repeat part (b) for methanol ($K = 33.0$).

d) For which fuel is this fuel gauge more practical?

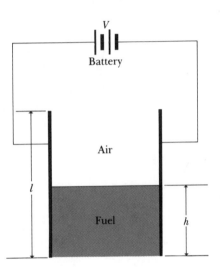

FIGURE 27–18

28

Current, Resistance, and Electromotive Force

In the preceding four chapters we have studied the interactions of electric charges at rest; now we're ready to study charges in motion. An electric current consists of motion of charge within a conductor forming a closed path called an electric circuit. Circuits are important; they are at the heart of all radio and television transmitters and receivers, household and industrial power distribution systems, computers, and the nervous systems of animals. In this chapter we describe the basic properties of conducting materials, using the concepts of resistivity and resistance and a relation called Ohm's law. We formulate the basic principles of circuit analysis in two principles called Kirchhoff's rules. Next we study energy and power considerations, which are vitally important in many practical applications of electric circuits. Finally, we discuss briefly a simple microscopic model of electrical conduction in metals.

28–1
Current

A **current** is any motion of charge from one region of a conductor to another. In an *electrostatic* situation there are no charges in motion, and the electric field everywhere within a conductor is zero. Conversely, to maintain a steady flow of charge in a conductor, we have to maintain a steady force on the mobile charges in the conductor, either with an electrostatic field or by other means that we'll come to later. For now, let's assume that there is an electric field E within the conductor, so a particle of charge q experiences a force $F = qE$.

When a charged particle such as an electron moves in an electric field *in vacuum*, it accelerates continuously. The motion of an electron inside a conducting material is very different because of frequent collisions with the atoms of the material. In a conductor a charge accelerates under the action of the electric field until it collides with a stationary particle. During each collision it gives up some of its kinetic energy; then it accelerates again until it bumps into something else, and so on. Thus there is a lot of back-and-forth motion, with a gradual *drift* in the direction of the electric-field force. The collisions with the atoms of the conductor increase their random motion, which we discussed in Section 20–6, and thus increase the temperature of the conductor.

Current is defined to be the amount of charge transferred per unit time. Let's consider a cross section of a conductor, such as a wire. We define the current through the area of this cross section as *the net charge flowing through the area per unit time*. Thus if a net charge ΔQ flows through an area in a time Δt, the current through the area, denoted by I, is

$$I = \frac{\Delta Q}{\Delta t}. \tag{28–1}$$

Current is a *scalar* quantity. The SI unit of current, *the coulomb per second*, is called the **ampere** (1 A = 1 C·s^{-1}), in honor of the French scientist André Marie Ampère (1775–1836). Currents in household electrical systems are of the order of a few amperes. Currents in radio and television circuits are usually expressed in *milliamperes* (1 mA = 10^{-3} A) or *microamperes* (1 μA = 10^{-6} A), and currents in computer circuits are expressed in *nanoamperes* (1 nA = 10^{-9} A) or *picoamperes* (1 pA = 10^{-12} A).

The current through an area can be expressed in terms of the drift velocity v of the moving charges. Let's consider the situation of Fig. 28–1, a conductor with cross-sectional area A and an electric field E directed from left to right. We assume first that the free charges in the conductor are positive; then the electric-field force is in the same direction as the field. Suppose there are n such particles per unit volume, all moving with a drift velocity v. In a time Δt, each particle moves a distance $v\,\Delta t$. The particles that flow through the right end of the shaded cylinder with length $v\,\Delta t$ during Δt are the particles that were within this cylinder at the beginning of Δt. The volume of the cylinder is $Av\,\Delta t$, and the

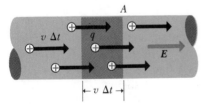

28–1
All the particles, and only those particles, within the shaded cylinder will cross its base in time Δt.

number of particles within it is $nAv \, \Delta t$. If each particle has a charge q, the charge ΔQ flowing through the end of the cylinder in time Δt is

$$\Delta Q = nqvA \, \Delta t,$$

and the current is

$$I = \frac{\Delta Q}{\Delta t} = nqvA. \tag{28-2}$$

The current *per unit cross-sectional area* is called the **current density** J. From Eq. (28–2),

$$J = \frac{I}{A} = nqv. \tag{28-3}$$

What if the moving charges are negative rather than positive? Then the electric-field force is opposite to E, and the drift velocity is right to left, *opposite* to the direction shown in Fig. 28–1. But the current is still left to right; negative charge moving right to left and positive charge moving left to right both increase the positive charge at the right of the section. We could generalize this formulation to include charges of both signs. In fact, the moving charges in metals are always (negative) electrons, while in an ionized gas (plasma), both electrons and positively charged ions are moving. In a semiconductor material such as germanium or silicon, conduction is partly by electrons and partly by motion of *vacancies*, also known as *holes*; these are sites of missing electrons and act like positive charges. We will study conduction in semiconductors in detail in Section 43–8.

It is customary to describe currents *as though* they consisted entirely of positive charge flow, even when we know that the current is really due to electrons. We will follow this convention consistently in the following sections. In Chapter 30, when we study the effect of a *magnetic* field on a moving charge, we will encounter a phenomenon called the Hall effect, in which the sign of the moving charges *is* important.

When there is a steady current in a closed loop (a "complete circuit"), the total charge in every segment of a conductor is constant. From the principle of conservation of charge (Section 24–2) the rate of flow of charge *out* at one end of a segment equals the rate of flow of charge *in* at the other end of the segment, and the current is the same at all cross sections.

Example 28–1   A copper conductor with a square cross section, 1.0 mm on a side, carries a constant current of 20 A to a 3-hp electric motor. The density of free electrons is 8.0×10^{28} electrons per cubic meter. Find the current density and the drift velocity.

Solution   The current density in the wire is

$$J = \frac{I}{A} = \frac{20 \text{ A}}{(1.0 \times 10^{-3} \text{ m})^2} = 20 \times 10^6 \text{ A·m}^{-2}.$$

From Eq. (28–3),

$$v = \frac{J}{nq} = \frac{20 \times 10^6 \ \text{A·m}^{-2}}{(8.0 \times 10^{28} \ \text{m}^{-3})(1.6 \times 10^{-19} \ \text{C})} = 1.6 \times 10^{-3} \ \text{m·s}^{-1},$$

or about $1.6 \ \text{mm·s}^{-1}$. At this speed an electron would require 625 s, or about 10 min, to travel the length of a wire 1 m long. The rms speed (defined in Section 20–3) of the random motion of the electrons is of the order of $10^5 \ \text{m·s}^{-1}$. So in this example the drift speed is around a hundred million times slower than the speed of random motion; picture the electrons bouncing around frantically, with a very slow and sluggish drift! ∎

28–2
Resistivity

The current density J in a conductor depends on the electric field E and on the properties of the material. For some materials, especially the metals, J is very nearly *directly proportional* to E, and the ratio of E to J is *constant*.

We define the **resistivity** ρ of a material as the ratio of electric field to current density:

$$\rho = \frac{E}{J}. \tag{28–4}$$

The greater the resistivity, the greater the field needed to cause a given current density, or the smaller the current density caused by a given field. Representative values of resistivity are given in Table 28–1. The

TABLE 28–1	Resistivities at room temperature		
Substance	**ρ, Ω·m**	**Substance**	**ρ, Ω·m**
Conductors		*Semiconductors*	
Metals — Silver	1.47×10^{-8}	Pure — Carbon	3.5×10^{-5}
Copper	1.72×10^{-8}	Germanium	0.60
Gold	2.44×10^{-8}	Silicon	2300
Aluminum	2.63×10^{-8}	*Insulators*	
Tungsten	5.51×10^{-8}	Amber	5×10^{14}
Steel	20×10^{-8}	Glass	10^{10}–10^{14}
Lead	22×10^{-8}	Lucite	$>10^{13}$
Mercury	95×10^{-8}	Mica	10^{11}–10^{15}
Alloys — Manganin	44×10^{-8}	Quartz (fused)	75×10^{16}
Constantan	49×10^{-8}	Sulfur	10^{15}
Nichrome	100×10^{-8}	Teflon	$>10^{13}$
		Wood	10^8–10^{11}

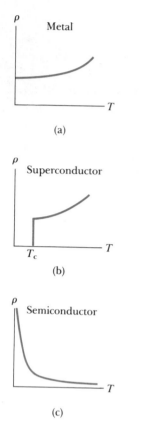

28–2
Variation of resistivity with temperature for three conductors: (a) an ordinary metal; (b) a superconducting metal, alloy, or compound; and (c) a semiconductor.

unit $\Omega \cdot m$ (ohm·meter) will be explained in the following section. A "perfect" conductor would have zero resistivity, and a "perfect" insulator would have an infinite resistivity. Metals and alloys have the lowest resistivities and are the best conductors. The resistivities of insulators are greater than those of the metals by an enormous factor, of the order of 10^{22}.

Good electrical conductors, such as the metals, are usually also good conductors of heat, while poor electrical conductors, such as ceramic and plastic materials, are also poor thermal conductors. In a metal the free electrons that carry charge in electrical conduction are also the principal mechanism for heat conduction, so we should expect a correlation between electrical and thermal conductivity.

The *semiconductors* have resistivities that are intermediate between those of metals and those of insulators. They are important particularly because of the way their resistivities are affected by temperature and by small amounts of impurities.

The proportionality of J to E for a metallic conductor at constant temperature was discovered by Georg Simon Ohm (1787–1854) and is called **Ohm's law.** A material that obeys Ohm's law is called an *ohmic* conductor or a *linear* conductor. Some materials *do not* obey Ohm's law; they are *nonohmic* or *nonlinear*. Ohm's law, like the ideal gas equation and Hooke's law, is an *idealized model* that describes the behavior of some materials quite well but is not a general description of *all* matter.

Analogies with fluid flow can be a big help in developing intuition about electric current and circuits. Here's an example. In wine making, the product is sometimes filtered to remove sediments. A pump forces the wine through the filter under pressure; if the flow rate is proportional to the pressure difference between the upstream and downstream sides, the behavior is analogous to Ohm's law. Maple syrup is also usually pressure-filtered.

The resistivity of a *metallic* conductor always increases with increasing temperature, as shown in Fig. 28–2a. Over a small temperature range (up to 100 C° or so), the resistivity of a metal can be represented approximately by the equation

$$\rho_T = \rho_0[1 + \alpha(T - T_0)], \qquad (28–5)$$

where ρ_0 is the resistivity at a reference temperature T_0 (often taken as 0°C or 20°C) and ρ_T is the resistivity at temperature T. The factor α is called the **temperature coefficient of resistivity.** Some representative values are given in Table 28–2. The resistivity of carbon (a nonmetal) *decreases* with increasing temperature, and its temperature coefficient of resistivity is negative. The resistivity of the alloy manganin is practically independent of temperature.

The resistivity of a *semiconductor* decreases rapidly with increasing temperature, as shown in Fig. 28–2c. A small semiconductor crystal called a *thermistor* can be used to make a sensitive electronic thermometer. Its resistivity is used as a thermometric property.

Some materials, including several metallic alloys, show a phenomenon called *superconductivity*. As the temperature decreases, the resistivity at first decreases smoothly, like that of any metal. But then at a certain transition temperature T_c, a phase transition occurs, and the resistivity

TABLE 28–2	Temperature coefficients of resistivity (Approximate values near room temperature)		
Material	α, C$^{\circ-1}$	Material	α, C$^{\circ-1}$
Aluminum	0.0039	Lead	0.0043
Brass	0.0020	Manganin (Cu 84, Mn 12, Ni 4)	0.000000
Carbon	−0.0005		
Constantan (Cu 60, Ni 40)	+0.000002	Mercury	0.00088
Copper (commercial annealed)	0.00393	Nichrome	0.0004
		Silver	0.0038
Iron	0.0050	Tungsten	0.0045

suddenly drops to zero, as shown in Fig. 28–2b. Once a current is established in a superconducting ring, it will continue indefinitely without the presence of any driving field. Until recently, transition temperatures for all superconducting materials were very low, 20 K and below. Recently (1987), however, materials with transition temperatures up to about 125 K have been found, and materials that are superconductors at room temperature may well become a reality. The implications of these discoveries for power-distribution systems, computer design, and transportation are enormous. We will discuss superconductivity in greater detail in Section 43–10.

28–3
Resistance

The current density J, at a point where the electric field is E in a conductor with resistivity ρ, is given by Eq. (28–4), which we can write as

$$E = \rho J. \tag{28–6}$$

Often we are more interested in the total current I in a conductor and the potential difference V between its ends. For example, suppose our conductor is a wire with uniform cross-sectional area A and length l, as shown in Fig. 28–3. If the current density J and the electric field E are uniform throughout the conductor, the total current I is given by $I = JA$, and the potential difference V between its ends is $V = El$. When we solve these equations for J and E, respectively, and substitute the results in Eq. (28–6), we obtain

$$\frac{V}{l} = \frac{\rho I}{A} \quad \text{or} \quad V = \frac{\rho l}{A}I. \tag{28–7}$$

This shows that the total current I is proportional to the potential difference V.

The quantity $\rho l / A$ for a particular conductor is called its **resistance** R:

$$R = \frac{\rho l}{A}. \tag{28–8}$$

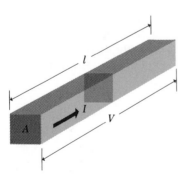

28–3
A conductor of uniform cross section. The current density is uniform over any cross section, and the electric field is constant along the length.

Equation (28–7) then becomes

$$V = IR. \tag{28–9}$$

This is the usual form of Ohm's law. It describes the behavior of a specific conductor, not a general property of a material as with Eq. (28–6). In the next section we'll show you what this relation is good for.

Equation (28–8) shows that the resistance of a wire or other conductor of uniform cross section is directly proportional to its length and inversely proportional to its cross-sectional area. It is also proportional to the resistivity of the material of which the conductor is made.

The SI unit of resistance is 1 *volt per ampere* (1 V·A^{-1}). This unit is called 1 **ohm** ($1\ \Omega$). The *kilohm* ($1\ k\Omega = 10^3\ \Omega$) and the *megohm* ($1\ M\Omega = 10^6\ \Omega$) are also in common use. From Eq. (28–8) the SI unit of resistivity is 1 ohm·meter ($1\ \Omega$·m).

Here's the flowing-fluid analogy again. The flow of water through a partly clogged pipe is approximately proportional to the pressure difference between the ends. Flow rate is analogous to current and pressure difference to potential difference ("voltage"). Let's not stretch this analogy too far, though; the water flow rate in a pipe is usually *not* proportional to its cross-sectional area, as Eq. (13–24) shows.

Because the resistivity of a material varies with temperature, the resistance of a specific conductor made of the material also varies with temperature. For temperature ranges that are not too great we can describe this variation as approximately a linear relation, analogous to Eq. (28–5):

$$R_T = R_0[1 + \alpha(T - T_0)]. \tag{28–10}$$

In this equation, R_T is the resistance at temperature T and R_0 is the resistance at the temperature T_0, often taken to be 20°C or 0°C. The temperature coefficient of resistivity α is the same constant that appears in Eq. (28–5). Table 28–2 gives values of α for several common materials. Within the limits of validity of Eq. (28–10) the *change* in resistance resulting from a temperature change $T - T_0$ is given by $R_0\alpha(T - T_0)$.

Example 28–2   In Example 28–1 (Section 28–1), find (a) the electric field, (b) the potential difference between two points 100 m apart, and (c) the resistance of a 100-m length of this copper conductor.

Solution

a) From Eq. (28–6) the electric field is given by

$$E = \rho J = (1.72 \times 10^{-8}\ \Omega\text{·m})(20 \times 10^6\ \text{A·m}^{-2}) = 0.344\ \text{V·m}^{-1}.$$

b) The potential difference is given by

$$V = El = (0.344\ \text{V·m}^{-1})(100\ \text{m}) = 34.4\ \text{V}.$$

c) The resistance of a piece of this wire 100 m in length is

$$R = \frac{V}{I} = \frac{34.4\ \text{V}}{20\ \text{A}} = 1.72\ \Omega.$$

We can also obtain this result directly from Eq. (28–8):

$$R = \frac{\rho l}{A} = \frac{(1.72 \times 10^{-8} \ \Omega\cdot m)(100 \ m)}{(1.00 \times 10^{-3} \ m)^2} = 1.72 \ \Omega. \quad \blacksquare$$

Example 28–3   In Example 28–2, suppose the resistance is 1.72 Ω at a temperature of 20°C. Find the resistance at 0°C and at 100°C.

Solution   We use Eq. (28–10), with $T_0 = 20°C$ and $R_0 = 1.72 \ \Omega$. From Table 28–2 the temperature coefficient of resistivity of copper is $\alpha = 0.00393 \ C^{\circ -1}$. At $T = 0°C$,

$$R = (1.72 \ \Omega)[1 + (0.00393 \ C^{\circ -1})(0°C - 20°C)]$$
$$= 1.58 \ \Omega,$$

and at $T = 100°C$,

$$R = (1.72 \ \Omega)[1 + (0.00393 \ C^{\circ -1})(100°C - 20°C)]$$
$$= 2.26 \ \Omega. \quad \blacksquare$$

Color	Digits	Multiplier
Black	0	1
Brown	1	10
Red	2	100
Orange	3	1,000
Yellow	4	10,000
Green	5	100,000
Blue	6	1,000,000
Violet	7	10,000,000
Gray	8	100,000,000
White	9	1,000,000,000

TABLE 28–3   **Resistor color code**

A circuit device made to have a specific value of resistance is called a **resistor.** Resistors used in electronic circuitry are often cylindrical in shape and a few millimeters in diameter and length, with wires coming out the ends. The resistance is marked with a standard code using three or four color bands near one end, according to the scheme shown in Table 28–3. The first two bands (counting in from the near end) are two digits, and the third is a power-of-ten multiplier. For example, yellow-violet-orange means $47 \times 1000 \ \Omega$, or 47 kΩ. The fourth band, if present, indicates the precision of the value; no band means ±20%, a silver band ±10%, and a gold band ±5%. Another important characteristic of a resistor is the maximum *power* it can dissipate without damage. We will return to this point in Section 28–5.

For a resistor that obeys Ohm's law, Eq. (28–9), a graph of current as a function of potential difference (voltage) is a straight line, as shown in Fig. 28–4a. Not all devices behave in such a simple way. The relation of voltage to current may not be a direct proportion, and it may be different for the two directions of current. Figure 28–4b shows the behavior of a vacuum diode, a vacuum tube used to convert high-voltage alternating current to direct current. For positive potentials of anode with respect to cathode, I is approximately proportional to $V^{3/2}$; for negative potentials the current is extremely small. The behavior of semiconductor diodes (Fig. 28–4c) is somewhat different but still strongly asymmetric, like a one-way valve in a circuit. Diodes are used to convert alternating current to direct current and to perform a wide variety of logic functions in computer circuitry. We will study the microscopic basis of diode behavior in later chapters.

Current-voltage relations are often temperature-dependent. At low temperatures the curve in Fig. 28–4c rises more steeply for positive V than at higher temperatures, and at successively higher temperatures the asymmetry in the curve becomes less and less pronounced.

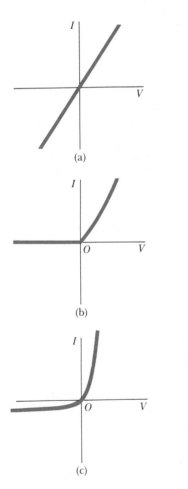

28–4
Current–voltage relations for (a) a resistor obeying Ohm's law, (b) a vacuum diode, and (c) a semiconductor diode.

28–4
Electromotive Force and Circuits

To have a steady current in a conductor, we need a path that forms a closed loop or **complete circuit.** But the path cannot consist entirely of resistance. In a resistor, charge always moves in the direction of decreasing potential energy. There must be some part of the circuit where the potential energy *increases*.

The problem is analogous to an ornamental water fountain that recycles its water. The water squirts out of openings at the top, cascades down over the terraces and spouts, and collects in a basin in the bottom. A pump then lifts the water back to the top for another trip. Without the pump, the water would just fall to the bottom and stay there.

In an electric circuit there must be a device somewhere in the loop in which a charge travels "uphill," from lower to higher potential, despite the fact that the electrostatic force is trying to push it from higher to lower potential. The influence that makes charge move from lower to higher potential is called **electromotive force.** Every complete circuit with a steady current must include some device that provides electromotive force (abbreviated emf, pronounced "ee-em-eff").

Batteries, electric generators, solar cells, thermocouples, and fuel cells are examples of sources of emf. All such devices convert energy of some form (mechanical, chemical, thermal, and so on) into electrical energy and transfer it into the circuit where it is connected. An ideal source of emf maintains a constant potential difference between its terminals, independent of the current through it. We define electromotive force quantitatively as the magnitude of this potential difference and denote it as $\mathcal{E}$. As we will see, such an ideal source is a mythical beast, like the unicorn, the frictionless plane, and the free lunch. We will discuss later how real-life sources of emf differ in their behavior from this idealized model.

Figure 28–5 is a schematic diagram of a source of emf that maintains a potential difference between conductors a and b, called the *terminals* of the device. Terminal a, marked with a plus sign, is maintained at *higher* potential than terminal b, marked with a minus sign. Associated with this potential difference is an electric field E in the region around the terminals, both inside and outside the source. The electric field inside the device is directed from a to b, as shown. A charge q within the source experiences an electrical force $F_e = qE$. The source has to provide some additional influence, which we represent as a force F_n, that pushes charge from b to a inside the device (opposite to the direction of F_e) and maintains the potential difference. The origin of this additional influence depends on what kind of source we are talking about. In a generator it results from magnetic-field forces on moving charges. In a battery or fuel cell it is associated with diffusion processes and varying electrolyte concentrations resulting from chemical reactions. In an electrostatic machine such as a Van de Graaff or Wimshurst generator an actual mechanical force is applied by a moving belt or wheel.

The potential V_{ab} of point a with respect to point b is defined, as always, as the work per unit charge performed by the electrostatic force

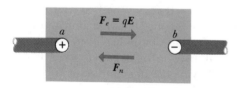

28–5
Schematic diagram of a source of emf in an "open-circuit" situation. The electric-field force $F_e = qE$ and the nonelectrostatic force F_n on a charge q are shown. The work done by F_n on a charge q moving from b to a is equal to $q\mathcal{E}$, where $\mathcal{E}$ is the electromotive force.

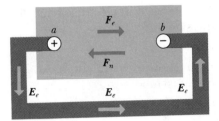

28–6
Schematic diagram of a source with a complete circuit. The vectors F_n and F_e represent the directions of the corresponding forces. The current is in the direction from a to b (the direction of E_e) in the external circuit and from b to a within the source. $V_{ab} = IR = \mathcal{E} - Ir$.

$F_e = qE$ on a charge q that moves from a to b. The emf $\mathcal{E}$ of the source is the energy per unit charge supplied by the source during the "uphill" displacement from b to a. For the ideal source of emf we have described, the potential difference V_{ab} is equal to the electromotive force $\mathcal{E}$:

$$V_{ab} = \mathcal{E}. \qquad (28\text{–}11)$$

The SI unit of emf is the same as that of potential or potential difference, namely, 1 J·C^{-1} or 1 V.

Now let's make a complete circuit by connecting a wire with resistance R to the terminals of a source, as shown in Fig. 28–6. The charged terminals a and b of the source set up an electric field in the wire, and this causes a current in the wire from a toward b. From Eq. (28–9) the current I in the circuit is determined by

$$\mathcal{E} = V_{ab} = IR. \qquad (28\text{–}12)$$

In other words, when a charge q flows around the circuit, the potential rise $\mathcal{E}$ as it passes through the source is numerically equal to the potential drop $V_{ab} = IR$ as it passes through the resistor. Once $\mathcal{E}$ and R are known, this relation determines the current in the circuit.

The current is the same at every point in the circuit. This follows from conservation of charge and from the fact that charge cannot accumulate in the circuit devices we have described. (Otherwise, the potential differences would change with time.) This is a special case of Kirchhoff's current rule, which states that, for any circuit junction, as much charge must flow in as out. We will apply this rule to more general circuits in Chapter 29.

Real sources do not behave exactly the way we have described because charge moving through any real source encounters *resistance*. We call this the **internal resistance** of the source, and we denote it by r. If this resistance behaves according to Ohm's law, the current through r has an associated drop in potential equal to Ir. The terminal potential difference V_{ab} under complete-circuit conditions is then given by

$$V_{ab} = \mathcal{E} - Ir. \qquad (28\text{–}13)$$

The current in the external circuit is still determined by the relation $V_{ab} = IR$; combining this with Eq. (28–13), we find

$$\mathcal{E} - Ir = IR,$$

or

$$I = \frac{\mathcal{E}}{R + r}. \qquad (28\text{–}14)$$

The current equals the source emf divided by the *total* circuit resistance $(r + R)$.

Thus we can describe the behavior of a source in terms of two properties, an emf $\mathcal{E}$, which supplies a constant potential difference independent of current, in series with an internal resistance r.

To summarize our discussion thus far, a circuit is a closed conducting path containing resistors, sources of emf, and possibly other circuit elements. The algebraic sum of the potential differences around the path is zero, and in a simple loop the current is the same at every point.

Now let's introduce the symbols usually used in electric-circuit diagrams. A resistor is represented by the symbol

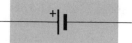

Conductors with negligible resistance are shown by straight lines.
A source of emf is represented by the symbol

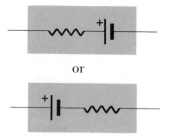

The longer vertical line always corresponds to the + terminal (ordinarily the terminal at higher potential). A source with internal resistance is represented by

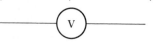

or

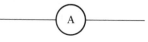

It doesn't matter on which side we draw the internal resistance.
We will use these symbols in circuit diagrams in the remainder of this chapter and the next. We will also include two types of idealized instruments. A **voltmeter,** represented by the circuit symbol

measures the potential difference between its terminals, and an **ammeter,** represented by the circuit symbol

measures the current through it. We assume that the presence of these instruments doesn't change the behavior of the circuit appreciably. This is an idealization; we will study the properties of real meters in greater detail in Chapter 29.

Example 28–4   Figure 28–7 shows a source with an emf $\mathcal{E}$ of 12 V and an internal resistance r of 2 Ω. (For comparison, the internal resistance of a commercial 12-V lead storage battery is only a few thousandths of an ohm.) Determine the readings of meters V and A in the following three cases:

a) Switches S_1 and S_2 are both open.

b) Switch S_1 is closed, permitting current through the resistor R.

c) Switches S_1 and S_2 are both closed; S_2 provides a zero-resistance path around the resistor R.

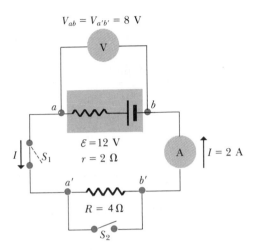

$V_{ab} = V_{a'b'} = 8$ V

$\mathcal{E} = 12$ V
$r = 2\ \Omega$

$I = 2$ A

$R = 4\ \Omega$

28–7
A source in a complete circuit.

Solution

a) There is no current because there is no complete circuit. (There is no current through our idealized voltmeter.) The ammeter A reads $I = 0$. Because there is no current in the battery, there is no potential difference across its internal resistance. The potential difference V_{ab} across its terminals is equal to the emf, $V_{ab} = \mathcal{E} = 12$ V, and the voltmeter reads $V = 12$ V.

b) There is now a complete circuit. The current I through the resistor R is determined by Eq. (28–14):

$$I = \frac{\mathcal{E}}{R + r} = \frac{12\ \text{V}}{4\ \Omega + 2\ \Omega} = 2\ \text{A}.$$

The ammeter A reads $I = 2$ A.

Our idealized conducting wires have zero resistance, so there is no potential difference between points a and a' or between b and b'. That is, $V_{ab} = V_{a'b'}$. We can find V_{ab} by considering a and b either as the terminals of the resistor or as the terminals of the source. Considering the terminals of the resistor, we use Ohm's law:

$$V_{a'b'} = IR = (2\ \text{A})(4\ \Omega) = 8\ \text{V}.$$

Considering the terminals of the source, we have

$$V_{ab} = \mathcal{E} - Ir = 12\ \text{V} - (2\ \text{A})(2\ \Omega) = 8\ \text{V}.$$

Either way, we conclude that the voltmeter reads $V_{ab} = 8$ V.

c) With switch S_2 closed, we have a zero-resistance path between points a and b, so we must have $V_{ab} = 0$, no matter what the current. Knowing this, we can find the current I from the relation

$$V_{ab} = \mathcal{E} - Ir = 12\ \text{V} - I(2\ \Omega) = 0,$$

$$I = 6\ \text{A}.$$

The ammeter reads $I = 6$ A, and the voltmeter reads $V_{ab} = 0$.

In all three cases we call V_{ab} the *terminal voltage*. Case (c) is called a *short circuit*. The short-circuit current is equal to the emf $\mathcal{E}$ divided by the internal resistance r. *Caution!* This can be an extremely dangerous situation. An automobile battery or a household power line has very small internal resistance (much less than in Example 28–4), and the short-circuit current can be great enough to cause a small wire actually to explode. Don't try it! ∎

We can generalize the reasoning that led to Eq. (28–14). Suppose we go around a loop, measuring potential differences across successive circuit elements. Because the electrostatic field is a *conservative* force field, the *algebraic sum* of these differences when we arrive back at the starting point must be zero.

Let's try this out in Fig. 28–7. With switch S_1 closed and S_2 open, we start at point b and travel counterclockwise (the same direction as I). We find a *rise* in potential (a *positive* change) due to the battery emf, a *drop* (a *negative* change) due to the battery's internal resistance, and an additional drop due to the 4-Ω resistor. The algebraic sum of these must be zero:

$$12 \text{ V} - I(2 \text{ }\Omega) - I(4 \text{ }\Omega) = 0, \qquad I = 2 \text{ A},$$

the same result that we obtained in Example 28–4b.

The algebraic sum of the potential differences around a complete circuit, including those corresponding to the emf's of the sources and those due to the IR products, must equal zero. This is called **Kirchhoff's loop rule.** In using it we need some sign conventions. First we assume a direction for the current and mark it on the diagram. Then, starting at any point in the circuit, we go around the circuit in the direction of the assumed current, adding emf's and IR products as we come to them. When we go through a source in the direction from $-$ to $+$, we count the emf as *positive* because the potential increases in this direction; when we go from $+$ to $-$, it is negative. The IR products are all negative because the direction of current is always that of *decreasing* potential.

We could also go around the loop in the direction *opposite* to that of the assumed current. In this case, all the emf's have opposite sign, and all the IR products are *positive* because in going in the opposite direction to the current we are going "uphill" from lower to higher potential. In Fig. 28–7, if we start at point b and go clockwise, the resulting equation is

$$I(4 \text{ }\Omega) + I(2 \text{ }\Omega) - 12 \text{ V} = 0.$$

This is just the previous equation multiplied through by (-1), and the value of I is the same. Or we can assume instead that I is clockwise. Then, starting at b and going counterclockwise around the loop, we find

$$12 \text{ V} + I(2 \text{ }\Omega) + I(4 \text{ }\Omega) = 0,$$

$$I = -2 \text{ A}.$$

The negative sign shows that our initial assumption was wrong; the actual direction of I is counterclockwise.

PROBLEM-SOLVING STRATEGY: *Electric Circuits*

1. Make an assumption about the direction of current in the circuit, and mark it clearly on your diagram. It doesn't matter whether the assumption is right or wrong. If it's wrong, your solution for I will give you a negative number, which means that the actual current direction is opposite to your assumption. But you *must* pick a direction at the start and use it consistently when you apply Kirchhoff's loop rule.

2. Decide the direction in which you will go around the loop when you add up the potential differences in applying Kirchhoff's loop rule. Again, it doesn't matter which way you go, but you *must* keep going the same way until you are back where you started.

3. Remember the sign rules: An emf is counted as positive if you go through the source from − to +, negative if from + to −. The change in potential going through a resistor (IR) is negative if you go through in the same direction as the

assumed current and positive if in the opposite direction.

4. You can use this same bookkeeping system to find the potential difference between *any* two points a and b in a circuit. To find $V_{ab} = V_a - V_b$ (the potential of a with respect to b), start at b, choose a path from b to a, and add the potential changes that you encounter in going from b to a, using the same sign rules that you used in item 3. The potential at a equals the potential at b plus the sum of the potential changes when we go from b to a. Thus $V_{ab} = V_a - V_b$ is just the sum of these changes. It may help to think of potential as analogous to altitude. Suppose we drive from Denver (elevation 5280 ft) to Loveland Pass (11,992 ft). Let Denver be b and the pass be a. The elevation at the pass (a) is the elevation in Denver (b) plus the amount we climbed (6712 ft) going from Denver to the pass.

Example 28–5   The circuit shown in Fig. 28–8 contains two batteries, each with an emf and an internal resistance, and two resistors. Find the current in the circuit and the potential difference V_{ab}.

Solution   We assume a direction for the current, as shown. Then, starting at a and going counterclockwise, we add potential increases and decreases and equate the sum to zero. The resulting equation is

$$-I(4\ \Omega) - 4\ \text{V} - I(7\ \Omega) + 12\ \text{V} - I(2\ \Omega) - I(3\ \Omega) = 0.$$

Collecting terms containing I and solving for I, we find

$$8\ \text{V} = I(16\ \Omega) \qquad \text{and} \qquad I = 0.5\ \text{A}.$$

The result for I is positive, showing that our assumed current direction is correct. For exercise, try assuming instead that I is clockwise; you should then get $I = -0.5$ A, showing that the actual current is opposite to this assumption.

To find V_{ab}, the potential at a with respect to b, we start at b and go toward a, adding potential changes. There are two possible paths from b to a; taking the lower one, we find

$$V_{ab} = (0.5\ \text{A})(7\ \Omega) + 4\ \text{V} + (0.5\ \text{A})(4\ \Omega) = 9.5\ \text{V}.$$

Point a is at 9.5 V higher potential than b. All the terms in this sum are

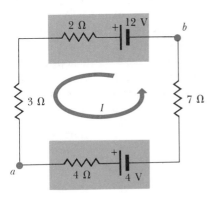

28–8
Circuit for Example 28–5.

positive because each represents an *increase* in potential as we go from b toward a. If instead we use the upper path, the resulting equation is

$$V_{ab} = 12 \text{ V} - (0.5 \text{ A})(2 \text{ }\Omega) - (0.5 \text{ A})(3 \text{ }\Omega) = 9.5 \text{ V}.$$

Here the IR terms are negative because our path goes in the direction of the current, with potential decreases through the resistors. The result is (and must be) the same as for the lower path.   ∎

28–5
Energy and Power in Electric Circuits

Let's now look at some energy and power relations in electric circuits. The box in Fig. 28–9 represents a circuit element with current I through it and potential difference $V_a - V_b = V_{ab}$ between its terminals. This might be a resistor, a source, or something else; the details don't matter. As charge passes through the circuit element, the electric field does work on the charge. In a source of emf, additional work is done by the force F_n that we mentioned in Section 28–4. In all cases the total work done on a charge ΔQ is equal to the product of the charge and the potential difference V_{ab} (work per unit charge). If the current is I, then in a time interval Δt, an amount of charge $\Delta Q = I \Delta t$ passes through. The work done on this charge is therefore

$$W = V_{ab} \Delta Q = V_{ab} I \Delta t.$$

This work represents electrical energy transferred into this circuit element. The time rate of energy transfer is *power*, denoted by P. Dividing the above equation by Δt, we obtain the *rate* at which the rest of the circuit delivers electrical energy to this circuit element:

$$\frac{\Delta W}{\Delta t} = P = V_{ab} I. \tag{28–15}$$

If the circuit element is a resistor, P represents the rate of conversion of electrical energy into heat in the resistor.

It may happen that the potential at b is higher than that at a; then V_{ab} is negative. The charge then *gains* potential energy (at the expense of some other form of energy). The circuit element is then acting as a source, delivering electrical energy into the circuit in which it is connected. This is the usual situation for a battery, which converts chemical energy into electrical energy and delivers it to the external circuit.

28–9
The power input P to the portion of the circuit between a and b is $P = V_{ab}I$.

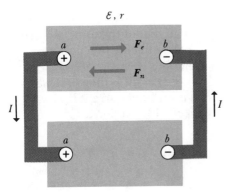

28–10
The rate of conversion of nonelectrical to electrical energy in the source equals $\mathcal{E}I$. The rate of energy dissipation in the source is I^2r. The difference $\mathcal{E}I - I^2r$ is the power output of the source.

The unit of V_{ab} is 1 V, or 1 J·C^{-1}, and the unit of I is 1 A, or 1 C·s^{-1}. We can confirm that the SI unit of power is 1 W:

$$(1 \text{ J·C}^{-1})(1 \text{ C·s}^{-1}) = 1 \text{ J·s}^{-1} = 1 \text{ W}.$$

Let's consider a few special cases.

1. *Pure resistance*. If the circuit element in Fig. 28–9 is a pure resistance, the potential difference is given by $V_{ab} = IR$. From Eq. (28–15) the electrical power delivered to the resistor by the circuit (and thus the rate of conversion of electrical energy to heat) is

$$P = V_{ab}I = I^2R = \frac{V_{ab}^{\,2}}{R}. \tag{28–16}$$

The moving charges collide with atoms in the resistor and transfer some of their energy to these atoms. The temperature of the resistor increases unless there is a flow of heat out of it. We say that energy is *dissipated* in the resistor at a rate I^2R. Because of this heat, every resistor has a *power rating*, the maximum power the device can dissipate without overheating. When this rating is exceeded, the resistance may change unpredictably; in extreme cases the resistor may melt or even explode. In practical applications the power rating of a resistor is often just as important a characteristic as its resistance value.

2. *Power output of a source*. The upper rectangle in Fig. 28–10 represents a source with emf $\mathcal{E}$ and internal resistance r, connected by ideal (resistanceless) conductors to an external circuit represented by the lower box. We assume that there is a current I in the direction shown and that point a is at higher potential than point b; $V_a > V_b$. The power delivered to the external circuit (i.e, the rate of conversion to electrical energy from energy of some other form and the rate of its delivery to the circuit) is given by Eq. (28–15):

$$P = V_{ab}I.$$

Considering the source, we also have, from Eq. (28–13),

$$V_{ab} = \mathcal{E} - Ir.$$

Multiplying this equation by I, we find

$$P = V_{ab}I = \mathcal{E}I - I^2r. \tag{28–17}$$

What do the terms $\mathcal{E}I$ and I^2r mean? In Section 28–4 we defined the emf $\mathcal{E}$ as the work per unit charge performed on the charges by the non-electrostatic force as the charges are pushed "uphill" from b to a in the source. So we see that $\mathcal{E}I$ is the rate at which work is done on the circulating charges by whatever agency causes the nonelectrostatic force in the source. This is therefore the rate of conversion of non-electrical energy to electrical energy within the source. The term I^2r is the rate at which electrical energy is *dissipated* (converted to heat) in the internal resistance of the source. The difference $\mathcal{E}I - I^2r$ is the *net* electrical power output of the source, that is, the rate at which the source delivers electrical energy to the remainder of the circuit.

3. *Power input to a source.* Suppose that the lower rectangle in Fig. 28–10 is itself a source, with an emf *larger* than that of the upper source and with its emf opposite to that of the upper source. A practical example would be an automobile battery (the upper box) being charged by the alternator (the lower box). The current I in the circuit is then *opposite* to that shown in Fig. 28–10; the lower source is pushing current backward through the upper source. Instead of Eq. (28–13), we have

$$V_{ab} = \mathcal{E} + Ir,$$

and instead of Eq. (28–17), we have

$$P = V_{ab}I = \mathcal{E}I + I^2r. \qquad (28\text{–}18)$$

Work is being done *on*, rather than *by*, the agent that causes the non-electrostatic force. There is a conversion of electrical energy into non-electrical energy in the source, at a rate $\mathcal{E}I$. The term I^2r is again the rate of dissipation of energy in the internal resistance of the source, and the sum $\mathcal{E}I + I^2r$ is the total electrical power *input* to the upper source. This is what happens when a rechargeable battery (a storage battery) is connected to a charger. The charger supplies electrical energy to the battery; part of it is converted to chemical energy, to be reconverted later, and the remainder is dissipated (wasted) as heat in the battery's internal resistance.

Example 28–6   In Example 28–4b, find the rate of energy conversion (chemical to electrical) and the rate of dissipation of energy (electrical energy to heat) in the battery, and its net power output.

Solution   The rate of energy conversion in the battery is

$$\mathcal{E}I = (12 \text{ V})(2 \text{ A}) = 24 \text{ W}.$$

The rate of dissipation of energy in the battery is

$$I^2r = (2 \text{ A})^2(2 \text{ } \Omega) = 8 \text{ W}.$$

The electrical power *output* of the source is the difference between these, or 16 W. The terminal voltage is $V_{ab} = 8$ V. The power output is also given by

$$V_{ab}I = (8 \text{ V})(2 \text{ A}) = 16 \text{ W}.$$

The electrical power input to the resistor is

$$V_{a'b'}I = (8 \text{ V})(2 \text{ A}) = 16 \text{ W}.$$

This equals the rate of dissipation of electrical energy (conversion to heat) in the resistor:

$$I^2R = (2 \text{ A})^2(4 \text{ } \Omega) = 16 \text{ W}.$$

Going back to Eq. (28–13), if we multiply through by I and rearrange, we get

$$\mathcal{E}I = V_{ab}I + I^2r,$$

showing again that the rate of energy conversion ($\mathcal{E}I$) equals the rate of dissipation in the source (I^2r) plus the net power output $V_{ab}I$ from the source. This is what we should expect from general energy-conservation considerations.   ■

We invite you to carry out a similar power analysis for the circuit in Example 28–5 (Fig. 28–8).

*28–6
Theory of Metallic Conduction

We can gain additional insight into electrical conduction by looking at the microscopic mechanisms of conductivity. We will consider only a crude and primitive model that treats the electrons as classical particles and ignores their quantum-mechanical, wavelike behavior in solids. Even though this model is not entirely correct conceptually, it will still help you to develop an intuitive idea of the microscopic basis of conduction.

In the simplest microscopic model of metallic conduction, each atom in the crystal lattice gives up one or more of its outer electrons. These electrons are then free to move through the crystal lattice, colliding at intervals with the stationary positive ions. The motion of the electrons is analogous to that of molecules of a gas moving through a porous bed of sand, and they are often referred to as an "electron gas." If there is no electric field, the electrons move in straight lines between collisions; but if an electric field is present, the paths curve slightly because of the acceleration caused by electric-field forces. Figure 28–11 shows a few free paths of an electron in an electric field directed from right to left. We assume that at each collision the electron loses *all* the energy it has acquired from the field and makes a fresh start. The energy given up in these collisions increases the energy of vibration of the positive ions and thus the temperature of the material.

The electric field E exerts a force with magnitude $F = eE$ on each electron, and this causes an acceleration a in the direction of the force, given by

$$a = \frac{F}{m} = \frac{eE}{m},$$

where m is the electron mass. Let u be the average *random* speed of an electron, and let λ be the **mean free path** (the average distance traveled between collisions). The average time t between collisions, called the **mean free time,** is

$$t = \frac{\lambda}{u}.$$

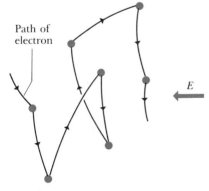

Path of electron

E

28–11
Random motion of an electron in a solid, superimposed on steady drift in direction opposite to the E field.

During this time the electron (assumed to start from rest after each collision) acquires a final velocity component v_f in the direction of the force, given by

$$v_f = at = \frac{eE}{m}\frac{\lambda}{u}.$$

The *average* velocity v_{av} in the direction of the force is superposed on its random velocity. This average value is one half the final velocity, so

$$v_{av} = \frac{1}{2}v_f = \frac{1}{2}\frac{e\lambda}{mu}E.$$

This is the *drift velocity* that we described in Section 28–1 (where we called it simply v), and this equation shows that it is *proportional* to the electric field magnitude E.

From Eq. (28–3) the current density J is given by

$$J = nev_{av},$$

where n is the number of electrons per unit volume. Combining this with the expression for v_{av}, we find

$$J = \frac{ne^2\lambda}{2mu}E.$$

Finally, from Eq. (28–4) the resistivity ρ is given by

$$\rho = \frac{E}{J} = \frac{2mu}{ne^2\lambda}. \tag{28–19}$$

Because the ratio of E to J is constant, this result predicts that the material obeys Ohm's law. When the temperature increases, the speed u of random motion increases, so this theory predicts that the resistivity of a metal increases with temperature.

We can estimate the value of u by assuming that the average electron kinetic energy at an absolute temperature T is given by the equipartition theorem (Section 20–4):

$$\frac{1}{2}mu^2 = \frac{3}{2}kT,$$

where k is Boltzmann's constant. At $T = 300$ K we get approximately $u = 1.2 \times 10^5$ m·s^{-1}. If we use the value of n for copper given in Example 28–1, $n = 8 \times 10^{28}$ m^{-3}, Eq. (28–19) gives a value of resistivity for copper that agrees with the experimental value given in Table 28–1 if the mean free path λ is about 6×10^{-9} m. This is around 30 times the size of an individual copper atom and is a reasonable value. We conclude that Eq. (28–19) gives resistivities for metals that are at least in the right ballpark. We invite you to fill in the details of this calculation.

We also note that the magnitude of the drift velocity v_{av} is *much* smaller than the speed of random motion u of the electrons— 10^{-3} m·s^{-1} or so compared with 10^5 m·s^{-1}. Thus conduction represents, relatively speaking, a very small change in the random motion of electrons in a metal.

In a semiconductor the number of charge carriers per unit volume, n, is not constant but increases very rapidly with increasing temperature.

This increase in n far outweighs the increase in the speed of random motion u, and the resistivity decreases rapidly with increasing temperature. At low temperatures, n is very small, and the resistivity becomes so large that the material can be considered an insulator.

*28–7
Physiological Effects of Currents

Electrical potential differences and currents play a vital role in the nervous systems of animals. Conduction of nerve impulses is basically an electrical process, although the mechanism of conduction is much more complex than in simple materials such as metals. A nerve fiber, or *axon*, along which an electrical impulse can travel includes a cylindrical membrane with one conducting fluid (electrolyte) inside and another outside. Chemical systems similar to those in batteries maintain a potential difference of the order of 0.1 V between these fluids.

When an electrical pulse is initiated, the nerve membrane temporarily becomes more permeable to the ions in the fluids, leading to a local drop in potential. As the pulse passes, with a typical speed of the order of $30 \ \mathrm{m \cdot s^{-1}}$, the membrane recovers, and the potential returns to its initial value. Some aspects of this process are not yet completely understood.

The basically electrical nature of nerve-impulse conduction is responsible for the great sensitivity of the body to externally supplied electrical currents. Currents through the body as small as 0.1 A, which are much too small to produce significant heating, are fatal because they interfere with nerve processes that are essential for vital functions such as heartbeat. The resistance of the human body is highly variable; body fluids are usually quite good conductors because of the substantial ion concentrations, but the conductivity of skin is relatively low. The resistance between two electrodes grasped by dry hands is of the order of 5 to 10 kΩ. For $R = 10$ kΩ a current of 0.1 A requires a potential difference $V = IR = (0.1 \ \mathrm{A})(10 \ \mathrm{k\Omega}) = 1000$ V. With wet hands the resistance can be considerably reduced.

Even much smaller currents can be very dangerous. A current of 0.01 A through an arm or leg causes strong, convulsive muscle action and considerable pain, and with 0.02 A a person holding the conductor that is inflicting the shock is typically unable to release it. Currents through the chest with this magnitude and even as small as 0.001 A can cause ventricular fibrillation, which is disorganized twitching of heart muscles that pumps very little blood. Surprisingly, very large currents (over 0.1 A) are somewhat *less* likely to cause fatal fibrillation because the heart muscle is "clamped" in one position and is more likely to resume normal beating when the current is removed. Severe burns are, of course, more likely with large currents.

The moral of this rather morbid story, if there is one, is that under certain conditions, voltages as small as 10 V can be dangerous and that they should not be regarded with anything but respect and caution.

On the positive side, rapidly alternating currents can have beneficial effects. Alternating currents with frequencies of the order of 10^6 Hz do not interfere appreciably with nerve processes and can be used for therapeutic heating for arthritic conditions, sinusitis, and a variety of other disorders. If one electrode is made very small, the resulting concentrated heating can be used for local destruction of tissue, such as tumors, or for cutting tissue in certain surgical procedures.

Study of particular nerve impulses is also an important *diagnostic* tool in medicine. The most familiar examples are electrocardiography (EKG) and electroencephalography (EEG). Electrocardiograms, obtained by attaching electrodes to the chest and back and recording the regularly varying potential differences, are used to study heart function. Similarly, electrodes attached to the scalp permit study of potentials in the brain, and the resulting patterns can be helpful in diagnosing epilepsy, brain tumors, and other disorders.

Questions

28–1 A rule of thumb used to determine the internal resistance of a source is that it is the open-circuit voltage divided by the short-circuit current. Is this correct?

28–2 The energy that can be extracted from a storage battery is always less than the energy that goes into it while it is being charged. Why?

28–3 In circuit analysis, one often assumes that a wire connecting two circuit elements has no potential difference between its ends; yet there must be an electric field within the wire to make the charges move, and so there must be a potential difference. How do you resolve this discrepancy?

28–4 Long-distance electric-power transmission lines always operate at very high voltage, sometimes as much as 750 kV. What are the advantages of such high voltages? The disadvantages?

28–5 Ordinary household electric lines usually operate at 120 V. Why is this a desirable voltage, rather than a value considerably larger or smaller? What about cars, which usually have 12-V electrical systems?

28–6 What is the difference between an emf and a potential difference?

28–7 Electric power for household and commercial use always uses *alternating current,* which reverses direction 120 times each second. A student claimed that the power conveyed by such a current would have to average out to zero, since it is going one way half the time and the other way the other half. What is your response?

28–8 As discussed in the text, the drift velocity of electrons in a good conductor is very slow. Why then does the light come on so quickly when the switch is turned on?

28–9 A fuse is a device designed to break a circuit, usually by melting, when the current exceeds a certain value. What characteristics should the material of the fuse have?

28–10 What considerations determine the maximum current-carrying capacity of household wiring?

28–11 The text states that good thermal conductors are also good electrical conductors. If so, why don't the cords used to connect toasters, irons, and similar heat-producing appliances get hot by conduction of heat from the heating element?

28–12 Eight flashlight batteries in series have an emf of about 12 V, similar to that of a car battery. Could they be used to start a car with a dead battery?

28–13 High-voltage power supplies are sometimes designed intentionally to have rather large internal resistance, as a safety precaution. Why is such a power supply with a large internal resistance safer than one with the same voltage but lower internal resistance?

28–14 How would you expect the resistivity of a good insulator such as glass or polystyrene to vary with temperature? Why?

28–15 A would-be inventor proposed to increase the power supplied by a battery to a light bulb by using thick wire near the battery and thinner wire near the bulb. In the thin wire the electrons from the thick wire would become more densely packed, more electrons per second would reach the bulb, and the energy received by the bulb would be greater than that emitted by the battery. What do you think of this scheme?

Exercises

Section 28–1 Current

28–1 For what interval of time must a current of 3.80 A flow to transfer 76.0 C of charge?

28–2 A glass tube filled with gas has electrodes at each end. When a sufficiently high potential difference is applied between the two electrodes, the gas ionizes; electrons move toward the positive electrode, and positive ions toward the negative electrode.

  a) What is the current in a hydrogen discharge if, in each second, 3.10×10^{18} electrons and 1.15×10^{18} protons move in opposite directions through a cross section of the tube?

  b) What is the direction of the current?

28–3 A silver wire 1.00 mm in diameter transfers a charge of 65.0 C in 1 hr, 15.0 min. Silver contains 5.80×10^{28} free electrons per cubic meter.

  a) What is the current in the wire?

  b) What is the magnitude of the drift velocity of the electrons in the wire?

Section 28–2 Resistivity

Section 28–3 Resistance

28–4 A copper wire has a square cross section 2.00 mm on a side. It is 4.00 m long and carries a current of 7.40 A. The density of free electrons is 8.00×10^{28} m^{-3}.

  a) What is the current density in the wire?

  b) What is the electric field?

  c) How much time is required for an electron to travel the length of the wire?

28–5 An aluminum wire carrying a current has diameter 0.800 mm. The electric field in the wire is 0.640 V·m^{-1}. What is

  a) the current carried by the wire?

  b) the potential difference between two points in the wire 12.0 m apart?

  c) the resistance of a 12.0-m length of this wire?

28–6 The potential difference between points in a wire 8.00 m apart is 7.20 V when the current density is 42.0×10^{6} A·m^{-2}. What is

  a) the electric field in the wire?

  b) the resistivity of the material of which the wire is made?

28–7 What length of copper wire 0.800 mm in diameter has a resistance of 1.00 Ω?

28–8 In household wiring, a copper wire commonly known as 12-gauge is often used. Its diameter is 2.05 mm. Find the resistance of a 40.0-m length of this wire.

28–9 What diameter must an aluminum wire have if its resistance is the same as an equal length of copper wire with diameter 2.60 mm?

28–10 An aluminum bar 3.80 m long has a rectangular cross section 1.00 cm by 5.00 cm.

  a) What is its resistance?

  b) What is the length of a copper wire 1.50 mm in diameter having the same resistance?

28–11

  a) What is the resistance of a Nichrome wire at 0.0°C if its resistance is 100.0 Ω at 16.0°C?

  b) What is the resistance of a carbon rod at 30.0°C if its resistance is 0.0220 Ω at 0.0°C?

28–12 A certain resistor has a resistance of 150.4 Ω at 20.0°C and a resistance of 152.8 Ω at 28.0°C. What is its temperature coefficient of resistivity?

28–13 A carbon resistor is to be used as a thermometer. On a winter day when the temperature is 4°C, the resistance of the carbon resistor is 217.3 Ω. What is the temperature on a hot summer day when the resistance is 214.2 Ω?

Section 28–4 Electromotive Force and Circuits

28–14 The following measurements of current and potential difference were made on a resistor constructed of Nichrome wire:

I, A	V_{ab}, V
0.50	2.18
1.00	4.36
2.00	8.72
4.00	17.44

  a) Make a graph of V_{ab} as a function of I.

  b) Does Nichrome obey Ohm's law?

  c) What is the resistance of the resistor in ohms?

28–15 The following measurements were made on a Thyrite resistor:

I, A	V_{ab}, V
0.50	4.76
1.00	5.81
2.00	7.05
4.00	8.56

Make a graph of V_{ab} as a function of I. Does Thyrite obey Ohm's law?

28–16 When switch S in Fig. 28–12 is open, the voltmeter V, connected across the terminals of the dry cell, reads 1.52 V. When the switch is closed, the voltmeter reading drops to 1.37 V, and the ammeter A reads 1.20 A. Find the emf and internal resistance of the cell. Assume that the two meters are ideal, so they don't affect the circuit.

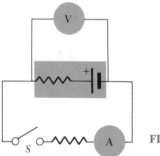

FIGURE 28–12

28–17 A complete circuit consists of a 12.0-V battery, a 4.70-Ω resistor, and a switch. The internal resistance of the battery is 0.30 Ω. The switch is opened. What does an ideal voltmeter read when placed

a) across the terminals of the battery?

b) across the resistor?

c) across the switch?

d) Repeat parts (a), (b), and (c) for the case when the switch is closed.

28–18 The internal resistance of a dry cell increases gradually with age, even though the cell is not used. The emf, however, remains fairly constant at about 1.5 V. Dry cells may be tested for age at the time of purchase by connecting an ammeter directly across the terminals of the cell and reading the current. The resistance of the ammeter is so small that the cell is practically short-circuited.

a) The short-circuit current of a fresh No. 6 dry cell (1.50-V emf) is 25.0 A. What is the internal resistance?

b) What is the internal resistance if the short-circuit current is only 10.0 A?

c) The short-circuit current of a 6.00-V storage battery may be as great as 1000 A. What is its internal resistance?

28–19 Consider the circuit shown in Fig. 28–13. The terminal voltage of the 24.0-V battery is 22.0 V, and the current in the circuit is 4.00 A. What is

a) the internal resistance r of the battery?

b) the resistance R of the circuit resistor?

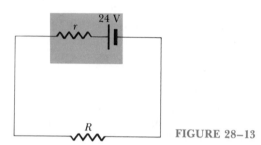

FIGURE 28–13

28–20 The circuit shown in Fig. 28–14 contains two batteries, each with an emf and an internal resistance, and two resistors. Find

a) the current in the circuit;

b) the terminal voltage V_{ab} of the 16.0-V battery;

c) the potential difference V_{ac} of point a with respect to point c.

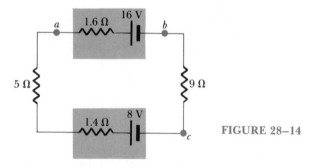

FIGURE 28–14

Section 28–5   Energy and Power in Electric Circuits

28–21 Consider a resistor of length L, uniform cross section A, and uniform resistivity ρ that is carrying a current of uniform current density J. Use Eq. (28–16) to find the electrical power dissipated *per unit volume, p.* Express your result in terms of

a) E and J,   b) J and ρ,   c) E and ρ.

28–22 A motor operating on 120 V draws a current of 2.50 A. How much electrical energy is delivered by the motor in 4.00 hr? (That is, how much electrical energy does the motor convert to other forms?)

28–23 A resistor develops heat at the rate of 360 W when the potential difference across its ends is 120 V. What is its resistance?

28–24 A "580-W" electric heater is designed to operate from 120-V lines.

a) What is its resistance?

b) What current does it draw?

c) If the line voltage drops to 110 V, what power does the heater take, in watts? (Assume that the resistance is constant. Actually, it will change because of the change in temperature.)

28–25 A typical small flashlight contains two batteries, each having an emf of 1.50 V, connected in series with a bulb having a resistance of 18.0 Ω.

a) If the internal resistance of the batteries is negligible, what power is delivered to the bulb?

b) If the batteries last for 5 hours, what is the total energy delivered to the bulb?

c) The resistance of real batteries increases as they run down. If the initial internal resistance is negligible, what is the combined internal resistance of the two batteries when the power to the bulb has decreased to half its initial value? (Assume that the resistance of the bulb is constant. Actually, it will change somewhat as the temperature of the filament changes, when the current through it changes.)

28–26 The capacity of a storage battery, such as those used in automobile electrical systems, is rated in ampere-hours (A·hr). A 50-A·hr battery can supply a current of 50 A for 1 hour, or 25 A for 2 hours, and so on.

a) What total energy is stored in a 12-V, 50-A·hr battery if its internal resistance is negligible?

b) What volume (in liters) of gasoline has a total heat of combustion equal to the energy obtained in part (a)? (See Section 15–5, near the end of the section. Take the density of gasoline to be 900 kg·m^{-3}.)

c) If a windmill-powered generator has an average electrical power output of 300 W, how much time would be required for it to charge the battery fully?

28–27 In the circuit in Fig. 28–15, find

a) the rate of conversion of internal (chemical) energy to electrical energy within the battery;

b) the rate of dissipation of electrical energy in the battery;

c) the rate of dissipation of electrical energy in the external resistor.

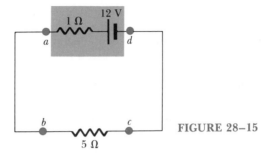

FIGURE 28–15

28–28 Consider the circuit of Example 28–5 (Fig. 28–8).

a) What is the total rate at which electrical energy is being converted to heat in the 3.00-Ω and 7.00-Ω resistors?

b) What is the power output of the 12.0-V battery?

c) At what rate is electrical energy being converted to other forms in the 4.00-V battery?

d) Show that the overall rate of conversion of non-electrical (chemical) energy to electrical energy equals the overall rate of dissipation of electrical energy (conversion to heat) in the circuit.

Section 28–6 Theory of Metallic Conduction

28–29 For copper the density of free electrons is $n = 8.00 \times 10^{28}$ m^{-3}. At a temperature of $T = 27°C$ the resistivity is 1.72×10^{-8} Ω·m, as given in Table 28–1. Calculate

a) the average random speed of a free electron in copper at this temperature;

b) the mean free path λ;

c) the mean free time t.

28–30 For silver the density of free electrons is $n = 5.80 \times 10^{28}$ m^{-3}. At a temperature of $T = 27°C$, what mean free path λ gives a value of the resistivity that agrees with the value given in Table 28–1?

Section 28–7 Physiological Effects of Currents

28–31 A person with body resistance between hands of 10 kΩ accidentally grasps the terminals of a 20-kV power supply.

a) If the internal resistance of the power supply is 2000 Ω, what is the current through the person's body?

b) What is the power dissipated in the body?

c) If the power supply is to be made safe by increasing its internal resistance, what should the internal resistance be in order for the maximum current in the above situation to be 0.001 A or less?

28–32 The average bulk resistivity of the human body (apart from surface resistance of the skin) is about 5.0 Ω·m. The conducting path between the hands can be represented approximately as a cylinder 1.6 m long and 0.10 m in diameter. The skin resistance can be made negligible by soaking the hands in salt water (or seawater).

a) What is the resistance between the hands if the skin resistance is negligible?

b) What potential difference between the hands is needed for a lethal shock current of 100 mA?

c) With the current in part (b), what power is dissipated in the body?

d) Does the result of part (b) increase your respect for electrical-shock hazards?

Problems

28–33 A vacuum diode (see Exercise 26–14) can be approximated by a plane cathode and a plane anode, parallel to each other and 5.00 mm apart. The area of each is 2.00 cm². In the region between cathode and anode the current is carried solely by electrons. If the electron current is 75.0 mA, and the electrons strike the anode surface with a speed of 1.20×10^7 m·s⁻¹, find the number of electrons per cubic millimeter in the space just outside the surface of the anode.

28–34 In the Bohr model of the hydrogen atom the electron makes 6.0×10^{15} rev·s⁻¹ around the nucleus. What is the average current at a point on the orbit of the electron?

28–35 A certain electrical conductor has a square cross section 2.00 mm on a side and is 12.0 m long. The resistance between its ends is 0.0580 Ω.

a) What is the resistivity of the material?

b) If the electric-field magnitude in the conductor is 0.160 V·m⁻¹, what is the total current?

c) If the material has 8.00×10^{28} free electrons per cubic meter, find the average drift speed under the conditions of part (b).

28–36 Two parallel plates of a capacitor have equal and opposite charges Q. The dielectric has a dielectric constant K and a resistivity ρ. Show that the "leakage" current carried by the dielectric is given by the relationship $i = Q/K\epsilon_0\rho$.

28–37 A toaster using a Nichrome heating element operates on 120 V. When it is switched on at 20°C, it carries an initial current of 1.50 A. A few seconds later the current reaches the steady value of 1.33 A. What is the final temperature of the element? The average value of the temperature coefficient of resistance for Nichrome over the temperature range is 0.000450 (C°)⁻¹.

28–38 A piece of wire has a resistance R. It is cut into three pieces of equal length, and the pieces are twisted together in parallel. What is the resistance of the resulting wire?

28–39 The potential difference across the terminals of a battery is 9.5 V when there is a current of 3.00 A in the battery from the negative to the positive terminal. When the current is 2.00 A in the reverse direction, the potential difference becomes 11.0 V.

a) What is the internal resistance of the battery?

b) What is the emf of the battery?

28–40

a) What is the potential difference V_{ad} in the circuit of Fig. 28–16?

b) What is the terminal voltage of the 4.00-V battery?

c) A battery with emf 15.0 V and internal resistance 0.500 Ω is inserted in the circuit at d, with its negative terminal connected to the negative terminal of the 8.00-V battery. What is now the difference of potential V_{bc} between the terminals of the 4.00-V battery?

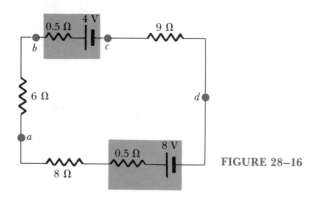

FIGURE 28–16

28–41 In the circuit of Fig. 28–17, find

a) the current through the 8.0 Ω resistor;

b) the total rate of dissipation of electrical energy (conversion to heat) in the 8.0 Ω resistor and in the internal resistance of the batteries.

c) In one of the batteries, chemical energy is being converted into electrical energy. In which one is this happening, and at what rate?

d) In one of the batteries, electrical energy is being

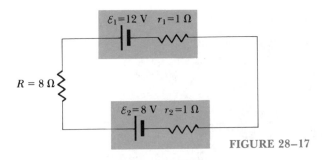

$\mathcal{E}_1 = 12\ V \quad r_1 = 1\ \Omega$

$R = 8\ \Omega$

$\mathcal{E}_2 = 8\ V \quad r_2 = 1\ \Omega$

FIGURE 28–17

converted into chemical energy. In which one is this happening, and at what rate?

e) Show that the overall rate of production of electrical energy equals the overall rate of consumption of electrical energy in the circuit.

28–42 A certain 12.0-V storage battery has a capacity of 60.0 A·hr. (See Exercise 28–26.) Its internal resistance is 0.300 Ω. The battery is charged by passing a 15.0-A current through it for 4.00 hr.

a) What is the terminal voltage during charging?

b) What total electrical energy is supplied to the battery during charging?

c) What electrical energy is dissipated in the internal resistance during charging?

The battery is now completely discharged through a resistor, again with a constant current of 15.0 A.

d) What is the external circuit resistance?

e) What total electrical energy is supplied to the external resistor?

f) What total electrical energy is dissipated in the internal resistance?

g) Why are the answers to parts (b) and (e) not equal?

28–43 Repeat Problem 28–42 with charge and discharge currents of 30.0 A. The charging and discharging times are now 2.00 hr rather than 4.00 hr. What differences in performance do you see?

Challenge Problems

28–44 A source with emf $\mathcal{E}$ and internal resistance r is connected to an external circuit. The short-circuit current is $\mathcal{E}/r$. In general, the circuit current I is some fraction of this, so it can be expressed as $I = a\mathcal{E}/r$, where a is a dimensionless number between 0 and 1.

a) Show that the power output of the source can be expressed as $P = (a - a^2)\mathcal{E}^2/r$.

b) Plot P versus a and determine the value of a for which P is a maximum. Your results should show that the power output of the source is maximum when the current in the circuit is one-half the short-circuit current of the source. (That is, when $a = 1/2$.)

c) If the external circuit consists of a resistance R, show that the power output is maximum when $R = r$ and that the maximum power is $\mathcal{E}^2/4r$.

28–45 The open-circuit terminal voltage of a source is 9.00 V, and its short-circuit current is 4.00 A.

a) What is the current when a resistor with resistance 2.00 Ω is connected to the terminals of the source? The resistor obeys Ohm's law.

b) What will be the current in the Thyrite resistor of Exercise 28–15 when it is connected across the terminals of this source?

c) What is the terminal voltage at this current?

28–46 A semiconductor diode is a nonlinear device whose current–voltage relationship is described by

$$I = I_0[\exp (eV/kT) - 1],$$

where I and V are, respectively, the current through and the voltage across the diode; I_0 is a constant characteristic of the device; e is the electron charge; k is Boltzmann's constant; and T is the Kelvin temperature. Such a diode is connected in series with a resistor with $R = 1.0\ \Omega$ and a battery with emf $\mathcal{E} = 2.00$ V. The polarity of the battery is such that the current through the diode is in the forward direction. (See Fig. 28–18.) The battery has negligible internal resistance.

a) Obtain an equation for V. Note that you cannot solve for V algebraically.

b) Since V cannot be solved for algebraically, the value of V must be obtained by using a numerical method. One approach is to try a value of V, see how the left- and right-hand sides of the equation compare for this V, and use this to refine your guess for V. Using $I_0 = 1.50$ A and $T = 293$ K, obtain a solution (accurate to three significant figures) for the voltage drop V across the diode and the current I through it.

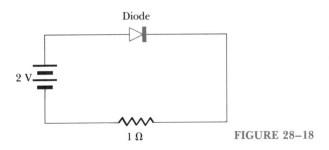

Diode

2 V

1 Ω

FIGURE 28–18

29

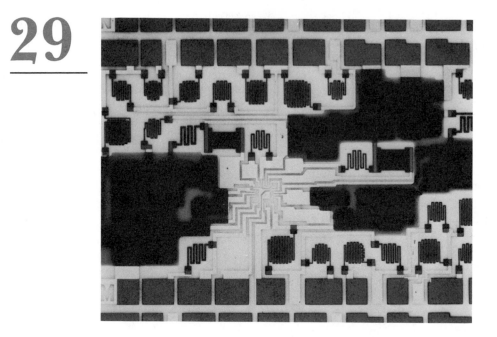

Direct-Current Circuits

In Chapter 28 we studied some of the basic principles of electric currents in simple circuits. But if you look inside your TV or your computer, you will find circuits of much greater complexity. Real-world circuits often contain several sources, resistors, and other circuit elements such as capacitors, transformers, and motors, interconnected in a *network*. In this chapter we study general methods for analyzing networks, including finding unknown voltages, currents, and properties of circuit elements. When several resistors are connected in series or in parallel, they can always be represented as a single equivalent resistor. To analyze more general networks, we need two rules called *Kirchhoff's rules*. One is basically the principle of conservation of charge applied to a junction; the other is based on energy conservation for a charge moving around a closed loop. We also discuss instruments for measuring various electrical quantities. We look at a circuit containing resistance and capacitance, in which the current varies with time. Finally, we look at how these principles are related to household wiring systems.

29–1
Resistors in Series and Parallel

Suppose we have three resistors with resistances R_1, R_2, and R_3. Figure 29–1 shows four different ways they might be connected between points a and b. In Fig. 29–1a, the resistors provide only a single path between these points. When circuit elements such as resistors, batteries, and motors are connected as in Fig 29–1a, where there is only a single current path between the points, we say they are connected in **series.** The *current* is the same in each element.

The resistors in Fig. 29–1b are said to be in **parallel** between points a and b. Each resistor provides an alternative path between the points. Any number of circuit elements similarly connected are in parallel with one another. The *potential difference* is the same across each element.

In Fig. 29–1c, resistors R_2 and R_3 are in parallel with each other, and this combination is in series with R_1. In Fig. 29–1d, R_2 and R_3 are in series, and this combination is in parallel with R_1.

For any combination of resistors it is always possible to find a single resistor that could replace the combination and result in the same total current and potential difference. The resistance of this single resistor is called the **equivalent resistance** of the combination. If any one of the networks in Fig. 29–1 were replaced by its equivalent resistance R, we could write

$$V_{ab} = IR \qquad \text{or} \qquad R = \frac{V_{ab}}{I},$$

where V_{ab} is the potential difference between terminals a and b of the network and I is the current at point a or b. To compute an equivalent resistance, all we have to do is to assume a potential difference V_{ab} across the actual network, compute the corresponding current I, and take the ratio V_{ab}/I.

For series and parallel combinations we can derive general equations for the equivalent resistance. If the resistors are in *series*, as in Fig. 29–1a, the current I must be the same in all of them. Applying Ohm's law to each, we have

$$V_{ax} = IR_1, \qquad V_{xy} = IR_2, \qquad V_{yb} = IR_3.$$

The potential difference V_{ab} is the sum of these three quantities:

$$V_{ab} = V_{ax} + V_{xy} + V_{yb} = I(R_1 + R_2 + R_3),$$

or

$$\frac{V_{ab}}{I} = R_1 + R_2 + R_3.$$

But V_{ab}/I is, by definition, the equivalent resistance R. Therefore

$$R = R_1 + R_2 + R_3. \tag{29–1}$$

29–1
Four different ways of connecting three resistors.

The equivalent resistance of *any number* of resistors in series equals the sum of their individual resistances.

It is interesting to compare this result with Eq. (27–5) for *capacitors* in series. Resistors in series add directly because the voltage across each is proportional to its resistance; capacitors in series add reciprocally because the voltage across each is *inversely* proportional to its capacitance.

If the resistors are in *parallel*, as in Fig. 29–1b, the potential difference between the terminals of each must be the same and equal to V_{ab}. Let's call the currents in the three resistors I_1, I_2, and I_3, respectively. Then from Ohm's law,

$$I_1 = \frac{V_{ab}}{R_1}, \qquad I_2 = \frac{V_{ab}}{R_2}, \qquad I_3 = \frac{V_{ab}}{R_3}.$$

Because charge is not accumulating or draining out of point a, the total current I must equal the sum of the three currents in the resistors:

$$I = I_1 + I_2 + I_3 = V_{ab}\left(\frac{1}{R_1} + \frac{1}{R_2} + \frac{1}{R_3}\right),$$

or

$$\frac{I}{V_{ab}} = \frac{1}{R_1} + \frac{1}{R_2} + \frac{1}{R_3}.$$

But, by definition of the equivalent resistance R, $I/V_{ab} = 1/R$, so

$$\frac{1}{R} = \frac{1}{R_1} + \frac{1}{R_2} + \frac{1}{R_3}. \qquad (29\text{–}2)$$

For *any number* of resistors in parallel the *reciprocal* of the equivalent resistance equals the *sum of the reciprocals* of their individual resistances.

For the special case of *two* resistors in parallel,

$$\frac{1}{R} = \frac{1}{R_1} + \frac{1}{R_2} = \frac{R_1 + R_2}{R_1 R_2} \qquad \text{and} \qquad R = \frac{R_1 R_2}{R_1 + R_2}.$$

The equivalent resistance is always *less* than either R_1 or R_2. Can you prove that?

Because $V_{ab} = I_1 R_1 = I_2 R_2$, it follows that

$$\frac{I_1}{I_2} = \frac{R_2}{R_1}. \qquad (29\text{–}3)$$

This shows that the currents carried by two resistors in parallel are *inversely proportional* to their resistances.

We can consider the networks in Figs. 29–1c and 29–1d as combinations of series and parallel arrangements. In Fig. 29–1c we first replace the parallel combination of R_2 and R_3 by its equivalent resistance; this then forms a series combination with R_1. In Fig. 29–1d the combination of R_2 and R_3 in series forms a parallel combination with R_1.

Example 29–1   Compute the equivalent resistance of the network in Fig. 29–2, and find the current in each resistor.

Solution   Figures 29–2b and 29–2c show successive stages in the reduction to a single equivalent resistance. From Eq. (29–2) the 6-Ω and the 3-Ω resistors in parallel in Fig. 29–2a are equivalent to the single 2-Ω

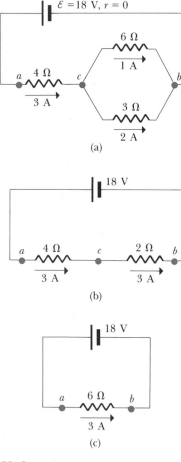

(a)

(b)

(c)

29–2
Steps in reducing a combination of resistors to a single equivalent resistor.

resistor in Fig. 29–2b. The series combination of this with the 4-Ω resistor results in the single equivalent 6-Ω resistor in Fig. 29–2c.

In the series circuit of Fig. 29–2c the current is 3 A, so the current in the 4-Ω and 2-Ω resistors in Fig. 29–2b is also 3 A. The potential difference V_{cb} is therefore 6 V. It must also be 6 V in Fig. 29–2a, so the currents in the 6-Ω and 3-Ω resistors in Fig. 29–2a are 1 A and 2 A, respectively.   ∎

29–2
Kirchhoff's Rules

Not all networks can be reduced to simple series–parallel combinations. An example is a resistance network with a cross connection, as in Fig. 29–3a. A circuit like that in Fig. 29–3b, which contains sources in parallel paths, is another example. We don't need any new *principles* to compute the currents in these networks, but there are some techniques that help us to handle such problems systematically. We will describe one of these, first developed by Gustav Robert Kirchhoff (1824–1887).

First, here are two terms that we will use often. A **branch point** in a network is a point where three or more conductors meet. A **loop** is any closed conducting path. In Fig. 29–3a, for example, points a, b, d, and e are branch points but points c and f are not. The circuit in Fig. 29–3b has two branch points, a and b. Some possible loops in Fig. 29–3a are the closed paths *aceda*, *defbd*, *hadbgh*, and *hadefbgh*.

Kirchhoff's rules consist of the following two statements.

Point rule: *The algebraic sum of the currents into any branch point is zero*:

$$\sum I = 0 \quad \text{(any branch point).} \quad (29\text{–}4)$$

Loop rule: *The algebraic sum of the potential differences in any loop*, including those associated with emf's and those of resistive elements, *must equal zero*:

$$\sum V = 0 \quad \text{(any closed loop).} \quad (29\text{–}5)$$

The point rule is based on *conservation of electric charge*. No charge can accumulate at a branch point, so the total current entering the point must equal the total current leaving. Or, if we consider currents entering as positive and those leaving as negative, the algebraic sum of currents into a branch point must be zero. We may as well confess that we used the point rule (without saying so) in the derivation of Eq. (29–2) for resistors in parallel in Section 29–1.

We have already seen the loop rule in Section 28–4. It is an expression of an *energy* relationship. As a charge goes around a loop and returns to its starting point, the algebraic sum of the changes in its potential energy must be zero. No matter what kinds of circuit elements are present, or whether they obey Ohm's law, the algebraic sum of potential differences around every closed loop must be zero.

These basic rules are all we need to solve a wide variety of network problems. Usually, some of the emf's, currents, and resistances are

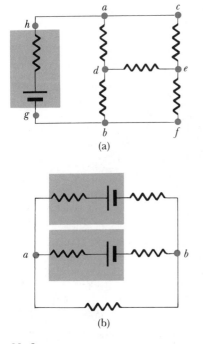

29–3
Two networks that cannot be reduced to simple series–parallel combinations of resistors.

known, and others are unknown. We must always obtain from Kirchhoff's rules a number of equations equal to the number of unknowns so that we can solve the equations simultaneously. Often the hardest part of the solution is not in understanding the basic principles but in keeping track of algebraic signs!

PROBLEM-SOLVING STRATEGY: *Kirchhoff's Rules*

1. Draw a *large* circuit diagram so that you have plenty of room for labels. Label all quantities, known and unknown, including an assumed sense of direction for each unknown current and emf. Often you will not know in advance the actual direction of an unknown current or emf, but this doesn't matter. Carry out your solution, using the assumed direction. If the actual direction of a particular quantity is opposite to your assumption, the result will come out with a negative sign. If you use Kirchhoff's rules correctly, they give you the directions as well as magnitudes of unknown currents and emf's. We made this point before, in Section 28–4; you may want to review that discussion now. We will illustrate it further in the following examples.

2. Usually, when you label currents, it is best to use the point rule immediately to express the currents in terms of as few quantities as possible. For example, Fig. 29–4a shows a circuit correctly labeled; Fig. 29–4b shows the same circuit, relabeled by applying the point rule to point a to eliminate I_3.

3. Choose any closed loop in the network, and designate a direction (clockwise or counterclockwise) to go around the loop in applying the loop rule. The direction doesn't have to be the same as any assumed current direction.

4. Go around the loop in the designated direction, adding potential differences as you cross them. An emf is counted as positive when it is traversed from $-$ to $+$ and negative when traversed from $+$ to $-$. An IR product is negative if your path passes through the resistor in the *same* direction as the assumed current and positive if in the opposite direction. "Uphill" potential changes are always positive; "downhill" changes are always negative.

5. Equate the sum in Step 4 to zero.

6. If necessary, choose another loop to get a different relation among the unknowns, and

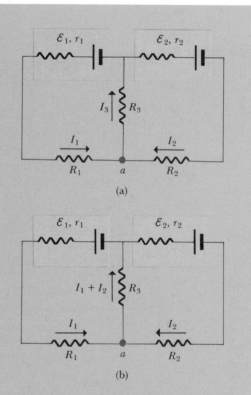

29–4
Application of the point rule to point a reduces the number of unknown currents from three to two.

continue until you have as many equations as unknowns or until every circuit element has been included in at least one of the chosen loops.

7. Finally, solve the equations simultaneously to determine the unknowns. This step is algebra, not physics, but it can be fairly complex. Be careful with algebraic manipulations; one sign error is fatal to the entire solution.

8. To find the potential V_{ab} of any point a with respect to any other point b, use the same method we outlined in item 4 of the Problem-Solving Strategy in Section 28–4.

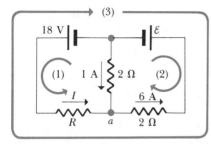

29–5
Circuit for Example 29–2.

Example 29–2   In the circuit shown in Fig. 29–5, find the unknown current I, the resistance R, and the emf $\mathcal{E}$.

Solution   First we apply the point rule to point a, obtaining

$$I + 1\text{ A} - 6\text{ A} = 0, \qquad I = 5\text{ A}.$$

To determine R, we apply the loop rule to the loop labeled (1); we find

$$18\text{ V} - (5\text{ A})R + (1\text{ A})(2\text{ }\Omega) = 0, \qquad R = 4\text{ }\Omega.$$

The term containing the resistance R is negative because our loop traverses that element in the same direction as the current and hence finds a potential *drop*. The term for the 2-Ω resistor is positive because in traversing it in the direction opposite to the current we find a potential *rise*. If we had chosen to traverse loop (1) in the opposite direction, every term would have had the opposite sign, and the result for R would have been the same.

To determine $\mathcal{E}$, we apply the loop rule to loop (2):

$$\mathcal{E} + (6\text{ A})(2\text{ }\Omega) + (1\text{ A})(2\text{ }\Omega) = 0, \qquad \mathcal{E} = -14\text{ V}.$$

This shows that the actual polarity of this emf is opposite to the assumption made in the figure; the positive terminal of this source is really on the left side. Alternatively, we could use loop (3), obtaining the equation

$$\mathcal{E} + (6\text{ A})(2\text{ }\Omega) + (5\text{ A})(4\text{ }\Omega) - 18\text{ V} = 0,$$

from which again $\mathcal{E} = -14$ V.   ■

Example 29–3   In Fig. 29–6, find the current in each resistor and the equivalent resistance of the network.

Solution   As we pointed out at the beginning of this section, this network cannot be represented in terms of series and parallel combinations. There are five different currents to determine, but by applying the point rule to junctions a and b we can represent them in terms of three unknown currents, as shown in the figure. The current in the battery is $(I_1 + I_2)$.

We apply the loop rule to the three loops shown, obtaining the following three equations:

$$13\text{ V} - I_1(1\text{ }\Omega) - (I_1 - I_3)(1\text{ }\Omega) = 0; \tag{1}$$

$$-I_2(1\text{ }\Omega) - (I_2 + I_3)(2\text{ }\Omega) + 13\text{ V} = 0; \tag{2}$$

$$-I_1(1\text{ }\Omega) - I_3(1\text{ }\Omega) + I_2(1\text{ }\Omega) = 0. \tag{3}$$

This is a set of three simultaneous equations for the three unknown currents. They may be solved by various methods; one straightforward procedure is to solve the third for I_2, obtaining $I_2 = I_1 + I_3$, and then substitute this expression into the first two equations to eliminate I_2. When this is done, we are left with the two equations

$$13\text{ V} = I_1(2\text{ }\Omega) - I_3(1\text{ }\Omega), \tag{1'}$$

$$13\text{ V} = I_1(3\text{ }\Omega) + I_3(5\text{ }\Omega). \tag{2'}$$

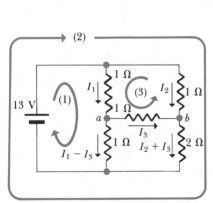

29–6
Circuit for Examples 29–3 and 29–4.

Now we can eliminate I_3 by multiplying Eq. (1′) by 5 and adding the two equations. We obtain

$$78 \text{ V} = I_1(13 \text{ }\Omega), \qquad I_1 = 6 \text{ A}.$$

We substitute this result back into Eq. (1′) to obtain $I_3 = -1$ A, and finally from Eq. (3) we find $I_2 = 5$ A. We note that the direction of I_3 is opposite to our initial assumption.

The total current through the network is $I_1 + I_2 = 11$ A, and the potential drop across it is equal to the battery emf, namely, 13 V. The equivalent resistance of the network is

$$R = \frac{13 \text{ V}}{11 \text{ A}} = 1.2 \text{ }\Omega. \qquad \blacksquare$$

To find $V_{ab} = V_a - V_b$ (the potential at a with respect to b), we can use the procedure we described in the Problem-Solving Strategy in Section 28–4 (item 4). We start at b and add the potential differences as we go from b to a. An emf is positive when we go from $-$ to $+$ and negative otherwise. An IR term is positive when we go "uphill," against the current direction, negative when in the same direction as the current.

Example 29–4   In the circuit of Fig. 29–6, find the potential difference V_{ab}.

Solution   Starting at point b, we follow a path to point a, adding potential rises and drops as we go. The simplest path is through the center 1-Ω resistor. We have found $I_3 = -1$ A, showing that the actual current direction in this branch is from right to left. Thus as we go from b to a, there is a drop of potential of magnitude $IR = (1 \text{ A})(1 \text{ }\Omega) = 1$ V, and $V_{ab} = -1$ V. Alternatively, we may go around the lower loop. We then have

$$I_2 + I_3 = 5 \text{ A} + (-1 \text{ A}) = 4 \text{ A},$$

$$I_1 - I_3 = 6 \text{ A} - (-1 \text{ A}) = 7 \text{ A},$$

and

$$V_{ab} = -(4 \text{ A})(2 \text{ }\Omega) + (7 \text{ A})(1 \text{ }\Omega) = -1 \text{ V}.$$

We suggest you try some other paths from b to a to verify that they also give this result. $\qquad \blacksquare$

29–3
Electrical Instruments

We've been talking about current and potential difference for two chapters; it's about time we said something about how to *measure* these quantities. Many familiar instruments for measuring potential difference

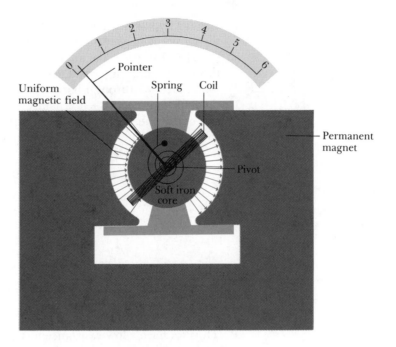

29–7
A d'Arsonval meter movement, showing pivoted coil with attached pointer, permanent magnet supplying uniform magnetic field, and spring to provide restoring torque, which opposes magnetic-field torque.

(voltage), current, or resistance use a device called a **d'Arsonval galvanometer.** A pivoted coil of fine wire is placed in the magnetic field of a permanent magnet, as shown in Fig. 29–7. Attached to the coil is a spring, similar to the hairspring on the balance wheel of a watch. In the equilibrium position, with no current in the coil, the pointer is at zero. When there is a current in the coil, the magnetic field exerts a torque on the coil that is proportional to the current. (We'll discuss this magnetic interaction in detail in Chapter 30.) As the coil turns, the spring exerts a restoring torque proportional to the angular displacement.

Thus the angular deflection of the coil and pointer is directly proportional to the coil current, and the device can be calibrated to measure current. The maximum deflection, typically 90° to 120°, is called *full-scale deflection*. The essential electrical characteristics of the meter are the current required for full-scale deflection (typically of the order of 10 μA to 10 mA) and the resistance R_c of the coil (typically of the order of 10 to 1000 Ω).

The meter deflection is proportional to the *current* in the coil, but if the coil obeys Ohm's law, the current is proportional to the *potential difference* between the terminals of the coil. Thus the deflection is also proportional to this potential difference. For example, consider a meter that has a coil with a resistance of 20 Ω and that deflects full scale with a current of 1 mA in its coil. The corresponding potential difference is

$$V_{ab} = IR = (10^{-3} \text{ A})(20 \ \Omega) = 0.020 \text{ V} = 20 \text{ mV}.$$

A current-measuring instrument is usually called an **ammeter** (or milliammeter, microammeter, etc., depending on the range). The instrument always measures the current passing through it. We can adapt such a meter to measure currents larger than its full-scale reading by connecting a resistor in parallel with it, as in Fig. 29–8a, so that some of the

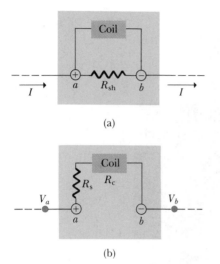

(a)

(b)

29–8
(a) Internal connections of an ammeter. (b) Internal connections of a voltmeter.

current bypasses the meter. The parallel resistor is called a **shunt resistor** or simply a *shunt*, denoted as R_{sh}.

How can we make an ammeter with a range of 0 to 10 A, based on the 1-mA meter described above? We must choose a shunt such that the total current I through both meter and shunt is 10 A when the current through the meter itself is 1 mA = 0.001 A. At full-scale deflection the current in the shunt is 9.999 A, and the potential difference across the shunt is the same as that across the meter, namely, 0.020 V. From Ohm's law the shunt resistance must be

$$R_{sh} = \frac{0.020 \text{ V}}{9.999 \text{ A}} = 0.00200 \text{ } \Omega.$$

The equivalent resistance R of the instrument is given by

$$\frac{1}{R} = \frac{1}{R_c} + \frac{1}{R_{sh}} = \frac{1}{20 \text{ } \Omega} + \frac{1}{0.00200 \text{ } \Omega},$$

and

$$R = 0.00200 \text{ } \Omega.$$

Thus we have a low-resistance instrument with the desired range of 0 to 10 A. If the current I is *less* than 10 A, the coil current and the deflection are correspondingly less, but the resistance R is still 0.00200 Ω. We note that in this case the 20-Ω path through the meter makes a negligible contribution to the overall resistance of the combination.

An *ideal* ammeter would have *zero* resistance, so including it in a branch of a circuit would not affect the current in that branch. Real ammeters always have some finite resistance, but it is always desirable for an ammeter to have as little resistance as possible.

This same 1-mA meter may also be used to measure potential difference or *voltage*. A voltage-measuring device is called a **voltmeter** (or millivoltmeter, etc., depending on the range). A voltmeter always measures the potential difference between two points, and its terminals must be connected to these points. Our 1-mA meter may be used as a voltmeter, but the maximum voltage it can measure is 0.020 V. We can extend the range by connecting a resistor R_s in *series* with the meter, as in Fig. 29–8b. Then only some fraction of the total potential difference appears across the meter itself, and the remainder appears across R_s.

For example, suppose we need a voltmeter with a maximum range of 10 V. Then when the voltage across the meter is 0.020 V, the voltage across the series resistor R_s must be 10 V − 0.020 V, or 9.98 V. The current through the meter at full-scale deflection is still 1 mA or 0.001 A, so from Ohm's law the value of R_s must be

$$R_s = \frac{9.98 \text{ V}}{0.001 \text{ A}} = 9980 \text{ } \Omega.$$

The equivalent resistance of the meter is then

$$R = R_c + R_s = 10{,}000 \text{ } \Omega.$$

An ideal voltmeter would have *infinite* resistance, so connecting it between two points in a circuit would not alter any of the currents. Real

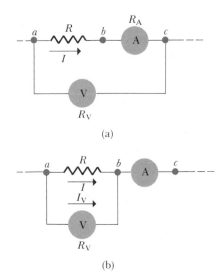

(a)

(b)

29–9

Ammeter–voltmeter method for measuring resistance or power.

voltmeters always have finite resistance, but a voltmeter should have resistance large enough that connecting it in a circuit does not change the other currents appreciably.

A voltmeter and an ammeter can be used together to measure *resistance* and *power*. The resistance R of a resistor is the potential difference V_{ab} between its terminals divided by the current I: $R = V_{ab}/I$. The power input P to any circuit element is the product of the potential difference across it and the current through it: $P = V_{ab}I$. In principle, the most straightforward way to measure R or P is to measure V_{ab} and I simultaneously.

With real-world ammeters and voltmeters this isn't quite as simple as it seems. In Fig. 29–9a, ammeter A reads the current I in the resistor R. Voltmeter V, however, reads the *sum* of the potential difference V_{ab} across the resistor and the potential difference V_{bc} across the ammeter. If we transfer the voltmeter terminal from c to b, as in Fig. 29–9b, then the voltmeter reads the potential difference V_{ab} correctly, but the ammeter now reads the *sum* of the current I in the resistor and the current I_V in the voltmeter. Either way, we have to correct the reading of one instrument or the other unless the corrections are small enough to be negligible.

Example 29–5 Suppose we want to measure an unknown resistance R using the circuit of Fig. 29–9a. The meter resistances are $R_V = 10,000\ \Omega$ and $R_A = 2.00\ \Omega$. If the voltmeter reads 12.0 V and the ammeter reads 0.100 A, what is the true resistance?

Solution If the meters were ideal (i.e., $R_V = \infty$ and $R_A = 0$), the resistance would be simply $R = V/I = (12.0\ \text{V})/(0.100\ \text{A}) = 120\ \Omega$. But the voltmeter reading includes the potential V_{bc} across the ammeter as well as that (V_{ab}) across the resistor. We have $V_{bc} = IR_A = (0.100\ \text{A})(2.00\ \Omega) = 0.200\ \text{V}$, so the actual potential drop V_{ab} across the resistor is 12.0 V $-$ 0.200 V = 11.8 V, and the resistance is

$$R = \frac{V_{ab}}{I} = \frac{11.8\ \text{V}}{0.10\ \text{A}} = 118\ \Omega. \qquad \blacksquare$$

Example 29–6 Suppose the meters of Example 29–5 are connected to a different resistor, in the circuit shown in Fig. 29–9b, and the above readings are obtained. What is the true resistance?

Solution In this case the voltmeter measures the potential across the resistor correctly; the difficulty is that the ammeter measures the voltmeter current I_V as well as the current I in the resistor. We have $I_V = V/R_V = (12.0\ \text{V})/(10,000\ \Omega) = 1.20\ \text{mA}$. The actual current I in the resistor is $I = 0.100\ \text{A} - 0.0012\ \text{A} = 0.0988\ \text{A}$, and the resistance is

$$R = \frac{V_{ab}}{I} = \frac{12.0\ \text{V}}{0.0988\ \text{A}} = 121\ \Omega. \qquad \blacksquare$$

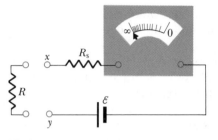

29–10
Ohmmeter circuit. The backward scale on the meter is calibrated to read resistance directly.

An alternative method for measuring resistance is to use a d'Arsonval meter in an arrangement called an **ohmmeter.** It consists of a meter, a resistor, and a source (often a flashlight cell) connected in series, as in Fig. 29–10. The resistance R to be measured is connected between terminals x and y.

The series resistance R_s is chosen so that when terminals x and y are short-circuited (that is, when $R = 0$), the meter deflects full scale. When the circuit between x and y is open (that is, when $R = \infty$), the meter shows no deflection. For a value of R between zero and infinity the meter deflects to some intermediate point depending on the value of R, and hence the meter scale can be calibrated to read the resistance R. Larger currents correspond to smaller resistances, so this scale reads backward in comparison to the current scale.

In situations in which high precision is required, instruments containing d'Arsonval meters have been supplanted by electronic instruments with direct digital readouts. These are more precise, stable, and mechanically rugged than d'Arsonval meters, but they are also considerably more expensive. Digital voltmeters can be made with extremely high internal resistance, of the order of 100 MΩ.

29–4
Resistance–Capacitance Circuits

In our discussion of circuits we have assumed that all the emf's and resistances are *constant.* As a result, all potentials and currents are constant, independent of time. Figure 29–11 shows a simple example of a circuit in which the current and voltages are *not* constant. The capacitor is initially uncharged; at some initial time $t = 0$ we close the switch, completing the circuit and permitting current around the loop to begin charging the capacitor. The current begins at the same instant in every part of the circuit, and at each instant the current is the same in every part.

To distinguish between quantities that vary with time and those that are constant, we will use lowercase letters for time-varying voltages, currents, and charges and capital letters for constants. Because the capacitor is initially uncharged, the potential difference v_{cb} across it is initially zero. At this time, from Kirchhoff's loop rule, the voltage v_{ac} across the resistor R is equal to the battery's terminal voltage V. We will neglect the internal resistance of the battery, so V is constant and equal to the battery emf $\mathcal{E}$. The initial current through the resistor, which we will call I_0, is given by Ohm's law: $I_0 = v_{ac}/R = V/R$.

As the capacitor charges, its voltage v_{cb} increases, and the potential difference v_{ac} across the resistor decreases, corresponding to a decrease in current. The sum of these two is constant and equal to V. After a long time the capacitor becomes fully charged, and the entire battery voltage V appears across the capacitor, $v_{cb} = V$. The current decreases to zero, and the potential difference v_{ac} across the resistor becomes zero.

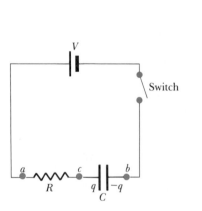

29–11
A capacitor C charged by a circuit containing a battery V and a resistor R.

We let q represent the charge on the capacitor and i the current in the circuit at some time t after the switch has been closed. The instantaneous potential differences v_{ac} and v_{cb} are given by

$$v_{ac} = iR, \qquad v_{cb} = \frac{q}{C}. \tag{29–6}$$

Therefore from Kirchhoff's loop rule,

$$V_{ab} = V = v_{ac} + v_{cb} = iR + \frac{q}{C}. \tag{29–7}$$

Solving this equation for i, we find

$$i = \frac{V}{R} - \frac{q}{RC}. \tag{29–8}$$

At time $t = 0$, when the switch is first closed, the capacitor is uncharged, so $q = 0$. From Eq. (29–8) the *initial* current I_0 is given by $I_0 = V/R$, as we have already noted. If the capacitor were not in the circuit, the last term in Eq. (29–8) would not be present; then the current would be *constant* and equal to V/R.

As the charge q increases, the term q/RC becomes larger, and the capacitor charge approaches its final value, which we will call Q_f. The current decreases and eventually becomes zero. When $i = 0$, Eq. (29–8) gives

$$\frac{V}{R} = \frac{q}{RC}, \qquad q = CV = Q_f. \tag{29–9}$$

We note that the final charge Q_f does not depend on R.

The current and the capacitor charge are shown as functions of time in Fig. 29–12. At the instant when the switch is closed ($t = 0$) the current jumps from zero to its initial value $I_0 = V/R$; after that it gradually approaches zero. The capacitor charge starts at zero and gradually approaches the final value $Q_f = CV$.

It is possible to derive expressions that describe the current i and the capacitor charge q as functions of time. The derivation requires calculus, and the results contain exponential functions; we won't go into the details. Figure 29–12a shows that after a time equal to RC the current has decreased to $1/e$ of its initial value, where e is the base of natural logarithms. ($e = 2.718$, $1/e = 0.368$.) At this time the capacitor charge has reached $(1 - 1/e) = 0.632$ of its final value $Q_f = CV$. The product RC is therefore a measure of how quickly the capacitor charges; it is called the **time constant,** or the **relaxation time,** of the circuit, denoted by τ:

$$\tau = RC. \tag{29–10}$$

When τ is small, the capacitor charges quickly; when τ is larger, the charging takes more time. The horizontal axis is an *asymptote* for the curve in Fig. 29–12a. Strictly speaking, i never becomes precisely zero. But the longer we wait, the closer it gets. For example, after a time equal to $10RC$ the current has decreased to 0.00005 of its initial value. Similarly, the curve in Fig. 29–12b approaches the horizontal broken line labeled Q_f as an asymptote. The charge q never attains precisely this value, but after a time equal to $10RC$ the difference between q and Q_f is $0.00005Q_f$. We invite you to verify that the product RC has units of time.

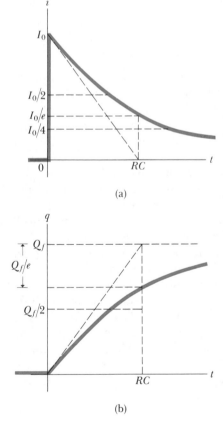

29–12
Current and capacitor charge as functions of time for the circuit of Fig. 29–11.

Example 29–7   A resistor with resistance $R = 10$ MΩ is connected in series with a capacitor with capacitance 1 μF. The time constant is

$$\tau = RC = (10 \times 10^6 \ \Omega)(10^{-6} \ \text{F}) = 10 \ \text{s}.$$

If $R = 10$ Ω, the time constant is only 10×10^{-6} s, or 10 μs. A capacitor charges more quickly through a small resistor; it is easier for the charge to get through.   ■

We could carry out a similar analysis for the *discharge* of a capacitor that is initially charged. Suppose, for example, that we charge the capacitor with the circuit of Fig. 29–11 and then connect points a and b directly together. We won't go into the details, but the results are very similar to the charging situation. Both the current i and the capacitor charge q decrease to $1/e = 0.368$ of their initial values after a time equal to $\tau = RC$, and after a time equal to $10\tau = 10RC$ they have both decreased to 0.00005 of their initial values. So after a time equal to a few time constants the capacitor is, for practical purposes, completely discharged.

*29–5
Power Distribution Systems

We conclude this chapter with a brief discussion of practical household and automotive electric-power distribution systems. Automobiles use direct-current (dc) systems, while nearly all household, commercial, and industrial systems use alternating current (ac). Most of the same basic wiring concepts apply to both. We will talk about alternating-current circuits in greater detail in Chapter 34.

The various lamps, motors, and other appliances to be operated are always connected in *parallel* to the power source, the wires from the power company for houses, the battery and alternator for a car. The basic idea of house wiring is shown in Fig. 29–13. One side of the "line," as the pair of conductors is called, is always connected to "ground." For houses this is an actual electrode driven into the earth (usually a good conductor) and also connected to the household water pipes. Electricians speak of the "hot" side and the "ground" side of the line.

The voltage–current–power relations are the same as those we saw in Section 28–5. Household voltage is nominally 120 V in the United States and Canada, often 240 V in Europe. (These are actually the "root-mean-square" voltages, as we will discuss in Section 34–1.) For example, we can determine the current in a 100-W light bulb from Eq. (28–15):

$$I = \frac{P}{V} = \frac{100 \ \text{W}}{120 \ \text{V}} = 0.833 \ \text{A}.$$

The resistance of this bulb at operating temperature is given by

$$R = \frac{V}{I} = \frac{120 \ \text{V}}{0.833 \ \text{A}} = 144 \ \Omega,$$

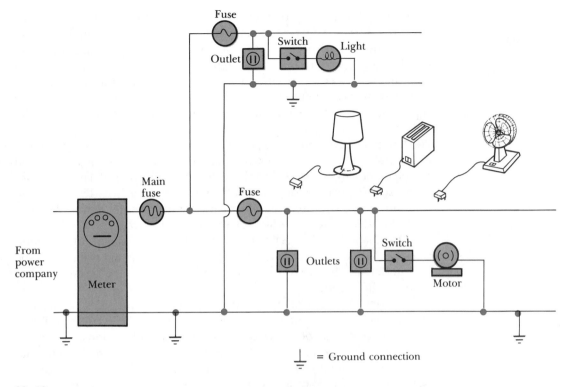

= Ground connection

29–13
Schematic diagram of a house wiring system. Only two branch circuits are shown; an actual system might have 4 to 30 branch circuits. The conventional symbol for ground is shown. Lamps and appliances may be plugged into the outlets. The grounding conductors, which normally carry no current, are not shown.

or

$$R = \frac{V^2}{P} = \frac{(120 \text{ V})^2}{100 \text{ W}} = 144 \ \Omega.$$

Similarly, a 1500-W waffle iron draws a current of $(1500 \text{ W})/(120 \text{ V}) = 12.5$ A and has a resistance, at operating temperature, of 9.6 Ω. Measuring the resistances of these devices with an ohmmeter would yield smaller values than these; the ohmmeter causes very little heating, and the resistance is substantially greater at operating temperature than at room temperature.

The maximum current available from an individual circuit is determined by the resistance of the wires; the power loss in the wires from I^2R heat causes them to become hot, and in extreme cases this heat can cause a fire or melt the wires. Ordinary lighting and outlet wiring in houses is usually 12-gauge wire. This has a diameter of 2.05 mm and is rated to carry a maximum current of 20 A safely, that is, without overheating. Larger sizes such as 8-gauge (3.26 mm) or 6-gauge (4.11 mm) are used for high-current appliances such as ranges and clothes dryers, and 2-gauge (6.54 mm) or larger is used for the main power lines entering a house.

Protection against overloading and overheating of circuits is provided by fuses or circuit breakers. A *fuse* contains a link of lead–tin alloy with a very low melting temperature; the link melts and breaks the circuit when its rated current is exceeded. A *circuit breaker* is an electromechanical device that performs the same function, using an electromagnet or a bimetallic strip to "trip" the breaker and interrupt the circuit when the current exceeds a specified value. Circuit breakers have the advantage that they can be reset after they are tripped; a blown fuse must be replaced, but fuses are somewhat more reliable in operation than circuit breakers.

You may have had the experience of blowing a fuse by plugging too many high-current appliances into the same outlet or into two outlets fed by the same circuit. *Do not* replace the fuse with one of larger rating; doing so risks overheating the wires and starting a fire. The only safe solution is to distribute the appliances among several circuits. Modern kitchens often have three or four separate 20-A circuits.

Overloaded and overheated wiring is one of the most common causes of house fires; because the fire often starts within walls, it can be well under way before it is detected and can consume a house in a few minutes. Be careful!

Accidental contact between the hot and ground sides of the line causes a *short circuit*. Such a situation, which can be caused by faulty insulation or by any of a variety of mechanical malfunctions, provides a very low-resistance current path, permitting a very large current that would quickly melt the wires and ignite their insulation if the current were not interrupted by a fuse or circuit breaker. The opposite situation, a broken wire that interrupts the current path, creates an **open circuit.** This can also be hazardous because of the sparking that can occur at the point of intermittent contact.

In approved wiring practice a fuse or breaker is placed *only* in the hot side of the line, never in the ground side. Otherwise, if a short circuit should develop because of faulty insulation or other malfunction, the ground-side fuse could blow. The hot side would still be live and would pose a shock hazard if you touched the live conductor and a grounded object such as a water pipe. For similar reasons the wall switch for a light fixture is always in the hot side of the line, never the ground side.

Further protection against shock hazard is provided by a third conductor called the *grounding wire*, which is included in all present-day wiring. This conductor corresponds to the long round or U-shaped prong of the three-prong connector plug on an appliance or power tool. It normally carries no current, but it connects the metal case or frame of the device to ground. If a conductor on the hot side of the line accidentally contacts the frame or case, the grounding conductor provides a current path, and the fuse blows. Without the ground wire the frame could become "live," that is, at a potential 120 V above ground. Then if you touched it and a water pipe (or even a damp basement floor) at the same time, you could get a dangerous shock. In some special situations, especially outlets located outdoors or near a sink or other water pipes, a special kind of circuit breaker called a *ground-fault interrupter* (GFI or GFCI) is used. This device senses the current in the grounding wire, which is normally zero, and trips when it exceeds some very small value, typically 10 mA.

All the above discussion can be applied directly to automobile wiring. The voltage is 12 V; the power is supplied by the battery and by the alternator, which charges the battery when the engine is running. The ground side of the circuits is connected to the body and frame of the vehicle. For this voltage, safety does not require a separate grounding conductor. The fuse or circuit breaker arrangement is the same in principle as in household wiring. Because of the lower voltage, more current is required for the same power; a 100-W headlight bulb requires a current of (100 W)/(12 V) = 8.3 A.

To help prevent wiring errors, household wiring uses a standardized color code in which the hot side of a line has black or red insulation, the ground side has white insulation, and the grounding conductor is bare or has green insulation. In electronic devices and equipment, on the other hand, the ground side of the line is usually black. Beware!

Most household wiring systems actually use a slight elaboration of the system described above. The power company provides *three* conductors. One is grounded or "neutral"; the other two are both at 120 V with respect to the neutral but with opposite polarity, giving a voltage between them of 240 V. Thus 120-V lamps and appliances can be connected between neutral and either hot conductor, and high-power devices requiring 240 V are connected between the two hot lines, as shown in Fig. 29–14. Ranges and dryers are usually designed for 240-V power input.

Although we have spoken of *power* in the above discussion, what we buy from the power company is *energy*. Power is energy transferred per unit time, so energy is power multiplied by time. The usual unit of energy sold by the power company is the kilowatt-hour (kWh):

$$1 \text{ kWh} = (10^3 \text{ W})(3600 \text{ s}) = 3.6 \times 10^6 \text{ W·s} = 3.6 \times 10^6 \text{ J}.$$

One kilowatt-hour typically costs 5 to 10 cents, depending on location and quantity of energy purchased. To operate a 1500-W (1.5-kW) waffle iron for 1 hour requires 1.5 kWh of energy and costs 7.5 to 15 cents (not including the cost of flour and eggs in the waffle batter). The cost of operating any lamp or appliance for a specified time can be calculated in the same way if the power rating is known.

29–14
Simplified schematic diagram of a 120–240-V house wiring system. Only one circuit on each side is shown; in actual systems there would be several 120-V circuits on each side of the neutral line. Grounding wires are not shown.

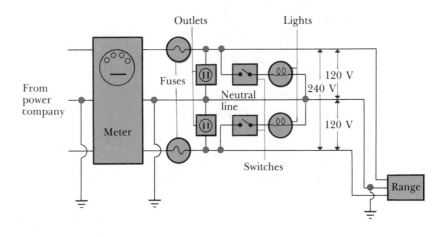

Questions

29–1 Can the potential difference between terminals of a battery ever be opposite in direction to the emf?

29–2 Why do the lights on a car become dimmer when the starter is operated?

29–3 What determines the maximum current that can be carried safely by household wiring? (Typical limits are 15 A for 14-gauge wire, 20 A for 12-gauge, and so on.)

29–4 Lights in a house often dim momentarily when a motor, such as a washing machine or a power saw, is turned on. Why does this happen?

29–5 Compare the formulas for resistors in series and parallel with those for capacitors in series and parallel. What similarities and differences do you see? Sometimes in circuit analysis, one uses the quantity *conductance*, denoted as *g* and defined as the reciprocal of resistance: $g = 1/R$. What is the corresponding comparison for conductance and capacitance?

29–6 Is it possible to connect resistors together in a way that cannot be reduced to some combination of series and parallel combinations? If so, give examples; if not, state why not.

29–7 In a two-cell flashlight the batteries are usually connected in series. Why not connect them in parallel?

29–8 Some Christmas-tree lights have the property that, when one bulb burns out, all the lights go out; in other sets of lights, only the burned-out bulb goes out. Discuss this difference in terms of series and parallel circuits.

29–9 What possible advantage could there be in connecting several identical batteries in parallel?

29–10 Two 120-V light bulbs, one 25-W and one 200-W, were connected in series across a 240-V line. It seemed like a good idea at the time, but one bulb burned out almost instantaneously. Which one burned out, and why?

29–11 When the direction of current in a battery reverses, does the direction of its emf also reverse?

29–12 Under what conditions would the terminal voltage of a battery be zero?

29–13 What sort of meter should be used to test the condition of a dry cell (such as a flashlight battery) having constant emf but internal resistance that increases with age and use?

29–14 For very large resistances it is easy to construct *RC* circuits having time constants of several seconds or minutes. How might this fact be used to measure very large resistances, too large to measure by more conventional means?

Exercises

Section 29–1   Resistors in Series and Parallel

29–1 Three resistors having resistances of 2.00 Ω, 3.00 Ω, and 4.00 Ω are connected in series to a 36.0-V battery that has negligible internal resistance.

  a) Find the equivalent resistance of the combination.

  b) Find the current in each resistor.

  c) Find the total current through the battery.

  d) Find the voltage across each resistor.

  e) Find the power dissipated in each resistor.

29–2 A 40.0-Ω resistor and a 90.0-Ω resistor are connected in parallel, and the combination is connected across a 120-V dc line.

  a) What is the resistance of the parallel combination?

  b) What is the total current through the parallel combination?

  c) What is the current through each resistor?

29–3 In Exercise 29–1 the same three resistors are connected in parallel to the same battery. Answer the same questions for this situation.

29–4 Compute the equivalent resistance of the network in Fig. 29–15, and find the current in each resistor. The battery has negligible internal resistance.

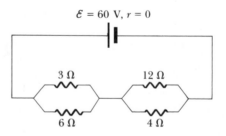

$\mathcal{E} = 60$ V, $r = 0$

3 Ω   12 Ω

6 Ω   4 Ω

FIGURE 29–15

29–5 Compute the equivalent resistance of the network in Fig. 29–16, and find the current in each resistor. The battery has negligible internal resistance.

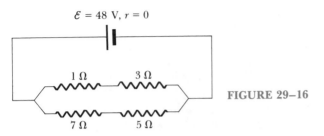

$\mathcal{E} = 48$ V, $r = 0$

1 Ω   3 Ω

7 Ω   5 Ω

FIGURE 29–16

29–6 A 25-W, 120-V light bulb and a 150-W, 120-V light bulb are connected in series across a 240-V line. Assume that the resistance of each bulb does not vary with current. (*Note:* This description of a light bulb gives the power it dissipates when connected to the stated potential difference; that is, a 25-W, 120-V light bulb dissipates 25 W when connected to a 120-V line.)

a) Find the current through the bulbs.

b) Find the power dissipated in each bulb.

c) One bulb burns out very quickly. Which one? Why?

29–7

a) The power rating of a 10,000-Ω resistor is 4.00 W. (The power rating is the maximum power the resistor can safely dissipate without too great a rise in temperature.) What is the maximum allowable potential difference across the terminals of the resistor?

b) We need a 20,000-Ω resistor, to be connected across a potential difference of 150 V. What power rating is required?

Section 29–2   Kirchhoff's Rules

29–8 In the circuit shown in Fig. 29–17, find

a) the current in resistor R;

b) the resistance R;

c) the unknown emf $\mathcal{E}$.

d) If the circuit is broken at point x, what is the current in the 28-V battery?

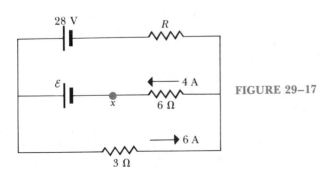

28 V R

$\mathcal{E}$ ← 4 A

x 6 Ω

→ 6 A

3 Ω

FIGURE 29–17

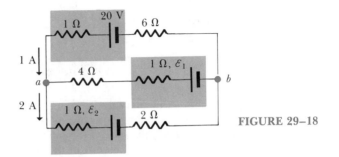

20 V

1 Ω   6 Ω

1 A

4 Ω   1 Ω, $\mathcal{E}_1$

a b

2 A

1 Ω, $\mathcal{E}_2$ 2 Ω

FIGURE 29–18

29–9 Find the emf's $\mathcal{E}_1$ and $\mathcal{E}_2$ in the circuit of Fig. 29–18 and the potential difference of point a relative to point b.

29–10 In the circuit shown in Fig. 29–19, find

a) the current in each branch;

b) the potential difference V_{ab} of point a relative to point b.

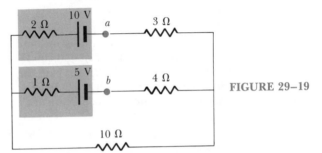

2 Ω   10 V a 3 Ω

1 Ω   5 V b 4 Ω

10 Ω

FIGURE 29–19

Section 29–3   Electrical Instruments

29–11 The resistance of a galvanometer coil is 50.0 Ω, and the current required for full-scale deflection is 400 μA.

a) Show in a diagram how to convert the galvanometer to an ammeter reading 5.00 A full-scale, and compute the shunt resistance.

b) Show how to convert the galvanometer to a voltmeter reading 150 V full-scale, and compute the series resistance.

29–12 The resistance of the coil of a pivoted-coil galvanometer is 12.0 Ω, and a current of 0.0200 A causes it to deflect full-scale. We want to convert this galvanometer to an ammeter reading 10.0 A full-scale. The only shunt available has a resistance of 0.0400 Ω. What resistance R must be connected in series with the coil? (See Fig. 29–20.)

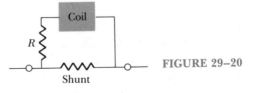

Coil

R

Shunt

FIGURE 29–20

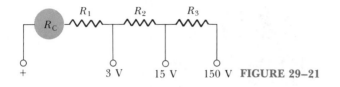

3 V   15 V   150 V **FIGURE 29–21**

29–13 Figure 29–21 shows the internal wiring of a "three-scale" voltmeter whose binding posts are marked +, 3 V, 15 V, and 150 V. The resistance of the moving coil, R_c, is 35.0 Ω, and a current of 1.00 mA in the coil causes it to deflect full-scale. Find the resistances R_1, R_2, and R_3.

29–14 A 100-V battery has an internal resistance of $r = 8.00$ Ω.

  a) What is the reading of a voltmeter having a resistance of $R_V = 500$ Ω when placed across the terminals of the battery?

  b) What maximum value may the ratio r/R_V have if the error in the reading of the emf of a battery is not to exceed 5.0%?

29–15 Two 150-V voltmeters, one with a resistance of 25,000 Ω and the other with a resistance of 250,000 Ω, are connected in series across a 120-V dc line. Find the reading of each voltmeter. (A 150-V voltmeter deflects full-scale when the potential difference between its two terminals is 150 V.)

29–16 In the ohmmeter in Fig. 29–22, M is a 1.00-mA meter having a resistance of 50.0 Ω. (This means that M deflects full-scale when the current through it is 1.00 mA.) The battery B has an emf of 3.00 V and negligible internal resistance. R is chosen so that, when the terminals a and b are shorted ($R_x = 0$), the meter reads full-scale. When a and b are open ($R_x = \infty$), the meter reads zero.

  a) What is the resistance of the resistor R?

  b) What current indicates a resistance R_x of 600 Ω?

  c) What resistances R_x correspond to meter deflections of 1/4, 1/2, and 3/4 full-scale if the deflection is proportional to the current through the galvanometer?

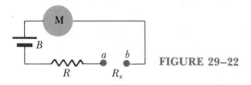

FIGURE 29–22

Section 29–4   Resistance–Capacitance Circuits

29–17 Verify that the product RC has units of time.

29–18 A resistor with resistance $R = 500$ Ω is connected in series with a capacitor. What must be the ca-

pacitance C of the capacitor to produce a time constant of 2.00 s?

29–19 A capacitor with capacitance $C = 2.50 \times 10^{-10}$ F is charged, with charge of magnitude 6.00×10^{-8} C on each plate. The capacitor is then connected to a voltmeter that has internal resistance 8.00×10^5 Ω.

  a) What is the current through the voltmeter just after the connection is made?

  b) What is the time constant of this RC circuit?

29–20 A 6.00-μF capacitor that is initially uncharged is connected in series with a 4.50×10^3 Ω resistor and an emf source with $\mathcal{E} = 500$ V and negligible internal resistance. Just after the circuit is completed, what is the

  a) voltage drop across the capacitor?

  b) voltage drop across the resistor?

  c) charge on the capacitor?

  d) current through the resistor?

  e) A long time after the circuit is completed (after many time constants), what are the values of the above four quantities?

Section 29–5   Power Distribution Systems

29–21 A 300-W driveway light is left on night and day for a year.

  a) What total energy is required? Express your results in joules and kilowatt-hours.

  b) What does this energy cost if the power company's rate is 10.0 cents per kWh?

29–22 An electric dryer is rated at 4.00 kW when connected to a 240-V line.

  a) What is the current in the dryer? Is 12-gauge wire large enough to supply this current?

  b) What is the resistance of the dryer's heating element?

  c) At 10 cents per kWh, how much does it cost per hour to operate the dryer?

29–23 An 1800-W toaster, a 1400-W electric frying pan, and a 75-W lamp are plugged into the same outlet in a 20-A, 120-V circuit. (*Note:* See the note in Exercise 29–6. When plugged into the same outlet, the three devices are in parallel, so the voltage across each is 120 V, and the total current in the circuit is the sum of the currents through each device.)

  a) What current is drawn by each device?

  b) Will this combination blow the fuse?

29–24 How many 60-W light bulbs can be connected to a 20-A, 120-V circuit without tripping the circuit breaker? (See the note in Exercise 29–23.)

Problems

29–25 Prove that when two resistors are connected in parallel, the equivalent resistance of the combination is always smaller than that of either resistor.

29–26

a) A resistance R_2 is connected in parallel with a resistance R_1. Derive an expression for the resistance R_3 that must be connected in series with the combination of R_1 and R_2 so that the equivalent resistance is equal to the resistance R_1. Draw a diagram.

b) A resistance R_2 is connected in series with a resistance R_1. Derive an expression for the resistance R_3 that must be connected in parallel with the combination of R_1 and R_2 so that the equivalent resistance is equal to R_1. Draw a diagram.

29–27 We want to connect an equivalent resistance of 1000 Ω across a potential difference of 180 V. A number of 10.0-W, 1000-Ω resistors are available. How should they be connected? How much power is dissipated by each resistor?

29–28 Each of three resistors in Fig. 29–23 has a resistance of 2.00 Ω and can dissipate a maximum of 32.0 W without becoming excessively heated. What is the maximum power the circuit can dissipate?

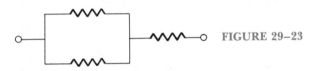

FIGURE 29–23

29–29 A 1000-Ω 2.00-W resistor is needed, but only several 1000-Ω 1.00-W resistors are available. (See Exercise 29–7.)

a) How can the required resistance and power rating be obtained by a combination of the available units?

b) What power is dissipated in each resistor when 2.00 W is dissipated by the combination?

29–30 Three identical resistors are connected in series. When a certain potential difference is applied across the combination, the total power dissipated is 20 W. What power would be dissipated if the three resistors were connected in parallel across the same potential difference?

29–31

a) Calculate the equivalent resistance of the circuit of Fig. 29–24 between x and y.

b) What is the potential of point a relative to point x if the current in the 8.0-Ω resistor is 0.600 A in the direction from left to right in the figure?

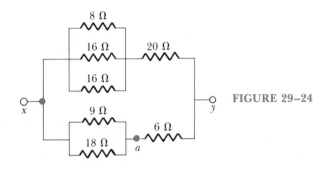

FIGURE 29–24

29–32 What must be the emf $\mathcal{E}$ in Fig. 29–25 in order for the current through the 7.00-Ω resistor to be 3.00 A? Each emf source has negligible internal resistance.

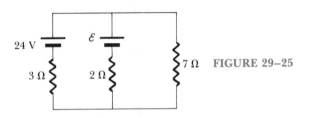

FIGURE 29–25

29–33 Find the current through each of the three resistors of the circuit of Fig. 29–26. The emf sources have negligible internal resistance.

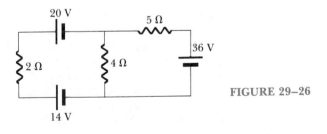

FIGURE 29–26

29–34 Calculate the three currents indicated in the circuit diagram of Fig. 29–27.

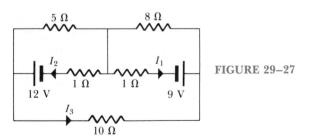

FIGURE 29–27

29–35

a) Find the potential of point a with respect to point b in Fig. 29–28.

b) If points a and b are connected by a wire with negligible resistance, find the current in the 12-V cell.

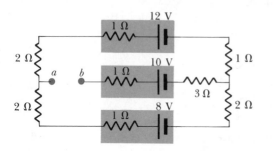

FIGURE 29–28

29–36 Find the current through the battery and each resistor for the circuit shown in Fig. 29–29.

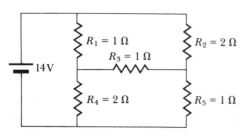

FIGURE 29–29

29–37 Figure 29–30 employs a convention often used in circuit diagrams. The battery (or other power supply) is not shown explicitly. It is understood that the point at the top, labeled "36 V," is connected to the positive terminal of a 36-V battery having negligible internal resistance and that the "ground" symbol at the bottom is connected to its negative terminal. The circuit is completed through the battery, even though it is not shown on the diagram.

a) In Fig. 29–30, what is the potential difference V_{ab}, the potential of point a relative to point b, when the switch is open?

b) What is the current through switch S when it is closed?

c) What is the equivalent resistance in Fig. 29–30 when switch S is open?

d) What is the equivalent resistance when switch S is closed?

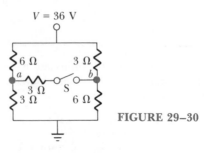

FIGURE 29–30

29–38 See Problem 29–37.

a) What is the potential of point a with respect to point b in Fig. 29–31 when switch S is open?

b) Which point, a or b, is at the higher potential?

c) What is the final potential of point b with respect to ground when switch S is closed?

d) How much does the charge on each capacitor change when S is closed?

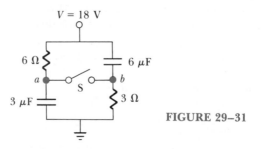

FIGURE 29–31

29–39 See Problem 29–37.

a) What is the potential of point a with respect to point b in Fig. 29–32 when switch S is open?

b) Which point, a or b, is at the higher potential?

c) What is the final potential of point b with respect to ground when switch S is closed?

d) How much charge flows through switch S when it is closed?

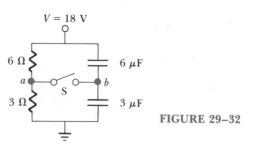

FIGURE 29–32

29–40 The resistance of the moving coil of the galvanometer G in Fig. 29–33 is 40.0 Ω, and the galvanome-

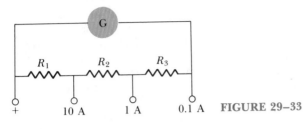

FIGURE 29–33

ter deflects full-scale with a current of 0.0100 A. Find the magnitudes of the resistances R_1, R_2, and R_3 required to convert the galvanometer to a multirange ammeter deflecting full-scale with currents of 10.0 A, 1.00 A, and 0.100 A. (When the meter is connected to the circuit being measured, one connection is made to the post marked + and the other to the post marked with the desired current range.)

29–41 A 600-Ω resistor and a 400-Ω resistor are connected in series across a 90.0-V line. A voltmeter connected across the 600-Ω resistor reads 50.0 V.

a) Find the voltmeter resistance.

b) Find the reading of the same voltmeter if connected across the 400-Ω resistor.

29–42 Point a in Fig. 29–34 is maintained at a constant potential of 500 V above ground. (See Problem 29–37.)

a) What is the reading of a voltmeter of the proper range and of resistance 3.00×10^4 Ω when it is connected between point b and ground?

b) What is the reading of a voltmeter of resistance 3.00×10^6 Ω?

c) What is the reading of a voltmeter of infinite resistance?

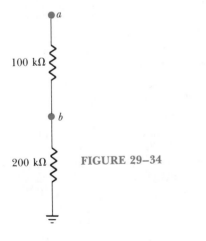

FIGURE 29–34

29–43 A 150-V voltmeter has a resistance of 20,000 Ω. When connected in series with a large resistance R across a 110-V line, the meter reads 80.0 V. Find the

resistance R. (This problem illustrates one method of measuring large resistances.)

29–44 Let V and I represent the readings of the voltmeter and ammeter, respectively, shown in Fig. 29–9, and let R_V and R_A be their equivalent resistances.

a) When the circuit is connected as in Fig. 29–9a, show that

$$R = \frac{V}{I} - R_A.$$

b) When the connections are as in Fig. 29–9b, show that

$$R = \frac{V}{I - (V/R_V)}.$$

c) Show that the power delivered to the resistor in part (a) is $IV - I^2 R_A$ and that in part (b) is $IV - (V^2/R_V)$.

29–45 In Fig. 29–35 a resistor of resistance 75.0 Ω is connected between points a and b. The resistance of the galvanometer G is 60.0 Ω. What should be the resistance between b and the sliding contact c if the galvanometer current I_G is to be 1/3 of the current I?

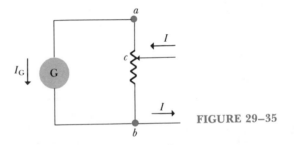

FIGURE 29–35

29–46 The circuit shown in Fig. 29–36, called a *Wheatstone bridge*, is used to determine the value of an unknown resistor X by comparison with three resistors M, N, and P whose resistance can be varied. For each

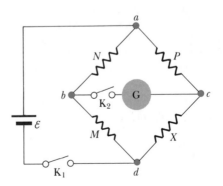

FIGURE 29–36

setting, the resistance of each resistor is precisely known. With switches K_1 and K_2 closed, these resistors are varied until the current in the galvanometer G is zero; the bridge is then said to be *balanced*.

a) Show that under this condition the unknown resistance is given by $X = MP/N$. (This method permits very high precision in comparing resistors.)

b) If the galvanometer G shows zero deflection when $M = 1000\ \Omega$, $N = 10.00\ \Omega$, and $P = 23.58\ \Omega$, what is the unknown resistance X?

29-47 The circuit shown in Fig. 29-37 is called a *potentiometer*. It permits measurements of potential differ-

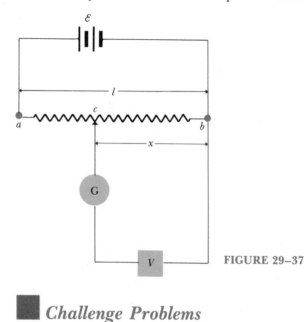

FIGURE 29-37

ence without drawing current from the circuit being measured and hence acts as an infinite-resistance voltmeter. The resistor between a and b is a uniform wire of length l, with a sliding contact c at a distance x from b. An unknown potential difference V is measured by sliding the contact until the galvanometer G reads zero.

a) Show that under this condition the unknown potential difference is given by $V = (x/l)\mathcal{E}$.

b) Why is the internal resistance of the galvanometer not important?

Now suppose that $\mathcal{E} = 12.00$ V and $l = 1.000$ m. The galvanometer G reads zero when $x = 0.654$ m.

c) What is the potential difference V?

d) Suppose that V is the emf of a battery. Can its internal resistance be determined by this method?

29-48 A $4.60 \times 10^3\ \Omega$ resistor is connected to the plates of a charged capacitor that has capacitance $C = 8.00 \times 10^{-10}$ F. The initial current through the resistor, just after the connection is made, is 0.250 A. What magnitude of charge was initially on each plate of the capacitor?

29-49 A capacitor that is initially uncharged is connected in series with a resistor and an emf source with $\mathcal{E} = 400$ V and negligible internal resistance. Just after the circuit is completed, the current through the resistor is 8.00×10^{-4} A, and the time constant for the circuit is 6.00 s. What are the resistance of the resistor and the capacitance of the capacitor?

Challenge Problems

29-50 A certain galvanometer has a resistance of $200\ \Omega$ and deflects full-scale with a current of 1.00 mA in its coil. We want to replace this with a second galvanometer that has a resistance of $30.0\ \Omega$ and deflects full-scale with a current of 50.0 μA in its coil. Devise a circuit incorporating the second galvanometer such that the equivalent resistance of the circuit equals the resistance of the first galvanometer and the second galvanometer deflects full-scale when the current through the circuit equals the full-scale current of the first galvanometer.

29-51 Prove that the resistance of the infinite network shown in Fig. 29-38 is equal to $(1 + \sqrt{3})r$.

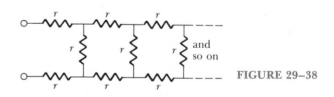

FIGURE 29-38

29-52 Suppose a resistor R lies along each edge of a cube (12 resistors in all) with connections at the corners. Find the equivalent resistance between two diagonally opposite corners of the cube.

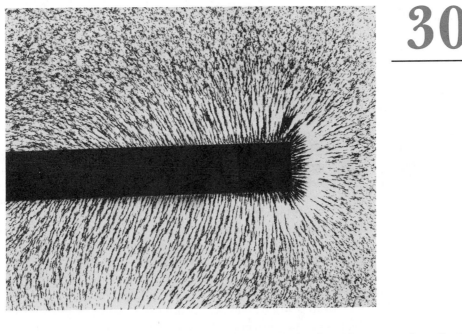

Magnetic Field
and Magnetic Forces

With this chapter we begin our exploration of magnetic interactions and their relationship to the electrical interactions we have been studying. The most familiar aspects of magnetism are those associated with permanent magnets, which attract unmagnetized iron objects and can also attract or repel other magnets. The fundamental nature of magnetism, however, is to be found in interactions involving electric charges in motion. A magnetic field is established by a permanent magnet, by an electric current in a conductor, or by moving charges. This magnetic field, in turn, exerts forces on moving charges and current-carrying conductors. In this chapter we study magnetic forces, and in Chapter 31 we look at the ways in which magnetic fields are produced by moving charges. Magnetic forces are an essential aspect of the interactions of electrically charged particles. Electric motors, TV picture tubes, high-energy particle accelerators, magnetrons in microwave ovens, and many other devices depend in part on magnetic forces for their operation.

30–1
Magnetism

Magnetic phenomena were first observed at least 2500 years ago in fragments of magnetized iron ore found near the ancient city of Magnesia (now Manisa, in western Turkey). It was discovered that when an iron rod is brought in contact with a natural magnet, the rod also becomes a magnet. When such a rod is suspended by a string from its center, it tends to line itself up in a north–south direction, like a compass needle. Magnets have been used for navigation at least since the eleventh century.

Before the relationship of magnetic interactions to moving charges was understood, the interactions of bar magnets and compass needles were described in terms of *magnetic poles*. The end of a bar magnet that points north is called a *north pole* or *N-pole*, and the other end is a *south* or *S-pole*. Two opposite poles attract each other, and two like poles repel each other. The concept of magnetic poles is of limited usefulness and is somewhat misleading because a single isolated magnetic pole has never been found; poles always appear in pairs. If a bar magnet is broken in two, each broken end becomes a pole. The existence of an isolated magnetic pole, or **magnetic monopole,** would have sweeping implications for theoretical physics. Extensive searches for magnetic monopoles have been carried out, so far without success.

A compass needle points north because the earth is a magnet; its north geographical pole is a magnetic *south* pole. The earth's magnetic axis is not quite parallel to its geographic axis (the axis of rotation), so a compass reading deviates somewhat from geographic north; this deviation, which varies with location, is called *magnetic declination*. At most points on the earth's surface the magnetic field is not horizontal; its inclination is described by the *angle of dip*.

A sketch of the earth's magnetic field is shown in Fig. 30–1. The lines show the direction a compass would point at each location. These lines are actually *magnetic-field lines*; we will discuss them in detail in Section 30–3. The direction of the field at any point can be defined as the

30–1
A sketch of the earth's magnetic field. A compass placed at any point in this field would point in the direction of the field line at that point. Representing the earth's field as that of a tilted bar magnet is only a crude approximation of the actual fairly complex field configuration.

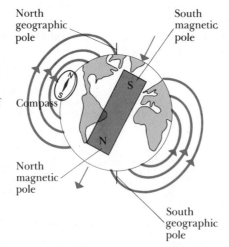

North geographic pole

South magnetic pole

Compass

North magnetic pole

South geographic pole

direction of the force the field would exert on a magnetic north pole. In Section 30–2 we will introduce a more fundamental way to define magnetic field.

In 1819 the Danish scientist Hans Christian Oersted (1777–1851) discovered that a compass needle was deflected by a current-carrying wire. Similar investigations were carried out in France by André Ampère. A few years later, Michael Faraday in England and Joseph Henry in the United States discovered that moving a magnet near a conducting loop can cause a current in the loop and that a changing current in one conducting loop can cause a current in another separate loop. These observations were the first evidence of the relationship of magnetism to moving charges.

30–2
Magnetic Field

We have described *electrical* interactions in two stages: A charge distribution sets up an electric field **E**, and the field exerts a force **F** = q**E** on any charge q that is present. We can follow this same pattern in describing magnetic interactions. A moving charge or a current sets up a **magnetic field** in the space around it, and this field exerts a force **F** on a moving charge. Like electric field, magnetic field is a *vector field*, that is, a vector quantity associated with each point in space. We will use the symbol **B** for magnetic field.

In this chapter we consider the *second* aspect of the interaction: Given the presence of a magnetic field, what force does it exert on a moving charge or a current? In Chapter 31 we will come back to the problem of how magnetic fields are *created* by moving charges and currents.

What are the characteristics of the magnetic force on a moving charge? First, its magnitude is proportional to the charge. If a 1-μC charge and a 2-μC charge move through a given magnetic field with the same velocity, the force on the 2-μC charge is twice as great as that on the 1-μC charge. The force is also proportional to the magnitude or "strength" of the field; if we double the magnitude of the field without changing the charge or its velocity, the force doubles.

The magnetic force is proportional to the particle's speed. This is quite different from the electric-field force, which is the same whether the charge is moving or not. A particle at rest experiences no magnetic force at all. Furthermore, the magnetic force **F** *does not* have the same direction as the magnetic field **B,** but instead is always *perpendicular* to both **B** and **v**. The magnitude F of the force is found to be proportional to the component of **v** perpendicular to the field; when that component is zero (that is, when **v** and **B** are parallel or antiparallel), the force is zero.

If this sounds confusing, Fig. 30–2 will help to clear things up. The direction of **F** is always perpendicular to the plane containing **v** and **B;** its magnitude is given by

$$F = |q|v_{\perp}B = |q|vB \sin \phi, \qquad (30\text{–}1)$$

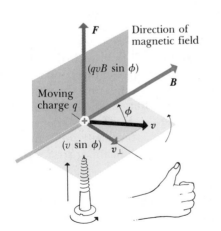

30–2

The magnetic force **F** acting on a charge q moving with velocity **v** is perpendicular to both the magnetic field **B** and to **v**.

where $|q|$ is the magnitude of the charge and ϕ is the angle measured from the direction of v to the direction of B, as shown in Fig. 30-2.

This description does not specify the direction of F completely; there are always two directions perpendicular to the plane of v and B but opposite to each other. To complete the description, we use the same right-hand-thread rule we used for angular mechanical quantities in Section 9-11. Imagine turning v until it points in the direction of B (turning through the smaller of the two possible angles). The direction of the force F on a *positive* charge is the direction in which a right-hand-thread screw would advance if turned the same way. Alternatively, wrap the fingers of your right hand around the line perpendicular to the plane of v and B so that they curl around with this sense of rotation from v to B; your thumb then points in the direction of F.

Equation (30-1) can be interpreted in a different but equivalent way. Recalling that ϕ is the angle between the direction of vectors v and B, we may interpret $(B \sin \phi)$ as the component of B perpendicular to v, that is, $B_\perp$. With this notation the force expression becomes

$$F = |q|vB_\perp. \tag{30-2}$$

This form is equivalent to Eq. (30-1), but it is sometimes more convenient, especially in problems involving currents rather than individual particles. We will discuss forces on currents in conductors later in this chapter.

From Eq. (30-1), the *units* of B must be the same as the units of F/qv. Therefore the SI unit of B is 1 N·s·C^{-1}·m^{-1}, or, since 1 ampere is 1 coulomb per second (1 A $= 1$ C·s^{-1}), 1 N·A^{-1}·m^{-1}. This unit is called 1 **tesla** (1 T), in honor of Nikola Tesla (1857–1943), the prominent Serbian-American scientist and inventor.

$$1 \text{ tesla} = 1 \text{ T} = 1 \text{ N·A}^{-1}\text{·m}^{-1}.$$

The cgs unit of B, the **gauss** (1 G $= 10^{-4}$ T), is also in common use. Instruments for measuring magnetic field are sometimes called gaussmeters.

When q is negative, the direction of F is opposite to the direction given by Fig. 30-2 and the right-hand rule. If two charges with equal magnitude and opposite sign move in the same B field with the same velocity, the forces have equal magnitude and opposite direction.

To explore an unknown magnetic field, we can measure the magnitude and direction of the force on a *moving* test charge. The cathode-ray tube, discussed in Section 26-7, is a convenient device for making such measurements. The electron gun shoots out a narrow beam of electrons at a known speed. If there is no force to deflect the beam, it strikes the center of the screen.

In general, when a magnetic field is present, the electron beam is deflected. However, if the beam is parallel or antiparallel to the field, then in Eq. (30-1), $\phi = 0$ and $F = 0$; there is no force and no deflection. If we find that the electron beam is undeflected when its direction is parallel to the z-axis, as in Fig. 30-3, the B-vector must point either up or down.

When we turn the tube 90°, so that its axis is along the x-axis in Fig. 30-3, the beam is deflected in a direction corresponding to a force

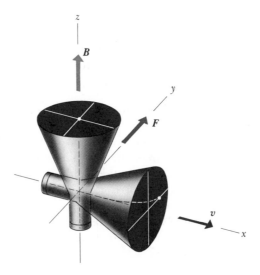

30–3
The electron beam of the cathode-ray tube is undeflected when the beam is parallel to the z-axis. The **B**-vector then points either up or down. When the tube axis is parallel to the x-axis, the beam is deflected in the positive y-direction. Then the **B**-vector points upward, and the force **F** on the electrons points along the positive y-axis, opposite to the rule of Fig. 30–2 because q is negative.

perpendicular to the plane of **B** and **v.** We can perform additional experiments in which the angle between **B** and **v** is between zero and 90° to confirm Eq. (30–1) and the accompanying discussion. We note that the electron has a negative charge; the force in Fig. 30–3 is opposite in direction to the force on a positive charge.

When a charged particle moves through a region of space where *both* electric and magnetic fields are present, both fields exert forces on the particle, and the total force is the vector sum of the electric-field and magnetic-field forces.

PROBLEM-SOLVING STRATEGY: *Magnetic-Field Forces*

The biggest difficulty is in relating the directions of the vector quantities. To find the direction of the magnetic-field force, draw the two vectors **v** and **B** with their tails together so that you can visualize and draw the plane in which they lie. This also helps you to identify the angle ϕ between the two

vectors and to avoid getting its complement or some other erroneous angle. Then remember that **F** is always perpendicular to this plane. The direction is determined by the right-hand rule; keep referring to Fig. 30–2 until you're sure you have this down cold.

Example 30–1   A proton beam moves through a region of space where there is a uniform magnetic field of magnitude 2.0 T directed along the positive z-axis, as in Fig. 30–4. The protons have a velocity of magnitude 3.0×10^5 m·s^{-1} in the xz-plane at an angle of 30° to the positive z-axis. Find the force on a proton. ($q = 1.6 \times 10^{-19}$ C.)

Solution   The right-hand rule shows that the direction of the force is along the negative y-axis. The magnitude of the force, from Eq. (30–1),

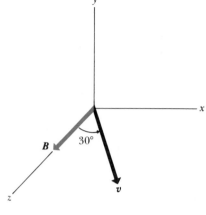

30–4
Directions of v and B for Example 30–1.

is

$$F = qvB \sin \phi$$
$$= (1.6 \times 10^{-19} \text{ C})(3.0 \times 10^5 \text{ m·s}^{-1})(2.0 \text{ T})(\sin 30°)$$
$$= 4.8 \times 10^{-14} \text{ N}.$$

If the beam consists of *electrons* rather than protons, the charge is negative ($q = -1.6 \times 10^{-19}$ C), and the direction of the force is reversed. The solution proceeds just as before. The force is now directed along the *positive* y-axis; the magnitude is the same as before, $F = 4.8 \times 10^{-14}$ N.

If the magnetic field in this example is along the +x-axis and the beam is along the +y-axis, the force on the proton beam is in the −z-direction, and the force on the electron beam is in the +z-direction; in each case the magnitude of the force is 9.6×10^{-14} N. We invite you to test your understanding by verifying these statements.   ■

30–3
Magnetic-Field Lines and Magnetic Flux

We can represent a magnetic field by *lines*, just as we did with electric fields in Section 25–3. We draw the lines so that the line through any point is tangent to the magnetic field vector B at that point and so that the *number* of lines per unit area (perpendicular to the lines at a given point) is proportional to the magnitude of the field at that point. We call these **magnetic-field lines.** They are sometimes called magnetic lines of force, but that's not a good name for them because, unlike electric-field lines, they *do not* point in the direction of the force on a charge.

In a uniform magnetic field, where the B vector has the same magnitude and direction at every point in a region, the field lines are straight, parallel, and equally spaced. If the poles of an electromagnet are large, flat, and close together, the magnetic field in the region between them is very nearly uniform. Figures 30–5 and 30–6 show magnetic-field lines produced by several sources of magnetic field.

The magnetic field of the earth is shown in Fig. 30–1; the field lines resemble those of a bar magnet with its axis tilted somewhat with respect to the earth's axis of rotation. The earth's field, thought to be caused by currents in its molten core, changes with time. There is geologic evidence that the earth's magnetic field has actually changed direction many times in the last 100 million years.

We define the **magnetic flux** Φ through a surface just as we defined electric-field flux in connection with Gauss's law in Section 25–4. We can divide any surface into elements of area ΔA, as shown in Fig. 30–7. For each element we determine the component of B normal to the surface, $B_\perp$, at the position of that element, as shown. From Fig. 30–7, $B_\perp = B \cos \theta$, where θ is the angle between the direction of B and a line perpendicular to the surface. In general, this component will vary from point to point on the surface. We define the magnetic flux $\Delta\Phi$ through

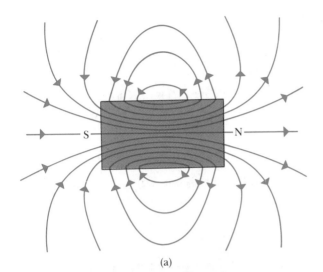

(a)

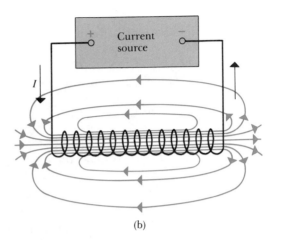

(b)

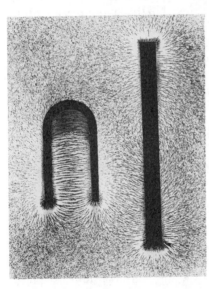

To dc
current
source

(c)

30–5
Magnetic-field lines produced by (a) a
bar-shaped permanent magnet, (b) a
coil of wire wound on a cylindrical
form, that is, a solenoid, and (c) a
laboratory electromagnet with an iron
core. In (c) the magnetic field is nearly
uniform in the gap in the core. In all
three cases the field lines are
continuous curves closing on
themselves; there are no endpoints.

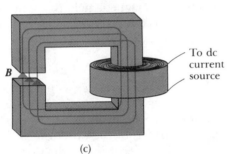

this area as

$$\Delta \Phi = B_\perp \, \Delta A = B \cos \theta \, \Delta A. \tag{30–3}$$

The *total* magnetic flux through the surface is the sum of the contributions from the individual area elements. In the special case in which B is uniform over a plane surface with total area A, $B_\perp$ and θ are the same at all points on the surface, and

$$\Phi = B_\perp A = BA \cos \theta. \tag{30–4}$$

If B happens to be perpendicular to the surface, $\cos \theta = 1$, and this

30–6
Magnetic fields can be visualized by use
of iron filings, which orient themselves
parallel to the field direction. This
photograph shows the concentration of
the fields near the poles. (Photo by
Fundamental Photographs, New York.)

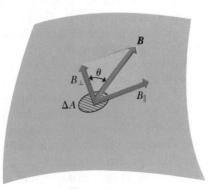

30–7
The magnetic flux through an area
element ΔA is defined to be
$\Phi = B_\perp \, \Delta A$.

expression reduces to $\Phi = BA$. We will use the concept of magnetic flux extensively during our study of electromagnetic induction in Chapter 32.

The SI unit of magnetic flux is the unit of magnetic field (1 T) times the unit of area (1 m^2):

$$(1\ T)(1\ m^2) = (1\ N \cdot A^{-1} \cdot m^{-1})(1\ m^2) = 1\ N \cdot m \cdot A^{-1}.$$

This unit is called 1 **weber** (1 Wb), in honor of Wilhelm Weber (1804–1891).

$$1\ weber = 1\ Wb = 1\ T \cdot m^2 = 1\ N \cdot m \cdot A^{-1}.$$

If the element of area ΔA in Eq. (30–3) is at right angles to the field lines, then $B_\perp = B$, and

$$B = \frac{\Delta \Phi}{\Delta A}. \tag{30–5}$$

That is, magnetic field is *flux per unit area* across an area at right angles to the magnetic field. For this reason, magnetic field **B** is sometimes called **magnetic flux density.** The unit of flux is 1 weber, so the unit of field, 1 tesla, is also equal to 1 *weber per square meter*:

$$1\ T = 1\ Wb \cdot m^{-2}.$$

We can picture the total flux through a surface as proportional to the number of field lines passing through the surface and the field (the flux density) as the number of lines *per unit area*.

The magnetic field of the earth is of the order of 10^{-4} T, or 1 G. Magnetic fields of the order of 10 T occur in the interior of atoms and are important in the analysis of atomic spectra. The largest values of steady magnetic field that have been achieved in the laboratory are of the order of 30 T. Some pulsed-current electromagnets can produce fields of the order of 120 T for short time intervals of the order of a millisecond.

30–4
Motion of Charged Particles in a Magnetic Field

Here is a simple example of the motion of a charged particle in a magnetic field. In Fig. 30–8 a particle with positive charge q is at point O, moving with velocity v in a uniform magnetic field **B** directed into the plane of the figure. The field and velocity are perpendicular. From Eq. (30–1) and the accompanying discussion an upward force **F** with magnitude $F = qvB$ acts on the particle at this point. The force is always perpendicular to v, so it cannot change the *magnitude* of the velocity, only its direction. Thus the magnitudes of both **F** and v are constant. At points such as P and Q the directions of force and velocity have changed as shown, but their magnitudes are the same. The particle therefore moves under the influence of a constant-magnitude force that is always at right angles to the velocity of the particle. Comparing these conditions with the discussion in Sections 3–5 and 6–1, we see that the particle's path is a *circle*, traced out with constant speed v. The centripetal acceleration is

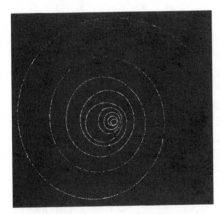

30–8

The orbit of a charged particle in a uniform magnetic field is a circle when the initial velocity is perpendicular to the field. The crosses represent a uniform magnetic field directed *away from* the reader.

v^2/R, and, from Newton's second law,

$$F = qvB = m\frac{v^2}{R}, \tag{30–6}$$

where m is the mass of the particle. The radius R of the circular path is given by

$$R = \frac{mv}{qB}. \tag{30–7}$$

In terms of the particle's magnitude of momentum $p = mv$ we can also write this as $R = p/qB$.

If the direction of the initial velocity is *not* perpendicular to the field, the velocity component parallel to the field is constant (because there is no force parallel to the field), and the particle moves in a helix. The radius of the helix is given by Eq. (30–7), where now v is the component of velocity perpendicular to the **B** field. This principle is used in plasma physics research; the charged particles in a hot plasma are confined by spiraling around magnetic-field lines.

The magnetic force acting on a charged particle can never do *work* because at every instant the force is perpendicular to the velocity. A magnetic force can change the *direction* of motion, but it can never increase or decrease the *magnitude* of the velocity. *Motion of a charged particle under the action of a magnetic field alone is always motion with constant speed.*

Figure 30–9 is a photograph of the track made in a liquid-hydrogen bubble chamber by a high-energy electron moving in a magnetic field perpendicular to the plane of the paper. As the particle loses energy (and speed), the radius of curvature decreases according to Eq. (30–7). Figure 30–10 shows electron–positron pair production, also in a bubble chamber. Similar experiments using a cloud chamber provided the first experimental evidence in 1932 for the existence of the *positron*, or positive electron.

30–9

A track in a liquid-hydrogen bubble chamber made by an electron with initial kinetic energy of about 27 MeV. The magnetic field strength is 1.8 T. As the particle loses energy, the radius of curvature decreases; the maximum radius is about 5 cm. (Courtesy of Lawrence Berkeley Laboratory, University of California.)

30–10

Electron–positron pair production in a liquid-hydrogen bubble chamber. A high-energy gamma ray coming in from above scatters on an atomic electron. The paths of the recoil electron and of the electron–positron pair can be seen; the directions of curvature in the magnetic field show the signs of the charges. (Courtesy of Lawrence Berkeley Laboratory, University of California.)

PROBLEM-SOLVING STRATEGY: *Motion in Magnetic Fields*

1. In analyzing the motion of a charged particle in electric and magnetic fields you are combining the use of Newton's laws of motion with what you have learned about electric and magnetic forces. You will be using $\Sigma F = ma$, and ΣF is in general the vector sum of the electric-field and magnetic-field forces. Many of the problems are similar to the trajectory problems we encountered in Sections 3–4, 3–5, and 6–1, and it wouldn't do any harm to review those sections.

2. Often, the use of components is the most efficient approach. Set up a coordinate system, and then express all the vector quantities (including E, B, v, F, and a) in terms of their components in this system. Then use $\Sigma F = ma$ in component form: $\Sigma F_x = ma_x$, and so forth. This approach is particularly useful when both electric and magnetic fields are present.

3. The next two sections, although not explicitly labeled as examples, are in fact applications of the principles introduced in this chapter and of the above strategy. Study them carefully!

30–5
Thomson's Measurement of e/m

One of the landmark experiments in modern physics at the turn of the century was the measurement of the charge-to-mass ratio of an electron, e/m. This quantity was first measured in 1897 by Sir Joseph John Thomson (1856–1940) at the Cavendish Laboratory in Cambridge, England. Thomson's experiment provided the best evidence available at that time of the existence of electrons, particles with definite mass and charge. Thomson's term for these particles was "cathode corpuscles." His experiment offers us an important and interesting example of magnetic-field forces.

Thomson's apparatus (Fig. 30–11) is very similar in principle to the cathode-ray tube we discussed in Section 26–7. (You may want to review that section before going ahead.) It consists of a highly evacuated glass tube with several metal electrodes sealed into it. Electrons from the hot

30–11
Thomson's apparatus for measuring the ratio e/m for cathode rays.

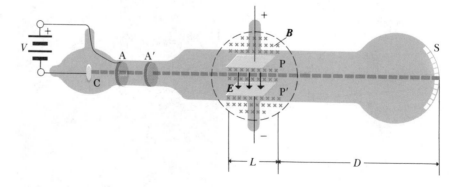

cathode C are accelerated and formed into a beam by the anodes A and A', and the beam passes into the region between the two plates P and P'. After passing between the plates the electrons strike the end of the tube, where they cause fluorescent material at S to glow. The speed v of the electrons is determined by the accelerating potential V, just as in the derivation of Eq. (26–26). The kinetic energy $\frac{1}{2}mv^2$ equals the loss of potential energy eV, where e is the magnitude of the electron charge:

$$\tfrac{1}{2}mv^2 = eV, \qquad \text{or} \qquad v = \sqrt{\frac{2eV}{m}}. \qquad (30\text{–}8)$$

Now if we establish a potential difference between the two deflecting plates P and P', as shown, the resulting downward electric field E exerts a force with magnitude eE that deflects the negatively charged electrons *upward*. Alternatively, we may impose a *magnetic* field B directed into the plane of the figure, as shown by the small crosses; this field results in a force with magnitude evB and a *downward* deflection of the beam. (Can you verify this direction?) Finally, if we apply the E and B fields simultaneously, we can adjust their relative magnitudes so that the two force magnitudes are equal; then the forces exactly cancel, and the beam is not deflected at all. The necessary condition is

$$eE = evB, \qquad \text{or} \qquad v = \frac{E}{B}. \qquad (30\text{–}9)$$

When we combine this with Eq. (30–8) to eliminate v, we obtain an expression for the charge-to-mass ratio e/m in terms of the other quantities:

$$\frac{E}{B} = \sqrt{\frac{2eV}{m}} \qquad \text{or} \qquad \frac{e}{m} = \frac{E^2}{2VB^2}. \qquad (30\text{–}10)$$

All the quantities on the right side can be measured, so e/m can be determined. We note that it is *not* possible to measure e or m separately by this method, only their ratio.

The most significant aspect of Thomson's e/m measurements was that he found a single value for this quantity. It did not depend on the cathode material, the residual gas in the tube, or anything else about the experiment. This independence showed that cathode corpuscles, which we now call electrons, are a common constituent of all matter. Thus Thomson is credited with discovery of the first subatomic particle, the electron. He also found that the *speed* of the electrons in the beam was about one tenth the speed of light, much larger than any previously measured material particle speed.

The most precise value of e/m available as of January 1990 is

$$e/m = 1.7588196(11) \times 10^{11} \ \text{C·kg}^{-1}.$$

As usual, (11) is the likely uncertainty in the last two digits, 96.

Fifteen years after Thomson's experiments, Millikan succeeded in measuring the charge of the electron precisely with his famous oil-drop experiment, described in Section 26–5. This value, together with the value of e/m, enables us to determine the *mass* of the electron.

30–6
Isotopes and Mass Spectroscopy

Thomson devised a method similar to the above e/m measurement for measuring the charge-to-mass ratio for *positive ions*. He assumed that each positive ion had a charge equal in magnitude to that of the electron because each ion was an atom that had lost one electron. He could then identify particular values of q/m with particular ions. Positive ions move more slowly than electrons and have lower values of q/m because they are much more massive. The *largest* q/m for positive particles is that for the *lightest* element, hydrogen. From the value of q/m for the hydrogen ion (i.e., the proton), Thomson found that its mass is 1836 times the mass of an electron. This showed for the first time that electrons make up only a small fraction of the total mass of an atom.

The most striking result of these experiments was that atoms of some elements had *more than one* value of q/m. An example was neon, which has an atomic mass of 20.2 g·mol^{-1}. Thomson obtained *two* values of q/m, corresponding to 20 and 22 g·mol^{-1}. After trying and discarding various explanations he concluded that there must be two kinds of neon atoms with different masses.

Soon afterward, Francis Aston (1877–1945), a student of Thomson, succeeded in separating these two atomic species by letting the gas diffuse repeatedly through a porous plug between two containers. Here's how the process works. We learned in Section 20–3, Eq. (20–12), that the rms speed of molecules in a gas at absolute temperature T is given by

$$v = \sqrt{\frac{3kT}{m}}, \qquad (30–11)$$

where m is the mass of an atom and k is Boltzmann's constant. In a mixture of atoms with different masses the more massive atoms have, on the average, somewhat smaller speeds. The gas emerging from the plug in Aston's experiment had a slightly greater concentration of the less massive atoms than the gas entering the plug. Thus Aston demonstrated directly the existence of two species of neon atoms with different masses.

Later experiments have shown that many elements have several kinds of atoms, identical in their chemical behavior but differing in mass. Such forms of an element are called **isotopes.** The mass differences are due to differing numbers of neutrons in the *nuclei* of the atoms; we will return to the subject of nuclear structure in Chapter 44.

A detailed search for the isotopes of all the elements required precise experimental technique. Aston built the first of many instruments called **mass spectrometers** in 1919; his instrument could measure masses of atoms with precision of one part in 10,000. A variation built by Bainbridge incorporates a *velocity selector* to produce a beam of ions all with the same speed. In Fig. 30–12 there is a source of ions (not shown) above apertures S_1 and S_2. Below these is the velocity selector, a region of crossed E and B fields in the same arrangement as in Thomson's e/m experiment. The E field is toward the right, and B points out of the plane of the figure. In this region the E-field force on a positive ion is toward

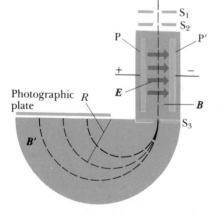

30–12
Bainbridge's mass spectrometer, utilizing a velocity selector. Both B and B' point out of the plane of the figure.

the right, and the **B**-field force is to the left. According to Eq. (30–9), only ions whose speed is equal to E/B can pass through this region undeflected; ions with other speeds are deflected and blocked by aperture S_3. All the ions that make it through S_3 have the same speed.

Below S_3 the ions enter a region where there is another magnetic field **B'**, perpendicular to the figure and pointing out of it, but no electric field. Here the magnetic-field force makes the ions move in circular paths of radius R. From Eq. (30–7),

$$m = \frac{qB'R}{v}. \qquad (30\text{--}12)$$

Assuming that the charge q is the same for all the ions, the mass m of each ion is proportional to the radius R of its path. Ions of different isotopes converge at different points on the photographic plate. The relative abundance of the various isotopes is determined from the densities of the photographic images they produce.

In present-day mass spectrometers the photographic plate is replaced by a more sophisticated particle detector. Figure 30–13 shows a modern mass spectrometer and a typical isotope analysis. For each isotope the number given represents the **mass number,** equal to the total number of protons and neutrons in the nucleus of the atom. Different isotopes of an element have the same number of protons but differing numbers of neutrons in the nucleus.

Masses of atoms are often expressed in **atomic mass units.** By definition, one atomic mass unit (1 u) is exactly 1/12 the mass of one atom of the most abundant isotope of carbon, ^{12}C. The mass of an atom in grams is equal to its atomic mass (mass per mole) divided by Avogadro's number

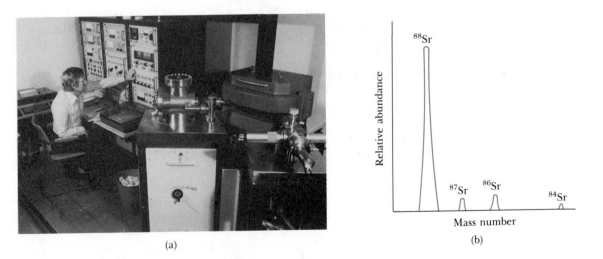

(a)   (b)

30–13
(a) A modern solid-source mass spectrometer. The specimen is placed in the cylindrical chamber in the center; the ion beam is deflected by the large magnet toward the collector and detector (right front). The instrument is controlled and the data processed by the equipment in front of the operator. (Courtesy of Institute of Geological Studies.) (b) A typical isotope analysis, showing several isotopes of strontium.

N_A (the number of atoms or molecules per mole). The mass of a carbon atom is $(12.0000 \text{ g·mol}^{-1})/N_A$, and one atomic mass unit is

$$1 \text{ u} = \frac{(1/12)(12.0000 \text{ g·mol}^{-1})}{6.02213 \times 10^{23} \text{ mol}^{-1}}$$

$$= 1.66054 \times 10^{-24} \text{ g} = 1.66054 \times 10^{-27} \text{ kg}.$$

30–7
Magnetic Force on a Conductor

What makes an electric motor work? The forces that make it turn are forces that a magnetic field exerts on a current-carrying conductor. The magnetic forces on the moving charges within the conductor are transmitted to the material of the conductor, and the conductor as a whole experiences a force distributed along its length. The moving-coil galvanometer we described in Section 29–3 also uses magnetic forces on conductors.

Figure 30–14 shows a segment of a conducting wire with length l and cross-sectional area A; the current is from left to right. The wire is in a magnetic field B, perpendicular to the plane of the diagram and directed *into* the plane. Let's assume first that the moving charges are positive. Later we will see what happens when they are negative.

The drift velocity v is to the right, perpendicular to B. The magnitude F of the magnetic-field force F on the charge is given by Eq. (30–2), with $\sin \phi = 1$: $F = qvB$. Using the rule shown in Fig. 30–2, we find that the direction of F is upward. Make sure you can confirm this direction.

We can derive an expression for the *total* force on all the moving charges in a length l of conductor with cross-sectional area A, using the same language that we used in Section 28–1, Eqs. (28–2) and (28–3). The number of charges per unit volume is n; the number of charges in a segment of conductor with length l is nAl. The total force F on *all* the charges, which is the total force on the conductor, has magnitude

$$F = (nAl)(qvB) = (nqv)(AlB). \tag{30–13}$$

The current density J, from Eq. (28–3), is $J = nqv$, and the product JA is the total current I, so we can rewrite Eq. (30–13) as

$$F = IlB. \tag{30–14}$$

If the B field is not perpendicular to the wire but makes an angle ϕ with it, we handle the situation the same way we did in Section 30–2 for a

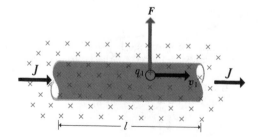

30–14

Forces on the moving charges in a current-carrying conductor. The magnetic field points into the plane of the figure; the force on a positive charge is shown.

single charge. The component of **B** parallel to the wire (and to the drift velocities of the charges) exerts no force; the component perpendicular to the wire is given by $B_\perp = B \sin \phi$. The general relation is

$$F = IlB_\perp = IlB \sin \phi. \tag{30–15}$$

The force is always perpendicular to both the conductor and the field, with the same right-hand rule that we used for a moving positive charge. Rotate a right-hand-thread screw from the direction of I toward **B**; the direction of advance is the direction of **F**. The situation is the same as that shown in Fig. 30–2, but with the direction of v replaced by the direction of I.

Finally, what happens when the moving charges are negative, such as electrons in a metal? Then in Fig. 30–14 a current to the right corresponds to a drift velocity to the left. But because q is now negative, the direction of the force **F** is opposite to the direction given by the right-hand rule for a positive charge. Thus the direction of **F** is the same as before. Therefore Eqs. (30–14) and (30–15) are valid for both positive and negative charges, even when *both* types of charge carry current. This happens in some semiconductor materials and in ionic solutions.

Example 30–2   A straight horizontal wire carries a current of 50.0 A from west to east in a region between the poles of a large electromagnet, where there is a horizontal magnetic field toward the northeast (i.e., 45° north of east) with magnitude 1.20 T. Find the magnitude and direction of the force on a 1-m section of wire.

Solution   The angle ϕ between the directions of current and field is 45°. From Eq. (30–15) we obtain

$$F = (50.0 \text{ A})(1.00 \text{ m})(1.20 \text{ T})(\sin 45°) = 42.4 \text{ N}.$$

To check consistency of units, we use the fact (from Section 30–2) that $1 \text{ T} = 1 \text{ N·A}^{-1}\text{·m}^{-1}$. The *direction* of the force is perpendicular to the plane of the current and the field, both of which lie in the horizontal plane. Thus the force must be along the vertical; the right-hand rule shows that it is vertically upward. We invite you to draw a diagram showing the various directions and confirm this conclusion.   ■

30–8
Force and Torque on a Current Loop

Current-carrying conductors usually form closed loops, so it is worthwhile to apply the results of Section 30–7 to find the total magnetic force and torque on a conductor in the form of a loop. As an example, let's look at a rectangular current loop in a uniform magnetic field. We can represent the loop as a series of straight line segments. We will find that the total *force* on the loop is zero but that there is a *torque* acting on the loop with some interesting properties.

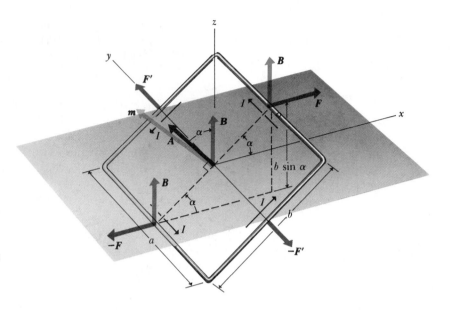

30–15
Forces on the sides of a current-carrying loop in a magnetic field. The resultant of the set of forces is a couple of moment $\Gamma = IAB \sin \alpha$.

Figure 30–15 shows a rectangular loop of wire with sides of lengths a and b. A line perpendicular to the plane of the loop (i.e., a *normal* to the plane) makes an angle α with the direction of the magnetic field $\boldsymbol{B}$, and the loop carries a current I. The wires leading the current into and out of the loop and the source of emf are omitted to keep the diagram simple.

The force $\boldsymbol{F}$ on the right side of the loop (length a) is in the direction of the x-axis, toward the right, as shown. On this side, $\boldsymbol{B}$ is perpendicular to the current direction, and the force on this side has magnitude

$$F = IaB.$$

A force $-\boldsymbol{F}$ with the same magnitude but opposite direction acts on the opposite side, as shown in the figure.

The sides with length b make an angle $(90° - \alpha)$ with the direction of $\boldsymbol{B}$. The forces on these sides are the vectors $\boldsymbol{F'}$ and $-\boldsymbol{F'}$; their magnitude F' is given by

$$F' = IbB \sin (90° - \alpha) = IbB \cos \alpha.$$

The lines of action of both lie along the y-axis.

The total force on the loop is zero because the forces on opposite sides cancel out in pairs. The two forces $\boldsymbol{F'}$ and $-\boldsymbol{F'}$ lie along the same lines, so they have no torque with respect to any axis. The two forces $\boldsymbol{F}$ and $-\boldsymbol{F}$ form a *couple*, as we defined it in Section 10–4. We showed there that the torque of a couple, with respect to any point, is the magnitude of either force multiplied by the distance between the lines of action of the two forces. From Fig. 30–15 this distance is $b \sin \alpha$, so the torque is

$$\Gamma = (IBa)(b \sin \alpha). \qquad (30-16)$$

The torque is greatest when $\alpha = 90°$ (i.e., when a line perpendicular to the plane of the coil is perpendicular to the field), and the torque is zero when α is zero or $180°$ and the line perpendicular to the coil is parallel to the field. The value $\alpha = 0$ is a stable equilibrium position. The torque is zero there, and when the coil is rotated slightly from this position, the resulting torque tends to rotate it back toward $\alpha = 0$. The position $\alpha = 180°$ is an *unstable* equilibrium position. We invite you to verify these statements.

The area A of the coil is equal to ab, so we can rewrite Eq. (30–16) as

$$\Gamma = IBA \sin \alpha. \qquad (30\text{--}17)$$

The product IA is called the **magnetic moment** m of the loop:

$$m = IA. \qquad (30\text{--}18)$$

The units of magnetic moment are current time area $(A \cdot m^2)$. We can also define a vector magnetic moment $\boldsymbol{m}$ as a vector quantity with magnitude given by Eq. (30–18). The direction of $\boldsymbol{m}$ is defined to be perpendicular to the plane of the loop, with a sense determined by the right-hand rule, as shown in Fig. 30–16. We can express the torque on a magnetic moment associated with a current loop as

$$\Gamma = mB \sin \alpha, \qquad (30\text{--}19)$$

where α is the angle between the vectors $\boldsymbol{m}$ and $\boldsymbol{B}$. The torque Γ tends to rotate the loop in the direction of *decreasing* α, that is, toward its stable equilibrium position, in which it lies in the *xy*-plane, perpendicular to the direction of the field $\boldsymbol{B}$. In that position the vector magnetic moment $\boldsymbol{m}$ is parallel to $\boldsymbol{B}$. The torque is greatest when $\boldsymbol{m}$ and $\boldsymbol{B}$ are perpendicular and zero when they are parallel or antiparallel.

When a magnetic dipole changes its orientation in a magnetic field, the field does work on it, and there is a corresponding potential energy U. Because $\alpha = 0$ (when $\boldsymbol{m}$ and $\boldsymbol{B}$ are parallel) is a stable equilibrium position, we expect this to be the position of *minimum* potential energy. Similarly, we expect U to be greatest when $\boldsymbol{m}$ and $\boldsymbol{B}$ are antiparallel. It can be shown that in *any* position the potential energy U of the interaction is given by

$$U = -mB \cos \alpha. \qquad (30\text{--}20)$$

We have derived Eqs. (30–17) through (30–20) for a *rectangular* current loop, but it is not hard to show that all these relations are valid for a plane loop of *any* shape. In particular, for a circular loop with radius R,

$$\Gamma = \pi IBR^2 \sin \alpha = IBA \sin \alpha. \qquad (30\text{--}21)$$

An arrangement of particular interest is the **solenoid,** a helical winding of wire such as a coil wound on a circular cylinder. If the windings are closely spaced, the solenoid can be approximated by a number of circular loops lying in planes at right angles to its long axis. The total torque on a solenoid in a magnetic field is simply the sum of the torques

30–16
A circular coil of wire and its associated magnetic moment in a magnetic field (Example 30–3).

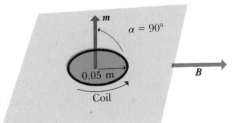

on the individual turns. For a solenoid with N turns in a uniform field B,

$$\Gamma = NIAB \sin \alpha, \tag{30--22}$$

where α is the angle between the axis of the solenoid and the direction of the field. The magnetic moment vector $\boldsymbol{m}$ is along the axis. The torque is greatest when the magnetic field is perpendicular to the solenoid axis and zero when they are parallel. The effect of this torque is to tend to rotate the solenoid into a position where its axis is parallel to the field.

The behavior of a solenoid in a magnetic field resembles that of a bar magnet or compass needle; both the solenoid and the magnet, if free to turn, orient themselves with their axes parallel to a magnetic field. We could use the torque on a solenoid for an alternative *definition* of magnetic field. The behavior of a bar magnet or compass needle is sometimes described in terms of magnetic forces on "poles" at its ends. For the solenoid, no such concept is needed. In fact, the moving electrons in a bar of magnetized iron play exactly the same role as the current in the windings of a solenoid, and the fundamental cause of the torque is the same in both cases. We will return to this subject later.

Example 30–3   A circular coil of wire 0.0500 m in radius, having 30 turns, lies in a horizontal plane, as shown in Fig. 30–16. It carries a current of 5.00 A in a counterclockwise sense when viewed from above. The coil is in a magnetic field directed toward the right with magnitude 1.20 T. Find the magnetic moment and the torque on the coil.

Solution   The area of the coil is

$$A = \pi R^2 = \pi (0.0500 \text{ m})^2 = 7.85 \times 10^{-3} \text{ m}^2.$$

The magnetic moment of each turn of the coil is

$$m = IA = (5.00 \text{ A})(7.85 \times 10^{-3} \text{ m}^2) = 3.93 \times 10^{-2} \text{ A·m}^2,$$

and the total magnetic moment of all 30 turns is

$$m_{\text{tot}} = (30)(3.93 \times 10^{-2} \text{ A·m}^2) = 1.18 \text{ A·m}^2.$$

The angle α between the direction of $\boldsymbol{B}$ and the normal to the plane of the coil is 90°. From Eq. (30–17) the torque on each turn of the coil is

$$\Gamma = IBA \sin \alpha = (5.00 \text{ A})(1.20 \text{ T})(7.85 \times 10^{-3} \text{ m}^2)(\sin 90°)$$
$$= 0.0471 \text{ N·m},$$

and the total torque on the coil is

$$\Gamma = (30)(0.0471 \text{ N·m}) = 1.41 \text{ N·m}.$$

Alternatively, from Eq. (30–19),

$$\Gamma = m_{\text{tot}} B \sin \alpha = (1.18 \text{ A·m}^2)(1.20 \text{ T})(\sin 90°)$$
$$= 1.41 \text{ N·m}.$$

The torque tends to rotate the right side of the coil down and the left side up, into a position where the normal to its plane is parallel to $\boldsymbol{B}$.   ■

Example 30–4   If the coil in Example 30–3 rotates from its initial position to a position where its magnetic moment is parallel to **B,** what is the change in potential energy?

Solution   From Eq. (30–20) the initial potential energy U_1 is

$$U_1 = -(1.18 \text{ A·m}^2)(1.20 \text{ T})(\cos 90°) = 0,$$

and the final potential energy U_2 is

$$U_2 = -(1.18 \text{ A·m}^2)(1.20 \text{ T})(\cos 0°) = -1.41 \text{ J}.$$

The change in potential energy is -1.41 J.   ■

Example 30–5   What vertical forces applied to the left and right edges of the coil of Fig. 30–16 would be required to hold it in equilibrium in its initial position?

Solution   An upward force of magnitude F at the right side and a downward force of equal magnitude on the left side would have a total torque of

$$\Gamma = (2)(0.0500 \text{ m})F.$$

This must be equal to the magnitude of the magnetic-field torque of 1.41 N·m, and we find that the required forces have magnitude 14.1 N.   ■

*30–9
The Direct-Current Motor

No one needs to be reminded of the importance of electric motors in contemporary society. Their operation depends on magnetic-field forces on current-carrying conductors. As an example, let's look at a simple type of direct-current motor, shown in Fig. 30–17. The center part A is the *armature* or *rotor*; it is a cylinder of soft steel that rotates about its axis (perpendicular to the plane of the figure).

Embedded in slots in the rotor surface (parallel to its axis) are insulated copper conductors C. Current is led into and out of these conductors through graphite brushes making contact with a segmented cylinder called the *commutator*, not shown in the figure. The commutator is an automatic switching arrangement that maintains the currents in the conductors in the directions shown in the figure as the rotor turns. The current in the field coils F and F' sets up a magnetic field in the motor frame M and in the gap between the pole pieces P and P' and the rotor. Some of the magnetic field lines are shown as broken lines. With the directions of field and rotor currents shown, the side thrust on each conductor in the rotor is such as to produce a *counterclockwise* torque on the rotor.

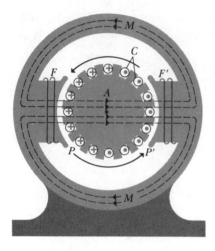

30–17
Schematic diagram of a dc motor. The armature or rotor A rotates on a shaft through its center, perpendicular to the plane of the figure. The conductors on the rotor are shown in cross section; those with dots at their centers carry current out of the plane; those with crosses carry current into the plane.

In a *series* motor the rotor and the field windings are connected in series; in a *shunt* motor they are connected in parallel.

A motor converts electrical energy to mechanical energy or work and requires electrical energy input. If the potential difference between its terminals is V_{ab} and the current is I, then the power input is $P = V_{ab}I$. Even if the motor coils have negligible resistance, there must be a potential difference between the terminals if P is to be different from zero. This potential difference results principally from magnetic forces exerted on the charges in the conductors of the rotor as they rotate through the magnetic field. The associated electromotive force (emf) $\mathcal{E}$ is called an *induced* emf or sometimes a *back* emf, referring to the fact that its sense is opposite to that of the current. In Chapter 32 we will study induced emf's resulting from motion of conductors in magnetic fields.

In a series motor with internal resistance r, V_{ab} is greater than $\mathcal{E}$, and the difference is the drop Ir across the internal resistance. That is,

$$V_{ab} = \mathcal{E} + Ir. \tag{30–23}$$

Because of the nature of the magnetic-field force, $\mathcal{E}$ is *not* constant but is proportional to the speed of rotation of the rotor.

A direct-current (dc) motor is analogous to a battery being charged, as we discussed in Section 28–5. In a battery, electrical energy is converted to chemical rather than mechanical energy.

Example 30–6   A dc motor with its rotor and field coils connected in series has an internal resistance of 2.00 Ω. When running at full load on a 120-V line, it draws a current of 4.00 A.

a) What is the emf in the motor?

b) What is the power delivered to the motor?

c) What is the rate of dissipation of energy in the resistance of the motor?

d) What is the mechanical power developed?

Solution

a) From Eq. (30–23),

$$V_{ab} = \mathcal{E} + Ir,$$

$$120 \text{ V} = \mathcal{E} + (4.0 \text{ A})(2.0 \ \Omega),$$

$$\mathcal{E} = 112 \text{ V}.$$

b)
$$P = V_{ab}I = (120 \text{ V})(4.0 \text{ A}) = 480 \text{ W}.$$

c)
$$P = I^2r = (4.0 \text{ A})^2(2.0 \ \Omega) = 32 \text{ W}.$$

d) The mechanical power output is the electrical power input minus the rate of dissipation of energy in the motor's resistance:

$$P = 480 \text{ W} - 32 \text{ W} = 448 \text{ W}. \quad \blacksquare$$

*30–10
The Hall Effect

Magnetic-field forces acting on the moving charges in a conductor are responsible for an interesting phenomenon called the **Hall effect.** To describe what this effect is, let's consider a conductor in the form of a flat strip, as shown in Fig. 30–18. The current is from left to right in the direction of the +x-axis, and there is a uniform magnetic field B perpendicular to the plane of the strip, in the +y-direction. The drift velocity of the moving charges (charge magnitude q) has magnitude v. Figure 30–18a shows the case of negative charges, such as electrons in a metal, and Fig. 30–18b shows positive charges. In both cases the magnetic-field force is upward, just as the magnetic force on a conductor is the same whether the moving charges are positive or negative. In either case a moving charge is driven toward the *upper* edge of the strip by the magnetic force $F_z = qvB$.

If the charge carriers are electrons, as in Fig. 30–18a, an excess negative charge accumulates at the upper edge of the strip, leaving an excess positive charge at its lower edge. This accumulation continues until the resulting transverse electrostatic field E_e becomes large enough to cause a force of magnitude qE_e that is equal and opposite to the magnetic-field force of magnitude qvB. After that there is no longer any net sideways force to deflect the moving charges. This electric field causes a transverse potential difference between opposite edges of the strip, called the *Hall voltage* or the *Hall emf*. The polarity depends on whether the moving charges are positive or negative. Experiments show that for metals the upper edge of the strip in Fig. 30–18a *does* become negatively charged, showing that the charge carriers in a metal are indeed negative electrons.

However, if the charge carriers are *positive*, as in Fig. 30–18b, then *positive* charge accumulates at the upper edge, and the potential differ-

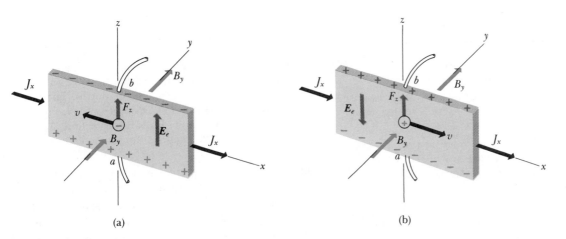

(a)   (b)

30–18
Forces on charge carriers in a conductor in a magnetic field. (a) Negative current carriers (electrons) are pushed toward top of slab, leading to charge distribution as shown. Point a is at higher potential than point b. (b) Positive current carriers; polarity of potential difference is opposite to that of (a).

ence is *opposite* to the situation with negative charges. Soon after the discovery of the Hall effect, in 1879, it was observed that some materials, particularly some *semiconductors*, show a Hall emf opposite to that of the metals, *as if* their charge carriers were *positively* charged. We now know that these materials conduct by a process known as *hole conduction*. Within such a material there are locations, called *holes*, that would normally be occupied by an electron but are actually empty. A missing negative charge is equivalent to a positive charge. When an electron moves in one direction to fill a hole, it leaves another hole behind it. The hole, equivalent to a positive charge, migrates in the direction opposite to that of the electron.

In terms of the coordinate axes in Fig. 30–18a the electrostatic field E_e for the negative-q case is in the +z-direction, and we write it as E_z. The magnetic field is in the +y-direction, and we write it as B_y. The magnetic-field force (in the +z-direction) is qvB_y. The current density J_x is in the x-direction. In the steady state, when the forces qE_z and qvB_y are equal in magnitude and opposite in direction,

$$E_z = vB_y.$$

The current density J_x is

$$J_x = nqv.$$

Eliminating v between these equations, we find that

$$nq = \frac{J_x B_y}{E_z}. \qquad (30\text{–}24)$$

We can measure J_x, B_y, and E_z, so we can compute the product nq. In both metals and semiconductors, q is equal in magnitude to the electron charge, so the Hall effect permits a direct measurement of n, the density of current-carrying charges in the material. The *sign* of the charges is determined by the polarity of the Hall emf, as we have described.

■ *Questions*

30–1 Does the earth's magnetic field have a significant effect on the electron beam in a TV picture tube?

30–2 If an electron beam in a cathode-ray tube travels in a straight line, can you be sure there is no magnetic field present?

30–3 If the magnetic-field force does no work on a charged particle, how can it have any effect on the particle's motion? Are there other examples of forces that do no work but have a significant effect on a particle's motion?

30–4 A permanent magnet can be used to pick up a string of nails, tacks, or paper clips, even though these are not magnets by themselves. How can this be?

30–5 How could a compass be used for a *quantitative* determination of magnitude and direction of magnetic field at a point?

30–6 The direction in which a compass points (magnetic north) is not in general exactly the same as the direction toward the north pole (true north). The difference is called *magnetic declination*; it varies from point to point on the earth and also varies with time. What are some possible explanations for magnetic declination?

30–7 Can a charged particle move through a magnetic field without experiencing any force? How?

30–8 Could the electron beam in an oscilloscope tube (cathode-ray tube) be used as a compass? How? What advantages and disadvantages would it have in comparison with a conventional compass?

30–9 Does a magnetic field exert forces on the electrons within atoms? What observable effect might such interaction have on the behavior of the atom?

30–10 How might a loop of wire carrying a current be used as a compass? Could such a compass distinguish between north and south?

30–11 How could the direction of a magnetic field be determined by making only *qualitative* observations of the magnetic force on a straight wire carrying a current?

30–12 Do the currents in the electrical system of a car have a significant effect on a compass placed in the car?

30–13 A student claimed that if lightning strikes a metal flagpole, the force exerted by the earth's magnetic field on the current in the pole can be large enough to bend it. Typical lightning currents are of the order of 10^4 to 10^5 A. Is the student's opinion justified?

30–14 A student tried to make an electromagnetic compass by suspending a coil of wire from a thread (with the plane of the coil vertical) and passing a current through it. He expected the coil to align itself perpendicular to the horizontal component of the earth's magnetic field; instead, the coil went into what ap-

peared to be angular simple harmonic motion (cf. Section 11–4), turning back and forth past the expected direction. What was happening? Was the motion truly simple harmonic?

30–15 When the polarity of the voltage applied to a dc motor is reversed, the direction of rotation *does not* reverse. Why not? How *could* the direction of rotation be reversed?

30–16 If an emf is produced in a dc motor, would it be possible to use the motor somehow as a *generator* or *source*, taking power out of it instead of putting power into it? How might this be done?

30–17 Hall-effect voltages are much *larger* for relatively poor conductors such as germanium than for good conductors such as copper for comparable currents, fields, and dimensions. Why?

30–18 Is it possible that, in a Hall-effect experiment, *no* transverse potential difference will be observed? Under what circumstances might this happen?

Exercises

Section 30–2   Magnetic Field

30–1 In a magnetic field directed vertically upward a particle initially moving north is deflected toward the east. What is the sign of the charge of the particle?

30–2 A particle with a mass of 5.00×10^{-3} kg and a charge of 3.50×10^{-8} C has at a given instant a velocity with a magnitude of 2.00×10^5 m·s^{-1} in the $+y$-direction. What are the magnitude and direction of the acceleration of the particle that is produced by a uniform magnetic field that has magnitude 0.8 T and is in the $-x$-direction?

30–3 A particle having a mass of 0.500 g carries a charge of 4.60×10^{-8} C. The particle is given an initial horizontal velocity that is due east and has a magnitude of 6.00×10^4 m·s^{-1}. What are the magnitude and direction of the magnetic field that will keep the particle moving in the earth's gravitational field in the same horizontal, eastward direction?

30–4 A particle with a charge of -2.50×10^{-8} C is moving with an instantaneous velocity of magnitude $v = 4.00 \times 10^4$ m·s^{-1} in the xy-plane at an angle of $50°$ counterclockwise from the $+x$-axis. What are the magnitude and direction of the force exerted on this particle by a magnetic field with magnitude 2.00 T in the

a) $-x$-direction?

b) $+z$-direction?

30–5 Each of the lettered circles at the corners of the cube in Fig. 30–19 represents a positive charge q

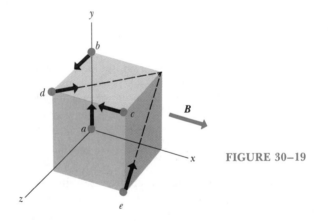

FIGURE 30–19

moving with a velocity of magnitude v in the direction indicated. The region in the figure is a uniform magnetic field B, parallel to the x-axis and directed toward the right. Copy the figure, find the magnitude and direction of the force on each charge, and show the force in your diagram.

Section 30–3   Magnetic-Field Lines and Magnetic Flux

30–6 A circular area with a radius of 0.400 m lies in the xy-plane. What is the magnetic flux through this circle due to a uniform magnetic field $B = 2.40$ T

a) in the $+z$-direction?

b) at an angle of 30.0° from the +z-direction?

c) in the +y-direction?

30-7 The magnetic field **B** in a certain region has magnitude 1.50 T, and its direction is that of the positive x-axis in Fig. 30–20.

a) What is the magnetic flux across the surface abcd in the figure?

b) What is the magnetic flux across the surface befc?

c) What is the magnetic flux across the surface aefd?

d) What is the net flux through all five surfaces that enclose the shaded volume?

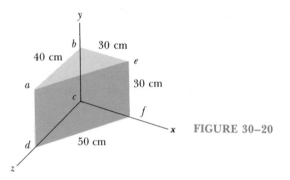

FIGURE 30–20

Section 30–4   Motion of Charged Particles in a Magnetic Field

30-8 A deuteron (the nucleus of an isotope of hydrogen) has a mass of 3.32×10^{-27} kg. It travels in a circular path with a radius of 0.0300 m in a magnetic field of magnitude 1.50 T.

a) Find the speed of the deuteron.

b) Find the time required for it to make one-half a revolution.

c) Through what potential difference would the deuteron have to be accelerated to acquire this speed?

30-9 An electron at point A in Fig. 30–21 has a speed v_0 of 6.00×10^6 m·s⁻¹. Find

a) the magnitude and direction of the magnetic field that will cause the electron to follow the semicircular path from A to B;

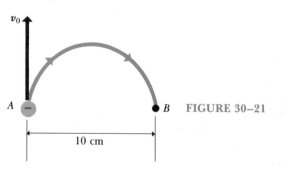

FIGURE 30–21

b) the time required for the electron to move from A to B.

30-10 In Exercise 30–9, suppose the particle is a proton rather than an electron. Answer the same questions as in that exercise.

30-11 A singly charged ^{7}Li ion has a mass of 1.16×10^{-26} kg. It is accelerated through a potential difference of 500 V and then enters a region of uniform magnetic field. The magnetic field has a magnitude of 0.600 T and is perpendicular to the path of the ion. What is the radius of the ion's path in the magnetic field?

30-12 In a TV picture tube an electron in the beam is accelerated by a potential difference of 20,000 V. Then it passes through a region of transverse magnetic field, where it moves in a circular arc with radius 0.180 m. What is the magnitude of the field?

Section 30–5   Thomson's Measurement of e/m

Section 30–6   Isotopes and Mass Spectroscopy

30-13 In the Bainbridge mass spectrometer (Fig. 30–12), suppose the magnetic field magnitude B in the velocity selector is 1.30 T, and ions having a speed of 4.00×10^6 m·s⁻¹ pass through undeflected.

a) What is the electric field between the plates P and P′?

b) If the separation of the plates is 0.500 cm, what is the potential difference between the plates?

30-14

a) What is the speed of a beam of electrons when the simultaneous influence of an electric field of 3.40×10^5 V·m⁻¹ and a magnetic field of 8.00×10^{-2} T, with both fields normal to the beam and to each other, produces no deflection of the electrons?

b) Show in a diagram the relative orientation of the vectors v, **E**, and **B**.

c) What is the radius of the electron path when the electric field is removed?

30-15 The electric field between the plates of the velocity selector in a Bainbridge mass spectrometer is 1.20×10^5 V·m⁻¹, and the magnetic field in both regions is 0.600 T. A stream of singly charged neon atoms moves in a circular path of 0.728-m radius in the magnetic field. Determine the mass of one neon atom and the mass number of this neon isotope.

Section 30–7   Magnetic Force on a Conductor

30-16 An electromagnet produces a magnetic field of 1.20 T in a cylindrical region of radius 4.00 cm between its poles. A straight wire carrying a current of

20.0 A passes through the center of this region, and is perpendicular to the magnetic field. What force is exerted on the wire?

30–17 A horizontal rod 0.200 m long is mounted on a balance and carries a current. At the location of the rod there is a uniform horizontal magnetic field with magnitude 0.0800 T and direction perpendicular to the rod. The magnetic force on the rod is measured by the balance and is found to be 0.240 N. What is the current?

30–18 In Exercise 30–17, suppose the magnetic field is horizontal but makes an angle of 30.0° with the rod. What is the current in the rod?

30–19 A wire along the x-axis carries a current of 6.00 A in the $+x$-direction. Calculate the force (magnitude and direction) on a 1.00-cm section of the wire exerted by the following uniform magnetic fields:

a) $B = 0.600$ T, in the $-y$-direction;

b) $B = 0.500$ T, in the $+z$-direction;

c) $B = 0.300$ T, in the $-x$-direction;

d) $B = 0.200$ T, in the xz-plane at an angle of 60.0° from the $+x$-axis and 30.0° from the $+z$-axis.

30–20 A straight, vertical wire carries a current of 8.00 A upward in a region between the poles of a large superconducting electromagnet, where the magnetic field has magnitude $B = 3.00$ T and is horizontal. What are the magnitude and direction of the magnetic force on a 1.00-cm section of the wire if the magnetic field direction is

a) east? b) south? c) 30.0° south of west?

Section 30–8 Force and Torque on a Current Loop

30–21 What is the maximum torque on a rectangular coil 5.00 cm × 12.0 cm and of 600 turns when carrying a current of 4.00×10^{-5} A in a uniform field with magnitude 0.300 T?

30–22 The plane of a rectangular loop of wire 5.00 cm × 8.00 cm is parallel to a magnetic field with magnitude 0.150 T. The loop carries a current of 8.00 A.

a) What torque acts on the loop?

b) What is the magnetic moment of the loop?

30–23 A circular coil of wire 8.00 cm in diameter has 12 turns and carries a current of 4.00 A. The coil is in a region where the magnetic field is 0.600 T.

a) What is the maximum torque on the coil?

b) In what position would the torque be one-half as great as in part (a)?

30–24 A coil with magnetic moment $m = 2.80$ A·m² is oriented initially with its magnetic moment parallel to a uniform magnetic field with $B = 0.750$ T. What is the change in potential energy of the coil when it is rotated 180° so that its magnetic moment is antiparallel to the field?

30–25 A circular coil with area A and N turns is free to rotate about a diameter that coincides with the x-axis. Current I is circulating in the coil. There is a uniform magnetic field B in the positive y-direction. Calculate the magnitude of the torque Γ and the value of the potential energy U, as given in Eq. (30–20), when the coil is oriented as shown in parts (a) through (d) of Fig. 30–22.

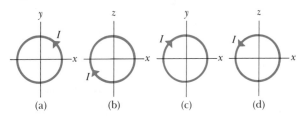

FIGURE 30–22

Section 30–9 The Direct-Current Motor

30–26 A dc motor with its rotor and field coils connected in series has an internal resistance of 5.00 Ω. When running at full load on a 12.0-V line, the emf in the rotor is 6.40 V.

a) What is the current drawn by the motor from the line?

b) What is the power delivered to the motor?

c) What is the mechanical power developed by the motor?

30–27 In a shunt-wound dc motor (Fig. 30–23) the resistance R_f of the field coils is 180 Ω, and the resistance R_r of the rotor is 6.00 Ω. When a potential difference of 120 V is applied to the brushes and the motor is running at full speed delivering mechanical power, the current supplied to it is 4.50 A.

a) What is the current in the field coils?

b) What is the current in the rotor?

c) What is the induced emf developed by the motor?

d) How much mechanical power is developed by this motor?

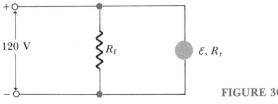

FIGURE 30–23

Section 30–10   The Hall Effect

30–28 Figure 30–24 shows a portion of a silver ribbon with $z_1 = 2.00$ cm and $y_1 = 1.00$ mm, carrying a current of 120 A in the positive *x*-direction. The ribbon lies in a

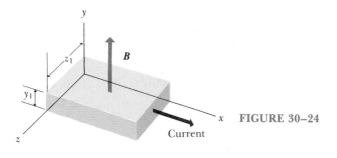

y

z_1

B

y_1

z

Current

x   **FIGURE 30–24**

uniform magnetic field, in the *y*-direction, with magnitude 1.50 T. If there are 7.40×10^{28} free electrons per m^3, find

a) the magnitude of the drift velocity of the electrons in the *x*-direction;

b) the magnitude and direction of the electric field in the *z*-direction due to the Hall effect;

c) the Hall emf.

30–29 Let Fig. 30–24 represent a strip of copper of the same dimensions as those of the silver ribbon in Exercise 30–28. When the magnetic field is 5.00 T and the current is 100 A, the Hall emf is found to be 45.4 μV. What is the density of free electrons in the copper?

Problems

30–30 A particle with initial velocity $v_0 = 6.00 \times 10^3$ m·s^{-1} in the +*x*-direction enters a region of uniform electric and magnetic fields. The magnetic field in the region is $B = 0.300$ T in the −*y*-direction. Calculate the magnitude and direction of the electric field in the region if the particle passes through undeflected for a particle of charge

a) $+0.400 \times 10^{-8}$ C;

b) -0.400×10^{-8} C.

Neglect the weight of the particle.

30–31 Estimate the effect of the earth's magnetic field on the electron beam in a TV picture tube. Suppose the accelerating voltage is 10,000 V. Calculate the approximate deflection of the beam over a distance of 0.36 m from the electron gun to the screen under the action of a transverse field with a magnitude of 5.0×10^{-5} T (comparable to the magnitude of the earth's field), assuming that there are no other deflecting fields. Is this deflection significant?

30–32 A particle carries a charge of 5.00×10^{-9} C. When it moves with a velocity v_1 of 3.00×10^4 m·s^{-1} at $45.0°$ from the +*x*-axis in the *xy*-plane, a uniform magnetic field exerts a force F_1 along the negative *z*-axis. When the particle moves with a velocity v_2 of

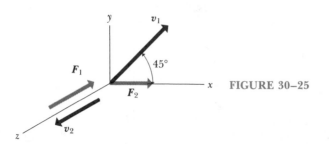

y v_1

F_1

$45°$

F_2

x   **FIGURE 30–25**

z v_2

2.00×10^4 m·s^{-1} along the *z*-axis, there is a force F_2 of 4.00×10^{-5} N exerted on it along the *x*-axis. What are the magnitude and direction of the magnetic field? (See Fig. 30–25.)

30–33 An electron moves in a circular path with radius 1.20 cm perpendicular to a uniform magnetic field. The speed of the electron is 4.00×10^6 m·s^{-1}. What is the total magnetic flux encircled by the path?

30–34 The force on a charged particle moving in a magnetic field can be computed as the vector sum of the forces due to each separate component of the magnetic field. A particle with a charge of 3.50×10^{-8} C has a velocity of $v = 8.00 \times 10^5$ m·s^{-1} in the −*x*-direction. It is moving in a uniform magnetic field with components $B_x = +0.200$ T, $B_y = -0.500$ T, and $B_z = +0.300$ T. What are the components of the force exerted on the particle by the magnetic field?

30–35 A particle having a charge $q = 2.00 \times 10^{-6}$ C is traveling with a velocity $v = 1.50 \times 10^3$ m·s^{-1} in the +*y*-direction. The particle experiences a force **F** due to a magnetic field **B**. The components of **F** are $F_x = 6.00 \times 10^{-4}$ N, $F_y = 0$, and $F_z = -8.00 \times 10^{-4}$ N.

a) Determine F, the magnitude of **F**.

b) Determine B_x, B_y, and B_z, or at least as many of the three components as possible from the information given. (See Problem 30–34.)

c) If it is given in addition that the magnitude of the magnetic field is 0.500 T, determine the remaining components of **B**.

30–36 An electron and an alpha particle (a doubly ionized helium atom) both move in a magnetic field in circular paths with the same tangential speed. Compute the ratio of the number of revolutions the electron makes per second to the number made per second by the alpha particle. The mass of the alpha particle is 6.68×10^{-27} kg.

30–37 A particle with mass m and charge q moves with velocity v in a magnetic field $\mathbf{B}$. The velocity of the particle is perpendicular to the field, and the particle moves in a circle with radius as given by Eq. (30–7).

a) Calculate the period of the motion (the time it takes for the particle to complete one revolution).

b) From your answer to part (a), obtain the frequency $f = 1/\tau$ of the circular motion. This frequency is called the *cyclotron frequency*.

30–38 Suppose the electric field between the plates P and P' in Fig. 30–12 is 1.50×10^4 V·m^{-1} and the magnetic field in both regions is 0.800 T. If the source contains the three isotopes of magnesium, ^{24}Mg, ^{25}Mg, and ^{26}Mg, and the ions are singly charged, find the distance between the lines formed by the three isotopes on the photographic plate. Assume that the atomic masses of the isotopes (in atomic mass units) are equal to their mass numbers.

30–39 The force on a charged particle moving in a magnetic field can be computed as the vector sum of the forces due to each separate component of the particle's velocity. (See Problem 30–34.) A particle with a charge of 7.60×10^{-8} C is moving in a region where there is a uniform magnetic field of 0.400 T in the $+x$-direction. At a particular instant of time the velocity of the particle has components $v_x = 2.50 \times 10^4$ m·s^{-1}, $v_y = 9.00 \times 10^4$ m·s^{-1}, and $v_z = -5.00 \times 10^4$ m·s^{-1}. What are the components of the force on the particle at this time?

30–40 A particle with positive charge q and mass $m = 1.00 \times 10^{-15}$ kg is traveling through a region containing a uniform magnetic field $\mathbf{B}$ with a magnitude of 0.150 T in the $-z$-direction. At a particular instant of time the velocity of the particle has components $v_x = 4.00 \times 10^6$ m·s^{-1}, $v_y = -3.00 \times 10^6$ m·s^{-1}, and $v_z = 12.0 \times 10^6$ m·s^{-1}, and the force $\mathbf{F}$ on the particle has a magnitude of 2.00 N. (See Problem 30–39.)

a) Determine the charge q.

b) Determine the components of the acceleration $\mathbf{a}$ of the particle.

c) Explain why the path of the particle is a helix, and determine the radius of curvature R of the circular component of the helical path.

d) Determine the cyclotron frequency of the particle. (See Problem 30–37.)

e) Although helical motion is not periodic in the full sense of the word, the x- and y-coordinates do vary in a periodic way. If the coordinates of the particle at $t = 0$ are $(x,y,z) = (R,0,0)$, determine the coordinates of the particle at a time $t = 2\tau$, where τ is the period of the motion in the xy-plane.

30–41 A wire 0.200 m long lies along the y-axis and carries a current of 10.0 A in the $+y$-direction. The magnetic field is uniform and has components $B_x = 0.300$ T, $B_y = -1.20$ T, and $B_z = 0.500$ T.

a) Find the components of force on the wire. (As in Problem 30–34, the resultant force is the vector sum of the forces due to each component of $\mathbf{B}$.)

b) What is the magnitude of the total force on the wire?

30–42 The cube in Fig. 30–26, 0.500 m on a side, is in a uniform magnetic field of 0.300 T, parallel to the x-axis. The wire $abcdef$ carries a current of 4.00 A in the direction indicated.

a) Determine the magnitude and direction of the force acting on segments ab, bc, cd, de, and ef.

b) What are the magnitude and direction of the total force on the wire?

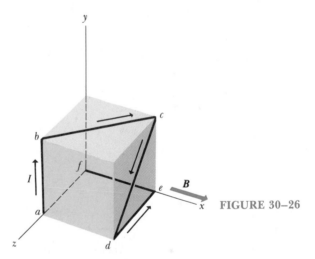

FIGURE 30–26

30–43 The rectangular loop in Fig. 30–27 is pivoted about the y-axis and carries a current of 10.0 A in the direction indicated.

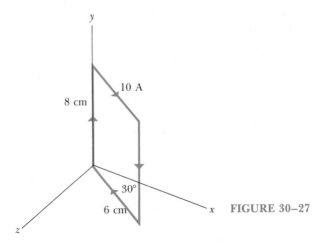

FIGURE 30–27

a) If the loop is in a uniform magnetic field of magnitude 0.400 T, parallel to the x-axis, find the magnitude of the torque required to hold the loop in equilibrium in the position shown.

b) Repeat part (a) for the case in which the field is parallel to the z-axis.

c) For each of the above magnetic fields, what magnitude of torque would be required if the loop were pivoted about an axis through its center, parallel to the y-axis?

30–44 The rectangular loop of wire in Fig. 30–28 has a mass of 0.200 g per centimeter of length and is

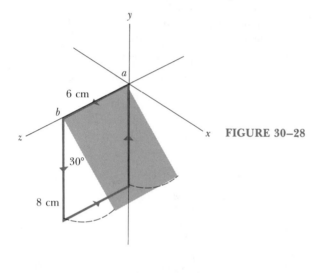

6 cm

8 cm

30°

x **FIGURE 30–28**

pivoted about side ab as a frictionless axis. The current in the wire is 15.0 A in the direction shown. Find the magnitude and direction of the magnetic field, parallel to the y-axis, that will cause the loop to swing up until its plane makes an angle of 30.0° with the yz-plane.

30–45 A shunt-wound dc motor (Figure 30–23) operates from a 120-V dc power line. The resistance of the field windings, R_f, is 250 Ω. The resistance of the rotor, R_r, is 5.00 Ω. When the motor is running, the rotor develops an emf $\mathcal{E}$. The motor draws a current of 4.50 A from the line. Friction losses amount to 50.0 W. Compute

a) the field current,

b) the rotor current,

c) the emf $\mathcal{E}$,

d) the rate of development of heat in the field windings,

e) the rate of development of heat in the rotor,

f) the power input to the motor,

g) the efficiency of the motor.

Challenge Problems

30–46 A particle with mass m and charge $+q$ starts from rest at the origin in Fig. 30–29. There is a uniform electric field E in the positive y-direction and a uniform magnetic field B directed toward the reader. It is shown in more advanced books that the path is a *cycloid* whose radius of curvature at the top points is twice the y-coordinate at that level.

a) Explain why the path has this general shape and why it is repetitive.

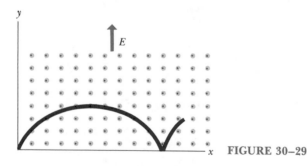

y

E

x **FIGURE 30–29**

b) Prove that the speed at any point is equal to $\sqrt{2qEy/m}$. (*Hint:* Use energy conservation.)

c) Applying Newton's second law at the top point and taking as given that the radius of curvature here equals $2y$, prove that the speed at this point is $2E/B$.

30–47 A particle with charge $q = 3.00 \times 10^{-6}$ C and mass $m = 1.00 \times 10^{-11}$ kg is initially traveling in the y-direction with a speed $v_0 = 2.00 \times 10^5$ m·s^{-1}. It then enters a region containing a uniform magnetic field directed away from the reader and perpendicular to the page in Fig. 30–30. The magnitude of the field is 0.500 T. The region extends a distance of 25 cm along the initial direction of travel; 75 cm from the point of entry into the magnetic field region is a wall. The length of the field-free region is thus 50 cm. When the charged particle enters the magnetic field, it will follow a curved path whose radius of curvature is R. It then leaves the magnetic field after a time t_1, having been deflected a distance Δx_1. The particle then travels in

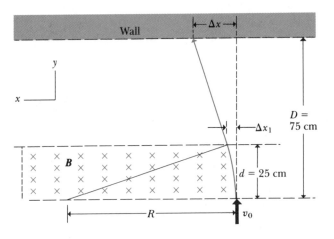

FIGURE 30–30

the field-free region and strikes the wall after undergoing a total deflection Δx.

a) Determine the radius R of the curved part of the path.

b) Determine t_1, the time the particle spends in the magnetic field.

c) Determine Δx_1, the horizontal deflection at the point of exit from the field.

d) Determine Δx, the total horizontal deflection.

30–48 Magnetic forces acting on conducting fluids provide a convenient means of pumping these fluids. This problem deals with such an electromagnetic pump. A horizontal tube of rectangular cross section (height h, width w) is placed at right angles to a uniform magnetic field of magnitude B so that a length l is in the field. (See Fig. 30–31.) The tube is filled with liquid sodium, and an electric current of density J is maintained in the third mutually perpendicular direction.

a) Show that the difference of pressure between a point in the liquid on a vertical plane through ab (Fig. 30–31) and a point in the liquid on another vertical plane through cd, under conditions in

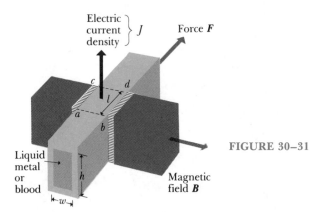

FIGURE 30–31

which the liquid is prevented from flowing, is $\Delta p = JlB$.

b) What current density is needed to provide a pressure difference of 1.00 atm between these two points if $B = 1.50$ T and $l = 0.0400$ m?

30–49 A wire with a length of 35.0 cm and mass $m = 9.79 \times 10^{-5}$ kg is bent into the shape of an inverted U such that the horizontal part has length $l = 25.0$ cm. The bent ends of the wire, which are each 5.0 cm long, are completely immersed in pools of mercury, and the entire structure is in a region containing a magnetic field with a magnitude of 0.0180 T and a direction into the page. (See Fig. 30–32.) An electrical connection from the mercury pools is made through wires that are connected to a 1.50-V battery and a switch S. Switch S is closed, and the wire jumps 0.800 m into the air, measured from its initial position.

a) Determine the speed v of the wire as it leaves the mercury.

b) Assuming that the current I through the wire was constant from the time the switch was closed until the wire left the mercury, determine I.

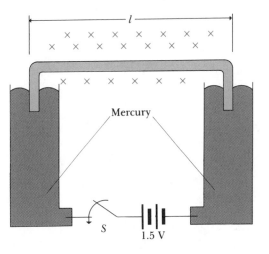

FIGURE 30–32

30–50 The neutron is a particle with zero charge but with a nonzero magnetic moment with magnitude $m = 9.66 \times 10^{-27}$ A·m². If the neutron is considered to be a fundamental entity with no internal structure, the two properties listed above seem to be contradictory. According to present theory in particle physics, a neutron is composed of three more fundamental particles called "quarks." (See the discussion of quarks in Section 44–10.) In this model the neutron consists of an "up quark" having a charge of $+2e/3$ and two "down quarks," each having a charge of $-e/3$. The combination of the three quarks produces a net charge of $2e/3 - e/3 - e/3 = 0$, as required, and if the quarks are in motion, they could also produce a nonzero magnetic moment. As a very simple model, suppose that the up quark is moving in a counterclockwise circular path and the down quarks are moving in a clockwise path, all of radius r and all with the same speed v. (See Fig. 30–33.)

a) Obtain an expression for the current due to the circulation of the up quark.

b) Obtain an expression for the magnitude m_u of the magnetic moment due to the circulating up quark.

c) Obtain an expression for the magnitude of the magnetic moment of the three-quark system. (Be careful to use the correct magnetic moment directions.)

d) With what speed v must the quarks move if this model is to reproduce the magnetic moment of the neutron? For the radius of the orbits, use $r = 1.20 \times 10^{-15}$ m, the radius of the neutron.

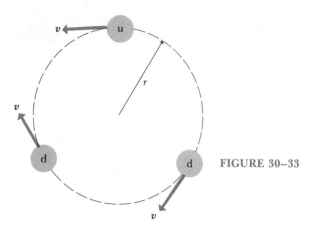

FIGURE 30–33

Sources of Magnetic Field

In Chapter 30 we studied one aspect of the magnetic interaction of moving charges: the *forces* that a magnetic field exerts on moving charges and on currents in conductors. We didn't worry about what caused the magnetic field; we simply took its existence as a given fact. Now we are ready to return to the question of how magnetic fields are *produced* by moving charges and by currents.

From a practical standpoint we are most often interested in magnetic fields produced by currents in wires or other conductors. We begin by studying the magnetic fields for a few simple configurations, such as a long, straight wire and a circular loop. Then we look at two general methods for calculating the magnetic fields produced by currents. In the first method, analogous to Coulomb's law in electrostatics, we find the field caused by a short segment of conductor, using a general rule called the *law of Biot and Savart*; then we take the vector sum of the contributions from all the segments to find the total field. The second method, called Ampere's law, is more closely analogous to Gauss's law in electrostatics; it is particularly useful in systems having a high degree of symmetry.

31–1
Magnetic Field of a Straight Conductor

In the first few sections of this chapter we will concentrate on *describing* the magnetic fields caused by a few simple conductor shapes, without attempting any detailed derivation. Then in Sections 31–5 and 31–6 we will derive some of the field relationships from basic principles. All of these relationships will be valid for situations in which current-carrying conductors are surrounded by *vacuum*. They are all very nearly correct (within 0.1% or so) when the conductors are surrounded by air or most materials. In Section 31–7 we will show how the relationships can be modified to include the properties of a surrounding *magnetic* material such as iron.

The simplest current configuration to describe is a very long, straight conductor carrying a steady current I. Biot and Savart found experimentally that the magnetic field produced by such a conductor has the general shape shown in Fig. 31–1. As the figure shows, the magnetic field B at each point is tangent to a circle centered on the conductor and lying in a plane perpendicular to it. The magnetic field lines are all *circles*; because of the axial symmetry, we know that B has the same *magnitude* at all points on a particular field line. Biot and Savart also found that the *magnitude B* of the magnetic field at a distance r from the conductor is inversely proportional to r and that it is directly proportional to the current I. The $1/r$ dependence can also be derived from more general considerations, as we will see in Section 31–5. The relationship is expressed symbolically by the equation

$$B = \frac{\mu_0 I}{2\pi r} \qquad \text{(long, straight wire).} \qquad (31\text{–}1)$$

In this equation, μ_0 is a constant that depends on the system of units we use. In SI units the units of μ_0 are (T·m·A^{-1}). Its numerical value, which is related to the definition of the unit of current, is defined to be *exactly*

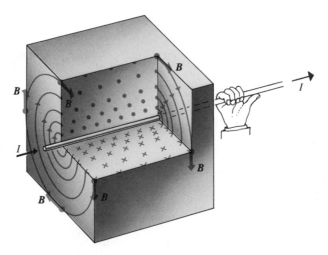

31–1
Magnetic field around a long, straight conductor. The field lines are circles, with directions determined by the right-hand rule.

$4\pi \times 10^{-7}$:

$$\mu_0 = 4\pi \times 10^{-7} \text{ T·m·A}^{-1}.$$

Also, from Eq. (30–14), 1 N = 1 A·m·T and 1 T = 1 N·A^{-1}·m^{-1}. So an alternative set of units for μ_0 is

$$\mu_0 = 4\pi \times 10^{-7} \text{ N·A}^{-2}.$$

Example 31–1   A long, straight conductor carries a current of 100 A. At what distance from the conductor is the magnetic field caused by the current equal in magnitude to the earth's magnetic field in Pittsburgh (about 0.5×10^{-4} T)?

Solution   We use Eq. (31–1). Everything except r is known, so we solve for r and insert the appropriate numbers:

$$r = \frac{\mu_0 I}{2\pi B} = \frac{(4\pi \times 10^{-7} \text{ T·m·A}^{-1})(100 \text{ A})}{2\pi(0.5 \times 10^{-4} \text{ T})} = 0.4 \text{ m}.$$

At smaller distances the field becomes stronger; for example, when $r = 0.2$ m, $B = 1.0 \times 10^{-4}$ T, and so on.   ∎

The shape of the magnetic-field lines is completely different from that of the electric-field lines in the analogous electrical situation. Electric-field lines radiate outward from the charges that are their sources (or inward for negative charges). By contrast, magnetic-field lines *encircle* the current that acts as their source. Electric-field lines begin and end at charges, while experiments have shown that magnetic-field lines *never* have endpoints, no matter what shape the conductor is. If lines *did* begin or end at a point, this point would correspond to a "magnetic charge" or a single magnetic pole. As we mentioned in Section 30–1, there is no experimental evidence that such a pole exists.

If we construct an imaginary closed surface in a magnetic field, no field line can start or end inside this surface. The number of lines emerging from the surface must therefore equal the number entering it. We have shown that the number of lines crossing a surface is proportional to the magnetic *flux* Φ through the surface. Therefore in a magnetic field the total flux through a *closed* surface is *always* zero. Compare this with Gauss's law for electrostatic fields, in which the total *electric* flux Ψ through a closed surface equals $1/\epsilon_0$ times the enclosed charge. There is no such thing as "magnetic charge" to act as a source of **B**. The sources of **B** are electric *currents* or other moving electric charges.

The direction of the **B** lines around a straight conductor is given by a right-hand rule: Grasp the conductor with your right hand, with your thumb extended in the direction of the current. Your fingers then curl around the conductor in the direction of the **B** lines. This rule is shown in Fig. 31–1.

Here's a final note on units. The choice of the numerical value for the constant μ_0 in Eq. (31–1) is related to the choice of the value of ϵ_0 in

Coulomb's law. We pointed out in Section 24–5 that the numerical value of ϵ_0 is related to the speed of light c; specifically,

$$\frac{1}{4\pi\epsilon_0} = 10^{-7}\, c^2.$$

This equation also has consistent units if we attach the units $(\mathrm{N\cdot A^{-2}})$ (the same units as μ_0) to the factor 10^{-7}; we invite you to verify this. Combining the above equation with the value of μ_0, we find that

$$\frac{1}{\epsilon_0\mu_0} = c^2. \tag{31-2}$$

Again, we invite you to verify that Eq. (31–2) has consistent units. This result is the real reason for the particular choice we made for the value of ϵ_0 in Chapter 24. We will explore the significance of this relation in greater detail in Chapter 35 in connection with electromagnetic waves.

31–2
Force between Parallel Conductors

Let's look at the interaction force between two long current-carrying conductors. This problem comes up in a variety of practical situations, and it also has fundamental significance in connection with the definition of the ampere. Figure 31–2 shows segments of two long, straight parallel conductors separated by a distance r and carrying currents I and I' in the same direction. Each conductor lies in the magnetic field set up by the other, so each experiences a force. The diagram shows some of the field lines set up by the current in the *lower* conductor.

From Eq. (31–1) the magnitude of the **B**-vector at the upper conductor is

$$B = \frac{\mu_0 I}{2\pi r}.$$

From Eq. (30–14) the force on a length l of the upper conductor is

$$F = I'Bl = \frac{\mu_0 l I I'}{2\pi r},$$

so the force *per unit length* F/l is

$$\frac{F}{l} = \frac{\mu_0 I I'}{2\pi r}. \tag{31-3}$$

The right-hand rule shows that the direction of the force on the upper conductor is *downward*. An equal and opposite (upward) force per unit length acts on the lower conductor; you can see that by looking at the field set up by the upper conductor. Therefore the conductors *attract* each other. If the direction of either current is reversed, the forces reverse also. Parallel conductors carrying currents in *opposite* directions *repel* each other.

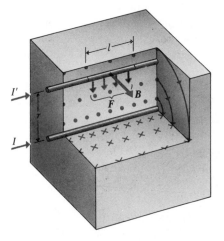

31–2
Parallel conductors carrying currents in the same direction attract each other.

Example 31–2   An electrical power cable containing two long, straight conductors 1.0 cm apart carries a current of 100 A to a large 40-hp electric motor used to run a ski lift. Find the force exerted on a 1.0-m length of one conductor by the other.

Solution   The two currents have opposite directions, so from the above discussion the forces are repulsive. From Eq. (31–3) the force per meter length is

$$\frac{F}{l} = \frac{(4\pi \times 10^{-7} \text{ N·A}^{-2})(100 \text{ A})^2}{2\pi(0.010 \text{ m})} = 0.20 \text{ N·m}^{-1}.$$

This is a relatively small force; the magnetic field caused by each conductor at the position of the other is only 2.0×10^{-3} T; we invite you to verify this. Much stronger fields, of the order of 1 to 2 T, are common in electrical machinery such as motors, generators, and transformers. The forces can amount to hundreds of newtons, and mechanical strength becomes a significant design consideration in such machinery.   ■

The forces that two straight parallel conductors exert on one another form the basis for the official SI definition of the ampere, as follows:

One ampere *is that unvarying current which, if present in each of two parallel conductors of infinite length and 1 meter apart in empty space, causes each conductor to experience a force of exactly 2×10^{-7} newtons per meter of length.*

This definition is consistent with the definition of the constant μ_0 as *exactly* $4\pi \times 10^{-7}$ N·A^{-2}, as we stated in Section 31–1.

In principle we can use this definition to *measure* current, using a meter stick and a spring balance. For high-precision standardization of the ampere, coils of wire a few centimeters apart are used instead of straight wires in an instrument called a *current balance*.

Our definition of the ampere is an *operational definition*; that is, it gives us an actual experimental procedure for measuring current and defining the unit of current. With this definition we can now return to electrostatics and define the **coulomb** as *the quantity of charge that in one second crosses a section of a circuit in which there is a constant current of one ampere.*

Mutual forces of attraction exist not only between *wires* carrying currents in the same direction, but also between the longitudinal elements of a single current-carrying conductor. If the conductor is a liquid or an ionized gas (a plasma), these forces result in a constriction of the conductor, just as though its surface were acted on by an external, inward pressure. The constriction of the conductor is called the *pinch effect*. The high temperature produced by the pinch effect in a plasma has been used in one technique for producing nuclear-fusion reactions.

31–3
Magnetic Field of a Circular Loop

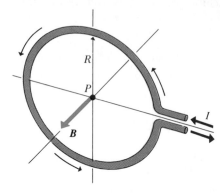

31–3
Field at the center of a circular loop.

In many practical devices such as transformers and electromagnets, in which a current is used to establish a magnetic field, the wire carrying the current is wound into a *coil* consisting of many circular loops. So an expression for the magnetic field produced by a single circular conducting loop carrying a current is very useful. Figure 31–3 shows a circular conductor with radius R, carrying a current I. The current is led into and out of the loop through two long, straight wires side by side; the currents in these straight wires are in opposite directions, so their magnetic fields cancel each other.

Biot and Savart found experimentally that the magnetic field at the center of a circular loop has the direction shown in the figure and that its magnitude is directly proportional to the current and inversely proportional to the radius of the loop. Specifically, they found that

$$B = \frac{\mu_0 I}{2R} \qquad \text{(center of circular loop)}. \tag{31–4}$$

If we have a coil of N loops instead of a single loop, and if the loops are closely spaced and all have the same radius, then each loop contributes equally to the field, and the field at the center is just N times Eq. (31–4):

$$B = \frac{\mu_0 N I}{2R} \qquad \text{(center of } N \text{ circular loops)}. \tag{31–5}$$

Some of the magnetic-field lines surrounding a circular loop and lying in planes through the axis are shown in Fig. 31–4. We see that the field lines encircle the conductor and that their directions are given by the same right-hand rule as for a long, straight conductor. The field lines for the circular loop are *not* circles, but they are closed curves that link the conductor.

31–4
Field lines surrounding a circular loop.

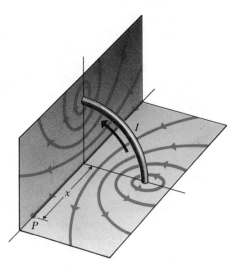

It's interesting to note the similarity of Eq. (31–4) for a circular loop to Eq. (31–1) for a long, straight conductor. The two expressions differ only by a factor of π; the field at the center of a circular loop with radius R is π times as great as the field at a distance R from a long, straight wire carrying the same current.

Example 31–3   A coil used to produce a magnetic field for an electron-beam experiment has a radius of 12 cm and has 200 turns. We need a magnetic field with a magnitude of 5.0×10^{-3} T at the center of the coil. What current is required?

Solution   We solve Eq. (31–5) for I, obtaining

$$I = \frac{2RB}{\mu_0 N} = \frac{2(0.12 \text{ m})(5.0 \times 10^{-3} \text{ T})}{(4\pi \times 10^{-7} \text{ T·m·A}^{-1})(200)} = 4.8 \text{ A}.$$

Can you verify that the units in this calculation come out correctly?   ■

31–4
Magnetic Field of a Solenoid

A **solenoid** is a helical winding of wire, usually wound around the surface of a cylindrical form. Ordinarily, the turns are so closely spaced that each one is very nearly a circular loop. There may be several layers of windings. The solenoid in Fig. 31–5 is drawn with only a few turns so that the field lines can be shown. All turns carry the same current I, and the total **B** field at every point is the vector sum of the fields caused by

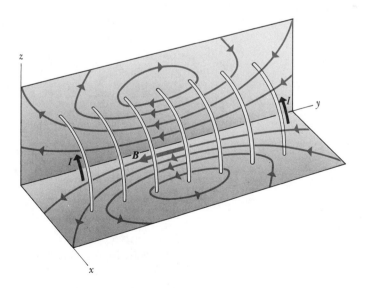

31–5
Magnetic-field lines surrounding a solenoid.

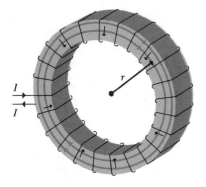

31–6

A toroidal solenoid. The field is very nearly zero at all points except those within the space enclosed by the windings.

the individual turns. Figure 31–5 shows field lines in the *xy*- and *yz*-planes. The field is found to be most intense in the center, less intense near the ends.

If the length L of the solenoid is large in comparison with its cross-sectional radius R, the ***B*** field inside the solenoid near its center is very nearly uniform and parallel to the axis, and the field outside, adjacent to the center, is very small. The magnetic-field magnitude B at the center depends on the number of turns *per unit length* of the solenoid; we'll call that quantity n. If there are N turns distributed uniformly over a total length L, then $n = N/L$. The field magnitude at the center of the solenoid is given by

$$B = \mu_0 nI \qquad \text{(solenoid).} \qquad (31\text{–}6)$$

The best way to derive this relation is to use Ampere's law; we'll return to the derivation in Section 31–6.

A more general expression for the field at the center of a solenoid with any length L and radius R is

$$B = \frac{\mu_0 NI}{\sqrt{4R^2 + L^2}} \qquad \text{(solenoid).} \qquad (31\text{–}7)$$

When $L = 0$, we have a circular loop with N turns, and Eq. (31–7) reduces to Eq. (31–5). When L is much greater than R, it reduces to Eq. (31–6). We invite you to verify these two statements.

A variation is the **toroidal** (doughnut-shaped) **solenoid,** shown in Fig. 31–6. This shape has the interesting property that when there are many very closely spaced windings, the magnetic field is confined entirely to the space enclosed by the windings; there is no field at all outside this region. If there are N turns in all, then the field magnitude B at a distance r from the center of the torus (*not* from the center of its cross section) is given by

$$B = \frac{\mu_0 NI}{2\pi r} \qquad \text{(toroidal solenoid).} \qquad (31\text{–}8)$$

The magnetic field is *not* uniform over a cross section of the core, but is inversely proportional to r. But if the radial thickness of the core is small in comparison with the overall radius of the torus, the field is *nearly* uniform over a section. In that case, considering that $2\pi r$ is the circumference of the toroid and that $N/2\pi r$ is the number of turns per unit length n, then we can rewrite Eq. (31–8) as

$$B = \mu_0 nI,$$

just as at the center of a long, *straight* solenoid.

31–5
Magnetic-Field Calculations

In the preceding sections we quoted without derivation several equations for the magnetic fields caused by various shapes of conductors. Now let's have a look at how some of these equations are derived. We begin with the basics, the magnetic field ***B*** caused by a single point charge q moving

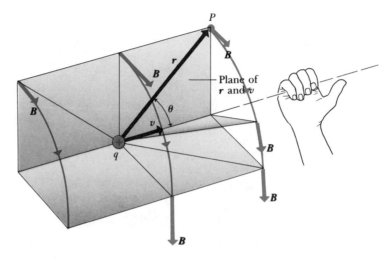

31–7
Magnetic-field vectors due to a moving positive point charge q. The field lines are circles with centers along the line of v.

with velocity v. We call the location of the charge the **source point,** and the point P where we want to find the field is called the **field point.** The distance between the two points is r.

Experiments show that the magnitude B of the field is proportional to q and to $1/r^2$. This reminds us of Coulomb's law. But the *direction* of B is *not* along the line from the source point to the field point. Instead, it is perpendicular to the plane containing this line and the particle's velocity vector v, as shown in Fig. 31–7. Furthermore, the field magnitude is proportional to the sine of the angle θ between these two directions. The magnitude B of the magnetic field at point P is given by

$$B = \frac{\mu_0}{4\pi} \frac{|q|v \sin \theta}{r^2}. \tag{31–9}$$

Figure 31–7 shows the magnetic field B at several points in the vicinity of the charge. At all points along a line through the charge parallel to the velocity v the field is zero because $\sin \theta = 0$ at all such points. At any distance r from q, B has its greatest magnitude at points lying in the plane through the charge perpendicular to v because at all such points $\theta = 90°$ and $\sin \theta = 1$. The charge also produces an *electric* field in its vicinity; the electric-field vectors are not shown in the figure.

The magnetic field lines are similar in character to those for a long, straight conductor; they are *circles* with centers along the line of v, lying in planes perpendicular to this line. We can also use the same right-hand rule as for the long straight conductor: Grasp the velocity vector v with your right hand so that your right thumb points in the direction of v; your fingers then curl around the line of v in the same sense as the magnetic field lines.

What if we have several point charges? For electric fields we could take the vector sum of the E fields of the individual charges; experiments show that this also works for magnetic fields. That is, the magnetic field obeys the **superposition principle:** *The total magnetic field caused by several moving charges is the vector sum of the fields caused by the individual charges.*

We can use the superposition principle to calculate the field caused by a current in a conductor. The magnetic field produced at any field

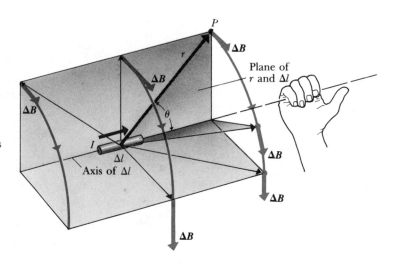

31–8
Magnetic-field vectors at various points due to a current segment. The field lines are circles with centers along the line of Δl.

point P by the current in a conductor is the vector sum of the fields due to all of the moving charges in the conductor. Let's think about the magnetic field produced by a short segment of conductor with length Δl and cross-sectional area A, carrying a current I, as shown in Fig. 31–8. The volume of the segment is $A\,\Delta l$. If we have n charges q per unit volume, then the total moving charge Q in the segment is

$$Q = nqA\,\Delta l.$$

These moving charges are equivalent to a single charge Q traveling with a velocity equal to the *drift* velocity v. From Eq. (31–9) the magnitude of the resulting field ΔB at any point caused by this segment of conductor is

$$\Delta B = \frac{\mu_0}{4\pi}\frac{Qv\,\sin\theta}{r^2} = \frac{\mu_0}{4\pi}\frac{nqvA\,\Delta l\,\sin\theta}{r^2}.$$

But $nqvA$ equals the current I in the element, as we found in Section 28–1, Eq. (28–2). Therefore

$$\Delta B = \frac{\mu_0}{4\pi}\frac{I\,\Delta l\,\sin\theta}{r^2}. \tag{31–10}$$

So a conductor segment Δl carrying a current I sets up a magnetic field ΔB with magnitude given by Eq. (31–10) and a direction perpendicular to the plane of Δl and the line joining the source and field points. Figure 31–8 shows that the field vectors ΔB are exactly like those set up by a positive charge Q moving in the direction of the drift velocity v. The field lines are circles lying in planes perpendicular to the axis of the segment of conductor. The direction of these lines is *clockwise* when viewed along the direction of the current. We can also describe this direction with the right-hand rule. Grasp the segment in your right hand with your thumb pointing in the direction of the current. Your fingers then encircle the element in the direction of the field lines.

We see from Eq. (31–10) that the field ΔB due to a segment of conductor is zero at all points on the axis of the segment because

$\sin \theta = 0$ at all such points. At any distance r from the segment the magnetic field is greatest at points in a plane passing through the segment perpendicular to its axis because for points in this plane, $\theta = 90°$ and $\sin \theta = 1$.

Equation (31–10) is called the **law of Biot and Savart.** To find the total magnetic field B at any point in space due to the current in a complete circuit, we have to find the *vector sum* of all the ΔB's due to all the segments of the conductor. This can become a sticky mathematical problem, but there are a few cases in which it is fairly simple.

We can't verify Eq. (31–10) directly because we can never experiment with an isolated segment of a current-carrying circuit. How would we get the current in and out? So we verify Eq. (31–10) indirectly by calculating B for various current configurations and comparing the results with experimental measurements.

As we remarked in Section 31–1, this formulation is strictly valid only when the conductors are surrounded with vacuum. When air or any nonmagnetic material is present, however, the formulation is in error by only about 0.1% or less. In Section 31–7 we will show how to modify the formulation to take account of material around the conductors.

PROBLEM-SOLVING STRATEGY: *Magnetic-Field Calculations*

1. Always make sure you can visualize the plane containing the segment Δl of conductor and the line joining it to the field point P; the field at P due to this segment is always perpendicular to this plane. Use the right-hand rule to find the direction of the field line passing through P.

2. In some problems the ΔB's at point P have the same direction for all the current elements. In that case the magnitude of the total B field is the sum of the magnitudes of the ΔB's. If the ΔB's have different directions for different current elements, then you have to set up a coordinate system and represent each ΔB in terms of its components. The vector sum for the total B is then expressed in terms of a sum for each component. Sometimes you can see from the symmetry of the situation that one component sums to zero. Be on the lookout for ways to use symmetry to simplify the problem.

3. You may need to use the superposition principle. Examples are several separated long, straight wires and several circular loops spaced out along an axis.

Example 31–4   Use the law of Biot and Savart to derive the expression for the magnetic field at the center of a circular conducting loop with radius R and current I.

Solution   We represent the loop as a large number of segments with lengths Δl_1, Δl_2, and so on. A typical segment with length Δl is shown in Fig. 31–9. All the segments are at the same distance R from the point P at the center, and each makes a right angle with the line joining it to P. The vectors ΔB_1, ΔB_2, and so on, due to the various segments, are all in the same direction, perpendicular to the plane of the loop, as shown. In

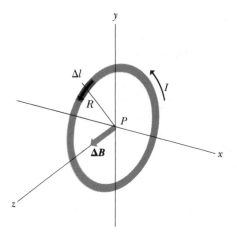

Magnetic field $\Delta \mathbf{B}$ caused by a segment Δl of a circular conducting loop. The segment, the radial line, and the direction of $\Delta \mathbf{B}$ are all mutually perpendicular.

Eq. (31-10), $\sin \theta = 1$ and $r = R$ for every segment. The total $\mathbf{B}$ magnitude is given by

$$B = \frac{\mu_0 I}{4\pi R^2}(\Delta l_1 + \Delta l_2 + \cdots).$$

But $\Delta l_1 + \Delta l_2 + \cdots$ is equal to the *circumference* of the loop, $2\pi R$, so

$$B = \frac{\mu_0 I}{2R}, \qquad (31\text{-}11)$$

in agreement with Eq. (31-4). ∎

Example 31-5   Use the law of Biot and Savart to find the magnetic field at a point on the axis of a circular loop with radius R and current I at a distance x from its center.

Solution   A typical segment Δl is shown in Fig. 31-10. This time the $\Delta \mathbf{B}$'s don't all have the same direction, but we can represent each one in terms of its components. As the figure shows, the segment Δl is always perpendicular to the line between it and the field point P; therefore $\sin \theta = 1$. The field $\Delta \mathbf{B}$ caused by the segment Δl shown lies in the xy-plane. Also, $r = (x^2 + R^2)^{1/2}$. For the segment Δl shown, Eq. (31-10) gives

$$\Delta B = \frac{\mu_0}{4\pi} \frac{I \Delta l}{(x^2 + R^2)}. \qquad (31\text{-}12)$$

To find the components of this $\Delta \mathbf{B}$, we first note from Fig. 31-10 that $\sin \alpha = R/(x^2 + R^2)^{1/2}$ and $\cos \alpha = x/(x^2 + R^2)^{1/2}$. The components of $\Delta \mathbf{B}$ are

$$\Delta B_x = \Delta B \sin \alpha = \frac{\mu_0}{4\pi} \frac{I \Delta l}{(x^2 + R^2)} \frac{R}{(x^2 + R^2)^{1/2}}, \qquad (31\text{-}13)$$

$$\Delta B_y = \Delta B \cos \alpha = \frac{\mu_0}{4\pi} \frac{I \Delta l}{(x^2 + R^2)} \frac{x}{(x^2 + R^2)^{1/2}}. \qquad (31\text{-}14)$$

Magnetic field of a circular loop. The segment Δl causes the field $\Delta \mathbf{B}$, lying in the xy-plane. Other Δl's have different components perpendicular to the x-axis; these add to zero, while the x-components combine to give the total $\mathbf{B}$ field at point P.

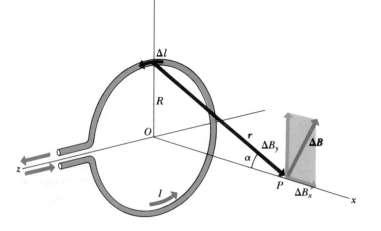

Because of symmetry about the x-axis, the components of $\boldsymbol{B}$ perpendicular to this axis must sum to zero. To see why this must be, consider a segment Δl on the opposite side of the loop. This element gives a contribution to the field with the same x-component as given by Eq. (31–13) but an *opposite* y-component. Similarly, all the components of $\boldsymbol{B}$ perpendicular to the x-axis set up by pairs of diametrically opposite elements cancel, leaving only the x-components.

To get the total x-component, we note that every Δl is multiplied by the same factor because x doesn't change as we go around the loop. Thus we obtain the total B_x by simply replacing Δl in Eq. (31–13) by the circumference of the circle, $2\pi R$. The result is

$$B = \frac{\mu_0 I R^2}{2(x^2 + R^2)^{3/2}}. \tag{31–15}$$

We get the corresponding result for N circular loops by inserting a factor of N in Eq. (31–15), the same way we obtained Eq. (31–5) from Eq. (31–4).

When $x = 0$, we are at the center of the loop, and Eq. (31–15) reduces to Eq. (31–4) when we set $x = 0$. We invite you to verify this. For points on the axis very far away from the center (compared to R) the R^2 in the denominator becomes negligible in comparison to x^2, and the expression becomes approximately equal to $\mu_0 I R^2/2x^3$. This says that at large distances the field magnitude along the axis is approximately proportional to $1/x^3$. ∎

Example 31–6   At what points along the axis of a circular loop does the magnetic field have half the magnitude it has at the center of the loop?

Solution   Using Eq. (31–15), we want to find a value of x for which

$$\frac{\mu_0 I R^2}{2(x^2 + R^2)^{3/2}} = \frac{1}{2}\frac{\mu_0 I R^2}{2R^3}.$$

We'll let you fill in the algebraic details of solving this for x; we first simplify the equation to obtain

$$(x^2 + R^2)^{3/2} = 2R^3.$$

Then we solve this for x; the result is

$$x = \pm\sqrt{2^{2/3} - 1}\,R = \pm 0.766R.$$

There are two points satisfying the requirement; they are located at opposite sides of the center at a distance of about three quarters of the radius from it. Is the direction of the field at these two points the same or opposite? ∎

31–6
Ampere's Law

Ampere's law provides an alternative formulation of the relationship between a magnetic field and its sources. In some problems it is more convenient than the law of Biot and Savart. Ampere's law is analogous to Gauss's law, which offers an alternative to Coulomb's law for electric-field calculations.

To introduce the basic idea, let's consider again the magnetic field caused by a long, straight conductor. We stated in Section 31–1, Eq. (31–1), that the field at a distance r from a long, straight conductor carrying a current I has magnitude

$$B = \frac{\mu_0 I}{2\pi r}$$

and that the magnetic field lines are circles centered on the conductor. The circumference of a circular field line with radius r is $2\pi r$. Now we note that for any r the product of B and the circumference is

$$B(2\pi r) = \frac{\mu_0 I}{2\pi r}(2\pi r) = \mu_0 I.$$

That is, this product is independent of r and depends only on the current I in the conductor.

This is a special case of Ampere's law. Here is the general statement: We construct an imaginary closed curve that encircles one or more conductors. We divide this curve into segments, calling a typical segment Δs. At each segment we take the component of $\boldsymbol{B}$ parallel to the segment; we call this component $B_\parallel$. We take all the products $B_\parallel \Delta s$ and add them as we go completely around the closed curve. The result of this sum is always equal to μ_0 times the total current in all the conductors that are encircled by the curve. Expressing this symbolically, we have

$$\sum B_\parallel \Delta s = \mu_0 I. \tag{31–16}$$

This is Ampere's law. Our initial example with the long, straight conductor used a circular path for which $B_\parallel$ was equal to B and was the same at each point of the path, so $\Sigma B_\parallel \Delta s$ was just equal to B multiplied by the circumference of the path. As with Gauss's law, the path that we use doesn't have to be the outline of any actual physical object; usually, it is a purely geometric curve that we construct to apply Ampere's law to a specific situation.

If several conductors pass through the surface bounded by the path, the total magnetic field at any point on the path is the vector sum of the fields produced by the individual conductors. Then we evaluate the sum in Eq. (31–16), using the *total* $\boldsymbol{B}$ field at each point. The result equals μ_0 times the *algebraic sum* of the currents. We need a sign rule for the currents; here it is: For the surface bounded by our Ampere's-law path, take a line perpendicular to the surface and wrap the fingers of your right hand around this line so that your fingers curl around in the same direction you plan to go around the path when you evaluate the $B_\parallel \Delta s$ sum.

Then your thumb indicates the positive current direction. Currents that pass through the surface in that direction are positive; those in the opposite direction are negative. Here's another way to say the same thing. Looking at the surface, proceed counterclockwise around the boundary to find the total current in Eq. (31–16). Any current moving toward you through the surface is counted as positive, and any current moving away from you as negative.

Ampere's law is particularly useful when you can use the symmetry of a situation to evaluate the sum $\Sigma B_\parallel \Delta s$. Following are several examples. Note that the problem-solving strategy we suggest is directly analogous to the strategy we suggested in Section 25–5 for applications of Gauss's law. We invite you to review that strategy now and compare the two methods.

PROBLEM-SOLVING STRATEGY: *Ampere's Law*

1. The first step is to select the path you will use with Ampere's law. If you want to learn something about the magnetic field at a certain point, then the path must pass through that point.

2. The path doesn't have to be any actual physical boundary. Usually, it is a purely geometric curve; it may be in empty space, embedded in a solid body, or some of each.

3. The path has to have enough *symmetry* to make it possible to evaluate the sum. If the problem itself has cylindrical symmetry, the path will usually be a circle coaxial with the cylinder axis.

4. If B is tangent to the path at every point and has the same magnitude B at every point, then $\Sigma B_\parallel \Delta s$ equals B multiplied by the circumference of the path.

5. If B is everywhere perpendicular to the path, for all or some portion of the path, that portion of the path makes no contribution to the sum.

6. In the sum $\Sigma B_\parallel \Delta s$, always obtain $B_\parallel$ from the *total* magnetic field B at each point on the path. In general, this field may be caused partly by currents enclosed by the path and partly by currents outside. Even when *no* net current is enclosed by the path, the field at points on the path need not be zero. In that case, however, $\Sigma B_\parallel \Delta s$ is always zero.

Example 31–7   *Field of a long straight conductor*. Because of the way we derived Ampere's law, we can reverse the process and use it to derive Eq. (31–1) for a long straight conductor. We take as our path a circle of radius r centered on the conductor and in a plane perpendicular to it. Then in Eq. (31–16), $\Sigma B_\parallel \Delta s = 2\pi r B$, and Eq. (31–1) follows immediately. ∎

Example 31–8   *Field inside a long cylindrical conductor*. To find the magnetic field *inside* a cylindrical conductor with radius R at a distance r from the axis, as in Fig. 31–11, we consider a circle of radius r. By symmetry, B has the same magnitude at every point on this circle and is tangent to it. Thus the sum in Ampere's law is simply $B(2\pi r)$. To find the current

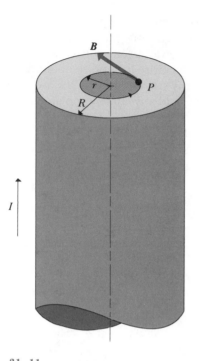

enclosed by the path, note that the current *density J* (current per unit area) is $J = I/\pi R^2$, so the current through the path is $I_r = J(\pi r^2) = Ir^2/R^2$. Ampere's law gives

$$2\pi rB = \mu_0 I \frac{r^2}{R^2} \qquad \text{or} \qquad B = \frac{\mu_0 I}{2\pi} \frac{r}{R^2}. \qquad (31\text{-}17)$$

Note that at $r = R$, that is, at the surface of the conductor, Eq. (31-1) (derived for $r > R$) and Eq. (31-17) (derived for $r < R$) agree. ■

31–11
The current through the color area is $(r^2/R^2)I$. To find the magnetic field at point P, we apply Ampere's law to the circle around the color area.

Example 31–9 *Field of a long solenoid.* In Section 31–4 we quoted the result $B = \mu_0 nI$ for the magnetic field at the center of a long solenoid. To derive this result from Ampere's law, we go counterclockwise around the path shown as a broken line in Fig. 31–12. Side ab, with length l, is parallel to the axis of the solenoid. We take sides bc and da to be very long, so side cd is far from the solenoid, and the field at this side is negligibly small.

From symmetry the **B** field along side ab is parallel to this side and is constant, so for this side, $B_\parallel = B$ and

$$\sum B_\parallel \Delta s = Bl.$$

Along sides bc and da, $B_\parallel = 0$ because B is perpendicular to these sides; along side cd, $B = 0$. The sum around the entire closed path therefore reduces to Bl.

If n is the number of turns *per unit length* in the windings, the number of turns in length l is nl. Each turn carries a current I, so the total current through the rectangle is nlI. From Ampere's law,

$$Bl = \mu_0 nlI \qquad \text{and} \qquad B = \mu_0 nI \qquad \text{(solenoid)}, \qquad (31\text{-}18)$$

31–12
Magnetic-field lines surrounding a solenoid. The dashed rectangle $abcd$ is used to compute the magnetic field **B** in the solenoid from Ampere's law.

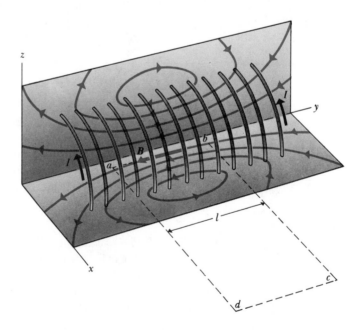

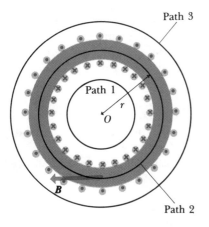

31–13
Closed paths (black circles) used to compute the magnetic field B set up by a current in a toroidal winding. The field is very nearly zero at all points except those within the space enclosed by the windings.

which agrees with Eq. (31–6). Note that we have not assumed that side ab lies along the axis but only that it is *parallel* to the axis. Thus the field is uniform across the entire cross section of the solenoid. ∎

Example 31–10   *Field of a toroidal solenoid.* Figure 31–13 shows a cross section of the toroidal solenoid we discussed in Section 31–4. To find the magnetic field inside the torus, we can apply Ampere's law to the black circles in the figure. Consider path 1 first. By symmetry, if there is any field at all in this region, it must be *tangent* to the path at all points, and $\Sigma B_{\parallel} \Delta s$ equals the product of B and the circumference $2\pi r$ of the path. The current through the path, however, is zero. From Ampere's law, then, the field B must be zero.

Similarly, if there is any field at path 3, it must also be tangent to the path at all points. Each turn of the winding passes *twice* through the area bounded by this path, carrying equal currents in opposite directions. The *net* current through this area is therefore zero, so again $B = 0$ at all points of the path. This corroborates our statement in Section 31–4 that the field of a toroidal solenoid is confined entirely to the space enclosed by the windings. (This is strictly true only in the limit of many very closely spaced windings.)

Finally, we consider path 2, a circle of radius r. Again, from symmetry the B field is tangent to the path, and $\Sigma B_{\parallel} \Delta s$ equals $2\pi rB$. Each turn of the winding passes *once* through the area bounded by path 2, and the total current through the area is NI, where N is the *total* number of turns in the winding. Then, from Ampere's law,

$$2\pi rB = \mu_0 NI,$$

and

$$B = \frac{\mu_0 NI}{2\pi r} \qquad \text{(toroidal solenoid).} \qquad (31\text{–}19)$$

This is the result we quoted at the end of Section 31–4, Eq. (31–8). ∎

*31–7
Magnetic Materials

In all the preceding discussion of magnetic fields caused by currents we assumed that the space surrounding the conductors contains only vacuum. If matter is present in the surrounding space, the magnetic field is changed. The atoms that make up all matter contain electrons in motion, and these electrons form microscopic current loops that produce magnetic fields of their own. In many materials these currents are randomly oriented, causing no net magnetic field. But in some materials the presence of an externally caused field can cause the loops to become oriented preferentially with the field so that their magnetic fields *add* to the external field. We then say that the material is *magnetized*.

TABLE 31–1 **Magnetic susceptibilities of paramagnetic and diamagnetic materials, at $T = 20°C$**	
Material	$\chi_m = K_m - 1$
Paramagnetic	
Iron ammonium	
alum	66×10^{-5}
Uranium	40×10^{-5}
Platinum	26×10^{-5}
Aluminum	2.2×10^{-5}
Sodium	0.72×10^{-5}
Oxygen gas	0.19×10^{-5}
Diamagnetic	
Bismuth	-16.6×10^{-5}
Mercury	-2.9×10^{-5}
Silver	-2.6×10^{-5}
Carbon	
(diamond)	-2.1×10^{-5}
Lead	-1.8×10^{-5}
Sodium chloride	-1.4×10^{-5}
Copper	-1.0×10^{-5}

A material showing this behavior is said to be **paramagnetic.** The result is that the magnetic field at any point in such a material is greater by a factor K_m than it would be if the material were not present. The value of K_m is different for different materials; it is called the **relative permeability** of the material. Values of K_m for common paramagnetic materials are typically 1.0001 to 1.0020.

All the equations in this chapter that relate magnetic fields to their sources can be adapted to the situation in which the conductor is embedded in a paramagnetic material by simply replacing μ_0 everywhere by $K_m\mu_0$. This product is usually denoted as μ; it is called the **permeability** of the material:

$$\mu = K_m\mu_0. \qquad (31-20)$$

The amount by which the relative permeability differs from unity is called the **magnetic susceptibility,** denoted by the symbol χ_m:

$$\chi_m = K_m - 1. \qquad (31-21)$$

Values of magnetic susceptibility for several materials are given in Table 31–1.

In some materials the total field due to the electrons in each atom sums to zero when there is no external field, and these materials have *no* net atomic current loops. But even in these materials, magnetic effects are present because an external field alters the electron motions to cause additional current loops. In this case the additional field caused by these current loops is always *opposite* in direction to that of the external field. (The reason for this is Faraday's law of induction, which we will study in Chapter 32. An induced current always tends to cancel the field change that caused it.) Such materials are said to be **diamagnetic;** they always have relative permeabilities slightly less than unity, typically of the order of 0.99990 to 0.99999. The susceptibility of a diamagnetic material is negative, as Table 31–1 shows.

There is a third class of materials, called **ferromagnetic** materials, in which the atomic current loops tend to line up parallel to each other even when no external field is present. This cooperative phenomenon leads to a relative permeability that is *much larger* than unity, typically of the order of 1,000 to 10,000. Iron, cobalt, nickel, and many alloys containing these elements are ferromagnetic.

Ferromagnetic materials differ in their behavior from paramagnetic and diamagnetic materials in two other important ways. First, the additional field caused by the microscopic current loops is *not* directly proportional to the external field except at relatively small field magnitudes. Thus for a ferromagnetic material, K_m is not constant. As the external field increases, a point is reached at which nearly all the microscopic current loops have their axes parallel to the external field. This condition is called *saturation magnetization*; after it is reached, a further increase in the external field causes no increase in magnetization or in the additional field caused by the material.

Second, some ferromagnetic materials retain their magnetization even when there is no externally caused field at all. These materials can thus become *permanent magnets*. Many kinds of steel and many alloys, such as Alnico, are commonly used for permanent magnets. The magnetic field in such a material, when it is magnetized to near saturation, is typically of the order of 1 T.

More generally, for many ferromagnetic materials the relationship of magnetization to magnetic field is different when the field is increasing from when it is decreasing. Thus the magnetization for a given field depends somewhat on the past history of the material. This phenomenon is called **hysteresis.** One consequence is the magnetization that remains when the field is reduced to zero, as we have mentioned. Magnetizing and demagnetizing a material that has hysteresis involve the dissipation of energy, and the temperature of such a material increases in this process.

Ferromagnetic materials are widely used in electromagnets, transformer cores, and motors and generators, in which it is desirable to have as large a magnetic field as possible for a given current. In these applications it is usually desirable for the material *not* to have permanent magnetization, that is, for it to have as little hysteresis as possible. Soft iron is often used; it has high permeability without appreciable hysteresis and permanent magnetization.

Questions

31–1 Streams of charged particles emitted from the sun during unusual sunspot activity create a disturbance in the earth's magnetic field. How does this happen?

31–2 A topic of current interest in physics research is the search (thus far unsuccessful) for an isolated magnetic pole, or magnetic *monopole*. If such an entity were found, how could it be recognized? What would its properties be?

31–3 What are the relative advantages and disadvantages of Ampere's law and the law of Biot and Savart for practical calculations of magnetic fields?

31–4 A student proposed to obtain an isolated magnetic pole by taking a bar magnet (N pole at one end, S at the other) and breaking it in half. Would this work?

31–5 Pairs of conductors carrying current into and out of the power-supply components of electronic equipment are sometimes twisted together to reduce magnetic-field effects. Why does this help?

31–6 The text discusses the magnetic field of an infinitely long, straight conductor carrying a current. Of course, there is no such thing as an infinitely long *anything*. How do you decide whether a particular wire is long enough to be considered infinite?

31–7 Suppose one has three long, parallel wires, arranged so that in cross section they are at the corners of an equilateral triangle. Is there any way to arrange the currents so that all three wires attract each other? So that all three wires repel each other?

31–8 Two parallel conductors carrying current in the same direction attract each other. If they are permitted to move toward each other, the forces of attraction do work. Where does the energy come from? Does this contradict the assertion in Chapter 30 that magnetic forces on moving charges do no work?

31–9 Considering the magnetic field of a circular loop of wire, would you expect the field to be greatest at the center or greater at some points in the plane of the loop but off-center?

31–10 Two concentric coplanar circular loops of wire, of different diameters, carry currents in the same direction. Describe the nature of the forces exerted on the inner loop.

31–11 A current was sent through a helical coil spring. The spring appeared to contract, as though it had been compressed. Why?

31–12 Using the fact that magnetic-field lines never have a beginning or an end, explain why it is reasonable for the field of a toroidal solenoid to be confined entirely to its interior, while a straight solenoid *must* have some field outside it.

31–13 A character in a popular comic strip has at various times proposed the possibility of "harnessing the earth's magnetic field" as a nearly inexhaustible source of energy. Comment on this concept.

31–14 Why should the permeability of a paramagnetic material be expected to decrease with increasing temperature?

31–15 In the discussion of magnetic forces on current loops in Section 30–8 it was found that no net force is exerted on a complete loop in a uniform magnetic field, only a torque. Yet magnetized materials, which

contain atomic current loops, certainly *do* experience net forces in magnetic fields. How is this discrepancy resolved?

31–16 What features of atomic structure determine whether an element is diamagnetic or paramagnetic?

31–17 The magnetic susceptibility of paramagnetic materials is quite strongly temperature dependent, while that of diamagnetic materials is nearly independent of temperature. Why the difference?

■ *Exercises*

Section 31–1   Magnetic Field of a Straight Conductor

31–1 Two hikers are reading a compass under an overhead transmission line that is 5.00 m above the ground and carries a current of 600 A in a horizontal direction from north to south.

a) Find the magnitude and direction of the magnetic field at a point on the ground directly under the conductor.

b) One hiker suggests that they walk on another 50 m to avoid inaccurate compass readings caused by the current. Considering that the magnitude of the earth's field is of the order of 0.5×10^{-4} T, is the current really a problem?

31–2 A long, straight telephone cable contains six wires, each carrying a current of 0.300 A. The distances between wires can be neglected.

a) If the currents in all six wires are in the same direction, what is the magnitude of the magnetic field 2.50 m from the cable?

b) If four wires carry currents in one direction and the other two carry currents in the opposite direction, what is the field magnitude 2.50 m from the cable?

31–3 We want to produce a magnetic field of magnitude 4.00×10^{-4} T at a distance of 0.050 m from a long, straight wire.

a) What current is required to produce this field?

b) With the current found in part (a), what is the magnitude of the field at a distance of 0.100 m from the wire? At 0.200 m?

31–4 A long, straight wire lies along the z-axis and carries a current of 4.00 A in the $-z$-direction. Determine the magnitude and direction of the magnetic field at the following points in the xy-plane:

a) $x = 0.200$ m, $y = 0$;

b) $x = 0$, $y = 0.200$ m;

c) $x = 0$, $y = -0.400$ m.

31–5 Two long, straight, horizontal parallel wires, one above the other, are separated by a distance $2a$. If the wires carry equal currents of magnitude I in opposite directions, what is the field magnitude in the plane of the wires at a point

a) midway between them?

b) at a distance a above the upper wire?

If the wires carry equal currents in the same direction, what is the field magnitude in the plane of the wires at a point

c) midway between them?

d) at a distance a above the upper wire?

Section 31–2   Force between Parallel Conductors

31–6 Two long, parallel wires are separated by a distance of 0.400 m, as shown in Fig. 31–14. The currents I_1 and I_2 have the directions shown.

a) Calculate the magnitude of the force exerted by each wire on a 0.500-meter length of the other. Is the force attractive or repulsive?

b) If each current is doubled, so that I_1 becomes 10.0 A and I_2 becomes 4.00 A, what is now the magnitude of the force each wire exerts on the other?

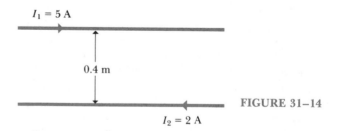

$I_1 = 5$ A

0.4 m

FIGURE 31–14

$I_2 = 2$ A

31–7 Two long, parallel wires are separated by a distance of 0.100 m. The force per unit length that each wire exerts on the other is 4.00×10^{-5} N·m^{-1}, and the wires repel each other. If the current in one wire is 2.00 A,

a) what is the current in the second wire?

b) are the two currents in the same or in opposite directions?

31–8 Three parallel wires each carry current I in the directions shown in Fig. 31–15. If the separation between adjacent wires is d, calculate the magnitude and direction of the resultant magnetic force per unit length on each wire.

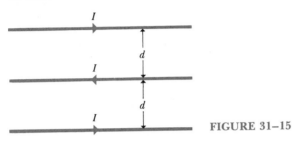

FIGURE 31–15

31–9 A long, horizontal wire AB rests on the surface of a table. (See Fig. 31–16.) Another wire CD vertically above the first is 0.400 m long and free to slide up and down on the two vertical metal guides C and D. The two wires are connected through the sliding contacts and carry a current of 30.0 A. The mass per unit length of the wire CD is 5.00×10^{-3} kg·m^{-1}. To what equilibrium height h will the wire CD rise, assuming that the magnetic force on it is due wholly to the current in the wire AB?

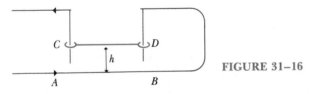

FIGURE 31–16

Section 31–3 Magnetic Field of a Circular Loop

31–10 A closely wound circular coil with a radius of 5.00 cm has 300 turns and carries a current of 0.200 A. What is the magnitude of the magnetic field at the center of the coil?

31–11 A closely wound coil has a diameter of 18.0 cm and carries a current of 2.50 A. How many turns does it have if the magnetic field at the center of the coil is 2.09×10^{-4} T?

Section 31–4 Magnetic Field of a Solenoid

31–12 A solenoid with a length of 20.0 cm and a radius of 3.00 cm is closely wound with 400 turns of wire. The current in the winding is 5.00 A. Compute the magnetic field at a point near the center of the solenoid.

31–13 Verify that Eq. (31–7) reduces to Eq. (31–5) when $L = 0$ and to Eq. (31–6) when L is much greater than R.

31–14 A toroidal solenoid (Fig. 31–6) has inner radius $r_1 = 0.200$ m and outer radius $r_2 = 0.280$ m. The solenoid has 300 turns and carries a current of 2.50 A. What is the magnetic field at each of the following distances from the center of the torus:

a) 0.150 m?   b) 0.240 m?   c) 0.350 m?

31–15 A solenoid is to be designed to produce a magnetic field of 0.180 T at its center. The radius is to be 2.50 cm and the length 50.0 cm, and the available wire can carry a maximum current of 10.0 A.

a) What is the minimum number of turns per unit length the solenoid must have?

b) What total length of wire is required?

31–16 A wooden ring whose mean diameter is 0.120 m is wound with a closely spaced toroidal winding of 500 turns. Compute the magnetic field at a point at the center of the cross section of the windings when the current in the windings is 0.300 A.

Section 31–5 Magnetic-Field Calculations

31–17 Refer to Fig. 31–4. Sketch a graph of the magnitude of the B field on the axis of the loop from $x = -3R$ to $x = +3R$.

31–18 A positive point charge with $q = 5.00$ μC has velocity in the $+x$-direction with magnitude $v = 7.00 \times 10^5$ m·s^{-1}. At the instant when the point charge is at the origin, what are the magnitude and direction of the magnetic field vector B it produces at the following points:

a) $x = 0.500$ m, $y = 0$, $z = 0$?

b) $x = 0$, $y = -0.500$ m, $z = 0$?

c) $x = 0$, $y = 0$, $z = +0.500$ m?

d) $x = 0$, $y = 0$, $z = -0.500$ m?

31–19 A pair of point charges, $q = +5.00$ μC and $q' = +3.00$ μC, are moving as shown in Fig. 31–17. At this instant, what are the magnitude and direction of

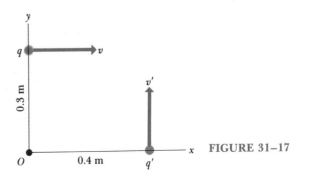

FIGURE 31–17

the magnetic field produced at the origin (point O)? Take $v = v' = 3.00 \times 10^5$ m·s^{-1}.

31–20 A long, straight wire carrying a current of 200 A runs through a cubical wooden box, entering and leaving through holes in the centers of opposite faces, as in Fig. 31–18. The length of each side of the box is 20.0 cm. Consider an element of the wire 1.00 cm long at the center of the box. Compute the magnitude ΔB of the magnetic field produced by this element at the points lettered a, b, c, d, and e in Fig. 31–18. Points a, c, and d are at the centers of the faces of the cube; point b is at the midpoint of one edge; and point e is at a corner. Copy the figure and show by vectors the directions and relative magnitudes of the field vectors. (*Note:* Assume that Δl is small in comparison to the distances from the current element to the points where $\mathbf{B}$ is to be calculated.)

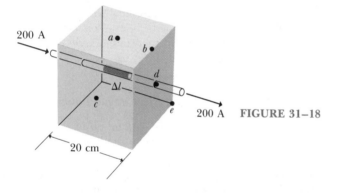

FIGURE 31–18

31–21 For the coil in Exercise 31–10, what is the magnitude of the magnetic field at a point on the axis of the coil 10.0 cm from its center?

31–22 Calculate the magnitude and direction of the magnetic field at point P due to the current in the semicircular section of wire shown in Fig. 31–19. (Does the current in the long, straight section of the wire produce any field at P?)

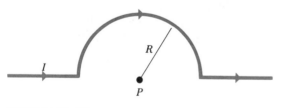

FIGURE 31–19

31–23 Calculate the magnitude of the magnetic field at point P of Fig. 31–20 in terms of R, I_1, and I_2. What does your expression give when $I_1 = I_2$?

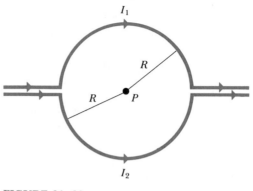

FIGURE 31–20

Section 31–6   Ampere's Law

31–24 A closed curve encircles several conductors. The sum of $B_\parallel \Delta s$ around this curve is 2.80×10^{-5} T·m. What is the net current in the conductors?

31–25 A coaxial cable consists of a solid conductor of radius R_1, supported by insulating disks on the axis of a tube with inner radius R_2 and outer radius R_3. If the central conductor and tube carry equal currents I in opposite directions, derive an expression for the magnetic field

a) at points outside the central solid conductor but inside the tube ($R_1 < r < R_2$);

b) at points outside the tube ($r > R_3$).

31–26 Repeat Exercise 31–25 for the case in which the current in the central solid conductor is I_1 and the current in the tube is I_2 in the opposite direction to I_1.

31–27 Repeat Exercise 31–25 for the case in which the current in the central solid conductor is I_1 and that in the tube is I_2. Also take these currents to be in the same direction rather than in opposite directions.

Section 31–7   Magnetic Materials

31–28 A toroidal solenoid having 500 turns of wire and a mean radius of 0.0800 m carries a current of 0.800 A. The relative permeability of the core is 600.

a) What is the magnetic field in the core?

b) What fraction of the magnetic field is due to atomic currents?

31–29 Experimental measurements of the magnetic susceptibility of iron ammonium alum are given below. Make a graph of $1/\chi$ against Kelvin temperature. What conclusion can you draw? (These data illustrate what is called the Curie law.)

T, °C	χ
−258.15	129×10^{-4}
−173	19.4×10^{-4}
−73	9.7×10^{-4}
27	6.5×10^{-4}

31–30 A toroidal solenoid with 400 turns is wound on a ring having a mean radius of 3.80 cm. Find the current in the winding that is required to set up a magnetic field of 0.100 T in the ring

 a) if the ring is of annealed iron ($K_m = 1400$);

 b) if the ring is of silicon steel ($K_m = 5200$).

Problems

31–31 Figure 31–21 is an end view of two long, parallel wires perpendicular to the *xy*-plane, each carrying a current *I*, but in opposite directions.

 a) Copy the diagram, and show by vectors the ***B*** field of each wire and the resultant ***B*** field at point *P*.

 b) Derive the expression for the magnitude of ***B*** at any point on the *x*-axis in terms of the coordinate *x* of the point. What is the direction of ***B***?

 c) Construct a graph of the magnitude of ***B*** at points on the *x*-axis, for *x* between 0 and 2*a*.

31–34 Two long, straight, parallel wires are 1.00 m apart, as in Fig. 31–22. The upper wire carries a current I_1 of 6.00 A into the plane of the paper.

 a) What must be the magnitude and direction of the current I_2 for the resultant field at point *P* to be zero?

 b) What are then the magnitude and direction of the resultant field at *Q*?

 c) What is then the magnitude of the resultant field at *S*?

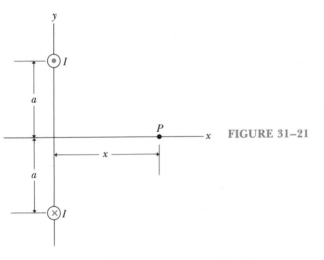

FIGURE 31–21

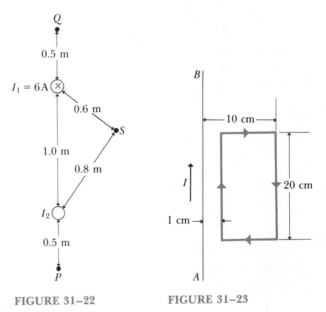

FIGURE 31–22   FIGURE 31–23

31–32 Same as Problem 31–31, except that the current in both wires is directed into the plane of the figure.

31–33 In Fig. 31–21, suppose a third long, straight wire, parallel to the other two, passes through point *P* and that each wire carries a current *I* = 15.0 A. Let *a* = 0.300 m and *x* = 0.400 m. Find the magnitude and direction of the force per unit length on the third wire

 a) if the current in it is directed into the plane of the figure;

 b) if the current is directed out of the plane of the figure.

(Use the results of Problem 31–31.)

31–35 The long, straight wire *AB* in Fig. 31–23 carries a current of 16.0 A. The rectangular loop whose long edges are parallel to the wire carries a current of 5.00 A. Find the magnitude and direction of the resultant force exerted on the loop by the magnetic field of the wire.

31–36 A long, straight wire carries a current of 1.50 A. An electron travels with a speed of $5.00 \times 10^4 \ \text{m·s}^{-1}$ parallel to the wire, 0.0600 m from it, and in the same direction as the current. What are the magnitude and direction of the force that the magnetic field of the current exerts on the moving electron?

31–37 Two long, parallel wires are hung by cords 4.00 cm long from a common axis, as shown in Fig. 31–24. The wires have a mass per unit length of 0.0300 kg·m^{-1} and carry the same current in opposite directions. What is the current if the cords hang at an angle of 6.00° with the vertical?

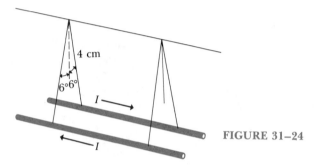

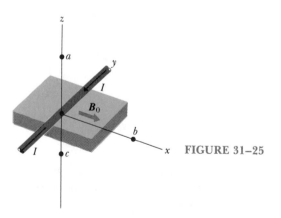

FIGURE 31–24

31–38 A long, straight wire carries a current of 8.00 A directed along the y-axis and in the $-y$-direction, as shown in Fig. 31–25. In addition to the magnetic field due to the current in the wire, a uniform magnetic field $\mathbf{B}_0$ with magnitude 8.00×10^{-7} T is directed parallel to the x-axis. Determine the resultant magnetic field (magnitude and direction) at the following points:

a) $x = 0$, $z = 2.00$ m;

b) $x = 2.00$ m, $z = 0$;

c) $x = 0$, $z = -2.00$ m.

31–39 Figure 31–26 is a sectional view of two circular coils of radius a, each wound with N turns of wire carrying a current I, circulating in the same direction in both coils. The coils are separated by a distance a equal

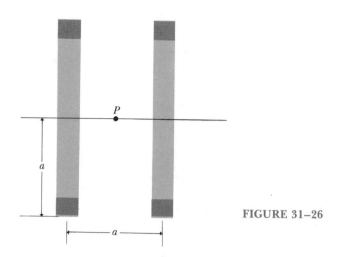

FIGURE 31–26

to their radii. In this configuration the coils are called Helmholtz coils; they produce a very uniform magnetic field in the region midway between the two coils.

a) Derive the expression for the magnetic field at a point on the axis a distance x to the right of point P that is midway between the coils.

b) Sketch a graph of B versus x for $x = 0$ to $x = a/2$. Compare this sketch to one for the magnetic field due to the right-hand coil alone.

c) From part (a), obtain an expression for the magnetic field at point P.

d) Calculate the magnitude of $\mathbf{B}$ at P if $N = 300$ turns, $I = 5.00$ A, and $a = 0.300$ m.

31–40 The wire semicircles in Fig. 31–27 have radii a and b. Calculate the resultant magnetic field (magnitude and direction) at point P.

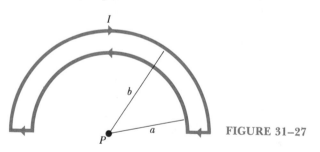

FIGURE 31–27

31–41 The current in the windings on a toroid is 2.00 A. There are 400 turns, and the mean radius is 0.0640 m. The magnetic field inside the windings is 1.40 T. Calculate

a) the relative permeability;

b) the magnetic susceptibility

of the material that fills the toroid.

31–42 A conductor is made in the form of a hollow cylinder with inner and outer radii a and b, respectively. It carries a current I, uniformly distributed over its cross section. Derive expressions for the magnitude of the magnetic field in the regions

   a) $r < a$,   b) $a < r < b$,   c) $r > b$.

31–43 Consider the coaxial cable of Exercise 31–25. Assume the currents to be uniformly distributed over the cross sections of the solid conductor and the tube. Calculate the magnitude of the magnetic field at

   a) $r < R_1$ (inside the central conductor; does your answer give the expected result for $r = R_1$?);

   b) $R_2 < r < R_3$ (inside the outer tube; does your answer give the expected results for $r = R_3$ and for $r = R_2$?).

Challenge Problems

31–44 The wire in Fig. 31–28 is infinitely long and carries current I. Calculate the magnitude and direction of the magnetic field this current produces at point P. (*Hint:* This problem can be done without detailed calculation!)

31–45 A thin disk of dielectric material with radius a has a total charge $+Q$ distributed uniformly over its surface. It rotates n times per second about an axis perpendicular to the surface of the disk and passing through its center. Find the magnetic field at the center of the disk. (*Hint:* Divide the disk into narrow concentric rings.)

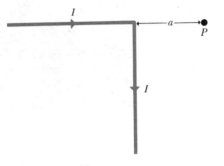

FIGURE 31–28

32

Electromagnetic Induction

We return in this chapter to the subject of electromotive force, a topic we studied in Chapter 28. Electromotive force is what keeps the charge going around and around in a circuit. Our main interest in this chapter is electromotive force of *magnetic* origin. The machinery for large-scale production, distribution, and use of electrical energy, including generators, transformers, and motors, all depend directly on magnetically induced emf's. Our present-day power distribution systems would not be possible if we had to depend on chemical sources of emf such as batteries.

We begin by studying the emf developed in a conductor moving in a magnetic field. Then we develop a more general relationship between emf and changing magnetic flux in a conducting loop; this relationship is called *Faraday's law*. We also discuss *Lenz's law*, which helps us to determine the directions of induced emf's and currents. This chapter provides the principles we need to understand electrical energy conversion devices, including motors, generators, and transformers, and it also paves the way for analysis of electromagnetic waves in Chapter 35.

32–1
Induction Phenomena

We begin our study of magnetically induced electromotive force with a look at several pioneering experiments carried out in the 1830s by Michael Faraday in England and Joseph Henry (first director of the Smithsonian Institution) in the United States. Figure 32–1a shows a coil of wire connected to a current-measuring device such as the d'Arsonval galvanometer we described in Section 29–3. Near the coil is a bar magnet. When the magnet is stationary, the meter shows no current, as we would expect with no source of emf in the circuit. But if we move the magnet either toward or away from the coil, the meter shows current in the circuit *while the magnet is moving*. If we hold the magnet stationary and move the coil and meter, the same thing happens. So something about the *changing* magnetic field through the coil is causing a current in the circuit. We call this an **induced current,** and the corresponding emf that has to be present to cause this current is called an **induced emf.**

The same effect occurs when the source of magnetic field is current in another circuit, as in Fig. 32–1b. We find that when the second coil is stationary, there is no current in the first coil. But when we move the second coil toward or away from the first or the first coil toward or away from the second, there is current in the first coil *during the motion*. In these experiments, as well as those with the bar magnet, the essential feature seems to be the *relative* motion of the two parts of the setup.

Finally, using the two-coil setup in Fig. 32–1c, we keep both coils stationary and vary the current in the second coil, either by opening and closing the switch or by changing the resistance R in its circuit. We find that as we open or close the switch, there is a momentary current pulse in

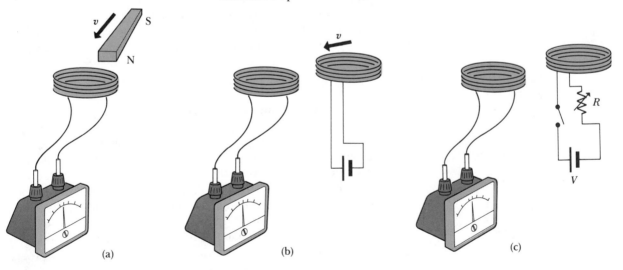

(a)   (b)   (c)

32–1
(a) A magnet moving near a coil of wire connected to a galvanometer induces a current in the coil. (b) A second coil carrying a current moves toward the coil connected to the galvanometer, inducing a current in it. (c) A changing current in the second coil induces a current in the first coil.

the first circuit. When we vary the current in the second coil, there is an induced current in the first circuit *while the current in the second circuit is changing*.

What do all these experiments have in common? The answer, which we will explore in detail in this chapter, is that *changing magnetic flux* in the meter circuit, from whatever cause, induces a current in that circuit. This statement forms the basis of Faraday's law of induction, the main subject of this chapter.

32–2
Motional Electromotive Force

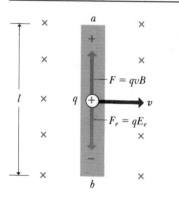

32–2
Conducting rod in a uniform magnetic field.

As the first step in our study of magnetically induced electromotive force, let's look at what happens when a conductor moves in a magnetic field. Figure 32–2 shows a conductor, such as a metal rod, with length l in a uniform magnetic field B perpendicular to the plane of the figure and directed *into* the page. We give the rod a constant velocity v to the right; a charged particle q in the rod then experiences a force F with magnitude $F = qvB$. If q is positive, the direction of this force is *upward* along the rod, from b toward a.

This force makes the free charges in the rod move, creating an excess of positive charge at the upper end a and of negative charge at the lower end b. This in turn creates an electric field E in the direction from a to b, which exerts a downward force qE on the charges. The accumulation of charge at the ends of the rod continues until E is large enough for the downward electric-field force (magnitude qE) to cancel exactly the upward magnetic-field force (magnitude qvB). Then $qE = qvB$, and the charges are in equilibrium, with point a at higher potential than point b.

What is the magnitude of the potential difference V_{ab}? It is the electric-field magnitude E multiplied by the distance l. From the above discussion, $E = vB$, so

$$V_{ab} = El = vBl, \tag{32–1}$$

with point a at higher potential than point b.

Now suppose the moving rod slides along a stationary U-shaped conductor, forming a complete circuit, as shown in Fig. 32–3. No magnetic force acts on the charges in the stationary conductor, but it lies in the electrostatic field caused by the charge accumulations at a and b. Under the action of this field a current is established in the counterclockwise sense around this complete circuit. The moving rod has become a source of electromotive force; within it, charge moves from lower to higher potential, and in the remainder of the circuit, charge moves from higher to lower potential. We call this a **motional electromotive force,** denoted by $\mathcal{E}$; we can write

$$\mathcal{E} = vBl. \tag{32–2}$$

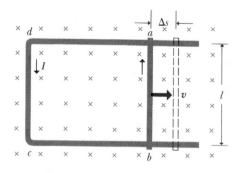

32–3
Current produced by the motion of a conductor in a magnetic field.

If the resistance of the sliding bar is negligible, then $\mathcal{E}$ is also equal to the potential difference V_{ab}. For a real rod with finite resistance r there is a potential drop Ir, and the potential difference between the ends of the bar is *less* than $\mathcal{E}$ by this amount:

$$V_{ab} = \mathcal{E} - Ir. \qquad (32\text{–}3)$$

If the external circuit has resistance R, then V_{ab} is also equal to IR. When we replace V_{ab} with IR in Eq. (32–3) and rearrange, we find that

$$I = \frac{\mathcal{E}}{R + r}. \qquad (32\text{–}4)$$

If the velocity v of the rod is not perpendicular to the field B but makes an angle ϕ with it, then we replace v in Eq. (32–2) by $v \sin \phi$, and the induced emf is

$$\mathcal{E} = v \sin \phi \, Bl. \qquad (32\text{–}5)$$

The emf associated with the moving rod in Fig. 32–3 is analogous to that of a battery with its positive terminal at a and negative terminal at b. Equation (32–3) has the same form as the corresponding relationship for a battery, Eq. (28–13), although the origins of the two emf's are completely different. In each case a non-electrostatic force acts on the charges in the device in the direction from b to a. When the device is connected to an external circuit, the direction of current is from a to b in the external circuit and from b to a in the device.

If we express v in meters per second, B in teslas, and l in meters, $\mathcal{E}$ is in joules per coulomb or volts; we invite you to verify this.

Example 32–1   Suppose the length l in Fig. 32–3 is 0.1 m, the velocity v is 0.1 m·s^{-1}, the total resistance of the loop is 0.01 Ω, and B is 1 T. Find $\mathcal{E}$, the induced current, the force acting on the rod, and the mechanical power needed to keep the rod moving.

Solution   From Eq. (32–2) the emf $\mathcal{E}$ is

$$\mathcal{E} = vBl = (0.1 \text{ m·s}^{-1})(1 \text{ T})(0.1 \text{ m}) = 0.01 \text{ V}.$$

From Eq. (32–4) the current in the loop is

$$I = \frac{0.01 \text{ V}}{0.01 \text{ Ω}} = 1 \text{ A}.$$

Because of this current, a force F acts on the rod in the direction *opposite* to its motion. From Eq. (30–14) this force is given by

$$F = IBl = (1 \text{ A})(1 \text{ T})(0.1 \text{ m}) = 0.1 \text{ N}.$$

To make the loop move with constant velocity, despite this resisting force, we have to apply an equal and opposite additional force. The rate at which this additional force does work is the *power P* needed to move the rod

$$P = Fv = (0.1 \text{ N})(0.1 \text{ m·s}^{-1}) = 0.01 \text{ W}.$$

The product $\mathcal{E}I$ is

$$\mathcal{E}I = (0.01 \text{ V})(1 \text{ A}) = 0.01 \text{ W}.$$

The rate at which electrical energy is delivered to the circuit, $\mathcal{E}I$, equals the mechanical power input, Fv, to the system, as we should expect. Finally, the rate of *dissipation* of electrical energy, that is, conversion to heat, is $P = I^2R = (1\ \text{A})^2(0.01\ \Omega) = 0.01\ \text{W}$, also as we should expect.   ∎

Example 32–2   The rectangular loop in Fig. 32–4, with length a and width b, rotates with constant angular velocity ω about the y-axis. The entire loop lies in a uniform, constant $\boldsymbol{B}$ field parallel to the z-axis. Calculate the induced emf in the loop from Eq. (32–2).

Solution   Each point on the sides with length a moves in a circle with radius $b/2$. From Eq. (9–12) the speed v of each of these sides is

$$v = \omega \frac{b}{2}.$$

The motional emf in each of these sides is

$$\mathcal{E} = vB \sin \theta\, a = \tfrac{1}{2}\omega B\, ab \sin \theta.$$

These two sides are in series, and their emf's add, just like two batteries in series. So the total emf due to these two sides is

$$\mathcal{E} = \omega B\, ab \sin \theta.$$

The magnetic forces on the other two sides of the loop (with length b) are transverse to these sides, and they don't contribute to the emf.

The product ab is the area A of the loop. If the loop lies in the xy-plane at $t = 0$ and turns with constant angular velocity ω, then $\theta = \omega t$ and

$$\mathcal{E} = \omega AB \sin \omega t. \tag{32–6}$$

The emf therefore varies *sinusoidally* with time. The *maximum* value of $\mathcal{E}$,

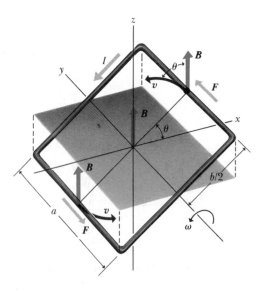

32–4
Rectangular loop rotating with constant angular velocity in a uniform magnetic field. The directions of the magnetic-field forces $\boldsymbol{F}$ on the moving charges are shown.

which we will call $\mathcal{E}_m$, occurs when $\sin \omega t = 1$:

$$\mathcal{E}_m = \omega AB,$$

so we can also write Eq. (32–6) as

$$\mathcal{E} = \mathcal{E}_m \sin \omega t. \qquad (32-7)$$

■

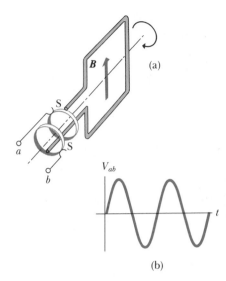

(a)

V_{ab}

(b)

32–5
(a) Schematic diagram of an alternator using a conducting loop rotating in a magnetic field. Connections to the external circuit are made by means of the slip rings S. (b) The resulting emf at terminals *ab*.

The rotating loop is the prototype of one type of alternating-current generator, or *alternator*; it develops a sinusoidally varying emf. The emf is greatest (in absolute value) when $\theta = 90°$ or $270°$ and the long sides are moving across (at right angles to) the field. The emf is zero when $\theta = 0$ or $180°$ and the long sides are moving parallel or antiparallel to the field. We will show in the next section that the emf depends only on the *area A* of the loop and not on its shape.

The rotating loop in Fig. 32–4 can serve as a source of emf in an external circuit by use of two *slip rings* S, which rotate with the loop, as shown in Fig. 32–5a. Stationary brushes sliding on the rings are connected to the output terminals *a* and *b*. Figure 32–5b is a graph of V_{ab} as a function of time.

We can use a similar scheme to obtain an emf that always has the same sign. The arrangement shown in Fig. 32–6a is called a *commutator*; it reverses the connections to the external circuit at angular positions where the emf reverses. The resulting emf is shown in Fig. 32–6b. This device is the prototype of a dc generator. Commerical dc generators have a large number of coils and commutator segments; this smooths out the bumps in the emf, so the terminal voltage is not only one-directional but also practically constant.

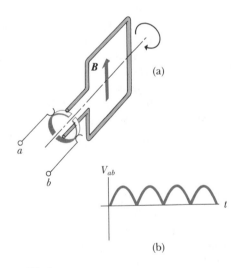

(a)

V_{ab}

(b)

32–6
(a) Schematic diagram of a dc generator using a split-ring commutator. (b) The resulting induced emf at terminals *ab*.

Example 32–3   A disk with radius R, shown in Fig. 32–7, lies in the *xy*-plane and rotates with constant angular velocity ω about the *z*-axis. The disk is in a uniform, constant **B** field parallel to the *z*-axis. Find the induced emf between the center and the rim of the disk.

Solution   The complicating feature of this problem is that different parts of the disk move at different speeds. Let's take as our moving conductor a narrow wedge or sector of the disk. We divide this thin sector into segments; the radial length of a typical segment is Δr, as shown. The speed v of this segment is $v = \omega r$, and the motional emf $\Delta \mathcal{E}$ due to the segment is

$$\Delta \mathcal{E} = vB \, \Delta r = \omega Br \, \Delta r.$$

The total emf between center and rim is the sum of all such contributions:

$$\mathcal{E} = \sum \omega Br \, \Delta r = \omega B \sum r \, \Delta r.$$

The segments Δr near the edge of the disk, where r is nearly equal to R, contribute more to the total emf than do those closer to the axis, where r

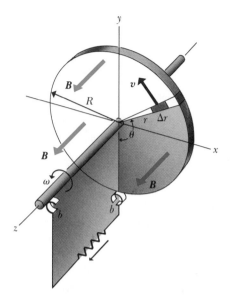

32–7
A Faraday disk dynamo. The emf is induced along radial lines of the rotating disk and is connected to an external circuit through the sliding contacts *bb*.

is smaller. The contributions increase proportionally with r, so to evaluate the sum, we simply replace r by its *average* value $R/2$; then

$$\sum r \, \Delta r = \sum \left(\frac{R}{2}\right) \Delta r = \left(\frac{R}{2}\right) \sum \Delta r = \left(\frac{R}{2}\right) R = \frac{1}{2} R^2,$$

and the total emf is

$$\mathcal{E} = \tfrac{1}{2}\omega B R^2. \tag{32–8}$$

All of the radial sectors of the disk are in *parallel*, so the emf between center and rim is the same as that in any sector. We can think of the entire disk as a single source, and the emf between center and rim is given by Eq. (32–8). We can use this device as a source in a circuit by completing the circuit through sliding contacts or brushes *bb*. The emf in such a disk was studied by Faraday; the device is a called a *Faraday disk dynamo* or a *homopolar generator*. ∎

We pointed out in Section 30–4 that the magnetic-field force on a moving charged particle never does any *work* on the particle because $\boldsymbol{F}$ and $\boldsymbol{v}$ are always perpendicular. Yet the motional emf has the effect of transporting charge from regions of lower to higher potential, so it appears that the upward force qvB in Fig. 32–2 must do work. How do we resolve this apparent paradox?

The resolution is somewhat subtle, and we can't go into it very deeply here. Briefly, what happens is that the vertical motion of the charges in the moving rod in Fig. 32–3 causes a transverse (horizontal) magnetic-field force and thus a transverse displacement of charge, corresponding to the Hall effect we discussed in Section 30–10. Thus there is a transverse *electrostatic* field in the rod, from left to right in the example of Fig. 32–3. As the rod moves to the right, it is this electrostatic force that actually does work on the moving charges. Detailed analysis shows that this work is the same *as though* it had been done by the vertical force qvB during the vertical displacement of the moving charges.

32–3
Faraday's Law

We analyzed the induced emf in the circuit of Fig. 32–3 by computing the magnetic-field forces on the mobile charges in the moving conductor. We can also look at this situation from a different viewpoint based on the changing *magnetic flux* through the circuit. When the conductor moves toward the right a distance Δs, the *area* enclosed by the circuit *abcd* increases by an amount $\Delta A = l \, \Delta s$, and the magnetic *flux* through the circuit increases by an amount $\Delta \Phi$ given by

$$\Delta \Phi = B \, \Delta A = Bl \, \Delta s.$$

The *rate of change* of flux is therefore

$$\frac{\Delta \Phi}{\Delta t} = \frac{\Delta s}{\Delta t} Bl = vBl. \tag{32–9}$$

The product vBl equals the induced emf $\mathcal{E}$, so this equation states that *the induced emf in a circuit is equal to the time rate of change of the magnetic flux through it.*

To state this relationship precisely, we need a sign rule. The rule is similar to the one we used with Ampère's law. As you look at the surface bounded by the circuit under consideration, an emf that causes a *counterclockwise* current is considered positive, and one that causes a *clockwise* current is negative. Flux is positive when the **B** field through the area points *toward* you and negative when it points away from you. Let's check these with Fig. 32–3. The field **B** points *into* the plane, so the magnetic flux is negative. As the bar moves, the flux becomes larger in magnitude, and hence more negative, and $\Delta\Phi/\Delta t$ is a *negative* quantity. But our previous analysis has shown that the induced current is *counterclockwise*; according to the above definition, the associated emf $\mathcal{E}$ is *positive*. So, at least in this situation, $\mathcal{E}$ and $\Delta\Phi/\Delta t$ have opposite sign, and we write

$$\mathcal{E} = -\frac{\Delta\Phi}{\Delta t}. \qquad (32\text{–}10)$$

Here is an alternative way to state the same rule. Hold your right hand with thumb extended perpendicular to the area. Go around the loop in the direction your fingers curl, and count the flux as positive if the field is in the direction your thumb points, negative if the field is opposite. If these sign rules seem a little obscure, don't despair; they will become clearer as we work out some examples. It's important to be precise about signs right from the start so that we can relate this equation to others that we will study later.

Equation (32–10) is called **Faraday's law,** or *Faraday's law of induction.* It may appear to be just an alternative form of Eq. (32–2) for the emf in a moving conductor. It turns out, though, that it has much broader significance than you might expect from this derivation. It is applicable to *any* circuit in which there is a varying flux, even when no part of the circuit is moving and thus there is no emf that we can attribute directly to a magnetic-field force.

For example, consider the two loops of wire in Fig. 32–8. A current in circuit 1 sets up a magnetic field, and the magnitude of the field at every point is proportional to the current. This field causes a magnetic flux through circuit 2; if the current in circuit 1 increases or decreases, the flux through circuit 2 also changes. Circuit 2 is not moving in a magnetic field, so no "motional" emf is induced in it. But the changing flux *does* cause an emf in circuit 2, and experiment shows that it is given by $\mathcal{E} = -\Delta\Phi/\Delta t$. In this situation the source of emf isn't localized in a particular portion of the circuit as it was in Fig. 32–3; we have to consider it as distributed around the entire circuit.

Here is another example. Suppose we set up a magnetic field in the toroidal solenoid of Fig. 32–9, link the toroid with a conducting ring, and vary the current in the winding of the toroid. We have shown that the magnetic field set up by a steady current in a toroidal winding is confined to the space enclosed by the winding. Not only is the ring not *moving* in a magnetic field, but if the current were steady, the ring would not even be *in* a magnetic field! However, field lines do pass through the area bounded by the ring, and the flux changes as the current in the

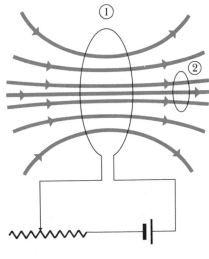

32–8
As the current in circuit 1 is varied, the magnetic flux through circuit 2 changes.

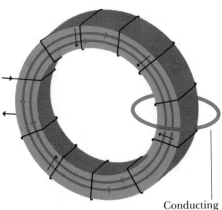

Conducting ring

32–9
An emf is induced in the ring when the flux in the toroid varies.

toroid winding changes. Equation (32–10) predicts an induced emf in the ring, and we find by experiment that the emf actually exists. We will discuss this class of induction phenomena more in Section 32–4. The apparatus in Fig. 32–9 illustrates the principle of operation of the *transformer*, which we will discuss in Section 34–7.

To sum up, then, an emf is induced in a circuit whenever the magnetic flux through the circuit varies with time. The flux may change in various ways, as Fig. 32–1 shows. For example, (1) a conductor may move through a stationary magnetic field, as in Figs. 32–2, 32–3, and 32–4, or (2) the magnetic field through a stationary conducting loop may change with time, as in Figs. 32–8 and 32–9. For case 1 we can compute the emf *either* from $\mathcal{E} = vBl$ or from $\mathcal{E} = -\Delta\Phi/\Delta t$. For case 2 we have to use $\mathcal{E} = -\Delta\Phi/\Delta t$.

If we have a coil with N turns and the flux varies at the same rate through each turn, the induced emf's in the turns are in *series* and must be added; the total emf is

$$\mathcal{E} = -N\frac{\Delta\Phi}{\Delta t}. \qquad (32\text{–}11)$$

PROBLEM-SOLVING STRATEGY: *Faraday's Law*

1. First, be sure that you understand what is making the flux change. Is the conductor moving? Is the magnetic field changing? Or both?

2. Remember the sign rule for the positive directions of magnetic flux and emf, and use it consistently when you implement Eq. (32–10). If your conductor has N turns in a coil, don't forget to multiply by N.

3. Use Faraday's law to get the emf. Interpret the sign of your result with reference to the sign rules to determine the direction of the induced current. If the circuit resistance is known, you can then calculate the current.

Example 32–4   A coil of wire containing 500 circular loops with a radius of 4.00 cm is placed between the poles of a large electromagnet, where the magnetic field is uniform, perpendicular to the plane of the coil, and increasing at a rate of 0.200 T·s^{-1}. What is the magnitude of the resulting induced emf?

Solution   The flux Φ at any time is given by $\Phi = BA$, and the rate of change of flux by $\Delta\Phi/\Delta t = (\Delta B/\Delta t)A$. In our problem, $A = \pi(0.0400 \text{ m})^2 = 0.00503 \text{ m}^2$, and

$$\frac{\Delta\Phi}{\Delta t} = \frac{\Delta B}{\Delta t}A = (0.200 \text{ T·s}^{-1})(0.00503 \text{ m}^2)$$

$$= 0.001006 \text{ T·m}^2\text{·s}^{-1} = 0.001006 \text{ Wb·s}^{-1}.$$

From Eq. (32–11) the magnitude of the induced emf is

$$|\mathcal{E}| = N\frac{\Delta\Phi}{\Delta t} = (500)(0.001006 \text{ Wb·s}^{-1}) = 0.503 \text{ V}.$$

If we view the coil from the side so that the flux points toward us, the sense of the induced emf is clockwise, according to our sign rule; if the ends of the wire are connected to a resistor, the direction of current in the coil is also clockwise. If the coil is tilted so that a line perpendicular to its plane makes an angle of 30° with **B,** then only the component $B \cos 30°$ contributes to the flux through the coil. In that case the induced emf has magnitude $\mathcal{E} = (0.503 \text{ V})(\cos 30°) = 0.436 \text{ V}$. ∎

Example 32–5   For the rotating rectangular loop in Example 32–2 (Fig. 32–4), determine the induced emf from Eq. (32–10).

Solution   The flux Φ through the loop equals its area $A = ab$ multiplied by the component of B perpendicular to the area, that is, $B \cos \theta$:

$$\Phi = BA \cos \theta = BA \cos \omega t.$$

Because Φ is a sinusoidal function of time, $\Delta\Phi/\Delta t$ is not constant. To derive an expression for $\Delta\Phi/\Delta t$ requires calculus, but we can make an educated guess even without calculus. Figure 32–10a is a graph of Φ as a function of time. The rate of change of Φ is proportional at each point to the *slope* of this curve. Where it is flat, Φ isn't changing at all; where it is steepest, Φ is changing most rapidly with time. So from the shape of the Φ versus t curve we can sketch the graph of $\Delta\Phi/\Delta t$ as a function of time. That sketch is shown in 32–10b; it looks like a *sine* curve, and indeed it is. The rate of change of Φ turns out to equal $-\omega BA \sin \omega t$, so from Eq.

32–10
Graphs of Φ and $\mathcal{E}$ as functions of time for a rotating loop. $\mathcal{E}$ is proportional to $-\Delta\Phi/\Delta t$. $\mathcal{E}$ has its maximum positive value when the slope of the Φ curve is most negative; $\mathcal{E}$ is zero when the slope of the Φ curve is zero.

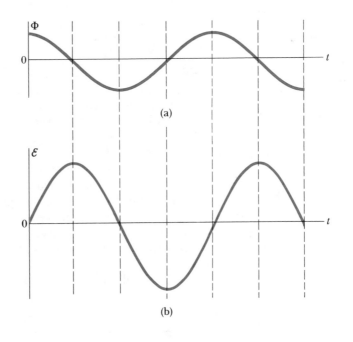

(a)

(b)

(32–10) the emf $\mathcal{E}$ is given by

$$\mathcal{E} = -\frac{\Delta\Phi}{\Delta t} = \omega BA \sin \omega t.$$

This is the same result that we derived in Example 32–2 from the "motional emf" approach.

The maximum value of $\mathcal{E}$ occurs when $\theta = \pm 90°$; at those positions the flux through the loop is zero and is changing most rapidly. When $\theta = 0$ or $180°$, the flux reaches its maximum and minimum values; at those instants it is neither increasing nor decreasing, and the emf is instantaneously zero. The emf depends not on the flux through the loop, but on its *rate of change*. Finally, we note that the induced emf does not depend on the *shape* of the loop, but only on its area. ∎

Example 32–6   Derive the emf of the rotating disk in Example 32–3 (Fig. 32–7), using Faraday's law, Eq. (32–10).

Solution   We take as our circuit the outline of the shaded areas in Fig. 32–7. There is no flux through the rectangular portion in the *yz*-plane because B is parallel to that plane. The shaded part of the disk in the *xy*-plane is a sector; its area is $\frac{1}{2}R^2\theta$, and the flux Φ through it is

$$\Phi = \tfrac{1}{2}BR^2\theta.$$

As the disk rotates, the shaded area increases. In a time Δt the angle θ increases by $\Delta\theta = \omega \, \Delta t$, and the flux increases by

$$\Delta\Phi = \tfrac{1}{2}BR^2 \, \Delta\theta = \tfrac{1}{2}BR^2\omega \, \Delta t.$$

The induced emf is

$$|\mathcal{E}| = \frac{\Delta\Phi}{\Delta t} = \tfrac{1}{2}BR^2\omega,$$

in agreement with Eq. (32–8). ∎

Example 32–7   One practical way to measure magnetic-field strength uses a small, closely wound coil with N turns called a *search coil*. If the area enclosed by the coil is A and its axis is initially aligned with a magnetic field with magnitude B, the flux Φ through it is $\Phi = BA$. Now if we quickly rotate the coil a quarter-turn about a diameter or snatch it out of the field, the flux decreases rapidly from BA to zero. While the flux is decreasing, there is a momentary induced emf, and a momentary induced current occurs in the external circuit connected to the coil. The rate of change of flux through the coil is proportional to the current, or rate of flow of charge, so it is easy to show that the *total* flux change is proportional to the total charge that flows around the circuit. We can build an instrument that measures this total charge, and from this we can compute B. We leave the details as a problem. Strictly speaking, this method gives only the *average* field over the area of the coil. But if the area is small, this is very nearly equal to the field at the center of the coil. ∎

32–4
Induced Electric Fields

The examples of induced emf that we have analyzed have been of two types, involving either a conductor moving in a magnetic field or changing flux through a stationary conductor. We need to think a little more about what is happening in the second type of situation. In particular, just what is it that pushes the charges around the circuit when we have a stationary conductor with changing flux?

Let's see how we can answer that question for the situation shown in Fig. 32–11. A long, thin solenoid with cross-sectional area A and n turns per unit length is encircled by a circular conducting loop with radius r. The galvanometer G measures the current in the loop. A current I in the winding of the solenoid sets up a magnetic field B along the solenoid axis, as shown, with magnitude B given by Eq. (31–6): $B = \mu_0 n I$. If we neglect the field outside the solenoid, then the magnetic flux Φ through the loop is given by

$$\Phi = BA = \mu_0 n I A.$$

When the current I changes with time, the magnetic flux Φ also changes, and according to Faraday's law, the induced emf in the loop is given by

$$\mathcal{E} = -\frac{\Delta\Phi}{\Delta t} = -\mu_0 n A \frac{\Delta I}{\Delta t}.$$

If the total resistance of the loop is R, the induced current in the loop, which we may call I', is given by $I' = \mathcal{E}/R$.

But what makes the charges move around the loop? There have to be forces on the charges in the conductor, but they can't be magnetic-field forces because the conductor isn't moving in a magnetic field and in fact isn't even *in* a magnetic field. So we are forced to conclude that there is an *electric* field in the conductor *caused by the changing magnetic flux.* This may be a little jarring; we are accustomed to thinking about electric charges as the sources of electric field, and now we are saying that a changing magnetic field somehow acts as a source of electric field. Furthermore, it's a strange sort of electric field. When a charge q goes once around the loop, the total work done on it by the electric field must be equal to q times the emf $\mathcal{E}$. That means that the electric field in the loop *is not conservative,* as we used the term in Chapter 26. To emphasize this, we call this field a **non-electrostatic field** and denote it as E_n. The emf is the *work per unit charge* done by E_n during one trip of a charge q around the loop. This is equal to the magnitude E_n multiplied by the circumference $2\pi r$ of the loop. That is, E_n is given by

$$E_n = \frac{\mathcal{E}}{2\pi r} = \frac{\mu_0 n A}{2\pi r}\frac{\Delta I}{\Delta t}. \tag{32–12}$$

The direction of E_n and the induced current are again given by the right-hand rule: Point the right thumb in the direction of the increasing B, and the direction the fingers curl is opposite (because of the negative sign in Faraday's law) to the direction of the induced emf and current.

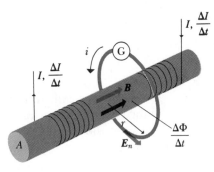

32–11
The windings of a long solenoid carry a current I that is increasing at a rate $\Delta I/\Delta t$. The magnetic flux in the solenoid is increasing at a rate $\Delta\Phi/\Delta t$, and this changing flux passes through a wire loop of arbitrary size and shape. An emf $\mathcal{E}$ is induced in the loop, given by $\mathcal{E} = -\Delta\Phi/\Delta t$.

Now let's try to put the pieces together. Faraday's law, Eq. (32–10), is valid for two rather different situations. In one an emf is induced by magnetic forces on charges when a conductor moves through a magnetic field. In the other a time-varying magnetic field induces an electric field of non-electrostatic nature in a stationary conductor and hence induces an emf. The E_n field in the latter case differs from an electro*static* field in an important way. It is nonconservative; the total work it does on a charge moving around a closed path is *not* zero. In contrast, an electro*static* field is *always* conservative, as we discussed in Section 26–1. Despite this difference, the fundamental effect of an electric field is to exert a force $F = qE$ on a charge q. This is the same whether the source of the field is a charge distribution or a changing magnetic field.

So a changing magnetic field acts as a source of electric field and can produce an electric field of a sort that we *cannot* produce with any static charge distribution. This may seem strange, but it's the way nature behaves. When we study electromagnetic waves, we will find that there is a similar relationship with the roles of the two fields reversed. That is, an *electric* field that changes with time acts as a source of *magnetic* field. We'll return to this concept in Chapter 35.

32–5
Lenz's Law

Lenz's law is a convenient alternative method for determining the sign or direction of an induced current or emf or the direction of the associated non-electrostatic field. It is not really an independent principle; it always gives the same results as the sign rules we introduced in connection with Faraday's law, but it is often easier to use. It also helps us to gain intuitive understanding of various induction phenomena. H. F. E. Lenz (1804–1865) was a German scientist who duplicated independently many of the discoveries of Faraday and Henry. **Lenz's law** states:

> *The direction of an induced current is such as to oppose the cause producing it.*

The "cause" of the current may be motion of a conductor in a magnetic field, or it may be a change of flux through a stationary circuit. In the first case the direction of the induced current in the moving conductor is such that the direction of the magnetic-field force on the conductor is opposite in direction to its motion. The motion of the conductor, which caused the induced current, is opposed.

In the second case the induced current sets up a magnetic field of its own. Within the area bounded by the circuit this field is *opposite* to the original field if the original field is *increasing* but is in the *same* direction as the original field if the latter is *decreasing*. That is, the induced current opposes the *change in flux* through the circuit, not the flux itself. In all these cases the induced current tries to preserve the *status quo* by opposing motion or a change of flux.

To have an induced current, of course, we need a complete circuit. If a conductor does not form a complete circuit, then we mentally complete the circuit between the ends of the conductor and use Lenz's law to determine the direction of the current. We can then deduce the polarity of the ends of the open-circuit conductor. The direction from the negative end to the positive end within the conductor is the direction in which current would flow if the circuit were complete.

Example 32–8   In Fig. 32–3, when the conducting bar moves to the right, a counterclockwise current is induced in the loop. The magnetic-field force exerted on the moving conductor as a result of this current is to the left, *opposing* the conductor's motion.   ■

Example 32–9   In Fig. 32–4 the magnetic field exerts forces on the induced current in the loop. The force on the right side of the loop (length a) is in the $+x$-direction, and the force on the left side is in the $-x$-direction. The resulting torque is opposite in direction to ω, and it opposes the rotational motion.   ■

Example 32–10   In the Faraday disk (or homopolar generator) shown in Fig. 32–7, the induced current in the disk is in the $-y$-direction, along a sector between the center of the disk and the contact (b) at the bottom of the rim. The magnetic-field force on this current is in the $-x$-direction; this force provides a torque that opposes the rotation of the disk. If we reverse the direction of rotation, the induced current also reverses direction, and again the magnetic-field force opposes the motion.   ■

Example 32–11   In Fig. 32–11, when the solenoid current is increasing, the induced current in the loop is counterclockwise, as shown. At points inside the loop, the additional field caused by this current is *opposite* in direction to the field inside the solenoid. The induced current opposes the increase in flux through the loop by causing flux in the opposite sense. If the solenoid current is *decreasing*, the induced current is clockwise. The additional flux caused by this current *adds* to the flux already present, so it opposes the decrease in flux.   ■

Lenz's law is also directly related to energy conservation. For example, in Section 32–1 and Example 32–8 the induced current in the loop dissipates energy at a rate I^2R, and this energy must be supplied by the force that keeps the conductor moving despite the magnetic force opposing its motion. The work done by this applied force must equal the energy dissipated in the circuit resistance, as we showed in Example 32–1. If the induced current were to have the opposite direction, the resulting force on the moving conductor would make it move faster and faster; this would certainly violate energy conservation.

*32–6
Eddy Currents

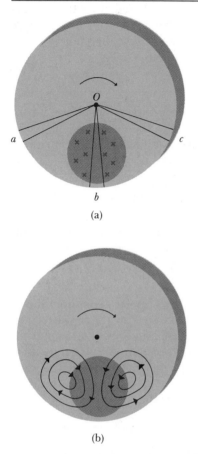

(a)

(b)

32–12
Eddy currents in a rotating disk.

In all the examples of induction phenomena that we have studied up until now, the induced currents have always been confined to well-defined paths in wires and other components forming a *circuit*. However, many pieces of electrical equipment contain masses of metal moving in magnetic fields or located in changing magnetic fields. In situations like these we can have induced currents that circulate throughout the volume of a material. Because their flow patterns resemble swirling eddies in a river, we call these **eddy currents.**

As an example, consider a disk that rotates in a magnetic field perpendicular to the plane of the disk but confined to a limited portion of the disk's area, as shown in Fig. 32–12a. Element *Ob* is moving across the field and has an emf induced in it. Elements *Oa* and *Oc* are not in the field, but they provide return conducting paths for charges displaced along *Ob* to return from *b* to *O*. The result is a circulation of eddy current in the disk, somewhat as sketched in Fig. 32–12b.

The downward current in the neighborhood of radius *Ob* experiences a sideways magnetic-field force toward the right that *opposes* the rotation of the disk, as Lenz's law predicts. The return currents lie outside the field, so they do not experience such forces. The interaction between the eddy currents and the field causes a braking action on the disk. This setup has several practical applications; it is called an *eddy-current brake*.

As a second example of eddy currents, consider the core of an alternating-current transformer, shown in Fig. 32–13a. The alternating current in the primary winding *P* sets up an alternating flux within the core, and an induced emf develops in the secondary winding *S* because of the continual change in flux through it. The iron core, however, is also a conductor, and any section such as *AA* can be pictured as several conducting circuits, one within the other (Fig. 33–13b). The flux through each of these circuits is continually changing, so eddy currents circulate in the entire volume of the core with lines of flow that form planes

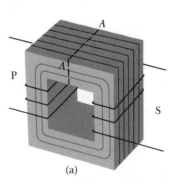

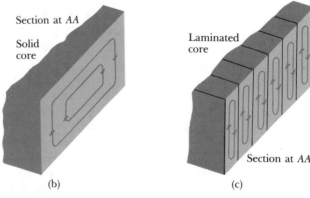

32–13
Reduction of eddy currents by use of a laminated core.

perpendicular to the flux. These eddy currents are very undesirable, both because they waste energy through I^2R heating and because of the opposing flux they themselves set up.

In all actual transformers the eddy currents are greatly reduced by the use of a *laminated* core, that is, a core built up of thin sheets, or laminae. The large electrical surface resistance of each lamina, due either to a natural coating of oxide or to an insulating varnish, effectively confines the eddy currents to individual laminae (Fig. 32–13c). The possible eddy-current paths are narrower, the induced emf in each path is smaller, and the eddy currents are greatly reduced.

In small transformers in which it is important to keep eddy-current losses to an absolute minimum, the cores are sometimes made of *ferrites*, which are complex oxides of iron and other metals. These materials are ferromagnetic, but they have much greater resistivity than pure iron.

Questions

32–1 In most parts of the northern hemisphere the earth's magnetic field has a vertical component directed *into* the earth. An airplane flying east generates an emf between its wingtips. Which wingtip acquires an excess of electrons and which a deficiency?

32–2 A sheet of copper is placed between the poles of an electromagnet, so the magnetic field is perpendicular to the sheet. When it is pulled out, a considerable force is required, and the force required increases with speed. What is happening?

32–3 In Fig. 32–4, if the angular velocity ω of the loop is doubled, then the frequency with which the induced current changes direction doubles, and the maximum emf also doubles. Why? Does the torque required to turn the loop change?

32–4 If we compare the conventional dc generator (Fig. 32–6) and the Faraday disk dynamo (Fig. 32–7), what are some advantages and disadvantages of each?

32–5 Some alternating-current generators use a rotating permanent magnet and stationary coils. What advantages does this scheme have? What disadvantages?

32–6 When a conductor moves through a magnetic field, the magnetic forces on the charges in the conductor cause an emf. But if this phenomenon is viewed in a frame of reference moving with the conductor, there is no motion, yet there is still an emf. How is this paradox resolved?

32–7 Two circular loops lie adjacent to each other. One is connected to a source that supplies an increasing current; the other is a simple closed ring. Is the induced current in the ring in the same direction as that in the ring connected to the source, or opposite? What if the current in the first ring is decreasing?

32–8 A farmer claimed that the high-voltage transmission lines running parallel to his fence induced dangerously large voltages on the fence. Is this within the realm of possibility?

32–9 Small one-cylinder gasoline engines sometimes use a device called a *magneto* to supply current to the spark plug. A permanent magnet is attached to the flywheel, and a stationary coil is mounted adjacent to it. What happens when the magnet passes the coil?

32–10 A current-carrying conductor passes through the center of a metal ring, perpendicular to its plane. If the current in the conductor increases, is a current induced in the ring?

32–11 A student asserted that if a permanent magnet is dropped down a vertical copper pipe, it eventually reaches a terminal velocity, even if there is no air resistance. Why should this be? Or should it?

Exercises

Section 32–2   Motional Electromotive Force

32–1 In Eq. (32–2), show that if v is in meters per second, B is in teslas, and l is in meters, then the units of the right-hand side of the equation are joules per coulomb or volts (the correct SI units for $\mathcal{E}$).

32–2 In Fig. 32–2 a rod with length $l = 0.250$ m moves with constant speed 6.00 m·s^{-1} in the direction shown. The induced emf is 1.50 V.

a) What is the magnitude of the magnetic field?

b) Which point is at higher potential, a or b?

32–3 In Fig. 32–3 a rod with length $l = 0.400$ m moves in a magnetic field with magnitude $B = 1.20$ T. The emf induced in the moving rod is 3.60 V.

a) What is the speed of the rod?

b) If the total circuit resistance is 0.900 Ω, what is the induced current?

c) What force (magnitude and direction) does the field exert on the rod as a result of this current?

32–4 In Fig. 32–14 a rod with length $l = 0.150$ m moves in a magnetic field $\mathbf{B}$ directed into the plane of the figure. $B = 0.600$ T, and the rod moves with velocity $v = 4.00$ m·s^{-1} in the direction shown.

a) What is the motional emf induced in the rod?

b) What is the potential difference between the ends of the rod?

c) Which point, a or b, is at higher potential?

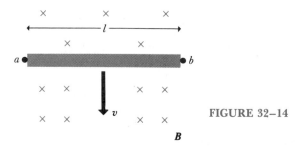

FIGURE 32–14

32–5 A conducting rod AB in Fig. 32–15 makes contact with the metal rails CA and DB. The apparatus is in a uniform magnetic field of 0.500 T, perpendicular to the plane of the diagram.

a) Find the magnitude of the emf induced in the rod when it is moving toward the right with a speed 8.00 m·s^{-1}.

b) In what direction does current flow in the rod?

c) If the resistance of the circuit $ABCD$ is 0.200 Ω (assumed to be constant), find the force (magnitude and direction) required to keep the rod moving to the right with a constant speed of 8.00 m·s^{-1}. Neglect friction.

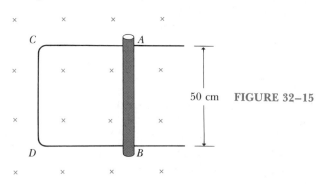

50 cm   FIGURE 32–15

d) Compare the rate at which mechanical work is done by the force (Fv) with the rate of development of heat in the circuit (I^2R).

32–6 A square loop of wire with resistance R is moved at constant speed v across a uniform magnetic field confined to a square region whose sides are twice the length of those of the square loop. (See Fig. 32–16.)

a) Sketch a graph of the external force F needed to move the loop at constant speed, as a function of the distance x, from $x = -2l$ to $x = +2l$. (The coordinate x is measured from the center of the magnetic-field region to the center of the loop. It is negative when the center of the loop is to the left of the center of the magnetic-field region. Take positive force to be to the right.)

b) Sketch a graph of the induced current in the loop as a function of x. Take clockwise currents to be positive.

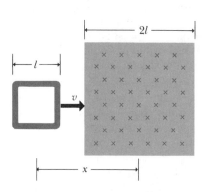

FIGURE 32–16

Section 32–3   Faraday's Law

32–7 A single loop of wire, with an area of 0.0900 m^2, is in a region of uniform magnetic field. The magnetic field has an initial value of 3.80 T and is decreasing at a constant rate of 0.190 T·s^{-1}. If the loop has a resistance of 0.600 Ω, what is the current induced in the loop?

32–8 A coil of wire with 200 circular turns of radius 3.00 cm is in a uniform magnetic field. The coil has a total resistance of 40.0 Ω. At what rate, in teslas per second, must the magnetic field be changing to induce a current of 0.150 A in the coil?

32–9 A coil with 800 turns enclosing an area of 20 cm^2 is rotated from a position where its plane is perpendicular to the earth's magnetic field to one where its plane is parallel to the field in 0.020 s. What average emf is induced if the earth's magnetic field is 6.0×10^{-5} T?

32–10 A closely wound rectangular coil with 50 turns has dimensions of 12.0 cm × 25.0 cm. The plane of the coil is rotated from a position where it makes an angle of 45.0° with a magnetic field of 1.60 T to a position perpendicular to the field in time $t = 0.0800$ s. What is the average emf induced in the coil?

32–11 A flat, square coil with 15 turns has sides of length 0.120 m. The coil rotates in a magnetic field of 0.0250 T.

a) What is the angular velocity of the coil if the maximum emf produced is 20.0 mV?

b) What is the average emf at this angular velocity?

32–12 A Faraday disk dynamo is used to supply current to a large electromagnet that requires 200 A at 6.00 V. The disk is 0.600 m in radius, and it turns in a magnetic field of 1.20 T, perpendicular to the plane of the disk, supplied by a smaller electromagnet.

a) How many revolutions per second must the disk turn?

b) What torque is required to turn the disk, assuming that all the mechanical energy is dissipated as heat in the large electromagnet?

32–13 Derive the equation that relates the total charge Q that flows through a search coil to the magnetic field strength B. The search coil has N turns, each of area A, and the flux through the coil is decreased from its initial maximum value to zero in a time Δt. The resistance of the coil is R, and the total charge is $Q = I \Delta t$, where I is the average current induced by the change in flux.

32–14 The cross-sectional area of a closely wound search coil (Exercise 32–13) having 20 turns is 1.50 cm^2, and its resistance is 6.00 Ω. The coil is connected through leads of negligible resistance to a charge-measuring instrument having an internal resistance of 16.0 Ω. Find the quantity of charge displaced when the coil is pulled quickly out of a region where $B = 1.80$ T to a point where the magnetic field is zero. The plane of the coil, when in the field, makes an angle of 90° with the magnetic field.

32–15 A closely wound search coil (Exercise 32–13) has an area of 4.00 cm^2, 160 turns, and a resistance of 50.0 Ω. It is connected to a charge-measuring instrument whose resistance is 30.0 Ω. When the coil is rotated quickly from a position parallel to a uniform magnetic field to one perpendicular to the field, the instrument indicates a charge of 9.00×10^{-5} C. What is the magnitude of the field?

32–16 A very long, straight solenoid with a cross-sectional area of 6.00 cm^2 is wound with 40 turns of wire per centimeter, and the windings carry a current of 0.250 A. A secondary winding of two turns encircles the solenoid at its center. When the primary circuit is opened, the magnetic field of the solenoid becomes zero in 0.0500 s. What is the average induced emf in the secondary?

Section 32–4   Induced Electric Fields

32–17 The magnetic field B at all points within the colored circle of Fig. 32–17 has an initial magnitude of 0.800 T. It is directed into the plane of the diagram and is decreasing at the rate of -0.0500 T·s^{-1}.

a) What is the shape of the field lines of the induced E_n field in Fig. 32–17, within the colored circle?

b) What are the magnitude and direction of this field at any point on the circular conducting ring with radius 0.100 m?

c) What is the current in the ring if its resistance is 2.00 Ω?

d) What is the potential difference between points a and b of the ring?

e) If the ring is cut at some point and the ends are separated slightly, what will be the potential difference between the ends?

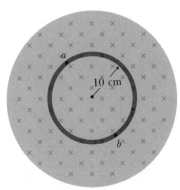

FIGURE 32–17

32–18 The magnetic field within a long, straight solenoid of circular cross section and radius R is increasing at a rate of $\Delta B/\Delta t$.

a) What is the rate of change of flux through a circle of radius r_1 inside the solenoid, normal to the axis of the solenoid, and with its center on the solenoid axis?

b) Find the induced electric field E_n inside the solenoid, at a distance r_1 from its axis. Show the direction of this field in a diagram.

c) What is the induced electric field *outside* the solenoid at a distance r_2 from the axis?

d) Sketch a graph of the magnitude of E_n, as a function of the distance r from the axis, from $r = 0$ to $r = 2R$.

e) What is the induced emf in a circular turn of radius $R/2$ that has its center on the solenoid axis?

f) Of radius R?

g) Of radius $2R$?

Section 32–5   Lenz's Law

32–19 A cardboard tube is wound with two windings of insulated wire that are wound in opposite directions, as in Fig. 32–18. Terminals a and b of winding A may be connected to a battery through a reversing switch. State whether the induced current in the resistor R is from left to right or from right to left in the following circumstances:

a) the current in winding A is from a to b and is increasing;

b) the current is from b to a and is decreasing;

c) the current is from b to a and is increasing.

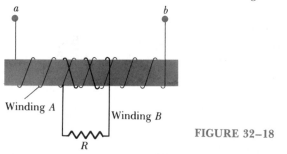

Winding A Winding B

R

FIGURE 32–18

32–20 A circular loop of wire is in a region of spatially uniform magnetic field, as shown in Fig. 32–17. The magnetic field is directed into the plane of the figure. Calculate the direction (clockwise or counterclockwise) of the induced current in the loop when

a) B is increasing,

b) B is decreasing,

c) B is constant with value B_0.

32–21 Using Lenz's law, determine the direction of the current in resistor ab of Fig. 32–19 when

a) switch S is opened after having been closed for several minutes;

b) coil B is brought closer to coil A with the switch closed;

c) the resistance of R is decreased while the switch remains closed.

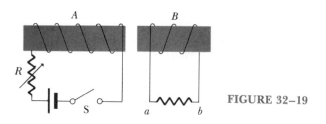

FIGURE 32–19

Problems

32–22 The cube in Fig. 32–20, 1.00 m on a side, is in a uniform magnetic field of 0.40 T, directed along the positive y-axis. Wires A, C, and D move in the directions indicated, each with a speed of 0.50 m·s^{-1}. (Wire A moves parallel to the xy-plane, C moves at an angle of 45° below the xy-plane, and D moves parallel to the xz-plane.) What is the potential difference between the ends of each wire?

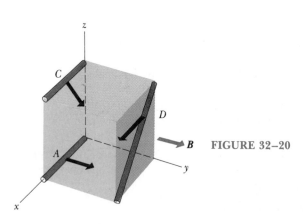

FIGURE 32–20

32–23 A conducting rod with length l, mass m, and resistance R moves without friction on metal rails as shown in Fig. 32–3. There is a uniform magnetic field B directed into the plane of the figure. The rod starts from rest and is acted on by a constant force F that is directed to the right. The rails have negligible resistance.

a) Sketch a graph of the speed of the rod as a function of time.

b) Find an expression for the terminal speed, the speed when the acceleration of the rod is zero.

32–24 A slender rod 0.760 m long rotates about an axis through one end and perpendicular to the rod with an angular velocity of 12.0 rad·s^{-1}. The plane of rotation of the rod is perpendicular to a uniform magnetic field with a magnitude of 0.500 T.

a) What is the induced emf in the rod?

b) What is the potential difference between its ends?

32–25 The rectangular loop in Fig. 32–21, with area A and resistance R, rotates at uniform angular velocity ω about the y-axis. The loop lies in a uniform magnetic field B in the direction of the x-axis. Sketch graphs of the following quantities, as functions of time. (Let $t = 0$

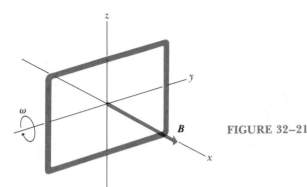

FIGURE 32–21

in the position shown in Fig. 32–21.)

a) the flux Φ through the loop;

b) the rate of change of flux $\Delta\Phi/\Delta t$;

c) the induced emf in the loop;

d) the torque Γ needed to keep the loop rotating at constant angular velocity;

e) the induced emf if the angular velocity is doubled.

32–26 In Problem 32–25 and Fig. 32–21, let $A = 400$ cm^2, $R = 2.00$ Ω, $\omega = 30.0$ rad·s^{-1}, and $B = 0.500$ T. Find

a) the maximum flux through the loop,

b) the maximum induced emf,

c) the maximum torque.

32–27 Suppose the loop in Fig. 32–21 is

a) rotated about the z-axis;

b) rotated about the x-axis;

c) rotated about an edge parallel to the y-axis.

What is the maximum induced emf in each case if the numerical values are those given in Problem 32–26?

32–28 A flexible circular loop 0.100 m in diameter lies in a magnetic field 1.80 T, directed into the plane of

the diagram in Fig. 32–22. The loop is pulled at the points indicated by the arrows, forming a loop of zero area in 0.200 s.

a) Find the average induced emf in the circuit.

b) What is the direction of the current in R, from a to b or from b to a?

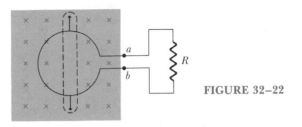

FIGURE 32–22

32–29 A search coil (Exercise 32–13) used to measure magnetic fields is to be made with a radius of 2.00 cm. It is to be designed so that flipping it 180° in a field of 0.100 T causes a total charge of 4.00×10^{-4} C to flow in a charge-measuring instrument when the total circuit resistance is 50.0 Ω. How many turns should the coil have?

32–30 A solenoid 0.500 m long and 0.0800 m in diameter is wound with 500 turns. A closely wound coil of 20 turns of insulated wire surrounds the solenoid at its midpoint, and the terminals of the coil are connected to a charge-measuring instrument. The total circuit resistance is 40.0 Ω.

a) Find the quantity of charge displaced through the instrument when the current in the solenoid is quickly decreased from 3.00 A to 1.00 A.

b) Draw a sketch of the apparatus, showing clearly the directions of the windings of the solenoid and coil and of the current in the solenoid. Show on your sketch the direction of the current in the coil when the solenoid current is decreased.

Challenge Problems

32–31 The magnetic field B at all points within a circular region of radius R is uniform in space and directed into the plane of Fig. 32–23. If the magnetic field is increasing at a constant rate $\Delta B/\Delta t$, what are the magnitude and direction of the force on a stationary point charge of positive charge q located at points a, b, and c? Point a is a distance r above the center of the region, point b is a distance r to the right of the center, and point c is at the center of the region.

32–32 A metal bar with length l, mass m, and resistance R is placed on frictionless metal rails that are inclined at an angle ϕ above the horizontal. The rails

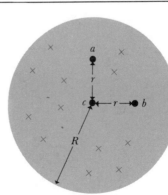

FIGURE 32–23

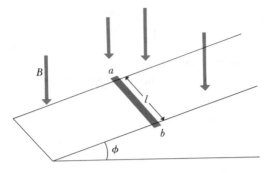

FIGURE 32-24

have negligible resistance. There is a uniform magnetic field of magnitude B directed downward in Fig. 32–24. The bar is released from rest and slides down the rails.

a) Is the direction of the current induced in the bar from a to b or from b to a?

b) What is the terminal speed of the bar?

c) What is the induced current in the bar when the terminal speed has been reached?

d) After the terminal speed has been reached, at what rate is electrical energy being converted to heat in the resistance of the bar?

e) After the terminal speed has been reached, at what rate is work being done on the bar by gravity? Compare your answer to that in part (d).

32–33 A square conducting loop, 20.0 cm on a side, is placed in the same magnetic field as in Exercise 32–17. (See Fig. 32–25. The center of the square loop is at the center of the magnetic-field region.)

a) Copy Fig. 32–25, and show by vectors the directions and relative magnitudes of the induced electric field E_n at points a, b, and c.

b) Prove that the component of E_n along the loop has the same value at every point of the loop and is equal to that of the ring of Fig. 32–17 (Exercise 32–17).

c) What is the current induced in the loop if its resistance is 2.00 Ω?

d) What is the potential difference between points a and b?

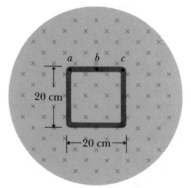

FIGURE 32–25

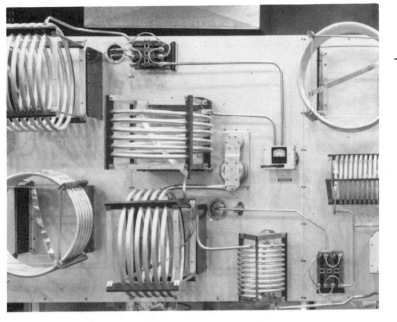

Inductance

The electromagnetic induction phenomena that we studied in Chapter 32 have several practical applications in electric-circuit devices, including transformers and inductors. When two coils are adjacent, a changing current in one induces an emf in the other; this is the operating principle of the *transformer*, and the coupling between the coils is characterized by their *mutual inductance*. A changing current in a single coil also causes an induced emf in that same coil, and the relationship of current to emf is described by the *self-inductance* of the coil. A study of energy relationships in inductors leads to the concept of energy stored in magnetic fields. We study several simple circuits containing inductors, including one that can undergo electrical *oscillations* analogous to those of a mechanical harmonic oscillator. This analysis forms part of the foundation for our study of alternating-current circuits in Chapter 34.

33–1
Mutual Inductance

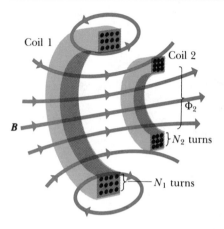

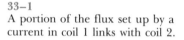

33–1
A portion of the flux set up by a current in coil 1 links with coil 2.

An emf is induced in a stationary circuit whenever the magnetic flux through the circuit varies with time. If this flux variation is caused by a varying current in a second circuit, we can express the induced emf in terms of the varying *current*, rather than in terms of the varying *flux*. In this analysis we will use lowercase letters to represent quantities that vary with time; for example, a time-varying current is i, often with a subscript to identify the circuit.

Figure 33–1 is a cross-sectional view of two coils of wire. A current i_1 in coil 1 sets up a magnetic field as indicated by the color lines, and some of these lines pass through coil 2. The resulting flux through coil 2 is Φ_2. The magnetic field is proportional to i_1, so Φ_2 is also proportional to i_1. When i_1 changes, Φ_2 changes; this changing flux induces an emf $\mathcal{E}_2$ in coil 2, given by

$$\mathcal{E}_2 = -N_2 \frac{\Delta \Phi_2}{\Delta t}. \tag{33–1}$$

We could represent the proportionality of Φ_2 and i_1 in the form $\Phi_2 =$ (constant) i_1, but instead it is more convenient to include the number of turns N_2 in the relation. Introducing a proportionality constant M, we write

$$N_2 \Phi_2 = M i_1. \tag{33–2}$$

From this,

$$N_2 \frac{\Delta \Phi_2}{\Delta t} = M \frac{\Delta i_1}{\Delta t},$$

and we can rewrite Eq. (33–1) as

$$\mathcal{E}_2 = -M \frac{\Delta i_1}{\Delta t}. \tag{33–3}$$

The constant M depends only on the geometry of the two coils; it is called their **mutual inductance.** It is defined by Eq. (33–2), which we may also write as

$$M = \frac{N_2 \Phi_2}{i_1}. \tag{33–4}$$

We can repeat this discussion for the opposite case in which a changing current i_2 in coil 2 causes a changing flux Φ_1 and an emf $\mathcal{E}_1$ in coil 1. We might expect that the constant M would be different in this case because in general the two coils are not identical and the flux through them is not the same. It turns out, however, that M is always the same in both cases. The mutual inductance M characterizes completely the induced-emf interaction of two coils.

The SI unit of mutual inductance, from Eq. (33–4), is *the weber per ampere*. An equivalent unit, obtained by reference to Eq. (33–3), is *the volt-second per ampere* or *the ohm-second*. These equivalent units are called

1 henry (1 H), in honor of Joseph Henry (1797–1878), one of the discoverers of electromagnetic induction. Thus the unit of mutual inductance is

$$1 \text{ H} = 1 \text{ Wb·A}^{-1} = 1 \text{ V·s·A}^{-1} = 1 \text{ }\Omega\text{·s}.$$

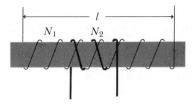

33-2
A long solenoid with cross-sectional area A and N_1 turns, surrounded by a small coil with N_2 turns.

Example 33–1   A long solenoid with length l and cross-sectional area A is closely wound with N_1 turns of wire. A coil with N_2 turns surrounds it at its center, as shown in Fig. 33–2. Find the mutual inductance.

Solution   A current i_1 in the solenoid sets up a $\boldsymbol{B}$ field at its center; from Eq. (31–6) the magnitude of $\boldsymbol{B}$ is

$$B = \mu_0 n i_1 = \frac{\mu_0 N_1 i_1}{l}.$$

The flux through the central section equals BA, and all of this flux links with the small coil. From Eq. (33–4) the mutual inductance M is

$$M = \frac{N_2 \Phi_2}{i_1} = \frac{N_2}{i_1} \frac{\mu_0 N_1 i_1}{l} A = \frac{\mu_0 A N_1 N_2}{l}.$$

Here's a numerical example to give you an idea of magnitudes. Suppose $l = 0.50$ m, $A = 10$ cm$^2 = 1.0 \times 10^{-3}$ m^2, $N_1 = 1000$ turns, and $N_2 = 10$ turns. Then

$$M = \frac{(4\pi \times 10^{-7} \text{ Wb·A}^{-1}\text{·m}^{-1})(1.0 \times 10^{-3} \text{ m}^2)(1000)(10)}{0.50 \text{ m}}$$

$$= 25 \times 10^{-6} \text{ Wb·A}^{-1} = 25 \times 10^{-6} \text{ H} = 25 \text{ }\mu\text{H}. \qquad \blacksquare$$

33–2
Self-Inductance

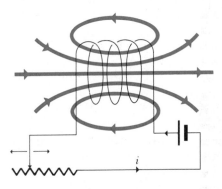

33-3
A flux Φ linking a coil of N turns. When the current in the circuit changes, the flux changes also, and a self-induced emf appears in the circuit.

In our discussion of mutual inductance we assumed that one circuit acted as the source of magnetic field. The emf under consideration was induced in a separate, independent circuit that linked some of the magnetic flux created by the first circuit. But whenever a current is present in any circuit, this current sets up a magnetic field that links with *the same* circuit and changes when the current changes. Any circuit that carries a varying current has an induced emf in it resulting from the variation in *its own* magnetic field. Such an emf is called a **self-induced electromotive force (emf).**

As an example, consider a coil with N turns of wire, as in Fig. 33–3, carrying a current i. As a result of this current, a magnetic flux Φ passes through each turn. In analogy to Eq. (33–4) we define the **self-inductance** L of the circuit, or simply its **inductance:**

$$L = \frac{N\Phi}{i}, \qquad \text{or} \qquad N\Phi = Li. \qquad (33\text{–}5)$$

If Φ and i change with time, then

$$N \frac{\Delta\Phi}{\Delta t} = L \frac{\Delta i}{\Delta t}.$$

From Eq. (32–11) the self-induced emf $\mathcal{E}$ is $-N\,\Delta\Phi/\Delta t$, so it follows that

$$\mathcal{E} = -L \frac{\Delta i}{\Delta t}. \qquad (33\text{--}6)$$

The self-inductance of a circuit is *the self-induced emf per unit rate of change of current*. The SI unit of self-inductance is 1 henry.

A circuit, or part of a circuit, that has inductance is called an **inductor** or a *choke*. The usual circuit symbol for an inductor is

We can find the direction of a self-induced emf and the associated non-electrostatic field from Lenz's law. The "cause" of the induced emf and the field is the *changing current* in the conductor. If the current is increasing, the direction of the induced field and emf are *opposite* to that of the current, to try to *decrease* the current. If the current is *decreasing*, the induced emf and field are in the *same* direction as the current. An inductor opposes a *change* in current, not current itself. So its circuit behavior is quite different from that of a resistor.

Example 33–2   An air-core toroidal solenoid with cross-sectional area A and mean radius r is closely wound with N turns of wire. Determine its self-inductance L. In calculating the flux, assume that B is uniform across a cross section; neglect the variation with distance from the toroid axis.

Solution   The field magnitude at distance r from the toroid axis is given by Eq. (31–8). If we assume that the field has this magnitude over the entire cross section, then the flux in the toroid is

$$\Phi = BA = \frac{\mu_0 N i A}{2\pi r}.$$

All of the flux links with each turn, and the self-inductance L is

$$L = \frac{N\Phi}{i} = \frac{\mu_0 N^2 A}{2\pi r}.$$

Here is a numerical example: Suppose $N = 100$ turns, $A = 10$ cm^2 = 1.0×10^{-3} m^2, and $r = 0.10$ m; then

$$L = \frac{(4\pi \times 10^{-7}\ \text{Wb·A}^{-1}\text{·m}^{-1})(100)^2(1.0 \times 10^{-3}\ \text{m}^2)}{2\pi(0.10\ \text{m})}$$

$$= 20 \times 10^{-6}\ \text{H} = 20\ \mu\text{H}. \qquad \blacksquare$$

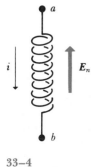

33–4
When $\Delta i / \Delta t$ is positive, the non-electrostatic induced field $\boldsymbol{E}_n$ is in the direction shown, and the emf is treated as a potential difference with V_{ab} positive; that is, a is at higher potential than b. When $\Delta i / \Delta t$ is negative, $\boldsymbol{E}_n$ has the opposite direction, and V_{ab} is negative.

When we use Kirchhoff's loop rule (Section 29–2) with circuits containing inductors, we treat this self-induced emf as though it were a potential difference, with a at higher potential than b. If we define the positive direction of the current i as from a to b in the inductor, as in Fig. 33–4, then

$$V_{ab} = L \frac{\Delta i}{\Delta t}. \qquad (33\text{–}7)$$

The self-inductance of a circuit depends on its size, shape, number of turns, and so on. It also depends on the magnetic properties of the material enclosed by the circuit. In the above examples we assumed that the conductor was surrounded by vacuum. If matter is present, then in the expression for B we must replace the constant μ_0, the permeability of vacuum, by the permeability of the material, $\mu = K_m \mu_0$, as we discussed in Section 31–7. If the material is diamagnetic or paramagnetic, this makes very little difference. If the material is *ferromagnetic*, however, the difference is of crucial importance. An inductor wound on a soft iron core having $K_m = 5000$ has an inductance approximately 5000 times as great as the same coil with an air core. Iron-core inductors are very widely used in a variety of electronic and electric-power applications.

An added complication is that with ferromagnetic materials the magnetization is not always a linear function of magnetizing current, especially as saturation is approached. As a result, the inductance can depend on current in a fairly complicated way. In our discussion we will ignore this complication and assume always that the inductance is constant. This is a reasonable assumption even for a ferromagnetic material if the magnetization remains well below the saturation level.

PROBLEM-SOLVING STRATEGY: *Self-Inductance*

1. In this chapter we view the inductor primarily as a *circuit* device, so circuit analysis is of primary importance. In general, all the voltages, currents, and capacitor charges are now functions of time, not constants as they have been in most of our previous analysis. But Kirchhoff's rules, which we studied in Chapter 29, are still valid. When the voltages and currents vary with time, Kirchhoff's rules hold at each instant of time.

2. As in all circuit analysis, getting the signs right is often more challenging than understanding the principles. We suggest that you review the strategy in Section 29–2 as preparation for study of the circuits in Sections 33–4 through 33–6. In addition, give close attention to the sign rule described with Eq. (33–7). Then look for the applications of Kirchhoff's loop rule in these discussions.

Example 33–3   If the current in the coil in Example 33–2 increases uniformly from zero to 1.0 A in 0.10 s, find the magnitude and direction of the self-induced emf.

Solution   From Eq. (33–6),

$$|\mathcal{E}| = L\frac{\Delta i}{\Delta t} = (20 \times 10^{-6}\ \text{H})\frac{1.0\ \text{A}}{0.10\ \text{s}} = 2.0 \times 10^{-4}\ \text{V}.$$

The current is increasing, so according to Lenz's law the direction of the emf is opposite to that of the current. In Fig. 33–4, suppose the inductor terminals are a and b and there is an *increasing* current from a to b in the inductor. Then the induced field $\boldsymbol{E}_n$ and the emf are in the direction from b to a, like a battery with a as the positive terminal and b the negative terminal.   ∎

33–3
Energy in an Inductor

An inductor carrying a current has energy stored in it because an input of energy is needed to establish the current. Why is this? A changing current in an inductor causes an emf. Because of this, the source that supplies the current must maintain a potential difference between its terminals while the current is changing, and therefore it must supply energy to the inductor. We can calculate the total energy input U needed to establish a final current I in an inductor with inductance L if the initial current is zero.

If the current at some instant is i and is changing at the rate $\Delta i/\Delta t$, the induced emf at that instant is $\mathcal{E} = L\,\Delta i/\Delta t$, and the instantaneous power P supplied by the current source is

$$P = \mathcal{E}i = Li\frac{\Delta i}{\Delta t}.$$

The energy ΔU supplied in a short time interval Δt is equal to $P\,\Delta t$, so

$$\Delta U = Li\,\Delta i.$$

To find the *total* energy supplied while the current increases from zero to a final value I, we note that the *average* value of Li during the entire increase is $LI/2$. The product of this and the *total* increase in current I gives the total energy U supplied, and we find

$$U = \tfrac{1}{2}LI^2. \qquad (33\text{–}8)$$

This result can also be derived (more easily) by use of integral calculus.

After the current has reached its final steady value I, $\Delta i/\Delta t = 0$, and the power input is zero. The energy U is needed to establish the magnetic field in and around the inductor. We can think of this as analogous to a *kinetic energy* associated with the current. This energy is zero when there is no current, and when the current is I, the energy has the value $\tfrac{1}{2}LI^2$. When the current decreases to zero, the inductor supplies a total amount of energy $\tfrac{1}{2}LI^2$ to the external circuit. If we interrupt the circuit suddenly by opening a switch, the current changes rapidly, the induced emf is very large, and the energy may be dissipated in an arc across the switch contacts. This is the electrical analog of a car running into a brick wall and stopping very suddenly, while very large forces act on it.

We can also consider the energy to be associated with the magnetic field itself, and we can develop a relation analogous to the one we obtained for electric-field energy in Section 27–4, Eqs. (27–10) and (27–18). We will concentrate on one simple case, the toroidal solenoid; this system has the advantage that its magnetic field is confined completely to a finite region of space in its interior. As in Example 33–2 (Section 33–2), we assume that the cross-sectional area A is small enough that we can pretend that the magnetic field is uniform over the area. The volume V in the toroid is approximately equal to the circumference $2\pi r$ multiplied by the area A: $V = 2\pi rA$. From Example 33–2 the self-inductance of the toroidal solenoid is

$$L = \frac{\mu_0 N^2 A}{2\pi r},$$

and the stored energy U when the current is I is

$$U = \frac{1}{2}LI^2 = \frac{1}{2}\frac{\mu_0 N^2 A}{2\pi r}I^2.$$

We can think of this energy as localized in the volume $V = 2\pi rA$ enclosed by the windings. The energy *per unit volume* or **energy density** $u = U/V$ is then

$$u = \frac{U}{2\pi rA} = \frac{1}{2}\mu_0\frac{N^2 I^2}{(2\pi r)^2}.$$

We can express this in terms of the magnetic field B inside the toroid. From Eq. (31–8),

$$B = \frac{\mu_0 NI}{2\pi r} \quad \text{and} \quad \frac{N^2 I^2}{(2\pi r)^2} = \frac{B^2}{\mu_0{}^2}.$$

When we substitute this into the above equation, we finally find

$$u = \frac{B^2}{2\mu_0}. \tag{33–9}$$

This is the analog of the expression for the energy per unit volume in the electric field of an air capacitor, $\frac{1}{2}\epsilon_0 E^2$, which we derived in Section 27–4. Although we have derived it only for one special situation, it turns out to be valid in general. That is, the energy per unit volume associated with *any* magnetic-field configuration is given by Eq. (33–9). We will need these expressions for electric- and magnetic-field energy densities when we study energy associated with electromagnetic waves in Chapter 35.

When the material inside the toroid is not vacuum but a material having magnetic permeability $\mu = K_m\mu_0$, we have to replace μ_0 by μ in Eq. (33–9). The energy per unit volume in the magnetic field is then

$$u = \frac{B^2}{2\mu}. \tag{33–10}$$

33–4
The *R–L* Circuit

An inductor is primarily a circuit device. Let's look at some examples of the circuit behavior of an inductor. One thing is clear already; we aren't going to see any sudden changes in the current through an inductor. In Eq. (33–6), $\Delta i/\Delta t$ is the rate of change of current, and this equation shows that the greater this is, the greater the potential difference between the inductor terminals must be.

We can learn some basic things about inductor behavior from the circuit of Fig. 33–5. The resistor R may be a separate circuit element, or it may be the resistance of the windings of the inductor; every real-life inductor has some resistance unless it is made of superconducting wire. By closing switch S_1 we can connect the $R–L$ combination to a source with constant terminal voltage V. (We assume that the source has zero internal resistance.) Or we can close switch S_2 and bypass the source. Suppose both switches are initially open, and then at some initial time $t = 0$ we close switch S_1. As we have mentioned, the current cannot change suddenly from zero to some final value because of the infinite emf that would be involved. Instead, it begins to grow at a definite rate that depends only on the value of L in the circuit.

Let i be the current at some time t after switch S_1 is closed; then $\Delta i/\Delta t$ is its rate of increase at that time. The potential difference v_{cb} across the inductor at that time is

$$v_{cb} = L \frac{\Delta i}{\Delta t},$$

and the potential difference v_{ac} across the resistor is

$$v_{ac} = iR.$$

From Kirchhoff's voltage rule,

$$V = L \frac{\Delta i}{\Delta t} + iR. \qquad (33–11)$$

Solving this for $\Delta i/\Delta t$, we find that the rate of increase of current is

$$\frac{\Delta i}{\Delta t} = \frac{V - iR}{L} = \frac{V}{L} - \frac{R}{L} i. \qquad (33–12)$$

At the instant the switch is first closed, $i = 0$ and the potential drop across R is zero. The initial rate of change of current is

$$\left(\frac{\Delta i}{\Delta t} \right)_{\text{initial}} = \frac{V}{L}.$$

The greater the inductance L, the more slowly the current increases.

As the current increases, the term $(R/L)i$ in Eq. (33–12) also increases, and the *rate* of increase of current becomes smaller and smaller. When the current reaches its final *steady-state* value I, its rate of increase is

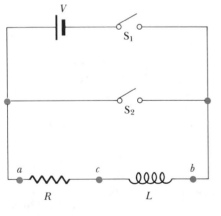

33–5
An *R–L* series circuit.

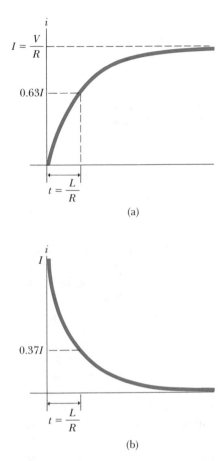

33–6
(a) Growth of current in a circuit containing inductance and resistance.
(b) Decay of current in a circuit containing inductance and resistance.

zero. Then Eq. (33–12) becomes

$$0 = \frac{V}{L} - \frac{R}{L}I \quad \text{and} \quad I = \frac{V}{R}.$$

That is, the *final* current I does not depend on the inductance L; it is the same as it would be in a pure resistance R connected to a source with emf V. The behavior of the current as a function of time is shown by the graph of Fig. 33–6a. We obtained this curve by deriving from Eq. (33–12) an equation that gives i as a function of time. Calculus is needed for the derivation, and we won't go into the details here.

To look at the energy relationships in this behavior of the *R–L* circuit, we multiply Eq. (33–11) by i, obtaining

$$Vi = Li\frac{\Delta i}{\Delta t} + i^2R. \tag{33–13}$$

The left side Vi is the instantaneous rate at which electrical energy is being added to the circuit by the source. This equals the rate of increase of energy in the inductor, $Li\,\Delta i/\Delta t$, plus the rate of dissipation of energy in the resistor, i^2R.

Equation (33–12) shows that the rate of change of i is proportional to i, with a proportionality factor R/L. Thus the larger this quantity is, the more quickly the current approaches its final value. Conversely, the *time* required for the current to reach its final value is proportional to the *reciprocal* of this factor, that is, to L/R. The greater the value of L, the more time is needed. It turns out that in a time equal to L/R the current reaches about 63% of its final value. The quantity L/R is called the **time constant** for the circuit, denoted by τ:

$$\tau = \frac{L}{R}. \tag{33–14}$$

In a time equal to 2τ the current reaches 86% of its final value, in 5τ it reaches 99.3%, and in 10τ it reaches 99.995%.

The graphs of i versus t have the same general shape for all values of L. When L is small, the current rises rapidly to its final value; when L is large, the current rises more slowly. For example, if $R = 100\ \Omega$ and $L = 10$ H,

$$\tau = \frac{L}{R} = \frac{10\text{ H}}{100\ \Omega} = 0.10\text{ s},$$

and the current increases to about 63% of its final value in 0.10 s. But if $L = 0.010$ H, $\tau = 1.0 \times 10^{-4}$ s $= 0.10$ ms, and the rise is much more rapid.

Now suppose that switch S_1 in the circuit of Fig. 33–5 has been closed for a long time, and the final current $I = V/R$ has been reached. Redefining our initial time, we close switch S_2 at time $t = 0$, bypassing the battery. (We can then open S_1 to save the battery from ruin.) The current through R and L does not instantaneously go to zero but decays smoothly, as shown in Fig. 33–6b. In a time equal to $\tau = L/R$ the current decreases to about 37% of its original value. In time 2τ it has dropped to 13.5%, in time 5τ to 0.67%, and in 10τ to 0.0045%. The energy needed to maintain the current during this decay is provided by the energy stored in the magnetic field of the inductor.

If this whole discussion looks familiar, it is because of the close similarity of this situation to a charging and discharging capacitor, which we analyzed in Section 29–4. You may want to review that section and compare it with our discussion of the L–R circuit.

33–5
The L–C Circuit

Here's another example of a circuit containing an inductor. This circuit shows an entirely new mode of behavior, characterized by *oscillating* current and charge. The **L–C circuit** in Fig. 33–7 contains an inductor with negligible resistance and a capacitor. We charge the capacitor to a potential difference V_m, as shown in Fig. 33–7a, and then close the switch. What happens?

The capacitor begins to discharge through the inductor. Figure 33–7b shows the situation at a later time when the capacitor has completely discharged and the potential difference between its terminals (and those of the inductor) has decreased to zero. During this discharge the increasing current in the inductor has established a magnetic field in the space around it, and the energy initially stored in the electric field in the capacitor is now stored in the magnetic field in the inductor. This magnetic field now begins to decrease, inducing an emf in the inductor in the same direction as the current. The current cannot change instantaneously, and it persists, although with decreasing magnitude, until the

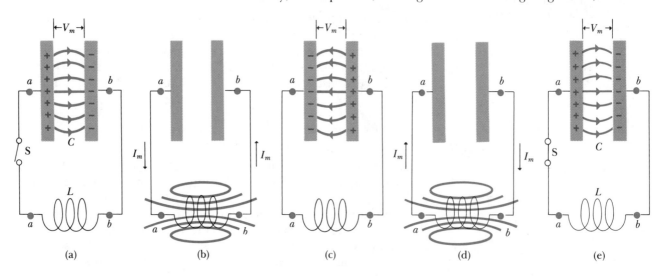

(a)   (b)   (c)   (d)   (e)

33–7
Energy transfer between electric and magnetic fields in an oscillating L–C circuit.

magnetic field has disappeared and the capacitor has been charged in the *opposite* sense to its initial polarity, as in Fig. 33–7c. The process now repeats itself in the reverse direction. If there are no energy losses, the charges on the capacitor surge back and forth indefinitely. This process is called an **electrical oscillation.**

From the energy standpoint the oscillations of an electrical circuit consist of a transfer of energy back and forth from the electric field of the capacitor to the magnetic field of the inductor. The *total* energy associated with the circuit is constant. This is analogous to the transfer of energy in an oscillating mechanical system from kinetic to potential and back, with constant total energy.

We can exploit this analogy with simple harmonic motion to determine the *frequency* of electrical oscillations in an *L–C* circuit. We suggest that you review the discussion of harmonic motion in Chapter 11 before going on. In the mechanical problem a body of mass m is attached to a spring with force constant k. Suppose we displace the body a distance A from its equilibrium position and release it from rest at time $t = 0$. Then, as shown in the left column of Table 33–1, the kinetic energy of the system at any later time is $\frac{1}{2}mv^2$, and its elastic potential energy is $\frac{1}{2}kx^2$. Because the system is conservative, the sum of these equals the initial energy of the system, $\frac{1}{2}kA^2$. The velocity v at any position is obtained just as in Section 11–2, Eq. (11–4):

$$v = \pm \sqrt{\frac{k}{m}}\sqrt{A^2 - x^2}. \tag{33–15}$$

The velocity v (strictly speaking, the x-component of velocity) equals $\Delta x/\Delta t$, and we found in Section 11–2 that the coordinate x varies with time t according to the function

$$x = A \cos\left(\sqrt{\frac{k}{m}}\,t\right) = A \cos \omega t, \tag{33–16}$$

where the angular frequency ω is

$$\omega = \sqrt{\frac{k}{m}}.$$

We recall also that the ordinary frequency f, the number of cycles per unit time, is given by $f = \omega/2\pi$.

In the electrical problem, also a conservative system, a capacitor with capacitance C is given an initial charge Q. At time $t = 0$ it is connected to the terminals of an inductor with self-inductance L. The magnetic energy of the inductor at any later time corresponds to the kinetic energy of the vibrating body and is given by $\frac{1}{2}Li^2$, where i is the current at any instant. The electrical energy of the capacitor corresponds to the elastic potential energy of the spring and is given by $q^2/2C$, where q is the charge on the capacitor at any instant. The sum of these energies equals the initial energy of the system, $Q^2/2C$. That is,

$$\frac{1}{2}Li^2 + \frac{q^2}{2C} = \frac{Q^2}{2C}.$$

TABLE 33-1 Oscillation of mass on a spring compared with the electrical oscillation in an L–C circuit	
Mass on a spring	**Circuit containing inductance and capacitance**
Kinetic energy $= \frac{1}{2}mv^2$	Magnetic energy $= \frac{1}{2}Li^2$
Potential energy $= \frac{1}{2}kx^2$	Electrical energy $= \dfrac{q^2}{2C}$
$\frac{1}{2}mv^2 + \frac{1}{2}kx^2 = \frac{1}{2}kA^2$	$\dfrac{1}{2}Li^2 + \dfrac{q^2}{2C} = \dfrac{Q^2}{2C}$
$v = \pm\sqrt{k/m}\,\sqrt{A^2 - x^2}$	$i = \pm\sqrt{1/LC}\,\sqrt{Q^2 - q^2}$
$v = \dfrac{\Delta x}{\Delta t}$	$i = \dfrac{\Delta q}{\Delta t}$
$x = A\cos\sqrt{k/m}\,t = A\cos\omega t$	$q = Q\cos\sqrt{1/LC}\,t = Q\cos\omega t$
$v = -\omega A\sin\omega t = -v_{max}\sin\omega t$	$i = -\omega Q\sin\omega t = -I\sin\omega t$

Solving for i, we find that when the charge on the capacitor is q, the current i is

$$i = \pm\sqrt{\frac{1}{LC}}\sqrt{Q^2 - q^2}. \qquad (33\text{--}17)$$

Comparing this with Eq. (33–15), we see that the relationship of current $i = \Delta q/\Delta t$ to charge q has exactly the same form as the relationship of velocity $v = \Delta x/\Delta t$ to position x in the mechanical problem. Continuing the analogy, we conclude from the form of Eq. (33–16) that q is given as a function of time by

$$q = Q\cos\left(\sqrt{\frac{1}{LC}}\,t\right) = Q\cos\omega t, \qquad (33\text{--}18)$$

with (k/m) in the mechanical problem replaced by $(1/LC)$. The angular frequency ω of the electrical oscillations is therefore

$$\omega = \sqrt{\frac{1}{LC}}. \qquad (33\text{--}19)$$

This is called the **natural frequency** of the L–C circuit. As Table 33–1 shows, it is analogous to the equation $\omega = \sqrt{k/m}$ for the angular frequency of a harmonic oscillator.

The striking parallel between the mechanical and electrical systems shown in Table 33–1 is only one of many such examples in physics. The parallel between electrical and mechanical (and acoustical) systems is so close that we can solve complicated mechanical and acoustical problems by setting up analogous electrical circuits and measuring the currents and voltages that correspond to the mechanical and acoustical quantities to be determined. This is the basic principle of one kind of *analog computer*. We see that in our comparison between the harmonic oscillator and the *L–C* circuit, *m* corresponds to *L*, *k* to $(1/C)$, *x* to *q*, and *v* to *i*. This analogy can be extended to *damped oscillations*, which we consider in the next section.

33–6
The *L–R–C* Circuit

In our discussion of the *L–C* circuit we did not include any *resistance*. This is an idealization, of course; every real inductor has resistance in its windings, and there may also be resistance in the connecting wires. The effect of resistance is to dissipate the electromagnetic energy in the circuit and convert it to heat. Resistance in an electric circuit is analogous to friction in a mechanical system.

Suppose an inductor with inductance *L* and a resistor with resistance *R* are connected in series across the terminals of a charged capacitor. As before, the capacitor starts to discharge as soon as the circuit is completed. But because of i^2R losses in the resistor, the energy of the inductor when the capacitor is completely discharged is *less* than the original energy of the capacitor. In the same way the energy of the capacitor when the magnetic field has collapsed is still smaller, and so on.

If the resistance *R* is relatively small, the circuit still oscillates, but with **damped harmonic motion,** as shown in Fig. 33–8a. If we increase *R*, the oscillations die out more rapidly. When *R* reaches a certain value, the circuit no longer oscillates, and we say that it is **critically damped,** as in Fig. 33–8b. For still larger values of *R* the circuit is **overdamped,** as in Fig. 33–8c, and the capacitor charge approaches zero more slowly.

It is possible, with appropriate electronic circuitry, to feed energy *into* an *L–R–C* circuit at the same rate that it is dissipated by i^2R losses. The behavior then is as though we had inserted a *negative resistance* into the circuit to make the *total* circuit resistance exactly zero. In this case the circuit oscillates with sustained oscillations of constant amplitude, just like the idealized *L–C* circuit with no resistance.

Still more interesting aspects of this circuit's behavior emerge when we include a sinusoidally varying source of emf in the circuit. This is analogous to the *forced oscillations* we discussed in Section 11–7, and there are analogous *resonance* effects. Such a circuit is called an *alternating-current (ac) circuit*; the analysis of ac circuits is the principal topic of Chapter 34.

33–8
Graphs of *q* versus *t* in an *L–R–C* circuit. (a) Small damping. (b) Critically damped. (c) Overdamped.

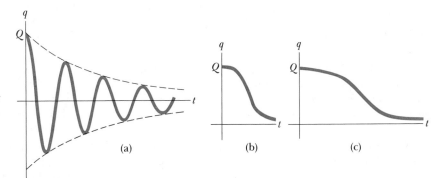

Questions

33–1 A resistor is to be made by winding a wire around a cylindrical form. To make the inductance as small as possible, it is proposed that we wind half the wire in one direction and the other half in the opposite direction. Would this achieve the desired result? Why or why not?

33–2 In Fig. 33–1b, if coil 2 is turned 90° so that its axis is vertical, does the mutual inductance increase or decrease?

33–3 The toroidal solenoid is one of the few configurations for which it is easy to calculate self-inductance. What features of the toroidal solenoid give it this simplicity?

33–4 Two identical closely wound circular coils, each having self-inductance L, are placed side by side, close together. If they are connected in series, what is the self-inductance of the combination? What if they are connected in parallel? Can they be connected so that the total inductance is zero?

33–5 If two inductors are separated enough that practically no flux from either links the coils of the other, show that the equivalent inductance of two inductors in series or parallel is obtained by the same rules for combining resistance.

33–6 Two closely wound circular coils have the same number of turns, but one has twice the radius of the other. How are the self-inductances of the two coils related?

33–7 One of the great problems in the field of energy resources and utilization is the difficulty of storing electrical energy in large quantities economically. Discuss the possibility of storing large amounts of energy by means of currents in large inductors.

33–8 In what regions in a toroidal solenoid is the energy density greatest? In what regions is it least?

33–9 Suppose there is a steady current in an inductor. If one attempts to reduce the current to zero instantaneously by opening a switch, a big fat arc appears at the switch contacts. Why? What happens to the induced emf in this situation? Is it physically possible to stop the current instantaneously?

33–10 In the R–L circuit of Fig. 33–5, is the current in the resistor always the same as that in the inductor? How do you know?

33–11 In the R–L circuit of Fig. 33–5, when switch S_1 is closed, the potential v_{ab} changes suddenly and discontinuously, but the current does not. Why can the voltage change suddenly but not the current?

33–12 In the R–L–C circuit, what criteria could be used to decide whether the system is overdamped or underdamped? For example, could one compare the maximum energy stored during one cycle to the energy dissipated during one cycle?

Exercises

Section 33–1   Mutual Inductance

33–1 From Eq. (33–4), 1 H = 1 Wb·A^{-1}, but from Eq. (33–3), 1 H = 1 Ω·s. Show that these two definitions are equivalent.

33–2 A toroidal solenoid has a radius of 10.0 cm and a cross-sectional area of 4.00 cm^2 and is wound uniformly with 1000 turns. A second coil with 500 turns is wound uniformly on top of the first. What is the mutual inductance?

33–3 A solenoid with a length of 10.0 cm and a radius of 2.00 cm is wound uniformly with 800 turns. A second coil with 50 turns is wound around the solenoid at its center. What is the mutual inductance of the two coils?

33–4 The flux from one coil links the turns of a second coil. When the current in the first coil is decreasing at a rate of -0.0850 A·s^{-1}, the induced emf in the

second coil has magnitude 2.00×10^{-3} V.

a) What is the mutual inductance of the pair of coils?

b) If the second coil has five turns, what is the flux through each turn when the current in the first coil equals 1.60 A?

c) If the current in the second coil increases at a rate of 0.0500 A·s^{-1}, what is the induced emf in the first coil?

33–5 Two coils have mutual inductance $M = 0.0200$ H. The current i_1 in the first coil increases at a uniform rate of 0.0500 A·s^{-1}.

a) What is the induced emf in the second coil? Is it constant?

b) Suppose that the current described is in the second coil rather than the first. What is the induced emf in the first coil?

Section 33–2   Self-Inductance

33–6

a) Show that the two expressions for self-inductance, namely,

$$\frac{N\Phi}{i} \quad \text{and} \quad \frac{\mathcal{E}}{\Delta i/\Delta t},$$

have the same units.

b) Show that L/R and RC both have units of time.

c) Show that 1 Wb·s^{-1} equals 1 V.

33–7 At the instant when the current in an inductor is increasing at a rate of 0.0600 A·s^{-1}, the self-induced emf is 0.0400 V.

a) What is the self-inductance of the inductor?

b) If the inductor is a solenoid with 300 turns, what is the magnetic flux through each turn when the current is 0.800 A?

33–8 An inductor with an inductance of 6.00 H carries a current that decreases at a uniform rate, $\Delta i/\Delta t = -0.0200$ A·s^{-1}. Find the self-induced emf. What is its polarity?

33–9

a) Find the self-inductance of the toroidal solenoid in Exercise 33–2 if only the 1000-turn coil is used.

b) If both coils are used, connected in series with each other, what is the self-inductance of the combination? The two coils are wound in the same sense, so the magnetic fields of the two windings are in the same direction.

33–10 A long, straight solenoid has N turns, uniform cross-sectional area A, and length l. Derive an expression for the self-inductance of the solenoid. Assume that the magnetic field is uniform inside the solenoid and zero outside. (This is a reasonable approximation if the solenoid is long and the turns are closely wound.)

33–11 A toroidal solenoid has a cross-sectional area of 4.00 cm^2, a radius of 5.00 cm, and 2000 turns. It is filled with a core with a relative permeability of 600. Calculate the self-inductance of the solenoid.

Section 33–3   Energy in an Inductor

33–12 It has been proposed to use large inductors as energy storage devices.

a) How much electrical energy is converted to light and heat by a 100-W light bulb in one day?

b) If the amount of energy calculated in part (a) is stored in an inductor in which the current is 50.0 A, what is the inductance?

33–13 A toroidal solenoid has a mean radius of 0.120 m and a cross-sectional area of 2.00×10^{-3} m^2.

When the current is 25.0 A, the energy stored is 0.350 J. How many turns does the winding have?

33–14 Derive in detail Eq. (33–10) for the energy density in a toroidal solenoid filled with a magnetic material.

33–15 An inductor used in a dc power supply has an inductance of 12.0 H and a resistance of 200 Ω and carries a current of 0.150 A.

a) What is the energy stored in the magnetic field?

b) At what rate is electrical energy converted to heat in the resistor?

33–16 A magnetic field with magnitude $B = 0.600$ T is uniform across a volume of 0.0200 m^3. Calculate the total magnetic energy in the volume if

a) the volume is free space;

b) the volume is filled with material with relative permeability 600.

Section 33–4   The R–L Circuit

33–17 The resistance of a 10.0-H inductor is 200 Ω. The inductor is suddenly connected across a potential difference of 40.0 V

a) What is the final steady current in the inductor?

b) What is the initial rate of increase of the current?

c) At what rate is the current increasing when its value is one-half the final current?

d) At what time after the circuit is closed does the current equal 99.3% of its final value?

33–18 An inductor with an inductance of 3.00 H and a resistance of 4.00 Ω is connected to the terminals of a battery with an emf of 12.0 V and negligible internal resistance. Find

a) the initial rate of increase of the current in the circuit;

b) the rate of increase of the current at the instant when the current is 1.00 A;

c) the final steady-state current.

33–19 In Fig. 33–5, let $V = 250$ V, $R = 500$ Ω, and $L = 0.300$ H. With switch S_2 open, switch S_1 is closed and left until a constant current is established. Then S_2 is closed and S_1 opened, taking the battery out of the circuit.

a) What is the initial current in the resistor, just after S_2 is closed and S_1 is opened?

b) What is the initial rate of change of the current in the resistor?

c) What is the current in the resistor after a large number of time constants?

33–20 In Fig. 33–5, let $V = 80.0$ V, $R = 400$ Ω, and $L = 0.200$ H. Initially, there is no current in the circuit.

With switch S_2 open, switch S_1 is closed.

a) Just after S_1 is closed, what are the potential differences v_{ac} and v_{cb}?

b) A long time (many time constants) after S_1 is closed, what are v_{ac} and v_{cb}?

c) What are v_{ac} and v_{cb} at an intermediate time when $i = 0.0500$ A?

33–21 Refer to Exercise 33–18.

a) What is the power input to the inductor at the instant when the current in it is 0.500 A?

b) What is the rate of dissipation of energy in the resistance of the inductor at this instant?

c) What is the rate at which the energy of the magnetic field is increasing?

d) How are the answers to parts (a), (b), and (c) related?

e) How much energy is stored in the magnetic field when the current has reached its final steady value?

Section 33–5   The L–C Circuit

33–22 An inductor having $L = 40.0$ mH is to be combined with a capacitor to make an L–C circuit with natural frequency 9.00×10^6 Hz. What capacitance should be used?

33–23 A capacitor with capacitance 6.00×10^{-4} F is charged by connecting it to a 50.0 V battery. The capacitor is disconnected from the battery and connected across an inductor with $L = 3.00$ H.

a) What is the angular frequency ω of the electrical oscillations and the period of these oscillations (the time for one oscillation)?

b) What is the initial charge on the capacitor?

c) How much energy is initially stored in the capacitor?

d) What is the charge on the capacitor 0.0444 s after the connection to the inductor is made?

e) At the time given in part (d), what is the current in the inductor?

f) At the time given in part (d), how much electrical energy is stored in the capacitor and how much is stored in the inductor?

33–24 The maximum capacitance of a variable air capacitor is 45.0 pF.

a) What is the self-inductance of a coil connected to this capacitor if the natural frequency of the L–C circuit is 550×10^3 Hz, corresponding to one end of the AM radio broadcast band, when the capacitor is set to its maximum capacitance?

b) The frequency at the other end of the broadcast band is 1550×10^3 Hz. What is the minimum capacitance of the capacitor if the natural frequency is adjustable over the range of the broadcast band?

■ Problems

33–25 The current in a coil of wire is initially zero but increases at a constant rate; after 10.0 s it is 50.0 A. The changing current induces an emf of 45.0 V in the coil.

a) Determine the self-inductance of the coil.

b) Determine the total magnetic flux through the coil when the current is 50.0 A.

c) If the resistance of the coil is 25.0 Ω, determine the ratio of the rate at which energy is being stored in the magnetic field to the rate at which electrical energy is being converted to heat by the resistance at the instant when the current is 50.0 A.

33–26 A solenoid has length l_1, radius r_1, and number of turns N_1. A second, smaller solenoid of length l_2, radius r_2, and number of turns N_2 is placed at the center of the first solenoid such that their axes coincide. Assume that the magnetic field of the first solenoid at the location of the second is uniform and has a magnitude given by Eq. (31–7).

a) What is the mutual inductance of the pair of solenoids?

b) If the current in the large solenoid is increasing at the rate $\Delta i_1/\Delta t$, what is the magnitude of the emf induced in the small solenoid?

c) If the current in the small solenoid is increasing at the rate $\Delta i_2/\Delta t$, what is the magnitude of the emf induced in the large solenoid?

33–27 The current in a resistanceless inductor is caused to vary with time as in the graph of Fig. 33–9. Sketch the pattern that would be observed on the screen of an oscilloscope connected to the terminals of

FIGURE 33–9

the inductor. (The oscilloscope spot sweeps horizontally across the screen at a constant speed, and its vertical deflection is proportional to the potential difference between the inductor terminals.)

33–28 A toroidal solenoid has two coils with N_1 and N_2 turns, both wound in the same direction. The solenoid has radius r and cross-sectional area A.

a) Derive an expression for the self-inductance L_1 when only the first coil is used and an expression for L_2 when only the second coil is used.

b) Derive an expression for the mutual inductance of the two coils.

c) Show that $M^2 = L_1L_2$. This result is valid whenever all the flux linked by one coil is also linked by the other.

33–29 A long, straight solenoid has N turns, uniform cross-sectional area A, and length l. The current in the solenoid is I.

a) Calculate the energy stored in the solenoid by multiplying the energy density, Eq. (33–9), by the volume Al enclosed by the solenoid. (This makes the assumption that the magnetic field is uniform inside the solenoid with the value given by Eq. (31–6) and zero outside. This assumption is reasonable if the length of the solenoid is much greater than its radius and if the turns are closely wound.)

b) Calculate the energy stored from Eq. (33–8) and the expression for L derived in Exercise 33–10. How does this result compare with that obtained in part (a)?

33–30 Uniform electric and magnetic fields E and B occupy the same region of free space. If $E = 600$ V·m^{-1}, what is B if the energy densities in the electric and magnetic fields are equal?

33–31 The 1000-turn toroidal solenoid described in Exercise 33–2 carries a current of 6.00 A.

a) What is the energy density in the magnetic field?

b) What is the total magnetic-field energy? Find this energy using Eq. (33–8) and also by multiplying the energy density from part (a) by the volume of the toroid, which is $2\pi rA$; compare the two results.

33–32 An L–C circuit consists of an inductor with $L = 0.800$ H and a capacitor with $C = 6.00 \times 10^{-4}$ F. The initial charge on the capacitor is 5.00 μC, and the initial current in the inductor is zero.

a) What is the maximum voltage across the capacitor?

b) What is the maximum current in the inductor?

c) What is the maximum energy stored in the inductor?

d) When the current in the inductor has half its maximum value, what is the charge on the capacitor and what is the energy stored in the inductor?

33–33 You are asked to design an L–C circuit in which the stored energy is 2.00×10^{-4} J and the natural frequency is $\omega = 8.00 \times 10^4$ rad·s^{-1}. The maximum voltage across the capacitor is to be 50.0 V. What values of C and L are required?

33–34 Consider the circuit of Fig. 33–10. Let $\mathcal{E} = 60.0$ V, $R_1 = 20.0$ Ω, $R_2 = 30.0$ Ω, and $L = 0.200$ H.

a) Just after the switch S is closed, what are the currents i_1 and i_2 through the resistors R_1 and R_2?

b) After the switch has been closed for a long time, what are i_1 and i_2?

c) After S has been closed for a long time it is opened again. Just after it is opened, what is the current through R_1?

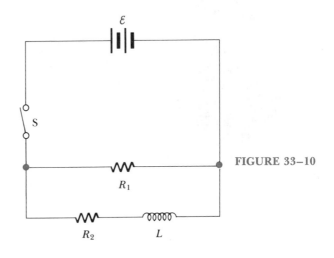

FIGURE 33–10

Challenge Problems

33–35 A tank containing a liquid has turns of wire wrapped around it, causing it to act as an inductor. The liquid content of the tank can be measured by using its inductance to determine the height of the liquid in the tank. The inductance of the tank changes

from a value of L_0, corresponding to a relative permeability of 1 when the tank is empty to a value of L_f, corresponding to a relative permeability of K_m (the relative permeability of the liquid), when the tank is full. The appropriate electronic circuitry can determine the inductance to five significant figures and hence the effective relative permeability of the combined air and liquid within the rectangular cavity of the tank. Each of the four sides of the tank has a width W and a height D. (See Fig. 33–11.) The height of the liquid in the tank is d. Neglect any fringing effects, and assume that the relative permeability of the tank material can be neglected.

a) Derive an expression for d as a function of L, the inductance corresponding to a certain fluid height, L_0, and L_f.

b) What is the inductance (to five significant figures) for a tank one-quarter full, one-half full, three-quarters full, and completely full if the tank contains liquid oxygen? Take $L_0 = 0.75000$ H. The magnetic susceptibility of liquid oxygen is $\chi_m = 1.52 \times 10^{-3}$.

c) Repeat part (b) for mercury. The magnetic susceptibility of mercury is given in Table 31–1.

d) For which material is this gauge more practical?

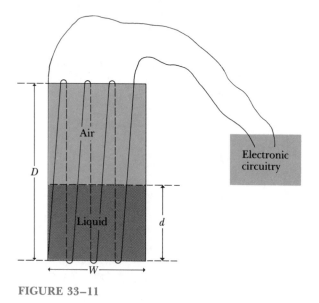

FIGURE 33–11

33–36 Consider the circuit of Fig. 33–12. Let $\mathcal{E} = 40.0$ V, $R_0 = 50.0$ Ω, $R = 150$ Ω, and $L = 5.00$ H.

a) Switch S_1 is closed, while S_2 is left open. Just after S_1 is closed, what are the current i_0 through R_0 and the potential differences v_{ac} and v_{cb}?

b) After S_1 has been closed a long time (S_2 is still open), so that the current in the circuit has reached its final steady value, what are i_0, v_{ac}, and v_{cb}?

c) After S_1 has been closed a long time, S_2 is closed as well. Just after S_2 has been closed, what are i_0, the current i through R, v_{ac}, and v_{cb}?

d) Repeat part (c) for when switch S_2 has been closed for a long time.

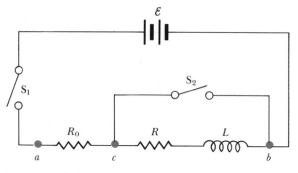

FIGURE 33–12

33–37 An inductor is made with two coils wound close together on a form so that all the flux linking one coil also links the other. The number of turns is the same in each. If the inductance of one coil is L, what is the inductance when the two coils are connected

a) in series?   b) in parallel?

In each case the current travels in the same sense around each coil.

c) If an L–C circuit using this inductor has natural frequency ω using one coil, what is the natural frequency when the two coils are used in series?

Alternating Currents

In our study of circuits in Chapters 28 and 29 we concentrated primarily on *direct-current* circuits, in which all the currents, voltages, and emf's are *constant*, that is, not functions of time. However, many electric circuits of practical importance, including most household and industrial power-distribution systems, use **alternating current,** in which the voltages and currents vary with time, often in a *sinusoidal* manner. Alternating currents are of utmost importance in technology and industry. Transmission of power over long distances is much more economical with alternating than with direct current. Circuits used in modern communication equipment, including radio and television, make extensive use of alternating current. In this chapter we study the behavior of circuits having sinusoidally varying voltages and currents. Many of the same principles that we used in Chapters 28, 29, and 33 are applicable here as well, and we also introduce several new concepts related to the circuit behavior of inductors and capacitors.

34–1

ac Sources and Phasors

We have already studied several sources of alternating emf or voltage. A coil of wire, rotating with constant angular velocity in a magnetic field, develops a sinusoidal alternating emf, as we discussed in Section 32–2. This simple device is the prototype of the commercial alternating-current generator, or **alternator.** An *L–C* circuit, which we discussed in Section 33–5, oscillates sinusoidally. With the proper circuitry it provides an alternating potential difference with a frequency that may range from a few hertz to many millions of hertz.

We will use the term **ac source** for an alternator or oscillator that maintains a sinusoidal alternating potential difference v between its terminals, where v is given by

$$v = V \cos \omega t. \tag{34–1}$$

In this expression, V is the maximum potential difference, which we call the **voltage amplitude;** v is the *instantaneous* potential difference; and ω is the *angular frequency*, equal to 2π times the frequency f. In the United States, commercial electric-power distribution systems always use a frequency of $f = 60$ Hz, corresponding to $\omega = 2\pi(60 \text{ s}^{-1}) = 377 \text{ s}^{-1}$. The usual circuit-diagram symbol for an ac source is ⎓⊘⎓.

In our analysis of alternating-current circuits we will often use rotating vector diagrams similar to those we used in the study of harmonic motion in Section 11–3. In these diagrams the instantaneous value of a quantity that varies sinusoidally with time is represented by the *projection* onto a horizontal axis of a vector with a length equal to the amplitude of the quantity. The vector rotates counterclockwise with constant angular velocity ω. These rotating vectors are called **phasors,** and diagrams containing them are called **phasor diagrams.**

A phasor is not a real physical quantity with a direction in space such as velocity, momentum, and electric field. Rather, it is a *geometric* entity that provides a language for describing and analyzing physical quantities that vary sinusoidally with time. In Section 11–3 we used a single phasor to represent the position and motion of a point mass undergoing simple harmonic motion. In this chapter we will use phasors to *add* sinusoidal voltages and currents. Combining sinusoidal quantities with phase differences then becomes a matter of vector addition. We will find a similar use for phasors in Chapter 39, in our study of interference phenomena in optics.

How do we measure a sinusoidally varying current? In Section 29–3 we used a d'Arsonval galvanometer to measure steady currents. But if we pass a *sinusoidal* current through a d'Arsonval meter, the torque on the moving coil varies sinusoidally. Both the current and the resulting torque have one direction half the time and the opposite direction the other half, and the average value of each quantity is zero. The needle may wiggle a little if the frequency is low enough, but its average deflection is zero. The *average* value of a sinusoidal current is always zero, so it isn't a very interesting quantity.

We need to get a one-way current through the meter; we can do this with the use of *diodes*, which we described in Section 28–3. An ideal

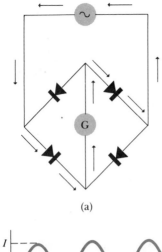

(a)

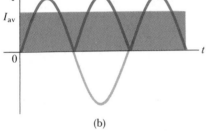

(b)

34–1
(a) A full-wave rectifier circuit.
(b) Graph of a full-wave rectified
current and its average value.

diode has zero resistance for one direction of current flow and infinite resistance for the other. One possible arrangement is shown in Fig. 34–1a; a little study shows that the current through the galvanometer G is always upward, regardless of the sign of the ac source voltage (i.e., which part of the cycle it is in). The current through the galvanometer then varies as shown by the graph in Fig. 34–1b. It pulsates, but it always has the same direction, and the meter deflection is *not* zero. The arrangement of diodes is called a *full-wave rectifier*.

The **average** current I_{av} is defined so that during any whole number of cycles the total charge that flows is the same as though the current were constant, with a value equal to the average value. For that to be true the area under the curve in Fig. 34–1b must be equal to the rectangular area with height I_{av}. We can see that I_{av} is about 2/3 the maximum current I; in fact, we can show, with the aid of a little calculus, that the two are related by

$$I_{av} = \frac{2}{\pi}I = 0.637I. \qquad (34\text{–}2)$$

The galvanometer deflection is proportional to I_{av}, and the scale can be calibrated to read either I or I_{av}. To emphasize that I_{av} is *not* the average of the original current, we call it the *rectified average* current.

A different and more generally useful way to deal with the average value of a quantity that is positive half the time and negative the other half is to use the concept of **root-mean-square** value. We discussed this concept in Section 20–3 in connection with describing the speeds of molecules in a gas. What we do is to *square* the instantaneous current i, take the average value of i^2, and take the square root of that average. The point is that i^2 is always positive, even when i is negative, so the average of i^2 is never zero. The result of this computation is the **root-mean-square current**, which we denote as I_{rms}.

Here's how we obtain I_{rms}. If the instantaneous current i is given by $i = I \cos \omega t$, where I is the maximum current (the current *amplitude*), then

$$i^2 = I^2 \cos^2 \omega t.$$

There is a double-angle formula that says that for any angle A,

$$\cos^2 A = \tfrac{1}{2}(1 - \cos 2A).$$

Using this in the expression for i^2, we find

$$i^2 = I^2 \tfrac{1}{2}(1 - \cos 2\omega t) = \tfrac{1}{2}I^2 - \tfrac{1}{2}I^2 \cos 2\omega t.$$

The average of $\cos 2\omega t$ is zero because it is positive half the time and negative half the time. Thus the average of i^2 is simply $I^2/2$, and the square root of this is I_{rms}:

$$I_{rms} = \frac{I}{\sqrt{2}}. \qquad (34\text{–}3)$$

In the same way the root-mean-square value of a sinusoidal voltage with amplitude (maximum value) V is

$$V_{rms} = \frac{V}{\sqrt{2}}. \qquad (34\text{–}4)$$

We can convert a rectifying ammeter into a voltmeter by adding a series resistor, just as we did for the dc case we discussed in Section 29–3. Meters used for ac voltage and current measurements are nearly always calibrated to read rms values, not maximum. Voltages and currents in power distribution systems are always described in terms of their rms values. The usual household power supply, "120-volt ac," has an rms voltage of 120 V. The voltage amplitude is

$$V = \sqrt{2}V_{\mathrm{rms}} = 170 \text{ V}.$$

34–2
Resistance, Inductance, and Capacitance

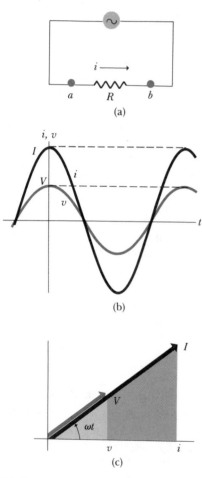

34–2
(a) Resistance R connected across an ac source. (b) Graphs of instantaneous voltage v and current i. (c) Phasor diagram; current and voltage are in phase.

The simplest problem in ac circuit analysis is a resistor with resistance R connected between the terminals of an ac source, as in Fig. 34–2a. Suppose the instantaneous potential v of point a with respect to point b is $v = V \cos \omega t$. From Ohm's law the instantaneous current i in the resistor is

$$i = \frac{v}{R} = \frac{V}{R} \cos \omega t. \qquad (34\text{–}5)$$

The maximum current I, also called the **current amplitude,** is

$$I = \frac{V}{R}, \qquad (34\text{–}6)$$

so we can also write

$$i = I \cos \omega t. \qquad (34\text{–}7)$$

The current i and voltage v are both proportional to $\cos \omega t$, so the current is *in phase* with the voltage. Equation (34–6) shows that the current and voltage amplitudes are related in the same way as in a dc circuit.

Figure 34–2b shows graphs of i and v as functions of time. The choice of vertical scales for i and v is arbitrary, so the relative heights of the two curves are not significant. The corresponding phasor diagram is given in Fig. 34–2c. Because i and v are *in phase* and have the same frequency, the current and voltage phasors rotate together; they are parallel at each instant. Their projections on the horizontal axis represent the instantaneous current and voltage, respectively.

Next, suppose we connect a capacitor with capacitance C across the source, as in Fig. 34–3a. From Eq. (27–1) the instantaneous charge q on the capacitor is

$$q = Cv = CV \cos \omega t. \qquad (34\text{–}8)$$

In this case the instantaneous current i is equal to the *rate of change* of the capacitor charge q and is thus proportional to the rate of change of voltage:

$$i = \frac{\Delta q}{\Delta t} = C \frac{\Delta v}{\Delta t}. \qquad (34\text{–}9)$$

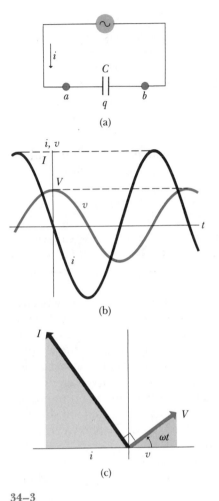

(a)

(b)

(c)

34–3
(a) Capacitor C connected across an ac source. (b) Graphs of instantaneous voltage v and current i. (c) Phasor diagram; voltage *lags* current by 90°.

Figure 34–3b shows v as a function of t. Because $i = \Delta q/\Delta t$, the current must be greatest when the v curve is rising or falling most steeply and zero when the v curve "levels off" at its maximum and minimum values. Thus the current i must vary with time as shown by the i curve in Fig. 34–3b. This curve has the same general shape as the graph of $-\sin \omega t$. In fact, it can be shown by use of calculus that the current i is given by

$$i = -\omega CV \sin \omega t. \tag{34–10}$$

Thus if the voltage is represented by a *cosine* function, the current is represented by a *negative sine* function, as shown in Fig. 34–3b. The voltage and current are "out of step" or *out of phase* by a quarter-cycle. The peaks of current occur a quarter-cycle *before* the corresponding voltage peaks. This result is also shown in the phasor diagram in Fig. 34–3c; the current phasor is ahead of the voltage phasor by a quarter-cycle or 90°.

We can also obtain this *phase difference* between current and voltage by rewriting Eq. (34–10), using the formula $\cos (A + 90°) = -\sin A$:

$$i = \omega CV \cos (\omega t + 90°). \tag{34–11}$$

We can think of the expression for i in a capacitor as a cosine function with a "head start" of 90° compared with that for the voltage. We say that the current *leads* the voltage by 90° or that the voltage *lags* the current by 90°. Alternatively, if i is given by $i = \omega CV \cos \omega t$, then $v = V \cos (\omega t - 90°)$.

For consistency in later discussions we will usually describe the phase of the voltage relative to the current. Thus if the current i in a circuit is given by

$$i = I \cos \omega t,$$

and the voltage v between two points is

$$v = V \cos (\omega t + \phi),$$

we call ϕ the **phase angle,** understanding that it gives the phase of the *voltage* relative to the *current*. For the capacitor we have $\phi = -90°$, and the voltage *lags* the current by 90°.

Equations (34–10) and (34–11) show that the *maximum* current I (the current amplitude) is given by

$$I = \omega CV. \tag{34–12}$$

We can put this expression in the same form as the maximum current in a resistor, $(I = V/R)$, if we write Eq. (34–12) as

$$I = \frac{V}{1/\omega C},$$

and define a quantity X_C, called the **capacitive reactance** of the capacitor, as

$$X_C = \frac{1}{\omega C}. \tag{34–13}$$

Then

$$I = \frac{V}{X_C}. \tag{34–14}$$

This has the same form as Ohm's law, with X_C playing the role of R. From Eq. (34–14) the SI unit of capacitive reactance is 1 *volt per ampere* (1 V·A^{-1}), or 1 *ohm* (1 Ω).

The reactance of a capacitor is inversely proportional both to the capacitance C and to the angular frequency ω; the greater the capacitance and the higher the frequency, the *smaller* the reactance X_C.

Example 34–1 When the angular frequency is 1000 rad·s^{-1} ($f = 1000$ s$^{-1}/2\pi = 159$ Hz) the reactance of a 1-μF capacitor is

$$X_C = \frac{1}{\omega C} = \frac{1}{(10^3 \text{ rad·s}^{-1})(10^{-6} \text{ F})} = 1000 \text{ Ω}.$$

At a frequency of 10,000 rad·s^{-1} the reactance of the same capacitor is only 100 Ω, and at a frequency of 100 rad·s^{-1} it is 10,000 Ω. ∎

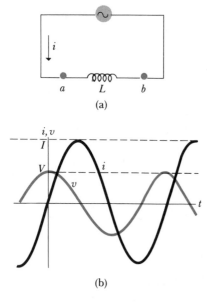

(a)

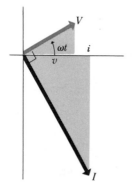

(b)

(c)

34–4

(a) Inductance L connected across an ac source. (b) Graphs of instantaneous voltage v and current i. (c) Phasor diagram; voltage *leads* current by 90°.

Finally, suppose we connect a pure inductor with self-inductance L and zero resistance to an ac source, as in Fig. 34–4a. The potential v of point a with respect to point b is given by Eq. (33–7): $v = L \, \Delta i/\Delta t$. The voltage at any instant is proportional to the *rate of change* of the current. The points of maximum voltage on the graph correspond to maximum steepness of the current curve, and the points of zero voltage are the points where the current curve levels off at its maximum and minimum values. In Fig. 34–4b, v is given by Eq. (34–1), and the general shape of the i curve is that of a *sine* function. Indeed, it can be shown by using calculus that in this case, i is given by

$$i = \frac{V}{\omega L} \sin \omega t. \qquad (34\text{–}15)$$

Again the voltage and current are a quarter-cycle out of phase, but this time the voltage *leads* the current by 90°. We can also see this by rewriting Eq. (34–15) using the formula $\cos (A - 90°) = \sin A$:

$$i = \frac{V}{\omega L} \cos (\omega t - 90°). \qquad (34\text{–}16)$$

This result and the phasor diagram of Fig. 34–4c show that the voltage can be viewed as a cosine function with a "head start" of 90°. Alternatively, if i is given by

$$i = \frac{V}{\omega L} \cos \omega t,$$

then the voltage v is

$$v = V \cos (\omega t + 90°).$$

The phase angle ϕ of the voltage with respect to the current is $\phi = +90°$.

From Eq. (34–15) or (34–16) the maximum current I is

$$I = \frac{V}{\omega L}. \qquad (34\text{–}17)$$

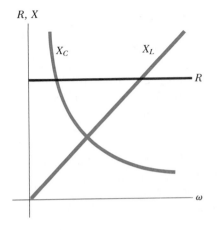

R, X

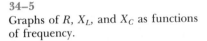

34–5
Graphs of R, X_L, and X_C as functions
of frequency.

We define the **inductive reactance** X_L of an inductor as

$$X_L = \omega L. \qquad (34\text{–}18)$$

Using X_L, we can write Eq. (34–17) in the same form as for a resistor:

$$I = \frac{V}{X_L}. \qquad (34\text{–}19)$$

The SI unit of inductive reactance is also 1 *ohm*.

The reactance of an inductor is directly proportional both to its inductance L and to the angular frequency ω; the greater the inductance and the higher the frequency, the *larger* the reactance.

Example 34–2   At an angular frequency of 1000 rad·s^{-1} the reactance of a 1-H inductor is

$$X_L = \omega L = (10^3 \text{ rad·s}^{-1})(1 \text{ H}) = 1000 \ \Omega.$$

At a frequency of 10,000 rad·s^{-1} the reactance of the same inductor is 10,000 Ω, while at a frequency of 100 rad·s^{-1} it is only 100 Ω.   ■

The graphs in Fig. 34–5 show how the resistance of a resistor and the reactances of an inductor and a capacitor vary with frequency. As the frequency increases, the reactance of the inductor approaches infinity, and that of the capacitor approaches zero. As the frequency decreases, the inductive reactance approaches zero, and the capacitive reactance approaches infinity. The limiting case of zero frequency corresponds to a dc circuit; in that case there is *no* current through a capacitor because $X_C \to \infty$, and there is no inductive effect because $X_L \to 0$.

34–3
The *L–R–C* Series Circuit

Many ac circuits used in real-life electronic systems include resistance, inductive reactance, and capacitive reactance. A series circuit containing a resistor, an inductor, and a capacitor is shown in Fig. 34–6a. To analyze this and similar circuits, we will use a phasor diagram that includes the voltage and current phasors for each of the components. In this circuit, because of Kirchhoff's loop rule, the instantaneous *total* voltage v_{ab} across all three components is equal to the source voltage at that instant. We will show that the phasor representing this total voltage is the *vector sum* of the phasors for the individual voltages. The complete phasor diagram for this circuit is shown in Fig. 34–6b. This diagram may appear complex, but we will explain it one step at a time.

The instantaneous current i has the same value at all points of the circuit. Thus a *single phasor I*, with length proportional to the current amplitude, represents the current in *all* circuit elements.

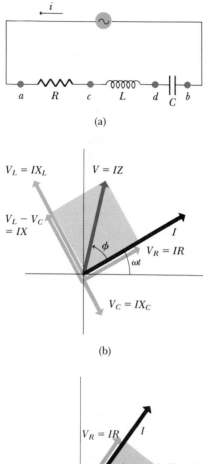

34–6
(a) A series L–R–C circuit. (b) Phasor diagram for the case $X_L > X_C$.
(c) Phasor diagram for the case $X_C > X_L$.

We use the symbols v_R, v_L, and v_C for the instantaneous voltages across R, L, and C and V_R, V_L, and V_C for their maximum values. We denote the instantaneous and maximum *source* voltages by v and V. Then $v = v_{ab}$, $v_R = v_{ac}$, $v_L = v_{cd}$, and $v_C = v_{db}$.

We have shown that the potential difference between the terminals of a resistor is *in phase* with the current in the resistor and that its maximum value V_R is

$$V_R = IR.$$

The phasor V_R in Fig. 34–6b, in phase with the current vector, represents the voltage across the resistor. Its projection on the horizontal axis at any instant gives the instantaneous potential difference v_R.

The voltage across an inductor *leads* the current by 90°. Its voltage amplitude is

$$V_L = IX_L.$$

The phasor V_L in Fig. 34–6b represents the voltage across the inductor, and its projection at any instant onto the horizontal axis equals v_L.

The voltage across a capacitor *lags* the current by 90°. Its voltage amplitude is

$$V_C = IX_C.$$

The phasor V_C in Fig. 34–6b represents the voltage across the capacitor, and its projection at any instant onto the horizontal axis equals v_C.

The instantaneous potential difference v between terminals a and b is equal at every instant to the (algebraic) sum of the potential differences v_R, v_L, and v_C. That is, it equals the sum of the *projections* of the phasors V_R, V_L, and V_C. But the sum of the projections of these phasors is equal to the *projection* of their *vector sum*. So the vector sum V must be the phasor that represents the source voltage v and the instantaneous voltage v_{ab} across the series of elements. To form this vector sum, we first subtract the phasor V_C from the phasor V_L. (These two phasors always lie along the same line.) This gives the phasor $V_L - V_C$. This is always at right angles to the phasor V_R, so from the Pythagorean theorem the magnitude of the phasor V is

$$V = \sqrt{V_R^2 + (V_L - V_C)^2} = \sqrt{(IR)^2 + (IX_L - IX_C)^2}$$
$$= I\sqrt{R^2 + (X_L - X_C)^2}. \qquad (34\text{--}20)$$

The quantity $X_L - X_C$ is called the **reactance** of the circuit, denoted by X:

$$X = X_L - X_C. \qquad (34\text{--}21)$$

Finally, we define the **impedance** Z of the circuit as

$$Z = \sqrt{R^2 + (X_L - X_C)^2} = \sqrt{R^2 + X^2}, \qquad (34\text{--}22)$$

so we can rewrite Eq. (34–20) as

$$V = IZ. \qquad (34\text{--}23)$$

Equation (34–23) again has the same form as Ohm's law, with impedance Z playing the same role as resistance R in a dc circuit. Note, however, that the impedance is actually a function of R, L, and C, as well as of the frequency ω. The complete expression for Z, for a series circuit, is

$$Z = \sqrt{R^2 + X^2} = \sqrt{R^2 + (X_L - X_C)^2}$$
$$= \sqrt{R^2 + [\omega L - (1/\omega C)]^2}. \tag{34–24}$$

From Eq. (34–22) or (34–23) the unit of impedance is 1 *volt per ampere* (1 V·A^{-1}) or 1 *ohm*.

Equation (34–24) gives the impedance Z only for a *series L–R–C* circuit. But we can *define* the impedance of *any* network, using Eq. (34–23), as the ratio of the voltage amplitude to the current amplitude.

The angle ϕ shown in Fig. 34–6b is the phase angle of the source voltage v with respect to the current i. From the diagram,

$$\tan \phi = \frac{V_L - V_C}{V_R} = \frac{I(X_L - X_C)}{IR} = \frac{X_L - X_C}{R} = \frac{X}{R}$$
$$= \frac{\omega L - 1/\omega C}{R}. \tag{34–25}$$

The source voltage leads the current by an angle ϕ. If the current i is a cosine function,

$$i = I \cos \omega t,$$

then the function for the source voltage v is

$$v = V \cos (\omega t + \phi).$$

Figure 34–6b shows the behavior of a circuit in which $X_L > X_C$. If $X_L < X_C$, as in Fig. 34–6c, vector V lies on the opposite side of the current vector I, and the voltage *lags* the current. In this case, $X = X_L - X_C$ is a *negative* quantity, $\tan \phi$ is negative, and ϕ is a negative angle between 0 and $-90°$.

Finally, we note that all the relations we have developed for an *L–R–C* series circuit are still valid if one of the circuit elements is missing. If the resistor is missing, we set $R = 0$; if the inductor is missing, we set $L = 0$. But if the capacitor is missing, we set $C = \infty$, corresponding to the absence of any potential difference ($v = q/C$) or any capacitive reactance ($X_C = 1/\omega C$).

PROBLEM-SOLVING STRATEGY: *Alternating-Current Circuits*

1. In ac circuit problems it is nearly always easiest to work with angular frequency ω. But you may be given the ordinary frequency f, expressed in hertz. Don't forget to convert, using $\omega = 2\pi f$.

2. Keep in mind a few basic facts about phase relationships. For a resistor, voltage and current are always *in phase*, and the two corresponding phasors in a phasor diagram always have the same direction. For a capacitor the voltage always *lags* the current by 90° (i.e., $\phi = -90°$), and the voltage phasor is always turned 90° clockwise from the current phasor. For an inductor the voltage always *leads* the current by 90° (i.e., $\phi = +90°$), and the voltage phasor is always turned 90° counterclockwise from the current phasor.

3. Remember that Kirchhoff's rules are just as applicable for ac circuits as for dc circuits. All the voltages and currents are sinusoidal functions of time instead of being constant, but Kirchhoff's rules hold at each instant. Thus in a series circuit

the instantaneous current is the same in all circuit elements; in a parallel circuit the instantaneous potential difference is the same across all circuit elements.

4. Reactance and impedance are analogous to resistance; each represents the ratio of voltage amplitude V to current amplitude I in a circuit element or combination of elements. But keep in mind that phase relations play an essential role; resistance, reactance, and impedance have to be combined by *vector* addition of the corresponding phasors. When you have several circuit elements in series, for example, you can't just *add* all the numerical values of resistance and reactance; that would ignore the phase relations.

Example 34–3   In the series circuit of Fig. 34–6a, suppose that $R = 300\ \Omega$, $L = 0.90$ H, $C = 2.0\ \mu$F, and $\omega = 1000$ rad·s^{-1}. Find the reactances X_L and X_C, the impedance Z, the current amplitude I, the phase angle ϕ, and the voltage amplitude across each circuit element.

Solution   From Eqs. (34–18) and (34–13),

$$X_L = \omega L = (1000\ \text{s}^{-1})(0.90\ \text{H}) = 900\ \Omega,$$

$$X_C = \frac{1}{\omega C} = \frac{1}{(1000\ \text{s}^{-1})(2.0 \times 10^{-6}\ \text{F})} = 500\ \Omega.$$

The reactance X of the circuit is

$$X = X_L - X_C = 400\ \Omega,$$

and the impedance Z is

$$Z = \sqrt{R^2 + X^2} = \sqrt{(300\ \Omega)^2 + (400\ \Omega)^2} = 500\ \Omega.$$

If the circuit is connected across an ac source with voltage amplitude $V = 50$ V, the current amplitude is

$$I = \frac{V}{Z} = \frac{50\ \text{V}}{500\ \Omega} = 0.10\ \text{A}.$$

The phase angle ϕ is

$$\phi = \arctan \frac{X_L - X_C}{R} = \arctan \frac{400\ \Omega}{300\ \Omega} = 53°.$$

From Eq. (34–6) the voltage amplitude V_R across the resistor is

$$V_R = IR = (0.10\ \text{A})(300\ \Omega) = 30\ \text{V}.$$

From Eq. (34–14) the voltage amplitude V_C across the capacitor is

$$V_C = IX_C = (0.10\ \text{A})(500\ \Omega) = 50\ \text{V}.$$

From Eq. (34–19) the voltage amplitude V_L across the inductor is

$$V_L = IX_L = (0.10\ \text{A})(900\ \Omega) = 90\ \text{V}.$$

Note that the source voltage amplitude $V = 50$ V is *not* equal to the sum of the voltage amplitudes across the separate circuit elements. Make sure you understand why not!   ∎

In this entire discussion we have described magnitudes of voltages and currents in terms of their *maximum* values, voltage and current *amplitudes*. But we remarked at the end of Section 34–1 that these quantities are usually described not in terms of their amplitudes but in terms of rms values. For any sinusoidally varying quantity the rms value is always $1/\sqrt{2}$ times the amplitude. All the relations between voltage and current that we have derived in this section and the preceding one are still valid if we use root-mean-square quantities throughout instead of amplitudes. For example, if we divide Eq. (34–23) by $\sqrt{2}$, we get

$$\frac{V}{\sqrt{2}} = \frac{I}{\sqrt{2}} Z,$$

which we can rewrite as

$$V_{\mathrm{rms}} = I_{\mathrm{rms}} Z. \qquad (34\text{--}26)$$

We can translate Eqs. (34–6), (34–14), and (34–19) in exactly the same way.

34–4
Series Resonance

The impedance of an $L-R-C$ series circuit depends on the frequency, as Eq. (34–24) shows. Figure 34–7a shows graphs of R, X_L, X_C, and Z as functions of ω. We have used a logarithmic frequency scale so that we can cover a wide range of frequencies. Because X_L increases and X_C decreases with increasing frequency, there is always one particular frequency where X_L and X_C are equal and $X = X_L - X_C$ is zero. At this frequency the impedance Z has its *smallest* value, equal simply to the resistance R.

Suppose we connect an ac source with constant voltage amplitude V but variable frequency ω across an $L-R-C$ series circuit. As we vary ω, the current amplitude I varies with frequency as shown in Fig. 34–7b; its *maximum* value occurs at the frequency where the impedance Z is *minimum*. This peaking of the current amplitude at a certain frequency is called **resonance.** The frequency ω_0 at which the resonance peak occurs is called the **resonance frequency.** This is the frequency at which the inductive and capacitive reactances are equal, so

$$X_L = X_C, \qquad \omega_0 L = \frac{1}{\omega_0 C}, \qquad \omega_0 = \frac{1}{\sqrt{LC}}. \qquad (34\text{--}27)$$

Note that this is equal to the natural frequency of oscillation of an $L-C$ circuit, which we derived in Section 33–5, Eq. (33–19).

Now let's look at what happens to the *voltages* in an $L-R-C$ series circuit at resonance. The current at any instant is the same in L and C. The voltage across an inductor always *leads* the current by 90° or 1/4 cycle, and the voltage across a capacitor always *lags* the current by 90°. Therefore the instantaneous voltages across L and C always differ in phase by 180° or 1/2 cycle; they have opposite signs at each instant. If the *amplitudes* of these two voltages are equal, then they add to zero at each instant, and the *total* voltage v_{cb} across the $L-C$ combination is exactly

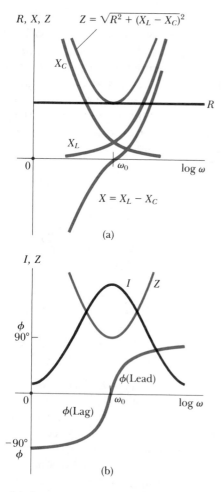

R, X, Z $Z = \sqrt{R^2 + (X_L - X_C)^2}$

X_C

R

X_L

0 ω_0 $\log \omega$

$X = X_L - X_C$

(a)

I, Z

I Z

ϕ
$90°$

$\phi(\text{Lead})$

0 ω_0 $\log \omega$

$\phi(\text{Lag})$

$-90°$
ϕ

(b)

34–7
(a) Reactance, resistance, and impedance as functions of frequency (logarithmic frequency scale). (b) Impedance, current, and phase angle as functions of frequency (logarithmic frequency scale).

zero! This occurs only at the resonance frequency. Depending on the numerical values of R, L, and C, the voltages across L and C individually can be larger than the voltage across R. At frequencies close to resonance the voltages across L and C individually can be much *larger* than the source voltage!

The *phase* of the voltage relative to the current is given by Eq. (34–25). At frequencies below resonance, X_C is greater than X_L; the capacitive reactance dominates, the voltage *lags* the current, and the phase angle ϕ is between zero and $-90°$. Above resonance the inductive reactance dominates; the voltage *leads* the current, and the phase angle is between zero and $+90°$. This variation of ϕ with frequency is shown in Fig. 36–7b.

If we can vary the inductance L or the capacitance C of a circuit, we can also vary the resonance frequency. This is exactly how a radio or television receiving set is "tuned" to receive a particular station. In the early days of radio this was accomplished by use of capacitors with movable metal plates whose overlap could be varied to change C. Nowadays it is more common to vary L by using a coil with a ferrite core that slides in or out.

Example 34–4   The series circuit in Fig. 34–8 is connected to the terminals of an ac source with a constant rms terminal voltage of 100 V and a variable frequency. Find (a) the resonance frequency, (b) the inductive and capacitive reactances and the impedance at the resonance frequency, (c) the rms current at resonance, and (d) the rms voltage across each circuit element at resonance.

Solution

a) The resonance frequency is

$$\omega_0 = \frac{1}{\sqrt{LC}} = \frac{1}{\sqrt{(2.0\ \text{H})(0.50 \times 10^{-6}\ \text{F})}} = 1000\ \text{rad·s}^{-1}.$$

b) At this frequency,

$$X_L = (1000\ \text{rad·s}^{-1})(2.0\ \text{H}) = 2000\ \Omega,$$

$$X_C = \frac{1}{(1000\ \text{rad·s}^{-1})(0.50 \times 10^{-6}\ \text{F})} = 2000\ \Omega,$$

$$X = X_L - X_C = 0.$$

From Eq. (34–24) the impedance Z at resonance is equal to the resistance: $Z = R = 500\ \Omega$.

c) At resonance the rms current is

$$I = \frac{V}{Z} = \frac{V}{R} = \frac{100\ \text{V}}{500\ \Omega} = 0.20\ \text{A}.$$

d) The rms potential difference across the resistor is

$$V_R = IR = (0.20\ \text{A})(500\ \Omega) = 100\ \text{V}.$$

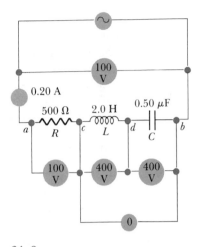

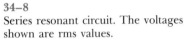

34–8
Series resonant circuit. The voltages shown are rms values.

The rms potential differences across the inductor and capacitor are, respectively,

$$V_L = IX_L = (0.20 \text{ A})(2000 \text{ }\Omega) = 400 \text{ V},$$

$$V_C = IX_C = (0.20 \text{ A})(2000 \text{ }\Omega) = 400 \text{ V}.$$

The rms potential difference across the inductor–capacitor combination (V_{cb}) is

$$V = IX = I(X_L - X_C) = 0.$$

The instantaneous potential differences across the inductor and the capacitor have equal amplitudes but are 180° out of phase, so they add to zero at each instant. Note also that at resonance, V_R is equal to the source voltage V, while V_L and V_C are both considerably *larger* than V. ∎

In a series L–R–C circuit the impedance reaches its minimum value and the current its maximum value at the resonance frequency. Figure 34–9 shows a graph of current as a function of frequency for the circuit in Fig. 34–8 (Example 34–4). This curve is called a *response curve* or a *resonance curve*. As we expect, the curve has a peak at $\omega = 1000 \text{ s}^{-1}$, the resonance frequency. The figure also shows graphs of I as a function of ω for $R = 200 \text{ }\Omega$ and for $R = 2000 \text{ }\Omega$. The curves are all similar for frequencies far away from resonance, where the impedance is dominated by X_L or X_C. But near resonance, where X_L and X_C nearly cancel each other, the curve is higher and more sharply peaked for small values of R than for larger values. The maximum height of the curve is in fact inversely proportional to R. A small value of R gives a sharply peaked response curve, and a large value of R gives a broad, flat curve.

34–9
Graph of rms current I as a function of frequency ω (the dark color curve) for the circuit of Example 34–4. The other curves show the relationship for different values of the circuit resistance R, 2000 Ω (black curve) and 200 Ω (light color curve).

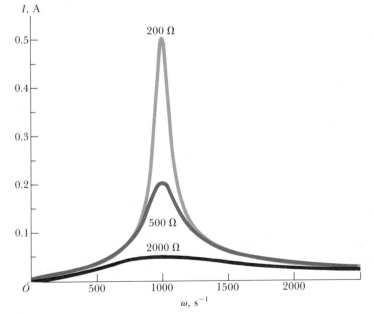

The shape of the response curve is important in the design of radio and television receiving circuits. The sharply peaked curve is what makes it possible to discriminate between two stations broadcasting on adjacent frequency bands. But if the peak is *too* sharp, some of the information in the received signal is lost, such as the high frequency sounds in music. The shape of the resonance curve is also related to the overdamped and underdamped oscillations we described in Section 33–6. A sharply peaked resonance curve corresponds to a small value of R and a lightly damped oscillating system; a broad, flat curve goes with a large value of R and a heavily damped system.

34–5
Parallel Resonance

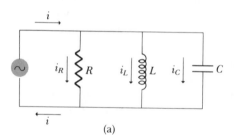

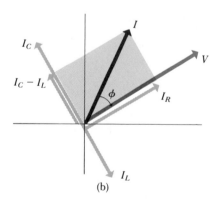

34–10

(a) A parallel L–R–C circuit. (b) Phasor diagram showing current phasors for the three branches. The single voltage phasor V represents the voltage across all three branches. The case $X_L > X_C$ is shown.

Figure 34–10a shows a circuit with a resistor, an inductor, and a capacitor in parallel. This circuit has resonance behavior similar to that of the L–R–C series circuit we analyzed in Section 34–4, but the roles of voltage and current are reversed. This time the instantaneous potential difference v is the same for all three circuit elements and is equal to the source voltage, but the current is different in each of the three elements. Figure 34–10b shows a phasor diagram; the phasor V represents this common voltage, and there are three current phasors. The phasor I_R, with amplitude V/R, is in phase with V; it represents the current in the resistor. Phasor I_L, with amplitude $V/X_L = V/\omega L$ and lagging V by 90°, represents the current in the inductor. Phasor I_C, with amplitude $V/X_C = V\omega C$ and leading V by 90°, represents the current in the capacitor.

The instantaneous current i, by Kirchhoff's point rule, equals the (algebraic) sum of the instantaneous currents i_R, i_L, and i_C. It is represented by the phasor I, the *vector sum* of phasors I_R, I_L, and I_C. Angle ϕ is the phase angle of source voltage with respect to current, as usual.

From Fig. 34–10, the magnitude I of the current phasor is

$$I = \sqrt{I_R^2 + (I_C - I_L)^2} = \sqrt{\left(\frac{V}{R}\right)^2 + \left(\omega C V - \frac{V}{\omega L}\right)^2}$$

$$= V\sqrt{\frac{1}{R^2} + \left(\omega C - \frac{1}{\omega L}\right)^2}. \qquad (34\text{–}28)$$

The current amplitude I is frequency-dependent, as expected. It is *minimum* when the quantity in parentheses in the radical is zero; this occurs when the two reactances have equal magnitudes, at the resonance frequency ω_0 given by Eq. (34–27).

Comparing this equation with Eq. (34–23), we see that the *impedance* Z of this parallel combination is given by

$$\frac{1}{Z} = \sqrt{\frac{1}{R^2} + \left(\omega C - \frac{1}{\omega L}\right)^2}. \qquad (34\text{–}29)$$

At resonance, $1/Z$ has its smallest value, equal to $1/R$, so Z itself has its *maximum* value at $\omega = \omega_0 = (1/LC)^{1/2}$. At this frequency, $Z = R$.

At resonance the total current in the parallel $L–R–C$ circuit is *minimum*, while the $L–R–C$ *series* circuit has *maximum* current at resonance. In the parallel circuit the currents in L and C are *always* exactly a half-cycle out of phase. When they also have equal *magnitudes*, they cancel each other completely, and the *total* current is simply the current through R. Indeed, when $\omega C = 1/\omega L$, Eq. (34–28) becomes simply $I = V/R$. This does *not* mean that there is *no* current in L or C at resonance, but only that the two currents cancel. If R is large, the impedance Z of the circuit near resonance is much *larger* than the individual reactances X_L and X_C.

34–6
Power in ac Circuits

Alternating currents play a central role in our systems for distributing, converting, and using electrical energy. Therefore it is worthwhile to look at power relationships in ac circuits. When a source with voltage amplitude V and instantaneous potential difference v supplies an instantaneous current i (current amplitude I) to an ac circuit, the instantaneous power p it supplies is given by

$$p = vi.$$

Let's see what this means for individual circuit elements.

Suppose first that the circuit consists of a pure resistance R, as in Fig. 34–2; then i and v are *in phase*. We obtain the graph representing p by multiplying the heights of the graphs of v and i in Fig. 34–2b at each instant. This graph is shown by the dark color curve in Fig. 34–11a. The product vi is always positive because v and i are always either both positive or both negative. Energy is supplied to the resistor at every instant, for both directions of i, although the power is not constant.

The power curve is symmetrical about a value equal to one-half its maximum value VI, so the *average power* P is

$$P = \tfrac{1}{2}VI. \tag{34–30}$$

An equivalent expression is

$$P = \frac{V}{\sqrt{2}} \frac{I}{\sqrt{2}} = V_{\text{rms}}I_{\text{rms}}. \tag{34–31}$$

Also, $V_{\text{rms}} = I_{\text{rms}}R$, so

$$P = I_{\text{rms}}^2 R. \tag{34–32}$$

Note that Eqs. (34–31) and (34–32) have the same form as the corresponding relations for a dc circuit.

Next we connect the source to a capacitor C, as in Fig. 34–3. The voltage lags the current by 90°. When we multiply the curves of v and i, the product vi is *negative* during the half of the cycle when v and i have *opposite* signs. We get the power curve in Fig. 34–11b, which is symmetrical about the horizontal axis. It is positive half the time and negative the other half, and the average power is zero. When p is positive, energy is

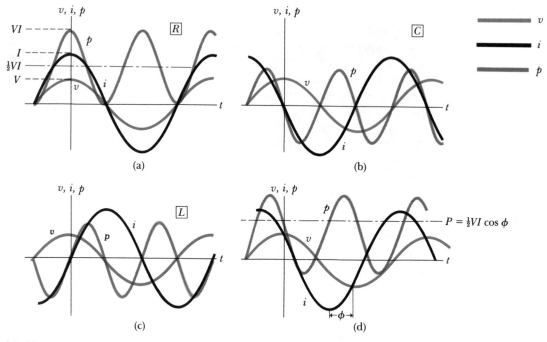

34–11
Graphs of voltage, current, and power as functions of time, for various circuits.
(a) Instantaneous power input to a resistor. The average power is $\frac{1}{2}VI$.
(b) Instantaneous power input to a capacitor. The average power is zero.
(c) Instantaneous power input to a pure inductor. The average power is zero.
(d) Instantaneous power input to an arbitrary ac circuit. The average power is $\frac{1}{2}VI \cos \phi = V_{rms}I_{rms} \cos \phi$.

being supplied to charge the capacitor; when p is negative, the capacitor is discharging and returning energy to the source. The net energy transfer over one cycle is zero.

Finally, we connect the source to an inductor L, as in Fig. 34–4. The voltage leads the current by 90°; Figure 34–11c shows the power curve; the average power is again zero. Energy is supplied to establish a magnetic field in the inductor and is returned to the source when the field collapses. The net energy transfer over one cycle is again zero.

In *any* circuit, with any combination of resistors, capacitors, and inductors, the current and voltage differ in phase by some angle ϕ, and the instantaneous power p is given by

$$p = [V \cos (\omega t + \phi)][I \cos \omega t]. \qquad (34–33)$$

The instantaneous power curve has the form shown in Fig. 34–11d. The area under the positive loops is greater than the area under the negative loops, and the average power is positive.

To derive an expression for the average power P, we use the identity for the cosine of the sum of two angles:

$$p = [V(\cos \omega t \cos \phi - \sin \omega t \sin \phi)][I \cos \omega t]$$
$$= VI \cos \phi \cos^2 \omega t - VI \sin \phi \cos \omega t \sin \omega t.$$

From the discussion leading to Eq. (34–3) in Section 34–1 we see that the average value of $\cos^2 \omega t$ (over one cycle) is 1/2. The average value of cos ωt sin ωt is zero because the two factors have the same sign half the time and opposite signs half the time, and the product averages out to zero. Thus the average value of the second term is zero, and the average power P is given by

$$P = \tfrac{1}{2}VI \cos \phi = V_{\text{rms}}I_{\text{rms}} \cos \phi. \qquad (34\text{–}34)$$

When v and i are *in phase*, the average power equals $\tfrac{1}{2}VI = V_{\text{rms}}I_{\text{rms}}$, and when v and i are 90° *out of phase*, the average power is zero. In the general case, when v and i differ by an angle ϕ, the average power equals $\tfrac{1}{2}I$ multiplied by $V \cos \phi$, the component of V that is *in phase* with I. For the L–R–C series circuit, $V \cos \phi$ is the voltage amplitude for the resistor, and Eq. (34–34) is the power dissipated in the resistor. The power dissipation in the inductor and capacitor is zero.

The factor $\cos \phi$ is called the **power factor** of the circuit. For a pure resistance, $\phi = 0$, $\cos \phi = 1$, and $P = V_{\text{rms}}I_{\text{rms}}$. For a pure (resistanceless) capacitor or inductor, $\phi = \pm 90°$, $\cos \phi = 0$, and $P = 0$.

A low power factor (large angle of lag or lead) is usually undesirable in power circuits because, for a given potential difference, a large current is needed to supply a given amount of power. This results in large heat losses in the transmission lines. Many types of ac machinery draw a lagging current; the power factor can be corrected by connecting a capacitor in parallel with the load. The leading current drawn by the capacitor compensates for the lagging current in the other branch of the circuit. The capacitor itself takes no net power from the line.

*34–7
Transformers

One of the great advantages of ac over dc for electric-power distribution is that it is much easier to step voltage levels up and down with ac than with dc. For long-distance power transmission it is desirable to use as high a voltage and as small a current as possible; this reduces I^2R heating losses in the transmission lines, and smaller wires can be used, saving on material costs. Present-day transmission lines routinely operate at rms voltages of the order of 500 kV. On the other hand, safety considerations and insulation requirements dictate relatively low voltages in generating equipment and in household and industrial power distribution. The standard voltage for household wiring is 120 V in the United States and Canada and 240 V in most of western Europe. The necessary voltage conversion is accomplished by use of **transformers.**

A transformer consists of two coils, electrically insulated from each other but wound on the same core so that they have mutual inductance, as we discussed in Section 33–1. The winding to which power is supplied is called the **primary;** the winding from which power is delivered is called the **secondary.** Transformers used in power-distribution systems have soft iron cores. The circuit symbol for an iron-core transformer is

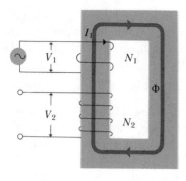

34–12
Schematic diagram of a transformer with secondary open.

Here's how a transformer works. An alternating current in either winding sets up an alternating flux in the core, and according to Faraday's law, this induces an emf in each winding. Energy is transferred from the current in one winding to the other via the core flux and its associated induced emfs.

An idealized transformer is shown in Fig. 34–12. We assume that all the flux is confined to the iron core, so the same flux links both primary and secondary. We also neglect the resistance of the windings. The primary winding has N_1 turns, and the secondary winding has N_2 turns. An ac source with voltage amplitude V_1 is connected to the primary. Because the same flux links both primary and secondary, the induced emf *per turn* is the same in each. The ratio of the primary emf $\mathcal{E}_1$ to the secondary emf $\mathcal{E}_2$ is therefore equal to the ratio of primary to secondary turns:

$$\frac{\mathcal{E}_1}{\mathcal{E}_2} = \frac{N_1}{N_2}.$$

If the windings have zero resistance, the induced emf's $\mathcal{E}_1$ and $\mathcal{E}_2$ are equal to the corresponding terminal voltages V_1 and V_2, and

$$\frac{V_2}{V_1} = \frac{N_2}{N_1}. \tag{34–35}$$

By choosing the appropriate turns ratio N_2/N_1 we may obtain any desired secondary voltage from a given primary voltage. If $V_2 > V_1$, we have a *step-up* transformer; if $V_2 < V_1$, we have a *step-down* transformer.

If the secondary circuit is completed by a resistance R, then $I_2 = V_2/R$. From energy considerations the power delivered to the primary equals that taken out of the secondary, so

$$V_1 I_1 = V_2 I_2. \tag{34–36}$$

If we use Eq. (34–35) and the relation $I_2 = V_2/R$ to eliminate V_2 and I_2, we obtain

$$I_1 = \frac{V_1}{(N_1/N_2)^2 R}. \tag{34–37}$$

This shows that when the secondary circuit is completed through a resistance R, the result is the same as if the *source* had been connected directly to a resistance equal to R multiplied by $(N_1/N_2)^2$. In other words, the transformer "transforms" not only voltages and currents, but resistances (more generally, impedances) as well.

Equation (34–37) has many practical consequences. The power supplied by a source to a resistor depends on its resistance and the internal resistance of the source. It can be shown that the power transfer is greatest when the two resistances are *equal*. The same principle applies in both dc and ac circuits. When a high-impedance ac source must be connected to a low-impedance circuit, the source impedance can be *matched* to that of the circuit by use of a transformer with an appropriate turns ratio.

Real transformers always have some energy losses. The windings have some resistance, although superconducting transformers may appear on the horizon in the next few years. There are also energy losses through hysteresis (Section 31–7) and eddy currents (Section 32–6) in the core. Hysteresis losses are minimized by the use of soft iron with a narrow hysteresis loop; and eddy currents are minimized by laminating the core. In spite of these losses, transformer efficiencies are usually well over 90%; in large installations they may reach 99%.

Questions

34–1 Some electric-power systems formerly used 25-Hz alternating current instead of the 60 Hz that is now standard. The lights flickered noticeably. Why is this not a problem with 60 Hz?

34–2 Power-distribution systems in airplanes sometimes use 400-Hz ac. What advantages and disadvantages does this have compared to the standard 60 Hz?

34–3 Fluorescent lights often use an inductor, called a "ballast," to limit the current through the tubes. Why is it better to use an inductor than a resistor for this purpose?

34–4 At high frequencies a capacitor becomes a short circuit. Discuss.

34–5 At high frequencies an inductor becomes an open circuit. Discuss.

34–6 Household electric power in most of Western Europe is 240 V, rather than the 120 V that is standard in the United States and Canada. What advantages and disadvantages does each system have?

34–7 The current in an ac-power line changes direction 120 times per second, and its average value is zero. So how is it possible for power to be transmitted in such a system?

34–8 Electric-power connecting cords, such as lamp cords, always have two conductors that carry equal currents in opposite directions. How might one determine, by using measurements only at the midpoints along the lengths of the wires, the direction of power transmission in the cord?

34–9 Are the equations for the average and rms values of current, Eqs. (34–2) and (34–3), correct when the variation with time is not sinusoidal? Explain.

34–10 Electric-power companies like to have their power factors (cf. Section 34–6) as close to unity as possible. Why?

34–11 Some electrical appliances operate equally well on ac or dc, while others work only on ac or only on dc. Give examples of each, and explain the differences.

34–12 When a series-resonant circuit is connected across a 120-V ac line, the voltage rating of the capacitor may be exceeded even if it is rated at 200 or 400 V. How can this be?

34–13 In a parallel-resonant circuit connected across a 120-V line it is possible for the maximum current rating in the inductor to be exceeded even if the total current through the circuit is very small. How can this be?

34–14 Can a transformer be used with dc? What happens if a transformer designed for 120-V ac is connected to a 120-V dc line?

34–15 During the last quarter of the nineteenth century there was great and acrimonious controversy over whether ac or dc should be used for power transmission. Edison favored dc, George Westinghouse ac. What arguments might each proponent have used to promote his scheme?

Exercises

Section 34–2   Resistance, Inductance, and Capacitance

34–1

a) What is the reactance of a 1.00-H inductor at a frequency of 50.0 Hz?

b) What is the inductance of an inductor whose reactance is 1.00 Ω at 50.0 Hz?

c) What is the reactance of a 1.00-μF capacitor at a frequency of 50.0 Hz?

d) What is the capacitance of a capacitor whose reactance is 1.00 Ω at 50.0 Hz?

34–2

a) Compute the reactance of a 5.00-H inductor at frequencies of 60.0 Hz and 600 Hz.

b) Compute the reactance of a 5.00-μF capacitor at the same frequencies.

c) At what frequency is the reactance of a 5.00-H inductor equal to that of a 5.00-μF capacitor?

34–3 A 3.00-μF capacitor is connected across an ac source whose voltage amplitude is kept constant at 50.0 V but whose frequency can be varied. Find the current amplitude when the angular frequency is

a) 100 rad·s^{-1},

b) 1000 rad·s^{-1},

c) 10,000 rad·s^{-1}.

d) Show the results of parts (a) through (c) in a plot of log I versus log ω.

34–4 The voltage amplitude of an ac source is 25.0 V, and its angular frequency is 1000 rad·s^{-1}. Find the current amplitude if the capacitance of a capacitor connected across the source is

a) 0.0100 μF,

b) 1.00 μF,

c) 100 μF.

d) Show the results of parts (a) through (c) in a plot of log I versus log C.

34–5 An inductor with a self-inductance of 5.00 H and with negligible resistance is connected across the source in Exercise 34–3. Find the current amplitude when the angular frequency is

a) 100 rad·s^{-1},

b) 1000 rad·s^{-1},

c) 10,000 rad·s^{-1}.

d) Show the results of parts (a) through (c) in a plot of log I versus log ω.

34–6 Find the current amplitude if the self-inductance of a resistanceless inductor connected across the source of Exercise 34–4 is

a) 0.0100 H,

b) 1.00 H,

c) 100 H.

d) Show the results of parts (a) through (c) in a plot of log I versus log L.

Section 34–3   The L–R–C Series Circuit

34–7 In an L–R–C series circuit the source has a voltage amplitude of 50.0 V and an angular frequency of 1000 rad·s^{-1}. $R = 200$ Ω, $L = 0.900$ H, and $C = 2.00$ μF. Suppose a series circuit contains only the resistor and the inductor in series.

a) What is the impedance of the circuit?

b) What is the current amplitude?

c) What are the voltage amplitudes across the resistor and across the inductor?

d) What is the phase angle ϕ of the source voltage

with respect to the current? Does the source voltage lag or lead the current?

e) Construct the phasor diagram.

34–8 Repeat Exercise 34–7, except that the circuit consists of only the capacitor and the inductor in series. For part (c), calculate the voltage amplitudes across the capacitor and across the inductor.

34–9 Repeat Exercise 34–7, except that the circuit consists of only the resistor and the capacitor in series. For part (c), calculate the voltage amplitudes across the resistor and across the capacitor.

34–10

a) Compute the impedance of an L–R–C series circuit at angular frequencies of 1000, 750, and 500 rad·s^{-1}. Take $R = 200$ Ω, $L = 0.900$ H, and $C = 2.00$ μF.

b) Describe how the current amplitude varies as the angular frequency of the source is slowly reduced from 1000 rad·s^{-1} to 500 rad·s^{-1}.

c) What is the phase angle of the source voltage with respect to the current when $\omega = 1000$ rad·s^{-1}?

d) Construct the phasor diagram when $\omega = 1000$ rad·s^{-1}.

e) Repeat parts (c) and (d) for $\omega = 500$ rad·s^{-1}.

34–11 A 200-Ω resistor is in series with a 0.100-H inductor and a 0.500-μF capacitor. Compute the impedance of the circuit and draw the phasor diagram

a) at a frequency of 500 Hz;

b) at a frequency of 1000 Hz.

Compute, in each case, the phase angle of the source voltage with respect to the current, and state whether the source voltage lags or leads the current.

Section 34–4   Series Resonance

34–12 In an L–R–C series circuit, $L = 0.200$ H and $C = 8.00 \times 10^{-5}$ F. The voltage amplitude of the source is 240 V.

a) What is the resonance angular frequency of the circuit?

b) When the source operates at the resonance angular frequency the current amplitude in the circuit is 0.600 A. What is the resistance R of the resistor?

c) At the resonance frequency, what are the peak voltages across the inductor, the capacitor, and the resistor?

34–13

a) Consider the L–R–C series circuit of Exercise 34–10. The voltage amplitude of the source is 150 V.

a) At what angular frequency is the circuit in resonance?

b) Sketch the phasor diagram at the resonance frequency.

c) What is the reading of each voltmeter in Fig. 34–13 when the source frequency equals the resonance frequency? The voltmeters are calibrated to read rms voltages.

d) What is the resonance angular frequency if the resistance is reduced to 100 Ω?

e) What is then the rms current at resonance?

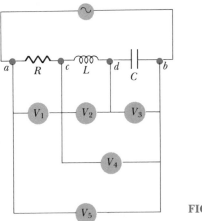

FIGURE 34–13

34–14 In an L–R–C series circuit, $R = 250\ \Omega$, $L = 0.500$ H, and $C = 0.0400\ \mu$F.

a) What is the resonance angular frequency of the circuit?

b) The capacitor can withstand a peak voltage of 350 V. If the voltage source operates at the resonance frequency, what maximum voltage amplitude can it have if the maximum capacitor voltage is not exceeded?

Section 34–5   Parallel Resonance

34–15 For the circuit of Fig. 34–10a, $R = 300\ \Omega$, $L = 0.500$ H, and $C = 0.600\ \mu$F. The voltage amplitude of the source is 120 V.

a) What is the resonance frequency of the circuit?

b) Sketch the phasor diagram at the resonance frequency.

c) At the resonance frequency, what is the current amplitude through the source?

d) At the resonance frequency, what is the current amplitude through the resistor? Through the inductor? Through the branch containing the capacitor?

34–16 For the circuit of Fig. 34–10a, $R = 200\ \Omega$, $L = 0.800$ H, and $C = 5.00\ \mu$F. When the source is operated at the resonance frequency the current amplitude in the inductor is 0.400 A. Determine

a) the current amplitude in the branch containing the capacitor;

b) the current amplitude through the resistor.

34–17 For the circuit of Fig. 34–10a, $R = 500\ \Omega$, $L = 0.200$ H, and $C = 0.200\ \mu$F. The source has voltage amplitude $V = 400$ V.

a) If the source is operated at an angular frequency of 500 rad·s^{-1}, what are the impedance of the circuit and the current amplitude through the source?

b) If the source is operated at the resonance angular frequency, what are the impedance of the circuit and the current amplitude through the source?

Section 34–6   Power in ac Circuits

34–18 An L–R–C series circuit has a resistance of $90.0\ \Omega$ and an impedance of $150\ \Omega$. The circuit is connected to a voltage source that has $V = 120$ V (rms). What average power is delivered to the circuit by the source?

34–19 The circuit in Exercise 34–11 carries an rms current of 0.250 A with a frequency of 100 Hz.

a) What is the average rate at which electrical energy is converted to heat in the resistor?

b) What average power is delivered by the source?

c) What is the average rate at which electrical energy is dissipated (converted to other forms) in the capacitor?

d) In the inductor?

34–20 Consider the circuit of Fig. 34–10a, with the same numerical values as in Exercise 34–15. At resonance, determine

a) the average rate at which electrical energy is being converted into heat in the resistor;

b) the average rate at which electrical energy is being delivered by the source.

c) Is the current through the inductor, and hence the energy stored in its magnetic field, zero at all times? If not, how can the result obtained in part (b) be explained?

d) Calculate the maximum energy stored in the inductor at the resonance frequency.

e) Calculate the maximum energy stored in the capacitor at the resonance frequency.

Section 34–7   Transformers

34–21 A transformer connected to a 120-V (rms) ac line is to supply 6.00 V (rms) to a low-voltage lighting system for a model-railroad village. The total equivalent resistance of the system is 8.00 Ω.

a) What should be the ratio of primary to secondary turns of the transformer?

b) What rms current must the secondary supply?

c) What average power is delivered to the load?

d) What resistance connected directly across the 120-V line would draw the same power as the transformer? Show that this is equal to 8.00 Ω times the square of the ratio of primary to secondary turns.

34–22 A step-up transformer connected to a 120-V (rms) ac line is to supply 15,600 V (rms) for a neon sign. To reduce shock hazard, a fuse is to be inserted in the primary circuit; the fuse is to blow when the rms current in the secondary circuit exceeds 10.0 mA.

a) What is the ratio of secondary to primary turns of the transformer?

b) What power must be supplied to the transformer when the secondary current is 10.0 mA?

c) What current rating should the fuse in the primary circuit have?

34–23 The internal resistance of an ac source is 9000 Ω.

a) What should be the ratio of primary to secondary turns of a transformer to match the source to a load with resistance 10.0 Ω? ("Matching" means that the effective load resistance equals the internal resistance of the source. Refer to Exercise 34–21d.)

b) If the voltage amplitude of the source is 100 V, what is the voltage amplitude in the secondary circuit under open circuit conditions?

Problems

34–24 At a certain frequency ω_1 the reactance of a certain capacitor equals that of a certain inductor.

a) If the frequency is changed to $\omega_2 = 2\omega_1$, what is the ratio of the reactance of the inductor to that of the capacitor? Which reactance is larger?

b) If the frequency is changed to $\omega_3 = \omega_1/3$, what is the ratio of the reactance of the inductor to that of the capacitor? Which reactance is larger?

34–25 A coil has a resistance of 50.0 Ω. At a frequency of 100 Hz the voltage across the coil leads the current in it by 30.0°. Determine the inductance of the coil.

34–26 Five infinite-impedance voltmeters, calibrated to read rms values, are connected as shown in Fig. 34–13. Take R, L, C, and V as given in Exercise 34–7. What is the reading of each voltmeter

a) if $\omega = 500$ rad·s^{-1}?

b) if $\omega = 1000$ rad·s^{-1}?

34–27 Consider the circuit sketched in Fig. 34–13. The source has a voltage amplitude of 240 V, $R = 150$ Ω, and the reactance of the capacitor is 600 Ω. The voltage amplitude across the capacitor is 720 V.

a) What is the current amplitude in the circuit?

b) What is the impedance?

c) What two values can the reactance of the inductor have?

34–28 An inductor having a reactance of 25.0 Ω and resistance R gives off heat at the rate of 16.0 J·s^{-1}

when it carries a current of 0.500 A (rms). What is the impedance of the inductor?

34–29 A circuit draws 330 W from a 110-V (rms), 60.0-Hz ac line. The power factor is 0.400, and the source voltage leads the current.

a) What is the resistance R of the circuit?

b) Find the capacitance of the series capacitor that will result in a power factor of unity when it is added to the original circuit.

c) What power will then be drawn from the supply line?

34–30 A series circuit has an impedance of 50.0 Ω and a power factor of 0.800 at 60.0 Hz. The source voltage lags the current.

a) Should an inductor or a capacitor be placed in series with the circuit to raise its power factor?

b) What size element will raise the power factor to unity?

34–31 In an L–R–C series circuit, $R = 300$ Ω, $X_C = 300$ Ω, and $X_L = 500$ Ω. The average power consumed in the resistor is 60.0 W.

a) What is the power factor of the circuit?

b) What is the rms voltage of the source?

34–32 A resistor with a resistance of 500 Ω and a capacitor with a capacitance of 2.00 μF are connected in parallel to an ac generator that supplies a rms voltage of 240 V at an angular frequency of 377 rad·s^{-1}. Find

a) the current amplitude in the resistor,

b) the current amplitude in the capacitor,

c) the phase angle (sketch the phasor diagram for the current phasors),

d) the amplitude of the current through the generator.

34–33 In an L–R–C series circuit the phase angle is 40.0°, with the source voltage leading the current. The reactance of the capacitor is $X_C = 400$ Ω, and the resistor resistance is $R = 200$ Ω. The average power delivered by the source is 150 W. Find

a) the reactance of the inductor,

b) the rms current,

c) the rms voltage of the source.

34–34 A 100-Ω resistor, a 0.100-μF capacitor, and a 0.300-H inductor are connected in *parallel* to a voltage source with amplitude 240 V.

a) What is the resonance angular frequency?

b) What is the maximum current through the source at the resonance frequency?

c) What is the maximum current in the resistor at resonance?

d) What is the maximum current in the inductor at resonance?

e) What is the maximum current in the branch containing the capacitor at resonance?

f) What is the maximum energy stored in the inductor at resonance? In the capacitor?

34–35 The same three components as in Problem

34–34 are connected in *series* to a voltage source with amplitude 240 V.

a) What is the resonance angular frequency?

b) What is the maximum current in the resistor at resonance?

c) What is the maximum voltage across the capacitor at resonance?

d) What is the maximum voltage across the inductor at resonance?

e) What is the maximum energy stored in the capacitor at resonance? In the inductor?

34–36 Consider the same circuit as in Problem 34–34, with the source operated at an angular frequency of 400 rad·s^{-1}.

a) What is the maximum current through the source?

b) What is the maximum current in the resistor?

c) What is the maximum current in the inductor?

d) What is the maximum current in the branch containing the capacitor?

e) What is the maximum energy stored in the inductor? In the capacitor?

34–37 Consider the same circuit as in Problem 34–35, with the source operated at an angular frequency of 400 rad·s^{-1}.

a) What is the maximum current in the resistor?

b) What is the maximum voltage across the capacitor?

c) What is the maximum voltage across the inductor?

d) What is the maximum energy stored in the capacitor? In the inductor?

Challenge Problem

34–38 Consider a series circuit connected to a source with terminal rms voltage $V = 120$ V and frequency ω. The inductor inductance is $L = 2.50$ H, the capacitor capacitance is $C = 0.800$ μF, and the resistor resistance is $R = 400$ Ω.

a) What is the resonance angular frequency ω_0 of the circuit?

b) What is the rms current through the source at resonance?

c) For what two values of the angular frequency, ω_1 and ω_2, is the current half the resonance value? The quantity $|\omega_1 - \omega_2|$ defines the *width* of the resonance.

d) Calculate the resonance width for $R = 4.00$ Ω, 40.0 Ω, and 400 Ω.

35

Electromagnetic Waves

An electromagnetic wave consists of time-varying electric and magnetic fields that travel or propagate through space with a definite speed. The theoretical basis for electromagnetic waves rests on two points. First, a time-varying magnetic field acts as a source of electric field, according to Faraday's law. Second, a time-varying electric field and its associated displacement current act as a source of magnetic field; Maxwell discovered this relationship in 1865. Electromagnetic waves carry energy and momentum and have the property of polarization. Among the simplest electromagnetic waves are sinusoidal waves, in which electric and magnetic fields vary sinusoidally with time. The spectrum of electromagnetic waves covers an extremely broad range of frequency and wavelength, and these waves play a central role in a wide variety of physical phenomena and life processes. Light consists of electromagnetic waves, and we can understand such basic optical concepts as reflection and refraction on the basis of the electromagnetic nature of light.

35–1
Displacement Current and Maxwell's Equations

In the last several chapters we studied various aspects of electric and magnetic fields. We can group these in two categories, fields that do not vary with time and those that do. The electrostatic field caused by charges at rest and the magnetic field of a steady current in a conductor are examples of fields that do not vary with time. (They may, however, vary from point to point in space.) For these situations we could discuss the electric and magnetic fields independently without worrying very much about interactions between the two fields.

But when fields *do* vary with time, it is *not* possible to treat the fields independently. Faraday's law tells us that a time-varying magnetic field acts as a source of electric field, as shown by induced emf's in inductances and transformers. It turns out that a time-varying *electric* field also acts as a source of *magnetic* field. This relationship is an essential part of the basis for electromagnetic waves, so exploring it is our first item of business in this chapter.

We start at what may seem an unlikely place, the charging of a parallel-plate capacitor, as shown in Fig. 35–1. Let's suppose that the plates are parallel round disks. We recall from Section 25–5, Eq. (25–11), that the electric field E between the plates of a capacitor with charge density of magnitude σ on each plate has a magnitude E given by

$$E = \frac{\sigma}{\epsilon_0}.$$

In terms of the plate area A and the total magnitude of charge Q on each plate we can also write this as

$$E = \frac{Q}{\epsilon_0 A}. \tag{35–1}$$

35–1
(a) A parallel-plate capacitor being charged. Charge flows into the left plate but not out of it. The increasing electric field and flux are identified with a fictitious current out of the left disk. (b) In applying Ampere's law to the circle, do we use the conduction current through the plane surface bounded by the circle or the displacement current through the bubble-shaped surface? The result has to be the same in both cases, so we have to consider displacement current as a source of magnetic field.

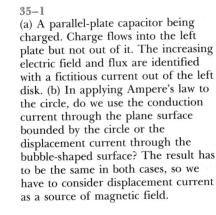

(a)

(b)

One of the interesting things about a charging capacitor is that if we look at an individual plate, Kirchhoff's point rule is not obeyed. This rule is based on the fact that charge ordinarily cannot accumulate at a point. But charge *does* accumulate on a capacitor plate. Charge flows in through the connecting wire, but no charge flows out the other side. It turns out, however, that we can invent an additional, fictitious current having the property that when we add it to the real conduction current, the *total* current does obey Kirchhoff's current rule. From Eq. (35–1) the rate of change of electric field between the plates, $\Delta E/\Delta t$, is given by

$$\frac{\Delta E}{\Delta t} = \frac{1}{\epsilon_0 A}\frac{\Delta Q}{\Delta t}, \qquad \text{or} \qquad \frac{\Delta Q}{\Delta t} = \epsilon_0 A\frac{\Delta E}{\Delta t}. \qquad (35\text{–}2)$$

Now we invent a fictitious current, or pseudocurrent, i_D, defined as

$$i_D = \epsilon_0 A\frac{\Delta E}{\Delta t} \qquad (35\text{–}3)$$

and a corresponding current density $j_D = i_D/A$:

$$j_D = \epsilon_0 \frac{\Delta E}{\Delta t}. \qquad (35\text{–}4)$$

This saves Kirchhoff's current rule. Conduction current comes in one side, pseudocurrent goes out the other side. The magnitudes of the two are equal, so when we count both real (conduction) current and our newly invented pseudocurrent, the net current into the capacitor plate is indeed zero, and we can speak of current *through* the capacitor. Of course, whether this new current has any real physical significance, or whether it is just a ruse to satisfy Kirchhoff's current rule, remains to be seen.

Before proceeding, we note that we can express the pseudocurrent i_D in yet another way, using the concept of *electric flux*, which we introduced in Section 25–4, Eq. (25–7). We haven't used that concept recently; you may want to review it. The total flux Ψ coming out of the capacitor plate is $\Psi = EA$, so $\Delta\Psi/\Delta t = (\Delta E/\Delta t)A$, and we can rewrite Eq. (35–3) as

$$i_D = \epsilon_0 \frac{\Delta\Psi}{\Delta t}. \qquad (35\text{–}5)$$

This fictitious current was invented by James Clerk Maxwell (1831–1879) in 1865; for historical reasons he called it **displacement current.** That's the reason for the subscript D. We will now try to convince you that it really does make physical sense. Let's think again about a single plate of a capacitor being charged. In particular, let's look at the magnetic field caused by the current in the wire that carries the charge onto the capacitor plate. We know from Chapter 31 that the magnetic-field lines are circles centered on the wire. Furthermore, Ampere's law, Eq. (31–16), tells us that if we go around one of these field lines, the sum $\Sigma B_\parallel \Delta s$ around the circle is equal to μ_0 times the total current I through the area bounded by the circle. But which area? If we take the area lying in the plane of the circle, then the current is just the conduction current in the wire. But suppose we distort the area so that it becomes bubble-shaped and goes to the right of the plate, as shown in Fig. 35–1b. Then there is *no* conduction current passing through the surface.

Does this mean that Ampere's law is wrong for this situation? Well, yes, and no. What it means is that if Ampere's law is to be correct, it has to include our newly invented displacement current as well as the real conduction current. In other words, to be consistent, we have to assume that *displacement current, as well as conduction current, acts as a source of magnetic field.*

This may sound implausible, but at least it is a conclusion we can test experimentally. If it is correct, then while a capacitor is charging, there ought to be a magnetic field in the region between its plates. In fact, the situation ought to be analogous to Example 31–8, in which we found the magnetic field inside a long, straight conductor. The space between the capacitor plates plays the role of "conductor" for the displacement current. Experiments have shown that this predicted magnetic field is really there. This confirms directly the role of displacement current as a source of magnetic field. It is now established beyond reasonable doubt that displacement current is far from being just an artifice; it is a fundamental fact of nature. Maxwell's discovery of it was the bold step of an extraordinary genius. Indeed, it was the missing link in the chain of electrodynamic theory that led Maxwell and others to the understanding of electromagnetic waves.

We are now in a position to wrap up in a wonderfully neat package all the relationships between electric and magnetic fields and their sources that we have studied in the past several chapters. The package consists of four equations, called **Maxwell's equations.**

Two of Maxwell's equations involve the flux of $\boldsymbol{E}$ or $\boldsymbol{B}$ out of a closed surface, that is, the sum $\Sigma E_\perp \, \Delta A$ or $\Sigma B_\perp \, \Delta A$ for a closed surface. The first is simply Gauss's law (Section 25–4), stating that the sum $\Sigma E_\perp \, \Delta A$ over any closed surface equals $1/\epsilon_0$ times the total charge Q enclosed within the surface:

$$\sum E_\perp \, \Delta A = \frac{Q}{\epsilon_0}. \tag{35–6}$$

The second is the analogous relation for *magnetic* fields; it states that the sum $\Sigma B_\perp \, \Delta A$ over any closed surface is always zero:

$$\sum B_\perp \, \Delta A = 0. \tag{35–7}$$

This statement means that there is no such thing as magnetic charge as a source of magnetic field, as we discussed in Section 31–1. There are no magnetic monopoles, or at least no one has ever found one.

The third equation is Ampere's law, including the displacement current that we just introduced, and the fourth is Faraday's law. Ampere's law, in its generalized form, states that both conduction current I_C and displacement current $\epsilon_0 \, \Delta\Psi/\Delta t$, where Ψ is electric flux, act as sources of magnetic field:

$$\sum B_\parallel \, \Delta s = \mu_0\!\left(I_C + \epsilon_0 \frac{\Delta\Psi}{\Delta t}\right). \tag{35–8}$$

Faraday's law, which we studied in Chapter 32, states that a changing magnetic field or magnetic flux Φ induces an electric field E_n such that for any closed path

$$\sum E_\parallel \, \Delta s = -\frac{\Delta \Phi}{\Delta t}. \qquad (35\text{--}9)$$

We have described this induced electric field as a *non-electrostatic* field, and we have denoted it as E_n. But if an *electrostatic* field, produced by electric charges at rest, is also present in the same region, it is always *conservative*, so for such a field, $\Sigma E_\parallel \, \Delta s$ around any closed path is always zero. So in Eq. (35–9), E is actually the *total* electric field, including both electrostatic and non-electrostatic contributions.

Comparing Eqs. (35–8) and (35–9), we see a remarkable symmetry. Equation (35–8) says that a changing electric field or electric flux creates a magnetic field, and Eq. (35–9) says that a changing magnetic field or magnetic flux creates an electric field. In empty space, where there is no conduction current and $I_C = 0$, the two equations have exactly the same form, apart from a numerical constant and a negative sign, with the roles of E and B reversed in the two equations. This same symmetry is evident in the first two equations; in empty space, where there is no charge, the equations are identical in form, one containing E, the other B. There is no term in Eq. (35–9) corresponding to the conduction current I_C in Eq. (35–8) because there is no "magnetic charge" analogous to electric charge; there are no isolated magnetic poles.

The fact that electromagnetism can be wrapped up so neatly and elegantly is a very satisfying discovery. In conciseness and generality, Maxwell's equations are comparable to Newton's laws of motion and to the laws of thermodynamics. But that's really what science is all about—learning how to express very broad and general physical laws in a concise and compact form. Maxwell's synthesis of electromagnetism stands as a towering intellectual achievement, comparable to the Newtonian synthesis we described at the end of Section 6–5 and to the development of relativity, quantum mechanics, and the understanding of DNA in our own century. They are all beautiful and all monuments to the achievements of which the human intellect is capable.

The most remarkable feature of Eqs. (35–8) and (35–9) is that a time-varying field of *either* kind induces a field of the other kind in neighboring regions of space. Maxwell recognized that these relationships predict the possible existence of electromagnetic disturbances consisting of time-varying electric and magnetic fields that travel or *propagate* from one region of space to another even if no matter is present in the intervening space. Such a disturbance is called an **electromagnetic wave.** Maxwell's analysis, which we will study in the following sections, included a prediction of the speed of propagation of these waves, and this prediction turned out to be identical to the measured value of the speed of light. This suggested very strongly that light is in fact an electromagnetic wave. By now it is a familiar fact that radio and television transmission, light, X-rays, and many other phenomena are examples of electromagnetic waves.

In 1887, Heinrich Hertz produced in the laboratory, for the first time, electromagnetic waves with macroscopic wavelengths. To produce the waves, he used oscillating L–C circuits of the sort we discussed in Section 33–5; he detected the waves with other circuits tuned to the same frequency. Hertz also produced electromagnetic *standing waves* and measured the distance between adjacent nodes (one-half wavelength) to determine the wavelength. Knowing the resonant frequency of his circuits, he then found the speed of the waves from the wavelength–frequency relation $c = \lambda f$. Hertz established that their speed was the same as that of light; this verified Maxwell's theoretical prediction directly. The SI unit of frequency, the cycle per second, is named the *hertz* in honor of Hertz.

The possible use of electromagnetic waves for long-distance communication does not seem to have occurred to Hertz. It remained for the enthusiasm and energy of Marconi and others to make radio communication a familiar household phenomenon.

35–2
Speed of an Electromagnetic Wave

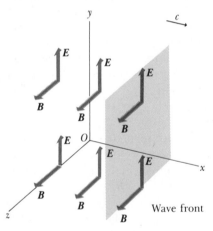

35–2
An electromagnetic wave front. The *E* and *B* fields are uniform over the region to the left of the plane but are zero everywhere to the right of it. The plane representing the wave front moves to the right with speed *c*.

We are now ready to develop the basic ideas of electromagnetic wave propagation and their relation to the principles summarized in Maxwell's equations. Our procedure will be to postulate a specific field configuration that has wavelike behavior; then we will test whether it is consistent with the principles mentioned above, particularly Faraday's law and Ampere's law including displacement current.

Using an *xyz*-coordinate system, as shown in Fig. 35–2, we imagine that all space is divided into two regions by a plane perpendicular to the *x*-axis (parallel to the *yz*-plane). At all points to the left of this plane we have a uniform electric field *E* in the +*y*-direction and a uniform magnetic field *B* in the +*z*-direction, as shown. Furthermore, we suppose that the boundary surface, which we will call the *wave front*, moves to the right with a constant speed *c*, as yet unknown. Thus the *E* and *B* fields travel to the right into previously field-free regions with a definite speed. The situation, in short, describes a rudimentary electromagnetic wave.

We won't concern ourselves with the problem of actually *producing* such a field configuration. Instead, we simply ask whether it is consistent with the laws of electrodynamics, that is, with Maxwell's equations. First we apply Faraday's law to a rectangle in the *xy*-plane, as in Fig. 35–3. The rectangle is located so that at some instant the wave front has progressed partway through it, as shown. In a time Δt the boundary surface moves a distance $\Delta x = c\,\Delta t$ to the right, sweeping out an area $ac\,\Delta t$ of the rectangle. In this time the magnetic flux through the rectangle increases by $B(ac\,\Delta t)$, so the rate of change of magnetic flux is given by

$$\frac{\Delta \Phi}{\Delta t} = Bac. \qquad (35\text{–}10)$$

According to Faraday's law, with the sign rule described in Section 32–3, this must equal the negative of $\Sigma E_{\parallel}\,\Delta s$. Because the flux points in the +*z*-direction in the figure, the sign rule specifies that in evaluating the sum we must go counterclockwise around the boundary of the area. The field at the right end is zero, and the top and bottom sides do not contribute because the component of *E* parallel to these sides is zero. Only the

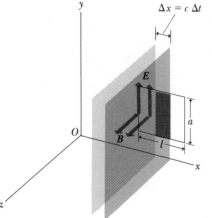

$\Delta x = c\,\Delta t$

E

a

O

B

l

35–3
In time Δt the wave front moves to the right a distance $\Delta x = c\,\Delta t$. The magnetic flux through the rectangle in the xy-plane increases by an amount $\Delta\Phi$ equal to the flux through the shaded rectangle of area $ac\,\Delta t$; that is, $\Delta\Phi = Bac\,\Delta t$.

left side contributes to the sum. On that side the direction of E is opposite to the direction in which we are traversing the boundary, so the total value of the sum is $-Ea$. When we equate this to the negative of Eq. (35–10) and divide out a, Faraday's law gives

$$E = cB. \qquad (35\text{–}11)$$

This shows that the wave we have postulated is consistent with Faraday's law only if E, B, and c are related as in Eq. (35–11).

Next we apply Ampere's law to a rectangle in the xz-plane, as shown in Fig. 35–4. There is no conduction current, so $I_C = 0$. From Eq. (35–8), Ampere's law with displacement current but no conduction current is

$$\sum B_{\parallel}\,\Delta s = \epsilon_0\mu_0\frac{\Delta\Psi}{\Delta t}. \qquad (35\text{–}12)$$

In Fig. 35–4 we evaluate the sum counterclockwise around the boundary of the area. The change in electric flux $\Delta\Psi$ through the area during time Δt is the area $bc\,\Delta t$ swept out by the wave front, multiplied by E. In evaluating $\sum B_{\parallel}\,\Delta s$ we note that B is zero on the right end of the rectangle and is perpendicular to the boundary on the front and back sides. Thus only the left end, where B is parallel to the end, contributes to the sum, and we find $\sum B_{\parallel}\,\Delta s = Bb$. Combining these results with Eq. (35–12) and dividing out the common factor b, we obtain

$$B = \epsilon_0\mu_0 cE. \qquad (35\text{–}13)$$

Ampere's law is obeyed only if B, c, and E are related as in Eq. (35–13).

For *both* Ampere's law and Faraday's law to be obeyed at the same time, Eqs. (35–11) and (35–13) must both be satisfied. This can happen only when $\epsilon_0\mu_0 c = 1/c$, or

$$c = \frac{1}{\sqrt{\epsilon_0\mu_0}}. \qquad (35\text{–}14)$$

Inserting the numerical values of these quantities, we find

$$c = \frac{1}{\sqrt{(8.85\times10^{-12}\ \mathrm{C^2\cdot N^{-1}\cdot m^{-2}})(4\pi\times10^{-7}\ \mathrm{N\cdot A^{-2}})}}$$
$$= 3.00\times10^8\ \mathrm{m\cdot s^{-1}}.$$

The postulated field configuration *is* consistent with the laws of electrodynamics, provided that the wave front moves with the speed given above; we recognize this as the speed of light!

We have chosen a simple and primitive wave for our study in order to avoid mathematical complications, but this special case illustrates several important features of *all* electromagnetic waves:

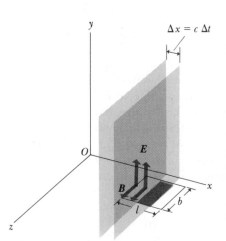

$\Delta x = c\,\Delta t$

y

O

E

B

l

b

x

z

35–4
In time Δt the electric flux through the rectangle in the xz-plane increases by an amount equal to E times the area $bc\,\Delta t$ of the shaded rectangle; that is, $\Delta\Psi = Ebc\,\Delta t$. Thus $\Delta\Psi/\Delta t = Ebc$.

1. The wave is **transverse;** both E and B are perpendicular to the direction of propagation of the wave and to each other. The fields and the direction obey a right-hand rule: Turn the E vector into the B vector; curl the fingers of the right hand in this direction, and the thumb gives the direction of propagation.

2. There is a definite ratio between the magnitudes of E and B.

3. The wave travels in vacuum with a definite and unchanging speed.

We can generalize this discussion to a more realistic situation. Suppose we have several wave fronts in the form of parallel planes perpendicular to the *x*-axis and all moving to the right with speed *c*. Suppose that, within a single region between two planes, the *E* and *B* fields are the same at all points in the region but that they differ from region to region. An extension of the above development shows that such a situation is also consistent with Ampere's and Faraday's laws, provided that the wave fronts all move with the speed *c* given by Eq. (35–14). From this picture it is only a short additional step to a wave picture in which the *E* and *B* fields at any instant vary smoothly, rather than in steps, as we move along the *x*-axis, and the entire field pattern moves to the right with speed *c*. In Section 35–5 we will consider waves in which the dependence of *E* and *B* on position and time is *sinusoidal*; first, however, we consider the *energy* associated with an electromagnetic wave.

35–3
Energy in Electromagnetic Waves

It is a familiar fact that there is energy associated with electromagnetic waves. Two simple examples are the energy in the sun's radiation and cooking with microwave ovens. To derive detailed relationships for the energy in an electromagnetic wave, we begin with the expressions derived in Sections 27–4 and 33–3 for the **energy densities** associated with electric and magnetic fields; we suggest you review those derivations now. Specifically, Eqs. (27–10) and (33–9) show that the total energy density *u* in a region of space where *E* and *B* fields are present is given by

$$u = \frac{1}{2}\epsilon_0 E^2 + \frac{1}{2\mu_0}B^2. \qquad (35\text{–}15)$$

For the simple wave we studied in Section 35–2, *E* and *B* are related by

$$B = \frac{E}{c} = \sqrt{\epsilon_0\mu_0}\,E. \qquad (35\text{–}16)$$

Combining this with Eq. (35–15), we can also express the energy density *u* as

$$u = \frac{1}{2}\epsilon_0 E^2 + \frac{1}{2\mu_0}(\sqrt{\epsilon_0\mu_0}\,E)^2 = \epsilon_0 E^2. \qquad (35\text{–}17)$$

This shows that the energy density associated with the *E* field in our simple wave is equal to that of the *B* field.

Because the *E* and *B* fields advance with time into regions where no fields were originally present, it is clear that the wave transports energy from one region to another. We can describe this energy transfer in terms of energy transferred *per unit time per unit cross-sectional area* for an area perpendicular to the direction of wave travel.

To see how the energy flow is related to the fields, consider a stationary plane, perpendicular to the x-axis, that coincides with the wave front at a certain time. In a time Δt after this the wave front moves a distance $\Delta x = c\,\Delta t$ to the right. Considering an area A on the stationary plane, we note that the energy in the space to the right of this area must have passed through it to reach its new location. The volume ΔV of the relevant region is the base area A times the length $c\,\Delta t$, and the energy ΔU in this region is the energy density u times this volume:

$$\Delta U = \epsilon_0 E^2 A c\,\Delta t. \qquad (35\text{--}18)$$

This energy passes through the area A in time Δt. The energy flow per unit time per unit area, which we will call S, is

$$S = \frac{1}{A}\frac{\Delta U}{\Delta t} = \epsilon_0 c E^2. \qquad (35\text{--}19)$$

Using Eqs. (35–14) and (35–16), we can derive the alternative forms

$$S = \frac{\epsilon_0}{\sqrt{\epsilon_0 \mu_0}} E^2 = \sqrt{\frac{\epsilon_0}{\mu_0}}\, E^2 = \frac{EB}{\mu_0}. \qquad (35\text{--}20)$$

The unit of S is energy per unit time per unit area. The SI unit of S is $1\ \mathrm{J\cdot s^{-1}\cdot m^{-2}}$ or $1\ \mathrm{W\cdot m^{-2}}$.

To describe both the magnitude and direction of the energy flow rate, we define a vector quantity S that points in the direction of propagation of the wave, with magnitude given by Eq. (35–19) or (35–20). We call S the **Poynting vector** (from the name of its inventor). The magnitude EB/μ_0 gives the flow of energy through a cross-sectional area perpendicular to the propagation direction per unit area and per unit time.

The electric and magnetic fields at any point in a wave vary with time, so the Poynting vector at any point is also a function of time. The *average* value of the magnitude of the Poynting vector at a point is called the **intensity** of the radiation at that point. As we mentioned above, the SI unit of intensity is the watt per square meter ($\mathrm{W\cdot m^{-2}}$). In Section 35–5 we will consider the relationship between the intensity of a sinusoidal wave and the amplitudes of the sinusoidally varying electric and magnetic fields.

Example 35–1   For the wave described in Section 35–2, suppose that
$$E = 100\ \mathrm{V\cdot m^{-1}} = 100\ \mathrm{N\cdot C^{-1}}.$$

Find the value of B, the energy density, and the rate of energy flow per unit area S.

Solution   From Eq. (35–11),
$$B = \frac{E}{c} = \frac{100\ \mathrm{V\cdot m^{-1}}}{3.00 \times 10^8\ \mathrm{m\cdot s^{-1}}} = 3.33 \times 10^{-7}\ \mathrm{T}.$$

From Eq. (35–17),
$$u = \epsilon_0 E^2 = (8.85 \times 10^{-12}\ \mathrm{C^2\cdot N^{-1}\cdot m^{-2}})(100\ \mathrm{N\cdot C^{-1}})^2$$
$$= 8.85 \times 10^{-8}\ \mathrm{N\cdot m^{-2}} = 8.85 \times 10^{-8}\ \mathrm{J\cdot m^{-3}}.$$

The magnitude of the Poynting vector is then given by

$$S = \frac{EB}{\mu_0} = \frac{(100 \text{ V·m}^{-1})(3.33 \times 10^{-7} \text{ T})}{4\pi \times 10^{-7} \text{ Wb·A}^{-1}·\text{m}^{-1}}$$
$$= 26.5 \text{ V·A·m}^{-2} = 26.5 \text{ W·m}^{-2}.$$

Alternatively,

$$S = \epsilon_0 c E^2$$
$$= (8.85 \times 10^{-12} \text{ C}^2·\text{N}^{-1}·\text{m}^{-2})(3.0 \times 10^8 \text{ m·s}^{-1})(100 \text{ N·C}^{-1})^2$$
$$= 26.5 \text{ W·m}^{-2}. \qquad \blacksquare$$

As we have seen, the fact that electromagnetic waves transport energy follows directly from the fact that energy is required to establish electric and magnetic fields. It can also be shown that electromagnetic waves carry *momentum p*, with a corresponding momentum density (momentum *p* per unit volume *V*) of magnitude:

$$\frac{p}{V} = \frac{EB}{\mu_0 c^2} = \frac{S}{c^2}. \qquad (35\text{–}21)$$

This momentum is a property of the field alone and is not associated with moving mass. There is also a corresponding momentum flow rate; just as the energy density u corresponds to S, the rate of energy flow per unit area, the momentum density given by Eq. (35–21) corresponds to the momentum flow rate per unit area:

$$(35\text{–}22)$$

which represents the momentum transferred per unit surface area per unit time.

This momentum is responsible for the phenomenon of **radiation pressure.** When an electromagnetic wave is completely absorbed by a surface perpendicular to the propagation direction, the time rate of change of momentum equals the *force* on the surface. Thus the force per unit area, or pressure, is equal to S/c. If the wave is totally reflected, the momentum change is twice as great, and the pressure is $2S/c$. For example, the value of S for direct sunlight is about 1.4 kW·m^{-2}, and the corresponding pressure on a completely absorbing surface is

$$\frac{S}{c} = \frac{1.4 \times 10^3 \text{ W·m}^{-2}}{3.0 \times 10^8 \text{ m·s}^{-1}} = 4.7 \times 10^{-6} \text{ Pa.}$$

The pressure on a totally reflecting surface is twice this, or 9.4×10^{-6} Pa. These are very small pressures, of the order of 10^{-10} atmospheres, but they can be measured with sensitive instruments.

Radiation pressure is important in the structure of stars. Gravitational attractions tend to shrink a star, but this tendency is balanced by radiation pressure in maintaining the size of the star through most stages of its evolution. The pressure of the sun's radiation is responsible for pushing the tail of a comet away from the sun.

35-4
Electromagnetic Waves in Matter

Our initial discussion of electromagnetic waves has been restricted to waves *in vacuum*, but it is easy to extend our analysis to electromagnetic waves in dielectrics. The wave speed is not the same as in vacuum, and we denote it by v instead of c. Faraday's law is unaltered, but Eq. (35-11), derived from Faraday's law, is replaced by $E = vB$. In Ampere's law the displacement current density j_D, defined initially by Eq. (35-4), is given not by $\epsilon_0 \, \Delta E/\Delta t$ but by $\epsilon \, \Delta E/\Delta t = K \epsilon_0 \, \Delta E/\Delta t$. Also, the constant μ_0 in Ampere's law must be replaced by $\mu = K_m \mu_0$, so Eq. (35-13) is replaced by

$$B = \epsilon \mu \, vE.$$

Following the same procedure as before, we find that the wave speed v is given by

$$v = \frac{1}{\sqrt{\epsilon\mu}} = \frac{1}{\sqrt{KK_m}} \frac{1}{\sqrt{\epsilon_0\mu_0}} = \frac{c}{\sqrt{KK_m}}. \qquad (35\text{-}23)$$

For most dielectrics the relative permeability K_m is very nearly equal to unity; in such cases we say that

$$v = \frac{1}{\sqrt{K}} \frac{1}{\sqrt{\epsilon_0\mu_0}} = \frac{c}{\sqrt{K}}.$$

Because K is always greater than unity, the speed v of electromagnetic waves in a dielectric is always *less* than the speed c in vacuum by a factor of $1/\sqrt{K}$. The ratio of the speed c in vacuum to the speed v in a material is known in optics as the **index of refraction** n of the material. For most dielectrics, where $K_m \approx 1$, this is given by

$$\frac{c}{v} = n = \sqrt{KK_m} \approx \sqrt{K}. \qquad (35\text{-}24)$$

Usually, we can't use values such as those in Table 27-1 in this equation because those values are measured by using *constant* electric fields. When the fields vary rapidly with time, there is usually not time for the reorienting of electric dipoles that occurs with steady fields. Values of K with rapidly varying fields are usually much *smaller* than the values in the table. For example, K for water is 80.4 for steady fields but only about 1.77 in the frequency range of visible light.

When a dielectric field is present, we need to modify the expressions for the energy density and the Poynting vector. The energy density is now given by

$$u = \frac{1}{2} \epsilon E^2 + \frac{1}{2\mu} B^2 = \epsilon E^2. \qquad (35\text{-}25)$$

The energy densities in the E and B fields are still equal. The Poynting vector magnitude S is now

$$S = \frac{EB}{\mu} = \sqrt{\frac{\epsilon}{\mu}} E^2. \qquad (35\text{-}26)$$

Electromagnetic waves cannot propagate any appreciable distance in a *conducting* material because the *E* field leads to currents that provide a mechanism for dissipating the energy of the wave. For an ideal conductor with zero resistivity, *E* must be zero everywhere inside the material. When an electromagnetic wave strikes such a material, it is totally reflected. Real conductors with finite resistivity permit some penetration of the wave into the material, with partial reflection. A polished metal surface is usually a good *reflector* of electromagnetic waves, but metals are not *transparent* to radiation.

35–5
Sinusoidal Waves

Sinusoidal electromagnetic waves are directly analogous to sinusoidal transverse mechanical waves on a stretched string. We studied these in Chapter 21; we suggest that you review that discussion now, especially Section 21–6. In a sinusoidal electromagnetic wave the *E* and *B* fields at any point in space are sinusoidal functions of time, and at any instant of time the *spatial* variation of the fields is also sinusoidal.

Some sinusoidal electromagnetic waves share with the waves described in Section 35–2 the property that at any instant the fields are uniform over any plane perpendicular to the direction of propagation (as shown in Fig. 35–2). Such a wave is called a **plane wave.** The entire pattern travels in the direction of propagation with speed c. The directions of *E* and *B* are perpendicular to the direction of propagation (and to each other), so the wave is *transverse*.

The frequency f, the wavelength λ, and the speed of propagation c are related by the usual wavelength–frequency relation $c = \lambda f$. If the frequency f is the power-line frequency of 60 Hz, the wavelength is

$$\lambda = \frac{c}{f} = \frac{3 \times 10^8 \text{ m·s}^{-1}}{60 \text{ Hz}} = 5 \times 10^6 \text{ m} = 5000 \text{ km},$$

which is of the order of the earth's radius! For a wave with this frequency, even a distance of many miles includes only a small fraction of a wavelength. But if the frequency is 10^8 Hz (100 MHz), typical of commercial FM radio stations, the wavelength is

$$\lambda = \frac{3 \times 10^8 \text{ m·s}^{-1}}{10^8 \text{ Hz}} = 3 \text{ m},$$

and a moderate distance can include many complete waves.

Figure 35–5 shows a sinusoidal electromagnetic wave traveling in the +*x*-direction. The *E* and *B* vectors are shown only for a few points on the *x*-axis. Imagine a plane perpendicular to the *x*-axis at a particular point at a particular time; the fields have the same values at all points in that plane. Of course, the values are different on different planes. In those planes where the *E* vector is in the +*y*-direction, *B* is in the +*z*-direction; where *E* is in the −*y*-direction, *B* is in the −*z*-direction.

We can describe electromagnetic waves by means of *wave functions*, just as we did in Section 21–6 for waves on a string. One form of the

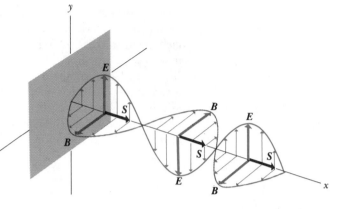

35–5
E, B, and *S* vectors in a sinusoidal electromagnetic wave traveling in the positive *x*-direction. The position of the wave at time $t = 0$ is shown.

equation of a transverse wave traveling to the right along a stretched string is Eq. (21–14):

$$y = A \sin (\omega t - kx),$$

where y is the transverse displacement from its equilibrium position, at time t, of a point with coordinate x on the string. The quantity A is the maximum displacement, or *amplitude*, of the wave; ω is its *angular frequency*, equal to 2π times the frequency f; and k is the wave number or *propagation constant*, equal to $2\pi/\lambda$, where λ is the wavelength.

Let E and B represent the instantaneous values and E_{max} and B_{max} the maximum values, or *amplitudes*, of the electric and magnetic fields in Fig. 35–5. The equations for the wave are then

$$E = E_{max} \sin (\omega t - kx), \qquad B = B_{max} \sin (\omega t - kx). \quad (35\text{–}27)$$

The sine curves in Fig. 35–5 represent instantaneous values of E and B, as functions of x, at time $t = 0$. The wave travels to the right with speed c.

We obtain the instantaneous value S of the magnitude of the Poynting vector by substituting Eq. (35–27) into Eq. (35–20):

$$S = \frac{EB}{\mu_0} = \frac{E_{max}B_{max}}{\mu_0} \sin^2 (\omega t - kx) = \frac{E_{max}B_{max}}{2\mu_0}[1 - \cos 2(\omega t - kx)].$$

The time average value of $\cos 2(\omega t - kx)$ is zero because at any point it is positive during half a cycle and negative during the other half. So the average value S_{av} of the Poynting vector magnitude is just

$$S_{av} = \frac{E_{max}B_{max}}{2\mu_0}.$$

This is the *average power* transmitted per unit area; as noted in Section 35–3, it is called the *intensity* of the radiation, denoted by I. By using the relations $E_{max} = B_{max}c$ and $\epsilon_0\mu_0 = 1/c^2$ we can express the intensity in several equivalent forms:

$$I = S_{av} = \frac{E_{max}B_{max}}{2\mu_0} = \frac{E_{max}{}^2}{2\mu_0 c} = \frac{1}{2}\sqrt{\frac{\epsilon_0}{\mu_0}}E_{max}{}^2 = \frac{1}{2}\epsilon_0 c E_{max}{}^2. \quad (35\text{–}28)$$

We invite you to verify that these expressions are all equivalent.

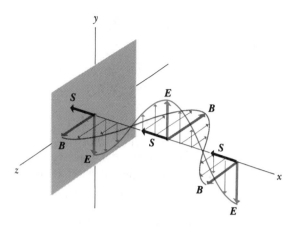

35–6
Electric and magnetic fields of a sinusoidal wave traveling in the negative x-direction. The position of the wave at time $t = \pi/2\omega$ is shown.

We can also obtain various expressions for the intensity of a wave in a material. In Eq. (35–28) we simply replace ϵ_0 by ϵ, μ_0 by μ, and c by v. Again, we will leave the details for you to work out.

Figure 35–6 shows the electric and magnetic fields of a wave traveling in the *negative x*-direction. At points where E is in the positive y-direction, B is in the *negative* z-direction; where E is in the negative y-direction, B is in the *positive* z-direction. The Poynting vector is in the negative x-direction at all points. This wave illustrates the right-hand rule for directions that we stated at the end of Section 35–2. (Compare this with Fig. 35–5, which shows a wave traveling in the *positive x*-direction.) The equations of the wave are

$$E = -E_{max} \sin (\omega t + kx), \qquad B = B_{max} \sin (\omega t + kx). \quad (35\text{--}29)$$

Example 35–2   A radio station radiates a sinusoidal wave with an average total power of 50 kW. Assuming that it radiates equally in all directions (which is unlikely in real-world situations), find the amplitudes E_{max} and B_{max} at a distance of 100 km from the antenna.

Solution   First we find the magnitude S of the Poynting vector. We surround the antenna with an imaginary sphere of radius 100 km $= 1.00 \times 10^5$ m. This sphere has area

$$A = 4\pi R^2 = 4\pi(1.00 \times 10^5 \text{ m})^2 = 12.6 \times 10^{10} \text{ m}^2.$$

All the power radiated passes through this surface, so the power per unit area is

$$S = \frac{P}{A} = \frac{P}{4\pi R^2} = \frac{5.00 \times 10^4 \text{ W}}{12.6 \times 10^{10} \text{ m}^2} = 3.98 \times 10^{-7} \text{ W·m}^{-2}.$$

But from Eq. (35–28),

$$S_{av} = \frac{E_{max}^{\;2}}{2\mu_0 c} \qquad \text{and} \qquad E_{max} = \sqrt{2\mu_0 c S_{av}},$$

so

$$E_{max} =$$

$$\sqrt{2(4\pi \times 10^{-7} \text{ Wb·A}^{-1}\text{·m}^{-1})(3.00 \times 10^8 \text{ m·s}^{-1})(3.98 \times 10^{-7} \text{ W·m}^{-2})}$$

$$= 1.73 \times 10^{-2} \text{ V·m}^{-1},$$

$$B_{max} = E_{max}/c = 5.77 \times 10^{-11} \text{ T}.$$

Note that the magnitude of E_{max} is comparable to many laboratory phenomena but that B_{max} is extremely *small* in comparison to $\boldsymbol{B}$ fields we have seen in previous chapters.   ■

Electromagnetic waves have the property of **polarization.** We introduced this concept at the end of Section 21–3 in the context of transverse waves on a string, and we suggest that you review that discussion now. In the present context we note that for a wave traveling in the x-direction the choice of the y-direction for $\boldsymbol{E}$ was arbitrary. We could just as well have specified the z-axis for $\boldsymbol{E}$; then when $\boldsymbol{E}$ is in the $+z$-direction, $\boldsymbol{B}$ is in the $-y$-direction, and so on.

A wave in which $\boldsymbol{E}$ always lies along a certain axis is said to be *linearly polarized* along that axis. More generally, we can think of *any* wave traveling in the x-direction as a superposition of waves linearly polarized in the y- and z-directions. A superposition of two linearly polarized waves with the same frequency and amplitude but a 90° phase difference yields a wave that is *circularly polarized*. We will study polarization phenomena in greater detail, with special emphasis on polarization of light, in Chapter 36.

*35–6
Standing Waves

Electromagnetic waves can be *reflected*; a conducting surface can serve as a reflector. The superposition principle holds for electromagnetic waves just as for all electric and magnetic fields, and the superposition of an incident wave and a reflected wave can form a **standing wave.** The situation is analogous to standing waves on a stretched string; we studied these in Section 22–2, and you should review that discussion now.

Suppose a sheet of an ideal conductor (zero resistivity) is placed in the yz-plane of Fig. 35–6 and that the wave shown, traveling in the negative x-direction, strikes it. There can never be an electric field inside an ideal conductor. Any attempt to establish a field is immediately cancelled by rearrangement of the mobile charges in the conductor. Thus $\boldsymbol{E}$ must always be zero everywhere in the yz-plane. The $\boldsymbol{E}$ field of the incident wave induces sinusoidal currents in the conductor in order to keep $\boldsymbol{E}$ zero everywhere inside it.

These induced currents produce a *reflected* wave, traveling out from the plane to the right. From the superposition principle the total $\boldsymbol{E}$ field at any point to the right of the plane is the vector sum of the E fields of the incident and reflected waves; the same is true for the total B field.

Suppose the incident wave is described by the wave functions of Eqs. (35–29) and the reflected wave by the wave functions of Eqs. (35–27). (Compare these with Eqs. (21–14) and (21–15) for transverse waves on a string.) From the superposition principle the total fields at any point are given by

$$E = E_{max}[-\sin(\omega t + kx) + \sin(\omega t - kx)],$$

$$B = B_{max}[\sin(\omega t + kx) + \sin(\omega t - kx)].$$

We can expand and simplify these expressions, using the identities

$$\sin(A \pm B) = \sin A \cos B \pm \cos A \sin B.$$

The results are

$$E = -2E_{max} \cos \omega t \sin kx, \tag{35–30a}$$

$$B = 2B_{max} \sin \omega t \cos kx. \tag{35–30b}$$

Equation (35–30a) is analogous to Eq. (22–1) for a stretched string. We see that at $x = 0$, E is *always* zero; this is required by the nature of the ideal conductor, which plays the same role as a fixed point at the end of the string. Furthermore, E is zero at all times in those planes for which $\sin kx = 0$; that is, $kx = 0, \pi, 2\pi, \ldots$, or

$$x = 0, \quad \frac{\lambda}{2}, \quad \lambda, \quad \frac{3\lambda}{2}, \quad \cdots.$$

These are called the **nodal planes** of the E field.

The total magnetic field is zero at all times in those planes for which $\cos kx = 0$. This occurs where

$$x = \frac{\lambda}{4}, \quad \frac{3\lambda}{4}, \quad \frac{5\lambda}{4}, \quad \cdots.$$

These are the nodal planes of the B field. The magnetic field is *not* zero at the conducting surface ($x = 0$), and there is no reason it should be. The surface currents that must be present to make E exactly zero at the surface cause magnetic fields at the surface. Figure 35–7 shows a standing-wave pattern at one instant of time.

35–7

E and *B* vectors in a standing wave. The pattern does not move along the x-axis, but the *E* and *B* vectors grow and diminish with time at each point. At each point, *E* is maximum when *B* is minimum, and conversely. The position of the wave at time $t = \tau/8$ is shown.

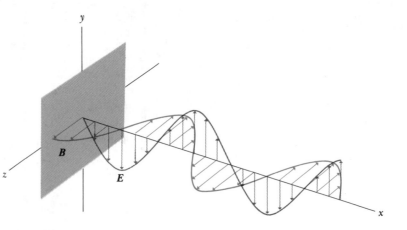

35–7
The Electromagnetic Spectrum

Electromagnetic waves cover an extremely broad spectrum of wavelength and frequency, as shown in Fig. 35–8. Radio and TV transmission, visible light, infrared and ultraviolet radiation, and gamma rays all form parts of the **electromagnetic spectrum,** a very broad class of electromagnetic radiations. All the members of this class have the general characteristics we have described in preceding sections, including the propagation speed (in vacuum) $c = 3.00 \times 10^8$ m·s^{-1}, but they differ in frequency f and wavelength λ. The relation $c = \lambda f$ holds for each.

The wavelengths of visible light (i.e., of electromagnetic waves that the human eye can perceive) can be measured by methods that we will study in Chapter 39; they are in the range 4 to 7×10^{-7} m (400 to 700 nm). The corresponding range of frequencies is about 7.5 to 4.3×10^{14} Hz.

Because of the very small magnitudes of light wavelengths, it is convenient to measure them in small units of length. The unit used most commonly is the nanometer (nm):

$$1 \text{ nm} = 10^{-9} \text{ m} = 10^{-7} \text{ cm}.$$

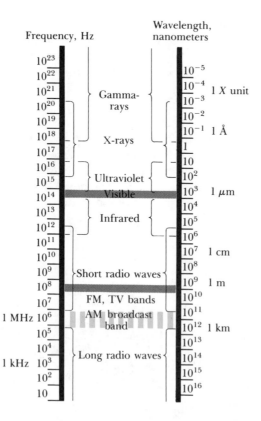

35–8
A chart of the electromagnetic spectrum.

Other units sometimes used are the micrometer (1 μm) and the angstrom (1 Å):

$$1 \ \mu m = 10^{-6} \ m = 10^{-4} \ cm,$$

$$1 \ \text{Å} = 10^{-10} \ m = 10^{-8} \ cm.$$

In older literature the micrometer is sometimes called the *micron*, and the nanometer is sometimes called the *millimicron*; these terms are now obsolete. The wavelength of the yellow light from a sodium-vapor lamp is 589 nm, but some older books on spectroscopy would identify this same wavelength as 5890 Å.

Different parts of the visible spectrum evoke in humans the sensations of different colors. Wavelengths for colors in the visible spectrum are (very approximately) as follows:

400 to 440 nm:	Violet	530 to 590 nm:	Yellow
440 to 480 nm:	Blue	590 to 630 nm:	Orange
480 to 530 nm:	Green	630 to 700 nm:	Red

By using special sources or special filters we can select a narrow band of wavelengths, with a range of, say, 1 to 10 nm. Such light is approximately *monochromatic* (single-color) light. Absolutely monochromatic light with only a single wavelength is an unattainable idealization. When we use the expression "monochromatic light of wavelength 550 nm" with reference to a laboratory experiment, we really mean a small band of wavelengths *around* 550 nm. One distinguishing characteristic of light from a *laser* is that it is much more nearly monochromatic than light obtainable in any other way.

*35–8
Radiation from an Antenna

Our discussion of electromagnetic waves in this chapter has centered mostly on *plane waves*. These waves have the property that they propagate in a single direction (often the *x*-axis of our coordinate system). In any plane perpendicular to the direction of propagation of the wave the *E* and *B* fields are uniform at any one instant of time. Plane waves are the simplest of all electromagnetic waves to describe and analyze, but they are by no means the simplest to produce experimentally. Any charge or current distribution that oscillates sinusoidally with time produces sinusoidal electromagnetic waves, but in general there is no reason to expect them to be plane waves.

An example of an oscillating charge distribution is an **oscillating dipole,** a pair of electric charges with equal magnitude and opposite sign, the charge magnitude varying sinusoidally with time. Such an oscillating dipole can be constructed in various ways, but we do not need to be concerned with the details.

The radiation from an oscillating dipole is *not* a plane wave but a wave that travels out in all directions from the source. The wave fronts

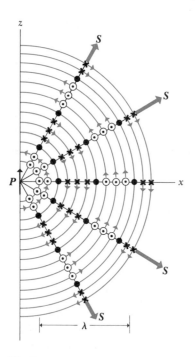

35–9

Cross section in the *xz*-plane of radiation from an oscillating electric dipole **P**. The wave fronts are expanding concentric spheres centered at **P**. The **E** field at every point lies in the plane; the colored lines show the directions of **E** at various points. The **B** field at every point is perpendicular to the plane. At points with circles, **B** comes out of the plane, and at points with crosses it is into the plane. The direction of the Poynting vector **S** is radially outward at every point. The magnitudes of the fields are not shown; they are strongest at points along the *x*-axis and become progressively weaker along lines closer to the *z*-axis. They also become weaker with increasing distance from **P**.

are not planes but expanding concentric spheres centered at the source. At points far from the source the **E** and **B** fields are perpendicular to the direction outward from the source and to each other; in this sense the wave is still transverse. The direction of the Poynting vector **S** at each point is radially outward from the source. The intensity *I* (the average value of the Poynting vector magnitude) is inversely proportional to the square of the distance from the source. The intensity also depends on the *direction* from the source; it is greatest in directions perpendicular to the dipole axis, and it is zero in directions parallel to the axis.

The radiation pattern from a dipole source is shown schematically in Fig. 35–9, which shows a cross section of the radiation pattern at one instant. The oscillating dipole **P** is located at the centers of the spheres. At each point in the plane of Fig. 35–9 the **E** field lies in the plane, and the **B** field is perpendicular to it. The **E** field is shown by colored arrows and the direction of **B** by crosses (where it points into the plane) and circles with dots (where it points out of the plane). The direction of the Poynting vector **S** is radially outward from the source at each point. As the wave travels outward, the spheres expand; the radius of each sphere increases at a constant rate *c*.

Electromagnetic waves can be *reflected* by conducting surfaces. When the surface is large in comparison to the wavelength of the radiation, the reflection behaves like reflection of light rays from a mirror, which we will study in Chapter 37. Large parabolic mirrors several meters in diameter are used as both transmitting and receiving antennas for microwave communications signals; typical wavelengths are a few centimeters. The transmitting reflector produces a wave that radiates in a narrow, well-defined beam; the receiving reflector gathers wave energy over its whole area and reflects it to the focus of the parabola, where a detecting device is placed. Figure 35–10 shows an antenna installation using a large parabolic reflector.

35–10

A microwave-receiving antenna 64 m in diameter at Goldstone Tracking Station, California, the prime station of a worldwide network of stations used by NASA to monitor unmanned interplanetary spacecraft.

Questions

35–1 In Ampere's law, is it possible to have both a conduction current and a displacement current at the same time? Is it possible for the effects of the two kinds of current to cancel each other exactly so that *no* magnetic field is produced?

35–2 By measuring the electric and magnetic fields at a point in space where there is an electromagnetic wave, can one determine the direction from which the wave came?

35–3 Sometimes neon signs located near a powerful radio station are seen to glow faintly at night, even though they are not turned on. What is happening?

35–4 Light can be *polarized;* is this a property of all electromagnetic waves, or is it unique to light? What about polarization of sound waves? What fundamental distinction in wave properties is involved?

35–5 How does a microwave oven work? Why does it heat materials that are conductors of electricity, including most foods, but not insulators such as glass or ceramic dishes? Why do the instructions forbid putting anything metallic in the oven?

35–6 Electromagnetic waves can travel through vacuum, where there is no matter. We usually think of vacuum as empty space, but is it *really* empty if electric and magnetic fields are present? What *is* vacuum, anyway?

35–7 Give several examples of electromagnetic waves that are encountered in everyday life. How are they all alike? How do they differ?

35–8 We are surrounded by electromagnetic waves emitted by many radio and television stations. How is a radio or television receiver able to select a single station among all this mishmash of waves? What happens inside a radio receiver when the dial is turned to change stations?

35–9 The metal conducting rods on a television antenna are always in a horizontal plane. Would they work as well if they were vertical?

35–10 If a light beam carries momentum, should a person holding a flashlight feel a recoil analogous to the recoil of a rifle when it is fired? Why is this recoil not actually observed?

35–11 The nineteenth century inventor Nikola Tesla proposed transmitting large quantities of electrical energy across space by using electromagnetic waves instead of conventional transmission lines. What advantages would this scheme have? What disadvantages?

35–12 Does an electromagnetic *standing wave* have energy? Momentum? What distinction can be drawn between a standing wave and a propagating wave on this basis?

35–13 If light is an electromagnetic wave, what is its frequency? Is this a proper question to ask?

35–14 When an electromagnetic wave is reflected from a moving reflector, the frequency of the reflected wave is different from that of the initial wave. Explain physically how this can happen. (Some radar systems used for highway-speed control operate on this principle.)

35–15 The ionosphere is a layer of ionized air 100 km or so above the earth's surface. It acts as a reflector of radio waves of frequency less than about 30 MHz but not of higher frequency. How does this reflection occur? Why does it work better for lower frequencies than for higher ones?

Exercises

Section 35–1 Displacement Current and Maxwell's Equations

35–1 A parallel-plate capacitor is being charged as in Fig. 35–1. The electric field between the plates is increasing at a uniform rate of 1.20×10^4 V·m^{-1}·s^{-1}, and each plate has an area of 20.0 cm^2.

a) What is the displacement current density j_D in the region between the plates?

b) What is the conduction current in the wires that are connected to the plates?

35–2 A parallel-plate capacitor is being charged as in Fig. 35–1. The circular plates have a radius of 0.0500 m, and at a particular instant the conduction current in the wires is 0.800 A.

a) What is the displacement current density j_D in the air space between the plates?

b) What is the rate at which the electric field between the plates is changing?

c) What is the induced magnetic field between the plates at a distance of 0.0250 m from the axis?

d) At 0.100 m from the axis?

Section 35–2   Speed of an Electromagnetic Wave

35–3 In a TV picture, ghost images are formed when the signal from the transmitter travels directly to the receiver and also indirectly after reflection from a building or other large metallic mass. In a 25-in. set the ghost is 1.0 cm to the right of the principal image if the reflected signal arrives 0.50 μs after the principal signal. In this case, what is the difference in path length for the two signals?

35–4 The maximum electric field in the vicinity of a certain radio transmitter is 4.00×10^{-3} V·m^{-1}. What is the maximum magnitude of the B field? How does this compare in magnitude with the earth's field?

35–5 A certain radio station broadcasts at a frequency of 1240 kHz. At a point some distance from the transmitter, the maximum magnetic field of the electromagnetic wave it emits is 3.20×10^{-11} T.

a) What is the wavelength of the wave?

b) What is the maximum electric field?

35–6

a) How much time does it take light to travel from the sun to the earth, a distance of 1.49×10^{11} m?

b) A star is 34.6 light years from the earth. (One light year is the distance light travels in one year.) What is this distance in kilometers?

Section 35–3   Energy in Electromagnetic Waves

Section 35–5   Sinusoidal Waves

35–7 Verify that all the expressions in Eq. (35–20) are equivalent.

35–8 A sinusoidal electromagnetic wave emitted by a microwave antenna has a wavelength of 5.00 cm and an electric field amplitude of 3.60×10^{-2} V·m^{-1} at a distance of 4.00 km from the antenna.

a) What is the frequency of the wave?

b) What is the magnetic field amplitude?

c) What is the intensity (average power per unit area) of the wave?

35–9 At a distance of 50.0 km from a radio station antenna the electric-field amplitude is $E_{max} = 0.0900$ V·m^{-1}.

a) What is the magnetic-field amplitude B_{max} at this same point?

b) Assuming that the antenna radiates equally in all directions (which is probably not the case), what is the total power output of the station?

c) At what distance from the antenna is $E_{max} = 0.0450$ V·m^{-1}, half the above value?

35–10 Consider each of the electric- and magnetic-field orientations given below. In each case, what is the direction of propagation of the wave?

a) E in the $+x$-direction, B in the $+y$-direction;

b) E in the $-y$-direction, B in the $+x$-direction;

c) E in the $+z$-direction, B in the $-x$-direction;

d) E in the $+y$-direction, B in the $-z$-direction.

35–11 Assume that 10% of the power input to a 100-W lamp is radiated uniformly as light of wavelength 500 nm (1 nm = 10^{-9} m). At a distance of 6.00 m from the source, the electric and magnetic fields vary sinusoidally according to the equations $E = E_{max} \sin (\omega t + \phi)$ and $B = B_{max} \sin (\omega t + \phi)$, where ϕ is a constant phase angle. Calculate E_{max} and B_{max} for the 500-nm light.

35–12 At the floor of a room the intensity of light from bright overhead lights is 800 W·m^{-2}. Find

a) the momentum density (momentum per unit volume);

b) the radiation pressure on a totally absorbing section of the floor.

35–13 The intensity at a certain distance from a bright light source is 600 W·m^{-2}. Find the radiation pressure (in pascals) on

a) a totally absorbing surface;

b) a totally reflecting surface.

Also express your results in atmospheres.

Section 35–4   Electromagnetic Waves in Matter

35–14 An electromagnetic wave with a frequency of 20.0 MHz propagates with a speed of 1.90×10^{8} m·s^{-1} in a certain piece of glass. Find

a) the wavelength of the wave in the glass;

b) the wavelength of a wave of the same frequency propagating in air;

c) the refractive index n of the glass for an electromagnetic wave with this frequency;

d) the dielectric constant for glass at this frequency, assuming that the relative permeability is unity.

35–15 An electromagnetic wave propagates in a ferrite material having $K = 10$ and $K_m = 1000$. For a wave with a frequency of 80.0 MHz, find

a) the speed of propagation;

b) the wavelength of the wave in the ferrite material.

Section 35–6   Standing Waves

35–16 An electromagnetic standing wave in air has a frequency of 6.00×10^{14} Hz.

a) What is the distance between nodal planes of the E field?

b) What is the distance between a nodal plane of E and the closest nodal plane of B?

35–17 An electromagnetic wave propagating in a certain material has a frequency of 2.00×10^{10} Hz. The nodal planes of the B field are 6.00 mm apart. What are

a) the wavelength of the wave in this material;

b) the distance between adjacent nodal planes of the E field;

c) the speed of propagation of the wave?

Section 35–7   The Electromagnetic Spectrum

35–18 For an electromagnetic wave propagating in air, determine the frequency of a wave with a wavelength of

a) 1.0 km,

b) 1.0 m,

c) 1.0 μm,

d) 1.0 nm.

35–19 For waves propagating in air, what is the wavelength in meters, micrometers, nanometers, and angstrom units of

a) soft X-rays with a frequency of 4.00×10^{17} Hz?

b) orange light with a frequency of 5.00×10^{14} Hz?

▇ Problems

35–20 A capacitor has two parallel plates with area A separated by a distance d. The capacitor is given an initial charge Q, but because the damp air between the plates is slightly conductive, the charge slowly leaks through the air. The charge initially changes at a rate $\Delta Q / \Delta t$.

a) In terms of $\Delta Q / \Delta t$, what is the initial rate of change of the electric field between the plates?

b) Show that the displacement current density has the same magnitude as the conduction current density but the opposite direction. Hence show that the magnetic field in the air between the plates is exactly zero at all times.

35–21 The energy flow to the earth associated with sunlight is about 1.4 kW·m^{-2}.

a) Find the maximum values of E and B for a sinusoidal wave of this intensity.

b) The distance from the earth to the sun is about 1.5×10^{11} m. Find the total power radiated by the sun.

35–22 For a sinusoidal electromagnetic wave in vacuum, such as that described by Eqs. (35–27), show that the average density of energy in the electric field is the same as that in the magnetic field.

35–23 A plane sinusoidal electromagnetic wave in air has a wavelength of 3.00 cm and an E-field amplitude of 60.0 V·m^{-1}.

a) What is the frequency?

b) What is the B-field amplitude?

c) What is the intensity?

d) What average force does this radiation exert on a totally absorbing surface with area 0.500 m^2 perpendicular to the direction of propagation?

35–24 A very long solenoid with n turns per unit length and radius a carries a current i that is increasing at a constant rate of $\Delta i / \Delta t$.

a) Calculate the magnitude of the induced electric field at a point inside the solenoid at a distance r from the solenoid axis.

b) Compute the magnitude and direction of the Poynting vector at this point. (The direction of S corresponds to flow of energy into the volume where energy is being stored in the magnetic field.)

35–25 A cylindrical conductor of circular cross section has a radius a and a resistivity ρ and carries a constant current I.

a) What are the magnitude and direction of the electric field vector E at a point inside the wire at a distance r from the axis?

b) What are the magnitude and direction of the magnetic field vector B at the same point?

c) What are the magnitude and direction of the Poynting vector S at the same point? (The direction of S corresponds to energy entering the volume of the conductor, the energy that is converted to heat in the conductor.)

d) Use the result in part (c) to find the rate of flow of energy into the volume occupied by a length l of the conductor, and compare this to the rate of generation of heat in the same volume.

35–26 A capacitor consists of two circular plates of radius r separated by a distance l. Neglecting fringing, show that while the capacitor is being charged, the rate at which energy flows into the space between the plates is equal to the rate at which the electrostatic energy stored in the capacitor increases. (*Hint:* Compute the Poynting vector at the surface of the volume between the plates. You will also need to use the relation $\Delta(Q^2)/\Delta t = 2Q\,\Delta Q/\Delta t$, which is easily shown to be true when Δt is small.)

35–27 A powerful searchlight shines on a man. The man has a cross-sectional area of 0.5 m² perpendicular to the light beam, and the intensity of the light at the man's location is 36.0 kW·m⁻². The man is wearing dark clothing, so you can assume that the light incident on him is totally absorbed. What is the magnitude of the force the light beam exerts on the man?

35–28 It has been proposed that to aid in meeting the energy needs of the United States, solar-power-collecting satellites could be placed in earth orbit, and the power they collect could be beamed down to earth as microwave radiation. For a microwave beam with a cross-sectional area of 36.0 m² and a total power of 1.00 kW at the earth's surface, what is the amplitude of the electric field of the beam at the earth's surface?

35–29 A space-walking astronaut has run out of fuel for her jet-pack and is floating 14.0 m from the space shuttle with zero relative velocity. The astronaut and all her equipment have a total mass of 200 kg. If she uses her 100-W flashlight as a light rocket, how long will it take her to reach the shuttle?

 Challenge Problems

35–30 Consider the standing wave given by Equations (35–30). Let *E* be parallel to the *y*-axis and *B* be parallel to the *z*-axis; the equations then give the components of *E* and *B* along each axis.

 a) Plot the energy density as a function of *x*, $0 < x < \pi/k$, for the times $t = 0$, $\pi/4\omega$, $\pi/2\omega$, $3\pi/4\omega$, and π/ω.

 b) Find the direction of *S* in the regions $0 < x < \pi/2k$ and $\pi/2k < x < \pi/k$ at the times $t = \pi/4\omega$, $3\pi/4\omega$.

 c) Use your results in part (b) to explain the plots obtained in part (a).

35–31 The concept of solar sailing has appeared in science fiction and proposals to NASA. A solar sailcraft uses a large low-mass sail and the energy and momentum of sunlight for propulsion. The total power output of the sun is 4.00×10^{26} W.

 a) Should the sail be absorbing or reflective? Why?

 b) How large a sail is necessary to propel a 5.00×10^4 kg spacecraft against the gravitational force of the sun? (Express your result in square miles.)

 c) Explain why your answer to part (b) is independent of the distance from the sun.

36

The Nature and
Propagation of Light

We begin this chapter with a general discussion of the nature and properties of light. Light is electromagnetic radiation; therefore it is fundamentally a *wave* phenomenon. Many aspects of the propagation of light can be described more simply by a *ray* model. Rays travel in straight lines in homogeneous materials; they are reflected and bent (*refracted*) at interfaces between materials. Like all transverse waves, light waves are *polarized*; we examine several aspects of polarization phenomena. Finally, Huygens' principle is the connecting link between the wave and ray descriptions of the behavior of light.

36–1
The Nature of Light

Until the time of Newton (1642–1727), most scientists thought that light consisted of streams of some sort of particles (called *corpuscles*) emitted by light sources. Galileo and others tried (unsuccessfully) to measure the speed of light. Around 1665, scientists began to discover evidence of wave properties of light. By the early nineteenth century, evidence that light is a wave phenomenon had grown very persuasive. We will study several optical wave phenomena in Chapter 39.

The next great step was taken in 1873 by Maxwell, who predicted the existence of electromagnetic waves and calculated their speed of propagation, as we learned in Chapter 35. This development, along with the experimental work of Hertz starting in 1887, showed conclusively that light is indeed an electromagnetic-wave phenomenon.

Successful as the wave picture of light is, it is not the whole story. Several phenomena associated with emission and absorption of light reveal a particle aspect, in the sense that the energy carried by light waves is packaged in discrete bundles called *photons* or *quanta*. We will explore some of these phenomena in Chapter 41. These apparently contradictory wave and particle properties have been reconciled only since 1930 with the development of quantum electrodynamics, a comprehensive theory that includes *both* wave and particle properties. *Propagation* of light is best described by a wave model, but emission and absorption phenomena require a particle approach.

All bodies emit electromagnetic radiation as a result of the thermal motion of their molecules; this radiation, called *thermal radiation*, is a mixture of different wavelengths. At sufficiently high temperatures, all matter emits enough visible light to be self-luminous; a very hot body appears "red hot" or "white hot." Thus hot matter in any form is a light source. Familiar examples are a candle flame, hot coals in a campfire, the coils in an electric room heater, and an incandescent lamp filament (which usually operates at a temperature of about 3000°C).

Light is also produced during electrical discharges through ionized gases. The bluish light of mercury-arc lamps, the orange-yellow of sodium-vapor lamps, and the various colors of "neon" signs are familiar. A variation of the mercury-arc lamp is the *fluorescent* lamp. This light source uses a material called a *phosphor* to convert the ultraviolet radiation from a mercury arc into visible light. This conversion makes fluorescent lamps more efficient than incandescent lamps in converting electrical energy to light.

A special light source that has attained prominence in the last 20 years is the *laser*. It can produce a very narrow beam of enormously intense radiation. High-intensity lasers have been used to cut through steel, to fuse high-melting-point materials, for microsurgery, and in many other applications. A significant characteristic of laser light is that it is much more nearly *monochromatic*, or single-frequency, than any other light source. We will study the operation of one type of laser in Chapter 41.

The speed of light in vacuum is a fundamental constant of nature. The first approximate measurement of the speed of light was made in 1676 by the Danish astronomer Olaf Roemer (1644–1710) from observations of the motion of one of Jupiter's satellites. The first successful *terrestrial* measurement was made by the French scientist Armand Fizeau (1819–1896) in 1849, using a reflected light beam interrupted by a notched rotating disk. More refined versions of this experiment were carried out by Foucault and by the American physicist Albert A. Michelson (1852–1931).

From analysis of all measurements up to 1983, the most probable value for the speed of light in vacuum at that time was

$$c = 2.99792458 \times 10^8 \text{ m·s}^{-1}.$$

As we explained in Section 1–2, the definition of the second based on the cesium clock is precise to within one part in 10 trillion (10^{13}). Up to 1983 the definition of the meter was much less precise, to about four parts in a billion (10^9). For this reason, in November 1983 the General Conference of Weights and Measures redefined the meter by *defining* the speed of light in vacuum to be precisely 299,792,458 m·s^{-1}. One meter is now defined to be the distance traveled by light in a time of 1/299,792,458 s, with the second defined by the cesium clock.

We often use the concept of a **wave front** to describe wave propagation. A familiar example is a crest of a water wave; when we drop a pebble in a calm pool, the expanding circles formed by the wave crests are wave fronts. Similarly, when sound waves spread out from a pointlike source, any spherical surface concentric with the source is a wave front. The surfaces over which the pressure is maximum and those over which it is minimum form sets of expanding spheres as the wave travels outward from the source. For a sinusoidal wave, wave fronts corresponding to maximum displacements in opposite directions are separated from each other by one-half wavelength.

For a light wave (or any other electromagnetic wave) the quantity that corresponds to the displacement of the surface in a water wave or the pressure in a sound wave is the electric or magnetic field. We will often use diagrams that show the shapes of the wave fronts or their intersections with some reference plane. For example, when electromagnetic waves are radiated by a small light source, we can represent the wave fronts as *spherical* surfaces concentric with the source or, as in Fig. 36–1a, by the intersections of these surfaces with the plane of the diagram. Far away from the source, where the radii of the spheres have become very large, a section of a spherical surface can be considered as a plane, and we have a *plane* wave, as in Fig. 36–1b.

It is sometimes convenient to represent a light wave by **rays** rather than by wave fronts. Rays were used to describe light long before its wave nature was firmly established, and in a particle theory of light, rays are the paths of the particles. From the wave viewpoint *a ray is an imaginary line along the direction of travel of the wave.* In Fig. 36–1a the rays are the radii of the spherical wave fronts, and in Fig. 36–1b they are straight lines perpendicular to the wave fronts. When waves travel in a homogeneous isotropic material, the rays are always straight lines normal to the

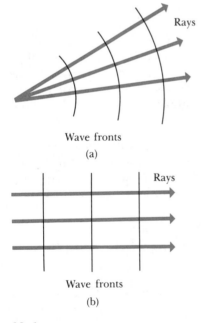

Rays

Wave fronts

(a)

Rays

Wave fronts

(b)

36–1
Wave fronts and rays. (a) When the wave fronts are spherical, the rays radiate out from the center of the spheres. (b) When the wave fronts are planes, the rays are parallel.

wave fronts. At a boundary surface between two materials, such as the surface of a glass plate in air, the direction of a ray changes, but the segments in the air and in the glass are straight lines.

The next several chapters will give you many opportunities to see the interplay of the ray, wave, and particle descriptions of light. The branch of optics for which the ray description is adequate is called **geometrical optics;** the branch dealing specifically with wave behavior is called **physical optics.** This chapter and the two following ones are concerned mostly with geometrical optics; in Chapter 39 we return to wave phenomena and physical optics.

36-2
Reflection and Refraction

When a light wave strikes a smooth interface between two optical materials, such as air and glass or water and glass, the wave is in general partly reflected and partly *refracted* (transmitted) into the second material, as shown in Fig. 36–2a. For example, when you look into a store window from the street, you see a reflection of the street scene, but a person in the store can look *through* the window at the same scene as light reaches him or her by refraction.

The segments of plane waves shown in Fig. 36–2a can be represented by bundles of rays forming *beams* of light, as in Fig. 36–2b. For simplicity we often draw only one ray in each beam, as in Fig. 36–2c. Representing these waves in terms of rays is the basis of *geometrical optics*.

At an interface between two optical materials we describe the directions of the incident, reflected, and refracted (transmitted) beams of light in terms of the angles they make with the *normal* to the surface at the point of incidence, as shown in Fig. 36–2c. Experimental studies of the directions of the incident, reflected, and refracted rays lead to the following conclusions:

1. *The incident, reflected, and refracted rays and the normal to the surface all lie in the same plane.* Thus if the incident ray is in the plane of the diagram and the boundary surface between the two materials is perpendicular to this plane, then the reflected and refracted rays are in the plane of the diagram.

2. *The angle of reflection ϕ_r is equal to the angle of incidence ϕ_a for all wavelengths and for any pair of substances.* That is,

$$\phi_r = \phi_a. \tag{36-1}$$

The experimental result that $\phi_r = \phi_a$ and that the incident and reflected rays and the normal all lie in the same plane is called the **law of reflection.**

3. For monochromatic light and for a given pair of substances, a and b, on opposite sides of the surface of separation, *the ratio of the sine of the angle ϕ_a* (between the ray in substance a and the normal) *and the sine of the angle ϕ_b* (between the ray in substance b

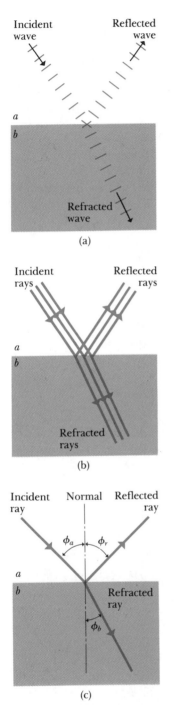

(a) A plane wave is in part reflected and in part refracted at the boundary between two media. (b) The waves in part (a) are represented by rays. (c) For simplicity, only one example of incident, reflected, and refracted rays is drawn.

and the normal) *is constant*. That is,

$$\frac{\sin \phi_a}{\sin \phi_b} = \text{constant}. \tag{36–2}$$

This experimental result, together with the fact that the incident and refracted rays and the normal to the surface all lie in the same plane, is known as the **law of refraction** or **Snell's law,** after Willebrord Snell (1591–1626). There is some doubt that Snell actually discovered it.

The *intensities* of the reflected and refracted rays depend on the angle of incidence. The fraction reflected is smallest at *normal* incidence (0°), where it is a few percent, and it increases with increasing angle of incidence to 100% at grazing incidence, when $\phi_a = 90°$.

When a ray of light approaches the interface from *below* in Fig. 36–2, there are again reflected and refracted rays; these two rays, the incident ray, and the normal to the surface all lie in the same plane. The laws of reflection and refraction apply whether the incident ray is in material a or b in the figure. The path of a refracted ray is reversible; it follows the same path when going from b to a as when going from a to b.

Now let's consider a beam of monochromatic light traveling *in vacuum*, making an angle of incidence ϕ_0 with the normal to the surface of a substance a, and let ϕ_a be the angle of refraction into the substance. In this case we call the constant in Snell's law the **index of refraction** of substance a, denoted by n_a:

$$\frac{\sin \phi_0}{\sin \phi_a} = n_a. \tag{36–3}$$

This definition of index of refraction may seem unrelated to the definition we encountered in Section 35–4. In fact, though, they are equivalent. We will discuss this equivalence in Section 36–7.

Most glasses used in optical instruments have indexes of refraction between about 1.4 and 2.0. A few substances have larger indexes; two examples are diamond (2.42) and rutile (crystalline titanium dioxide) (2.62). The index of refraction (also called *refractive index*) depends not only on the substance but also on the wavelength of the light. The dependence on wavelength is called *dispersion*; we will consider it in Section 36–4. Indexes of refraction for several solids and liquids are given in Table 36–1.

The index of refraction of *air* at standard conditions is about 1.0003, and we will usually take it to be exactly unity. The index of refraction of a gas increases uniformly as its density increases.

As Table 36–1 shows, the index of refraction is always greater than unity. When a ray passes from vacuum into a material, the angle of refraction ϕ_a is always *less than* the angle of incidence ϕ_0. The ray is always bent *toward* the normal. When light travels in the opposite direction, from a material into vacuum, the reverse is true, and the ray is always bent *away from* the normal.

We can express the constant in Eq. (36–2) in terms of the indexes of refraction n_a and n_b of the two materials. To develop this relation, we

TABLE 36–1   Index of refraction for yellow sodium light (λ = 589 nm)

Substance	Index of refraction
Solids	
Ice (H_2O)	1.309
Fluorite (CaF_2)	1.434
Polystyrene	1.49
Rock salt (NaCl)	1.544
Quartz (SiO_2)	1.544
Zircon ($ZrO_2 \cdot SiO_2$)	1.923
Diamond (C)	2.417
Fabulite ($SrTiO_3$)	2.409
Rutile (TiO_2)	2.62
Glasses (typical values)	
Crown	1.52
Light flint	1.58
Medium flint	1.62
Dense flint	1.66
Lanthanum flint	1.80
Liquids at 20°C	
Methyl alcohol (CH_3OH)	1.329
Water (H_2O)	1.333
Ethyl alcohol (C_2H_5OH)	1.36
Carbon tetrachloride (CCl_4)	1.460
Turpentine	1.472
Glycerine	1.473
Benzene	1.501
Carbon disulfide (CS_2)	1.628

consider two parallel-sided plates of substances a and b placed parallel to each other with space between them, as in Fig. 36–3a. We assume that the surrounding medium is vacuum. A ray of monochromatic light starts at the lower left with an angle of incidence ϕ_0. The angle between the ray and the normal in substance a is ϕ_a, and the light emerges from substance a at an angle ϕ_0 equal to its incident angle. The light ray then enters plate b with an angle of incidence ϕ_0, makes an angle ϕ_b in substance b, and emerges again at an angle ϕ_0. The angles are independent of the thickness of the space between the two plates and are the same when the space shrinks to nothing, as in Fig. 36–3b.

Applying Snell's law to the refractions at the surface between vacuum and substance a and at the surface between vacuum and substance b, we have

$$\frac{\sin \phi_0}{\sin \phi_a} = n_a,$$

$$\frac{\sin \phi_0}{\sin \phi_b} = n_b.$$

Dividing the second equation by the first, we find

$$\frac{\sin \phi_a}{\sin \phi_b} = \frac{n_b}{n_a}. \tag{36–4}$$

This shows that the constant in Snell's law for refraction between substances a and b is the inverse of the ratio of the indexes of refraction. The simplest way to express Snell's law for any two substances a and b is to rewrite Eq. (36–4) as

$$n_a \sin \phi_a = n_b \sin \phi_b. \tag{36–5}$$

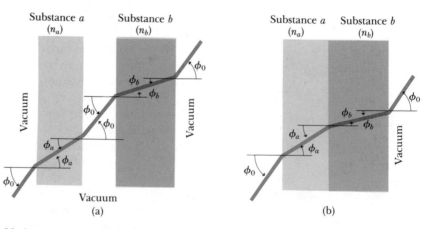

36–3
The transmission of light through parallel plates of different substances. The incident and emerging rays are parallel, regardless of direction and regardless of the thickness of the space between adjacent slabs.

Example 36–1   In Fig. 36–2, material *a* is water and material *b* is a glass with an index of refraction of 1.50. If the incident ray makes an angle of 60° with the normal, find the directions of the reflected and refracted rays.

Solution   According to Eq. (36–1), the angle the reflected ray makes with the normal is the same as that of the incident ray, Hence $\phi_r = \phi_a = 60°$. To find the direction of the refracted ray, we use Eq. (36–5), with $n_a = 1.33$, $n_b = 1.50$, and $\phi_a = 60°$. We find

$$n_a \sin \phi_a = n_b \sin \phi_b,$$

$$(1.33)(\sin 60°) = (1.50)(\sin \phi_b),$$

$$\phi_b = 50.2°.$$

The second material has a larger refractive index than the first, and the refracted ray is bent toward the normal. As Eq. (36–5) shows, this is always the case when the second index is larger than the first. In the opposite case, in which the second index is *smaller* than the first, the ray is always bent *away from* the normal.   ■

The index of refraction of a material is closely related to the speed of light in the material. We will develop this relationship in detail in Section 36–7, but we state the principal results here for reference. Light always travels *more slowly* in a material than in vacuum. The ratio of the two speeds is equal to the index of refraction. The speed of light *v* in a material with index of refraction *n* is given by

$$v = \frac{c}{n}, \qquad \text{or} \qquad n = \frac{c}{v}. \tag{36–6}$$

When light passes from one material to another, its frequency *f* does not change. The electrons in the material absorb energy from the light and undergo vibrational motion with the same frequency as the light. This motion causes reradiation of the energy *with the same frequency*. In any material, $v = \lambda f$. Because *f* is the same in any material as in vacuum and *v* is always less than the wave speed *c* in vacuum, λ is also correspondingly reduced. Thus the wavelength λ of light in a material is *less than* the wavelength λ_0 of the same light in vacuum by a factor *n*:

$$\lambda = \frac{\lambda_0}{n}. \tag{36–7}$$

Here are two final comments about reflection and refraction. First, reflection also occurs at a polished surface of an *opaque* material such as a metal. There is no refracted ray, but the reflected ray behaves according to Eq. (36–1). Second, if the reflecting surface (of either a transparent or an opaque material) is rough, with irregularities on a scale comparable to the wavelength of light, reflection does not occur in a single direction but in all directions. This is called *diffuse* reflection, in contrast to the *specular* reflection described above.

■ **PROBLEM-SOLVING STRATEGY:** *Reflection and Refraction*

1. In geometrical optics problems involving rays and angles, *always* start by drawing a large, neat diagram. Use a ruler and protractor. Label all known angles and indexes of refraction.

2. Don't forget that by convention we always measure the angles of incidence, reflection, and refraction from the *normal* to the surface where the reflection and refraction occur, *never* from the surface itself.

3. You will often have to use some simple geometry or trigonometry in working out angular relations. The sum of the interior angles in a triangle is 180°, vertical angles are equal, and so on. Often it helps to think through the problem, asking yourself "What information am I given?" "What do I need to know in order to find this angle?" or "What other angles or other quantities can I compute using the information given in the problem?"

36–3
Total Internal Reflection

Figure 36–4a shows several rays diverging from a point source P in material a with index of refraction n_a. The rays strike the surface of a second material b with index n_b, where $n_a > n_b$. From Snell's law,

$$\sin \phi_b = \frac{n_a}{n_b} \sin \phi_a.$$

Because n_a/n_b is greater than unity, $\sin \phi_b$ is larger than $\sin \phi_a$. Thus there must be some value of ϕ_a *less than* 90° for which $\sin \phi_b = 1$ and

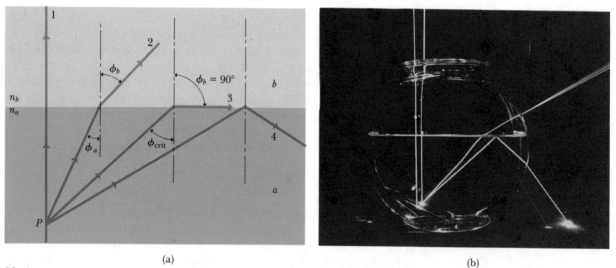

(a)   (b)

36–4
(a) Total internal reflection. The angle of incidence ϕ_a for which the angle of refraction is 90°, is called the critical angle. (b) Rays of laser light enter the water in the fishbowl from above; they are reflected at the bottom by mirrors tilted at slightly different angles, and one ray undergoes total internal reflection at the air–water interface. (Nancy Roger, The Exploratorium.)

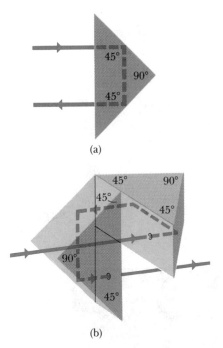

(a)

(b)

36–5
(a) A Porro prism. (b) A combination of two Porro prisms.

$\phi_b = 90°$. This is shown by ray 3 in the diagram, which emerges just grazing the surface at an angle of refraction of 90°. The angle of incidence for which the refracted ray emerges tangent to the surface is called the **critical angle** and is denoted by ϕ_{crit} in the diagram. If the angle of incidence is *greater than* the critical angle, the sine of the angle of refraction, as computed by Snell's law, would have to be greater than unity, and this is impossible. Beyond the critical angle the ray *cannot* pass into the upper material; it is trapped in the lower material and is completely reflected internally at the boundary surface. **Total internal reflection** occurs only when a ray is incident on the surface of a material whose index of refraction is *smaller* than that of the material in which the ray is traveling.

We can find the critical angle for two given materials by setting $\phi_b = 90°$ ($\sin \phi_b = 1$) in Snell's law. We then have

$$\sin \phi_{crit} = \frac{n_b}{n_a}. \qquad (36\text{–}8)$$

For a glass–air surface, with $n = 1.50$ for the glass,

$$\sin \phi_{crit} = \frac{1}{1.50} = 0.67, \qquad \phi_{crit} = 42°.$$

The fact that this angle is slightly less than 45° makes it possible to use a prism with angles of 45°–45°–90° as a totally reflecting surface. Totally reflecting prisms have some advantages over metallic surfaces, such as ordinary coated-glass mirrors, as reflectors. The light is *totally* reflected, while no metallic surface reflects 100% of the light incident on it. Also, the reflecting properties are permanent and not affected by tarnishing.

A 45°–45°–90° prism, used as in Fig. 36–5a, is called a *Porro* prism. Light enters and leaves at right angles to the hypotenuse and is totally reflected at each of the shorter faces. The total change of direction of the rays is 180°. Binoculars often use combinations of two Porro prisms, as in Fig. 36–5b.

If a beam of light enters at one end of a transparent rod, as in Fig. 36–6, the light is totally reflected internally and is "trapped" within the rod even if the rod is curved, provided that the curvature is not too great. Such a rod is sometimes called a *light pipe*. A bundle of fine glass fibers behaves in the same way and has the advantage of being flexible. A bundle may consist of thousands of individual fibers, each of the order of 0.002 mm to 0.01 mm in diameter. If the fibers are assembled in the bundle so that the relative positions of the ends are the same (or mirror images) at both ends, the bundle can transmit an image, as shown in Fig. 36–7.

Fiber-optic devices have found a wide range of medical applications in instruments called *endoscopes*, which can be inserted directly into the bronchial tubes, the bladder, the colon, and other parts of the body for direct visual examination. A bundle of fibers can be enclosed in a hypodermic needle for study of tissues and blood vessels far beneath the skin.

Fiber optics are now also finding applications in communication systems, in which they are used to transmit a modulated laser beam. Be-

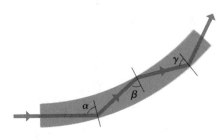

36–6
A light ray "trapped" by internal reflections.

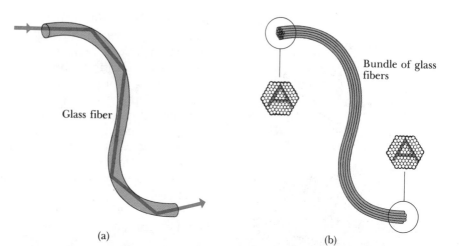

Glass fiber

Bundle of glass
fibers

(a)

(b)

(c)

36–7

(a) Total internal reflection in a single fiber. (b) Image transmission by a bundle
of fibers. (c) A fiber-optic cable used to transmit a modulated laser beam for
communication purposes compared to a larger copper cable that has equal
information-transmitting capacity. (Photo courtesy of Corning Incorporated.)

cause the frequency of the modulated beam is very much higher than
those used in wire or radio communication, an enormous amount of
information can be transmitted through one fiber-optic cable. For example, the Carnegie-Mellon University computer system, which includes
several thousand networked personal computers, is linked partly by
fiber-optic cables of the type shown in Fig. 36–7c. Some telephone systems are connected by fiber optics.

36–4
Dispersion

Most light beams are superpositions of waves with wavelengths extending throughout the visible spectrum. The speed of light *in vacuum* is the same for all wavelengths, but the speed of light in a material substance is different for different wavelengths. Therefore the index of refraction of a material depends on wavelength. Any wave medium in which the speed of a wave varies with wavelength is said to show **dispersion.** Figure 36–8 shows the variation of index of refraction with wavelength for a few common optical materials. The value of *n* usually *decreases* with increasing wavelength and thus *increases* with increasing frequency. Light of longer wavelength usually has greater speed in a material than light of shorter wavelength.

Figure 36–9 shows a ray of white light (a superposition of all visible wavelengths) incident on a prism. The deviation (change of direction) produced by the prism increases with increasing index of refraction and decreasing wavelength. Violet light is deviated most and red is deviated least, with other colors in intermediate positions. When it comes out of the prism, the light is spread out into a fan-shaped beam, as shown. The light is said to be *dispersed* into a spectrum. The amount of dispersion depends on the *difference* between the refractive indexes for violet light and for red light. From Fig. 36–8 we can see that for a substance such as fluorite, whose refractive index for yellow light is small, the difference between the indexes for red and violet is also small. For silicate flint glass, both the index for yellow light and the difference between extreme indexes are larger.

The brilliance of diamond is due in part to its large dispersion and in part to its unusually large refractive index. In recent years, synthetic crystals of titanium dioxide and of strontium titanate, with about eight times the dispersion of diamond, have been produced.

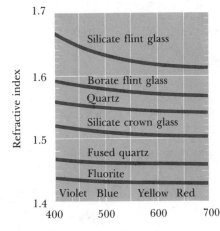

36–8
Variation of index of refraction with wavelength.

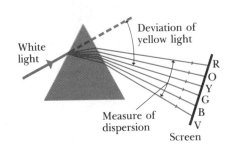

36–9
Dispersion by a prism. The band of colors on the screen is called a spectrum.

36–5
Polarization

Polarization occurs with all transverse waves. This chapter is about light, but to introduce basic polarization concepts, let's go back to Chapter 21, in which we studied transverse waves on a string. For a string whose equilibrium position is along the x-axis the displacements may be along the y-direction, as in Fig. 36–10a. In this case the string always lies in the xy-plane. But the displacements might instead be along the z-axis, as in Fig. 36–10b; then the string lies in the xz-plane.

When a wave has only y-displacements, we say that it is **linearly polarized** in the y-direction; a wave with only z-displacements is linearly polarized in the z-direction. We can build a mechanical *filter* that permits only waves with a certain polarization direction to pass. In Fig. 36–10c the string can slide vertically in the slot without friction, but no horizon-

36–10
(a) Transverse wave on a string, polarized in the y-direction. (b) Wave polarized in the z-direction. (c) Barrier with a frictionless vertical slot passes components polarized in the y-direction but blocks those polarized in the z-direction, acting as a polarizing filter.

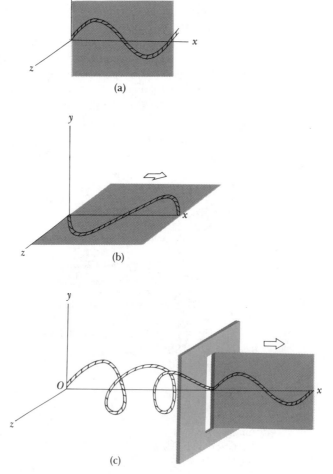

(a)

(b)

(c)

tal motion is possible. This filter passes waves polarized in the y-direction but blocks those polarized in the z-direction.

This same language can be applied to electromagnetic waves, which also have polarization. As we learned in Chapter 35, an electromagnetic wave is a *transverse* wave; the fluctuating electric and magnetic fields are perpendicular to each other and to the direction of propagation. We always define the direction of polarization of an electromagnetic wave to be the direction of the *electric*-field vector, not the magnetic field, because most common electromagnetic-wave detectors depend on the electric-field forces on electrons in materials, not the magnetic forces.

Polarizing filters can be made for electromagnetic waves; the details of construction depend on the wavelength. For microwaves with a wavelength of a few centimeters a grid of closely spaced, parallel conducting wires insulated from each other will pass waves whose E-fields are perpendicular to the wires but not those with E-fields parallel to the wires. For light the most common polarizing filter is a material known by the trade name Polaroid, which is widely used for sunglasses and polarizing filters for camera lenses. This material, developed originally by Edwin H. Land, incorporates substances that have **dichroism,** a selective absorption in which one of the polarized components is absorbed much more strongly than the other. A Polaroid filter transmits 80% or more of the intensity of a wave polarized parallel to a certain axis in the material (called the **polarizing axis**) but only 1% or less for waves polarized perpendicular to this axis. The action of such a polarizing filter is shown schematically in Fig. 36–11.

Waves emitted by a radio transmitter are usually linearly polarized; a vertical rod antenna of the type widely used for CB radios emits waves that, in a horizontal plane around the antenna, are polarized in the vertical direction (parallel to the antenna). Light from ordinary sources is *not* polarized, for a slightly subtle reason. The "antennas" that radiate light waves are the molecules that make up the sources. The waves emitted by

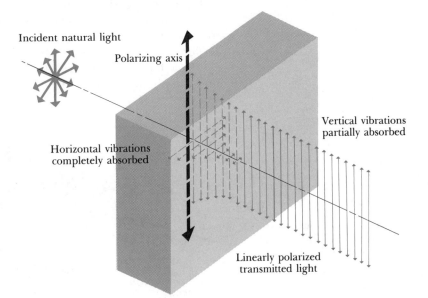

36–11
Linearly polarized light transmitted by a polarizing filter.

Incident natural light

Polarizing axis

Vertical vibrations partially absorbed

Horizontal vibrations completely absorbed

Linearly polarized transmitted light

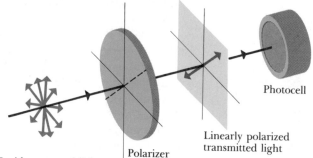

36-12
The intensity of the transmitted linearly polarized light, measured by the photocell, is the same for all orientations of the polarizing filter.

Photocell

Linearly polarized transmitted light

Polarizer

Incident natural light

any one molecule may be linearly polarized, like those from a radio antenna. But any actual light source contains a tremendous number of molecules with random orientations, so the light emitted is a random mixture of waves that are linearly polarized in all possible transverse directions.

An ideal polarizing filter or **polarizer** passes 100% of the incident light polarized in the direction of the filter's **polarizing axis** but blocks completely all light polarized perpendicular to this axis. Such a device is an unattainable idealization, but the concept is useful in clarifying the basic ideas. In Fig. 36-12, unpolarized light (a random mixture of all polarization states) is incident on a polarizer in the form of a flat plate. The polarizing axis is represented by the broken line. The polarizer transmits the components of the incident waves in which the *E*-vector is parallel to the polarizing axis. The light emerging from the polarizer is linearly polarized parallel to the polarizing axis.

When we measure the intensity (power per unit area) of the light transmitted through the polarizer, using the photocell in Fig. 36-12, we find that it is exactly half that of the incident light, no matter how the polarizing axis is oriented. Here's why: We can resolve the incident light into components polarized parallel to the polarizer axis and components polarized perpendicular to it. Because the incident light is a random mixture of all states of polarization, these two components are, on the average, equal. The ideal polarizer transmits only the component parallel to the polarizer axis, so half the incident intensity is transmitted.

Now suppose we insert a second polarizer between the first polarizer and the photocell, as in Fig. 36-13. The polarizing axis of the second

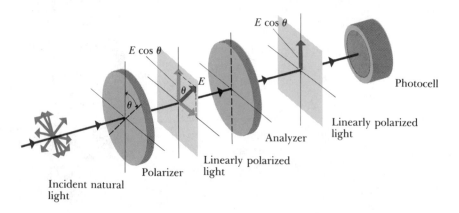

$E \cos \theta$

$E \cos \theta$

θ

E

θ

Photocell

36-13
The analyzer transmits only the component parallel to its transmission direction or polarizing axis.

Analyzer

Linearly polarized light

Linearly polarized light

Polarizer

Incident natural light

polarizer, or **analyzer,** is vertical, and the axis of the first polarizer makes an angle θ with the vertical. That is, θ is the angle between the polarizing axes of the two polarizers. We can resolve the linearly polarized light transmitted by the first polarizer into two components as shown, one parallel and the other perpendicular to the axis of the analyzer. Only the parallel component, with amplitude $E \cos \theta$, is transmitted by the analyzer. The transmitted intensity is greatest when $\theta = 0$; it is zero when $\theta = 90°$, that is, when the polarizer and analyzer are *crossed*.

To find the transmitted intensity at intermediate angles, we use Eq. (35–28). This equation shows that the intensity is proportional to the *square* of the amplitude; the ratio of transmitted to incident *amplitude* is $\cos \theta$, so the ratio of transmitted to incident *intensity* is $\cos^2 \theta$, and we have

$$I = I_{\max} \cos^2 \theta, \tag{36–9}$$

where $I_{\max}$ is the maximum intensity of light transmitted (at $\theta = 0$) and I is the amount transmitted at angle θ. This relation, discovered experimentally by Etienne Louis Malus in 1809, is called **Malus's law.**

■ **PROBLEM-SOLVING STRATEGY:** *Linear Polarization*

1. Remember that in light or any other electromagnetic wave the E field is perpendicular to the propagation direction and is the direction of polarization (or opposite to that direction). The polarization direction can be thought of as a two-headed arrow. When working with polarizing filters, you are really dealing with components of E parallel and perpendicular to the polarizing axis. Everything you know about components of vectors is applicable here.

2. The intensity (average power per unit area) of a wave is proportional to the *square* of its amplitude, as shown by Eq. (35–28). If you find that two waves differ in amplitude by a certain factor, their intensities differ by the square of that factor.

3. Later in this section we will encounter problems in which two linearly polarized waves with perpendicular directions of polarization are superposed. Their relative phase is crucial; if they are in phase, the resultant is again linearly polarized, but if they are not, the resultant is circularly or elliptically polarized. In such cases, pay close attention to phase relationships.

Example 36–2   In Fig. 36–13 the incident unpolarized light has intensity I_0. Find the intensity transmitted by the first polarizer and by the second if the angle θ is $30°$.

Solution   As explained above, the intensity after the first filter is $I_0/2$. According to Eq. (36–9), the second filter reduces the intensity by a factor of $\cos^2 30° = 3/4$. Thus the intensity transmitted by the second polarizer is $(I_0/2)(3/4) = 3I_0/8$.   ■

Unpolarized light can be partially polarized by *reflection*. When unpolarized light strikes a reflecting surface between two optical materials, preferential reflection occurs for those waves in which the electric-field

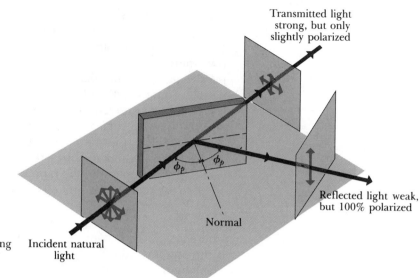

Transmitted light
strong, but only
slightly polarized

Reflected light weak,
but 100% polarized

Normal

Incident natural
light

36–14
When light is incident at the polarizing
angle, the reflected light is linearly
polarized.

vector is parallel to the reflecting surface (perpendicular to the plane of
incidence). At one particular angle of incidence, called the **polarizing
angle** ϕ_p, *no* light is reflected except that in which the E vector is perpendicular to the plane of incidence. This case is shown in Fig. 36–14.

When light is incident at the polarizing angle, *none* of the component
parallel to the plane of incidence is reflected; this component is 100%
transmitted in the *refracted* beam. So the *reflected* light is *completely* polarized. The *refracted* light is a mixture of the parallel component, all of
which is refracted, and the remainder of the perpendicular component;
it is therefore *partially* polarized.

In 1812, Sir David Brewster noticed that when the angle of incidence
is equal to the polarizing angle ϕ_p, the reflected ray and the refracted ray
are perpendicular to each other, as shown in Fig. 36–15. In this case the
angle of refraction ϕ_b becomes the complement of ϕ_p, so $\sin \phi_b = \cos \phi_p$.
From the law of refraction,

$$n_a \sin \phi_p = n_b \sin \phi_b, \qquad (36\text{–}10)$$

so we find

$$n_a \sin \phi_p = n_b \cos \phi_p,$$

and

$$\tan \phi_p = \frac{n_b}{n_a}, \qquad (36\text{–}11)$$

a relation known as **Brewster's law.**

Polaroid sheet is widely used in sunglasses. When sunlight is reflected from a horizontal surface, the plane of incidence is vertical, and
the reflected light contains a preponderance of light polarized in the
horizontal direction. When the reflection occurs at a smooth asphalt
road surface or the surface of a lake, it causes unwanted "glare," and
vision is improved by eliminating it. The polarizing axis of the sunglasses

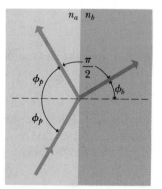

36–15
At the polarizing angle the reflected
and transmitted rays are perpendicular
to each other.

is vertical, so none of the horizontally polarized light is transmitted to the eyes. The glasses also reduce the overall intensity in the transmitted light to somewhat less than 50% of the incident intensity. The sensitivity of the eye is independent of the state of polarization of the light.

Light and other electromagnetic radiation can also have *circular* or *elliptical* polarization. To introduce these concepts, let's return once more to mechanical waves on a stretched string. In Fig. 36–10, suppose the two linearly polarized waves in parts (a) and (b) are in phase and have equal amplitude. When they are *superposed*, each point in the string has simultaneous y- and z-displacements of equal magnitude, and a little thought shows that the resultant wave lies in a plane oriented at 45° to the y- and z-axes (i.e., in a plane making a 45° angle with the xy- and xz-planes). The amplitude of the resultant wave is larger by a factor of $\sqrt{2}$ than that of either component wave, and the resultant wave is linearly polarized.

But now suppose one of the equal-amplitude component waves differs in phase by a quarter-cycle from the other. Then the resultant motion of each point corresponds to a superposition of two simple harmonic motions at right angles, with a quarter-cycle phase difference. The motion is then no longer confined to a single plane; the y-displacement at a point is greatest at times when the z-displacement is zero and vice versa, and it can be shown that each point on the rope moves in a *circle* in a plane parallel to the yz-plane. Successive points on the rope have successive phase differences, and the overall motion of the string has the appearance of a rotating helix. This particular superposition of two linearly polarized waves is called **circular polarization.** By convention the wave is said to be *right circularly polarized* when the sense of motion of a particle of the string, to an observer looking *backward* along the direction of propagation, is *clockwise* and *left circularly polarized* when the sense of motion is *counterclockwise*.

If the phase difference between the two component waves is something other than a quarter-cycle, or if the two component waves have different amplitudes, then each point on the string traces out not a circle but an *ellipse*. The resulting wave is said to be **elliptically polarized.**

For electromagnetic waves with radio frequencies, circular or elliptical polarization can be produced by using two antennas at right angles, fed from the same transmitter but with a phase-shifting network that introduces the appropriate phase difference. For light the phase shift can be introduced by use of a **birefringent** material, a material that has different indexes of refraction for different directions of polarization. A common example is calcite; when a calcite crystal is oriented appropriately in a beam of unpolarized light, its refractive index (for $\lambda = 589$ nm) is 1.658 for one direction of polarization and 1.486 for the perpendicular direction. When two waves with perpendicular directions of polarization enter such a material, they travel with different speeds. If they are in phase when they enter the material, then in general they are no longer in phase when they emerge. If the crystal is just thick enough to introduce a quarter-cycle phase difference, then the crystal converts linearly polarized light to circularly polarized light. Such a crystal is called a **quarter-wave plate.** This plate also converts circularly polarized light to linearly polarized light. Can you prove this?

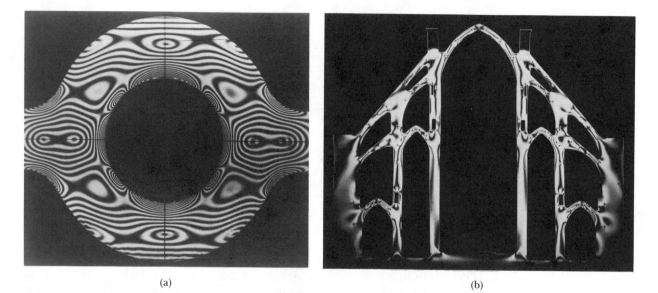

(a)   (b)

36–16

(a) Photoelastic stress analysis of a plastic model of a machine part. (Courtesy of
Dr. W. M. Murray, Massachusetts Institute of Technology.) (b) Stress analysis of a
model of a cross section of a Gothic cathedral. The masonry construction used for
this kind of building had great strength in compression but very little in tension.
Inadequate buttressing and high winds sometimes caused tensile stresses in
normally compressed structural elements, leading to some spectacular collapses.
(Sepp Seitz/Woodfin Camp.)

Some optical materials that are not normally doubly refracting become so when they are subjected to mechanical stress. This is the basis of
the science of **photoelasticity**. Stresses in girders, boiler plates, gear
teeth, and cathedral pillars can be analyzed by constructing a transparent
model of the object, usually of a plastic material, subjecting it to stress,
and examining it between a polarizer and an analyzer in the crossed
position. Very complicated stress distributions can be studied by these
optical methods. Figure 36–16 shows two photographs of photoelastic
models under stress.

Liquids are not normally doubly refracting, but some become so
under the action of a strong electric field perpendicular to the transmission direction. This phenomenon, called the *Kerr effect*, can be used to
make an electrically controlled "light valve." A cell with transparent walls
contains the liquid, often nitrobenzene, between a pair of parallel plates.
The cell is inserted between crossed polarizing filters. Light is transmitted when an electric field is set up between the plates and is cut off when
the field is removed.

Some crystals and liquids have the effect of *rotating* the direction of
polarization of a beam of linearly polarized light. Substances that have
this effect are said to be *optically active*. Those that rotate the direction of
polarization to the right, looking along the advancing beam, are called
dextrorotatory or right-handed; those that rotate it to the left are *levorota-
tory* or left-handed. In some cases, optical activity results from an asymmetry of the molecules of a substance. The molecules of the sugars
dextrose and levulose are mirror images, and the optical activities of

these sugars in solution are opposite. Crystalline quartz is also optically active; some natural crystals are right-handed, and others are left-handed. When the quartz is melted and allowed to resolidify into a glassy, noncrystalline state called fused quartz, the optical activity disappears; therefore it is associated with the crystal structure of the material.

*36–6
Scattering of Light

The sky is blue. Sunsets are red. Skylight is partially polarized, as you can verify by looking at the sky directly overhead through a polarizing filter. It turns out that one phenomenon is responsible for all three of these effects.

In Fig. 36–17, sunlight (unpolarized) comes from the left along the x-axis and passes over an observer looking vertically upward along the y-axis. Molecules of the earth's atmosphere are located at point O. The electric field in the beam of sunlight sets the electric charges in the molecules into vibration. Light is a transverse wave; the direction of the electric field in any component of the sunlight lies in the yz-plane, and the motion of the charges takes place in this plane. There is no field, and hence no vibration, in the direction of the x-axis.

An incident light wave with its electric field at an angle θ with the z-axis sets the electric charges in the molecules vibrating in the same direction, as indicated by the heavy line through point O. We can resolve this vibration into two components, one along the y-axis and the other along the z-axis. Each component in the incident light produces the equivalent of two molecular "antennas," oscillating with the same frequency as the incident light and lying along the y- and z-axes.

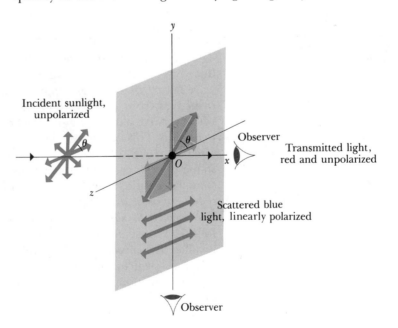

36–17
Scattered light is linearly polarized.

We mentioned in Section 35–8 that an antenna does not radiate in the direction of its own length. The antenna along the y-axis does not send any light to the observer directly below it, although it does emit light in other directions. Therefore the only light reaching this observer comes from the component of vibration along the z-axis; this light is linearly polarized, with its electric field parallel to the antenna. The vectors on the y-axis below point O show the direction of polarization of the light reaching the observer.

The process we have just described is called **scattering.** The energy of the scattered light is removed from the original beam, reducing its intensity. Detailed analysis of the scattering processes shows that the intensity of the scattered light increases with increasing frequency. That is, the scattered light contains more blue light than red, and it appears blue. That's why the sky is blue!

Because skylight is partially polarized, polarizers are useful in photography. The sky can be darkened in a photograph by appropriate orientation of the polarizer axis. The effect of atmospheric haze can be reduced in exactly the same way, and unwanted reflections can be controlled just as with polarizing sunglasses (discussed in Section 36–5).

Toward evening, when sunlight has to travel a long distance through the earth's atmosphere, a substantial fraction of the blue light is removed by scattering. White light minus blue light appears yellow or red. Thus when sunlight, with the blue component removed, is incident on a cloud, the light reflected from the cloud to the observer has the yellow or red hue we see so often at sunset. If the earth had no atmosphere, we would receive *no* skylight at the earth's surface, and the sky would appear as black in the daytime as it does at night. To an astronaut in a spaceship or on the moon the sky appears black, not blue.

*36–7
Huygens' Principle

The principles of reflection and refraction of light rays that we introduced in Section 36–2 were discovered experimentally long before the wave nature of light was firmly established. However, we can *derive* these principles from wave considerations and show that they are consistent with the wave nature of light. We begin with a principle called **Huygens' principle.** This principle, stated originally by Christian Huygens (1629–1695) in 1678, is a geometrical method for finding, from the known shape of a wave front at some instant, the shape of the wave front at some later time. Huygens assumed that *every point of a wave front may be considered the source of secondary wavelets that spread out in all directions with a speed equal to the speed of propagation of the wave.* The new wave front is then found by constructing a surface *tangent* to the secondary wavelets or, as it is called, the *envelope* of the wavelets. All the results that we obtain from Huygens' principle can also be obtained from Maxwell's equations. Thus it is not an independent principle, but it is often very convenient for calculations with wave phenomena.

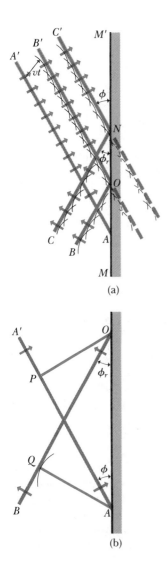

36–18
Geometric construction illustrating Huygens' principle.

36–19
(a) Successive positions of a plane wave AA' as it is reflected from a plane surface. (b) A portion of part (a).

Huygens' principle is shown in Fig. 36–18. The original wave front AA' is traveling as indicated by the small arrows. We want to find the shape of the wave front after a time interval t. Let v be the speed of propagation of the wave; then in time t it travels a distance vt. We construct several circles (traces of spherical wavelets) with radius $r = vt$, centered along AA'. The trace of the envelope of these wavelets, which is the new wave front, is the curve BB'. The speed v is assumed to be the same at all points and in all directions.

To derive the law of reflection from Huygens' principle, we consider a plane wave approaching a plane reflecting surface. In Fig. 36–19a the lines AA', BB', and CC' represent successive positions of a wave front approaching the surface MM'. Point A on the wave front AA' has just arrived at the reflecting surface. We can use Huygens' principle to find the position of the wave front after a time interval t. With points on AA' as centers we draw several secondary wavelets with radius vt, where v is the speed of propagation of the wave. The wavelets that originate near the upper end of AA' spread out unhindered, and their envelope gives the portion OB' of the new wave surface. The wavelets originating near the lower end of AA', however, strike the reflecting surface. If the surface had not been there, they would have reached the positions shown by the dashed circular arcs. The effect of the reflecting surface is to *reverse the direction* of travel of those wavelets that strike it, so that part of a wavelet that would have penetrated the surface actually lies to the left of it, as shown by the lower solid arcs. The envelope of these reflected wavelets is then the portion OB of the wave front. The trace of the entire wave front at this instant is the bent line BOB'. A similar construction gives the line CNC' for the wave front after another interval t.

The angle ϕ between the incident *wave front* and the *surface* is the same as that between the incident *ray* and the *normal* to the surface and is therefore the angle of incidence. Similarly, ϕ_r is the angle of reflection. To find the relation between these angles, we consider Fig. 36–19b. From O we draw $OP = vt$, perpendicular to AA'. Now OB, by construction, is tangent to a circle of radius vt with center at A. If we draw AQ from A to the point of tangency, the triangles APO and OQA are equal because they are right triangles with the side AO in common and with $AQ = OP$. The angle ϕ therefore equals the angle ϕ_r, and we have the law of reflection.

We can derive the law of *refraction* by a similar procedure. In Fig. 36–20a we consider a wave front, represented by line AA', for which point A has just arrived at the boundary surface SS' between two transparent materials a and b, with indexes of refraction n_a and n_b and wave speeds v_a and v_b. (The *reflected* waves are not shown in the figure; they proceed exactly as in Fig. 36–19.) We can apply Huygens' principle to find the position of the refracted wave fronts after a time t.

With points on AA' as centers we draw several secondary wavelets. Those originating near the upper end of AA' travel with speed v_a and, after a time interval t, are spherical surfaces of radius $v_a t$. The wavelet originating at point A, however, is traveling in the second material b with speed v_b and at time t is a spherical surface of radius $v_b t$. The envelope of the wavelets from the original wave front is the plane whose trace is the

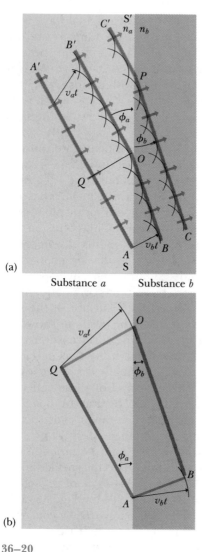

(a)

Substance a Substance b

(b)

36–20
(a) Successive positions of a plane wave front AA' as it is refracted by a plane surface. (b) A portion of part (a). The case $v_b < v_a$ is shown.

line BOB'. A similar construction leads to the trace CPC' after a second interval t.

The angles ϕ_a and ϕ_b between the surface and the incident and refracted wave fronts are the angle of incidence and the angle of refraction, respectively. To find the relation between these angles, refer to Fig. 36–20b. Draw $OQ = v_a t$, perpendicular to AQ, and draw $AB = v_b t$, perpendicular to BO. From the right triangle AOQ,

$$\sin \phi_a = \frac{v_a t}{AO},$$

and from the right triangle AOB,

$$\sin \phi_b = \frac{v_b t}{AO}.$$

Combining these, we find

$$\frac{\sin \phi_a}{\sin \phi_b} = \frac{v_a}{v_b}. \tag{36–12}$$

The quantity v_a/v_b is constant, so Eq. (36–12) is Snell's law. We have derived Snell's law from a wave theory! This result emphasizes that the general wave theory gives the same results as the more specialized ray picture in cases in which the ray picture is applicable.

The most general form of Snell's law is given by Eq. (36–4), namely,

$$\frac{\sin \phi_a}{\sin \phi_b} = \frac{n_b}{n_a}.$$

Comparing this with Eq. (36–12), we see that

$$\frac{v_a}{v_b} = \frac{n_b}{n_a}, \quad \text{and} \quad n_a v_a = n_b v_b.$$

When either material is vacuum, $n = 1$ and $v = c$. In that case we have

$$n_a = \frac{c}{v_a} \quad \text{and} \quad n_b = \frac{c}{v_b}. \tag{36–13}$$

This shows that *the index of refraction of any material is the ratio of the speed of light in a vacuum to the speed in the material.* We stated Eq. (36–13) without proof at the end of Section 36–2, and now we have proved it. The speed of light in a material is always *less* than that in vacuum, so n is always greater than unity.

In Fig. 36–20, if we choose t to be the period τ of the wave, the spacing is $v\tau$, which is equal to the wavelength λ. The figure shows that when v_b is less than v_a, the wavelength in the second material is smaller than in the first. When a light wave proceeds from one material to another, where the speed is different, the wavelength changes, *but not the frequency*, as we discussed in Section 36–2. We have $v_a = \lambda_a f$ and $v_b = \lambda_b f$, so

$$\frac{\lambda_a}{v_a} = \frac{\lambda_b}{v_b}, \quad \lambda_a \frac{c}{v_a} = \lambda_b \frac{c}{v_b}.$$

Finally, using Eqs. (36–13), we obtain

$$\lambda_a n_a = \lambda_b n_b.$$

If either material is vacuum, the index is 1, and the wavelength in vacuum is λ_0. Therefore

$$\lambda_a = \frac{\lambda_0}{n_a}, \qquad \lambda_b = \frac{\lambda_0}{n_b}. \tag{36–14}$$

This shows that *the wavelength in any material is the wavelength in vacuum divided by the index of refraction of the medium.* We stated this without proof in Section 36–2, and now we have proved it.

■ *Questions*

36–1 During a thunderstorm, one always sees the flash of lightning before hearing the accompanying thunder. Discuss this in terms of the various wave speeds. Can this phenomenon be used to determine how far away the storm is?

36–2 When hot air rises around a radiator or from a heating duct, objects behind it appear to shimmer or waver. What is happening?

36–3 Light requires about 8 min to travel from the sun to the earth. Is it delayed appreciably by the earth's atmosphere?

36–4 Sometimes when looking at a window, one sees two reflected images, slightly displaced from each other. What causes this?

36–5 An object submerged in water appears to be closer to the surface than it actually is. Why? Swimming pools are always deeper than they look; is this the same phenomenon?

36–6 A ray of light in air strikes a glass surface. Is there a range of angles for which total reflection occurs?

36–7 As shown in Table 36–1, diamond has a much larger refractive index than glass. Is there a larger or smaller range of angles for which total internal reflection occurs for diamond than for glass? Does this have anything to do with the fact that a real diamond has more sparkle than a glass imitation?

36–8 Sunlight or starlight passing through the earth's atmosphere is always bent toward the vertical. Why? Does this mean that a star is not really where it appears to be?

36–9 The sun or moon usually appears flattened just before it sets. Is this related to refraction in the earth's atmosphere, mentioned in Question 36–8?

36–10 A student claimed that, because of atmospheric refraction (cf. Question 36–8), the sun can be seen after it has set and that the day is therefore longer than it would be if the earth had no atmosphere. First, what does the student mean by saying the sun can be seen after it has set? Second, comment on the validity of the conclusion.

36–11 It has been proposed that automobile windshields and headlights should have polarizing filters to reduce the glare of oncoming lights during night driving. Would this work? How should the polarizing axes be arranged? What advantages would this scheme have? What disadvantages?

36–12 A salesperson at a bargain counter claims that a certain pair of sunglasses has Polaroid filters; you suspect that they are just tinted plastic. How could you find out for sure?

36–13 When unpolarized light is incident on two crossed polarizers, no light is transmitted. A student asserted that if a third polarizer is inserted between the other two, some transmission may occur. Does this make sense? How can adding a third filter *increase* transmission?

36–14 How could you determine the direction of the polarizing axis of a single polarizer?

36–15 In three-dimensional movies, two images are projected on the screen, and the viewers wear special glasses to sort them out. How does this work?

36–16 In Fig. 36–17, since the light scattered out of the incident beam is polarized, why is the transmitted beam not also partially polarized?

36–17 Light from blue sky is strongly polarized because of the nature of the scattering process described in Section 36–6. But light scattered from white clouds is usually *not* polarized. Why not?

36–18 When a sheet of plastic food wrap is placed

between two crossed polarizers, no light is transmitted. When the sheet is stretched in one direction, some light passes through. What is happening?

36–19 Television transmission usually uses plane-polarized waves. It has been proposed to use circularly polarized waves to improve reception. Why?

36–20 Can sound waves be reflected? Refracted? Give examples. Does Huygens' principle apply to sound waves?

36–21 Why should the wavelength of light change, but not its frequency, in passing from one material to another?

36–22 When light is incident on an interface between two materials, the angle of the refracted ray depends on the wavelength, but the angle of the reflected ray does not. Why should this be?

Exercises

Section 36–2   Reflection and Refraction

36–1 The speed of light with a wavelength of 656 nm in heavy flint glass is $1.82 \times 10^8 \ \text{m·s}^{-1}$. What is the index of refraction of this glass at this wavelength?

36–2 Light with a frequency of 5.00×10^{14} Hz travels in a block of plastic that has an index of refraction of 2.00. What is the wavelength of the light while it is in the plastic? In vacuum?

36–3 A parallel-sided plate of glass having a refractive index of 1.60 is in contact with the surface of water in a tank. A ray coming from above makes an angle of incidence of 32.0° with the top surface of the glass.

a) What angle does the ray make with the normal in the water?

b) What is the dependence of this angle on the refractive index of the glass?

36–4 A ray of light is incident on a plane surface separating two transparent substances with refractive indices 1.60 and 1.40. The angle of incidence is 40.0°, and the ray originates in the medium of higher index. Compute the angle of refraction.

36–5 The density of the earth's atmosphere increases as the surface of the earth is approached. This increase in density is accompanied by a corresponding increase in refractive index.

a) Draw a diagram showing how the rays of light from a star or planet bend as they pass through the atmosphere. Indicate the apparent position of the light source.

b) Explain how one can see the sun after it has set.

c) Explain why the setting sun appears flattened.

36–6 A parallel beam of light in air makes an angle of 30.0° with the surface of a glass plate having a refractive index of 1.60.

a) What is the angle between the reflected part of the beam and the surface of the glass?

b) What is the angle between the refracted beam and the surface of the glass?

36–7 A beam of light has a wavelength of 500 nm in vacuum.

a) What is the speed of light in a piece of glass whose index of refraction at this wavelength is 1.60?

b) What is the wavelength in the glass?

36–8 Light of a certain frequency has a wavelength in water of 524 nm. What is the wavelength of this light in carbon disulfide?

36–9 A parallel beam of light is incident on a prism, as shown in Fig. 36–21. Part of the light is reflected from one face and part from another. Show that the angle θ between the two reflected beams is twice the angle A between the two reflecting surfaces.

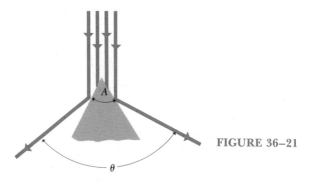

FIGURE 36–21

36–10 Prove that a ray of light reflected from a plane mirror rotates through an angle of 2θ when the mirror rotates through an angle θ about an axis perpendicular to the plane of incidence.

Section 36–3   Total Internal Reflection

36–11 A ray of light in glass with an index of refraction of 1.60 is incident on an interface with air. What is the *largest* angle the ray can make with the normal and not be totally reflected back into the glass?

36–12 The critical angle for total internal reflection at a liquid–air interface is 37.0°

a) If a ray of light traveling in the liquid has an angle of incidence at the interface of 28.0°, what angle does the refracted ray in the air make with the normal?

b) If a ray of light traveling in air has an angle of incidence at the interface of 28.0°, what angle does the refracted ray in the liquid make with the normal?

36–13 The speed of a sound wave is 344 m·s^{-1} in air and 1320 m·s^{-1} in water.

a) Which medium has the higher "index of refraction" for sound?

b) What is the critical angle for a sound wave incident on the surface between air and water?

36–14 A point source of light is 40.0 cm below the surface of a body of water. Find the diameter of the largest circle at the surface through which light can emerge from the water.

Section 36–5   Polarization

36–15 Unpolarized light with intensity I_0 is incident on a polarizing filter, and the emerging light strikes a second polarizing filter with its axis at 55.0° to that of the first. Determine

a) the intensity of the beam after it has passed through the second polarizer;

b) its state of polarization.

36–16 A polarizer and an analyzer are oriented so that the maximum amount of light is transmitted. To what fraction of its maximum value is the intensity of the transmitted light reduced when the analyzer is rotated through

a) 30.0°?   b) 45.0°?   c) 60.0°?

36–17 Three polarizing filters are stacked, with the polarizing axes of the second and third at 30.0° and 90.0°, respectively, with that of the first.

a) If unpolarized light of intensity I_0 is incident on the stack, find the intensity and state of polarization of light emerging from each filter.

b) If the second filter is removed, how does the situation change?

36–18 The critical angle for light at an interface be-

tween certain substances is 54.2°. What is the polarizing angle at this same interface?

36–19 The polarizing angle for light in air incident on a glass plate is 57.6°. What is the index of refraction of the glass?

36–20 A parallel beam of unpolarized light is incident in air at an angle of 59.4° (with respect to the normal) on a plane glass surface. The reflected beam is completely linearly polarized.

a) What is the refractive index of the glass?

b) What is the angle of refraction of the transmitted beam?

36–21

a) At what angle above the horizontal is the sun if sunlight reflected from the surface of a calm body of water is completely polarized?

b) What is the plane of the E vector in the reflected light?

Section 36–6   Scattering of Light

36–22 A beam of light, after passing through the Polaroid disk P_1 in Fig. 36–22, traverses a cell containing a scattering medium. The cell is observed at right angles through another Polaroid disk P_2. Originally, the disks are oriented until the brightness of the field as seen by the observer is at maximum.

a) Disk P_2 is now rotated through 90°. Is extinction produced? Explain.

b) Disk P_1 is now rotated through 90°. Is the field bright or dark? Explain.

c) Disk P_2 is then restored to its original position. Is the field bright or dark? Explain.

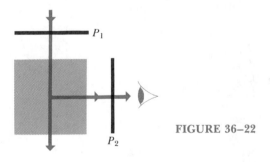

FIGURE 36–22

Problems

36–23 A thick layer of oil is floating on the surface of water in a tank. A beam of light traveling in the oil is incident on the water interface at an angle of 30.0° from the normal. The refracted beam travels in the

water at an angle of 45.0° from the normal. What is the index of refraction of the oil?

36–24 A parallel beam of light in air is incident on the surface of a glass plate having a refractive index of

1.60. What is the angle of incidence ϕ with this plate for which the angle of refraction is $\phi/2$, where both angles are measured relative to the normal?

36–25 High frequency ($f = 1$ to 5 MHz) sound waves, called ultrasound, are now being used by physicians to image internal organs. The speed of these ultrasound waves is 1480 m·s^{-1} in muscle and 344 m·s^{-1} in air.

a) At what angle from the normal does an ultrasound beam enter the heart if it leaves the lungs at an angle of $9.54°$ from the normal to the heart wall? (Assume that the speed of sound in the lungs is 344 m·s^{-1}.)

b) What is the critical angle for sound waves in air incident on muscle?

36–26 A glass plate 3.00 mm thick, with an index of refraction of 1.50, is placed between a point source of light with wavelength 500 nm (in vacuum) and a screen. The distance from the source to the screen is 3.00 cm. How many wavelengths are there between the source and the screen?

36–27 Old photographic plates were made of glass with a light-sensitive emulsion on the front surface. This emulsion was somewhat transparent. When a bright point source is focused on the front of the plate, the developed photograph will show a halo around the image of the spot. If the glass plate is 3.00 mm thick and the halos have a radius of 4.80 mm, what is the index of refraction of the glass? (*Hint:* Light from the spot on the front surface is totally reflected at the back surface of the plate and comes back to the front surface.)

36–28 The prism of Fig. 36–23 has a refractive index of 1.52, and the angles A are $30.0°$. Two light rays m and n are parallel as they enter the prism. What is the angle between them after they emerge?

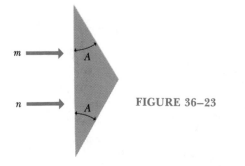

m → A

n → A **FIGURE 36–23**

36–29 A $45°$–$45°$–$90°$ prism is immersed in water. A ray of light is incident normally on one of its shorter faces. What is the minimum index of refraction the prism must have if this ray is to be totally reflected within the glass at the long face of the prism?

36–30 A beaker filled with a liquid whose index of refraction is 2.00 has a mirrored bottom that reflects the light incident on it. A light beam strikes the top surface of the liquid at an angle of $50.0°$ from the normal. At what angle from the normal will the beam exit from the liquid after traveling down through the liquid, reflecting from the mirrored bottom, and returning to the surface?

36–31 A ray of light traveling in a block of glass ($n = 1.60$) is incident on the top surface at an angle of $55.0°$ with respect to the normal. If a layer of oil is placed on the top surface of the glass, the ray is totally reflected. What is the maximum index of refraction of the oil?

36–32 The glass vessel shown in Fig. 36–24a contains a large number of small, irregular pieces of glass and a liquid. The dispersion curves of the glass and of the liquid are shown in Fig. 36–24b. Explain the behavior of a parallel beam of white light as it traverses the vessel. (This is known as a *Christiansen filter*.)

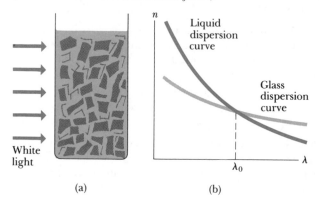

(a)   (b)

FIGURE 36–24

36–33 A block of glass has a polarizing angle of $60.0°$ for red light and $70.0°$ for blue light for light traveling in air and reflecting from the glass.

a) What is the index of refraction for red light and for blue light?

b) Which color is refracted more on entering the glass for the same incident angle?

36–34 Light is incident normally on the short face of a $30°$–$60°$–$90°$ prism, as in Fig. 36–25. A drop of liquid is placed on the hypotenuse of the prism. If the index of refraction of the prism is 1.60, find the maximum

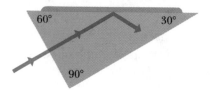

FIGURE 36–25

index the liquid may have if the light is to be totally reflected.

36–35 It is desired to rotate the direction of polarization of linearly polarized light through 90°, using two Polaroid filters. Explain how this can be done, and find the maximum possible final intensity in terms of the incident intensity I_0.

36–36 Three polarizing filters are stacked, the polarizing axes of the second and third being at angles θ and 90.0°, respectively, with that of the first. Unpolarized light with intensity I_0 is incident on the stack.

a) Derive an expression for the intensity of light transmitted through the stack as a function of I_0 and θ.

b) For what value of θ does the maximum transmission occur?

36–37 The refractive index of a certain flint glass is 1.58. For what incident angle is light reflected from the surface of this glass completely polarized if the glass is immersed in

a) air?   b) water?

36–38 A beam of light traveling horizontally is made of an unpolarized component of intensity I_0 and a polarized component of intensity I_p. The plane of polarization of the polarized component is oriented at an angle of θ with respect to the vertical. The following data give the intensity measured through a polarizer with an orientation of ϕ with respect to the vertical.

ϕ (°)	I_{total} (W·m^{-2})
0.0	18.4
10.0	21.4
20.0	23.7
30.0	24.8
40.0	24.8
50.0	23.7
60.0	21.4
70.0	18.4
80.0	15.0
90.0	11.6
100.0	8.6
110.0	6.3
120.0	5.2
130.0	5.2
140.0	6.3
150.0	8.6
160.0	11.6
170.0	15.0
180.0	18.4

a) What is the orientation of the polarized component? (That is, what is the angle θ?)

b) What are the values of I_0 and I_p?

36–39 Many biologically active molecules are also optically active. When plane polarized light traverses a solution of these compounds, its plane of polarization is rotated. Some compounds rotate the polarization clockwise, while others rotate the polarization counterclockwise. The amount of rotation depends on the amount of material in the light path. The following data give the amount of rotation through two amino acids over a path length of 100 cm. From this data, find the relationship between the concentration C in grams per 100 mL and the rotation in degrees of the polarization for each amino acid.

| Rotation (°) | | Concentration |
l-Leucine	*d*-Glutamic acid	(g/100 mL)
− 0.11	0.124	1.0
− 0.22	0.248	2.0
− 0.55	0.620	5.0
− 1.10	1.24	10.0
− 2.20	2.48	20.0
− 5.50	6.20	50.0
−11.0	12.4	100.0

36–40 A certain birefringent material has indexes of refraction n_1 and n_2 for the two perpendicular components of linearly polarized light passing through it. The corresponding wavelengths are $\lambda_1 = \lambda_0/n_1$ and $\lambda_2 = \lambda_0/n_2$, where λ_0 is the wavelength in vacuum.

a) If the crystal is to function as a quarter-wave plate, the number of wavelengths of each component within the material must differ by $\frac{1}{4}$. Show that the minimum thickness for a quarter-wave plate is

$$d = \frac{\lambda_0}{4(n_1 - n_2)}.$$

b) Find the minimum thickness of a quarter-wave plate made of calcite if the indexes of refraction are 1.658 and 1.486 and the wavelength in vacuum is $\lambda_0 = 422$ nm.

36–41 A quarter-wave plate converts linearly polarized light to circularly polarized light. Prove that a quarter-wave plate also converts circularly polarized light to linearly polarized light.

Challenge Problems

36–42 Light passes symmetrically through a prism with refractive index n and apex angle A, as shown in Fig. 36–26.

a) Show that the angle of deviation δ (the angle between the initial and final directions of the ray) is given by

$$\sin \frac{A + \delta}{2} = n \sin \frac{A}{2}.$$

b) Use the result of part (a) to find the angle of deviation for a ray of light passing symmetrically through a prism having three equal angles ($A = 60°$) and $n = 1.50$.

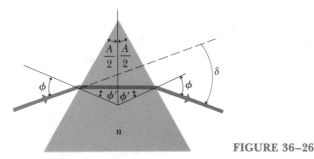

FIGURE 36–26

c) A certain glass has a refractive index of 1.50 for red light (700 nm) and 1.54 for violet light (400 nm). If both colors pass through symmetrically, as described in part (a), and if $A = 60°$, find the difference between the angles of deviation for the two colors.

36–43 Light is incident in air at an angle ϕ_1 (as in Fig. 36–27) on the upper surface of a transparent plate, the surfaces of the plate being plane and parallel to each other.

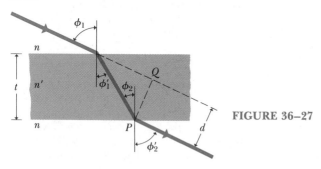

FIGURE 36–27

a) Prove that $\phi_1 = \phi_2'$.

b) Show that this is true for any number of different parallel plates.

c) Prove that the lateral displacement d of the emergent beam is given by the relation

$$d = t \, \frac{\sin (\phi_1 - \phi_1')}{\cos \phi_1'},$$

where t is the thickness of the plate.

d) A ray of light is incident at an angle of 60.0° on one surface of a glass plate 1.40 cm thick with an index of refraction of 1.50. The medium on either side of the plate is air. Find the lateral displacement between the incident and emergent rays.

36–44 Consider two vibrations, one along the x-axis,

$$x = a \sin (\omega t - \alpha),$$

and the other along the y-axis, of equal amplitude and frequency, but differing in phase,

$$y = a \sin (\omega t - \beta).$$

Let us write them as follows:

$$\frac{x}{a} = \sin \omega t \cos \alpha - \cos \omega t \sin \alpha, \qquad (1)$$

$$\frac{y}{a} = \sin \omega t \cos \beta - \cos \omega t \sin \beta. \qquad (2)$$

a) Multiply Eq. (1) by $\sin \beta$ and Eq. (2) by $\sin \alpha$ and then subtract the resulting equations.

b) Multiply Eq. (1) by $\cos \beta$ and Eq. (2) by $\cos \alpha$ and then subtract the resulting equations.

c) Square and add the results of parts (a) and (b).

d) Derive the equation $x^2 + y^2 - 2xy \cos \delta = a^2 \sin^2 \delta$, where $\delta = \alpha - \beta$.

e) Use the above result to justify each of the diagrams in Fig. 36–28. In the figure the angle given is the phase difference between two simple harmonic motions, one horizontal (along the x-axis) and the other vertical (along the y-axis), of the same frequency and amplitude. The figure thus shows the resultant motion from the superposition of the two perpendicular harmonic motions.

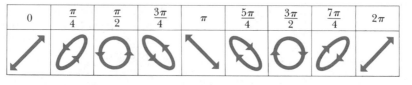

0	$\frac{\pi}{4}$	$\frac{\pi}{2}$	$\frac{3\pi}{4}$	π	$\frac{5\pi}{4}$	$\frac{3\pi}{2}$	$\frac{7\pi}{4}$	2π

FIGURE 36–28

Images Formed by a Single Surface

In the preceding chapter we discussed reflection and refraction of a ray of light at an interface between two materials. We are now ready to analyze the behavior of several rays that diverge from a common point and strike a reflecting or refracting surface. A central idea in this discussion is the concept of *image*. After the rays are reflected or refracted, their directions are the same as though they had passed through some other common point called the *image point*. In this chapter we analyze the formation of images by a single surface. This discussion lays the foundation for analysis of many familiar optical instruments, including camera lenses, magnifiers, the human eye, microscopes, and telescopes. We will study these instruments in Chapter 38.

37–1
Reflection at a Plane Surface

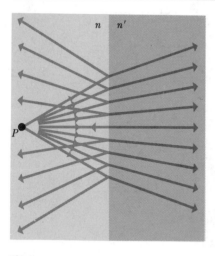

37–1

Reflection and refraction of rays at a plane interface between two transparent materials.

To introduce the concept of image, let's consider the situation shown in Fig. 37–1. Rays diverge from point P, called an **object point,** and are reflected or refracted (or both) at an interface between two transparent materials. The direction of each *reflected* ray is given by the law of reflection, and that of each transmitted or *refracted* ray is given by the law of refraction. Here and in the following discussion we denote the two indexes of refraction as n and n', rather than n_a and n_b as we did in Chapter 36.

We look first at the *reflected* rays. Reflection can occur at an interface between two transparent materials or at a polished surface of an opaque material such as a metal. We will use the term *mirror* to include both of these possibilities.

As we have mentioned, the key concept is that of **image.** After reflection the rays appear to have diverged from some common point, which we call the *image point*. In some cases the rays coming from the surface after reflection really *do* meet at a common point and then diverge again after passing it; we call this a **real image** point. In other cases the rays diverge *as though* they had passed through such a point; then we call the point a **virtual image** point. In Fig. 37–1 the reflected rays appear to diverge from a virtual image point on the right side, and the refracted rays appear to diverge from a virtual image point on the left side. Often the image point exists only in an approximate sense, that is, when we can use certain approximations in the calculations. This chapter and the next are mostly about the formation and properties of images.

Figure 37–2a shows two rays diverging from a point P at a distance s to the left of a plane mirror. The ray PV is incident normally on the mirror (i.e., it is perpendicular to the mirror surface), and it returns along its original path. The ray PB makes an angle u with PV. It strikes the mirror at an angle of incidence $\phi = u$ and is reflected at an angle $r = \phi = u$. When we extend the two reflected rays backward, they intersect at point P'. The angle u' is equal to r and therefore also to u.

Figure 37–2b shows several rays diverging from P. We can repeat the construction of Fig. 37–2a for each of these rays. We see that the directions of all the outgoing rays are the same *as though* they had originated at point P'; therefore P' is the *image* of P. The rays do not, of course, actually pass through point P'. In fact, if the mirror is opaque, there is no light at all on the right side. Thus P' is a *virtual* image, not a real image. Nevertheless, P' is a very real point in the sense that it describes the final directions of all the rays that originally came from P.

The point P' lies on a line perpendicular to the mirror, passing through P. Also, because the angles u, u', and ϕ are all equal, P and P' are at the same distance from the mirror, on opposite sides. Thus for a plane mirror the image of an object point lies on the extension of the normal line from the object point to the mirror, and the object and image points are the same distance from the mirror.

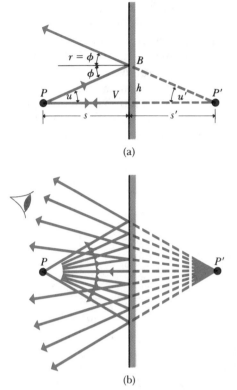

(a)

(b)

37–2
After reflection at a plane surface, all rays originally diverging from the object point P now diverge from the point P', although they do not *originate* at P'. Point P' is called the *virtual image* of point P. The eye sees some of the outgoing rays and perceives them as having come from point P'.

Before proceeding further, we pause to introduce some sign rules. These rules are general enough that they will also cover later situations in which the object and image may be on *either* side of a reflecting or refracting surface. Here are the rules:

1. When the object is on the same side of the reflecting surface as the incoming light, the object distance s is positive; otherwise, it is negative.

2. When the image is on the same side of the reflecting surface as the outgoing light, the image distance s' is positive; otherwise, it is negative.

For a mirror the incoming and outgoing sides are always the same; in Fig. 37–2 they are both the left side. We have stated the rules so that we can apply them also to *refracting* surfaces, in which light comes in one side and goes out the opposite side.

In Fig. 37–2 the object distance s is *positive* because the object point P is on the incoming side (the left side) of the reflecting surface. The image distance s' is *negative* because the image point P' is *not* on the outgoing side (the left side) of the surface. The object and image distances s and s' are related simply by

$$s = -s'. \qquad (37\text{–}1)$$

Next we consider an object with finite size, parallel to the mirror, as represented by the arrow PQ with height y in Fig. 37–3. Two of the rays from Q are shown; *all* the rays from Q diverge from its image point Q' after reflection. The image of the arrow is the line $P'Q'$, with height y'. Other points of the object PQ have image points between P' and Q'. The triangles PQV and $P'Q'V$ are mirror images, so the object PQ and image $P'Q'$ have the same size and orientation, and $y = y'$.

The ratio of image to object size, y'/y, in *any* image-forming situation, is called the **lateral magnification** m; that is,

$$m = \frac{y'}{y}. \qquad (37\text{–}2)$$

For the plane mirror, therefore, the lateral magnification m is unity. When you look at yourself in a plane mirror, you don't look any larger or smaller than you really are.

In general, if an object is represented by an arrow, its image may point in the same direction as the object or in the opposite direction. When the directions are the same, as in Fig. 37–3, we say that the image is **erect;** when they are opposite, the image is **inverted.** The image formed by a plane mirror is always erect. A positive value of lateral magnification m corresponds to an erect image, a negative value to an inverted image. That is, for an erect image y and y' always have the *same* sign, and for an inverted image they always have *opposite* signs.

The three-dimensional virtual image of a three-dimensional object, formed by a plane mirror, is shown in Fig. 37–4. The images $P'Q'$ and $P'S'$ are parallel to their objects, but $P'R'$ is reversed in relation to PR. The image of a three-dimensional object formed by a plane mirror is the

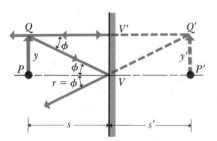

37–3
Construction for determining the height of an image formed by reflection at a plane surface.

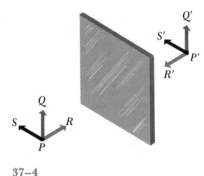

37–4
The image formed by a plane mirror is virtual, erect, and reversed and is the same size as the object.

same *size* as the object in all its dimensions, but the image and object are *not* identical. They are related in the same way as a right hand and a left hand, and indeed we speak of a pair of objects with this relationship as "mirror-image" objects. To verify this object-image relationship, point your two thumbs along PR and $P'R'$, your forefingers along PQ and $P'Q'$, and your middle fingers along PS and $P'S'$. When an object and its image are related in this way, the image is said to be **reversed.** When the transverse dimensions of object and image are in the same direction, the image is erect. Thus a plane mirror always forms an erect but reversed image.

37–2
Reflection at a Spherical Surface

Continuing our analysis of reflecting surfaces, we consider next the formation of an image by a *spherical* mirror. Figure 37–5a shows a spherical mirror with radius of curvature R, with its concave side facing the incident light. The **center of curvature** of the surface (the center of the sphere of which the surface is a part) is at C. Point P is an object point; for the moment we assume that the distance from P to V is greater than R. The ray PV, passing through C, strikes the mirror normally and is reflected back on itself. Point V, at the center of the mirror surface, is called the **vertex** of the mirror, and the line PCV is the **optic axis.**

Ray PB, at an angle u with the axis, strikes the mirror at B, where the angle of incidence is ϕ and the angle of reflection is $r = \phi$. The reflected ray intersects the axis at point P'. We will show that *all* rays from P intersect the axis at the *same* point P', as in Fig. 37–5b, no matter what u is, provided that u is a *small* angle. Point P' is therefore the *image* of object point P. The object distance, measured from the vertex V, is s, and the image distance is s'. The object point P is on the same side as the incident light, so the object distance s is positive. The image point P' is on the same side as the reflected light, so the image distance s' is also positive.

Unlike the reflected rays in Fig. 37–2, the reflected rays in Fig. 37–5b actually do intersect at point P'; then they diverge from P' *as if* they had originated at this point. The image P' is a *real* image point, and the corresponding image distance s' is *positive*.

An exterior angle of a triangle equals the sum of the two opposite interior angles. Using this with triangles PBC and $P'BC$ in Fig. 37–5a, we have

$$\theta = u + \phi, \qquad u' = \theta + \phi.$$

Eliminating ϕ between these equations gives

$$u' + u = 2\theta. \tag{37–3}$$

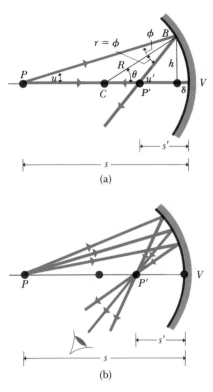

37–5
(a) Construction for finding the position of the image P' of a point object P, formed by a concave spherical mirror. (b) If the angle u is small, *all* rays from P intersect at P'. The eye sees some of the outgoing rays and perceives them as having come from P'.

Now we need a sign rule for the radii of curvature of spherical surfaces:

When the center of curvature C is on the same side as the outgoing (reflected) light, the radius of curvature is positive; otherwise, it is negative.

In Fig. 37–5, R is positive because the center of curvature C is on the same side of the mirror as the reflected light. This is always the case when reflection occurs at the *concave* side of a surface. For a *convex* surface the center of curvature is on the opposite side from the reflected light, and R is negative.

We may now compute the image distance s'. Let h represent the height of point B above the axis, and δ the short distance from V to the foot of this vertical line. We now write expressions for the tangents of u, u', and θ, remembering that s, s', and R are all positive quantities:

$$\tan u = \frac{h}{s - \delta}, \qquad \tan u' = \frac{h}{s' - \delta}, \qquad \tan \theta = \frac{h}{R - \delta}.$$

These trigonometric equations cannot be solved as simply as the corresponding algebraic equations for a plane mirror. However, *if the angle u is small*, the angles u' and θ are also small. The tangent of a small angle is nearly equal to the angle itself (in radians), so we can replace $\tan u'$ by u', and so on, in the equations above. Also if u is small, we can neglect the distance δ compared with s' s, and R. So for small angles we have the approximate relations

$$u = \frac{h}{s}, \qquad u' = \frac{h}{s'}, \qquad \theta = \frac{h}{R}.$$

Substituting these into Eq. (37–3) and dividing out h, we obtain a general relation among s, s', and R:

$$\frac{1}{s} + \frac{1}{s'} = \frac{2}{R}. \tag{37–4}$$

This equation does not contain the angle u. This means that *all* rays from P that make sufficiently small angles with the axis intersect at P' after they are reflected. Such rays, nearly parallel to the axis, are called **paraxial** rays.

Make sure you understand that Eq. (37–4), as well as many similar relations that we will derive later in this chapter and the next, is only *approximately* correct. It results from a calculation containing approximations, and it is valid only for paraxial rays. (The term **paraxial approximation** is often used for the approximations we have just described.) As the angle u increases, the point P' moves somewhat closer to the vertex; a spherical mirror, unlike a plane mirror, does not form a precise point image of a point object. This property of a spherical mirror is called *spherical aberration*.

If $R = \infty$, the mirror becomes *plane*, and Eq. (37–4) reduces to Eq. (37–1), which we derived previously for a plane reflecting surface.

37–6
Construction for determining the position, orientation, and height of an image formed by a concave spherical mirror.

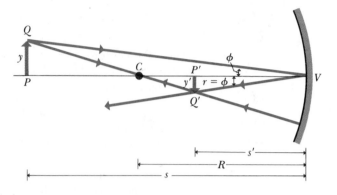

Now suppose we have an object with finite size, represented by the arrow PQ in Fig. 37–6, perpendicular to the axis PV. The image of P formed by paraxial rays is at P'. The object distance for point Q is very nearly equal to that for the point P, so the image of $P'Q'$ is nearly straight and is perpendicular to the axis. Note that object and image have different sizes, y and y', respectively, and that they have opposite orientation. We have defined the *lateral magnification m* as the ratio of image size y' to object size y:

$$m = \frac{y'}{y}.$$

Because triangles PVQ and $P'VQ'$ in Fig. 37–6 are *similar*, we also have the relation $y/s = -y'/s'$. The negative sign is needed because object and image are on opposite sides of the optic axis; if y is positive, y' is negative. Therefore

$$m = \frac{y'}{y} = -\frac{s'}{s}. \qquad (37-5)$$

A negative value of m indicates that the image is *inverted* relative to the object, as Fig. 37–6 shows. In cases that we will consider later, in which m may be either positive or negative, a positive value always corresponds to an erect image, a negative value to an inverted one. For a *plane* mirror, $s = -s'$, so $y' = y$ and the image is erect, as we have already shown.

Although the ratio of image size to object size is called the *magnification*, the image formed by a mirror or lens may be either larger or smaller than the object. If it is smaller, then the magnification is less than unity. The image formed by an astronomical telescope mirror, or by a camera lens, is *much* smaller than the object. For three-dimensional objects the ratio of image-to-object distances measured *along* the optic axis is different from the ratio of *lateral* distances (the lateral magnification). In particular, if m is a small fraction, the three-dimensional image of a three-dimensional object is reduced *longitudinally* much more than it is reduced *transversely*. Figure 37–7 shows this effect. Also, the image formed by a spherical mirror, like that of a plane mirror, is always reversed.

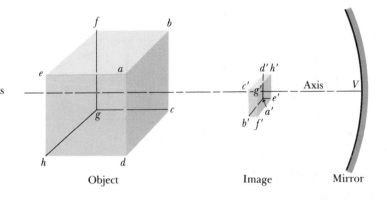

37-7
Schematic diagram of an object and its real, inverted, reduced image formed by a concave mirror.

Example 37–1   A concave mirror forms an image, on a wall 3.0 m from the mirror, of the filament of a headlight lamp 10 cm in front of the mirror.

a) What is the radius of curvature of the mirror?

b) What is the height of the image if the height of the object is 5 mm?

Solution

a) Both object distance and image distance are positive; we have $s = 10$ cm and $s' = 300$ cm. From Eq. (37–4),

$$\frac{1}{10 \text{ cm}} + \frac{1}{300 \text{ cm}} = \frac{2}{R}, \qquad R = 19.4 \text{ cm.}$$

The radius is positive, which confirms that the mirror is concave.

b) From Eq. (37–5),

$$m = \frac{y'}{y} = -\frac{s'}{s} = -\frac{300 \text{ cm}}{10 \text{ cm}} = -30.$$

The image is inverted (because m is negative); its height is 30 times the height of the object, or $(30)(5 \text{ mm}) = 150$ mm.   ■

In Fig. 37–8a the *convex* side of a spherical mirror faces the incident light, so R is negative. Ray PB is reflected with the angle of reflection r equal to the angle of incidence ϕ. The reflected ray, projected backward, intersects the axis at P'. As is the case with a concave mirror, *all* rays from P that are reflected by the mirror diverge from the same point P', provided that the angle u is small. Therefore P' is the image of P. The object distance s is positive, the image distance s' is negative, and the radius of curvature R is negative.

Figure 37–8b shows two rays diverging from the head of the arrow PQ and the virtual image $P'Q'$ of this arrow. We leave it to you to show,

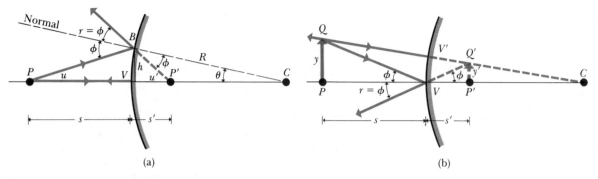

37–8
Construction for finding (a) the position and (b) the magnification of the image formed by a convex mirror.

by the same procedure that we used for a concave mirror, that

$$\frac{1}{s} + \frac{1}{s'} = \frac{2}{R}$$

and that the lateral magnification is

$$m = \frac{y'}{y} = -\frac{s'}{s}.$$

These expressions are exactly the same as those for a concave mirror, as they must be when we use consistent sign rules.

37–3
Focus and Focal Length

When an object point is very far away from a spherical mirror (in comparison to its radius of curvature), all rays from that point that strike the mirror are (in the paraxial approximation) parallel to one another. The object distance is $s = \infty$, and from Eq. (37–4),

$$\frac{1}{\infty} + \frac{1}{s'} = \frac{2}{R}, \qquad s' = \frac{R}{2}.$$

When R is positive (concave mirror), the situation is as shown in Fig. 37–9a. A beam of incident parallel rays converges after reflection at a point F at a distance $R/2$ from the vertex of the mirror. Point F is called the *focal point* or simply the **focus,** and its distance from the vertex, denoted by f, is called the **focal length.**

When R is negative (convex mirror), as in Fig. 37–9b, the image point is behind the mirror, and f is negative. In that case the outgoing rays do not converge at a point, but instead diverge as though they had come from the point F behind the mirror. In this case, F is called a *virtual focus.*

The entire discussion may be reversed, as shown in Fig. 37–10. When the *image* distance s' is very large, the outgoing rays are parallel to

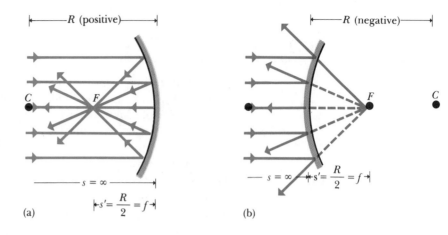

37–9
Incident rays parallel to the axis
(a) converge to the focus F of a
concave mirror, (b) diverge as though
coming from the focus F of a convex
mirror.

the optic axis. The object distance s is then given by

$$\frac{1}{s} + \frac{1}{\infty} = \frac{2}{R}, \qquad s = \frac{R}{2}.$$

In Fig. 37–10a, rays coming in toward the mirror pass through the focus and diverge from it, and after reflection they are parallel to the optic axis. In Fig. 37–10b the incoming rays are converging as though they would meet at the virtual focus F, and they are reflected parallel to the optic axis.

Thus for both concave and convex mirrors the focal length f is related to the radius of curvature R by

$$f = \frac{R}{2}. \tag{37–6}$$

For a concave mirror, both f and R are positive, and for a convex mirror, both are negative.

We can now express the relation between object and image distances for a mirror, Eq. (37–4), as

$$\frac{1}{s} + \frac{1}{s'} = \frac{1}{f}. \tag{37–7}$$

37–10
Rays from a point object at the focus
of a spherical mirror are parallel to the
axis after reflection. The object in part
(b) is virtual.

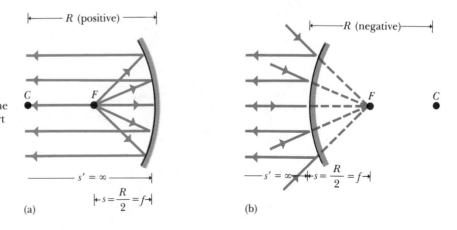

37–4
Graphical Methods

We can find the position and size of the image formed by a mirror by a simple graphical method. This method consists of finding the point of intersection of a few particular rays that diverge from a point of the object (such as point Q in Fig. 37–11) and are reflected by the mirror. Then (neglecting aberrations) *all* rays from this point that strike the mirror will intersect at the same point. For this construction we always choose an object point that is *not* on the optic axis. Four rays that we can always draw easily are shown in Fig. 37–11. These are called **principal rays.**

1. *A ray parallel to the axis*, after reflection, passes through the focus F of a concave mirror or appears to come from the (virtual) focus of a convex mirror.

2. *A ray through (or proceeding toward) the focus F* is reflected parallel to the axis.

3. *A ray along the radius* through the center of curvature C (extended if necessary) intersects the surface normally and is reflected back along its original path.

4. *A ray to the vertex V* is reflected forming equal angles with the optic axis.

37–11

Rays used in the graphical method of locating an image. (a) The object is farther from the mirror than the focus. The reflected rays converge at Q' and then diverge from it. A real image of Q is formed at Q'. (b) The object is closer to the mirror than the focus. The reflected rays diverge as though they had come from point Q', located by extending the outgoing rays backward. A virtual image of Q is formed at Q'.

(a)

(b)

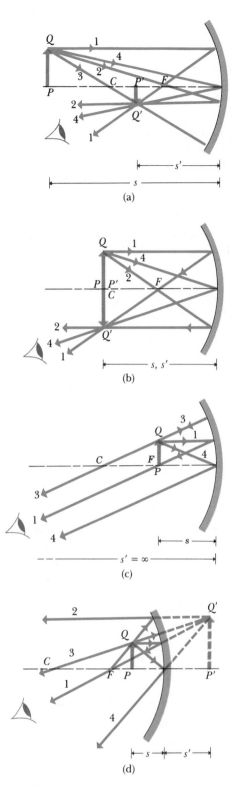

(a)

(b)

(c)

(d)

37–12
Image of an object at various distances from a concave mirror, showing principal-ray construction. (a) Real image, smaller than object. (b) Real image, same size as object. (c) Image at infinity. (d) Virtual image.

Once we have found the position of the image point by means of the intersection of any two of these principal rays (1, 2, 3, 4), we can draw the path of any other ray from the object point to the same image point.

Example 37–2   A concave mirror has a radius of curvature with a magnitude of 20 cm. Find graphically the image of an object in the form of an arrow perpendicular to the axis of the mirror at each of the following object distances: 30 cm, 20 cm, 10 cm, and 5 cm. Check the construction by *computing* the size and magnification of each image.

Solution   The graphical constructions are shown in the four parts of Fig. 37–12. Study each of these diagrams carefully, comparing each numbered ray with the description above. Several points are worth noting. First, in Fig. 37–12b the object and image distances are equal; ray 3 cannot be drawn in this case because a ray from Q through the center of curvature C does not strike the mirror. For the same reason, ray 2 cannot be drawn in Fig. 37–12c; in this case the outgoing rays are parallel, corresponding to an infinite image distance. In Fig. 37–12d the outgoing rays have no real intersection point; they must be extended backward to find the point from which they appear to diverge, that is, from the *virtual image point Q'*.

Measurements of the figures, with appropriate scaling, give the following approximate image distances: (a) 15 cm, (b) 20 cm, (c) ∞ or $-\infty$, (d) -10 cm. To *compute* these distances, we first note that $f = R/2 = 10$ cm; then we use Eq. (37–7):

a) $\dfrac{1}{30 \text{ cm}} + \dfrac{1}{s'} = \dfrac{1}{10 \text{ cm}}$, $s' = 15$ cm,

b) $\dfrac{1}{20 \text{ cm}} + \dfrac{1}{s'} = \dfrac{1}{10 \text{ cm}}$, $s' = 20$ cm,

c) $\dfrac{1}{10 \text{ cm}} + \dfrac{1}{s'} = \dfrac{1}{10 \text{ cm}}$, $s' = \infty$ (or $-\infty$),

d) $\dfrac{1}{5 \text{ cm}} + \dfrac{1}{s'} = \dfrac{1}{10 \text{ cm}}$, $s' = -10$ cm.

In case (c) the outgoing rays are parallel, and we can think of the image as either a real image at $s' = \infty$ or a virtual image at $s' = -\infty$. The lateral magnifications measured from the figures are approximately (a) $-1/2$, (b) -1, (c) ∞ or $-\infty$, (d) $+2$. *Computing* the magnifications from Eq. (37–5), we find

a) $m = -\dfrac{15 \text{ cm}}{30 \text{ cm}} = -\dfrac{1}{2}$,   b) $m = -\dfrac{20 \text{ cm}}{20 \text{ cm}} = -1$,

c) $m = -\dfrac{\pm\infty \text{ cm}}{10 \text{ cm}} = \mp\infty$,   d) $m = -\dfrac{-10 \text{ cm}}{5 \text{ cm}} = +2$.

In cases (a) and (b) the image is inverted; in case (d) it is erect.   ■

■ **PROBLEM-SOLVING STRATEGY:** *Image Formation by Mirrors*

1. The principal-ray diagram is to geometrical optics what the free-body diagram is to mechanics. When you attack a problem involving image formation by a mirror, *always* draw a principal-ray diagram first if you have enough information. The same advice should be applied to lenses in the next chapter. It is usually best to orient your diagrams consistently with the incoming rays traveling from left to right. Don't draw a lot of other rays at random; stick with the principal rays, the ones you know something about. If your principal rays don't converge at a real image point, you may have to extend them straight backward to locate a virtual image point. We recommend drawing the extensions with dashed lines. Another useful aid is to color-code your principal rays, using red for (1) in the above list, green for (2), black for (3), and blue for (4) or something like that.

2. Pay careful attention to signs on object and image distances, radii of curvature, and object and image heights. Make certain you understand that the same sign rules work for all four cases in this chapter: reflection and refraction from plane and spherical surfaces. A negative sign on any one of these quantities mentioned above *always* has significance; use the equations and the sign rules carefully and consistently, and they will tell you the truth!

3. In the next section we will get into refraction. Remember that when a ray passes from a material of smaller index of refraction to one of larger index, it is always bent *toward* the normal; when going from larger to smaller, it is bent *away from* the normal.

37–5
Refraction at a Plane Surface

Suppose we want to find the image of a point object formed by rays *refracted* at a plane or spherical interface between two materials. The method is the same as for reflection; the only difference is that we use the law of refraction (Snell's law) instead of the law of reflection. We let n represent the refractive index of the material on the "incoming" side of the surface and n' that of the material on the "outgoing" side, and we use the same sign rules as for reflection.

Consider first a plane surface, shown in Fig. 37–13, and assume that $n' > n$. This is not a necessary restriction, but the picture looks a little different if $n' < n$. A ray from the object point P toward point V is normal (perpendicular) to the interface and passes into the second material without deviation. A ray making an angle u with the axis is incident at

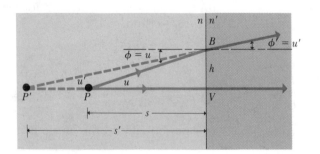

37–13
Construction for finding the position of the image P' of a point object P, formed by a refraction at a plane surface.

B with an angle of incidence $\phi = u$. We find the angle of refraction, ϕ', from the law of refraction:

$$n \sin \phi = n' \sin \phi'.$$

The two rays both appear to come from the image point P' after refraction. From the triangles PVB and $P'VB$,

$$\tan \phi = \frac{h}{s}, \qquad \tan \phi' = \frac{h}{-s'}. \tag{37–8}$$

We have to write $-s'$ because according to our sign rules, s' is negative; the image point is on the side *opposite* to that of the refracted (outgoing) light.

If the angle u is small, the angles ϕ, u', and ϕ' are small also, and we can use the approximations

$$\sin \phi = \tan \phi, \qquad \sin \phi' = \tan \phi'.$$

Then we can write the law of refraction as

$$n \tan \phi = n' \tan \phi'.$$

Using Eq. (37–8) and dividing out h, we find

$$\frac{n}{s} = -\frac{n'}{s'}, \qquad \text{or} \qquad \frac{s'}{s} = -\frac{n'}{n}. \tag{37–9}$$

Because we have used the approximation $\tan \phi = \sin \phi$, this is an *approximate* relation, *valid for paraxial rays only*. That is, a plane refracting surface does *not* image all rays from a point object precisely at the same image point, but only those rays that are nearly perpendicular to the refracting surface, that is, nearly parallel to the optic axis

Now let's consider the image of a finite object, as in Fig. 37–14. The two rays diverging from point Q appear to diverge from its image Q' after refraction, so $P'Q'$ is the image of the object PQ. As the figure shows, the object and the image have the same size and orientation, so the lateral magnification is unity:

$$m = \frac{y'}{y} = 1. \tag{37–10}$$

The image *distance* is greater than the object distance, but image and object are the same *height*.

Here is a familiar example of refraction at a plane surface. When you look vertically downward into the quiet water of a pond or swimming

37–14
Construction for determining the height of an image formed by refraction at a plane surface.

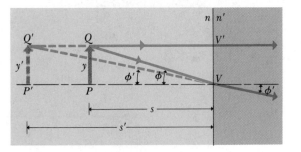

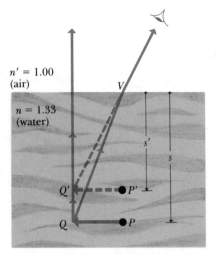

37–15
Arrow $P'Q'$ is the image of the underwater object PQ. The angles of the rays with the vertical are exaggerated for clarity.

pool, the apparent depth is less than the actual depth. Figure 37–15 shows this situation. Two rays diverge from a point Q at a distance s below the surface. Here, n' (air) is less than n (water), and the ray through V is deviated *away from* the normal. The rays after refraction appear to diverge from Q', and the arrow PQ, to an observer looking vertically downward, appears to be lifted to the position $P'Q'$. From Eq. (37–9),

$$s' = -\frac{n'}{n}s = -\frac{1.00}{1.33}s = -0.75s.$$

The apparent depth s' is therefore only three fourths of the actual depth s. The same phenomenon accounts for the apparent sharp bend in an oar when a portion of it extends below a water surface. The submerged portion appears to be lifted above its actual position.

37–6
Refraction at a Spherical Surface

37–16
Construction for finding the position of the image P' of a point object P formed by refraction at a spherical surface.

Our final topic in this chapter is refraction at a spherical surface. This will prepare the way for the analysis of lenses in Chapter 38. In Fig. 37–16, P is an object point at a distance s to the left of a spherical surface with radius R. The center of curvature C is on the outgoing side of the surface, so R is positive. The indexes of refraction of the materials to the left and right of the surface are n and n', respectively. Ray PV is perpendicular to the surface (that is, to the tangent plane to the surface at the point of incidence V), and it passes into the second material without deviation. Ray PB, making an angle u with the axis, is incident at an angle ϕ with the normal and is refracted at an angle ϕ'. These rays intersect at P' at a distance s' to the right of the vertex. The figure is drawn for the case $n' > n$. The object and image distances are both positive.

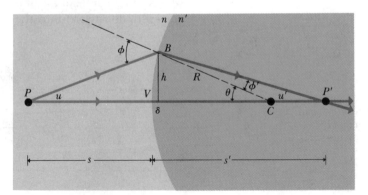

We are going to prove that if the angle u is small, *all* rays from P intersect at the same point P', so P' is the *real image* of P. From the triangles PBC and $P'BC$ we have

$$\phi = \theta + u, \qquad \theta = u' + \phi'. \qquad (37\text{--}11)$$

From the law of refraction,

$$n \sin \phi = n' \sin \phi'.$$

Also, the tangents of u, u', and θ are

$$\tan u = \frac{h}{s + \delta}, \qquad \tan u' = \frac{h}{s' - \delta}, \qquad \tan \theta = \frac{h}{R - \delta}. \qquad (37\text{--}12)$$

For paraxial rays we may approximate both the sine and tangent of an angle by the angle itself and neglect the small distance δ. The law of refraction then gives

$$n\phi = n'\phi'.$$

Combining this with the first of Eqs. (37–11), we obtain

$$\phi' = \frac{n}{n'}(u + \theta).$$

When we substitute this into the second of Eqs. (37–11), we get

$$nu + n'u' = (n' - n)\,\theta. \qquad (37\text{--}13)$$

Now we use the approximations $\tan u = u$, and so on, in Eqs. (37–12) and neglect δ; these equations then become

$$u = \frac{h}{s}, \qquad u' = \frac{h}{s'}, \qquad \theta = \frac{h}{R}.$$

Finally, we substitute these into Eq. (37–13) and divide out the common factor h, and we obtain

$$\frac{n}{s} + \frac{n'}{s'} = \frac{n' - n}{R}. \qquad (37\text{--}14)$$

This equation does not contain the angle u, so the image distance is the same for *all* paraxial rays from P.

If the surface is plane, $R = \infty$. In this case, Eq. (37–14) reduces to Eq. (37–9), which we have already derived for refraction at a plane surface.

We can obtain the magnification from the construction in Fig. 37–17. We draw two rays from point Q, one through the center of curvature C and the other incident at the vertex V. From the triangles PQV and $P'Q'V$,

$$\tan \phi = \frac{y}{s}, \qquad \tan \phi' = \frac{-y'}{s'},$$

and from the law of refraction,

$$n \sin \phi = n' \sin \phi'.$$

For small angles,

$$\tan \phi = \sin \phi, \qquad \tan \phi' = \sin \phi',$$

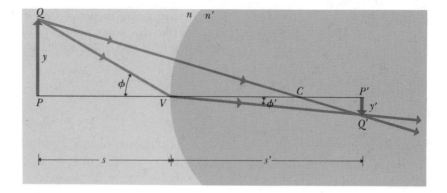

37-17
Construction for determining the height of an image formed by refraction at a spherical surface.

so finally

$$\frac{ny}{s} = -\frac{n'y'}{s'},$$

or

$$m = \frac{y'}{y} = -\frac{ns'}{n's}. \tag{37-15}$$

In the special case of a *plane* refracting surface, Eq. (37–9) gives $ns' = -n's$; combining this with Eq. (37–15), we find $m = 1$, in agreement with Eq. (37–10).

Example 37–3   A cylindrical glass rod (Fig. 37–18) has index of refraction 1.50. One end is ground to a hemispherical surface with radius $R = 20$ mm. Find the image distance of a point object on the axis of the rod, 80 mm to the left of the vertex. The rod is in air.

Solution   We are given

$$n = 1, \qquad\qquad n' = 1.50,$$
$$R = +20 \text{ mm}, \qquad s = +80 \text{ mm}.$$

From Eq. (37–14),

$$\frac{1}{80 \text{ mm}} + \frac{1.50}{s'} = \frac{1.50 - 1}{+20 \text{ mm}},$$
$$s' = +120 \text{ mm}.$$

$n = 1.00$ (air)

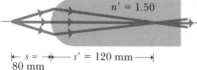

$n' = 1.50$

$s = 80$ mm $s' = 120$ mm

37-18
Image formation by the glass rod in Example 37–3.

The image is formed to the right of the vertex (because s' is positive), at a distance of 120 mm from it. Suppose that the object is an arrow 1 mm high, perpendicular to the axis. Then, from Eq. (37–15),

$$m = -\frac{ns'}{n's} = -\frac{(1)(120 \text{ mm})}{(1.5)(80 \text{ mm})} = -1.$$

The image is the same height as the object, but it is inverted.   ∎

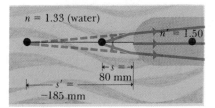

37–19
Image formation by a glass rod immersed in water (Example 37–4).

Example 37–4   The rod in Example 37–3 is immersed in water of index 1.33; the other quantities have the same values as before. Find the image distance (Fig. 37–19).

Solution   From Eq. (37–14),

$$\frac{1.33}{80 \text{ mm}} + \frac{1.50}{s'} = \frac{1.50 - 1.33}{+20 \text{ mm}},$$

$$s' = -185 \text{ mm}.$$

The fact that s' is negative means that after the rays are refracted by the surface, they are not converging but *appear* to diverge from a point 185 mm to the *left* of the vertex. We saw a similar case in the refraction of spherical waves by a plane surface; we called the point a *virtual image*. In this example the surface forms a virtual image 185 mm to the left of the vertex.   ∎

Equations (37–14) and (37–15) can be applied to both convex and concave refracting surfaces, provided that you use the sign rules consistently, and they apply whether n' is greater or less than n. We suggest that you construct diagrams like Figs. 37–16 and 37–17 when R is negative and when $n' < n$ and use them to derive Eqs. (37–14) and (37–15) for these cases.

Here's a final note on the sign rule for the radius of curvature R of a surface. For the convex reflecting surface in Fig. 37–8 we considered R to be negative, but in Fig. 37–16 the refracting surface with the same orientation has a *positive* value of R. This may seem inconsistent, but it isn't. Both cases are consistent with the rule that R is positive when the center of curvature is on the "outgoing" side of the surface and negative when it is *not* on the "outgoing" side. When both reflection and refraction occur at a spherical surface, R has one sign for the reflected light and the opposite sign for refracted light. This may seem strange, but it is consistent with our sign rules.

All the formulas for object distance s and image distance s' for plane and spherical mirrors and refracting surfaces are summarized in Table 37–1. The equation for a plane surface can be obtained from the corresponding equation for a spherical surface by setting $R = \infty$.

The following sign rules are used with all spherical reflecting and refracting surfaces.

s is positive when the object is on the incoming side of the surface and negative otherwise.

s' is positive when the image is on the outgoing side of the surface and negative otherwise.

R is positive when the center of curvature is on the outgoing side of the surface and negative otherwise.

m is positive when the image is erect and negative when it is inverted.

TABLE 37–1

	Plane mirror	Spherical mirror	Plane refracting surface	Spherical refracting surface
Object and image distances	$\dfrac{1}{s} + \dfrac{1}{s'} = 0$	$\dfrac{1}{s} + \dfrac{1}{s'} = \dfrac{2}{R} = \dfrac{1}{f}$	$\dfrac{n}{s} + \dfrac{n'}{s'} = 0$	$\dfrac{n}{s} + \dfrac{n'}{s'} = \dfrac{n' - n}{R}$
Lateral magnification	$m = -\dfrac{s'}{s} = 1$	$m = -\dfrac{s'}{s}$	$m = -\dfrac{ns'}{n's} = 1$	$m = -\dfrac{ns'}{n's}$

Questions

37–1 Can a person see a real image by looking backward along the direction from which the rays come? A virtual image? Can you tell by looking whether an image is real or virtual? How *can* the two be distinguished?

37–2 Why does a plane mirror reverse left and right but not top and bottom?

37–3 For a spherical mirror, if $s = f$, then $s' = \infty$, and the lateral magnification m is infinite. Does this make sense? If so, what does it mean?

37–4 According to the discussion of the preceding chapter, light rays are reversible. Are the formulas in Table 37–1 still valid if object and image are interchanged? What does reversibility imply with respect to the *forms* of the various formulas?

37–5 If a spherical mirror is immersed in water, does its focal length change?

37–6 For what range of object positions does a concave spherical mirror form a real image? What about a convex spherical mirror?

37–7 If a piece of photographic film is placed at the location of a real image, the film will record the image. Can this be done with a virtual image? How might one record a virtual image?

37–8 When a room has mirrors on two opposite walls, an infinite series of reflections can be seen. Discuss this phenomenon in terms of images. Why do the distant images appear darker?

37–9 When observing fish in an aquarium filled with water, one can see clearly only when looking nearly perpendicularly to the glass wall; objects viewed at an oblique angle always appear blurred. Why? Do the fish have the same problem when looking at you?

37–10 Can an image formed by one reflecting or refracting surface serve as an object for a second reflection or refraction? Does it matter whether the first image is real or virtual?

37–11 A concave mirror (sometimes surrounded by lights) is often used as an aid for applying cosmetics to the face. Why is such a mirror always concave rather than convex? What considerations determine its radius of curvature?

37–12 A student claimed that one can start a fire on a sunny day by use of the sun's rays and a concave mirror. How is this done? Is the concept of image relevant? Could one do the same thing with a convex mirror?

37–13 A person looks at her reflection in the concave side of a shiny spoon. Is it right side up or inverted? What if she looks in the convex side?

37–14 In Example 37–2 (Section 37–4) there appears to be an ambiguity for the case $s = 10$ cm, as to whether s' is ∞ or $-\infty$ and as to whether the image is erect or inverted. How is this resolved? Or is it?

37–15 "See yourself as others see you." Can you do this with an ordinary plane mirror? If not, how *can* you do it?

37–16 The shadow formed under a tree by sunlight partially blocked by leaves ordinarily is sprinkled with small circles of light and irregular patterns. During a solar eclipse, however, the shadow is sprinkled instead with a pattern of overlapping crescents that copy the shape of the occluded sun. Why?

Exercises

Section 37–1   Reflection at a Plane Surface

37–1 A candle 6.0 cm tall is 40 cm to the left of a plane mirror. Where is the image formed by the mirror, and what is the height of this image?

37–2 The image of a tree just covers the length of a 5.0-cm plane mirror when the mirror is held 30 cm from the eye. The tree is 70 m from the mirror. What is its height?

Section 37–2   Reflection at a Spherical Surface

Section 37–3   Focus and Focal Length

Section 37–4   Graphical Methods

37–3 A spherical concave shaving mirror has a radius of curvature of 30 cm.

   a) What is the magnification of a person's face when it is 12 cm from the vertex of the mirror?

   b) Where is the image? Is the image real or virtual?

   c) Draw a principal-ray diagram showing formation of the image.

37–4 The diameter of the moon is 3480 km, and its distance from the earth is 386,000 km. Find the diameter of the image of the moon formed by a spherical concave telescope mirror with a focal length of 3.60 m.

37–5 An object 2.00 cm high is placed 14.0 cm to the right of a concave spherical mirror having a radius of curvature of 20.0 cm.

   a) Draw a principal-ray diagram showing formation of the image.

   b) Calculate the position, size, orientation, and nature (real or virtual) of the image.

37–6 A concave mirror has a radius of curvature of 16.0 cm.

   a) What is its focal length?

   b) If the mirror is immersed in water (refractive index 1.33), what is its focal length?

37–7 Repeat Exercise 37–5 for the case in which the mirror is convex.

37–8 Prove that the image formed of a real object by a convex mirror is always virtual, no matter what the object position.

37–9 An object 1.50 cm tall is placed 6.00 cm to the left of the vertex of a convex spherical mirror whose radius of curvature has a magnitude of 20.0 cm.

   a) Draw a principal-ray diagram showing formation of the image.

   b) Determine the position, size, orientation, and nature (real or virtual) of the image.

37–10 Equations (37–4) and (37–5) were derived in the text for the case of a concave mirror. Repeat the similar derivation for a convex mirror, and show that the same equations result if you use the sign convention established in the text.

Section 37–5   Refraction at a Plane Surface

37–11 A speck of dirt is embedded 3.0 cm below the surface of a sheet of ice ($n = 1.309$). What is its apparent depth when viewed at normal incidence?

37–12 A skin diver is 2.0 m below the surface of a lake. A bird flies overhead 7.0 m above the surface of the lake. When the bird is directly overhead, how far above the diver does it appear to be?

37–13 A tank whose bottom is a mirror is filled with water to a depth of 20.0 cm. A small object hangs motionless 6.0 cm under the surface of the water.

   a) What is the apparent depth of the object when viewed at normal incidence?

   b) What is the apparent depth of the image of the object formed by the mirror?

37–14 To a person swimming 0.80 m beneath the surface of the water in a swimming pool, the diving board directly overhead appears to be a height of 5.20 m above the swimmer. What is the actual height of the diving board above the surface of the water?

Section 37–6   Refraction at a Spherical Surface

37–15 Equations (37–14) and (37–15) were derived in the text for the case in which R is positive and $n < n'$. (See Figs. 37–16 and 37–17.)

   a) Carry through the derivation of these two equations for the case in which $R > 0$ and $n > n'$.

   b) Carry through the derivation for $R < 0$ and $n < n'$.

37–16 The left end of a long glass rod 6.00 cm in diameter has a convex hemispherical surface 3.00 cm in radius. The refractive index of the glass is 1.50. Determine the position of the image if an object is placed on the axis of the rod at the following distances to the left of the vertex of the curved end:

   a) infinitely far,   b) 16.0 cm,   c) 4.00 cm.

37–17 The rod of Exercise 37–16 is immersed in a liquid. An object 60.0 cm from the vertex of the left end of the rod and on its axis is imaged at a point 100 cm inside the rod. What is the refractive index of the liquid?

37–18 The left end of a long glass rod 10.0 cm in diameter, with an index of refraction of 1.50, is ground and polished to a convex hemispherical surface with a radius of 5.0 cm. An object in the form of an arrow 4.0 mm tall, at right angles to the axis of the rod, is located on the axis 30.0 cm to the left of the vertex of the convex surface. Find the position and height of the image of the arrow formed by paraxial rays incident on the convex surface. Is the image erect or inverted?

37–19 Repeat Exercise 37–18 for the case in which the end of the rod is ground to a *concave* hemispherical surface with radius 5.00 cm.

37–20 A small tropical fish is at the center of a spherical fish bowl 26.0 cm in diameter.

a) Find the apparent position and magnification of the fish to an observer outside the bowl. The effect of the thin walls of the bowl may be neglected.

b) A friend advised the owner of the bowl to keep it out of direct sunlight to avoid blinding the fish, which might swim into the focal point of the parallel rays from the sun. Is the focal point actually within the bowl?

Problems

37–21 If you run toward a plane mirror at 2.00 m·s^{-1}, at what speed is your image approaching you?

37–22 An object is placed between two plane mirrors arranged at right angles to each other such that the object is a distance d_1 from the surface of one mirror and a distance d_2 from the other.

a) How many images are formed? Show the location of the images in a diagram.

b) Draw the paths of rays from the object to the eye of an observer.

37–23 What is the size of the smallest vertical plane mirror in which a man with height h standing erect can see his full-length image?

37–24 Where must you place an object in front of a concave mirror with radius R so that the image is real and one-half the size of the object? Where is the image?

37–25 A luminous object is 4.00 m from a wall. You are to use a concave mirror to project an image of the object on the wall, with the image three times the size of the object. How far should the mirror be from the wall, and what should its radius of curvature be?

37–26 A mirror on the passenger side of your automobile is convex and has a radius of curvature with magnitude 20.0 cm. Another automobile is 5.0 m behind you and is seen in this side mirror. If this auto is 1.5 m high, what is the height of the image? (These mirrors usually have a warning attached that objects viewed in them are closer than they appear. Why is this so?)

37–27 A concave mirror is to form an image of the filament of a headlight lamp on a screen 4.00 m from the mirror. The filament is 5.0 mm high, and the image is to be 30.0 cm high.

a) How far in front of the vertex of the mirror should the filament be placed?

b) What should be the radius of curvature of the mirror?

37–28 An object is 12.0 cm from the center of a silvered spherical glass Christmas tree ornament 8.0 cm in diameter. What are the position and magnification of its image?

37–29 If light incident from the left onto a convex mirror does not diverge from an object point but instead converges toward a point at a (negative) distance s to the right of the mirror, this point is called a *virtual object*.

a) For a convex mirror having a radius of curvature of 8.00 cm, from what range of virtual-object positions is a real image formed?

b) What is the orientation of this real image?

c) Draw a principal-ray diagram showing formation of such an image.

37–30 A microscope is focused on the upper surface of a glass plate. A second plate is then placed over the first. In order to focus on the bottom surface of the second plate the microscope must be raised 0.800 mm. In order to focus on the upper surface it must be raised 1.60 mm *farther*. Find the index of refraction of the second plate. (This problem illustrates one method of measuring index of refraction.)

37–31 A solid glass hemisphere having a radius of 10.0 cm and a refractive index of 1.50 is placed with its flat face downward on a table. A parallel beam of light with a circular cross section 0.500 cm in diameter travels straight down and enters the hemisphere at the center of its curved surface.

a) What is the diameter of the circle of light formed on the table?

b) How does your result depend on the radius of the hemisphere?

37–32 What should be the index of refraction of a transparent sphere in order for paraxial rays from an infinitely distant object to be brought to a focus at the vertex of the surface opposite the point of incidence?

37–33 For refraction at a spherical surface the first focal length f is defined as the value of s corresponding to $s' = \infty$, as shown in Fig. 37–20a. The second focal length f' is defined as the value of s' when $s = \infty$, as shown in Fig. 37–20b.

a) Prove that $n/n' = f/f'$.

b) Prove that the general relation between object and image distance is

$$\frac{f}{s} + \frac{f'}{s'} = 1.$$

37–34 A transparent rod 40.0 cm long is cut flat at one end and rounded to a hemispherical surface with 8.00-cm radius at the other end. A small object is embedded within the rod along its axis and halfway between its ends, 20.0 cm from the flat end and 20.0 cm from the vertex of the curved end. When viewed from the flat end of the rod, the apparent depth of the object is 12.5 cm from the flat end. What is its apparent depth from the vertex of the curved end when viewed from the curved end?

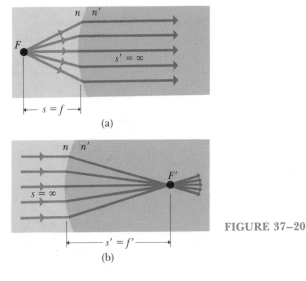

(a)

(b)

FIGURE 37–20

▮ *Challenge Problems*

37–35 Two mirrors are placed together as shown in Fig. 37–21.

a) Show that a point source in front of these mirrors and its two images lie on a circle.

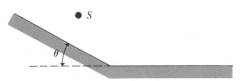

FIGURE 37–21

b) Find the center of the circle.

c) Draw a diagram to show where an observer should stand so as to be able to see both images.

37–36 A wire frame in the form of a small cube 1.00 cm on a side is placed with its center on the axis

of a concave mirror with radius of curvature 40.0 cm. The sides of the cube are all either parallel or perpendicular to the axis. The cube face toward the mirror is 80.0 cm to the left of the mirror vertex.

a) Compute the lateral magnification for an object 80.0 cm from the mirror.

b) From the result of part (a), what is the vertical distance between the images of the top and bottom faces of the cube?

c) Find the locations of the images of objects 80.0 and 81.0 cm from the mirror. From this, find the horizontal distance between the image of the face of the cube facing the mirror and the image of the opposite face.

d) From the result of part (c), what is the longitudinal magnification? (The longitudinal magnification is defined as the ratio of the width of the image along the optic axis to the corresponding width of the object.)

e) Repeat these calculations for a cube 100 cm from the mirror. From these results, can you deduce a relation between the magnitude of the lateral magnification $|m|$ and the magnitude of the longitudinal magnification $|m'|$?

37–37 A convex spherical mirror with a focal length with a magnitude of 20.0 cm is placed 15.0 cm to the left of a plane mirror. An object 0.80 cm tall is placed midway between the surface of the plane mirror and the vertex of the spherical mirror. The spherical mirror forms multiple images of the object. Where are the two images of the object formed by the spherical mirror that are closest to this mirror, and how tall is each of them?

37–38 Spherical aberration is a blurring of the image formed by a mirror or lens because parallel rays strik-ing the mirror far from the optic axis are focused at a different point than rays near the axis. This problem is usually minimized by using only the center of a spherical mirror.

a) Show that for a spherical concave mirror the focus moves toward the mirror as the parallel rays move toward the outer edge of the mirror. (*Hint:* Derive an expression for the distance from the vertex to the focus of the ray for a particular parallel ray in terms of the radius of curvature R of the mirror and the angle θ; θ is the angle between the incident ray and the line connecting the center of curvature of the mirror and the point where the ray strikes the mirror.)

b) What value of θ produces a 5.0% change in the location of the focus compared to the $\theta \approx 0$ value?

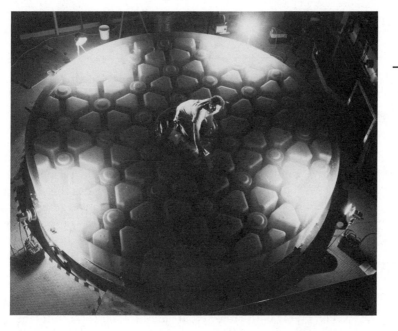

Lenses and Optical Instruments

The most familiar and widely used optical device (after the plane mirror) is the *lens*. We introduce the concepts of focus and focal length for a lens, and then we study the formation of *images* by lenses. We develop graphical methods, analogous to those we used for spherical mirrors, to analyze image formation by lenses. Lenses are central to the operation of many familiar optical devices, including the human eye, cameras, projectors, and magnifiers. Other devices, such as telescopes and compound microscopes, use combinations of lenses or of lenses and mirrors. Here, as in the preceding chapter, the concept of *image* provides the key to analyzing and understanding these optical devices. We again base our analysis on the *ray* model of light. The content of this chapter, as well as that of the previous one, comes under the heading of *geometrical optics*.

38–1
The Thin Lens

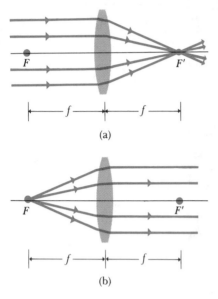

(a)

(b)

38–1
Focal points of a thin lens.

A lens is an optical system with two refracting surfaces. The simplest example is a lens with two *spherical* surfaces close enough together that we can neglect the distance between them (the thickness of the lens). Such a device is called a **thin lens.** We can analyze this system in detail, using the results of Section 37–6 for refraction by a single spherical surface. We postpone this analysis until Section 38–3 so that we can move immediately into a discussion of the properties of thin lenses.

A lens of the type shown in Fig. 38–1 has the property that when a beam of parallel rays strikes it, the rays converge after passing through the lens at a point F', as shown in Fig. 38–1a. Similarly, rays passing through point F emerge from the lens as a beam of parallel rays, as shown in Fig. 38–1b. The points F and F' are called the first and second *focal points* or *foci* (plural form of **focus**), and the distance f is called the **focal length.** We have already used the concepts of focus and focal length for spherical mirrors in Section 37–3. The two focal lengths in Fig. 38–1, both labeled f, *are always equal* for a thin lens, even when the two sides have different curvatures. We will derive this somewhat surprising result in Section 38–3. The central horizontal line is called the **optic axis,** as with spherical mirrors. The centers of curvature of the two spherical surfaces lie on and define the optic axis.

The focal length f is determined by the index of refraction n of the lens material (and that of the surrounding matter if it is not vacuum) and by the radii of curvature of the spherical surfaces. We will derive this relationship, called the *lensmaker's equation*, in Section 38–3.

A thin lens forms an *image* of an object of finite size. Figure 38–2 shows how we can determine the position of the image. Let s and s' be the object and image distances, respectively, and let y and y' be the object and image heights. This is the same notation that we used in Chapter 37. Ray QA, parallel to the optic axis before refraction, passes through the second focus F' after refraction. Ray QOQ' passes undeflected straight through the center of the lens because at the center the two surfaces are parallel and (we have assumed) very close together. There is refraction where the ray enters and leaves the material, but no net change in direction.

38–2
Construction used to find the image position for a thin lens. The ray QAQ' is shown as bent at the midplane of the lens rather than at the two surfaces to emphasize that the thickness of the lens is assumed to be very small.

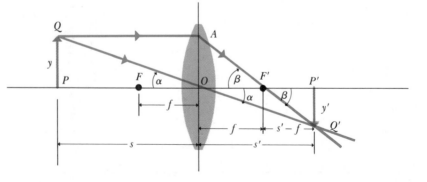

In the following analysis we will use the sign rules that we introduced in Chapter 37. These are summarized at the end of Section 37–6, and we suggest that you review them.

The angles labeled α in Fig. 38–2 are vertical angles and are equal. Therefore the two right triangles PQO and $P'Q'O$ are *similar*, and ratios of corresponding sides are equal. Thus

$$\frac{y}{s} = -\frac{y'}{s'}, \quad \text{or} \quad \frac{y'}{y} = -\frac{s'}{s}. \tag{38–1}$$

(The reason for the negative sign is that the image is below the optic axis and y' is negative.) Also, the two angles labeled β are equal, and the two right triangles OAF' and $P'Q'F'$ are similar, so

$$\frac{y}{f} = -\frac{y'}{s'-f} \quad \text{or} \quad \frac{y'}{y} = -\frac{s'-f}{f}. \tag{38–2}$$

We now equate Eqs. (38–1) and (38–2), divide by s', and rearrange to obtain

$$\frac{1}{s} + \frac{1}{s'} = \frac{1}{f}. \tag{38–3}$$

This analysis also gives us the lateral magnification $m = y'/y$ of the system; from Eq. (38–1),

$$m = -\frac{s'}{s}. \tag{38–4}$$

The negative sign tells us that when s and s' are both positive, the image is *inverted*, and y and y' have opposite signs.

Equations (38–3) and (38–4) are the basic equations for thin lenses. It is pleasing to note that their *form* is exactly the same as the corresponding equations for spherical mirrors, Eqs. (37–7) and (37–5), respectively. As we will see, the sign rules that we used for spherical mirrors are also applicable to lenses.

The three-dimensional image of a three-dimensional object formed by a lens is shown in Fig. 38–3. Point R is nearer the lens than point P. Its image, from Eq. (38–3), is farther from the lens than is point P', and the image $P'R'$ points in the same direction as the object PR. Arrows $P'S'$ and $P'Q'$ are reversed in space in relation to PS and PQ.

We invite you to compare Fig. 38–3 with Fig. 37–4, which shows the image formed by a plane *mirror*. Note that the image formed by a lens is inverted, but it is *not* reversed. That is, if the object is a left hand, its image is also a left hand. You can verify this by pointing your left thumb along PR, your left forefinger along PQ, and your left middle finger along PS. Then rotate your hand 180°, using your thumb as an axis; this brings the fingers into coincidence with $P'Q'$ and $P'S'$. In other words, *inversion* of an image is equivalent to a rotation of 180° about the lens axis.

A bundle of parallel rays incident on the lens shown in Figure 38–1 converges to a real image after passing through the lens. This lens is called a **converging lens.** Its focal length is a positive quantity, and it is also called a *positive lens.*

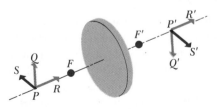

38–3
A lens forms a three-dimensional image of a three-dimensional object.

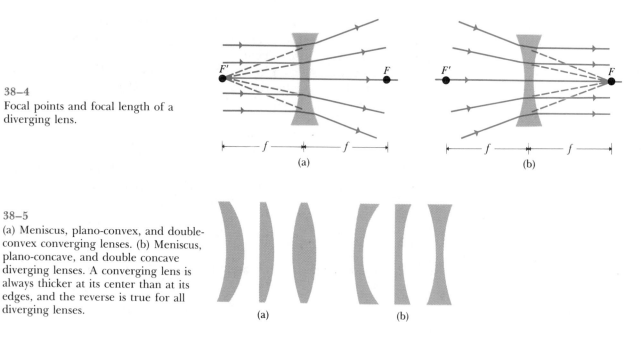

38–4
Focal points and focal length of a diverging lens.

(a)

(b)

38–5
(a) Meniscus, plano-convex, and double-convex converging lenses. (b) Meniscus, plano-concave, and double concave diverging lenses. A converging lens is always thicker at its center than at its edges, and the reverse is true for all diverging lenses.

(a)

(b)

A bundle of parallel rays incident on the lens in Fig. 38–4 *diverges* after refraction, and this lens is called a **diverging lens.** Its focal length is a negative quantity, and the lens is also called a *negative lens*. The foci of a negative lens are reversed in relation to those of a positive lens. The second focus, F', of a negative lens is the point from which rays, originally parallel to the axis, *appear to diverge* after refraction, as in Fig. 38–4a. Incident rays converging toward the first focus F, as in Fig. 38–4b, emerge from the lens parallel to its axis.

Equations (38–3) and (38–4) apply to *both* negative and positive lenses. Various types of lenses, both converging and diverging, are shown in Fig. 38–5. Equation (38–6), to be derived in Section 38–3, can be used to show that any lens that is thicker at the center than at the edges is a converging lens with positive f and that any lens thicker at the edges than at the center is a diverging lens with negative f.

38–2
Graphical Methods

We can determine the position and size of an image formed by a thin lens by using a graphical method that is very similar to the one we used in Section 37–4 for spherical mirrors. Again we draw a few special rays, called **principal rays,** diverging from a point of the object that is *not* on the optic axis. The intersection of these rays, after they pass through the lens, determines the position and size of the image. In using this graphical method we will consider the entire deviation of a ray as occurring at the midplane of the lens, as shown in Fig. 38–6; this is consistent with the assumption that the distance between the lens surfaces is negligible.

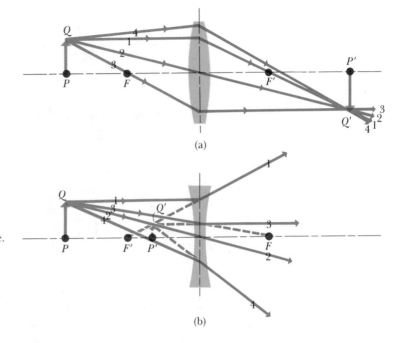

38–6
Principal-ray diagram, showing graphical method of locating an image. (a) A converging lens; (b) a diverging lens.

The three principal rays whose paths are easy to trace are shown in Fig. 38–6. They are as follows.

1. *A ray parallel to the axis*, after refraction by the lens, passes through the second focus F' of a converging lens or appears to come from the second focus of a diverging lens.

2. *A ray through the center of the lens* is not appreciably deviated because at the center of the lens the two surfaces are parallel and close together.

3. *A ray through (or proceeding toward) the first focus F* emerges parallel to the axis.

The position of the image point is determined by the intersection of any two of rays 1, 2, and 3. Once the image position is known, we can draw any other ray from the same point, such as ray 4 in Fig. 38–6 (not a principal ray). There is usually no point in drawing a lot of additional rays.

Figure 38–7 shows several principal-ray diagrams for various object positions. The unnumbered rays are not principal rays. We suggest that you study each of these diagrams (drawn for several different object distances) very carefully, comparing each numbered ray with the above description. Several points are worth noting. In Fig. 38–7d the object is at the focus; ray 3 cannot be drawn because it does not pass through the lens. In Fig. 38–7e the object distance is less than the focal length. The outgoing rays are divergent, and the *virtual image* is located by extending the outgoing rays backward. In this case the image distance s' is negative. Figure 38–7f corresponds to a *virtual object*. The incoming rays do not diverge from a real object point O but are *converging* as though they

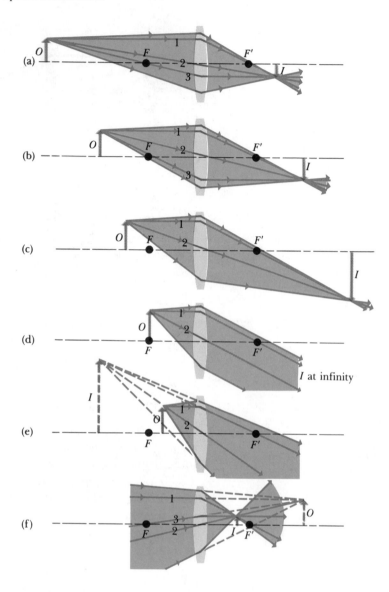

38-7
Formation of an image by a thin lens. The principal rays are labeled.

would meet at the virtual object point O on the right side. The object distance s is negative in this case. The image is real; the image distance s' is positive and less than f.

Example 38–1 A converging lens has a focal length of 20 cm. Find graphically the image location for an object at each of the following distances from the lens: 50 cm, 20 cm, 15 cm, and −40 cm. Determine the magnification in each case. Check your results by calculating the image position and magnification from Eqs. (38–3) and (38–4).

Solution The appropriate principal-ray diagrams are shown in Figs. 38–7a, 38–7d, 38–7e, and 38–7f. The approximate image distances, from measurements of these diagrams, are 35 cm, ∞, −40 cm, and 15 cm, and the approximate magnifications are −2/3, ∞, +3, and +1/3.

Calculating the image positions from Eq. (38–3), we find

$$\frac{1}{s} + \frac{1}{s'} = \frac{1}{f},$$

a) $\dfrac{1}{50 \text{ cm}} + \dfrac{1}{s'} = \dfrac{1}{20 \text{ cm}},$ $s' = 33.3$ cm,

d) $\dfrac{1}{20 \text{ cm}} + \dfrac{1}{s'} = \dfrac{1}{20 \text{ cm}},$ $s' = \infty,$

e) $\dfrac{1}{15 \text{ cm}} + \dfrac{1}{s'} = \dfrac{1}{20 \text{ cm}},$ $s' = -60$ cm,

f) $\dfrac{1}{-40 \text{ cm}} + \dfrac{1}{s'} = \dfrac{1}{20 \text{ cm}},$ $s' = 13.3$ cm.

The graphical results are fairly close to these except for part (e) (Fig. 38–7e), in which the precision of the diagram is limited because the rays extended backward have nearly the same direction.

From Eq. (38–4) the magnifications are

$$m = -\frac{s'}{s},$$

a) $m = -\dfrac{33.3 \text{ cm}}{50 \text{ cm}} = -\dfrac{2}{3},$ d) $m = -\dfrac{\infty}{20 \text{ cm}} = -\infty,$

e) $m = -\dfrac{-60 \text{ cm}}{15 \text{ cm}} = +4,$ f) $m = -\dfrac{13.3 \text{ cm}}{-40 \text{ cm}} = +\dfrac{1}{3}.$ ■

PROBLEM-SOLVING STRATEGY: *Image Formation by a Thin Lens*

1. The strategy outlined at the end of Section 37–4 is equally applicable here, and we suggest that you review it now. Always begin with a principal-ray diagram; orient your diagrams consistently so that light travels from left to right. For a lens there are only three principal rays, compared to four for a mirror. Don't just sketch these diagrams; draw the rays with a ruler and measure the distances carefully. Draw the rays so that they bend at the midplane of the lens, as shown in Fig. 38–6. Be sure to draw *all three* principal rays. The intersection of any two determines the image, but if the third doesn't pass through the same intersection point, you know you have made a mistake. Redundancy can be useful in spotting errors. When there is a virtual image, you will have to extend the outgoing rays backward; in that case the image lies on the *incoming* side of the lens.

2. The set of sign rules that we used in Chapter 37 is still applicable for thin lenses, and we will extend it in the next section to include radii of curvature of lens surfaces. Be extremely careful to get your signs right and to interpret the signs of results correctly.

3. Always determine the image position and size *both* graphically and by calculating. This gives an extremely useful consistency check.

4. An additional point that we will encounter in the next section is that the *image* from one lens or mirror may serve as the *object* for another. In that case, be careful in finding the object and image *distances* for this intermediate image; be sure that you include the distance between the two elements (lenses and/or mirrors) correctly.

38–3
Images as Objects

An image formed by one reflecting or refracting surface can serve as the object for a second reflecting or refracting surface. We can use this principle to derive the thin-lens equation, Eq. (38–3), from the single-surface equation, Eq. (37–14). For this derivation, consider the situation of Fig. 38–8. Rays diverge from point Q of an object PQ. The first surface of the lens forms a virtual image of Q at Q'. This virtual image serves as a real object for the second surface of the lens, which forms a real image of Q' at Q''. Distance s_1 is the object distance for the first surface, and s_1' is the corresponding image distance. The object distance for the second surface is s_2. The difference between the magnitudes of s_1' and s_2 is the lens thickness t, and s_2' is the image distance for the second surface.

If the lens is thin enough that its thickness t is negligible in comparison with the distances s_1, s_1', s_2, and s_2', then we may assume that $s_1' = -s_2$. (The negative sign is needed because s_1' is a virtual image distance and is negative.) Also, we can measure object and image distances from the midplane of the lens. We will also assume that the material on both sides of the lens is vacuum, with an index of refraction of 1.00. For the first refraction, Eq. (37–14) gives

$$\frac{1}{s_1} + \frac{n}{s_1'} = \frac{n-1}{R_1}.$$

Applying Eq. (37–14) to the second surface yields

$$\frac{n}{s_2} + \frac{1}{s_2'} = \frac{1-n}{R_2}.$$

Adding these two equations and using the thin-lens assumption, $s_2 = -s_1'$, we find

$$\frac{1}{s_1} + \frac{1}{s_2'} = (n-1)\left(\frac{1}{R_1} - \frac{1}{R_2}\right).$$

Now s_1 is the original object distance for the thin lens, which we have previously called s, and s_2' is the final image distance, previously called s'. Omitting the subscripts, we finally obtain

$$\frac{1}{s} + \frac{1}{s'} = (n-1)\left(\frac{1}{R_1} - \frac{1}{R_2}\right). \tag{38–5}$$

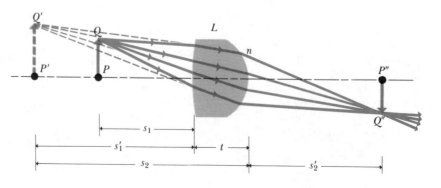

38–8
The image formed by the first surface of a lens serves as the object for the second surface.

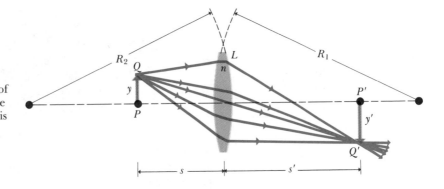

38–9
A thin lens. The radius of curvature of the first surface is R_1, and that for the second surface is R_2. In this case, R_1 is positive but R_2 is negative. The focal length f is positive, and the lens is a converging lens. The figure is not to scale for the data of Example 38–2.

The usual sign conventions apply to this equation. These are illustrated in Fig. 38–9, in which we see that s, s', and R_1 are positive quantities but R_2 is negative.

Comparing Eq. (38–5) with our previous form of the thin-lens equation, Eq. (38–3), we see that the focal length f is given by

$$\frac{1}{f} = (n - 1)\left(\frac{1}{R_1} - \frac{1}{R_2}\right). \qquad (38\text{–}6)$$

This is known as the **lensmaker's equation.** In the process of rederiving the thin-lens equation we have also derived an expression for the focal length f of the lens in terms of the index of refraction n and the radii of curvature R_1 and R_2 of the surfaces.

We can also obtain the focal length f directly from Eq. (38–5) by recalling that the focus is the image of an infinitely distant object; when $s = \infty$, $s' = f$. Inserting these values into Eq. (38–5) yields Eq. (38–6) immediately.

Example 38–2   In Fig. 38–9, suppose that the magnitudes of the radii of curvature of the lens surfaces are 20 cm and 5 cm, respectively, and the index of refraction is $n = 1.50$. What is the focal length f of the lens?

Solution   The center of curvature of the first surface is on the outgoing side, so R_1 is positive: $R_1 = +20$ cm. The center of curvature of the second surface is *not* on the outgoing side, so R_2 is negative: $R_2 = -5$ cm. From Eq. (38–6),

$$\frac{1}{f} = (1.50 - 1)\left(\frac{1}{20 \text{ cm}} - \frac{1}{-5 \text{ cm}}\right), \qquad f = 8.0 \text{ cm.} \qquad \blacksquare$$

It is not hard to generalize Eq. (38–6) to the situation in which the lens is immersed in a material with an index of refraction greater than unity. We invite you to work out the lensmaker's equation for this more general situation.

We can extend this same method of analysis to a system consisting of one or more *thick* lenses; an example is shown in Fig. 38–10. The arrow

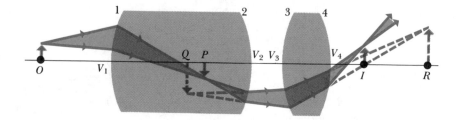

38–10
The object for each surface, after the first, is the image formed by the preceding surface.

at point O represents a small object at right angles to the optic axis. A narrow cone of rays diverging from the head of the arrow is traced through the system. Surface 1 forms a real image of the arrow at point P. Distance OV_1 is the object distance for the first surface, and distance V_1P is the image distance. Both of these distances are positive.

The image at P, formed by surface 1, serves as the object for surface 2. The object distance is PV_2; it is positive because the object for surface 2 is on its incoming side. This surface forms a virtual image at point Q. The image distance is V_2Q; it is negative because the image is *not* on the outgoing side for surface 2.

The image at Q, formed by surface 2, serves as the object for surface 3. The object distance is QV_3; it is positive. The image at Q, although virtual, is a *real object* as far as surface 3 is concerned. The rays passing through surface 3 become convergent; if surface 4 were not present, they would converge to a real image at point R. Even though this image is never formed, distance V_3R is the image distance for surface 3; it is positive.

The rays incident on surface 4 are *converging*; there is no point at the left of the vertex from which they diverge or appear to diverge. The *image at R, toward which the rays are converging*, is the *object* for surface 4. Because it is not on the incoming side of this surface, the object distance RV_4 is negative. The image at R is called a **virtual object** for surface 4. Whenever a *converging* cone of rays is incident on a surface, the point toward which the rays are converging serves as the object, the object distance is negative, and the point is called a virtual object.

Finally, surface 4 forms a real image at I. The image distance is V_4I; it is positive.

Many optical systems, such as camera lenses, microscopes, and telescopes, use more than one lens. In each case the image formed by any one lens serves as the object for the next lens. We will use this principle in our analysis of compound microscopes and telescopes in Sections 38–9 and 38–10. Figure 38–11 shows various possibilities. Lens 1 forms a real image at P of a real object at O. This real image serves as a real object for lens 2. The virtual image at Q formed by lens 2 is a real object for lens 3.

38–11
The object for each lens after the first is the image formed by the preceding lens.

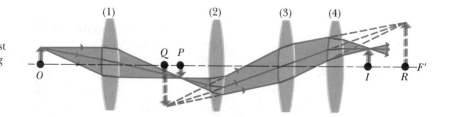

If lens 4 were not present, lens 3 would form a real image at R. Although this image is never formed, it serves as a *virtual object* for lens 4, which forms a real image at I.

*38–4
Lens Aberrations

The equations we have derived for object and image distances, focal lengths, radii of curvature, and so on, have been based upon the *paraxial approximation*; all rays were assumed to be *paraxial*, that is, to make small angles with the axis. In general, however, a lens must form images not only of points on its axis, but also of points that lie off the axis. Furthermore, because of the finite size of the lens, the cone of rays that forms the image of any point is of finite size. In general, nonparaxial rays that proceed from a given object point *do not* all intersect at precisely the same point after they are refracted by a lens. For this reason the image formed by these rays is never a perfectly sharp one. Furthermore, the focal length of a lens depends upon its index of refraction, which varies with wavelength. Therefore if the light proceeding from an object is a mixture of wavelengths, different wavelengths are imaged at different points.

The failures of an actual image to conform to the predictions of our simple theory are called **aberrations.** Those caused by the variation of index with wavelength are the **chromatic aberrations.** Others, which occur even with monochromatic light, are **monochromatic aberrations.** Lens aberrations are not caused by faulty construction of the lens, such as irregularities in its surfaces, but are inevitable consequences of the laws of refraction at spherical surfaces.

Monochromatic aberrations are all related to the limitations of the paraxial approximation. *Spherical aberration* is the failure of rays from a point object on the optic axis to converge to a point image. Instead, the rays converge within a circle of minimum radius, called *the circle of least confusion*, and then diverge again, as shown in Fig. 38–12. The corresponding effect for points off the axis produces images that are comet-shaped figures rather than circles; this is called *coma*.

Astigmatism is the imaging of a point off the axis as two perpendicular *lines*. In this aberration the rays from a point object converge, at a certain distance from the lens, to a line in the plane defined by the optic axis and the object point. At a somewhat different distance from the lens they converge to a second line *perpendicular* to this plane. The circle of least

38–12
Spherical aberration. The circle of least confusion is shown by C–C.

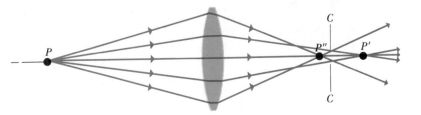

confusion appears between these two positions, at a location that depends on the object point's distance from the axis as well as its distance from the lens. As a result, object points lying in a plane are, in general, imaged not in a plane but in some curved surface; this effect is called *curvature of field*. Finally, the image of a straight line that does not pass through the optic axis may be curved. As a result, the image of a square with the axis through its center may resemble a barrel (sides bent outward) or a pincushion (sides bent inward). This effect, called *distortion*, is not related to lack of sharpness of the image but results from a change in lateral magnification with distance from the axis.

Chromatic aberrations result directly from the variation of index of refraction with wavelength. When an object is illuminated with white light containing a mixture of wavelengths, different wavelengths are imaged at different points. The magnification of a lens also varies with wavelength; this effect is responsible for the rainbow-fringed images seen with inexpensive binoculars or telescopes.

It is impossible to eliminate all these aberrations from a single lens, but in a compound lens of several elements, the aberrations of one element may partially cancel those of another element. Design of such lenses is an extremely complex problem, aided greatly in recent years by the use of computers. It is still impossible to eliminate all aberrations, but it *is* possible to decide which ones are most troublesome for a particular application and to design accordingly.

38–5
The Eye

The essential parts of the human eye, considered as an optical system, are shown in Fig. 38–13. The eye is nearly spherical in shape and about 2.5 cm in diameter. The front portion is somewhat more sharply curved and is covered by a tough, transparent membrane C, called the *cornea*. The region behind the cornea contains a liquid A called the *aqueous humor*. Next comes the *crystalline lens L*, a capsule containing a fibrous jelly, hard at the center and progressively softer at the outer portions. The crystalline lens is held in place by ligaments that attach it to the ciliary muscle M, which encircles it. Behind the lens the eye is filled with a thin watery jelly V, called the *vitreous humor*. The indexes of refraction of both the aqueous humor and the vitreous humor are nearly equal to that of water, about 1.336. The crystalline lens, while not homogeneous, has an average index of 1.437. This is not very different from the indexes of the aqueous and vitreous humors; most of the refraction of light entering the eye occurs at the outer surface of the cornea.

Refraction at the cornea and the surfaces of the lens produces a *real image* of the object being viewed; the image is formed on the light-sensitive *retina R*, lining the rear inner surface of the eye. The *rods* and *cones* in the retina act like an array of miniature photocells; they sense the image and transmit it via the *optic nerve O* to the brain. Vision is most acute in a

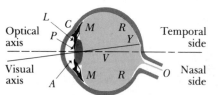

38–13
The eye.

TABLE 38–1	
Age, years	Near point, cm
10	7
20	10
30	14
40	22
50	40
60	200

small central region called the *fovea centralis Y*, which is about 0.25 mm in diameter.

In front of the lens is the *iris*. It contains an aperture with variable diameter called the *pupil P*, which opens and closes to adapt to changing light intensity. The receptors of the retina also have intensity adaptation mechanisms.

For an object to be seen sharply the image must be formed exactly at the location of the retina. The lens-to-retina distance, corresponding to s', does not change, but the eye accommodates to different object distances s by changing the focal length of its lens. When the ciliary muscle surrounding the lens contracts, the lens bulges, and the radii of curvature of its surfaces *decrease*; this decreases the focal length. For the normal eye an object at infinity is sharply focused when the ciliary muscle is relaxed. With increasing tension the focal length decreases to permit sharp imaging on the retina of closer objects. This process is called *accommodation*.

The extremes of the range over which distinct vision is possible are known as the *far point* and the *near point* of the eye. The far point of a normal eye is at infinity. The position of the near point depends on the amount by which the ciliary muscle can increase the curvature of the crystalline lens. The range of accommodation gradually diminishes with age as the crystalline lens loses its flexibility. For this reason the near point gradually recedes as one grows older. This recession of the near point is called *presbyopia*. Table 38–1 lists the approximate position of the near point for an average person at various ages. For example, an average person 50 years of age cannot focus on an object closer than about 40 cm.

Several common defects of vision result from incorrect distance relations in the eye. A normal eye forms an image on the retina of an object at infinity when the eye is relaxed, as in Fig. 38–14a. In the *myopic* (nearsighted) eye the eyeball is too long from front to back in comparison with the radius of curvature of the cornea, and rays from an object at infinity are focused in front of the retina (Fig. 38–14b). The most distant object for which an image can be formed on the retina is then nearer than infinity. In the *hyperopic* (farsighted) eye the eyeball is too short, and the image of an infinitely distant object is behind the retina (Fig. 38–14c). The myopic eye produces *too much* convergence in a parallel bundle of rays for an image to be formed on the retina; the hyperopic eye produces *not enough* convergence.

Astigmatism refers to a defect in which the surface of the cornea is not spherical but is more sharply curved in one plane than another. Astigmatism makes it impossible, for example, to focus clearly on the horizontal and vertical bars of a window at the same time.

These defects can be corrected by the use of corrective lenses (glasses or contact lenses). The near point of either a presbyopic or a hyperopic eye is farther from the eye than normal. To see clearly an object at normal reading distance (usually assumed to be 25 cm), we need a lens that forms a virtual image of the object at or beyond the near point. The lens does not make the object appear larger, but in effect it moves the object farther away from the eye to a point where a sharp retinal image can be formed.

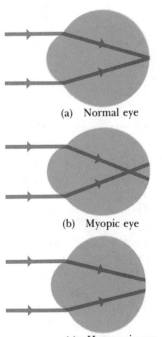

(a)   Normal eye

(b)   Myopic eye

(c)   Hyperopic eye

38–14
Viewing a very distant object with (a) a normal eye; (b) a myopic eye; (c) a hyperopic eye.

Example 38–3   The near point of a certain hyperopic eye is 100 cm in front of the eye. What lens should be used to see clearly an object 25 cm in front of the eye?

Solution   We want the lens to form a virtual image of the object at a location corresponding to the near point of the eye, 100 cm from it. That is, when $s = 25$ cm, we want s' to be -100 cm. From Eq. (38–3),

$$\frac{1}{f} = \frac{1}{s} + \frac{1}{s'} = \frac{1}{+25 \text{ cm}} + \frac{1}{-100 \text{ cm}},$$

$$f = +33 \text{ cm}.$$

We need a converging lens with focal length $f = 33$ cm.   ∎

The far point of a *myopic* eye is nearer than infinity. To see clearly objects beyond the far point, we need a lens that forms a virtual image of such objects, no farther from the eye than the far point.

Example 38–4   The far point of a certain myopic eye is 1.0 m in front of the eye. What lens should be used to see clearly an object at infinity?

Solution   Assume that the virtual image is formed at the far point. Then when $s = \infty$, we want s' to be -1.0 m $= -100$ cm. From Eq. (38–3),

$$\frac{1}{f} = \frac{1}{s} + \frac{1}{s'} = \frac{1}{\infty} + \frac{1}{-100 \text{ cm}},$$

$$f = -100 \text{ cm}.$$

We need a *diverging* lens with a focal length of 100 cm.   ∎

Astigmatism is corrected by use of a *cylindrical* lens. For example, suppose the curvature of the cornea in a horizontal plane is correct to focus rays from infinity on the retina, but the curvature in the vertical plane is not great enough to form a sharp retinal image. When a cylindrical lens with its axis horizontal is placed before the eye, the rays in a horizontal plane are unaffected, but the additional convergence of the rays in a vertical plane causes these to be sharply imaged on the retina.

Optometrists describe the converging or diverging effect of lenses in terms of the *reciprocal* of the focal length, $1/f$. This is called the *power* of the lens. If the focal length is in meters, the power is in **diopters.** If $f = 0.50$ m, the power is $+2.0$ diopters; if $f = -0.25$ m, the power is -4.0 diopters. Prescriptions for glasses are usually given to the nearest 1/4 diopter. In Examples 38–3 and 38–4 the powers of the lenses needed are $+3.0$ diopters and -1.0 diopter, respectively.

38–6
The Camera

Object

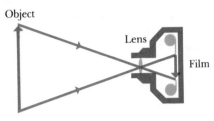

38–15
Essential elements of a camera.

The essential elements of a camera are a lens equipped with a shutter, a light-tight enclosure, and a light-sensitive film to record an image. An example is shown in Fig. 38–15. The lens forms an inverted real image on the film of the object being photographed, just as the lens of the human eye forms a real image on the retina, the eye's "film." The lens may be moved closer to or farther from the film to provide proper image distances for various object distances. All but the most inexpensive lenses have several elements to permit partial correction of various aberrations. A classic design is the Zeiss "Tessar" design, shown in Fig. 38–16.

For the film to record the image properly, the total light energy per unit area reaching the film (the "exposure") must fall within certain limits. This is controlled by the *shutter* and the *lens aperture.* The shutter controls the time interval during which light enters the lens. This is usually adjustable in steps corresponding to factors of about 2, often from 1 s to $\frac{1}{1000}$ s. The light-gathering capacity of the lens is proportional to its effective area; this may be varied by means of an adjustable aperture or *diaphragm,* a nearly circular hole with variable diameter. The aperture size is usually described in terms of its "*f*-number," which is the focal length of the lens divided by the diameter of the aperture. That is,

$$f\text{-number} = \frac{\text{focal length}}{\text{diameter}}.$$

A lens with a focal length $f = 50$ mm and an aperture diameter of 25 mm has an aperture of $f/2$ or an f-number of 2.

Because the light-gathering capacity of a lens is proportional to its area and thus to the *square* of its diameter, changing the diameter by a factor of $\sqrt{2}$ changes the exposure by a factor of 2. Adjustable apertures usually have scales labeled with successive numbers related by factors of $\sqrt{2}$, such as

$$f/2, \quad f/2.8, \quad f/4, \quad f/5.6, \quad f/8, \quad f/11, \quad f/16,$$

and so on. The larger numbers represent smaller apertures and exposures, and each step corresponds to a factor of 2 in exposure.

The choice of focal length for a camera lens depends on the film size and the desired angle of view, or *field.* The popular 35-mm cameras have an image size on the film of 24 × 36 mm. The normal lens usually has a focal length of about 50 mm; this permits an angle of about 45°. A longer-focal-length lens, often 135 mm or 200 mm, provides a *smaller* angle of view and a larger image of *part* of the object, compared with a normal lens. This gives the impression that the camera is *closer* than it really is, and such a lens is called a *telephoto* lens. At the other extreme, a lens with shorter focal length, such as 35 mm or 28 mm, permits a wider angle of view and is called a *wide-angle* lens.

The optical system for a television camera is the same in principle as that for an ordinary camera. The film is replaced by an electronic system

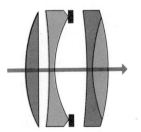

38–16
Zeiss "Tessar" lens design.

that scans the image with a series of 525 parallel lines. The image brightness at points along these lines is translated into electrical impulses that can be broadcast, using electromagnetic waves with frequencies of the order of 100 to 400 MHz. The entire picture is scanned 30 times each second, so 30×525 or 15,750 lines are scanned each second. Some TV receivers emit a faint high-pitched sound at this scanning frequency (two octaves above the highest B on the piano).

38–7
The Projector

A projector for slides or motion pictures operates very much like a camera in reverse. The essential elements are shown in Fig. 38–17. Light from the source (an incandescent lamp bulb or, in large motion-picture projectors, a carbon-arc lamp) shines through the film, and the projection lens forms a real, enlarged, inverted image of the film on the projection screen. Additional lenses called *condenser* lenses are placed between lamp and film. Their function is to direct the light from the source so that most of it enters the projection lens after passing through the film. A concave mirror behind the lamp also helps to direct the light. The condenser lenses must be large enough to cover the entire area of the film. The image on the screen is always inverted; this is why slides have to be put into a projector upside-down.

The position and size of the image projected on the screen are determined by the position and focal length of the projection lens.

Example 38–5   An ordinary 35-mm color slide has a picture area of 24×36 mm. What focal-length projection lens would be needed to project an image 1.2 m $\times$ 1.8 m on a screen 5.0 m from the lens?

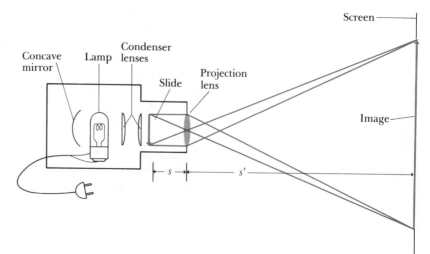

38–17
A slide projector. The concave mirror and condenser lenses gather and direct the light from the lamp so that it will enter the projection lens after passing through the slide. The cooling fan, usually needed to take away excessive heat from the lamp, is not shown.

Solution We need the lateral magnification (apart from sign) to be (1.2 m)/(24 mm) = 50. From Eq. (38–4) the ratio s'/s must also be 50. We are given $s' = 5.0$ m, so $s = 5$ m/50 = 0.10 m. From Eq. (38–3),

$$\frac{1}{f} = \frac{1}{0.10 \text{ m}} + \frac{1}{5.0 \text{ m}}, \qquad f = 0.098 \text{ m} = 98 \text{ mm}.$$

A commercially available lens would probably have $f = 100$ mm; this is a popular focal length for home slide projectors. ∎

*38–8
The Magnifier

The apparent size of an object is determined by the size of its retinal image. If the eye is unaided, this size depends upon the *angle* subtended by the object at the eye, called its **angular size.** To look closely at a small object, such as an insect or a tiny crystal, you bring it close to your eye to make the subtended angle and the retinal image as large as possible. But your eye cannot focus sharply on objects closer than the near point, so the angular size of an object is greatest (i.e., it subtends the largest possible viewing angle) when it is placed at the near point. In the following discussion we will assume that the near point is 25 cm from the eye.

A converging lens can be used to form a virtual image that is larger and farther from the eye than the object itself. Then the object can be moved closer to the eye, and the angular size of the image may be substantially larger than the angular size of the object at 25 cm without the lens. A lens used in this way is called a *magnifying glass* or simply a **magnifier.** The virtual image is most comfortable to view when it is placed at infinity, and in the following discussion we assume that this is done.

The principle of the magnifier is shown in Fig. 38–18. In Fig. 38–18a the object is at the near point, where it subtends an angle u at the eye. In Fig. 38–18b a magnifier in front of the eye forms an image at infinity, and the angle subtended at the magnifier is u'. The **angular magnification** M (not to be confused with the *lateral magnification* m) is defined as the ratio of the angle u' to the angle u:

$$M = \frac{u'}{u}. \tag{38–7}$$

We can find the value of M as follows. We assume that the angles are small enough that each angle (in radians) is equal to its sine and its tangent. From Fig. 38–18, u and u' are given (in radians) by

$$u = \frac{y}{25 \text{ cm}}, \qquad u' = \frac{y}{f}.$$

Combining these expressions with Eq. (38–7), we find

$$M = \frac{u'}{u} = \frac{y/f}{y/25 \text{ cm}} = \frac{25 \text{ cm}}{f}. \tag{38–8}$$

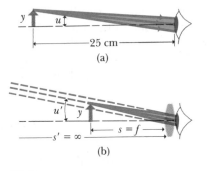

(a)

(b)

38–18
A simple magnifier.

It may seem that we can make the angular magnification as large as we like by decreasing the focal length f. In fact, the aberrations of a simple double convex lens set a limit to M of about $2\times$ or $3\times$. If these aberrations are corrected, the angular magnification may be made as great as $20\times$. When greater magnification than this is needed, we usually use a compound microscope, which we will discuss in the next section.

*38–9
The Microscope

When we need greater magnification than we can get with a simple magnifier, the instrument we usually use is the **microscope,** sometimes called a *compound microscope*. The essential elements of a microscope are shown in Fig. 38–19. The object O to be viewed is placed just beyond the first focus F_1 of the **objective** lens, which forms a real and enlarged image I. This image lies just inside the first focus F_2 of the **eyepiece** (also called the *ocular*), which forms a final virtual image of I at I'. The position of I' may be anywhere between the near and far points of the eye. Both the objective and eyepiece of an actual microscope are highly corrected compound lenses, but for simplicity they are shown here as simple thin lenses.

The objective lens forms an enlarged real image that is viewed through the eyepiece. The overall angular magnification M of the compound microscope is the product of the *lateral* magnification m_1 of the objective and the *angular* magnification M_2 of the eyepiece. The first is given by

$$m_1 = -\frac{s_1'}{s_1},$$

where s_1 and s_1' are the object and image distances, respectively, for the objective lens. Ordinarily, the object is very close to the focus, and the resulting image distance s_1' is very great in comparison to the focal length f_1 of the objective lens. Thus s_1 is approximately equal to f_1, and $m_1 = -s_1'/f_1$.

The eyepiece functions as a simple magnifier, as we discussed in Section 38–8. From Eq. (38–8) its angular magnification is $M_2 = (25 \text{ cm})/f_2$, where f_2 is the focal length of the eyepiece, considered as a simple lens. The overall magnification M of the compound microscope (apart from a negative sign, which is customarily ignored) is the product of the two magnifications, that is,

$$M = m_1 M_2 = \frac{(25 \text{ cm})s_1'}{f_1 f_2}, \tag{38–9}$$

where s_1', f_1, and f_2 are measured in centimeters. Microscope manufacturers usually specify the values of m_1 and M_2 for microscope components rather than the focal lengths of the objective and eyepiece.

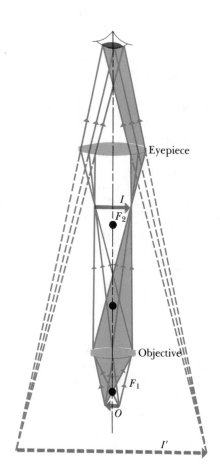

38–19
The optical system of a microscope.

*38–10
Telescopes

The optical system of a refracting **telescope** is similar to that of a compound microscope. In both instruments the image formed by an objective is viewed through an eyepiece. The difference is that the telescope is used to view large objects at large distances, and the microscope is used to view small objects close at hand.

The *astronomical* telescope is shown in Fig. 38–20. The objective lens forms a real, reduced image I of the object, and a virtual image of I is formed by the eyepiece. As with the microscope, the image I' may be formed anywhere between the near and far points of the eye. Objects viewed with a telescope are usually so far away from the instrument that the first image I is formed very nearly at the second focus of the objective lens. This image is the object for the eyepiece lens. If the final image I' formed by the eyepiece is at infinity, the first image must be at the first focus of the eyepiece. The distance between objective and eyepiece, which is the length of the telescope, is therefore the *sum* of the focal lengths of objective and eyepiece, $f_1 + f_2$.

The angular magnification M of a telescope is defined as the ratio of the angle subtended at the eye by the final image I' to the angle subtended at the (unaided) eye by the object. We can express this ratio in terms of the focal lengths of objective and eyepiece. In Fig. 38–20 the ray passing through F_1, the first focus of the objective, and through F_2', the second focus of the eyepiece, has been emphasized. The object (not shown) subtends an angle u at the objective and would subtend essentially the same angle at the unaided eye. Also, since the observer's eye is placed just to the right of the focal point F_2', the angle subtended at the eye by the final image is very nearly equal to the angle u'. Because bd is parallel to the optic axis, the distances ab and cd are equal to each other and also to the height y' of the image I. Since u and u' are small, they may be approximated by their tangents. From the right triangles $F_1 ab$ and $F_2' cd$,

$$u = \frac{-y'}{f_1}, \qquad u' = \frac{y'}{f_2},$$

and the angular magnification M is

$$M = \frac{u'}{u} = -\frac{y'/f_2}{y'/f_1} = -\frac{f_1}{f_2}. \qquad (38\text{--}10)$$

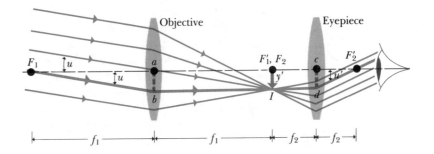

38–20
Optical system of a telescope; final image at infinity.

38–21
The prism binocular. (Courtesy of Bushnell Division of Bausch & Lomb Optical Co.)

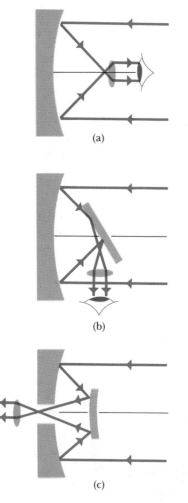

(a)

(b)

(c)

38–22
Optical systems for reflecting telescopes.

The angular magnification M of a telescope is equal to the ratio of the focal length of the objective to that of the eyepiece. The negative sign shows that the final image is inverted.

An inverted image is no particular disadvantage for astronomical observations. When we use a telescope or binoculars on earth, though, we want the image to be right-side up. Inversion of the image is accomplished in *prism binoculars* by a pair of 45°–45°–90° totally reflecting prisms inserted between objective and eyepiece, as shown in Fig. 38–21. The image is inverted by the four reflections from the inclined faces of the prisms. The prisms also have the effect of folding the optical path and making the instrument shorter and more compact than it would otherwise be. Binoculars are usually described by two numbers separated by a multiplication sign, such as 7×50. The first number is the angular magnification M, and the second is the diameter of the objective lenses (in millimeters); this determines the light-gathering capacity of the objective lenses and thus the brightness of the image.

In the *reflecting telescope* the objective lens is replaced by a concave mirror, as shown in Fig. 38–22. In large telescopes this scheme has many advantages, both theoretical and practical. The mirror is inherently free of chromatic aberrations, and spherical aberrations are much easier to correct than with a lens. The material need not be transparent, and the reflector can be made more rigid than a lens, which has to be supported only at its edges. The largest reflecting telescope in the world has a mirror over 5 m in diameter, while lenses larger than 1 m in diameter are not practical.

Because the image is formed in a region traversed by incoming rays, this image can be observed directly with an eyepiece only by blocking off part of the incoming beam; this is practical only for the very largest telescopes. Alternative schemes use a mirror to reflect the image out the side or through a hole in the mirror, as shown in Figs. 38–22b and 38–22c. This scheme is also used in some long-focal-length telephoto lenses for cameras. In the context of photography, such a system is called a *catadioptric lens*, an optical system containing both reflecting and refracting elements. The reflector for a large astronomical telescope is shown in Fig. 38–23.

38–23
The reflector of the 200-inch Hale telescope at Palomar Observatory being cleaned in preparation for the application of a new aluminum reflective surface. (Palomar Observatory Photograph.)

Questions

38–1 Sometimes a wine glass filled with white wine forms an image of an overhead light on a white tablecloth. Would the same image be formed with an empty glass? With a glass of gin? Of gasoline?

38–2 How could one very quickly make an approximate measurement of the focal length of a converging lens? Could the same method be applied if we wished to use a diverging lens?

38–3 If you look closely at a shiny Christmas tree ball, you can see nearly the entire room. Does the room appear right side up or upside down? Discuss your observations in terms of images.

38–4 A student asserted that any lens with spherical surfaces has a positive focal length if it is thicker at the center than at the edge and a negative focal length if it is thicker at the edge. Do you agree?

38–5 The focal length of a simple lens depends on the color (wavelength) of light passing through it. Why? Is it possible for a lens to have a positive focal length for some colors and negative for others?

38–6 The human eye is often compared to a camera. In what ways is it similar to a camera? In what ways does it differ?

38–7 How could one make a lens for sound waves?

38–8 A student proposed to use a plastic bag full of air, immersed in water, as an underwater lens. Is this possible? If the lens is to be a converging lens, what shape should the air pocket have?

38–9 When a converging lens is immersed in water, does its focal length increase or decrease in comparison with the value in air?

38–10 You are marooned on a desert island and want to use your eyeglasses to start a fire. Can this be done if you are nearsighted? If you are farsighted?

38–11 While lost in the mountains, a person who was nearsighted in one eye and farsighted in the other made a crude emergency telescope from the two lenses of his eyeglasses. How did he do this?

38–12 In using a magnifying glass, is the magnification greater when the glass is close to the object or when it is close to the eye?

38–13 When a slide projector is turned on without a slide in it, and the focus adjustment is moved far enough in one direction, a gigantic image of the light-bulb filament can be seen on the screen. Explain how this happens.

38–14 A spherical air bubble in water can function as a lens. Is it a converging or diverging lens? How is its focal length related to its radius?

38–15 As discussed in the text, some binoculars use prisms to invert the final image. Why are prisms better than ordinary mirrors for this purpose?

38–16 There have been reports of round fishbowls starting fires by focusing the sun's rays coming in a window. Is this possible?

38–17 How does a person judge distance? Can a person with vision in only one eye judge distance? What is meant by "binocular vision"?

38–18 Zoom lenses are widely used in television cameras and conventional photography. Such a lens has, effectively, a variable focal length; changes in focal length are accomplished by moving some lens elements relative to others. Try to devise a scheme to accomplish this effect.

38–19 Why can't you see clearly when your head is under water? Could you wear glasses so that you *could*

see under water? Would the lenses be converging or diverging?

Exercises

Section 38–1   The Thin Lens

Section 38–2   Graphical Methods

38–1 A converging lens has a focal length of 15.0 cm. For an object to the left of the lens, at distances of 30.0 cm, 20.0 cm, 10.0 cm, and 5.00 cm, determine

  a) the image position;

  b) the magnification;

  c) whether the image is real or virtual;

  d) whether the image is erect or inverted.

Be sure to draw a principal-ray diagram in each case.

38–2 Repeat Exercise 38–1 for the case in which the lens is diverging, with a focal length of −10.0 cm.

38–3 A converging lens with a focal length of 10.0 cm forms a real image 1.00 cm tall, 14.0 cm to the right of the lens. Determine the position and size of the object. Is the image erect or inverted? Draw a principal-ray diagram for this situation.

38–4 An object is 10.0 cm to the left of a lens. The lens forms an image 20.0 cm to the right of the lens.

  a) What is the focal length of the lens? Is the lens converging or diverging?

  b) If the object is 1.00 cm tall, how tall is the image? Is it erect or inverted?

  c) Draw a principal-ray diagram.

38–5 A lens forms an image of an object. The object is 20.0 cm from the lens. The image is 5.00 cm from the lens on the same side as the object.

  a) What is the focal length of the lens? Is the lens converging or diverging?

  b) If the object is 2.00 cm tall, how tall is the image? Is it erect or inverted?

  c) Draw a principal-ray diagram.

38–6 A converging lens with a focal length of 2.00 cm forms an image of a 40.0-cm tall object that is to the left of the lens. The image is 5.00 cm tall and inverted. Where are the object and image located in relation to the lens? Is the image real or virtual?

38–7 A converging lens with a focal length of 2.00 cm forms an image of a 5.00-cm tall object that is to the left of the lens. The image is 40.0 cm tall and erect.

Where are the object and image located? Is the image real or virtual?

38–8 You are standing to the left of a lens that projects an image of you onto a wall 1.80 m to your right. The image is three times your height.

  a) How far are you from the lens?

  b) Is your image erect or inverted?

  c) What is the focal length of the lens? Is the lens converging or diverging?

38–9 Prove that the image of a real object formed by a diverging lens is *always* virtual.

Section 38–3   Images as Objects

38–10 A layer of benzene ($n = 1.50$) 3.00 cm deep floats on water ($n = 1.33$) that is 4.00 cm deep. What is the apparent distance from the upper benzene surface to the bottom of the water layer when it is viewed at normal incidence?

38–11 Sketch the various possible thin lenses that can be obtained by combining two surfaces whose radii of curvature are 10.0 cm and 20.0 cm in absolute magnitude. Which are converging and which are diverging? Find the focal length of each if the lenses are made of glass with index of refraction 1.60.

38–12 A diverging meniscus lens (see Fig. 38–5b) with a refractive index of 1.48 has spherical surfaces whose radii are 4.00 and 2.50 cm. What is the position of the image if an object is placed 18.0 cm to the left of the lens?

38–13 Both ends of a glass rod 10.0 cm in diameter, with an index of 1.50, are ground and polished to convex hemispherical surfaces. The radius of curvature at the left end is 5.00 cm, and the radius of curvature at the right end is 10.0 cm. The length of the rod between vertexes is 50.0 cm. An arrow 1.00 mm long, at right angles to the axis and 20.0 cm to the left of the first vertex, constitutes the object for the first surface.

  a) What constitutes the object for the second surface?

  b) What is the object distance for the second surface?

  c) Is the object for the second surface real or virtual?

  d) What is the position of the image formed by the second surface?

38–14 A transparent rod 40.0 cm long and with a refractive index of 1.50 is cut flat at the right-hand end and rounded to a hemispherical surface with a 12.0-cm radius at the left-hand end. An object is placed on the axis of the rod 12.0 cm to the left of the vertex of the hemispherical end.

a) What is the position of the final image?

b) What is its magnification?

38–15 A narrow beam of parallel rays enters a solid glass sphere in a radial direction. At what point outside the sphere are these rays brought to a focus? The radius of the sphere is 2.00 cm, and its index of refraction is 1.50.

38–16 The rod in Exercise 38–13 is now shortened to a distance of 15.0 cm between its vertexes; the curvatures of its ends remain the same. As in Exercise 38–13, an arrow 1.00 mm tall and 20.0 cm to the left of the first vertex constitutes the object for the first surface.

a) What is the object distance for the second surface?

b) Is the object for the second surface real or virtual?

c) What is the position of the image formed by the second surface?

d) Is the final image real or virtual? Is it erect or inverted with respect to the original object?

e) What is the height of the final image?

38–17 The radii of curvature of the surfaces of a thin converging meniscus lens are $R_1 = +10.0$ cm and $R_2 = +30.0$ cm. The index of refraction is 1.50.

a) Compute the position and size of the image of an object in the form of an arrow 1.00 cm high, perpendicular to the lens axis, and 50.0 cm to the left of the lens. Is this image erect or inverted?

b) A second converging lens with the same focal length is placed 120 cm to the right of the first. Find the position and size of the final image. Is the final image erect or inverted?

c) Repeat part (b) except that the second lens is 40.0 cm to the right of the first.

d) Repeat part (c) except that the second lens, of focal length −30.0 cm, is diverging.

38–18 Three thin lenses, each with a focal length of 20.0 cm, are aligned on a common axis; adjacent lenses are separated by 30.0 cm. Find the position of the image of a small object on the axis, 40.0 cm to the left of the first lens.

38–19 An eyepiece consists of two converging thin lenses, each with a focal length of 9.00 cm, separated by a distance of 3.00 cm. Where are the first and second focal points of the eyepiece?

38–20 Two thin lenses with a focal length of magnitude 10.0 cm, the first converging and the second diverging, are placed 8.00 cm apart. An object 2.00 mm tall is placed 20.0 cm to the left of the first (converging) lens.

a) How far from this first lens is the final image formed?

b) Is the final image real or virtual?

c) What is the height of the final image? Is the final image erect or inverted?

Section 38–5   The Eye

38–21

a) Where is the near point of an eye for which a lens with a power of +2.50 diopters is prescribed?

b) Where is the far point of an eye for which a lens with a power of −0.750 diopter is prescribed for distant vision?

38–22 In a simplified model of the human eye the aqueous and vitreous humors and the lens all have a refractive index of 1.40, and all the refraction occurs at the cornea, whose vertex is 2.60 cm from the retina. What should be the radius of curvature of the cornea in order to focus on the retina the image of an infinitely distant object?

38–23 For the model of the eye described in Exercise 38–22, what should be the radius of curvature of the cornea in order to focus on the retina the image of an object 25.0 cm from the cornea?

38–24 Determine the power of the corrective lenses required

a) by a hyperopic eye whose near point is at 75.0 cm,

b) by a myopic eye whose far point is at 60.0 cm.

Section 38–6   The Camera

38–25 A camera lens has a focal length of 135 mm. How far from the lens should the subject for the photo be if the lens is 14.8 cm from the film?

38–26 During a lunar eclipse, a picture of the moon (diameter 3.48×10^6 m, distance from earth 3.86×10^8 m) is taken with a camera whose lens has a focal length of 300 mm. What is the diameter of the image on the film?

38–27 The picture size on ordinary 35-mm camera film is 24×36 mm. Focal lengths of lenses available for 35-mm cameras typically include 28, 35, 50 (the "standard" lens), 85, 100, 135, 200, and 300 mm, among others. Which of these lenses should be used to photograph the following objects, assuming that the object is to fill most of the picture area?

a) A cathedral 100 m high and 150 m long at a distance of 150 m.

b) An eagle with a wingspan of 2.0 m at a distance of 12.0 m.

38–28 When a camera is focused, the lens is moved away from or toward the film. If you take a picture of your friend who is standing 4.00 m from the lens, with a camera with a 50 mm focal length lens, how far from the film is the lens? Will the whole image of your friend who is 175 cm tall fit on film that is 24 × 36 mm?

38–29 Camera *A*, having an *f*/8 lens with an aperture diameter of 2.50 cm, photographs an object using the correct exposure time of 1/60 s. What exposure time should camera *B* use in photographing the same object if it has an *f*/4 lens with an aperture diameter of 5.00 cm?

38–30 The focal length of an *f*/2.8 camera lens is 10.0 cm.

a) What is the aperture diameter of the lens?

b) If the correct exposure of a certain scene is 1/100 s at *f*/2.8, what is the correct exposure at *f*/5.6?

Section 38–7   The Projector

38–31 In Example 38–5, for a lens with a 98.0-mm focal length, it was found that the slide needs to be placed 10.0 cm in front of the lens to focus the image on a screen 5.00 m from the lens. Now assume instead that a 100-mm-focal-length lens is used.

a) If the screen remains 5.00 m from the lens, how far should the slide be in front of the lens?

b) Could the distance between the slide and lens be kept at 10.0 cm and the screen moved to achieve focus? If so, how far and in what direction would it have to be moved?

38–32 The dimensions of the picture on a 35-mm color slide are 24 × 36 mm. An image of the slide is projected on a screen 8.00 m from the projector lens. The focal length of the projector lens is 12.0 cm.

a) How far is the slide from the lens?

b) What are the dimensions of the image on the screen?

Section 38–8   The Magnifier

38–33 You are examining a flea with a magnifying lens that has a focal length of 2.50 cm. If the image of the flea is ten times the size of the flea, how far is the flea from the lens? Where is the image in relation to the lens?

38–34 A thin lens with a focal length of 5.0 cm is used as a simple magnifier.

a) What maximum angular magnification is obtainable with the lens?

b) When an object is examined through the lens, how close may it be brought to the lens?

Assume that the image viewed by the eye is at infinity.

38–35 The focal length of a simple magnifier is 15.0 cm.

a) How far in front of the magnifier should an object be placed if the image is formed at the observer's near point, 25.0 cm in front of her eye?

b) If the object is 1.00 mm high, what is the height of its image formed by the magnifier?

Assume the magnifier to be a thin lens placed very close to the eye.

Section 38–9   The Microscope

38–36 The focal length of the eyepiece of a certain microscope is 2.50 cm. The focal length of the objective is 16.0 mm. The distance between objective and eyepiece is 20.5 cm. The final image formed by the eyepiece is at infinity. Treat all lenses as thin.

a) What is the distance from the objective to the object being viewed?

b) What is the magnitude of the linear magnification produced by the objective?

c) What is the overall magnification of the microscope?

38–37 A certain microscope is provided with objectives that have focal lengths of 16.0 mm, 4.00 mm, and 1.90 mm and with eyepieces that have angular magnifications of 5× and 10×. Determine

a) the largest magnification obtainable,

b) the least magnification obtainable.

Each objective forms an image 120 mm beyond its second focal point.

38–38 The image formed by a microscope objective with a focal length of 4.00 mm is 180 mm from its second focal point. The eyepiece has a focal length of 26.0 mm.

a) What is the magnification of the microscope?

b) The unaided eye can distinguish two points at its near point as separate if they are about 0.10 mm apart. What is the minimum separation that can be resolved with this microscope?

Section 38–10   Telescopes

38–39 The eyepiece of a refracting telescope (Fig. 38–20) has a focal length of 5.00 cm. The distance between objective and eyepiece is 2.05 m, and the final image is at infinity. What is the angular magnification of the telescope?

38–40 The moon subtends an angle at the earth of approximately $\frac{1}{2}°$. What is the diameter of the image of the moon produced by the objective of the Lick Observatory telescope, a refractor having a focal length of 18.0 m?

38–41 A reflecting telescope (Fig. 38–22a) is made by using a spherical mirror with a radius of curvature of 0.600 m and an eyepiece with a focal length of 1.00 cm. The final image is at infinity.

a) What is the angular magnification?

b) What is the distance between the eyepiece and the mirror vertex if the object is taken to be at infinity?

38–42 The proposed space telescope (Fig. 1–1b) uses an optical system similar to that shown in Fig. 38–24 (Cassegrain system). The image of a far distant object is focused on the detector through a hole in the large (primary) mirror. The primary mirror has a focal length of 2.50 m, the distance between the vertexes of

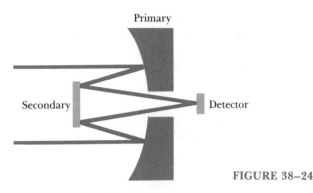

FIGURE 38–24

the two mirrors is 1.50 m, and the distance from the vertex of the primary mirror to the detector is 0.25 m. Should the smaller mirror (the secondary) be concave or convex? What is its radius of curvature? (*Note:* The space telescope is planned to be placed in earth orbit. A telescope in space, above the earth's atmosphere, would give much better viewing of astronomical objects than an earth-based telescope.)

Problems

38–43 An object is placed 16.0 cm from a screen.

a) At what two points between object and screen may a converging lens with a 3.00-cm focal length be placed to obtain an image on the screen?

b) What is the magnification of the image for each position of the lens?

38–44 An object to the left of a lens is imaged by the lens on a screen 8.00 cm to the right of the lens. When the lens is moved 2.00 cm to the right, the screen must be moved 2.00 cm to the left to refocus the image. Determine the focal length of the lens.

38–45 When an object is placed at the proper distance to the left of a converging lens, the image is focused on a screen 25.0 cm to the right of the lens. A diverging lens is now placed 12.5 cm to the right of the converging lens, and it is found that the screen must be moved 25.0 cm farther to the right to obtain a sharp image. What is the focal length of the diverging lens?

38–46

a) Prove that when two thin lenses with focal lengths f_1 and f_2 are placed *in contact*, the focal length f of the combination is given by the relation

$$\frac{1}{f} = \frac{1}{f_1} + \frac{1}{f_2}.$$

b) A converging meniscus lens (Fig. 38–5a) has an index of refraction of 1.50, and the radii of its sur-

faces are 4.00 and 8.00 cm. The concave surface is placed upward and filled with water. What is the focal length of the water–glass combination?

38–47 A lens operates via Snell's Law, bending light rays at each surface an amount determined by the index of refraction of the lens and the index of the medium in which the lens is located.

a) Equation (38–6) assumes that the lens is surrounded by air. Consider instead a thin lens immersed in a liquid with refractive index n_{liq}. Prove that the focal length f' is then given by Eq. (38–6) with n replaced by n/n_{liq}.

b) A thin lens with index n has a focal length f in vacuum. Use the result of part (a) to show that when this lens is immersed in a liquid of index n_{liq}, it will have a new focal length

$$f' = \left[\frac{n_{liq}(n-1)}{n - n_{liq}} \right] f.$$

38–48 In the arrangement shown in Fig. 38–25 the candle is at the center of curvature of the concave mirror whose focal length is 10.0 cm. The converging lens has a focal length of 35.0 cm and is 85.0 cm to the right of the candle. The candle is viewed looking through the lens from the right. The lens forms two images of the candle. The first is formed by light passing directly through the lens. The second image is formed from the light that goes from the candle to the mirror, is reflected, and then passes through the lens. For *each* of these two images, answer the following questions:

a) Draw a principal-ray diagram that locates the image.

b) Where is the image?

c) Is the image real or virtual?

d) Is the image erect or inverted?

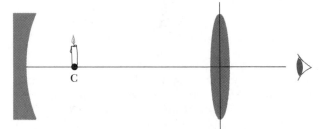

FIGURE 38–25

38–49 Your camera has a lens with a 50.0-mm focal length and a viewfinder that is 20.0 mm (high) by 30.0 mm (long). In taking a picture of a 3.50-m-long automobile you find that the image of the auto fills only two-thirds of the viewfinder.

a) How far are you from the auto?

b) How close should you stand if you want to fill the viewfinder frame with the auto's image?

38–50 A thin-walled glass sphere with radius R is filled with water. An object is placed a distance $3R$ from the surface of the sphere. Determine the position of the final image. The effect of the glass wall may be neglected. The refractive index of the water is 4/3.

38–51 A glass rod with a refractive index of 1.50 is ground and polished at both ends to hemispherical surfaces with a radius of 5.00 cm. When an object is placed on the axis of the rod, 20.0 cm to the left of one end, the final image is formed 50.0 cm to the right of the opposite end. What is the length of the rod measured between the vertexes of the two hemispherical surfaces?

38–52 Rays from a lens are converging toward a point image P located to the right of the lens. What thickness t of glass with an index of refraction of 1.50 must be interposed between the lens and P for the image to be formed at P', located 0.3 cm to the right of P? The location of the piece of glass and of points P and P' are shown in Fig. 38–26.

38–53 A glass plate 2.00 cm thick, with an index of refraction of 1.50, and having plane parallel faces is held with its faces horizontal and its lower face 6.00 cm above a printed page. Find the position of the image of

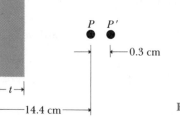

FIGURE 38–26

the page formed by rays making a small angle with the normal to the plate.

38–54

a) Show that when two thin lenses are placed in contact, the *power* of the combination in diopters, as defined in Section 38–5, is the sum of the powers of the separate lenses. Is this relation valid even when one lens has positive power and the other negative?

b) Two thin converging lenses with 20.0-cm and 40.0-cm focal lengths are in contact. What is the power of the combination?

38–55 The *resolution* of a camera lens can be defined as the maximum number of lines per millimeter in the image that can barely be distinguished as separate lines. A certain lens has a focal length of 50.0 mm and a resolution of 100 lines·mm^{-1}. What is the minimum separation of two lines in an object 40.0 m away if they are to be visible in the image as separate lines?

38–56 A certain very nearsighted person cannot focus anything farther than 20.0 cm from the eye. Consider the simplified model of the eye described in Exercise 38–22. If the radius of curvature of the cornea is 0.70 cm when the eye is focusing on an object 20 cm from the cornea vertex and the indexes of refraction are as described in Exercise 38–22, what is the cornea-vertex-to-retina distance? What does this tell you about the shape of the nearsighted eye?

38–57 A microscope with an objective that has a focal length of 8.00 mm and an eyepiece that has a focal length of 5.00 cm is used to project an image on a screen 1.00 m from the eyepiece. Let the image distance of the objective be 18.0 cm.

a) What is the lateral magnification of the image?

b) What is the distance between the objective and the eyepiece?

38–58 A crude telescope is constructed of two eyeglass lenses with focal lengths of 80.0 cm and 20.0 cm, the 80.0-cm lens being used as the objective. Both the object being viewed and the final image are at infinity.

a) Find the angular magnification for the telescope.

b) Find the height of the image formed by the objective of a building 80.0 m high, 2.00 km away.

c) What is the angular size of the final image as viewed by an eye very close to the eyepiece?

38–59 Figure 38–27 is a diagram of a *Galilean telescope*, or *opera glass*, with both object and final image at infinity. The image I serves as a virtual object for the eyepiece. The final image is virtual and erect.

a) Prove that the angular magnification $M = -f_1/f_2$.

b) A Galilean telescope is to be constructed with the same objective lens as in Problem 38–58. What focal length should the eyepiece have if this tele-

scope is to have the same magnification as the one in Problem 38–58?

c) Compare the lengths of the telescopes.

38–60 A certain reflecting telescope, constructed as in Fig. 38–22a, has a mirror that is 10.0 cm in diameter with a radius of curvature of 0.800 m and an eyepiece with a focal length of 1.00 cm. If the angular magnification has a magnitude of 36 and the object is at infinity, find the position of the lens and the position and nature (real or virtual) of the final image. (*Note:* $|M|$ is *not* equal to $|f_1/f_2|$, so the image formed by the eyepiece is *not* at infinity.)

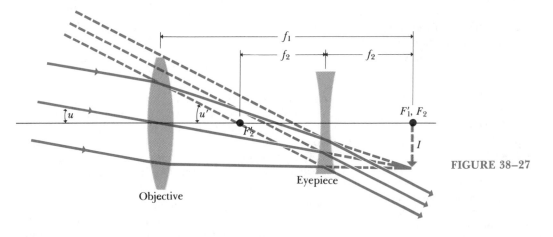

Objective   Eyepiece

FIGURE 38–27

Challenge Problems

38–61 A thick-walled wine goblet sitting on a table can be considered to be a glass sphere with an outer radius of 4.00 cm and having a spherical cavity with a radius of 3.00 cm. The index of refraction of the goblet glass is 1.50.

a) A beam of parallel light rays enters the side of the empty goblet along a horizontal radius. Where, if anywhere, will an image be formed?

b) The goblet is now filled with white wine ($n = 1.37$). Where is the image now formed?

38–62 A 20.0-cm-long pencil is placed at a 45° angle, with its center 15.0 cm above the optic axis and 45.0 cm from a 20.0-cm-focal-length lens, as shown in Fig. 38–28.

a) Where is the image of the pencil? (Give the location of the images of the points A, B, and C on the object, which are located at the eraser, point, and center of the pencil, respectively.)

b) What is the length of the image, the distance between the images of points A and B?

c) Show the orientation of the image in a sketch. Neglect aberration effects.

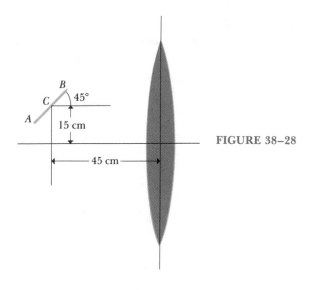

FIGURE 38–28

38–63 A person with normal vision cannot focus his or her eyes underwater.

a) Why not?

b) With the simplified model of the eye described in Exercise 38–22, what corrective lens (specified by focal length, as measured in air) would be needed to enable a person underwater to focus an infinitely distant object? (Be careful—the focal length of a lens underwater is not the same as that in air! See Problem 38–47. Assume that the corrective lens has a refractive index in air of 1.60.)

38–64 A solid glass sphere with radius R and an index of refraction of 1.60 is silvered over one hemisphere, as in Fig. 38–29. A small object is located on the axis of the sphere at a distance $2R$ to the left of the vertex of the unsilvered hemisphere. Find the position of the final image after all refractions and reflections have taken place.

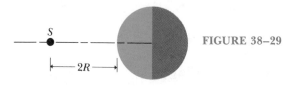

FIGURE 38–29

38–65 A convex mirror and a concave mirror are placed on the same optic axis, separated by a distance $L = 0.600$ m. The radius of curvature of each mirror has a magnitude of 0.400 m. A light source is located a distance x from the concave mirror, as shown in Fig. 38–30.

a) What distance x will result in the rays from the source returning to the source after reflecting first from the convex mirror and then from the concave mirror?

b) Repeat part (a), but now let the rays reflect first from the concave mirror and then from the convex one.

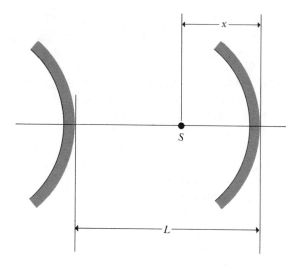

FIGURE 38–30

38–66 A symmetric double-convex thin lens made of glass with an index of refraction of 3/2 has a focal length in air of 30.0 cm. The lens is sealed into an opening in the left end of a tank filled with water. At the right-hand end of the tank, opposite the lens, is a plane mirror 80.0 cm from the lens. The index of refraction of the water is 4/3.

a) Find the position of the image formed by the lens–water–mirror system of a small object outside the tank on the lens axis and 120 cm to the left of the lens.

b) Is the image real or virtual?

c) Is it erect or inverted?

d) If the object has a height of 4.00 mm, what is the height of the image?

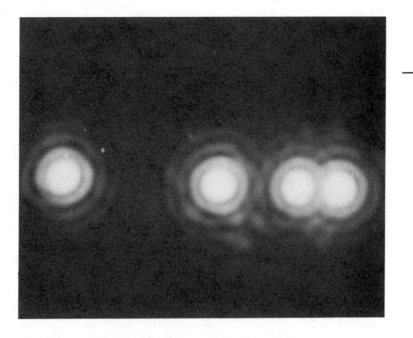

39

Interference and Diffraction

In our analysis of lenses and mirrors we have represented light as *rays* that travel in straight lines in a homogeneous material and are bent at a reflecting or refracting surface. This is the model of *geometrical optics*, and it is all we need to understand the formation of images by lenses and mirrors.

In this chapter we will study *interference* and *diffraction* phenomena. These are inherently *wave* phenomena, and they *cannot* be understood on the basis of geometrical optics. Instead, we must return to the more general view that light is a *wave motion*. When several waves overlap at a point, their total effect depends on the *phases* of the waves as well as their amplitudes. When light passes through apertures or around obstacles, patterns are formed that result from the wave nature of light and cannot be understood on the basis of rays. We will look at several practical applications of physical optics, including diffraction gratings, X-ray diffraction, and holography.

39–1
Interference and Coherent Sources

In our discussions of mechanical waves in Chapter 21 and electromagnetic waves in Chapter 35 we often talked about *sinusoidal* waves with a single frequency and a single wavelength. In optics, such a wave is called a **monochromatic** (single-color) wave. Common sources of light, such as an incandescent light bulb or a flame, *do not* emit monochromatic light but rather a continuous distribution of wavelengths.

A precisely monochromatic light wave is an idealization, but monochromatic light can be *approximated* in the laboratory. There are filters that block all but a narrow range of wavelengths. Gas-discharge lamps, such as the mercury-vapor lamp, emit light with a discrete set of colors, each having a narrow band of wavelengths. The bright green line in the spectrum of a mercury-vapor lamp has a wavelength of about 546.1 nm, with a spread of the order of ±0.001 nm. By far the most nearly monochromatic source available at present is the *laser*, which we will study in Chapter 41. The familiar helium-neon laser, inexpensive and readily available, emits visible light at 632.8 nm with a line width (wavelength range) of the order of ±0.000001 nm, or about one part in 10^9. When we analyze interference and diffraction phenomena in this chapter, we will always assume that we are working with monochromatic waves.

The term **interference** refers to any situation in which two or more waves overlap in space. When this occurs, the total displacement at any point at any instant of time is governed by the **principle of linear superposition.** This is the most important principle in all of physical optics. It states that *when two or more waves overlap, the resultant displacement at any point and at any instant may be found by adding the instantaneous displacements that would be produced at the point by the individual waves if each were present alone.*

We use the term *displacement* in a general sense. With waves on the surface of a liquid we mean the actual displacement of the surface above or below its normal level. With sound waves the term refers to the excess or deficiency of pressure. For electromagnetic waves we mean the magnitude of the electric or magnetic field.

To introduce the essential ideas of interference, consider first the problem of two identical sources of monochromatic waves, S_1 and S_2, separated in space by a certain distance. The two sources are permanently *in phase*; they vibrate in unison. They might be two agitators in a ripple tank, two loudspeakers driven by the same amplifier, two radio antennas powered by the same transmitter, or two small apertures in an opaque screen illuminated by the same monochromatic light source.

We position the sources S_1 and S_2 along the y-axis, equidistant from the origin, as shown in Fig. 39–1. Let P_0 be any point on the x-axis. From symmetry the two distances S_1P_0 and S_2P_0 are equal; waves from the two sources thus require equal times to travel to P_0. Waves that leave S_1 and S_2 in phase arrive at P_0 in phase. The total amplitude at P_0 is then *twice* the amplitude of each individual wave.

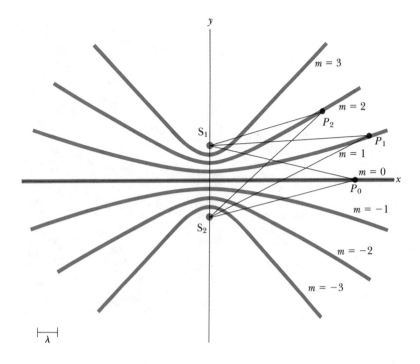

Curves of maximum intensity in the interference pattern of two monochromatic point sources. In this example the distance between sources is four times the wavelength.

Similarly, the distance from point P_1 to S_2 is exactly one wavelength greater than the distance from P_1 to S_1; that is,

$$S_2P_1 - S_1P_1 = \lambda.$$

A wave crest from S_1 arrives at P_1 exactly one cycle earlier than the crest emitted at the same time from S_2, and again the two waves arrive *in phase*. For point P_2 the path difference is *two* wavelengths, $(S_2P_2 - S_1P_2 = 2\lambda)$, and again the two waves arrive in phase. And so on.

The addition of amplitudes that results when waves from two or more sources arrive at a point *in phase* is called **constructive interference** or *reinforcement*. Constructive interference occurs whenever the path difference for the two sources is an integral multiple of the wavelength:

$$S_2P - S_1P = m\lambda \qquad (m = 0, \pm 1, \pm 2, \pm 3, \ldots). \qquad (39-1)$$

In our example the points satisfying this condition lie on the set of curves shown in Fig. 39–1.

Intermediate between these curves is another set of curves for which the path difference for the two sources is a *half-integer* number of wavelengths. Waves from the two sources arrive at a point on one of these lines exactly a half-cycle out of phase, and the resultant amplitude is the *difference* between the two individual amplitudes. If the amplitudes are equal, the *total* amplitude is zero! This condition is called **destructive interference** or *cancellation*. In our example the condition for destructive interference is

$$S_2P - S_1P = (m + \tfrac{1}{2})\lambda \qquad (m = 0, \pm 1, \pm 2, \pm 3, \ldots). \qquad (39-2)$$

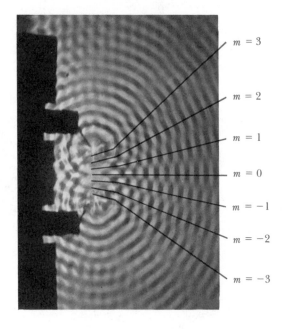

39–2
Photograph of an interference pattern produced by water waves in a shallow ripple tank. The two wave sources are small balls moved up and down by the same vibrating mechanism. As waves move outward from the sources, they overlap and produce an interference pattern. The lines of maximum amplitude in the pattern are shown by the superposed color lines. (*PSSC Physics,* second edition, 1965; D. C. Heath and Co., with Educational Development Center, Inc., Newton, Mass.)

An example of this interference pattern is the familiar ripple-tank pattern shown in Fig. 39–2. The two wave sources are two agitators driven by the same vibrating mechanism. The regions of both maximum and zero amplitude are clearly visible. The superimposed color lines, corresponding to those in Fig. 39–1, show the lines of maximum amplitude.

The constant *phase* relationship between the sources is essential. When the wave is light, there is no practical way to achieve such a relationship with two separate sources because of the way light is emitted. In ordinary light sources, atoms gain excess energy by thermal agitation or by impact with accelerated electrons. An atom thus "excited" begins to radiate energy and continues until it has lost all the energy it can, typically in a time of the order of 10^{-8} s. The many atoms in a source ordinarily radiate in an unsynchronized and random phase relationship, and the light emitted from *two* such sources has no definite phase relation.

However, the light from a single source can be split so that parts of it emerge from two or more regions of space, forming two or more *secondary sources.* Then any random phase change in the source affects these secondary sources equally and does not change their *relative* phase. Two such sources that are derived from a single primary source and have a definite phase relation are said to be **coherent.**

The distinguishing feature of light from a *laser* is that the emission of light from many atoms is *synchronized* in frequency and phase by mechanisms that we will discuss in Chapter 41. As a result, the random phase changes mentioned above occur *much* less frequently. Definite phase relations are preserved over correspondingly much greater lengths in the beam, and laser light is much more *coherent* than ordinary light.

39–2
Two-Source Interference

One of the earliest quantitative experiments with interference of light was performed in 1800 by the English scientist Thomas Young (1773–1829). His experiment involved interference of light from two sources, which we discussed in Section 39–1.

Young's apparatus is shown schematically in Fig. 39–3a. Monochromatic light emerging from a narrow slit S_0 (0.1 mm or so wide) falls on a screen with two other narrow slits S_1 and S_2, each 0.1 mm or so wide and 1.0 mm or less apart. According to Huygens' principle (Section 36–7), cylindrical wave fronts spread out from slit S_0 and reach slits S_1 and S_2 *in phase* because they travel equal distances from S_0. The waves emerging from the two slits are therefore in phase, and they act as two *coherent* sources (Fig. 39–3b). But the waves do not necessarily arrive at point P in phase because of the path difference $(r_2 - r_1)$.

To simplify the following analysis, we will assume that the distance R from the slits to the screen is so large in comparison to the slit spacing d that the lines from S_1 and S_2 to P are very nearly parallel, as shown in Fig. 39–3c. In this case the difference in path length is given by

$$r_1 - r_2 = d \sin \theta. \tag{39–3}$$

We found in Section 39–1 that constructive interference (reinforcement) occurs at point P when the path difference $d \sin \theta$ is an integral

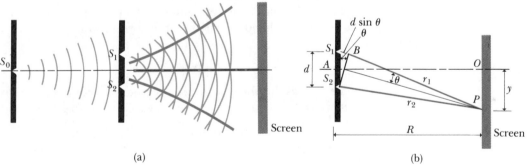

(a)   (b)

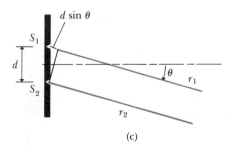

(c)

39–3
(a) Interference of light waves passing through two slits. (b) Geometrical analysis of Young's experiment. (c) Approximate geometry when R is much larger than d.

Zeroth fringe

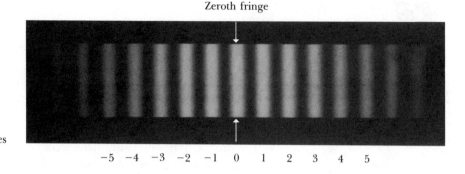

39–4
Interference fringes produced by
Young's double-slit experiment. Values
of m are shown.

$$-5 \quad -4 \quad -3 \quad -2 \quad -1 \quad 0 \quad 1 \quad 2 \quad 3 \quad 4 \quad 5$$

number of wavelengths, $m\lambda$, where $m = 0$, ± 1, ± 2, ± 3, ... So constructive interference occurs at angles θ for which

$$d \sin \theta = m\lambda \qquad (m = 0, \pm 1, \pm 2, \ldots). \qquad (39\text{–}4)$$

Similarly, complete cancellation or destructive interference occurs when the path difference is a half-integral number of wavelengths, $(m + \frac{1}{2})\lambda$:

$$d \sin \theta = (m + \tfrac{1}{2})\lambda \qquad (m = 0, \pm 1, \pm 2, \ldots). \qquad (39\text{–}5)$$

Thus the pattern on the screen of Fig. 39–3b is a succession of bright and dark bands. An actual photograph of such a pattern is shown in Fig. 39–4.

We can derive an expression for the positions of the centers of the bright bands. In Fig. 39–3b, y is the distance from the center of the pattern, corresponding to horizontal distance from the center of Fig. 39–4. Let y_m be the distance from the center of the pattern ($\theta = 0$) to the center of the mth bright band. We denote the corresponding value of θ as θ_m; then

$$y_m = R \tan \theta_m.$$

In experiments such as this the y_m's are always much smaller than R. This means that θ_m is very small, $\tan \theta_m$ is very nearly equal to $\sin \theta_m$, and

$$y_m = R \sin \theta_m.$$

Combining this with Eq. (39–4), we find

$$y_m = R\,\frac{m\lambda}{d} \qquad (39\text{–}6)$$

and

$$\lambda = \frac{y_m d}{mR}. \qquad (39\text{–}7)$$

We can measure R and d as well as the positions y_m of the bright fringes. Thus this experiment provides a direct measurement of the wavelength λ.

Example 39–1 In a two-slit interference experiment with the slits 0.20 mm apart and a screen at a distance of 1.0 m, the third bright fringe (not counting the central bright fringe straight ahead from the slits) is found to be displaced 7.5 mm from the central fringe. Find the wavelength of the light used.

Solution From Eq. (39–7),

$$\lambda = \frac{y_m d}{mR} = \frac{(0.75 \text{ cm})(0.020 \text{ cm})}{(3)(100 \text{ cm})} = 5.0 \times 10^{-5} \text{ cm}$$
$$= 500 \times 10^{-9} \text{ m} = 500 \text{ nm.} \qquad \blacksquare$$

We have described the experiment that Young performed with visible light, but a completely analogous experiment can be done with any other electromagnetic waves, such as radio waves.

Example 39–2 A radio station operating at a frequency of 1500 kHz = 1.5×10^6 Hz (the top end of the AM broadcast band) has two identical vertical dipole antennas spaced 400 m apart. In what directions is the intensity greatest in the resulting radiation pattern?

Solution The two antennas, seen from above, correspond to slits S_1 and S_2 in Fig. 39–3. The wavelength is $\lambda = c/f = 200$ m. The directions of the intensity *maxima* are the values of θ for which the path difference is zero or an integer number of wavelengths, as given by Eq. (39–4). Inserting the numerical values, with $m = 0, \pm 1, \pm 2$, we find

$$\sin\theta = \frac{m\lambda}{d} = \frac{m}{2}, \qquad \theta = 0, \pm 30°, \pm 90°.$$

In this example, values of m greater than 2 or less than -2 give values of $\sin\theta$ greater than 1 or less than -1, which is impossible. There is *no* direction for which the path difference is three or more wavelengths. Thus values of m of ± 3 and beyond have no physical meaning in this example.

The angles for zero intensity (complete destructive interference) are given by Eq. (39–5), with $m = -2, -1, 0, 1$:

$$\sin\theta = \frac{(m + \frac{1}{2})\lambda}{d} = \frac{m + \frac{1}{2}}{2}, \qquad \theta = \pm 14.5°, \pm 48.6°.$$

Other values of m have no physical significance in this example. $\blacksquare$

39–3
Interference in Thin Films

You often see bright bands of color when light is reflected from a soap bubble or from a thin layer of oil floating on water. These are the results of interference effects. Light waves are reflected from opposite surfaces of the thin films, and constructive interference between the two reflected

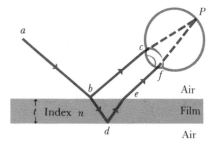

39–5
Interference between rays reflected from the upper and lower surfaces of a thin film.

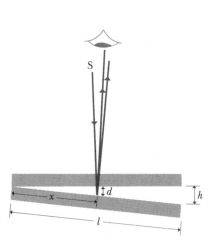

39–6
Interference between two light waves reflected from the two sides of an air wedge separating two glass plates. The path difference is 2*d*. Reflections from the top surface of the top plate and the bottom surface of the bottom plate are not shown.

waves occurs in different places for different wavelengths. The situation is shown schematically in Fig. 39–5. Light shining on the upper surface of a thin film is partly reflected at the upper surface (path *abc*). Light *transmitted* at the upper surface is partly reflected at the lower surface (path *abdef*). The two reflected waves come together at point *P* on the retina of the eye. Depending on the phase relationship, they may interfere constructively or destructively. Different colors have different wavelengths, so the interference may be constructive for some colors and destructive for others. That's why we see colored rings or fringes.

Here is an example involving *monochromatic* light reflected from two nearly parallel surfaces at nearly normal incidence. Figure 39–6 shows two plates of glass separated by a thin wedge of air; we want to consider interference between the two light waves reflected from the surfaces adjacent to the air wedge, as shown. (There are also reflections from the top surface of the upper plate and the bottom surface of the lower plate; to keep our discussion simple, we won't include those.) The situation is the same as in Fig. 39–5 except that the film thickness is not uniform. The path difference between the two waves is just twice the thickness *d* of the air wedge at each point. At points where 2*d* is an integer number of wavelengths, we expect to see constructive interference and a bright area; where it is a half-integer number of wavelengths, we expect destructive interference and a dark area. Along the line where the plates are in contact there is *no* path difference, and we expect a bright area.

When we carry out the experiment, the bright and dark fringes appear as expected, but they are interchanged! Along the line of contact we find a *dark* fringe, not a bright one. What happened? Somehow one of the waves has undergone a half-cycle phase shift during its reflection, so the two reflected waves are a half-cycle out of phase even though they have the same path length.

Further experiments show that a half-cycle phase change *does* occur whenever the material in which the wave is initially traveling (before reflection) has a *smaller* index of refraction than the second material forming the interface. But when the first material has a *greater* index of refraction than the second, such as a wave in glass reflected internally at a glass–air interface, *no* phase change occurs. In Fig. 39–5 the wave reflected at point *b* is shifted by a half cycle, while the wave reflected at *d* is not. Similarly, in Fig. 39–6 the wave reflected from the lower surface of the air wedge is shifted half a cycle, but the other wave is not.

Example 39–3   Suppose the two glass plates in Fig. 39–6 are two microscope slides 10 cm long. At one end they are in contact; at the other end they are separated by a piece of paper 0.020 mm thick. What is the spacing of the interference fringes? Is the fringe adjacent to the line of contact bright or dark? Assume monochromatic light with $\lambda = 500$ nm.

Solution   The fringe at the line of contact is dark because the wave reflected from the lower surface of the air wedge has a half-cycle phase shift, while the wave from the upper surface has none. So the condition for *destructive* interference (a dark fringe) is that the path difference (2*d*) should be an integer number of wavelengths:

$$2d = m\lambda \qquad (m = 0, 1, 2, 3, \ldots). \qquad (39\text{–}8)$$

From similar triangles in Fig. 39–6, d is proportional to the distance x from the line of contact:

$$\frac{d}{x} = \frac{h}{l}.$$

Combining this with Eq. (39–8), we find

$$\frac{2xh}{l} = m\lambda,$$

or

$$x = m\frac{l\lambda}{2h} = m\frac{(0.10 \text{ m})(500 \times 10^{-9} \text{ m})}{(2)(0.020 \times 10^{-3} \text{ m})} = m(1.25 \text{ mm}).$$

Successive dark fringes, corresponding to successive integer values of m, are spaced 1.25 mm apart.

In this example, if the space between plates contains water ($n = 1.33$) instead of air, the phase changes are the same but the wavelength is $\lambda = \lambda_0/n = 376$ nm, and the fringe spacing is 0.94 mm. But what if the top plate is glass with $n = 1.4$, the wedge is filled with a silicone grease having $n = 1.5$, and $n = 1.6$ for the bottom plate? In this case there are half-cycle phase shifts at *both* surfaces adjacent to the wedge, and the line of contact corresponds to a *bright* fringe, not a dark one. The fringe spacing is again determined by the wavelength *in the wedge* (i.e., in the silicone grease), $\lambda = 500$ nm/1.5 = 333 nm; we invite you to show that the fringe spacing is 0.83 mm. ∎

39–7
Air film between a convex and a plane surface.

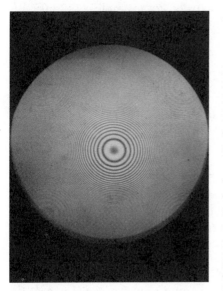

39–8
Newton's rings formed by interference in the air film between a convex and a plane surface. (Courtesy of Bausch & Lomb.)

If you place the convex surface of a lens in contact with a plane glass plate, as in Fig. 39–7, a thin film of air is formed between the two surfaces. If you now view the setup with monochromatic light, you see circular interference fringes, as shown in Fig. 39–8. These were studied by Newton and are called *Newton's rings*. When viewed by reflected light, the center of the pattern is black. Can you use the discussion of this section to show why this should be expected?

The surface of an optical part that is being ground to some desired curvature may be compared with another surface that is known to be correct by bringing the two in contact and observing the interference fringes. Figure 39–9 is a photograph made during the grinding of a telescope objective lens. The lower, larger-diameter, thicker disk is the master, and the smaller upper disk is the lens under test. The "contour lines" are Newton's interference fringes; each one indicates an additional distance between the specimen and the master of $\frac{1}{2}$ wavelength. At ten lines from the center spot the distance between the two surfaces is five wavelengths, or about 0.0001 inch. This isn't very good; high-quality lenses are routinely ground with a precision of less than one wavelength.

Thin-film interference occurs in nonreflective coatings for lenses. A thin layer or film of hard transparent material with an index of refrac-

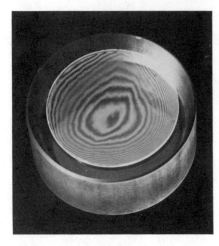

39–9
The surface of a telescope objective under inspection during manufacture. (Courtesy of Bushnell Division, Bausch & Lomb.)

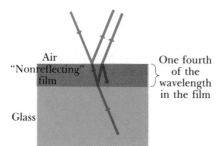

Air
"Nonreflecting" film

Glass

One fourth of the wavelength in the film

39–10
Destructive interference results when the film thickness is one quarter of the wavelength in the film.

tion smaller than that of the glass is deposited on the surface of the glass, as in Fig. 39–10. If the coating has the proper index of refraction, equal amounts of light are reflected from its outer surface and from the boundary surface between it and the glass. Furthermore, since in both reflections the light is reflected from a medium of greater index than that in which it is traveling, the same phase change occurs in each reflection. If the film thickness is $\frac{1}{4}$ wavelength *in the film* (assuming normal incidence), the light reflected from the first surface is one-half cycle out of phase with light reflected from the second, and there is complete destructive interference.

Of course, the thickness can be $\frac{1}{4}$ wavelength for only one particular wavelength. This is usually chosen in the central yellow-green portion of the spectrum (550 nm), where the eye is most sensitive. Then there is some reflection at both longer and shorter wavelengths, and the reflected light has a purple hue. The overall reflection from a lens or prism surface can be reduced in this way from 4 to 5% to less than 1%. This treatment is particularly important in eliminating stray reflected light in highly corrected lenses with many air–glass surfaces. A commonly used coating material is magnesium fluoride, MgF_2, with an index of 1.38. With this coating, the wavelength λ of green light in the coating is

$$\lambda = \frac{\lambda_0}{n} = \frac{550 \times 10^{-9} \text{ m}}{1.38} = 4.0 \times 10^{-5} \text{ cm},$$

and the thickness of a "nonreflecting" film of MgF_2 is 1.0×10^{-5} cm.

If a material with an index of refraction *greater* than that of glass is deposited on glass to a thickness of $\frac{1}{4}$ wavelength, then the reflectivity is *increased*. In this case there is a half-cycle phase shift at the air–film interface but none at the film–glass interface, and reflections from the two sides of the film interfere constructively. For example, a coating with an index of 2.5 allows 38% of the incident energy to be reflected, compared with 4% or so with no coating. By use of multiple-layer coatings, it is possible to achieve reflectivity for a particular wavelength of almost 100%. These coatings are used for "one-way" windows and reflecting sunglasses.

39–4
The Michelson Interferometer

The **Michelson interferometer** played an interesting role in the history of science during the latter part of the nineteenth century, and it has also had an important role in establishing high-precision length standards. In contrast to the Young two-slit experiment, which uses light from two very narrow sources, the Michelson interferometer uses light from a broad, spread-out source. Figure 39–11 is a diagram of its principal components. The figure shows the path of one ray from a point A of an extended monochromatic source. This ray strikes a glass plate C, whose right side has a thin coating of silver. Part of the light (ray 2) is reflected from the silvered surface at point P to the mirror M_2 and back through C to the observer's eye. The remainder of the light (ray 1) passes through

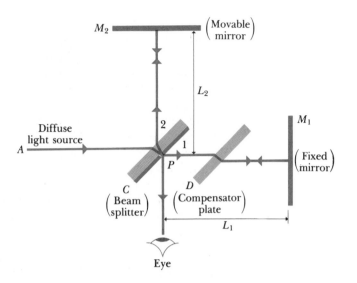

39–11
The Michelson interferometer.

the silvered surface and the compensator plate D and is reflected from mirror M_1. It then returns through D and is reflected from the silvered surface of C to the observer. The compensator plate D is cut from the same piece of glass as plate C, so its thickness is identical to that of C within a fraction of a wavelength. Its purpose is to ensure that rays 1 and 2 pass through the same thickness of glass. Plate C is called a *beam splitter*.

The whole apparatus is mounted on a very rigid frame, and a fine, very accurate micrometer screw is used to move mirror M_2. A common commercial model of the interferometer is shown in Fig. 39–12. The light source is placed to the left, and the observer is directly in front of the handle that turns the screw.

If the distances L_1 and L_2 in Fig. 39–11 are exactly equal, and the mirrors M_1 and M_2 are exactly at right angles, the virtual image of M_1 formed by reflection at the silvered surface of plate C coincides with

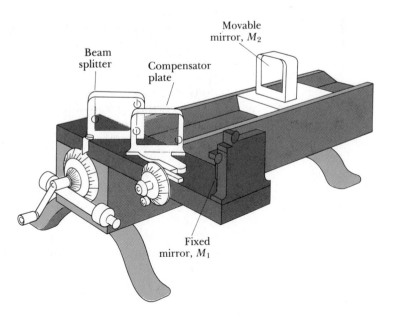

39–12
A common type of Michelson interferometer.

mirror M_2. If L_1 and L_2 are *not* exactly equal, the image of M_1 is displaced slightly from M_2; and if the mirrors are not exactly perpendicular, the image of M_1 makes a slight angle with M_2. Then the mirror M_2 and the virtual image of M_1 play the same roles as the two surfaces of a thin film, discussed in Section 39–3, and light reflected from these surfaces forms the same sort of interference fringes.

Suppose the angle between mirror M_2 and the virtual image of M_1 is just great enough that five or six vertical fringes are present in the field of view. If we now move the mirror M_2 slowly either backward or forward a distance $\lambda/2$, the effective film thickness changes by λ, and each fringe moves to the left or right a distance equal to the fringe spacing. If we observe the fringe positions through a telescope with a crosshair eyepiece, and m fringes cross the crosshair when we move the mirror a distance x, then

$$x = m\frac{\lambda}{2}, \qquad \text{or} \qquad \lambda = \frac{2x}{m}. \qquad (39\text{–}9)$$

If m is several thousand, the distance x is large enough that it can be measured with good precision, and we can obtain a precise value for the wavelength λ.

Until recently, the meter was defined as a length equal to 1,650,763.73 wavelengths of the orange-red light of krypton-86. Interferometers similar to the one we have described were used to calibrate other length-measuring instruments. As we mentioned in Section 1–2, this definition of the meter has recently been superseded by a new length standard based on the unit of *time* as defined by the cesium clock.

Another application of the Michelson interferometer with considerable historical interest is the **Michelson-Morley experiment.** To understand the purpose of this experiment, recall that before the electromagnetic theory of light and Einstein's special theory of relativity became established, most physicists believed that the propagation of light waves occurred in a medium called the **ether,** which was believed to permeate all space. In 1887, Michelson and Morley used the Michelson interferometer in an attempt to detect the motion of the earth through the ether. Suppose the interferometer in Fig. 39–11 is moving from left to right in relation to the ether. According to nineteenth-century theory, this would lead to changes in the speed of light in the portions of the path shown as horizontal lines in the figure. There would be fringe shifts relative to the positions the fringes *would have* if the instrument were at rest in the ether. Then when the entire instrument was rotated 90°, the other portions of the paths would be similarly affected, giving a fringe shift in the opposite direction.

Michelson and Morley expected that the motion of the earth through the ether would cause a fringe shift of about four tenths of a fringe when the instrument was rotated. The shift actually observed was less than a hundredth of a fringe and, within the limits of experimental uncertainty, appeared to be exactly zero. Despite its orbital motion around the sun, the earth appeared to be *at rest* relative to the ether. This negative result baffled physicists until Einstein developed the special theory of relativity in 1905. Einstein recognized that the speed of a light wave has the same magnitude c relative to *all* reference frames, no matter what their velocity may be relative to each other. The presumed ether then plays no role, and the concept of an ether has been abandoned.

The theory of relativity is a well-established cornerstone of modern physics, and we will study it in detail in Chapter 40. In retrospect, the negative result of the Michelson-Morley experiment gives strong experimental support to the special theory of relativity, and it is often called the most significant "negative-result" experiment ever performed.

39–5
Fresnel Diffraction

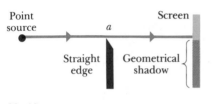

39–13
Geometrical shadow of a straight edge.

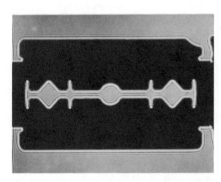

39–14
Shadow of a razor blade.

39–15
Shadow of a straight edge. The arrows show the position of the *geometric* shadow.

According to *geometrical* optics, when an opaque object is placed between a point light source and a screen, as in Fig. 39–13, the shadow of the object forms a sharp line. No light at all strikes the screen at points within the shadow, and the area outside the shadow is uniformly illuminated. But geometrical optics is an idealized model, and there are many situations in which the ray model of light is inadequate. An important class of such phenomena is grouped under the heading **diffraction.**

Here is an example. The photograph in Fig. 39–14 was made by placing a razor blade halfway between a pinhole illuminated by monochromatic light and a photographic film so that the film made a record of the shadow cast by the blade. Figure 39–15 is an enlargement of a region near the shadow of an edge of the blade. The *geometrical* shadow line is indicated by arrows. It is bordered by alternating bright and dark bands. There is some light in the shadow region, although this is not visible in the figure. The first bright band, just outside the geometrical shadow, is actually *brighter* than in the region of uniform illumination to the extreme left. This simple experimental setup gives us some idea of the complexity of what might seem to be a simple phenomenon, the casting of a shadow by an opaque object.

We don't often observe diffraction patterns such as that in Fig. 39–14 in everyday life because most ordinary light sources are not point sources of monochromatic light. If we use a frosted light bulb instead of a point source in Fig. 39–13, the light from every point of the bulb forms its own diffraction pattern, but the patterns overlap to such an extent that no individual pattern can be observed.

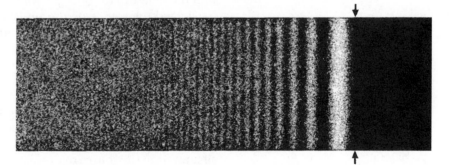

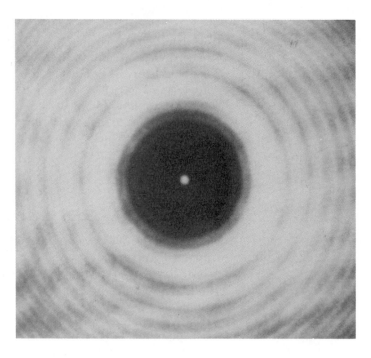

39-16
Fresnel diffraction pattern formed by a steel ball 3 mm in diameter. The Poisson bright spot is seen at the center of the shadow area. (From Eugene Hecht, *Optics*, 2nd edition, © 1987, Addison-Wesley Publishing Co., Inc., Reading, MA. Fig. 10.56. Reprinted by permission of the publisher.)

Diffraction is sometimes described as "the bending of light around an obstacle." But the process by which diffraction effects are produced is going on continuously in the propagation of *every* wave. When part of the wave is cut off by some obstacle, we observe diffraction effects. Every optical instrument uses only a limited portion of a wave; for example, a telescope uses only the part of a wave admitted by its objective lens. Thus diffraction plays a role in nearly all optical phenomena.

Figure 39-16 shows a diffraction pattern formed by a steel ball about 3 mm in diameter. Note the rings in the pattern, both outside and inside the geometrical shadow area, and the bright spot at the very center of the shadow. The existence of this spot was predicted in 1818 by the French mathematician Poisson. Ironically, Poisson himself was *not* a believer in the wave theory of light, and he published this *apparently* absurd result to ridicule the wave theory. But almost immediately after that, the bright spot was actually observed by Arago. It had in fact been seen in 1723 by Maraldi, but its significance was not recognized then.

The fringe patterns formed by diffraction effects can be analyzed with the help of Huygens' principle: Every point of a wave front can be considered the source of a secondary wave that spreads out in all directions. At every point we must combine all the individual displacements produced by these secondary waves, taking into account their amplitudes and relative phases. The mathematical operations can become quite complicated.

In Fig. 39-13, both the point source and the screen are at finite distances from the obstacle forming the diffraction pattern. This situation is described as **Fresnel diffraction** (after Augustin Jean Fresnel, 1788-1827). If the source, obstacle, and screen are far enough away that all lines from the source to the obstacle can be considered parallel and all lines from the obstacle to a point in the pattern can be considered parallel, the phenomenon is called **Fraunhofer diffraction** (after Joseph von Fraunhofer, 1787–1826). These situations are simpler to analyze in detail than Fresnel diffraction, and we will restrict our discussion to Fraunhofer diffraction.

39–6
Fraunhofer Diffraction from a Single Slit

In this section we consider the diffraction pattern formed by monochromatic light emerging from a long, narrow slit, as shown in Fig. 39–17. According to geometrical optics, the transmitted beam should have the same cross section as the slit, as in Fig. 39–17a. What is *actually* observed is the pattern shown in Fig. 39–17b. The beam spreads out vertically after passing through the slit. The diffraction pattern consists of a central bright band, which may be much *wider* than the slit width, bordered by alternating dark and bright bands with rapidly decreasing intensity. About 85% of the total intensity is in the central bright band. You can easily observe a similar diffraction pattern by looking at a point source such as a distant street light through a narrow slit formed between two fingers in front of your eye. The retina of your eye then corresponds to the screen.

Figure 39–18 shows a side view of the same setup; the long sides of the slit are perpendicular to the figure. According to Huygens' principle,

39–17
(a) Geometrical "shadow" of a slit.
(b) Diffraction pattern of a slit. The slit width has been greatly exaggerated.

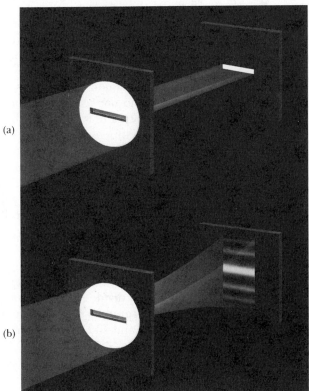

(a)

(b)

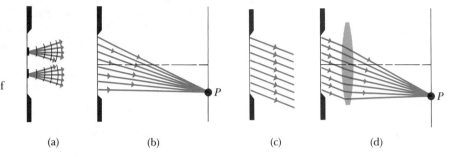

39–18
Diffraction by a single slit. Relation of
Fresnel diffraction to Fraunhofer
diffraction by a single slit.

(a)   (b)   (c)   (d)

each element of area of the slit opening can be considered as a source of
secondary waves. In particular, imagine dividing the slit into narrow
strips parallel to the long edges, perpendicular to the page in Fig.
39–18a. From each strip, cylindrical secondary wavelets spread out, as
shown in cross section.

In Fig. 39–18b a screen is placed to the right of the slit. We can
calculate the resultant intensity at a point P by adding the contributions
from the individual wavelets, taking proper account of their various
phases and amplitudes. The problem is much simpler if the screen is far
away; in this case the rays from the slit to the screen are parallel, as in
Fig. 39–18c. An equivalent situation is Fig. 39–18d, in which the rays to
the lens are parallel and the lens forms a reduced *image* of the same
pattern that would be formed on an infinitely distant screen without the
lens. We might expect that the various light paths through the lens
would introduce additional phase shifts, but in fact it can be shown that
all the paths have *equal* phase shifts, so this is not a problem.

The situation of Fig. 39–18b is Fresnel diffraction; those in Figs.
39–18c and 39–18d, in which the outgoing rays can be considered parallel, are Fraunhofer diffraction. We can derive quite simply the most
important characteristics of the Fraunhofer diffraction pattern from a
single slit. First consider two narrow strips, one just below the top edge
of the slit and one at its center, as in Fig. 39–19. The difference in path
length to point P is $(a/2) \sin \theta$, where a is the slit width. Suppose this path
difference happens to be equal to $\lambda/2$; then light from these two strips
arrives at point P with a half-cycle phase difference, and cancellation
occurs. Similarly, light from two strips immediately *below* these two also
arrives a half-cycle out of phase. In fact, the light from *every* strip in the
top half cancels out the light from a corresponding strip in the bottom
half. The result is complete cancellation for the entire slit, giving a dark
fringe in the interference pattern. That is, a dark fringe occurs whenever

$$\frac{a}{2} \sin \theta = \pm\frac{\lambda}{2}, \quad \text{or} \quad \sin \theta = \pm\frac{\lambda}{a}. \qquad (39\text{--}10)$$

We may also divide the screen into quarters, sixths, and so on, and use
the above argument to show that a dark fringe occurs whenever $\sin \theta =$
$2\lambda/a$, $3\lambda/a$, and so on. Thus the condition for a *dark* fringe is

$$\sin \theta = \frac{n\lambda}{a} \qquad (n = \pm 1, \pm 2, \pm 3, \ldots). \qquad (39\text{--}11)$$

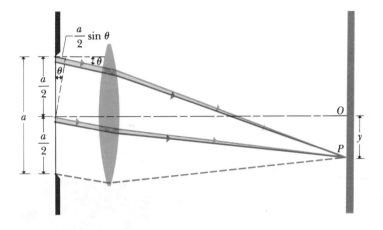

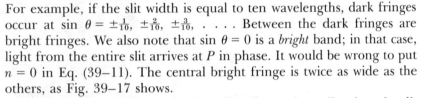

39–19
The wave front is divided into a large number of narrow strips.

For example, if the slit width is equal to ten wavelengths, dark fringes occur at $\sin \theta = \pm\frac{1}{10}, \pm\frac{2}{10}, \pm\frac{3}{10}, \ldots$. Between the dark fringes are bright fringes. We also note that $\sin \theta = 0$ is a *bright* band; in that case, light from the entire slit arrives at P in phase. It would be wrong to put $n = 0$ in Eq. (39–11). The central bright fringe is twice as wide as the others, as Fig. 39–17 shows.

With light the wavelength λ is ordinarily much smaller than the slit width a. The wavelength is of the order of 5×10^{-5} cm, and a typical slit width is 10^{-2} cm. Therefore the values of θ in Eq. (39–11) are so small that the approximation $\sin \theta = \theta$ is very good, and we can rewrite this equation as

$$\theta = \frac{n\lambda}{a}, \qquad n = \pm 1, \pm 2, \pm 3, \ldots.$$

Also, if the distance from lens to screen is R, and the height of the nth dark band above the center of the pattern is y_n, then $\tan \theta = y_n/R$. For small θ we may approximate $\tan \theta \simeq \theta$, and we then find

$$y_n = \frac{Rn\lambda}{a}. \tag{39–12}$$

This equation has the same form as the equation for the two-slit pattern, Eq. (39–6), but here it gives the positions of the *dark* fringes in a *single-slit* pattern rather than the *bright* fringes in a *double-slit* pattern. Be careful!

Figure 39–20a is a graph of intensity as a function of y for a single-slit diffraction pattern, and Fig. 39–20b is an actual photograph of such a pattern. As we have noted, 85% of the total intensity is in the central bright fringe. The photograph in Fig. 39–20c shows the Fraunhofer diffraction pattern of *two* slits, each with the same width a as for Fig. 39–20b but separated by a distance $d = 4a$. (The left ends of the figures show the slit patterns.) The two-slit interference pattern, represented by the narrow fringes, is modified by the diffraction curve of Fig. 39–20a because of the finite widths of the slits. Thus the first minimum in the single-slit pattern in Fig. 39–20c completely extinguishes the $m = 4$ bright fringe of the two-slit pattern.

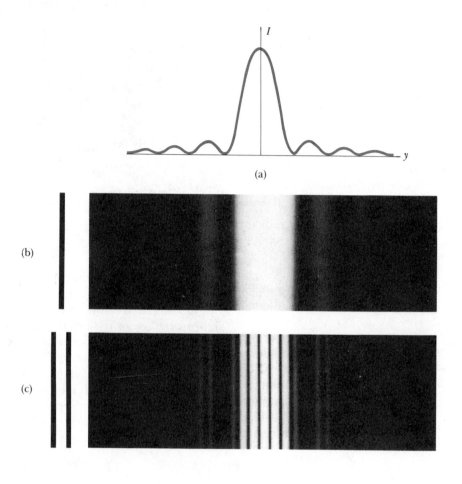

39-20
(a) Intensity distribution.
(b) Photograph of the Fraunhofer diffraction pattern of a single slit.
(c) Photograph of the Fraunhofer diffraction pattern of a double slit.

39-7
The Diffraction Grating

Suppose that instead of a single slit or two slits side by side, we have a large number of parallel slits, all with the same width and spaced equal distances apart. Such an arrangement is called a **diffraction grating;** the first one was constructed by Fraunhofer using fine wires. Gratings are now made by using a diamond point to scratch many equally spaced grooves on a glass or metal surface or by photographic reduction of a black-and-white pattern drawn with a pen. The interference pattern produced by a grating has some similarities to the two-slit pattern we studied in Section 39-2 and some interesting differences.

In Fig. 39-21, GG' is a cross section of the grating; the slits are perpendicular to the plane of the page. Only five slits are shown in the diagram, but an actual grating may contain several thousand slits. The spacing d between centers of adjacent slits is called the *grating spacing*; it is typically about 0.002 mm. A plane monochromatic wave is incident normally on the grating from the left side. The lens is included so that we can view the pattern on a screen at a finite distance from the grating and still meet the conditions for Fraunhofer diffraction, that is, parallel rays

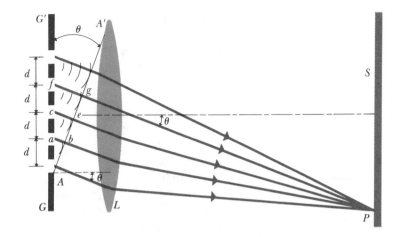

39-21

The plane diffraction grating. From the right triangle *Aab* the path difference *ab* is equal to *d* sin θ.

emerging from the grating. What does the pattern on the screen look like?

We will assume that the slits are very narrow, so we don't have to worry about phase differences for light coming from opposite sides of an individual slit. Suppose the angle θ in Fig. 39-21 happens to be just the right size so that the distance *ab* equals λ, the wavelength of the incident light. Then *ce* = 2λ, *fg* = 3λ, and so on. The waves from all these slits are in phase at the plane of the grating. Because of the integer-wavelength path differences, they are also in phase along the plane *AA'* and therefore reach the point *P* in phase.

If we increase the angle θ slightly, the waves from the various grating slits no longer arrive at *AA'* in phase. If there are many slits, even a small change in angle results in almost complete destructive interference among them. The phase difference for two adjacent slits may be small, but for two slits separated by 100 other slits the phase difference is substantial. If we have a very large number of slits, the phase differences are nearly random, and the waves sum to zero unless the phase difference for adjacent slits is *exactly* an integer number of cycles. Thus the maximum is a very sharp one, in contrast to the rather broad maxima in a two-slit pattern.

As we increase the angle θ still further, we eventually reach a position where the distance *ab* in Fig. 39-21 is equal to 2λ. Then *ce* equals 4λ, *fg* equals 6λ, and so on. The waves at *AA'* are again all in phase; the path difference for waves from adjacent slits is now 2λ, and we find another intensity maximum. Still others appear when *ab* = 3λ, 4λ, ... We also find maxima at corresponding angles on the opposite side of the grating normal and along the normal itself. Along the normal the phase difference between waves reaching *AA'* is zero.

The general condition for an intensity maximum is that the path difference *ab* for adjacent slits must be an integer number of wavelengths, that is, *m*λ, where *m* = 0, ±1, ±2, ±3, ... From Fig. 39-21 we also see that the path difference *ab* is equal to *d* sin θ. So the general condition for an intensity maximum is

$$d \sin \theta = m\lambda \qquad (m = 0, \pm 1, \pm 2, \ldots). \qquad (39\text{-}13)$$

This equation has the same form as Eq. (39–4), which we derived for two-slit interference. The intensity maxima are indeed in the same positions in both cases; the crucial difference is that the grating maxima are sharp and narrow, while the two-slit maxima are broad and fuzzy, as Fig. 39–4 shows.

When a grating is illuminated by monochromatic light, the pattern is a series of sharp lines at angles determined by Eq. (39–13). The $m = 1$ lines are called the *first-order lines*, the $m = 2$ lines the *second-order* lines, and so on. If the grating is illuminated by white light with a continuous distribution of wavelengths, each value of m corresponds to a continuous spectrum in the pattern. The angle for each wavelength is determined by Eq. (39–13), which shows that for a given value of m, long wavelengths (the red end of the spectrum) lie at larger angles (i.e., are deviated more from the straight-ahead direction) than the shorter wavelengths at the violet end of the spectrum.

As Eq. (39–13) shows, the sines of the deviation angles of the maxima are proportional to the ratio λ/d. For substantial deviation to occur, the grating spacing d should be of the same order of magnitude as the wavelength λ. Gratings for use in the visible spectrum usually have about 500 to 1500 lines per millimeter, so d is of the order of 1000 nm.

The diffraction grating is widely used in spectrometry as a means of dispersing a light beam into spectra. If the grating spacing is known, then we can measure the angles of deviation and use Eq. (39–13) to compute the wavelength. A prism can also be used to disperse the various wavelengths through different angles because the index of refraction always varies with wavelength. But there is no simple relationship that describes this variation, so a spectrometer using a prism has to be calibrated with known wavelengths that are determined in some other way. Another difference is that a prism deviates red light the least and violet the most, while a grating does the opposite.

Example 39–4   The wavelengths of the visible spectrum are approximately 400 nm (violet) to 700 nm (red). Find the angular width of the first-order visible spectrum produced by a plane grating with 6000 lines per centimeter when white light falls normally on the grating.

Solution   The first-order spectrum corresponds to $m = 1$. The grating spacing d is

$$d = \frac{1}{6000 \text{ lines}\cdot\text{cm}^{-1}} = 1.67 \times 10^{-6} \text{ m}.$$

From Eq. (39–13), with $m = 1$, the angular deviation of the violet (400 nm or 4.00×10^{-7} m) is

$$\sin \theta = \frac{400 \times 10^{-9} \text{ m}}{1.67 \times 10^{-6} \text{ m}} = 0.240,$$

$$\theta = 13.9°.$$

The angular deviation of the red (700 nm) is

$$\sin \theta = \frac{700 \times 10^{-9} \text{ m}}{1.67 \times 10^{-6} \text{ m}} = 0.419, \qquad \theta = 24.8°$$

So the first-order visible spectrum includes an angle of

$$24.8° - 13.9° = 10.9°.$$ ■

Example 39–5   In the situation of Example 39–4, show that the violet end of the third-order spectrum overlaps the red end of the second-order spectrum.

Solution   From Eq. (39–13) the angular deviation of the third-order violet ($m = 3$) is

$$\sin \theta = \frac{(3)(400 \times 10^{-9} \text{ m})}{d} = \frac{1.20 \times 10^{-6} \text{ m}}{d}.$$

The deviation of the second-order red ($m = 2$) is

$$\sin \theta = \frac{(2)(700 \times 10^{-9} \text{ m})}{d} = \frac{1.40 \times 10^{-6} \text{ m}}{d}.$$

This shows that no matter what the grating spacing d is, the largest angle (at the red end) for the second-order spectrum is always greater than the smallest angle (at the violet end) for the third-order spectrum, so the second and third orders *always* overlap. ■

PROBLEM-SOLVING STRATEGY: *Diffraction*

Here are several general comments about the kinds of problems you will encounter in this chapter. You may want to refer back to earlier sections and look for applications of these ideas.

1. Always draw a diagram; label all the distances and angles clearly. Several of the equations derived in this chapter contain an angle θ. Make absolutely sure that you know where θ is on your diagram.

2. The equations for an intensity *maximum* in the two-source or grating pattern, Eqs. (39–4) and (39–13), look very much like the equation for an intensity *minimum* in the single-slit pattern, Eq. (39–11). Be careful not to get these confused, and be sure that you understand why the same equation gives intensity maxima in some situations and minima in others.

3. In X-ray diffraction, discussed in the next section, the angle θ is traditionally defined differently from the angles of incidence and reflection in geometrical optics. In this case, θ is the angle of the incoming beam relative to the crystal planes, not their normals. Be careful! Also notice that there are *two* conditions for an intensity maximum in X-ray diffraction: The incident and scattering angles are equal, and the Bragg condition, Eq. (39–14) in Section 39–8, must be satisfied.

4. One more time we caution you about units. Light wavelengths are usually expressed in nanometers (1 nm = 10^{-9} m), but if you refer to other books, you may also find Ångstrom units; 1 Å = 10^{-10} m = 1/10 nm. Dimensions of slits and apertures may be expressed in millimeters, and lens-to-screen distances may be in centimeters or meters. Lens focal lengths are traditionally expressed in millimeters. Be very careful not to drop any powers of ten!

39–8
X-ray Diffraction

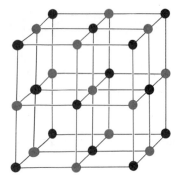

39–22
Model of arrangement of ions in a crystal of NaCl. Black circles, Na; color circles, Cl. The spacing of adjacent atom is 0.282 nm.

X-rays were discovered by Wilhelm Röntgen (1845–1923) in 1895, and early experiments suggested that they were electromagnetic waves with wavelengths of the order of 10^{-10} m. At about the same time the idea began to emerge that in a crystalline solid the atoms are arranged in a lattice in a regular repeating pattern, with spacing between adjacent atoms of the order of 10^{-10} m. Putting these two ideas together, Max von Laue (1879–1960) suggested in 1912 that a crystal might serve as a kind of three-dimensional diffraction grating for X-rays. That is, a beam of X-rays might be scattered (i.e., absorbed and re-emitted) by the individual atoms in a crystal, and the scattered waves might interfere just like waves from a diffraction grating.

The first **X-ray diffraction** experiments were performed in 1912 by Friederich, Knipping, and von Laue, and interference effects *were* observed. These experiments verified that X-rays *are* waves, or at least have wavelike properties, and also that the atoms in a crystal *are* arranged in a regular pattern. Since that time, X-ray diffraction has proved an invaluable research tool, both for measuring X-ray wavelengths and for the study of crystal structure. Figure 39–22 is a diagram of the structure of a familiar crystal, sodium chloride.

To introduce basic ideas, we consider first a two-dimensional scattering situation, as shown in Fig. 39–23a, where a plane wave is incident on a square array of scattering centers. The situation might be a ripple tank with an array of small posts, 3-cm microwaves with an array of small conducting spheres, or X-rays with an array of atoms. In the case of electromagnetic waves the wave induces an oscillating electric dipole moment in each scatterer. These dipoles act like little antennas, emitting scattered waves. The interference pattern is the superposition of all these scattered waves. The situation is different from the diffraction grating, in which the waves from all the slits are emitted *in phase*. Here the scattered waves *are not* all in phase because their distances from the source are different. To compute the interference pattern, we have to consider the *total* path differences for the scattered waves, including the distances both from source to scatterer and from scatterer to observer.

39–23
Scattering of radiation from a square array. Interference from successive scatterers in a row is constructive when the angles of incidence and reflection are equal. Interference from adjacent rows is also constructive when Eq. (39–14) is satisfied.

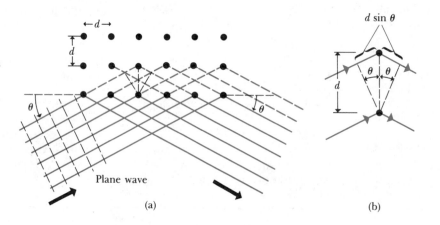

Plane wave

(a)

(b)

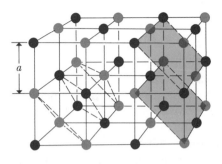

39–24
Cubic crystal lattice, showing two different families of crystal planes. The spacing of the planes on the left is $a/\sqrt{3}$; that of the planes on the right is $a/\sqrt{2}$. There are also three sets of planes parallel to the cube faces, with spacing a.

As Fig. 39–23a shows, the path length from source to observer is the same for all the scatterers in a single row if the two angles θ are equal, as shown. Scattered radiation from adjacent rows is *also* in phase if the path difference for adjacent rows is an integer number of wavelengths. Figure 39–23b shows that this path difference is $2d \sin \theta$. Therefore the conditions for radiation from the *entire array* to reach the observer in phase are that (1) the angle of incidence must equal the angle of scattering and (2) the path difference for adjacent rows must equal $n\lambda$, where n is an integer. We can express the second condition as

$$2d \sin \theta = n\lambda \qquad (n = 1, 2, 3, \ldots). \qquad (39\text{–}14)$$

In directions for which this condition is satisfied, we see a strong maximum in the interference pattern. We can describe this interference in terms of *reflections* of the wave from the horizontal rows of scatterers in Fig. 39–23a. Strong interference occurs at angles such that the incident and scattered angles are equal and Eq. (39–14) is satisfied.

We can extend this discussion to a three-dimensional array. Instead of *rows*, we consider *planes* of scatterers. Figure 39–24 shows several different sets of parallel planes that pass through all the scatterers. Waves from all the scatterers in a given plane interfere constructively if the angles of incidence and scattering are equal. There is also constructive interference between planes when Eq. (39–14) is satisfied, where d is now the distance between adjacent planes. Because there are many different sets of parallel planes, there are also many values of d and many sets of angles that give constructive interference for the whole crystal lattice. This phenomenon is called **Bragg reflection,** and Eq. (39–14) is called the **Bragg condition,** in honor of Sir William Bragg and his son Laurence Bragg, two pioneers in X-ray analysis. *Caution:* Don't let the term *reflection* obscure the fact that we are dealing with an *interference* effect.

Figure 39–25 is a photograph made by directing a narrow beam of X-rays at a thin section of a quartz crystal and letting the scattered beam strike a photographic film. Nearly complete cancellation occurs for all but certain very specific directions, in which constructive interference occurs and forms bright spots. Such a pattern is usually called an X-ray *diffraction* pattern, although there is no fundamental distinction between *interference* and *diffraction*. Such patterns are also called Laue patterns.

If the crystal lattice spacing is known, we can determine the wavelength, just as we determined wavelengths of visible light by measuring diffraction patterns from slits or gratings. For example, we can determine the crystal lattice spacing for sodium chloride from its density and Avogadro's number. Conversely, if we know the X-ray wavelength, we can use X-ray diffraction to explore the structure and lattice spacing of crystals with unknown structure.

X-ray diffraction is by far the most important experimental tool in the investigation of crystal structure of solids. Atomic spacings in crystals can be measured precisely, and the lattice structure of complex crystals can be determined. X-ray diffraction also plays an important role in studies of the structures of liquids and of organic molecules.

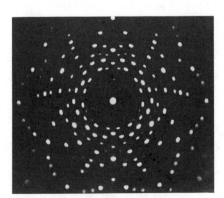

39–25
Laue diffraction pattern formed by directing a beam of X-rays at a thin section of quartz crystal. (Courtesy of Dr. B. E. Warren.)

*39–9
Circular Apertures and Resolving Power

The diffraction pattern formed by a *circular* aperture is of special interest because of its role in limiting the resolving power of optical instruments. Computing the details of the pattern is fairly complex; we will only *describe* the pattern and quote a few relevant numbers.

The pattern consists of a central bright spot surrounded by a series of bright and dark rings, as shown in Fig. 39–26. We can describe the pattern in terms of the angle θ, representing the angular size of each ring. If the aperture diameter is d and the wavelength is λ, the angular size θ_1 of the first *dark* ring is given by

$$\sin \theta_1 = 1.22 \frac{\lambda}{d}. \tag{39-15}$$

The angular sizes of the next two dark rings are given by

$$\sin \theta_2 = 2.23 \frac{\lambda}{d}, \qquad \sin \theta_3 = 3.24 \frac{\lambda}{d}. \tag{39-16}$$

Between these are bright rings with angular sizes given by

$$\sin \theta = 1.63 \frac{\lambda}{d}, \quad 2.68 \frac{\lambda}{d}, \quad 3.70 \frac{\lambda}{d}, \tag{39-17}$$

and so on. The central bright spot is called the **Airy disk,** in honor of Sir George Airy (1801–1892), Astronomer Royal of England, who first derived the expression for the intensity in the pattern. The angular size of the Airy disk is that of the first dark ring, given by Eq. (39–15). Most of the light energy falls in the Airy disk; only about 15% of the light is in the bright rings. Figure 39–27 shows a diffraction pattern from a circular aperture 1.0 mm in diameter.

All of this has far-reaching implications for image formation of lenses and mirrors. In our study of optical instruments in Chapter 38 we assumed that a lens of focal length f focuses a parallel beam (plane wave) to a *point* at a distance f from the lens. This assumption ignored diffraction effects. We now see that what we get is not a point but the diffraction

39–26
Diffraction pattern formed by a circular aperture of diameter d, consisting of a central bright spot and alternating dark and bright rings. The angular size θ_2 of the second dark ring is shown.

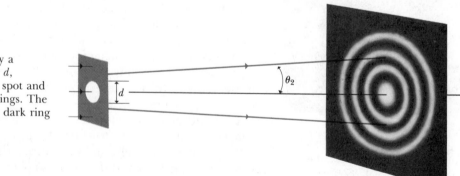

39–27
Diffraction pattern formed by a circular aperture 1.0 mm in diameter.

pattern just described. If we have two point objects, their images are not two points but two diffraction patterns. When the objects are close together, their diffraction patterns overlap; if they are close enough, their patterns overlap almost completely and cannot be distinguished. The effect is shown in Fig. 39–28, which shows the patterns for four (very small) "point" objects. In Fig. 39–28(a) the two images on the right have merged; in Fig. 39–28(b), with a larger aperture diameter and resulting smaller Airy disks, the two right images are barely resolved. In Fig. 39–28(c), with a still larger aperture, they are well resolved.

A widely used criterion for resolution of two point objects, proposed by Lord Rayleigh and called **Rayleigh's criterion,** is that the points are just barely resolved (i.e., distinguishable) if the center of one diffraction pattern coincides with the first minimum of the other. In that case the

39–28
Diffraction patterns of four "point" sources with a circular opening in front of the lens. In part (a) the opening is small enough that the patterns at the right are barely resolved, by Rayleigh's criterion. Increasing the aperture decreases the size of the diffraction patterns, as in parts (b) and (c).

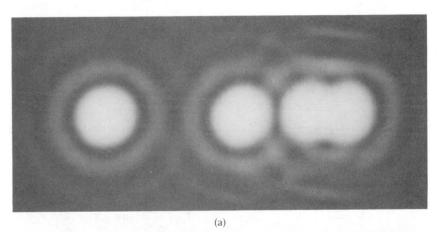

(a)

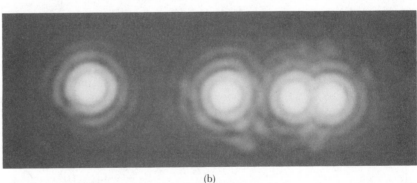

(b)

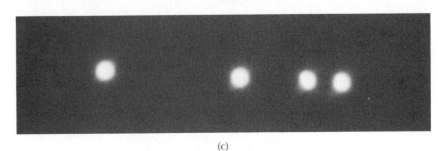

(c)

angular separation of the image centers is given by Eq. (39–15). The angular separation of the *objects* is the same as that of the *images*, so two point objects are barely resolved, according to Rayleigh's criterion, when their angular separation is given by Eq. (39–15).

The minimum separation of two points that can just be resolved by an optical instrument is called the **limit of resolution** of the instrument. The smaller the limit of resolution, the greater the **resolution** or *resolving power* of the instrument. Diffraction sets the ultimate limits on resolution of lenses. *Geometrical* optics may make it seem that we can make images as large as we like. Eventually, though, we always reach a point at which the image becomes larger but does not gain in detail. The images in Fig. 39–28 would not become sharper with further enlargement.

Example 39–6   A camera lens with focal length $f = 50$ mm and maximum aperture $f/2$ forms an image of an object 10 m away.

a) If the resolution is limited by diffraction, what is the minimum distance between two points on the object that are barely resolved, and what is the corresponding distance between image points?

b) How does the situation change if the lens is "stopped down" to $f/16$? Assume that $\lambda = 500$ nm in both cases.

Solution

a) The aperture diameter is $d = (50 \text{ mm})/2 = 25 \text{ mm} = 25 \times 10^{-3}$ m. From Eq. (39–15) the angular separation θ of two object points that are barely resolved is given by

$$\sin \theta \simeq \theta = 1.22 \frac{\lambda}{d} = 1.22 \frac{500 \times 10^{-9} \text{ m}}{25 \times 10^{-3} \text{ m}} = 2.44 \times 10^{-5}.$$

Let y be the separation of the object points and y' the separation of the corresponding image points. We know from our thin-lens analysis in Section 38–1 that, apart from sign, $y/s = y'/s'$. Thus the angular separations of the object points and the corresponding image points are both equal to θ. The image distance s' is approximately equal to the focal length, $f = 50$ mm. Thus

$$\frac{y}{10 \text{ m}} = 2.44 \times 10^{-5}, \qquad y = 2.44 \times 10^{-4} \text{ m} = 0.244 \text{ mm};$$

$$\frac{y'}{50 \text{ mm}} = 2.44 \times 10^{-5}, \qquad y' = 1.22 \times 10^{-3} \text{ mm} = 0.00122 \text{ mm}$$

$$\simeq \frac{1}{800} \text{ mm}.$$

b) The aperture is now $(50 \text{ mm})/16$, or one eighth as large as before. The angular separation is eight times as great, and the values of y and y' are also eight times as great as before:

$$y = 1.95 \text{ mm}, \qquad y' = 0.0098 \text{ mm} \simeq \frac{1}{100} \text{ mm.} \qquad \blacksquare$$

Setups to test the resolution of lenses often use series of parallel lines with varying spacing, and the resolution in the image is often described in "lines per millimeter." Our lens would be described as having a resolution of about 800 lines per mm when "wide open" and about 100 lines per mm when stopped down to $f/16$. Only the best-quality camera lenses approach this resolution. Photographers who always use the smallest possible aperture for maximum depth of focus and (presumably) maximum sharpness should be aware that diffraction effects become more significant at small apertures. One cause of fuzzy images has to be balanced against another.

Another lesson to be learned is that resolution improves with shorter wavelengths. Ultraviolet microscopes have higher resolution than visible-light microscopes. In electron microscopes, which we will study in Chapter 42, the resolution is limited by the wavelengths associated with wavelike behavior of electrons. These wavelengths can be made 100,000 times smaller than wavelengths of visible light, with a corresponding gain in resolution. Finally, one reason for building very large reflecting telescopes is to increase the aperture diameter and thus minimize diffraction effects. This also provides greater light-gathering area for viewing very faint stars.

*39–10
Holography

Holography is a technique for recording and reproducing an image of an object without the use of lenses. Unlike the two-dimensional images recorded by an ordinary photograph or television system, a holographic image is truly three-dimensional. Such an image can be viewed from different directions to reveal different sides and from various distances to reveal changing perspective. If you had never seen a hologram, you wouldn't believe it was possible!

The basic procedure for making a hologram is shown in Fig. 39–29a. We illuminate the object to be holographed with monochromatic light, and we place a photographic film so that it is struck by scattered light from the object and also by direct light from the source. In practice, the source must be a laser, for reasons we will discuss later. Interference between the direct and scattered light leads to the formation and recording of a complex interference pattern on the film.

To form the images, we simply project laser light through the developed film, as shown in Fig. 39–29b. Two images are formed, a virtual image on the side of the film nearer the source, and a real image on the opposite side.

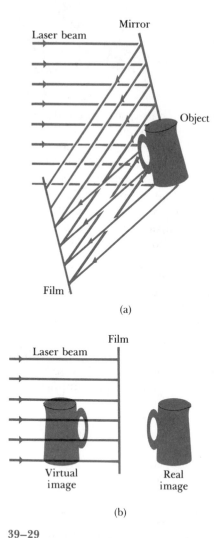

(a)

(b)

39-29
(a) The hologram is the record on film of the interference pattern formed with light directly from the source and light scattered from the object. (b) Images are formed when light is projected through the hologram.

A complete analysis of holography is beyond our scope, but we can gain some insight into the process by looking at how a single point is holographed and imaged. Consider the interference pattern formed on a photographic film by the superposition of an incident plane wave and a spherical wave, as shown in Fig. 39–30a. The spherical wave originates at a point source P at a distance d_0 from the film; P may in fact be a small object that scatters part of the incident plane wave. We assume that the two waves are monochromatic and coherent and that the phase relation is such that constructive interference occurs at point O on the diagram. Then constructive interference will *also* occur at any point Q on the film

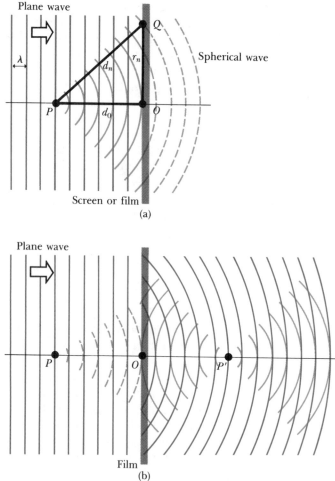

39-30
(a) Constructive interference of the plane and spherical waves occurs in the plane of the film at every point Q for which the distance d_n from P is greater than the distance d_0 from P to O by an integer number of wavelengths $n\lambda$. For the point shown, $n = 2$. (b) When a plane wave strikes the developed film, the diffracted wave consists of a wave converging to P' and then diverging again and a diverging wave that appears to originate at P. These waves form the real and virtual images, respectively.

that is farther from P than O is, by an integer number of wavelengths. That is, if $d_n - d_0 = n\lambda$, where n is an integer, then constructive interference occurs. The points where this condition is satisfied form circles centered at O, with radii r_n given by

$$d_n - d_0 = \sqrt{d_0^2 + r_n^2} - d_0 = n\lambda \qquad (n = 1, 2, 3, \ldots). \quad (39\text{--}18)$$

Solving this for r_n^2, we find

$$r_n^2 = \lambda(2nd_0 + n^2\lambda).$$

Ordinarily, d_0 is very much larger than λ, so we neglect the second term in parentheses, obtaining

$$r_n = \sqrt{2n\lambda d_0} \qquad (n = 1, 2, 3, \ldots). \quad (39\text{--}19)$$

The interference pattern consists of a series of concentric bright circular fringes with radii given by Eq. (39–19). Between these bright fringes are dark fringes.

Now we develop the film and make a transparent positive print, so the bright-fringe areas have the greatest transparency on the film. Then we illuminate it with monochromatic plane-wave light of the same wavelength that we used initially. In Fig. 39–30b, consider a point P' at a distance d_0 along the axis from the film. The centers of successive bright fringes differ in their distances from P' by an integer number of wavelengths, and therefore a strong *maximum* in the diffracted wave occurs at P'. That is, light converges to P' and then diverges from it on the opposite side. Therefore P' is a *real image* of point P.

This is not the entire diffracted wave, however; there is also a diverging spherical wave, which would represent a continuation of the wave originally emanating from P if the film had not been present. Thus the *total* diffracted wave is a superposition of a converging spherical wave forming a real image at P' and a diverging spherical wave shaped as though it had originated at P, forming a *virtual image* at P.

Because of the principle of linear superposition, what is true for the imaging of a single point is also true for the imaging of any number of points. The film records the superposed interference pattern from the various points, and when light is projected through the film, the various image points are reproduced simultaneously. Thus the images of an extended object can be recorded and reproduced just as for a single point object.

In making a hologram we have to overcome several practical problems. First, the light used must be *coherent* over distances that are large in comparison to the dimensions of the object and its distance from the film. Ordinary light sources *do not* satisfy this requirement, for reasons that we discussed in Section 39–1, and laser light is essential. Second, extreme mechanical stability is needed. If any relative motion of source, object, or film occurs during exposure, even by as much as a wavelength, the interference pattern on the film is blurred enough to prevent satisfactory image formation. These obstacles are not insurmountable, however, and holography promises to become increasingly important in research, entertainment, and a wide variety of technological applications.

Questions

39–1 Could an experiment similar to Young's two-slit experiment be performed with sound? How might this be carried out? Does it matter that sound waves are longitudinal and electromagnetic waves are transverse?

39–2 At points of constructive interference between waves of equal amplitude the intensity is four times that of either individual wave. Does this violate energy conservation? If not, why not?

39–3 In using the superposition principle to calculate intensities in interference and diffraction patterns, could one add the intensities of the waves instead of their amplitudes? What is the difference?

39–4 A two-slit interference experiment is set up, and the fringes are displayed on a screen. Then the whole apparatus is immersed in the nearest swimming pool. How does the fringe pattern change?

39–5 Would the headlights of a distant car form a two-source interference pattern? If so, how might it be observed? If not, why not?

39–6 A student asserted that it is impossible to observe interference fringes in a two-source experiment if the distance between sources is less than half the wavelength of the wave. Do you agree? Explain.

39–7 An amateur scientist proposed to record a two-source interference pattern by using only one source, placing it first in position S_1 in Fig. 39–1 and turning it on for a certain time, then placing it at S_2 and turning it on for an equal time. Does this work?

39–8 When a thin oil film spreads out on a puddle of water, the thinnest part of the film looks lightest in the resulting interference pattern. What does this tell you about the relative magnitudes of the refractive indexes of oil and water?

39–9 A glass windowpane with a thin film of water on it reflects less than when it is perfectly dry. Why?

39–10 In high-quality camera lenses the resolution in the image is determined by diffraction effects. Is the resolution best when the lens is "wide open" or when it is "stopped down" to a smaller aperture? How does this behavior compare with the effect of aperture size on the depth of focus, that is, on the limit of resolution due to imprecise focusing?

39–11 If a two-slit interference experiment were done with white light, what would be seen?

39–12 Why is a diffraction grating better than a two-slit setup for measuring wavelengths of light?

39–13 Would the interference and diffraction effects described in this chapter still be seen if light were a longitudinal wave instead of transverse?

39–14 One sometimes sees rows of evenly spaced radio antenna towers. A student remarked that these act like diffraction gratings. What did she mean? Why would one *want* them to act like a diffraction grating?

39–15 Could X-ray diffraction effects with crystals be observed by using visible light instead of X-rays? Why or why not?

39–16 Does a microscope have better resolution with red light or blue light?

39–17 How could an interference experiment, such as one using a Michelson interferometer or fringes caused by a thin air space between glass plates, be used to measure the refractive index of air?

Exercises

Section 39–2   Two-Source Interference

39–1 Two slits are spaced 0.300 mm apart and are placed 75.0 cm from a screen. What is the distance between the second and third dark lines of the interference pattern when the slits are illuminated with light with a wavelength of 600 nm?

39–2 Light from a mercury-arc lamp is passed through a filter that blocks everything except for one spectrum line in the blue region of the spectrum. It then falls on two slits separated by 0.600 mm. In the resulting interference pattern on a screen 2.50 m away, adjacent bright fringes are separated by 1.92 mm. What is the wavelength?

39–3 Young's experiment is performed with sodium light ($\lambda = 589$ nm). Fringes are measured carefully on a screen 1.50 m away from the double slit, and the center of the twentieth bright fringe (not counting the central bright fringe) is found to be 11.9 mm from the center of the central bright fringe. What is the separation of the two slits?

39–4 An FM radio station has a frequency of 100 MHz and uses two identical antennas mounted at the same elevation, 9.00 m apart. The resulting radiation pattern has maximum intensity at points along a horizontal line perpendicular to the line joining the antennas and midway between them.

a) At what other angles (measured from the line of maximum intensity) is the intensity maximum?

b) At what angles is it zero?

Assume that the intensity is observed at distances from the antennas that are much larger than 9.00 m.

Section 39–3   Interference in Thin Films

39–5 Light with wavelength 500 nm is incident perpendicularly from air on a film 0.833×10^{-4} cm thick and with refractive index 1.35. Part of the light is reflected from the first surface of the film, and part enters the film and is reflected back at the second surface, where the film is again in contact with air.

a) How many wavelengths are contained along the path of this second part of the light in the film?

b) What is the phase difference between these two parts of the light as they leave the film?

39–6 In Example 39–3, suppose the top plate is glass with $n = 1.40$, the wedge is filled with silicone grease having $n = 1.50$, and the bottom plate is glass with $n = 1.60$. Calculate the spacing between the dark fringes.

39–7 A plate of glass 10.0 cm long is placed in contact with a second plate and is held at a small angle with it by a metal strip 0.100 mm thick placed under one end. The space between the plates is filled with air. The glass is illuminated from above with light having a wavelength of 635 nm. How many interference fringes are observed per centimeter in the reflected light?

39–8 Two rectangular pieces of plane glass are laid one upon the other on a table. A thin strip of paper is placed between them at one edge so that a very thin wedge of air is formed. The plates are illuminated by a beam of sodium light at normal incidence ($\lambda = 589$ nm). Interference fringes are formed, with 15 fringes per centimeter length of wedge measured normal to the edges in contact. Find the angle of the wedge.

39–9

a) Is a thin film of polystyrene suitable as a non-reflecting coating for fabulite? (See Table 36–1.)

b) If so, what is the minimum thickness of the film required? Assume that the wavelength of the light is 550 nm.

39–10 What is the thinnest film of a 1.40 refractive index coating on glass ($n = 1.50$) for which destructive interference of the green component (500 nm) of an incident white light beam in air can take place by reflection?

Section 39–4   The Michelson Interferometer

39–11 How far must the mirror M_2 (Fig. 39–11) of the Michelson interferometer be moved so that 2000 fringes of krypton-86 light ($\lambda = 606$ nm) move across a line in the field of view?

39–12 A Mach-Zehnder interferometer is shown in Fig. 39–31. The mirrors at B and C are totally reflecting, while the beam-splitters at A and D are half-silvered so that they reflect half of the light and transmit half of the light. The reflection occurs at the silvered surfaces shown, the left surface of A and the right surface of D. Light polarized in the plane of the mirrors is used. Remember that light undergoes a half-cycle (180°) phase change on reflection at an interface where the refractive index increases, in this case air to glass, but no phase change occurs when the refractive index decreases across the interface (glass to air). Show that if the optical paths are such that the output at F is zero (total destructive interference), then the output at E will show total constructive interference.

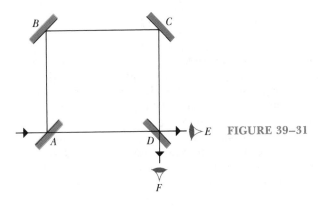

FIGURE 39–31

Section 39–6   Fraunhofer Diffraction from a Single Slit

39–13 Light with a wavelength of 589 nm from a distant source is incident on a slit 0.720 mm wide, and the resulting diffraction pattern is observed on a screen 2.00 m away. What is the distance between the two dark fringes on either side of the central bright fringe?

39–14 Parallel rays of green mercury light with a wavelength of 546 nm pass through a slit with a width of 0.437 mm covering a lens with a focal length of 60.0 cm. In the focal plane of the lens, what is the distance from the central maximum to the first minimum?

39–15 Monochromatic light from a distant source is incident on a slit 0.800 mm wide. On a screen 3.00 m away, the distance from the central maximum of the diffraction pattern to the first minimum is measured to be 2.42 mm. Calculate the wavelength of the light.

Section 39–7   The Diffraction Grating

39–16 A plane transmission grating is ruled with 4500 lines·cm^{-1}. Compute the angular separation in degrees between the α and δ lines of atomic hydrogen in the second-order spectrum. The wavelengths of these lines are 656 nm and 410 nm, respectively. Assume normal incidence.

39–17 Plane monochromatic waves with wavelength 600 nm are incident normally on a plane transmission grating having 400 lines·mm^{-1}. Find the angles of deviation in the first, second, and third orders.

39–18

a) What is the wavelength of light that is deviated in the first order through an angle of 18.0° by a transmission grating having 6000 lines·cm^{-1}?

b) What is the second-order deviation for this wavelength? Assume normal incidence.

Section 39–8   X-Ray Diffraction

39–19 X-rays with a wavelength of 1.20 nm are scattered from the square lattice of a crystal. The fifth-order maximum in the Bragg reflection occurs when the angle θ in Fig. 39–23 is 21.4°. What is the spacing between adjacent atoms in the crystal?

39–20 Monochromatic X-rays are incident on a crystal for which the atomic spacing is 0.40 nm. The first-order maximum in the Bragg reflection occurs when the incident and reflected X-rays make an angle of 38.0° with the normal to the crystal. What is the wavelength of the X-rays?

Section 39–9   Circular Apertures and Resolving Power

39–21 A converging lens 8.00 cm in diameter has a focal length of 40.0 cm. If the resolution is diffraction limited, how far away can an object be if points on it 3.00 mm apart are to be resolved (according to Rayleigh's criterion)? (Use $\lambda = 550$ nm.)

39–22 In Fig. 39–32, two point sources of light, a and b, at a distance of 50.0 m from lens L and 8.00 mm apart produce images at c that are just resolved according to Rayleigh's criterion. The focal length of the lens is 20.0 cm. What is the diameter of the diffraction circles at c?

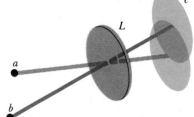

FIGURE 39–32

39–23 A telescope is used to observe two distant point sources 1.00 m apart. ($\lambda = 500$ nm.) The objective of the telescope is covered with a slit having a width of 0.600 mm. What is the maximum distance in meters at which the two sources may be distinguished?

Section 39–10   Holography

39–24 A hologram is made using 600-nm light and is then viewed using continuous-spectrum white light from an incandescent bulb. What will be seen?

39–25 If a hologram is made using 600-nm light and then viewed using 500-nm light, how will the images look compared to those observed with 600-nm light?

39–26 Ordinary photographic film reverses black and white, in the sense that the most brightly illuminated areas become blackest upon development (hence the term *negative*). Suppose a hologram negative is viewed directly, without making a positive transparency. How will the resulting images differ from those obtained with the positive hologram?

Problems

39–27 Parallel light rays with wavelength $\lambda = 600$ nm fall on a single slit. On a screen 3.00 m away, the distance between the dark fringes on either side of the central maximum is 4.50 mm. What is the width of the slit?

39–28 In Exercise 39–1, suppose the entire apparatus (slits, screen, and space in between) is immersed in water. Then what is the distance between the second and third dark lines?

39–29 Two identical audio speakers connected to the same amplifier produce sound waves with a frequency between 400 and 800 Hz. The speed of sound is 340 m·s^{-1}. You find that where you are standing, you hear no sound.

a) Explain why you hear no sound.

b) To help you, a friend moves one of the speakers toward you. When the speaker has been moved 0.34 m, the sound you hear has maximum intensity. What is the frequency of the sound?

c) How much closer to you from the position in part (b) must the speaker be moved to the next position at which you hear maximum intensity?

39–30 What is the thinnest soap film that appears black when illuminated by light with a wavelength of 590 nm? The index of refraction of the film is 1.45, and there is air on both sides of the film.

39–31 An oil tanker spills a large amount of oil ($n = 1.40$) into the sea. Assume that the refractive index of seawater is 1.33.

a) If you are overhead and look down onto the oil spill, what predominant visible wavelength do you see at a point where the oil is 390 nm thick?

b) If you swim under the slick and look up at the same place in the slick as in part (a), what visible wavelength (as measured in air) is predominant in the transmitted light?

39–32 A glass plate that is 0.375 μm thick and surrounded by air is illuminated by a beam of white light normal to the plate. The index of refraction of the glass is 1.50. What wavelengths within the limits of the visible spectrum ($\lambda = 400$ nm to $\lambda = 700$ nm) are intensified in the reflected beam?

39–33 In a Young's two-slit experiment a piece of glass with an index of refraction n and a thickness L is placed in front of the upper slit.

a) Describe qualitatively what happens to the interference pattern.

b) Derive an expression for the values of θ that locate the maxima in the interference pattern. That is, derive an equation that is analogous to Eq. (39–4) but that also involves L and n for the glass plate.

39–34 The radius of curvature of the convex surface of a plano-convex lens is 1.40 m. The lens is placed convex side down on a glass plate that is perfectly flat and illuminated from above with red light having a wave-length of 650 nm. Find the diameter of the third bright ring in the interference pattern.

39–35 Newton's rings can be seen when a plano-convex lens is placed on a flat glass surface (Problem 39–34). If the lens has an index of refraction of $n = 1.50$ and the glass plate has an index of $n = 1.80$, the diameter of the second bright ring is 0.650 mm. If a liquid with an index of 1.30 is added to the space between the lens and the plate, what is the new diameter of this ring?

39–36 In Exercise 39–13, suppose the entire apparatus (slits, screen, and space in between) is immersed in water ($n = 1.333$). Then what is the distance between the two dark fringes?

39–37 What is the longest wavelength that can be observed in the fourth order for a transmission grating having 4000 lines per centimeter? Assume normal incidence.

39–38 A slit with width a is placed in front of a lens with focal length 0.800 m. The slit is illuminated by parallel light with wavelength 500 nm, and the diffraction pattern of Fig. 39–20b is formed on a screen in the focal plane of the lens. If the photograph of Fig. 39–20b represents an enlargement to twice the actual size, what is the slit width?

39–39 An astronaut in the space shuttle can just resolve two point sources on earth that are 65.0 m apart. Assume that the resolution is diffraction limited and use Rayleigh's criterion. What is the astronaut's altitude above the earth? Treat his eye as a circular aperture with a diameter of 4.00 mm (the diameter of his pupil), and take the wavelength of the light to be 550 nm.

39–40 A Michelson interferometer can be used to measure the index of refraction of gases by placing an initially evacuated tube in one arm of the interferometer. The gas is then slowly added to the tube, and the number of fringes that cross the telescope crosshairs are counted. If the length of the tube is 4.00 cm and the light source is a sodium lamp (589 nm), what is the index of refraction of the gas if 45 fringes are seen to pass the view of the telescope? (*Note:* For gases it is convenient to give the value of $n - 1$ rather than n itself, since the index differs little from unity.)

Challenge Problems

39–41 The index of refraction of a glass rod is 1.48 at $T = 20.0°C$ and varies linearly with temperature, with a coefficient of 3.00×10^{-5} $(C°)^{-1}$. The coefficient of linear expansion of the glass is 5.00×10^{-6} $(C°)^{-1}$. At 20.0°C the length of the rod is 2.00 cm. A Michelson interferometer has this glass rod in one arm, and the rod is being heated so that its temperature increases at a rate of 5.00 C°·min^{-1}. The light source has wavelength $\lambda = 589$ nm, and the rod initially is at $T = 20.0°C$. How many fringes cross the field of view each minute?

39–42 During the Battle of Britain (World War II) it was found that aircraft flying at certain low altitudes over the English Channel could not receive radio signals from transmission towers located on the Cliffs of Dover, 200 m above the water. At other altitudes the signals received were very strong. For an airplane flying 10.0 km from England and a radio signal with a wavelength of 4.00 m, at what altitudes above the water will the received signal be the strongest? (Consider only altitudes much less than 10 km. Interference occurs between radio waves that travel directly to the plane and those that first reflect off the water.)

39–43 The yellow sodium D lines are a doublet with wavelengths of 589.0 and 589.6 nm and equal intensities.

a) How many lines per centimeter are required for a diffraction grating to resolve these two lines in the second-order spectrum? Assume that the grating is placed 0.500 m from a screen and that the source image is 0.100 mm wide so that resolution of the lines means that their centers are 0.100 mm apart on the screen.

b) The sodium D lines are used as a source in a Michelson interferometer. As the mirror is moved, it is noted that in addition to moving across the field of view, the interference fringes periodically appear and disappear. Why? How far is the mirror moved between disappearances of the fringes?

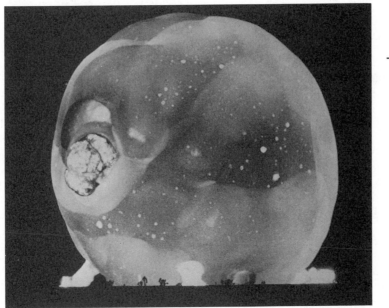

Relativistic Mechanics

In earlier chapters, especially in mechanics, we stressed the importance of inertial frames of reference. In an inertial frame a body acted on by no forces moves with constant velocity. Newton's laws of motion are valid *only* in inertial frames, but they are valid in *all* inertial frames. Any frame moving with constant velocity with respect to an inertial frame is itself an inertial frame, so there are infinitely many inertial frames. As far as the laws of mechanics are concerned, all inertial frames are equivalent. *The laws of mechanics are the same in every inertial frame of reference.*

In 1905, Einstein proposed that this principle should include *all* the basic laws of physics, including electromagnetism as well as mechanics. This innocent-sounding proposition, often called the *principle of relativity*, has far-reaching and startling consequences. For example, we will find that if the principle of conservation of momentum is to be valid in all inertial systems, we have to revise the *definition* of momentum for particles moving at speeds comparable to the speed of light. The definition of kinetic energy also has to be modified. Equally fundamental are the modifications needed in the *kinematic* aspects of motion. These generalizations of the laws of mechanics are part of the **special theory of relativity,** the subject of this chapter. In studying this material you have to be ready to confront some ideas that at first sight will seem too strange to be believed. You will find that your intuition is often unreliable when you are considering phenomena far removed from everyday experience.

Our discussion will center mostly on *mechanical* concepts, but the theory of relativity has far-reaching consequences in *all* areas of physics, including thermodynamics, electromagnetism, optics, atomic and nuclear physics, and high-energy physics.

40–1
Invariance of Physical Laws

Einstein's **principle of relativity** states that *the laws of physics are the same in every inertial frame of reference.* A familiar example in electromagnetism is the electromotive force (emf) induced in a coil of wire by a nearby moving permanent magnet. In the frame of reference where the *coil* is stationary, the moving magnet causes a change of magnetic flux through the coil, and this induces an emf. In a frame of reference where the *magnet* is stationary, the motion of the coil through a magnetic field causes magnetic-field forces on the mobile charges in the conductor, inducing an emf. According to the principle of relativity, both of these points of view have equal validity, and both must predict the same induced emf. As we saw in Chapter 32, Faraday's law of electromagnetic induction can be applied to either description, and it does indeed satisfy this requirement. If the moving-magnet and moving-coil situations *did not* give the same results, we could use this experiment to distinguish one inertial frame from another, and this would contradict the principle of relativity.

Equally significant is the prediction of the speed of electromagnetic radiation, emerging from the development in Chapter 35. Light and all other electromagnetic waves travel with a constant speed $c = 299{,}792{,}458$ m·s^{-1}. (We will often use the approximate value $c = 3.00 \times 10^8$ m·s^{-1}, which is within one part in 1000 of the exact value.) The principle of relativity requires that this speed must be the same in all inertial frames of reference and must be independent of the motion of the source. As we will see, the speed of light plays a very special role in the theory of relativity.

During the nineteenth century, most physicists believed that light traveled through a hypothetical medium called the *ether*, just as sound waves travel through air. If so, the speed of light would depend on the motion of the observer relative to the ether and would therefore be different in different directions. The Michelson–Morley experiment, described in Section 39–4, was an effort to detect motion of the earth relative to the ether. No such motion was ever detected, and the ether concept has been discarded. These negative results paved the way for the prediction, from the principle of relativity, that the speed of light is the same in all frames of reference.

Let's think about what this means. Suppose two observers measure the speed of light. One is at rest with respect to the light source, and the other is moving away from it. Both are in inertial frames of reference. According to the principle of relativity, the two observers must obtain the same speed, despite the fact that one is moving with respect to the other.

If this seems too easy, consider the following situation. A spaceship moving away from earth at 1000 m·s^{-1} fires a missile with a speed of 2000 m·s^{-1} in a direction directly away from earth. What is the missile's speed relative to earth? This is an elementary problem in relative velocity. The correct answer, according to Newtonian mechanics, is 3000 m·s^{-1}. But now suppose there is a searchlight in the spaceship,

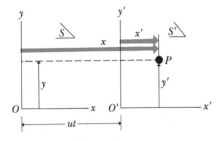

40–1
The position of point P can be described by the coordinates x and y in frame of reference S or by x' and y' in S'. S' moves relative to S with constant velocity u along the common x–x'-axis. The two origins O and O' coincide at time $t = t' = 0$.

pointing in the same direction that the missile was fired. An observer on the spaceship measures the speed of light emitted by the searchlight and obtains the value c. According to our previous discussion, the observer on earth who measures the speed of this same light must also obtain the value c. This contradicts our elementary notion of relative velocities, and it may not appear to agree with common sense. But "common sense" is intuition based on everyday experience, and this does not usually include measurements of the speed of light.

Let's restate this argument symbolically, using the two inertial frames of reference, labeled S for the observer on earth and S' for the moving spaceship, shown in Fig. 40–1. To keep things as simple as possible, we have omitted the z-axes. The x-axes of the two frames lie along the same line, but the origin O' of frame S' moves relative to the origin O of frame S with constant velocity u along the common x–x'-axis. We set our clocks so that the two origins coincide at time $t = 0$, so their separation at a later time t is ut.

Now think about how we describe the motion of a particle P. This might be an exploratory vehicle launched from the spaceship or a flash of light from a searchlight. We can describe the *position* of this point by using the earth coordinates (x, y, z) in S or the spaceship coordinates (x', y', z') in S'. The figure shows that these are related by

$$x = x' + ut, \qquad y = y', \qquad z = z'. \tag{40–1}$$

These equations, based on the familiar Newtonian notions of space and time, are called the **Galilean coordinate transformation.**

If point P moves in the x-direction, its velocity v as measured by an observer stationary in S is given by $v = \Delta x/\Delta t$. Its velocity v' measured by an observer at rest in S' is $v' = \Delta x'/\Delta t$. From our discussion of relative velocities in Sections 2–6 and 3–6 we know that these are related by

$$v = v' + u, \tag{40–2}$$

which agrees with the relative velocity equation we derived at the end of Chapter 2. We can also derive this relation from Eqs. (40–1). Suppose that the particle is at a point described by coordinate x_1 or x_1' at time t_1 and by x_2 or x_2' at time t_2. Then $\Delta t = t_2 - t_1$. From Eq. (40–1),

$$\Delta x = x_2 - x_1 = (x_2' - x_1') + u(t_2 - t_1) = \Delta x' + u\,\Delta t,$$

$$\frac{\Delta x}{\Delta t} = \frac{\Delta x'}{\Delta t} + u,$$

and

$$v = v' + u,$$

in agreement with Eq. (40–2).

Now here's the fundamental problem. Applied to the speed of *light*, Eq. (40–2) says that $c = c' + u$. Einstein's principle of relativity, supported by experimental evidence, says that $c = c'$. This is a genuine inconsistency, not an illusion, and it demands resolution. If we accept the principle of relativity, we are forced to conclude that Eqs. (40–1) and (40–2), intuitively appealing as they are, *cannot* be correct. They have to be modified to bring them into harmony with this principle.

The resolution involves some very fundamental modifications in our kinematic concepts. First is the seemingly obvious assumption that the observers in frames S and S' use the same *time scale*. We can state this formally by adding to Eqs. (40–1) a fourth equation:

$$t = t'.$$

Alas, we are about to show that the assumption $t = t'$ cannot be correct; the two observers *must* have different time scales. The difficulty lies in the concept of *simultaneity*, which is our next topic. A careful analysis of simultaneity will help us to develop the appropriate modifications of our notions about space and time.

40–2
Relative Nature of Simultaneity

Measuring times and time intervals involves the concept of **simultaneity.** When you say that you awoke at seven o'clock, you mean that two *events* (your awakening and the arrival of the hour hand of your clock at the number seven) occurred *simultaneously*. The fundamental problem in measuring time intervals is that, in general, two events that are simultaneous in one frame of reference *are not* simultaneous in a second frame if it is moving in relation to the first, even if both are inertial frames.

Here is a hypothetical experiment, devised by Einstein, that illustrates this point. Consider a long train moving with uniform velocity, as shown in Fig. 40–2a. Two lightning bolts strike the train, one at each end. Each bolt leaves a mark on the train and one on the ground at the same instant. The points on the ground are labeled A and B in the figure, and the corresponding points on the train are A' and B'. An observer is standing on the ground at O, midway between A and B. Another observer is at O' at the middle of the train, midway between A' and B', moving with the train. Both observers see both light flashes emitted from the points where the lightning strikes.

Suppose the two light flashes reach the observer at O simultaneously. He knows he is the same distance from A and B, so he concludes that the two bolts struck A and B simultaneously. But the observer at O' is moving to the right, with the train, with respect to the observer at O, and the light flash from B' reaches her before the light flash from A' does. Because the observer at O' is the same distance from A' and B', she concludes that the lightning bolt at the front of the train struck *earlier* than the one at the rear. The two events appear simultaneous to observer O but not to observer O'! *Whether two events at different space points are simultaneous depends on the state of motion of the observer.*

You may want to argue that in this example the lightning bolts really *are* simultaneous and that if the observer at O' could communicate with the distant points without the time delay caused by the finite speed of light, she would realize this. But that would be erroneous; the finite speed of information transmission is not the real issue. If O' is midway between A' and B', then, in her frame of reference, the time for a signal

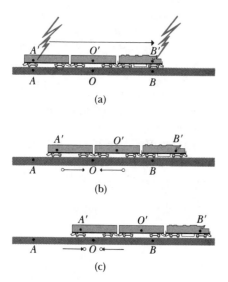

40–2
(a) To the stationary observer at point O, two lightning bolts appear to strike simultaneously. (b) The moving observer at point O' sees the light from the front of the train first and thinks that the bolt at the front struck first. (c) The two light pulses arrive at O simultaneously.

to travel from A' to O' is the same as from B' to O'. Two signals arrive simultaneously at O' only if they were emitted simultaneously at A' and B'. In this example they *do not* arrive simultaneously at O', and so O' must conclude that the events at A' and B' were *not* simultaneous.

Furthermore, there is no basis for saying that O is right and O' is wrong or the reverse. According to the principle of relativity, no inertial frame of reference is preferred over any other in the formulation of physical laws. Each observer is correct *in his or her own frame of reference*. In other words, simultaneity is not an absolute concept. Whether two events are simultaneous depends on the frame of reference. Because of the essential role of simultaneity in measuring time intervals, it also follows that *the time interval between two events depends on the frame of reference*. So our next task is to learn how to compare time intervals in different frames of reference.

40–3
Relativity of Time

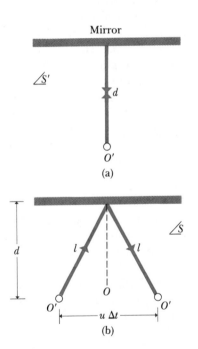

40–3
(a) Light pulse emitted from source at O' and reflected back along the same line, as observed in S'. (b) Path of the same light pulse, as observed in S. The positions of O' at the times of departure and return of the pulse are shown. The speed of the pulse is the same in S as in S', but the path is longer in S.

To derive a quantitative relation between time intervals in different coordinate systems, we consider another thought experiment. As before, a frame of reference S' moves along the common x–x'-axis with constant speed u relative to a frame S. For reasons that will become clear later, we assume that u is always less than the speed of light c. An observer O' in S' with a light source directs a flash of light at a mirror a distance d away, as shown in Fig. 40–3a. He measures the time interval $\Delta t'$ for light to make the "round trip" to the mirror and back. The total distance is $2d$, so the time interval is

$$\Delta t' = \frac{2d}{c}. \qquad (40\text{–}3)$$

The time for the round trip as measured in frame S is a different interval Δt. During this time the source moves in relation to S a distance $u\,\Delta t$. The total round-trip distance as seen in S is not just $2d$ but is $2l$, where

$$l = \sqrt{d^2 + \left(\frac{u\,\Delta t}{2}\right)^2}.$$

In writing this expression we have used the fact that the distance d looks the same to both observers. This can (and indeed must) be justified by other thought experiments, but we won't go into this now. The speed of light is the same for both observers, so the relation in S analogous to Eq. (40–3) is

$$\Delta t = \frac{2l}{c} = \frac{2}{c}\sqrt{d^2 + \left(\frac{u\,\Delta t}{2}\right)^2}. \qquad (40\text{–}4)$$

We would like to have a relation between Δt and $\Delta t'$ that doesn't contain d. To get this, we solve Eq. (40–3) for d and substitute the result into Eq. (40–4), obtaining

$$\Delta t = \frac{2}{c}\sqrt{\left(\frac{c\,\Delta t'}{2}\right)^2 + \left(\frac{u\,\Delta t}{2}\right)^2}.$$

Now we square this and solve for Δt; the result is

$$\Delta t = \frac{\Delta t'}{\sqrt{1 - u^2/c^2}}. \qquad (40\text{–}5)$$

We may generalize this important result: If two events (in our case, the departure and arrival of the light signal at O') occur at the same space point in a frame of reference S' and are separated in time by an interval $\Delta t'$, then the time interval Δt between these two events as observed in S is given by Eq. (40–5). Because the denominator is always smaller than unity, Δt is always *larger* than $\Delta t'$. Thus when the rate of a clock at rest in S' is measured by an observer in S, the rate measured in S is *slower* than the rate observed in S'. This effect is called **time dilation.** We note that Eq. (40–5) makes sense only when $u < c$; otherwise, the denominator is imaginary.

It is important to note that the time interval Δt in frame S cannot be measured by a single observer. In Fig. 40–3 the points of departure and return of the light pulse are different space points in S, although they are the same point in S'. To avoid complications from the finite time of communication between these two points, we can use two observers, each with his own clock, at the two points. We can synchronize these two clocks without difficulty, as long as they are at rest in the same frame of reference. For example, we could send a light pulse simultaneously to the two clocks from a point midway between them. When the pulses arrive, the observers set their clocks to a prearranged time. When a clock is moving in relation to a given frame of reference, then we have to watch for ambiguities of synchronization or simultaneity.

Example 40–1   A spaceship flies past earth with a speed of $0.99c$ (about 2.97×10^8 m·s^{-1}) relative to earth. A high-intensity signal light (perhaps a pulsed laser) blinks on and off; each pulse lasts 2.00×10^{-6} s, as measured on the spaceship. At a certain instant the ship is 1000 km above an observer on earth and is traveling perpendicular to the line of sight. What is the duration of each light pulse, as measured by the observer on earth, and how far does the ship travel in relation to the earth during each pulse?

Solution   Let S be the earth's frame of reference, S' that of the spaceship. Then, in the notation of Eq. (40–5), $\Delta t' = 2.00 \times 10^{-6}$ s. This interval refers to two events occurring at the same point relative to S', namely, the starting and stopping of the pulse. The corresponding interval Δt in S is given by Eq. (40–5):

$$\Delta t = \frac{\Delta t'}{\sqrt{1 - u^2/c^2}} = \frac{2.00 \times 10^{-6} \text{ s}}{\sqrt{1 - (0.99)^2}} = 14.2 \times 10^{-6} \text{ s}.$$

Thus the time dilation in S is about a factor of 7. During this interval the spaceship travels a distance d in S, given by

$$d = u\,\Delta t = (0.99)(3.00 \times 10^8 \text{ m·s}^{-1})(14.2 \times 10^{-6} \text{ s})$$
$$= 4220 \text{ m} = 4.22 \text{ km.} \qquad \blacksquare$$

Example 40–2   An airplane flies from San Francisco to New York (about 4800 km or 4.80×10^6 m) at a steady speed of 300 m·s^{-1} (about 670 mi·hr^{-1}). How much time does the trip take, as measured by observers on the ground? By an observer in the plane?

Solution   The time measured by the ground observers corresponds to Δt in Eq. (40–5); it is simply the distance divided by the speed:

$$\Delta t = \frac{4.80 \times 10^6 \text{ m}}{300 \text{ m·s}^{-1}} = 1.60 \times 10^4 \text{ s,}$$

or about 4 1/2 hours. We need two observers with synchronized clocks to measure this interval, one in San Francisco and one in New York, because the two events (takeoff and landing) occur at different space points in the ground frame of reference. In the airplane's frame they occur at the *same* point. The time interval in the airplane, which can be measured by a single observer, corresponds to $\Delta t'$ in Eq. (40–5). We have

$$\frac{u^2}{c^2} = \frac{(300 \text{ m·s}^{-1})^2}{(3.00 \times 10^8 \text{ m·s}^{-1})^2} = 10^{-12},$$

and from Eq. (40–5),

$$\Delta t' = (1.60 \times 10^4 \text{ s})\sqrt{1 - 10^{-12}} = (1.60 \times 10^4 \text{ s})(1 - 0.500 \times 10^{-12}).$$

The time measured in the airplane is very slightly less (by less than one part in 10^{12}) than the time measured on the ground. We don't notice such effects in everyday life. But as we mentioned in Section 1–2, present-day atomic clocks can attain a precision of about one part in 10^{13}, and measurements similar to this example have been carried out, verifying Eq. (40–5) directly. $\qquad \blacksquare$

The derivation of Eq. (40–5) and Examples 40–1 and 40–2 show that a time interval between two events that occur *at the same point* in a given frame of reference has a special significance. We use the term **proper time** for an interval between two events at the same space point. We can use Eq. (40–5) *only* when $\Delta t'$ is a proper time interval in S'; then Δt is *not* a proper time interval in S. If, instead, Δt is proper in S, then we interchange Δt and $\Delta t'$ in Eq. (40–5).

When the relative velocity u of the two frames of reference S and S' is very small, the factor $(1 - u^2/c^2)$ is very nearly equal to unity, and Eq. (40–5) approaches the Newtonian relation $\Delta t = \Delta t'$ (i.e., the same time scale for all frames of reference).

Equation (40–5) suggests an apparent paradox called the **twin paradox.** Consider two identical-twin astronauts named Eartha and Astro.

Eartha remains on earth, while Astro takes off on a high-speed trip through the galaxy. Because of time dilation, Eartha sees Astro's heartbeat and all other life processes proceeding more slowly than his own. Thus Eartha thinks that Astro ages more slowly, so when Astro returns to earth, he is younger than Eartha.

Now here is the paradox: All inertial frames are equivalent. Can't Astro make exactly the same arguments to conclude that Eartha is in fact the younger? Then each twin thinks that the other is younger, and that's a paradox.

To resolve the paradox, we recognize that the twins are *not* identical in all respects. If Eartha remains in an inertial frame at all times, Astro must have an acceleration with respect to inertial frames during part of his trip in order to turn around and come back. Eartha remains always at rest in the same inertial frame; Astro does not. Thus there is a real physical difference between the circumstances of the twins. Careful analysis shows that Eartha is correct; when Astro returns, he *is* younger than Eartha.

40–4
Relativity of Length

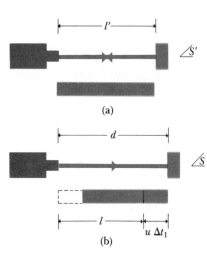

40–4

(a) A light pulse is emitted from a source at one end of a ruler, reflected from a mirror at the opposite end, and returned to the source position, as seen by an observer in S'. (b) Motion of the light pulse as seen by an observer in S. The distance traveled from source to mirror is greater than the length l measured in S, by the amount $u\,\Delta t_1$, as shown.

Just as the time interval between two events depends on the observer's frame of reference, the *distance* between two points also depends on the observer's frame of reference. To measure a distance, one must, in principle, observe the positions of two points, such as the two ends of a ruler, simultaneously; but what is simultaneous in one reference frame is not simultaneous in another.

To develop a relationship between lengths in various coordinate systems, we consider another thought experiment. We attach a source of light pulses to one end of a ruler and a mirror to the other end, as shown in Fig. 40–4. The ruler is at rest in reference frame S', and its length in this frame is l'. Then the time $\Delta t'$ required for a light pulse to make the round trip from source to mirror and back is given by

$$\Delta t' = \frac{2l'}{c}. \tag{40–6}$$

This is a proper time interval because departure and return occur at the same point in S'.

In S the ruler is moving to the right with speed u during this travel of the light pulse. The length of the ruler in S is l, and the time of travel from source to mirror, as measured in S, is Δt_1. During this interval the ruler, with source and mirror attached, moves a distance $u\,\Delta t_1$. The total length of path d from source to mirror is not l but

$$d = l + u\,\Delta t_1. \tag{40–7}$$

The light pulse travels with speed c, so it is also true that

$$d = c\,\Delta t_1. \tag{40–8}$$

Combining Eqs. (40–7) and (40–8) to eliminate d, we find

$$c \, \Delta t_1 = l + u \, \Delta t_1 \qquad \text{or} \qquad \Delta t_1 = \frac{l}{c - u}. \qquad (40\text{--}9)$$

In the same way we can show that the time Δt_2 for the return trip from mirror to source is

$$\Delta t_2 = \frac{l}{c + u}. \qquad (40\text{--}10)$$

The *total* time $\Delta t = \Delta t_1 + \Delta t_2$ for the round trip, as measured in S, is

$$\Delta t = \frac{l}{c - u} + \frac{l}{c + u} = \frac{2l}{c(1 - u^2/c^2)}. \qquad (40\text{--}11)$$

We also know that Δt and $\Delta t'$ are related by Eq. (40–5) because $\Delta t'$ is proper in S'. Thus Eq. (40–6) becomes

$$\Delta t \sqrt{1 - \frac{u^2}{c^2}} = \frac{2l'}{c}. \qquad (40\text{--}12)$$

Finally, combining this with Eq. (40–11) to eliminate Δt, and simplifying, we obtain

$$l = l' \sqrt{1 - \frac{u^2}{c^2}}. \qquad (40\text{--}13)$$

Thus the length l measured in S, in which the ruler is moving, is *shorter* than the length l' measured in S', where it is at rest. A length measured in the rest frame of the body is called a proper length; thus l' above is a proper length in S', and the length measured in any other frame is less than l'. This effect is called **length contraction.**

Example 40–3   In Example 40–1 (Section 40–3) a crew member on the spaceship measures its length, obtaining the value 400 m. What is the length measured by observers on earth?

Solution   The length of the spaceship in the frame in which it is at rest (400 m) corresponds to l' in Eq. (40–13), and we want to find the length l measured by observers on earth. From Eq. (40–13),

$$l = l' \sqrt{1 - \frac{u^2}{c^2}} = (400 \text{ m}) \sqrt{1 - (0.99)^2} = 56.4 \text{ m}.$$

To measure this quantity requires two observers; we have to observe the positions of the two ends of the spaceship simultaneously in the earth's reference frame. (These two observations will *not* appear simultaneous to an observer in the spaceship.)   ■

When u is very small in comparison to c, the contraction factor in Eq. (40–13) approaches unity, and in the limit of small speeds we recover the

Newtonian relation $l = l'$. This and the corresponding result for time dilation show that Eqs. (40–1) retain their validity in the limit of speeds much smaller than c; only at speeds comparable to c are modifications needed.

We have derived Eq. (40–13) for lengths measured in the direction *parallel* to the relative motion of the two frames of reference. Lengths measured *perpendicular* to the direction of motion are *not* contracted. To prove this, consider two identical rulers. One ruler is at rest in frame S and lies along the y-axis with one end at O, the origin of S. The other ruler is at rest in frame S' and lies along the y'-axis with one end at O', the origin of S'. At the instant the two origins coincide, observers in the two frames of reference S and S' simultaneously observe the positions of the upper ends of the rulers. (Note that because the observations occur at the same space point for both observers, they agree that they are simultaneous. If the observer in S thinks that her ruler is shorter, the observer in S' must think that his ruler is longer, or the reverse. But this would mean that there is some distinction between the two frames of reference, and this violates our basic premise that all inertial frames of reference are equivalent. Thus both observers must conclude that the two rulers have the same length, even though to each observer, one of them is stationary and one is moving. So *there is no length contraction perpendicular to the direction of relative motion of the coordinate systems*. In fact, we used this result in our derivation of Eq. (40–5) when we assumed that the distance d is the same in both frames of reference.

40–5
The Lorentz Transformation

In Section 40–1 we discussed the Galilean coordinate transformation, which relates the coordinates (x, y, z) of a point in frame of reference S to the coordinates (x', y', z') of the point in a second frame S' moving with constant velocity u relative to S, along the common x–x'-axis. The transformation is given by Eqs. (40–1). Embedded in this formulation is the assumption that the time scale is the same in the two frames of reference, as expressed by the additional relation $t = t'$. This transformation, as we have seen, is valid only in the limit when u is much smaller than c. We are now ready to derive a more general transformation that is consistent with the principle of relativity. The more general relations are called the *Lorentz transformation*. In the limit of very small u they reduce to the Galilean transformation, but they may also be used when u is comparable to c.

The basic problem is this: When an event occurs at point (x, y, z) at time t, as observed in a frame of reference S, what are the coordinates (x', y', z') and time t' of the event as observed in a second frame S' moving relative to S with constant velocity u along the x-direction?

To derive the transformation equations, we refer to Fig. 40–5, which is the same as Fig. 40–1. As before, we assume that the origins coincide at the initial time $t = t' = 0$. Then in S the distance from O to O' at time t is still ut. The coordinate x' is a *proper length* in S', so in S it appears

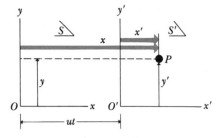

40–5

The distance x' is a proper length in S'. In S it appears contracted by the factor $\sqrt{1 - u^2/c^2}$. The distance between O and O', as seen in S, is ut, and x is a proper length in S. Thus $x = ut + x'\sqrt{1 - u^2/c^2}$.

contracted by the factor given in Eq. (40–13). Thus the distance x from O to P in S is given not simply by $x = ut + x'$ as in the Galilean transformation, but by

$$x = ut + x'\sqrt{1 - \frac{u^2}{c^2}}. \tag{40–14}$$

Solving this equation for x', we obtain

$$x' = \frac{x - ut}{\sqrt{1 - u^2/c^2}}. \tag{40–15}$$

This is half of the Lorentz transformation; the other half is the equation giving t' in terms of x and t. To obtain this, we note that the principle of relativity requires that the *form* of the transformation from S to S' must be identical to that from S' to S; the only difference is a change in the sign of the relative velocity u. Thus from Eq. (40–14) it must be true that

$$x' = -ut' + x\sqrt{1 - \frac{u^2}{c^2}}. \tag{40–16}$$

We now equate Eqs. (40–15) and (40–16) to eliminate x'. This gives us an equation for t' in terms of x and t. We will leave the algebraic details for you to work out; the result is

$$t' = \frac{t - ux/c^2}{\sqrt{1 - u^2/c^2}}. \tag{40–17}$$

As we discussed previously, lengths perpendicular to the direction of relative motion are not affected by the motion, so $y' = y$ and $z' = z$.

Collecting all the transformation equations, we have

$$x' = \frac{x - ut}{\sqrt{1 - u^2/c^2}}, \qquad y' = y,$$

$$z' = z, \qquad t' = \frac{t - ux/c^2}{\sqrt{1 - u^2/c^2}}. \tag{40–18}$$

These are the **Lorentz transformation** equations, the relativistic generalization of the Galilean transformation, Eqs. (40–1). When u is much smaller than c, the radicals in the denominators become unity, and the second term in the numerator of the t' equation becomes zero. In this limit, Eqs. (40–18) become identical to Eqs. (40–1), and $t = t'$. In general, though, both the coordinates and time of an event in one frame depend on its coordinates and time in another frame. Space and time have become intertwined; we can no longer say that length and time have absolute meanings, independent of frame of reference.

We can use Eqs. (40–18) to obtain relations for distance and time *intervals* between two events in the two coordinate systems. Suppose the distance interval is $\Delta x = x_2 - x_1$ and the time interval is $\Delta t = t_2 - t_1$ for two events as observed in frame S, and the corresponding intervals as seen in the moving frame S' are $\Delta x'$ and $\Delta t'$. Then by using Eqs. (40–18) for each event and subtracting, we find

$$\Delta x' = \frac{\Delta x - u\,\Delta t}{\sqrt{1 - u^2/c^2}}, \qquad \Delta t' = \frac{\Delta t - u\,\Delta x/c^2}{\sqrt{1 - u^2/c^2}}. \tag{40–19}$$

The Galilean velocity transformation equation, Eq. (40–2), is valid only in the limit when u is very small. We can use Eqs. (40–19) to derive the appropriate relativistic generalization. We use v and v' for the x-components of velocity of a particle, as measured in S and S', respectively. In S', if a point moves a distance $\Delta x'$ in a time $\Delta t'$, its velocity v' is $v' = \Delta x'/\Delta t'$. Using the expressions for $\Delta x'$ and $\Delta t'$ given by Eqs. (40–19), we find

$$v' = \frac{\Delta x - u\,\Delta t}{\Delta t - u\,\Delta x/c^2} = \frac{(\Delta x/\Delta t) - u}{1 - (u/c^2)(\Delta x/\Delta t)}.$$

But $\Delta x/\Delta t$ equals v, the x-component of velocity as measured in S, so we finally obtain

$$v' = \frac{v - u}{1 - uv/c^2}. \tag{40–20}$$

When u and v are much smaller than c, the denominator in Eq. (40–20) approaches unity, and we obtain the nonrelativistic result $v' = v - u$. The opposite extreme is the case $v = c$; then we find

$$v' = \frac{c - u}{1 - uc/c^2} = c.$$

This says that anything moving with speed c relative to S also has speed c relative to S', despite the relative motion of the two frames. So Eq. (40–20) is consistent with our initial assumption that the speed of light is the same in all frames of reference.

We can also rearrange Eq. (40–20) to give v in terms of v'. We leave the algebraic details as a problem; the result is

$$v = \frac{v' + u}{1 + uv'/c^2}. \tag{40–21}$$

Example 40–4   A spaceship moving away from the earth with speed $0.90c$ fires a missile in the same direction as its motion, with speed $0.70c$ relative to the spaceship. What is the missile's speed relative to the earth?

Solution   Let the earth's frame of reference be S, the spaceship S'. Then $u = 0.90c$ and $v' = 0.70c$. The nonrelativisitic velocity addition formula would give a velocity relative to earth of $1.60c$. The correct relativistic result, from Eq. (40–21), is

$$v = \frac{0.70c + 0.90c}{1 + (0.90c)(0.70c)/c^2} = 0.98c. \qquad \blacksquare$$

When u is less than c, a body moving with a speed less than c in one frame of reference also has a speed less than c in *every other* frame of reference. This is one reason for thinking that no material body may travel with a speed greater than that of light relative to *any* frame of reference. The relativistic generalizations of energy and momentum, which we will consider in the following sections, give further support to this hypothesis.

PROBLEM-SOLVING STRATEGY: *Lorentz Transformation*

1. Try hard to understand the concepts of proper time and proper length. A time interval between two events that happen at the same space point in a particular frame of reference is a proper time in that frame, and the time interval between the same two events is longer in any other frame. The length of a body measured in a frame in which it is at rest is a proper length in that frame, and the length is less in any other frame.

2. The Lorentz transformation equations tell you how to relate measurements made in different inertial frames of reference. When you use them, it helps to make a list of coordinates and times of events in the two frames, such as x_1, x_1', t_2, and so on. List and label carefully what you know and don't know. Do you know the coordinates in one frame? The time of an event in one frame? What are your knowns and unknowns?

3. In velocity-transformation problems, if you have two observers measuring the motion of a body, decide which you want to call S and which S', identify the velocities v and v' clearly, and make sure you know the velocity u of S' relative to S. Use either form of the velocity transformation equation, Eq. (40–20) or (40–21), whichever is more convenient.

4. Don't be discouraged if some of your results don't seem to make sense or if they disagree with your intuition. Reliable intuition about relativity takes time to develop. Keep trying to develop intuitive understanding; it will come.

40–6
Momentum

Newton's laws of motion have the same form in all inertial frames of reference. When we transform coordinates from one inertial frame to another, using the Galilean coordinate transformation, the laws are *invariant* (unchanging). But we have just learned that the principle of relativity forces us to replace the Galilean transformation with the more general Lorentz transformation. As we will see, this requires corresponding generalizations in the laws of motion and the definitions of momentum and energy.

The principle of conservation of momentum states that *when two bodies collide, the total momentum is constant*, provided that they are an *isolated* system (that is, provided that they interact only with each other, not with anything else). If conservation of momentum is a valid physical law, it must be valid in *all* inertial frames of reference. Now, here's the problem: Suppose we look at a collision in one inertial coordinate system S and find that momentum is conserved. Then we use the Lorentz transformation to obtain the velocities in a second inertial system S'. We find that if we use the Newtonian definition of momentum ($p = mv$), momentum is *not* conserved in the second system! If we are convinced that the principle of relativity and the Lorentz transformation are correct, the only way to save momentum conservation is to generalize the *definition* of momentum.

Deriving the correct relativistic generalization of momentum is beyond our scope, and we simply quote the result. The **relativistic momentum p** of a particle with mass m moving with velocity v is given by

$$p = \frac{mv}{\sqrt{1 - v^2/c^2}}. \qquad (40\text{--}22)$$

When the particle's speed v is much less than c, this is approximately equal to the Newtonian expression $p = mv$, but in general the momentum is greater in magnitude than mv.

In Eq. (40–22), m is a *constant* that describes the inertial properties of a particle. Because $p = mv$ is still valid in the limit of very small velocities, m must be the same quantity we used (and learned to measure) in our study of Newtonian mechanics. In relativistic mechanics, m is often called the **rest mass** of a particle.

What about the relativistic generalization of Newton's second law? In Newtonian mechanics, one form of the second law is

$$F = \frac{\Delta p}{\Delta t}, \qquad (40\text{--}23)$$

that is, force equals time rate of change of momentum. Experiments show that this result is still valid in relativistic mechanics, provided that we use the relativistic momentum given by Eq. (40–22). An interesting aspect of this relation is that, because momentum is no longer directly proportional to velocity, the rate of change of momentum is no longer directly proportional to acceleration. As a result, *constant force does not cause constant acceleration.* We can show, by combining Eqs. (40–22) and (40–23) and using methods of calculus, that when the force and velocity are both along the x-axis, the acceleration a is given by

$$F = \frac{m}{(1 - v^2/c^2)^{3/2}}\, a \qquad \text{or} \qquad a = \frac{F}{m}\left(1 - \frac{v^2}{c^2}\right)^{3/2}. \qquad (40\text{--}24)$$

As a particle's speed increases, the acceleration caused by a given force continuously *decreases.* As the speed approaches c, the acceleration approaches zero, no matter how great a force is applied. Thus it is impossible to accelerate a particle from a state of rest to a speed equal to or greater than c, and the speed of light is sometimes called "the ultimate speed."

Equation (40–22) is sometimes interpreted to mean that a rapidly moving particle undergoes an increase in mass. If the mass at zero velocity (the rest mass) is denoted by m, then the "relativistic mass" m_{rel} is given by

$$m_{rel} = \frac{m}{\sqrt{1 - v^2/c^2}}.$$

Indeed, when we consider the motion of a system of particles (such as gas molecules in a moving container), the total mass of the system is the sum of the relativistic masses of the particles, not the sum of their rest masses.

The concept of relativistic mass also has its pitfalls, however. As Eq. (40–24) shows, it is *not* correct to say that the relativistic generalization of Newton's second law is $\boldsymbol{F} = m_{\text{rel}}\boldsymbol{a},$ and it is *not* correct that the relativistic kinetic energy of a particle is $K = \frac{1}{2}m_{\text{rel}}v^2.$ Thus this concept must be approached with great caution. For our discussion it is best to think of Eq. (40–22) as a generalized definition of momentum and to retain the meaning of m as a constant for each particle, independent of its state of motion. We will derive the correct relativistic kinetic-energy expression in Section 40–7.

40–7
Work and Energy

When we developed the relationship between work and kinetic energy in Chapter 7, we used Newton's laws of motion. But these laws have to be generalized to bring them into harmony with the principle of relativity, so we also need to generalize the definition of kinetic energy.

As Eq. (40–24) shows, a constant force on a body does not cause a constant acceleration (except when the speed of the body is very small). For this reason, even the simplest dynamics problems require the use of calculus, and we will not be able to carry out a detailed derivation of the relativistic work–energy theorem (the relativistic version of Section 7–4). Instead, we have to be content with quoting the result. We retain the classical definition of work W done by a force F:

$$W = \sum_i F_i \, \Delta x_i.$$

The derivation yields the result that

$$W = \frac{mc^2}{\sqrt{1 - v_2^2/c^2}} - \frac{mc^2}{\sqrt{1 - v_1^2/c^2}},$$

where v_1 and v_2 are the initial and final speeds of the particle, respectively.

This result suggests that we might define kinetic energy as

$$K = \frac{mc^2}{\sqrt{1 - v^2/c^2}}. \tag{40–25}$$

But this expression is not zero when the particle is at rest. Instead, when $v = 0,$ it becomes equal to $mc^2.$ Thus the correct relativistic generalization of kinetic energy K must be

$$K = \frac{mc^2}{\sqrt{1 - v^2/c^2}} - mc^2. \tag{40–26}$$

If this expression is correct, it must reduce to the Newtonian expression $K = \frac{1}{2}mv^2$ when v is much smaller than $c.$ It does, although it's not obvious. To prove it, we expand the radical using the binomial theorem:

$$\left(1 - \frac{v^2}{c^2}\right)^{-1/2} = 1 + \frac{1}{2}\frac{v^2}{c^2} + \frac{3}{8}\frac{v^4}{c^4} + \frac{5}{16}\frac{v^6}{c^6} + \cdots.$$

Combining this with Eq. (40–26), we find

$$K = mc^2\left(1 + \frac{1}{2}\frac{v^2}{c^2} + \frac{3}{8}\frac{v^4}{c^4} + \cdots\right) - mc^2$$

$$= \frac{1}{2}mv^2 + \frac{3}{8}\frac{v^4}{c^2} + \cdots. \tag{40–27}$$

When v is much smaller than c, all the terms in the series except the first are negligibly small, and we obtain the classical $\frac{1}{2}mv^2$.

But what is the significance of the term mc^2 that we had to subtract in Eq. (40–26)? Although Eq. (40–25) does not give the *kinetic energy* of the particle, perhaps it represents some kind of *total* energy, including both the kinetic energy and an additional energy mc^2, which the particle possesses even when it is not moving. Calling this total energy E and using Eq. (40–26), we find

$$E = K + mc^2 = \frac{mc^2}{\sqrt{1 - v^2/c^2}}. \tag{40–28}$$

The energy mc^2 associated with mass rather than motion is called the **rest energy** of the particle.

There is direct experimental evidence that rest energy really does exist. The simplest example is the decay of the π^0 meson, an unstable particle that undergoes a decay process in which the particle disappears and electromagnetic radiation appears. When the particle, with mass m, is at rest (and therefore has no kinetic energy) before its decay, the total energy of the radiation produced is found to be exactly equal to mc^2. There are many other examples of fundamental particle transformations in which the total mass of the system changes; in every case a corresponding energy change occurs, consistent with the assumption of a rest energy mc^2 associated with a rest mass m.

Historically, the principles of conservation of mass and of energy developed quite independently. The theory of relativity now shows that they are actually two special cases of a single broader conservation principle, the *principle of conservation of mass and energy*. In some physical phenomena, neither mass nor energy is separately conserved, but the changes in these quantities are related by a more general conservation principle: When a change in rest mass m occurs in an isolated system, an opposite change mc^2 in the total energy of other types must accompany this change.

The conversion of mass into energy is the fundamental principle involved in the generation of power through nuclear reactions, a subject we will discuss in Chapter 44. When a uranium nucleus undergoes fission in a nuclear reactor, the total mass of the resulting fragments is *less than* that of the parent nucleus, and the total kinetic energy of the fragments is equal to this mass deficit multiplied by c^2. This kinetic energy can be used in a variety of ways, such as producing steam to operate turbines for electric power generators.

We can also relate the total energy E (kinetic plus rest) of a particle directly to its momentum by combining Eqs. (40–22) and (40–28) to eliminate the particle's velocity. The simplest procedure is to rewrite these equations in the following forms:

$$\left(\frac{E}{mc^2}\right)^2 = \frac{1}{1 - v^2/c^2}; \qquad \left(\frac{p}{mc}\right)^2 = \frac{v^2/c^2}{1 - v^2/c^2}.$$

Subtracting the second of these from the first and rearranging, we find

$$E^2 = (mc^2)^2 + (pc)^2. \qquad (40\text{--}29)$$

Again we see that for a particle at rest ($p = 0$), $E = mc^2$.

Equation (40–29) also suggests that a particle may have energy and momentum even when it has no rest mass. In such a case, $m = 0$ and

$$E = pc. \qquad (40\text{--}30)$$

In fact, massless particles do exist. One example is the *photon*, the quantum of electromagnetic radiation. We will study these particles in greater detail in later chapters. They always travel with the speed of light; they are emitted and absorbed during changes of state of an atomic or nuclear system when the energy and momentum of the system changes.

40–8
Relativity and Newtonian Mechanics

The sweeping changes required by the principle of relativity go to the very roots of Newtonian mechanics, including the concepts of length and time, the equations of motion, and the conservation principles. Thus it may appear that we have destroyed the foundations on which Newtonian mechanics is built. In one sense this is true, and yet the Newtonian formulation is still valid whenever speeds are small in comparison with the speed of light. In such cases, time dilation, length contraction, and the modifications of the laws of motion are so small that they are unobservable. In fact, every one of the principles of Newtonian mechanics survives as a special case of the more general relativistic formulation.

The laws of Newtonian mechanics are not *wrong*; they are *incomplete*. They are a limiting case of relativistic mechanics; they are *approximately* correct when all speeds are small in comparison to c, and in the limit when all speeds approach zero they become exactly correct. Thus relativity does not completely destroy the laws of Newtonian mechanics but *generalizes* them. Newton's laws rest on a very solid base of experimental evidence, and it would be very strange to advance a new theory that is inconsistent with this evidence. This is a common pattern in the development of physical theory. Whenever a new theory is in partial conflict with an older, established theory, it still must yield the same predictions as the old in areas in which the old theory is supported by experimental evidence. Every new physical theory must pass this test, called the **correspondence principle.** This principle is a fundamental procedural rule in all of physics. There are many situations for which Newtonian mechanics is clearly inadequate, including all phenomena in which particle speeds are comparable to that of light or direct conversion of mass to energy occurs. But there is still a large area, including nearly all the behavior of macroscopic bodies in mechanical systems, in which Newtonian mechanics is still perfectly adequate.

At this point we may ask whether relativistic mechanics is the final word on this subject or whether *further* generalizations are possible or necessary. For example, inertial frames of reference have occupied a privileged position in our discussion. Should the principle of relativity be extended to noninertial frames as well?

Here is an example that illustrates some implications of this question. A student decides to go over Niagara Falls while enclosed in a large wooden box. During his free fall he can perform experiments inside the box. An object released inside the box does not fall to the floor because both the box and the object are in free fall with a downward acceleration of 9.8 m·s^{-2}. But an alternative interpretation, from the student's point of view, is that the gravitational interaction with the earth, which causes his weight, has suddenly been turned off. As long as he remains in the box and it remains in free fall, he cannot tell whether he is indeed in free fall or whether the gravitational interaction has vanished. A similar problem appears in a space station in orbit around the earth. Objects in the spaceship appear to be weightless, but without looking outside the ship there is no way to determine whether gravitational interactions have disappeared or whether the spaceship is in an accelerated (i.e., noninertial) frame of reference.

These considerations form the basis of Einstein's **general theory of relativity.** If we cannot distinguish experimentally between a gravitational field at a particular location and an accelerated reference system, then there cannot be any real distinction between the two. Pursuing this concept, we may try to represent *any* gravitational field in terms of special characteristics of the coordinate system. This turns out to require even more sweeping revisions of our space–time concepts than did the special theory of relativity, and we find that, in general, the geometric properties of space are non-Euclidean.

The basic ideas of the general theory of relativity are now well established, but some of the details remain speculative in nature. Its most significant applications are in cosmological investigations of the structure of the universe, the formation and evolution of stars, and related matters. In recent years a few attempts have been made to test this theory with purely terrestrial experiments, and no major surprises have turned up.

Questions

40–1 What do you think would be different in everyday life if the speed of light were 10 m·s^{-1} instead of its actual value?

40–2 The average life span in the United States is about 70 years. Does this mean that it is impossible for an average person to travel a distance greater than 70 light-years away from the earth? (A light-year is the distance light travels in a year.)

40–3 What are the fundamental distinctions between an inertial frame of reference and a noninertial frame?

40–4 A physicist claimed that it is impossible to define what is meant by a rigid body in a relativistically correct way. Why?

40–5 Two events occur at the same space point in a particular frame of reference and appear to be simultaneous in that frame. Is it possible that they may not appear to be simultaneous in another frame?

40–6 Does the fact that simultaneity is not an absolute concept also destroy the concept of *causality*? If event *A* is to *cause* event *B*, *A* must occur first. Is is possible that in some frames *A* may appear to cause *B* and in others *B* may appear to cause *A*?

40–7 A social scientist who has done distinguished work in fields far removed from physics has written a book purporting to refute the special theory of relativity. He begins with a premise that might be paraphrased as follows: "Either two events occur at the same time, or they don't; that's just common sense." How would you respond to this in the light of our discussion of the relative nature of simultaneity?

40–8 When an object travels across an observer's field of view at a relativistic speed, it appears not only foreshortened but also slightly rotated, with the side toward the observer shifted in the direction of motion relative to the side away from her. How does this come about?

40–9 According to the twin paradox mentioned in Section 40–3, if one twin stays on earth while the other takes off in a spaceship at relativistic speed and then returns, one will be older than the other. Can you think

of a practical experiment, perhaps using two very precise atomic clocks, that would test this conclusion?

40–10 When a monochromatic light source moves toward an observer, its wavelength appears to be shorter than the value measured when the source is at rest. Does this contradict the hypothesis that the speed of light is the same for all observers? What about the apparent frequency of light from a moving source?

40–11 A student asserted that a massive particle must always have a speed less than that of light, while a massless particle must always travel at exactly the speed of light. Is he correct? If so, how do massless particles such as photons and neutrinos acquire this speed? Can they not start from rest and accelerate?

40–12 The theory of relativity sets an upper limit on the speed a particle can have. Are there also limits on its energy and momentum?

40–13 In principle, does a hot gas have more mass than the same gas when it is cold? Explain. In practice, would this be a measurable effect?

40–14 Why do you think the development of Newtonian mechanics preceded the more refined relativistic mechanics by so many years?

Exercises

Section 40–2   Relative Nature of Simultaneity

40–1 For the train discussed in Section 40–2, suppose the two lightning bolts appear to be simultaneous to an observer on the train. Show that they *do not* appear to be simultaneous to an observer on the ground. Which appears to come first?

Section 40–3   Relativity of Time

40–2 A spaceship flies past Mars with a speed of $0.964c$ relative to the surface of Mars. When the spaceship is directly overhead at an altitude of 1500 km, a very bright signal light on the Martian surface blinks on and then off. An observer on Mars measures that the signal light was on for 8.00×10^{-5} s. What is the duration of the light pulse measured by the pilot of the spaceship?

40–3 The π^+ meson, an unstable particle, lives on the average about 2.6×10^{-8} s (measured in its own frame of reference) before decaying.

   a) If such a particle is moving with respect to the laboratory with a speed of $0.992c$, what lifetime is measured in the laboratory?

   b) What distance, measured in the laboratory, does the particle move before decaying?

40–4 The μ^+ meson (or positive muon) is an unstable particle with a lifetime of about 2.3×10^{-6} s (measured in the rest frame of the muon).

   a) If the muon is made to travel at very high speed relative to a laboratory, its lifetime is measured in the laboratory to be 1.2×10^{-5} s. Calculate the speed of the muon expressed as a fraction of c.

   b) What distance, measured in the laboratory, does the particle travel during its lifetime?

40–5 An advanced space probe in the twenty-first century travels from the earth with a speed of 2.00×10^6 m·s^{-1} relative to the earth and then returns at the same speed. The probe carries an atomic clock that has been carefully synchronized with an identical clock that remains at rest on earth. The probe returns after 1 year, as measured on earth, has passed. What is the difference in the elapsed times on the two clocks? Which clock, the one in the probe or the one on earth, shows the smallest elapsed time?

40–6 An alien spacecraft is flying overhead at a great distance as you stand in your backyard. You see its searchlight blink on for 5.00×10^{-4} s. The first officer on the spacecraft measures that the searchlight is on for 8.00×10^{-5} s.

a) Which of these two measured times is the proper time?

b) What is the speed of the spacecraft relative to the earth, expressed as a fraction of the speed of light c?

Section 40–4   Relativity of Length

40–7 You measure the length of a futuristic car to be 3.60 m when the car is at rest relative to you. If you measure the length of the car as it zooms past you at a speed of $0.900c$, what result do you get?

40–8 A meter stick moves past you at great speed. If you measure the length of the moving meter stick to be 0.840 m—for example, by comparing it to a meter stick that is at rest relative to you—what is the speed with which the meter stick is moving relative to you?

40–9 In the year 2010 a spacecraft flies over Moon Station III at a speed of $0.800c$. A scientist on the moon measures the length of the moving spacecraft to be 140 m. The spacecraft later lands on the moon, and the same scientist measures the length of the now stationary spacecraft. What value does she get?

40–10 An unstable particle is created in the upper atmosphere from a cosmic ray and travels straight down toward the surface of the earth with a speed of $0.9992c$ relative to the earth. A scientist in a laboratory on the surface of the earth measures that the particle is created at an altitude of 60.0 km.

a) As measured by the scientist, how much time does it take the particle to travel the 60.0 km to the surface of the earth?

b) Use the length contraction formula to calculate the distance from where the particle is created to the surface of the earth as measured in the particle's frame.

c) In the particle's frame, how much time does it take the particle to travel from where it is created to the surface of the earth? Calculate this time both by the time dilation formula and from the distance calculated in part (b). Do the two results agree?

40–11 A muon created 20.0 km above the surface of the earth (as measured in the earth's frame) is traveling with a speed relative to the earth of $0.996c$. The lifetime of the muon, measured in its own rest frame, is 2.3×10^{-6} s. In the frame of the muon the earth is moving toward the muon with a speed of $0.996c$.

a) In the muon's frame, what is its height above the surface of the earth?

b) In the muon's frame, how much closer does the earth get during the lifetime of the muon? What fraction is this of the muon's original height, as measured in the muon's frame?

c) In the earth's frame, what is the lifetime of the muon? In the earth's frame how far does the muon travel during its lifetime? What fraction is this of the muon's original height in the earth's frame?

40–12 Two events are observed in a frame of reference S to occur at the same space point, the second occurring 2.00 s after the first. In a second frame S' moving relative to S, the second event is observed to occur 2.50 s after the first. What is the distance between the positions of the two events as measured in S'?

Section 40–5   The Lorentz Transformation

40–13 Show in detail the derivation of Eq. (40–17) from Eqs. (40–15) and (40–16).

40–14 Solve Eqs. (40–18) to obtain x and t in terms of x' and t', and show that the resulting transformation has the same form as the original one except for a change of sign for u.

40–15 Show the details of the derivation of Eq. (40–21) from Eq. (40–20).

40–16 An enemy spaceship is moving toward your starfighter with a speed, as measured in your frame, of $0.600c$. The enemy ship fires a missile toward you at a speed of $0.800c$ relative to the enemy ship.

a) What is the speed of the missile relative to you? Express your answer in terms of the speed of light.

b) If you measure that the enemy ship is 4.00×10^6 km away from you when the missile is fired, how much time, measured in your frame, will it take the missile to reach you?

40–17 A spaceship moving relative to the earth at a large speed fires a missile toward the earth with a speed of $0.840c$ relative to the spaceship. An earth-based observer measures that the missile is approaching him with a speed of $0.400c$. What is the speed of the spaceship relative to the earth? Is the spaceship moving toward or away from the earth?

40–18 Two particles emerge from a high-energy accelerator in opposite directions, each with a speed $0.700c$ as measured in the laboratory. What is the magnitude of the relative velocity of the particles?

40–19 A rebel fighter is in hot pursuit of a starfleet cruiser. As measured by an observer on earth, the starfleet cruiser is traveling with a speed of $0.800c$ and the rebel fighter at $0.900c$ in the same direction. What is the speed of the cruiser relative to the fighter?

40–20 Two particles are created in a high-energy accelerator and move off in opposite directions. The speed of one of the particles, as measured in the laboratory, is $0.700c$, and the speed of each particle relative to the other is $0.900c$. What is the speed of the second particle, as measured in the laboratory?

Section 40–6 Momentum

40–21 At what speed is the momentum of a particle three times as great as the result obtained from the nonrelativistic expression mv?

40–22

a) At what speed does the momentum of a particle differ by 2.0% from the value obtained by using the nonrelativistic expression mv?

b) Is the correct relativistic value of the momentum greater or less than that obtained from the nonrelativistic expression?

Section 40–7 Work and Energy

40–23 Compute the kinetic energy of an electron using both the nonrelativistic and relativistic expressions, and compute the ratio of the two results (relativistic divided by nonrelativistic), for speeds of

a) $5.00 \times 10^7 \ \mathrm{m\cdot s^{-1}}$;

b) $2.60 \times 10^8 \ \mathrm{m\cdot s^{-1}}$.

40–24 What is the speed of a particle whose kinetic energy is equal to

a) its rest energy?

b) five times its rest energy?

40–25 In *positron annihilation* an electron and a positron (a positively charged electron) collide and disappear, producing electromagnetic radiation. If each particle has a mass of 9.109×10^{-31} kg and they are at rest just before the annihilation, find the total energy of the radiation.

40–26

a) How much work must be done on a particle with mass m to accelerate it from rest to a speed of $0.0900c$? (Express the answer in terms of mc^2.)

b) From a speed $0.900c$ to a speed $0.990c$?

40–27 In a hypothetical nuclear-fusion reactor, two deuterium nuclei combine or "fuse" to form one helium nucleus. The mass of a deuterium nucleus, expressed in atomic mass units (u), is 2.0136 u; that of a helium nucleus is 4.0015 u. (1 u = 1.661×10^{-27} kg.)

a) How much energy is released when 1.0 kg of deuterium undergoes fusion?

b) The annual consumption of electrical energy in the United States is of the order of 1.0×10^{19} J. How much deuterium must react to produce this much energy?

40–28 The total consumption of electrical energy per year in the United States is of the order of 1.0×10^{19} J. If matter could be converted completely into energy, how many kilograms of matter would have to be converted to produce this much energy?

40–29 A particle has a rest mass of 3.32×10^{-27} kg and a momentum of $9.00 \times 10^{-19} \ \mathrm{kg\cdot m\cdot s^{-1}}$.

a) What is the total energy (kinetic plus rest energy) of the particle?

b) What is the kinetic energy of the particle?

c) What is the ratio of the kinetic energy to the rest energy of the particle?

40–30 Calculate relativistically the amount of work in MeV that must be done

a) to bring an electron from rest to a speed of $0.450c$;

b) to increase its speed from $0.450c$ to $0.900c$.

c) What is the ratio of the kinetic energy of the electron at the speed of $0.900c$ to that of $0.450c$ when computed (i) from relativistic values and (ii) from classical values?

 ## Problems

40–31 The starships of the Solar Federation are marked with the symbol of the Federation, a circle, while starships of the Denabian Empire are marked with the Empire's symbol, an ellipse whose major axis is 1.50 times its minor axis. How fast relative to an observer does a Federation ship have to travel for its markings to be confused with those of the Empire?

40–32 A space probe is sent to the star Vega, which is 26.5 light-years from earth. The probe travels with a speed of $0.999c$ and leaves earth containing a single

bacterium, which reproduces on earth with a doubling time of 2.16×10^5 s. (The doubling time is the time it takes the number of bacteria to double.) If the bacteria reproduce unchecked during the flight, how many bacteria are on board when the probe reaches Vega?

40–33 The Stanford Linear Accelerator Center (SLAC) uses a 3.00-km-long tube in accelerating subatomic particles. The π^+ meson has a lifetime of 2.6×10^{-8} s.

a) How fast must a π^+ meson travel if it is not to decay before it reaches the end of the tube? (Since

v will be very close to c, write $v = [1 - \Delta]c$ and give your answer in terms of Δ rather than v.)

b) With a rest mass of 139.6 MeV, what is the π^+ meson's total energy at the speed calculated in part (a)?

40–34 A cube of metal with sides of length a sits at rest in a frame S_1 with one edge parallel to the x-axis. Therefore in S_1 the cube has volume a^3. Frame S_2 moves along the x-axis with a velocity $\mathbf{v}$. To an observer in frame S_2, what is the volume of the metal cube?

40–35 Use the Lorentz transformation equations, Eq. (40–18), to show that $x^2 + y^2 + z^2 - c^2t^2 = x'^2 + y'^2 + z'^2 - c^2t'^2$. The expression $x^2 + y^2 + z^2 - c^2t^2$ is thus the same in any reference frame. Such quantities are called *relativistic invariants*.

40–36 Two atomic clocks are carefully synchronized. One remains in New York while the other is loaded on a supersonic airplane that travels at an average speed of 400 m·s^{-1} and then returns to New York. When the plane returns, the elapsed time on the clock that stayed behind is 5.00 hr. By how much will the readings of the two clocks differ, and which clock will show the smaller elapsed time? (*Hint:* Use the fact that $u \ll c$ to simplify $\sqrt{1 - u^2/c^2}$ by making a binomial expansion.)

40–37 By what amount does the mass of 1.00 kg of ice increase when the ice melts?

40–38 Starting from Eq. (40–29), show that in the classical limit ($pc \ll mc^2$) the energy approaches the classical kinetic energy plus the rest mass energy.

40–39 A photon with energy E is emitted by an atom with mass m, which recoils in the opposite direction.

a) Assuming that the atom can be treated nonrelativistically, compute the recoil speed of the atom.

b) From the result of part (a), show that the recoil speed is much smaller than c whenever E is much smaller than the rest energy mc^2 of the atom.

40–40 A radioactive isotope of cobalt, ^{60}Co, emits an electromagnetic photon (gamma ray) with energy of 1.33 MeV. The cobalt nucleus contains 27 protons and 33 neutrons, each with a mass of about 1.66×10^{-27} kg.

a) If the nucleus is at rest before emission, what is the speed afterward?

b) Is it necessary to use the relativistic generalization of momentum?

40–41 In Problem 40–40, suppose that the cobalt atom is in a metallic crystal containing 0.0100 mol of cobalt (6.02×10^{21} atoms) and that the entire crystal recoils as a unit, rather than just the single nucleus. Find the recoil speed. (This recoil of the entire crystal rather than a single nucleus is called the *Mössbauer effect* in honor of its discoverer, who first observed it in 1958.)

40–42 A particle is said to be in the *extreme relativistic range* when its kinetic energy is much larger than its rest energy.

a) What is the speed of a particle (expressed as a fraction of c) such that the total energy is five times the rest energy?

b) What is the percentage difference between the left and right sides of Eq. (40–29) if $(mc^2)^2$ is neglected for a particle with the speed calculated in part (a)?

40–43 A nuclear bomb containing 15.0 kg of plutonium explodes. The rest mass of the products of the explosion is less than the original rest mass by one part in 10^4.

a) How much energy is released in the explosion?

b) If the explosion takes place in 2.00 μs, what is the average power developed by the bomb?

c) What mass of water could the released energy lift to a height of 1.00 km?

40–44 Electrons are accelerated through a potential difference of 7.50×10^5 V so that their kinetic energy is 7.50×10^5 eV.

a) What is the ratio of the speed v of an electron having this energy to the speed of light c?

b) What would the speed be if it were computed from the principles of classical mechanics?

40–45 An electron in a certain X-ray tube is accelerated from rest through a potential difference of 160,000 V in going from the cathode to the anode. When it arrives at the anode, what is

a) its kinetic energy in electronvolts?

b) its total energy in electronvolts?

c) its speed?

d) What is the speed of the electron, calculated classically?

40–46 Construct a right triangle in which one of the angles is α, where $\sin \alpha = v/c$ (v is the speed of a particle, c the speed of light). If the base of the triangle (the side adjacent to α) is the rest energy mc^2, show that

a) the hypotenuse is the total energy;

b) the side opposite α is c times the relativistic momentum.

c) Describe a simple graphical procedure for finding the kinetic energy K.

40–47 The Soviet physicist P. A. Cerenkov discovered that a charged particle traveling in a solid with a speed exceeding the speed of light in that material radiates electromagnetic radiation. What is the minimum kinetic energy (in electronvolts) an electron must have while traveling inside a slab of crown glass ($n = 1.52$) to create this Cerenkov radiation?

40–48 An astronaut, her jet pack, and her spacesuit have a combined rest mass of 100 kg and a speed of 5.00×10^4 m·s^{-1}.

a) What is the difference between her correct relativistic kinetic energy and her Newtonian kinetic energy? Note that you cannot simply calculate both values and subtract, since the precision of most calculators is insufficient. Instead, use the binomial theorem to expand the square root that appears in the relativistic expression.

b) What fraction of the Newtonian energy is this difference?

Challenge Problems

40–49 In high-energy physics, new particles are created by collisions of fast-moving projectile particles with stationary particles. Some of the kinetic energy of the incident particle is used to create the mass of the new particle. A proton–proton collision can result in the creation of 2 pions (π^- and π^+):

$$p + p \rightarrow p + p + \pi^- + \pi^+.$$

a) Calculate the threshold kinetic energy of the incident proton that will allow this reaction to occur if the second proton is initially at rest. The rest mass of each π is 139.6 MeV. (*Hint:* Working in the center-of-mass frame is useful here. See Challenge Problem 8–58. But now the Lorentz transformation must be used to relate the velocities in the laboratory and the center-of-mass frames.)

b) How does this calculated threshold kinetic energy compare with the total rest mass energy of the created particles?

40–50 The French physicist Fizeau was the first to measure the speed of light accurately. (See Section 36–1.) He also found experimentally that the speed relative to the lab frame of light traveling in a tank of water that is itself moving at a speed V relative to the lab frame is

$$v = c/n + kV.$$

Fizeau called k the dragging coefficient and obtained an experimental value of $k = 0.44$. What value of k would you calculate from relativistic transformations?

40–51 Two events observed in a frame of reference S have positions and times given by (x_1, t_1) and (x_2, t_2), respectively.

a) Show that in a frame S' moving along the x-axis just fast enough that the two events occur at the same point in S', the time interval $\Delta t'$ between the two events is given by

$$\Delta t' = \sqrt{(\Delta t)^2 - \left(\frac{\Delta x}{c}\right)^2},$$

where $\Delta x = x_2 - x_1$, and $\Delta t = t_2 - t_1$. Hence show that if $\Delta x \geq c\,\Delta t$, there is *no* frame S' in which the two events occur at the same point. The interval $\Delta t'$ is sometimes called the *proper-time interval* for the events. Is this term appropriate?

b) Show that if $\Delta x > c\,\Delta t$, there is a frame of reference S', in which the two events occur *simultaneously*. Find the distance between the two events in S'. This distance is sometimes called a *proper length*. Is this term appropriate?

c) Two events are observed in a frame of reference S' to occur simultaneously at points separated by a distance of 1.00 m. In a second frame S moving relative to S' along the line joining the two points in S', the two events appear to be separated by 3.00 m. What is the time interval between the events as measured in S? (*Hint:* Apply the result obtained in part (b).)

41

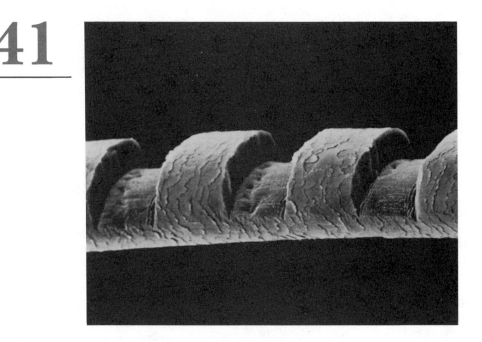

Photons, Electrons, and Atoms

The work of Maxwell, Hertz, and others established that light is an electromagnetic wave. Optical phenomena such as interference, diffraction, and polarization show the wave nature of light. When interference effects can be neglected, we can use the simpler *ray* model to analyze the behavior of lenses and mirrors.

But there are many phenomena in which light seems to behave as a stream of *particles*. Among these are the photoelectric effect (the emission of electrons from a surface when light strikes it); the emission of line spectra of elements; and the production and scattering of X-rays. In all these phenomena the energy of light appears to be carried in packages with a definite size, called *photons* or *quanta*. The energy of a single photon is proportional to the frequency of the radiation. The existence of line spectra also suggests the existence of *energy levels* in atoms. These can be deduced from the frequencies of the spectrum lines, but there is also the problem of how to *calculate* the levels from fundamental principles. The search for understanding of these matters takes us to the threshold of *quantum mechanics*, which involves some radical changes in our views of the nature of radiation and of matter itself.

41–1
Emission and Absorption of Light

How is light produced? In Chapter 35 we discussed the electromagnetic-wave experiments of Hertz. He produced waves using oscillations in a resonant L–C circuit similar to those we studied in Chapter 33. His frequencies were of the order of 10^8 Hz. Frequencies of visible light are of the order of 10^{15} Hz, far higher than the highest frequencies that can be attained with conventional electronic circuits.

In the mid-nineteenth century theorists speculated that waves in this frequency range might be produced by oscillating electric charges within individual atoms. One of the great challenges was to understand the production of *line spectra*. A prism or a diffraction grating can be used to separate the various wavelengths in a beam of light into a *spectrum*. If the light source is an incandescent solid or liquid, the spectrum is *continuous*; light of all wavelengths is present. But if the source is a gas carrying an electrical discharge or a volatile salt heated in a flame, only a few colors appear, in the form of isolated sharp parallel lines. (Each "line" is an image of the spectrograph slit, deviated through an angle that depends on the frequency of the light forming the image.) A spectrum of this sort is called a **line spectrum.** Each line corresponds to a definite wavelength and frequency.

It was discovered early in the nineteenth century that each element has a certain set of wavelengths in its line spectrum. Hydrogen always gives a set of lines with the same set of wavelengths; sodium produces a different set, iron still another, and so on. The existence of a characteristic spectrum for each element showed that the characteristics and internal structure of an atom are directly related to its spectrum. However, attempts to understand this relation on the basis of classical mechanics and electrodynamics were not successful.

There were also mysteries associated with *absorption* of light. In 1887, Hertz discovered the **photoelectric effect** during his electromagnetic-wave experiments. When light strikes the surface of a conductor, some electrons near the surface absorb energy and escape from the surface into the surrounding space. Detailed investigation of this effect revealed some puzzling features that could *not* be understood on the basis of classical optics. We will discuss these in the next section.

Still another area of unsolved problems centered around the production and scattering of *X-rays*, electromagnetic radiation with wavelengths shorter than those of visible light by a factor of the order of 10^4 and with correspondingly greater frequencies. These rays were produced in high-voltage glow discharge tubes, but no one understood how or why. Even worse, when these rays collided with matter, the scattered rays sometimes had a longer wavelength than the original ray. This is analogous to a beam of blue light striking a mirror and reflecting back as red!

All these phenomena and several others pointed forcefully to the conclusion that classical optics, successful though it was in explaining ray optics, interference, and polarization, nevertheless had its limitations. Understanding these phenomena would require at least some generalization of classical theory. In fact, it has required something much more radical than that. All these phenomena are concerned with the *quantum theory* of radiation. Despite the *wave* nature of electromagnetic radiation, some of its properties resemble those of *particles*. In particular, the *energy* in an electromagnetic wave always comes in packages with a magnitude proportional to the *frequency* of the wave. These units of energy are called *photons* or *quanta*. In the remainder of this chapter we will apply this dual wave–particle view to some of the phenomena mentioned above.

41–2
The Photoelectric Effect

The **photoelectric effect** is the emission of electrons from the surface of a conductor when light strikes the surface. The liberated electrons have absorbed energy from the incident radiation and are thus able to overcome the potential-energy barrier that normally confines them inside the material. Think of this barrier as a curb separating a flat street from a sidewalk. A ball rolling on the street can bounce against a curb and back into the street, but if it has enough kinetic energy it can hop up onto the sidewalk, gaining potential energy (proportional to the height of the curb) and losing an equal amount of kinetic energy.

The photoelectric effect was first observed in 1887 by Hertz, quite by accident. He noticed that a spark would jump more readily between two electrically charged spheres when their surfaces were illuminated by the light from another spark. Light shining on the surfaces somehow facilitated the escape of electrons. This idea in itself was not revolutionary. The existence of the surface potential-energy barrier was already known. In 1883, Edison had discovered **thermionic emission,** in which the escape energy is supplied by heating the material to a very high temperature, liberating electrons by a process analogous to boiling a liquid. The amount of energy an individual electron has to gain in order to escape from a particular surface is called the **work function** for that surface, denoted by ϕ.

The photoelectric effect was investigated in detail by Hallwachs and Lenard, with quite unexpected results. We will describe their work in terms of a modern phototube, shown schematically in Fig. 41–1. A beam of light, indicated by the arrows, falls on a photosensitive surface K called the *cathode*. The battery or other source of potential difference creates an electric field in the direction from A (called the *collector* or *anode*) toward K, and electrons emitted from K are pushed by this field to the anode A. Anode and cathode are enclosed in a container with a high vacuum; a residual pressure of 0.01 Pa (10^{-7} atm) or less is needed, in order to avoid collisions of electrons with gas molecules. The circuit is completed by electron flow from K to A in the tube, and the photoelectric current is measured by the galvanometer G.

It is found that, for each emitter material, no photoelectrons at all are emitted unless the wavelength of the light is *less than* some critical value. The corresponding *minimum* frequency is called the **threshold fre-**

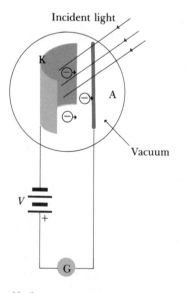

41–1
Schematic diagram of a photocell circuit.

quency for the surface. The threshold frequency for most metals is in the ultraviolet range (corresponding to wavelengths of 200 to 300 nm), but for potassium and cesium oxides it is in the visible spectrum (400 to 700 nm). This result suggests that each liberated electron absorbs an amount of energy E proportional to the frequency f of the light. When f is not great enough, the energy E is not great enough for the electron to surmount the potential-energy barrier at the surface.

When the frequency f is *greater than* the threshold value, some electrons are emitted from the cathode with substantial initial speeds. This is shown by the fact that, even with *no* emf in the external circuit, a few electrons reach the collector, causing a small current in the external circuit. Indeed, even when the polarity of the potential difference V is reversed and the associated electric-field force on the electrons is back toward the cathode, some electrons still reach the anode. Only when the reversed potential V is made large enough that the potential energy eV is greater than the maximum kinetic energy $\frac{1}{2}mv_{\max}^2$ of the emitted electrons does the electron flow stop completely. The reversed potential required to stop the flow completely is called the **stopping potential,** denoted by V_0. From the above discussion,

$$\tfrac{1}{2}mv_{\max}^2 = eV_0. \qquad (41\text{–}1)$$

Measuring the stopping potential V_0 therefore gives us a direct measurement of the maximum kinetic energy electrons have when they leave the cathode. We might guess that when we increase the *intensity*, the electrons come off with greater energy and the stopping potential is greater. But that isn't what actually happens. The maximum kinetic energy of an emitted electron *does not* depend on the *intensity* of the incident light, but it *does* depend on the *wavelength* or *frequency*. When the light intensity increases, the photoelectric current also increases, but only because the *number* of emitted electrons increases, not the energy of an individual electron.

The correct analysis of the photoelectric effect was developed by Einstein in 1905. Extending a proposal made two years earlier by Planck, Einstein postulated that a beam of light consists of small bundles of energy called **quanta** or **photons.** The energy E of a photon is equal to a constant times its frequency f:

$$E = hf, \qquad (41\text{–}2)$$

where h is a universal constant called **Planck's constant.** Its numerical value is

$$h = 6.6260755(40) \times 10^{-34}\ \text{J·s.}$$

A photon striking the surface is absorbed by an electron at the surface of the conductor. The energy transfer is an "all-or-nothing" process; the electron gets all the photon's energy or none at all. If this energy is greater than the surface potential-energy barrier (the work function ϕ), the electron can escape from the surface.

Then the *maximum* kinetic energy $\frac{1}{2}mv_{\max}^2$ for an emitted electron is the energy hf gained from a photon minus the work function ϕ:

$$\tfrac{1}{2}mv_{\max}^2 = hf - \phi. \qquad (41\text{–}3)$$

Combining this with Eq. (41–1), we find

$$eV_0 = hf - \phi. \tag{41-4}$$

We can measure the stopping potential V_0 for each of several values of frequency f for a given cathode material. From these measurements and Eq. (41–4) we can determine both the work function ϕ for the material and the value of the quantity h/e. Thus this experiment provides a direct confirmation of Einstein's interpretation of photoelectric emission and also a direct measurement of the value of Planck's constant.

In energy relations involving electrons it is often convenient to use the *electronvolt* as a unit of energy. We introduced this unit in Section 26–6, and we suggest that you review that section now. Remember that the volt, equal to $1\,\mathrm{J \cdot C^{-1}}$, is a unit of *electrical potential*, but the electronvolt (eV) is a unit of *energy*. If V is in volts and e is measured in units of the electron charge, then the product eV is in electronvolts. When an electron accelerates through a potential difference of 5 V, it gains 5 eV of energy. That is, if $V = 5$ V, then $eV = 5$ eV. The conversion factor is

$$1 \text{ eV} = 1.602 \times 10^{-19} \text{ J.}$$

Typical work functions are of the order of 1 to 5 eV.

Example 41–1   For a certain cathode material used in a photoelectric-effect experiment a stopping potential of 3.0 V was required for light of wavelength 300 nm, 2.0 V for 400 nm, and 1.0 V for 600 nm. Determine the work function for this material and the value of Planck's constant.

Solution   According to Eq. (41–4), a graph of V_0 as a function of f should be a straight line. We rewrite this equation as

$$V_0 = \frac{h}{e}f - \frac{\phi}{e}.$$

In this form we see that the *slope* of the line is h/e and the *intercept* on the vertical axis (corresponding to $f = 0$) is at $-\phi/e$. The frequencies, obtained from $f = c/\lambda$ and $c = 3.00 \times 10^8$ m·s^{-1}, are 1.0, 0.75, and 0.5×10^{15} s^{-1}. The graph is shown in Fig. 41–2. From it we find

$$-\frac{\phi}{e} = -1.0 \text{ V}, \qquad \phi = 1.0 \text{ eV} = 1.60 \times 10^{-19} \text{ J,}$$

and

$$\frac{h}{e} = \frac{1.0 \text{ V}}{0.25 \times 10^{15} \text{ s}^{-1}} = 4.0 \times 10^{-15} \text{ J·C}^{-1}\text{·s,}$$

$$h = (4.0 \times 10^{-15} \text{ J·C}^{-1}\text{·s})(1.60 \times 10^{-19} \text{ C}) = 6.4 \times 10^{-34} \text{ J·s.}$$

This experimental value differs by about 3% from the currently accepted value cited above. ∎

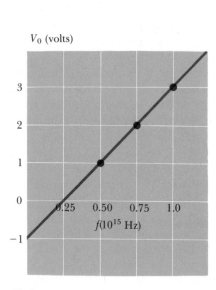

V_0 (volts)

$f(10^{15}$ Hz)

41–2
Stopping potential as a function of frequency. For a different cathode material having a different work function the line would be displaced up or down but would have the same slope.

Figure 41–3 shows a very direct illustration of the particle aspects of light.

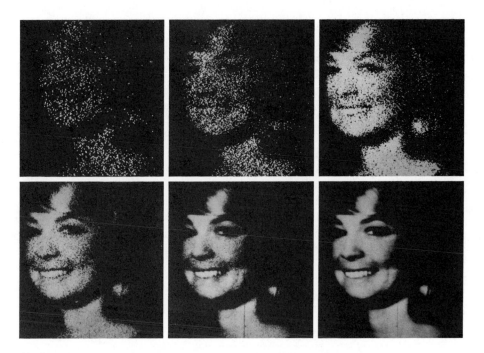

41–3
These photographs are images made by small numbers of photons, using electronic image amplification. In the upper pictures, each spot corresponds to one photon; under extremely faint light (few photons) the pattern seems almost random, but it emerges more distinctly as the light level increases (lower pictures). (Used with permission of RCA Corporation.)

A photon of electromagnetic radiation with frequency f and wavelength $\lambda = c/f$ has energy E given by

$$E = hf = \frac{hc}{\lambda}. \tag{41–5}$$

Furthermore, according to relativity theory, every particle that has energy must also have momentum, even if it has no rest mass. Photons have zero rest mass. According to Eq. (40–30), a photon with energy E has momentum with magnitude p given by $E = pc$. Thus the wavelength λ of a photon and its momentum p are related simply by

$$p = \frac{h}{\lambda}. \tag{41–6}$$

41–3
Line Spectra and Energy Levels

The photon concept that we used to analyze the photoelectric effect also plays an important role in understanding atomic *spectra*, particularly the *line spectra* we described in Section 41–1. One of the key principles was discovered in 1913 by the Danish physicist Niels Bohr (1885–1962). According to Bohr's hypothesis, every atom has some internal structure and internal motion and consequently also some *internal energy*. But this energy cannot change from any arbitrary value to any other. Instead, each atom has a set of possible **energy levels.** An atom can have an amount of internal energy corresponding to any one of these levels, but it *cannot* have an energy *intermediate* between two levels. All atoms of a given element have the same set of energy levels, but atoms of different elements have different sets. For the simplest atom, hydrogen, Bohr pictured these levels in terms of the electron revolving in various circular orbits. Only certain orbit radii were permitted. We'll come back to this picture in Section 41–5.

While an atom is in one of these permitted energy states, it does not radiate. However, an atom can make a transition from one energy level to a lower level by emitting a photon with energy equal to the energy *difference* between the initial and final states. If E_i is the initial energy of the atom, before such a transition, E_f is its final energy, after the transition, and the photon's energy is hf, then

$$hf = E_i - E_f. \tag{41–7}$$

For example, a photon of orange light with wavelength $\lambda = 600$ nm has a frequency f given by

$$f = \frac{c}{\lambda} = \frac{3.00 \times 10^8 \ \text{m·s}^{-1}}{600 \times 10^{-9} \ \text{m}} = 5.00 \times 10^{14} \ \text{s}^{-1}.$$

The corresponding photon energy is

$$E = hf = (6.63 \times 10^{-34} \ \text{J·s})(5.00 \times 10^{14} \ \text{s}^{-1})$$
$$= 3.31 \times 10^{-19} \ \text{J} = 2.07 \ \text{eV}.$$

This photon must be emitted in a transition between two states of the atom that differ in energy by 2.07 eV.

Let's see how this fits in with what was known about spectra in 1913. The spectrum of hydrogen, the least massive atom, had been studied intensively. Under proper conditions, atomic hydrogen emits the series of lines shown in Fig. 41–4. The line with longest wavelength or lowest frequency, in the red, is called H_α; the next line, in the blue-green, is H_β, and so on. In 1885, Johann Balmer (1825–1898) found (by trial and error) a formula that gives the wavelengths of these lines, which are now called the **Balmer series.** Balmer's formula is

$$\frac{1}{\lambda} = R\left(\frac{1}{2^2} - \frac{1}{n^2}\right), \tag{41–8}$$

41–4
The Balmer series of atomic hydrogen. (Reproduced by permission from *Atomic Spectra and Atomic Structures* by Gerhard Herzberg. Copyright 1937 by Prentice-Hall, Inc.)

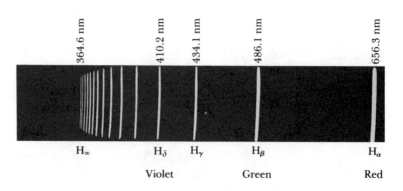

where λ is the wavelength, R is a constant called the **Rydberg constant,** and n may have the integer values 3, 4, 5, etc. If λ is in meters, the numerical value of R is

$$R = 1.097 \times 10^7 \ \mathrm{m}^{-1}.$$

Letting $n = 3$ in Eq. (41–8), we obtain the wavelength of the H_α line:

$$\frac{1}{\lambda} = (1.097 \times 10^7 \ \mathrm{m}^{-1})\left(\frac{1}{4} - \frac{1}{9}\right), \qquad \lambda = 656.2 \ \mathrm{nm}.$$

For $n = 4$ we obtain the wavelength of the H_β line, and so on. For $n = \infty$ we obtain the shortest wavelength in the series, $\lambda = 364.6$ nm.

What does this have to do with Bohr's hypothesis about energy levels? Let's find the *photon energies* corresponding to the wavelengths of the Balmer series, using the relations $f = c/\lambda$ and $E = hf$. Multiplying Eq. (41–8) by hc, we find

$$\frac{hc}{\lambda} = hf = E = hcR\left(\frac{1}{2^2} - \frac{1}{n^2}\right) = \frac{hcR}{2^2} - \frac{hcR}{n^2}. \qquad (41\text{–}9)$$

Now we compare Eqs. (41–7) and (41–9). The two agree if we identify $-hcR/n^2$ as the initial energy E_i of the atom and $-hcR/2^2$ as its final energy E_f, in a transition where a photon with energy $hf = E_i - E_f$ is emitted. The Balmer series therefore suggests that the hydrogen atom has a series of energy levels, which we may call E_n, given by

$$E_n = -\frac{hcR}{n^2}, \qquad n = 2, 3, \ldots . \qquad (41\text{–}10)$$

Each wavelength in the Balmer series corresponds to a transition from a state having n equal to 3 or greater to the state where $n = 2$.

The numerical value of the product hcR is

$$\begin{aligned}
hcR &= (6.626 \times 10^{-34} \ \mathrm{J\cdot s})(2.998 \times 10^8 \ \mathrm{m\cdot s}^{-1})(1.097 \times 10^7 \ \mathrm{m}^{-1}) \\
&= 2.179 \times 10^{-18} \ \mathrm{J} = 13.6 \ \mathrm{eV}.
\end{aligned}$$

Thus the magnitudes of the energy levels given by Eq. (41–10) are approximately -13.6 eV, -3.40 eV, -1.51 eV, $\ldots$.

Other series spectra for hydrogen have since been discovered. These are known, after their discoverers, as the Lyman, Paschen, Brackett, and Pfund series. Their wavelengths are represented by formulas similar to the Balmer formula:

Lyman series:

$$\frac{1}{\lambda} = R\left(\frac{1}{1^2} - \frac{1}{n^2}\right), \qquad n = 2, 3, \ldots,$$

Paschen series:

$$\frac{1}{\lambda} = R\left(\frac{1}{3^2} - \frac{1}{n^2}\right), \qquad n = 4, 5, \ldots,$$

Brackett series:

$$\frac{1}{\lambda} = R\left(\frac{1}{4^2} - \frac{1}{n^2}\right), \qquad n = 5, 6, \ldots,$$

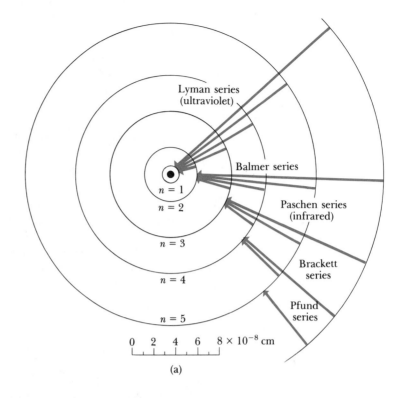

Lyman series
(ultraviolet)

Balmer series

Paschen series
(infrared)

$n = 1$
$n = 2$
$n = 3$
$n = 4$
$n = 5$

Brackett
series

Pfund
series

0   2   4   6 8×10^{-8} cm

(a)

41–5
(a) "Permitted" orbits of an electron in the Bohr model of a hydrogen atom. The transitions responsible for some of the lines of the various series are indicated by arrows. (b) Energy-level diagram, showing transitions corresponding to the various series.

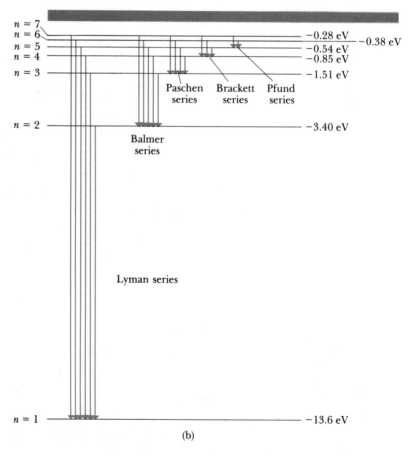

$n = 7$
$n = 6$
$n = 5$
$n = 4$

$n = 3$

-0.28 eV
-0.38 eV
-0.54 eV
-0.85 eV
-1.51 eV

Paschen   Brackett   Pfund
series   series   series

$n = 2$

-3.40 eV

Balmer
series

Lyman series

$n = 1$

-13.6 eV

(b)

Pfund series:

$$\frac{1}{\lambda} = R\left(\frac{1}{5^2} - \frac{1}{n^2}\right), \qquad n = 6, 7, \ldots.$$

The Lyman series is in the ultraviolet, and the Paschen, Brackett, and Pfund series are in the infrared. We see that the Balmer series fits into the scheme between the Lyman and Paschen series.

If we assume that the possible energy levels for the hydrogen atom are given by Eq. (41–10), and if we let n be any positive integer 1, 2, 3, . . ., then *all* the spectral series of hydrogen can be understood on the basis of Bohr's picture of transitions from one energy level (and corresponding electron orbit) to another. For the Lyman series the final state is always $n = 1$; for the Paschen series it is $n = 3$; and so on. Taken together, these spectral series give very strong support to Bohr's picture of energy levels in atoms. The relation of the various spectral series to the energy levels and electron orbits is shown in Fig. 41–5.

In case you're still not convinced of the reality of energy levels, here's even more direct experimental evidence. In 1914, Franck and Hertz were studying the motion of electrons through mercury vapor under the action of an electric field. They found that when the electron kinetic energy was greater than 4.9 eV, the vapor emitted a spectrum line at 254 nm. This suggests the existence of an energy level 4.9 eV above the lowest energy state. A mercury atom is raised to this level by collision with an electron; it later decays back to the lowest energy state by emitting a photon. According to Eq. (41–2), the energy of the photon should be

$$E = hf = \frac{hc}{\lambda} = \frac{(6.63 \times 10^{-34}\ \text{J·s})(3.00 \times 10^8\ \text{m·s}^{-1})}{254 \times 10^{-9}\ \text{m}}$$

$$= 7.82 \times 10^{-19}\ \text{J} = 4.9\ \text{eV},$$

the same value as the measured electron energy.

Only a few elements (hydrogen, singly ionized helium, doubly ionized lithium) have spectra that can be represented by a formula of the Balmer type. But it is *always* possible to analyze the more complicated spectra of other elements in terms of transitions between various energy levels. For hydrogen the numerical values of the energy levels can be *calculated* from theoretical considerations, as we will see in Section 41–5 and Chapter 42. For complex atoms they must usually be deduced from the spectrum wavelengths. This is often an extremely complex problem, but nevertheless nearly all atomic spectra have been analyzed and the resulting energy levels tabulated. The energy levels for sodium are shown in Fig. 41–6.

Every atom has a lowest energy level, representing the *minimum* energy the atom can have. This is called the **ground state,** and all higher levels are called **excited states.** A photon corresponding to a particular spectrum line is emitted when an atom makes a transition from an excited state to a lower state.

From Fig. 41–6 we can see that a sodium atom emits its characteristic yellow light with wavelengths 589.0 and 589.6 nm when it makes transitions from the two closely spaced levels labeled *resonance levels* to the ground state. But a sodium atom in the ground state can also *absorb* a

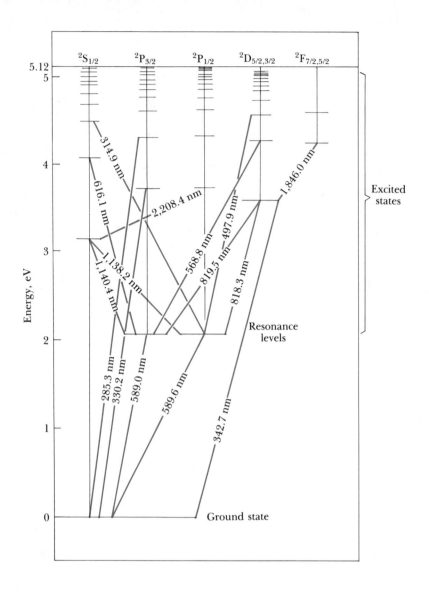

41–6
Energy levels of the sodium atom.
Numbers on the lines between levels
are wavelengths. The column labels,
such as $^2S_{1/2}$, refer to the quantum
states of the valence electron, to be
discussed in Chapter 43.

photon with wavelength 589.0 or 589.6 nm. It then undergoes a transition in the opposite direction and is raised to one of the resonance levels. After a short time the atom spontaneously returns to the ground state, emitting a photon. The average time spent in the excited state is called the *lifetime* of the state; for the resonance levels of the sodium atom the lifetime is about 1.6×10^{-8} s.

The radiation emitted in this process is called **resonance radiation;** we can demonstrate it as follows. We pump the air out of a glass bulb and then introduce a small amount of pure metallic sodium. Then we concentrate a strong beam of yellow light from a sodium-vapor lamp on the bulb. When we warm the bulb to evaporate some of the sodium, the atoms in the vapor absorb the 589-nm photons from the beam and then re-emit them in all directions. This causes the vapor to glow with the characteristic yellow light of sodium.

More generally, a photon *emitted* when a sodium atom makes a transition from an excited state to the ground state can also be *absorbed* by another sodium atom in the ground state. If we pass white (continuous-spectrum) light through sodium vapor and look at the *transmitted* light

41–7
Absorption spectrum of sodium. This is an image on photographic film. Black and white are reversed; the bright regions of the spectrum show as black, and the dark absorption lines show as light lines.

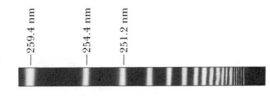

with a spectroscope, we find series of dark lines, corresponding to the wavelengths that have been absorbed, as shown in Fig. 41–7. This is called an **absorption spectrum.**

The spectrum of sunlight is an absorption spectrum. The main body of the sun emits a continuous spectrum, but absorption by cooler vapors in the sun's atmosphere causes many faint *dark* lines in the continuous spectrum. These were first observed by Fraunhofer and are called *Fraunhofer lines*. Figure 41–8 shows Fraunhofer lines in a portion of the sun's spectrum.

Line spectra are produced by matter in the gaseous state, in which the atoms are far apart and interactions between atoms are negligible. If the atoms are all identical, their spectra are also identical. But in condensed states of matter (liquid or solid) there are strong interactions between atoms. These interactions cause shifts in the energy levels, and levels are shifted by different amounts for different atoms. Because of the very large numbers of atoms, practically any photon energy is possible. Therefore hot condensed matter always emits a spectrum with a *continuous* distribution of wavelengths, not a line spectrum. This is called a **continuous spectrum.** The total rate of radiation of energy is proportional to the fourth power of the absolute temperature T, as we learned in Section 16–3. The radiation is most intense in the vicinity of a certain wavelength that is *inversely* proportional to the absolute temperature. As the material's temperature increases, the intensity peak shifts to shorter wavelengths, and the total intensity increases. When a body that is glowing dull red is heated further, it gets brighter and more orange or yellow.

Although the Bohr hypothesis is successful in relating line spectra to energy levels of atoms, it is not complete because it provides no basis for *predicting* what the energy levels should be for any particular kind of atom. Bohr did provide a partial solution for this problem for the hydrogen atom; we will discuss this in Section 41–5. Then in Chapter 42 we will introduce some general principles of quantum mechanics that are needed for more general understanding of the structure and energy levels of atoms.

41–8
A portion of the solar spectrum, between 390 and 460 nm, showing the Fraunhofer lines corresponding to the absorption spectrum. (Courtesy of the Observatories of the Carnegie Institute of Washington.)

PROBLEM-SOLVING STRATEGY: *Photons and Energy Levels*

1. Remember that with photons, as with any other periodic wave, the wavelength λ and frequency f are related by $f = c/\lambda$. The energy E of a photon can be expressed as hf or hc/λ, whichever is more convenient for the problem at hand. Be careful with units; if E is in joules, h must be in joule-seconds, λ in meters, and f in $\sec^{-1}$ or hertz. The magnitudes are in such unfamiliar ranges that common sense may not help if your calculation is wrong by a factor of 10^{10}, so be careful with powers of 10.

2. It is often convenient to measure energy in electronvolts. The conversion 1 eV = 1.602 × 10^{-19} J is often useful. When energies are in eV, you may want to express h in electronvolt-seconds; in those units, $h = 4.136 \times 10^{-15}$ eV·s. We invite you to verify this value.

3. Keep in mind that an electron moving through a potential difference of 1 V gains or loses an amount of energy equal to 1 eV. You will use the electronvolt a lot in this chapter and the next three, so it's important that you get familiar with it now.

41–4
The Nuclear Atom

What does the inside of an atom look like? In one sense this is a silly question; we know that atoms are much smaller than wavelengths of visible light and that there is no hope of actually *seeing* an atom. But we can still describe how the mass and electric charge are distributed through the volume of the atom.

Here's where things stood in 1910. J. J. Thomson had discovered the electron and measured its charge-to-mass ratio in 1897; by 1910, Millikan had completed his first measurements of the electron charge. These and other experiments showed that most of the mass of an atom had to be associated with the *positive* charge, not with the electrons. It was also known that the overall size of atoms is of the order of 10^{-10} m and that all atoms except hydrogen contain more than one electron. What was *not* known was how the mass and charge were distributed in the atom. Thomson had proposed a model of the atom that included a sphere of positive charge, of the order of 10^{-10} m in diameter, with the electrons embedded in it like chocolate chips in a cookie.

The first experiments designed to probe the inner structure of the atom were the **Rutherford scattering** experiments, carried out in 1910–1911 by Sir Ernest Rutherford and two of his students, Hans Geiger and Ernest Marsden, at Cambridge University, England. Rutherford's experiment consisted of projecting other charged particles at the atoms under study. Observations of the ways these particles were deflected or *scattered* provided information about the internal structure and charge distribution of the atoms. The particle accelerators now in common use in high-energy physics laboratories had not yet been invented, and Rutherford's projectiles were *alpha particles* emitted from naturally radioactive elements. We now know that alpha particles are identical with the nuclei of

41–9
The scattering of alpha particles by a thin metal foil.

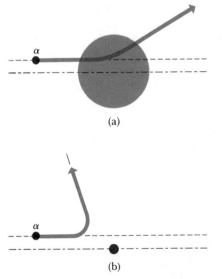

(a)

(b)

41–10
(a) Alpha particle scattered through a small angle by the Thomson atom.
(b) Alpha particle scattered through a large angle by the Rutherford nuclear atom.

helium atoms, two protons and two neutrons bound together. They are ejected from unstable nuclei with speeds of the order of 10^7 m·s^{-1}, and they can travel several centimeters through air or 0.1 mm or so through solid matter before they are brought to rest by collisions.

Rutherford's experimental setup is shown schematically in Fig. 41–9. A radioactive material at the left emits alpha particles. Thick lead screens stop all particles except those in a narrow *beam* defined by small holes. The beam then passes through a target consisting of a thin gold, silver, or copper foil and strikes a screen coated with zinc sulfide, similar in principle to the screen of a TV picture tube. A momentary flash or *scintillation* can be seen on the screen whenever it is struck by an alpha particle. (This is the same phenomenon that makes your TV screen glow when the electron beam strikes it.) Rutherford counted the numbers of particles deflected through various angles.

Think of the atoms of the target material as packed together like marbles in a box. An alpha particle can pass through a thin sheet of metal foil, so the alpha particle must actually penetrate into the interiors of atoms. The *total* electric charge of the atom is zero, so outside the atom there is no force on the alpha particle. Within the atom there are electrical forces caused by the electrons and by the positive charge. But the mass of an alpha particle is about 7400 times that of an electron. Momentum considerations show that the alpha particle can be scattered only a very small amount by its interaction with the much lighter electrons. It's like driving a car through a hailstorm; the hailstones don't deflect the car very much. Only interactions with the *positive* charge, which is tied to most of the mass of the atom, can deflect the alpha particle appreciably.

In the Thomson model the positive charge is distributed through the whole atom. We can calculate the maximum deflection angle an alpha particle can have in this situation. It turns out that the interaction potential energy is much *smaller* than the kinetic energy of the alpha particles and that the maximum deflection to be expected is only a few degrees, as Fig. 41–10a suggests.

The results were very different from this and were totally unexpected. Some alpha particles were scattered by nearly 180°, that is, almost straight backward. Rutherford wrote later:

> It was quite the most incredible event that ever happened to me in my life. It was almost as incredible as if you had fired a 15-inch shell at a piece of tissue paper and it came back and hit you.

Back to the drawing board! Suppose the positive charge, instead of being distributed through a sphere with atomic dimensions (of the order of 10^{-10} m), is all concentrated in a much *smaller* space. Rutherford called this concentration of positive charge the **nucleus.** Then it would act like a point charge down to much smaller distances. The maximum repulsive force on the alpha particle would be much larger, and large-angle scattering would be possible, as in Fig. 41–10b. Rutherford again computed the numbers of particles expected to be scattered through various angles. Within the precision of his experiments the computed and measured results agreed, down to distances of the order of 10^{-14} m. His experiments therefore established that the atom does have a nucleus, a very small, very dense structure, no larger than 10^{-14} m in diameter, containing all the positive charge and most of the mass of the atom.

41–5
The Bohr Model

We remarked at the end of Section 41–3 that Bohr's picture of the relation of spectra to energy levels of atoms was incomplete because it didn't offer any insight into *why* the energy levels have the values they have or how to *calculate* them. But Bohr also proposed a mechanical model of the hydrogen atom, with which he was able to calculate the energy levels and obtain agreement with values determined from spectra. This description is called the **Bohr model** of the hydrogen atom.

Rutherford's discovery of the atomic nucleus raised a serious question. What kept the negatively charged electrons at relatively large distances from the positively charged nucleus despite their electrostatic attraction? Rutherford suggested that perhaps the electrons *revolve* about the nucleus in orbits, more or less as the planets in the solar system revolve around the sun, with the electrical attraction of the nucleus providing the necessary centripetal force. The problem with this picture is that, according to classical electromagnetic theory, any accelerating electric charge, either oscillating or revolving, radiates electromagnetic waves. The total energy of the revolving electrons should therefore decrease continuously, their orbits should become smaller and smaller, and they should eventually spiral into the nucleus and come to rest. Even worse, the *frequency* of the electromagnetic waves emitted by a revolving electron, according to classical theory, should equal the frequency of revolution. As the electrons radiated energy, their angular velocities would change continuously, and they would emit a *continuous* spectrum (a mixture of all frequencies), not the *line* spectrum actually observed.

To solve this problem, Bohr made a revolutionary proposal. He postulated that an electron in an atom can revolve in certain **stable orbits,** with a definite energy associated with each orbit, *without* emitting radiation, contrary to the predictions of classical electromagnetic theory. According to Bohr, an atom radiates only when it makes a transition from one of these stable orbits to another, at the same time emitting (or absorbing) a photon with appropriate energy and frequency, as given by Eq. (41–7).

To determine the radii of the "permitted" orbits, Bohr introduced what we have to regard in hindsight as a brilliant intuitive guess. He noted that the *units* of Planck's constant h, usually written as J·s, are the same as the units of angular momentum, usually written as kg·m^2·s^{-1}. He postulated that only those orbits are permitted for which the angular momentum is an integral multiple of $h/2\pi$. Recall from Section 9–9, Eq. (9–35), that the angular momentum L of a particle with mass m, moving with speed v in a circle of radius r, is $L = mvr$. So Bohr's assumption may be stated as

$$mvr = n\frac{h}{2\pi},$$

where $n = 1, 2, 3, \ldots$. Each value of n corresponds to a permitted value of the orbit radius, which we denote from now on by r_n, and a corresponding speed v_n. With this notation the above equation becomes

$$mv_n r_n = n\frac{h}{2\pi}. \tag{41–11}$$

Now let's make a mechanical model of the hydrogen atom that incorporates this condition. This atom consists of a single electron with mass m and charge $-e$, revolving around a single proton with charge $+e$. The proton is nearly 2000 times as massive as the electron, so we will assume that the proton does not move. We learned back in Chapter 6 that when a particle with mass m moves with speed v_n in a circular orbit with radius r_n, its acceleration is v_n^2/r_n. According to Newton's second law, a force with magnitude $F = mv_n^2/r_n$ is needed to cause this acceleration. The force F is provided by the electrical attraction between the two charges:

$$F = \frac{1}{4\pi\epsilon_0}\frac{e^2}{r_n^2},$$

so the $F = ma$ equation is

$$\frac{1}{4\pi\epsilon_0}\frac{e^2}{r_n^2} = \frac{mv_n^2}{r_n}. \tag{41–12}$$

When we solve Eqs. (41–11) and (41–12) simultaneously for r_n and v_n, we obtain

$$r_n = \epsilon_0 \frac{n^2 h^2}{\pi m e^2}, \tag{41–13}$$

$$v_n = \frac{1}{\epsilon_0}\frac{e^2}{2nh}. \tag{41–14}$$

Equation (41–13) shows that the orbit radius r_n is proportional to n^2; the smallest orbit r_1 corresponds to $n = 1$. With the notation

$$r_1 = \epsilon_0 \frac{h^2}{\pi m e^2} \qquad (41\text{–}15)$$

we can rewrite Eq. (41–13) as

$$r_n = n^2 r_1. \qquad (41\text{–}16)$$

The permitted, nonradiating orbits have radii r_1, $4r_1$, $9r_1$, and so on. The value of n for each orbit is called the **quantum number** for the orbit.

The numerical values of the quantities on the right side of Eq. (41–15) are

$$\epsilon_0 = 8.854 \times 10^{-12}\ \text{C}^2\cdot\text{N}^{-1}\cdot\text{m}^{-2},$$

$$h = 6.626 \times 10^{-34}\ \text{J}\cdot\text{s},$$

$$m = 9.109 \times 10^{-31}\ \text{kg},$$

$$e = 1.602 \times 10^{-19}\ \text{C}.$$

Using these values in Eq. (41–15), we find that the radius r_1 of the smallest Bohr orbit is

$$r_1 = \frac{(8.854 \times 10^{-12}\ \text{C}^2\cdot\text{N}^{-1}\cdot\text{m}^{-2})(6.626 \times 10^{-34}\ \text{J}\cdot\text{s})^2}{(3.142)(9.109 \times 10^{-31}\ \text{kg})(1.602 \times 10^{-19}\ \text{C})^2}$$

$$= 0.5293 \times 10^{-10}\ \text{m}.$$

This result is consistent with atomic dimensions estimated by various other methods.

The kinetic energy K_n of the electron in the orbit with quantum number n can be expressed in terms of n with the help of Eq. (41–14):

$$K_n = \frac{1}{2} m v_n^2 = \frac{1}{\epsilon_0^2} \frac{m e^4}{8 n^2 h^2},$$

and we can use Eq. (41–13) to express the potential energy U_n in terms of n:

$$U_n = -\frac{1}{4\pi\epsilon_0} \frac{e^2}{r_n} = -\frac{1}{\epsilon_0^2} \frac{m e^4}{4 n^2 h^2}.$$

The total energy E_n is the sum of the kinetic and potential energies:

$$E_n = K_n + U_n = -\frac{1}{\epsilon_0^2} \frac{m e^4}{8 n^2 h^2}. \qquad (41\text{–}17)$$

This expression has a negative sign because we have taken the reference level of potential energy to be zero when the electron is at an infinite distance from the nucleus. We are interested only in energy *differences*, so this doesn't matter.

The energy levels and orbits are displayed graphically in Fig. 41–5. The possible states of the atom are labeled by values of n, the *quantum number* for the system. For each value of n there are corresponding values of orbit radius r_n, speed v_n, angular momentum $L_n = nh/2\pi$, and total energy E_n. The energy of the atom is least when $n = 1$ and E_n has its largest negative value. This is the *ground state* of the atom; it is the state with the smallest orbit, with radius r_1. For $n = 2, 3, \ldots$, the absolute value of E_n is smaller, and the energy is progressively larger (less negative). The orbit radius increases as n^2, as shown by Eq. (41–13).

The expression for E_n in Eq. (41–17) has exactly the same form as Eq. (41–10), deduced from analysis of the spectrum of hydrogen. Furthermore, it shows us how to *calculate* the value of the Rydberg constant from the fundamental physical constants m, c, e, h, and ϵ_0. Equating coefficients in Eqs. (41–10) and (41–17), we find

$$hcR = \frac{1}{\epsilon_0{}^2} \frac{me^4}{8h^2},$$

or

$$R = \frac{me^4}{8\epsilon_0{}^2 h^3 c}. \tag{41-18}$$

Every quantity in Eq. (41–18) can be determined quite independently of the Bohr theory. When we substitute the numerical values of these quantities, the value of R that we obtain is the same value that we deduced from spectrum wavelengths. This is a very strong and direct confirmation of Bohr's theory. We invite you to substitute the numerical values into Eq. (41–18) and compute the value of R to confirm these statements.

We can also predict the *ionization energy* of the hydrogen atom (the energy required to remove the electron completely) from the Bohr theory. Ionization corresponds to a transition from the ground state ($n = 1$) to an infinitely large orbit radius ($n = \infty$). The predicted energy is 13.6 eV. The ionization energy can also be measured directly, and the two values agree within 0.1%.

The Bohr model can be extended to other one-electron atoms, such as the singly ionized helium atom, the doubly ionized lithium atom, and so on. If the nuclear charge is Ze (where Z is the atomic number) instead of just e, the effect in the above analysis is to replace e^2 everywhere by Ze^2. In particular, the orbit radii r_n given by Eq. (41–13) become smaller by a factor of Z, and the energy levels E_n given by Eq. (41–17) are multiplied by Z^2. We invite you to verify these statements.

Although the Bohr model was successful in predicting the energy levels of the hydrogen atom, it raised as many questions as it answered. It combined elements of classical physics with new postulates that were inconsistent with classical ideas. It provided no insight into what happens *during* a transition from one orbit to another. The stability of certain orbits was achieved at the expense of discarding the only picture available at the time of the electromagnetic mechanism for the atom to radiate energy. There was no clear justification for restricting the angular momentum to multiples of $h/2\pi$, except that it led to the right answer. Attempts to extend the model to atoms with two or more electrons were not successful. In Chapter 42 we will find that an even more radical departure from classical concepts was needed before the understanding of atomic structure could progress further.

*41–6
The Laser

The **laser** is a light source that produces a beam of highly coherent light as a result of cooperative emission from many atoms, through a process called *stimulated emission.* If the energy difference between the ground state and the first excited state of an atom is E, the atom can absorb a photon whose frequency f is given by the Planck equation $E = hf$. This process is shown schematically in Fig. 41–11a. After absorbing the photon, the atom becomes an excited atom $A*$. A short time later, *spontaneous emission* takes place, and the excited atom returns to the ground state by emitting a photon with the same frequency as the one originally absorbed. The direction and phase of this photon are random, as shown in Fig. 41–11b. But in **stimulated emission,** shown schematically in Fig. 41–11c, an incident photon encounters an excited atom and forces it to emit *another* photon with the same frequency, the same direction, the same phase, and the same polarization as the incident photon. The two photons thus have a definite phase relation and emerge together as *coherent* radiation. The **laser** makes use of stimulated emission to produce a beam consisting of a large number of such coherent photons.

Here's how one kind of laser works. Suppose we have a large number of identical atoms in a gas or vapor in a container with transparent walls, as in Fig. 41–11a. At moderate temperatures, if no radiation is incident on the container, most of the atoms are in the ground state, and only a few are in excited states. If there is an energy level E above the ground state, the ratio of the number n_E of atoms in this state (the *population* of the state) to the number of atoms n_0 in the ground state is very small.

Now suppose we send through the container a beam of radiation with frequency f corresponding to the energy difference E. Some of the atoms absorb photons of energy E and are raised to the excited state, and the population ratio n_E/n_0 increases. Because n_0 is originally so much larger than n_E, an enormously intense beam of light would be required to increase n_E to a value comparable to n_0. Therefore the rate at which energy is absorbed from the beam by the n_0 ground-state atoms far out-

41–11
Three interaction processes between an atom and radiation. The heavier waves on the right side of part (c) show the presence of additional photons from stimulated emission.

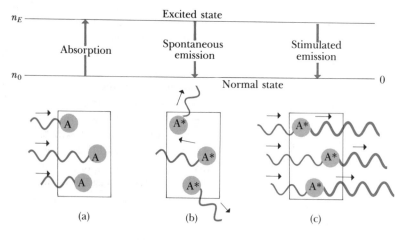

weighs the rate at which energy is added to the beam by stimulated emission from the relatively rare (n_E) excited atoms.

But now suppose that we can create a situation in which n_E is substantially increased in comparison to the normal equilibrium value; this condition is called a **population inversion.** In this case the rate of energy radiation by stimulated emission may actually *exceed* the rate of absorption. The system then acts as a *source* of radiation with photon energy E. Furthermore, because the photons are the result of stimulated emission, they all have the same frequency, phase, polarization, and direction. The resulting radiation is therefore very much more *coherent* than light from ordinary sources, in which the emissions of individual atoms are *not* coordinated. This coherent emission is exactly what happens in a laser.

The necessary population inversion can be achieved in a variety of ways. As an example, consider the helium–neon laser, a common and inexpensive laser available in many undergraduate laboratories. A mixture of helium and neon, each typically at a pressure of the order of 10^2 Pa (10^{-3} atm), is sealed in a glass enclosure provided with two electrodes. When a sufficiently high voltage is applied, a glow discharge occurs. Collisions between ionized atoms and electrons carrying the discharge current excite atoms to various energy states.

Figure 41–12 shows an energy-level diagram for the system. The notation used to label the various energy levels, such as $1s$, $3p$, and $5s$, refers to the energy states of the electrons in the atoms. We will discuss this notation in Chapter 43. A helium atom with an electron excited to

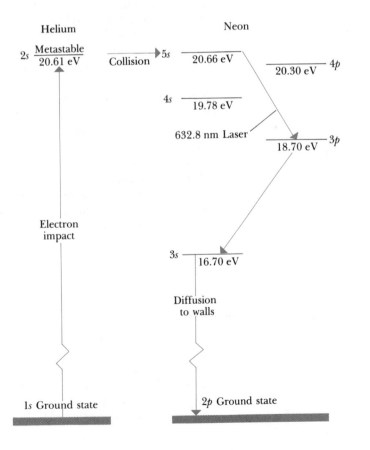

41–12
Energy-level diagram for a helium–neon laser.

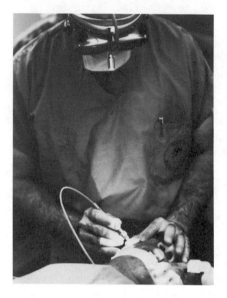

41–13
A laser beam, directed by a fiber-optic conductor, is used to treat a skin malignancy. (Photo by Dan McCoy/Rainbow.)

the 2s state cannot return to the ground (1s) state by emitting a 20.61-eV photon, as you might expect. We can't discuss the reason in detail; it is related to restrictions imposed by conservation of angular momentum. Such a state, in which single-photon emission is impossible, is called a **metastable state.**

However, excited helium atoms *can* lose energy by energy-exchange collisions with neon atoms initially in the ground state. A 2s helium atom, with its internal energy of 20.61 eV and a little additional kinetic energy, can collide with a neon atom in the ground state, exciting the neon atom to its 5s excited state at 20.66 eV and leaving the helium atom in its 1s ground state. Thus we have the necessary mechanism for a population inversion in neon, greatly enhancing the population in the 5s state compared to the 3p state. Stimulated transitions from the 5s to the 3p state then result in the emission of highly coherent light at 632.8 nm, as shown in the diagram. In practice the beam is sent back and forth through the gas many times by a pair of parallel mirrors, to stimulate emission from as many excited atoms as possible. One of the mirrors is partially transparent, so a portion of the beam emerges as an external beam. The net result of all these processes is a beam of light that is (1) very intense, (2) almost perfectly parallel, (3) almost monochromatic, and (4) spatially *coherent* at all points within a given cross section.

In recent years, lasers have found a wide variety of practical applications. The high intensity of a laser beam makes it a convenient drill. For example, a laser beam can drill a very small hole in a diamond for use as a die in drawing very small-diameter wire. Because the photons in a laser beam are strongly correlated in their directions, a laser beam can travel long distances without appreciable spreading. This makes it a very useful tool for surveyors, especially in situations in which great precision is required, such as a long tunnel drilled from both ends.

Lasers are finding increasing application in medical science. A laser can produce a very *narrow* beam with extremely high *intensity*, high enough to vaporize anything in its path. This property is used in the treatment of a detached retina; a short burst of radiation damages a small area of the retina, and the resulting scar tissue "welds" the retina back to the choroid from which it has become detached. Laser beams are also used in surgery; blood vessels cut by the beam tend to seal themselves off, making it easier to control bleeding. Lasers are also used for selective destruction of tissue, as in the removal of tumors. An example is shown in Fig. 41–13.

41–7
X-ray Production and Scattering

The production and scattering of **X-rays** gives additional support to the quantum view of electromagnetic radiation. X-rays are produced when rapidly moving electrons that have been accelerated through a potential difference of the order of 10^3 to 10^6 V strike a metal target. They were first produced by Röntgen in 1895, using an apparatus similar in principle to that shown in Fig. 41–14a. Electrons are "boiled off" from the

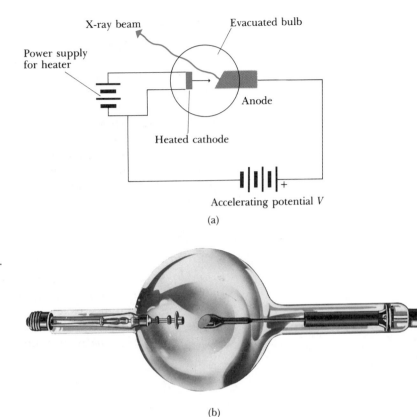

X-ray beam

Evacuated bulb

Power supply
for heater

Anode

Heated cathode

Accelerating potential *V*

(a)

41-14
(a) Apparatus used to produce X-rays. Electrons are emitted thermionically from the heated cathode and are accelerated toward the anode; when they strike it, X-rays are produced. (b) A Coolidge-type X-ray tube.

(b)

heated cathode by thermionic emission and are accelerated toward the anode (the target) by a large potential difference V. Most of the air is pumped out of the bulb so that electrons can travel from cathode to anode with only a small probability of collisions with air molecules. The residual gas pressure is of the order of 0.01 Pa (10^{-7} atm). When V is a few thousand volts or more, a very penetrating radiation is emitted from the anode surface. A common X-ray tube of the type invented by Coolidge is shown in Fig. 41-14b.

Because of their origin, it is clear that X-rays are electromagnetic waves; like light, they are governed by quantum relations in their interaction with matter. Thus we can talk about X-ray photons or quanta, and the energy of an X-ray photon is related to its frequency and wavelength in the same way as for photons of light, $E = hf = hc/\lambda$. Typical X-ray wavelengths are 0.001 to 1 nm (10^{-12} to 10^{-9} m). X-ray wavelengths can be measured quite precisely by crystal diffraction techniques, which we discussed in Section 39-8.

X-ray emission is the inverse of the photoelectric effect. In photoelectric emission the energy of a photon is transformed into kinetic energy of an electron; in X-ray production the kinetic energy of an electron is transformed into energy of a photon. The energy relation is exactly the same in both cases. In X-ray production we can neglect the work function of the target because it is ordinarily very small in comparison to the other energies.

Two distinct processes are involved in X-ray emission. Some electrons are stopped by the target (anode), and all their kinetic energy is converted directly to a continuous spectrum of photons, including X-rays. Other electrons transfer their energy partly or completely to individual atoms in the target. These atoms are left in excited states, and when they decay back to the ground state, they emit X-ray photons with energies characteristic of the element in the target. The atomic energy levels associated with excitation by X-rays are rather different in character from those associated with visible spectra. They are associated with vacancies in the inner electron configurations of complex atoms. The energy levels can be hundreds or thousands of electronvolts above the ground state, rather than a few electronvolts as is typical with optical spectra. We will return to X-ray energy levels in Section 43–2.

Example 41–2   Electrons are accelerated by a potential difference of 10.0 kV. If an electron produces a photon on impact with the target, what is the minimum wavelength of the resulting X-rays?

Solution   The *maximum* photon energy $hf = hc/\lambda$ is equal to the kinetic energy eV of the electron just before impact:

$$eV = hf = \frac{hc}{\lambda}, \tag{41–19}$$

and

$$\lambda = \frac{hc}{eV} = \frac{(6.626 \times 10^{-34} \text{ J·s})(3.00 \times 10^8 \text{ m·s}^{-1})}{(1.602 \times 10^{-19} \text{ C})(1.00 \times 10^4 \text{ V})}$$
$$= 1.24 \times 10^{-10} \text{ m} = 0.124 \text{ nm}.$$

We can measure the X-ray wavelength by crystal diffraction and confirm this prediction directly.   ■

A phenomenon called **Compton scattering,** first observed in 1924 by A. H. Compton, provides additional direct confirmation of the quantum nature of electromagnetic radiation. When X-rays impinge on matter, some of the radiation is *scattered*, just as visible light falling on a rough surface undergoes diffuse reflection. Compton discovered that some of the scattered radiation has smaller frequency (longer wavelength) than the incident radiation and that the change in wavelength depends on the angle through which the radiation is scattered. Specifically, if the scattered radiation emerges at an angle ϕ with respect to the incident direction, as shown in Fig. 41–15, and if λ and λ' are the wavelengths of the incident and scattered radiation, respectively, we find that

$$\lambda' - \lambda = \frac{h}{mc}(1 - \cos \phi), \tag{41–20}$$

where m is the electron mass.

Compton scattering cannot be understood on the basis of classical electromagnetic theory, which would predict that the scattered wave has

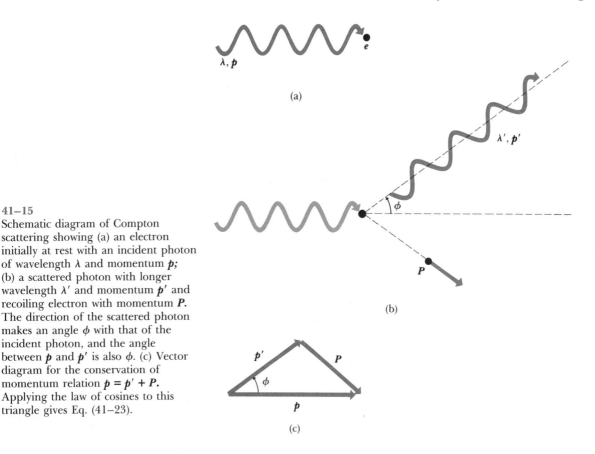

41–15
Schematic diagram of Compton scattering showing (a) an electron initially at rest with an incident photon of wavelength λ and momentum $\boldsymbol{p}$; (b) a scattered photon with longer wavelength λ' and momentum $\boldsymbol{p}'$ and recoiling electron with momentum $\boldsymbol{P}$. The direction of the scattered photon makes an angle ϕ with that of the incident photon, and the angle between $\boldsymbol{p}$ and $\boldsymbol{p}'$ is also ϕ. (c) Vector diagram for the conservation of momentum relation $\boldsymbol{p} = \boldsymbol{p}' + \boldsymbol{P}$. Applying the law of cosines to this triangle gives Eq. (41–23).

the same wavelength as the incident wave. In contrast, the quantum theory provides a beautifully clear explanation. We imagine the scattering process as a collision of two *particles*, the incident photon and an electron initially at rest, as in Fig. 41–15a. The photon gives up some of its energy and momentum to the electron, which recoils as a result of this impact. The final scattered photon has less energy, smaller frequency, and longer wavelength than the initial one (Fig. 41–15b).

We can derive Eq. (41–20) from the principles of conservation of energy and momentum. We outline the derivation below; we invite you to fill in the details. The electron energy may be in the relativistic range, so we have to use the relativistic energy–momentum relations, Eqs. (40–29) and (40–30). The initial photon has momentum $\boldsymbol{p}$ and energy pc; the final photon has momentum $\boldsymbol{p}'$ and energy $p'c$. The electron is initially at rest, so its initial momentum is zero, and its initial energy is mc^2. The final electron momentum has magnitude P, and the final electron energy E is given by $E^2 = (mc^2)^2 + (Pc)^2$. Then energy conservation gives us the relation

$$pc + mc^2 = p'c + E,$$

or

$$(pc - p'c + mc^2)^2 = E^2 = (mc^2)^2 + (Pc)^2. \qquad (41\text{–}21)$$

We may eliminate the electron momentum $\boldsymbol{P}$ from this equation by using momentum conservation:

$$p = p' + P, \quad \text{or} \quad p - p' = P. \tag{41-22}$$

By using the law of cosines with the vector diagram in Fig. 41–15c we find

$$P^2 = p^2 + p'^2 - 2pp' \cos \phi. \tag{41-23}$$

We now substitute this expression for P^2 into Eq. (41–21) and multiply out the left side. We divide out a common factor c^2; several terms cancel, and when the resulting equation is divided through by (pp'), the result is

$$\frac{mc}{p'} - \frac{mc}{p} = 1 - \cos \phi. \tag{41-24}$$

Finally, we substitute $p = h/\lambda$ and $p' = h/\lambda'$ and rearrange again to obtain Eq. (41–20).

X-rays have many practical applications in medicine and industry. Because they can penetrate several centimeters of solid matter, they can be used to visualize the interiors of materials that are opaque to ordinary light, such as broken bones or defects in structural steel. The object to be visualized is placed between an X-ray source and a large sheet of photographic film; the darkening of the film is proportional to the radiation exposure. A crack or air bubble allows greater transmission and shows as a dark area. Bones appear lighter than the surrounding flesh because they contain greater proportions of elements with high atomic number (and greater absorption) than flesh, where the light elements carbon, hydrogen, and oxygen predominate.

In the past decade, several vastly improved X-ray techniques have been developed. One widely used system is *computerized axial tomography*; the corresponding instrument is called a CAT-scanner. The X-ray source produces a thin, fan-shaped beam that is detected on the opposite side of the subject by an array of several hundred detectors in a line. Each detector measures absorption along a thin line through the subject. The entire apparatus is rotated around the subject in the plane of the beam during a few seconds. The changing photon-counting rates of the detectors are recorded digitally; a computer processes this information and reconstructs a picture of density over an entire cross section of the subject. Density differences as small as 1% can be detected with CAT-scans, and tumors and other anomalies much too small to be seen with older X-ray techniques can be detected.

X-rays cause damage to living tissues. As X-ray photons are absorbed in tissues, they break molecular bonds and create highly reactive free radicals (such as neutral H and OH), which in turn can disturb the molecular structure of proteins and especially genetic material. Young and rapidly growing cells are particularly susceptible; hence X-rays are useful for selective destruction of cancer cells. However, a cell may be damaged by the radiation but survive, continue dividing, and produce generations of defective cells; hence X-rays can *cause* cancer. Even when the organism itself shows no apparent damage, excessive radiation exposure can cause changes in the reproductive system that will affect the organism's offspring. The use of X-rays in medical diagnosis has become an area of great concern in recent years; a careful assessment of the balance between risks and benefits of radiation exposure is essential in each individual case.

Questions

41-1 In analyzing the photoelectric effect, how can we be sure that each electron absorbs only *one* photon?

41-2 In what ways do photons resemble other particles such as electrons? In what ways do they differ? Do they have mass? Electric charge? Can they be accelerated? What mechanical properties do they have?

41-3 Considering a two-slit interference experiment, if the photons are not synchronized with each other (i.e., are not coherent) and if half go through each slit, how can they possibly interfere with each other? Is there any way out of this paradox?

41-4 Can you devise an experiment to measure the work function of a material?

41-5 How might the energy levels of an atom be measured directly, that is, without recourse to analysis of spectra?

41-6 Would you expect quantum effects to be generally more important at the low-frequency end of the electromagnetic spectrum (radio waves) or at the high-frequency end (X-rays and gamma rays)? Why?

41-7 Most black-and-white photographic film (with the exception of some special-purpose films) is less sensitive at the far red end of the visible spectrum than at the blue end and has almost no sensitivity to infrared. How can these properties be understood on the basis of photons?

41-8 Human skin is relatively insensitive to visible light, but ultraviolet radiation can be quite destructive to skin. Does this have anything to do with photon energies?

41-9 Does the concept of photon energy shed any light (no pun intended) on the question of why X-rays are so much more penetrating than visible light?

41-10 The phosphorescent materials that coat the inside of a fluorescent lamp tube convert ultraviolet radiation (from the mercury-vapor discharge inside the tube) to visible light. Could one also make a phosphor that converts visible light to ultraviolet?

41-11 As a body is heated to very high temperature and becomes self-luminous, the apparent color of the emitted radiation shifts from red to yellow and finally to blue as the temperature increases. What causes the color shift?

41-12 Elements in the gaseous state emit line spectra with well-defined wavelengths; but hot solid bodies usually emit a continuous spectrum, that is, a continuous smear of wavelengths. Can you account for this difference?

41-13 Could Compton scattering occur with protons as well as electrons? Suppose, for example, one directed a beam of X-rays at a liquid-hydrogen target. What similarities and differences in behavior would be expected?

Exercises

Section 41-2   The Photoelectric Effect

41-1 A photon has a momentum of 1.65×10^{-27} kg·m·s^{-1}.

a) What is the energy of this photon? Give your answer in joules and in electronvolts.

b) What is the wavelength of this photon? In what region of the electromagnetic spectrum does it lie?

41-2 A nucleus in an excited state emits a gamma-ray photon with energy of 1.40 MeV.

a) What is the photon frequency?

b) What is the photon wavelength?

c) How does the wavelength compare with typical nuclear radii (of the order of 10^{-15} m)?

41-3 A sodium-vapor lamp emits light with a wavelength of 589 nm. If the total power of the emitted light is 15.0 W, how many photons are emitted per second?

41-4 A photon of blue light has a wavelength of 460 nm. Find the frequency, momentum, and energy of the photon; express the energy both in joules and in electronvolts.

41-5 A laser used to weld detached retinas emits light with a wavelength of 633 nm in pulses that are 30.0 ms in duration. The average power during each pulse is 0.500 W.

a) How much energy is in each pulse in joules? In electronvolts?

b) What is the energy of one photon in joules? In electronvolts?

c) How many photons are in each pulse?

41–6 A radio station broadcasts at a frequency of 92.0 MHz with a power output of 50.0 kW.

a) What is the energy of each emitted photon in joules? In electronvolts?

b) How many photons are emitted per second?

41–7 In the photoelectric effect, what is the relation between the threshold frequency f_0 and the work function ϕ?

41–8 The photoelectric threshold wavelength of tungsten is 273 nm. Calculate the maximum kinetic energy of the electrons ejected from a tungsten surface by ultraviolet radiation with a wavelength of 140 nm. (Express the answer in electronvolts.)

41–9 A photoelectric surface has a work function of 4.00 eV. What is the maximum speed of the photoelectrons emitted by light with a frequency of 3.60×10^{15} Hz?

41–10 When ultraviolet light with a wavelength of 254 nm from a mercury arc falls upon a clean copper surface, the retarding potential necessary to stop emission of photoelectrons is 0.590 V. What is the photoelectric threshold wavelength for copper?

41–11 The photoelectric work function of potassium is 2.25 eV. If light having a wavelength of 360 nm falls on potassium, find

a) the stopping potential in volts;

b) the kinetic energy in electronvolts of the most energetic electrons ejected;

c) the speeds of these electrons.

Section 41–3   Line Spectra and Energy Levels

41–12 The silicon–silicon single bond that forms the basis of the (mythical) silicon-based creature the Horta has a bond strength of 3.80 eV. What wavelength photon would you need in a (mythical) phaser distintegration gun to destroy the Horta?

41–13 Calculate (a) the frequency and (b) the wavelength of the H_β-line of the Balmer series for hydrogen. This line is emitted in the transition from $n = 4$ to $n = 2$.

41–14 Find the longest and shortest wavelengths in the Lyman and Paschen series for hydrogen. In what region of the electromagnetic spectrum does each series lie?

41–15 The energy-level scheme for the mythical one-electron element Searsium is shown in Fig. 41–16. The potential energy of an electron is taken to be zero at an infinite distance from the nucleus.

a) How much energy (in electronvolts) does it take to ionize an electron from the ground state?

b) A 15-eV photon is absorbed by a Searsium atom. When the atom returns to its ground state, what possible energies can the emitted photons have?

c) What will happen if a photon with an energy of 8 eV strikes a Searsium atom? Why?

d) If photons emitted from Searsium transitions $n = 4$ to $n = 2$ and from $n = 2$ to $n = 1$ will eject photoelectrons from an unknown metal, but the photon emitted from the transition $n = 3$ to $n = 2$ will not, what are the limits (maximum and minimum possible values) of the work function of the metal?

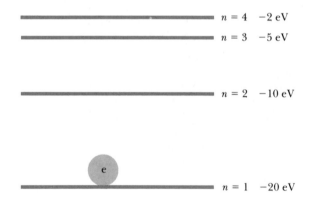

FIGURE 41–16

Section 41–4   The Nuclear Atom

41–16 A 4.20-MeV alpha particle from a radium ^{226}Ra decay makes a head-on collision with a gold nucleus.

a) What is the distance of closest approach of the alpha particle to the center of the nucleus? Assume that the gold nucleus remains at rest.

b) What is the force on the alpha particle at the instant when it is at the point of closest approach?

41–17 A beam of alpha particles is incident on a gold nucleus. A particular alpha particle comes in "head-on" and stops 5.00×10^{-14} m away from the center of the gold nucleus. Assume that the gold nucleus remains at rest. The mass of the alpha particle is 6.65×10^{-27} kg.

a) Calculate the electrostatic potential energy of the alpha particle when it has stopped. Express your result in joules and in MeV.

b) What initial kinetic energy did the alpha particle have? Express your result in joules and in MeV.

c) What was the initial speed of the alpha particle?

Section 41–5   *The Bohr Model*

41–18 According to the Bohr model, the Rydberg constant R is equal to $me^4/8\epsilon_0^2h^3c$.

a) Calculate R in m^{-1} and compare with the experimental value.

b) Calculate the energy (in electronvolts) of a photon whose wavelength equals R^{-1}. (This quantity is known as the Rydberg energy.)

41–19 For a hydrogen atom in the ground state, determine in electronvolts:

a) the kinetic energy of the electron;

b) its potential energy;

c) its total energy;

d) the minimum energy required to remove the electron completely.

e) What wavelength does a photon with the energy calculated in part (d) have? In what region of the electromagnetic spectrum does it lie?

41–20

a) Calculate the Bohr-model speed of the electron in a hydrogen atom in the $n = 1, 2,$ and 3 states.

b) Calculate the orbital period in each of these states.

c) The average lifetime of the first excited state of a hydrogen atom is 1.0×10^{-8} s. How many orbits does an electron in an excited atom complete before returning to the ground state?

41–21 A hydrogen atom initially in the ground state absorbs a photon, which excites it to the $n = 4$ state. Determine the wavelength and frequency of the photon.

41–22 A singly ionized helium ion (a helium atom with one electron removed) behaves very much like a hydrogen atom, except that the nuclear charge is twice as great.

a) How do the energies of the levels differ in magnitude from those of the hydrogen atom?

b) Which spectral series for He$^+$ have lines in the visible spectrum? (Refer to Exercise 41–14.)

c) For a given value of n, how does the radius of an orbit in He$^+$ relate to that for H?

Section 41–6   *The Laser*

41–23 In Fig. 41–12, compute the energy difference for the $5s$–$3p$ transition in neon; express your result in electronvolts and in joules. Compute the wavelength of a photon having this energy, and compare your result with the observed wavelength of the laser light.

41–24 In the helium–neon laser, what wavelength corresponds to the $3p$–$3s$ transition in neon? Why is this not observed in the beam with the same intensity as the 632.8-nm laser line?

41–25 How many photons per second are emitted by a 2.50-mW He–Ne laser that has a wavelength of 633 nm?

Section 41–7   *X-ray Production and Scattering*

41–26 Complete the derivation of the Compton-scattering formula, Eq. (41–20), following the outline given in Eqs. (41–21) through (41–24).

41–27

a) What is the minimum potential difference between the filament and the target of an X-ray tube if the tube is to produce X-rays with a wavelength of 0.0800 nm?

b) What is the shortest wavelength produced in an X-ray tube operated at 4.00×10^4 V?

41–28 The cathode-ray tubes that generated the picture in early color television sets were sources of X-rays. If the acceleration voltage in a TV tube is 25.0 kV, what are the shortest-wavelength X-rays produced by the television? (Modern TV tubes contain shielding to stop these X-rays.)

41–29 An X-ray with a wavelength of 0.100 nm collides with an electron that is initially at rest. The X-ray's final wavelength is 0.110 nm. What is the final kinetic energy of the electron?

41–30 X-rays with an initial wavelength of 0.900×10^{-10} m undergo Compton scattering. For what scattering angle is the wavelength of the scattered X-rays greater by 1.0% than that of the incident X-rays?

41–31 X-rays are produced in a tube operating at 30.0 kV. After emerging from the tube, X-rays with the minimum wavelength produced strike a target and are Compton-scattered through an angle of 60.0°.

a) What is the original X-ray wavelength?

b) What is the wavelength of the scattered X-rays?

c) What is the energy of the scattered X-rays (in electronvolts)?

Problems

41–32 The directions of emission of photons from a source of radiation are random. According to the wave theory, the intensity of radiation from a point source varies inversely as the square of the distance from the source. Show that the number of photons from a point source passing out through a unit area is also given by an inverse-square law.

41–33

a) If the average wavelength emitted by a 250-W light bulb is 600 nm, and 10% of the input power is emitted as visible light, approximately how many visible light photons are emitted per second?

b) At what distance does this correspond to 1.00×10^6 photons per square centimeter per second if the light is emitted uniformly in all directions?

41–34 From the kinetic-molecular theory of an ideal gas (Chapter 20) we know that the average kinetic energy of an atom is $\frac{3}{2}kT$. What is the wavelength of a photon that has this energy for $T = 300$ K (room temperature)?

41–35 The light-sensitive compound on most photographic films is silver bromide, AgBr. A film is "exposed" when the light energy absorbed dissociates this molecule into its atoms. (The actual process is more complex, but the quantitative result does not differ greatly.) The energy of dissociation of AgBr is 1.00×10^5 J·mol^{-1}. For a photon that is just able to dissociate a molecule of silver bromide, find

a) the photon energy in electronvolts,

b) the wavelength of the photon,

c) the frequency of the photon.

d) What is the energy in electronvolts of a quantum of radiation having a frequency of 100 MHz?

e) Explain the fact that light from a firefly can expose a photographic film, whereas the radiation from a TV station transmitting 50,000 W at 100 MHz cannot.

41–36 The photoelectric work functions for particular samples of certain metals are as follows: cesium, 2.00 eV; copper, 4.00 eV; potassium, 2.25 eV; and zinc, 3.60 eV.

a) What is the threshold wavelength for each metal?

b) Which of these metals *could not* emit photoelectrons when irradiated with visible light?

41–37 What is the change in the stopping potential for photoelectrons emitted from a surface if the wavelength of the incident light is reduced from 400 nm to 340 nm?

41–38 When a certain photoelectric surface is illuminated with light of different wavelengths, the stopping potentials in the table below are observed.

Wavelength (nm)	Stopping potential (V)
366	1.48
405	1.15
436	0.93
492	0.62
546	0.36
579	0.24

Plot the stopping potential as ordinate against the frequency of the light as abscissa. Determine

a) the threshold frequency,

b) the threshold wavelength,

c) the photoelectric work function of the material (in electronvolts),

d) the value of Planck's constant h (assuming that the value of e is known).

41–39 An unknown element is found to have an absorption spectrum with lines at 3.0, 7.0, and 9.0 eV, and its ionization potential is 10.0 eV.

a) Draw an energy-level diagram for this element.

b) If a 9.0-eV photon is absorbed, what energies can the subsequently emitted photons have?

41–40

a) What is the least amount of energy in electronvolts that must be given to a hydrogen atom initially in its ground state so that it can emit the H_β-line (see Exercise 41–13) in the Balmer series?

b) How many different possibilities of spectral line emissions are there for this atom when the electron starts in the $n = 4$ level and eventually ends up in the ground state? Calculate the wavelength of the emitted photon in each case.

41–41 If hydrogen were monatomic, at what temperature would the average translational kinetic energy be equal to the energy required to ionize a hydrogen atom initially in the ground state?

41–42 If electrons in a metal had the same energy distribution as molecules in a gas at the same temperature (which is not actually the case), at what temperature would the average electron kinetic energy equal 1.0 eV, which is typical of work functions of metals? Comment on the relevance of your result to thermionic emission.

41–43 A sample of hydrogen atoms is irradiated with light with a wavelength of 40.0 nm, and electrons are observed leaving the gas. If the hydrogen atoms are initially in their ground state, what is the maximum kinetic energy in electronvolts of these photoelectrons?

41–44 Consider a hydrogenlike atom with nuclear charge Z. (Refer to Exercise 41–22.)

a) For what value of Z (rounded to the nearest integer value) is the Bohr speed of the electron in the ground state equal to 10.0% of the speed of light?

b) For what value of Z (rounded to the nearest integer value) is the ionization energy of the ground state equal to 1.0% of the rest mass energy of the electron?

41–45 The negative μ-meson (or muon) has a charge equal to that of an electron but a mass about 207 times as great. Consider a hydrogenlike atom consisting of a proton and a muon. (For simplicity, assume that the muon orbits around the proton, which is stationary. In reality, both revolve about the center of mass of the system.)

a) What is the ground-state energy (in electronvolts)?

b) What is the radius of the $n = 1$ Bohr orbit?

c) What is the wavelength of the radiation emitted in the transition from the $n = 2$ state to the $n = 1$ state?

41–46

a) Calculate the maximum increase in X-ray wavelength that can occur during Compton scattering.

b) What is the energy (in electronvolts) of the smallest-energy X-ray photon for which Compton scattering could result in doubling the original wavelength?

41–47 An X-ray tube is operating at 1.50×10^5 V and 20.0 mA.

a) If only 1.0% of the electric power supplied is converted into X-rays, at what rate is the target being heated in joules per second?

b) If the target has a mass of 0.300 kg and a specific heat of 147 $J \cdot kg^{-1} \cdot (C°)^{-1}$, at what average rate would its temperature rise if there were no thermal losses?

c) What must be the physical properties of a practical target material? What would be some suitable target elements?

41–48 A photon with $\lambda = 0.100$ nm collides with an electron at rest. After the collision the photon's wavelength is 0.115 nm.

a) What is the kinetic energy of the electron after the collision?

b) If the electron is suddenly stopped (for example, in a solid target), it emits a photon. What is the minimum wavelength of this photon?

41–49 A photon with a wavelength of 0.1400 nm is Compton-scattered through an angle of 180°.

a) What is the wavelength of the scattered photon?

b) How much energy is given to the electron?

c) What is the recoil speed of the electron? Is it necessary to use the relativistic kinetic-energy relationship?

Challenge Problems

41–50 An X-ray collides with an electron at rest. The final wavelength of the X-ray is 0.00600 nm, and the final velocity of the struck electron is 1.20×10^8 m·s^{-1}.

a) What was the original wavelength of the X-ray before the collision?

b) Through what angle is the X-ray scattered in the collision?

41–51

a) Show that the frequency of revolution of an electron in its circular orbit in the Bohr model of the hydrogen atom is $f = me^4/4\epsilon_0{}^2 n^3 h^3$.

b) Show that when n is very large, the frequency of revolution equals the radiated frequency calculated from Eq. (41–7) for a transition from

$$n_1 = n + 1 \quad \text{to} \quad n_2 = n.$$

(This problem illustrates Bohr's *correspondence principle*, which is often used as a check on quantum calculations. When n is small, quantum physics gives results that are very different from those of classical physics. When n is large, the differences are not significant, and the two methods then "correspond." In fact, when Bohr first tackled the hydrogen atom problem, he sought to determine f as a function of n such that it would correspond to classical physics for large n.)

42

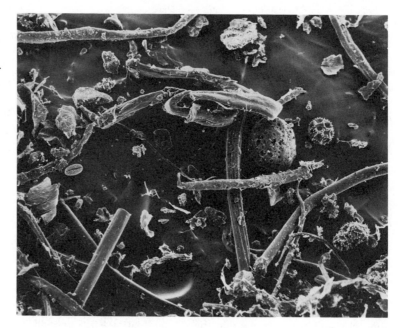

Quantum Mechanics

We saw in the preceding chapter that some aspects of emission and absorption of light, including atomic spectra, can be understood on the basis of the photon concept, together with the concept of discrete energy levels in atoms. But a complete theory should also offer some means of *predicting*, on theoretical grounds, the values of these energy levels for any particular atom. The Bohr model of the hydrogen atom is a step in this direction, but it cannot be generalized to atoms with more than one electron. More sweeping revisions of nineteenth-century ideas are needed. The wave–particle duality that has been firmly established for electromagnetic radiation has to be extended to include particles as well as radiation. The entities (such as electrons) that we are accustomed to calling *particles* may in some situations exhibit *wavelike* behavior.

The new theory, called *quantum mechanics*, requires fundamental changes in the language we use to describe the state of a mechanical system. A particle can no longer be described as a single point moving in space. Instead, it is an inherently spread-out entity. As the particle moves, the spread-out character has some of the properties of a *wave*; for example, particles can undergo *diffraction*. Quantum mechanics is the key to understanding the structure of atoms and molecules, including their spectra, chemical behavior, and many other properties. It has the happy effect of restoring unity to our description of both particles and radiation, and *wave* concepts are central to the entire theory.

42–1
The Wave Nature of Particles

A major advance in the understanding of atomic structure began in 1924, about 10 years after the Bohr theory, with a proposition made by a young French physicist, Louis de Broglie. His reasoning, freely paraphrased, went like this. Nature loves symmetry. Light is dualistic in nature, behaving in some situations like waves and in others like particles. Therefore the same thing ought to be true of matter. Electrons and protons, which are usually thought of as *particles*, may in some situations behave like *waves*.

Specifically, de Broglie postulated that a free electron with mass m, moving with speed v, should have a wavelength λ related to its momentum $p = mv$ in exactly the same way as for a photon, as expressed by Eq. (41–6), $\lambda = h/p$. The **de Broglie wavelength** of an electron is given by

$$\lambda = \frac{h}{mv}, \tag{42–1}$$

where h is the same Planck's constant that appears in the frequency–energy relation for photons.

This wave hypothesis, unorthodox though it seemed at the time, almost immediately received direct experimental confirmation. We described in Section 39–8 how the atoms in a crystal can function as a three-dimensional diffraction grating for X-rays. An X-ray beam is strongly reflected when it strikes a crystal at an angle that gives constructive interference in the various scattered waves. The existence of these strong reflections is evidence for the *wave* nature of X-rays.

In 1927, Davisson and Germer, working in the Bell Telephone Laboratories, were studying the surface of a crystal of nickel by directing a beam of *electrons* at the surface and observing how many electrons were reflected at various angles. It might be expected that even the smoothest surface attainable would still look rough to an electron and that the electron beam would be diffusely reflected. But the **Davisson-Germer experiment** showed that the electrons were reflected in almost the same way that X-rays would be reflected from the same crystal; that is, they were being *diffracted*.

Davisson and Germer could determine the speeds of the electrons from the accelerating voltage, so they could compute the de Broglie wavelength from Eq. (42–1). They found that the angles at which strong reflection took place were the same as those at which X-rays with the same wavelength would be reflected. This phenomenon is called **electron diffraction,** and its discovery gave strong support to de Broglie's hypothesis.

This wave hypothesis requires sweeping revisions of our fundamental concepts of the description of matter. What we are accustomed to calling a *particle* actually behaves like a particle only if we don't look too closely. In general, a particle is not a geometric point but has to be described as an entity that is spread out in space. In some cases this spreading appears as a periodic pattern suggesting *wavelike* properties. The wave and particle aspects are not inconsistent; the particle model is a special case of a more general wave picture. The situation is comparable to the ray model of geometrical optics, a special case of the more general wave model of physical optics. Indeed, there is a very close analogy between optics and the description of the motion of particles.

Within a few years after 1924 the wave hypothesis of de Broglie was developed by Heisenberg, Schrödinger, Dirac, Born, and many others into a complete theory called **quantum mechanics.** In the following sections we will sketch the main lines of thought in a nonmathematical way and describe some of the experimental evidence for the wave nature of material particles. We will show how the quantum numbers that were introduced in a somewhat artificial way in the Bohr model now enter naturally into the theory of atomic structure.

One of the essential features of quantum mechanics is that a particle is no longer described as located at a single point, but is described instead in terms of a *function* that has various values at various points in space. The spatial distribution describing a *free* electron may have a recurring pattern characteristic of a wave that propagates through space. Electrons *in atoms* can be visualized as diffuse clouds surrounding the nucleus. The idea that the electrons in an atom move in definite orbits such as those in Fig. 41–5 is an oversimplification and should not be taken too seriously. The orbits themselves were never an essential part of Bohr's theory. The frequencies of the emitted photons are determined by the *energies* of the states that we pictured in terms of orbits. The new theory still assigns definite energy states to an atom. In the hydrogen atom the energies turn out to be the same as those given by Bohr's theory; in more complicated atoms, for which the Bohr theory does not work, the quantum mechanical picture is in excellent agreement with observation.

To show how quantization (the existence of discrete energy levels) arises in atomic structure, we can use an analogy with the classical mechanical problem of a vibrating string held at its ends. We worked out the normal modes of this system in Section 22–3, and we suggest that you review that discussion. When the string vibrates, the ends are always nodes, and there may be other nodes along the string. The general requirement is that the length of the string must equal some *integral* number of half-wavelengths.

In a similar way the principles of quantum mechanics lead to an equation (the Schrödinger equation) that must be satisfied by an electron in an atom, subject also to certain boundary conditions. For the moment, think of an electron as a wave wrapped around in a circle around the nucleus. In order for the wave to "come out even" and join onto itself smoothly, the circumference of this circle must include some *integral number* of wavelengths, as suggested by Fig. 42–1. For an orbit with radius r and circumference $2\pi r$ we must have $2\pi r = n\lambda$, where $n = 1, 2, 3, \ldots$. According to the de Broglie relation, Eq. (42–1), the wavelength λ of a particle with mass m, moving with speed v, is $\lambda = h/mv$. Combining these two equations, we find

$$2\pi r = n\frac{h}{mv} \quad \text{and} \quad mvr = n\frac{h}{2\pi}. \quad (42\text{–}2)$$

But mvr is the *angular momentum L* of the electron! The wave-mechanical

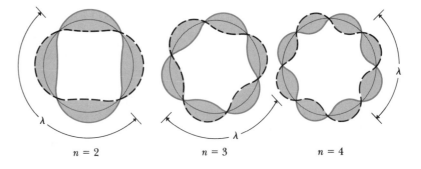

42–1

Diagrams showing the idea of wrapping a standing wave around a circular orbit. For the wave to join onto itself smoothly the circumference of the orbit must be an integral number n of wavelengths. Examples are shown for $n = 2$, 3, and 4.

$n = 2$ $n = 3$ $n = 4$

picture leads naturally to Bohr's postulate that the angular momentum must be an integer multiple of $h/2\pi$.

The idea of wrapping a wave around in a circular orbit is a rather vague notion. But the agreement of Eq. (42–2) with Bohr's hypothesis is much too remarkable to be a coincidence. It strongly suggests that the wave properties of electrons do indeed have something to do with atomic structure.

PROBLEM-SOLVING STRATEGY: *Atomic Physics*

1. In atomic physics the orders of magnitude of physical quantities are so unfamiliar that often common sense isn't much help in judging the reasonableness of a result. It helps to remind yourself of some typical magnitudes of various quantities:

Size of an atom: 10^{-10} m

Mass of an atom: 10^{-26} kg

Mass of an electron: 10^{-30} kg

Energy of an atomic state: 1 to 10 eV or 10^{-18} J for outer electrons (but some interaction energies are much smaller)

Speed of an electron in the Bohr atom: 10^6 m·s^{-1}

Electron charge: 10^{-19} C

kT at room temperature: 1/40 eV

and so on. You may want to add items to this list. These values will also help you in Chapter 44, in which we have to deal with magnitudes characteristic of *nuclear* rather than atomic structure, often different by factors of 10^4 to 10^6. In working out problems, be very careful to handle powers of ten properly. A gross error may not be obvious.

2. As in the last chapter, energies may be expressed either in joules or in electronvolts. Be sure that you use consistent units. Lengths, such as wavelengths, are always in meters if you use the other quantities consistently in SI units, such as $h = 6.626 \times 10^{-34}$ J·s. If you want nanometers or something else, don't forget to convert.

3. Aside from these calculational details, the main challenges of this chapter are conceptual, not computational. Try to keep an open mind when you encounter new and sometimes jarring ideas. Eventually, you will come to appreciate the fact that a photon *can* have both wavelike and particlelike properties. Don't get discouraged; intuitive understanding of quantum mechanics takes some time to develop. Keep trying!

Example 42–1 Find the speed and kinetic energy of a neutron ($m = 1.675 \times 10^{-27}$ kg) that has a de Broglie wavelength $\lambda = 0.100$ nm, typical of atomic spacing in crystals. Compare the energy with the average kinetic energy of a gas molecule at room temperature ($T = 20°C$).

Solution   From Eq. (42–1),

$$v = \frac{h}{\lambda m} = \frac{6.626 \times 10^{-34} \text{ J·s}}{(0.100 \times 10^{-9} \text{ m})(1.675 \times 10^{-27} \text{ kg})}$$
$$= 3.96 \times 10^3 \text{ m·s}^{-1};$$

$$K = \tfrac{1}{2}mv^2 = \tfrac{1}{2}(1.675 \times 10^{-27} \text{ kg})(3.96 \times 10^3 \text{ m·s}^{-1})^2$$
$$= 1.31 \times 10^{-20} \text{ J} = 0.0818 \text{ eV}.$$

The average translational kinetic energy of a molecule of an ideal gas is given by Eq. (20–10):

$$K = \tfrac{3}{2}kT = \tfrac{3}{2}(1.38 \times 10^{-23} \text{ J·K}^{-1})(293 \text{ K})$$
$$= 6.06 \times 10^{-21} \text{ J} = 0.0378 \text{ eV}.$$

Thus the two energies are comparable in magnitude. In fact, a neutron with kinetic energy in this range is called a *thermal neutron*. Diffraction of thermal neutrons can be used to study crystal and molecular structure in the same way as X-ray diffraction. Neutron diffraction has proved especially useful in the study of large organic molecules. ■

42–2
The Electron Microscope

An electron beam can be used to form an image of an object in exactly the same way as a light beam. A ray of light is bent by reflection or refraction, and an electron trajectory is bent by an electric or magnetic field. Rays of light diverging from a point on an object can be brought to convergence by a converging lens, and electrons diverging from a small region can be brought to convergence by an electrostatic or magnetic lens. Figures 42–2a and 42–2b show the behavior of a simple type of electrostatic lens, and Fig. 42–2c shows the analogous optical system. In each case the image can be made larger than the object, so both devices can act as magnifiers.

The analogy between light rays and electrons goes deeper. The *ray* model of geometrical optics is an approximate representation of the more general *wave* model. Geometrical optics is valid whenever interference and diffraction effects can be neglected. Similarly, we saw in Section 42–1 that the model of an electron as a point particle following a line trajectory is an approximate description of the actual behavior of the electron; this model is useful when we can neglect effects associated with the wave nature of electrons.

How is an **electron microscope** superior to an optical microscope? The *resolution* of an optical microscope is limited by diffraction effects, as we discussed in Section 39–9. Using wavelengths around 500 nm, an optical microscope can't resolve objects smaller than a few hundred nanometers, no matter how carefully its lenses are made. The resolution of

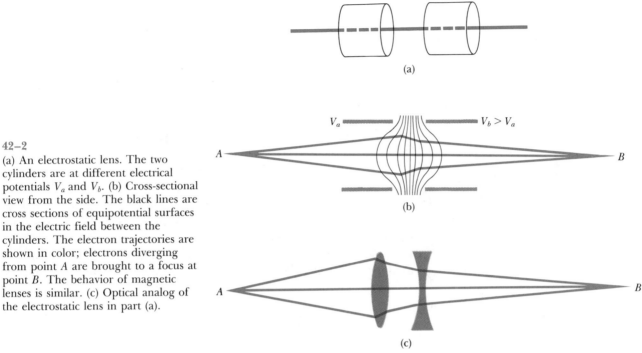

42–2
(a) An electrostatic lens. The two cylinders are at different electrical potentials V_a and V_b. (b) Cross-sectional view from the side. The black lines are cross sections of equipotential surfaces in the electric field between the cylinders. The electron trajectories are shown in color; electrons diverging from point A are brought to a focus at point B. The behavior of magnetic lenses is similar. (c) Optical analog of the electrostatic lens in part (a).

an electron microscope is similarly limited by the wavelengths of the electrons, but these may be many thousands of times *smaller* than wavelengths of visible light. The useful magnification of an electron microscope can be thousands of times as great as that of an optical microscope.

Be sure that you understand that the ability of the electron microscope to form an image *does not* depend on the wave properties of electrons. We can compute their trajectories by treating them as classical charged particles under the action of electric- and magnetic-field forces. Only when we talk about *resolution* do the wave properties become important.

Example 42–2   An electron beam is formed by a setup similar to that of the cathode-ray tube, discussed in Section 26–7. If the accelerating voltage is 10 kV, what is the wavelength of the electrons?

Solution   The wavelength is determined by Eq. (42–1). To find the speed, we use conservation of energy. The kinetic energy is much smaller than the electron's rest energy, so we can use the nonrelativistic kinetic expression $\frac{1}{2}mv^2$. The gain of kinetic energy of an electron equals the loss of potential energy eV. That is,

$$\frac{1}{2}mv^2 = eV, \qquad v = \sqrt{\frac{2eV}{m}}.$$

Using this result in Eq. (42–1), we find

$$\lambda = \frac{h}{m}\sqrt{\frac{m}{2eV}} = \frac{h}{\sqrt{2meV}}$$

$$= \frac{6.63 \times 10^{-34}\ \text{J·s}}{\sqrt{2(9.11 \times 10^{-31}\ \text{kg})(1.60 \times 10^{-19}\ \text{C})(1.00 \times 10^4\ \text{V})}} \quad (42\text{–}3)$$

$$= 1.23 \times 10^{-11}\ \text{m} = 0.0123\ \text{nm}.$$

This is about 40,000 times smaller than typical wavelengths of visible light. ■

Most practical electron microscopes use magnetic rather than electrostatic lenses. A common setup includes three lenses in a compound-microscope arrangement, as shown in Fig. 42–3. Electrons are emitted from a hot cathode and accelerated by a potential difference, typically 10 to 100 kV. The electrons pass through a condenser lens and are formed

42–3
An electron microscope. The magnetic lenses, consisting of coils of wire carrying currents, are shown in cross section. The condensing lens forms a parallel beam of electrons that strikes the object. The objective lens forms an intermediate image that serves as the object for the final image formed by the projection lens. All images are *real*. The final image is projected on photographic film or a fluorescent screen. The magnification of each lens may be of the order of 100×, and the overall magnification of the order of 10,000×. For greater magnification an additional intermediate lens may be used. The color lines are not continuous electron trajectories through the instrument but are drawn from lens to lens to show the formation of images. The angles of the electron paths with the optic axis are greatly exaggerated; in actual instruments these angles are usually less than 0.01 rad or 0.5°. The entire apparatus is enclosed in a vacuum chamber, not shown in the diagram.

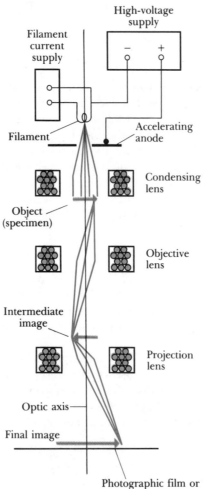

42–4
A scanning electron microscope, showing a vacuum chamber in the background and cathode-ray tube monitors in the foreground. (Courtesy of General Electric.)

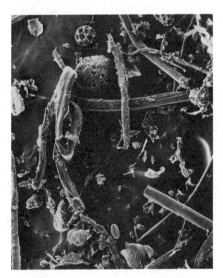

42–5
Scanning electron micrograph of house dust, including fibers, soot particles, and pollen. The overall magnification is 575×. (Photo by Prof. G. F. Leedale, Biophoto Associates. Courtesy of Photo Researchers, Inc.)

into a parallel beam before passing through the specimen or object to be viewed. The objective lens then forms an intermediate image of this object, and the projection lens produces a final real image of that image. The latter two lenses play the roles of the objective and eyepiece lenses, respectively, of a compound optical microscope. The final image is recorded on photographic film or projected onto a fluorescent screen for viewing or photographing. The entire apparatus, including the specimen, must be enclosed in a vacuum container, just as in the case of the cathode-ray tube; otherwise, electrons would collide with air molecules and muddle up the image. The specimen to be viewed is very thin, typically 10 to 100 nm, so the electrons are not slowed appreciably as they pass through.

We might think that when the electron wavelength is 0.01 nm, as in the above example, the resolution would also be about 0.01 nm. In fact, it is seldom better than 0.5 nm, for several reasons. Large-aperture magnetic lenses have aberrations analogous to those of optical lenses, as we discussed in Section 38–4. The focal length of a magnetic lens depends on the current in the coil, which must be controlled precisely. It also depends on the electron speed, which is never exactly the same for all electrons in the beam. This effect is the equivalent of chromatic aberration.

An important variation is the *scanning electron microscope*. The electron beam is focused to a very fine line and is swept across the specimen, just as the electron beam in a TV picture tube traces out the picture. As the beam scans the specimen, electrons are knocked off and are collected by a collecting anode that is kept at a potential a few hundred volts positive with respect to the specimen. The current in the collecting anode is amplified and used to modulate the electron beam in a cathode-ray tube, which is swept in synchronism with the microscope beam. Thus the cathode-ray tube traces out a greatly magnified image of the specimen. This scheme has the advantages that the beam need not pass through the specimen and that the knockoff electron production depends on the *angle* at which the beam strikes the surface. Thus scanning electron micrographs have a much greater three-dimensional appearance than conventional ones. The resolution is not as great, typically of the order of 10 nm, but still much greater than the best optical microscopes. A scanning electron microscope is shown in Fig. 42–4, and a photograph made with such an instrument is shown in Fig. 42–5.

42–3
Probability and Uncertainty

The discovery of the dual wave–particle nature of matter has forced us to revise drastically the language we use to describe the behavior of a particle. In classical Newtonian mechanics we think of a particle as a point. At any instant of time it has a definite position and a definite velocity. We can describe its state of motion completely with three coordinates and three components of velocity. As we will see, such a specific description is, in general, not possible. When we look on a small enough scale, there are fundamental limitations on the precision with which we can describe the position and velocity of a particle. Many aspects of a particle's behavior can be stated only in terms of *probabilities*.

To try to get some insight into the nature of the problem, let's review the optical single-slit diffraction experiment we described in Section 39–6. Most (85%) of the intensity in the diffraction pattern is concentrated in the central maximum, bounded on either side by the first intensity *minimum*. We use θ_1 to denote the angle between the central maximum and the first minimum. Using Eq. (39–11), with $n = 1$, we find that θ_1 is given by $\sin \theta_1 = \lambda/a$, where a is the slit width. If λ is much smaller than a, then θ_1 is very small, $\sin \theta_1$ is very nearly equal to θ_1 (in radians), and we can say

$$\theta_1 = \frac{\lambda}{a}. \tag{42–4}$$

Now we perform the same experiment again, but using a beam of *electrons* instead of a beam of monochromatic light. We have to do the experiment in vacuum (10^{-7} atm or less) so that the electrons don't bump into air molecules. We can produce the electron beam with a setup similar in principle to the electron gun in a cathode-ray tube. This produces a narrow beam of electrons that all have the same direction and speed and therefore also the same *wavelength*. Such an experiment is shown schematically in Fig. 42–6.

The result of this experiment, recorded on photographic film or by use of more sophisticated detectors, is a diffraction pattern identical to the one shown in Fig. 39–20b. This gives us additional direct evidence of the *wave* nature of electrons. Most (85%) of the electrons strike the film in the region of the central maximum, but a few strike farther from the center, in the subsidiary maxima on both sides.

If we really believe that electrons are waves, the wave behavior in this experiment isn't surprising. But if we try to interpret it in terms of *particles*, we run into very serious problems. First, the electrons don't all follow the same path, even though they all have the same initial state of motion. In fact, we can't predict the trajectory of an individual electron from knowledge of its initial state. The best we can do is to say that most

42–6
An electron diffraction experiment. The graph at the right shows the degree of blackening of the film, which in any region is proportional to the number of electrons striking that region. The components of momentum of an electron striking the outer fringe of the central maximum are shown.

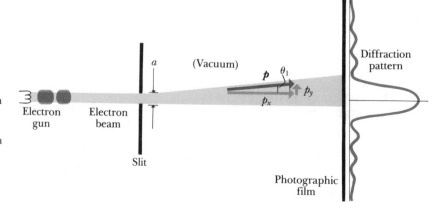

of the electrons go to a certain region, fewer go to other regions, and so on. That is, we can describe only the *probability* that an individual electron will strike each of various areas on the film. This fundamental indeterminacy has no counterpart in Newtonian mechanics, in which the motion of a particle or a system can always be predicted if we know the initial position and motion with great enough precision.

Second, there are fundamental *uncertainties* in both position and momentum of an individual particle, and these two uncertainties are related inseparably. To clarify this point, let's go back to Fig. 42–6. An electron that strikes the film at the outer edge of the central maximum, at angle θ_1, has to have a component of momentum p_y in the y-direction, as well as a component p_x in the x-direction, despite the fact that initially the beam was directed along the x-axis. From the geometry of the situation the two components are related by $p_y/p_x = \tan\theta_1$; and if θ_1 is small, we may approximate $\tan\theta_1 = \theta_1$, obtaining

$$p_y = p_x\theta_1. \tag{42–5}$$

Neglecting those 15% of the electrons that strike the film outside the central maximum (that is, at angles greater than λ/a), we see that the y-component of momentum may be as large as

$$p_y = p_x\frac{\lambda}{a}. \tag{42–6}$$

So the *uncertainty* Δp_y in the y-component of momentum is at least as great as $p_x\lambda/a$:

$$\Delta p_y \geq p_x\frac{\lambda}{a}. \tag{42–7}$$

The narrower the slit width a, the broader the diffraction pattern and the greater the uncertainty in the y-component of momentum p_y.

Now the electron wavelength λ is related to the momentum $p_x = mv_x$ by the de Broglie relation, Eq. (42–1), which we may rewrite as $\lambda = h/p_x$. Using this relation in Eq. (42–7) and simplifying, we find

$$\Delta p_y \geq p_x\frac{h}{p_x a} = \frac{h}{a},$$

or

$$\Delta p_y a \geq h. \tag{42–8}$$

What does this result mean? The slit width a represents the uncertainty in *position* of an electron as it passes through the slit. We don't know exactly *where* in the slit each particle passes through. So both the y position and the y-component of momentum have uncertainties, and the two uncertainties are related by Eq. (42–8). We can reduce the *momentum* uncertainty Δp_y only by reducing the width of the diffraction pattern. To do this, we have to increase the slit width, which increases the *position* uncertainty. Conversely, when we *decrease* the position uncertainty by narrowing the slit, the diffraction pattern broadens, and the corresponding momentum uncertainty *increases*.

You may well want to protest that it doesn't make sense for a particle not to have a definite position and momentum. We reply that what we call common sense is based on familiarity gained through experience. Our usual experience includes very little contact with the microscopic behavior of particles. Sometimes we have to accept conclusions that violate our intuition when we are dealing with areas that are far removed from everyday experience.

In more general discussions of uncertainty relations the uncertainty of a quantity is usually described in terms of the statistical concept of *standard deviation*, a measure of the spread or dispersion of a set of numbers around their average value. If a coordinate x has an uncertainty Δx defined in this way, and if the corresponding momentum component p_x has an uncertainty Δp_x, then the two uncertainties are found to be related in general by the inequality

$$\Delta x \, \Delta p_x \geq \frac{h}{2\pi}. \qquad (42-9)$$

Equation (42–9) is one form of the **Heisenberg uncertainty principle.** It states that, in general, neither the momentum nor the position of a particle can be predicted with arbitrarily great precision, as classical physics would predict. Instead, the uncertainties in the two quantities play complementary roles, as we have described. It is tempting to suppose that we could get greater precision by using more sophisticated particle detectors in various areas of the slit. This turns out not to be possible. To detect a particle, the detector must *interact* with it, and this interaction unavoidably changes the state of motion of the particle, introducing uncertainty about its original state. A more detailed analysis of such hypothetical experiments shows that the uncertainties we have described are fundamental and intrinsic. They *cannot* be circumvented *even in principle* by any experimental technique, no matter how sophisticated.

There is also an uncertainty principle involving *energy*. It turns out that the energy of a system has inherent uncertainty. The uncertainty ΔE depends on the *time interval* Δt during which the system remains in the given state. The relation is

$$\Delta E \, \Delta t \geq \frac{h}{2\pi}. \qquad (42-10)$$

A system that remains in a certain state for a very long time (large Δt) can have a very well-defined energy (small ΔE), but if it remains in that state for only a short time (small Δt), the uncertainty in energy must be correspondingly greater (large ΔE).

Example 42–3   A sodium atom in one of the "resonance levels" shown in Fig. 41–6 (Section 41–3) remains in that state for an average time of 1.6×10^{-8} s before it makes a transition back to the ground state by emitting a photon with a wavelength of 589 nm and energy of 2.109 eV. What is the uncertainty in energy of the resonance level? What is the wavelength spread of the corresponding spectrum line?

Solution   From Eq. (42–10),

$$\Delta E = \frac{h}{2\pi\,\Delta t} = \frac{6.626 \times 10^{-34}\ \text{J·s}}{(2\pi)(1.6 \times 10^{-8}\ \text{s})}$$
$$= 6.6 \times 10^{-27}\ \text{J} = 4.1 \times 10^{-8}\ \text{eV}.$$

The atom remains an indefinitely long time in the ground state, so there is *no* uncertainty there; the uncertainty of the resonance level energy and of the corresponding photon energy amounts to about two parts in 10^8. The corresponding spread in wavelength, or "width," of the spectrum line is approximately

$$\Delta\lambda = (2 \times 10^{-8})(589\ \text{nm}) = 0.000012\ \text{nm}.$$

This irreducible uncertainty is called the *natural line width* of this particular spectrum line. Though very small, it is within the limits of resolution of present-day spectrometers. Ordinarily, the natural line width is much smaller than line broadening from other causes such as collisions among atoms. ■

Now let's take a brief look at a quantum interpretation of a *two-slit* optical interference pattern. We studied these patterns in detail for light in Section 39–2. In terms of photons the intensity–distribution pattern must correspond to the numbers of photons striking various regions of the screen where the pattern is formed. In fact, it is possible to detect individual photons with a device called a *photomultiplier*. Using the setup shown in Fig. 42–7, we can place the photomultiplier at various positions for equal time intervals, count photons at each position, and plot out the intensity distribution. We find that *on the average*, the distribution of photons agrees with our predictions from Section 39–2.

If we now reduce the light intensity to a level at which only a few photons per second pass through the slits, there is no way to predict where an individual photon will go. Thus the interference pattern has to

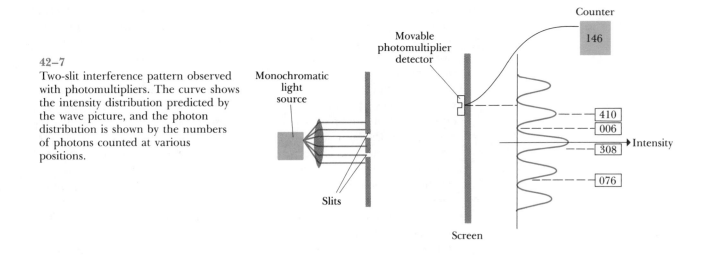

42–7

Two-slit interference pattern observed with photomultipliers. The curve shows the intensity distribution predicted by the wave picture, and the photon distribution is shown by the numbers of photons counted at various positions.

be viewed as a *statistical distribution* of photons. It tells us what fraction of the incident photons will go in each direction, or the *probability* that an individual photon will go in each of various directions, but *not* precisely where any particular photon will go.

It is tempting to think that each individual photon must pass through one or the other of the slits. But if this were the case, we would be able to record the interference pattern on film by opening one slit for awhile, then closing it and opening the other. This doesn't work; to form an interference pattern, the waves from the two slits have to be *coherent*. To resolve this apparent paradox, we are forced to conclude that *every* photon goes partly through *both* slits and that *each photon interferes only with itself.* If this sounds like nonsense, remember that the photon is *not* a single point in space; it is a conceptual framework to describe the quantization of energy in electromagnetic waves. There is nothing conceptually wrong with saying that every photon passes through both slits; indeed, this is the *only* consistent viewpoint.

Finally, what happens when we do a two-slit interference experiment with electrons? Exactly the same thing as with photons! Again we can do a particle-counting experiment to trace out the interference pattern, as we did with photons, but we *cannot* predict where in the pattern an individual electron will land. Furthermore, again because of the coherence requirement, we have to assume that *every electron goes through both slits*! This conclusion may be even more disturbing than the idea of a photon passing through both slits. But remember that the electron is *not* a point; it is an inherently spread-out entity. There is nothing conceptually wrong with having it pass through both slits. Like photons, each electron interferes only with itself.

42–4
Wave Functions

We have now seen ample evidence for the conclusion that on an atomic scale we have to replace the classical kinematic language for a particle (three coordinates, three velocity components) by some more general language. But what language? In our search for the appropriate generalizations we are guided by the language of classical wave motion. In Chapter 21, when we studied transverse waves on a string, we described the motion of the string by specifying the position of each point in the string at each instant of time. To do this, we used a **wave function,** which we introduced in Section 21–6. If y represents the displacement from equilibrium at time t of a point on the string at a distance x from the origin, then the function $y = f(x, t)$ or $y(x, t)$ represents the displacement of point x at time t. Once we know the wave function for a particular wave motion, we know everything there is to know about the motion. We can find the position and velocity of any point on the string at any time, and so on.

We followed a similar pattern for sound waves in Chapter 23. The wave function $p(x, t)$ for a wave traveling along the x-direction represented the pressure variation at any point x at any time t. The same pattern reappeared once more in the description of *electromagnetic* waves in Section 35–5, in which we used two wave functions to describe the electric and magnetic fields at any point in space at any time.

Thus it is natural to use a wave function as the central element of our generalized language for describing particles. The symbol usually used for this wave function is Ψ. In general, Ψ is a function of all the space coordinates and time. Just as the wave function $y(x, t)$ for mechanical waves on a string provides a complete description of the motion, the wave function $\Psi(x, y, z, t)$ for a particle contains all the information that can be known about the particle.

It is tempting to ask "What is the wave medium for this wave?" Unfortunately, there is no answer to that question. The wave function for a particle is not a wave that propagates through some material medium. Ultimately, all we can really say is that the wave function *is* the particle. We can't define it in terms of anything material; we can only describe how it is related to physically observable effects.

Two more questions arise. First, how do we relate the wave function to observable behavior of the particle? Second, how do we determine what Ψ is for any given physical situation? With reference to the first question, the wave function describes the distribution of the particle in space. It is related to the *probability* of finding the particle in each of various regions; the particle is most likely to be found in regions where Ψ is large, and so on. We have already used this interpretation in our discussion of electron diffraction experiments. If the particle has charge, the wave function can be used to find the *charge density* at any point in space. In addition, from Ψ we can calculate the *average* position of the particle, its average velocity, and dynamic quantities such as momentum, energy, and angular momentum. The required techniques are far beyond the scope of this discussion, but they are well established and well supported by experimental results.

The answer to the second question is that the wave function must be one of a set of solutions of a certain differential equation called the **Schrödinger equation,** developed by Erwin Schrödinger (1887–1961) in 1925. In principle we can set up a Schrödinger equation for any given physical situation, such as the electron in a hydrogen atom. The wave functions that are solutions of this equation represent various possible physical states of the system. Furthermore, it turns out for some systems that it is not even *possible* to find acceptable solutions of this equation unless some physical quantity, such as the energy of the system, has certain special values. The solutions of the Schrödinger equation for any particular system also yield a set of allowed *energy levels*. This discovery is of the utmost importance. Before the development of the Schrödinger equation there was no way to predict energy levels from any fundamental theory, except for the very limited success of the Bohr model for hydrogen.

Soon after the Schrödinger equation was developed, it was applied to the problem of the hydrogen atom. The predicted energy levels E_n for the simplest model turned out to be identical to those from the Bohr model, Eq. (41–17). Therefore these results agreed with experimental values obtained from spectrum analysis.

In addition, the solutions have quantized values of *angular momentum*; that is, only certain discrete values of the magnitude and components of angular momentum are possible. Recall that quantization of angular momentum was put into the Bohr model as an ad hoc assumption with no fundamental justification; with the Schrödinger equation it appears automatically. Specifically, it is found that the magnitude L of the angular momentum of an electron in the hydrogen atom in a state with energy E_n and quantum number n must be given by

$$L = \sqrt{l(l + 1)}\, \frac{h}{2\pi}, \qquad (42\text{--}11)$$

where l is zero or a positive integer no larger than $n - 1$. The *component* of L in a given direction, say the z-component L_z, can have only the set of values

$$L_z = m\frac{h}{2\pi}, \qquad (42\text{--}12)$$

where m can be zero or a positive or negative integer up to but no larger in magnitude than l. That is, $|m| \le l$.

The quantity $h/2\pi$ appears so often in quantum mechanics that we give it a special symbol, $\hbar$, pronounced "h-bar." That is,

$$\hbar = \frac{h}{2\pi} = 1.054 \times 10^{-34}\ \text{J}\cdot\text{s}.$$

In terms of $\hbar$ the two preceding equations become

$$L = \sqrt{l(l + 1)}\,\hbar \qquad (l = 0, 1, 2, \ldots, n - 1) \qquad (42\text{--}13)$$

and

$$L_z = m\hbar \qquad (m = 0, \pm 1, \pm 2, \ldots, \pm l). \qquad (42\text{--}14)$$

Note that the component L_z can never be quite as large as L. For example, when $l = 4$ and $m = 4$, we find

$$L = \sqrt{4(4 + 1)}\,\hbar = 4.47\hbar, \qquad L_z = 4\hbar.$$

This inequality arises from the uncertainty principle, which makes it impossible to predict the *direction* of the angular momentum vector with complete certainty. Thus the component of $\boldsymbol{L}$ in a given direction can never be quite as large as the magnitude L, except when $l = 0$; then both L and L_z are zero. Unlike the Bohr model, the Schrödinger equation gives values for the magnitude L of angular momentum that are *not* integer multiples of $\hbar$.

Another interesting feature of Eqs. (42–13) and (42–14) is that there are states for which the angular momentum is *zero*. This result has no classical analog; in the Bohr model the electron always moved in an orbit and thus had nonzero angular momentum. But in the new mechanics we find states having zero angular momentum.

The possible wave functions for the hydrogen atom are labeled according to the values of the three integers n, l, and m, called the **principal quantum number** (n), the **angular momentum quantum number** (l),

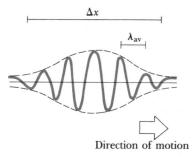

Δx

λ_{av}

Direction of motion

42–8
A wave pulse or packet. There is an average wavelength λ_{av}, the distance between adjacent peaks, but the wave is localized at any instant in a region with length of the order of Δx. The dashed lines are called the envelope of the pulse; all the peaks lie on the envelope curves, which approach zero at both ends of the pulse.

and the **magnetic quantum number** (m). For each energy level E_n there are several distinct states having the same energy but different values of l and m. The only exception is the ground state ($n = 1$), for which the only possibility is $l = 0$, $m = 0$. More detailed inspection of the wave functions also shows that in each case the wave function is concentrated primarily in a region around the nucleus with a radius equal to the Bohr radius for the same value of n.

Finally, let's think briefly about how we can use the concept of a wave function to reconcile wave and particle properties. Figure 42–8 shows a *wave pulse*, a possible wave function for a *free* particle such as an electron in the beams we have used for electron diffraction experiments. This wave function has both wave and particle properties. The regular spacing λ_{av} between successive maxima is characteristic of a wave, but there is also a particle-like localization in space. To be sure, the wave pulse is not localized at a single point, but in any experiment that detects only dimensions much larger than Δx, the wave pulse will appear to be a localized particle. Wave functions such as this show that wave and particle properties aren't incompatible.

It would *not* be correct to regard the wave of Fig. 42–8 as having only a single wavelength. A sinusoidal wave with a definite wavelength has no beginning and no end. To make a wave *pulse* with a finite length, we have to superpose many sinusoidal waves with various wavelengths. According to de Broglie's hypothesis, this also means that we have a superposition of various values of *momentum*. Thus both position and momentum have uncertainties, and their complementary nature is described by Eq. (42–9). The wave function shown in Fig. 42–8 corresponds to a range of wavelengths, and λ_{av} is an average value.

The new mechanics described above, which we call quantum mechanics, is much more complex, both conceptually and mathematically, than Newtonian mechanics. It deals with probabilities rather than certainties, and it predicts discrete rather than continuous behavior. However, quantum mechanics enables us to understand physical phenomena and to analyze physical problems for which classical mechanics is completely powerless. Added complexity is the price we pay for this greatly expanded understanding.

*42–5
The Zeeman Effect

The **Zeeman effect** is the shifting of atomic energy levels and the associated spectrum lines when the atoms are placed in a magnetic field. Atoms contain charges in motion, so it should not be surprising that the resulting magnetic-field forces cause changes in the motion and in the energy levels. As early as 1862, Faraday had placed light sources in a magnetic field in an attempt to observe this effect. His spectroscopic techniques were not refined enough to observe any effect. But in 1896 the Dutch physicist Pieter Zeeman (1865–1943), using improved instruments, *was* able to detect small shifts in spectrum wavelengths, and the effect now bears his name.

Let's first look at the interaction of a hydrogen atom with a magnetic field, using the Bohr model. We can describe the interaction energy in terms of the atom's *magnetic moment*, a concept we introduced in Section 30–8. There is a danger of having too many m's in this discussion. To avoid confusion in notation, we denote magnetic moment by $\boldsymbol{\mu}$, the electron mass by m_e, and the magnetic quantum number by m. Be careful to keep these symbols straight in the analysis that follows. We looked at the interaction energy U of a magnetic moment $\boldsymbol{\mu}$ in a magnetic field $\boldsymbol{B}$ in Section 30–8, Eq. (30–20). It is given by

$$U = -\mu B \cos \alpha, \qquad (42\text{--}15)$$

where α is the angle between the directions of the vectors $\boldsymbol{\mu}$ and $\boldsymbol{B}$.

We can compute the magnetic moment of the orbiting electron in the Bohr model. It is equivalent to a current loop with radius r and area πr^2. The average current I is the average charge per unit time passing a point of the orbit, and this is given by e/τ, where τ is the time for one revolution: $\tau = 2\pi r/v$. Thus $I = ev/2\pi r$, and from Eq. (30–18) the magnetic moment μ is given by

$$\mu = IA = \frac{ev}{2\pi r}\pi r^2 = \frac{evr}{2}. \qquad (42\text{--}16)$$

We can also express this in terms of the angular momentum L, which from Eq. (9–35) is given by $L = m_e vr$:

$$\mu = \frac{e}{2m_e}L. \qquad (42\text{--}17)$$

The ratio of magnetic moment to angular momentum, $e/2m_e$, is called the **gyromagnetic ratio.**

In the Bohr model, $L = nh/2\pi = n\hbar$, where $n = 1, 2, \ldots$. For the $n = 1$ state (the ground state) we find

$$\mu = \frac{e}{2m_e}\hbar = \frac{1}{2}(1.759 \times 10^{11}\ \text{C·kg}^{-1})(1.054 \times 10^{-34}\ \text{J·s})$$
$$= 9.27 \times 10^{-24}\ \text{A·m}^2.$$

Example 42–4   Find the interaction potential energy when the hydrogen atom described above is placed in a magnetic field with a magnitude of 2.00 T.

Solution   According to Eq. (42–15), the interaction energy U when $\boldsymbol{B}$ and $\boldsymbol{\mu}$ are parallel is

$$U = -\mu B = -(9.27 \times 10^{-24}\ \text{A·m}^2)(2.00\ \text{T})$$
$$= -1.85 \times 10^{-23}\ \text{J} = -1.16 \times 10^{-4}\ \text{eV}.$$

This is the amount by which the energy level of the state is shifted by the magnetic-field interaction. When $\boldsymbol{\mu}$ and $\boldsymbol{B}$ are antiparallel, the energy is $+1.16 \times 10^{-4}$ eV. These energy shifts are *smaller* than the energy levels of the atom by a factor of the order of 10^{-4}. ∎

We can generalize the above discussion to states described by Schrödinger wave functions. It turns out that electrons described by the Schrödinger equation have the same ratio of μ to B (gyromagnetic ratio) as in the Bohr model, namely, $e/2m_e$. Suppose the magnetic field $\boldsymbol{B}$ is directed along the $+z$-axis; then the interaction energy of the atom's magnetic moment with the field is given by

$$U = -\mu B \cos \alpha = -\mu_z B, \qquad (42\text{--}18)$$

where $\mu_z = \mu \cos \alpha$ is the z-component of the vector $\boldsymbol{\mu}$.

From the above discussion,

$$\mu_z = \frac{e}{2m_e} L_z. \qquad (42\text{--}19)$$

For the Schrödinger wave functions, $L_z = m\hbar$, with $m = 0, \pm 1, \pm 2, \ldots, \pm l$, so

$$\mu_z = \frac{e}{2m_e} L_z = m \frac{e\hbar}{2m_e}. \qquad (42\text{--}20)$$

Finally, we can express the interaction energy, Eq. (42–18), as

$$U = -\mu_z B = -m \frac{e\hbar B}{2m_e} \qquad (m = 0, \pm 1, \pm 2, \ldots, \pm l). \quad (42\text{--}21)$$

The effect of the magnetic field is to shift each energy level by an amount U, given by Eq. (42–21). The magnitude of the shift depends on the value of the magnetic quantum number m, which is determined by the orientation of the angular-momentum vector. For each value of l there are $(2l + 1)$ values of m. An energy level with a certain value of the angular-momentum quantum number l is split into $(2l + 1)$ sublevels, with adjacent sublevels differing in energy by $e\hbar B/2m_e$. Spectrum lines corresponding to transitions involving this energy level are correspondingly split and appear as a series of closely spaced spectrum lines replacing a single line. The Zeeman effect is a very direct experimental confirmation of the quantization of angular momentum.

Example 42–5   An atom in a state with $l = 1$ emits a photon with a wavelength of 600.000 nm as it decays to its ground state (with $l = 0$). If the atom is placed in a magnetic field of magnitude $B = 1.00$ T, determine the shifts in the energy level and in the wavelength.

Solution   The energy of a 600-nm photon, as we obtained in Section 41–2, is 3.31×10^{-19} J or 2.07 eV. The ground-state level has $l = 0$ and is not split by the field. The splitting of levels in the $l = 1$ state is given by Eq. (42–21):

$$U = -m \frac{e\hbar B}{2m_e}$$

$$= -m \frac{(1.60 \times 10^{-19}\ \text{C})(1.054 \times 10^{-34}\ \text{J·s})(1.00\ \text{T})}{2(9.11 \times 10^{-31}\ \text{kg})}$$

$$= -m(9.26 \times 10^{-24}\ \text{J}) = -m(5.79 \times 10^{-5}\ \text{eV}).$$

When $l = 1$, the possible values of m are -1, 0, and $+1$, and the three resulting levels are split by equal intervals of 5.79×10^{-5} eV. This is a small fraction of the photon energy: $(5.79 \times 10^{-5}$ eV$)/(2.07$ eV$) = 2.80 \times 10^{-5}$. The corresponding *wavelength* shifts are approximately $(2.80 \times 10^{-5})(600$ nm$) = 0.017$ nm. The original 600-nm line is split into a triplet with wavelengths of 599.983, 600.000, and 600.017 nm. This splitting is well within the limit of resolution of modern spectrometers. ∎

42–6
Electron Spin

Some of the observed Zeeman-effect energy level splittings are not completely explained by the analysis we sketched in Section 42–5. And some energy levels show splitting that resembles the Zeeman effect even when there is no external magnetic field. It was suggested in 1925 that perhaps the electron behaves like a spinning sphere of charge. In that case it would have additional angular momentum and magnetic moment that might help in understanding these energy-level anomalies.

To introduce this concept, let's start with an analogy. The earth travels in a nearly circular orbit around the sun, and at the same time it *rotates* on its axis. Each motion has its associated angular momentum, which we call the *orbital* and *spin* angular momentum, respectively. The total angular momentum of the system is the sum of the two. If we were to model the earth as a single point, it could not have spin angular momentum. But when our model includes an earth of finite size, spin angular momentum becomes possible.

This discussion can be translated into the language of the Bohr model. Suppose the electron is not a point charge moving in an orbit, but a small spinning sphere in orbit. Then the electron has not only orbital angular momentum, but also spin angular momentum associated with its rotation on its axis. The sphere carries an electric charge, so the spinning motion leads to current loops and to a magnetic moment, as we discussed in Section 30–8. When the atom is placed in a magnetic field, there should be an interaction energy. This is in addition to the interaction energy of the *orbital* magnetic moment with a magnetic field, which we discussed in Section 42–5. We should see additional small Zeeman-effect shifts in the energy levels of the atom and in the wavelengths of the associated spectrum lines.

Such shifts *are* indeed observed in precise spectroscopic analysis; this and a variety of other experimental evidence have shown conclusively that the electron *does* have angular momentum and a magnetic moment that do not depend on its orbital motion but are intrinsic to the particle itself. Like orbital angular momentum, spin angular momentum (usually denoted by S) is found to be *quantized*. Suppose we have some apparatus that measures the component of S in a particular direction, which we will call the z-axis. Denoting the z-component of S by S_z, we find that the only possible values are

$$S_z = \pm\frac{1}{2}\hbar. \tag{42–22}$$

This relation is reminiscent of Eq. (42–14) for L_z, the z-component of orbital angular momentum, except that S_z is *one half* of $\hbar$ instead of an *integral* multiple.

In quantum mechanics, in which the Bohr orbits are superseded by wave functions, we can't really *picture* electron spin. If we visualize the wave functions as clouds surrounding the nucleus, then we can imagine many tiny arrows distributed throughout the cloud, all pointing in the same direction, either all +z or all −z. But don't take this picture too seriously.

In any event the concept of electron spin is well established by a variety of experimental evidence. To label completely the state of the electron in a hydrogen atom, we now need a fourth quantum number s to specify the electron spin orientation. If s can take the value +1 or −1, then the z-component of spin angular momentum is given by

$$S_z = \frac{1}{2}s\hbar \qquad (s = \pm 1). \tag{42–23}$$

The corresponding component of magnetic moment, which we again denote by μ_z, turns out to be related to S_z by

$$\mu_z = \frac{e}{m_e}S_z, \tag{42–24}$$

where e and m_e are the charge and mass of the electron, respectively. This shows that for electron spin the gyromagnetic ratio (μ_z/S_z) is just *twice* the value for *orbital* angular momentum and magnetic moment. When the atom is placed in a magnetic field, the interaction of the electron spin magnetic moment with the field causes further splittings in energy levels and in the corresponding spectrum lines.

The electron spin magnetic moment also causes splitting of energy levels even when there is *no* external field. This effect is somewhat more subtle. In the Bohr model an observer moving with the electron would see the positively charged nucleus moving around him or her. This moving charge causes a magnetic field at the location of the electron (as seen in the electron's frame of reference). The resulting interaction energy with the spin magnetic moment causes a twofold splitting of this level, corresponding to the two possible orientations of electron spin.

We know that the validity of the Bohr model is limited, but a similar result can be derived from a more complete quantum-mechanical treatment based on the Schrödinger equation. The effect is called **spin-orbit coupling;** it is responsible for the small energy difference between the two closely spaced "resonance levels" of sodium shown in Fig. 41–6 and for the corresponding familiar doublet (589.0, 589.6 nm) in the spectrum of sodium.

The various line splittings resulting from these magnetic interactions are collectively called *fine structure*. There are also additional, much smaller splittings that result from the fact that the *nucleus* of the atom also has a magnetic moment, and it interacts with the orbital and spin magnetic moments of the electrons. These effects are called *hyperfine structure*.

Questions

42–1 In analyzing the absorption spectrum of hydrogen at room temperature, one finds absorption lines corresponding to wavelengths in the Lyman series but not to those in the Balmer series. Why not?

42–2 A singly ionized helium atom has one of its two electrons removed, and the energy levels of the remaining electron are closely related to those of the hydrogen atom. The nuclear charge for helium is $+2e$ instead of just $+e$; exactly how are the energy levels related to those of hydrogen? How is the size of the ion in the ground state related to that of the hydrogen atom?

42–3 Consider the line spectrum emitted from a gas discharge tube such as a neon sign or a sodium-vapor or mercury-vapor lamp. It is found that when the pressure of the vapor is increased, the spectrum lines spread out, that is, are less sharp and less monochromatic. Why?

42–4 Suppose a two-slit interference experiment is carried out by using an electron beam. Would the same interference pattern result if one slit at a time is uncovered instead of both at once? If not, why not? Does not each electron go through one slit or the other? Or does every electron go through both slits? Does the latter possibility make sense?

42–5 Is the wave nature of electrons significant in the function of a television picture tube? For example, do diffraction effects limit the sharpness of the picture?

42–6 A proton and an electron have the same speed. Which has longer wavelength?

42–7 A proton and an electron have the same kinetic energy. Which has longer wavelength?

42–8 Does the uncertainty principle have anything to do with marksmanship? That is, is the accuracy with which a bullet can be aimed at a target limited by the uncertainty principle?

42–9 Is the Bohr model of the hydrogen atom consistent with the uncertainty principle?

42–10 If the energy of a system can have uncertainty, as stated by Eq. (42–10), does this mean that the principle of conservation of energy is no longer valid?

42–11 If quantum mechanics replaces the language of Newtonian mechanics, why do we not have to use wave functions to describe the motion of macroscopic objects such as baseballs and cars?

42–12 Why is analysis of the helium atom much more complex than that of the hydrogen atom, either in a Bohr type of model or using the Schrödinger equation?

42–13 Do gravitational forces play a significant role in atomic structure?

Exercises

Section 42–1   The Wave Nature of Particles

Section 42–2   The Electron Microscope

42–1

a) An electron moves with a speed of 4.00×10^6 m·s^{-1}. What is its de Broglie wavelength?

b) A proton moves with the same speed. Determine its de Broglie wavelength.

42–2 Approximately what range of photon energies (in electronvolts) corresponds to the visible spectrum? Approximately what range of wavelengths would electrons in this energy range have?

42–3 For crystal diffraction experiments, wavelengths of the order of 0.50 nm are often appropriate. Find the

energy in electronvolts for a particle with this wavelength if the particle is

a) a photon;   b) an electron.

42–4

a) What is the de Broglie wavelength of an electron that has been accelerated through a potential difference of 120 V?

b) Would this electron exhibit particlelike or wavelike characteristics on meeting an obstacle or opening 1.0 mm in diameter?

42–5

a) What is the de Broglie wavelength of an electron accelerated through 900 V?

b) What is the de Broglie wavelength of a proton accelerated through the same potential difference?

Section 42–3 Probability and Uncertainty

42–6

a) The uncertainty in the y-component of the position of a proton is 5.0×10^{-12} m. What is the minimum uncertainty in the y-component of the velocity of the proton?

b) The uncertainty in the z-component of the velocity of an electron is 0.200 m·s^{-1}. What is the minimum uncertainty in the z-coordinate of the electron?

42–7 A certain atom has an energy level 3.50 eV above the ground state. When excited to this state, it remains on the average 4.0×10^{-6} s before emitting a photon and returning to the ground state.

a) What is the energy of the photon? What is its wavelength?

b) What is the smallest possible uncertainty in energy of the photon?

42–8

a) Suppose that the uncertainty in position of a particle is of the order of its de Broglie wavelength. Show that in this case the uncertainty in its momentum is of the order of its momentum.

b) Suppose that the uncertainty in position of an electron is equal to the radius of the $n = 1$ Bohr orbit, about 0.5×10^{-10} m. Estimate the uncertainty in its momentum, and compare this with the magnitude of the momentum of the electron in the $n = 1$ Bohr orbit.

42–9 An unstable particle produced in a high-energy collision has a mass that is four times that of the proton and an uncertainty in mass that is 1.0% of the particle's mass. Assuming that mass and energy are related by $E = mc^2$, estimate the lifetime of the particle.

Section 42–4 Wave Functions

42–10 Make a chart showing all the possible sets of quantum numbers l and m for the states of the electron

in the hydrogen atom when $n = 3$. How many combinations are there?

42–11 Consider states with $l = 3$.

a) In units of $\hbar$, what is the largest possible value of L_z?

b) In units of $\hbar$, what is the value of L? Which is larger, L or the maximum possible L_z?

c) Assume a model in which $\mathbf{L}$ is described as a classical vector. For each allowed value of L_z, what angle does the vector $\mathbf{L}$ make with the $+z$-axis?

Section 42–5 The Zeeman Effect

42–12 Consider an atom in an $l = 2$ state. In the absence of an external magnetic field the states with different m have (approximately) the same energy. (We say that the states are *degenerate*.)

a) If the effect of electron spin can be ignored (which is not actually the case), calculate the splitting (in electronvolts) of the m-levels when the atom is put in a 0.800-T magnetic field that is in the $+z$-direction.

b) Which m-level will have the lowest energy?

c) Draw an energy-level diagram that shows the $l = 2$ levels with and without the external magnetic field.

Section 42–6 Electron Spin

42–13 If you treat an electron as a classical spherical particle with a radius of 1.0×10^{-17} m, what is the angular velocity necessary to produce a spin angular momentum of $\hbar$?

42–14 A hydrogen atom in the $n = 1$, $s = 1$ state is placed in a magnetic field with a magnitude of 1.80 T in the $+z$-direction. Find the interaction energy (in electronvolts) of the atom with the field due to the electron spin.

Problems

42–15 The average kinetic energy of a thermal neutron is $\tfrac{3}{2}kT$. What is the de Broglie wavelength associated with the neutrons in thermal equilibrium with matter at 300 K? (The mass of a neutron is 1.68×10^{-27} kg.)

42–16 A 40.0-kg satellite circles the earth once every 2.00 hr in an orbit having a radius of 8060 km.

a) Assuming that Bohr's angular-momentum postulate $(L = n\hbar)$ applies to satellites just as it does to an electron in the hydrogen atom, find the quantum number n of the orbit of the satellite.

b) Show from Bohr's angular-momentum postulate and Newton's law of gravitation that the radius of an earth-satellite orbit is directly proportional to the square of the quantum number, $r = kn^2$, where k is a constant of proportionality.

c) Using the result from part (b), find the distance between the orbit of the satellite in this problem and its next "allowed" orbit. (Calculate a numerical value.)

d) Comment on the possibility of observing the separation of the two adjacent orbits.

e) Do quantized and classical orbits correspond for this satellite? Which is the "correct" method for calculating the orbits?

42–17 What is the de Broglie wavelength of a red blood cell with a mass of 1.00×10^{-11} g that is moving with a speed of 0.500 cm·s^{-1}? Do we need to be concerned with the wave nature of the blood cells when we describe the flow of blood in the body?

42–18

a) If the transition energy E is shifted by an amount ΔE, there is a corresponding shift $\Delta\lambda$ in the wavelength of the emitted photon. Show that $\Delta E/E = -\Delta\lambda/\lambda$ when $|\Delta\lambda/\lambda|$ is small. (*Hint:* Use the relation $E = hc/\lambda$ and apply it to a photon with energy E' and wavelength λ', where $E' = E + \Delta E$ and $\lambda' = \lambda + \Delta\lambda$.)

b) Refer to Exercise 42–7. Use the results you obtained to calculate the magnitude of the smallest possible uncertainty in the wavelength of the photon.

42–19 A hydrogen atom in the $n = 2$, $l = 1$, $m = -1$ state emits a photon when it decays to the $n = 1$, $l = 0$, $m = 0$ ground state.

a) In the absence of an external magnetic field, what is the wavelength of this photon?

b) If the atom is in a magnetic field in the $+z$-direction with a magnitude of $B = 2.50$ T, what is the shift in the wavelength of the photon from the zero-field value? Does the magnetic field increase or decrease the wavelength? (Use the result of Problem 42–18(a). Disregard the effect of electron spin.)

42–20 A hydrogen atom makes a transition from the $n = 3$ state to the $n = 2$ state (the Balmer H_α line at 656 nm) while in a magnetic field in the $+z$-direction with magnitude 1.50 T. If the magnetic quantum number is $m = 2$ in the initial ($n = 3$) state and $m = 1$ in the final ($n = 2$) state,

a) by how much is each energy level shifted from the zero-field value?

b) By how much is the wavelength of the spectrum line shifted from the zero-field value? Is the wavelength increased or decreased? Disregard the effect of electron spin. (Use the result of Problem 42–18(a).)

42–21 The radii of atomic nuclei are of the order of 1.0×10^{-15} m.

a) Estimate the minimum uncertainty in the momentum of an electron if it is confined within a nucleus.

b) Take this uncertainty in momentum to be an estimate of the magnitude of the momentum. (Refer to Exercise 42–8.) Use the relativistic expression of Eq. (40–29) to obtain an estimate of the kinetic energy of an electron confined within a nucleus.

c) Compare the energy calculated in part (b) to the magnitude of the Coulomb potential energy of a proton and an electron separated by 1.0×10^{-15} m. On the basis of your result, could there be electrons within the nucleus?

42–22 The radii of atomic nuclei are of the order of 1.0×10^{-15} m.

a) Estimate the minimum uncertainty in the momentum of a proton if it is confined within a nucleus.

b) Take this uncertainty in momentum to be an estimate of the magnitude of the momentum. (Refer to Exercise 42–8.) Use the relativistic expression of Eq. (40–29) to obtain an estimate of the kinetic energy of a proton confined within a nucleus.

(*Note:* It is interesting to compare this result to that of Problem 42–21.)

42–23 In another universe the value of Planck's constant is 6.63×10^{-12} J·s. Assume that the physical laws and all other physical constants are the same as in our universe. In this other universe an atom is in an excited state 25.0 eV above the ground state. The lifetime of this excited state (the average time the electron stays in this state) is 1.50×10^{-3} s. What is the uncertainty in the energy of the photon emitted when the atom makes the transition from this excited state to the ground state?

42–24 In a television picture tube the accelerating voltage is 1.50 kV, and the electron beam passes through an aperture 0.500 mm in diameter to a screen 0.300 m away.

a) What is the uncertainty in position of the point where the electrons strike the screen?

b) Does this uncertainty affect the clarity of the picture significantly?

(Use nonrelativistic expressions for the motion of the electrons. This is fairly accurate and is certainly adequate for obtaining an estimate of uncertainty-principle effects.)

42–25 Show that the total number of hydrogen-atom states (including different spin states) for a given value of the principal quantum number n is $2n^2$. (*Hint:* The sum of the first N integers $1 + 2 + 3 + \cdots + N$ is given by $N[N + 1]/2$.)

42–26 The π^0 meson is an unstable particle produced in high-energy particle collisions. Its mass is about 264 times that of the electron, and it exists for an average lifetime of 0.8×10^{-16} s before decaying into two gamma-ray photons. Assuming that the mass and energy of the particle are related by the Einstein relation $E = mc^2$, find the uncertainty in the mass of the particle and express it as a fraction of the mass.

42–27 In another universe the value of Planck's constant is 0.0663 J·s. Assume that the physical laws and all other physical constants are the same as in our universe. In this other universe, two physics students are playing catch with a baseball. They are 50 m apart, and one throws a 0.10-kg ball with a speed of 5.0 m·s^{-1}.

a) What is the uncertainty in the ball's horizontal momentum in a direction perpendicular to that in which it is being thrown if the student throwing the ball knows that it is located within a cube with volume 1000 cm^3 at the time she throws it?

b) By what horizontal distance could the ball miss the second student?

Challenge Problems

42–28 The wave nature of particles results in the quantum mechanical situation that a particle confined in a box can have only wavelengths that result in standing waves in the box, with nodes at the box walls.

a) Show that an electron confined in a one-dimensional box of length L will have energy levels given by

$$E_n = \frac{n^2h^2}{8mL^2}.$$

(*Hint:* Recall that the relation between de Broglie wavelength and the speed of a particle is $mv = h/\lambda$. The energy of the particle is $\frac{1}{2}mv^2$.)

b) If a hydrogen atom is modeled as a one-dimensional box with a length equal to the Bohr radius, what is the energy (in electronvolts) of the ground state of the electron?

42–29 When a photon is emitted by an atom, the atom must recoil to conserve momentum. This means that the photon and the recoiling atom share the transition energy. For a hydrogen atom, calculate the correction due to recoil to the wavelength of the photon emitted when an electron in the $n = 5$ state returns to the ground state. (*Hint:* The correction is very small, so $|\Delta\lambda/\lambda| \ll 1$. Use this fact to help you obtain an approximate but very accurate expression for $\Delta\lambda$.)

43

Atoms, Molecules, and Solids

The basic concepts of quantum mechanics that we studied in Chapter 42 enable us to understand many aspects of the structure of atoms, molecules, and solid materials. We need one additional principle, the *exclusion principle*, which states that two electrons may not occupy the same quantum-mechanical state. With this principle we can derive the most important features of the structure and chemical behavior of multielectron atoms, including the periodic table of the elements.

The nature of *molecular bonds*, by which two or more atoms combine in a stable structure, can be understood on the basis of the electron configurations of the atoms. Transitions among vibrational and rotational energy states of molecules give rise to *molecular spectra*. Interatomic forces are also responsible for the large-scale binding of atoms into solid structures. Several different types of interactions are possible, and many properties of solid materials can be understood at least qualitatively on the basis of the types of bonding that are present. *Semiconductors*, a particular class of solid materials, are discussed in some detail because of their inherent interest and their great practical importance in present-day technology. Finally, we look briefly at the phenomenon of *superconductivity*, the complete disappearance of electrical resistance at low temperatures.

43–1
The Exclusion Principle

The hydrogen atom is the simplest atom in structure; it contains one electron and one proton. Analysis of atoms with more than one electron increases in complexity very rapidly. Each electron interacts not only with the positively charged nucleus but also with all the other electrons. In principle the motion of the electrons is governed by the Schrödinger equation, which we mentioned in Section 42–4. But the mathematical problem of finding appropriate solutions of this equation is so complex that it has not been solved exactly even for the helium atom, which has two electrons.

There are various approximation schemes for applying the Schrödinger equation to multielectron atoms. The most drastic is to *ignore* the interactions between electrons and consider the motion of each electron under the electric field of the nucleus, considered to be a point charge. A less drastic and more useful approximation is to think of all the electrons together as making up a charge cloud that is, on the average, *spherically symmetric*. We can then think of each individual electron as moving in the total electric field due to the nucleus and this averaged-out electron cloud. This is called the **central-field approximation;** it provides a useful starting point for the understanding of atomic structure.

An additional principle is also needed, the **exclusion principle.** To understand the role this principle plays, we need to consider the lowest-energy state or *ground state* of a multielectron atom. In the central-field model there is a lowest energy state (corresponding roughly to the $n = 1$ state for the hydrogen atom). We might expect that, in the ground state of a complex atom, all the electrons should be in this lowest state. If so, then the behavior of atoms with increasing numbers of electrons should show gradual changes in physical and chemical properties as the number of electrons in the atoms increases.

A variety of evidence shows conclusively that this is *not* what happens at all. For example, the elements fluorine, neon, and sodium have 9, 10, and 11 electrons per atom, respectively. Fluorine is a *halogen*; it tends strongly to form compounds in which each atom acquires an extra electron. Sodium, an *alkali metal*, forms compounds in which it *loses* an electron, and neon is an *inert gas*, forming no compounds at all. This and many other observations show that in the ground state of a complex atom the electrons *cannot* all be in the lowest energy states.

The key to this puzzle, discovered by the Swiss physicist Wolfgang Pauli (1900–1958) in 1925, is called the **Pauli exclusion principle.** Briefly, it states that *no two electrons in an atom can occupy the same quantum-mechanical state*. Different states correspond to different spatial distributions, including different distances from the nucleus. Therefore in a complex atom there is not enough room for all the electrons in the states nearest the nucleus; some electrons are forced into states farther away, with higher energies.

To apply the Pauli principle to atomic structure, let's first review some results that we quoted in Sections 42–4 and 42–6. The quantum-mechanical state of the electron in the hydrogen atom is identified by the

TABLE 43–1

n	l	m	Spectroscopic notation	Maximum number of electrons		Shell
1	0	0	$1s$	2		K
2	0	0	$2s$	2		
2	1	−1			8	L
2	1	0	$2p$	6		
2	1	1				
3	0	0	$3s$	2		
3	1	−1				
3	1	0	$3p$	6		
3	1	1				
3	2	−2			18	M
3	2	−1				
3	2	0	$3d$	10		
3	2	1				
3	2	2				
4	0	0	$4s$	2		
4	1	−1				
4	1	0	$4p$	6	32	N
4	1	1				
	etc.					

four quantum numbers $n, l, m,$ and s, which determine the energy, angular momentum, and components of orbital and spin angular momentum in a particular direction. It turns out that we can still use this scheme when the electron moves in the electric field of *any spherically symmetric charge distribution*, as in the central-field approximation. One important difference is that the *energy* of a state is no longer given by Eq. (41–17); in general it depends on *both* the quantum numbers n and l. Usually, for a given value of n the energy increases with increasing l.

We can now make a list of all the possible sets of quantum numbers and thus of the possible states of electrons in an atom. Such a list is given in Table 43–1, which also indicates two alternative notations. It is customary to designate the value of l by a letter, according to this scheme:

$l = 0$: s state

$l = 1$: p state

$l = 2$: d state

$l = 3$: f state

$l = 4$: g state

This peculiar code originated in the early days of spectroscopy, before atomic structure was understood, when spectral series were classified as "sharp," "principal," "diffuse," and "fundamental." A state for which $n = 2$ and $l = 1$ is called a $2p$ state, and so on, as shown in Table 43–1. This table also shows the relationship between values of n and the X-ray levels ($K, L, M, \ldots$) that we will describe in Section 43–2. The $n = 1$ levels are designated as K, $n = 2$ as L, and so on.

Because the average electron distance from the nucleus increases with n, each value of n corresponds roughly to a region of space around the nucleus in the form of a spherical **shell.** Hence we speak of the K *shell* as the region occupied by the electrons in the $n = 1$ states, the L shell as the region of the $n = 2$ states, and so on. States with the same n but different l form *subshells*, such as the $3p$ subshell.

We are now ready for a more precise statement of the exclusion principle: *In any atom, only one electron can occupy any given quantum state.* That is, no two electrons in an atom can have the same values of all four quantum numbers. Each quantum state corresponds to a certain distribution of the electron "cloud" in space. Therefore the principle says in effect: "No more than two electrons (with opposite values of the spin quantum number s) can occupy the same region of space." We shouldn't take this statement too seriously because the clouds and associated wave functions that describe electron distributions don't have sharp, definite boundaries. But the exclusion principle limits the degree of overlap of electron wave functions that is permitted. The maximum number of electrons in each shell and subshell are shown in Table 43–1.

The exclusion principle plays an essential role in the understanding of the structure of complex atoms. In the next section we will see how the periodic table of the elements can be understood on the basis of this principle.

43–2
Atomic Structure

We are now ready to use the exclusion principle and the electron energy states we described in Section 43–1 to understand some of the main features of atomic structure. The number of electrons in an atom in its normal (electrically neutral) state is called the **atomic number,** denoted by Z. The nucleus contains Z protons and some number of neutrons. The neutron has no charge; the proton and electron charges have the same magnitude but opposite sign, so in the normal atom the total electric charge is zero. Because the electrons are attracted to the nucleus, the quantum states corresponding to regions nearest the nucleus have the lowest energies. We may imagine constructing an atom by starting with a bare nucleus with Z protons and adding Z electrons, one by one. To obtain the ground state, we fill the lowest-energy states (ordinarily those with the smallest values of n and l) first, and we use successively higher states until all the electrons are in place. The chemical properties of an atom are determined principally by interactions involving the *outermost* electrons, so we particularly want to learn how these electrons are arranged.

Let's look at the ground-state electron configurations for the first few atoms (in order of increasing Z). For hydrogen the ground state is $1s$; the single electron is in the state $n = 1$, $l = 0$, $m = 0$, and $s = \pm 1$. In the helium atom ($Z = 2$), *both* electrons are in $1s$ states, with opposite spins;

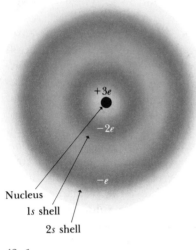

Nucleus

1s shell

2s shell

43–1
Schematic representation of charge distribution in a lithium atom. The nucleus has a charge $3e$; the two $1s$ electrons are closer to the nucleus than the $2s$ electron, which moves in a field approximately equal to that of a point charge of $3e - 2e$, or simply e.

we denote this state as $1s^2$. For helium the K shell is completely filled, and all others are empty.

Lithium ($Z = 3$) has three electrons; in the ground state, two are in the $1s$ state, and one is in a $2s$ state. We denote this state as $1s^2 2s$. On the average, the $2s$ electron is considerably farther from the nucleus than the $1s$ electrons, as shown schematically in Fig. 43–1. According to Gauss's law, the *net* charge influencing the $2s$ electron is $+e$, rather than $+3e$ as it would be without the $1s$ electrons present. The $2s$ electron is loosely bound; only 5.4 eV is required to remove it, compared with 13.6 eV needed to ionize the hydrogen atom. In chemical behavior, lithium is an alkali metal. It forms ionic compounds in which each atom loses an electron and has a valence of $+1$.

Next is beryllium ($Z = 4$); its ground-state configuration is $1s^2 2s^2$, with two electrons in the L shell. Beryllium is the first of the *alkaline-earth* elements, forming ionic compounds in which they have a valence of $+2$.

Table 43–2 shows the ground-state electron configurations of the first 30 elements. The L shell can hold a total of eight electrons; we invite you to verify this from the rules in Section 43–1. At $Z = 10$, both the K and L shells are filled, and there are no electrons in the M shell. We expect this to be a particularly stable configuration with little tendency to gain or lose electrons. This element is neon, a noble gas with no known compounds. The next element after neon is sodium ($Z = 11$), with filled K and L shells and one electron in the M shell. Its "filled-shell-plus-one-electron" structure resembles that of lithium; both are alkali metals. The element *before* neon is fluorine, with $Z = 9$. It has a vacancy in the L shell and has an affinity for an extra electron to fill the shell. Fluorine forms ionic compounds in which it has a valence of -1. This behavior is characteristic of the *halogens* (fluorine, chlorine, bromine, iodine, and astatine), all of which have "filled-shell-minus-one" configurations.

Proceeding down the list, we can understand all the regularities in chemical behavior displayed by the **periodic table of the elements** (found in Appendix D) on the basis of electron configurations. A slight complication occurs with the M and N shells because the $3d$ and $4s$ subshells ($n = 3$, $l = 2$ and $n = 4$, $l = 0$, respectively) overlap in energy. Argon ($Z = 18$) has all the $1s$, $2s$, $2p$, $3s$, and $3p$ states filled, but in potassium ($Z = 19$) the additional electron goes into a $4s$ level rather than a $3d$ level. The next several elements have one or two electrons in the $4s$ states and increasing numbers in the $3d$ states. These elements are all metals with rather similar chemical and physical properties; they form the first *transition series*, starting with scandium ($Z = 21$) and ending with zinc ($Z = 30$), for which the $3d$ and $4s$ levels are filled.

The similarity of elements in each *group* (vertical column) of the periodic table reflects corresponding similarity in outer electron configuration. All the noble gases (helium, neon, argon, krypton, xenon, and radon) have filled-shell configurations. All the alkali metals (lithium, sodium, potassium, rubidium, cesium, and francium) have "filled-shell-plus-one" configurations. All the alkaline-earth metals (beryllium, magnesium, calcium, strontium, barium, and radium) have "filled-shell-plus-two" configurations, and all the halogens (fluorine, chlorine, bromine, iodine, and astatine) have "filled-shell-minus-one" structures.

TABLE 43–2	**Ground-state electron configurations**		

Element	Symbol	Atomic number (Z)	Electron configuration
Hydrogen	H	1	$1s$
Helium	He	2	$1s^2$
Lithium	Li	3	$1s^2 2s$
Beryllium	Be	4	$1s^2 2s^2$
Boron	B	5	$1s^2 2s^2 2p$
Carbon	C	6	$1s^2 2s^2 2p^2$
Nitrogen	N	7	$1s^2 2s^2 2p^3$
Oxygen	O	8	$1s^2 2s^2 2p^4$
Fluorine	F	9	$1s^2 2s^2 2p^5$
Neon	Ne	10	$1s^2 2s^2 2p^6$
Sodium	Na	11	$1s^2 2s^2 2p^6 3s$
Magnesium	Mg	12	$1s^2 2s^2 2p^6 3s^2$
Aluminum	Al	13	$1s^2 2s^2 2p^6 3s^2 3p$
Silicon	Si	14	$1s^2 2s^2 2p^6 3s^2 3p^2$
Phosphorus	P	15	$1s^2 2s^2 2p^6 3s^2 3p^3$
Sulfur	S	16	$1s^2 2s^2 2p^6 3s^2 3p^4$
Chlorine	Cl	17	$1s^2 2s^2 2p^6 3s^2 3p^5$
Argon	Ar	18	$1s^2 2s^2 2p^6 3s^2 3p^6$
Potassium	K	19	$1s^2 2s^2 2p^6 3s^2 3p^6 4s$
Calcium	Ca	20	$1s^2 2s^2 2p^6 3s^2 3p^6 4s^2$
Scandium	Sc	21	$1s^2 2s^2 2p^6 3s^2 3p^6 3d 4s^2$
Titanium	Ti	22	$1s^2 2s^2 2p^6 3s^2 3p^6 3d^2 4s^2$
Vanadium	V	23	$1s^2 2s^2 2p^6 3s^2 3p^6 3d^3 4s^2$
Chromium	Cr	24	$1s^2 2s^2 2p^6 3s^2 3p^6 3d^5 4s$
Manganese	Mn	25	$1s^2 2s^2 2p^6 3s^2 3p^6 3d^5 4s^2$
Iron	Fe	26	$1s^2 2s^2 2p^6 3s^2 3p^6 3d^6 4s^2$
Cobalt	Co	27	$1s^2 2s^2 2p^6 3s^2 3p^6 3d^7 4s^2$
Nickel	Ni	28	$1s^2 2s^2 2p^6 3s^2 3p^6 3d^8 4s^2$
Copper	Cu	29	$1s^2 2s^2 2p^6 3s^2 3p^6 3d^{10} 4s$
Zinc	Zn	30	$1s^2 2s^2 2p^6 3s^2 3p^6 3d^{10} 4s^2$

The *outer* electrons of an atom are responsible for optical spectra. Their excited states are usually only a few electronvolts above the ground state. In transitions from excited states to the ground state they usually emit photons in or near the visible region. There are also **X-ray energy levels,** corresponding to vacancies in the *inner* shells of a complex atom. We mentioned these levels in Section 41–7. In an X-ray tube the electrons may strike the target with enough energy to knock electrons out of the inner shells of the target atoms. These inner electrons are much closer to the nucleus than the electrons in the outer shells; they are much more tightly bound, and hundreds or thousands of electronvolts may be required to remove them.

Suppose an electron is knocked out of the *K* shell. This leaves a vacancy, which is then filled by an electron from one of the outer shells,

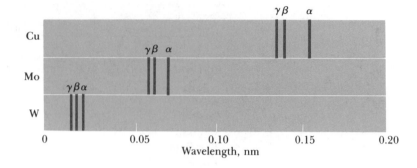

43–2
Wavelengths of the K_α, K_β, and K_γ lines of copper, molybdenum, and tungsten.

such as the L, M, N, . . . shell. This transition is accompanied by a decrease in the energy of the atom, and an X-ray photon is emitted with energy equal to this decrease. The energy change is perfectly definite for atoms of any specific element, so the emitted X-rays have definite wavelengths, and the spectrum is a *line spectrum*.

If the outermost electrons are in the N shell, there are three lines in the series, resulting from transitions in which the vacancy in the K shell is filled by an L, M, or N electron. This series is called a K series. Figure 43–2 shows the K series for copper, molybdenum, and tungsten. The three lines in each series are called the K_α, K_β, and K_γ lines. The K_α line is produced by the transition of an L electron to the vacancy in the K shell, the K_β line by an M electron, and the K_γ line by an N electron.

There are other series of X-ray lines, called the L, M, and N series, produced by the ejection of electrons from the L, M, and N shells rather than the K shell. Electrons in these outer shells are farther away from the nucleus and are not held as tightly as those in the K shell. Their removal requires less energy, and the X-ray photons emitted when these vacancies are filled have lower energy than those in the K series.

PROBLEM-SOLVING STRATEGY: Atomic Structure

1. Be sure you know how to count the energy levels for electrons in the central-field approximation. There are four quantum numbers: n, l, m, and s, all integers; n is always positive, l can be zero or positive, m can be zero, positive, or negative, and $s = \pm 1$. Be sure you know how to count the number of levels in each shell and subshell; study Tables 43–1 and 43–2 carefully.

2. As in Chapter 42, familiarizing yourself with some numerical magnitudes is useful. Here are two examples to work out: The electrical potential energy of a proton and an electron 0.10 nm apart (typical of atomic dimensions) is 14.4 eV or $2.31 \times$ 10^{-18} J. The moment of inertia of two protons 0.10 nm apart (about an axis through the center of mass, perpendicular to the line joining them) is 0.84×10^{-47} kg·m². Think of other examples like this and work them out to help you know what kinds of magnitudes to expect in atomic physics.

3. As in Chapter 42, you will need to use both electronvolts and joules. The conversion 1 eV = 1.602×10^{-19} J and Planck's constant in eV, $h = 4.136 \times 10^{-15}$ eV·s, are useful. Nanometers are convenient for atomic and molecular dimensions, but don't forget to convert to meters in calculations.

43–3
Diatomic Molecules

The study of electron configurations in atoms provides valuable insight into the nature of *chemical bonds*, the interactions that hold atoms together to form stable structures such as molecules and solids. There are several types of chemical bonds. We consider first the **ionic bond,** also called the *electrovalent* or *heteropolar* bond. The most familiar example is sodium chloride (NaCl), in which the sodium atom gives its one $3s$ electron to the chlorine atom, filling the vacancy in the $3p$ subshell of chlorine.

Let's look at the energy balance in this transaction. Removing the $3s$ electron from the sodium atom requires 5.1 eV of energy; this is called the **ionization energy** or *ionization potential* of sodium. Chlorine has an **electron affinity** of 3.8 eV. That is, the neutral chlorine atom can attract an extra electron; once this electron takes its place in the $3p$ level, 3.8 eV of energy is required to remove it. Thus creating the separated Na$^+$ and Cl$^-$ ions requires a net expenditure of only $5.1 - 3.8$ eV $= 1.3$ eV. When the two mutually attracting ions come together, they have negative potential energy with magnitude determined by the closeness to which they can approach each other. This in turn is determined by the electrical interactions and by the exclusion principle, which forbids extensive overlap of the electron clouds of the two atoms.

The minimum potential energy turns out to be -5.5 eV at a separation of 0.24 nm. At distances less than this the interaction becomes repulsive. The net energy given up by the system in creating the ions and letting them come together to the equilibrium separation of 0.24 nm is $(-5.5 + 1.3)$ or -4.2 eV, and this is the binding energy of the molecule. That is, 4.2 eV of energy is needed to dissociate the molecule into separate atoms.

Ionic bonds can involve more than one electron per atom. The alkaline-earth elements form ionic compounds in which an atom loses *two* electrons; an example is Mg^{++}Cl$_2{}^-$. Loss of more than two electrons is relatively rare; instead, a different kind of bond comes into operation.

The **covalent** or *homopolar* bond is characterized by a more nearly symmetric participation of the two atoms, as contrasted with the complete asymmetry involved in the electron-transfer process of the ionic bond. An example of a covalent bond is the hydrogen molecule, a structure containing two protons and two electrons. As a prelude to understanding this bond, consider first the interaction of two electric dipoles, as in Fig. 43–3. In Fig. 43–3a the dipoles are far apart; in Fig. 43–3b the like charges are farther apart than the unlike charges, and there is a net *attractive* force. In Figs. 43–3c and 43–3d the interaction is repulsive.

The charges in a molecule are not at rest, but Fig. 43–3b at least makes it seem plausible that if the electrons are localized primarily in the region *between* the protons, the electrons exert an attractive force on each proton that may more than counteract the repulsive interactions of the protons on each other and the electrons on each other. In the covalent

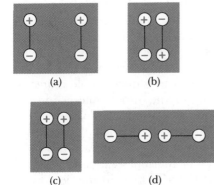

43–3
When two dipoles (a) are brought together, the interaction may be (b) attractive or (c and d) repulsive.

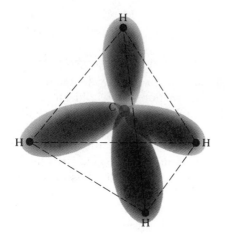

43–4
Methane (CH₄) molecule, showing four covalent bonds. The electron cloud between the central carbon atom and each of the four hydrogen nuclei represents the two electrons of a covalent bond. The hydrogen nuclei are at the corners of a regular tetrahedron.

bond the attractive interaction is supplied by a *pair* of electrons, one contributed by each atom, with charge clouds that are concentrated primarily in the region between the two atoms. This bond is also called a shared-electron or electron-pair bond.

According to the exclusion principle, two electrons can occupy the same region of space only when they have opposite spins. When the spins are parallel, the state that would be most favorable from energy considerations is forbidden by the exclusion principle, and the lowest-energy state permitted is one in which the electron clouds are concentrated *outside* the central region between atoms. The nuclei then repel each other, and the interaction is repulsive rather than attractive. Opposite spins are an essential requirement for an electron-pair bond, and no more than two electrons can participate in such a bond.

However, an atom with several electrons in its outermost shell can form several electron-pair bonds. The bonding of carbon and hydrogen atoms, of central importance in organic chemistry, is an example. In the *methane* molecule (CH_4) the carbon atom is at the center of a regular tetrahedron, with a hydrogen atom at each corner. The carbon atom has four electrons in its L shell, and one of these electrons forms a covalent bond with each of the four hydrogen atoms, as shown in Fig. 43–4. Similar patterns occur in more complex organic molecules.

Ionic and covalent bonds represent two extremes in the nature of molecular bonds, but there is no sharp division between the two types. In many situations there is a *partial* transfer of one or more electrons (corresponding to a greater or smaller distortion of the electron wave functions) from one atom to another. As a result, many molecules having dissimilar atoms have electric dipole moments, that is, a preponderance of positive charge at one end and of negative charge at the other. Such molecules are called *polar* molecules. Water molecules have large dipole moments; these are responsible for the exceptionally large dielectric constant of liquid water.

The bonds discussed so far typically have energies in the range of 1 to 5 eV. They are called *strong bonds* to distinguish them from several types of much *weaker* bonds having energies typically of the order of 0.1 eV or less. One of these, the **van der Waals bond,** is an interaction between the electric dipole moments of two atoms or molecules. Even when an atom or molecule has no permanent dipole moment, fluctuating charge densities in the interior of the structure can lead to fluctuating dipole moments; these in turn can induce dipole moments in neighboring structures. The resulting dipole–dipole interaction can be attractive and can lead to weak bonding of atoms or molecules. The low-temperature liquefaction and solidification of such molecules as H_2, O_2, and N_2 and of the noble gases is due to interaction of the induced-dipole type. Not much energy of thermal agitation is needed to break these weak bonds, so these substances exist in the liquid and solid states only at very low temperatures.

A second type of important weak bond is the **hydrogen bond,** which is analogous to the covalent bond. In the latter an electron pair serves to bind two positively charged structures together. In the hydrogen bond a hydrogen atom acts as the glue to bond two negatively charged structures. Again the bond energy is only about 0.1 eV, but nevertheless the hydrogen bond plays an essential role in many organic molecules, including, for example, cross-link bonding between the two strands of the famous double-helix DNA molecule.

All these bond types play roles in the structure of *solids* as well as of molecules. Indeed, a solid is in many respects a giant molecule. Still another type of bonding, the *metallic bond*, comes into play in the structure of metallic solids. We will return to this subject in Section 43–5.

43–4
Molecular Spectra

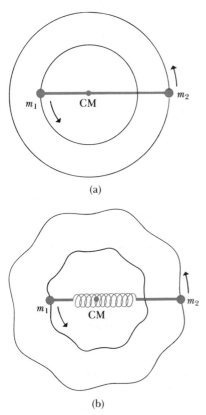

(a)

(b)

43–5
(a) Model of a diatomic molecule as a rigid dumbbell that rotates about an axis through its center of mass (CM). (b) Model of a diatomic molecule as a nonrigid dumbbell that can also vibrate along the line joining the atoms. The motion of each atom is a combination of vibration and rotation. Each atom is shown as a point mass, corresponding to the concentration of most of the mass of each atom in its nucleus.

The energy levels of atoms are associated with the kinetic energy of electron motion and with the potential energy of interaction of the electrons with the nucleus and with each other. Energy levels of *molecules* have additional features that result from motion of the *nuclei* of the atoms relative to each other. Associated with transitions among these energy levels are **molecular spectra.**

We consider *diatomic* molecules first. In the model shown in Fig. 43–5a we picture a diatomic molecule as a rigid dumbbell that can *rotate* about an axis through its center of mass. According to classical mechanics, when a rigid body with moment of inertia I rotates with angular velocity ω, its kinetic energy is $K = \frac{1}{2}I\omega^2$. This is Eq. (9–16); you may want to review its derivation in Section 9–4. We can also express the kinetic energy in terms of the magnitude L of angular momentum, which is given by Eq. (9–36): $L = I\omega$. Combining these two equations, we find $K = L^2/2I$. If the molecule is rigid, there is no potential energy, and the kinetic energy K is equal to the total energy E:

$$E = \frac{L^2}{2I}. \qquad (43–1)$$

In a quantum-mechanical discussion of molecular rotation a reasonable guess is that the angular momentum is quantized in the same way as for electrons in an atom, as given by Eq. (42–13):

$$L^2 = l(l + 1)\hbar^2 \qquad (l = 0, 1, 2, \ldots). \qquad (43–2)$$

Combining Eqs. (43–1) and (43–2), we obtain the **rotational energy levels:**

$$E = l(l + 1)\frac{\hbar^2}{2I} \qquad (l = 0, 1, 2, \ldots). \qquad (43–3)$$

A more detailed analysis, using the Schrödinger equation, confirms our guess that the angular momentum is given by Eq. (43–2) and that the energy levels are given by Eq. (43–3).

Let's look at some magnitudes: The moment of inertia of an oxygen (O_2) molecule is about $I = 5 \times 10^{-46}$ kg·m². We'll leave the derivation of this number as a problem. For this molecule the constant $\hbar^2/2I$ in

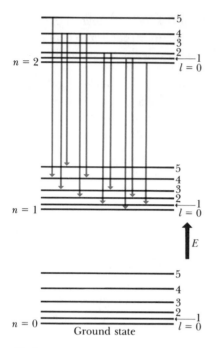

43–6

Energy-level diagram for vibrational and rotational energy levels of a diatomic molecule. For each vibrational level (n) there is a series of more closely spaced rotational levels (l). Several transitions corresponding to a single band in a band spectrum are shown.

Eq. (43–3) is approximately equal to

$$\frac{\hbar^2}{2I} = \frac{(1.05 \times 10^{-34}\ \text{J·s})^2}{2(5 \times 10^{-46}\ \text{kg·m}^2)}$$

$$= 1.1 \times 10^{-23}\ \text{J}$$

$$= 0.7 \times 10^{-4}\ \text{eV}.$$

This amount of energy is much *smaller* than atomic energy levels (a few eV) typically associated with optical spectra. Photon energies for transitions among rotational levels are correspondingly small, and they fall in the *far infrared* region of the spectrum.

In a more realistic model of a diatomic molecule we represent the connection between atoms not as a rigid rod but as a *spring*, as in Fig. 43–5b. Then in addition to rotating, the molecule can also *vibrate* along the line joining the atoms. There is additional kinetic and potential energy associated with this motion. Analysis using the Schrödinger equation (which we won't go into) shows that the corresponding **vibrational energy levels** are given by

$$E = (n + \tfrac{1}{2})hf, \qquad (n = 0, 1, 2, \ldots). \qquad (43\text{–}4)$$

where f is the frequency of vibration. For typical diatomic molecules this turns out to be of the order of 10^{13} Hz; the constant hf in Eq. (43–4) is then of the order of

$$hf = (6.6 \times 10^{-34}\ \text{J·s})(10^{13}\ \text{s}^{-1})$$

$$= 6.6 \times 10^{-21}\ \text{J} = 0.041\ \text{eV}.$$

Thus the vibrational energies, while much smaller than those of atomic spectra, are usually much *larger* than the rotational energies.

An energy-level diagram for a diatomic molecule has the general appearance of Fig. 43–6. For each value of n there are many values of l, forming a series of closely spaced levels. Transitions between different pairs of n values give different series of spectrum lines, and the resulting spectrum has a series of *bands*. Each band corresponds to a particular vibrational transition, and each individual line in a band represents a particular rotational transition. A typical **band spectrum** is shown in Fig. 43–7.

We can apply these same principles to more complex molecules. A molecule with three or more atoms has several different kinds or *modes* of vibratory motion. Each mode has its own set of energy levels, related to its frequency by Eq. (43–4). In nearly all cases the associated radiation lies in the infrared region of the electromagnetic spectrum. Analysis of molecular spectra has proved to be an extremely valuable analytical tool, providing information about the strength and rigidity of molecular bonds and the structure of complex molecules.

43–7

Typical band spectrum. (Courtesy of R. C. Herman.)

43–5
Structure of Solids

At ordinary temperatures and pressures, most materials are in the *solid state*. This is a condensed state of matter in which the interactions among the atoms or molecules are strong enough to give the material definite volume and shape that change relatively little with stress. The distances between adjacent atoms in a solid are of the same order of magnitude as the diameters of the electron clouds of the atoms, typically around 10^{-10} m.

A solid may be **amorphous** or **crystalline.** A crystalline solid is characterized by *long-range order*, a recurring pattern of atomic positions that extends over many atoms. This pattern is called the *crystal structure* or the *lattice structure.* Liquids have *short-range order* (correlations between neighboring atoms or molecules) but not long-range order. There are also amorphous (noncrystalline) solids. In general, these have more in common with liquids than with crystalline solids.

In some cases the forces responsible for the regular arrangement of atoms in a crystal are the same as those involved in molecular bonds. Ionic and covalent molecular bonds are found in ionic and covalent crystals, respectively. The most familiar **ionic crystals** are the alkali halides, such as ordinary salt (NaCl). The positive sodium ions and the negative chlorine ions occupy alternate positions in a cubic crystal lattice, as in Fig. 43–8. The forces are the familiar Coulomb's-law forces between charged particles. These forces have no preferred direction, and the arrangement in which the material crystallizes is determined by the relative size of the two ions.

An example of a **covalent crystal** is the *diamond structure*, a structure found in the diamond form of carbon and also in silicon, germanium, and tin. All these elements are in Group IV of the periodic table, with four electrons in the outermost shell. In the diamond structure, each atom is situated at the center of a regular tetrahedron, with four nearest-neighbor atoms at the corners, and it forms a covalent bond with each of these four atoms. These bonds are strongly directional because of the asymmetrical electron distributions, and the result is a tetrahedral structure.

A third crystal type, less directly related to the chemical bond than are ionic or covalent crystals, is the **metallic crystal.** In this structure the outermost electrons are not localized at individual atomic lattice sites, but are detached from their parent atoms and free to move through the crystal. The corresponding charge clouds (and their associated wave functions) extend over many atoms. Thus we can picture a metallic crystal roughly as an array of positive ions (atoms from which one or more electrons have been removed) immersed in a sea of electrons whose attraction for the positive ions holds the crystal together. This "sea" has many of the properties of a gas, and indeed we speak of the *electron-gas model* of metallic solids.

In a metallic crystal the situation is as though the atoms would like to form shared-electron bonds but do not have enough valence electrons.

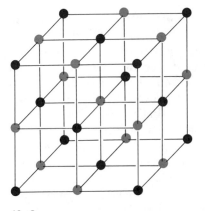

43–8
Symbolic representation of a sodium chloride crystal with exaggerated distances between ions.

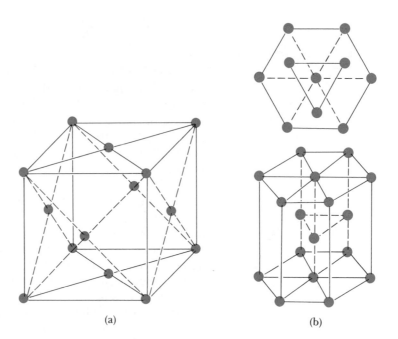

43–9
Close-packed crystal lattice structures.
(a) Face-centered cubic; (b) hexagonal
close-packed.

(a)   (b)

Instead, electrons are shared among *many* atoms. This bonding is not
strongly directional. The shape of the crystal lattice is determined primarily by considerations of **close packing,** that is, the maximum number
of atoms that can fit into a given volume. The two most common metallic
crystal lattices, the face-centered cubic and the hexagonal close-packed,
are shown in Fig. 43–9. In each of these lattices, each atom has 12 nearest neighbors.

As we mentioned in Section 43–3, van der Waals interactions and
hydrogen bonding also play a role in the structure of some solids. In
polyethylene and similar polymers, covalent bonding of atoms forms
long-chain molecules, and hydrogen bonding forms cross-links between
adjacent chains. In solid water, both van der Waals forces and hydrogen
bonds are significant, and together they determine the crystal structure
of ice. Many other examples might be cited.

The discussion in this section has centered around *perfect crystals,*
crystals in which the crystal lattice extends uninterrupted throughout the
entire material. Real crystals show a variety of departures from this idealized structure. Materials are often *polycrystalline*, composed of many small
perfect single crystals bonded together at *grain boundaries*. Within a single crystal, *interstitial* atoms may occur in places where they do not belong, and there may be *vacancies*, lattice sites that should be occupied by
an atom but are not. An imperfection of particular interest in semiconductors, which we will discuss in Section 43–8, is the *impurity atom*, a
foreign atom (e.g., arsenic in a silicon crystal) occupying a regular lattice
site.

A more complex kind of imperfection is the *dislocation*, shown schematically in Fig. 43–10, in which one plane of atoms slips in relation to
another. The mechanical properties of metallic crystals are influenced
strongly by the presence of dislocations. The ductility and malleability of
some metals depend on the presence of dislocations that move through
the lattice during plastic deformations.

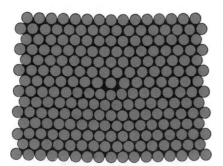

43–10
A dislocation. The concept is seen most
easily by viewing the figure from
various directions at a grazing angle
with the page.

43–6
Properties of Solids

We can understand many *macroscopic* properties of solids, including mechanical, thermal, electrical, magnetic, and optical properties, by considering their relation to the *microscopic* structure of the material. Following are a few examples that indicate the kinds of insights we can gain through study of the microscopic structure of solids.

We discussed heat capacities of crystals in Section 20–6, using the principle of equipartition of energy from the kinetic theory of gases. With this approach we were able to understand the empirical rule of Dulong and Petit on the basis of a microscopic model. This analysis has its limitations, to be sure. It does not include the energy of electron motion, which in metals makes a small additional contribution to specific heat. And it does not predict the temperature dependence of specific heats resulting from the *quantization* of the lattice-vibration energy we discussed in Section 20–6. But these additional refinements *can* be included in the model to improve the agreement of observed macroscopic properties with theoretical predictions.

The electrical resistivity of a material depends on the mobility or lack of mobility of electrons in the material. In a *metallic* crystal the valence electrons are not bound to individual lattice sites, but are free to move through the crystal. Metals are usually good conductors. In a *covalent* crystal the valence electrons are tied up in the bonds responsible for the crystal structure and are therefore *not* free to move. There are no mobile charges available for conduction, and such materials are usually insulators. Similarly, an ionic crystal such as NaCl has no charges that are free to move, and solid NaCl is an insulator. However, when salt is melted, the ions are no longer locked to their individual lattice sites but are free to move, and *molten* NaCl is a good conductor. There are, of course, no perfect conductors (except for superconductors at low temperatures) or perfect insulators, but the resistivities of good insulators are greater than those of good conductors by an enormous factor, of the order of at least 10^{15}.

In addition, the resistivities of all materials depend on temperature; in general, the large resistivity of an insulator *decreases* with temperature, but that of a good conductor usually *increases* at increased temperatures. Two competing effects are responsible for this difference. In metals the *number* of electrons available for conduction is nearly independent of temperature, and the resistivity is determined by the frequency of collisions between electrons and the lattice. As the temperature increases, the average speed of the electrons increases, and they collide more frequently with ion cores in the lattice. This effect causes the resistivities of most metals to *increase* with temperature.

In insulators the small amount of conduction that does take place is due to electrons that have gained enough energy from thermal motion of the lattice to break away from their "home" atoms and wander through the lattice. The number of electrons able to gain this much energy is very strongly temperature-dependent; a twofold increase in number of mobile electrons for a 10 C° temperature rise is typical.

Partially offsetting this is the increased frequency of collisions at higher temperatures, as with metals, but the increased *number* of carriers is a far larger effect. Resistivities of insulators invariably *decrease* rapidly (i.e., they become better conductors) as the temperature increases.

A similar analysis can be made for *thermal* conductivity, which involves transport of microscopic mechanical energy rather than electric charge. Wave motion associated with lattice vibrations is one mechanism for energy transfer, and in metals the mobile electrons also carry kinetic energy from one region to another. This effect turns out to be much larger than that of the lattice vibrations. As a result, metals are usually much better thermal conductors than are nonmetals, which have very few free electrons.

Optical properties are also related directly to microscopic structure. Good electrical conductors *cannot* be transparent to electromagnetic waves because the electric fields of the waves induce currents in the material. These induced currents dissipate the wave energy into heat as the electrons collide with the atoms in the lattice. All transparent solid materials are very good insulators. Metals are good *reflectors* of radiation because of the presence of free electrons at the surface of the material, which can move in response to the incident wave and generate a reflected wave. Reflection from the polished surface of an insulator depends on dielectric polarization of the material caused by the incident wave.

43–7
Band Theory of Solids

The concept of **energy bands** in solids offers us additional insight into some of the properties of solids we discussed in Section 43–6. To introduce the idea, suppose we have a large number N of identical atoms, far enough apart that their interactions are negligible. Every atom has the same energy-level diagram. We can draw an energy-level diagram for the *entire system*. It looks just like the diagram for a single atom, but the exclusion principle, applied to the entire system, permits each state to be occupied by N electrons instead of just one.

Now we begin to push the atoms closer together. Because of the electrical interactions and the exclusion principle, the wave functions begin to distort, especially those of the outer, or *valence*, electrons. The energy levels also shift somewhat; some move upward and some downward, depending on the environment of each individual atom. Thus each valence electron state for the *system*, formerly a sharp energy level that can accommodate N electrons, splits into a *band* containing N closely spaced levels, as shown in Fig. 43–11. Ordinarily, N is very large, of the order of Avogadro's number (10^{23}), so we can think of the levels as forming a *continuous* distribution of energies within a band. Between adjacent energy bands are gaps or forbidden regions where there are *no* allowed energy levels. The inner electrons in an atom are affected much less by nearby atoms than the valence electrons, and their energy levels remain relatively sharp.

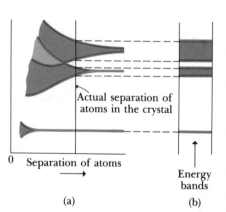

43–11

Origin of energy bands in a solid. (a) As the atoms are pushed together, the energy levels spread into bands. The vertical line shows the actual atomic spacing in the crystal lattice. (b) Symbolic representation of energy bands.

43–12
Three types of energy-band structure.
(a) An insulator; a completely full band
is separated by a gap of several
electronvolts from a completely empty
band, and electrons in the full band
cannot move. At finite temperatures a
few electrons can reach the upper
"conduction band." (b) A conductor;
there is a partially filled band, and
electrons in this band are free to move
when an electric field is applied. (c) A
semiconductor; a completely filled
band is separated by a small gap of
1 eV or less from an empty band; at
finite temperatures, substantial
numbers of electrons can reach the
upper "conduction band," where they
are free to move.

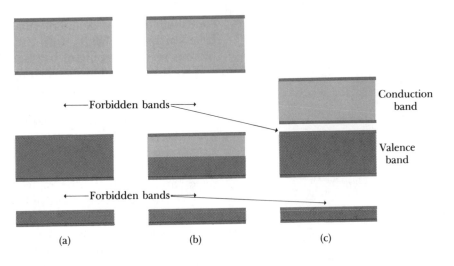

What does this have to do with electrical conductivity? In insulators
and semiconductors the valence electrons completely fill the highest occupied band, called the **valence band.** The next higher band, called the
conduction band, is completely empty. The energy gap separating the
two may be of the order of 1 to 5 eV. This situation is shown in Fig.
43–12a. The electrons in the valence band are not free to move in response to an applied electric field; to move, an electron would have to go
to a different quantum-mechanical state with slightly different energy,
but all the neighboring states are already occupied. The only way an
electron can move is to jump into the conduction band. This would require an additional energy of a few electronvolts, and that much energy
is ordinarily not available. The situation is like a completely filled parking lot; none of the cars can move because there is no place to go. If a
car could jump over the others, it could move!

However, at any temperature above absolute zero the crystal lattice
has some vibrational motion, and there is some probability that an electron can gain enough energy from thermal motion to jump to the conduction band. Once in the conduction band, an electron is free to move
in response to an applied electric field because there are plenty of nearby
empty states available. There are always a few electrons in the conduction band, so no material is a perfect insulator. Furthermore, as the temperature increases, the population in the conduction band increases very
rapidly. A doubling of the number of conduction electrons for a temperature rise of 10 C° is typical.

With metals the situation is different because the valence band is
only partly filled. The metal sodium is an example. The energy-level
diagram for sodium in Fig. 41–6 shows that for an isolated atom the $3p$
"resonance-level" states for the valence electron are about 2.1 eV above
the $3s$ ground state. But in the crystal lattice of solid sodium the $3s$ and $3p$
bands spread out enough that they actually overlap, forming a single
band that is only one quarter filled. The situation is similar to the one
shown in Fig. 43–12b. Electrons in states near the top of the filled portion of the band have many adjacent unoccupied states available, and
they can easily gain or lose small amounts of energy in response to an
applied electric field. Therefore these electrons are mobile and can

contribute to electrical and thermal conductivity. Metallic crystals always have partly filled bands. In the *ionic* NaCl crystal, on the other hand, there is no overlapping of bands; the valence band is completely filled, and solid sodium chloride is an insulator.

The band picture also adds insight to the phenomenon of *dielectric breakdown*, in which insulators subjected to a large enough electric field become conductors. If the electric field in a material is so large that there is a potential difference of a few volts over a distance comparable to atomic sizes (i.e., a field of the order of 10^{10} V·m^{-1}), then the field can do enough work on a valence electron to boost it over the forbidden region and into the conduction band. Real insulators usually have dielectric strengths much *less* than this because of structural imperfections that provide some energy states in the forbidden region.

The concept of energy bands is very useful in understanding the properties of semiconductors, which we will study in the next section.

*43–8
Semiconductors

As the name implies, a **semiconductor** has an electrical resistivity that is intermediate between those of good conductors and those of good insulators. There are also many other important aspects of the behavior of this class of materials, so vital to present-day electronics. We will discuss the basic concepts using the semiconductor elements silicon and germanium as examples.

Both silicon and germanium have four electrons in the outermost electron subshell, and both crystallize in the diamond structure we described in Section 43–5. Each atom lies at the center of a regular tetrahedron, with four nearest neighbors at the corners and a covalent bond with each. All the valence electrons are involved in the bonding, and the materials should be insulators. However, an unusually small amount of energy is needed to break one of the bonds and set an electron free to roam around the lattice: 1.1 eV for silicon and only 0.7 eV for germanium. This energy corresponds to the energy gap between the valence and conduction bands in Fig. 43–12c. Thus even at room temperature a substantial number of electrons are dissociated from their parent atoms, and this number increases rapidly with temperature.

Furthermore, when an electron is removed from a covalent bond, it leaves a vacancy where there would ordinarily be an electron. An electron from a neighboring atom can drop into this vacancy, leaving the neighbor with the vacancy. In this way the vacancy, usually called a **hole,** can travel through the lattice and serve as an additional current carrier. A hole behaves like a positively charged particle. In a pure semiconductor, holes and electrons are always present in equal numbers; the resulting conductivity is called *intrinsic conductivity* to distinguish it from conductivity due to impurities, which we will discuss later.

The parking-lot analogy we mentioned in Section 43–7 helps to clarify the mechanisms of conduction in a semiconductor. A crystal with no bonds broken is like a completely filled floor of a parking garage. No cars (electrons) can move because there is nowhere for them to go. But if one car is removed to the empty floor above, it can move freely, and the empty space it leaves also permits other cars to move on the nearly filled floor. In fact, we can describe the motion in terms of *motion of the vacant space*. This corresponds to a vacancy or hole in the normally filled valence band.

Now suppose we mix into melted germanium a small amount of arsenic, an element in Group V of the periodic table (Appendix D), with *five* valence electrons. When one of these electrons is removed, the remaining electron structure is essentially that of germanium; the only difference is that it is scaled down in size by the insignificant factor 32/33 because the arsenic nucleus has a charge of $+33e$ rather than $+32e$. An arsenic atom can comfortably take the place of a germanium atom in the lattice. Four of its five valence electrons form the necessary covalent bonds with the nearest neighbors. The fifth valence electron is very loosely bound, with a binding energy of only about 0.01 eV. This corresponds in the band picture to an isolated energy level lying in the gap, 0.01 eV below the bottom of the conduction band. Even at ordinary temperatures this electron can very easily gain enough energy to climb into the conduction band, where it is free to wander through the lattice. The corresponding positive charge is associated with the nuclear charge ($+33e$ instead of $+32e$). It is *not* free to move, in contrast to the situation with electrons and holes in pure germanium.

At ordinary temperatures, only a very small fraction of the valence electrons in germanium are able to escape their sites and participate in conduction. A concentration of arsenic atoms as small as one part in 10^{10} can increase the conductivity so drastically that conduction due to impurities becomes by far the dominant mechanism. In this case the conductivity is due almost entirely to *negative* charge (electron) motion. We call the material an **n-type semiconductor,** with *n*-type impurities.

Adding atoms of an element in Group III, with only *three* valence electrons, has an analogous effect. An example is gallium; placed in the germanium lattice, the gallium atom would like to form four covalent bonds, but it has only three outer electrons. It can, however, steal an electron from a neighboring germanium atom to complete the bonding. This leaves the neighboring atom with a *hole*, or missing electron, and this hole can then move through the lattice just as in intrinsic conductivity. This situation is characteristic of **p-type semiconductors,** materials with *p*-type impurities. In this case the corresponding negative charge is associated with the deficiency of positive charge of the gallium nucleus ($+31e$ instead of $+32e$), so it is *not* free to move. The two types of impurities, *n* and *p*, are also called *donors* and *acceptors*, respectively, and the deliberate addition of these impurity elements is called *doping*.

We can verify the assertion that the current in *n* and *p* semiconductors really *is* carried by electrons and holes, respectively, by using the Hall effect (Section 30–10). The direction of the Hall emf is opposite in the two cases. Measurements of the Hall emf in various semiconductor materials confirm our analysis of the conduction mechanisms.

*43–9
Semiconductor Devices

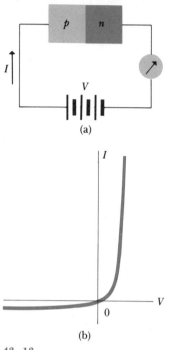

(a)

(b)

43–13
(a) A semiconductor $p-n$ junction in a circuit; (b) graph showing the asymmetric voltage–current relationship.

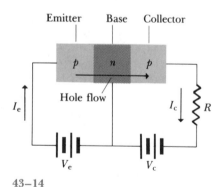

43–14
Schematic diagram of a $p-n-p$ transistor and circuit. When $V_e = 0$, the current in the collector circuit is very small. When a potential V_e is applied between emitter and base, holes travel from emitter to base, as shown; when V_c is sufficiently large, most of them continue into the collector. The collector current I_c is controlled by the emitter current I_e.

Semiconductor devices play an indispensable role in contemporary electronics. Radio and TV transmitting and receiving equipment originally relied on vacuum tubes, but these have been almost completely replaced in the last two decades by transistors, diodes, integrated circuits, and other semiconductor devices. The only surviving vacuum tubes in radio and TV equipment are the picture tube in a TV receiver, imaging devices in TV cameras, and some microwave equipment. Equally significant are large-scale integrated circuits that incorporate the equivalent of many thousands of transistors, capacitors, resistors, and diodes on a silicon chip less than 1 cm square. Such chips form the heart of every pocket calculator, personal computer, and mainframe computer.

The role of semiconductor materials in these devices is tied directly to the fact that the conductivity of the material is controlled by impurity concentrations, which can be varied within wide limits and changed from one region of a device to another. An example is the **$p-n$ junction,** a crystal of germanium or silicon with p-type impurities in one region and n-type impurities in another. The two regions meet in a boundary region called the *junction*. Originally, such junctions were produced by growing a crystal, usually by pulling a seed crystal very slowly away from the surface of a melted semiconductor. If the concentration of impurities in the melt is changed as the crystal is grown, the result is a crystal with two or more regions with different magnitudes of conductivity and conductivity types (n or p). There are now much better ways to fabricate $p-n$ junctions, but we do not need to go into the details.

When a $p-n$ junction is connected in an external circuit, as shown in Fig. 43–13a, and the potential V across the device is varied, the behavior of the current is as shown in Fig. 43–13b. The device conducts much more readily in the direction $p \rightarrow n$ than the reverse, in striking contrast to the symmetric behavior of materials that obey Ohm's law. Such a one-way device is called a **diode.**

We can understand the behavior of a $p-n$ junction diode qualitatively on the basis of the conductivity mechanisms in the two regions. When the p region is at higher potential than the n region, the resulting electric field is in the direction p to n. This is called the *forward* direction. Holes in the p region flow into the n region, and electrons in the n region move into the p region; this flow constitutes a *forward* current. When the polarity is reversed, the field tends to push electrons from p to n and holes from n to p. But there are very few mobile electrons in the p region, only those associated with intrinsic conductivity and some that diffuse over from the n region. Similarly, there are very few holes in the n region. As a result, the current in the *reverse* direction is much smaller than with the same potential in the forward direction.

A **transistor** includes two $p-n$ junctions in a "sandwich" configuration, which may be either $p-n-p$ or $n-p-n$. A $p-n-p$ transistor is shown in Fig. 43–14. The three regions are called the emitter, base, and collector, as shown. When there is no current in the left loop of the circuit, there is only a very small current through the resistor R because the

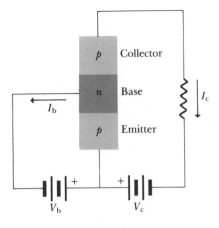

43–15

A common-emitter circuit. When $V_b = 0$, I_c is very small, and most of the voltage V_c appears across the base–collector junction. As V_b increases, the base–collector potential decreases, and more holes can diffuse into the collector; thus I_c increases. Ordinarily, I_c is much larger than I_b.

voltage across the base–collector junction is in the reverse direction. But when a voltage is applied between emitter and base, as shown, the holes traveling from emitter to base can travel *through* the base to the second junction, where they come under the influence of the collector-to-base potential difference and flow on through the resistor.

In this way the current in the collector circuit is *controlled* by the current in the emitter circuit. Furthermore, V_c may be considerably larger than V_e, so the *power* dissipated in R may be much larger than the power supplied to the emitter circuit by the battery V_e. Thus the device functions as a *power amplifier*. If the potential drop across R is greater than V_e, it may also be a voltage amplifier.

In this configuration the *base* is the common element between the "input" and "output" sides of the circuit. Another widely used arrangement is the *common-emitter* circuit, shown in Fig. 43–15. In this circuit the current in the collector side of the circuit is much larger than that in the base side, and the result is current amplification.

The first semiconductor devices were invented in 1948. Since then, they have completely revolutionized the electronics industry, including applications in communications, computer systems, control systems, and many other areas.

A further refinement in semiconductor technology is the **integrated circuit.** By successively depositing layers of material and etching patterns to define current paths we can combine the functions of several transistors, capacitors, and resistors on a single square of semiconductor material that may be only a few millimeters on a side. An elaboration of this idea leads to *large-scale integrated circuits* and *very-large-scale integration* (VLSI). Starting on a silicon chip base, various layers are built up, including evaporated metal layers for conducting paths and silicon-dioxide layers for insulators and for dielectric layers in capacitors. Appropriate patterns are etched into each layer by use of photosensitive etch-resistant materials onto which optically reduced patterns are projected. A circuit containing the functional equivalent of many thousands of transistors, diodes, resistors, and capacitors can be built up on a single chip. These so-called MOS (metal-oxide-semiconductor) chips are the heart of pocket calculators and nearly all present-day computers, large and small. An example is shown in Fig. 43–16.

Semiconductors have many other practical applications. A thin slab of pure silicon or germanium can serve as a *photocell*. When the material is irradiated with light whose photons have at least as much energy as the gap between the valence and conduction bands, an electron in the valence band can absorb a photon and jump to the conduction band, where it contributes to the conductivity. The conductivity therefore increases when the material is exposed to light, and the current in the circuit containing the device changes accordingly. Detectors for charged particles operate on the same principle. A high-energy charged particle passing through the semiconductor material interacts with the electrons, and as it loses energy, some of the electrons are excited from the valence to the conduction band, creating pairs of holes and conduction electrons. The conductivity increases momentarily, causing a pulse of current in the external circuit. Solid-state detectors are widely used in nuclear and high-energy physics research.

43–16

A large-scale integrated circuit. This dime-sized chip is a 32-bit microprocessor chip containing the equivalent of 150,000 transistors. (Courtesy of AT&T Archives.)

The inverse of the semiconductor photocell is the light-emitting diode (LED), which acts as a source of light. When a diode such as the one shown in Fig. 43–13a is given a large *forward* voltage, many holes are injected across the junction into the *n*-region and electrons into the *p*-region. When these minority carriers recombine with majority carriers in their respective regions, they lose energy. Under appropriate conditions this can be radiated as photons of visible light. Light-emitting diodes are widely used for digital displays in clocks, electronic equipment, automobile instrument panels, and many other applications.

*43–10
Superconductivity

At very low temperatures, some materials show a complete disappearance of all electrical resistance. Such materials are called **superconductors.** Superconductivity was discovered in 1911 by the Dutch physicist H. Kamerlingh Onnes (1853–1926) during experiments on the variation of electrical resistivity with temperature. Three years earlier, he had succeeded in liquefying helium for the first time, attaining lower temperatures than were available by any other means. Helium boils at 4.2 K at a pressure of 1 atm and at lower temperatures under reduced pressure. Using liquid-helium cooling, Kamerlingh Onnes found that when very pure solid mercury was cooled to 4.16 K, it underwent a phase transition in which its resistivity suddenly dropped to zero.

In more recent years, many other superconducting metals, alloys, and other materials have been found. Each one has a characteristic superconducting transition temperature T_c called its **critical temperature.** The highest critical temperature found so far for a *metallic* alloy is 23 K for a niobium–germanium alloy. Recently discovered *ceramic* materials have critical temperatures of over 90 K (about −180°C or −300°F).

Below the superconducting transition temperature the resistivity of a material is believed to be *exactly* zero. Experimental upper limits are of the order of 10^{-25} Ω·m, compared with typical values of 10^{-8} Ω·m for good conductors such as silver and copper at ordinary temperatures. When a current is magnetically induced in a superconducting ring, the current continues without measurable decrease for years!

A magnetic field can never exist inside a superconducting material. When we place a superconductor in a magnetic field, eddy currents are induced that exactly cancel the applied field everywhere inside the material (except for a surface layer a hundred or so atoms thick). Related to this behavior is the fact that an applied magnetic field lowers the critical temperature, as shown in Fig. 43–17. A sufficiently strong field eliminates the superconducting phase transition completely. Figure 43–17 is a *phase diagram* for the superconducting transition.

Although superconductivity was discovered in 1911, it was not well understood on a theoretical basis until 1957. In that year, Bardeen, Cooper, and Schrieffer published the theory, now called the BCS theory, that was to earn them the Nobel Prize in 1972. The key to the BCS theory is an interaction between *pairs* of conduction electrons, called

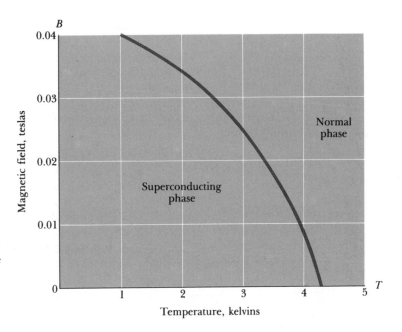

43–17

Phase diagram for pure mercury, showing the superconducting transition critical temperature and its dependence on magnetic field. Other superconducting materials have similar curves but with different scales.

Cooper pairs, caused by an interaction with the positive ion cores of the crystal lattice. Here is a rough qualitative picture of what happens. An electron exerts attractive forces on the positive ion cores, distorting the lattice slightly. The resulting slight concentration of positive charge then exerts an attractive force on another electron with momentum opposite to the first. At ordinary temperatures this electron-pair interaction is very small in comparison to energies of thermal motion, but at very low temperatures it becomes significant.

Thus bound together, the pairs of electrons cannot *individually* gain or lose very small amounts of energy, as they would ordinarily be able to do in a partly filled conduction band. There is an energy gap in the allowed quantum states of the electron pairs, and at low temperatures there is not enough energy for a pair to jump this gap. Therefore the electrons can move freely through the lattice without any energy exchange through collisions.

Another class of materials are the *type*-II *superconductors*. When such a material is placed in a magnetic field, the bulk of the material is superconducting, but there are thin filaments of material in the normal state, running parallel to the field. Currents circulate around the boundaries of these filaments, and there *is* magnetic flux inside the filaments. Type-II superconductors are used for electromagnets because much larger magnetic fields can usually be present without destroying the superconducting state than is possible with ordinary superconductors.

Still another type of material is the group of high-temperature superconductors, first discovered in 1987. These are not metals or alloys but *ceramic* materials that combine rare-earth metals, other metals, and nonmetals. An example is a compound of yttrium, barium, copper, and oxygen with a critical temperature of 93 K. This temperature is very significant because it is above the boiling temperature of liquid nitrogen, 77 K. Until 1987, superconductivity had been achieved only at liquid helium temperatures, requiring sophisticated and expensive equipment.

The critical temperatures of some of the new ceramics can be reached with liquid nitrogen, which is relatively cheap and easy to handle.

Many important and exciting applications of superconductors are under development. Superconducting electromagnets have been used in research laboratories for several years. Once a current is established in the coil of such a magnet, no additional power input is required because there is no resistive energy loss. The coils can also be made more compact because there is no need to provide channels for the circulation of cooling fluids. Thus superconducting magnets can attain very large fields much more easily and economically than conventional magnets; fields of the order of 10 T are fairly routine. These considerations also make superconductors attractive for long-distance electric-power transmissions, an active area of development.

One of the most glamorous applications of superconductors is in the field of magnetic levitation. Imagine a superconducting ring mounted on a railroad car that runs on a magnetized rail. The current induced in the ring leads to a repulsive interaction with the rail, and levitation is possible. Magnetically levitated trains have been running on an experimental basis in Japan for several years, and similar development projects are also under way in Germany.

There are reasons to think that in the future, materials may be developed that have critical temperatures at or above room temperature. The potential implications of such developments for long-distance power transmission, magnetic levitation, and many other applications are fairly breathtaking. The high-temperature superconductors discovered thus far are mechanically weak and brittle, like many ceramics, and are often chemically unstable. Fabricating conductors from them will pose very difficult technological problems.

Questions

43–1 In the ground state of the helium atom the electrons must have opposite spins. Why?

43–2 The central-field approximation is more accurate for alkali metals than for transition metals (Group IV of the periodic table). Why?

43–3 The outermost electron in the potassium atom is in a $4s$ state. What does this tell you about the relative positions of the $3d$ and $4s$ states for this atom?

43–4 A student asserted that any filled shell (i.e., all the levels for a given n occupied by electrons) must have zero total angular momentum and hence must be spherically symmetric. Do you believe this? What about a filled *subshell* (all values of m for given values of n and l)?

43–5 What factors determine whether a material is a conductor of electricity or an insulator?

43–6 The nucleus of a gold atom contains 79 protons. How would you expect the energy required to remove a $1s$ electron completely from a gold atom to compare with the energy required to remove the electron from a hydrogen atom? In what region of the electromagnetic spectrum would a photon of the appropriate energy lie?

43–7 Elements can be identified by their visible spectra. Could analogous techniques be used to identify compounds from their molecular spectra? In what region of the electromagnetic spectrum would the appropriate radiation lie?

43–8 The ionization energies of the alkali metals (i.e., the energy required to remove an outer electron) are in the range from 4 to 6 eV, while those of the inert gases are in the range from 15 to 25 eV. Why the difference?

43–9 The energy required to remove the 3s electron from a sodium atom in its ground state is about 5 eV. Would you expect the energy required to remove an additional electron to be about the same, more, or less? Why?

43–10 Electrical conductivities of most metals decrease gradually with increasing temperature, but the intrinsic conductivity of semiconductors always *increases* rapidly with increasing temperature. Why the difference?

43–11 What are some advantages of transistors compared to vacuum tubes for electronic devices such as amplifiers? What are some disadvantages? Are there any situations in which vacuum tubes *cannot* be replaced by solid-state devices?

Exercises

Section 43–1   The Exclusion Principle

Section 43–2   Atomic Structure

43–1 Make a list of the four quantum numbers n, l, m, and s for each of the ten electrons in the ground state of the neon atom.

43–2

a) List the different possible combinations of quantum numbers l and m for the $n = 5$ shell.

b) How many electrons can be placed in the $n = 5$ shell?

43–3 For bromine ($Z = 35$), make a list of the number of electrons in each state (1s, 2s, 2p, etc.).

43–4 The energies of an electron in the K, L, and M shells of the tungsten atom are $-69,500$ eV, $-12,000$ eV, and -2200 eV, respectively. Calculate the wavelengths of the K_α and K_β X-rays of tungsten.

43–5 Work the two examples described in Problem-Solving Strategy step 2 in Section 43–2. That is,

a) show that the magnitude of the electrical potential energy of a proton and an electron 0.100 nm apart is 14.4 eV, or 2.31×10^{-18} J;

b) show that the moment of inertia of two protons 0.100 nm apart about an axis through the center of mass and perpendicular to the line joining them is 0.836×10^{-47} kg·m².

Section 43–3   Diatomic Molecules

Section 43–4   Molecular Spectra

43–6

a) Calculate the electrical potential energy for a K^+ and a Br^- ion separated by a distance of 0.29 nm, the equilibrium separation in the KBr molecule.

b) The ionization energy of the potassium atom is 4.3 eV. Atomic bromine has an electron affinity of 3.5 eV. Use these data and the results of part (a) to *estimate* the binding energy of the KBr molecule.

Do you expect the actual binding energy to be larger or smaller than your estimate?

43–7 Show that the frequencies in a pure rotation spectrum (no change in vibrational level) are all integer multiples of the quantity $\hbar/2\pi I$. (Assume that the rotational quantum number l changes by ± 1 in the rotational transitions.)

43–8 If the distance between atoms in a diatomic oxygen molecule is 0.20 nm, calculate the moment of inertia about an axis through the center of mass perpendicular to the line joining the atoms. The mass of an oxygen atom is 2.66×10^{-26} kg.

43–9 The distance between atoms in a hydrogen molecule is 0.0740 nm.

a) Calculate the moment of inertia of a hydrogen molecule about an axis through the center of mass and perpendicular to the line joining the nuclei.

b) Find the energies (in electronvolts) of the $l = 0$, $l = 1$, and $l = 2$ rotational states.

c) Find the wavelength and frequency of the photon emitted in the transition from $l = 2$ to $l = 1$.

43–10 The vibrational frequency of the hydrogen molecule is 1.29×10^{14} Hz.

a) What is the spacing of adjacent vibrational energy levels in electronvolts?

b) What is the wavelength of radiation emitted in the transition from the $n = 1$ to $n = 0$ vibrational state of the hydrogen molecule?

c) From what initial values of n do transitions to the ground state of vibrational motion yield radiation in the visible spectrum (400 to 700 nm)?

Section 43–5   Structure of Solids

Section 43–6   Properties of Solids

43–11 The spacing of adjacent atoms in a sodium-chloride crystal is 0.282 nm. Calculate the density of sodium chloride. The mass of a sodium atom is

3.82×10^{-26} kg, and the mass of a chlorine atom is 5.89×10^{-26} kg.

43–12 Potassium bromide, KBr, has a density of 2.75×10^3 kg·m^{-3}, and the same crystal structure as NaCl. The mass of a potassium atom is 6.49×10^{-26} kg, and the mass of a bromine atom is 1.33×10^{-26} kg.

a) Calculate the average spacing between adjacent atoms in a KBr crystal.

b) How does the value calculated in part (a) compare with the spacing in NaCl (Exercise 43–11)? Is the relation between the two values qualitatively what you would expect?

Section 43–8   Semiconductors

Section 43–9   Semiconductor Devices

43–13

a) Suppose a piece of very pure germanium is to be used as a light detector by observing by absorption of photons the increase in conductivity resulting from generation of electron-hole pairs. If each pair requires 0.70 eV of energy, what is the maximum wavelength that can be detected? In what portion of the spectrum does it lie?

b) What are the answers to part (a) if the material is silicon, with an energy requirement of 1.10 eV per pair, corresponding to the gap between valence and conduction bands in silicon?

■ *Problems*

43–14 For magnesium the first ionization potential is 7.6 eV; the second (additional energy required to remove a second electron) is almost twice this, 15 eV, and the third ionization potential is much larger, about 80 eV. How can these numbers be understood?

43–15 The vibration frequency for the molecule HCl is 8.60×10^{13} Hz.

a) If this molecule can be regarded as a simple harmonic oscillator with the Cl atom stationary (because it is much more massive than the H atom), what is the effective "spring constant" k corresponding to the interatomic force?

b) What is the spacing between adjacent vibrational energy levels in joules? In electronvolts?

c) What is the wavelength of a photon emitted in a transition between two adjacent vibrational levels? In what region of the spectrum does it lie?

43–16 In Problem 43–15, suppose the hydrogen atom is replaced by an atom of deuterium, an isotope of hydrogen with a mass of 3.32×10^{-27} kg. The effective spring constant k is determined by the electron configuration, so it is the same as for the normal HCl molecule. Assume, as in Problem 43–15, that the Cl atom is stationary.

a) What is the vibrational frequency of this molecule?

b) What is the wavelength of light emitted in the transition $n = 2$ to $n = 1$? In what region of the spectrum does it lie?

43–17

a) For the sodium chloride molecule (NaCl) discussed at the beginning of Section 43–3, what is the maximum separation of the ions for stability if they may be regarded as point charges? That is, what is the largest separation for which the energy of Na$^+$ + Cl$^-$, calculated in this model, is lower than the energy of the two separate atoms Na and Cl?

b) Calculate this distance for the potassium bromide (KBr) molecule (Exercise 43–6).

43–18 The rotational spectrum of HCl contains the following wavelengths:

> 60.4 μm
> 69.0 μm
> 80.4 μm
> 96.4 μm
> 120.4 μm

Find the moment of inertia of the HCl molecule about an axis through the center of mass and perpendicular to the line joining the two nuclei.

43–19 The dissociation energy of the hydrogen molecule (i.e., the energy required to separate the two atoms) is 4.72 eV. In the gas phase (treated as an ideal gas), at what temperature is the average kinetic energy of a molecule equal to this energy?

Challenge Problems

43–20

a) If we consider the hydrogen molecule (H_2) to be a simple harmonic oscillator with an equilibrium spacing of $r_0 = 0.0740$ nm, estimate the vibrational energy-level spacing for H_2. (*Hint:* Estimate the force constant k by equating the change in Coulomb repulsion of the protons, when the atoms move slightly closer together than r_0, to the "spring" force. That is, assume that the chemical binding force remains approximately constant as r is decreased slightly from r_0.)

b) Use the results of part (a) to calculate the vibrational energy level spacing for the deuterium molecule, D_2. As in Problems 43–15 and 43–16, assume that the spring constant is the same for these two molecules.

(In each case the spring constant is related to the angular frequency ω by $\omega = \sqrt{k/\mu}$, where $\mu = m_A m_B / [m_A + m_B]$ is the *reduced mass* for the diatomic molecule whose atoms have masses m_A and m_B.)

43–21

a) Use the result of Problem 43–18 to calculate the equilibrium separation of the atoms in HCl. The mass of the chlorine atom is 5.81×10^{-26} kg.

b) Given that l changes by ± 1 in rotational transitions, what is the value of l for the upper level of the transition that gives rise to each of the wavelengths listed in Problem 43–18?

c) What will be the longest-wavelength line in the rotational spectrum of HCl?

d) Calculate the wavelengths of the emitted light for the corresponding transitions in the DCl molecule. Assume that the equilibrium separation between the atoms is the same as for HCl.

44

Nuclear and
High-Energy Physics

Every atom contains at its center an extremely dense, positively charged *nucleus*, much smaller than the overall size of the atom but containing most of its total mass. We begin this chapter by describing several important properties of nuclei. The stability or instability of a particular nucleus is determined by the competition between the attractive nuclear force among the protons and neutrons and the repulsive electrical interactions among the protons. Unstable nuclei *decay*, transforming themselves spontaneously into other structures, by a variety of decay processes. Structure-altering nuclear reactions can also be induced by impact on a nucleus of a particle or an-

other nucleus. Two classes of reactions of special interest are *fission* and *fusion*.

Protons and neutrons are not fundamental particles, but are composed of more basic entities called *quarks*, which play a fundamental role in the relationships among the four basic interactions: strong, electromagnetic, weak, and gravitational. Research into the nature and interactions of fundamental particles has required the construction of very large experimental facilities such as particle accelerators, as scientists probe more and more deeply into this most fundamental aspect of the nature of our physical universe.

44–1
Properties of Nuclei

The most obvious feature of the atomic nucleus is its size; the nucleus is 20,000 to 200,000 times smaller than the atom itself. Since Rutherford's initial experiments, which we described in Section 41–4, many additional scattering experiments have been performed, using high-energy protons, electrons, and neutrons as well as alpha particles (helium nuclei). The radius of a nucleus is found to depend on the mass, which in turn depends on the total number A of neutrons and protons in the nucleus, called the **mass number.** The radii of most nuclei are represented fairly well by the empirical equation

$$r = r_0 A^{1/3}, \qquad (44-1)$$

where r_0 is an empirical constant equal to 1.2×10^{-15} m and is the same for all nuclei.

The volume V of a sphere is equal to $4\pi r^3/3$, so Eq. (44–1) shows that the *volume* of a nucleus is proportional to A (i.e., to the total mass). Therefore *the mass per unit volume* (proportional to A/r^3) is the same for all nuclei. That is, *all nuclei have approximately the same density.* This fact is of crucial importance in understanding nuclear structure.

Two additional important properties of nuclei are *angular momentum* and *magnetic moment*, associated with the motions of the particles within the nucleus. Evidence for the existence of nuclear angular momentum (often called **nuclear spin**) and nuclear magnetic moment came originally from spectroscopy. Some spectrum lines are found to be split into series of very closely spaced lines, called *hyperfine structure*, which can be understood on the basis of interactions between electrons and the nuclear magnetic moment. Nuclear angular momentum is *quantized*, just as it is for electrons and for molecular rotation. The component of angular momentum in a specified axis direction is a multiple of $\hbar$. Some nuclei have *integral* multiples (as with orbital angular momentum of electrons) and some *half-integral* multiples of $\hbar$ (as with electron spin).

The basic building blocks of the nucleus are the **proton** and the **neutron.** The total number of protons, equal in a neutral atom to the number of electrons, is the **atomic number** Z. The number of neutrons, denoted by N, is called the **neutron number.** For any nucleus the mass number (or nucleon number) A is the sum of these:

$$A = Z + N. \qquad (44-2)$$

Table 44–1 lists values of A, Z, and N for several nuclei. The table shows some nuclei with the same Z but different N. The electron structure of an atom, which determines its chemical properties, depends on the charge Ze of the nucleus, so these are nuclei of the same element. They have different masses, however, and they can be distinguished in precise experiments. Nuclei of a given element with different mass numbers are called **isotopes** of the element, and a single nuclear species (unique values of both Z and N) is called a **nuclide.** We studied the experimental investigation of *isotopes* through mass spectroscopy in Section 30–6, and we suggest that you review this section.

Table 44–1 also shows the usual notation for individual nuclides; we write the symbol of the element, with a pre-subscript equal to the atomic number Z and a pre-superscript equal to the mass number A. For example, $^{13}_{6}C$ denotes the isotope of carbon with $Z = 6$, $A = 13$, and $N = 7$. This notation is redundant because the name of the element determines the atomic number, but it is a useful aid to memory. The pre-subscript (the value of Z) is often omitted.

The proton and neutron masses are

$$m_p = 1.6726 \times 10^{-27} \text{ kg}, \qquad m_n = 1.6750 \times 10^{-27} \text{ kg}.$$

These are nearly equal, so it is not surprising that many nuclear masses are approximately integer multiples of the proton or neutron mass. We could define a new mass unit equal to the proton or neutron mass. For reasons of precision of measurement it turns out to be more convenient to define a new mass unit equal to 1/12 the mass of the neutral carbon atom with mass number $A = 12$. This mass is called one **atomic mass unit** (1 u). It turns out that

$$1 \text{ u} = 1.660566 \times 10^{-27} \text{ kg}.$$

In atomic mass units the masses of the proton, neutron, and electron are

$$m_p = 1.007276 \text{ u}, \qquad m_n = 1.008665 \text{ u}, \qquad m_e = 0.000549 \text{ u}.$$

We can find the energy equivalent of 1 u from the relation $E = mc^2$:

$$E = (1.660566 \times 10^{-27} \text{ kg})(2.9979 \times 10^8 \text{ m·s}^{-1})^2$$
$$= 1.4924 \times 10^{-10} \text{ J} = 931.5 \text{ MeV}.$$

TABLE 44–1   Compositions of some common nuclei

Nucleus	Mass number (total number of nuclear particles), A	Atomic number (number of protons), Z	Neutron number, $N = A - Z$
$^{1}_{1}H$	1	1	0
$^{2}_{1}D$	2	1	1
$^{4}_{2}He$	4	2	2
$^{6}_{3}Li$	6	3	3
$^{7}_{3}Li$	7	3	4
$^{9}_{4}Be$	9	4	5
$^{10}_{5}B$	10	5	5
$^{11}_{5}B$	11	5	6
$^{12}_{6}C$	12	6	6
$^{13}_{6}C$	13	6	7
$^{14}_{7}N$	14	7	7
$^{16}_{8}O$	16	8	8
$^{23}_{11}Na$	23	11	12
$^{65}_{29}Cu$	65	29	36
$^{200}_{80}Hg$	200	80	120
$^{235}_{92}U$	235	92	143
$^{238}_{92}U$	238	92	146

TABLE 44–2   **Atomic masses of light elements**

Element	Atomic number, Z	Neutron number, N	Atomic mass, u	Mass number, A
Hydrogen H	1	0	1.00783	1
Deuterium H	1	1	2.01410	2
Helium He	2	1	3.01603	3
Helium He	2	2	4.00260	4
Lithium Li	3	3	6.01512	6
Lithium Li	3	4	7.01600	7
Beryllium Be	4	5	9.01218	9
Boron B	5	5	10.01294	10
Boron B	5	6	11.00931	11
Carbon C	6	6	12.00000	12
Carbon C	6	7	13.00336	13
Nitrogen N	7	7	14.00307	14
Nitrogen N	7	8	15.00011	15
Oxygen O	8	8	15.99491	16
Oxygen O	8	9	16.99913	17
Oxygen O	8	10	17.99916	18

Source: Encyclopedia of Physics, Lerner and Trigg, eds. (Reading, Mass.: Addison-Wesley, 1981.)

The masses of some common atoms, including their electrons, are shown in Table 44–2. The masses of the bare nuclei are obtained by subtracting Z times the electron mass.

The total mass of a nucleus is always *less* than the total mass of its constituent parts because of the mass equivalent ($E = mc^2$) of the (negative) potential energy associated with the attractive forces that hold the nucleus together. This mass difference is called the **mass defect.** We can determine the total potential energy, or **binding energy,** of a nucleus by comparing its mass with the total mass of its constituents.

Example 44–1   Find the mass defect, the total binding energy, and the binding energy per nucleon for the common isotope of carbon, ^{12}C.

Solution   The mass of the neutral carbon atom, including the nucleus and the six electrons, is, according to Table 44–2, 12.00000 u. We obtain the mass of the bare nucleus by subtracting the mass of the six electrons:

$$m = 12.00000 \text{ u} - (6)(0.000549 \text{ u}) = 11.996706 \text{ u}.$$

The total mass of the six protons and six neutrons in the nucleus is

$$(6)(1.007276 \text{ u}) + (6)(1.008665 \text{ u}) = 12.095646 \text{ u}.$$

The mass defect is therefore

$$12.095646 \text{ u} - 11.996706 \text{ u} = 0.09894 \text{ u}.$$

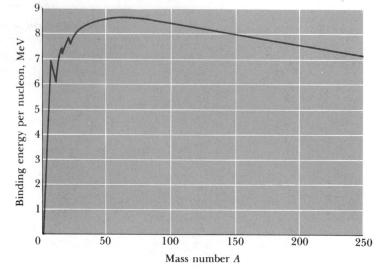

44–1
Binding energy per nucleon as a function of mass number A (the total number of nucleons). The curve reaches a peak of about 8.7 MeV at about $A = 60$, corresponding to the element iron. The spike at $A = 4$ shows the unusual stability of the alpha particle structure.

The energy equivalent of this mass is

$$(0.09894 \text{ u})(931.5 \text{ MeV·u}^{-1}) = 92.16 \text{ MeV}.$$

Thus the total binding energy for the 12 nucleons is 92.16 MeV. To pull the carbon nucleus completely apart into 12 separate nucleons would require a minimum of 92.16 MeV. The binding energy *per nucleon* is 1/12 of this, or 7.68 MeV per nucleon. Nearly all stable nuclei, from the lightest to the most massive, have binding energies in the range of 6 to 9 MeV per nucleon. Figure 44–1 is a graph of binding energy per nucleon as a function of the mass number A. ∎

The energy of internal motion of a nucleus is quantized. Each nucleus has a set of allowed energy levels, including a *ground state* (state of lowest energy) and several *excited states*. Because of the great strength of nuclear interactions, excitation energies of nuclei are typically of the order of 1 MeV, compared with a few electronvolts for atomic energy levels. In ordinary physical and chemical transformations the nucleus always remains in its ground state. When a nucleus is placed in an excited state, either by bombardment with high-energy particles or by a radioactive transformation, it can decay to the ground state by emission of one or more photons, called in this case **gamma rays** or *gamma-ray photons*.

The forces that hold protons and neutrons together in the nucleus, despite the electrical repulsion of the protons, are an example of the strong interactions we mentioned in Section 5–1. In the present context this kind of interaction is called the **nuclear force.** Here are some of its characteristics. First, it does not depend on charge; neutrons as well as protons must be bound, and the binding is the same for both. Second, it has short range, of the order of nuclear dimensions, 10^{-15} m. (Otherwise, the nucleus would pull in additional protons and neutrons.) But within its range the nuclear force is much stronger than electrical forces; otherwise, the nucleus could never be stable. Third, the nearly constant density of nuclear matter and the nearly constant binding energy per nucleon show that a particular nucleon cannot interact simultaneously with *all* the other nucleons in a nucleus, but only with those few in its immediate vicinity. This is different from electrical forces; *every* proton in the nucleus repels every other one. This limited number of interactions is called *saturation*; it is analogous in some respects to covalent bonding in solids. Finally, the nuclear force favors binding of *pairs* of protons or neutrons with opposite spins and of *pairs of pairs*, a pair of protons and a pair of neutrons, with each pair having a total spin of zero. For example, the alpha particle (two protons and two neutrons) is an exceptionally stable nucleus.

These qualitative features of the nuclear force are helpful in understanding the various kinds of nuclear instability, which are discussed in the following sections.

PROBLEM-SOLVING STRATEGY: *Nuclear Structure*

1. Once again, as in Chapters 42 and 43, some familiarity with numerical magnitudes is helpful. The scale of things in nuclear structures is very different from atomic structures. The size of a nucleus is of the order of 10^{-15} m; the potential energy of interaction of two protons at this distance is 2.31×10^{-13} J or 1.44 MeV. Typical nuclear energies are of the order of a few MeV, rather than a few eV as with atoms. Protons and neutrons are about 1840 times as massive as electrons. The binding energy per nucleon is roughly 1% of the rest energy of a nucleon; compare this with the ionization energy of the hydrogen atom, which is only 0.003% of the electron rest energy. Angular momentum is of the same order of magnitude in both atoms and nuclei because it is determined by the value of Planck's constant. But magnetic moments of nuclei are typically much *smaller* than those of electrons in atoms because the nuclear gyromagnetic ratio (the ratio of magnetic moment to angular momentum) is $e/2m_{\mathrm{p}}$ instead of $e/2m_{\mathrm{e}}$, smaller than for orbital electron motion by a factor of the order of 2000. Check out all these numbers, and try to think of other magnitudes to check.

2. In energy calculations involving the mass defect, binding energies, and so on, mass tables nearly always list the masses of *neutral* atoms, including their full complements of electrons. To get the mass of a bare nucleus, you have to subtract the masses of these electrons. The binding energies of the electrons are much smaller, and we won't worry about them. Binding energy calculations often involve subtracting two nearly equal quantities. To get enough precision in the difference, you often have to carry five or six significant figures, if that many are available. If not, you may have to be content with an approximate result.

44–2
Nuclear Stability

Of about 1500 different nuclides now known, only about one fifth are stable. The others are **radioactive;** this means that they are unstable structures that decay to form other nuclides by emitting particles and electromagnetic radiation. The time scale of these decay processes ranges from a small fraction of a microsecond to billions of years. The *stable* nuclides are shown by dots on the graph in Fig. 44–2, where the neutron number N and proton number (or atomic number) Z for each

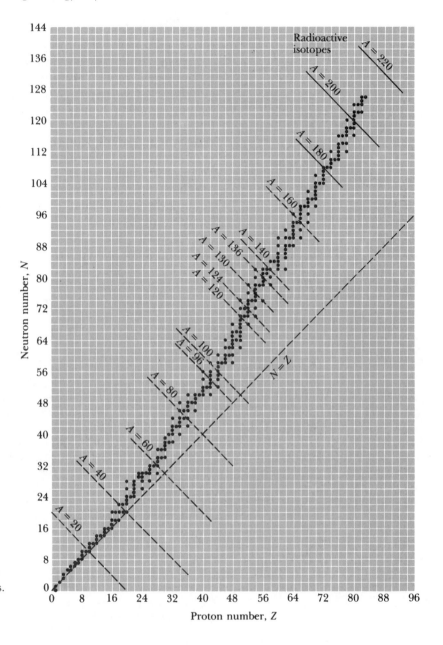

44–2
Segrè chart, showing neutron number and proton number for stable nuclides.

nuclide are plotted. Such a chart is called a *Segrè chart*, after its inventor, Emilio Segrè.

Each broken line perpendicular to the line $N = Z$ represents a specific value of the mass number $A = Z + N$. Most lines of constant A pass through only one or two stable nuclides; that is, there are usually only one or two stable nuclides with a given mass number. The lines at $A = 20$, $A = 40$, $A = 60$, and $A = 80$ are examples. In four cases these lines pass through *three* stable nuclides, namely, at $A = 96$, 124, 130, and 136. Only four stable nuclides have both odd Z and odd N:

$$\ _{1}^{2}\text{H}, \quad \ _{3}^{6}\text{Li}, \quad \ _{5}^{10}\text{B}, \quad \ _{7}^{14}\text{N};$$

these are called *odd-odd nuclides*. Also, there is *no* stable nuclide with $A = 5$ or $A = 8$.

The points representing stable nuclides define a rather narrow stability region. For low mass numbers the numbers of protons and neutrons are approximately equal; $N = Z$. The ratio N/Z increases gradually with A, up to about 1.6 at large mass numbers. Points to the right of the stability region represent nuclides that have too many protons, or not enough neutrons, to be stable. To the left are nuclei with too many neutrons or not enough protons. The graph also shows that no nuclide with A greater than 209 or Z greater than 83 is stable.

The most important reason that some nuclei are stable and others are not is the competition between the attractive nuclear force and the repulsive electrical force. As we mentioned in Section 44–1, the nuclear force favors *pairs* of nucleons and *pairs of pairs*. If there were no electrical interactions, the most stable nuclei would be those with equal numbers of neutrons and protons, $N = Z$. The electrical repulsion shifts the balance to favor greater numbers of neutrons, but a nucleus with *too many* neutrons is unstable because not enough of them are paired with protons. A nucleus with too many *protons* has too much repulsive electrical interaction, compared with the attractive nuclear interaction, to be stable.

As the number of nucleons increases, the total energy of electrical interaction increases faster than that of the nuclear interaction. To understand this, recall the discussion of electrostatic energy in Section 27–4. The energy of a capacitor with charge Q is proportional to Q^2. The energy required to bring a total charge Q together to form a spherical charge distribution is also proportional to Q^2. For this reason the (positive) electric potential energy in the nucleus increases approximately as Z^2, while the (negative) nuclear potential energy increases approximately as A, with corrections for pairing effects. At large A the positive electric energy *per nucleon* grows faster than the negative nuclear energy per nucleon until the point is reached at which stability is impossible. Thus the competition of electric and nuclear forces accounts for the fact that the neutron–proton ratio in stable nuclei increases with Z and also for the fact that a nucleus cannot be stable if A or Z is too large. In the next section and several later ones we will describe various ways in which unstable nuclei decay.

44–3
Radioactive Transformations

The study of natural radioactivity began in 1896, one year after Röntgen discovered X-rays. Henri Becquerel discovered a radiation from uranium salts that seemed similar to X-rays. Intensive investigation in the following two decades by Marie and Pierre Curie, Rutherford, and many others revealed that the emissions consist of positively and negatively charged and neutral particles, which were christened **alpha, beta,** and **gamma** particles. It was found that alpha particles are helium nuclei (two protons and two neutrons bound together), betas are high-energy electrons, and gammas are high-energy electromagnetic-wave photons. The

Curies discovered the elements radium and polonium. They showed that the emission of radiation from radium, per unit mass, is of the order of a million times more intense than that from uranium.

Some radioactive elements emit alphas; others emit betas. Gammas can accompany both. No change in physical or chemical environment, such as chemical reactions or heating or cooling, affects the rate of decay. After the existence of the nucleus was established by Rutherford, it was suspected that radioactivity was a nuclear process. Emission of a charged particle from a nucleus leaves a nucleus with a different charge, belonging to a different chemical element. Radioactivity transforms one element into another!

Identifying the alpha particle involved some very challenging scientific detective work. To measure its charge, Rutherford and Geiger counted the number of alpha particles emitted from a radium source in a known time interval and then collected other alpha particles from the same source on a conducting plate and measured its charge. They found that the charge of the alpha particle is $+2e$, where e is the magnitude of the electron charge. They measured the ratio of charge to mass by the Thomson electric and magnetic deflection method that we described in Section 30–5. This determined the *mass* of the alpha particle, which they found to be 6.62×10^{-27} kg, almost exactly four times the mass of a hydrogen atom.

It seemed certain that alpha particles are helium nuclei. To clinch the identification, Rutherford and Royds collected alpha particles in an evacuated glass tube for several days and then established an electric discharge in the tube. They were able to identify the spectrum of helium and thus establish beyond doubt that alpha particles *are* helium nuclei.

The speed of an alpha particle can be determined from the curvature of its path in a transverse magnetic field. The alpha particles emitted by radium, ^{226}Ra, have speeds of about 1.5×10^7 m·s^{-1}. The corresponding kinetic energy is

$$K = \tfrac{1}{2}(6.62 \times 10^{-27} \text{ kg})(1.5 \times 10^7 \text{ m·s}^{-1})^2$$
$$= 7.4 \times 10^{-13} \text{ J} = 4.6 \times 10^6 \text{ eV} = 4.6 \text{ MeV}.$$

This speed, although large, is only 5% of the speed of light, so we can use the nonrelativistic kinetic-energy expression. Alpha particles can travel several centimeters in air or a few tenths or hundredths of a millimeter through solids before they are brought to rest by collisions.

Beta particles were identified by experiments similar to the Thomson experiments that we described in Section 30–5. They are electrons, emitted with tremendous speeds, up to 0.9995 that of light. Energy and momentum conservation considerations suggest strongly that in beta emission an additional neutral particle is emitted along with the beta. This particle, called a **neutrino** (symbol ν), has zero rest mass and zero charge and therefore produces very little observable effect when it passes through matter. It evaded detection until 1953, when Reines and Cowan succeeded in observing it directly. We now know that there are at least three varieties of neutrinos, the one associated with beta decay and two others associated with the decay of unstable particles, the μ mesons and the τ particles.

Gamma rays are not deflected by a magnetic field, so they cannot be charged particles. However, they are diffracted at the surface of a crystal in a manner similar to X-rays. Diffraction experiments and other evidence led to the conclusion that gamma rays are high-energy photons with the same basic nature as X-rays.

A gamma-ray photon is emitted during a transition between two nuclear energy levels. For example, alpha particles emitted from radium have a kinetic energy of either 4.879 MeV or 4.695 MeV. When an alpha particle with the smaller energy is emitted, the resulting nucleus (which corresponds to the element *radon*) is left in an excited state. It can then decay to its ground state by emitting a gamma-ray photon with energy

$$(4.879 - 4.695) \text{ MeV} = 0.184 \text{ MeV}.$$

A photon with this energy is observed during this decay.

When a radioactive nucleus decays, the resulting nucleus may also be unstable. There may be a *series* of successive decays until a stable configuration is reached. The most abundant radioactive nucleus found on earth is uranium ^{238}U, which undergoes a series of 14 decays, including eight alpha emissions and six beta emissions, terminating at the stable isotope of lead, ^{206}Pb.

In alpha decay, the neutron number N and the charge number Z each decrease by two, and the mass number A decreases by four, corresponding to the values $N = 2$, $Z = 2$, and $A = 4$ for the alpha particle. Beta decay is less obvious; how can a nucleus made up of protons and neutrons emit an *electron*? The answer is that in beta decay a neutron in the nucleus is transformed into a proton, an electron, and a neutrino. We will study such transformations in Section 44–10. The effect is to *increase* the charge number Z by one, decrease the neutron number N by one, and leave the mass number A unchanged. Gamma emission leaves all three numbers unchanged.

The number of radioactive nuclei in any sample of radioactive material decreases continuously as the nuclei decay, but the rate of decay varies widely for different kinds of nuclei. Let N be the number of radioactive nuclei in a sample at time t, and let ΔN be the (negative) change in that number during a short time interval Δt. The rate of change of N is $\Delta N / \Delta t$. The larger the number of nuclei in the sample, the larger the number that decay during any interval, so the rate of change of N is proportional to N. That is, it is equal to a constant λ multiplied by N:

$$\frac{\Delta N}{\Delta t} = -\lambda N. \tag{44–3}$$

The constant λ is called the **decay constant,** and it has different values for different nuclides. A large value of λ corresponds to rapid decay, a small value to slower decay. The situation is reminiscent of a discharging capacitor, which we studied in Section 29–4. Figure 44–3 shows the number of nuclei N as a function of time for the decay of polonium ^{214}Po.

The **half-life** $t_{1/2}$ is the time required for the number of radioactive nuclei to decrease to half the original number N_0. Then half of those remaining decay during a second interval $t_{1/2}$, and so on. The numbers remaining after successive intervals of $t_{1/2}$ are $N_0/2$, $N_0/4$, $N_0/8$, ...

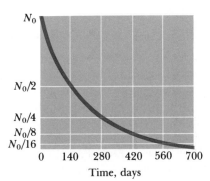

44–3
Decay curve for the radioactive element polonium. Polonium has a half-life of 140 days.

The half-life $t_{1/2}$ and decay constant λ are related by

$$t_{1/2} = \frac{\ln 2}{\lambda} = \frac{0.693}{\lambda}. \qquad (44\text{--}4)$$

The **lifetime** (or mean lifetime) t_{mean} of a nucleus or unstable particle is proportional to the half-life $t_{1/2}$:

$$t_{\text{mean}} = \frac{1}{\lambda} = \frac{t_{1/2}}{\ln 2} = \frac{t_{1/2}}{0.693}. \qquad (44\text{--}5)$$

In particle physics the life of an unstable particle is usually described by the lifetime, not the half-life.

The **activity** of a specimen is the number of decays per unit time. A common unit is the **curie,** abbreviated Ci, defined to be 3.70×10^{10} decays per second. This is approximately equal to the activity of 1 g of radium. The number of decays is proportional to the number of radioactive nuclei, so the activity decreases with time. Thus Fig. 44–3 is also a graph of the activity of polonium, ^{210}Po, which has a half-life of 140 days.

The SI unit of activity is the **becquerel,** abbreviated Bq. One becquerel is one disintegration per second, so

$$1 \text{ Ci} = 3.70 \times 10^{10} \text{ Bq}.$$

Radioactive decay series can be represented on a Segrè chart, as in Fig. 44–4. The neutron number N is plotted vertically, and the atomic number (or charge number) Z horizontally. In alpha emission, both N and Z decrease by two. In beta emission, N decreases by one and Z increases by one. The half-lives are given in years (y), days (d), hours (h), minutes (m), or seconds (s).

Figure 44–4 shows the uranium decay series, which begins with the common uranium isotope ^{238}U and ends with an isotope of lead, ^{206}Pb. The decays can also be represented in equation form; the first two decays in the series are written as

$$^{238}\text{U} \longrightarrow {}^{234}\text{Th} + \alpha,$$

$$^{234}\text{Th} \longrightarrow {}^{234}\text{Pa} + \beta,$$

or more briefly as

$$^{238}\text{U} \xrightarrow{\ \alpha\ } {}^{234}\text{Th},$$

$$^{234}\text{Th} \xrightarrow{\ \beta\ } {}^{234}\text{Pa}.$$

In the second decay, the beta decay leaves the daughter nucleus ^{234}Pa in an excited state, from which it decays to the ground state by emitting a gamma-ray photon.

An interesting feature of the ^{238}U decay series is the branching that occurs at ^{214}Bi. This nuclide decays to ^{210}Pb by emission of an alpha and a beta, which can occur in either order. We also note that the series includes unstable isotopes of several elements that also have stable isotopes, including Tl, Pb, and Bi. The unstable isotopes of these elements that occur in the ^{238}U series all have too many neutrons to be stable, as we discussed in Section 44–2.

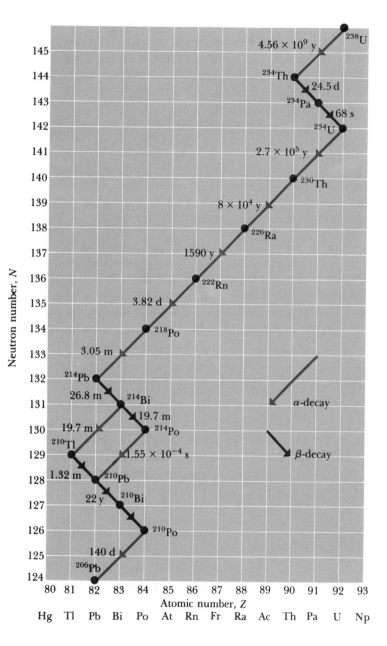

44–4
Segrè chart showing the uranium ^{238}U decay series, terminating with the stable nuclide $^{206}_{82}$Pb.

Three other decay series are known; two of these occur in nature, one starting with the uncommon isotope ^{235}U, the other with thorium (^{232}Th). The fourth series starts with neptunium ^{237}Np, an element that is not found in nature but is produced in nuclear reactors. In each case the series continues until a stable nucleus is reached; for these series the final members are ^{207}Pb, ^{208}Pb, and ^{209}Bi, respectively.

An interesting application of radioactivity is the dating of archeological and geological specimens by measuring the concentration of radioactive isotopes. The most familiar example is carbon dating. The unstable isotope ^{14}C is produced by nuclear reactions in the atmosphere caused by cosmic-ray bombardment, and there is a small proportion of ^{14}C in the CO_2 in the atmosphere. Plants that obtain their carbon from this source contain the same proportion of ^{14}C as the atmosphere. When a plant dies, it stops taking in carbon, and the ^{14}C it has already absorbed decays, with a half-life of 5568 years. By measuring the proportion of ^{14}C in the remains we can determine how long ago the organism died. Similar techniques are used with other isotopes for dating geologic specimens. One difficulty is that the ^{14}C concentration in the atmosphere changes over long time intervals.

*44–4
Radiation and the Life Sciences

The interaction of radiation with living organisms is a topic that grows daily in interest and usefulness. In this discussion we define **radiation** to include radioactivity (alpha, beta, gamma, and neutrons) and electromagnetic radiation such as X-rays. As these particles pass through matter, they lose energy, breaking molecular bonds and creating ions, hence the term *ionizing radiation*. Charged particles interact through direct electrical forces on the electrons in the material. X-rays and gamma-rays can interact by photoelectric effect, in which an electron absorbs a photon and is freed from its molecular bond, or by Compton scattering, which is discussed in Section 41–7. Neutrons cause ionization indirectly through absorption by nuclei with subsequent alpha or beta decay of the resulting unstable nucleus.

The interactions of radiation with living tissue are extremely complex. It has been known for many years that excessive exposure to radiation, including sunlight, X-rays, and all the nuclear radiations, can cause destruction of tissues. In mild cases this destruction is manifested as a burn, as with common sunburn. Greater exposure can cause very severe illness or death by a variety of mechanisms, one of which is the destruction of the components in bone marrow that produce red blood cells.

Radiation dosimetry is the quantitative description of the effect of radiation on living tissue. The *absorbed dose* of radiation is defined as the energy delivered to the tissue per unit mass. The SI unit of absorbed dose, the joule per kilogram, is called the *gray* (Gy); that is, 1 Gy = 1 J·kg^{-1}. Another unit, in more common use at present, is the *rad*, defined as 0.01 J·kg^{-1}:

$$1 \text{ rad} = 0.01 \text{ J·kg}^{-1} = 0.01 \text{ Gy}. \qquad (44–6)$$

Absorbed dose by itself is not an adequate measure of biological effect because equal energies of different kinds of radiation cause different extents of biological effect. This variation is described by a numerical factor called the **relative biological effectiveness (RBE),** also called the *quality factor* (QF), of each specific radiation. X-rays with 200 keV energy are defined to have an RBE of unity, and the effects of other radiations can be compared experimentally. The RBE also depends somewhat on the kind of tissue in which the radiation is absorbed. Table 44–3 shows approximate values of RBE for several radiations. All these values depend somewhat on the *energy* of the radiation.

TABLE 44–3   Relative biological effectiveness (RBE) for several radiations

Radiation	RBE
X-rays and gamma-rays	1
Electrons	1.0–1.5
Protons	10
Alpha particles	20
Heavy ions	20
Slow neutrons	3–5

The biological effect is described by the *product* of the absorbed dose and the RBE of the radiation; this quantity is called the *biologically equivalent dose*, or simply equivalent dose. The SI unit of equivalent dose for humans is the Sievert (Sv):

$$\text{equivalent dose (Sv)} = \text{RBE} \times \text{absorbed dose (Gy).} \quad (44\text{–}7)$$

A more common unit, corresponding to the rad, is the rem:

$$\text{equivalent dose (rem)} = \text{RBE} \times \text{absorbed dose (rad).} \quad (44\text{–}8)$$

The unit millirem (1 mrem = 10^{-3} rem) is also in common use.

Example 44–2   During a diagnostic X-ray a broken leg with a mass of 5 kg receives an equivalent dose of 50 mrem. What total energy is absorbed, and how many X-ray photons are absorbed if the X-ray energy is 50 keV?

Solution   For X-rays, RBE = 1, so the absorbed dose is

$$50 \text{ mrad} = 0.050 \text{ rad} = (0.050)(0.01 \text{ J·kg}^{-1})$$
$$= 5.0 \times 10^{-4} \text{ J·kg}^{-1}.$$

The total energy absorbed is

$$(5.0 \times 10^{-4} \text{ J·kg}^{-1})(5 \text{ kg}) = 2.5 \times 10^{-3} \text{ J}$$
$$= 1.56 \times 10^{16} \text{ eV.}$$

The number of X-ray photons is

$$\frac{1.56 \times 10^{16} \text{ eV}}{5.0 \times 10^4 \text{ eV}} = 3.1 \times 10^{11} \text{ photons.}$$

If the ionizing radiation had been a beam of alpha particles, for which RBE = 20, the absorbed dose needed for an equivalent dose of 50 mrem would be 2.5 mrad, corresponding to a total absorbed energy of 1.25×10^{-4} J. ∎

Here are a few numbers for perspective. An ordinary chest X-ray delivers about 20 to 40 mrem to about 5 kg of tissue. A whole-body dose of up to about 20 rem causes no immediately detectable effect. A short-term whole-body dose of 500 rem or more usually causes death within a few days or weeks. A localized dose of 10,000 rem causes complete destruction of the exposed tissue. Radiation exposure from cosmic rays and natural radioactivity in soil, building materials, and so on is of the order of 0.1 rem per year at sea level and twice that at an elevation of 5000 ft.

The long-term hazards of radiation exposure in causing various cancers and genetic defects have been widely publicized, and the question of whether there is any "safe" level of radiation exposure has been hotly debated. U.S. government regulations are based on a maximum *yearly* exposure, from all except natural sources, of 0.2 to 0.5 rem. Workers with occupational exposure to radiation are permitted 5 rem per year.

Recent studies suggest that these limits are too high and that even extremely small exposures carry hazards. One study suggests that a single chest X-ray may induce leukemia in one of 10 million individuals. It has become clear that any use of X-rays for medical diagnosis should be preceded by a very careful consideration of the relation of risk to possible benefit.

Another sharply debated question is that of radiation hazards from nuclear power plants. The radiation level from these plants is *not* negligible. To make a meaningful evaluation of hazards, we have to compare these levels with the alternatives, such as coal-powered plants. The health hazards of coal smoke are serious and well documented, and the radioactivity in the smoke from a coal-fired power plant is believed to be roughly 100 times as great as that from a properly operating nuclear plant with equal capacity. Disposal of radioactive waste from nuclear plants is a very serious problem. It is clearly impossible to eliminate *all* hazards to health. The best we can do is to try to take a rational approach to the problem of *minimizing* hazards.

Radiation is widely used in medicine for intentional selective destruction of tissue such as tumors. The hazards are considerable, but if the disease would be fatal without treatment, the radiation hazard may be preferable. Artificially produced isotopes are often used as sources. An example is an isotope of cobalt, ^{60}Co. This is prepared by bombarding the stable isotope ^{59}Co with neutrons in a nuclear reactor. Neutron absorption leads to the unstable ^{60}Co, with $Z = 27$ and $N = 33$. This is an "odd-odd" nucleus, and it decays to ^{60}Ni by beta and gamma emission, with a half-life of about 5 years. Such artificial sources have several advantages over naturally radioactive sources. They have shorter half-lives and correspondingly greater activity. They do not emit alpha particles, which are usually not wanted, and the electrons they emit are easily stopped by thin metal sheets without blocking the desired gamma radiation. Beams of π mesons produced with cyclotron beams have also been used. In a different line, radiation is being used to sterilize and preserve some food products.

Here are several examples of the expanding field called *nuclear medicine*. Radioactive isotopes have the same electron configurations and chemical behavior as stable isotopes of the same element. But the location and concentration of radioactive isotopes can easily be detected by measurements of the radiation they emit. A familiar example is the use of an unstable isotope of iodine for thyroid studies. Nearly all the iodine ingested that is not eliminated eventually reaches the thyroid, and the body does not discriminate between the unstable isotope ^{131}I and the stable isotope ^{127}I. A minute quantity of ^{131}I is fed or injected, and the speed with which it becomes concentrated in the thyroid provides a measure of thyroid function. The half-life is about 8 days, so there are no long-lasting radiation hazards. By use of more sophisticated scanning detectors, one can also obtain a "picture" of the thyroid, which shows enlargement and other abnormalities. This procedure, a type of *autoradiography*, is comparable to photographing the glowing filament of an incandescent light bulb using the light emitted by the filament itself.

Similar techniques are used to visualize coronary arteries. A thin tube or *catheter* is threaded through a vein in the arm into the heart, and a radioactive material is injected. Narrowed or blocked arteries can actually be photographed by use of a scanning detector; such a picture is called an *angiogram* or *arteriogram*. A useful isotope for such purposes is technicium ^{99}Tc, formed in the beta decay of molybdenum ^{99}Mo. It is formed in an excited state, from which it decays to the ground state by gamma emission with a half-life of about 6 hours, unusually long for gamma emission. Scanning detectors, often called *gamma cameras*, have been used for studies of the brain, kidneys, and numerous other organs.

Radioactive isotopes are used in *tracer* techniques. We have mentioned radioactive iodine in the thyroid. Tritium, a hydrogen isotope, ^{3}H, is used to tag molecules in complex organic reactions. In the world of machinery, radioactive iron can be used to study piston ring wear; radioactive tags on pesticide molecules can be used to trace their passage through food chains. Laundry detergent manufacturers test the effectiveness of their products using radioactive dirt.

Ionizing radiation is a two-edged sword; it poses very serious health hazards, yet it also provides many benefits to humankind, including the diagnosis and treatments of disease and a wide variety of analytical techniques. Many direct effects of radiation are also useful, such as strengthening of polymers by cross-linking, sterilizing of food and surgical tools, and dispersion of unwanted static electricity in the air.

44–5
Nuclear Reactions

In Section 44–3 we studied the decay of unstable nuclei. The processes we described were spontaneous emission of an alpha or beta particle, sometimes followed by gamma emission. Nothing was done to initiate this emission, and nothing could be done to control it. Rutherford suggested in 1919 that a massive particle with sufficient kinetic energy might be able to penetrate a nucleus. The result would be either a new nucleus with greater atomic number and mass number or a decay of the original nucleus. Rutherford bombarded nitrogen with alpha particles and obtained an oxygen nucleus and a proton, according to the reaction

$$_2^4\text{He} + _7^{14}\text{N} \rightarrow _8^{17}\text{O} + _1^1\text{H}. \tag{44–9}$$

The sum of the initial atomic numbers is equal to the sum of the final atomic numbers. This is required by conservation of charge. The sum of the initial mass numbers is also equal to the sum of the final mass numbers, but the initial rest mass is *not* equal to the final rest mass. Such a process is called a **nuclear reaction,** a rearrangement of nuclear components that results from bombardment by a particle rather than a spontaneous natural process.

The difference between the rest masses before and after the reaction corresponds to the **reaction energy,** according to the mass–energy relation $E = mc^2$. If the sum of the final rest masses is greater than the sum of the initial rest masses, energy is *absorbed* in the reaction. If the final sum is *less than* the initial sum, energy is released in the form of kinetic energy of the final particles. (1 u is equivalent to 931.5 MeV.)

In the nuclear reaction represented by Eq. (44–9) the rest masses of the various particles (from Table 44–2) are

$$^{4}_{2}\text{He:}\quad 4.00260\text{ u}\qquad ^{17}_{8}\text{O:}\quad 16.99913\text{ u}$$
$$\underline{^{14}_{7}\text{N:}\quad 14.00307\text{ u}}\qquad \underline{^{1}_{1}\text{H:}\quad 1.00783\text{ u}}$$
$$18.00567\text{ u}\qquad\qquad 18.00696\text{ u}$$

(These values include nine electron masses in each case.) The total rest mass of the final products exceeds that of the initial particles by 0.00129 u, which is equivalent to 1.20 MeV. This amount of energy is *absorbed* in the reaction. If the initial particles do not have at least this much kinetic energy, the reaction cannot take place.

Here is another example. When lithium is bombarded by a proton, two alpha particles are produced.

$$^{1}_{1}\text{H} + ^{7}_{3}\text{Li} \rightarrow ^{4}_{2}\text{He} + ^{4}_{2}\text{He}. \qquad (44\text{–}10)$$

The sum of the final masses is *smaller* than the sum of the initial values, as shown by the following data:

$$^{1}_{1}\text{H:}\quad 1.00783\text{ u}\qquad ^{4}_{2}\text{He:}\quad 4.00260\text{ u}$$
$$\underline{^{7}_{3}\text{Li:}\quad 7.01600\text{ u}}\qquad \underline{^{4}_{2}\text{He:}\quad 4.00260\text{ u}}$$
$$8.02383\text{ u}\qquad\qquad 8.00520\text{ u}$$

Four electron masses are included on each side. The decrease in mass is 0.01863 u. The equivalent energy, $(0.01863\text{ u})(931.5\text{ MeV·u}^{-1}) =$ 17.4 MeV, is liberated and appears as kinetic energy of the two separating alpha particles.

For positively charged particles such as the proton and the alpha particle to penetrate nuclei of other atoms, they must have enough initial kinetic energy to overcome the potential-energy barrier caused by the repulsive electrostatic forces. For example, in the reaction of Eq. (44–10), if the lithium nucleus has a radius of the order of 2.3×10^{-15} m, as suggested by Eq. (44–1), the repulsive potential energy of the proton (charge $+e$) and the lithium nucleus (charge $+3e$) at this distance is

$$U = \frac{1}{4\pi\epsilon_0}\frac{(e)(3e)}{r} = \frac{3(9.0 \times 10^9\text{ N·m}^2\text{·C}^{-2})(1.6 \times 10^{-19}\text{ C})^2}{2.3 \times 10^{-15}\text{ m}}$$
$$= 3.01 \times 10^{-13}\text{ J} = 1.88 \times 10^6\text{ eV} = 1.88\text{ MeV}.$$

Even though energy is liberated in this reaction, the proton must have a minimum or **threshold** energy of about 1.9 MeV for the reaction to occur.

Absorption of *neutrons* by nuclei forms an important class of nuclear reactions. Heavy nuclei bombarded by neutrons in a nuclear reactor can undergo a series of neutron absorptions alternating with beta decays, in which the mass number A increases by as much as 25. The *transuranic elements*, elements having Z larger than 92, are produced in this way. These elements do not occur in nature. Seventeen transuranic elements, having Z up to 109 and A up to about 265, have been identified.

The analytical technique of *neutron activation analysis* uses similar reactions. When stable nuclei are bombarded by neutrons, some absorb neutrons and then undergo beta decay. The energies of the beta and gamma emissions depend on the parent nucleus and provide a means of identifying it. The presence of elements in quantities far too small for conventional chemical analysis can be detected in this way.

44–6
Nuclear Fission

In 1939, Hahn and Strassman discovered a new nuclear phenomenon. They bombarded uranium ($Z = 92$) with neutrons, and by chemical analysis they found barium ($Z = 56$) and krypton ($Z = 36$) among the products. Uranium nuclei were splitting into two massive fragments. The process is called **nuclear fission,** and the two pieces resulting from the split are called *fission fragments*. The energy released during fission, about 200 MeV, emerges as kinetic energy of the fission fragments. A few free neutrons usually appear along with the fission fragments. Both ^{238}U and ^{235}U can be split by neutron bombardment, ^{235}U by slow neutrons and ^{238}U only by neutrons with at least 1.2 MeV of energy.

Over 100 different nuclides representing more than 20 different elements have been found among the fission products. Most of these are in the middle of the periodic table, with atomic numbers ranging from 34 to 58. Because the neutron–proton ratio needed for stability in this range is much *smaller* than that of the original uranium nucleus, the fission fragments always have too many neutrons for stability. A few free neutrons are liberated during fission, and the fission fragments undergo a series of beta decays (each of which increases Z by one and decreases N by one) until a stable structure is attained. During these decays an average of 15 MeV of additional energy is liberated.

The fact that fission of a uranium nucleus is triggered by neutron bombardment and that other neutrons are liberated during fission suggested the possibility of a **chain reaction,** a self-sustaining series of fissions that would continue until the uranium is used up. A neutron causes fission of one uranium nucleus, during which a large amount of energy and several neutrons are emitted. These neutrons then cause fission of neighboring uranium nuclei, which produce more energy and more neutrons. The chain reaction may be made to proceed slowly and in a controlled manner in a **nuclear reactor,** or explosively in a bomb.

The probability of neutron absorption by a nucleus is much larger for low-energy (less than 1 eV) neutrons than for the higher-energy neutrons liberated during fission. In a nuclear reactor the neutrons emitted during fission are slowed down by collisions with nuclei in the surrounding material, called the *moderator*, so that they can cause further fissions. In nuclear power plants the moderator is often water. On the average, each fission of a ^{235}U nucleus produces about 2.5 free neutrons, so 40% of the neutrons are needed to sustain a chain reaction. The *rate* of the reaction is controlled by inserting or withdrawing *control rods* made of elements (often cadmium) whose nuclei *absorb* neutrons without undergoing any additional reaction. The isotope ^{238}U can also absorb neutrons, leading to ^{239}U, and it cannot by itself sustain a chain reaction. Uranium used in reactors must be "enriched" by increasing the proportion of ^{235}U through isotope-separation processing.

The most familiar application of nuclear reactors is the generation of electric power. To illustrate some of the numbers involved, consider a hypothetical nuclear power plant with a generating capacity of 1000 MW; this figure is typical of large plants currently being built. As we noted above, the fission energy appears as kinetic energy of the fission fragments, and its immediate result is to heat the fuel elements and the surrounding water. This heat generates steam to drive turbines, which drive the electrical generators. The turbines are heat engines and are subject to the efficiency limitations imposed by the second law of thermodynamics, as we discussed in Chapter 19. In modern nuclear plants the overall efficiency is about one third, so 3000 MW of thermal power from the fission reaction are needed to generate 1000 MW of electrical power.

How much uranium has to undergo fission per unit time to provide 3000 MW of thermal power? Each second, we need 3000 MJ or 3000×10^6 J. Each fission provides 200 MeV, which is

$$200 \text{ MeV} = (200 \text{ MeV})(1.6 \times 10^{-13} \text{ J·MeV}^{-1}) = 3.2 \times 10^{-11} \text{ J}.$$

The number of fissions needed per second is

$$\frac{3000 \times 10^6 \text{ J}}{3.2 \times 10^{-11} \text{ J}} = 0.94 \times 10^{20}.$$

Each uranium atom has a mass of about $(235)(1.67 \times 10^{-27} \text{ kg}) = 3.9 \times 10^{-25}$ kg, so the mass of uranium needed per second is

$$(0.94 \times 10^{20})(3.9 \times 10^{-25} \text{ kg}) = 3.7 \times 10^{-5} \text{ kg} = 37 \text{ mg}.$$

In one day (86,400 seconds) the total consumption of uranium is

$$(3.7 \times 10^{-5} \text{ kg·s}^{-1})(86,400 \text{ s·d}^{-1}) = 3.2 \text{ kg·d}^{-1}.$$

For comparison, note that the 1000-MW coal-fired power plant we described in Section 19–9 burns 10,600 tons (about 10^7 kg) of coal per day. Combustion of one carbon atom yields about 2 eV of energy, while fission of one uranium nucleus yields 200 MeV, 10^8 times as much!

Nuclear fission reactors have many other practical uses. Among these are the production of artificial radioactive isotopes for medical and other research, production of high-intensity neutron beams for research in nuclear structure, and production of fissionable transuranic elements such as plutonium from the common isotope ^{238}U. The last is the function of *breeder reactors*.

We mentioned above that about 15 MeV of the energy from fission of a ^{235}U nucleus comes from the beta decays of the fission fragments rather than from the kinetic energy of the fragments themselves. This fact poses a serious problem with respect to control and safety of reactors. Even after the chain reaction has been completely stopped by insertion of control rods into the core, heat continues to be evolved by the beta decays, which cannot be stopped. For a 1000-MW reactor this heat power amounts to about 200 MW, which, in the event of total loss of cooling water, is more than enough to cause a catastrophic "meltdown" of the reactor core and possible penetration of the containment vessel. The difficulty in achieving a "cold shutdown" following an accident at the Three Mile Island nuclear power plant in Pennsylvania in March 1979 was a result of the continued evolution of heat due to beta decays.

Fission appears to set an upper limit on the production of transuranic nuclei, which we mentioned in Section 44–5. When a nucleus with $Z = 109$ is bombarded with neutrons, fission occurs essentially instantaneously; no $Z = 110$ nucleus is formed even for a short time. There are theoretical reasons to expect that nuclei in the vicinity of $Z = 114$, $N = 184$ might be stable with respect to spontaneous fission. These numbers correspond to *filled shells* in the nuclear energy-level structure, analogous to the filled shells of electrons in the noble gases, as discussed in Section 43–2. Such nuclei, called *superheavy nuclei*, would still be unstable with respect to alpha emission, but they might live long enough to be identified. Attempts to produce superheavy nuclei in the laboratory have not been successful; whether they exist in nature is still an open question.

44–7
Nuclear Fusion

In any nuclear reaction in which the total rest mass of the products is less than the original rest mass, energy is liberated. The fission of uranium, which we have just described, is an example of one type of energy-liberating reaction. Another type involves the *combination* of two light nuclei to form a nucleus that is more complex but whose rest mass is less than the sum of the rest masses of the original nuclei. Such a process is called **nuclear fusion.** Here are three examples of energy-liberating fusion reactions:

$$^1_1H + {^1_1}H \rightarrow {^2_1}H + \beta^+ + \nu,$$

$$^2_1H + {^1_1}H \rightarrow {^3_2}He + \gamma,$$

$$^3_2He + {^3_2}He \rightarrow {^4_2}He + {^1_1}H + {^1_1}H.$$

In the first reaction, two protons combine to form a deuteron and a β^+ or *positron* (a positively charged electron, to be discussed in Section 44–9). In the second a proton and a deuteron (a proton and a neutron bound together, forming the nucleus of deuterium or ^2H) unite to form the light isotope of helium, ^3He. In the third, two ^3He nuclei unite to form ordinary helium (^4He) and two protons. These fusion reactions, known as the *proton–proton* chain, are believed to take place in the interior of the sun and other stars.

The positrons produced during the first step of the proton–proton chain collide with electrons; mutual annihilation takes place, and their energy is converted into gamma radiation. The net effect of the chain is therefore the combination of four hydrogen nuclei into a helium nucleus and gamma radiation. We can calculate the net energy release from the mass balance:

Mass of four hydrogen atoms (including electrons):	4.03132 u
Mass of one helium atom plus two electrons:	4.00370 u
Mass difference:	0.02762 u
	= 25.7 MeV.

Considering the sun, 1 g of its mass contains about 2×10^{23} protons. If all of these protons were fused into helium, the energy released would be about 57,000 kWh. If the sun were to continue to radiate at its present rate, it would take about 30 billion years to exhaust its supply of protons.

For fusion of two nuclei to occur they must come together to within the range of the nuclear force, typically of the order of 2×10^{-15} m. To do this, they must overcome the electrical repulsion of their positive charges. For two protons at this distance the corresponding potential energy is of the order of 1.1×10^{-13} J or 0.7 MeV; this represents the initial *kinetic* energy the fusion nuclei must have.

Such energies are available at extremely high temperatures. According to Section 20–3, the average translational kinetic energy of a gas molecule at temperature T is $\frac{3}{2}kT$, where k is Boltzmann's constant. For this to be equal to 1.1×10^{-13} J the temperature must be of the order of 5×10^9 K. Not all the nuclei have to have this energy, but the temperature must be of the order of millions of kelvins if any appreciable fraction of the nuclei are to have enough kinetic energy to surmount the electrical repulsion and achieve fusion.

Intensive efforts are underway in many laboratories to achieve controlled fusion reactions, which potentially represent an enormous new energy resource. In one kind of experiment a plasma is heated to extremely high temperature by an electrical discharge, while being contained by appropriately shaped magnetic fields. In another experiment, pellets of the material to be fused are heated by a high-intensity laser beam. One current laser experiment set-up is shown in Fig. 44–5. Some of the reactions being studied are

$${}_1^2\text{H} + {}_1^2\text{H} \rightarrow {}_1^3\text{H} + {}_1^1\text{H} + 4 \text{ MeV}, \qquad (1)$$

$${}_1^3\text{H} + {}_1^2\text{H} \rightarrow {}_2^4\text{He} + {}_0^1\text{n} + 17.6 \text{ MeV}, \quad (2)$$

$${}_1^2\text{H} + {}_1^2\text{H} \rightarrow {}_2^3\text{He} + {}_0^1\text{n} + 3.3 \text{ MeV}, \qquad (3)$$

$${}_2^3\text{He} + {}_1^2\text{H} \rightarrow {}_2^4\text{He} + {}_1^1\text{H} + 18.3 \text{ MeV}. \quad (4)$$

44–5

The Novette laser system at Lawrence Livermore National Laboratory, used for fusion research. This system went into operation in January 1983; it can deliver a power of 50×10^{12} W for a period of the order of 1 ns. (Courtesy of Lawrence Livermore National Laboratory.)

In the first reaction, two deuterons combine to form tritium (a proton plus two neutrons bound together, the nucleus of ^{3}H) and a proton. In the second the tritium nucleus combines with another deuteron to form helium and a neutron. The result of both of these reactions together is the conversion of three deuterons into a helium-4 nucleus, a proton, and a neutron, with the liberation of 21.6 MeV of energy. Reactions (3) and (4) together achieve the same conversion. In a plasma containing deuterium the two pairs of reactions occur with roughly equal probability. As yet, no one has succeeded in producing these reactions under controlled conditions in such a way as to yield a net surplus of usable energy, but the practical problems do not appear to be insurmountable.

44-8
Particle Accelerators

Many important experiments in nuclear and high-energy physics during the last 60 years or so have made use of beams of charged particles, such as protons or electrons, that have been accelerated to high speeds. Any device that uses electric and magnetic fields to guide and accelerate a beam of charged particles is called a **particle accelerator.** In a sense the cathode-ray tubes of Thomson and his contemporaries were the first accelerators. In more recent times, accelerators have grown enormously in size, complexity, and energy range.

The **cyclotron,** developed in 1931 by Lawrence and Livingston at the University of California, was the first accelerator to use a magnetic field to guide particles in a nearly circular path so that they could be accelerated repeatedly by an electric field in a cyclic process.

In the cyclotron, shown schematically in Fig. 44–6, particles with mass m and charge q move inside a vacuum chamber in a uniform magnetic field B perpendicular to the plane of their trajectories. We learned in Section 30–4 that in such a situation a particle with speed v moves in a circular path with radius r given by

$$r = \frac{mv}{qB}. \qquad (44\text{–}11)$$

The angular velocity ω of the particles is

$$\omega = \frac{v}{r} = \frac{qB}{m}. \qquad (44\text{–}12)$$

Note that ω is independent of r and that v is directly proportional to r.

Now we apply an alternating potential difference between the two hollow electrodes D_1 and D_2, which are called *dees.* If this potential difference has the same frequency as the circular motions of the particles, the resulting electric field gives them a push twice each revolution, as they pass the gaps between the dees, boosting them into paths with larger radius, proportionately larger speed, and greater kinetic energy. The maximum radius is determined by the radius R of the electromagnet poles. We can find the corresponding maximum kinetic energy $K_{max} =$

High-frequency alternating voltage

B

D_1 r_1 D_2

44–6
Schematic diagram of a cyclotron.

$\frac{1}{2}mv_{\max}^2$ by solving Eq. (44–11) for v. The result is

$$K_{\max} = \frac{1}{2}mv_{\max}^2 = \frac{q^2 B^2 R^2}{2m}. \qquad (44-13)$$

If the particles are protons, $q = 1.60 \times 10^{-19}$ C and $m = 1.67 \times 10^{-27}$ kg. For a typical early (1930's) cyclotron, $B = 1.50$ T and $R = 0.500$ m. From Eq. (44–13) the maximum kinetic energy is

$$K_{\max} = \frac{(1.60 \times 10^{-19} \text{ C})^2 (1.50 \text{ T})^2 (0.500 \text{ m})^2}{2(1.67 \times 10^{-27} \text{ kg})}$$

$$= 4.31 \times 10^{-12} \text{ J} = 2.69 \times 10^7 \text{ eV} = 26.7 \text{ MeV}.$$

This energy is considerably larger than the average binding energy per nucleon; it is enough to cause a variety of interesting nuclear reactions.

The maximum energy that can be attained with the cyclotron is limited by relativistic effects. For Eq. (44–12) to be relativistically correct, m should be replaced by $m/(1 - v^2/c^2)^{1/2}$. As the particles speed up, their angular velocity ω *decreases*, and the particle motion is no longer in phase with the alternating dee voltage. In a variation called the *synchrocyclotron* the particles are accelerated in bursts. For each burst, the frequency of the alternating voltage is decreased at just the right rate to maintain the correct phase relation with the particles' motion. Another limitation of the cyclotron is the difficulty of building very large electromagnets. The largest synchrocyclotron ever built has a vacuum chamber about 8 m in diameter and accelerates protons to energies of about 600 MeV.

To attain higher energies, another type of machine, called the **synchrotron,** is more practical. In a synchrotron the particles move in a vacuum chamber in the form of a thin doughnut, called the *accelerating ring*. The particle beam is bent around by a series of electromagnets around the ring. As the particles speed up, the magnetic field is increased so that the particles retrace the same trajectory over and over. The synchrotron at the Fermi National Accelerator Laboratory (Fermilab) in Batavia, Illinois, was originally designed to accelerate protons to an energy of 800 GeV (800×10^9 eV), and modifications have recently been completed to permit a maximum energy of 1000 GeV. The accelerating ring is 2 km in diameter; the accelerator and associated facilities cost about \$400 million to build. In each machine cycle, a few seconds long, it accelerates approximately 10^{13} protons. An aerial view of the Fermilab accelerator is shown in Fig. 44–7.

As higher and higher energies are needed to investigate new phenomena in particle interactions, a new problem emerges. When a beam of high-energy particles collides with a stationary target, not all the kinetic energy of the incident particles is *available* to form new particle states. Because momentum must be conserved, the particles emerging from the collision must have some motion and thus some kinetic energy. The energy E_a available for creating new particles or particle configurations is the *difference* between initial and final kinetic energies.

In the extreme-relativistic range, in which the kinetic energies of the particles are large in comparison to their rest energies, this is a very severe limitation. When beam and target particles have equal mass, as in the case of protons bombarding a hydrogen target, it can be shown from

44–7
An aerial view of the 1000-GeV accelerator at the Fermi National Accelerator Laboratory, Batavia, Illinois. (Courtesy of Fermilab Visual Media Services.)

relativistic mechanics that the available energy E_a is related to the total energy E of the bombarding particle and to its mass m by

$$E_a = \sqrt{2mc^2E}. \tag{44-14}$$

For example, for the proton, $mc^2 = 931$ MeV $= 0.931$ GeV. If $E = 800$ GeV, as for the original Fermilab accelerator, then

$$E_a = \sqrt{2(0.931 \text{ GeV})(800 \text{ GeV})} = 38.6 \text{ GeV}.$$

If $E = 1000$ GeV, $E_a = 43.1$ GeV. Increasing the beam energy by 200 GeV increases the available energy by only 4.5 GeV!

This limitation is circumvented in *colliding-beam* experiments. In these experiments there is no stationary target; beams of particles and their antiparticles (such as electrons and positrons or protons and antiprotons) circulate in opposite directions in an arrangement called a *storage ring*. In regions where the beams intersect, they are focused sharply onto one another, and collisions can occur. Because the total momentum in such a two-particle collision is zero, the available energy E_a is the total kinetic energy of the two particles.

An example is the storage ring facility at the Stanford Linear Accelerator Center (SLAC), where electron and positron beams collide with total available energy of up to 36 GeV. Other storage-ring facilities are located at DESY (German Electron Synchrotron) in Hamburg, West Germany (E_a up to 42 GeV total in electron-positron collisions), and at the Cornell Electron Storage Ring Facility (CESR), with 16 GeV maximum total available energy. At the CERN (European Council for Nuclear Research) laboratory in Geneva, Switzerland, construction has begun for a large electron–positron storage ring that will transport beams of particles with energies of 50 GeV or more for a total available energy of at least 100 GeV. As this book goes to press, that facility is expected to have usable beams in late 1989.

The highest-energy accelerator project currently under way is the Superconducting Supercollider (SSC). In December 1988 the U.S. Department of Energy selected a site near Waxahachie, Texas, for this project. In two ring-shaped vacuum chambers in the collider's underground tunnel, 85 km (about 53 miles) in circumference, beams of protons will be steered in opposite directions by rings of superconducting magnets, accelerated to an energy of 20 TeV (20×10^{12} eV), and brought together for head-on collisions. Construction of this facility will require 8 to 10 years and about $6 billion. When completed, it will have an operating budget of the order of $250 million per year. This experimental facility will be a significant new tool for research into the most fundamental levels of the structure of matter.

*44–9

Fundamental Particles

What are the most fundamental building blocks of matter? This question is at least 2000 years old, yet we keep finding new answers. The electron and proton were known by 1900, but the neutron was not discovered until 1930. In that year, two German physicists, Bothe and Becker, observed that when beryllium, boron, or lithium was bombarded by fast alpha particles, the bombarded material emitted *something*, either particles or electromagnetic waves, with much greater penetrating power than the original alpha particles. Further experiments by these and other physicists established that *uncharged* particles with mass approximately equal to that of the proton were emitted from the nuclei of the target material. Chadwick christened these particles *neutrons*. A typical reaction, using a beryllium target, is

$$ {}^{4}_{2}\text{He} + {}^{9}_{4}\text{Be} \rightarrow {}^{12}_{6}\text{C} + {}^{1}_{0}\text{n}, \qquad (44\text{--}15) $$

where ${}^{1}_{0}\text{n}$ denotes a neutron.

Because neutrons have no charge, they produce no ionization when they pass through gases, and they are not deflected by electric or magnetic fields. They can be slowed down only by a direct hit with a nucleus. When this happens, neutrons may either undergo elastic collisions or penetrate the nucleus. Once the neutrons are moving slowly, they may be detected by means of another nuclear reaction, the ejection of an alpha particle from the nucleus of a boron atom, according to the reaction

$$ {}^{1}_{0}\text{n} + {}^{10}_{5}\text{B} \rightarrow {}^{7}_{3}\text{Li} + {}^{4}_{2}\text{He}. \qquad (44\text{--}16) $$

The ejected alpha particle can be detected in a Geiger counter or other particle detector.

The discovery of the neutron cleared up a mystery about the composition of the nucleus. Before 1930 it had been thought that the total mass of a nucleus was due only to protons, but it was hard to understand why the charge-to-mass ratio was not the same for all nuclei. We now know that all nuclei (except hydrogen) contain both protons and neutrons.

In the early days of particle physics the *cloud chamber* and the *bubble chamber* were used to visualize paths of charged particles. In the cloud chamber, supercooled vapor condenses around a line of ions created by passage of a charged particle; the result is a visible track. In the bubble chamber, superheated liquid boils locally around a similar line of ions, creating a visible track of tiny bubbles. In either case the density of the track depends on the particle's speed v, which can therefore be determined by measuring the track. By imposing a magnetic field and measuring the radius of curvature of a track we can determine the momentum $p = mv$ of the particle. Knowing v and p, we can determine the particle's mass.

The positive electron, or **positron,** was first observed during an investigation of cosmic rays by Carl D. Anderson in 1932, in a historic cloud-chamber photograph reproduced in Fig. 44–8. The photograph was made with the cloud chamber in a magnetic field perpendicular to the plane of the picture. A lead plate crosses the chamber, and the particle has passed through it. The curvature of the track is greater above the plate than below it, so the velocity is less above than below. Therefore the particle had to be moving upward; it could not have *gained* energy going through the lead.

The density and curvature of the track suggested a mass equal to that of the electron. But the directions of the magnetic field and the

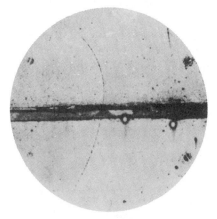

44–8
Track of a positive electron traversing a lead plate 6 mm thick. (Photograph by C. D. Anderson.)

velocity showed that the particle had *positive* charge. Anderson concluded that the track had been made by a positive electron or **positron.** The mass of the positron is equal to that of an ordinary (negative) electron; its charge is equal in magnitude but opposite in sign to the electron charge. Pairs of particles related to each other in this way are said to be *antiparticles* of each other.

Positrons do not form a part of ordinary matter. They are produced in high-energy collisions of charged particles or gamma rays with matter in a process called **pair production,** in which an ordinary electron and a positron are produced simultaneously. Electric charge is conserved in this process, but enough energy E must be available to account for the energy equivalent of the rest masses m of the two particles. The minimum energy for pair production is

$$E = 2mc^2 = 2(9.11 \times 10^{-31} \text{ kg})(3.00 \times 10^8 \text{ m·s}^{-1})^2$$
$$= 1.64 \times 10^{-13} \text{ J} = 1.02 \text{ MeV}.$$

The inverse process, e^+e^- *annihilation*, occurs when a positron and an electron collide. Both particles disappear, and two or three gamma-ray photons appear, with total energy $2mc^2$. Decay into a *single* photon is impossible because such a process cannot possibly conserve both energy and momentum.

Positrons also occur in the decay of some unstable nuclei. Recall that nuclei with *too many* neutrons for stability often emit a beta particle (electron), decreasing N by one and increasing Z by one. A nucleus with *too few* neutrons for stability may respond by converting a proton to a neutron, emitting a positron, increasing N by one and decreasing Z by one. Such nuclides do not occur in nature, but they can be produced artificially by neutron bombardment of stable nuclides in nuclear reactors. An example is the unstable odd-odd nuclide ^{22}Na, which has one less neutron than the stable ^{23}Na. It emits a positron, leaving the stable even-even nuclide ^{22}Ne with the same mass number $A = 22$.

In 1935 the Japanese physicist Hideki Yukawa (1907–1981) proposed a hypothetical particle he called a **meson,** with mass intermediate between that of the electron and the proton. This particle was intended to provide a mechanism for transmitting nuclear forces. Yukawa suggested that nucleons could interact by emitting and absorbing mesons, just as two basketball players interact by tossing the ball back and forth or by grabbing it away from each other.

Particles with intermediate mass, but *not* the one predicted by Yukawa, were discovered a year later by Anderson and Neddermeyer as a component of cosmic radiation. These particles are now called μ *mesons* or **muons.** The μ^- has charge equal to that of the electron, and its antiparticle, the μ^+, has a positive charge with equal magnitude. The two particles have equal mass, about 207 times the electron mass. Muons are unstable; each decays into an electron with the same sign, plus two neutrinos, with a lifetime of about 2.2×10^{-6} s. It was established soon after the discovery of the muons that they *could not* be Yukawa's particles because their interactions with nuclei were far too weak.

In 1947, *another* family of mesons, called π *mesons* or **pions,** were discovered; they have charges $+e$, $-e$, and zero. The charged pions have masses of about 273 times the electron mass and decay into muons with the same sign, plus a neutrino, with a lifetime of about 2.6×10^{-8} s. The neutral pion has a smaller mass, about 264 electron masses, and decays, with a very short lifetime of about 0.8×10^{-16} s, into two gamma-ray photons. The pions interact strongly with nuclei, and they *are* the particles predicted by Yukawa.

*44–10
High-Energy Physics

In the years since 1947, *high-energy physics* has emerged as a distinct branch of physics. These years have witnessed the attainment of higher and higher energies in particle accelerators, the discovery of many new particles, and intensive efforts to understand the properties of these new particles and their interactions.

A basic truth in high-energy physics is that fundamental particles are not *permanent* entities. They can be created or destroyed during interactions with other particles. In Section 44–9 we mentioned electron–positron pairs, which are *created* in high-energy collisions and can be *annihilated* with the emission of two or three gamma-ray photons. This transitory nature of the fundamental particles may seem disturbing, but in one sense it is a welcome development. Photons and electrons (and indeed all particles) share the dual wave–particle nature we discussed in Section 42–1. Photons are created and destroyed (or emitted and absorbed) in atomic and nuclear transitions. So it is not unreasonable that other particles can also be created and destroyed.

As an example, it was speculated as early as 1932 that there might be an *antiproton,* bearing the same relation to the ordinary proton as the positron does to the electron, that is, a particle with the same mass as the proton but negatively charged. In 1955, proton–antiproton pairs were created by impact on a stationary target of a beam of protons with kinetic energy 6 GeV (6×10^9 eV) from the Bevatron at the University of California at Berkeley.

In the years after 1960, as higher-energy accelerators and more sophisticated detectors were developed, a veritable blizzard of new unstable particles were identified. To describe them, we have to create a small blizzard of new terms. Initially, the particles were classified according to *mass.* The particles with the smallest masses (electrons, muons, and their associated neutrinos) are called **leptons.** Particles with masses between those of muons and nucleons are called **mesons.** (The recently discovered tau particles are also classified as leptons, even though their masses are greater than those of nucleons; and some particles more massive than nucleons are called mesons. We will return to these points later.) Particles that resemble nucleons but are more massive are called **hyperons,** and nucleons and hyperons collectively are called **baryons.** Particles are further classified according to electric charge, spin, and two additional quantum numbers, *isospin* (the number that determines the number of different charges a particular type of particle can have) and *strangeness* (a number needed to account for the production and decay modes of certain particles).

A partial list of some known particles is shown in Table 44–4. All particles with zero or integer spin (including photons and π and K mesons) are called **bosons,** and all particles having half-integer spin (including all leptons and baryons) are called **fermions.** These terms are derived from the names Bose and Fermi. Fermions obey the exclusion principle; bosons do not. This difference leads to different statistical energy distribution functions for the two classes of particles.

A more fundamental approach is to classify particles according to their *interactions* and the conservation laws associated with these interactions. We spoke briefly in Section 5–1 about kinds of interactions. The four known classes of interactions, in order of decreasing strength, are

1. Strong interactions
2. Electromagnetic interactions
3. Weak interactions
4. Gravitational interactions

Particles that experience strong interactions are called **hadrons;** these include all the particles grouped in Table 44–4 as mesons and baryons. The strong interactions are responsible for the nuclear force and also for the creation of pions, heavy mesons, and hyperons in high-energy collisions. Leptons, including electrons, muons, tau particles, and

TABLE 44–4   Some known particles and their properties

	Particle	Mass, MeV/c^2	Charge	Spin	Isopin	Strangeness	Mean lifetime, s	Typical decay modes	Quark content
Leptons	e^-	0.511	-1	$\frac{1}{2}$	—	0	stable	—	—
	ν_e	$0\ (<5 \times 10^{-5})$	0	$\frac{1}{2}$	—	0	stable	—	—
	μ^-	105.7	-1	$\frac{1}{2}$	—	0	2.2×10^{-6}	$e^- \bar{\nu}_e \nu_\mu$	—
	ν_μ	$0\ (<0.52)$	0	$\frac{1}{2}$	—	0	stable	—	—
	τ^-	1784	-1	$\frac{1}{2}$	—	0	5×10^{-13}	$\mu^- \bar{\nu}_\mu \nu_\tau$	—
	ν_τ	$0\ (<80)$	0	$\frac{1}{2}$	—	0	stable	—	—
Mesons	π^0	135.0	0	0	1	0	0.83×10^{-16}	$\gamma\gamma$	$u\bar{u},\ d\bar{d}$
	π^+	139.6	$+1$	0	1	0	2.6×10^{-8}	$\mu^+ \nu_\mu$	$u\bar{d}$
	π^-	139.6	-1	0	1	0	2.6×10^{-8}	$\mu^- \bar{\nu}_\mu$	$\bar{u}d$
	K^+	493.7	$+1$	0	$\frac{1}{2}$	$+1$	1.24×10^{-8}	$\mu^+ \nu_\mu$	$u\bar{s}$
	K^-	492.67	-1	0	$\frac{1}{2}$	-1	1.24×10^{-8}	$\mu^- \bar{\nu}_\mu$	$\bar{u}s$
	η^0	548.8	0	0	0	0	$\sim 10^{-18}$	$\gamma\gamma$	$u\bar{u},\ d\bar{d},\ s\bar{s}$
Baryons	p	938.3	$+1$	$\frac{1}{2}$	$\frac{1}{2}$	0	stable	—	uud
	n	939.6	0	$\frac{1}{2}$	$\frac{1}{2}$	0	917	$pe^- \bar{\nu}_e$	udd
	Λ	1115	0	$\frac{1}{2}$	0	-1	2.63×10^{-10}	$p\pi^-$ or $n\pi^0$	uds
	Σ^+	1189	$+1$	$\frac{1}{2}$	1	-1	0.80×10^{-10}	$p\pi^0$ or $n\pi^+$	uus
	Δ^{++}	1232	$+2$	$\frac{3}{2}$	$\frac{3}{2}$	0	$\sim 10^{-23}$	$p\pi^+$	uuu
	Ξ^-	1321	-1	$\frac{1}{2}$	$\frac{1}{2}$	-2	1.64×10^{-10}	$\Lambda\pi^-$	dss
	Ω^-	1672	-1	$\frac{3}{2}$	0	-3	0.82×10^{-10}	ΛK^-	sss
	Λ_c^+	2273	1	$\frac{1}{2}$	0	0	$\sim 7 \times 10^{-13}$	$\Lambda\pi\pi\pi$	udc

neutrinos, have *no* strong interactions, and they are therefore *not* hadrons.

The *electromagnetic* interactions are those associated directly with electric charge. At distances of the order of nuclear dimensions the electromagnetic interaction between two protons is weaker than the strong interaction, but the electromagnetic interaction has longer range. Neutral particles have no electromagnetic interactions, except for effects due to the magnetic moments of neutral baryons.

The *weak* interaction is responsible for beta decay, such as the conversion of a neutron into a proton, an electron, and a neutrino. It is also responsible for the decay of many unstable particles (pions into muons, muons into electrons, Λ particles into protons, and so on).

The *gravitational* interaction, although of central importance for the large-scale structure of celestial bodies, is not thought to play a significant role in fundamental-particle interactions at currently attainable energies. For example, the gravitational attraction of two electrons is smaller than their electrical repulsion by a factor of about 2.4×10^{-43}.

Several conservation laws are believed to be obeyed in *all* of the above interactions. These include the classical conservation laws: energy, momentum, angular momentum, and electrical charge. In addition, several new quantities that have no classical analog have been introduced to help characterize the properties of particles. These include *baryon number* (the number of baryons involved in an interaction minus the number of antibaryons), *lepton number* (the number of leptons minus the number of antileptons), *isospin* (used to describe the charge independence of nuclear forces), *parity* (the comparative behavior of two systems that are mirror images of each other), and *strangeness* (a quantum number used to classify particle production and decay reactions). Baryon number and lepton number are conserved in *all* interactions (hence the conservation of A in all nuclear reactions); isospin is conserved in strong interactions but not in electromagnetic or weak interactions. Parity and strangeness are conserved in strong and electromagnetic interactions but not in weak interactions. Unlike the classical laws, these conservation laws are not absolute. Instead, they serve as a means for *classifying* interactions.

The large number of supposedly fundamental particles discovered since 1960 (well over 100) suggests strongly that these particles *do not* represent the most fundamental level of the structure of matter, but that there is at least one additional level of structure. Our present understanding of the nature of this level is described by what is called the **standard model;** it is based on a proposal made initially in 1964 by Murray Gell-Mann and his collaborators. We cannot discuss this theory in detail, but here is a very brief sketch of some of its features.

Leptons are indeed fundamental particles. In addition to the electrons and muons and their associated neutrinos a third, much more massive lepton called the *tau* (τ), with spin $\frac{1}{2}$ and mass 1784 MeV was discovered in 1974. The τ neutrino has not been observed directly, but there is strong indirect evidence for its existence. Neutrinos with zero rest mass are postulated in most theories, but small masses cannot be ruled out. Table 44–4 gives experimental upper limits for the masses of the three neutrinos. If neutrinos *do* have mass, oscillations in which one type of neutrino changes into another type are theoretically possi-

44–9
Brookhaven National Laboratory's solar neutrino experiment, located 4900 feet underground in a gold mine in South Dakota to shield out cosmic rays and all other particles except neutrinos. The tank contains 100,000 gallons of perchloroethylene. Neutrinos from the interior of the sun are captured by ^{37}Cl nuclei, which then beta-decay into ^{37}A. The argon is then trapped and measured.

ble, and these oscillations allow for experimental detection of finite neutrino mass. Experiments designed to detect neutrino oscillations are under way, but no positive results have yet been obtained. Meanwhile, neutrino research continues; an example is shown in Fig. 44–9.

It now appears that hadrons are *not* fundamental particles but are composite structures whose constituents are spin $= \frac{1}{2}$ fermions called **quarks.** In fact, all known hadrons can be constructed as follows: baryons are composed of three quarks (qqq), and mesons are composed of quark–antiquark pairs ($q\bar{q}$). No other combinations seem to be necessary. This scheme requires that quarks have electric charges with magnitudes $\frac{1}{3}$ and $\frac{2}{3}$ of the electron charge, previously thought to be the fundamental unit of charge.

Quarks have a strong affinity for each other through a new kind of charge known as "color" charge. Thus color charge is responsible for strong interactions, and the force is known as the color force. The color force is mediated (transmitted) by exchange of color *gluons,* massless spin-one bosons. These play the same role in strong interactions that the pions played in the Yukawa theory of nuclear force and the photon plays in a quantum theory of electromagnetic interactions.

The weak and gravitational forces are also mediated by exchange of particles. In these cases the particles exchanged are the weak bosons ($W^{\pm}$ and Z^0) and the graviton, respectively. The graviton has not yet been observed experimentally.

The theory of strong interactions is known as **quantum chromodynamics** (QCD). To date, isolated free quarks have not been observed. A few experimenters have reported the observation of fractional electric charge. Other researchers have not been able to duplicate these results, and their validity is doubtful. In most QCD theories there are phenomena associated with the creation of quark–antiquark pairs that make it impossible to observe a single free, isolated quark. However, many indirect observations lead us to believe that the quark structure of hadrons is correct and that quantum chromodynamics may be the key to understanding the strong interactions.

The first quark theory included three types (flavors) of quarks, labeled **u** (up), **d** (down), and **s** (strange), as shown in Table 44–5. Protons, neutrons, π and K mesons, and several hyperons can be constructed from these three quarks. (For convenience we describe the charge Q of a

TABLE 44–5	**Properties of quarks**						
Symbol	Q/e	Spin	Baryon number	Strange-ness	Charm	Bottom-ness	Top-ness
u	$\frac{2}{3}$	$\frac{1}{2}$	$\frac{1}{3}$	0	0	0	0
d	$-\frac{1}{3}$	$\frac{1}{2}$	$\frac{1}{3}$	0	0	0	0
s	$-\frac{1}{3}$	$\frac{1}{2}$	$\frac{1}{3}$	-1	0	0	0
c	$\frac{2}{3}$	$\frac{1}{2}$	$\frac{1}{3}$	0	$+1$	0	0
b	$-\frac{1}{3}$	$\frac{1}{2}$	$\frac{1}{3}$	0	0	$+1$	0
t	$\frac{2}{3}$	$\frac{1}{2}$	$\frac{1}{3}$	0	0	0	$+1$

particle as a multiple of the magnitude e of the electron charge.) For example, a proton has $Q/e = +1$, baryon number $(B) = +1$, and strangeness $(S) = 0$. From Table 44–5 the u quark has $Q/e = \frac{2}{3}$ and $B = \frac{1}{3}$, and the d quark has $Q/e = -\frac{1}{3}$ and $B = \frac{1}{3}$. The proton quark content is uud. The neutron has quark content udd, the π^+ meson is $u\bar{d}$, and the K^+ meson is $u\bar{s}$. Antiparticles fit nicely into this scheme; the antiproton is $\bar{p} = \overline{uud}$, the negative pion is $\pi^- = \bar{u}d$, and so on. Particles can be arranged according to quark content, and families of particles can be classified according to intrinsic orbital angular momentum, spin, and parity. A state $q\bar{q}$, for example, can represent particles in different families, depending on the spin configuration and orbital angular momentum of the quarks.

The Pauli exclusion principle (Section 43–1) requires quarks to have a property that distinguishes one quark from another of the same flavor in order to permit three-quark states such as uud. This new property is labeled *color*; each quark flavor comes in three colors. This "color charge" is responsible for the strong interaction between quarks.

For symmetry and other compelling reasons, theorists later predicted the existence of a fourth quark flavor. This quark is labeled c (charm); it has $Q/e = \frac{2}{3}$, $B = \frac{1}{3}$, $S = 0$, and a new quantum number $C = +1$. This prediction was confirmed in 1974 at both the SLAC and Brookhaven accelerator laboratories by the observation of a meson with a mass of 3100 MeV. This meson, named Ψ at SLAC and J at Brookhaven, was found to have several decay modes, decaying into e^+e^-, $\mu^+\mu^-$, or hadrons. The mean lifetime was found to be about 10^{-20} s. This is consistent with J/Ψ being the ground state of a bound $c\bar{c}$ system, just as the hydrogen atom is a bound p–e system. Immediately after this, excited states of the $c\bar{c}$ system, with higher energy, were observed. A few years later, individual mesons with the charm quantum number were also observed. These mesons, D^0 $(c\bar{u})$ and D^+ $(c\bar{d})$, and their excited states are now firmly established. A charmed baryon, Λ_c^+, has been observed.

In 1977 a meson with a mass of 9460 MeV, called upsilon (Υ), was discovered at Brookhaven. Because it had properties similar to J/Ψ, it was conjectured that the meson was really the bound system of a new quark b and its antiquark, $\bar{b}$. Excited states of Υ were soon observed, and the B^+ $(\bar{b}u)$ and B^0 $(\bar{b}d)$ mesons are now well established also.

So far, we have five flavors of quarks (u, d, s, c, and b), and six flavors of leptons (e, μ, τ, ν_e, ν_μ, and ν_τ). We can understand many aspects of the strong and weak interactions of hadrons and mesons and the weak interactions of leptons on the basis of these fundamental particles. But it is an appealing conjecture that nature is symmetric in its building blocks and that there is therefore a *sixth* quark. This quark, labeled t (top), should have $Q/e = \frac{2}{3}$, $B = \frac{1}{3}$, and a new quantum number, $T = 1$. No direct experimental evidence for the existence of the t quark has yet been found. Table 44–5 lists some properties of the six quarks.

It has long been a dream of particle theorists to be able to combine all four interactions of nature into a single unified theory. In 1967, Weinberg and Salam proposed a theory that unifies the weak and electromagnetic forces. This electro-weak theory was successfully verified in 1983 with the discovery of the weak-force intermediary particles, the Z^0 and $W^\pm$ bosons, by two experimental groups working at the $p\bar{p}$ collider at CERN, Geneva. Not only were these particles found experimentally, but their observed masses agreed with the predictions of the electro-weak theory.

It is possible that the theory of strong interaction and the electro-weak theory can be unified to give a comprehensive theory of strong, weak, and electromagnetic interactions. Such schemes, called grand unified theories (GUT), are still speculative in nature. One interesting feature of some grand unified theories is that they predict the decay of the proton, with an estimated lifetime of the order of 10^{30} to 10^{31} years. Experiments are under way that should have detected the decay of the proton if its lifetime is 10^{30} years or less, but such decays have not been observed. The entire area is a very active field of present-day theoretical and experimental research.

Questions

44–1 How can you be sure that nuclei are not made of protons and electrons, rather than of protons and neutrons?

44–2 In calculations of nuclear binding energies such as those in the examples of Sections 44–1 and 44–5, should the binding energies of the *electrons* in the atoms be included?

44–3 If different isotopes of the same element have the same chemical behavior, how can they be separated?

44–4 In beta decay a neutron becomes a proton, an electron, and a neutrino. This decay also occurs with free neutrons, with a half-life of about 15 min. Could a free *proton* undergo a similar decay?

44–5 Since lead is a stable element, why doesn't the ^{238}U decay series shown in Fig. 44–4 stop at lead, ^{214}Pb?

44–6 In the ^{238}U decay chain shown in Fig. 44–4, some nuclides in the chain are found much more abundantly in nature than others, despite the fact that every ^{238}U nucleus goes through every step in the chain before finally becoming ^{206}Pb. Why are the abundances of the intermediate nuclides not all the same?

44–7 Radium has a half-life of about 1600 years. If the universe was formed five billion or more years ago, why is there any radium left now?

44–8 Why is the decay of an unstable nucleus unaffected by the *chemical* situation of the atom, such as the nature of the molecule in which it is bound, and so on?

44–9 Fusion reactions, which liberate energy, occur only with light nuclei, and fission reactions only with heavy nuclei. A student asserted that this shows that the binding energy per nucleon increases with A at small A but decreases at large A and hence must have a maximum somewhere in between. Do you agree?

44–10 Nuclear power plants use nuclear fission reactions to generate steam to run steam-turbine generators. How does the nuclear reaction produce heat?

44–11 There are cases in which a nucleus having too few neutrons for stability can capture one of the electrons in the K shell of the atom. What is the effect of this process on N, A, and Z? Is this the same effect as that of β^+ emission? Might there be situations in which K capture is energetically possible while β^+ emission is not? Explain.

44–12 Is it possible that some parts of the universe contain antimatter whose atoms have nuclei made of antiprotons and antineutrons, surrounded by positrons? How could we detect this condition without actually going there? What problems might arise if we actually *did* go there?

44–13 When X-rays are used to diagnose stomach disorders such as ulcers, the patient first drinks a thick mixture of (insoluble) barium sulfate and water. What does this do? What is the significance of the choice of barium for this purpose?

44–14 Why are so many health hazards associated with fission fragments that are produced during fission of heavy nuclei?

Exercises

Section 44–1   Properties of Nuclei

44–1 How many protons and how many neutrons are there in a nucleus of

a) neon, $^{21}_{10}$Ne?   b) zinc, $^{65}_{30}$Zn?   c) silver, $^{108}_{47}$Ag?

44–2 Consider the three nuclei of Exercise 44–1.

a) Estimate the radius of each nucleus.

b) Estimate the surface area of each.

c) Estimate the volume of each.

d) Determine the mass density (in kilograms per cubic meter) for each. (Assume that the mass is A atomic mass units.)

e) Determine the particle density (in particles per cubic meter) for each.

44–3 Calculate

a) the mass defect,

b) the binding energy, and

c) the binding energy per nucleon for the common isotope of nitrogen, ^{14}N.

44–4 Calculate the binding energy (in MeV) and the binding energy per nucleon of

a) the deuterium nucleus, $^{2}_{1}$H;

b) the helium nucleus, $^{4}_{2}$He.

c) How do the results of parts (a) and (b) compare?

Section 44–2   Nuclear Stability

Section 44–3   Radioactive Transformations

44–5 Tritium is an unstable isotope of hydrogen, $^{3}_{1}$H; its mass, including one electron, is 3.01605 u.

a) Show that it must be unstable with respect to beta decay because $^{3}_{2}$He plus an emitted electron has less total mass.

b) Determine the total kinetic energy of the decay products, taking care to account for the electron masses correctly.

44–6 A radium (^{226}Ra) nucleus undergoes alpha emission, leading to radon (^{222}Rn). The masses, including all electrons in each atom, are 226.0254 u and 222.0163 u, respectively. Find the maximum kinetic energy that the emitted alpha particle can have. Neglect the small recoil kinetic energy of the ^{222}Rn nucleus.

44–7 A radioactive isotope has a half-life of 76.0 min. A sample is prepared that has an initial activity of 16.0×10^{10} Bq.

a) How many radioactive nuclei are initially present in the sample?

b) How many are present after 76.0 min? What is the activity at this time?

c) Repeat part (b) for a time of 152 min after the sample is first prepared.

44–8 The common isotope of uranium, ^{238}U, has a half-life of 4.56×10^9 years, decaying to ^{234}Th by alpha emission.

a) What is the decay constant?

b) What mass of uranium is required for an activity of 1 curie?

c) How many alpha particles are emitted per second by 10.0 g of uranium?

44–9 The common isotope of radium, ^{226}Ra, has a half-life of 1590 yr, decaying to ^{222}Rn by alpha emission.

a) What is the decay constant?

b) What mass of radium is required for an activity of 1 curie?

c) How many alpha particles are emitted per second by 10.0 g of radium?

Section 44–4   Radiation and the Life Sciences

44–10 In an experimental radiation therapy an equivalent dose of 0.400 rem is given to a localized area of tissue with a mass of 0.150 kg by 0.800-MeV protons.

a) What is the absorbed dose in rad?

b) How many protons are absorbed by the tissue?

c) How many alpha particles of the same energy of 0.800 MeV are required to deliver the same equivalent dose of 0.400 rem?

44–11 In a diagnostic X-ray procedure, 5.00×10^{10} photons are absorbed by tissue with a mass of 0.600 kg. The X-ray wavelength is 0.0200 nm.

a) What is the total energy absorbed by the tissue?

b) What is the equivalent dose in rem?

Section 44–5   Nuclear Reactions

Section 44–6   Nuclear Fission

Section 44–7   Nuclear Fusion

44–12 Consider the nuclear reaction

$$^{4}_{2}\text{He} + ^{7}_{3}\text{Li} \rightarrow ^{10}_{5}\text{B} + ^{1}_{0}\text{n}.$$

Is energy absorbed or liberated? How much?

44–13 Consider the nuclear reaction

$$^{2}_{1}H + ^{9}_{4}Be \rightarrow ^{7}_{3}Li + ^{4}_{2}He.$$

a) How much energy is liberated?

b) Estimate the threshold energy for this reaction.

44–14 In the fission of one ^{238}U nucleus, 200 MeV of energy are released. Express this energy in joules per mole and compare with typical heats of combustion, which are of the order of 1.0×10^{5} J·mol^{-1}.

44–15 Consider the fusion reaction

$$^{2}_{1}H + ^{2}_{1}H \rightarrow ^{3}_{2}He + ^{1}_{0}n.$$

a) Compute the energy liberated in this reaction in MeV and in joules.

b) Compute the energy *per mole* of deuterium, remembering that the gas is diatomic, and compare it with the heat of combustion of diatomic molecular hydrogen, about 2.9×10^{5} J·mol^{-1}.

44–16 Calculate the energy released in the fusion reaction

$$^{2}_{1}H + ^{3}_{1}H \rightarrow ^{4}_{2}He + ^{1}_{0}n.$$

The atomic mass of $^{3}_{1}H$ (tritium) is 3.01605 u.

Section 44–8   Particle Accelerators

44–17 Deuterons in a cyclotron travel in a circle with radius 32.0 cm just before emerging from the dees. The frequency of the applied alternating voltage is 4.00 MHz. Find

a) the magnetic field;

b) the speed and energy of the deuterons upon emergence.

44–18 The magnetic field in a cyclotron that is accelerating protons is 0.750 T.

a) How many times per second should the potential across the dees reverse? (This is twice the frequency of the oscillating potential.)

b) The maximum radius of the cyclotron is 0.250 m. What is the maximum speed of the proton?

c) Through what potential difference would the proton have to be accelerated to give it the same speed as calculated in part (b)?

44–19 A high-energy beam of alpha particles collides with a stationary helium gas target. What must be the total energy of a beam particle if the available energy in the collision is 12.0 GeV?

Section 44–9   Fundamental Particles

Section 44–10   High-Energy Physics

44–20 A neutral pion at rest decays into two gamma-ray photons. Find the energy, frequency, and wavelength of each photon.

44–21 If two gamma-ray photons of the same energy are produced in $e^{+}e^{-}$ annihilation, find the energy, frequency, and wavelength of each photon.

44–22 Determine the electric charge, baryon number, strangeness quantum number, and charm quantum number for the following quark combinations:

a) *uus*,   b) $c\bar{s}$,   c) $\overline{ddu}$,   d) $\bar{c}b$.

44–23 Beams of π^{-} mesons are being used experimentally in the treatment of cancer. What is the minimum total energy a pion can release in a tumor? (That is, what energy is released when a π^{-} at rest decays to stable products? The actual energy deposited will be increased over this by the initial kinetic energy of the π^{-}.)

 Problems

44–24 Compute the approximate density of nuclear matter, and compare your result with typical densities of ordinary matter.

44–25 The starship *Enterprise*, of television and movie fame, is powered by the controlled combination of matter and antimatter. If the entire 400-kg antimatter fuel supply of the *Enterprise* combines with matter, how much energy is released?

44–26 A 70.0-kg person experiences a whole-body exposure to alpha radiation with energy of 1.50 MeV. A total of 5.00×10^{12} alpha particles are absorbed.

a) What is the absorbed dose in rad?

b) What is the equivalent dose in rem?

c) If the source is 0.0100 g of ^{226}Ra (half-life 1590 years) somewhere in the body, what is the activity of this source?

d) If all the alpha particles produced are absorbed, what time is required for this dose to be delivered?

44–27 A ^{60}Co source with activity 15.0 Ci is imbedded in a tumor that has a mass of 0.500 kg. The Co source emits gamma-ray photons with average energy of 1.25 MeV. Half the photons are absorbed in the tumor, and half escape.

a) What energy is delivered to the tumor per second?

b) What absorbed dose (in rad) is delivered per second?

c) What equivalent dose (in rem) is delivered per second if the RBE for these gamma rays is 0.70?

d) What exposure time is required for an equivalent dose of 200 rem?

44–28 The nucleus $^{15}_{8}O$ has a half-life of 2.0 min. $^{19}_{8}O$ has a half-life of 0.50 min.

a) If at some time a sample contains equal amounts of $^{15}_{8}O$ and $^{19}_{8}O$, what is the ratio of $^{15}_{8}O$ to $^{19}_{8}O$ after 2.0 min?

b) After 10.0 min?

44–29 The unstable isotope ^{40}K is used for dating rock samples. Its half-life is 2.40×10^8 years.

a) How many decays occur per second in a sample containing 6.00×10^{-6} g of ^{40}K?

b) What is the activity of the sample in curies?

44–30 An unstable isotope of cobalt, ^{60}Co, has one more neutron in its nucleus than the stable ^{59}Co and is a beta emitter with a half-life of 5.30 years. This isotope is widely used in medicine. A certain radiation source in a hospital contains 0.0400 g of ^{60}Co.

a) What is the decay constant for this isotope?

b) How many atoms are in the source?

c) How many decays occur per second?

d) What is the activity of the source in curies? How does this compare with the activity of an equal mass of radium (^{226}Ra; half-life 1590 yr)?

44–31 A free neutron at rest decays into a proton, an electron, and a neutrino, with a half-life of about 15 min. Calculate the total kinetic energy of the decay products.

44–32

a) What is the binding energy of the least strongly bound proton in $^{12}_{6}C$?

b) The least strongly bound neutron in $^{13}_{6}C$?

44–33 Consider the nuclear reaction

$$^{2}_{1}H + ^{14}_{7}N \rightarrow ^{6}_{3}Li + ^{10}_{5}B.$$

Is energy absorbed or liberated? How much?

44–34 The atomic mass of $^{56}_{26}Fe$ is 55.934939 u, and the atomic mass of $^{56}_{27}Co$ is 55.939847 u.

a) Which of these nuclei will decay into the other?

b) What type of decay will occur?

c) How much kinetic energy will the products of the decay have?

44–35 A K^+ meson at rest decays into two π mesons.

a) What are the allowed combinations of π^0, π^+, and π^- as decay products?

b) Find the total kinetic energy of the π mesons.

44–36 The measured energy width of the ϕ meson is 4.0 MeV, and its mass is 1020 MeV/c^2. Using the uncertainty principle, Eq. (42–10), estimate the lifetime of the ϕ meson.

44–37 A ϕ meson (Problem 44–36) at rest decays via $\phi \rightarrow K^+ K^-$.

a) Find the kinetic energy of the K^+ meson. (Assume that the two decay products share kinetic energy equally, since their masses are almost equal.)

b) Suggest a reason why the decay $\phi \rightarrow K^+ K^- \pi^0$ has not been observed.

c) Suggest reasons why the decays $\phi \rightarrow K^+ \pi^-$ and $\phi \rightarrow K^+ \mu^-$ have not been observed.

Challenge Problems

44–38 A patient is given a 2.0 μCi dose of radioactively labeled calcium; the radioactive isotope has a half-life of 2.0 hr. Assuming that the entire dose remains in the body, how much time must elapse before the activity of the radioactive calcium is 8.5 counts·min^{-1}, which is about three times the normal background of 3 counts·min^{-1}?

44–39 An Ω^- particle at rest decays into a Λ and a K^-. (See Table 44–4.)

a) Find the total kinetic energy of the decay products.

b) What fraction of the energy is carried off by each particle? (For simplicity, use nonrelativistic momentum and kinetic-energy expressions.)

APPENDIXES

Appendix A

THE INTERNATIONAL SYSTEM OF UNITS

The Système International d'Unités, abbreviated SI, is the system developed by the General Conference on Weights and Measures and adopted by nearly all the industrial nations of the world. It is based on the mksa (meter-kilogram-second-ampere) system. The following material is adapted from NBS Special Publication 330 (1981 edition) of the National Bureau of Standards.

Quantity	Name of unit	Symbol	
SI base units			
length	meter	m	
mass	kilogram	kg	
time	second	s	
electric current	ampere	A	
thermodynamic temperature	kelvin	K	
luminous intensity	candela	cd	
amount of substance	mole	mol	
SI derived units			**Equivalent units**
area	square meter	m^2	
volume	cubic meter	m^3	
frequency	hertz	Hz	s^{-1}
mass density (density)	kilogram per cubic meter	$kg \cdot m^{-3}$	
speed, velocity	meter per second	$m \cdot s^{-1}$	
angular velocity	radian per second	$rad \cdot s^{-1}$	
acceleration	meter per second squared	$m \cdot s^{-2}$	
angular acceleration	radian per second squared	$rad \cdot s^{-2}$	
force	newton	N	$kg \cdot m \cdot s^{-2}$
pressure (mechanical stress)	pascal	Pa	$N \cdot m^{-2}$
kinematic viscosity	square meter per second	$m^2 \cdot s^{-1}$	
dynamic viscosity	newton-second per square meter	$N \cdot s \cdot m^{-2}$	
work, energy, quantity of heat	joule	J	$N \cdot m$
power	watt	W	$J \cdot s^{-1}$
quantity of electricity	coulomb	C	$A \cdot s$
potential difference, electromotive force	volt	V	$W \cdot A^{-1}$, $J \cdot C^{-1}$
electric field strength	volt per meter	$V \cdot m^{-1}$	$N \cdot C^{-1}$
electric resistance	ohm	Ω	$V \cdot A^{-1}$
capacitance	farad	F	$A \cdot s \cdot V^{-1}$

Quantity	Name of unit	Symbol	Equivalent units
magnetic flux	weber	Wb	$V \cdot s$
inductance	henry	H	$V \cdot s \cdot A^{-1}$
magnetic flux density	tesla	T	$Wb \cdot m^{-2}$
magnetic field strength	ampere per meter	$A \cdot m^{-1}$	
magnetomotive force	ampere	A	
luminous flux	lumen	lm	$cd \cdot sr$
luminance	candela per square meter	$cd \cdot m^{-2}$	
illuminance	lux	lx	$lm \cdot m^{-2}$
wave number	1 per meter	m^{-1}	
entropy	joule per kelvin	$J \cdot K^{-1}$	
specific heat capacity	joule per kilogram kelvin	$J \cdot kg^{-1} \cdot K^{-1}$	
thermal conductivity	watt per meter kelvin	$W \cdot m^{-1} \cdot K^{-1}$	
radiant intensity	watt per steradian	$W \cdot sr^{-1}$	
activity (of a radioactive source)	becquerel	Bq	s^{-1}
radiation dose	gray	Gy	$J \cdot kg^{-1}$
radiation dose equivalent	sievert	Sv	$J \cdot kg^{-1}$
SI supplementary units			
plane angle	radian	rad	
solid angle	steradian	sr	

DEFINITIONS OF SI UNITS

meter (m)   The *meter* is the length equal to the distance traveled by light, in vacuum, in a time of 1/299,792,458 second.

kilogram (kg)   The *kilogram* is the unit of mass; it is equal to the mass of the international prototype of the kilogram. (The international prototype of the kilogram is a particular cylinder of platinum-iridium alloy that is preserved in a vault at Sèvres, France, by the International Bureau of Weights and Measures.)

second (s)   The *second* is the duration of 9,192,631,770 periods of the radiation corresponding to the transition between the two hyperfine levels of the ground state of the cesium-133 atom.

ampere (A)   The *ampere* is that constant current that, if maintained in two straight parallel conductors of infinite length, of negligible circular cross section, and placed 1 meter apart in vacuum, would produce between these conductors a force equal to 2×10^{-7} newton per meter of length.

kelvin (K)   The *kelvin*, unit of thermodynamic temperature, is the fraction 1/273.16 of the thermodynamic temperature of the triple point of water.

ohm (Ω)   The *ohm* is the electric resistance between two points of a conductor when a constant difference of poten-

tial of 1 volt, applied between these two points, produces in this conductor a current of 1 ampere, this conductor not being the source of any electromotive force.

coulomb (C)   The *coulomb* is the quantity of electricity transported in 1 second by a current of 1 ampere.

candela (cd)   The *candela* is the luminous intensity, in a given direction, of a source that emits monochromatic radiation of frequency 540×10^{12} hertz and that has a radiant intensity in that direction of 1/683 watt per steradian.

mole (mol)   The *mole* is the amount of substance of a system that contains as many elementary entities as there are carbon atoms in 0.012 kg of carbon 12. The elementary entities must be specified and may be atoms, molecules, ions, electrons, other particles, or specified groups of such particles.

newton (N)   The *newton* is that force that gives to a mass of 1 kilogram an acceleration of 1 meter per second per second.

joule (J)   The *joule* is the work done when the point of application of 1 newton is displaced a distance of 1 meter in the direction of the force.

watt (W)   The *watt* is the power that gives rise to the production of energy at the rate of 1 joule per second.

volt (V)   The *volt* is the difference of electric potential between two points of a conducting wire carrying a constant current of 1 ampere, when the power dissipated between these points is equal to 1 watt.

weber (Wb)   The *weber* is the magnetic flux that, linking a circuit of one turn, produces in it an electromotive force of 1 volt as it is reduced to zero at a uniform rate in 1 second.

lumen (lm)   The *lumen* is the luminous flux emitted in a solid angle of 1 steradian by a uniform point source having an intensity of 1 candela.

farad (F)   The *farad* is the capacitance of a capacitor between the plates of which there appears a difference of potential of 1 volt when it is charged by a quantity of electricity equal to 1 coulomb.

henry (H)   The *henry* is the inductance of a closed circuit in which an electromotive force of 1 volt is produced when the electric current in the circuit varies uniformly at a rate of 1 ampere per second.

radian (rad)   The *radian* is the plane angle between two radii of a circle that cut off on the circumference an arc equal in length to the radius.

steradian (sr)   The *steradian* is the solid angle that, having its vertex in the center of a sphere, cuts off an area of the surface of the sphere equal to that of a square with sides of length equal to the radius of the sphere.

SI Prefixes   The names of multiples and submultiples of SI units may be formed by application of the prefixes listed in Table 1–1, page 6.

Appendix B

USEFUL MATHEMATICAL RELATIONS

ALGEBRA

$$a^{-x} = \frac{1}{a^x} \qquad a^{(x+y)} = a^x a^y \qquad a^{(x-y)} = \frac{a^x}{a^y}$$

Logarithms: If $\log a = x$, then $a = 10^x$. $\log a + \log b = \log (ab)$ $\log a - \log b = \log (a/b)$ $\log (a^n) = n \log a$

If $\ln a = x$, then $a = e^x$. $\ln a + \ln b = \ln (ab)$ $\ln a - \ln b = \ln (a/b)$ $\ln (a^n) = n \ln a$

Quadratic formula: If $ax^2 + bx + c = 0$, $x = \dfrac{-b \pm \sqrt{b^2 - 4ac}}{2a}$.

BINOMIAL THEOREM

$$(a + b)^n = a^n + na^{n-1}b + \frac{n(n-1)a^{n-2}b^2}{2!} + \frac{n(n-1)(n-2)a^{n-3}b^3}{3!} + \cdots$$

TRIGONOMETRY

In the right triangle ABC, $x^2 + y^2 = r^2$.

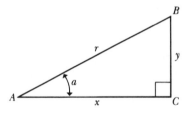

Definitions of the trigonometric functions: $\sin a = y/r$ $\cos a = x/r$ $\tan a = y/x$

Identities: $\sin^2 a + \cos^2 a = 1$ $\tan a = \dfrac{\sin a}{\cos a}$

$\sin 2a = 2 \sin a \cos a$ $\cos 2a = \cos^2 a - \sin^2 a = 2 \cos^2 a - 1$

$\sin \frac{1}{2}a = \sqrt{\dfrac{1 - \cos a}{2}}$ $\cos \frac{1}{2}a = \sqrt{\dfrac{1 + \cos a}{2}}$

$\sin (-a) = -\sin a$ $\sin (a \pm b) = \sin a \cos b \pm \cos a \sin b$

$\cos (-a) = \cos a$ $\cos (a \pm b) = \cos a \cos b \mp \sin a \sin b$

$\sin (a \pm \pi/2) = \pm\cos a$ $\sin a + \sin b = 2 \sin \frac{1}{2}(a + b) \cos \frac{1}{2}(a - b)$

$\cos (a \pm \pi/2) = \mp\sin a$ $\cos a + \cos b = 2 \cos \frac{1}{2}(a + b) \cos \frac{1}{2}(a - b)$

GEOMETRY

Circumference of circle of radius r: $C = 2\pi r$

Area of circle of radius r: $A = \pi r^2$

Volume of sphere of radius r: $V = 4\pi r^3/3$

Surface area of sphere of radius r: $A = 4\pi r^2$

Volume of cylinder of radius r and height h: $V = \pi r^2 h$

Appendix C

THE GREEK ALPHABET

Name	Capital	Lowercase	Name	Capital	Lowercase
Alpha	A	α	Nu	N	ν
Beta	B	β	Xi	Ξ	ξ
Gamma	Γ	γ	Omicron	O	o
Delta	Δ	δ	Pi	Π	π
Epsilon	E	ϵ	Rho	P	ρ
Zeta	Z	ζ	Sigma	Σ	σ
Eta	H	η	Tau	T	τ
Theta	Θ	θ	Upsilon	Υ	υ
Iota	I	ι	Phi	Φ	ϕ
Kappa	K	κ	Chi	X	χ
Lambda	Λ	λ	Psi	Ψ	ψ
Mu	M	μ	Omega	Ω	ω

Appendix D

PERIODIC TABLE OF THE ELEMENTS

Period	IA	IIA	IIIB	IVB	VB	VIB	VIIB	VIIIB	VIIIB	VIIIB	IB	IIB	IIIA	IVA	VA	VIA	VIIA	Noble gases
1	1 **H** 1.008																	2 **He** 4.003
2	3 **Li** 6.941	4 **Be** 9.012											5 **B** 10.811	6 **C** 12.011	7 **N** 14.007	8 **O** 15.999	9 **F** 18.998	10 **Ne** 20.179
3	11 **Na** 22.990	12 **Mg** 24.305											13 **Al** 26.982	14 **Si** 28.086	15 **P** 30.974	16 **S** 32.064	17 **Cl** 35.453	18 **Ar** 39.948
4	19 **K** 39.098	20 **Ca** 40.08	21 **Sc** 44.956	22 **Ti** 47.90	23 **V** 50.942	24 **Cr** 51.996	25 **Mn** 54.938	26 **Fe** 55.847	27 **Co** 58.933	28 **Ni** 58.70	29 **Cu** 63.546	30 **Zn** 65.38	31 **Ga** 69.72	32 **Ge** 72.59	33 **As** 74.922	34 **Se** 78.96	35 **Br** 79.904	36 **Kr** 83.80
5	37 **Rb** 85.468	38 **Sr** 87.62	39 **Y** 88.906	40 **Zr** 91.22	41 **Nb** 92.906	42 **Mo** 95.94	43 **Tc** (99)	44 **Ru** 101.07	45 **Rh** 102.905	46 **Pd** 106.4	47 **Ag** 107.868	48 **Cd** 112.41	49 **In** 114.82	50 **Sn** 118.69	51 **Sb** 121.75	52 **Te** 127.60	53 **I** 126.905	54 **Xe** 131.30
6	55 **Cs** 132.905	56 **Ba** 137.33	57 **La** 138.905	72 **Hf** 178.49	73 **Ta** 180.948	74 **W** 183.85	75 **Re** 186.2	76 **Os** 190.2	77 **Ir** 192.22	78 **Pt** 195.09	79 **Au** 196.966	80 **Hg** 200.59	81 **Tl** 204.37	82 **Pb** 207.19	83 **Bi** 208.2	84 **Po** (210)	85 **At** (210)	86 **Rn** (222)
7	87 **Fr** (223)	88 **Ra** (226)	89 **Ac** (227)	104 **Rf(?)** (261)	105 **Ha(?)** (262)	106 (257)	107 (260)											

58 **Ce** 140.12	59 **Pr** 140.907	60 **Nd** 144.24	61 **Pm** (145)	62 **Sm** 150.35	63 **Eu** 151.96	64 **Gd** 157.25	65 **Tb** 158.925	66 **Dy** 162.50	67 **Ho** 164.930	68 **Er** 167.26	69 **Tm** 168.934	70 **Yb** 173.04	71 **Lu** 174.96
90 **Th** (232)	91 **Pa** (231)	92 **U** (238)	93 **Np** (239)	94 **Pu** (239)	95 **Am** (240)	96 **Cm** (242)	97 **Bk** (245)	98 **Cf** (246)	99 **Es** (247)	100 **Fm** (249)	101 **Md** (256)	102 **No** (254)	103 **Lr** (257)

For each element the average atomic mass of the mixture of isotopes occurring in nature is shown. For elements having no stable isotope, the approximate atomic mass of the most common isotope is shown in parentheses.

Appendix E

UNIT CONVERSION FACTORS

LENGTH

$1\ m = 100\ cm = 1000\ mm = 10^6\ \mu m = 10^9\ nm$
$1\ km = 1000\ m = 0.6214\ mi$
$1\ m = 3.281\ ft = 39.37\ in.$
$1\ cm = 0.3937\ in.$
$1\ in. = 2.540\ cm$
$1\ ft = 30.48\ cm$
$1\ yd = 91.44\ cm$
$1\ mi = 5280\ ft = 1.609\ km$
$1\ \text{Å} = 10^{-10}\ m = 10^{-8}\ cm = 10^{-1}\ nm$
$1\ \text{nautical mile} = 6080\ ft$
$1\ \text{light year} = 9.461 \times 10^{15}\ m$

AREA

$1\ cm^2 = 0.155\ in^2$
$1\ m^2 = 10^4\ cm^2 = 10.76\ ft^2$
$1\ in^2 = 6.452\ cm^2$
$1\ ft^2 = 144\ in^2 = 0.0929\ m^2$

VOLUME

$1\ \text{liter} = 1000\ cm^3 = 10^{-3}m^3 = 0.03531\ ft^3 = 61.02\ in^3$
$1\ ft^3 = 0.02832\ m^3 = 28.32\ \text{liters} = 7.477\ \text{gallons}$
$1\ \text{gallon} = 3.788\ \text{liters}$

TIME

$1\ min = 60\ s$
$1\ hr = 3600\ s$
$1\ da = 86{,}400\ s$
$1\ yr = 365.24\ da = 3.156 \times 10^7\ s$

ANGLE

$1\ rad = 57.30° = 180°/\pi$
$1° = 0.01745\ rad = \pi/180\ rad$
$1\ \text{revolution} = 360° = 2\pi\ rad$
$1\ rev \cdot min^{-1}\ (rpm) = 0.1047\ rad \cdot s^{-1}$

SPEED

$1\ m \cdot s^{-1} = 3.281\ ft \cdot s^{-1}$
$1\ ft \cdot s^{-1} = 0.3048\ m \cdot s^{-1}$
$1\ mi \cdot min^{-1} = 60\ mi \cdot hr^{-1} = 88\ ft \cdot s^{-1}$
$1\ km \cdot hr^{-1} = 0.2778\ m \cdot s^{-1} = 0.6214\ mi \cdot hr^{-1}$
$1\ mi \cdot hr^{-1} = 1.466\ ft \cdot s^{-1} = 0.4470\ m \cdot s^{-1} = 1.609\ km \cdot hr^{-1}$
$1\ furlong \cdot fortnight^{-1} = 1.662 \times 10^{-4}\ m \cdot s^{-1}$

ACCELERATION

$1\ m \cdot s^{-2} = 100\ cm \cdot s^{-2} = 3.281\ ft \cdot s^{-2}$
$1\ cm \cdot s^{-2} = 0.01\ m \cdot s^{-2} = 0.03281\ ft \cdot s^{-2}$
$1\ ft \cdot s^{-2} = 0.3048\ m \cdot s^{-2} = 30.48\ cm \cdot s^{-2}$
$1\ mi \cdot hr^{-1} \cdot s^{-1} = 1.467\ ft \cdot s^{-2}$

MASS

$1\ kg = 10^3\ g = 0.0685\ slug$
$1\ g = 6.85 \times 10^{-5}\ slug$
$1\ slug = 14.59\ kg$
$1\ u = 1.661 \times 10^{-27}\ kg$
$1\ kg$ has a weight of $2.205\ lb$ when $g = 9.80\ m \cdot s^{-2}$

FORCE

$1\ N = 10^5\ dyn = 0.2248\ lb$
$1\ lb = 4.448\ N = 4.448 \times 10^5\ dyn$

PRESSURE

$1\ Pa = 1\ N \cdot m^{-2} = 1.451 \times 10^{-4}\ lb \cdot in^{-2} = 0.209\ lb \cdot ft^{-2}$
$1\ bar = 10^5\ Pa$
$1\ lb \cdot in^{-2} = 6891\ Pa$
$1\ lb \cdot ft^{-2} = 47.85\ Pa$
$1\ atm = 1.013 \times 10^5\ Pa = 1.013\ bar$
$\quad\quad = 14.7\ lb \cdot in^{-2} = 2117\ lb \cdot ft^{-2}$
$1\ mm\ Hg = 1\ torr = 133.3\ Pa$

ENERGY

$1\ J = 10^7\ ergs = 0.239\ cal$
$1\ cal = 4.186\ J$ (based on 15° calorie)
$1\ ft \cdot lb = 1.356\ J$
$1\ Btu = 1055\ J = 252\ cal = 778\ ft \cdot lb$
$1\ eV = 1.602 \times 10^{-19}\ J$
$1\ kWh = 3.600 \times 10^6\ J$

MASS–ENERGY EQUIVALENCE

$1\ kg \leftrightarrow 8.988 \times 10^{16}\ J$
$1\ u \leftrightarrow 931.5\ MeV$
$1\ eV \leftrightarrow 1.073 \times 10^{-9}\ u$

POWER

$1\ W = 1\ J \cdot s^{-1}$
$1\ hp = 746\ W = 550\ ft \cdot lb \cdot s^{-1}$
$1\ Btu \cdot hr^{-1} = 0.293\ W$

Appendix F

NUMERICAL CONSTANTS

FUNDAMENTAL PHYSICAL CONSTANTS

Name	Symbol	Value
Speed of light	c	$2.9979 \times 10^8 \text{ m} \cdot \text{s}^{-1}$
Charge of electron	e	$1.602 \times 10^{-19} \text{ C}$
Gravitational constant	G	$6.673 \times 10^{-11} \text{ N} \cdot \text{m}^2 \cdot \text{kg}^{-2}$
Planck's constant	h	$6.626 \times 10^{-34} \text{ J} \cdot \text{s}$
Boltzmann's constant	k	$1.381 \times 10^{-23} \text{ J} \cdot \text{K}^{-1}$
Avogadro's number	N_0	$6.022 \times 10^{23} \text{ molecules} \cdot \text{mol}^{-1}$
Gas constant	R	$8.314 \text{ J} \cdot \text{mol}^{-1} \cdot \text{K}^{-1}$
Mass of electron	m_e	$9.110 \times 10^{-31} \text{ kg}$
Mass of neutron	m_n	$1.675 \times 10^{-27} \text{ kg}$
Mass of proton	m_p	$1.673 \times 10^{-27} \text{ kg}$
Permittivity of free space	ϵ_0	$8.854 \times 10^{-12} \text{ C}^2 \cdot \text{N}^{-1} \cdot \text{m}^{-2}$
	$1/4\pi\epsilon_0$	$8.987 \times 10^9 \text{ N} \cdot \text{m}^2 \cdot \text{C}^{-2}$
Permeability of free space	μ_0	$4\pi \times 10^{-7} \text{ Wb} \cdot \text{A}^{-1} \cdot \text{m}^{-1}$

OTHER USEFUL CONSTANTS

Name	Symbol	Value
Mechanical equivalent of heat		$4.186 \text{ J} \cdot \text{cal}^{-1}$ (15° calorie)
Standard atmospheric pressure	1 atm	$1.013 \times 10^5 \text{ Pa}$
Absolute zero	0 K	$-273.15°\text{C}$
Electronvolt	1 eV	$1.602 \times 10^{-19} \text{ J}$
Atomic mass unit	1 u	$1.661 \times 10^{-27} \text{ kg}$
Electron rest energy	mc^2	0.511 MeV
Energy equivalent of 1 u	Mc^2	931.5 MeV
Volume of ideal gas (0°C and 1 atm)	V	$22.4 \text{ liter} \cdot \text{mol}^{-1}$
Acceleration due to gravity (sea level, at equator)	g	$9.78049 \text{ m} \cdot \text{s}^{-2}$

ASTRONOMICAL DATA

Body	Mass, kg	Radius, m	Orbit radius, m	Orbit period
Sun	1.99×10^{30}	6.95×10^8	—	—
Moon	7.36×10^{22}	1.74×10^6	0.38×10^9	27.3 d
Mercury	3.28×10^{23}	2.57×10^6	5.8×10^{10}	88.0 d
Venus	4.82×10^{24}	6.31×10^6	1.08×10^{11}	224.7 d
Earth	5.98×10^{24}	6.38×10^6	1.49×10^{11}	365.3 d
Mars	6.34×10^{23}	3.43×10^6	2.28×10^{11}	687.0 d
Jupiter	1.88×10^{27}	7.18×10^7	7.78×10^{11}	11.86 y
Saturn	5.63×10^{26}	6.03×10^7	1.43×10^{12}	29.46 y
Uranus	8.61×10^{25}	2.67×10^7	2.87×10^{12}	84.02 y
Neptune	9.99×10^{25}	2.48×10^7	4.49×10^{12}	164.8 y
Pluto	5×10^{23}	4×10^5	5.90×10^{12}	247.7 y

Answers to
Odd-Numbered Problems

CHAPTER 1

1–1 0.621 mi

1–3 153 in.^{3}

1–5 8.64×10^4 s; 3.15×10^7 s

1–7 35.3 mi·gal^{-1}

1–9 a) 0.2%   b) 0.007%   c) 0.06%

1–11 0.00382

1–13 5.50×10^3 kg·m^{-3}

1–15 10,000

1–17 1 km on a side

1–19 4000

1–21 6 km; 1 m

1–23 10^{15} dollars

1–25 10^{12}; no

1–27 12 in., at 45° to initial direction of line

1–29 a) 15 m, 53°   b) 26 m, 210°

1–31 a) 4.70 m, 8.14 m
   b) 10.6 km, -10.6 km
   c) -3.67 cm, 2.77 cm

1–33 a) 6.06 cm, 302°   b) 11.0 m, 240°
   c) 7.16 km, 107°

1–35 6.95 km, 63.2° N of E

1–37 a) 15 m, 53°   b) 26 m, 210°

1–39 a) 5.80 cm, 0.0°   b) 10.0 cm, 90.0°
   c) 10.0 cm, 270°

1–41 a) 1.17 cm, -1.04 cm
   b) 1.57 cm, 318°

1–43 $\sqrt{(x_2 - x_1)^2 + (y_2 - y_1)^2}$; arctan $\left(\dfrac{y_2 - y_1}{x_2 - x_1}\right)$

1–45 3.61 km, 18.3° S of E

1–47 b) $\theta = 120°$ or 240°
   c) $\sqrt{A^2 + B^2 - 2AB \cos \theta}$
   d) $\theta = 60°$ or 300°

CHAPTER 2

2–1 a) 15.0 mi·hr^{-1} b) 22.0 ft·s^{-1}

2–3 41 min

2–5 a) $+5.00$ m·s^{-1} b) $+12.0$ m·s^{-1}
   c) $+19.0$ m·s^{-1}

2–7 a) 5.0 m·s^{-1}; 10.0 m·s^{-1} b) 20.0 m·s^{-1}

2–9 a) 0; 1.00 m·s^{-2}; 1.50 m·s^{-2};
   2.50 m·s^{-2}; 2.50 m·s^{-2}; 1.00 m·s^{-2}; 0
   b) 2.5 m·s^{-2}; 0.8 m·s^{-2}; 0

2–11 12.0 m·s^{-2}

2–15 a) 5.13 ft·s^{-2} b) 477 ft

2–17 a) 52.7 ft·s^{-2} b) 373 ft·s^{-1} c) 1.53 s

2–19 a) 0; 6.25 m·s^{-2}; -11.2 m·s^{-2} b) 100 m;
   230 m; 320 m

2–21 a) 1.20×10^4 m·s^{-1} (12.0 km·s^{-1})   b) 96.4%
   c) 576 min

2–23 980 m

2–25 a) 122 m   b) 49.0 m·s^{-1}

2–27 a) 34.6 m·s^{-1} b) 49.6 m   c) 20.5 m·s^{-1}

2–29 a) 56.0 ft·s^{-1} b) 49.0 ft   c) 0
   d) 32.0 ft·s^{-2}, downward

2–31 a) 815 ft·s^{-2} b) $25.5g$ c) 1320 ft
   d) No, $a = 20.6g$ if constant

2–33 a) 6.0 m·s^{-1}, to the right   b) 13.5 m·s^{-1}, to
   the left   c) 12.0 m·s^{-1}, to the left

2–35 Man on shore: 29.0 min; man in boat: 41.6 min

2–37 3.6 m·s^{-2}

2–39 a) 9.0 m·s^{-1}; 11.0 m·s^{-1}; 13.0 m·s^{-1}
   b) 1.00 m·s^{-2} c) 8.0 m·s^{-1} d) 8.00 s
   e) 8.50 m

2–41 5.26 m from point directly below you

2–43 a) 180 m   b) 30.0 m·s^{-1}

2–45 a) 11.2 s   b) 38 m   c) Truck: 22.4 m·s^{-1};
   auto: 29.1 m·s^{-1}

2–47 a) 22.3 m   b) 1.22 s
2–49 a) 3.33 m·s^{-2} b) 5.00 m·s^{-1} c) 3.75 m
2–51 0.47 m
2–53 15.7 m
2–55 a) 12.3 s; 73.5 m   b) 2.21 m·s^{-1}
d) 9.79 m·s^{-1} e) No   f) 4.65 m·s^{-1};
25.8 s; 120 m
2–57 a) 27   b) 109

CHAPTER 3

3–1 a) -2.04 m·s^{-1}, $+1.17$ m·s^{-1} b) 2.36 m·s^{-1},
150°
3–3 a) -3.50 m·s^{-2}, 8.00 m·s^{-2} b) 8.73 m·s^{-2},
114°
3–5 a) 0.452 s   b) 5.76 m·s^{-1} c) 7.26 m·s^{-1},
37.6° below horizontal
3–7 a) 20.2 s   b) 3030 m   c) 150 m·s^{-1},
-198 m·s^{-1} d) Directly above where the box
lands
3–9 a) 0.64 ft   b) 5.76 ft
3–11 a) 0.682 s, 7.48 s   b) 30.0 m·s^{-1}, 33.3 m·s^{-1};
30.0 m·s^{-1}, -33.3 m·s^{-1} c) 50.0 m·s^{-1} at
53.1° below the horizontal
3–13 a) 1.04 m above ground   b) 0.668 m above
ground   c) Arrow hits ground before
reaching apple
3–15 a) 5.40 m·s^{-2}, upward   b) 10.5 s
3–17 a) 2.97×10^4 m·s^{-1} b) 5.92×10^{-3} m·s^{-2}
3–19 8.74 knots
3–21 a) 3.35 m·s^{-1}, 26.6° N of E   b) 333 s
c) 500 m
3–23 a) 5.00 m·s^{-1}, 143°   b) 7.21 m·s^{-1}, 124°
3–25 9.87 m·s^{-1}
3–27 a) 145 ft·s^{-1} b) 201 ft
3–29 a) 26.2 m·s^{-1} b) 17.1 m·s^{-1}, 40.1° below
horizontal
3–33 17.8 m·s^{-1}
3–35 91.1 km·hr^{-1} relative to hero; 140 km·hr^{-1}
relative to earth
3–37 a) 157 km·hr^{-1}, 26.6° N of W   b) 68.0° W
of N
3–39 $2v_0^2 \cos^2 (\phi + \theta)[\tan (\phi + \theta) - \tan \theta]/g \cos \theta = 2v_0^2 \sin \phi[\cos \phi - \tan \theta \sin \phi]/g \cos \theta$
3–41 $\Delta t = 0.500$ s: 23.40 m·s^{-2}, 54.2°; $\Delta t = 0.100$ s:
24.93 m·s^{-2}, 82.8°; $\Delta t = 0.0500$ s: 24.98 m·s^{-2},
86.4°; $\Delta t \rightarrow 0$: 25.0 m·s^{-2}, 90.0°

CHAPTER 4

4–1 30.3 N (right), 17.5 N (down)
4–3 a) 32.3 N   b) 16.2 N
4–5 a) 0.306 kg   b) 118 N
4–7 4.59 kg; 17.0 N
4–9 a) Gravity   b) Gravity force of earth on bottle

(downward) equal and opposite to gravity force
of bottle on earth (upward)
4–11 1200 N (270 lb)
4–13 a) 11.7 ft·s^{-2} b) 583 ft   c) 117 ft·s^{-1}
4–15 a) 8.44 kg   b) 160 m
4–17 a) 8.00×10^{14} m·s^{-2} b) 5.00×10^{-9} s
c) 7.29×10^{-16} N
4–19 46.6 N, at 90.0° clockwise from $+x$-direction
4–21 a) 200 N: $+173$ N, $+100$ N; 300 N: -212 N,
$+212$ N; 155 N: -93 N, -124 N   b) 230 N,
125°   c) 230 N, 305°
4–23 1770 N (398 lb)
4–25 a) 7.92 m·s^{-1} b) 52.3 m·s^{-2}, upward
c) 4970 N = 6.33w
4–27 0.150 N

CHAPTER 5

5–1 a) 5.1 lb   b) 2.3 s
5–3 a) 14 N   b) 16 N   c) (a) 2.3 N; (b) 4.5 N
5–5 a) 30.9 m   b) 12.3 m·s^{-1}
5–7 Low pressure: 0.0302; high pressure: 0.00646
5–9 a) 20.0 N   b) 40.0 N
5–11 a) 1350 N   b) 0.912°
5–13 a) 21.2 N, 21.2 N   b) 21.2 N
5–15 a) $w \sin \theta$ b) $2w \sin \theta$
5–17 a) $\mu_k(w_A + w_B)$ b) $\mu_k w_A$
5–19 61°
5–21 a) Held back   b) 600 N
5–23 a) $\mu_k w/(\cos \theta - \mu_k \sin \theta)$ b) $1/\tan \theta$
5–27 1.46×10^4 N
5–29 a) 48.0 N   b) $a = 2.65$ m·s^{-2}, downward   c) 0
5–33 a) 38.7°   b) 3.06 m·s^{-2} c) 2.29 s
5–35 a) String is vertical   b) String is
perpendicular to ceiling in each stage of motion
5–37 a) 1.40 m·s^{-2} b) 50.4 N
5–39 a) 4.90 m·s^{-2}, upward   b) 4.08 m·s^{-2},
downward   c) Yes, free fall
5–41 621 N; 161 N
5–43 $w \tan \theta$
5–45 26.7 N
5–47 a) 16.1 N   b) 9.71 N
5–49 b) 0.251
5–51 6.30 N
5–53 2.80 s; 7.84 m
5–55 a) Yes   b) 1.58 m·s^{-2}, down incline
5–57 a) 100-kg block descends   b) 0.658 m·s^{-2}
c) 424 N
5–59 $a_1 = 2m_2 g/(4m_1 + m_2)$, $a_2 = m_2 g/(4m_1 + m_2)$
5–61 a) 2.70 m·s^{-2} b) 112.5 N   c) 87.5 N
5–63 2.50 m above the floor
5–65 g/μ_s
5–67 a) Move up   b) Remains constant
c) Remains constant   d) Stop falling, just like
the monkey
5–69 a) $\mu_k w/(\cos \phi + \mu_k \sin \phi)$ b) 17°

CHAPTER 6

6–1 12.6 m·s^{-1}
6–3 $12.7°$
6–5   a) 7.11 s   b) No
6–7   a) 21.6 ft·s^{-2}, upward   b) 26.8 lb
6–9   a) 551 m   b) 6170 N
6–11   87.3 N; 2.54%
6–13 $6.14 \times 10^{24} \text{ kg}$
6–15 $2.35 \times 10^{-12} \text{ N}$, to the left
6–17 -39.5 m·s^{-2}; $+25.6 \text{ m·s}^{-2}$
6–19 $4G(m_2 - m_1)/d^2$, toward m_2
6–21 $7.40 \times 10^3 \text{ m·s}^{-1}$
6–23   a) $4230 \text{ rev·min}^{-1}$ b) $2.94 \times 10^4 \text{ m·s}^{-2}$
6–25   a) 20.0 m·s^{-1} b) 6.42 m·s^{-1}
6–27   b) 0.17   c) No
6–29   a) To the right   b) 42 m
6–31   a) $2.9 \times 10^{15} \text{ kg}$; $7.7 \times 10^{-3} \text{ m·s}^{-2}$
       b) 6.2 m·s^{-1}; yes
6–33 $2.58 \times 10^8 \text{ m}$
6–35   a) $+4.56 \times 10^{-10} \text{ m·s}^{-2}$; $+4.56 \times 10^{-10} \text{ m·s}^{-2}$
       b) $1.61 \times 10^{-11} \text{ N}$, $45.0°$
6–37 $3.59 \times 10^7 \text{ m}$
6–39 $\tau_{\max} = \left[\dfrac{4\pi^2 h \tan\theta}{g} \dfrac{\tan\theta + \mu_s}{1 - \mu_s \tan\theta} \right]^{1/2}$;
       $\tau_{\min} = \left[\dfrac{4\pi^2 h \tan\theta}{g} \dfrac{\tan\theta - \mu_s}{1 + \mu_s \tan\theta} \right]^{1/2}$

CHAPTER 7

7–1   320 J
7–3 $2.82 \times 10^4 \text{ J}$
7–5   a) 165 N   b) 1150 J   c) -1150 J
       d) 0; 0
7–7   a) 270 ft·lb   b) -210 ft·lb
       c) 0   d) 62 ft·lb
7–9   a) kx_1 b) kx_2 c) $\frac{1}{2}k(x_2^2 - x_1^2)$
7–11   1350 J
7–13   a) $1.85 \times 10^4 \text{ J}$ b) 4
7–15   159 J
7–17   a) 11.5 m·s^{-1} b) 11.5 m·s^{-1}
7–19   0.400 m
7–21   a) $v_0^2/2\mu_k g$ b) 353 ft
7–23 $3.35 \times 10^6 \text{ J}$
7–25   a) 277 N   b) 538 J
7–27 -0.426 J
7–29 8.33 m·s^{-1}
7–31 7.31 m·s^{-1}; yes
7–33 $1.59 \times 10^6 \text{ m}$
7–35   34.6 J
7–37   0.103 m
7–39   a) 0.866 m·s^{-1} b) 0.693 m·s^{-1}
7–41   2.55 m
7–43   a) 6.12 m·s^{-1} b) 3.16 m·s^{-1}
7–45   0.927 hp

7–47   a) $1.25 \times 10^4 \text{ J}$ b) 625 W
7–49   58 kW
7–51 $1.20 \times 10^3 \text{ m}^3\text{·s}^{-1}$
7–53   a) $1.61 \times 10^3 \text{ N}$ b) 51.8 hp   c) 25.6 hp
       d) 14%
7–55 $(v_0 \sin\theta)^2/2g$
7–57 2.21 m·s^{-1}
7–59   a) 294 N   b) 1764 J
7–61 6.93 m·s^{-1}
7–65   a) 0.233   b) -31.0 J
7–67   a) $1.20 \times 10^5 \text{ J}$ b) 1.39 W
7–69 $\sqrt{2Gm_E h/[R_E(R_E + h)]}$
7–71   a) 6.71 m·s^{-1} b) 1.25 cm
7–73   a) 3.87 m·s^{-1} b) 0.100 m
7–75 $0.01R_E = 63.8 \text{ km}$
7–77 $\sqrt{gR_E} = 7.91 \times 10^3 \text{ m·s}^{-1}$

CHAPTER 8

8–1   a) $3.00 \times 10^5 \text{ kg·m·s}^{-1}$ b) 60.0 m·s^{-1};
       42.4 m·s^{-1}
8–3   a) $-1.00 \times 10^6 \text{ m·s}^{-2}$ b) $-5.00 \times 10^3 \text{ N}$
       c) $4.00 \times 10^{-4} \text{ s}$
8–5 $5.48 \times 10^3 \text{ N}$; $1.72 \times 10^3 \text{ N}$
8–7   a) 7.80 m·s^{-1} b) -16.2 J
8–9   a) 0.0746 m·s^{-1} b) 0.150 m·s^{-1}
8–11   a) 3.40 m·s^{-1}, in Gretzky's direction
       b) -6790 J
8–13 2.73 m·s^{-1}
8–15   a) A: 14.6 m·s^{-1}; B: 10.4 m·s^{-1} b) 19.6%
8–17   a) 1.67 m·s^{-1} b) $8.33 \times 10^4 \text{ J}$
       c) 2.50 m·s^{-1}
8–19   a) 15.0 m·s^{-1} b) 25.0%
8–21 257 m·s^{-1}
8–23   a) 0.0732 m   b) 1800 J   c) 3.59 J
8–25   0.300-kg block: 0.840 m·s^{-1}, to the left;
       0.200-kg block: 0.960 m·s^{-1}, to the right
8–27 $4.6 \times 10^6 \text{ m}$ from the center of the earth
8–29   a) 20.0 m in front of the 1000-kg auto
       b) $7.00 \times 10^4 \text{ kg·m·s}^{-1}$ c) 23.3 m·s^{-1}
       d) $7.00 \times 10^4 \text{ kg·m·s}^{-1}$
8–31   75.0 kg
8–33   12.0 N
8–35 2.75 m·s^{-1}; 0.866 m·s^{-1}
8–37 244 m·s^{-1}
8–39   a) 0.653   b) 480 J   c) 1.28 J
8–41   a) 0.160 m·s^{-1} b) 0.150 kg
8–43   a) $m_A v_A/m_B$
8–47 0.885 m·s^{-1}, to the left
8–49   2.91 m
8–51 0.300 m·s^{-1}
8–55 $1.74 \times 10^6 \text{ m·s}^{-1}$; $7.40 \times 10^5 \text{ m·s}^{-1}$;
       $v_{Kr} = 1.53 v_{Ba}$
8–57   a) 3390 m   b) $6.40 \times 10^4 \text{ J}$
8–59   b) $\frac{1}{2}MV^2$

CHAPTER 9

9–1 a) 2.50 rad; 143°   b) 0.900 m   c) 61.4 cm
9–3 a) 3.20 rad·s^{-1}; 4.25 rad·s^{-1} b) 3.60 rad·s^{-1}; 6.75 rad·s^{-1}
9–7 a) 12.5 s   b) 7.96 rev
9–9 40.0 rad·s^{-2}; 405 rad
9–11 a) 16.0 rad·s^{-1} b) 30.7 rad·s^{-2}
9–13 1.34×10^5 rpm
9–15 a) 0.225 m·s^{-2}; 0; 0.225 m·s^{-2}
b) 0.225 m·s^{-2}; 0.471 m·s^{-2}; 0.522 m·s^{-2}
c) 0.225 m·s^{-2}; 0.942 m·s^{-2}; 0.969 m·s^{-2}
9–17 a) 0.0960 kg·m^2 b) 0.0480 kg·m^2
9–19 a) 4.00 kg·m^2 b) 16.0 kg·m^2
c) 2.40×10^{-3} kg·m^2
9–21 a) 398 J   b) 13.5 m
9–23 2.05 lb
9–25 a) 8.75 rad·s^{-1} b) 13.0 kg·m^2
9–27 a) 120 ft·lb, counterclockwise   b) 104 ft·lb, counterclockwise   c) 60.0 ft·lb, counterclockwise   d) 52.0 ft·lb, clockwise   e) 0   f) 0
9–29 2.65 N·m, counterclockwise
9–31 1.20 m·s^{-1}
9–33 3.75 rad·s^{-2}
9–35 a) 65.3 N   b) 16.2 m·s^{-1} c) 2.47 s   d) 261 N
9–37 3.92 m·s^{-2}; 7.85 N; 0.250
9–39 a) 15.7 N·m   b) 157 rad   c) 2.47×10^3 J   d) 2.47×10^3 J
9–41 a) 8.98 rad·s^{-1} b) 9.88×10^3 J   c) 494 W
9–43 a) 9550 N·m   b) 3.82×10^4 N   c) 62.8 m·s^{-1}
9–45 6.54×10^{-5} kg·m^2·s^{-1}
9–47 46 kg·m^2·s^{-1}
9–49 a) 25.8 kg·m^2·s^{-1} b) 4.78 rad·s^{-1} c) 38.7 J; 61.6 J; work done by the woman
9–51 a) 22.5 rad·s^{-1} b) 0.113 J   c) 0.113 J
9–53 0.827 rad·s^{-1}
9–55 0.297 rad·s^{-1}
9–57 a) 1.76 N   b) 5.36×10^3 rev·min^{-1}
9–59 b) 49.6°
9–61 $\sqrt{4g/3R}$
9–63 a) 362 rev·min^{-1} b) 500 W
9–65 $\sqrt{2gd(m_B - \mu_k m_A)/(m_A + m_B + I/R^2)}$
9–67 a) 82.8 N   b) 32.5 N   c) 45.2 s
9–69 0.710 s
9–71 0.730 m·s^{-2}; 6.09 rad·s^{-2}; 36.3 N; 21.1 N
9–73 $a = F/2M$; $\mathcal{F}_s = F/2$
9–75 2.45 m
9–77 0.576 J
9–79 4500 J
9–81 $0.371MR^2$
9–83 a) 4.49 rad·s^{-1} b) 1.37 cm   c) 1150 m·s^{-1}

CHAPTER 10

10–1 0.405 m to right of center of the 1.00-kg ball
10–3 (0.133 m, 0.133 m)
10–5 1200 N; 0.833 m from end where the 700-N force acts
10–7 a) 2040 N   b) 1360 N
10–11 a) 1.73w; 2.00w at 30.0° above horizontal (along strut)   b) 2.73w; 3.35w at 45.0° above horizontal (along strut)
10–13 53.3 N; 53.3 N
10–15 a) 1.12 m   b) Clockwise
10–17 2.13 m
10–19 b) 2.22 m   c) 2.68 m
10–21 4.05 m along the ladder, measured from the floor
10–23 a) 2.89 m   b) 161 N
10–25 a) 21.8°   b) 0.112 m   c) 0.529
10–27 a) 30 N (to left); 50 N (up)   b) 59°   c) 58 N   d) 4.0 m from the left-hand end
10–29 a) 960 N   b) 753 N
10–31 a) 390 N   b) 173 N
10–33 You: 1176 N; friend: 784 N; above
10–35 a) Slip: 16.7°; tip: 26.6°; slips first   b) Yes, tips first
10–37 a) A: 120 N; B: 480 N   b) 2.50 m
10–39 a) Left: 489 N; right: 561 N   b) 336 N   c) 354 N   d) 976 N

CHAPTER 11

11–1 0.125 s
11–3 a) 208 N·m^{-1} b) 120 N
11–5 a) 0.0513 J   b) 0.0160 m   c) 0.453 m·s^{-1}
11–7 54.8 N·m^{-1}
11–9 a) 0.167 s   b) 37.7 rad·s^{-1} c) 0.141 kg
11–11 0.118 m
11–13 a) 1.80 m   b) $-90.0° = -\dfrac{\pi}{2}$ rad   c) 162 J
d) $x(t) = (1.80 \text{ m}) \sin [(5.00 \text{ rad·s}^{-1})t]$
11–15 a) 75.8 m·s^{-2}; 3.02 m·s^{-1} b) −31.6 m·s^{-2}; 2.74 m·s^{-1} c) 0.0337 s
11–17 8.11 kg
11–19 0.0621 m
11–21 a) 2.70×10^{-7} kg·m^2 b) 4.26×10^{-5} N·m
11–23 1.21 s
11–25 a) 0.0419 kg·m^2 b) 1.26 rad·s^{-1}
11–27 a) 8530 m·s^{-2} b) 3410 N   c) 22.6 m·s^{-1}
11–29 0.852 s
11–31 1.33 s
11–33 a) 0.419 m·s^{-1} b) 0.877 m·s^{-2}, downward   c) 0.250 s   d) 0.559 m
11–35 a) 1.88 kg   b) 0.0693 m below equilibrium and moving upward   c) 22.0 N, upward

11–37 a) $m[g - 4\pi^2 f^2 A \cos(\omega t + \phi_0)]$ b) $4\pi^2 f_b^2 A$
11–39 1.08 m
11–41 a) $k_1 + k_2$ b) $k_1 + k_2$ c) $k_1 k_2/(k_1 + k_2)$
  d) $\sqrt{2}$
11–43 a) New period $= 2\pi\sqrt{(m_1 + m_2)/k}$;
  new amplitude $= A\sqrt{m_1/(m_1 + m_2)}$
  b) Yes, due to friction work; $m_1/(m_1 + m_2)$
  c) New period $= 2\pi\sqrt{(m_1 + m_2)/k}$;
  new amplitude $= A$ (unchanged)

CHAPTER 12

12–1 6.0×10^{11} Pa
12–3 a) 2.31×10^8 Pa   b) 0.072 mm
12–5 5.6×10^5 N·m^{-1}
12–7 2.0 mm
12–9 a) 6.4 Hz   b) 6.5×10^{10} Pa
12–11 a) -0.0503 m^3 b) 1.08×10^3 kg·m^{-3}
12–13 3.02×10^4 N
12–15 a) 1.4×10^3 N   b) 9.0×10^{-3} m
  c) 4.4×10^3 N
12–17 a) 1.0×10^{11} Pa   b) 1.02×10^8 Pa
12–19 a) 0.788 m   b) 0.700 m
12–21 a) 0.727 m   b) Copper: 2.5×10^8 Pa;
  steel: 5.0×10^8 Pa   c) Copper: 2.3×10^{-3};
  steel: 2.5×10^{-3}
12–23 5.0 cm
12–25 a) 9.8×10^{-4} m   b) 0.0294 J   c) 0.0090 J
  d) -0.0384 J   e) $+0.0384$ J

CHAPTER 13

13–1 1.11×10^3 kg·m^{-3}
13–3 0.0641 kg
13–5 a) 9.08×10^6 Pa   b) 1.61×10^5 N
13–7 1.66×10^5 Pa; 1.64 atm
13–9 a) 1.09×10^5 Pa   b) 1.05×10^5 Pa
  c) 1.05×10^5 Pa   d) 8.00×10^3 Pa; 60.0 torr
13–11 a) 1.90×10^{-3} m^3 b) 141 N
13–13 89.3%
13–15 a) 2940 N   b) 218 kg   c) 72.8%
13–17 2.86 Pa
13–19 a) 3.18 m·s^{-1} b) 0.166 m
13–21 30.7 m·s^{-1}
13–23 1.52×10^5 Pa
13–25 2.94×10^5 Pa
13–27 2.22×10^3 N, upward
13–29 24.1 Pa
13–31 9.59 cm·s^{-1}
13–33 a) 1.10×10^8 Pa   b) 1.08×10^3 kg·m^{-3};
  $+5.3\%$
13–35 a) 30.0%   b) 70.0%
13–37 a) 1.25×10^4 m^3 b) 13,900 kg

13–39 a) $M/\rho A$ b) $F/\rho Ag$ c) $2\pi\sqrt{m/\rho Ag}$
  d) 0.193 m   e) 3.42 s   f) 0.385 s
13–41 a) 1250 kg·m^{-3} b) D: 7.50 kg; E: 2.50 kg
13–43 a) 0.025 m   b) 490 Pa
13–45 a) 63.2%   b) 0.397 L
13–47 7.19×10^{-5} m
13–49 0.131 m
13–51 a) 0.250 m^3·s^{-1} b) 5.88×10^4 Pa
13–53 165 m·s^{-1}
13–55 b) 3.06 m
13–57 a) 4.33 cm·s^{-1} b) 10.7 cm·s^{-1}
13–59 a) 6.86×10^5 m^3·s^{-1} b) 0.686 m·s^{-1};
  1.37 m·s^{-1}; 3.43 m·s^{-1} c) 0.576 m;
  0.504 m; 0   d) 0.220 m   e) 0.879 m
  f) 1.37 m·s^{-1}; 2.74 m·s^{-1}; 6.86 m·s^{-1}
13–61 Air bubbles cause inaccuracies
13–63 7.02 N·m

CHAPTER 14

14–1 a) 16.7°C   b) 33.3°C   c) -7.8°C
14–3 77.3 K
14–5 600.46 K
14–7 0.065 m
14–9 -0.060%
14–11 0.4009 cm
14–13 499.73 mL
14–15 4.6×10^{-5} (C°)$^{-1}$
14–17 -5×10^{-5} (C°)$^{-1}$; 6.86×10^{-4} (C°)$^{-1}$
14–19 a) 7.4 mm   b) 1.1×10^8 Pa
14–21 a) 911 atm   b) 46.4°C
14–23 a) $+2.9 \times 10^{-6}$ m^3 b) -7.8 kg·m^{-3}
14–25 76.6 m
14–29 31.1 cm; 8.9 cm
14–31 5.07×10^7 Pa
14–33 27.2°C
14–35 a) -0.024% b) Gains 10 s   c) 1.9 C°

CHAPTER 15

15–1 4.80×10^4 J
15–3 1.91×10^5 J
15–5 a) 6.70×10^4 J   b) 447 s
15–7 a) 50.7 J   b) 3.65×10^4 J
15–9 3.07×10^3 J·kg^{-1}·(C°)$^{-1}$
15–11 1.25×10^5 J; 2.99×10^4 cal; 118 Btu
15–13 a) 2.53×10^4 J   b) 2.77×10^3 J
15–15 a) 38.3 min   b) 356 min
15–17 357 m·s^{-1}
15–19 3.50×10^3 W; 1.19×10^4 Btu·hr^{-1}
15–21 32.6°C
15–23 2.29 kg

15–25 11.5°C
15–27 33.0
15–29 0.234 C°
15–31 a) 300 J·s^{-1} b) 0.13 C°·s^{-1}
15–33 0.0551 kg
15–35 14.3°C
15–37 52.8°C
15–39 a) 44.7 m^3 b) 10.5 m^3
15–41 a) 77.3°C   b) Steady state
15–43 89.7°C; 119.2°C

CHAPTER 16

16–1 1.7 × 10^5 J
16–3 113.5°C
16–5 a) −6.7°C   b) 8.9 J·s^{-1}·m^{-2}
16–7 1320 Btu
16–9 a) 5.78 J·s^{-1} b) 0.304 m
16–11 3.10 × 10^6 J
16–13 a) 13.5 J·s^{-1} b) 13.5 J·s^{-1} c) 0.10 C°
16–15 166 W
16–17 111 m^2
16–19 0.0573 m^3 (57.3 L)
16–21 a) 1.9 × 10^7 J   b) 4.7 × 10^6 J
16–25 0.027 J·s^{-1}·m^{-1}·(C°)$^{-1}$
16–27 69
16–29 Steel to aluminum: 27.3°C; aluminum to copper: 9.5°C
16–31 170 min
16–33 a) 53.3°C   b) Copper: 7.82 J·s^{-1}; steel: 2.98 J·s^{-1}; brass: 4.84 J·s^{-1}
16–35 a) 10.0 J·s^{-1} b) 175 C°·m^{-1}
16–37 48.5°C
16–39 20.09 K

CHAPTER 17

17–1 4.00 atm
17–3 a) 899°C   b) 8.00 L
17–5 a) 3.74 × 10^3 mol   b) 120 kg
17–7 5.00 × 10^4 Pa
17–9 1.09 atm
17–11 3.75
17–13 0.258 L
17–15 18 cm^3; 56 cm^3
17–17 a) 51.1%   b) 0.0119 × 10^5 Pa   c) 8.79 × 10^{-3} kg·m^{-3}
17–19 23.0%
17–21 6.73 × 10^{-4} g
17–23 9.6 cm
17–25 a) 0.362 kg   b) 0.053 kg
17–27 a) 7.60 × 10^4 Pa   b) 1.56 g

17–29 a) 5.77 cylinders   b) 600 kg   c) 556 kg
17–31 8.67 kg
17–33 a) 18.4 m·s^{-1} b) 8.34 m·s^{-1}; 4.49 m·s^{-1} c) 1.40 m

CHAPTER 18

18–1 0
18–3 3.33 × 10^3 J
18–5 a) Yes   b) No   c) Negative
18–7 280 J
18–9 a) 1.67 × 10^5 J   b) 2.03 × 10^6 J
18–11 a) −8.00 × 10^4 J   b) −2.40 × 10^5 J   c) No
18–13 b) 1.66 × 10^3 J   c) On piston
d) 4.22 × 10^3 J   e) 5.88 × 10^3 J
f) 1.66 × 10^3 J
18–15 a) 2.51 atm; 189 K   b) 3.03 atm; 227 K
18–17 159°C
18–19 a) 169 J   b) 0
18–21 a) 34.4 mol   b) 3.57 × 10^4 J
c) 1.43 × 10^4 J   d) 3.57 × 10^4 J
18–23 a) 800 J; 0   b) 0; −800 J
18–25 a) 9.98 × 10^3 J   b) 5.56 × 10^3 J
c) Isobaric   d) Isobaric   e) Isobaric
18–27 b) 600 K   c) 8.00 × 10^5 Pa
18–29 a) 0.182 m   b) 222°C   c) 1.21 × 10^5 J

CHAPTER 19

19–1 a) 33.3%   b) 6000 J   c) 0.180 g
d) 1.50 × 10^5 W; 201 hp
19–3 a) 40.0%   b) 300 MW
19–5 a) 1.40 × 10^4 J   b) 57.1%
19–7 331°C
19–9 a) 7.50 × 10^3 J   b) 2.25 × 10^4 J
19–13 a) 258 K   b) 35.6%   c) 185 J
19–15 a) 3750 J   b) 1250 J   c) 25.0%
19–17 a) 488 J·K^{-1} b) −454 J·K^{-1} c) 34 J·K^{-1}
19–19 −3.02 × 10^3 J·K^{-1}
19–21 5.70%
19–23 a) p_1 = 1.01 × 10^5 Pa, V_1 = 9.85 × 10^{-3} m^3;
p_2 = 2.03 × 10^5 Pa, V_2 = 9.85 × 10^{-3} m^3;
p_3 = 1.01 × 10^5 Pa, V_3 = 1.49 × 10^{-2} m^3;
b) Process 1 → 2: Q = 1496 J, W = 0,
ΔU = 1496 J; Process 2 → 3: Q = 0, W = 723 J,
ΔU = −723 J; Process 3 → 1: Q = −1288,
W = −515 J, ΔU = −773 J   c) 208 J
d) 208 J
19–25 10.6%
19–27 a) −178 J·K^{-1} b) 244 J·K^{-1} c) 0
d) 66 J·K^{-1}
19–29 63.9%

CHAPTER 20

20–1 16.7 mol; 1.00×10^{25} molecules
20–3 a) 3.34×10^{-9} m   b) About a factor of 10 larger
20–5 3510°C
20–7 1.006
20–9 a) 1.10 cm·s^{-1} b) No
20–11 1.01×10^{4} J·kg^{-1}·K^{-1}; factor of 2.4 larger
20–13 a) m^{2}·s^{-1}
20–15 4.41×10^{-11} mol·s^{-1}
20–17 20.8 mol·m^{-3}
20–19 6.0×10^{27} atoms
20–21 10^{8} Pa (1000 atm)
20–23 a) 4.56×10^{-23} J   b) 2.20 K
20–25 a) 1.22×10^{4} m·s^{-1} b) 6.18×10^{5} m·s^{-1}
   c) No
20–27 a) 1.82×10^{3} J   b) 0.00535%
20–29 a) 1.03×10^{3} mol·m^{-3} b) 2.50×10^{6} Pa
   c) 2.50×10^{6} Pa

CHAPTER 21

21–1 a) 10.8 m   b) 282 Hz
21–3 a) 17.2 m; 0.0172 m   b) 74.0 m; 0.740 m
21–5 a) 1.0 m·s^{-1} b) 1.5 m
21–7 73.7 N
21–9 8.00×10^{8} Pa
21–11 60.2 m
21–13 a) 323 m·s^{-1} b) 1320 m·s^{-1}
21–17 a) 25.0 Hz; 0.0400 s; 10.5 m^{-1} b) $y(x, t) =$
   $-(0.0800 \text{ m}) \sin 2\pi \left(\dfrac{t}{0.0400 \text{ s}} - \dfrac{x}{0.600 \text{ m}} \right)$
   c) -0.0693 m
21–19 a) 126 m·s^{-1}; 12.6 m   b) Increase by a factor of $\sqrt{2}$
21–21 0.683
21–23 $Y/400$
21–25 a) 0.625 Hz; 3.93 rad·s^{-1}; 3.93 m^{-1} b) $y(x, t) =$
   $-(0.120 \text{ m}) \sin [(3.93 \text{ s}^{-1})t - (3.93 \text{ m}^{-1})x]$
   c) $y(0, t) = -(0.120 \text{ m}) \sin [(3.93 \text{ s}^{-1})t]$
   d) $y(1.2 \text{ m}, t) = -(0.120 \text{ m}) \cos [(3.93 \text{ s}^{-1})t]$
   e) 0.471 m·s^{-1} f) 0.120 m
21–27 1030 m due west

CHAPTER 22

22–1 a) 0; 0.60 m; 1.20 m; 1.80 m; 2.40 m
   b) 0.30 m; 0.90 m; 1.50 m; 2.10 m
22–3 a) 224 Hz   b) 44
22–5 a) 54.0 m·s^{-1} b) 146 N
22–7 a) Fundamental: 2.4 m; first overtone: 0.8 m,

2.4 m; second overtone: 0.48 m, 1.44 m, 2.40 m
   b) Fundamental: 0; first overtone: 0, 1.6 m; second overtone: 0, 0.96 m, 1.92 m
22–9 a) 478 Hz; 956 Hz; 1430 Hz; 1910 Hz
   b) 239 Hz; 717 Hz; 1190 Hz; 1670 Hz
   c) 41; 83
22–11 1520 Hz
22–13 1.27
22–15 a) 40 m·s^{-1} b) Four times per second
22–17 a) 200 N   b) 12.2%
22–19 Diatomic
22–21 a) 4.30 m   b) 6, 7
22–23 a) 0.656 m   b) 56.2°C
22–25 5.88 m; 1.52 m; 0.38 m

CHAPTER 23

23–1 a) 4   b) 3
23–3 a) 18.2 Pa; below pain threshold   b) 726 Pa; well above pain threshold
23–5 a) 40.0 dB   b) 81.5 dB
23–7 437.2 Hz; 442.8 Hz
23–9 a) 0.714 m   b) 0.850 m   c) 482 Hz
   d) 405 Hz   e) 503 Hz   f) 387 Hz
23–11 a) 408.0 Hz   b) 412.1 Hz   c) 4.1 beats·s^{-1}
23–13 a) 0.287 Pa   b) 2.52×10^{-7} m   c) 80.0 m
23–15 b) 27.0 dB
23–17 17.5 dB
23–19 9.9 m·s^{-1}
23–21 a) 0.40 m·s^{-1} b) 1.80 m
23–23 a) 0.0370 m   b) 344 Hz
23–25 c) 4800 m·s^{-1}
23–27 a) ct b) $(c - v_1)/f_0$ c) $f_0 t(c + v_2)/(c - v_1)$
   d) c e) $(c - v_2)(c - v_1)/f_0(c + v_2)$
   f) $f_0 c(c + v_2)/(c - v_2)(c - v_1)$ g) 1420 Hz
23–29 a) 180°   b) 4.48×10^{-6} W·m^{-2}; 66.5 dB
   c) 1.06×10^{-5} W·m^{-2}; 70.3 dB
   d) 1.30×10^{-6} W·m^{-2}; 61.2 dB

CHAPTER 24

24–1 9.3×10^{5} C
24–3 2.02 N; repulsive
24–5 1.07×10^{-14} m; 1.07×10^{-14} m
24–7 6980
24–9 a) 1.10×10^{26} b) 1.32×10^{16}
   c) 1.20×10^{-8}%
24–11 6.38×10^{-7} N; +y-direction
24–13 0.259 N; +x-direction
24–15 a) $(1/4\pi\epsilon_0)2q^2/a^2$; +$y$-direction
   b) $(1/4\pi\epsilon_0)2aq^2/(a^2 + x^2)^{3/2}$; +$y$-direction
24–17 a) 5.06×10^{7} N   b) 1.43×10^{8} N; toward the center of the earth

24–19 a) 3.24×10^{-5} N; -1.30×10^{-5} N
  b) 3.49×10^{-5} N; 338°
24–21 a) $F = (1/4\pi\epsilon_0)2aq^2/x^3$; $+y$-direction
  b) $F = (1/4\pi\epsilon_0)4aq^2/y^3$; $-y$-direction
24–23 a) 5.29×10^{-11} m   b) 1.09×10^6 m·s^{-1}
24–25 b) 2.15×10^{-6} C   c) 31.7°

CHAPTER 25

25–1 1.08×10^5 N·C^{-1}; upward
25–3 3.35 m
25–5 a) 2.50 N·C^{-1} b) 4.00×10^{-19}; upward
25–7 5.57×10^{-11} N·C^{-1}
25–9 3.55×10^3 N·C^{-1}
25–11 a) 1050 N·C^{-1}; $-x$-direction   b) 312 N·C^{-1}; $+x$-direction   c) 845 N·C^{-1}; $+x$-direction
25–13 35.7 N·C^{-1}; 245°
25–15 a) 4.49×10^4 N·C^{-1}; $-x$-direction
  b) 2.00×10^4 N·C^{-1}; $+x$-direction
  c) 8.34×10^3 N·C^{-1}; 110°
  d) 1.59×10^4 N·C^{-1}; $-x$-direction
25–17 2.82×10^5 N·C^{-1}·m^2
25–19 7.97×10^{-11} C·m^{-2}
25–21 6.37×10^{-10} C
25–25 a) 0   b) $(1/4\pi\epsilon_0)q/r^2$ c) 0
  d) $(1/4\pi\epsilon_0)q/r^2$ e) $-q$ f) $+q$
25–27 55.2°
25–29 a) 5.12 cm   b) 35.5 cm
25–31 -31.2×10^{-9} C
25–33 -2.66×10^{-10} C
25–35 a) $r < a$: $E = Q/4\pi\epsilon_0 r^2$; $a < r < b$: $E = 0$; $r > b$: $E = 3Q/4\pi\epsilon_0 r^2$
  b) $-Q/4\pi\epsilon_0 a^2$ c) $-3Q/4\pi\epsilon_0 b^2$
25–37 b) $q_1 < 0$, $q_2 < 0$ c) 3.12×10^4 N·C^{-1}

CHAPTER 26

26–1 0.218 m
26–3 -0.481 J
26–5 a) 14.9 m·s^{-1} b) 0.274 m
26–7 a) 0.0599 m   b) 0.0300 m
26–9 a) 359 V   b) -786 V   c) -2.86×10^{-6} J
26–11 b) $2q/4\pi\epsilon_0 a$ e) $\pm\sqrt{3}a$
26–13 a) 0   b) -1.80×10^{-3} J
  c) $+4.14 \times 10^{-3}$ J
26–15 a) 20.0 V   b) Plate with positive charge
26–17 1.75 mm
26–19 a) 157 V   b) 157 V
26–21 a) 0.433 mm·s^{-1} b) 0.008 mm·s^{-1}
26–23 939 MeV
26–25 a) 5.11×10^3 V   b) $0.141c$
  c) 9.39×10^6 V; $0.141c$
26–27 a) 1.32 cm   b) 33.4°   c) 9.23 cm
26–29 a) -3.00×10^5 J   b) -1.36×10^4 V
  c) 2.73×10^5 V·m^{-1}

26–33 a) Remains at rest   b) Returns to origin
  c) Moves off to infinity along the $+x$-axis
26–35 a) 4.00 m   b) 3.56×10^{-7} C
26–37 a) 5.6×10^7 V·m^{-1} b) 0.28 V
26–39 2.27×10^{-14} m
26–41 a) -539 V; $+60$ V   b) -3.00×10^{-6} J
26–43 $Q/4\pi\epsilon_0 a$
26–45 a) 1/3   b) 3
26–47 a) 667 m·s^{-1} c) -3.59 J   d) No
  e) 25.1 mm   f) (c) 9.61 J; (d) yes;
  (e) 981 m·s^{-1}

CHAPTER 27

27–3 a) 400 V   b) 3.39×10^{-2} m^2
  c) 6.67×10^5 V·m^{-1} d) 5.90×10^{-6} C·m^{-2}
27–5 a) $Q_1 = 1.15 \times 10^{-4}$ C; $Q_2 = 1.15 \times 10^{-4}$ C
  b) $V_1 = 28.8$ V; $V_2 = 19.2$ V
27–7 a) $Q_1 = 4.32 \times 10^{-5}$ C; $Q_2 = 8.64 \times 10^{-5}$ C;
  $Q_3 = 1.30 \times 10^{-4}$ C   b) $V_1 = 21.6$ V;
  $V_2 = 21.6$ V; $V_3 = 14.4$ V   c) 21.6 V
27–9 2.16 J
27–11 a) 7.50×10^{-11} F   b) 0.0148 m^2
  c) 1.50×10^{-6} J   d) 1.40×10^3 V
27–13 a) 4.00×10^3 V   b) 8.00×10^3 V
  c) 8.00×10^{-3} J
27–17 a) 0.723 m^2 b) 2.00×10^3 V
27–19 a) 1.12×10^{-4} C·m^{-2} b) 8.68×10^{-5} C·m^{-2}
27–21 a) 4.43×10^{-11} F   b) 5.31×10^{-9} C
  c) 1.50×10^4 V·m^{-1} d) 3.19×10^{-7} J
  e) (a) 2.21×10^{-11} F; (b) 5.31×10^{-9} C;
  (c) 1.50×10^4 V·m^{-1}; (d) 6.37×10^{-7} J
27–23 a) $xq^2/2\epsilon_0 A$ b) $(x + \Delta x)q^2/2\epsilon_0 A$
27–25 a) 2.00 μF   b) $Q_3 = 1.80 \times 10^{-3}$ C;
  $Q_2 = 1.20 \times 10^{-3}$ C   c) 100 V
27–27 a) 2 μF: 1.44×10^{-3} C; 720 V
  3 μF: 1.44×10^{-3} C; 480 V
  b) 2 μF: 1.15×10^{-3} C; 576 V
  3 μF: 1.73×10^{-3} C; 576 V
27–29 2.30×10^{-3} J
27–31 a) $\epsilon_0 A/(d - a)$ b) $[d/(d - a)]C_0$
27–35 9.44×10^{-10} F

CHAPTER 28

28–1 20.0 s
28–3 a) 0.0144 A   b) 1.98×10^{-6} m·s^{-1}
28–5 a) 12.2 A   b) 7.68 V   c) 0.628 Ω
28–7 29.2 m
28–9 3.22 mm
28–11 a) 99.4 Ω   b) 0.0217 Ω
28–13 33°C
28–15 No
28–17 a) 12.0 V   b) 0   c) 12.0 V
  d) (a) 11.3 V; (b) 11.3 V; (c) 0

28–19 a) 0.500 Ω   b) 5.50 Ω

28–21 a) EJ b) ρJ^2 c) E^2/ρ

28–23 40.0 Ω

28–25 a) 0.500 W   b) 9000 J   c) 7.46 Ω

28–27 a) 24.0 W   b) 4.0 W   c) 20.0 W

28–29 a) 1.2×10^5 m·s^{-1} b) 6.0×10^{-9} m
c) 5.2×10^{-14} s

28–31 a) 1.67 A   b) 2.78×10^4 W
c) 2.00×10^7 Ω

28–33 1.95 electrons·mm^{-3}

28–35 a) 1.93×10^{-8} Ω·m   b) 33.1 A
c) 6.46×10^{-4} m·s^{-1}

28–37 304°C

28–39 a) 0.30 Ω   b) 10.4 V

28–41 a) 0.40 A   b) 1.6 W   c) 12-V battery; 4.8 W
d) 8-V battery; 3.2 W

28–43 a) 21.0 V   b) 4.54×10^6 J   c) 1.94×10^6 J
d) 0.100 Ω   e) 0.65×10^6 J
f) 1.94×10^6 J

28–45 a) 2.12 A   b) 1.3 A   c) 6.2 V

CHAPTER 29

29–1 a) 9.00 Ω   b) 4.00 Ω in each   c) 4.00 A
d) 2 Ω: 8.0 V; 3 Ω: 12.0 V; 4 Ω: 16.0 V
e) 2 Ω: 32.0 W; 3 Ω: 48.0 W; 4 Ω: 64.0 W

29–3 a) 0.923 Ω   b) 2 Ω: 18.0 A; 3 Ω: 12.0 A;
4 Ω: 9.0 A   c) 39.0 A   d) 36.0 V across
each   e) 2 Ω: 648 W; 3 Ω: 432 W; 4 Ω:
324 W

29–5 3 Ω; 1 Ω: 12 A; 3 Ω: 12 A; 7 Ω: 4 A; 5 Ω: 4 A

29–7 a) 200 V   b) 1.12 W

29–9 $\mathcal{E}_1 = 18$ V; $\mathcal{E}_2 = 7$ V; $V_{ab} = 13$ V

29–11 a) 4.00×10^{-3} Ω   b) 3.75×10^5 Ω

29–13 2.96×10^3 Ω; 1.20×10^4 Ω; 1.35×10^5 Ω

29–15 25,000 Ω: 10.9 V; 250,000 Ω: 109.1 V

29–19 a) 3.00×10^{-4} A   b) 2.00×10^{-4} s

29–21 a) 9.47×10^9 J; 2.63×10^3 kWh   b) $263

29–23 a) Toaster: 15.0 A; frypan: 11.7 A;
lamp: 0.625 A   b) Yes

29–27 Two in parallel in series with two in parallel;
8.1 W

29–29 a) Two in series in parallel with two in series
b) 0.50 W

29–31 a) 8 Ω   b) −14.4 V

29–33 2 Ω: 5.21 A; 4 Ω: 1.11 A; 5 Ω: 6.32 A

29–35 a) +0.222 V   b) 0.464 A

29–37 a) −12 V   b) (12/7) A   c) 4.5 Ω
d) 4.2 Ω

29–39 a) −6 V   b) b c) +6 V   d) +54 μC,
in the direction of b to a

29–41 a) 3000 Ω   b) 33.3 V

29–43 7.50×10^3 Ω

29–45 45.0 Ω

29–47 b) No current through galvanometer

c) 7.85 V   d) No

29–49 5.00×10^5 Ω; 1.20×10^{-5} F

CHAPTER 30

30–1 Positive

30–3 1.78 T; north

30–5 a: qvB, in the −z-direction; b: qvB, in the
+y-direction; c: 0; d: $qvB/\sqrt{2}$, in the
−y-direction; e: qvB, directed midway between
the −y-axis and the −z-axis

30–7 a) 0.180 Wb   b) 0   c) 0.180 Wb   d) 0

30–9 a) 6.82×10^{-4} T; into the plane of the figure
b) 2.62×10^{-8} s

30–11 0.0142 m

30–13 a) 5.20×10^6 V·m^{-1} b) 2.60×10^4 V

30–15 3.50×10^{-25} kg; 21

30–17 15.0 A

30–19 a) 0.0360 N; −z-direction   b) 0.0300 N;
−y-direction   c) 0   d) 0.0104 N;
−y-direction

30–21 4.32×10^{-5} N·m

30–23 a) 0.145 N·m   b) Plane of coil at 60° to the
field

30–25 a) $NIBA$; 0   b) 0; −$NIBA$ c) $NIBA$; 0
d) 0; +$NIBA$

30–27 a) 0.667 A   b) 3.83 A   c) 97 V
d) 372 W

30–29 6.87×10^{28} electrons·m^{-3}

30–31 9.6×10^{-3} m; yes

30–33 8.57×10^{-7} Wb

30–35 a) 1.00×10^{-3} N   b) $B_x = +0.267$ T;
$B_z = +0.200$ T   c) $B_y = \pm 0.373$ T

30–37 a) $2\pi m/qB$ b) $qB/2\pi m$

30–39 $F_x = 0$; $F_y = -1.52 \times 10^{-3}$ N;
$F_z = -2.74 \times 10^{-3}$ N

30–41 a) $F_x = +1.00$ N; $F_y = 0$; $F_z = -0.600$ N
b) 1.17 N

30–43 a) 0.0166 N·m   b) 0.00960 N·m
c) 0.0166 N·m; 0.00960 N·m

30–45 a) 0.480 A   b) 4.02 A   c) 99.9 V
d) 57.6 W   e) 80.8 W   f) 540 W
g) 65.1%

30–47 a) 1.33 m   b) 1.26×10^{-6} s   c) 0.0236 m
d) 0.119 m

30–49 a) 3.83 m·s^{-1} b) 3.41 A

CHAPTER 31

31–1 a) 2.40×10^{-5} T   b) Yes

31–3 a) 100 A   b) 2.00×10^{-4} T; 1.00×10^{-4} T

31–5 a) $\mu_0 I/\pi a$ b) $\mu_0 I/3\pi a$ c) 0
d) $2\mu_0 I/3\pi a$

31–7 a) 10.0 A   b) Opposite

31–9 3.67 mm

31–11 12 turns

31–15 a) 7200 turns   b) 1.13×10^3 m

31–19 1.10×10^{-6} T; $-z$-direction

31–21 6.74×10^{-5} T

31–23 $\mu_0 |I_1 - I_2|/4R$; 0

31–25 a) $\mu_0 I/2\pi r$ b) 0

31–27 $\mu_0 I_1/2\pi r$ b) $\mu_0 (I_1 + I_2)/2\pi r$

31–31 b) $\mu_0 Ia/\pi (a^2 + x^2)^{3/2}$; $+x$-direction

31–33 a) 1.08×10^{-4} N·m^{-1}; $-y$-direction
b) 1.08×10^{-4} N·m^{-1}; $+y$-direction

31–35 2.88×10^{-4} N; toward the wire

31–37 35.9 A

31–39 a) $(N\mu_0 Ia^2/2) \left\{ 1 \Big/ \left[a^2 + \left(\dfrac{a}{2} + x \right)^2 \right]^{3/2} \right.$

$\left. + 1 \Big/ \left[a^2 + \left(\dfrac{a}{2} - x \right)^2 \right]^{3/2} \right\}$

c) $8N\mu_0 I/a\sqrt{125}$ d) 4.50×10^{-3} T

31–41 a) 560   b) 559

31–43 a) $\mu_0 Ir/2\pi R_1^2$
b) $(\mu_0 I/2\pi r)[(R_3^2 - r^2)/(R_3^2 - R_2^2)]$

31–45 $\mu_0 Qn/a$

CHAPTER 32

32–3 a) 7.50 m·s^{-1} b) 4.00 A   c) 1.92 N, to the left

32–5 a) 2.00 V   b) From B to A c) 2.50 N, to the right   d) Both equal 20.0 W

32–7 0.0285 A

32–9 4.8×10^{-3} V

32–11 a) 3.70 rad·s^{-1} b) 0

32–13 NAB/R

32–15 0.112 T

32–17 a) Concentric circles   b) 2.50×10^{-3} V·m^{-1}; tangent to ring in clockwise direction   c) 7.85×10^{-4} A   d) 0   e) 1.57×10^{-3} V

32–19 a) Right to left   b) Right to left   c) Left to right

32–21 a) a to b b) b to a c) b to a

32–23 b) $FR/B^2 l^2$

32–27 a) 0.600 V   b) 0   c) 0.600 V

32–29 80 turns

32–31 a) $\frac{1}{2} qr(\Delta B/\Delta t)$, to left in plane of figure
b) $\frac{1}{2} qr(\Delta B/\Delta t)$, upward in plane of figure
c) Force is zero

32–33 c) 1.00×10^{-3} A   d) 0

CHAPTER 33

33–3 5.15×10^{-4} H

33–5 a) 1.00×10^{-3} V; yes   b) 1.00×10^{-3} V

33–7 a) 0.667 H   b) 1.78×10^{-3} Wb

33–9 a) 8.00×10^{-4} H   b) 1.80×10^{-3} H

33–11 3.84 H

33–13 580 turns

33–15 a) 0.135 J   b) 4.50 W

33–17 a) 0.200 A   b) 4.00 A·s^{-1} c) 2.00 A·s^{-1}
d) 0.250 s

33–19 a) 0.500 A   b) 833 A·s^{-1} c) 0

33–21 a) 6.00 W   b) 1.00 W   c) 5.00 W
d) (a) = (b) + (c)   e) 13.5 J

33–23 a) 23.6 rad·s^{-1}; 0.267 s   b) 0.0300 C
c) 0.750 J   d) 0.0150 C   e) 0.612 A
f) 0.187 J; 0.563 J

33–25 a) 9.00 H   b) 450 Wb   c) 0.0360

33–29 a) $\mu_0 N^2 I^2 A/2l$ b) $\mu_0 N^2 I^2 A/2l$; same

33–31 a) 57.3 J·m^{-3} b) 0.0144 J

33–33 $C = 1.60 \times 10^{-7}$ F; $L = 9.77 \times 10^{-4}$ H

33–35 a) $D(L - L_0)/(L_f - L_0)$ b) 0.75028 H; 0.75057 H; 0.75086 H; 0.75114 H
c) 0.74999 H; 0.74999 H; 0.74998 H; 0.74998 H   d) Oxygen

33–37 a) $4L$ b) L c) $\omega_1/2$

CHAPTER 34

34–1 a) 314 Ω   b) 3.18×10^{-3} H
c) 3.18×10^3 Ω   d) 3.18×10^{-3} F

34–3 a) 0.0150 A   b) 0.150 A   c) 1.50 A

34–5 a) 0.100 A   b) 0.0100 A   c) 0.00100 A

34–7 a) 922 Ω   b) 0.0542 A   c) 10.8 V; 48.8 V
d) 77.5°; lead

34–9 a) 539 Ω   b) 0.0928 A   c) 18.6 V; 46.4 V
d) $-68.2°$; lag

34–11 a) 379 Ω; $-58.2°$; lags   b) 369 Ω; $+57.2°$; leads

34–13 a) 745 rad·s^{-1} c) V_1: 106 V; V_2: 356 V; V_3: 356 V; V_4: 0; V_5: 106 V   d) 745 rad·s^{-1}
e) 1.06 A

34–15 a) 1.83×10^3 rad·s^{-1} c) 0.400 A
d) 0.400 A; 0.131 A; 0.131 A

34–17 a) 99.0 Ω; 4.04 A   b) 500 Ω; 0.800 A

34–19 a) 12.5 W   b) 12.5 W   c) 0   d) 0

34–21 a) 20   b) 0.750 A   c) 4.50 W
d) 3200 Ω

34–23 a) 30   b) 3.33 V

34–25 0.0459 H

34–27 a) 1.20 A   b) 200 Ω   c) 468 Ω; 732 Ω

34–29 a) 5.87 Ω   b) 1.97×10^{-4} F   c) 2060 W

34–31 a) 0.832   b) 161 V

34–33 a) 568 Ω   b) 0.866 A   c) 266 V

34–35 a) 5.77×10^3 rad·s^{-1} b) 2.40 A
c) 4.16×10^3 V   d) 4.16×10^3 V
e) 0.864 J; 0.864 J

34–37 a) 9.65×10^{-3} A   b) 241 V   c) 1.16 V
d) 2.91×10^{-3} J; 1.40×10^{-5} J

CHAPTER 35

35–1 a) 1.06×10^{-7} A·m^{-2} b) 2.12×10^{-10} A
35–3 150 m
35–5 a) 242 m   b) 9.59×10^{-3} V·m^{-1}
35–9 a) 3.00×10^{-10} T   b) 3.38×10^5 W
 c) 100 km
35–11 4.08 V·m^{-1}; 1.36×10^{-8} T
35–13 a) 2.00×10^{-6} Pa   b) 4.00×10^{-6} Pa
35–15 a) 3.00×10^6 m·s^{-1} b) 0.0375 m
35–17 a) 1.20×10^{-2} m   b) 6.00 mm
 c) 2.40×10^8 m·s^{-1}
35–19 a) 7.50×10^{-10} m; 7.50×10^{-4} μm;
 7.50×10^{-1} nm; 7.50 Å   b) 6.00×10^{-7} m;
 6.00×10^{-1} μm; 6.00×10^2 nm; 6.00×10^3 Å
35–21 a) 1.03×10^3 V·m^{-1}; 3.43×10^{-6} T
 b) 4.0×10^{26} W
35–23 a) 9.99×10^9 Hz   b) 2.00×10^{-7} T
 c) 4.78 W·m^{-2} d) 7.97×10^{-9} N
35–25 a) $\rho I/\pi a^2$; in the direction of the current
 b) $\mu_0 r I/2\pi a^2$; tangential   c) $\rho I^2 r/2\pi^2 a^4$;
 radially inward   d) Both equal $\rho l I^2/\pi a^2$
35–27 6.00×10^{-5} N
35–29 36.0 hr
35–31 a) Reflecting; gives twice the radiation pressure
 b) 12.1 mi^2 c) Both gravitational force and
 radiation force are proportional to r^{-2}

CHAPTER 36

36–1 1.65
36–3 a) 23.4°   b) Is independent
36–7 a) 1.87×10^8 m·s^{-1} b) 312 nm
36–11 38.7°
36–13 a) Air   b) 15.1°
36–15 a) $0.164 I_0$ b) Linearly polarized, in the
 direction parallel to the axis of the second
 polarizer
36–17 a) First filter: $0.500 I_0$, linearly polarized; second
 filter: $0.375 I_0$, linearly polarized; third filter:
 $0.0938 I_0$, linearly polarized   b) No light
 passed by third filter
36–19 1.58
36–21 a) 36.9°   b) Horizontal
36–23 1.89
36–25 a) 45.5°   b) 13.4°
36–27 1.18
36–29 1.89
36–31 1.31
36–33 a) Red: 1.73; blue: 2.75   b) Blue
36–35 $\frac{1}{4} I_0$
36–37 a) 57.7°   b) 49.8°
36–39 *l*-leucine: $-0.11C$; *l*-glutamic acid: $0.124C$
36–43 d) 0.717 cm

CHAPTER 37

37–1 40 cm to the right of the mirror; 6.0 cm tall
37–3 a) $+5.0$ b) 60 cm behind the mirror; virtual
37–5 b) 35.0 cm to the right of the mirror; 5.00 cm;
 inverted; real
37–7 b) 5.83 cm to the left of the mirror; 0.833 cm;
 erect; virtual
37–9 b) 3.75 cm to the right of the mirror; 0.938 cm;
 erect; virtual
37–11 2.3 cm
37–13 a) 4.5 cm   b) 25.5 cm
37–17 1.39
37–19 11.2 cm to the left of the vertex; 1.0 mm; erect
37–21 4.00 m·s^{-1}
37–23 $h/2$
37–25 6.00 m; 3.00 m
37–27 a) 6.67 cm   b) 13.1 cm
37–29 a) $|s| < 4.00$ cm   b) Erect
37–31 a) 0.333 cm   b) Independent
37–35 b) At the point where the mirrors join
37–37 5.45 cm to the left of the vertex of the spherical
 mirror, 0.58 cm tall; 10.6 cm to the left of the
 vertex of the spherical mirror, 0.38 cm tall

CHAPTER 38

38–1 30.0 cm: a) 30.0 cm to the right of the lens
  b) -1.00 c) Real   d) Inverted
 20.0 cm: a) 60.0 cm to the right of the lens
  b) -3.00 c) Real   d) Inverted
 10.0 cm: a) 30.0 cm to the left of the lens
  b) $+3.00$ c) Virtual   d) Erect
 5.00 cm: a) 7.50 cm to the left of the lens
  b) $+1.50$ c) Virtual   d) Erect
38–3 35.0 cm to the left of the lens; 2.50 cm tall;
 inverted
38–5 a) -6.67 cm; diverging   b) 0.500 cm; erect
38–7 1.75 cm to the left of the lens; 14.0 cm to the
 left of the lens; virtual
38–11 $f = \pm 33.3$ cm, ± 11.1 cm
38–13 a) Image formed by the first surface
 b) $+20.0$ cm   c) Real   d) Inside rod,
 40.0 cm to the left of the second vertex
38–15 3.00 cm from the center of the sphere
38–17 a) 75.0 cm to the right of the lens; 1.50 cm;
 inverted   b) 90.0 cm to the right of the
 second lens; 3.00 cm; erect   c) 16.2 cm to the
 right of the second lens; 0.692 cm; inverted
 d) 210 cm to the left of the second lens;
 9.00 cm; erect.
38–19 3.60 cm from either end of the eyepiece
38–21 a) 66.7 cm in front of the eye   b) 133 cm in
 front of the eye

38–23 0.691 cm

38–25 1.54 m

38–27 a) 35 mm   b) 200 mm

38–29 1/240 s

38–31 a) 10.2 cm   b) No

38–33 2.25 cm; 22.5 cm from the lens

38–35 a) 9.38 cm   b) 2.67 mm

38–37 a) 642   b) 42.5

38–39 −40

38–41 a) −30   b) 31.0 cm

38–43 a) 4.0 cm from the screen; 12.0 cm from the screen   b) 4.0 cm from the screen: $m = -0.333$; 12.0 cm from the screen: $m = -3.00$

38–45 −18.8 cm

38–49 a) 8.80 m   b) 5.88 m

38–51 48.8 cm

38–53 5.33 cm below the lower face of the plate

38–55 7.99 mm

38–57 a) +408   b) 23.3 cm

38–59 b) 20.0 cm   c) Telescope of Problem 38–58: 100.0 cm; Galilean telescope: 60.0 cm

38–61 a) 18.0 cm from the center of the goblet, on the same side as the incident rays   b) 8.03 cm from the center of the goblet, on the side opposite from the incident rays

38–63 a) Water affects the refractive properties of the eye   b) +0.993 cm

38–65 a) 0.276 m   b) 0.276 m

CHAPTER 39

39–1 1.50 mm

39–3 1.48 mm

39–5 a) 4.50   b) none (0°)

39–7 31.5 fringes·cm^{-1}

39–9 a) Yes   b) 92.3 nm

39–11 0.606 mm

39–13 3.27 mm

39–15 645 nm

39–17 13.9°; 28.7°; 46.1°

39–19 8.22 nm

39–21 358 m

39–23 1200 m

39–27 0.800 mm

39–29 a) Destructive interference   b) 500 Hz   c) 0.68 m

39–31 a) 437 nm   b) 546 nm

39–33 a) The interference pattern is shifted downward on the screen   b) $\sin \theta = [m\lambda - L(n - 1)]/d$

39–35 0.570 mm

39–37 625 nm

39–39 387 km

39–41 5.50 fringes

39–43 a) 1.67×10^3 lines·cm^{-1} b) 0.14 mm

CHAPTER 40

40–1 Bolt at A

40–3 a) 2.06×10^{-7} s   b) 61.3 m

40–5 11.7 min; the one in the probe

40–7 1.57 m

40–9 233 m

40–11 a) 1.79 km   b) 0.687 km; 38.4%   c) 2.57×10^{-5} s; 7.69 km; 38.4%

40–17 $0.663c$; moving away

40–19 $0.357c$

40–21 $0.943c$

40–23 a) 1.14×10^{-15} J; 1.16×10^{-15} J; 1.02   b) 3.08×10^{-14} J; 8.26×10^{-14} J; 2.68

40–25 1.64×10^{-13} J

40–27 a) 5.74×10^{14} J   b) 1.74×10^4 kg

40–29 a) 4.02×10^{-10} J   b) 1.04×10^{-10} J   c) 0.348

40–31 $0.745c$

40–33 a) $\Delta = 3.38 \times 10^{-6}$ b) 5.57×10^4 MeV

40–37 3.72×10^{-12} kg

40–39 a) E/mc

40–41 1.19×10^{-18} m·s^{-1}

40–43 a) 1.35×10^{14} J   b) 6.74×10^{19} W   c) 1.38×10^{10} kg

40–45 a) 1.60×10^5 eV   b) 6.71×10^5 eV   c) 1.94×10^8 m·s^{-1} d) 2.37×10^8 m·s^{-1}

40–47 1.68×10^5 eV

40–49 a) 600 MeV   b) Larger by a factor of 2.15

40–51 c) 9.43×10^{-9} s

CHAPTER 41

41–1 a) 4.95×10^{-19} J; 3.09 eV   b) 402 nm; ultraviolet

41–3 6.72×10^{18} photons·s^{-1}

41–5 a) 0.0150 J; 9.36×10^{16} eV   b) 3.14×10^{-19} J; 1.96 eV   c) 4.78×10^{16} photons

41–7 $\phi = hf_0$

41–9 1.96×10^6 m·s^{-1}

41–11 a) 1.19 V   b) 1.19 eV   c) 6.48×10^5 m·s^{-1}

41–13 a) 6.17×10^{14} Hz   b) 486 nm

41–15 a) 20 eV   b) 5 eV; 10 eV; 15 eV   c) The photon is not absorbed; its energy is not equal to an energy level difference   d) 5 eV ≤ ϕ ≤ 8 eV

41–17 a) 7.29×10^{-13} J; 4.55 MeV   b) 7.29×10^{-13} J; 4.55 MeV   c) 1.48×10^7 m·s^{-1}

41–19 a) 13.6 eV   b) −27.2 eV   c) −13.6 eV   d) 13.6 eV   e) 91.2 nm; ultraviolet

41–21 97.2 nm; 3.08×10^{15} Hz

41–23 1.96 eV; 3.14×10^{-19} J; 633 nm

41–25 7.97×10^{15} photons·s^{-1}

41–27 a) 15.5 kV   b) 0.0310 nm

41–29 1.13 keV

41–31 a) 0.0413 nm   b) 0.0425 nm   c) 29.1 keV

41–33 a) 7.6×10^{19} photons·s^{-1} b) 25 km

41–35 a) 1.04 eV   b) 1200 nm   c) 2.51×10^{14} Hz
d) 4.14×10^{-7} eV   e) TV photons each have
too little energy

41–37 0.547 V

41–39 b) 2 eV, 3 eV, 4 eV, 6 eV, 7 eV, 9 eV

41–41 1.05×10^5 K

41–43 17.4 eV

41–45 a) -2820 eV   b) 2.56×10^{-13} m
c) 0.587 nm

41–47 a) 2.97×10^3 W   b) 67.3 C°·s^{-1} c) High
melting point and good thermal conductivity;
iron, nickel, tungsten

41–49 a) 0.145 nm   b) 297 eV
c) 1.02×10^7 m·s^{-1}; no

CHAPTER 42

42–1 a) 1.82×10^{-10} m   b) 9.90×10^{-14} m

42–3 a) 2480 eV   b) 6.02 eV

42–5 a) 4.09×10^{-11} m   b) 9.54×10^{-13} m

42–7 a) 3.50 eV; 354 nm   b) 1.65×10^{-10} eV

42–9 1.8×10^{-23} s

42–11 a) $3\hbar$ b) $3.46\hbar$; L is larger   c) $3\hbar$: 30.0°;
$2\hbar$: 54.7°; $\hbar$: 73.2°; $0\hbar$: 90.0°; $-\hbar$: 106.8°;
$-2\hbar$: 125.3°; $-3\hbar$: 150.0°

42–13 2.89×10^{30} rad·s^{-1}

42–15 0.145 nm

42–17 1.33×10^{-17} m; no

42–19 a) 122 nm   b) -0.00172 nm; decreased

42–21 a) 1.1×10^{-19} kg·m·s^{-1} b) 200 MeV
c) No

42–23 4×10^9 eV

42–27 a) 0.1 kg·m·s^{-1} b) 10 m

42–29 6.60×10^{-16} m

CHAPTER 43

43–1 $n = 1, l = 0, m = 0, s = 1/2$;
$n = 1, l = 0, m = 0, s = -1/2$;
$n = 2, l = 0, m = 0, s = 1/2$;
$n = 2, l = 0, m = 0, s = -1/2$;

$n = 2, l = 1, m = 1, s = 1/2$;
$n = 2, l = 1, m = 1, s = -1/2$;
$n = 2, l = 1, m = 0, s = 1/2$;
$n = 2, l = 1, m = 0, s = -1/2$;
$n = 2, l = 1, m = -1, s = 1/2$;
$n = 2, l = 1, m = -1, s = -1/2$

43–3 $1s^2 2s^2 2p^6 3s^2 3p^6 3d^{10} 4s^2 4p^5$

43–9 a) 4.58×10^{-48} kg·m^2 b) 0; 0.0151 eV;
0.0454 eV   c) 41.0 μm; 7.32×10^{12} Hz

43–11 2.16×10^3 kg·m^{-3}

43–13 a) 1770 nm; infrared   b) 1130 nm; infrared

43–15 a) 489 N·m^{-1} b) 5.70×10^{-20} J; 0.356 eV
c) 3490 nm; infrared

43–17 a) 1.11 nm   b) 1.80 nm

43–19 3.65×10^4 K

43–21 a) 0.129 nm   b) 8, 7, 6, 5, 4   c) 484 μm
d) 117 μm, 134 μm, 156 μm, 187 μm, 234 μm

CHAPTER 44

44–1 a) 10, 11   b) 30, 35   c) 47, 61

44–3 a) 0.112 u   b) 105 MeV
c) 7.48 MeV·nucleon^{-1}

44–5 b) 0.02 MeV

44–7 a) 1.05×10^{15} nuclei   b) 5.26×10^{14} nuclei;
8.00×10^{10} Bq   c) 2.63×10^{14} nuclei;
4.00×10^{10} Bq

44–9 a) 4.36×10^{-4} yr^{-1} b) 1.01 g
c) 3.68×10^{11} decays·s^{-1}

44–11 a) 4.97×10^{-4} J   b) 0.0828 rem

44–13 a) 7.15 MeV   b) 2.3 MeV

44–15 a) 3.26 MeV; 5.23×10^{-13} J
b) 3.15×10^{11} J·mol^{-1}

44–17 a) 0.525 T   b) 8.04×10^6 m·s^{-1}; 0.675 MeV

44–19 19.2 GeV

44–21 0.511 MeV; 1.24×10^{20} Hz; 2.43×10^{-3} nm

44–23 139.1 MeV

44–25 7.19×10^{19} J

44–27 a) 0.0556 J·s^{-1} b) 11.1 rad·s^{-1}
c) 7.78 rem·s^{-1} d) 25.7 s

44–29 a) 8.26 decays·s^{-1} b) 2.23×10^{-10} Ci

44–31 0.782 MeV

44–33 Absorbed; 10.1 MeV

44–35 a) $\pi^0 + \pi^+$ b) 219 MeV

44–37 a) 17 MeV   b) Not energetically allowed
c) Violate strangeness conservation

44–39 a) 64 MeV   b) Λ: 31%; K^-: 69%

Index

Appendix E

UNIT CONVERSION FACTORS

LENGTH

1 m = 100 cm = 1000 mm = 10^6 μm = 10^9 nm
1 km = 1000 m = 0.6214 mi
1 m = 3.281 ft = 39.37 in.
1 cm = 0.3937 in.
1 in. = 2.540 cm
1 ft = 30.48 cm
1 yd = 91.44 cm
1 mi = 5280 ft = 1.609 km
1 Å = 10^{-10} m = 10^{-8} cm = 10^{-1} nm
1 nautical mile = 6080 ft
1 light year = 9.461×10^{15} m

AREA

1 cm^2 = 0.155 in^2
1 m^2 = 10^4 cm^2 = 10.76 ft^2
1 in^2 = 6.452 cm^2
1 ft^2 = 144 in^2 = 0.0929 m^2

VOLUME

1 liter = 1000 cm^3 = 10^{-3}m^3 = 0.03531 ft^3 = 61.02 in^3
1 ft^3 = 0.02832 m^3 = 28.32 liters = 7.477 gallons
1 gallon = 3.788 liters

TIME

1 min = 60 s
1 hr = 3600 s
1 da = 86,400 s
1 yr = 365.24 da = 3.156×10^7 s

ANGLE

1 rad = 57.30° = 180°/π
1° = 0.01745 rad = π/180 rad
1 revolution = 360° = 2π rad
1 rev·min^{-1} (rpm) = 0.1047 rad·s^{-1}

SPEED

1 m·s^{-1} = 3.281 ft·s^{-1}
1 ft·s^{-1} = 0.3048 m·s^{-1}
1 mi·min^{-1} = 60 mi·hr^{-1} = 88 ft·s^{-1}
1 km·hr^{-1} = 0.2778 m·s^{-1} = 0.6214 mi·hr^{-1}
1 mi·hr^{-1} = 1.466 ft·s^{-1} = 0.4470 m·s^{-1} = 1.609 km·hr^{-1}
1 furlong·fortnight^{-1} = 1.662×10^{-4} m·s^{-1}

ACCELERATION

1 m·s^{-2} = 100 cm·s^{-2} = 3.281 ft·s^{-2}
1 cm·s^{-2} = 0.01 m·s^{-2} = 0.03281 ft·s^{-2}
1 ft·s^{-2} = 0.3048 m·s^{-2} = 30.48 cm·s^{-2}
1 mi·hr^{-1}·s^{-1} = 1.467 ft·s^{-2}

MASS

1 kg = 10^3 g = 0.0685 slug
1 g = 6.85×10^{-5} slug
1 slug = 14.59 kg
1 u = 1.661×10^{-27} kg
1 kg has a weight of 2.205 lb when g = 9.80 m·s^{-2}

FORCE

1 N = 10^5 dyn = 0.2248 lb
1 lb = 4.448 N = 4.448×10^5 dyn

PRESSURE

1 Pa = 1 N·m^{-2} = 1.451×10^{-4} lb·in^{-2} = 0.209 lb·ft^{-2}
1 bar = 10^5 Pa
1 lb·in^{-2} = 6891 Pa
1 lb·ft^{-2} = 47.85 Pa
1 atm = 1.013×10^5 Pa = 1.013 bar
$\qquad$ = 14.7 lb·in^{-2} = 2117 lb·ft^{-2}
1 mm Hg = 1 torr = 133.3 Pa

ENERGY

1 J = 10^7 ergs = 0.239 cal
1 cal = 4.186 J (based on 15° calorie)
1 ft·lb = 1.356 J
1 Btu = 1055 J = 252 cal = 778 ft·lb
1 eV = 1.602×10^{-19} J
1 kWh = 3.600×10^6 J

MASS–ENERGY EQUIVALENCE

1 kg $\leftrightarrow$ 8.988×10^{16} J
1 u $\leftrightarrow$ 931.5 MeV
1 eV $\leftrightarrow$ 1.073×10^{-9} u

POWER

1 W = 1 J·s^{-1}
1 hp = 746 W = 550 ft·lb·s^{-1}
1 Btu·hr^{-1} = 0.293 W